Twentieth-Century Britain

Twentieth-Century Britain
An Encyclopedia

Editor
F. M. Leventhal

GARLAND PUBLISHING, INC.
New York & London
1995

Library of Congress Cataloging-in-Publication Data

Twentieth-century Britain : an encyclopedia / editor, F.M. Leventhal.
        p.   cm. — (Garland reference library of the humanities ; vol.
1378)
    Includes bibliographical references (p.) and index.
    ISBN 0-8240-7205-7 (hardcover : alk. paper)
    1. Great Britain—History—20th century—Encyclopedias.   2. Great
Britain—Civilization—20th century—Encyclopedias.   I. Leventhal, F. M.,
1938– . II. Series.
DA566.T835   1995
941.082'03—dc20   95-30749
                                              CIP

Cover design by Lawrence Wolfson Design, New York. Photoresearch: Margery Trenk.
Cover photographs courtesy of Bettman Archive.

Printed on acid-free, 250-year-life paper
Manufactured in the United States of America

Contents

Topical Contents

Illustrations

The editor and publishers are grateful to the following for permission to reproduce illustrations:

Britain on View (British Tourist Authority), p. 469

Robert M. Craig, pp. 30, 378, 477, 736, 804

Crown Copyright (Public Record Office), p. 286

Greater London Photograph Library, pp. 199, 723

Hulton Deutsch Collection, pp. 64, 77, 117, 123, 188, 193, 296, 323, 409, 432, 535, 708

Imperial War Museum, pp. 88, 275, 657, 847

Museum of London, p. 855

University of Kent and *Evening Standard*/Solo Syndication, pp. 151, 474, 487

Preface

When Gary Kuris invited me to edit an encyclopedia on twentieth-century Britain approximately five years ago, my initial response was one of mingled skepticism and derision. The task seemed monumental and perhaps ultimately self-defeating. Was it possible within the span of a single volume to encompass enough of the history and culture of the century for the work to be useful to its intended audience of college students, professors, and general readers? Could a single reference work be of value to diverse constituencies? After initial hesitation, I accepted the challenge and have been grateful ever since for the opportunity to compile my own version of twentieth-century Britain. My task as editor has been, above all, to select the topics and contributors, recognizing that another editor might well have chosen differently. The range of subjects covered has been partly determined by my own interests in social and cultural history, in the history of the labor movement, and in music and art. However, while I am ultimately responsible for the contents of this work, I have not sought to impose a uniform style on authors, preferring to encourage diversity of approach and independent judgment.

It might be presumptuous to anticipate the end of the century and to contrive a purportedly comprehensive volume five years before its conclusion. For that editorial decision we beg the indulgence of readers. Other editorial policies, however idiosyncratic, warrant explanation rather than apology. Many of the articles may be loosely described as biographical, but no effort has been made to ensure that they include all of the factual information provided in *Who's Who* or in the *Dictionary of National Biography*. Instead they have been intended as interpretive assessments, including whatever biographical detail authors deemed pertinent. Writers, artists, and politicians whose careers fell primarily in the nineteenth century but who lived on into the twentieth have mostly been excluded. Thus there are no entries on Thomas Hardy or Henry James, on Lord Rosebery or Lord Salisbury, on Alfred Marshall or John Singer Sargent. At the other end of the century it seemed advisable to exclude individuals—particularly those in the political realm—whose ongoing careers preclude retrospective assessment, such as John Major or the present monarch. For purposes of this volume the political century begins with Arthur Balfour and ends with Margaret Thatcher.

Although the title *Twentieth-Century Britain* has been chosen deliberately to connote something broader than England, I have certainly not given equal space to all of the components that lay claim to the term "British." Some attempt—admittedly inadequate—has been made to include Scottish, Welsh, and Irish literature, to discuss the rise of nationalism in constituent parts of the United Kingdom, and to recognize that economic and social developments have had distinctive impacts on different parts of the British Isles. This may appear to disregard the current debate over what constitutes national identity, but it seemed a reasonable solution to the problem of keeping the volume within manageable dimensions. In the case of writers, in particular, emphasis has been placed on individuals—for example, George Bernard Shaw, William Butler Yeats, and Dylan Thomas—who became part of a metropolitan British culture, partly because they left Ireland or Wales to live in London, but mostly because they are major figures within twentieth-century English literature. This has also justified the inclusion of the American-born T.S. Eliot and American-born artists like Jacob Epstein and R.B. Kitaj, whose professional work was largely identified with England. Little attention has been paid to the Empire and Commonwealth except insofar as it affected developments in Britain. Articles on some former colonies and current Commonwealth members focus on their relationship with Britain, rather than on internal developments.

A single volume imposes constraints not merely on the number of subjects permissible but on the amount of space that can be allocated to each. These articles range from 500 to nearly 3,000 words, and my own judgment has largely determined the length of each entry. It has been an intriguing process to decide whether a particular politician or event merited a 1,000-word or a 2,500-word entry and to persuade contributors that such limitations needed to be imposed. This has not been done with the intention of slighting any individuals but in the recognition that certain events or professional lives warrant greater attention than others.

Following the model of the preceding volume in this series, Sally Mitchell's *Victorian Britain: An Encyclopedia* (1988), this work is arranged alphabetically, but with occasional accommodation to enable readers to find articles more easily. Thus New Universities (under the title Universities, New) appears just before University Education, not after New Towns. Wars and battles are referred to using the most familiar designation: the Boer War, not the Anglo-Boer War or the South African War; the Battle of Passchendaele, not the Third Battle of Ypres. The First World War and the Second World War, which figure so prominently throughout this work, are identified consistently in that way rather than as World War I or World War II, although occasionally the First World War is noted in articles as the Great War. Individuals appear under the name by which they are best known: Lord Beaverbrook, not William Maxwell Aitken; Samuel Hoare, not Viscount Templewood; George Orwell, not Eric Blair. Within articles, words in bold type cross-reference other articles, but I have limited the use of "see also" to an absolute minimum. The topical contents at the beginning of the book organize most of the entries within twenty broad categories to provide the reader with an alternative method of discovering the range of subjects.

Each entry contains a short bibliography—usually books rather than articles—of critical, biographical, or related studies to enable the reader to pursue further investigation of the topic. In the case of literary figures it seemed sensible to avoid listing their own collected works, even where an authoritative edition exists. A brief guide to research material at the end of the encyclopedia indicates other sources for locating books and articles on the period, as well as general studies.

In the process of editing this volume I have had the rewarding experience of becoming acquainted with large numbers of scholars working on aspects of twentieth-century Britain. There are more than two hundred contributors, not to mention those approached who declined to participate. Negotiating over word count and deadlines is not always calculated to solidify friendships, but despite my importuning and cajoling, I have survived the years in which this book came together having made many new friends and remarkably few enemies. In selecting authors I have inevitably drawn on old friends both in the United States and in Britain, but I have had to depend on the advice of others in locating scholars with whose work I was not familiar. I have relied extensively on my Associate Editors, Robert L. Caserio of Temple University, Christopher Lawrence of the Wellcome Institute for the History of Medicine in London, and Peter Stansky of Stanford University, for suggestions as to topics and contributors and for some of the editing of articles. Other scholars, some of them not directly connected with this project, have provided names of potential authors. Space permits mention only of a few of these, but I would like to thank Stephen Banfield, Kathleen Burk, Michael Dintenfass, Vera Gottlieb, David Howell, Tony Mason, David Mellor, Sally Mitchell, Jonathan Rose, Barry Supple, and David Vaughan.

I am also grateful to Boston University and to Garland Publishing for providing financial assistance during the course of the project.

My greatest debts are to three individuals, without whose support its completion would have been unimaginable. Gary Kuris of Garland Publishing, who commissioned the encyclopedia, proved to be a model editor, offering wise counsel, a wry sense of humor, and occasional lunches, all of which sustained my sometimes flagging spirits. James T. Dutton, my friend and departmental administrator at Boston University, provided technical assistance on a wholly voluntary basis over several years, converting diskettes, devising a database, and solving unforeseen computer problems, which enormously facilitated my task. My son David became an invaluable editorial and research assistant, word-processing dozens of articles and checking innumerable bibliographical references, which, although often tedious, involved skills that would, I suggested, ultimately prove useful.

F.M. Leventhal

Chronology

1900

Labour Representation Committee
    established in February
Relief of Mafeking in May
Conservatives win October
    "khaki" election
W.G. Grace ends cricket career
George Cadbury founds Bourneville
    Village trust
Joseph Conrad, *Lord Jim*
Arthur Thomas Quiller-Couch, ed.
    Oxford Book of English Verse
Edward Elgar, *The Dream of Gerontius*

1901

Queen Victoria dies 22 January;
    Edward VII becomes King
Taff Vale judgment issued
Commonwealth of Australia established
First British submarine launched
Order of Merit established
Ronald Ross wins Nobel Prize for Medicine
Rudyard Kipling, *Kim*
Seebohm Rowntree, *Poverty:*
    A Study of Town Life
The World's Classics reprint series started
Edwin Lutyens, The Deanery Garden

1902

Treaty of Vereeniging concludes Boer War
    in May
Arthur Balfour becomes Prime Minister
Education Act abolishes school boards,
    transfers powers to local authorities
Anglo-Japanese Naval Treaty signed
Committee of Imperial Defence formed
British Academy incorporated

Arthur Conan Doyle, *The Hound*
    of the Baskervilles
J.A. Hobson, *Imperialism*
The Times Literary Supplement
    begins publication

1903

King Edward VII visits Paris
Emmeline Pankhurst creates Women's
    Social and Political Union
Albert Mansbridge establishes Workers'
    Educational Association
Letchworth developed as the first garden city
Universities of Liverpool and
    Manchester founded
W. Randal Cremer wins Nobel Peace Prize
Samuel Butler, *The Way of All Flesh*
George Bernard Shaw, *Man and Superman*
G.E. Moore, *Principia Ethica*

1904

Anglo-French Entente signed
London Symphony Orchestra gives
    first concert
Rolls-Royce Company founded
J.W. Strutt, Lord Rayleigh, wins
    Nobel Prize for Physics
William Ramsay wins Nobel Prize
    for Chemistry
James Barrie, *Peter Pan*
G.K. Chesterton, *The Napoleon*
    of Notting Hill

1905

Henry Campbell-Bannerman becomes Prime
    Minister after Arthur Balfour resigns

Aliens Act attempts to curb immigration
from Eastern Europe
Austin Motor Company formed
Piccadilly and Bakerloo Underground lines
open in London
George Bernard Shaw, *Major Barbara*

1906
Liberals win 400 seats in February
election victory
HMS *Dreadnought* launched
J.J. Thompson wins Nobel Prize
for Physics
John Galsworthy, *The Man of Property*

1907
Anglo-Russian Entente signed
New Zealand becomes a Dominion
within the British Empire
United Methodist Church established
SS *Lusitania* and *Mauretania* launched
Robert Baden-Powell launches
Boy Scout movement
Rudyard Kipling wins Nobel Prize
for Literature
Joseph Conrad, *The Secret Agent*
Edmund Gosse, *Father and Son*

1908
H.H. Asquith becomes Prime Minister
Old-Age Pensions Act passed
by Parliament
Olympic Games held in London
Lord Northcliffe buys *The Times*
Ernest Rutherford wins Nobel Prize
for Chemistry
Arnold Bennett, *The Old Wives' Tale*
Graham Wallas, *Human Nature in Politics*

1909
David Lloyd George presents
People's Budget
Forcible feeding of suffragette prisoners
introduced
Morley-Minto Reforms in India
Anglo-Persian Oil Company formed
H.G. Selfridge opens department store
in Oxford Street
Minority report of the Poor Law
Commission issued
H.G. Wells, *Tono-Bungay*

William Beveridge, *Unemployment:
A Problem for Industry*
Frederick Delius, *A Mass of Life*

1910
Liberals win February election
with reduced majority
King Edward VII dies 6 May;
George V becomes King
First labor exchanges open
Conciliation bill on women's suffrage fails
Liberals win second 1910 election
in December over Peers vs. People
Roger Fry organizes Post-Impressionist
Exhibition in London
Arthur Evans completes excavation
of Cnossus, Crete
Norman Angell, *The Great Illusion*
E.M. Forster, *Howards End*
John Galsworthy, *Justice*
Ralph Vaughan Williams, *Fantasia
on a Theme of Tallis*

1911
Parliament Act limits powers of the House
of Lords
Canadian-born Andrew Bonar Law replaces
Arthur Balfour as Conservative leader
National Insurance Act provides health
and unemployment insurance
Ford begins manufacturing automobiles
in Manchester
Ernest Rutherford formulates theory
of atomic structure
Official Secrets Act becomes law
Diaghilev's *Ballets Russes* performs
first London season
Max Beerbohm, *Zuleika Dobson*
J.L. and Barbara Hammond,
The Village Labourer

1912
Suffragette violence escalates
London dock strike
Marconi scandal
Lilian Baylis assumes control
of Old Vic theater
Robert F. Scott reaches South Pole
SS *Titanic* sinks after colliding
with iceberg on maiden voyage
Royal Flying Corps established
Second Post-Impressionist Exhibition

1913

"Cat and Mouse" Act allows temporary
discharge of suffragette prisoners
Suffragette Emily Wilding Davison dies
after being trampled by King's horse
at Derby, 9 June
Miners, Railwaymen, and Transport
Workers form Triple Alliance
Trade Union Act allows unions to finance
Labour Party through political fund
New Statesman founded by Sidney
and Beatrice Webb
D.H. Lawrence, *Sons and Lovers*
Bertrand Russell and Alfred North
Whitehead, *Principia Mathematica*

1914

Mutiny at Curragh garrison in Ireland
in March
Britain declares war on Germany,
4 August
H.N. Brailsford, *The War of Steel and Gold*
Compton Mackenzie, *Sinister Street*
Robert Tressell, *The Ragged Trousered
Philanthropists*

1915

Gallipoli campaign
Rupert Brooke dies of blood poisoning
en route to the Dardanelles
Douglas Haig becomes British
Commander-in-Chief in France
Edith Cavell executed in Brussels
W.H. and W.L. Bragg share Nobel Prize
for Physics
Ford Madox Ford, *The Good Soldier*
Somerset Maugham, *Of Human Bondage*
Dorothy Richardson, *Pointed Roofs*
(first volume of *Pilgrimage*)

1916

Military Service Act imposes conscription
Battle of Jutland, 31 May
Lord Kitchener drowns when HMS
Hampshire hits a mine, 5 June
Battle of the Somme, 1 July–19 November
David Lloyd George replaces
H.H. Asquith as Prime Minister
Summer Time introduced
James Joyce, *Portrait of the Artist
as a Young Man*
Gustav Holst, *The Planets*

1917

British Royal Family adopts
the name Windsor
Battle of Passchendaele (Third Battle
of Ypres), 31 July–17 November
Leonard and Virginia Woolf establish
the Hogarth Press

1918

Labour Party approves new constitution
British troops intervene in Russia
against Soviet government
Wilfred Owen killed in action
in France, 4 November
Armistice signed, 11 November
David Lloyd George leads coalition to
victory in December "coupon" election
Universal male suffrage and votes
for women over age thirty enacted
Education Act raises school-leaving age
to fourteen
Lytton Strachey, *Eminent Victorians*
Marie Stopes, *Married Love*

1919

Nancy Astor takes seat in Parliament
as first woman MP
British troops massacre Indians at Amritsar
in April
Sankey Commission investigates
the coal industry
London dockers refuse to load munitions
for Poland on the *Jolly George*
John Maynard Keynes, *The Economic
Consequences of the Peace*
George Bernard Shaw, *Hearbreak House*
William Butler Yeats,
The Wild Swans at Coole
Edward Elgar, *Cello Concerto*
Paul Nash, *The Menin Road*

1920

British mandate over Palestine
Government of Ireland Act partitions island
General Council of the Trades Union
Congress formed
Communist Party of Great Britain founded
Women admitted as full members
of the University of Oxford
Medical Research Council chartered
Royal Institute of International Affairs
(Chatham House) begun

Agatha Christie, *The Mysterious Affair*
 at Styles
D.H. Lawrence, *Women in Love*
H.G. Wells, *Outline of History*
Stanley Spencer, *Christ Carrying the Cross*

1921
Parliament approves treaty creating
 Irish Free State
Threatened Triple Alliance strike abandoned
 on Black Friday, 15 April
Frederick Soddy wins Nobel Prize
 for Chemistry
R.H. Tawney, *The Acquisitive Society*

1922
Washington Treaty establishes
 Anglo-American parity in capital ships
Conservatives win November election with
 majority of eighty-eight seats
Andrew Bonar Law replaces David Lloyd
 George as Prime Minister
Transport and General Workers'
 Union founded
Francis Aston wins Nobel Prize
 for Chemistry
Archibald Hill shares Nobel Prize
 for Medicine
New tennis stadium opens at Wimbledon
T.S. Eliot, *The Waste Land*
James Joyce, *Ulysses*
Ludwig Wittgenstein,
 Tractatus Logico-Philosophicus

1923
Stanley Baldwin becomes Prime Minister
 after resignation of Andrew Bonar Law
Conservative Party loses majority
 in December election fought over issue
 of free trade
First Football Association Cup Final played
 at Wembley
John Macleod shares Nobel Prize
 for Medicine
William Butler Yeats wins Nobel Prize
 for Literature
George Bernard Shaw, *Saint Joan*

1924
Ramsay MacDonald becomes Prime Minister
 in first Labour goverment

Britain grants diplomatic recognition
 to Soviet Union in February
John Wheatley's Housing Act increases
 state subsidy for rental housing
Foreign Office publishes Zinoviev Letter,
 25 October
Conservatives win October election with
 majority of 221; Stanley Baldwin
 returns to Downing Street
British Empire Exhibition held at Wembley
British Imperial Airways begins operations
Noel Coward, *The Vortex*
E.M. Forster, *A Passage to India*

1925
Chancellor of the Exchequer Winston
 Churchill restores gold standard
Britain signs Locarno Pact
Government offers subsidy after threat
 of united trade union action on behalf
 of coal miners, Red Friday, 31 July
Samuel Commission on coal
 industry convened
Austen Chamberlain shares Nobel Peace Prize
George Bernard Shaw wins Nobel Prize
 for Literature
T.S. Eliot, "The Hollow Men"
Virginia Woolf, *Mrs. Dalloway*

1926
British Broadcasting Corporation chartered
 as public corporation
Imperial Chemical Industries formed
General Strike, 3-12 May
T.E. Lawrence, *The Seven Pillars of Wisdom*
A.A. Milne, *Winnie the Pooh*
Beatrice Webb, *My Apprenticeship*

1927
Trade Disputes Act bans sympathetic strikes
W.H. Auden and Cecil Day Lewis, eds.
 Oxford Poetry
Rosamond Lehmann, *Dusty Answer*
Virginia Woolf, *To the Lighthouse*

1928
Britain signs General Pact
 for the Renunciation of War
Representation of the People Act concedes
 votes to women at age twenty-one
Scottish Nationalist Party founded

Alexander Fleming discovers penicillin
Owen Richardson wins Nobel Prize
    for Physics
Radclyffe Hall, *The Well of Loneliness*
Aldous Huxley, *Point Counter Point*
D.H. Lawrence, *Lady Chatterley's Lover*
Evelyn Waugh, *Decline and Fall*
William Butler Yeats, *The Tower*

1929
Neville Chamberlain's Local Government Act
    abolishes Poor Law guardians and
    restructures public assistance
Labour emerges as largest party in May
    election; Ramsay MacDonald forms
    second Labour government; Arthur
    Henderson becomes Foreign Secretary
Robert Graves, *Goodbye to All That*
Lewis Namier, *The Structure of Politics
    at the Accession of George III*
J.B. Priestley, *The Good Companions*
I.A. Richards, *Practical Criticism*
R.C. Sherriff, *Journey's End*
Virginia Woolf, *A Room of One's Own*
John Grierson's *Drifters* initiates British
    documentary film movement
Alfred Hitchcock's *Blackmail*,
    the first British talking movie
Henry Moore, *Reclining Figure*

1930
First Round Table Conference on India held
London Naval Conference sets limits
    on cruisers
Pilgrim Trust started with £2 million grant
    from American E.S. Harkness
Siegfried Sassoon,
    Memoirs of an Infantry Officer

1931
Naval force at Invergordon mutinies
    over pay cuts
Second Labour government collapses
    after Cabinet rejects cuts in rate
    of unemployment benefit
Tory-dominated National government
    formed under Ramsay MacDonald;
    confirmed in landslide election victory
    with majority of 497
Ramsay MacDonald expelled
    from Labour Party
Britain abandons gold standard

Statute of Westminster defines
    Dominion status
Vic-Wells Ballet begins performing
    at Sadler's Wells Theatre
Virginia Woolf, *The Waves*
William Walton, *Belshazzar's Feast*
Jacob Epstein, *Genesis*

1932
Disarmament Conference opens at Geneva
    under Arthur Henderson's presidency
Free trade ends as government introduces
    import duties and imperial preference
Lytton Commission on Japanese invasion
    of Manchuria
Independent Labor Party (ILP) disaffiliates
    from Labour Party
Oswald Mosley forms British Union
    of Fascists
John Galsworthy wins Nobel Prize
    for Literature
Edgar Adrian and Charles Sherrington share
    Nobel Prize for Medicine
Shakespeare Memorial Theatre opens
    in Stratford-upon-Avon
Thomas Beecham founds London
    Philharmonic Orchestra
Aldous Huxley, *Brave New World*
John Strachey, *The Coming Struggle
    for Power*
Charles Holden, Senate House,
    University of London

1933
London Passenger Transport Board created
Paul Dirac wins Nobel Prize for Physics
Norman Angell wins Nobel Peace Prize
Oxford Union "King and Country" debate,
    9 February
Vera Brittain, *Testament of Youth*
Walter Greenwood, *Love on the Dole*
Oxford English Dictionary
Alexander Korda,
    The Private Life of Henry VIII

1934
Unemployment Act imposes means test
    on family basis
Britain ceases war debt payments
    to United States
Fascists rally at Olympia, London, 7 June
Road Traffic Act introduces driving tests

Arthur Henderson wins Nobel Peace Prize
Canon Dick Sheppard organizes
    Peace Pledge campaign
SS *Queen Mary* launched
John Christie establishes opera festival
    at Glyndebourne
J.B. Priestley, *English Journey*

1935
Peace Ballot organized by League
    of Nations Union
Stanley Baldwin succeeds Ramsay
    MacDonald as Prime Minister, 7 June
Clement Attlee becomes leader
    of Labour Party
Conservatives win November election;
    National government majority of 247
Cabinet disavows Hoare-Laval Pact
    on Abyssinia
Anthony Eden succeeds Samuel Hoare
    as Foreign Secretary
Government of India Act provides
    for greater provincial autonomy
British Council founded
Allen Lane launches Penguin Books
James Chadwick wins Nobel Prize
    for Physics
T.S. Eliot, *Murder in the Cathedral*
Christopher Isherwood,
    Mr. Norris Changes Trains
Sidney and Beatrice Webb, *Soviet
    Communism: A New Civilisation?*
Alfred Hitchcock, *The Thirty-Nine Steps*

1936
King George V dies on 20 January;
    Edward VIII becomes King
Oswald Mosley leads anti-Jewish
    demonstration in Whitechapel
Britain signs Nonintervention Agreement,
    pledging neutrality in Spain
Ellen Wilkinson leads Jarrow unemployed
    march to London in October
Left Book Club founded by Victor Gollancz,
    Harold Laski, and John Strachey
King Edward VIII abdicates on 11 December;
    George VI becomes King
Henry Dale shares Nobel Prize for Medicine
A.J. Ayer, *Language, Truth, and Logic*
Winifred Holtby, *South Riding*
John Maynard Keynes, *General Theory
    of Employment, Interest, and Money*
Terence Rattigan, *French without Tears*

1937
Neville Chamberlain succeeds Stanley
    Baldwin as Prime Minister in May
Duke of Windsor marries
    Mrs. Wallis Simpson
Matrimonial Causes (Herbert) Act
    extends grounds for divorce
Mass-Observation founded
George Thomson shares Nobel Prize
    for Physics
Walter Haworth shares Nobel Prize
    for Chemistry
Viscount Cecil wins Nobel Peace Prize
W.H. Auden and Christopher Isherwood,
    The Ascent of F6
George Orwell, *The Road to Wigan Pier*
Dorothy L. Sayers, *Gaudy Night*

1938
Anthony Eden resigns as Foreign Secretary
    over appeasement policy
Munich Conference begins, 29 September
Air Raid Precautions (ARP) implemented
    in England
National Marriage Guidance Council
    founded to promote marriage
    and family life
Women's Voluntary Services founded
    by Lady Reading
Edward Hulton launches *Picture Post*
Elizabeth Bowen,
    The Death of the Heart
Graham Greene, *Brighton Rock*
Henry Moore, *Recumbent Figure*

1939
British Overseas Airways Corporation
    (BOAC) founded
Radar stations put in operation
White Paper pledges end to Jewish
    immigration to Palestine
King George VI and Queen Elizabeth visit
    the United States
Evacuation of children from cities begins,
    1 September
Britain declares war on Germany,
    3 September
Myra Hess organizes lunchtime concerts
    in National Gallery
Council for the Encouragement of Music
    and the Arts (CEMA) formed
Christopher Isherwood, *Goodbye to Berlin*
James Joyce, *Finnegans Wake*

Ellen Wilkinson,
   The Town That Was Murdered

Michael Powell and Emeric Pressburger,
   The Life and Death of Colonel Blimp
Henry Moore, *Madonna and Child*

1940
Winston Churchill succeeds Neville
   Chamberlain as Prime Minister, 10 May
British troops evacuate Dunkirk,
   26 May–June 4
Winston Churchill offers France union
   with Britain
Local Defence Volunteers formed
Battle of Britain begins in August;
   London Blitz continues until May 1941
SS *City of Benares* sunk in Atlantic, killing
   seventy-three evacuated children
Coventry bombed in November
Oswald Mosley imprisoned under
   Defence Regulations
"Cato," *Guilty Men*
Graham Greene, *The Power and the Glory*

1941
Virginia Woolf commits suicide,
   28 March
Franklin D. Roosevelt introduces Lend-Lease
Winston Churchill and Franklin D. Roosevelt
   issue Atlantic Charter, 14 August
Britain declares war on Japan, 8 December
Conscription of women introduced
   in December
Michael Tippett, *A Child of Our Time*
Henry Moore, *The Shelter Sketchbook*
Paul Nash, *Totes Meer*

1942
Singapore falls to Japanese forces in February
British win North African victory in Battle
   of El Alamein
Beveridge Report calls for comprehensive
   social services
Cripps mission to India; Mohandas Gandhi
   demands independence
Noel Coward, *In Which We Serve*

1943
British Eighth Army reaches Tripoli
Winston Churchill confers with Franklin
   D. Roosevelt at Casablanca, Quebec,
   Cairo, and Tehran
T.S. Eliot, *Four Quartets*
Humphrey Jennings, *Fires Were Started*

1944
Education Act provides secondary education
   for all in tripartite structure
Allies land in Normandy on D-Day, 6 June
V-2 rockets attack in September
William Beveridge, *Full Employment
   in a Free Society*
Joyce Cary, *The Horse's Mouth*
G.M. Trevelyan, *English Social History*
Francis Bacon, *Three Studies for Figures
   at the Base of a Crucifixion*

1945
British bomb Dresden, 14 February
Montgomery's forces cross Rhine, 23 March
VE-Day, 8 May
Family Allowances Act passed
Labour wins 393 seats in July election
   landslide; Clement Attlee becomes
   Prime Minister
Lend-Lease ends after Japanese surrender;
   John Maynard Keynes negotiates
   American loan
Ernst Chain, Alexander Fleming, and
   Howard Florey share Nobel Prize
   for Medicine for discovery of penicillin
George Orwell, *Animal Farm*
Evelyn Waugh, *Brideshead Revisited*
Benjamin Britten, *Peter Grimes*
Noel Coward, *Brief Encounter*
Laurence Olivier, *Henry V*

1946
National Health Service Act passed
Bank of England, coal, and civil aviation
   nationalized
Anglo-American Palestine Committee favors
   visas for 100,000 Jewish immigrants
Britain Can Make It Exhibition held
Sadler's Wells Ballet reopens Covent Garden
   with *The Sleeping Beauty*
Arts Council of Great Britain established
   by Royal Charter
British Broadcasting Corporation (BBC)
   Third Programme begins broadcasting
Cabinet mission to India fails to reconcile
   communal divisions
Burma gains independence

Frederick Ashton, *Symphonic Variations*
(for Sadler's Wells Ballet)

1947

Convertibility of sterling restored in July
Indian independence proclaimed on
August 15; communal strife compels
partition into India and Pakistan
Town and Country Planning Act applies
planning control to entire country
Railways nationalized
Edinburgh International Festival launched
Edward Appleton wins Nobel Prize
for Physics
Robert Robinson wins Nobel Prize
for Chemistry

1948

Bread rationing ends
Marshall Plan begins
Representation of the People Act abolishes
university seats and plural voting
University of Cambridge admits women
to degrees
London Olympiad held
P.M.S. Blackett wins Nobel Prize for Physics
T.S. Eliot wins Nobel Prize for Literature
F.R. Leavis, *The Great Tradition*
Terence Rattigan, *The Winslow Boy*
Michael Powell and Emeric Pressburger,
The Red Shoes

1949

Britain joins North Atlantic
Treaty Organization
Britain devalues pound from $4.03 to $2.80
John Boyd Orr wins Nobel Peace Prize
Elizabeth Bowen, *The Heat of the Day*
Christopher Fry,
The Lady's Not for Burning
George Orwell, *Nineteen Eighty-Four*
Carol Reed, *The Third Man*
Henry Moore, *Family Group*

1950

Labour wins February election
with majority of six seats
British join United States in Korean War
Bertrand Russell wins Nobel Prize
for Literature
T.S. Eliot, *The Cocktail Party*

1951

Aneurin Bevan and Harold Wilson resign
from Cabinet over imposition of health
service charges
Festival of Britain held
Labour outpolls Conservatives but loses
October election; Winston Churchill re-
places Clement Attlee as Prime Minister
Guy Burgess and Donald Maclean defect
to Soviet Union
John Cockcroft shares Nobel Prize for Physics
Benjamin Britten, *Billy Budd*
Anthony Powell, *A Question of Upbringing*
(first volume in *A Dance to the Music
of Time* series)
C.P. Snow, *The Masters*
The Archers first broadcast
on Light Programme
Robert Matthew and Leslie Martin,
Royal Festival Hall

1952

King George VI dies; Elizabeth II
becomes Queen
British atomic bomb announced
Archer Martin and Richard Synge share
Nobel Prize for Chemistry
Samuel Beckett, *Waiting for Godot*
Agatha Christie, *The Mousetrap*
Evelyn Waugh, *Men at Arms* (first volume
of *Sword of Honour* trilogy)

1953

Edmund Hillary climbs Mt. Everest
Winston Churchill wins Nobel Prize
for Literature
Hans Krebs shares Nobel Prize for Medicine
L.P. Hartley, *The Go-Between*

1954

Commercial television begins in Britain
Max Born shares Nobel Prize for Physics
Roger Bannister breaks four-minute
mile record
Kingsley Amis, *Lucky Jim*
William Golding, *Lord of the Flies*
Dylan Thomas, *Under Milk Wood*

1955

Winston Churchill retires in April; Anthony
Eden becomes Prime Minister

Conservatives increase majority in May
    election to fifty-eight seats
Hugh Gaitskell elected leader of
    Labour Party on Clement Attlee's
    retirement
British forces battle EOKA in Cyprus
Mary Quant opens boutique
    in King's Road, Chelsea
Michael Tippett,
    The Midsummer Marriage

1956
Suez crisis erupts
Cyril Inshelwood shares Nobel Prize
    for Chemistry
Anthony Crosland,
    The Future of Socialism
John Osborne, *Look Back in Anger*
Angus Wilson, *Anglo-Saxon Attitudes*

1957
Anthony Eden resigns in January; Harold
    Macmillan becomes Prime Minister
Britain explodes thermonuclear bomb
    in central Pacific
Wolfenden Report on homosexuality
    and prostitution issued
Ghana becomes independent
Archbishop Makarios released from
    imprisonment
Alexander Todd wins Nobel Prize
    for Chemistry
Lawrence Durrell, *Justine* (first volume
    of *The Alexandria Quartet*)
Richard Hoggart, *The Uses of Literacy*
John Osborne, *The Entertainer*
David Lean, *The Bridge on the River
    Kwai*

1958
Campaign for Nuclear
    Disarmament launched
First Aldermaston march for nuclear
    disarmament
Notting Hill riots
Life peerages introduced
Frederick Sanger wins Nobel Prize
    for Chemistry
Alan Sillitoe, *Saturday Night
    and Sunday Morning*
Raymond Williams, *Culture and Society*
Henry Moore, *Reclining Figure*

1959
Harold Macmillan leads Conservatives
    to third straight electoral victory
    in October
Hugh Gaitskell challenges Clause Four
    of Labour constitution
Obscene Publications Act limits censorship
Alex Issigonis introduces Mini car
Philip Noel-Baker wins Nobel Peace Prize
John Arden, *Sergeant Musgrave's Dance*
Boulting Brothers, *I'm All Right Jack*

1960
Macmillan government abandons British
    ballistic missile, Blue Streak
Agreement allows United States
    to use Holy Loch for Polaris missiles
Military conscription ends
European Free Trade Area formed
Cyprus and Nigeria become independent
Obscenity trial of *Lady Chatterley's Lover*
Peter Medawar shares Nobel Prize
    for Medicine
New Left Review founded
Olivia Manning, *The Great Fortune*
    (first volume of *The Balkan Trilogy*)
Alan Bennett, Jonathan Miller et al.,
    Beyond the Fringe
Robert Bolt, *A Man for All Seasons*
Harold Pinter, *The Caretaker*

1961
Britain's application to join Common
    Market rebuffed by French President
    Charles DeGaulle
South Africa expelled
    from Commonwealth
University of Sussex opens
Espionage trials of Gordon Lonsdale,
    George Blake, and the Krogers
Iris Murdoch, *A Severed Head*
Muriel Spark, *The Prime of Miss Jean
    Brodie*

1962
Commonwealth Immigrant Act restricts
    entry to Britain
Conservatives lose Orpington by-election
National Economic Development Council
    (Neddy) sets targets for economic growth
John Kendrew and Max Perutz share
    Nobel Prize for Chemistry

Francis Crick, Maurice Wilkins,
   and American James Watson share
   Nobel Prize for Medicine for research
   on structure of DNA
Coronation Street television serial begins
Anthony Burgess, *A Clockwork Orange*
Doris Lessing, *The Golden Notebook*
Arnold Wesker, *Chips with Everything*
Benjamin Britten, *War Requiem*
Basil Spence, University of Sussex
   and Coventry Cathedral

1963
Hugh Gaitskell dies; Harold Wilson elected
   Labour leader
Kim Philby granted asylum in Soviet Union
Profumo scandal rocks Tory government
Harold Macmillan resigns as Prime Minister;
   Alec Douglas-Home succeeds him
Robbins Report on higher education issued
Kenya becomes independent
Alan Hodgkin and Andrew Huxley share
   Nobel Prize for Medicine
John Le Carré, *The Spy Who Came
   in from the Cold*
E.P. Thompson, *The Making of the English
   Working Class*
Joan Littlewood, *Oh What a Lovely War*

1964
Labour wins general election with majority
   of four seats; Harold Wilson becomes
   Prime Minister
Mods and Rockers battle at seaside resorts
Dorothy Hodgkin wins Nobel Prize
   for Chemistry
Terence Conran opens first Habitat store
Philip Larkin, *The Whitsun Weddings*
Peter Shaffer,
   The Royal Hunt of the Sun
Barbara Hepworth, *Single Form*
Peter and Alison Smithson, *The Economist*
   building, London

1965
Winston Churchill dies at age ninety,
   24 January
Edward Heath elected Conservative
   Party leader
Labour government promotes
   comprehensive secondary schools
Death penalty abolished

Race Relations Act tackles discrimination
   and racism
Ian Smith issues Unilateral Declaration
   of Independence in Rhodesia
Universities of Kent and Warwick open
Edward Bond, *Saved*
Kenneth MacMillan, *Romeo and Juliet*
   (for Royal Ballet)

1966
Labour increases majority to ninety-six
   in March election
England defeats West Germany to win
   World Cup in football
Paul Scott, *The Jewel in the Crown*
   (first volume of *The Raj Quartet*)
Tom Stoppard, *Rosencrantz and
   Guildenstern Are Dead*
Richard Seifert, Centrepoint Tower, London

1967
Abortion legalized
Sexual Offences Act decriminalizes
   homosexuality
Wilson government's application to join
   Common Market rejected
Pound devalued
Milton Keynes designated as a New Town
Ronald Norrish and George Porter share
   Nobel Prize for Chemistry
Alan Ayckbourn, *Relatively Speaking*
The Beatles, *Sergeant Pepper's Lonely Hearts
   Club Band*

1968
Restrictions imposed on immigration from
   India, Pakistan, and West Indies
Civil rights marches held in Ulster

1969
Voting qualification lowered to age eighteen
Employment Secretary Barbara Castle issues
   In Place of Strife White Paper on
   industrial relations
British send troops to Londonderry and
   Belfast
Divorce Act abandons principle of marital
   fault
Open University founded
Student unrest temporarily closes London
   School of Economics

Rupert Murdoch acquires the *Sun*
Derek Barton shares Nobel Prize
    for Chemistry
Samuel Beckett wins Nobel Prize
    for Literature
John Fowles,
    The French Lieutenant's Woman

1970
Labour defeated in June election; Edward
    Heath becomes Prime Minister
Conservative government introduces
    internment without trial in Ulster
Bernard Katz shares Nobel Prize
    for Medicine

1971
Industrial Relations Act passed
Dennis Gabor wins Nobel Prize
    for Physics

1972
Coal strike lasts forty-seven days
Northern Ireland government at Stormont
    suspended; replaced by direct rule
    from Westminster
Rodney Porter shares Nobel Prize
    for Medicine
John Hicks shares Nobel Prize
    for Economics

1973
Britain joins European Economic Community
Sunningdale Agreement proposes
    power-sharing arrangement in Ulster
Brian Josephson shares Nobel Prize
    for Physics
Geoffrey Wilkinson shares Nobel Prize
    for Chemistry
Nikolaas Tinbergen shares Nobel Prize
    for Medicine
Alan Ayckbourn, *The Norman Conquests*

1974
Miners strike in February; three-day work
    week imposed to save power
Conservatives defeated in February election;
    Harold Wilson returns as Prime Minister
Labour wins October general election by
    narrow majority

Martin Ryle and Antony Hewish share Nobel
    Prize for Physics

1975
Margaret Thatcher succeeds Edward Heath
    as Conservative leader
First North Sea oil production
Referendum on membership in European
    Economic Community
David Lodge, *Changing Places*
Anthony Powell, *Hearing Secret Harmonies*
    (concluding volume of *A Dance
    to the Music of Time* series)

1976
Harold Wilson retires; James Callaghan
    becomes Prime Minister
Denys Lasdun's National Theatre opens
    on London's South Bank

1977
Lib-Lab (Liberal-Labour) pact in House
    of Commons
Nevill Mott shares Nobel Prize for Physics
James Meade shares Nobel Prize
    for Economics
Margaret Drabble, *The Ice Age*

1978
Scottish and Welsh Devolution Acts passed
Peter Mitchell wins Nobel Prize
    for Chemistry
David Hare, *Plenty*
Kenneth MacMillan, *Mayerling*
    (for Royal Ballet)

1979
Referendums on Scottish and Welsh
    devolution fail to win sufficient votes
Winter of Discontent: public service strikes
Conservative election victory in May;
    Margaret Thatcher becomes
    Prime Minister
Lord Mountbatten assassinated by Irish
    Republican Army (IRA) terrorists,
    27 August
Geoffrey Hounsfield shares Nobel Prize
    for Medicine
Arthur Lewis shares Nobel Prize
    for Economics

1980

Michael Heseltine's Housing Act promotes
   sale of council housing
James Callaghan resigns as Labour leader;
   Michael Foot replaces him
Zimbabwe becomes independent under
   leadership of Robert Mugabe

1981

Social Democratic Party founded; Shirley
   Williams wins Crosby by-election
Urban riots in Brixton, Southall, Toxteth
D.M. Thomas, *The White Hotel*
David Puttnam, *Chariots of Fire*

1982

Britain wages Falklands War against
   Argentina, May–June
Employment Act outlaws secondary strikes
   and restricts closed shops
Channel Four established as second
   commercial television channel
Terrence Higgins Trust launched to provide
   support for people with AIDS
John Vane shares Nobel Prize for Medicine

1983

Falklands factor helps Conservatives win
   June general election with 144-seat
   majority despite mounting
   unemployment
Neil Kinnock elected Labour leader
   in October
Graham Swift, *Waterland*

1984

Miners strike
British Telecom privatized
Urban riots in Handsworth, Brixton,
   and Toxteth
Hillsborough Agreement in Ulster calls
   for Anglo-Irish consultation
Richard Stone wins Nobel Prize
   for Economics
Julian Barnes, *Flaubert's Parrot*

1986

Local Government Act abolishes
   metropolitan authorities, including
   Greater London Council (GLC)

Michael Heseltine resigns from Cabinet
   over Westland affair
Big Bang in City of London, 27 October
British Gas privatized
The Independent begins publication
Andrew Lloyd Webber,
   The Phantom of the Opera
Richard Rogers, Lloyd's Bank building

1987

Margaret Thatcher continues in office
   as Conservatives win third
   straight election
Britain signs Single European Act
Margaret Drabble, *The Radiant Way*
Penelope Lively, *Moon Tiger*
James Stirling, Clore Gallery

1988

Community Charge ("poll tax") enacted
Section 28 of Local Government Act bans
   promotion of homosexuality
Social Democrats merge with Liberal Party
   to form Liberal Democrats
James Black shares Nobel Prize for Medicine
Stephen Hawking, *A Brief History of Time*
Salman Rushdie, *The Satanic Verses*

1989

House of Commons sessions televised
   for first time
Kazuo Ishiguro, *The Remains of the Day*

1990

Anti-poll-tax riots in London
Margaret Thatcher fails to defeat Michael
   Heseltine's leadership challenge in
   November, resigns prime ministership
   after eleven-year tenure
John Major wins Tory leadership on second
   ballot to become Prime Minister
A.S. Byatt, *Possession*
Robert Venturi, Sainsbury Wing
   of National Gallery
Canary Wharf, Docklands, First Phase

1992

John Major leads Conservatives to fourth
   straight election victory in April with
   reduced majority of twenty-one

John Smith replaces Neil Kinnock
as Labour leader
Church of England votes to ordain women
as priests
Queen Elizabeth II voluntarily agrees
to pay tax on private income
Prince and Princess of Wales separate
after eleven years of marriage

1993
Parliament ratifies Maastricht treaty
on European unity

Anglo-Irish Peace Declaration
in Northern Ireland

1994
Channel Tunnel opens
Multiracial government under Nelson
Mandela elected in South Africa,
applies to rejoin Commonwealth
Labour Party leader John Smith dies;
Tony Blair becomes leader
Conservatives suffer defeats in local
government and European elections
IRA declares truce in Northern Ireland

Abbreviations

BBC	British Broadcasting Corporation
CBE	Commander of the Order of the British Empire
CEMA	Council for the Encouragement of Music and the Arts
CH	Companion of Honour
CND	Campaign for Nuclear Disarmament
CPGB	Communist Party of Great Britain
DBE	Dame Commander of the Order of the British Empire
DORA	Defence of the Realm Act
EC	European Community
ENSA	Entertainments National Service Association
EU	European Union
FRS	Fellow of the Royal Society
GCE	General Certificate of Education
GLC	Greater London Council
ICA	Institute of Contemporary Arts
ICI	Imperial Chemical Industries
ILEA	Inner London Education Authority
ILP	Independent Labour Party
IRA	Irish Republican Army
ITA	Independent Television Authority
KC	King's Counsel
LCC	London County Council
LSE	London School of Economics and Political Science
MI5	Security Service
MI6	Secret Intelligence Service
MP	Member of Parliament
MRC	Medical Research Council
NATO	North Atlantic Treaty Organization
NCF	No-Conscription Fellowship
NEC	National Executive Committee of the Labour Party
NFRB	New Fabian Research Bureau
NHS	National Health Service
NUM	National Union of Mineworkers
NUR	National Union of Railwaymen
PC	Privy Councillor
OM	Order of Merit
QC	Queen's Counsel
RIBA	Royal Institute of British Architects
SDP	Social Democratic Party

SSIP   Society for Socialist Inquiry and Propaganda
T&GWU   Transport and General Workers' Union
TUC   Trades Union Congress
UDC   Union of Democratic Control
UGC   University Grants Committee
UNESCO   United Nations Economic and Social Council
WSPU   Women's Social and Political Union

The Encyclopedia

A

Abortion

English abortion law is based on theological belief, and late abortion was always condemned on grounds that a fetus was a human life created by God. The stage at which the fetus was thought to be infused with God's spirit has, however, been a subject of controversy over the centuries. In 1803 abortion became an offense from the time of conception, but it was more severely punished after quickening in the second half of pregnancy. In 1861 the Offenses Against the Person Act was passed. This act made attempted abortion at any stage a felony, with a uniform maximum punishment of life imprisonment. There were subsequent minor changes to abortion legislation, notably the 1929 Infant Life Preservation Act, which made it an offense, except to save the life of the mother, to destroy the life of a child "capable of being born alive," presumed to be at around twenty-eight weeks' gestation.

The practice of abortion continued to grow and reached epidemic proportions by the early twentieth century. In 1933 nearly 500 women were officially stated to have died in England and Wales as a result of abortion, a figure recognized in the Chief Medical Officer's report for that year to be an underestimate. The social stigma attached to the subject ensured its systematic underreporting. The Abortion Law Reform Association was founded in 1936 by a group of radical women who campaigned to legalize abortion in the interests of the health and welfare of women. The following year the British Medical Association established a committee on abortion that also recommended reform of the law. In 1938 a celebrated trial took place after Aleck Bourne, an eminent gynecologist, carried out an abortion on a fourteen-year-old girl who had been raped by two soldiers. In that case, *Rex v. Bourne,* the judge ruled that abortion was lawful if the woman would otherwise die. He also argued that abortion might be lawful if a woman's health were so adversely affected as to endanger her life. The government, under heavy pressure, set up its own inquiry, the Birkett Committee, which reported in 1939, recommending a measure of abortion law reform. Several subsequent legal cases seemed to confirm the legality of abortion to preserve the mental or physical health of the mother.

After the Second World War reformers became politically active in promoting private members' legislation in the House of Commons with the aim of obtaining clear statute law in this field. There were six such attempts between 1952 and 1965 to reform the abortion laws, all successfully resisted by **Roman Catholic** members of Parliament (MPs), who used all available parliamentary procedures to defeat reform. In 1967, however, David Steel, MP, with the assistance of Lord Silkin in the **House of Lords**, piloted the 1967 Abortion Reform Act to a successful conclusion. The act permits legal abortion in England, Wales, and Scotland where it is necessary to preserve the mental or physical health of the pregnant woman, where a child would otherwise be born seriously handicapped, or where an additional child would affect adversely the health of the existing children of the family (the "medico-social" clause). The time limit was derived from the Infant Life Preservation Act and was generally taken to be about twenty-eight weeks' gestation.

During the next twenty-five years Roman Catholic MPs, other MPs representing largely Roman Catholic constituencies, and right-wing **Conservative** MPs made twenty unsuccessful attempts to amend, limit, or destroy the Abortion Act, using all possible parliamentary procedural devices. In 1990 the Human Fertilisation and Embryology Act was passed to regulate multiple births. One of its clauses (Clause 37) slightly amended the 1967 Abortion Act. Abortion where the woman's life or health was at stake or where the child would be born handicapped was now legal without gestation limit (as it had always been in Scotland). Other abortions were now legal only within the first twenty-four weeks of gestation. Since nonurgent abortions had hardly ever been performed after twenty-four weeks, the practical effect of this amendment was negligible.

Legal abortions in Britain as a whole (excluding Northern Ireland, where the Abortion Act does not apply) rose from 90,000 in 1970, to 170,000 in 1980, to nearly 200,000 in 1990. This included 11,000, 32,000, and 14,000 Irish and foreign women in those years, respectively, who came to Britain for legal and safe abortions they were unable to obtain in their own countries where abortion was still illegal or difficult to obtain. These numbers declined as countries overseas reformed their own abortion laws. Before the Abortion Act, estimates of the extent of illegal abortions in Britain varied from 40,000 a year to 250,000 a year, with the government accepting a likely figure of about 100,000 a year. Whether there really are more abortions now than in the past, allowing for population growth, is a subject of some controversy. Illegal abortion seems to have been eliminated, and there are now no deaths from this cause. Nearly 90 percent of women who obtain abortions obtain them in the first trimester of pregnancy. Half obtain them free within the National Health Service. Others pay to obtain them in one of seventy private clinics that are licensed to carry out abortions. There are also nonprofit consumer-oriented agencies that run their own clinics subject to government inspection.

It seems likely that attacks will continue to be made on the Abortion Act by extremist pressure groups but with diminishing parliamentary support. Public opinion surveys over many years have shown that between two-thirds and three-quarters of all electors support liberal abortion legislation. In the 1990s it is likely that parliamentary attempts will be made to align the abortion law in Northern Ireland with that in the rest of the United Kingdom.

Madeleine Simms

Bibliography

Brookes, Barbara. *Abortion in England, 1900–1967.* 1988.

Hindell, Keith, and Madeleine Simms. *Abortion Law Reformed.* 1971.

HMSO. *Report of the Inter-Departmental Committee on Abortion* (Birkett Report). 1939.

Office of Population Censuses and Surveys. *Abortion Statistics,* series AB, no. 17. 1990.

Williams, Glanville. *The Sanctity of Life and the Criminal Law.* 1958.

Abyssinian Crisis (1935–1936)

Italy invaded Abyssinia on 3 October 1935, using a minor border incident at Walwal as a pretext. The appeals of the Abyssinian Emperor Haile Selassie for protection under the Covenant of the **League of Nations** turned a local, colonial dispute into a major international crisis. Anxious to retain Italy as an ally against Hitler's Germany, Britain and France pursued a policy of making territorial concessions in the vain hope of appeasing the Fascist dictator Benito Mussolini. The Abyssinian crisis represented a singular defeat for the League and the first notable act of **appeasement**.

More than a year before the Italian invasion of Abyssinia a firm stand by Mussolini had thwarted a Nazi takeover of Austria. In early 1935 France and Italy agreed to condemn German rearmament and to guarantee the independence of Austria. Three months later Britain, France, and Italy met at Stresa, Italy, to form an anti-German front. Britain's silence on the issue of Abyssinia at the conference convinced Mussolini that he had a free hand in Africa.

The events leading to the crisis coincided with the release of the results of the controversial **Peace Ballot** in Britain. More than 11 million people participated, with 10 million voting to endorse the League and support economic sanctions if one nation attacked another. After the offer of concessions was rejected by Mussolini, the British government moved unenthusiastically to embrace the League in order to pacify public opinion in an election year. Behind the scenes Foreign Secretary **Sir Samuel Hoare** made it clear to Mussolini that Britain rejected the use of force or the closure of the Suez Canal to stop Italy. Driven by his dreams of creating another Roman Empire and desiring military success to heighten his international reputation, Mussolini was set on war.

The full-scale invasion of Abyssinia prompted the League to vote for limited sanctions. Mussolini threatened war if the vital flow of oil were placed under embargo. Hoare and his French counterpart, Pierre Laval, concluded the **Hoare-Laval Pact** (1935) in December, proposing to turn more than half of Abyssinia over to Italy. After details of the agreement were leaked to the French press, a public outcry in Britain coupled with a **Conservative** revolt in Parliament forced the British **Cabinet** to repudiate the plan and ask for Hoare's resignation. German reoccupation of the Rhineland (March 1936) diverted attention from Abyssinia, enabling the Italians to complete the conquest of Abyssinia by May. League sanctions were discontinued by midsummer.

The Abyssinian crisis shattered the illusion that the League of Nations was capable of maintaining international order. The principle of collective security lay in ruins. Encouraged by the weakness of the Western democracies, Germany and Italy increasingly relied on force to destroy the post-war order based on the League and the Versailles settlement. The Abyssinian crisis was one of the most significant steps on the road to the Second World War.

Van Michael Leslie

Bibliography
Baer, George W. *The Coming of the Italian-Ethiopian War*. 1967.
Chukumba, Stephen U. *The Big Powers against Ethiopia: Anglo-French-American Maneuvers during the Italo-Ethiopian Dispute, 1934–1938*. 1977.
Hardie, Frank M. *The Abyssinian Crisis*. 1974.
Parker, R.A.C. "Great Britain, France, and the Ethiopian Crisis, 1935–1936," *English Historical Review*, vol. 89 (1974), pp. 293–332.
Waley, Daniel. *British Public Opinion and the Abyssinian War*. 1975.

Actors and Acting

British acting was dominated until the mid-1950s by actors who had made their names playing the great Shakespearean roles, although, in fact, the end of the actor-manager tradition, which had sustained most of the great Shakespearean actors since the eighteenth century, was signaled by the death of Sir Henry Irving in 1903. While flamboyant and eccentric personalities like Sir Herbert Beerbohm Tree and Mrs. Patrick Campbell were the stars of the Edwardian theater, younger actors like Harley Granville Barker (1877–1946), Lillah McCarthy (1875–1960), and Sir Lewis Casson (1875–1969) developed simpler and more colloquial acting styles in response to the new drama of Henrik Ibsen (1828–1906) and **George Bernard Shaw**, which they championed for its progressive views of society and art.

The work of the actor-manager Sir Frank Benson and the scholar William Poel had a major impact on the actor-centered, less spectacular Shakespeare productions at the **Old Vic**, which under the forceful management of **Lilian Baylis** between 1914 and 1937 became the breeding ground of the first generation of twentieth-century British theater stars. The early reputations of Dame Sybil Thorndike (1882–1976), Dame Gwen Ffrangçon-Davies (1896–1992), Sir John Gielgud (1904–), Sir Ralph Richardson (1902–83), Dame Peggy Ashcroft (1907–91), **Sir Laurence (Lord) Olivier**, and Sir Michael Redgrave (1908–85) were made in Old Vic productions; Dame Edith Evans (1888–1976), Charles Laughton (1899–1962), Dame Flora Robson (1902–84), Sir Alec Guinness (1914–), Paul Scofield (1922–), Richard Burton (1925–84), and many others achieved prestige through their appearances at the Old Vic.

Gielgud's first great success in Shakespeare was as Richard II (1929) at the Old Vic. He consolidated his reputation as the leading poetic actor of his generation with his great Hamlet (1930), a role he repeated several times until 1946 with enormous success. Gielgud is regarded as the finest verse speaker in the English language, excelling in roles that allow him to express his sensitivity, wit, and vocal agility. In the late 1960s he embarked on a career as a character actor in film and television, employing his patrician manner and brilliant timing to create cameos of rare distinction. The only real challenge to Gielgud's preeminence came from Olivier, a more virile and romantic actor, who was always determined to be as much an international film star as a great classical actor. A master of physical disguise, Olivier excelled in full-blooded impersonations of Romeo, Henry V, Macbeth, Coriolanus, Titus Andronicus, Richard III, and Othello. His vigorous style of vocal delivery was matched by his athleticism and charm. The very successful films of *Ham-*

let, *Henry V*, and *Richard III*, which he directed and in which he starred, popularized Shakespeare for a cinema-going public.

Together with Richardson and John Burrell, he ran the Old Vic between 1944 and 1949 and became the first Director of the **National Theatre** (1963–73). His performance as the seedy music hall comedian Archie Rice in *The Entertainer* made him the first actor of his generation to embrace the new drama of the 1950s. Troubled by ill health in the last seventeen years of his life, he continued to play major roles on film and **television**.

Richardson is usually regarded as the third in the triumvirate of preeminent male actors. Possessed of an endearingly eccentric stage persona, he had a unique gift for investing the character of the average man with transcendent qualities of spirit or imagination that brilliantly complemented the talents of his two peers.

Without doubt, Edith Evans and Peggy Ashcroft were the two greatest female stars of this generation. While Evans excelled at portraying upper-class characters who were either witty or poignant in their inability directly to express their feelings, Ashcroft's apparently artless performances were unparalleled in their capacity to illuminate the soul of a character, whether beautiful or malignant.

Sir Donald Wolfit (1902–68) was a barnstorming eccentric whose heroic performances as a touring actor-manager occasionally achieved greatness. Redgrave and Guinness both learned a great deal from working with Gielgud in the 1930s. Redgrave, a handsome and intelligent actor who projected a quality of understated emotionalism, was a popular film star in the 1940s and 1950s. Guinness was a subtle character actor whose dry and self-effacing personality was unrecognizable beneath the mask of a given role. This talent, making him one of the most versatile actors in British films of the 1950s, guaranteed him enormous success in Hollywood films since the 1960s. One of the greatest actors to work at the Old Vic in the 1930s was Charles Laughton, an imaginative character actor of extraordinary intensity, who became the most successful British film star of his day in Hollywood. The most glamorous British star to achieve success in the classical theater and in Hollywood films was Vivien Leigh (1913–67), who acted opposite her husband, Olivier, between 1937 and 1956.

Paul Scofield and Richard Burton appeared in the 1950s as the natural heirs of Gielgud and Olivier: Each possessed a beautiful voice and fine physique, but although each gave a number of brilliant performances on stage and film, neither seemed able to sustain the consistent level of achievement of their predecessors.

The "throwaway" style of witty understated acting characteristic of West End commercial theater was perfected by Sir Gerald du Maurier (1873–1934) and given a tone of clipped 1920s modishness by **Sir Noel Coward** and his costar Gertrude Lawrence (1898–1952). Coward's plays and his persona exerted a great influence on actors and playwrights until the 1950s, establishing a tradition of stiff-upper-lip reticence that was developed in films and television drama to produce the reserved and subtle naturalism characteristic of contemporary British television acting. Among the stars of British films who had mastered this understated style between 1930 and 1960 were Robert Donat, Celia Johnson, Trevor Howard, Sir Rex Harrison, Sir John Mills, Dame Wendy Hiller, Dirk Bogarde, Glynis Johns, Richard Todd, Laurence Harvey, Kenneth More, and Sir Richard Attenborough.

Britain has always had a strong tradition of comic actors, most of whom have performed successfully in legitimate theater and revue, on radio, film, and television. Among the most memorable are Dame Margaret Rutherford, Alastair Sim, Hermione Gingold, Hermione Baddeley, Beatrice Lillie, Joyce Grenfell, Peter Ustinov, Norman Wisdom, Robert Morley, Kenneth Williams, Beryl Reid, Peter Sellers, Peter Cook, Dudley Moore, John Cleese, Rik Mayall, Rowan Atkinson, and Stephen Fry.

Another tradition of serious acting reflecting a more egalitarian approach to social class was created in the wake of the "Royal Court revolution" of 1956 by young actors whose acting became associated with the work of contemporary dramatists (on stage and screen). Among those who achieved fame in the 1960s the most enduring have been Albert Finney, Peter O'Toole, Joan Plowright, Alan Bates, and Tom Courtenay.

Since the early 1960s inheritors of the great tradition of classical acting have usually come to prominence through the **Royal Shakespeare Company** or the National Theatre, although most modern British actors now establish their reputations with the public by appearing in television drama, which has consequently had a great impact on contemporary acting styles. Among the actors who achieved star status during Olivier's regime at the National are Dame Maggie Smith, Sir Anthony Hopkins, Sir Derek Jacobi, and Sir Robert Stephens; those who established or consolidated their reputations with the Royal Shakespeare Company include Vanessa Redgrave, Dorothy Tutin, Ian Holm, Dame Judi Dench, Sir Ian McKellan, Glenda Jackson, Janet Suzman, Alan Howard, Michael Gambon, Jeremy Irons, Antony Sher, Brian Cox, and Kenneth Branagh.

Robert Gordon

Bibliography

Barnes, Philip. *A Companion to Post-War British Theatre.* 1986.
Burton, Hal, ed. *Great Acting.* 1967.
Findlater, Richard. *These Our Actors.* 1983.
Gielgud, John. *An Actor and His Time.* 1979.
Tynan, Kenneth. *A View of the English Stage.* 1984.
Wardle, Irving. *The Theatres of George Devine.* 1979.

Adult Education

Many Victorian centers for adult education continued their work into the twentieth century. In **London** the Working Men's College (founded 1854) and Morley College (1889) have survived to the present day; and Leicester's Working Men's College (1862) became Vaughan College, the extramural center of Leicester University College. Some cooperative societies carried on their tradition of devoting up to 2.5 percent of their profits to libraries, lectures, and other education services, although most branches spent little or nothing. The YMCA provided reading rooms, extension courses, lectures, and (during the **First World War**) army education. The National Home Reading Union (founded 1889) assisted autodidacts with reading lists and discussion circles. Victorian **Quakers** had taught basic literacy through their Adult Schools; after 1899 the movement became more interdenominational and turned to teaching literature, current events, sports, arts, and crafts.

Every twentieth-century venture in adult education consciously strove to overcome the failure of the mechanics' institutes and the university extension movement to attract large numbers of working people. One of the more successful efforts was the Workers' Educational Association (WEA), created by Albert Mansbridge (1876–1952) in 1903, and governed jointly by committees of academics and work-ers. The pride of the WEA was the innovative tutorial class, first taught with brilliant success by **R.H. Tawney** at Longton and Rochdale in 1908. These three-year courses strove to attain a university-level schedule of reading and essay writing. The WEA also offered shorter courses and university summer schools, and from 1919 it provided classes for organized labor through the Workers' Educational Trade Union Committee.

In 1916 Mansbridge set up the Central Library for Students (later renamed the National Central Library) to loan out textbooks for adult classes. He went on to launch the World Association for Adult Education (1918) and the British Institute of Adult Education (1921). He founded as well the Seafarers' Education Service (1919), which offered libraries for merchant ships and, via the College of the Sea (1938), tutoring by mail for sailors.

In 1899 two Americans, Walter Vrooman and Charles Beard, set up Ruskin College at **Oxford** to provide residential correspondence courses for working men. Some Marxist students at Ruskin, fearing that the college would fall under the control of the neighboring capitalist university, organized the Plebs League in 1908. The following year they staged a student strike and set up their own Central Labour College, which relocated to London in 1911. By 1921 the Plebs League had organized its local branches into the National Council of Labour Colleges. These groups offered a strictly Marxist program of classes, lectures, and correspondence courses explicitly designed to prepare workers for class warfare; and they continually attacked Ruskin College and the WEA for their more liberal approach to education.

Perhaps the most impressive ventures in worker-run adult education were the miners' institutes, which blossomed in the South Wales coalfields between 1890 and 1920. Though assisted by mine owners and local authorities, they were funded primarily by deductions from miners' wages and, after 1920, by the Miners' Welfare Fund. There were more than 100 such institutes by the Second World War, when the Tredegar Workmen's Institute (founded 1861) was offering courses, lectures, celebrity concerts; debating, theatrical, choral, operatic, and film societies; and a library issuing 100,000 volumes a year. By the 1970s most miners' institutes had fallen victim to the decline of the coal industry, competition from public libraries, and television.

A

Toynbee Hall, opened as the world's first **settlement** house in 1884, sponsored concerts, classes, literary societies, and (from 1901) the Whitechapel Art Gallery. By 1914 there were at least forty-six settlement houses in the United Kingdom, most of them offering courses for slum dwellers. Nonresidential settlements specifically devoted to education began in 1909 with Swarthmore in Leeds and St. Mary's in York. By 1918 there were also ten residential educational settlements in the Midlands and northern counties, including Woodbrooke (1903) and Fircroft (1909). Wales would be served by Coleg Harlech (1927), Scotland by Newbattle Abbey (1937). Hillcroft (1920) was the first residential college for working women.

Local Education Authorities (LEAs) subsidized university extension and WEA courses, and awarded adult bursaries and scholarships. They had their own Evening Institutes, which mainly offered classes in vocational subjects, crafts, homemaking, and athletics. The liberal arts were available as well, through such institutions as London's City Literary Institute. Some LEAs set up residential colleges, among them Grantley Hall (1949) and Wrea Head (1950).

The Women's Institutes, which emerged during the First World War, had almost a half-million members by 1953. The institutes brought lectures and classes to rural areas, and sponsored dance, music, and drama groups. Their urban counterparts, the Townswomen's Guilds (1929), had a more feminist slant.

The University College of Hull set up the first department of adult education in 1928. By 1939 most English universities had a full-time director or department of extramural studies, usually working in cooperation with the WEA.

The universities and the WEA both contributed greatly to **army education** during the **Second World War**. The Army Educational Corps, a tiny unit in peacetime, was expanded enormously. The Army Bureau of Current Affairs (ABCA), begun in August 1941, introduced libraries, educational films, and compulsory classes for His Majesty's Forces. Leftist instructors and Conservative officers alike complained of political bias in the curriculum, and the large soldiers' vote for **Labour** in 1945 has been partly attributed to ABCA discussion sessions on post-war reconstruction.

The **British Broadcasting Corporation** **(BBC)** had experimented with educational broadcasting as early as 1924, initially with little success. With the **Open University**, radio and **television** have been used effectively in conjunction with correspondence courses and meetings with tutors. Since it took in its first students in 1971, the Open University has been open to any resident of the United Kingdom eighteen or over, regardless of academic qualifications. By 1990 it had awarded 100,000 B.A. degrees, as well as higher degrees, and it had a flourishing Open Business School.

Jonathan Rose

Bibliography

Blyth, John A. *English University Adult Education, 1908–1958.* 1983.

Davies, J.H., and J.E. Thomas, eds. *A Select Bibliography of Adult Continuing Education.* 5th ed. 1988.

Jennings, Bernard. *Knowledge Is Power: A Short History of the WEA, 1903–78.* 1979.

Kelly, Thomas. *A History of Adult Education in Great Britain.* 3rd ed. 1992.

Marriott, Stuart. *Extramural Empires: Service and Self-Interest in English University Adult Education, 1873–1983.* 1984.

Advertising

Public advertising in the twentieth century has developed from a relatively humble marketing tool into an omnipresent fact of life and the driving force behind the major communications media. In the later years of the nineteenth century a great deal of advertising still took the form of posted bills, but ads constituted an important part of the revenue of newspapers and periodicals, and there were even some experiments with direct mail. By the turn of the century misleading advertising had become sufficiently widespread to alarm both citizen's groups and Parliament: The 1907 Advertisements Regulation Act was passed in direct response to the lobbying of the National Society for Controlling the Abuses of Advertising. This group was preoccupied with possible social implications of advertising, but there were also others increasingly concerned about ads for drugs and various sorts of cures. Products routinely claimed to cure everything from asthma to baldness (an ad campaign for one brand of cigarettes as late as the 1930s confidently assured the consumer that its smoke was a sure cure for throat cancer), and there were few if any regulations as yet. But as the century progressed, ads for medicines would become more closely policed. The relation of advertising to **public health** continues to be controversial, especially with regard to cigarettes: as of 1992 Britain remained one of only three **European Union** countries not supporting a proposed Europe-wide ban on cigarette advertisements.

While laws were beginning to restrict advertisers' activities, advertisers themselves were increasingly concerned about the reputation of their young profession as well as its direction. In 1917 a group subsequently named the Institute of Incorporated Practitioners in Advertising (IPA) was formed and sought to work together with the government in ways mutually beneficial. The sale of war bonds and recruitment for the **army** were both greatly aided by the voluntary efforts of IPA members, while the public's attitude toward **conscription** was also molded by professional advertisers. This trend intensified, so that today the biggest single advertiser in Great Britain is the government, producing print and television ads on topics ranging from the use of seat belts to energy conservation, from conversion to decimal currency to military recruitment.

During the 1920s advertising expenditures nearly doubled, becoming a £60 million industry by the decade's end. New, more specific targets, such as the housewife, were identified, and new techniques in market research and audience targeting were pioneered, some of them imported from the United States by firms like the J. Walter Thompson agency, a powerful force in British advertising for decades. As the industry grew in power and influence, other organizations emerged, such as the Advertising Association (first formed in 1925), which came to wield considerable influence. The Depression of the 1930s retarded the growth of the industry, but phenomena such as the newspaper wars of that decade only served to show that effective advertising was crucial to a paper's success. While billings were down in the 1930s, the prestige and importance of advertising continued to increase. The new medium of radio was also attracting the advertisers' attention; even though the government would not officially sanction commercial radio until 1976, stations such as Radio Luxembourg and Radio Normandy welcomed ads and regarded the British listener as a major target audience.

During the **Second World War** the government again made heavy use of advertising, primarily in newspapers. Despite the paper shortages (or perhaps because of them), newspapers became even more widely read during the war, and the impact of advertising, whether official or commercial, was even stronger. The government alone is believed to have spent £10 million on ads during the war years in both national and local papers, even as it issued orders regulating the amount of space in a newspaper that could be allotted to ads.

The slow recovery of the post-war period impeded the steady progress of the British advertising industry. Into this situation stepped American ad agencies, which began locating in **London**—twenty-four American agencies had London offices by 1970, controlling nearly half of all billings in the country. Americans bought up many smaller British agencies, and eventually (1974) even the Masius agency, then the most prestigious and largest of all the British firms.

The new medium of **television**, like radio before it, was quickly seen as an important marketing arena. Television ads made up 3 percent of industry expenditure in 1956, but within fifteen years the figure grew to more than 50 percent. Research showed that television ads were far more successful than those in print or radio, and British advertisers (often accompanied by their American Madison Avenue mentors) flocked to this new outlet.

Demands for more controls and restraints continued to grow as well, and the industry tried to police itself from within by means of its new British Code of Advertising Practice (1961). Government continued to respond to public demands also, and by 1961 there were more than sixty separate laws and statutes regulating ads. The threat of more and tougher legislation moved the industry in 1974 to strengthen the Advertising Standards Authority (ASA), a private body, but one meant to be highly sensitive to government pressures and views. The ASA created a committee to enforce the Code, which it does often stringently (one of its first targets was the alcohol industry, which many felt was going too far in directly associating sexual fulfillment with consumption of alcohol). The goal of self-policing, of course, is to stave off further and more onerous government control.

During the 1980s the American-British industry relationship reversed itself. The most dynamic of the new British agencies by this time was Saatchi and Saatchi. Formed in 1970, it had begun by 1974 to buy other agencies and scored a great success with its campaign for the **Conservative Party** in 1978–9; soon it was buying American agencies as well. It raised more than £300 million in the 1980s in public stock offering, money it used for further acquisitions. Several other British agencies followed Saatchi's lead in going public, including Wire and Plastics Products (WPP), which even bought up the venerable J. Walter Thompson agency in 1987, paying more than £225 million.

Both Saatchi and WPP, however, like many high-flying firms of the 1980s, came to grief following the 1987 stock market crash. Their huge debts became even more burdensome in the recession of the early 1990s. The IPA estimated that 10 percent of the 15,000 British people employed in advertising were laid off in 1990. And once again, foreign companies—American and Japanese—were beginning to dominate. London itself had long been the first stop for an American or Japanese company seeking to expand in Europe, but the trend in the 1990s is to work directly with Continental agencies. Paris and Brussels are becoming the centers of European advertising activity, leaving the industry in a depressed state in London.

The British advertising industry, however, can take solace in its own highly cyclical history: It is an industry in which a decade or less can make an enormous difference. Advertising in Britain has gone from a matter of bill posting and small newspaper announcements to a multimillion-dollar industry deeply involved in the world economy.

Raymond N. MacKenzie

Bibliography

Kleinman, Philip. *Advertising Inside Out.* 1977.
Nevett, T.R. *Advertising in Britain: A History.* 1982.
Southan, Malcolm. "The Adman Cometh" in Richard Boston, ed. *The Press We Deserve.* 1970. pp. 57–72.
West, Douglas. "Multinational Competition in the British Advertising Agency Business, 1936–1987," *Business History Review*, vol. 62 (1988), pp. 467–501.

Ageing

During the twentieth century, for the first time in history, living into and beyond one's sixties became a normal expectation. This was due to reduced rates of mortality in younger age groups, especially among infants. Old people were not extreme rarities in earlier societies; in the 350 years before 1900 the median proportion of persons over age sixty fluctuated between 6 percent and 10 percent of the population, but many people younger in years were prematurely aged by poverty and hard work.

Life expectancy at birth for **women** in the early 1990s was 77.4 years, for men 71.4, and both were rising. It is not useful to compare life expectancy at birth over the whole century, because the very high **infant mortality** rates at the beginning of the century dramatically influence the figures. Those who did survive the hazardous years of infancy had a very good chance of living at least well into middle age, and here the comparisons are useful: While a woman who was fifty years old in 1901 could expect to live to be about 71.6, and a man about 67.5, in 1931 the respective ages were 74.1 and 71.6; in 1961, 77.4 and 72.6.

The numbers living to very old age began to show a significant rise in the 1980s. In 1981 there were 400,000 women and 100,000 men over the age of eighty-five; in 1991, 600,000 and 200,000, respectively. Among females over sixty-five in 1991, 11.3 percent were over eighty-five; among males the comparable figure was 5.7 percent. In the total population of England and Wales those over the age of sixty were 7.6 percent in 1901, 11.7 percent in 1931, 16.8 percent in 1961, and 20.7 percent in 1991. These rising percentages are largely attributable to the falling birthrate over most of the century, though falling mortality rates obviously influenced the absolute numbers.

Throughout the century class differences in life expectancy narrowed only slightly. This is important to emphasize in view of the tendency to stereotype the old as an undifferentiated and usually marginalized category, as though differences of class, ethnicity, gender, income, power, and personal attractiveness ceased around the age of sixty-five. If the old are often perceived as poor, it is partly because so many of them are female, who are more likely to be poor due to their lesser opportunities to accumulate wealth, other than by **marriage** or inheritance, when younger. Also, social surveys of older people, which flourished from the 1950s, tended to focus upon and publicize the poverty, loneliness, and marginality of older people partly because social scientists generally seemed to find the poor more rivetting, or more vulnerable to academic intrusion, than the rich and partly due to a desire to improve their conditions through public exposure. The elderly are likely to be perceived as white because large-scale Black **immigration** began only in the 1950s, and so only in the 1980s and 1990s were significant numbers of older **Black people** becoming visible.

Cultural imagery of the old throughout the century has been generally negative and has occasioned little protest from older people in comparison with resistence to ageism in the United States. At the same time such imagery has steadily become less appropriate since fewer fitted the stereotype. As people age, their physical and their material resources are inevitably depleted. But such depletion occurred at later ages as the century progressed. Better diet, health care, and **health** awareness meant that by the early 1990s most people who survived past the age of sixty remained fit into their later seventies; and most of those who survived into their eighties and nineties did not suffer a long period of severe ill health and dependency before death. Research from the 1950s onward persistently showed that most people could continue to be highly efficient at their accustomed tasks, both mental and physical, including surprisingly heavy labor, into their sixties and could acquire new mental skills even in their eighties. Financially over time, more older people acquired occupational in addition to state **old-age pensions** and owned property that could be converted into additional income. Retirement from work before the onset of physical decline, almost unknown for manual workers before the twentieth century, quickly became the norm in the 1940s and 1950s and, combined with greater prosperity, allowed more people a period of **leisure** later in life. The loneliness of old people is often "proved" by reference to the steadily increasing numbers living alone. But there is evidence that many choose to live alone in preference to the tensions of dependency upon their children. Nor does solitary living necessarily imply isolation from friends or kin. Old people in the 1990s were far more likely to have surviving children and to be in contact with them than in the days of high mortality and poor communications at the beginning of the century.

This is to stress the optimistic view to counter the stereotype. Still, as more people live to be very old, more suffer from Alzheimer's or other incurable diseases. **Unemployment** in the 1980s and 1990s hit older workers at least as hard as younger ones, and large numbers were effectively retired in their fifties to face a very long period of marginality as a result of declining health and deteriorating public services. Among older as well as younger age groups there was discernible social polarization at the end of the century.

Pat Thane

Bibliography
Jefferys, Margot. *Growing Old in the Twentieth Century.* 1989.
Laslett, Peter. *A Fresh Map of Life: The Emergence of the Third Age.* 1989.

Allen, (Reginald) Clifford (1889–1939)

Clifford Allen was a politician who never held elective office and who ended his career without meaningful party affiliation, an advocate for socialism who made his living speculating on the stock exchange, an enemy of the class system who became Lord Allen of Hurtwood (1931), a globe-trotting diplomat who was never accredited by any government, and a courageous martyr for peace who died prematurely as the result of a self-appointed mission in support of **Neville Chamberlain**'s cringing policy of **appeasement**.

When he crowned an impressive school career by winning an exhibition to Peterhouse, **Cambridge**, in 1907, Allen seemed on the way to fulfilling the dream of his **Conservative** Monmouthshire family that he become an **Anglican** priest. At Cambridge, however, he read history, debated at the Union, and converted to socialism, joining and eventually presiding over both the University Socialist Federation and the University **Fabian Society**. Allen's socialist creed certainly undermined his religious beliefs, and his political activism probably interfered with his studies, but a disappointing third-class degree did not seem to dim his prospects. Upon leaving Cambridge, he was appointed Secretary and General Manager of the *Daily Citizen*, a short-lived Labour newspaper. Even before the prosaic *Citizen*'s demise in 1915, Allen had become absorbed in the pacifist struggle against the **First World War** as one of the founders of the **No-Conscription Fellowship** (NCF). Under Allen's leadership, the NCF, which drew most of its membership from the **Independent Labour Party** (ILP) and other socialist bodies, became the largest and most effective anti**conscription**, antiwar organization in modern British history.

As chairman and spokesman for the NCF, Allen acquired a national forum in which to display his considerable abilities as speaker, organizer, and leader of men; as an "absolutist" **conscientious objector** who endured over fifteen months imprisonment on account of his refusal to make any compromise with the warrior state, Allen achieved the status of left-wing martyr/saint. But while his obvious ability and courageous **pacifism** seemed to assure him a bright future in socialist politics, the **tuberculosis** he contracted in prison made him a semi-invalid who could never follow a normal working career.

Despite this setback Allen secured a place in left-wing politics. After returning from a Labour-sponsored trip to the Soviet Union, where he interviewed Lenin, lost his enthusiasm for Bolshevism, and nearly died of pneumonia, he was elected Treasurer, then Chairman, of the ILP. But by 1925 renewed ill health had cost him the chance for a safe seat in the House of Commons, and ideological divisions had caused him to resign as leader of the ILP. For the next few years Allen eschewed politics for Labour journalism as a director of the *Daily Herald*. Then, in 1931, he gained a peerage by supporting **Ramsay MacDonald**'s decision to form a National government, but he also lost his credibility in the **Labour Party** as well as most of his former friends and allies.

Without party or influence (MacDonald effectively ignored him after 1931), Allen attempted to "plough my own furrow" as an independent representative for "progressive," nonparty politics. With **Harold Macmillan** and others, he formed the Next Five Years Group (NFYG), which in 1935 published a much-praised scheme for inter-party cooperation to carry out a fully integrated domestic and foreign policy that could, according to its authors, lift Britain out of the economic doldrums while establishing a comprehensive peace settlement. When the NFYG inevitably foundered, dragged down by political weakness and tactical disputes, Allen turned to personal diplomacy as a means of making his mark on Britain and the world.

During the inter-war period Allen had abandoned absolute pacifism for collective security under the **League of Nations** as humanity's best hope for peace. But as an inveterate activist (some, like **Anthony Eden**, would say busybody) with sincere convictions and enormous confidence, Allen believed in bold initiatives. So in January 1935 he used his status and charm to secure a personal interview with Adolf Hitler. In the course of their conversation Allen presented the German Chancellor with a plan for securing Nazi agreement to halt persecution of Jews and other minorities as *quid pro quo* for the satisfaction of all German grievances arising from the "wicked" Versailles treaty. This was to be the first step toward a comprehensive European peace settlement. Hitler feigned interest, and a second invitation from the Nazis inspired hope, but these were cynical ploys that, while they produced no results, encouraged Allen's illusions. Thus, even though by late 1938 Allen had lost faith in the efficacy of collective security under the League, he still believed he could use his German contacts to make a vital contribution to the best remaining hope for peace, Chamberlain's policy of appeasement.

In September 1938, in the midst of the Czech crisis and against his physician's advice, Allen undertook his final journey for peace, visiting Berlin and Prague and emphasizing to German and Czech officials the necessity for a four-power conference to resolve the Sudeten question as the first step toward an all-round European settlement. Because the **Munich** agreement emerged from just such a conference, Allen went to his grave in March 1939 believing he had, at last, made a difference in the struggle for peace.

Sadly, for all of Allen's courage and devotion to sweet reason, his best efforts could neither shorten the First World War nor prevent the Second. Likewise, his belief in, and work for, the implementation of democratic socialism brought no personal or political triumphs. Yet, despite the ultimate frustration of his plans and hopes, Allen deserves to be remembered for the unselfish idealism and uncompromising honesty that made him a substantial contributor to the politics of conscience in twentieth-century Britain.

Thomas C. Kennedy

Bibliography

Gilbert, Martin, ed. *Plough My Own Furrow: The Story of Lord Allen of Hurtwood as Told through His Writings and Correspondence.* 1965.

Kennedy, Thomas C. "The Next Five Years Group and the Failure of the Politics of Agreement in Britain," *Canadian Journal of History*, vol. 9 (1974), pp. 45–68.

———. "'Peace In Our Time': The Personal Diplomacy of Lord Allen of Hurtwood, 1933–38" in Solomon Wank, ed. *Doves* and *Diplomats*. 1978. pp. 217–39.

Marwick, Arthur. *Clifford Allen: The Open Conspirator*. 1964.

Amritsar Massacre (1919)

In April 1919 British troops opened fire, without warning, upon a peaceful crowd of demonstrators in India, killing 379 and wounding 1,200. As a result **Indian nationalism** took a militant turn, and Mohandas Gandhi (1869–1948) emerged as a brilliant new force in the independence movement.

India was in turmoil in the post-war period. Most Indian nationalists had supported the war effort, believing that dominion status would be their reward. They were encouraged by London officials, who announced in 1917 that the British intended to create responsible government in India. But reforms were slow in coming once the war was over, and in 1919 the Indian government's emergency war powers were extended through the Rowlatt Acts. These events led to serious protests throughout India in 1919, especially the Punjab, where martial law was soon declared. The local military commander, Brigadier-General R.E.H. Dyer, decided to teach the militants a lesson and ordered his troops to open fire upon protesters in Amritsar.

A commission of inquiry was established to investigate the event. Dyer was forced to resign his commission but otherwise returned to a hero's welcome in Britain. Indian public opinion was horrified, both by the bloody deed and by the callous response of many British officials and citizens. The Indian National Congress established its own committee of inquiry, with Gandhi one of the key members. His work there, and in the ongoing protests against the Rowlatt Acts, catapulted him to a commanding position in the nationalist movement.

Lynn Zastoupil

Bibliography
Brown, Judith M. *Gandhi's Rise to Power: Indian Politics, 1915–1922*. 1972.

Moore, R.J. *Liberalism and Indian Politics, 1872–1922*. 1966.

Angell (Lane), (Ralph) Norman (1872–1967)

Norman Angell was a prolific antiwar writer and activist. Born Ralph Norman Angell Lane,

he dropped Lane after his first book. He spent most of his life elaborating and promoting the idea that war would, in the modern world of economic interdependence, harm the victor as much as the vanquished. His most famous book was *The Great Illusion* (1910). In 1914 he helped to found the **Union of Democratic Control** (UDC); in 1920 he joined the **Independent Labour Party** (ILP). He served in Parliament in 1929–31, was knighted in 1931, and won the 1933 Nobel Peace Prize.

Despite a Conservative, middle-class background, Angell was a restless and radical youth. At the age of seventeen he emigrated to the United States, where he worked as a farm laborer, cowboy, and journalist. In 1897 he took a job on a Paris newspaper, where he remained until returning to England in 1912.

Angell's public career began with the publication of *Europe's Optical Illusion* (1908). Lord Esher, the chairman of the **Committee of Imperial Defence**, introduced it to many influential people, including King **Edward VII** and Sir Richard Garton, an industrialist, who donated funds to establish the Garton Foundation in order to promote Angell's ideas. *War and Peace*, a monthly devoted to "Norman Angellism," was established in 1913. Politically, its contributors ranged from **Conservatives** to revolutionary socialists.

Angell's popularity plummeted during the **First World War**, partly because he was widely misinterpreted as having argued that war had actually become impossible, and partly because of his involvement (albeit limited) in the UDC, which opposed the government's war policy and advocated a negotiated peace.

Angell was one of the first critics of the Versailles treaty, which he thought embodied the fallacies he had exposed in his pre-war work and would lead to economic catastrophe. His views regained popularity—among leftists especially—as the international economy deteriorated. Angell moved sharply left immediately after the war, arguing, uncharacteristically, that capitalism was responsible for the flawed postwar settlement. These views took him into the ILP, but he soon gravitated toward **Labour's** moderate wing.

Between the wars he contributed to many journals and was active on a host of committees. He entered Parliament in 1929 on his fourth attempt and was disappointed not to be offered any government post by his UDC comrade **Ramsay MacDonald**. He was never comfortable in Parliament and was secretly relieved to lose his seat in the 1931 election. He spent most of the **Second World War** in the United States promoting Britain's cause and urging American participation. After the war he moved further to the right, dismayed by many socialists' endorsement of Soviet expansionism.

Angell's theories influenced the outlook of an entire generation throughout Europe and the English-speaking world. They contributed to the growth of public hostility to the Versailles treaty and helped to create the climate of opinion that produced the generous settlement after the Second World War.

D.P. Blaazer

Bibliography
Angell, Norman. *After All.* 1951.
Miller, J.D.B. *Norman Angell and the Futility of War.* 1986.

Anglicanism
See CHURCH OF ENGLAND

Anglo-American Relations
During the twentieth century Britain and the United States became close allies. Their relationship stabilized before the Second World War, peaked during the 1940s and 1950s, cooled during the 1960s and 1970s, and recovered during the 1980s.

As the century dawned, European imperial rivalries convinced Britain to improve relations with America in order to safeguard its Western Hemisphere interests. Britain urged negotiation to settle the Venezuelan border dispute, voted with the United States and against Canada in arbitration of the Alaska boundary dispute, supported the United States' Open Door notes on China, and recognized Washington's right to build and fortify a Central American canal. Britain maintained neutrality in the Spanish-American War of 1898, and Washington refrained from criticizing London during the **Boer War**. In 1906 Britain withdrew its military and naval forces from Canada and the Caribbean, signaling its reliance on the United States to police the Western Hemisphere.

The **First World War** threatened this rapprochement. From 1914 to 1917 President Woodrow Wilson exhorted Americans to remain "impartial in thought as well as action," expressed disdain for British and German vio-

lations of American neutral rights, and equated Britain's war aims with Germany's. British officials fumed at Wilson's mediation efforts and resented American inroads into Britain's trade and financial interests.

America entered the war in 1917, according to Wilson, associated, not allied, with Britain. He refused to integrate military operations as the Allies urged. Freedom of the seas, one of his Fourteen Points, challenged Britain's naval dominance. In late 1918 Wilson negotiated an armistice with Germany and compelled Britain to comply. At the Paris Peace Conference the British regretted Wilson's idealism, arrogance, and insensitivity to their wartime sacrifices. Rejection of the Versailles treaty by the U.S. Senate compounded British frustration.

During the inter-war years Britain and the United States only partially composed their disagreements. To avoid a post-war naval race, both powers signed the Washington treaty (1922) that established parity between them on capital ships. Negotiations in 1927, however, failed to limit noncapital ships, and mutual mistrust resulted. Limits on cruisers were set during the London Naval Conference of 1930, but the distance between the two countries became evident in their incoherent response to Japan's invasion of Manchuria in 1931.

Financial problems also beset Anglo-American relations. Washington insisted that London repay wartime loans, rejecting pleas to forgive the debts as a contribution to victory over Germany. American approval of Anglo-French terms for collecting **reparations** from Germany and of the Dawes Plan to restore Germany's economy pleased London, and American and British bankers and industrialists cooperated in financial, petroleum, and communications enterprises. The Great Depression, however, strained relations. London blamed its general economic misery on Washington's collection of war debts, its record-high tariff of 1930, and the refusal of American banks to provide credits. Britain renounced the **gold standard** in 1931, raised its tariff and developed the **imperial preference** trade system, and defaulted on war-debts payments in 1933. Britain organized the London Economic Conference in 1933 to restore world currencies, but President Franklin D. Roosevelt refused to abide by any agreement until he achieved domestic recovery. Bilateral negotiations from 1934 to 1938 failed to reduce tariffs, and the two powers traded mutual recriminations. In that atmosphere Congress passed neutrality laws to isolate the United States from political and military turmoil in Europe.

The discord in Anglo-American relations evaporated in the glaring heat of the **Second World War**. In 1938 American and British naval officers secretly discussed joint tactics in the impending war in Europe. In 1939 Congress revised the neutrality laws to allow arms sales to London and Paris. The fall of France in 1940 convinced many Americans that they must fight against Nazi Germany, and Roosevelt exchanged destroyers for rights at British bases, resumed Selective Service, and extended **Lend-Lease** aid. The retreat from **Dunkirk** shattered British illusions that the war could be won without American assistance. Prime Minister **Winston Churchill** cultivated Roosevelt's friendship and encouraged him to enter the war. In late 1941 the two statesmen issued the Atlantic Charter, and Roosevelt waged unofficial naval warfare against Germany.

From 1941 to 1945 the United States and Great Britain developed a special wartime relationship. They declared an alliance and agreed to follow a Germany-first strategy. American and British officials established the Combined Chiefs of Staff, integrated military commands, established joint boards for allocating resources, dovetailed intelligence operations, collaborated in the Manhattan Project, and cooperated in dispensing Lend-Lease aid.

Beneath the surface of the Anglo-American alliance loomed disputes over numerous matters. Despite the Germany-first strategy, American and British officers bickered repeatedly over how and when to take the war to Berlin. Americans suspected the British of designing war plans to recover their imperial interests after the war. Commercial issues such as control of Middle East oil, trade with Argentina, and post-war opportunities for American firms in the British Empire generated tension. Roosevelt frustrated Churchill at the Tehran Conference of 1943 by trying to mediate Anglo-Soviet differences. Debates over policy toward East Asia, the Middle East, and occupied Europe diminished Anglo-American harmony.

Relations cooled as the Axis peril vanished in 1945. The United States abruptly terminated Lend-Lease, dismantled the Combined Chiefs of Staff, and abolished the Middle East Supply Center. Secretary of State James Byrnes refused to consult Foreign Secretary **Ernest Bevin** while preparing for Foreign Ministers' meetings. The United States offered Britain a generous loan but forced London to agree to make sterling convertible.

The escalation of the Cold War, however, convinced the United States to strike an alliance with Britain. In 1946 London and Washington jointly pressured Moscow to withdraw from Iran and merged their occupation zones in Germany. Washington declared the Truman Doctrine at London's invitation. Britain facilitated European acceptance of the **Marshall Plan** and gratefully accepted American largesse.

Ties became especially close on security matters. American and British military officers resumed wartime collaboration, shared contingency war plans, standardized weapons, traded intelligence, coordinated the Berlin airlift, and established the North Atlantic Treaty Organization (NATO) in 1949. They also coordinated covert operations against Iranian Prime Minister Mohammed Mossadegh in 1953. The weakest link in the strategic alliance developed when Congress passed the McMahon Act (1946), forbidding dissemination of atomic secrets abroad.

Despite Anglo-American unity regarding the Cold War in Europe, problems in other regions beset the relationship. Britain resented President Harry S. Truman's pro-Zionism and American control of occupied Japan, and it recognized Beijing in January 1950 over American protests. Britain supported American military action in Korea but protested Truman's remark that **nuclear weapons** might be employed and blocked an American plan to have the **United Nations** brand the Chinese as aggressors. Washington excluded London from the Australia-New Zealand-United States Pact and criticized Britain's response to the nationalization of the Anglo-Iranian Oil Company.

Problems continued to develop despite the accession to office of Churchill in 1951 and Dwight Eisenhower in 1953. London protested Washington's consideration of force to rescue French troops at Dienbienphu and negotiated the Geneva accords with the Soviets. Britain objected to American covert operations in Guatemala and handling of the Quemoy-Matsu crisis. Washington criticized London's policies toward the Buraimi oasis and Egypt. Anglo-American divergence peaked during the **Suez crisis** of 1956, when Britain attacked Egypt over American opposition and Eisenhower condemned his ally.

In the late 1950s American and British officials repaired their alliance. Strategic coopera-

A

tion was reaffirmed at the NATO ministers meeting in December 1956. Prime Minister **Harold Macmillan**, a wartime associate of Eisenhower, met him at Bermuda in March 1957 to continue the healing. Eisenhower promised Macmillan sixty Thor missiles, the first time the United States ever provided missiles to another state. After Congress repealed the McMahon Act in 1957, Eisenhower shared nuclear secrets with the British and eventually exchanged nuclear components and Skybolt missiles for Polaris submarine base rights in Scotland. In addition, the British coordinated with the Americans their occupations of Jordan and Lebanon in 1958, backed Washington during the 1958–9 showdown over Berlin, and stood by Eisenhower during the U-2 debacle in 1960.

In the early 1960s Macmillan provided solace to President John F. Kennedy after his unnerving experiences at the Bay of Pigs and the Vienna summit. When the United States cancelled development of the Skybolt missile system in 1962, Kennedy averted an Anglo-American rupture by selling London Polaris missiles. America embraced the Nuclear Test Ban Treaty of 1963, which Macmillan had advocated for six years.

The Anglo-American relationship cooled after 1963. Prime Minister **Harold Wilson** and President Lyndon B. Johnson invested little in it. Britain's financial problems reduced its relative importance to many American officials, who encouraged London to join the **European Community** (EC). Washington protested Britain's evacuation of military bases east of Suez, and quarrels erupted over policy in Cuba and Malaysia. The Vietnam War seriously tested the Atlantic alliance. London refused Washington's pleas to send troops, disputed American assessments of Communist China's role in the war, eventually doubted that the United States could win and therefore questioned the destruction, and mediated between Moscow and Washington.

President Richard M. Nixon tried but failed to restore closer relations because Prime Minister **Edward Heath** practiced Europeanism in the hope of entering the EC. Heath denied any special relationship with Washington and refused to serve as mediator between the United States and European powers after Henry Kissinger announced his "Year of Europe" plan in 1973. Nixon reciprocated by launching initiatives in China, the Soviet Union, arms control, and currency conversions without consult-

ing London. During the 1973 Arab-Israeli War, London refused to participate in the airlift of supplies to Israel, criticized Nixon's alert of American forces, and endorsed EC negotiation of an oil deal with Arab states.

In the late 1970s President Jimmy Carter tried with little success to improve relations with London. The British worried about his diplomatic naivete, evident in his alienation of Moscow over human rights; his consideration of a no-first-use pledge on nuclear weapons; his exclusion of intermediate-range missiles, the type aimed at British territory, from SALT II; and his excessive reaction to the Soviet invasion of Afghanistan. Anglo-American military ties remained close in the 1960s and 1970s despite the political disharmony. Both powers remained firmly committed to NATO, and London continued to welcome the American military presence in Britain while other NATO states pressed the United States to withdraw. Washington and London shared intelligence, integrated tactical military planning, and jointly developed the base at Diego Garcia.

Anglo-American political relations dramatically improved in the 1980s because Prime Minister **Margaret Thatcher** sought to strengthen ties with America rather than the EC. President Ronald Reagan backed Thatcher during the **Falklands War** with weapons supplies, satellite and signals intelligence, and access to the American airbase on Ascension Island. Washington sold London Trident missiles in 1982. Defying domestic opposition, Thatcher deployed Cruise missiles in 1983, participated in Strategic Defense Initiative research, allowed American aircraft to use bases in Britain in the raid on Libya in 1986, and supported Reagan's policies in Central America. Thatcher did not support the American effort to boycott construction of a Soviet pipeline, protest of the Soviet radar at Krasnoyarsk, and invasion of Grenada. Yet she remained close to Reagan, gained influence in American-Soviet arms control talks in the late 1980s, and emerged in the eyes of many as the senior partner of the alliance once Reagan lost prestige in the Iran-Contra scandal. The closeness of the relationship was revealed in the unity of purpose and action during the Persian Gulf War of 1990–1.

Peter L. Hahn

Bibliography
Bartlett, C.J. *The "Special Relationship": A Political History of Anglo-American Re-*

lations since 1945. 1992.

Dimbleby, David, and David Reynolds. *An Ocean Apart: The Relationship between Britain and America in the Twentieth Century*. 1988.

Hathaway, Robert M. *Great Britain and the United States: Special Relations since World War II*. 1990.

Louis, William Roger, and Hedley Bull, eds. *The "Special Relationship": Anglo-American Relations since 1945*. 1986.

Watt, D. Cameron. *Succeeding John Bull: America in Britain's Place, 1900–1975*. 1984.

Anglo-Soviet Relations (1917–1956)

Anglo-Soviet relations were most significant after the First World War when Britain was in a key position to decide on the possible future survival of the new "Russia" (as it was always called before 1939). The Bolshevik leaders, who set enormous store on friendly relations with Britain, had great hopes for economic reconstruction and the promotion of world revolution through the relationship, an inherent contradiction that aroused suspicion in British circles. Until Joseph Stalin's death in 1953, relations were rarely amicable, except during the Second World War, and were usually fraught with difficulties. If relations between the United States and Russia have reflected ideological considerations, those between Britain and Russia have been dominated by a curious mixture of distaste and *realpolitik*.

Until 1917 Russia was regarded by successive British governments and by wider public opinion as a threat to the Empire, especially India, and disparaged for its semifeudal political system and oppression of its people. The revolution of February 1917 was greeted with some enthusiasm in Britain, especially in the **Labour Party**. It was hoped that Aleksandr Kerensky would keep Russia in the war on the Allied side and introduce democracy. Reaction to the Bolshevik revolution of October 1917 and the subsequent separate peace with Germany varied from **Winston Churchill**'s warnings of the "plague bacillus of Bolshevism" to an enthusiastic welcome from a small band of "fellow travellers" like Arthur Ransome of the *Manchester Guardian*. The official policy of the **David Lloyd George** coalition government was to sanction limited intervention, organized through the Allied Supreme Council, the Brit-

ish contributions consisting of a contingent of troops in Archangel and support for the Whites in southern Russia. There was some limited support from workers for Councils of Action to force British withdrawal from Russia, but the main impetus for this came from general war weariness and a lack of enthusiasm for the intervention within the **Cabinet**.

By early 1920 Lloyd George decided to try a more conciliatory approach, which led to the signing of an Anglo-Soviet Trade Agreement in March 1921 and eventually to the convening of a British-led conference at Genoa in April 1922 to discuss the modalities of settling the post-war status of Soviet Russia. The meeting ended in acrimony and failure, due to the signing of a treaty between Russia and Germany at Rapallo, Soviet refusal to pay czarist debts or compensate Westerners who had lost property after the revolution, and Allied disagreement on how to deal with Russia.

During the rest of the 1920s and 1930s both the **Conservative** and Labour leaderships were suspicious about the impact of Comintern propaganda, especially in the Empire, the activities of the **Communist Party of Great Britain** (CPGB), and disruptive activities of the Soviet Union in international relations. **Ramsay MacDonald**'s 1924 Labour government recognized the Soviet Union and initialed a comprehensive treaty to settle debt and other questions in the hope of great trade benefits, while continuing the Lloyd George tradition of "civilization through trade." But Labour lost the 1924 general election in the wake of the **Zinoviev letter** scandal. The treaty was not ratified by **Stanley Baldwin**'s Conservative government, which also broke diplomatic relations in 1927 after a raid on Arcos, the Russian trading company in London, revealed evidence of subversive activity by the Soviet delegation.

There were no prominent Conservative supporters of Russia, and many diehards who advocated isolation in the same terms as those used by Churchill. The **Foreign Office** mirrored this distaste, despite a minority sympathetic to Labour's more conciliatory, yet still suspicious, attitude. The Labour rank and file were generally enthusiastic about the Soviet experiment, as were a small but significant group of intellectuals (notably **Sidney and Beatrice Webb, George Bernard Shaw**, and **H.G. Wells**). Much of the rest of British public opinion viewed the Soviet repression of religion and support for such events as the 1926 **General Strike** with distaste.

Although diplomatic relations were resumed in 1929, a temporary commercial agreement was signed in 1930, Russia joined the **League of Nations** in 1934, and Foreign Secretary **Anthony Eden** visited Moscow in 1935, official relations remained cool until 1941, whereas trade never reached important levels. The National government preferred trying to conciliate Germany to regarding Russia as a potential ally, and no Anglo-Soviet treaty emerged to match that signed by Russia with France. The Foreign Office feared a Franco-Soviet pact and was alarmed as much by Soviet intervention in Spain as by that of Germany and Italy, even if by 1939 **Neville Chamberlain** was probably resigned to the necessity of an Anglo-Soviet agreement of some sort to restrain Germany. Britain's concessions over Czechoslovakia in 1938 at **Munich**, a meeting to which Soviet Russia was not invited, convinced Stalin that he could not count on collective security pacts to guarantee Soviet security and led to the signature of a Soviet pact with Nazi Germany in August 1939, even though British negotiators were already on their way to Moscow.

The signing of the pact and the Russian invasion of Finland in 1939 spurred widespread revulsion in Britain, especially within the Labour Party. Even the CPGB vacillated before condoning Soviet actions. But it also prompted a reappraisal of Anglo-Soviet relations in the interests of defeating Germany. The pro-Soviet **Stafford Cripps** went to Russia in February 1940 as an unofficial mediator, with the knowledge but not yet the offical support of the government. In May 1940 he was sent back with the rank of ambassador. Stalin met Cripps, and the Russians made it clear that they wished to retain normal relations with Britain despite their alliance with Germany. However, Stalin refused to believe British information about the forthcoming Operation Barbarossa, which had been obtained by breaking German codes, probably because he feared British duplicity. The Foreign Office refuted Cripps' appeal for a rapprochment with Russia and discounted fears of a German attack.

When Hitler invaded Russia in June 1941 the ground had thus been prepared for a change of policy. Churchill, now Prime Minister, announced British support for Russia. Cripps, who had been recalled, was sent back, and an Anglo-Soviet treaty was signed in May 1942. Most negotiations after Russia's entry into the war were conducted by Eden and at summit

conferences at Moscow (1942), Tehran (1943), Yalta (1945), and Potsdam (1945) directly by Churchill and Stalin. The drawing up of a blueprint for a post-war world could not hide the fact that the alliance held together only because of the existence of a common foe, with Churchill increasingly convinced that post-war Anglo-Soviet relations would be cool if not hostile. Meanwhile, British public opinion was encouraged to view Soviet Russia as a heroic friend by the Ministry of Information, helped by a groundswell of spontaneous popular enthusiasm, especially during the battle of Stalingrad. The discovery of thousands of murdered Polish officers in the Katyn forest soured public relations after 1943, as did Russian inaction during the Warsaw uprising in 1944.

After 1945, in spite of the election of a Labour government, "Left" did not "speak to Left" as **Ernest Bevin**, the new Foreign Secretary, had promised. There were fears on the Left of the Labour Party that British policy was becoming too pro-American during the 1945–51 **Attlee** government. Bevin never shed his trade-unionist dislike for Soviet authoritarianism and the CPGB, a dislike shared by others in the Cabinet. Despite firm support for the Atlantic Alliance, Britain in the post-war period proved a moderating influence on American attitudes about Soviet actions in Europe, advocating arms control talks with Moscow just after the repression of Hungary in 1956.

Andrew J. Williams

Bibliography

Gorodetsky, Gabriel. *Stafford Cripps' Mission to Moscow, 1940–42.* 1984.

Northedge, F.S., and Audrey Wells. *Britain and Soviet Communism.* 1982.

Ullman, Richard. *Anglo-Soviet Relations.* 3 vols. 1961–72.

White, Stephen. *Britain and the Bolshevik Revolution.* 1979.

Williams, Andrew J. *Labour and Russia.* 1989.

Anthropology

Anthropology, the study of humankind, was established as a field of intellectual endeavor during the nineteenth century. In Britain the term included the study of archaeology and prehistory, biological variation and evolution, accounts of "savage" custom and the history of customs (ethnology), and language (philology), rather than being restricted, as in Continental Europe, to the physical study of humans. The value of the study of other cultures lay in reconstructing from contemporary primitive life the origin and evolution of European society.

In 1900 anthropology in Britain maintained a broad, cohesive approach to the evolution of humankind, but divisions were emerging. **Archaeology** was becoming a separate discipline; linguistics was poorly developed. Concern with racial variation based on studies of human anatomy gradually declined in the early decades of the century. The study of custom, especially social and cultural variation, as an end in itself, was to become the dominant focus. Studies of history, culture contact, and diffusionism shifted interest away from studies of the Australian Aborigines toward more complex agrarian groups, especially in Melanesia. Eventually a more ahistorical (synchronic) and ethnographically based social and cultural anthopology emerged. This change in intellectual approaches to the study of other cultures was accompanied by changes in the institutional base of anthropology and its professionalization.

Until the twentieth century anthropology was weakly established in universities. Activities centered around learned societies, especially the (Royal) Anthropological Institute, and museums. The major figures were men of letters such as E.B. Tylor (1832–1917) and Sir James George Frazer (1854–1940), colonial officers, and the professional middle classes. During the 1890s a number of natural scientists associated with university teaching and research entered anthopology, bringing new methodologies, academic standards, and a degree of professionalism. They included A.C. Haddon (1855–1940) and W.H.R. Rivers (1864–1922). During the period before 1914, with the support of colonial governments interested in training imperial officials, anthropology began to be taught at **Oxford**, **Cambridge**, and London universities. Among the new recruits were Bronislaw C. Malinowski (1884–1942), a Polish scholar who carried out research in Melanesia and who emphasized the importance of field research, and A.R. Radcliffe-Brown (1881–1955), who emphasized the need for theory. Both were instrumental in the establishment of synchronic, functional studies of society and culture in Britain and the Empire during the inter-war years. Physical anthropology failed to keep pace with this new professionalism in sociocultural an-

thropology. Interest in history degenerated into the extreme diffusionism of G. Elliot Smith (1872–1937), who viewed all culture as originating in ancient Egypt.

From his base at the **London School of Economics** Malinowski trained a new generation of researchers in field methods and functional anthropology. In the 1930s support from America allowed researchers, under the auspices of the International African Institute, to carry out research in Africa, particularly in British colonies. The emphasis was on culture contact and the study of practical issues: education, economics and diet, kinship, politics, and jural relations. Radcliffe-Brown, operating outside Britain but mainly within the Empire, also promoted fieldwork but instilled in his students the need to develop a distinctive, theoretical discipline of "social" anthropology. The anthropologists who emerged in this period were influenced, directly or indirectly, by the theoretical writings of French sociologist Emile Durkheim (1858–1917) and by Malinowski and Radcliffe-Brown. They included E.E. Evans-Pritchard (1902–73); Raymond Firth (1901–), a New Zealander; and Meyer Fortes (1906–84), a South African. In academic life anthropology, still a marginal subject, attracted a number of women, including Audrey Richards (1899–1985) and Lucy Mair (1901–86), as well as Central Europeans such as Siegfried Nadel (1903–56).

Changes in colonial policy in the late 1930s promised increased employment for anthropologists, but official support for research became generally available only after the Second World War. During this period new departments of social anthropology were established or reestablished in British and colonial universities, staffed largely by students of Malinowski and Radcliffe-Brown. The foundation of an Association of Social Anthropologists of the Commonwealth in 1946 marked the professionalization of the discipline of social anthropology.

The emphasis on functional studies of social systems, however, was challenged from within the discipline during the 1950s. Max Gluckman (1911–75), a South African based at Manchester, suggested that conflict is an important feature of social systems, and Edmund Leach (1910–89) at London and later Cambridge challenged the normative basis of theoretical models. Evans-Pritchard disputed Radcliffe-Brown's claims that social anthropology was a natural science, suggesting it was more related to the arts, especially **history**. More important, there was a shift away from structural and functional studies of society, toward questions of meaning and culture. During the 1960s studies of ritual and symbolism by Victor Turner (1920–83), and of classification by Mary Douglas (1921–), revived older anthropological interest in religion and symbolism. The influence of the French anthropologist Claude Lévi-Strauss (1908–) added to these concerns, and structuralist ideas became popular.

The development of these new approaches occurred in conjunction with **decolonization** and changes in both research funding and the rationale for research and teaching. An interest in cultural issues also led to a rediscovery of older anthropology and archaeology as well as of physical anthropology (human biology), which had survived in a few universities and developed new interests in genetic variation, human adaptation, and primatology. Materialist and Marxist ideas became popular in the 1970s. Since the 1980s interest in history, evolution, and wider comparative studies has been revived and new concerns with **psychology**, medical anthropology, and gender studies have been promoted. Ethnographic field research is still emphasized, although complex as well as small-scale societies have been studied.

Anthropology, however, is still dominated by sociocultural anthropologists, most located in universities, although a few are employed in areas of public policy and development programs. The old imperial connection to Commonwealth countries has weakened, replaced by closer connections with North American anthropology and, in recent years, with the new Continental European anthropology.

James Urry

Bibliography

Kuklick, Henrika. *The Savage Within: The Social History of British Anthropology, 1885–1945.* 1992.

Kuper, Adam. *Anthropology and Anthropologists: The Modern British School.* 1983.

Stocking, George W. Jr. "The Ethnographer's Magic: Fieldwork in British Anthropology from Tylor to Malinowski" in George W. Stocking Jr., ed. *Observers Observed: Essays on Ethnographic Fieldwork.* 1983. pp. 50–120.

———. "Radcliffe-Brown and British Social Anthropology" in George W. Stocking Jr., ed. *Functionalism Historicized: Essays on British Social Anthropology.* 1984. pp. 131–91.

Urry, James. *Before Social Anthropology: Essays on the History of British Anthropology.* 1993.

Anti-Semitism

Anti-Semitism, a hostility toward **Jews** as Jews, is often supposed to be absent from Britain. Commentators who celebrate British tolerance tend to underplay the presence of racial and ethnic conflict. However, hostility toward Jews has been a persistent feature of British social life in the twentieth century both in the form of ideas (written or spoken) and in anti-Semitic behavior. Such hostility became more restrained after the Holocaust, but its tenacity meant that it did not altogether disappear. Even so, it is often difficult, both before and after the Holocaust, to identify such hostility, occurring as it often does under the more respectable facade of anti-alienism.

Anti-Semitism has been a constant feature on the fringe of British politics. It surfaced in the early twentieth century in the campaign mounted against the immigration of Russian Polish Jews. Some of the fiercest anti-Semitism expressed anywhere in Europe at this time appeared in Joseph Banister's *England under the Jews*, which was first published in 1901. It also remained an integral component in the ideology of the racial nationalist group The Britons, which was founded in 1919, as it did of the **Fascist** groups that developed in the 1920s and 1930s. Among the Fascists, Arnold Leese of the Imperial Fascist League (IFL) offered a brand of racial, conspiratorial anti-Semitism that embraced a complete belief in *The Protocols of the Elders of Zion* and advanced older elements of anti-Semitic ideology. However, the IFL was not the only extreme anti-Semitic organization in existence in the 1930s. The Nordic League was the most significant: One German observer regarded it as "the English branch of international Nazism." Anti-Semitism was also present in the 1930s within the larger Fascist group, the British Union of Fascists (BUF). Although BUF founder **Oswald Mosley** denied that he had ever been an anti-Semite, he articulated anti-Semitic sentiments under pressure. Other members of his organization—such as William Joyce, expelled eventually from the BUF in 1937, and A.K. Chesterton, an early biographer of Mosley—were more overt in their hostility toward Jews. At times the anti-Semitic sentiments of the Fascists could be translated into action, particularly in East **London**.

It might be expected that between 1939 and 1945, with Britain engaged in war against Germany, anti-Semitism in Britain would not be advocated or tolerated. In fact, anti-Semitic beliefs continued to circulate in Britain throughout the Second World War. A number of Fascist and related organizations were proscribed by the government, but some anti-Semitic groups continued to function.

Following the war anti-Semitism in various guises has continued to appear in Fascist and racist speeches and publications despite the experience of the Holocaust. A move began in Britain and other countries to develop revisionist perspectives on the Holocaust, suggesting that it was a myth, manufactured by a powerful international Jewish community for political advantage.

This shadowy world of racial nationalism and Fascism, where psychopaths and fanatics operate, is inseparable from anti-Semitism in twentieth-century Britain. But hostility toward Jews has stretched into other areas of society. Before 1914 anti-Semitism, in what has been categorized as its "commonsense" rather than scientific form, circulated widely in the East End. Moreover, violence directed against Jews in Tredegar in South Wales in 1911 and various examples of anti-Semitic discrimination reported at regular intervals in the newspaper the *Jewish Chronicle* serve as reminders that anti-Semitism was reflected in forms of behavior toward Jews as well as in attitudes.

Following the Holocaust a greater degree of restraint has often been shown by the wider public in its response toward Jews. The persistence of stereotypes, evident in the publicity surrounding the death of Robert Maxwell, is significant in revealing the continuity of anti-Semitic sentiment. Violence directed toward Jews in Lancashire in 1947 at a time of tension in the Middle East as well as more recent attacks on Jewish cemeteries, property, and people, particularly in London, reveal the persistence of anti-Semitic conduct.

Nor has the state been entirely guiltless in condoning or perpetuating anti-Semitism, although official sentiment has often been masked as anti-alienism. Opposition to the naturalization of Russian Polish Jews, policies of deportation that followed the 1919 Aliens Act, entry barriers erected against potential refugees from Central Europe in the 1930s, and discriminatory policies pursued by the London County Council in the 1920s—all mitigate the benevolent image of official policy in Britain.

Whether the emphasis is on official or popular responses, anti-Semitic thought and behavior have been recurrent features of twentieth-century Britain. The fact that anti-Semitism has assumed greater significance in other countries should not be allowed to obscure its tenacity in Britain.

Colin Holmes

Bibliography

Cesarani, David, ed. *The Making of Modern Anglo-Jewry.* 1990.

Garrard, J.A. *The English and Immigration: A Comparative Study of the Jewish Influx, 1880–1910.* 1971.

Holmes, Colin. *Anti-Semitism in British Society, 1876–1939.* 1979.

Kushner, Tony. *The Persistence of Prejudice: Anti-Semitism in British Society during the Second World War.* 1989.

Apostles, The

The Cambridge Conversazione Society, its proper name, was founded in 1820 as a secret undergraduate discussion society. During its first century the Society, as its members refer to it, had some of the most prominent people at the University of **Cambridge** as members, from Alfred Tennyson to **John Maynard Keynes**. The purpose of its discussions was self-formation, and, as a consequence, the subjects considered were religious, philosophical, and literary, issues of personal, rather than academic, importance. This was a *Lernfreiheit*, a society for the unrestricted pursuit of truth. Absolute candor, as Apostles were fond of saying, was the only tradition the Society enforced. In their most prominent conceit, the Apostles considered themselves as Reality; all else was Phenomenal. However, rather than turning themselves inward, this conceit allowed them to have a particular view of the world that they could be in, but not of.

Many nineteenth-century Apostles were clerics, albeit often of a heterodox sort, and many went to the Bar. In the twentieth century these trends were replaced by the tendency of

Apostles to enter the civil service, public school teaching, and university education. George Rylands remarked after the deaths of Lytton Strachey, Roger Fry, and Goldsworthy Lowes Dickinson, whom the Apostles had elected before 1914, that he was left in a world of petty men. Strong feelings of personal loss of this sort, however, ought not obscure an extensive tradition of distinguished service. Of the Apostles elected after 1914, 14 percent entered the civil service. These included Andrew Cohen at the Colonial Office, Frederic Harmer and Dennis Proctor at the Treasury, Henry Lintott at the Board of Trade, and Victor Rothschild as head of Edward Heath's think tank as well as in other official capacities. Of the Apostles elected after 1914, 10 percent became public school masters, including Francis Crusoe at Eton, Wilfred Noyce at Charterhouse, Lancelot Rolleston at Sherborne and Marlborough, and A.R.D. Watkins at Harrow.

A much higher proportion (64 percent) returned to the university as dons: 35 percent in letters and 29 percent in the sciences. Anthony Blunt distinguished himself as the greatest art historian of his time. John Gross, who lectured at the University of London, has been editor of the *Times Literary Supplement* and the literary editor of the *New Statesman*. Matthew Hoggart has been a University Lecturer in English at Cambridge and Professor of English at the University of Sussex. Richard Llewelyn Davies, a modernist much influenced by J.D. Bernal in the 1930s, became Professor of urban planning at the University of London. Gary Runciman left his mark on sociological theory, and Quentin Skinner on the history of political thought. Hugh Sykes Davies, who distanced himself from F.R. Leavis as University Lecturer in English at Cambridge from 1936 to 1974, also was prominent as a poet and novelist. Stephen Toulmin became a major figure, both in Britain and the United States, in the history and philosophy of science.

The Apostles also did significant work in scientific and medical subjects: James Doggart in ophthalmology, Robin Gandy in mathematics, Alan Hodgkin in biophysics, John Mitchison in zoology, Victor Rothschild on the study of sperm speeds by the mathematical technique called probability-after-effect. Bertrand Russell, G.E. Moore, and Ludwig Wittgenstein were Apostles, and Richard Braithwaite and Frank Ramsey made more recent contributions to philosophy. Ramsey died young, but Braithwaite went on to distinction in the philosophy of science and to hold the Knightsbridge Chair of Moral Philosophy, the chair F.D. Maurice and Henry Sidgwick had held. There was another kind of continuity between the Apostles elected before the First World War and those after. W.H. Thompson, Montagu Butler, and G.M. Trevelyan were Masters of Trinity; Norman McLean was Master of Christ's College; John Sheppard was Provost of King's College. Of the Apostles who were elected to the Society after 1919, Alan Hodgkin became Master of Trinity, Noel Annan became Provost of King's, and Geoffrey E.R. Lloyd, the Professor of Ancient Philosophy and Science, became Master of Darwin College.

In a group that included Keynes, it is not surprising that the twentieth-century Apostles should be drawn to economics, as David Champernowne, Harry Johnson, Dennis Robertson, and Robert Henry Scanes Spicer were. Psychology was born at the margins of moral philosophy, and James Strachey, whom the Apostles elected in 1906, went to Vienna, was analyzed by Freud, and returned to Britain to practice. Leonard and Virginia Woolf's Hogarth Press published his translation of Freud's works. Lionel Penrose also studied with Freud, became a physician and a Fellow of the Royal Society, conducted research into the causes of Down's syndrome, and became Galton Professor of eugenics at University College, London. Sebastian Sprott was a demonstrator at the Cambridge Psychological Laboratory and lectured at the University of Nottingham.

Noel Annan has described such groups as an "intellectual aristocracy." But it was an aristocracy of talent rather than of birth or privilege. With an outlook shaped by the spirited discussion of speculative matters, the Apostles were a clerisy of intellectuals and professionals who spoke to the physical and moral well-being of the nation by criticizing narrow, materialistic, and specializing impulses. Operating in what Jurgen Habermas called the "bourgeois public sphere," they were a collection of equals involved in unrestricted rational debate outside the ambit of the state and in a social realm between popular culture and the ruling elite.

W.C. *Lubenow*

Bibliography

Allen, Richard. *The Cambridge Apostles: The Early Years*. 1978.

Deacon, Richard. *The Cambridge Apostles: A History of Cambridge University's Elite Intellectual Secret Society.* 1985.

Appeasement

Broadly defined, appeasement refers to a method of diplomacy whereby a state engages in compromise and negotiation with a potential antagonist in order to alleviate grievances and preserve peace. But within the context of modern British history, appeasement has acquired a negative connotation and become a term of abuse and condemnation. During the 1930s appeasement was the label attached to the conduct of British foreign policy in regard to the Fascist dictatorships. According to critics, the appeasers totally misjudged the evil intentions of the Fascist leaders, negotiated with them out of fear and from a position of military weakness, yielded to diplomatic bullying and cravenly made unilateral concessions, rendering themselves vulnerable to charges of stupidity, cowardice, and moral bankruptcy.

Admittedly, British diplomats faced an unenviable task in the 1930s. **Fascism** appeared to be the wave of the future, and Adolf Hitler and Benito Mussolini demonstrated verve and energy as they furiously rearmed and launched an assault upon existing treaties and territorial boundaries. Despite their personal detestation of Fascism, British diplomats were determined to avoid another war, and acknowledging that the Versailles treaty had been too vindictive, they believed that the legitimate grievances of the Fascist states had to be met. Still, they might have moved more cautiously in view of Hitler's withdrawal from the Disarmament Conference and the **League of Nations** in 1933, and his subsequent attempted subversion of the Austrian state in 1934. Hitler's first major challenge to Britain came in March 1935, when he violated the Versailles treaty by announcing Germany's intention to rearm and reintroduce conscription. But Britain offered only tepid diplomatic protests and then proceeded to negotiate the Anglo-German Naval Agreement. This treaty allowed the German navy to exceed the limits imposed upon it by Versailles, thereby giving the impression that Britain was conniving with Germany behind the back of France in a major breach of treaty. In the autumn of 1935 Italy invaded **Abyssinia**, and Britain, anxious to keep Mussolini as a potential ally against Germany, was apparently willing to make extensive

territorial concessions to Italy under the terms of the infamous **Hoare-Laval Pact**, but when the terms leaked out, an outraged House of Commons forced the government to scrap the deal. Economic sanctions were eventually imposed upon Italy by the League of Nations, but Britain along with most members did not pursue that policy with any tenacity or enthusiasm. When Hitler remilitarized the Rhineland in March 1936, Britain condemned the action but showed no inclination to expel German troops from indisputable German territory, telling the French that no military assistance could be expected in the event of hostilities. When Hitler annexed Austria in early 1938 in a most brutal fashion, Britain showed a marked reluctance to get involved in Central European affairs. The epitome of appeasement was reached during the Czechoslovakian crisis of 1938 when Hitler demanded the German-speaking portions of the Czech state. Britain readily accepted the principle of partition, gave France no encouragement to stand firm, and placed pressure upon the Czechs to accept this humiliating solution. The final agreement involving Czechoslovakia was signed at **Munich** in September 1938, and that name has since become synonymous with surrender and betrayal. It was only after Hitler occupied the remainder of the Czech state in early 1939 that the British government finally began to address itself with some urgency to rearming, negotiating alliances with allies, and taking a firmer line with Germany. Even then, the British **Cabinet** hesitated to declare war upon Germany following its attack upon Poland in September 1939, thus giving the impression that appeasement had not been totally abandoned. Blame for this tragic series of events has fallen mostly upon a relatively small group of Tories, hardly surprising since the **Conservative Party** commanded large majorities in the House of Commons during the 1930s. Two Prime Ministers, **Stanley Baldwin** and **Neville Chamberlain**, have been marked for special censure, especially the latter. Chamberlain was appeasement's principal architect and practitioner and has been savaged by critics as being vain, devious, reluctant to accept expert advice from the **Foreign Office**, and guilty of totally misjudging the personality of Hitler and the inner dynamics of Nazism. Perhaps the most serious criticism is that he continued to pursue appeasement after it became apparent that the policy was ineffective and that Hitler was not interested in honorable negotiations and reasonable compromises but only in diplomatic intimidation and military conquest. Other advocates of appeasement were **Lord Halifax**, the Foreign Secretary at the time of Munich, and two former foreign secretaries, **Sir Samuel Hoare** and **Sir John Simon**. A particularly notorious appeaser was Sir Nevile Henderson, the British ambassador to Germany 1937–9, who has been accused of exceeding his instructions in slavishly trying to accommodate the Germans. A shadowy figure in the appeasement drama was Sir Horace Wilson, the government's industrial adviser, but a man who had an important personal influence upon Chamberlain. Particularly useful to the Prime Minister was **Geoffrey Dawson**, who as editor of *The Times* could use his influential newspaper to sway opinion. But it cannot be emphasized too strongly that support for appeasement, at least up to and including Munich, went well beyond a small clique of Britain's governing elites; this policy found wide acceptance among the general public, including pacifists, university dons, trade unionists, businessmen, newspaper editors, and elements of the **Liberal Party** and **Labour Party**.

Since the Second World War a vast amount of literature has been produced on the topic, generating much controversy and debate. In the immediate post-war period historians and polemicists came down hard on the appeasers, sometimes indulging in personal, vitriolic attacks. But during the 1960s a newer generation of scholars came to the forefront, and more sober and objective scholarship began to assert itself. This was due partly to the release of important government documents as well as the fact that many of the participants began to write their memoirs or at least open their papers to established scholars. The results revealed a more complex situation, less amenable to simplistic analysis and banal cliches, and the end result was that there was now considerably more appreciation of the cruel dilemmas and hard realities facing the appeasers in the 1930s.

Much of this new scholarship revolved around the question of motivation: Why did the appeasers appease? While there was a vast range of answers given to this question and writers frequently hedged their conclusions with qualifications and exceptions, the collective response was that there were several reasons to account for appeasement, some admittedly reprehensible but most understandable under the

circumstances. To begin with, there was the memory of the First World War with all its frightful slaughter and the fear that a future war, made more hideous by the addition of terrifying new weapons, might well destroy civilization. In this respect the appeasers faithfully reflected the sentiments of the general public—anti-war sentiment was pervasive, and peace organizations experienced much growth and popularity—during this period. There was also considerable guilt over the harsh nature of the Versailles treaty, particularly in regard to its economic provisions and the questionable territorial arrangements of Central Europe. By the early 1930s it was inconceivable that Britain would go to war in order to defend such a discredited treaty, especially if the dictators invoked the Wilsonian principle of the self-determination of peoples in order to acquire territory.

Then there was the problem of allies. Historically, there were racial, religious, political, and dynastic bonds linking Britain and Germany, but the French were still viewed with suspicion. Ironically, Britain feared French aggressiveness and power in the 1920s, while by the 1930s France was seen as a nation lacking resolve and will power, riddled with pacifism, defeatism, and political factionalism. Nor could Britain automatically count upon the Empire and Commonwealth; in fact, Britain's leaders were warned that if they got involved in a Continental war over questionable boundary disputes, they could not expect military assistance from the Commonwealth. The United States was viewed at this time as isolationist at best and untrustworthy at worst, too involved with its domestic economic problems to play a decisive role on the international scene. There was always the possibility of a military alliance with the Soviet Union, but aside from the Tories' ideological distaste for Bolshevism, it was believed that the Soviets were militarily weak after the ghastly purges of the officer corps, and that Joseph Stalin would demand too high a price for his support, mainly in the form of territorial annexations in Eastern Europe. In turn, **Marxist historians** claim that the appeasers encouraged Hitler to move eastward, seeing in Hitler a bulwark against Bolshevism and a valuable ally in maintaining the power of capitalism. Lacking reliable allies meant that Britain would have to look after its own defenses, and a rearmament program was launched, though rather belatedly. At the time of the Munich crisis, Britain was woefully short of almost every conceivable weapon, especially modern fighter aircraft, and the military chiefs informed the Cabinet that the armed forces could not prevent Germany from smashing Czechoslovakia in the event of war. Some historians have placed the blame for the nation's sorry state of defenses upon the stinginess of the Treasury, which feared that Britain could never recover from the Great Depression and might well experience an economic catastrophe if it spent vast sums of money on "unproductive" expenditures, such as armaments. Nor should it be forgotten that the Labour Party had consistently voted against defense expenditures up to the summer of 1937, mainly on the grounds that weapons were socially wasteful, economically disastrous, and likely to generate another armaments race with Germany.

Another way of understanding appeasement is to see it in larger historical perspective instead of confining the analysis narrowly to the 1930s. There are historians who argue that appeasement is a traditional policy, going back to the mid-nineteenth century when Britain, for selfish, not altruistic motives, pursued a policy of peace and free trade as being the best guarantor of its continued economic and political predominance. Others taking the long view see Britain as a declining power since the nineteenth century; by the 1930s it was confronted by a menacing coalition of Japan, Italy, and Germany. Faced with such a perilous threat, lacking adequate armaments and allies, Britain either had to pursue a policy of peace at almost any price or risk defeat and disaster in a war. Another argument is that historically Britain never felt compelled to intervene in Central European affairs, the very areas where Hitler was particularly active; the areas of greatest concern to Britain, namely the Low Countries and the Suez Canal, were initially marginal in Hitler's scheme of things. Given these long-range historical considerations as well as the specific forces at work in the 1930s, it is not surprising to find those who would argue that regardless of who was Prime Minister or what political party was in power, the outcome might well have been the same.

This vast amount of scholarship has produced no consensus, but in the midst of conflicting interpretations and partisan explanations, certain broad trends have begun to emerge. It is no longer fashionable to attack the appeasers personally as stupid, craven, or spineless; by and large even critics concede that the appeasers were decent, educated, and well-intentioned, motivated by a love of country and detestation of war, willing to risk personal unpopularity in order to avert the calamity of another conflict. Their guilt consisted more in misjudgment, self-deception, and bungling rather than unashamed cowardice or evil intent. There is also a greater appreciation of the constraints imposed upon the appeasers by strategic, economic, military, and political realities. But despite all this revisionism, few writers have sought to defend or approve what actually transpired during this period; explaining appeasement has not led to justifying it, and Munich will probably always be regarded as a national humiliation for Britain, a shameful surrender to brutality and force, a disgraceful betrayal of principles and peoples.

After the 1930s politicians and nations tried to avoid the label of appeasement, believing correctly or incorrectly that the lesson of Munich was never to accommodate dictators but rather to confront their aggression immediately and directly, especially since they might well be bluffing. This led to a tendency among government leaders to draw historical parallels between Munich and a number of subsequent events. One of the most famous examples occurred in 1956, involving **Sir Anthony Eden,** who was then Prime Minister and, significantly, had been a well-known antiappeaser during the 1930s. When Egypt's President Gamal Abdel Nasser nationalized the Suez Canal, Eden and some of his colleagues believed they saw a parallel with Hitler's bold diplomatic moves, and, disdaining any compromise, they launched an attack against Egypt—with disastrous results for Eden's career and British diplomacy.

David C. Lukowitz

Bibliography

Adams, R.J.Q. *British Politics and Foreign Policy in the Age of Appeasement, 1935–39.* 1993.

Gilbert, Martin. *The Roots of Appeasement.* 1966.

Robbins, Keith. *Appeasement.* 1988.

Rock, William. *British Appeasement in the 1930s.* 1977.

Taylor, A.J.P. *The Origins of the Second World War.* 1961.

Archaeology

While archaeology entered the English language by the beginning of the seventeenth century, it was reserved for the mid-nineteenth century to extend the term to identify the scientific study of the remains and monuments of the prehistoric period. By the twentieth century, British usage increasingly saw archaeology as an alternative scientific method for gaining historical information by obtaining and studying the material remains of the human past, including the relatively recent.

The coming of age of archaeology in Britain and by British scholars worldwide carried with it in the twentieth century not only developments in techniques, methods, and related auxillary disciplines, but also some sense of a requisite ethic in the context in which excavation of the past by necessity implies the destruction of that past. Sir (William Matthew) Flinders Petrie (1853–1942), working at forty sites in Egypt and on its borders, elaborated the principles of stratification and developed pottery classification as an "archaeological chronometer," thereby achieving "sequence dating" as the main tool of the archaeologist. Osbert Guy Stanhope Crawford (1886–1957) introduced the results of aerial reconnaissance photography, developed during the First World War, into archaeological investigation, by the publishing in 1928, with Alexander Keiller, of *Wessex from the Air*; he went on to edit from its inception in 1927 until his death the major British periodical *Antiquity: A Quarterly Review of Archaeology*.

Experimentation has led to such developments as the Weald and Downland Open Air Museum (Singleton, near Chichester, West Sussex), launched in 1967 to rescue representative examples of vernacular buildings from diverse historical periods, and the Butser Iron Age Farm (near Petersfield, Hampshire), originated in 1972, where persons have attempted to live in facilities and under conditions demonstrating the probable validity of archaeological reconstruction.

The work of archaeology is centered upon academic institutions, museums, and societies— learned and amateur, national and local—and reported upon in their various publications. The Society of Antiquaries is the oldest (1707) and most elite, electing members as fellows; its periodical—*Archaeologia, or Miscellaneous Tracts, Relating to Antiquity*—dates from 1770. At least 160 county or local societies originated over the past two centuries, beginning with the Maidstone Historical (1825), the Oxfordshire Architectural and Historical (1839), and the Cambridge Antiquarian (1840), which antedate the greater national organizations: The British Archaeological Association and the Royal Archaeological Institute of Great Britain and Northern Ireland began together (1844) before separating (1846).

British archaeology abroad, funded by the government through the British Academy, is mostly represented by eight schools or institutes: at Athens (1886), Rome (1901), Jerusalem (1919), Iraq (1932), Ankara (1948), Nairobi (1960), Tehran (1963), and Amman (1980). Others promoting archaeological research, headquartered in London, include: the Palestine Exploration Fund (1865), the Society for the Promotion of Hellenic Studies (1879), the Society for the Promotion of Roman Studies (1910), the Egypt Exploration Society (1914), the Society for South Asian Studies (1973), and the Anglo-Israel Archaeological Society (1981). National societies concerned with British archaeology by "period" include: for Roman Studies (1910, but from 1970 also a separate periodical *Britannia*), the Prehistoric (1935), for Medieval Archaeology (1957), for Post-Medieval Archaeology (1967), and for Industrial Archaeology (1974).

Major British names in twentieth-century archaeology include: Sir Arthur John Evans (1851–1941), Sir Charles Leonard Woolley (1880–1960), Robin George Collingwood (1889–1943), Sir Robert Eric Mortimer Wheeler (1890–1976), Vere Gordon Childe (1892–1957), Sir Ian Archibald Richmond (1902–65), Sir Max Edgar Lucien Mallowan (1904–78), Dame Kathleen Mary Kenyon (1906–78), Joan Liversidge (1914–84), and Glyn Edmund Daniel (1914–86, second editor of *Antiquity*). The most impressive British find might well be the Sutton Hoo seventh-century East Anglian royal burial ship, discovered in 1939, whose treasures are in the **British Museum**.

Clyde Curry Smith

Bibliography

Bacon, Edward, ed. *The Great Archaeologists.* 1976.

Daniel, Glyn. *A Hundred and Fifty Years of Archaeology.* 1975.

Selkirk, Andrew. "The *Current Archaeology* Down to Earth Guide to British Archaeology," *Current Archaeology*, vol. 11 (1990), Supplement, pp. 1–32.

Architecture

Twentieth-century architecture in Britain is determined by the competing forces of design traditionalism, material and technological expression, and freestyle innovation that reflect both national and international developments in building. Late Victorian and Edwardian domestic design and public building extend nineteenth-century themes into the opening years of the twentieth century in late manifestations of the arts and crafts movement, high Edwardian baroque classicism, neo-Georgian design, and other traditional, especially classical, revivals that by late century found a symbiotic relationship with modernism in a phenomenon that architectural critic Charles Jencks has called **postmodernism**. Simultaneously, a restrained formalism affecting what **Nikolaus Pevsner** has called "pioneer modernism" prepared the soil for a more abstract and technological avant-garde. During the 1930s both foreign and native practitioners of International Style modernism established a machinist aesthetic that by mid-century had manifested itself in significant housing, university, and multiuse complexes, evolved through a phase of "New Brutalism," and culminated in a high-tech expressionism of international acclaim and native royalist controversy.

A generation of turn-of-the-century arts and crafts architects rediscovered the free style designs of Richard Norman Shaw and the restrained "nonstyle" of Philip Webb and encouraged a veneration for the vernacular in domestic and occasionally commercial design. Webb's Standon (1891–2), East Grinstead, is rooted in local Sussex building traditions but characterized by a picturesque composition of traditional and innovative arts and crafts elements: grouped gables, exaggerated chimney stacks, variegated color and texture, individuality of expression, and a distinctly human scale effected by the diversity of forms and surfaces enriching this large and rambling country house. Stoneywell Cottage (1898–9) in Leicestershire discloses Ernest Gimson's unique translation of native building method and natural materials in a cottage so much a part of its locale it appears to have grown out of the ground several centuries ago.

Edwardian house designers would follow these traditions. **Sir Edwin Lutyens'** series of 1890s masterpieces of residential architecture continued after 1900 with Deanery Garden (1901), nestled behind aged brick walls in the heart of the Berkshire village of Sonning, while Marsh Court, of the same year, translates more historicist forms of Tudor architecture to its native Hampshire chalk walls with flint and red tile accents. This English reference of materials, which looks backward to John Ruskin and forward to New Brutalism and late-century high-tech architecture, finds particular expressiveness at the hand of Detmar Blow, whose butterfly-plan composition for Happisburgh House (1900) in Norfolk combines a roof of local Norfolk reed thatch with traditional wall patterns of local flint. Home Place (originally Kelling Place) (1903–5) by Edward S. Prior is a masterpiece of this local flint and pebble-faced patterning and of arts and crafts artisan handicraft and pictorial colorism.

William Lethaby, at his Liverpool Cathedral competition design (1903), envisioned concrete forms of particularly expressive shapes. Lethaby had just erected an experimental concrete vault at All Saints Church, Brockhampton (1901–2), a Herefordshire church rich in symbolism, innovative in its use of materials and traditional in its exterior formal language, despite its almost German expressionist interior. Randall Wells' restrained Church of St. Edmund the Confessor, Kempley, Gloucestershire (1903), appeared similarly proto-modern in its simplified forms, while C. Harrison's Townsend St. Mary the Virgin Church, Great Warley, Essex (1903–4), looked to Art Nouveau decorative expression as the basis for its displacement of traditional Gothic revivalism with a history-free modernism.

Any move toward restrained surfaces and a machine-efficient aesthetic at the expense of traditional architectural languages would be presaged in the rationalized traditionalism of C.F.A. Voysey (The Orchard, Chorleywood, Hertfordshire, 1900–1) and C.R. Mackintosh (Hill House, Helensburgh, Scotland, 1902–4). Although both of these architects, and these works specifically, were viewed by spokesmen of the new modernism as pioneers of the machine aesthetic, the works of Voysey and Mackintosh more correctly embody individualism, craftsmanship, a simplified traditionalism, and a morality linked to Ruskin and the Gothic. At Upmeads, Stafford (1908), Edgar Wood would cap a flat facade of banded and grouped windows with a flat concrete roof in a house that

A

looks forward in its logical expression of structure and freer interior planning to modern architecture. But Britain would await the arrival of foreigners such as Peter Behrens, Erich Mendelsohn, and Walter Gropius before a full-blown European modernism was felt in England in the late 1920s and especially 1930s.

The mood of the early century in Britain remained a freestyle eclecticism, and nowhere was this more imaginatively expressed within traditional formal elements than by the high Edwardian baroque classicism of A. Brumwell Thomas and John Belcher. At both Belfast City Hall (1897–1906) and Stockport Town Hall, Cheshire (1904–8), Thomas displays the Edwardians' admiration for the innovative English baroque of Christopher Wren, John Vanbrugh, and Nicholaus Hawksmoor. The Belfast City Hall places an elaborate dome on a French palace form accented with corner towers based on Wren's west towers at St. Paul's Cathedral. At Stockport Thomas translates Wren's open, wedding-cake steeple designs into an extravagant Edwardian baroque. The government buildings at Parliament Square in Westminster, London (1898–1912), evidence John Brydon's close reliance on such details as Vanbrugh's towers at Blenheim for source material for his own more English-inspired Edwardian baroque. Perhaps the most extravagant is Belcher's tower for Royal London House, Finsbury Square (1904–5), although his Ashton Memorial in Lancaster (designed 1904, built 1907–9) is a bombastic fanfare of truly Edwardian splendor.

A Continental European baroque (more than English baroque) is reflected at Cardiff Hall and Law Courts (1897–1906) by H.V. Lancaster and Edwin Rickards, an expansive layout of Beaux Arts planning. While Richard Norman Shaw's Piccadilly Hotel, Regent's Street (1905–8), may be said to be "free baroque," the slightly earlier Ritz Hotel (1903–6) by Charles Mèwes and Arthur J. Davis is distinctly Parisian, and their Royal Automobile Club, London (1908–11), contained an entry hall reminiscent of Parisian *passages*, a monumental public gathering place embodying traditional French neo-classicism. Davis redressed Luton Hoo (1903) and Polesden Lacey (1906) in the new French fashion as well.

It was precisely this design method and historicist formalism, by which a popular architectural dress was put on buildings like fashions of clothing, that disengaged the avant-garde

from the practices of previous generations of builders. The trend toward a more technological expression of modern materials and methods was evidenced earliest in Britain in works of the early 1910s. In 1914 the Trussed Concrete Steel Company built a factory of three parallel blocks of reinforced concrete frame for the Birmingham Small Arms Ltd. This work was preceded and then followed by two functionally expressive designs behind classical facades: in 1910–11, John Burnet's Kodak Building, Kingsway, London, and in 1916 the Heal Furniture Store, Tottenham Court Road, a steel frame structure by Dunbar Smith and Cecil Brewer.

Even before the arrival in Britain of European modernists, a more rational modern aesthetic found a basis in the restrained freestyle classicism of such works as H.S. Goodhart Rendel's 1931–2 Hays Wharf and Charles Holden's monumental Senate House, University of London (1932). Moreover, within the streamlined envelope of black and transparent glass of the *Daily Express* Building (Ellis and Clark with Owen Williams, 1931–2), Ronald Atkinson's extravagant lobby ornamented with Egyptian-inspired wall relief sculpture provided London's best Art Deco work of the period. The style, including its streamlined modern phase, is seen well in London cinemas (the Leicester Square Odeon by Harry Weedon dates from 1936–7), and found particularly direct inspiration from transportation forms, as characterizes streamlined moderne, in A. Pleydell Bouverie's 1937 Ramsgate Airport. Some of the finest examples of the period's Deco/modernist eclecticism were in factories of the 1930s, including Wallis Gilbert and Partners' Hoover Factory (1932–5) and the superb row of factories on the Great West Road out of London, including Banister Fletcher's Gillette Factory (1936) and two by Wallis Gilbert and Partners: the Pyrene Factory (1930) and the Firestone Factory (1929).

Once transplanted European modernists arrived in Britain, the influence of the European avant-garde was immediately manifested in a series of classic British monuments of International Style modernism. Behrens built the first modern house in Britain at New Ways (1925–6) in Northampton, and in 1930 the Russian Berthold Lubetkin became the first European modernist to emigrate to Britain. Lubetkin founded Tecton in 1932 and built a series of innovative modernist works from 1933 to late decade. His first projects for the London Zoo include the Gorilla House (1933–4) and the Penguin Pool (1934–5), the latter featuring steel reinforced concrete ramps of structural expressiveness designed with the assistance of Ove Arup and innovative for their time. Tecton's Highpoint I Flats (1933–5) displayed the Le Corbusier five points of the new architecture and manifestly presented to Britain what Le Corbusier called "one of the first vertical garden cities of the future." It is significant, however, that already by 1937–8 at Highpoint II (with its Erechtheum caryatid casts at the entry), the modernist block was marked by mannerisms that would later cause Jencks to include the work in his defining essay on postmodernism.

Modernism was evidenced in private houses (the first expensive London modern house was E. Maxwell Fry's Sun House (1935) at 9 Frognal Way), in blocks of flats, in factory design, and in socialist experiments at health clinics of interest both in and out of London. The machine aesthetic was immediately adapted for industrial and transportation design and for at least one little-known institutional design of precocious structural expressiveness reminiscent of August Perret in France: The Royal Horticultural Society Hall, Westminster (1929), by Stanley Hall and Easton and Robertson, displays a wide-span, reinforced concrete construction to shape a monumental interior space. Further, the reinforced concrete and glass factory in Beeston for Boots Pharmaceutical Company (1930–2) by E. Owen Williams rivals the noted Van Nelle Factory built by J.A. Brinkman and L.C. Van Vlugt outside Rotterdam in 1927–30 in its expression of frame and amount of exposed exterior glass. While hints of the new forms appeared in the work of Holden for London Transport, particularly for such stations as Arnos Grove (1932–3) built for the Piccadilly Line (1930–3), it would be Joseph Emberton who would provide, in his Royal Corinthian Yacht Club, Burnham-on-Crouch (1931), England's only work recognized by Henry Russell-Hitchcock and Philip Johnson as worthy of inclusion in their defining modern architecture exhibition and book *The International Style* (1932). Emberton's best-known London work of the period is the 1935 Simpson Department Store, which he designed with engineer Felix Samuely and designer Lazlo Maholy-Nagy. The year before, Samuely had built the first all-welded-steel frame in England for Erich Mendelsohn's famous pavilion at Bexhill-on-Sea, the only portion constructed of the De La Warr Resort Cure intended to include shops, a cinema, and hotel as well as the pavilion. The year *after* Emberton's Simpson Store, J.A. Slater and A.H. Moberly (with W. Crabtree and Charles Reilly) constructed on Sloane Square the Peter Jones Department Store (1936–8), a work that displays one of London's first glass curtain walls in an expressive curved envelope wrapping around its corner site.

As noted, Behrens introduced Britain to residential modernism at New Ways, and English architects were soon to follow with their own interpretations. The often traditionalist Oliver Hill replaced Webb's 1873 Joldwynds in Surrey with a Modern 1930 version, and the same year Amyas Connell built Ashmole House in Amersham, Buckinghamshire, both early expressions of the stark, rectangular white concrete forms of high modernism. Connell continued the language at Grayswood (1931–2) and "High and Over" (1934), near Ashmole, and in London, near Fry's Sun House, at 66 Frognal Way (1936–8, Connell Ward and Lucas). Modernist houses by Europeans included Tecton's Six Pillars (1935), a house on pilotis with roof terrace expressive of Corbusian modernism and three works of 1936: Serge Chermayeff's house for himself at Bentley Wood, which included a Christopher Tunnard garden; Walter Gropius' (with Maxwell Fry) house for Benn Levy at 66 Old Church Street; and Erich Mendelsohn's and Chermayeff's house next door at 64. Gropius' best known work with Fry was the Impington College complex in Cambridgeshire of 1936. Denys Lasdun, whose work in cluster housing and university design would be noteworthy in the 1960s, had been one of the young English architects gathered by Lubetkin to form Tecton, and at the age of twenty-four Lasdun built a surviving house in London at 32 Newton Road (1938), a work that echoes Le Corbusier's 1926 Maison Cook in Paris.

The socialist intentions of the new architecture were evident especially in blocks of flats and pioneer health centers, the most important of the latter including the Peckham Experiment (Owen Williams' 1934–6 Pioneer Health Center) and Tecton's 1938 Health Center at Finsbury. Among noteworthy designs by native British architects were Wells Coates' Isokon Flats (1933), Maxwell Fry's Ladbroke Grove Flats (c. 1933), Frederick Gibberd's (who would later build Heathrow Airport (1951) three- and seven-story picturesquely sited block of flats called Pullman Court (1935), and Wells Coates' 10 Palace Flats of 1938 based on Le Corbusier's Swiss Pavilion model.

The spatial potential of the new architecture was especially brought to public notice in the Royal Festival Hall (1949–51), South Bank, London, designed by Robert Matthew and Sir Leslie Martin. Its open riverfront facade (the exterior was later remodeled) revealed restaurant and gallery space and free circulation in a modern expression of the new architecture. The later South Bank design by Lasdun for the National Theatre (1967–76) layers stepped terraces in a more form-giving architectural exercise. The exposed aggregate concrete panels and rough-shuttered reinforced concrete of the slightly earlier Queen Elizabeth Hall and Hayward Gallery (1964) are brutal reflections of a new dimension of late modernism.

"Brutal," indeed, was the telling label, as Britain had already initiated an international architectural movement, New Brutalism. The final period of British twentieth-century modern architecture is informed by this movement and produced noteworthy designs for **housing, new universities,** cathedrals, and "Americanized" late modern office buildings and multiuse, large-scale development (and redevelopment), including, at Canary Wharf in the late 1980s and 1990s, Europe's largest construction project.

With the work of Peter and Alison Smithson and James Stirling (1926–92) and James Gowan, designs based on the late-career architectural languages of Le Corbusier, Mies van der Rohe, and, to a lesser extent, Alvar Aalto, informed a British-born movement known as New Brutalism. The Brutalists admired the *beton brut* of late-Corbu and the *art brut* of Jean Dubuffet, the technologically expressive steel and glass of Mies, and the sculptural vitality and rough textural reality of Aalto's forms and brickwork at MIT's Baker House dormitory (1947–51). At Hunstanton Elementary School, Norfolk (1949–53), the Smithsons extended Mies' technological language to a steel-frame, glass, and corrugated metal construction that gloried in its "unfinished" interiors, crude plumbing and electrical fixtures, and exposed heating, ventilation, and air-conditioning systems. Their *Economist* Building in London (1964) grouped three office buildings of varying height around a small piazza integrating pedestrian street life, the civility of the adjacent Boodles Club, and a nonaxial, more inviting contextual link of old and new. Stirling and

The Economist Building, St. James's Street, London (Peter and Alison Smithson, completed 1964).

Gowan's Langham House Flats (1958) were clearly based on Le Corbusier's Maisons Jaoul (1956) and paralleled the tactile, tectonic gruffness of mainstream Brutalism.

Between 1961 and 1965 seven **new universities** were built in England (Sussex, East Anglia, York, Lancaster, Essex, Warwick, and Kent) and an eighth in Scotland, Stirling. **Basil Spence**'s designs for Sussex combined traditional and new materials and forms of concrete frame and brick in distinctly modern works of a classic monumentality, even reflecting beyond its sweeping arches the cloistered traditions of quadrangles. At East Anglia University, Lasdun, on the other hand, turned to the late modern megastructure tradition in a linear arrangement of classrooms and administrative units: The complex picturesquely rambles across open Norfolk countryside and is distinguished especially for its stepped-pyramid student dormitory blocks. Stirling's Andrew Melville Hall at St. Andrews University (1964) and the History Faculty Building at Cambridge (1965–7) were noteworthy, if not wholly successful, additions to academic architecture.

During this same period an "Americanization" of the modern urban skyline began to be felt in Britain as elsewhere in Europe. The slab-on-podium model of Gordon Bunshaft's Lever House influenced both Andrew Renton's design for Thorn House (Basil Spence and Partners, 1957–9) and Sir Robert Matthew, Johnson-Marshall's New Zealand House (1960), the latter, one of the first completely air-conditioned glass-curtain-wall office buildings in London. The more formalist Centrepoint Tower (R. Seifert and Partners, 1967) stood vacant for over a decade, an unintentional monument to the failure of speculative development.

Finally, some noteworthy modern cathedrals continued Britain's historic line of noble ecclesiastical building. The Liverpool Anglican Cathedral, whose competition of 1903 was won by Giles Gilbert Scott with altered designs of 1910 by Scott, was modified again during construction throughout the mid-century. It is one of Britain's great Gothic revival works. Guildford Cathedral (1932–66) by Sir Edward Maufe displays a cool, modern spaciousness, sharp profiles, minimal ornament, and more restrained neo-Gothic lines. Spence won the 1951 competition for the rebuilding of Coventry Cathedral (1956–62). Finally, a distinctly contemporary image for Christ the King Roman Catholic Cathedral, Liverpool (1960–7), by Frederick Gibberd, presents a pavilion as a symbolic "crown of thorns" in a highly derivative work borrowing from Oscar Niemeyer, Auguste Perret, and Marcel Breuer.

Robert M. Craig

Bibliography

Curtis, William J.R. *Modern Architecture since 1900*. 2nd ed. 1982.

Jackson, Anthony. *The Politics of Architecture: A History of Modern Architecture in Britain*. 1970.

Jencks, Charles. *Late-Modern Architecture*. 1980.

Landau, Royston. *New Directions in British Architecture*. 1968.

Murray, Peter, and Stephen Trombley. *Modern British Architecture since 1945*. 1984.

Service, Alastair. *Edwardian Architecture: A Handbook to Building Design in Britain, 1890–1914*. 1977.

Army

The **Boer War** dramatically exposed both Britain's diplomatic isolation and its army's inadequacy. The Anglo-Japanese Naval Treaty of 1902 and the Entente Cordiale of 1904 corrected the former; repairing the latter meant redesign of the size, structure, command system weaponry, and mission of the army. In 1902 the **Committee of Imperial Defence** was established to survey the strategic military needs of the Empire, giving Britain a singularly effective defense planning capability. In 1904 the report of the War Office (Reconstruction) Committee, familiarly known as the Esher Committee, recommended an Army Council mirroring the Admiralty structure, a general staff, and redistribution of function in the War Office on clear and logistical bases. These and other reforms were carried out by Secretary for War **R.B. Haldane,** by whose name they are generally known. He saw to the production of field service manuals that set out regulations specifying staff responsibilities and procedures. His predecessors in the **Cabinet** had variously envisioned a Regular Army of three corps (about 120,000 men) in addition to militia and reserves or a long-service Regular Army supplemented by a short-service home defense army. To rationalize the structure of the forces and save money, Haldane abolished the militia and reserves, creating in 1908 a **Territorial Army** of fourteen divisions, fourteen cavalry brigades, and corps troops for home defense. In addition to this force, whose members could volunteer for overseas service in wartime, the army now had an expeditionary force able to land in Europe in fifteen days from mobilization, as well as colonial forces. Introduction of khaki full dress, new weaponry, tactics, and training methods completed the army's transformation. On the eve of the **First World War** the Regular Army numbered 247,432 with 209,280 reserves and the Territorial Army stood at 268,777.

At the outbreak of European hostilities the United Kingdom sent four divisions immediately to France to play a prearranged role guarding the left flank of the French army's planned advance into Lorraine. Within a few weeks the British had committed two additional divisions and sustained 89,000 casualties of the approximately 108,000 troops fighting. Territorial volunteers plugged the gaps: By December 69,000 of them were serving in France. **Lord Kitchener,** who had been made Secretary for War at the outset of the conflict, set out to create a mass volunteer army known as "the New Army," or "Kitchener's Army." Nearly 1.2 million volunteers had come forward by the end of 1914, swamping the army's training and logistical capabilities. Huge difficulties in transport, supply, medical treatment, and troop welfare had to be mastered. In March 1916 **conscription** was introduced, and by June of that year the British Expeditionary Force in France numbered fifty-seven divisions divided into five armies. Though British army units were used in other theaters, the vast majority fought on the Western Front in a horrifying war of attrition. By war's end, 2.1 million men were serving outside the United Kingdom, nearly 1.4 million inside. Of 1.8 million casualties sustained, 744,702 were killed.

With the **Cabinet's** insistence in 1919 that military planning should proceed on the basis that no major war was anticipated for a decade, the army lost its mission and reverted to a small force for putting down civil disturbances in places as disparate as Ireland and India, as well as guarding the **Royal Air Force** bases by which the Middle East was controlled. This period of the ten-year rule, during which the army had neither plans nor equipment and largely abandoned the professional orientation it had in the pre-1914 reform years, lasted until 1934. Despite the concepts and urging of the tactical visionaries, J.F.C. Fuller and Basil Liddell Hart, the army engaged in only desultory experiments in tank warfare, and, though these were enough to make it the world leader in that department, found it necessary to abandon such experiments after 1934 due to lack of money and equipment. In that year the Cabinet set the course for military spending in austere times by deciding to maintain a first-class navy and develop a first-class air force. Fiscal retrenchment, belief in the efficacy of naval and air forces, and reluctance to commit a mass army to the risk of continental carnage experienced in the First World War, combined to mandate an indefinite future for the army as a colonial police force. After **Munich** the mood changed rapidly, and in February 1939 the Cabinet decided on an army of thirty-two divisions, six regular and twenty-six territorial, to be supplemented by twenty-three Commonwealth divisions. Conscription was introduced in May, and by July the army numbered 237,736 regulars, 212,000 reserves, and 249,000 territorials.

The coming of the **Second World War** caught the army in the midst of an awkward and difficult expansion. As in 1914 it sent four divisions to France on mobilization and was able to add another half dozen by the time of the German attack in the West in May 1940. These were smaller than the 1914 divisions, with three infantry brigades of only three battalions, a total of 13,600 men, as against three brigades of four battalions, 18,073 men, in 1914. They were also better armed, with fifty machine guns to a battalion as against two in 1914, and where the earlier division had fifty-four 18–pound field pieces, eighteen 4.5–inch howitzers and four 60–pound field guns, the 1939 division had seventy-two 25–pound howitzers, forty-eight antitank guns, twenty-eight light tanks and forty-four Bren gun carriers. Yet the German breakthrough was swift and decisive: 199,000 British troops minus their equipment were evacuated from **Dunkirk** by 3 June, and the army was left without a toehold on the Continent. This spared the British a repetition of the horrors of trench warfare and provided both the necessity and the opportunity for rapid re-creation of the army as an offensive force.

The conflict saw not only huge expansion in the Regular Army's size, some of it achieved by incorporating the Territorial Army at the beginning of the war, but significant change in its shape and functioning. From a force of two armored divisions and one brigade in 1939, the army developed a total of twenty-eight armored brigades in 1945. Communications were largely switched from telephone and telegraph to radio early in the war; engineers added airfield construction and problems of amphibious warfare to their agenda; ordnance solved complex difficulties in supplying armies in deserts and jungles with millions of items; medical services became more flexible to accommodate the modern battlefield; and close air/ground cooperation was developed. The human problems of command, multiplied by resistance to mindless discipline by a more educated and sophisticated conscript, were addressed. As the war progressed, it became evident that the decisive theater was once again the West. Since the Allied invasion of France came only after the German army had been thoroughly battered on the Russian front, the British army came out of the war with only 144,079 killed.

At the end of the war the potential for confrontation with the Soviets in Europe combined with unrest in the colonies presented a continuing complex mission for the army. In the immediate post-war years the British maintained an army in Germany, fought a full-scale guerrilla war in Malaya, and contributed a brigade to **United Nations** forces in the Korean War. To counter the effects of massive demobilization, conscription was retained, the term of service set at two years for the regulars and three-and-a-half years for the territorials or reserves. The Territorial Army was assigned the antiaircraft defense of the realm and served as a strategic reserve, even though it was not at full strength until 1952. The beginnings of imperial retreat and the advent of nuclear weaponry made for widespread changes in the army in the mid-1950s. The Royal Air Force assumed complete responsibility for the air defense of Britain, and Territorial Army air defenses were scrapped, with units reassigned or disbanded. Two territorial divisions were earmarked to flesh out North Atlantic Treaty Organization (NATO) forces in wartime, the remainder being assigned to civil defense.

The **Suez crisis** of 1956 exposed the hollowness of Britain's pretense at being able to project force in pursuit of national interests and led to the Defense White Paper of 1957 that deemphasized conventional land forces. Britain would rely on nuclear deterrence in major crises. Garrisons in the colonies were to be downsized, with flareups met by airlifting troops from the United Kingdom. Divisions were scrapped in favor of brigade-group organization. In light of this drastic change of mission and structure, conscription was ended in 1960. The Regular Army was limited thereafter to 185,000 long-service volunteers, while the Territorial Army was pegged at 123,000, with a reserve of nearly 70,000. Through the 1960s the army experimented with organizational forms in an attempt to retain the tradition-laden regiments, cope with worldwide postings of troops, and deal with recruitment problems and fiscal retrenchment. This process produced first "administrative brigades" in which regiments constituted the battalions, then "administrative divisions" of eleven or twelve battalions. By the 1970s most of the historic regiments were no more. Moreover, the Territorial Army had disappeared into a Territorial and Army Volunteer Reserve of 50,000 created in 1966. Despite the presence in Germany of a British Army of the Rhine, the United Kingdom had abandoned the capacity for extended conventional land war in Europe, expecting any clash to be solved by diplomacy or escalate to a nuclear exchange in days. The collapse of the Soviet Union, the reunification of Germany, and progress toward European unity have validated the strategy just as the swift and successful **Falklands War** jus-

tified reliance on deploying a highly trained and mobile force for small conflicts.

Joseph M. McCarthy

Bibliography
Barnett, Correlli. *Britain and Her Army, 1509–1970: A Military, Political, and Social Survey.* 1970.
Barthorp, Michael. *The Armies of Britain, 1485–1980.* 1980.
Blaxland, William Gregory. *The Regiments Depart: A History of the British Army, 1945–1970.* 1971.
Carver, Michael. *The Seven Ages of the British Army.* 1984.
Strawson, John. *Gentlemen in Khaki: The British Army, 1890–1990.* 1989.

Army Education

Education for the rank and file of the British **army**, as distinct from military training and officer education, dates back into the nineteenth century. It was only in the twentieth century, however, that it assumed major proportions and became a subject of political controversy.

During the first fifteen years of the century army education remained the responsibility of the Army Corps of Schoolmasters, which was formed in 1846 to teach those soldiers who needed help with the rudiments of reading, writing, and calculation. In the course of the **First World War**, concern over the morale of wartime volunteer and conscript troops led in 1917–18 to the creation of a new educational scheme designed to improve fighting spirit and avoid unrest through special unit lectures and discussions on the reasons for the conflict, the better world that would arise out of it, and the responsibilities of the citizen-soldier. Largely the work of Lord Gorell, this scheme had barely got under way before the end of the war, and the subsequent demobilization brought it to an end.

In the inter-war years army education returned to its pre-war form, this time under the Army Educational Corps (AEC), which replaced the Army Corps of Schoolmasters in 1922. The **Second World War**, however, witnessed a revival of interest in the idea of current affairs and citizenship schemes with the advent of a new mass army and concerns over its morale. With the overall aim of improving morale by explaining what the war was about and what victory would bring, large-scale educational efforts were undertaken, with strong backing from Sir Ronald

Adam (Adjutant-General). In August 1941 the Army Bureau of Current Affairs (ABCA) was formed under the direction of W.E. Williams, charged with providing pamphlets and other material for unit junior officers to use as a basis for weekly current affairs discussions with the men under their command. In 1942 came the British Way and Purpose (BWP), a compulsory course in citizenship run by the AEC. By 1944, quite apart from the remedial reading and writing work undertaken by the AEC, current affairs and citizenship work had become so prevalent that virtually every man and woman in the British army was being exposed to special civilian lectures, ABCA discussions, and BWP classes in one form or another.

Controversy, however, arose over the impact of what was being taught, especially in the wake of the stunning Conservative defeat in the general election of July 1945. Tory critics charged that schemes such as ABCA had been covertly left wing in nature and had inculcated a bias against the Conservatives in the minds of soldiers—thereby swinging the vote decisively in favor of Labour. Though it was true that many of those involved in wartime army education were left-wingers, there is no real evidence to suggest that the ABCA or BWP classes seriously affected the election.

Meanwhile, the apparent success of the wartime citizenship and current affairs schemes in keeping up morale had led to the adoption of modified versions in the post-war National Service army. The advent of the Cold War, however, coupled with official concerns over the pro-Soviet tone of the material being produced by Williams' new civilian Bureau of Current Affairs, had by the end of the 1940s led to the abandonment of this form of education. Since then army education, under the supervision of the Royal Army Educational Corps ("Royal" was added in 1946) has focused on basic technical and remedial instruction.

S.P. MacKenzie

Bibliography

Hawkins, T.H., and L.J.F. Brimble. *Adult Education: The Record of the British Army.* 1947.
MacKenzie, S.P. *Politics and Military Morale: Current Affairs and Citizenship Education in the British Army, 1914–1950.* 1992.
White, A.C.T. *The Story of Army Education, 1643–1963.* 1963.
Wilson, N. Scarlyn. *Education in the Forces, 1939–46: The Civilian Contribution.* 1948.

Arts Council of Great Britain

When the war came to an end in 1945 the Council for the Encouragement of Music and the Arts (CEMA) had not only earned its citation for meritorious achievement in fulfilling its original terms of reference to prevent the blackout of the arts in wartime; it also had shown that there was a continuing role in making the arts more accessible to the population.

On 12 June 1945 the Chancellor of the Exchequer announced in the House of Commons that the government would incorporate the Arts Council of Great Britain to be financed by the Treasury. The Royal Charter, dated 9 August 1946, constituted the Arts Council of not more than sixteen persons, selected by the Chancellor, after consultation with the Minister for Education and the Secretary of State for Scotland, together with separate and autonomous committees for Scotland and Wales. There is a separate Arts Council for Northern Ireland. The council does not comprise persons representing other organizations, but members are chosen for their professional knowledge of, or concern for, one or more of the fine arts. Members retire on a system of rotation so as to prevent any solidification of interest.

Supporting the council are advisory panels, initially for music, drama, art, and poetry, their membership changing every three years. These have since been extended to include advisory panels for dance, literature, photography, and film. No one taking part in this network of policy-making is paid for the work. The Arts Council is not a government department and bears little resemblance to those ministries of fine arts that exist in other countries. No minister directs policies or decides how, and to whom, its grants shall be made. There is no single instance on record of a minister requiring or directing, or even advising, the Arts Council to do this or not to do that. And when from time to time some action of the Arts Council is criticized in the House of Commons, successive governments have invariably declared that they will not interfere with the Arts Council's discretion.

This liberty of action carries with it the obligation upon the Arts Council to discharge its duties within the objectives set out in its Royal Charter:

(1) To develop and improve the knowledge, understanding and practice of the arts;

(2) To increase the accessibility of the arts to the public throughout Great Britain;

(3) To advise and cooperate with departments of government, local authorities, and other bodies to achieve these objectives.

As a recipient of public funds, the Arts Council publishes an annual report, containing its audited accounts, to provide Parliament and the general public with an overview of the year's work and to record all grants and guarantees offered in support of the arts in England, Scotland, and Wales.

The first years's grant-in-aid from the Treasury totaled £235,000 (for 1945–6), and this has increased annually to £820,000 (1955–6), £3.91 million (1965–6), £28.85 million (1975–6), £106.05 million (1985–6) and to £221.2 million (1992–3).

The first Chairman of the council was Sir Ernest Pooley, who was succeeded by Sir **Kenneth Clark** (later Lord Clark) in 1952. Sir William Emrys Williams, who had been a member of CEMA and the Arts Council from 1940 to 1951, was appointed Secretary-General in 1951, the start of the most significant period of development for the arts in Great Britain and served until his retirement in 1963. In 1965 Lord Goodman was named the council's Chairman. Together with the appointment of Jennie Lee as Great Britain's first Minister for the Arts, the council was granted a new Royal Charter of Incorporation by the Queen on 7 February 1967. This increased the membership of the council from a maximum of sixteen to twenty and redesignated the Scottish and Welsh committees as councils. By the time Lord Goodman retired from the council in 1972, the major national arts institutions in **London** had been supplemented by the development of the arts resources to major regional companies throughout the rest of the United Kingdom.

The two most significant periods of office since the new Royal Charter have been those of Sir Hugh Willatt as Secretary-General (1968–75), and his successor, Sir Roy Shaw (1975–83). As the most-senior paid employees, both developed even more ambitious policies throughout these periods, placing great emphasis on supporting the work of creative artists, playwrights, and composers. Since 1983, appointments to the council have tended to be administrators, accountants, academics, and lawyers rather than creative artists, and the council's officers have shifted policy from developing the arts and entertainments profession, maintaining and improving standards, and making the arts increasingly accessible to the population generally to a more value-for-money efficient business as required by government directives during **Margaret Thatcher**'s regime. This, in turn, has led to the Arts Council becoming a much less important force in the arts world since 1981 and, in 1990, delegating increasing responsibilities to newly created Regional Arts Boards.

It is too early to tell whether this change from primarily central-government funding to more commercial sponsorship will enable Britain to maintain the high level of international earnings and benefits derived by the Treasury from the previous government investment in the arts.

The grant that Parliament annually votes to the Arts Council is offered in response to its application for funds based upon a precise appraisal of the needs of the hundreds of organizations it supports. The government grant invariably falls far short of the total Arts Council requirements, but if the council were to decide to withdraw its subsidy completely from any major organization, its total Treasury grant could well be reduced. It was originally hoped that the Arts Council would be given a quinquennial grant, so as to enable it to conduct long-term planning. Although a number of attempts have been made to institute at least a triennial grant, the national financial situation has obstructed that aspiration, and, consequently, for nearly half a century the council has been compelled to practice hand-to-mouth policies.

One of the most fundamental changes of policy that has occurred in the Arts Council's history has been the diminution of directly provided activities and the consequent development of self-governing, nonprofit distributing companies, registered as charities, to provide the arts activities in Great Britain. This ensures that creative artists (playwrights, composers, choreographers, artists, sculptors, writers, poets, and so on) are twice-removed from political control—once by the autonomous Arts Council, protected by its Royal Charter, and again by the independent producing companies.

The primary responsibility imposed by the Royal Charter is to preserve and improve standards of performance in the various arts. Thus, the Arts Council established the principal national institutions and helped preserve them with regular, annual subsidies: the Royal Opera, the Royal Ballet, the **Royal National Theatre** and the **Royal Shakespeare Company**. Next came the development of the Welsh National and the Scottish Opera Companies and the major symphony **orchestras** both in London and in the regions (in Liverpool, Manchester, Birmingham, Bournemouth, and Glasgow). Finally came the establishment of the network of regional drama companies in all the main cities and towns, with the help of Housing the Arts funds to provide new and refurbished buildings.

Since 1980 there has been increasing encouragement to move toward a mixed economy, so that the commercial world of the arts can help exploit subsidized activities to the benefit of both areas of work. For example, over half of the West End theater productions in recent years originated in subsidized companies. Further, most commercial productions, film, radio, and **television** programs, videos and cassette discs, and many British productions seen worldwide have been wholly dependent on talent trained and developed by subsidized drama, dance, and **opera** companies and orchestras.

Anthony Field

Bibliography

Harris, John S. *Government Patronage of the Arts in Great Britain*. 1970.
Hutchison, Robert. *The Politics of the Arts Council*. 1982.
Landstone, Charles. *Off-Stage*. 1953.
Shaw, Roy. *The Arts and the People*. 1987.
White, Eric Walter. *The Arts Council of Great Britain*. 1975.

Ashton, Frederick (1904–1988)

Frederick Ashton, one of the handful of great ballet choreographers of the twentieth century, was largely responsible for formulating the British style of classic **ballet**, in "chamber" ballets made for the tiny stage of Marie Rambert's Ballet Club, then in larger works for the company founded by **Ninette de Valois** and known first as the Vic-Wells, then as the Sadler's Wells Ballet, and finally in ballets on a grand scale that he created for that company after it moved to the Royal Opera House, Covent Garden, in 1946. In 1963 he succeeded de Valois as Director of the company, which had become the Royal Ballet in 1956. He retired from that position in 1970.

Ashton had been inspired to become a dancer by seeing the great Russian ballerina Anna Pavlova in 1917, in Lima, Peru, where he grew up, but it was not until the early 1920s that he was able to pursue this ambition, when he began to study in London, first with the Russian choreographer Leonide Massine, then with Rambert. She encouraged Ashton to try his hand at choreography, and his first ballet, *A Tragedy of Fashion*, was presented in a London revue in 1926. Another major influence was Bronislava Nijinska, the sister of Vaslav Nijinsky, who was the choreographer of a company formed by Ida Rubinstein in Paris in 1928, in which Ashton was briefly employed as a dancer.

Returning to London, Ashton continued to choreograph both for Rambert's dancers and for the Camargo Society, an organization formed to fill the gap left in London dance seasons by the disbandment of the Ballets Russes following the death of Serge Diaghilev. He also worked in the commercial theater, staging dance numbers for musical comedy, revue, and cabaret, and for films. His first major successes were *Capriol Suite* (1930), a suite of court and country dances, and *Façade* (1931), which satirized various social and theatrical dance forms.

In 1934 he traveled to the United States to stage the Virgil Thomson-Gertrude Stein opera *Four Saints in Three Acts*, first in Hartford, then in New York. This gave him his first taste of international fame, but he returned to London, where in the following year he was invited by de Valois to join the Vic-Wells Ballet. He had previously worked for her as a guest dancer and choreographer, notably of *Les Rendezvous* (1933), which showed the beginnings of a personal neo-classical style, but now he was to be the company's resident choreographer. The association continued for the rest of his life.

During the rest of that decade Ashton created a series of ballets notable for the distinction of his collaborations with Constant Lambert, who, as Musical Director of the company, was responsible for arranging and sometimes composing scores; with designers such as Sophie Fedorovitch, **Cecil Beaton**, and William Chappell; and with the ballerina **Margot Fonteyn**, who emerged from the *corps de ballet* at the age of sixteen to become Ashton's muse for the next twenty-five years.

During the **Second World War** British choreographers felt the need to celebrate the nation's literary heritage, as in Robert Helpmann's *Comus* (1942) and *Hamlet* (1942). Ashton also contributed to this trend with *The Quest* (1943), derived from Edmund Spenser's *The Faerie Queene*. But his first ballet at Covent Garden, *Symphonic Variations* (1946), was an affirmation of the supremacy of the classic dance. From then on dance was of primary importance in his work, even when he told a story, as he did in his first three-act ballet, *Cinderella* (1948), *Daphnis and Chloe* (1951), *Sylvia* (1952), and *Ondine* (1956), all of which were created with Fonteyn in mind.

Ashton also developed the talents of younger dancers, such as Nadia Nerina and David Blair in his new version of the old ballet *La Fille mal gardée* (1960), Lynn Seymour and Christopher Gable in *The Two Pigeons* (1961), and Antoinette Sibley and Anthony Dowell in *The Dream* (1964), each of them a masterpiece, as well as setting the seal on the new partnership of Fonteyn with Rudolf Nureyev in *Marguerite and Armand* (1963). The two trios that comprise *Monotones* (1965–6) represent the purest distillation of Ashton's classicism.

After his retirement Ashton contented himself for several years with choreographing small *pièces d'occasion*—small, that is, in scale, though *Thais* (1971) for Sibley and Dowell, *The Walk to the Paradise Garden* (1972) for Merle Park and David Wall, and *Five Brahms Waltzes in the Manner of Isadora Duncan* (1975–6) for Seymour, are perfect works of art. In 1976 he returned to the larger scale with a long one-act ballet, *A Month in the Country*, based on Ivan Turgenev's play, also for Seymour, which showed no diminution in his powers.

His last major work was *Rhapsody* (1980), fulfilling a long-held wish to choreograph Serge Rachmaninov's *Rhapsody on a Theme of Paganini,* to which he made a piece that celebrated the virtuosity of Mikhail Baryshnikov and the Royal Ballet ballerina Lesley Collier. Ashton always felt that he was more appreciated in New York than he was at home, and for the opening of the 1983 Royal Ballet season at the Metropolitan Opera House he confected a *bonne bouche, Varii capricci.* He continued to involve himself in revivals of his ballets, such as the *Romeo and Juliet* he had choreographed for the Royal Danish Ballet in 1955, revived by the London Festival Ballet in 1985, and *Ondine*, restored to the Royal Ballet repertory in 1988.

Ashton was a master of choreographic structure, building what he called the "scaffolding" of his ballets on the foundation of the musical score; in his realization of Igor Stravinsky's *Scènes de ballet* (1948), perhaps his greatest work, every step is related to the whole structure. But even a seemingly light *divertissement* like *Les Patineurs* (1937) can serve as an object lesson in putting a ballet together. Ashton may not have accomplished what the critic Alan M. Kriegsman called the "radical transfiguration" of the vocabulary of classic dance proposed by George Balanchine; his great contribution was to enlarge the use of classic dance as a poetic language, to encompass subject matter of such subtlety and psychological complexity as he addressed in *Enigma Variations* (1968) and *A Month in the Country*, and yet preserve the autonomy of the dance itself.

David Vaughan

Bibliography

Dominic, Zoë, and John Selwyn Gilbert. *Frederick Ashton: A Choreographer and His Ballets.* 1971.

Macaulay, Alastair. *Some Views and Reviews of Ashton's Choreography.* 1987.

Manchester, P.W. *Vic-Wells: A Ballet Progress.* 1942.

Vaughan, David. *Frederick Ashton and His Ballets.* 1977.

Asquith, H(erbert) H(enry) (1852–1928)

As Liberal Prime Minister from April 1908 to May 1915 and head of a coalition government thereafter until December 1916, H.H. Asquith was the central figure in an era of intense political passion and turbulence. His premiership saw the breaking of the power of the **House of Lords**, the introduction of social reforms that laid the foundation of the **welfare state**, legislation for self-government in Ireland that brought the nation to the brink of civil war, and foreign and defense policies that ensured that Germany's war in Europe would not be quickly triumphant.

Asquith's parliamentary career from 1886 onward was of such apparently ineluctable success that many students of his life were inclined to underestimate the ambition and application that had propelled him forward. His father, a Yorkshire wool merchant, died when Herbert was eight. In spite of a much disrupted youth, the self-help, radicalism, and pragmatism of

Yorkshire's business Liberals were deeply imprinted. A Balliol College fellowship followed a succession of academic honors at Oxford and presidency of the Oxford Union. But politics was Asquith's vocation. The **legal profession** had to be the path to financial security. While still a junior barrister, supplementing his income with lecturing and journalism, he married Helen Melland, the daughter of a prominent Manchester doctor. When she died fourteen years later, leaving him with five children, he had begun to recognize that she was "a restricting rather than a stimulating influence." His second wife, Margot Tennant, brought an appetite for society and politics that more than matched his own. Her father's wealth also relieved Asquith of the full burden of supporting the life-style of a prospective party leader.

Making his mark as Liberal MP for East Fife, he was invited to join W.E. Gladstone's last government as Home Secretary in 1892. In an increasingly discordant **Cabinet** after Lord Rosebery succeeded Gladstone, Asquith was an effective departmental chief, a forceful debater, and a respected contributor to collective deliberations. By the time the government fell, he and many colleagues realized that it was only a matter of time and the avoidance of calamity before he reached the top.

The opportunity to step forward came when Sir William Harcourt relinquished the Liberal leadership in the House of Commons. But, foreseeing only years of dismal opposition ahead, Asquith resisted pressure to claim the prize. Expecting that **Sir Henry Campbell-Bannerman** would stand aside after the next general election, he set himself to put by funds sufficient to allow his undivided attention to party affairs.

Having allowed Campbell-Bannerman (who preferred the designation C.B.) to come to the fore, Asquith showed him scant loyalty. During the **Boer War** and afterward he did not hesitate to advertise their differences or to organize friends and followers to fight for control of the party. He conspired to have C.B. removed to the House of Lords in the event of a Liberal ministry being formed. But when the **Conservative** government collapsed in 1905, it was unthinkable that he would decline the offer of the Chancellorship of the Exchequer. The compact he had made with **Sir Edward Grey** and **R.B. Haldane** was dissolved, and these three Liberal Imperialists became key members of the new government.

On his unchallenged accession to the premiership in May 1908 he shifted the balance of the ministry by promoting **David Lloyd George** to the Exchequer and **Winston Churchill** to the Board of Trade. The Liberals were already in conflict with the House of Lords, yet no one foresaw the upheaval that was to be precipitated by the Lords' rejection of Lloyd George's 1909 budget. The ensuing constitutional crisis tested all of Asquith's capacity to hold his Cabinet and party together, to withstand the robust bargaining of the Irish Nationalists who held the balance of power in the Commons after January 1910, and to face repeated onslaughts from a bitter opposition.

Asquith relied on his colleagues for the initiatives and energy that sustained the government. He could declare policy emphatically but was rarely its creator. Nevertheless, the Liberal reform program—from the proposed abolition of plural voting to the introduction of national insurance against **unemployment** and invalidity, from trades boards and labor exchanges to Welsh disestablishment and land taxes—could not have proceeded without his blessing and at times his decisive intervention.

Beset by growing industrial unrest, suffragette militancy, and vehement Conservative resistance to Irish Home Rule, Asquith's position as party leader was strengthened even as his ministry's hold on power grew more precarious. Liberal fortunes had not been helped by quarrels over naval estimates, incompetent preparation of the 1914 budget, the continuing unpopularity of national insurance, and unresolved wrangling over Lloyd George's land campaign. But the German invasion of Belgium brought instant clarity to a political situation of ominous uncertainty.

Asquith's grip on power was progressively eroded as expected early victories did not materialize. The creation of a coalition with the Conservatives in May 1915 alienated many of his own party. It also set him on a path of compromise over manpower, **conscription**, and economic mobilization that continually dismayed a minority of Liberals while rarely satisfying a majority of their coalition partners.

In some respects, more significant than policy difficulties in undermining the premier's authority was the manifest deterioration in his personal dedication and capability. Excessive drinking, noted a decade or more earlier, had by 1916 seriously diminished his capacity to cope with the unprecedented demands of wartime political management. An overlapping succession of friendships with younger women did not compensate for the lost companionship of Venetia Stanley, whose decision to marry his colleague **Edwin Montagu** was a devastating blow. The final emotional trauma was the death in action of his eldest son, Raymond, in September 1916.

From the outbreak of the **First World War** Asquith had placed great reliance on the presence at the War Office of **Lord Kitchener**. Kitchener's death in June 1916 robbed the ministry of a symbol of national unity. Meanwhile, Lloyd George was widely recognized as the embodiment of a spirit of full-hearted commitment to victory. Asquith was increasingly perceived as an impediment to overdue institutional changes and drastic policy solutions. There was enough truth in this to shake the loyalties even of some senior Liberal colleagues. When Lloyd George, **Andrew Bonar Law**, and **Sir Edward Carson** made common cause late in 1916 to insist on changes at the top, Asquith at first overestimated the strength of his own position. Concluding within a few days that he was likely to be reduced to a figurehead as Prime Minister, he resigned.

By refusing to take a subordinate place in the ministry while clinging to the leadership of the **Liberal Party**, Asquith ensured that the party itself would lose the benefit of association with the government in power when Germany was finally defeated. The next twelve years of his life were a melancholy coda. Rejected by the electors in 1918, he returned to the Commons in 1920 to lead a greatly depleted party. After the fall of the Lloyd George coalition in 1922 an uneasy reconciliation of Liberal forces was effected. Asquith retained the titular leadership of the Liberal Party after losing his seat in 1924 and accepting a peerage. He resigned at last in 1926, leaving Lloyd George to lead the Liberal remnant.

In retirement he wrote his *Memories and Reflections* (1928). Complementing earlier works on *The Genesis of the War* (1923) and *Fifty Years of Parliament* (1926), the autobiography was an austere but still revealing record. At the height of his powers Asquith had been a formidable parliamentarian. But there was no hiding the lack of vision to focus and sustain the outstanding qualities that had so impressed his contemporaries.

Cameron Hazlehurst

Bibliography

Brock, Michael, and Eleanor Brock, eds. *H.H. Asquith: Letters to Venetia Stanley*. 1985.

Hazlehurst, Cameron. "Herbert Henry Asquith," in John P. Mackintosh, ed. *British Prime Ministers in the Twentieth Century*. vol. 1. 1977. pp. 78–117.

Jenkins, Roy. *Asquith*. rev. ed. 1978.

Koss, Stephen. *Asquith*. 1976.

Searle, G.R. *The Liberal Party: Triumph and Disintegration, 1886–1929*. 1992.

Spender, J.A., and Cyril Asquith. *Life of Herbert Henry Asquith, Lord Oxford and Asquith*. 2 vols. 1932.

A

Astor, Nancy Witcher Langhorne (1879–1964)

American-born Nancy Langhorne of Virginia became, as Viscountess Astor, the first woman to sit in the House of Commons. Emigrating to Britain in her twenties as a young divorcee with a small child, she married the rising Conservative politician Waldorf Astor. Her 1919 victory in the by-election followed her husband's retirement from the Commons after inheriting his father's title and exemplified the success of the feminist movement in claiming women's political equality to men. She subsequently enjoyed a long career in Parliament, representing her Plymouth constituency for the **Conservative Party** until her retirement in 1945. During that time her tenacious and ebullient personality carved out a place for herself and the women who followed her in a seemingly irredeemably masculine institution.

Lady Astor's political achievements evidenced a deeply felt, personal feminist commitment. Astor worked on behalf of the legislation that equalized the grounds for **divorce** (1923) and lowered the voting age of women from thirty to twenty-one (1928). She consistently defended the right of married women to work and supported the principle of **equal pay**. She warmly welcomed women MPs of all parties who joined her in the Commons, creating a small community for them and encouraging their careers.

Nancy Astor's **feminism** exhibited a moralistic and socially conservative point of view, but it also reflected her own personal experience and her sympathy for human suffering. Her first marriage, to an alcoholic and abusive husband, gave her a lively appreciation of the plight of many women similarly circumstanced. Her interest in education issues, especially nursery schools, derived much of its energy from her experience as a mother and her love of children. She also continued to be an ardent champion of temperance throughout her life. Temperament, personal experience, and religious conviction—she was an unwavering Christian Scientist—underlay her views, but she lacked either a comprehensive political agenda or a coherent philosophical system.

Nancy Astor's political career manifested major historical developments in two other respects. Her prominent position as a wealthy political hostess and her support of **Neville Chamberlain**'s policy of **appeasement** led the popular press of the 1930s to attribute to her and her social circle, known as the **Cliveden Set**, undue influence on the course of British foreign policy. No substantive evidence supports this conspiratorial theory, although it enjoyed wide circulation at the time. Upon the outbreak of war Astor candidly admitted her misjudgment of the situation and became a staunch supporter of **Winston Churchill**'s war **Cabinet**, despite the notorious and long-standing antipathy between these two strong personalities of the Conservative Party.

Astor's close identification with her constituency in Plymouth, which suffered heavily during the **Blitz**, and her work to bolster public morale defined the final stage of her public career. Seemingly tireless, her ubiquitous presence and jaunty manner became emblematic of England's continued will to resist attack and carry on the war effort to victory.

Nancy Astor's election to Parliament had great symbolic significance. She also enjoyed real, if limited, success as a parliamentarian. A prominent public figure throughout the 1920s, 1930s, and 1940s, she had a decisive impact on developing and shaping the possibilities available to **women** entering the English political system after the **First World War**.

Gail L. Savage

Bibliography

Grigg, John. *Nancy Astor: A Lady Unashamed*. 1980.
Harrison, Brian. "Nancy Astor: Publicist and Communicator" in *Prudent Revolutionaries*. 1987. pp. 73–97.
Sykes, Christopher. *Nancy: The Life of Lady Astor*. 1972.

Atomic Weapons
See NUCLEAR WEAPONS

Attlee, Clement Richard (1883–1967)

Clement Attlee was leader of the **Labour Party** between 1935 and 1955, Deputy Prime Minister during the **Second World War** in the **Churchill** coalition, and Prime Minister of the Labour government between 1945 and 1951. He became Earl Attlee in 1955.

Attlee was born on 3 January 1883, in Putney, the seventh child of a successful upper-middle-class family. He was educated at Haileybury School between 1896 and 1901 and then proceeded to University College, **Oxford**, where in 1904 he took a degree in **history**. After spending a desultory period working in a law office, Attlee committed himself to **settlement** work among the poor in the East End of **London** at Haileybury House, Stepney, which prompted his conversion to socialism. He joined the **Independent Labour Party** in 1907, becoming parliamentary candidate for Limehouse. When the **First World War** broke out, Attlee joined the South Lancashire regiment, serving with distinction at **Gallipoli** and in Mesopotamia, where he was wounded, and ending the war with the rank of major.

In 1919, after Labour gained control of the Stepney council, he was co-opted as Mayor, his first political office. He served successfully in this post until 1920, joining **George Lansbury**'s Poplar campaign against tax cuts. In the general election of 1922 Attlee won Limehouse for Labour and was immediately given a post in the Parliamentary Labour Party, serving as Private Secretary to the leader, **Ramsay MacDonald**. He held his seat in the election of December 1923 and, when Labour formed its first government, was rewarded with a junior office, Undersecretary at the War Office. In 1927 MacDonald recommended his appointment to the **Simon** Commission on constitutional reform in India. Despite some hesitations, Attlee served enthusiastically, gaining first-hand experience of India and becoming committed to a gradual move toward self-government. His position on the Simon Commission disqualified him for office when MacDonald formed his second government in 1929. But after **Oswald Mosley** resigned in May 1930, Attlee replaced him as Chancellor of the Duchy of Lancaster. Though less aggressive in this post than Mosley, Attlee did use it to make a study of economic affairs, putting together his own memorandum on economic policy, which was duly ignored by the **Cabinet**. In February 1931 he was shifted to his first administrative position, becoming Postmaster-General.

Attlee was on holiday in August 1931 when the government broke apart. In the election that followed in October, which cut Labour's parliamentary strength to a handful and decimated its leadership, Attlee retained his seat in Limehouse with a majority of only 551. He and **Stafford Cripps**, though both junior, were the only former ministers left in the Parliamentary Labour Party and were, therefore, natural choices to be lieutenants of the new parliamentary leader, George Lansbury. Attlee, who became deputy leader, worked tirelessly, making an enormous number of speeches both in Parliament and throughout the country. When Lansbury resigned from the leadership in 1935 over foreign-policy disagreements, Attlee was made interim leader for the election and, in November 1935, won the permanent leadership, against challenges from **Herbert Morrison** and Arthur Greenwood. Drawing upon the support of the core Parliamentary Party of 1931–5, Attlee took 58 votes on the first ballot, to Morrison's 44 and Greenwood's 33. Greenwood then dropped out, and Attlee won the second ballot by 88 to 48.

Attlee's style of leadership differed considerably from that of his predecessors. He was, first of all, ready to follow collective decisions rather than initiate them. In the revision of domestic and international policy during the 1930s, for instance, Attlee supported the shift in Labour's outlook, generally to the left in domestic policy and toward support for rearmament in foreign policy, but he did not really leave his imprint on policy, as **Hugh Dalton, Ernest Bevin**, and Morrison did in different ways. Attlee did help ease Labour toward these developments, but he was not willing to sacrifice party unity for a clear lead on his part. This was particularly true over the question of nonintervention in the **Spanish Civil War**. By 1937 and 1938 he was, however, taking a very firm line against the National government over Spain and the **Munich** agreement. He effectively articulated Labour's socialism in two works, *The Will and the Way to Socialism* (1935) and *The Labour Party in Perspective* (1937). Throughout this period his bland leadership within the party was questioned by those who envisaged Morrison or Dalton as inevitable successors.

It was the Second World War that strengthened his position within the party. First of all, Labour participation in Churchill's coalition from May 1940 gave him an opportunity to demonstrate his considerable administrative talents. Attlee may not have been a born leader, but he was a born committee man. Serving as Lord Privy Seal, Lord President, Dominions Secretary, and, unofficially at first and then officially from February 1942, as Deputy Prime Minister, he proved his skills at running a Cabinet. In many ways it was a dry run for his premiership in 1945. Attlee also showed his abilities at balancing the often volatile personalities of the coalition. His relationship with the party outside of Westminster was less happy, since he faced sustained criticism thoughout the war from the Left, particularly from **Harold Laski**, the most prominent left-wing intellectual. Through the war Attlee contributed importantly to both the coalition and the party. Within the government he played an important role both in the shape of reconstruction policy and on such issues as India and post-war planning for foreign relations.

Attlee's strengthened position became evident during the 1945 election campaign, particularly in the contrasting image of calm he presented against Churchill's more hysterical stance. There was a brief and abortive attempt by Morrison to unsaddle Attlee after the election results, which was largely stymied by Bevin, a pillar of Attlee's strength. The experience of premiership between 1945 and 1951 demonstrated most of Attlee's virtues and some of his weaknesses. His choice of Cabinet was adroit, particularly in placing Bevin at the Foreign Office and **Aneurin Bevan** at the Ministry of Health. He also proved capable at drawing upon younger talent in the parliamentary party, such as **Harold Wilson** and **Hugh Gaitskell**. Attlee quickly asserted his particular style of effective and clear Cabinet administration, generally following the drift of opinion within the Cabinet and using that to secure collective decisions.

In foreign affairs he lent considerable support to Bevin, his Foreign Secretary (and received Bevin's support at home). He shared the latter's opposition to the Soviet Union and his desire to bring the Americans toward commitment on the world stage, cemented with the establishment of the North Atlantic Treaty Organization in 1949. Attlee put much emphasis upon building up the **United Nations**; in

A

this regard, for instance, he supported the use of military sanctions against North Korea in 1950. Attlee also took a controversial decision, with Bevin, in 1946 to build a British **nuclear weapon**. His real triumph on the international stage, and one for which he can claim almost sole credit, was the independence of India, granted on 15 August 1947. Attlee's personal interventions in this sphere hastened the movement toward independence; replacing **Archibald Wavell** as Viceroy with **Earl Mountbatten** in 1947, setting a definite date for independence, and keeping the new republic within the Commonwealth were masterstrokes. The speed with which independence was effected in both India and Burma after the war stands as the greatest testament to Attlee's skill at governing.

On the home front, Attlee was less obviously prominent, delegating responsibility to the relevant ministers. The economic crises of 1947 shook Attlee's position within the government and, in September of that year, he was faced with what amounted to a palace coup engineered by Cripps. Attlee's deceptive strength, and the support of Bevin, helped him foil the most significant challenge to his leadership during the years of government, defusing Cripps' threat with the offer of higher office. The dollar-gap crisis, trade union unrest, and arguments over the **nationalization** of the **steel industry** during 1949 nonetheless helped to undermine Attlee's position and the reputation of the government.

In March 1950 Attlee called an election, which Labour won narrowly, its majority reduced to only fifteen. The following twenty months put a great strain on Labour and Attlee himself. He was, first of all, faced with a growing split that turned largely on a rivalry between his favored successor for the leadership, the left-winger Bevan, and Gaitskell and Morrison on the Right of the party. The conflict was precipitated by the Korean War. Though restraining President Harry S. Truman and General Douglas MacArthur in the escalation of the war, and, in particular, in the use of nuclear weapons, Attlee supported U.N. action in Korea and called for rearmament in Britain. According to Gaitskell, the Chancellor, this rearmament program called for charges to be imposed on certain provisions of the **National Health Service**, something Bevan vehemently opposed. Though favoring Bevan, Attlee could not avoid a split within his Cabinet over the issue. Attlee and the party were seriously weakened by Bevan's 1951 resignation and by the deaths of Cripps and Bevin. In 1951, Attlee called another election, which the party lost.

Between 1951 and 1955 Attlee remained as leader of the opposition, enduring a widening fissure within the Labour Party. Bevan and the "Bevanites" were the main cause of these splits, though those in the right wing, under Gaitskell and Morrison, were also culpable. Attlee was left in the middle, trying to keep the party together. Though often under attack from the Bevanites, Attlee attempted to protect them from reprisals by the Right and the unions. After four years of squabbling, Labour lost another election in 1955. Attlee wished to stand down from the leadership at this point, but he was persuaded, largely by Bevan, to stay on in order to frustrate the leadership aspirations of Morrison. In December of that year, however, convinced that Morrison was no longer a contender for the leadership, Attlee resigned, to be succeeded by Gaitskell. It may be to Attlee's credit, in part, that his resignation was followed by a period of reconciliation between Gaitskell and Bevan. Upon retiring, Attlee was given a peerage and became Earl Attlee. He devoted his declining years to journalism and to the promotion of world government. He lived to see the formation of two Labour governments in the 1960s and died on 8 October 1967.

Attlee's achievement lies not only in the remarkable and record-setting twenty years he spent as leader of a fractious Labour Party, but also as the symbol in many ways of the Labour achievement of the 1940s—one of "sensible" socialism, bloodless, perhaps, but effective, democratic, and constructive. His role in granting India independence would alone guarantee Attlee's historical reputation, but his skills of administration and the quiet force of his personality within two dynamic governments, the coalition of 1940–5 and the Labour government of 1945–51, certainly mark Attlee as one of the most impressive politicians and Prime Ministers of the century.

Stephen Brooke

Bibliography
Attlee, Clement. *As It Happened*. 1954.
Burridge, Trevor. *Clement Attlee*. 1985.
Harris, Kenneth. *Attlee*. 1982.
Tiratsoo, Nick, ed. *The Attlee Years*. 1991.
Williams, Francis. *A Prime Minister Remembers*. 1961.

Auden, W(ystan) H(ugh) (1907–1973)

W.H. Auden, one of the most distinguished and influential English poets of the century, was the third son of a cultivated doctor and a highly religious mother. He grew up outside Birmingham, attended the relatively progressive Gresham's School in Norfolk, and in 1925 went up to Christ Church, **Oxford**, where he read English (thus incidentally becoming one of the first major poets to study English literature academically). Especially excited by the forms of Anglo-Saxon and Middle English poetry he read at Oxford, Auden rapidly established himself as a writer with a keen interest in the intricate mechanisms of verse. A pamphlet by Auden, *Poems*, appeared in 1928, the same year he received his degree. He spent ten months in Germany writing and reading widely in **psychology**, and in 1930 he published a full-length verse collection, again austerely titled *Poems*. Although Auden's taut, cryptic free-verse poems were mostly about love, after 1930 he started to write a more public form of verse in which he castigated Britain's spiritual and public torpor. *The Orators* (1932) is a fusion of the love poetry and the public-minded stirrings. Despite his early work's obscurity, Auden was hailed as the leader of a group of left-wing poets that included **Louis MacNeice, Stephen Spender**, and **Cecil Day Lewis**.

In the autumn of 1932 Auden started teaching at the Downs School in Herefordshire, and his poetry opened out, becoming more accessible. This is the start of the second phase in his career, the years when, drawing on Marx and Freud, he made uncanny connections between middle-class life and the political crisis gripping Europe. In 1935 the avowedly **homosexual** Auden married Erika Mann, Thomas Mann's daughter and a fugitive from Nazi persecution, so that she could obtain a British passport. The same year he left the Downs and worked briefly in **documentary film**. Then, for six years, Auden lived as a free-lance writer. A second collection of lyrics, *Look, Stranger!* (1936), extended his fame, as did his plays. In the later 1930s he and one of his lovers, the novelist **Christopher Isherwood**, produced a string of dramas: *The Dog Beneath the Skin* (1935), *The Ascent of F6* (1936), and *On the Frontier* (1938).

The pre-war years were a period of continuous wandering. In 1936 he traveled with MacNeice to Iceland, a trip that resulted in *Letters from Iceland* (1937). In January 1937 he went to observe the **Spanish Civil War**. Although Auden was a leftist, he never joined the **Communist Party**, and he was shunted aside by the party bosses in Spain. In spite of being disturbed by internecine violence in the Republican ranks, immediately after he returned home, he wrote his most famous call to action, "Spain." In early 1938 Auden went abroad again, this time with Isherwood. They traveled to China to write about the Sino-Japanese War, but their *Journey to a War* (1939) became a parable about the difficulties of politically engaged writing. The problem is developed in the volume's sonnet sequence, "In Time of War," which shows a change in Auden's moral imagination. Christian symbolism comes to the surface.

On their way back to England in mid-1938 Auden and Isherwood stopped off in New York. Returning to America in 1939, on the eve of the Second World War, was another turning point. The next period in Auden's career, initiated by a series of elegies and psychological portraits, is a phase of strenuous existential inwardness. He had fallen in love with a younger American writer, Chester Kallman, and his happiness released a flood of other feelings, including intensifying religious impulses. *Another Time* (1940) contains some of his best work, though, as the title indicates, the poems already seemed to him to belong to a vanished era. The book includes the celebrated "September 1, 1939," a poem that tries to come to terms with the failures of a "low dishonest decade." Auden became a practicing Anglican in 1940. The suggestions of a religious and poetic conversion are heightened in *The Double Man* (1941). "New Year Letter," a long neo-Augustan verse epistle, ends with a petition for aid from a numinous—though still unnamed—power.

Although Auden stayed a Christian for the rest of his life, he never was narrowly dogmatic, at least in his poems. In fact, his faith seemed to increase his intellectual curiosity. By inclination his mind was speculative, synthesizing, and eclectic—he was intensely acquainted with the advanced psychological, religious, and philosophical thought of his day—and Christianity allowed him to order this knowledge into a harmonious world view. But his reputation suffered in Britain during and after the war, partly because he was accused by fanatics of the Left and the Right of abandoning his country, and partly because his writing developed in subtle and not immediately assimilable ways.

A

From 1941 to 1946 he produced three long poems, each of which addresses the situation created by the crisis of the war and by a breach in his relationship with Kallman (who nonetheless remained Auden's companion for the rest of his life). Two of these long poems, "For the Time Being," a Christmas oratorio dedicated to the memory of his mother who had died in 1941, and "The Sea and the Mirror," a commentary on *The Tempest* that Auden called his *ars poetica*, were published in *For the Time Being* (1944). His final long poem, the ambitious *The Age of Anxiety* (1947), is an interior portrait of the average twentieth-century city dweller, cast in the form of a meeting between four New Yorkers in a bar on All Souls' Night.

In 1945 Auden spent a few months in Germany with the U.S. Air Force's Strategic Bombing Survey, studying the effects of aerial bombardment. Among the ruins of Darmstadt and Munich, his interest in the problems of contemporary civilization took on renewed urgency. The most important post-war works in this respect are the poem "Memorial for the City" (1949) and a series of lectures, *The Enchafèd Flood* (1950).

Like many of his generation, Auden was dissatisfied with the stagnant cultural and political life of Britain—he once compared his decision to emigrate to New York to the odyssey that lead his contemporary, Guy Burgess, to Moscow. In 1946 he became an American citizen. But he still wandered: From 1948 until 1957 Auden summered on Ischia, an island in the Bay of Naples. This period was inaugurated by the elegiac "In Praise of Limestone" in *Nones* (1951). The Mediterranean breathed a feeling of classical elegance into Auden's work and renewed his interest in nature and history. This phase culminates in a pair of major sequences from mid-decade: "Bucolics" and "Horae Canonicae" in *The Shield of Achilles* (1955). The final pieces from the period were gathered in *Homage to Clio* (1960).

By this time Auden's verse had become very wry and conversational. His contrasting grand style continued its life, however, by finding an outlet in opera libretti. (He had already worked on an operetta, *Paul Bunyan*, with **Benjamin Britten** in 1941.) He and Kallman wrote the words for Igor Stravinsky's *The Rake's Progress* (1951) and later also collaborated on *Elegy for Young Lovers* (1961) and *The Bassarids* (1966), both by Hans Werner Henze, and *Love's Labours Lost* (1973), by

Nicolas Nabokov. From 1956 to 1961 he was Professor of Poetry at Oxford. His late poetry came under the Horatian influence of George Herbert and John Dryden. His Horatian persona is represented in *About the House* (1965), that contains another major sequence, a poem for every room in his new summer home, outside Vienna, that he and Kallman had established in 1958. Auden's final books, *City without Walls* (1969), *Epistle to a Godson* (1972), and the posthumous *Thank You, Fog* (1974), each contains important poems—restrained meditations in which extinction is a frequent subject. In 1972, feeling frail, Auden decided to leave New York and spend his winters back at Christ Church. On 28 September 1973 in Vienna he suffered a fatal heart attack.

Since his death, Auden's polemical aura, whether in its early political form or in its later High Church style, has faded. Towering over the mid-century's poetic landscape, he was a protean, didactic, virtuosic writer (he produced many distinguished prose collections), a restless, rigorously intellectual man who mingled a love of clinical exactness with an acute knowledge of human folly. In literary-historical terms his importance partly lies in his work's reaction against modernism's aesthetic of crisis and fragmentation and in his far-reaching insistence that "The pious fable and the dirty story / Share in the total literary glory."

Nicholas Jenkins

Bibliography

Bloomfield, B.C., and Edward Mendelson. *W.H. Auden: A Bibliography 1924–1969*. 2nd ed. 1972.

Carpenter, Humphrey. *W.H. Auden: A Biography*. 1981.

Fuller, John. *A Reader's Guide to W.H. Auden*. 1970.

Hecht, Anthony. *The Hidden Law: The Poetry of W.H. Auden*. 1993.

Mendelson, Edward. *Early Auden*. 1981.

Osborne, Charles. *W.H. Auden: The Life of a Poet*. 1980.

Australia

Founded in 1788 as a British penal colony superimposed on a scattered, heterogeneous, technologically primitive Aboriginal population, Australia by 1901 had become a federation of six states, largely self-governing internally, but in virtually all external matters subject to the

British imperial government in London. The constitution of the Commonwealth of Australia was an act of the British Parliament. The white population, predominantly British in origin, now numbered just under 3 million (the Aborigines, uncounted, probably numbered several hundred thousand), occupying a continent of 3 million square miles. By the time of the bicentennial celebrations in 1988, Australia was a sovereign state in all respects, a partner but no longer a dependency. The population had grown to nearly 17 million, of which about 1.5 percent declared themselves to be Aborigines. Probably no more than 70 percent of the people could now claim to be of substantially British and Irish descent. The culture was still predominantly British, though with regional emphases and accents and American overtones.

At the turn of the century, when Australia became a single nation, armed forces from its component six colonies, moved by imperial sentiment, were fighting as part of British formations in the **Boer War** in South Africa. When Britain declared war on Germany in August 1914, Australian political leaders competed in their **patriotism**. The Australian naval squadron was put under British command, and expeditionary forces (ANZAC) were assembled. Australia eventually sent 330,000 members of its armed services overseas—to the Middle East, including the Dardanelles, and to Europe, as part of the imperial war effort. It lost nearly 60,000 men in the war—more than the United States. Despite initial enthusiasm, the continuing war, with mounting and massive casualty lists, was not supported by all Australians, especially not by those (nearly a quarter of the population) of Irish descent. Thus, two referenda on conscripting troops to fight in Europe were defeated. Participation in the war helped foster a sense of nationhood, of national identity, and Australia signed the peace treaty, and became a member of the **League of Nations**, in its own right even though part of the British Empire.

In September 1939 the Australian Conservative government declared that because Britain was at war with Germany, Australia was as well. Naval forces were again put under British command, and expeditionary forces were raised to participate in British operations in North Africa, Greece, Crete, and Syria, while thousands of Australian airmen served with the **Royal Air Force** in the defense of Britain and the invasion of Europe. When Japan entered the war in December 1941, Australian units were part of British forces in Malaya and **Singapore**, quickly defeated by the Japanese in their sweep southward that took them to within a few miles of Port Moresby, capital of the Australian colonial territory of Papua on the island of New Guinea. In these circumstances, Australia withdrew its divisions from the Middle East for the defense of the homeland and sought an active partnership with the United States without discarding its imperial links and obligations.

The imperial links were re-emphasized after the war, first through Australia's providing the commander and about a third of the British Commonwealth Occcupation Force in Japan, then in 1950 in limited air assistance to the British campaign against terrorism in Malaya. When North Korea invaded South Korea in June of that year, Australia provided naval and air units to the **United Nations** force, then one battalion and eventually two to a (British) Commonwealth formation.

In 1950–1 Australia negotiated a security treaty with the United States and New Zealand (ANZUS). At American insistence, Britain (to its chagrin) was excluded from this agreement, and Australia was not prepared to force the issue. In the following forty years, Australia maintained close defense relations with Britain, especially over the defense of Malaya and then Malaysia, over the exchange of information, and general military liaison. But the United States soon replaced Britain as the major source of defense equipment and the acknowledged ultimate guarantor of Australian security. When in 1965 Australia committed forces to the war in Vietnam alongside the Americans, it was the first time Australians had served overseas other than in cooperation with the British, something they have not done since except as parts of U.N. forces.

Since 1887 Britain had from time to time convened meetings of the colonial Prime Ministers, and during the 1920s those leaders (especially from **Canada, South Africa**, and Ireland) pressed increasingly for greater degrees of independence in foreign affairs. At the 1926 conference the autonomous status of Britain and the Dominions was defined, and it was subsequently legislated in the Imperial **Statute of Westminster** (1931). Unlike the others, Australia did not ratify the statute until eleven years later. In 1939 Australia declared war on Germany an hour after Britain did, following a Cabinet meeting, but as a direct consequence of the British declaration. In 1941 the Australian government, now under the Australian Labour Party, felt it must make its own decision about war with Japan, and did so, separately advising King George VI to declare war on its behalf.

The period of the Second World War was a growing-up time for Australian foreign policy. Until 1940 Australia had had no overseas diplomatic posts other than in London, and its external relations were channeled through the British Foreign Office. A separate Australian Department of External Affairs was created in 1935, and during the war diplomatic posts were established in the United States and nine other countries. For several years an Australian representative in London, unlike his Empire and Commonwealth counterparts, attended meetings of the British War Cabinet.

Australia sought increasingly, but on the whole ineffectively, to influence the conduct of the war. In August 1943 and again the following year Prime Minister John Curtin proposed more formal machinery for Commonwealth consultation. Winston Churchill was too busy fighting the war, and was too much an imperialist, to entertain it. Australia was somewhat more effective in influencing the post-war arrangements through active diplomacy at the San Francisco conference that produced the U.N. Charter.

In almost every formal sense, Australia achieved during the war the sovereignty and independence defined in the Statute of Westminster. Australian law still provided for appeals from the High Court of Australia to the Judicial Committee of the Privy Council in London. This right was restricted in 1968, further restricted in 1975, and abolished in 1986. In that year, the British and Australian Parliaments each enacted an Australia Act, in virtually identical terms, severing all remaining constitutional links other than those involving the position of the Queen as Queen of Australia. A republican movement was given a boost by the constitutional crisis of 1975 and gained further momentum during the early 1990s, raising the possibility of further constitutional modifications.

The white convicts and free settlers from the British Isles after 1788 were predominantly working-class and lower-middle-class people. This had its effects: on the quest for egalitarianism, on the Australian accent, on the desire for an adequate minimum wage, universal suffrage, an unestablished church, a racially homogeneous (white) population, and a sense of re-moteness, vulnerability, and dependence. In the 1901 census, out of a population of 3.8 million, 2.9 million were born in Australia (presumably mostly of British stock), and 680,000 in the British Isles. Along with continuing (and preferred) migration from Britain, there was an influx of Germans and Italians after the First World War, and of Europeans generally (many of them displaced persons) after the Second World War. The "White Australia" policy was progressively discarded from the early 1950s, with admission especially of Asians from Asian Commonwealth countries and (after 1975) from Indochina. In the period 1971–86 the net gain of migrants from Asia was 399,000, compared with 302,000 from the British Isles. These figures also reflect the propensity of Australians of British descent to return to Britain either as tourists or as settlers. By the 1990s Australia had become a mosaic of peoples and cultures from many parts of the world, although with Anglo-Celtic elements still predominant.

Just as Australia was initially peopled mainly by British migrants, Britain was the principal external source of capital for development throughout the nineteenth century, and well into the twentieth. British investment built a high proportion of the towns, the railways, the roads, and the factories, and developed the farms and the mines whose products were exported to Britain in return for capital and consumer goods. These processes gradually diversified as Australia was able to produce much of its own capital, the United States and Japan becoming important trading partners and the United States a valuable source of investment. By the late 1940s Britain still supplied about half of Australia's imports and took about the same proportion of exports. These proportions then began to decline, as Australia found new markets in Asia and Europe and Britain entered the European Community, until by the late 1980s Britain supplied only 7 percent of Australia's imports and took 3 percent of its exports. Britain has continued to provide capital investment, for a long time offering Australia preferred access to the London capital market, and is still often the largest individual supplier, with nearly a quarter of the total of all foreign investment in Australia. For their part, Australian enterprises have come to use Britain as a springboard into the European Community.

The multiplicity of personal relationships between British and Australians has underlaid the many institutional links—in government, academia, commerce, industry, the arts, the armed forces, and sports. Despite a degree of stridency on the Australian side and of nonchalance on the British, few countries or peoples are as close, in most respects, as the former imperial power and its former remote colony of settlement.

T.B. Millar

Bibliography

Madden, A.F., and W.H. Morris-Jones. *Australia and Britain: Studies in a Changing Relationship*. 1980.

Millar, T.B. *Australia in Peace and War: External Relations since 1788*. 2nd ed. 1991.

Automobile Industry

In 1896 the Daimler Motor Company, housed in a converted cotton mill in Coventry, became the first commercial manufacturer of motor vehicles in Britain and began a process that would transform the economic and social contours of British society. The million people employed directly and indirectly in the industry by the late 1930s not only pioneered new forms of collective organization, but also revised expectations of consumption levels. The 2 million vehicles in operation by 1938 required extensive public road works, which in turn altered the spatial configuration of British society. The size of the industry made it an obvious candidate for manipulation by the state in its attempts to implement Keynesian demand-management schemes after 1945. More recently, the automobile has become the symbol of growing concerns regarding the environment and sustainable development.

In 1896 the industry had barely moved beyond the experimental stage. There was still resistance to the thought of mechanized vehicles propelling along British roads at excessive speeds. The Red Flag Act, which required a person to walk in front of any motorized vehicle, had recently been repealed, and the official speed limit had been raised to fourteen miles an hour. Initial technical breakthroughs came from Europe. Daimler relied on the German patents of Gottlieb Daimler for its early designs. The lack of standardization in the industry required the extensive use of highly skilled male fitters and turners using the techniques of the nineteenth-century craft worker.

By 1910 the technical lead in this industry had shifted toward the Americans. Their invasion of the British market began in earnest in 1911, when Ford commenced manufacturing vehicles in Manchester. Despite pre-1914 production levels of less than 10,000, Ford's Manchester shop implemented many of the labor practices perfected in Detroit. The influence of the trade unions was reduced after an extended **strike** in 1913. Work tasks were simplified and made suitable for less-skilled workers, and the moving assembly line was introduced in late 1914. During this same period the hourly wages of Ford workers more than doubled, bringing an example of the American high-wage and high-productivity strategy to Britain. By 1914 Ford was the largest producer of vehicles in Britain.

British producers responded quickly to the American challenge. New grinding and milling machines, developed in the United States, were widely adopted. These machines were less demanding of the skills of the operator but more precise in machining critical components such as pistons and blocks. New entrants such as Rover, Sunbeam, and Morris built on their experience in bicycle production, an industry that had implemented many of the principles of interchangeable mass production by the turn of the century. By 1914 many motor vehicle producers had reduced their dependence on skilled workers and had moved toward mass production.

The initial success of Ford in the pre-1914 era did not translate into American dominance of the British industry after the First World War. While the early British industry is best known for its luxury vehicles, manufactured by firms such as Daimler, Rolls Royce, and Sunbeam, there were a number of British firms producing less-expensive cars, including Standard, Belsize, Swift, and Vulcan. But it was two other firms, Morris, which began producing the Morris Cowley in 1915, and Austin, which began producing the Austin 7 in 1922, that were the most successful in challenging Ford. Neither Ford nor General Motors, which began producing Chevrolets in Britain in 1924 and acquired Vauxhall in 1925, were able to match Austin and Morris. Designing cars better suited to British tastes, British roads, and especially British taxes, which penalized the high-horsepower and fuel-inefficient American designs, and sheltered by the 1915 McKenna import duties on foreign luxury goods, Austin and Morris captured 60 percent of the British market by 1929.

While British firms adopted much of the mass production system perfected in the United States, there remained important differences. Levels of output were generally lower, and there was less emphasis on mechanization and sequential or moving assembly. On paper, skilled labor was still extensively used, but at least outside of body shops the differences between the American and the British systems should not be exaggerated. Firms such as Morris pioneered automated transfer techniques with their block and cylinder lines in the 1920s. These early automated lines failed in large part because of weaknesses in hydraulic clamping technology, but they were clearly precursors of the automated systems perfected in the United States during the Second World War.

The most significant difference between the British and American systems of mass production was the continued reliance by British producers on shop-floor workers to perform many of the duties that in the United States had been transferred to management. Operating under piece work payment systems, which closely tied earnings to output, British workers retained significant responsibility for preventive maintenance, chasing stock, and ensuring the smooth running of the shops. The pinnacle of this British combination of mechanized production techniques and continued dependence on shop-floor workers for decision making came at Standard, where the gang system of production was employed. There, contrary to the overall thrust of Fordism and Scientific Management, workers retained control over staffing levels and task assignment and even played a role in selecting machinery and plant layout. Management dictated model design and output levels. In the early 1950s the gang system allowed Standard to earn above-average profits and pay above-average wages. In the 1960s and 1970s the shop stewards at Austin played a central role in overcoming sectional disputes and managerial incompetence to keep the plant running so as to ensure high bonus earnings for workers.

The 1950s were boom years for British producers. The European industry had been destroyed, and the American producers were preoccupied with satisfying domestic demand. British firms, encouraged by state rationing policies that rewarded exporters, dominated world export markets and enjoyed healthy profits. The strong position of producers provided openings for the resurrection of trade unionism in the industry, which had been all but elimi-

nated in the early 1920s. Motor vehicles had come to represent a major component of British exports and domestic demand and became the focus of government attempts to manage aggregate demand and stimulate regional development.

The period of success was short-lived. British manufacturers continued to follow conservative investment strategies, distributing much of their profits as dividends and expanding output by employing more labor rather than investing in new plants. By the late 1950s American advances in capital-intensive automated methods could no longer be ignored. British firms began the transition to this new system of production and, by the early 1970s, were facing bankruptcy.

Two problems surfaced in the transition to a more capital-intensive process. The first was the small size of British firms. Compared with the United States, where three companies dominated the industry, the British market had six major firms satisfying a much smaller market. The small British firms had difficulty raising the capital needed to finance the expensive new production systems and, even when the capital was found, had trouble producing at a level of output that justified the new investment. Equally serious, the stillbirth of managerial capitalism in Britain in the 1920s and the continued dependence on workers to coordinate shop-floor activity made management vulnerable to labor slowdowns and stoppages. Unable to afford peace with labor in an increasingly competitive industry, but also unable to manage without the labor input that was a key to the inter-war success of the major producers, the transition to a more capital-intensive and managerial-directed system of production proved to be a disaster. A series of mergers, some under state pressure, was executed, giving birth to major new players such as the British Motor Corporation in 1952 and Leyland Motors in 1961, who in turn merged to form British Leyland Motor Corporation in 1968. Given the independent-minded British producers, they had limited effect in rationalizing product lines or capacity.

On the shop floor a wholesale shift from piece work to measured day work took place. Management was to take greater responsibility for coordinating production, a task at which it proved to be inept. The government was forced to bail out and effectively take control of what little remained of the British industry in the late

1960s and early 1970s, but the dominance of the British producers in their own market had ended. By the end of the 1970s over 50 percent of the British car market was satisfied by imports. The British-based operations of the American giants Ford and General Motors enjoyed new success. BL Ltd., which had absorbed most of what remained of the British producers, was forced to enter into a partnership with Honda to survive. By the early 1980s and despite over a billion pounds of cash infusion from the government, BL Ltd. captured less than 20 percent of the British market and was a minor player in Europe. In 1988, in a deal that generated significant criticism from the **European Community**, BL Ltd., now known as the Rover Group, was returned to private control under the ownership of British Aerospace, only to be sold in 1994 to the German automobile manufacturer BMW.

Wayne Lewchuk

Bibliography
Church, Roy, and Herbert Austin. *The British Motor Car Industry to 1941.* 1979.
Dunnett, Peter. *The Decline of the British Motor Industry.* 1980.
Foreman-Peck, James, Sue Bowden, and Alan McKinlay. *The British Motor Industry.* 1994.
Lewchuk, Wayne. *American Technology and the British Vehicle Industry.* 1987.
Melman, Seymour. *Decision-Making and Productivity.* 1958.
Whipp, Richard, and Peter Clark. *Innovation and the Auto Industry: Product, Process, and Work Organization.* 1986.

Aviation
Britain is historically a world leader in the innovation and construction of both military and commercial aircraft. Its factories and studios have produced some of the most famous names in aviation history, and Britain has always been an important center for civil aviation. In the 1990s Britain builds large aircraft with its European partners as well as smaller airplanes at home.

Early British aircraft were flown by many inventors and builders who went on to form their own companies. The **First World War** provided the real impetus for aircraft development, and Britain produced war planes such as the Sopwith Camel, the DeHavilland DH4, and the Bristol Fighter. The wartime technical advances in both land and seaborne aircraft led to the creation of the **Royal Air Force** in 1918 out of the previous Royal Naval Air Service and Royal Flying Corps.

Commercial aviation in Britain began soon after the war, using surplus war aircraft. A DeHavilland DH4 operated the first true airline service, between London and Paris, as early as 1919. A number of small airlines grew up in the early 1920s as air travel became fashionable. Most of these services were between London (especially the new Croydon airport, opened in 1920) and cities in France, Belgium, and the Netherlands. In order to rationalize commercial aviation, many small firms were combined into the new Imperial Airways in 1924. Through Royal Mail contracts and various other kinds of official support, Imperial Airways became Britain's international standard bearer of the inter-war years. It was most famous for its empire services, which by the 1930s connected Britain to the Middle East, India, **Australia**, and **New Zealand**, and through Egypt and East Africa to Capetown, **South Africa**. Most of the commercial aircraft of the period, including the famous Empire flying boats, were cumbersome and slow, and their interiors often resembled the ocean liners with which they competed.

For a time airships seemed to provide a possible alternative to land aircraft. The British government experimented with airships in the years after the First World War, and in 1924 the first **Labour** government agreed to construct a large airship in tandem with a similar design built by Vickers. The two ships, the R100 and R101, were completed by 1930, but the British airship program ended abruptly with the crash of the R101 in France on its maiden voyage to India, when 48 people, including the Secretary of State for Air, were killed (1930).

British rearmament during the 1930s led to the first of the monoplane fighter aircraft, the Hawker Hurricane of 1938, that was the first true departure from the biplanes of the 1914–18 era. Its famous contemporary, the Supermarine Spitfire, established an international standard for fighter aircraft that was matched only by the German Messerschmitt 109. The **Second World War** provided another opportunity for innovation, and types such as the Mosquito fighter-bomber and Lancaster heavy bomber were among the finest and most versatile aircraft of their time. Advances in aircraft design in the 1940s saw the introduction of the first British jet

A

fighter, the Gloster Meteor, in 1944. British commercial flying effectively ended with the outbreak of war, but in 1939 Imperial Airways was combined with a smaller, private competitor to form a new national airline, British Overseas Airways Corporation (BOAC).

BOAC reintroduced commercial services on imperial routes in 1945, making use of old converted Lancasters and flying boats that were not competitive with new American transport aircraft such as the Douglas DC-6 and Lockheed Constellation. The new Labour government also decided to create two new national airline companies: British European Airways (BEA) and British South American Airways (BSAA), both in 1945. Britain led the way in developing new types of aircraft against fierce competition from the United States. Although large land aircraft such as the Bristol Brabazon (late 1940s) were failures, the Bristol Britannia and the Vickers Viscount (1950s) were successful medium- and short-range turbine-powered airliners that enjoyed a speed and comfort advantage over their piston-engine competitors. As national airlines BOAC (which absorbed BSAA in 1949) and BEA were expected to fly the new British aircraft. The most innovative of these was the DeHavilland Comet, which was the first jet-powered transport aircraft in the world to enter commercial service, with BOAC in 1952. A series of fatal crashes led to the grounding of the type in 1954, when investigations revealed metal fatigue. Although the Comet was totally revamped and reentered service in 1958, the United States had by then developed jet transports that were able to take the lead in the world airline market.

Until the 1960s Britain was able to produce aircraft of every type in competition with American and European designs. The British government (both Labour and Conservative) was deeply involved with aircraft development and supported most programs. In an attempt to rationalize the aviation industry, the British Aircraft Corporation was created out of a number of smaller private companies in 1960; it later amalgamated with most of the remaining independents to form British Aerospace in the late 1970s.

The British government also supported collaborative projects with France, including the Jaguar fighter-bomber (1970s) and the Concorde supersonic transport. The latter began development in the early 1960s but, due to technical problems and vast cost overruns, did not enter commercial service until 1976. The Concorde is the prestige aircraft of British Airways, the national company formed out of BOAC and BEA in 1973.

Due to persistent sterling crises and the decay of British industry, major British aircraft projects since the Concorde have tended to be in cooperation with partners. An Anglo-German-Italian consortium produced the Tornado fighter-bomber (1980s), and British Aerospace owns 20 percent of, and produces the wings for, the European Airbus series of airliners. Airbus has become the only major competitor for the powerful American Boeing Company.

The Conservative government of **Margaret Thatcher** partially reversed the tradition of government involvement with the airline and aircraft industries by privatizing British Airways in 1987. British Aerospace is a highly diversified military and commercial aviation company and a profitable exporter. British commercial aviation and its supporting aircraft industry have returned to health in the 1990s, and British Airways maintains one of the world's largest route networks. British aviation expertise, alone or in cooperation with other countries, continues a long tradition of technical excellence.

David R. Devereux

Bibliography

Hayward, Keith. *The British Aircraft Industry.* 1989.

Higham, Robin. *Britain's Imperial Air Routes, 1918 to 1939.* 1960.

Hudson, Kenneth. *Air Travel: A Social History.* 1972.

Hyde, H. Montgomery. *British Air Policy between the Wars, 1918–1939.* 1976.

Ayckbourn, Alan (1939–)

Alan Ayckbourn, the most prolific comic playwright currently working in Britain, was born in 1939 in Hampstead and educated at Haileybury. His first work in the theater was as assistant stage manager in 1956, his career continuing in repertory theatre. His first four plays, produced at Scarborough, were written under the name of "Roland Allen." Since his first success, *Relatively Speaking* (1967), he has written more than forty plays, among which the most popular have been *How the Other Half Loves* (1969), *Absurd Person Singular* (1972), *The Norman Conquests* (1973), *Bedroom Farce*

(1975), *A Chorus of Disapproval* (1984), *A Small Family Business* (1987), and *Man of the Moment* (1990). He has won numerous drama awards, and in 1987 he was named a CBE. Since 1971 he has been based in Scarborough at the Steven Joseph Theatre-in-the-Round, where his plays are first performed before being staged in London.

Ayckbourn satirizes contemporary middle-class society with a blend of astute observation and biting humor similar to that with which **Noel Coward** satirized the upper classes of an earlier generation. Stressing the need for theater as entertainment, Ayckbourn has deliberately set himself apart from the political drama of the 1970s. Yet Ayckbourn has shown that farce at its most entertaining can also be profound. He describes his work as "black farce"—dark comedies that reveal pathos and tragedy beneath their ebullient surface. Ayckbourn speaks of "exploring attitudes to death, loneliness, etc.—themes not generally dealt with in comedy." His farce revolves around family rituals, dinner parties, birthdays, wedding anniversaries, reunions, and picnics, all of which teeter on the brink of personal and collective catastrophe. The forms of Ayckbourn's farces reveal a taste for experimental and symmetrical patterns: *Absurd Person Singular* has three scenes, featuring three married couples on three consecutive Christmas Eves, in three different kitchens. In *How the Other Half Loves* the separate lives and conversations of a middle-class couple and a lower-middle-class couple are superimposed on each other. Thus the plays combine realistic and detailed observation of middle-class life in formally inventive and even surrealistic explorations of time and space. Sir Peter Hall, former artistic director, justified the inclusion of Ayckbourn's work in the **National Theatre** repertoire as an "accurate reflection of English life . . . [and] a very important social document."

Brian Pearce

Bibliography

Billington, Michael. *Alan Ayckbourn*. 1983.
Page, Malcolm, ed. *File on Ayckbourn*. 1989.
Watson, Ian. *Conversations with Ayckbourn*. 1981.

Ayer, A(lfred) J(ules) (1910–1989)

A highly influential twentieth-century British philosopher, A.J. Ayer was educated at Eton, where he was a King's scholar, and at Christ Church, **Oxford**, where he studied under the linguistic philosopher Gilbert Ryle.

On graduating, Ayer considered studying at **Cambridge** under the Austrian philosopher Ludwig Wittgenstein, but on Ryle's suggestion he went instead to Vienna in 1932 to learn about the work of the Vienna Arde. Ayer endorsed the **logical positivism** of the Vienna Circle and, on his return in 1933, wrote *Language, Truth, and Logic*, which was published in 1936. It became the manifesto of logical positivism and a classic of twentieth-century philosophy.

Ayer advocated the verification principle as a theory of meaning. This implied that all and only sentences expressing propositions are literally significant. A sentence expresses a proposition if and only if that sentence is (at least in principle) verifiable. All verifiable sentences are verifiable in only one of two ways: a priori (that is, intellectually) or a posteriori (that is, by observation). All and only a priori truths are analytic, and all and only a posteriori propositions are synthetic and contingent (informative and although true, not necessarily true). In common with the other logical positivists, Ayer thought that the application of the verification principle to the sentences of metaphysics showed that they are meaningless. Hence a putative sentence such as "God exists" is nonsensical because it expresses no genuine proposition. This, in turn, is because it is not even in principle verifiable.

In his moral philosophy Ayer was an emotivist. He held that ethical sentences are not literally significant but are expressions and excitements of emotion. It follows that contradictions may not obtain between different ethical positions because a contradiction may only obtain between a proposition and its negation and there are no ethical propositions.

In his philosophy of perception Ayer was a phenomenalist; he held that physical objects may be "reduced" to sense contents. This means that any sentence or set of sentences about physical objects may be translated without loss of meaning into a sentence or set of sentences about actual or possible sense contents.

Ayer was a radically antimetaphysical empiricist philosopher, in the British empiricist tradition of John Locke, George Berkeley, David Hume, John Stuart Mill, and **Bertrand Russell**. He was Grote Professor of the Philosophy of Mind and Logic at the University of London from 1946 and Wykeham Professor of Logic at the University of Oxford from 1959. A.J. Ayer was knighted in 1970 and died in 1989.

Stephen Priest

Bibliography

Ayer, A.J. *Language, Truth, and Logic.* 1936.
———. *The Central Questions of Philosophy.* 1973.
———. *Part of My Life.* 1977.
———. *More of My Life.* 1984.
Priest, Stephen. *The British Empiricists.* 1990.

B

Bacon, Francis (1909–1992)

Irish-born Francis Bacon's paintings show the violence of life with an uncompromising relish and beauty that is often unsettling. Certainly, when the triptych *Three Studies for Figures at the Base of the Crucifixion* (1944, Tate Gallery, London) was seen at the Lefevre Gallery, London, in a group exhibition, "visitors," as John Russell recounted, "were brought up short by images so unrelievedly awful that the mind shut with a snap at the sight of them." At a time when the dominant stream in British art was a lyrical neo-romanticism exemplified by the work of **Graham Sutherland,** John Craxton, or **John Piper,** the directness of Bacon's triptych was seen as a violation of those aesthetic values.

Although the exhibition of this painting effectively marked the start of his career at the age of thirty-six, he had been painting since at least 1929. When he left Ireland for London in 1925, he had first worked as an interior designer, making abstract rug designs and tubular steel furniture. He took up painting in oils, after returning from a period in Paris and Berlin, and, rather than attend an art school, received advice from his friend, painter Roy de Maistre. Despite the inclusion in **Herbert Read's** *Art Now* of one of three versions of a *Crucifixion* (1933), he was largely unsuccessful during this period, and his painting received scant recognition.

It was with other painters, especially Michael Andrews, **Lucian Freud,** Frank Auerbach, and Leon Kossoff—loosely termed the "School of London"—that Bacon has come to be identified. Even though these artists held no common set of preoccupations, beyond an adherence to the continued value of figurative painting, there was a pattern of friendship, signaled especially in the portraits that Bacon and Freud made of each other.

Portraits assumed a major part of Bacon's *oeuvre*, but rather than aim for a likeness he tried, as with all his paintings, to convey his perceptions of the nature of existence, which hinged on his pessimism about the condition of life. This attempt found a parallel in his general adoption of strategies of accident and chance, while his use of the unprimed side of a canvas, on which he painted directly without any preliminary drawing, along with his often unorthodox handling of paint, testify to his attempts at unlocking images that could approximate this primal immediacy. Between 1946 and 1950 he lived mostly in Monte Carlo, where the lure of the casino unlocked the urge to gamble that is all too apparent in his paintings.

Nevertheless, despite the distortions that Bacon wrought within his self-portraits or his portraits of friends and patrons, there remains a tangible likeness, not so much of that person's features (although the subject is always recognizable), but rather the likeness that derives from a contact between artist and subject, an event, a sense of existence distilled through memory. His paintings, apart from the portraits, rarely refer to actual narrative. The figures in *Three Studies for a Crucifixion* (1962, Solomon R. Guggenheim Museum, New York) are not intended to be read as being Goebbels or Himmler; neither is the swastika armband on one of the figures in *Crucifixion* (1965, Staatsgalerie Moderner Kunst, Munich) to be read literally in terms of Nazism. In this way his recurring motif of the crucifixion is used as a potent image of the mechanics of inhumanity rather than a comment on Christ's crucifixion; the paintings of popes are images of regression and alienation. Bacon's symbolism, vague rather than specific, is universal in its attack.

Similarly, although Bacon draws inspiration from a wide range of writers and artists, his attraction to such sources is a result of a recognition of the articulation of tragedy and extreme emotion rather than the urge directly to transcribe a painting's external compositional and aesthetic values or a writing's sense of plot. The result of his 1957 series of paintings derived from a Van Gogh self-portrait was such as to de-particularize the source, *The Painter on the Road to Tarascon*, so that an image of solitary quest could stand on its own terms.

By the time of his death Bacon was widely held to be one of the world's most important painters. He had received two full-scale retrospectives at the Tate Gallery, London (1962 and 1985), as well as retrospective exhibitions at museums around the world.

Andrew Wilson

Bibliography
Ades, Dawn, and Andrew Forge. *Francis Bacon*. 1985.
Alley, Ronald, and John Rothenstein. *Francis Bacon*. 1964.
Alphen, Ernst van. *Francis Bacon and the Loss of Self*. 1993.
Leiris, Michel. *Francis Bacon, Full Face and in Profile*. 1983.
Russell, John. *Francis Bacon*. rev. ed. 1993.
Sylvester, David. *The Brutality of Fact: Interviews with Francis Bacon, 1962–1979*. 3rd ed. 1988.
Trucchi, Lorenza. *Francis Bacon*. 1976.

Baden-Powell, Robert (1857–1941)

Robert Baden-Powell was a British army officer who during the **Boer War** commanded the besieged garrison at Mafeking 1899–1900, holding out for seven months before being relieved. Back in Britain he was celebrated as the "hero of Mafeking." He later founded the Boy Scouts in 1907 and the Girl Guides in 1910. A baronet from 1922, Baden-Powell became the first Baron Baden-Powell of Gilwell in 1929.

Baden-Powell's father, who died when he was three, taught geometry at **Oxford**; his mother, Henrietta Grace Baden-Powell, would have a strong influence on him throughout his life. He attended Charterhouse School and then joined the Thirteenth Hussars, serving in India from 1876 to 1883. He participated in the 1888 Zulu War, the 1895 Ashanti War in West Africa, and the 1896 Matabele uprising in Central Africa. In 1897 Baden-Powell was promoted to colonel, commanding the Fifth Dragoon Guards, a cavalry regiment posted in India. From there he went to South Africa to raise some cavalry and to organize the police forces along the frontier of Cape Colony. Then came Mafeking, which forever became linked with Baden-Powell, standing for British determination and "pluck." To honor the hero, British composers came up with songs such as "Our Hero B-P," "The Hero of Mafeking Waltz," and "Major-General British Pluck." Baden-Powell capitalized on his fame to help establish and promote his great scheme for character building among the boys of the British Empire, **scouting**, which he started with a trial camp on Brownsea Island, off Poole, Dorset, in 1907. A year later he published his famous *Scouting for Boys*, which went through many editions. He retired from the army in 1910 to devote himself full time to his beloved scouts.

The Boer War hero wanted above all to promote character, **patriotism**, and manliness through scouting, so that the British Empire could avoid the fate of the Roman Empire. In Britain the fear of the decline and fall of the British Empire gave scouting its initial stimulus. Just as the "hero of Mafeking" had lifted sagging spirits during the Boer War, now after the war, with Britain's poor performance against an overmatched foe, Edwardian society seemed to be afflicted with pessimism and anxiety about the future. Baden-Powell's scouting seemed to offer to many in the middle class the hope of regeneration. The phenomena of Mafeking and scouting touched deep nerves in British society, and both came from the complex personality of Baden-Powell. To a society wracked by fears of impending decline through a lack of virility, his program of character development had a potent appeal. Baden-Powell did not marry until he was fifty-five, taking a wife thirty-two years younger than he. Olave, Lady Baden-Powell (1889–1977), worked tirelessly on behalf of the Girl Guides, the female counterpart to the scouts, giving them the kind of strong authority figure that Baden-Powell was for the Boy Scouts. Throughout his life Baden-Powell wrote numerous books, including *Quick Training for War* (1914), *My Adventures as a Spy* (1915), *Recovering to Success* (1922), *Life's Snags and*

How to Meet Them: Talks to Young Men (1927), his autobiography *Lessons of a Lifetime* (1933), *Adventuring to Manhood* (1936), and *Paddle Your Own Canoe, or Tips for Boys* (1939). Baden-Powell spent the last years of his life in Kenya, where he died on 8 January 1941.

Richard A. Voeltz

Bibliography

Baden-Powell, Robert. *Scouting for Boys.* 1908.

————. *Lessons of a Lifetime.* 1933.

Hillcourt, William, and Olave, Lady Baden-Powell. *Baden-Powell: The Two Lives of a Hero.* 1964.

Jeal, Tim. *The Boy-Man: The Life of Lord Baden-Powell.* 1990.

Rosenthal, Michael. *The Character Factory: Baden-Powell and the Origins of the Boy Scout Movement.* 1986.

Baldwin, Stanley (1867–1947)

Stanley Baldwin was the dominant figure in British politics between the wars. He led the **Conservative Party** from 1923 to 1937, establishing an image of moderation that contributed to its electoral success. He was Prime Minister three times, in 1923–4, 1924–9, and 1935–7, and played a crucial role during the National government of 1931–5. He retired from the premiership after the abdication crisis, and was created the first Earl Baldwin of Bewdley in 1937. Baldwin's desire to promote social harmony and industrial reconciliation has been credited with the "appeasement of Labour" in the 1920s, while he has been accused of laziness, lack of resolution, and responsibility for the **appeasement** of the dictators in the 1930s. After Baldwin's death his reputation fell to a low ebb, but in more recent years he has become a symbol of "one-nation" paternalist Conservatism and his domestic achievements have received greater recognition.

Baldwin's political vision was formed by two factors during his early years in semirural Worcestershire. The first of these was industrial: the communal spirit between employer and worker in the family business, an ironworks of moderate size and prosperity. This influenced his quest to re-create this mood upon the national stage and gave substance as well as passion to his oratory. The second element was rural: Baldwin developed an abiding love of the English countryside, and his ability to evoke this traditional heritage made a powerful appeal in a society gravely shaken by the **First World War** and the dislocations of the 1920s. His public image of the pipe-smoking English squire, honest but not clever, was both reassuring and popular. Baldwin was able to make a wide appeal across normal party lines and was acknowledged to be his party's greatest electoral asset. He established cordial relations with the Labour opposition in the House of Commons, without which the formation or continuation of the National government of 1931 would have been unlikely.

Baldwin entered the House of Commons in 1908 for the seat formerly represented by his father and made little impact during his first ten years. In 1917 he was given junior office by **Andrew Bonar Law,** and in the April 1921 reshuffle following Bonar Law's retirement he came into the **Cabinet** in the post of President of the Board of Trade. His rise from this position of relative obscurity to the premiership in the space of two years was both extraordinarily rapid and entirely unexpected. The cause was the revolt from below within the Conservative Party against the continuation of the **Lloyd George** coalition in 1922. Baldwin was the only Cabinet minister openly and vigorously to come out against Lloyd George: He expected this action to end his career, when in fact it made it. In October 1922 the coalition was overthrown, and into the wilderness with it went almost all the Conservative leaders. Bonar Law, who at the eleventh hour had consented to lead the revolt, became Prime Minister and had little choice but to make Baldwin Chancellor of the Exchequer. When in May 1923 Bonar Law's ill health forced a final retirement with the party still divided, Baldwin succeeded him as both Prime Minister and party leader. Baldwin's image as the antithesis of antidemocratic reaction and his position in the House of Commons led to his selection instead of the more experienced Foreign Secretary, **Lord Curzon.**

Baldwin's rejection of the tarnished Lloyd George coalition had established his reputation for honesty. His determination to keep Lloyd George out of power and to thwart any revival of coalitionism was shared by his followers. Anticoalitionism was a dominant theme of the next decade, with the former coalitionists constantly suspected of intrigue and disloyalty. Ironically, such fears may have led to Baldwin's greatest blunder and the swift demise of his first

B

premiership, yet also may have saved him from the consequences. In November 1923 he raised the banner of **tariff reform** partly to outflank Lloyd George, but slid instead into a general election in which the Conservatives lost their majority. He survived the period of opposition during the resulting 1924 Labour government mainly because no other credible noncoalitionist leader was available. Tariffs were dropped, and the moderate outlook known as the "New Conservatism" promoted in their place. In the election of November 1924 this pragmatism paid off, and Baldwin won a landslide victory.

Baldwin was at the height of his powers during his second premiership of 1924–9. During 1925 he established his authority over the **Cabinet** and over the parliamentary party with his appeal for "peace and goodwill in industry." Baldwin was concerned during this period with the connected problems of educating the new democratic electorate, the challenge from the **Labour Party**, industrial strife, and **unemployment**. He sought to buy time to resolve the conflict in the **coal mining** industry by providing a subsidy in 1925, to the dismay of much of his party. However, when that conflict spread to cause the **General Strike** in May 1926 his combination of firmness but fairness ensured that public opinion remained mainly on the government side. After the defeat of the General Strike, Baldwin's public reputation stood at its peak. The second half of the government was less successful than the first. The 1927 Trade Disputes and Trade Unions Act was not harsh enough for many Conservatives, but it aroused great Labour and trade union opposition. The Tory rank and file were alienated by the granting of the vote to women at age twenty-one, by agricultural policy, and by failures to take action on protection for iron and **steel** and on **House of Lords** reform. The government gave much emphasis to social reform, with widows' pensions, Poor Law reform, and, finally in 1928, the de-rating policy to reduce the tax burden on industry. In May 1929 Baldwin led a united if rather tired Cabinet into the election on a moderate platform that drew together all these themes. The most famous Conservative slogan from this campaign, "Safety First," was thereafter held to sum up Baldwin's approach to politics and all its supposed defects.

The Conservative defeat in 1929 led to the most serious crisis of Baldwin's career. There was great pressure from below to abandon the moderate pledges that had failed to secure victory, especially over tariff reform. Baldwin resisted because he was aware that the Conservatives had to win back the industrial seats in the Midlands and North if they were to return to power, but this pragmatic approach led to great tensions in the party. During 1929 and 1930 his position came under sustained pressure from the Conservative strongholds, mainly in the South, where resentment was encouraged and vocalized by the "Empire Crusade" campaign waged against Baldwin by the press magnates Lords **Beaverbrook** and Rothermere. The crisis reached its peak in the summer of 1930, but the steam was taken out of the critics when Baldwin made a substantial move toward a "free hand" policy on protection in October. The press lords continued their attacks with little effect until their final defeat in the St. George's by-election in March 1931.

In the crisis of August 1931 Baldwin agreed to serve under **Ramsay MacDonald** in a temporary emergency cross-party team to save the pound, and then found himself locked into a permanent coalition. Baldwin had not sought this, but he came to find the arrangement politically and personally agreeable. As leader of by far the biggest party in the National government, he was in many ways its most important figure without having the formal responsibility of the premiership. Baldwin concentrated his energies upon two areas. The first was keeping the coalition together, and especially coordinating its parliamentary work; the second was India. Between 1929 and 1935 Baldwin provoked further rebellions from the Conservative right wing, led this time by **Winston Churchill**, over his determination to follow the bipartisan line on India foreshadowed by the Irwin Declaration of 1929. The 1935 **Government of India Act**, placed on the statute book after a long struggle, though directly the work of **Sir Samuel Hoare**, is in many ways Baldwin's most concrete personal achievement.

In June 1935 he changed positions with MacDonald and became Prime Minister for the third time, winning a comfortable victory in the November 1935 election. The remainder of Baldwin's premiership was dominated by two crises: problems abroad with the Fascist dictators and problems at home with the new monarch. The hostile public reaction to the **Hoare-Laval Pact** in December 1935 gravely shook the government and the ditching of Hoare as Foreign Secretary reflected badly on Baldwin. In early 1936 he suffered a form of nervous break-down, and the government drifted uneasily for several months. Toward the end of 1936 Baldwin recovered to handle the abdication crisis with tact and skill, to great public approval. He decided to retire at the coronation of **George VI** in May 1937, handing over to his heir-apparent for many years, **Neville Chamberlain**.

Only one area of politics consistently aroused Baldwin's interest: threats to the general political stability enshrined in the parliamentary constitution. All his major battles were fought in this area, from the cynicism and corruption of the Lloyd George coalition, through the General Strike, the pretensions of the press barons, and the future of India to the abdication crisis. Once he shifted political conflict to this ground he was unbeatable, a fact found to their cost by apparently more able politicians such as Lloyd George and Churchill, who constantly underestimated his reserves of strength.

Stuart Ball

Bibliography

Baldwin, Stanley. *On England, and Other Addresses.* 1926.
Ball, Stuart. *Baldwin and the Conservative Party: The Crisis of 1929–1931.* 1988.
Campbell, John. "Stanley Baldwin" in John P. Mackintosh, ed. *British Prime Ministers in the Twentieth Century.* vol 1. 1977. pp. 188–218.
Hyde, H. Montgomery. *Baldwin.* 1973.
Middlemas, Keith, and John Barnes. *Baldwin.* 1969.

Balfour, Arthur James (1848–1930)

One of Britain's wealthiest and most powerful politicians, Arthur James Balfour led the **Conservatives** in the House of Commons while his uncle, Lord Salisbury, served as Prime Minister. When Balfour held that position from 1902 to 1905, he enjoyed no great popularity in the aftermath of the war in South Africa, demonstrating more initiative in foreign and imperial affairs than in domestic matters. Equivocating on **tariff reform**, Balfour tried to bridge deep divisions within his party until he resigned as Tory leader in 1911, later serving as a minister in coalition and Conservative **Cabinets**. As the Foreign Secretary from 1916 to 1919, he promoted closer ties with the United States and greater cooperation among the white Dominions.

At the age of eight, when his father died, Balfour inherited a Scottish estate and fortune that his grandfather had amassed as a contractor in India. Balfour's mother, a sister of the Marquess of Salisbury, the Prime Minister for most of the period from 1885 to 1902, inculcated religious devotion and bookish pursuits in her near-sighted, frail son. Balfour's years at Eton and Trinity College, **Cambridge,** had less impact on him than the brilliant family circle of brothers, sisters, and their spouses, which broadened Balfour's philosophical and scientific interests. Unwavering in his religious and political beliefs, the skeptical Balfour had a low opinion of humanity's past and little expectation that humans could do much better in the future.

Elected to the House of Commons in 1876, Balfour served his political apprenticeship under his uncle, Lord Salisbury, who first made Balfour his Parliamentary Private Secretary, then Minister in turn for Local Government, Scotland, and Ireland. Balfour used the carrot and the stick in Ireland, which gained him praise from Conservatives and Unionists, but the title "Bloody Balfour" from the Irish and their Liberal supporters. He led the House of Commons, serving as First Lord of the Treasury under his uncle in the 1890s and during the **Boer War**. Never an impressive orator, Balfour was more effective in parliamentary debate and in the Cabinet room.

When Salisbury resigned the premiership, Balfour moved into 10 Downing Street in July 1902. Balfour's party was weakened in the aftermath of the Boer War by **Lord Milner**'s employment of Chinese "coolie" labor in South Africa, by the conflict between Lords **Curzon** and **Kitchener** in India, and especially because prices increased more rapidly than wages, all of which eclipsed Balfour success in piloting his education and licensing bills through Parliament. In foreign affairs, Balfour and his Foreign Secretary, Lord Lansdowne, negotiated an agreement with France and a treaty with Japan, both of which were designed to contain Russian expansionism. Balfour also established the **Committee of Imperial Defence**, which brought together civilian, military, and bipartisan figures to determine priorities. When the Unionist Joseph Chamberlain pressed for a scheme of tariff reform favoring the British Empire over other protectionist powers, Balfour tried to keep the free traders in the party, conscious that Tory protectionism had earlier been a liability and that Sir Robert Peel's free-trade policy had split the Conservative Party. Balfour's efforts failed, and the Tories were badly defeated early in 1906. He even lost his own parliamentary seat in East Manchester but was soon returned for the safe seat of the City of London. Until 1911, when Balfour stepped down as Conservative leader, he had increasing difficulty in holding his party together in opposition to Liberal legislation, particularly their budget of 1909, advocacy of Home Rule for Ireland, and reform of the House of Lords. To "die-hard" Conservatives, Balfour appeared weak, while others found him politically ineffectual.

The outbreak of war in 1914 gave Balfour a new political lease on life, when he was asked by H.H. Asquith, the Liberal Prime Minister, to serve on a war-policy committee that had evolved from the Committee of Imperial Defence. In 1915 Balfour joined the Asquith coalition, taking charge of the Admiralty and reluctantly presiding over British evacuation from the Gallipoli Peninsula. At the end of 1916 Balfour joined the coalition formed by David Lloyd George, this time as Foreign Secretary. After the United States entered the war in the spring of 1917, Balfour visited Washington and promoted closer Anglo-American relations. Later that year he sent a public letter to Lord Rothschild, on behalf of the Zionists, affirming British support of a Jewish homeland in Palestine.

In the post-war years, Balfour assumed the mantle of "elder statesman" and left his mark on foreign and imperial affairs. He generally deferred to Lloyd George on Germany, Russia, the Middle East, and Ireland, but he played a bigger role in the settlement with Austria. Balfour also led the British delegation to the Washington Naval Conference in 1921. When Lloyd George's second coalition fell in 1922, Balfour was out of office until he joined the ministry of Stanley Baldwin. In 1926 he chaired a committee on inter-imperial relations, recognizing the equality of all British Dominions and paving the way for the Statute of Westminster of 1931, a year after his death.

Roger Adelson

Bibliography

Egremont, Max. *Balfour: A Life of Arthur James Balfour*. 1980.
Mackay, Ruddock F. *Balfour, Intellectual Statesman*. 1985.
Young, Kenneth. *Arthur James Balfour*. 1963.
Zebel, Sydney H. *Balfour: A Political Biography*. 1973.

Balfour Declaration

The public letter Arthur James Balfour, then British Foreign Secretary, addressed to Lord Rothschild, who represented British Zionists, was dated 2 November 1917. This wartime declaration gave the British and Zionists grounds for the League of Nations recognition of the British mandate over Palestine from 1922 to 1947 and fostered the Zionist aim of making Palestine a Jewish state.

Zionism, the movement started in the 1890s by European Jews to establish a national escape for Jews suffering from anti-Semitism throughout Europe, was largely ignored by most British politicians before the First World War. As Prime Minister from 1902 to 1905 Balfour associated with several British Jews who were prominent in financial and political circles. Although conscious of the plight of European Jewry, he doubted the utility of Zionism. The British Empire decision to declare war on the Ottoman Empire, which allied with Germany late in 1914, encouraged Zionists to renew their quest for support in London and other capitals. Herbert Samuel, the Liberal Home Secretary, approached the Foreign Office as a Jew sympathetic to Zionist aspirations in Palestine, but his overtures were rebuffed in 1914 and 1915. After the British evacuated Gallipoli at the end of 1915, the idea of advancing into Palestine to safeguard Egypt prompted Mark Sykes, a Tory MP involved with Middle East policy and Allied diplomacy, to take Zionism much more seriously. Once David Lloyd George became Prime Minister, resistance to concentrating the army on the Western Front grew, especially after revolution broke out in Russia in March 1917. Chaim Weizmann, a Zionist emigré from Russia, encouraged Sykes' belief that the opposition of Russian Jews to the czar could be counteracted by promising them a return to Zion. Some members of the government also believed that American Jews might be induced to support the Allies more vigorously if the British sanctioned Zionist objectives. Sykes' draft of a public declaration in support of Zionism provoked opposition from within the government: Some feared a Muslim backlash, while others feared compromising the citizenship of Jews living outside Palestine. Lloyd George and the majority believed they could indicate the British had no specific Jewish state in mind, but merely a national center for world Jewry, whose influence might significantly affect the Allied war efforts. After Balfour learned in the autumn of 1917 that Germany was contemplating such a commitment to Zionists, the Cabinet agreed that the following carefully phrased note from the Foreign Secretary to Rothschild be made public: "His Majesty's Government view with favour the establishment in Palestine of a national home for the Jewish people, and will use their best endeavours to facilitate the achievement of this object, it being clearly understood that nothing shall be done which may prejudice the civil and religious rights of existing non-Jewish communities in Palestine, or the rights and political status enjoyed by Jews in any other country."

Roger Adelson

Bibliography

Adelson, Roger. *Mark Sykes: Portrait of an Amateur.* 1975.
Friedman, Isaiah. *The Question of Palestine, 1914–1918.* 1973.
Reinharz, Jehuda. "The Balfour Declaration and Its Maker: A Reassessment," *Journal of Modern History*, vol. 64 (1992), pp. 455–99.
Stein, Leonard. *The Balfour Declaration.* 1961.

Ballard, J(ames) G(raham) (1930–)

J.G. Ballard is recognized as one of the most influential of New Wave science fiction writers and "experimental" novelists. He was born in Shanghai and lived with his parents in the International Settlement during his childhood. There he was exposed to the continual confrontation of the wealthy community of Western industrialists and businessmen with the poverty, overcrowding, and violence of much of Shanghai. In 1942 he was interned with his parents in a Japanese prison camp where he remained until the Japanese were expelled at the end of the Second World War. This period, represented in two of Ballard's novels, *Empire of the Sun* (1985) and *The Kindness of Women* (1991), forms the background for many of his depictions of the fragility of Western culture. His family returned to Britain in 1946. Ballard's education included two years of medical school at Cambridge where he developed an interest in, and knowledge of, anatomy, an abortive year

studying literature at the University of London, and training as a pilot in the Royal Air Force. By the late 1950s he was publishing regularly in science fiction magazines. In 1964 his wife, Mary, died, leaving him with three children, whom he raised in Shepperton, his current home.

Ballard's early interest in science fiction derived from his desire to represent what was implied in the rapidly changing technology and social organization of the world in the mid-twentieth century. His novels return repeatedly to the question of a world devastated by ecological disasters brought about by technological achievements: the floods of *The Drowned World* (1962), the drought of *The Burning World* (also published as *The Drought*, 1964), and the climatic rearrangements of *Hello America* (1981). By 1966 his early interest in the style of James Joyce's late writing, surrealist painters (Francis Bacon, Salvador Dali), and other late modernists found expression in the short stories in *The Atrocity Exhibition* (1970). This collection disturbingly juxtaposes obsessions of contemporary life—violence, politics, fame, sex, science—in such stories as "Love and Napalm: Export USA" and "The Assassination of John Fitzgerald Kennedy Considered as a Downhill Motor Race." These writings reject psychological explanations of character, focusing instead on external determinants of action expressed through collage-like effects typical of much postmodernist art and writing.

Ballard describes his most controversial novel, *Crash!* (1973), not entirely accurately as "the first pornographic novel based on technology." This novel proposes a near-future world in which lives have become so deeply intertwined with cinema and automobiles that the only erotic bodies are those most reshaped and disfigured by filmic images and crashes. In Ballard's novels, internal and external landscapes are closely allied and reinforce each other, as in his story of a man trapped within a freeway interchange (*Concrete Island* 1974) or of life reduced to primitive levels in an apartment complex (*High Rise* 1975). Ballard's most compelling and consistent theme concerns the ways in which the most horrific aspects of contemporary life can be embraced by its victims. This situation is represented in the semi-autobiographical *Empire of the Sun* (made into a film by Steven Spielberg, 1987), in which the young hero thrives on wartime violence, the terrorism of prison camp, and the spectacle of the atomic explosion. The result is a powerful dramatization of the relations between violence and modern technologies by one of the few writers to cross science fiction and fantasy with mainstream fiction.

Dennis A. Foster

Bibliography

Pringle, David. *J.G. Ballard: A Primary and Secondary Bibliography.* 1984.
Re/Search: J.G. Ballard. 1984.

Ballet

A colorful hybrid of foreign influences and native talent, classical ballet in Britain traces its ancestry to the elaborate masques staged at the Tudor and Stuart courts and the riotous Harlequin pantomimes of the eighteenth century. The academic classicism of France and Italy arrived in Britain during the nineteenth century, when the most acclaimed European dancers regularly performed at Her Majesty's Theatre, London. The greatest ballerinas of the romantic era made their only joint appearance there, in the legendary *Pas de Quatre* (1845) Jules Perrot created for them.

At the beginning of the twentieth century British ballet was the sparkling centerpiece of the music-hall variety show and an enormous commercial draw at the Alhambra and the Empire theatres. The latter usually staged two extravagent new productions annually and ran them for six months, often with the delicate Danish ballerina, Adeline Genée, in the starring role. So many people wanted to see Genée dance that the Empire offered daily matinees for several months in 1907 to satisfy the demand for tickets.

Before the First World War England had its first glimpse of Russian ballet when Anna Pavlova and Mikhail Mordkin brought a small troupe to the Palace and Tamara Karsavina performed at the Coliseum. With the arrival of Serge Diaghilev's exotic Ballets Russes, ballet exchanged mere prettiness for primitive, dramatic, and sometimes shocking effects, and artists like Karsavina and Vaslav Nijinsky infused steps, mime, and characterization with passionate conviction.

Diaghilev's troupe also nurtured the founders of Britain's own ballet companies: **Ninette de Valois** (born Edris Stannus), Alicia Markova (born Alicia Marks), Anton Dolin

(born Patrick Healey-Kay), and Marie Rambert (born Cyvia Rambam) all danced for him, although Rambert was employed primarily to help Nijinsky, as choreographer, untangle the rhythms of Igor Stravinsky's *Rite of Spring*. Inspired by the daring choreography and mesmeric performers of the Ballets Russes, and imagining a time when native dancers would make their own artistic impact, Rambert opened a ballet school in 1920, and de Valois did the same in 1926.

The Cecchetti Society was founded in 1921 to perpetuate the methods of the great teacher Enrico Cecchetti, and the Association of Teachers of Operatic Dancing (the Royal Academy of Dancing from 1936) was formed in 1920. Although the Ballets Russes continued to appear, performing opportunities for most British dancers during the 1920s lay in the commercial theater, in pantomime or in revues, where two of Diaghilev's choreographers, Leonide Massine and George Balanchine, also found work before and after his death in 1929.

Part of a revue called "Riverside Nights," *The Tragedy of Fashion* (1926) marked the choreographic debut of **Frederick Ashton**, whose works eventually formed the bedrock of the native British repertory. In 1930 the first public performances of Rambert's students, as the Ballet Club, marked the first steps of a native company. Led in its early seasons by Karsavina, the Ballet Club gave Sunday evening performances in the school's premises in Notting Hill. Markova succeeded Karsavina in 1931, and by 1934 the company had moved to the tiny Mercury Theatre and added weekday performances to the schedule.

Two extraordinary English choreographers created the remarkable repertory. Until 1934 Ashton provided a stream of short works stamped with the lyricism, eloquent musicality, and sunny humor that would characterize his mature works and define the British style of dancing. Having made his debut with a comic piece, *Cross Garter'd* (1931), Antony Tudor discovered a unique and powerfully dramatic vocabulary from which he shaped his masterpieces, *Jardin aux Lilas* (1936) and *Dark Elegies* (1937).

Launched the same year as the Ballet Club, the Camargo Society was founded to further the interests of English ballet and fill the void left for both dancers and public when Diaghilev's company disbanded. Although it survived only until 1933 and produced only sixteen new ballets, it supplied another important breeding ground for British choreographers. Ashton made his witty *Façade* (1931), which is still widely danced today, and, having left Diaghilev to choreograph in Cambridge, Dublin, and London, de Valois created the starkly dramatic *Job* (1931).

She also made one piece, *Bar aux Folies Bergère* (1934), for the Ballet Club, but choreography was not her primary goal. In 1928 the producer **Lilian Baylis** hired her to arrange the dances for the operas and plays at the **Old Vic**. With Baylis' support, in 1931 de Valois moved her school into the Sadler's Wells Theatre as the nucleus of a new company devoted exclusively to ballet. Called the Vic-Wells Ballet when it arrived, the minuscule troupe initially danced complete evenings of ballet only every two weeks. With Ashton as her resident choreographer from 1935 and the young **Margot Fonteyn** as her ballerina after Markova departed the same year, de Valois built a company of international stature at Sadler's Wells. It drew its strength from traditional productions of the nineteenth-century classics—*The Sleeping Beauty*, *Swan Lake*, and *Giselle*—and from the innovative choreography of Ashton, de Valois herself—*The Rake's Progress* (1935) and *Checkmate* (1937)—and, later, John Cranko and **Kenneth MacMillan**.

De Valois, Baylis, and Rambert created British ballet from a combination of vision, courage, and tenacity. Until the Second World War, their fledgling efforts had to compete for an audience with several glamorous Russian companies, which visited **London** regularly. But no foreign companies appeared in England between 1939 and 1946, and British ballet flourished as a result.

Ballet Rambert performed in factories and office cafeterias around the country and, in 1940–1, at the Arts Theatre in London, offering programs of "Lunch Ballet," "Tea Ballet," and "Sherry Ballet," along with the appropriate beverage. Tudor, who had formed the London Ballet in 1938, left England when the war broke out to join Ballet Theatre in America, where he spent the rest of his life, and his company merged with the Arts Theatre Ballet and shared performances with Ballet Rambert. Tudor's deliciously sardonic *Gala Performance* (1938) entered Rambert's repertory, as did new works by Andrée Howard and Frank Staff.

The Sadler's Wells Ballet, as the Vic-Wells was named in 1940, traveled outside the capital to civilian and military theaters and briefly visited Holland. It found a new home in the New Theatre, London, and a new, sometimes controversial choreographer in its *premier danseur* Robert Helpmann, who created *Hamlet* (1942) and *Miracle in the Gorbals* (1944) after Ashton joined the **Royal Air Force**.

Although **conscription** depleted the onstage forces and money was scarce, several new companies—International Ballet and the Anglo-Polish Ballet among them—emerged during the **Second World War** and toured extensively for some time. Ballet Rambert closed for 18 months (1941–3), but when it reappeared, it was supported for the first time by government funds. Under the direction of economist **John Maynard Keynes**, the **Council for the Encouragement of Music and the Arts** (CEMA) financed and managed Rambert for four years (1943–7), during which time the company staged an acclaimed production of *Giselle* starring its compelling ballerina, Sally Gilmour.

Thanks also to the assistance of CEMA (the **Arts Council of Great Britain** from 1945), de Valois' Sadler's Wells Ballet was invited to make the Royal Opera House its permanent home. Reopening the theatre in 1946, with Fonteyn in a splendid new production of *The Sleeping Beauty*, sealed the company's future at Covent Garden. Later that year, a second branch of the company, called Sadler's Wells Opera (later Theatre) Ballet, was established to foster new choreographic and performing talent for Covent Garden. In only fifteen years, de Valois had realized her dream of creating a company to represent the nation both at home and abroad.

Artistic triumph marked the post-war years. At Covent Garden, Ashton created a timeless masterpiece, *Symphonic Variations* (1946), and Massine appeared as a guest artist. Resident ballerina Moira Shearer starred in **Michael Powell**'s film, *The Red Shoes* (1948), which introduced ballet to a vast new audience. And on its first transatlantic tour (1949), the company captivated the American public and press with its noble dancing and sumptuous full-evening productions of *The Sleeping Beauty* and *Swan Lake*, then only known there in abbreviated versions.

Meanwhile, another important company was finding its feet in England. When Markova left the Vic-Wells Ballet, she and Anton Dolin organized their own company, the Markova-Dolin Ballet (1935–8). Having spent the war years dancing with Ballet Theatre in America, they returned to England to guest at Covent

Garden in 1948 and founded a second small troupe with which they toured the country.

Encouraged by its touring success and backed by an experienced impresario, Julian Braunsweg, in 1950 the company adopted the name Festival Ballet (anticipating the **Festival of Britain** the following year) and gave its first London season. Markova left in 1952, but the Festival Ballet had quickly found an audience by offering international stars and an eclectic repertory at popular prices.

The company's artistic director until 1960, Dolin chose to concentrate on nineteenth-century classics—*The Nutcracker*, his production of *Giselle*, and eventually *Swan Lake*—and on the Diaghilev repertory; during the 1950s, Nicholas Beriosoff revived many of Russian choreographer Mikhail Fokine's works, and Massine revived his own in the 1970s. Led by an English *danseur*, John Gilpin, the principal artists hailed from Russia, Denmark, France, and Hungary.

Over the years the repertory grew rapidly with contributions by Balanchine, Harald Lander, Jack Carter, and Ronald Hynd, and new productions of the well-loved classics from Russia and Denmark. Renamed English National Ballet in 1989, the company still pursues Dolin's original policy, mixing choreographic novelty with classics and casting foreign dancers alongside British ones.

In 1956 the two Sadler's Wells companies were incorporated by Royal Charter as the Royal Ballet. They maintained their separate identities, however, and from the smaller company came the first memorable works of MacMillan, who changed the face of British ballet by reshaping the classical vocabulary in order to explore modern and psychological subjects.

Just as de Valois' enterprise took a firmer hold on the capital, a small regional ballet company was taking shape, and in 1957 Western Theatre Ballet gave its debut performance in Bristol. Directed by Elizabeth West, this group was interested, like MacMillan, in applying classical technique to contemporary themes. With the Arts Council's help, it toured Europe as well as Britain, often performing the topical ballets of codirector Peter Darrell, who took charge after West's untimely death (1962).

Having first visited Scotland in 1960, the company moved its home to Glasgow in 1969, took the name Scottish Theatre Ballet, and began building a community following for tradi-tional dance and theatrical daring. By 1974, when the troupe was renamed the Scottish Ballet, it had developed an international reputation and was generally accepted as the national ballet of Scotland.

The spotlights of the 1960s focused on Rudolf Nureyev's matchless partnership with Margot Fonteyn and on the Royal Ballet's young stars: Antoinette Sibley, Anthony Dowell, and Lynn Seymour. Ballet Rambert made headlines in 1966 by abandoning classical ballet entirely and transforming itself into a contemporary company. Directed since 1986 by choreographer Richard Alston and called simply the Rambert Dance Company, it is the only British company that performs the seminal modern works of Merce Cunningham.

The second regional company to take root was the Northern Dance Theatre, which was founded in Manchester in 1969 by Laverne Meyer. Originally a lively blend of small-scale classical and modern works, the repertory leans heavily on full-evening narrative ballets with a strong, theatrical slant and a broad popular appeal. Called Northern Ballet Theatre since 1977 and operating out of Halifax, it was until 1990 the only classical English company based outside London.

In that year the smaller Royal Ballet company, then known as the Sadler's Wells Royal Ballet, transferred its home base to Birmingham and changed its title to the Birmingham Royal Ballet. With that move, nearly sixty years after its founding, the national company represented the provinces and the capital equally at last, as de Valois always hoped it would.

Barbara Newman

Bibliography

Bland, Alexander. *The Royal Ballet: The First Fifty Years.* 1981.

Clarke, Mary. *Dancers of Mercury: The Story of Ballet Rambert.* 1962.

———. *The Sadler's Wells Ballet: A History and an Appreciation.* 1955.

Vaughan, Mary, and David Vaughan, eds. *The Encyclopedia of Dance and Ballet.* 1977.

White, Joan W., ed. *Twentieth-Century Dance in Britain.* 1985.

Battle of Britain

See Blitz and Battle of Britain

Baylis, Lilian Mary (1874–1937)

A unique figure in the British theater, Lilian Baylis served as manager of the **Old Vic** for forty years, the restorer of Sadler's Wells, and the woman responsible for bringing Shakespeare, **opera**, and later **ballet** to ordinary people in **London** at affordable prices. The eldest of ten children born to performing musicians, she received erratic and incomplete schooling but solid musical training. She performed as a child prodigy on the violin, mandolin, and banjo in recitals and with the St. James' Ladies Orchestra. At seventeen she accompanied her parents to **South Africa**, where the Baylis family toured as a concert party known as "The Gypsy Revellers," Lilian supplementing the often precarious family income by giving music lessons. After being hospitalized in Johannesburg for a kidney operation, she returned to England to convalesce in 1897 and began to help her aunt Emma Cons to manage the Old Vic.

Seventeen years earlier Emma Cons (1837–1912), a protegée of Octavia Hill, had opened the Royal Victoria Coffee and Music Hall to provide uplifting, teetotal entertainment for the respectable poor at the former Royal Coburg, known for drunken rowdyism in an already blighted neighborhood. During its early years theater offerings included lectures and concerts of opera excerpts, while part of the building was reserved for workingmen's **adult education** in what became known as Morley College. Lilian Baylis became manager of the Old Vic in 1898, working in her aunt's shadow until 1912, when she assumed sole control over its operations.

After the death of Emma Cons, the Old Vic obtained a theater license, which enabled it finally to present full-length operas and plays, although for some years it continued to intersperse lectures and temperance meetings in the weekly billings. Relying on wealthy benefactors and what she believed was her personal ability to intercede with God, the deeply religious, High Anglican Baylis survived recurrent financial crises to establish the foundations of a people's theater with a loyal community following. Although she lacked commercial theatrical experience or private income, she managed by improvisation, frugality, and her domineering personality to keep the Old Vic open, however difficult it proved to combine artistry and philanthropy. Her tactlessness, explosive temper, and legendary stinginess were coupled with unremitting hard work and steely determination. Despite the minimal salaries, her initial reluctance to employ stars, and technically impoverished productions, often using borrowed costumes, her single-mindedness attracted many leading actors of their generation, who welcomed the opportunity to perform Shakespeare, under directors like Robert Atkins and Tyrone Guthrie, free of the commercial constraints of the West End. The Old Vic in the Baylis years produced all of Shakespeare's plays plus a range of other dramatic classics, including Ibsen and Chekhov with, among others, Sybil Thorndike, Lewis Casson, Edith Evans, John Gielgud, Charles Laughton, and **Laurence Olivier**, acquiring an unmatched reputation for artistic integrity that widened its audience base.

In 1926 Baylis engaged **Ninette de Valois** to teach movement to Old Vic drama students, to choreograph Shakespeare productions, and eventually to establish a ballet school and company at the derelict Sadler's Wells, whose freehold Baylis acquired in 1925 with a grant from the Carnegie United Kingdom Trust. The slow progress of renovations meant that it was not until 1931 that the theater reopened as a North London version Old Vic. At first, drama, opera, and ballet alternated at both theaters, but that proved impractical, and in 1936 Sadler's Wells was reserved for opera and the so-called Vic-Wells Ballet, launched when the theater opened. In their own building the ballet company and the Sadler's Wells Opera flourished, the latter performing in English many operas outside the restricted repertory hitherto attempted at the Old Vic.

In 1924 Baylis received an honorary M.A. at Oxford, and in 1929 she was named a Companion of Honour. She died suddenly of a heart attack at the age of sixty-three, having made a singular contribution to the arts in Britain and paved the way for what would eventually become the **National Theatre**, the Royal Ballet, and the English National Opera. A portrait of Baylis in the academic robes that became her trademark hangs prominently at the Coliseum in London.

F.M. Leventhal

Bibliography

Dent, E.J. *A Theatre for Everybody: The Story of the Old Vic and Sadler's Wells.* 1945.

Findlater, Richard. *Lilian Baylis: The Lady of the Old Vic.* 1975.

Williams, Harcourt, ed. *Vic-Wells: The Work of Lilian Baylis.* 1938.

Beatles, The

The Beatles were the first and perhaps most important global **popular music** group. They capitalized on the 1950s mass media explosion of rock 'n' roll, especially the star-making machinery that had catapulted Elvis Presley to fame. As the "Fab Four," they comprised John Lennon (guitar, vocals), Paul McCartney (bass, vocals), George Harrison (guitar, vocals), and Ringo Starr (drums, vocals). All came from Liverpool and consequently popularized Merseyside clubs, such as the Cavern, and guitar-group music that became labeled "Merseybeat." They emerged into the media spotlight in 1962 and had a first British chart hit with "Love Me Do." Subsequent worldwide chart single hits included "From Me To You," "She Loves You," "Yellow Submarine," "All You Need Is Love," "Strawberry Fields Forever," "Penny Lane," "Hey Jude," "Let It Be," and "Get Back." Numerous album chart successes were also notched up, including *Beatles for Sale, Rubber Soul, Revolver, Sgt.* *Pepper's Lonely Hearts Club Band, The Beatles* (a double LP known as "The White Album"), *Abbey Road,* and *Let It Be.* Managed for a long while by Brian Epstein until his suicide and inspired by the arrangements and production of George Martin, the Beatles played live concert tours only until 1966, concentrating mainly on recording and songwriting. Their success was measured in later years by huge global record sales, their controversial involvement in films (such as their own *Magical Mystery Tour*) and the 1960s "counterculture," and the continued prolific songwriting of Lennon and McCartney.

By the end of the 1960s the group was in turmoil, as evidenced in the scenes recorded for the film *Let It Be* that chart the personal disillusionment of group members and the growing attachment of Lennon to Yoko Ono. The end came in 1970 amid threats of expensive legal wrangles over the group's affairs. All members subsequently embarked on variable solo careers and, despite constant media rumors over many years, the Beatles never played together again. Their last public performance was a famous free concert that included a rendition of "Get Back" played on the open-air roof of the offices of their company, Apple, in

The Beatles in 1963.

central London in 1970. The 1970s saw continuing coverage of their songs by many other artists and ever more intractable court cases over their financial affairs. At the beginning of the 1980s Lennon, who had successfully applied to be allowed to live in the United States in the previous decade, was shot dead in front of the Dakota apartment building in New York where he and Yoko Ono lived. His killer, Mark Chapman, claimed he was a fan and had pursued Lennon for his autograph. Lennon had just finished recording a comeback LP after several years of musical inactivity, and it was released to considerable commercial success. The rest of the ex-Beatles continued their involvement in various branches of the entertainment industry.

Steve Redhead

Bibliography

Lewisohn, Mark. *The Beatles: 25 Years in the Life.* 1987.
Norman, Philip. *Shout! The True Story of the Beatles.* 1982.
Stokes, Geoffrey. *The Beatles.* 1988.

Beaton, Cecil Walter Hardy (1904–1980)

Cecil Beaton described himself as "the first photographer whose work caught the imagination of the general public." That was apropos of his first exhibition in London, at Cooling Galleries in November 1927. Educated at Harrow and at St. John's College, **Cambridge**, he was introduced to photography and to gardening by his nanny. His interests in art and the theater were encouraged at Harrow and sustained at Cambridge, which he left without a degree in 1925. After a brief period in business he became a photographer, with the encouragement of Osbert Sitwell and the advice of professional photographer Paul Tanqueray (1905–). From 1927 Beaton became a regular contributor of articles, **caricatures**, illustrations, and photographs to *Vogue*, for which he continued to work until the late 1960s. In 1929 he was the only British photographer represented at the Stuttgart *Film und Photo* exhibition.

Beaton was influenced by a 1926 trip to Venice, where he met ballet producer Serge Diaghilev and saw the painted ceilings of the Tiepolos. In 1933 he met Jean Cocteau, Pavel Tchelichew, and Christian Bérard in Paris, but he was, above all, a man of the theater and of the film world and, for *Vanity Fair*, made his first trip to Hollywood in 1929. His first book, *The Book of Beauty*, was published in 1930, followed by *Cecil Beaton's Scrapbook* in 1937. During the 1930s he continued to design for **musical revues** and **ballets** and to photograph in Hollywood. In 1939 he became a royal portraitist and in 1940 was employed by the Ministry of Information to take pictures of war leaders and of the north of England. During the **Second World War** he published eight books on wartime themes, including *Air of Glory* (1941) and *Winged Squadrons* (1942).

After the war Beaton's interest in design intensified, and although his *Photobiography* appeared in 1951, it was the theater that held his interest. In 1951 his first play, *The Gainsborough Girls*, was staged at the Theatre Royal, Brighton, to no great acclaim. In 1955 he worked on the American stage version of *My Fair Lady*, which led to his Oscar-winning designs for the film in 1963. During the 1950s he became something of a celebrity in his own right, while gaining a reputation as a photographer of celebrities, serving as official photographer at the wedding of Antony Armstrong-Jones and Princess Margaret. In 1961 he designed costumes and sets for *Turandot* at the Metropolitan Opera, and the first volume of his diaries, *The Wandering Years, 1922–1939*, was published. Knighted in 1972, he suffered a disabling stroke in 1974 but continued to photograph until 1979. Devoted as he was to celebrity and to publicity, he functioned as a British laureate of the intertwined milieux of high society, fashion, and pop. He was the last heroic, national representative of that nexus.

Ian Jeffrey

Bibliography

Buckle, Richard, ed. *Self-Portrait with Friends: The Selected Diaries of Cecil Beaton, 1926–74.* 1979.
Mellor, David. *Cecil Beaton.* 1986.
Vickers, Hugo. *Cecil Beaton.* 1985.

Beaverbrook, Lord (William Maxwell Aitken) (1879–1964)

Lord Beaverbrook was the leading "press baron" of the twentieth century and a maverick, but periodically influential, Conservative politician. Born William Maxwell "Max" Aitken in Canada, he was created the first Baron Beaverbrook in 1917. He was a personal friend of **Andrew Bonar Law** and **Winston Churchill** but vigorously opposed the leadership of **Stanley Baldwin** in 1929–31. He held ministerial office during both world wars, but his most significant contribution was as an energetic Minister of Aircraft Production in 1940–1.

In his early years in Canada Beaverbrook acquired the fortune that was the basis of his later business success. In 1910 he moved to Britain, where he remained domiciled for the rest of his life, although he retained links with Canadian statesmen. An ardent believer in Joseph Chamberlain's crusade for **tariff reform**, Beaverbrook was elected as a Conservative MP in December 1910, mainly as a result of his developing friendship with Bonar Law. He made little impact in the House of Commons but acquired a reputation as a manipulator behind the scenes with a taste for intrigue.

There are three significant aspects to Beaverbrook's career. Typically, all revolved around a highly personalized form of political allegiance or antipathy. The first of these was Beaverbrook's role as confidant and supporter of Bonar Law from 1910 to 1923. He was among those who encouraged Bonar Law to maintain his candidacy for the Conservative leadership in November 1911. Beaverbrook played a still more important role in bringing together Bonar Law and **David Lloyd George** in December 1916 and thus precipitating the fall of **H.H. Asquith** from the premiership. Although Beaverbrook was also an intimate of Lloyd George after 1916, he encouraged Bonar Law to come out against the continuation of the coalition at the Carlton Club meeting of October 1922. Thus was his reputation as a political "kingmaker" established.

The second strand in Beaverbrook's life was of the most lasting importance: his preeminent position in the British national **press**. In 1916 Beaverbrook acquired control of the *Daily Express*, which he built up during the inter-war years first to rival the *Daily Mail* and then to surpass it in the mass-circulation popular market. The *Daily Express* formed the heart of Beaverbrook's press empire and remained the focus of his attention: He closely monitored both content and appearance, with a constant stream of instructions to his editorial staff. In 1918 he founded the *Sunday Express*, and in 1923 he completed his coverage with the acquisition of the London afternoon paper, the *Evening Standard*. Partly as a result of his media interests, he was made Minister of Information in 1918–19, but the appointment attracted

press and parliamentary criticism. In the early twentieth century it was believed that the press wielded enormous influence over its readers, and thus politicians were both resentful and fearful of the power of press "barons" such as Lords **Northcliffe**, Rothermere, and Beaverbrook. After the Conservative election defeat of 1929, the latter two put this power to the test in an attempt first to force a protectionist policy upon the party and second to oust its unresponsive leader, Baldwin. Beaverbrook was the active force in their "Empire Crusade" campaign, which enlisted members and contested by-elections. Baldwin found the press lords' attempt at "power without responsibility" to be an easy target for counterattack in the spring of 1931. However, rank-and-file support for "Empire Free Trade" had forced Baldwin to make substantial concessions on policy in October 1930: Beaverbrook's defeat was more apparent than real.

The final element of Beaverbrook's career revolved around his friendship with Churchill, which was especially close after 1940. Beaverbrook filled the vital post of Minister of Aircraft Production from May 1940 to May 1941, and his energy and willingness to innovate resulted in significantly higher output at a critical moment for national survival. He served as Minister of Supply (1941–2) but then left the government for eighteen months and campaigned vigorously for greater support for the Russian war effort and an early second front in Europe. He returned as Lord Privy Seal (1943–5), in which role he was regarded by many in the **Conservative Party** as a mischievous and reactionary influence upon Churchill and was blamed for contributing to the 1945 election defeat.

Stuart Ball

Bibliography

Ball, Stuart. *Baldwin and the Conservative Party: The Crisis of 1929–1931.* 1988.

Beaverbrook, Lord. *The Decline and Fall of Lloyd George.* 1963.

———. *Politicians and the War, 1914–1916.* 2nd ed. 1960.

Chisholm, Anne, and Michael Davie. *Lord Beaverbrook: A Life.* 1992.

Koss, Stephen. *The Rise and Fall of the Political Press in Britain.* vol. 2: *The Twentieth Century.* 1984.

Taylor, A.J.P. *Beaverbrook.* 1972.

Beckett, Samuel (1906–1989)

Samuel Beckett is one of the most significant writers of the twentieth century, not only because of the originality and power of his work, but also because his novels and theater pieces, his one film (called simply *Film* (1965), starring Buster Keaton), and his plays for radio and television have had such a profoundly transforming effect on the various genres to which they belong. *Waiting for Godot* (1952) is the most striking example of this. A *succès de scandale* when it was first performed in Paris in 1953, it quickly made its way around the world and changed the reigning conception of what theater was, or ought to be, forever.

The elder son of Irish Protestant parents, Beckett was born in Foxrock, County Dublin, and died in Paris. He was educated at Portora Royal School, Enniskillen, and Trinity College, Dublin, where he was greatly influenced by his French Professor, T.B. Rudmose Brown, graduating with academic distinction in 1927. He was *lecteur d'anglais* at the Ecole Normale Supérieure in Paris for the years 1928–30, during which he was befriended by **James Joyce**. Beckett's first published text, the essay "Dante . . . Bruno. Vico . . . Joyce," was written at Joyce's request. He returned to Ireland to take up a three-year appointment as Lecturer in modern languages at Trinity in 1930 but resigned abruptly in December 1931 and turned to writing, to which he devoted the rest of his life.

Beckett's monograph on *Proust* (1931) was followed by a collection of stories, *More Pricks than Kicks* (1934) and a novel, *Murphy* (1938), but none of these was widely read, and Beckett was still an obscure young writer when he took up residence definitively in Paris in 1937. It was there, between 1947 and 1950, that he wrote the trilogy of novels—*Molloy* (1951), *Malone Meurt* (1951), *L'Innommable* (1953)—and the play—*En Attendant Godot* (1952)—that made him famous. All of these works were originally written in French. (The first collected edition in English of the trilogy, entitled *Molloy, Malone Dies, and The Unnamable*, appeared in 1959.) After *Molloy*, translated by Patrick Bowles in collaboration with the author and published separately in 1955, Beckett translated all his work himself, and it is the consistently bilingual character of his *oeuvre* that makes him unique among twentieth-century writers. (After the one-act play *Fin de partie* (1957)—in English, *Endgame* (1958)—Beckett did most of his writ-ing for the theater in English but continued to do his own translating.)

The austerity of Beckett's writing, and of the worldview it is believed to express, is legendary and is reinforced by the increasing brevity of his texts over the course of his career. Thus, what has been called his "post-trilogy" writing consists of a series of short, enigmatic pieces whose flavor is accurately conveyed by titles such as *Stories and Texts for Nothing* (1967)—the English version of *Nouvelles et textes pour rien* (1958)—and *Fizzles* (1976), as well as numerous plays for stage, radio, and television. Among those, for the stage are *Krapp's Last Tape* (1960), *Happy Days* (1961), *Not I* (1973), and *Rockaby* (1980); for radio, *All That Fall* (1957), *Eh Joe* (1965), and *Lessness* (1970); and for television, *. . . but the clouds, . . .* (1976), *Ghost Trio* (1977), and *Quad* (1980).

Critics increasingly acknowledge that Beckett's work is as much concerned with writing itself and with the relation of human beings to language as it is with depicting in bleak, but by no means humorless, terms the human condition. It should be noted also that for all his declared difficulty with writing as an enterprise, and his alleged desire for silence, Beckett was not only a prolific, but an unusually inventive, writer. His willingness to explore different media and his great skill in exploiting the particular characteristics of each are quite remarkable, suggesting that far from being the reclusive figure he was often taken to be, he was thoroughly and happily a man of his time. Beckett was awarded the Nobel Prize for Literature in 1969.

Mary Lydon

Bibliography

Bair, Deirdre. *Samuel Beckett: A Biography.* 1978.

Brater, Enoch. *Why Beckett.* 1989.

Federman, Raymond, and John Fletcher. *Samuel Beckett: His Works and His Critics: An Essay in Bibliography.* 1970.

O'Brien, Eoin. *The Beckett Country: Samuel Beckett's Ireland.* 1986.

Trezise, Thomas. *Into the Breach: Samuel Beckett and the Ends of Literature.* 1990.

Beecham, Thomas (1879–1961)

Born in St. Helens, Lancashire, 29 April 1879, Thomas Beecham became the most celebrated

British **conductor** of the twentieth century, exerting a considerable influence over British musical life. He founded a number of organizations, some of which—the London Philharmonic Orchestra and the Royal Philharmonic Orchestra—were to become permanent and major institutions, and was associated with several British and foreign **orchestras** and opera companies.

Beecham's father, Sir Joseph Beecham, owned a highly successful pharmaceutical business, and Thomas was educated at Rossall School and **Oxford**. The family fortune enabled him to finance many of his early projects himself. His first important venture was the formation of the Beecham Symphony Orchestra in 1909. In 1915 he formed the Beecham Opera Company, which performed in London and the provinces in the war years. The company became the British National Opera Company in 1923; by then it was no longer under Beecham's direction and was amalgamated with Covent Garden in 1929.

The formation of the London Philharmonic Orchestra in 1932 was intended to serve the joint interests of the Royal Philharmonic Society and the **British Broadcasting Corporation** (BBC). When it became a self-governing orchestra, reluctant to offer any conductor the exclusive status and rights that Beecham enjoyed, he founded, in 1946, the Royal Philharmonic Orchestra. This orchestra was the vehicle for his most conspicuous and meritorious achievements after the Second World War. Beecham's taste in music was eclectic. He championed the works of many composers before they had wide popular appeal, including **Frederick Delius** and Richard Strauss. He also brought to British audiences the work of foreign artists such as Serge Diaghilev's Ballets Russes.

Many of Beecham's recordings testify to his understanding of orchestral and vocal textures; this is evident in his performances of works by composers as diverse as Mozart and Puccini. A figure of titanic energy, Beecham, who was knighted in 1916 for his contributions to British music, was frequently involved in controversy and was known for his caustic wit. More than any other figure in British musical life in the twentieth century, he was the subject of humorous quote and anecdote. Such reminiscences should not overshadow the lasting importance that his work had on British musical life.

Trevor Herbert

Bibliography

Beecham, Thomas. *A Mingled Chime: Leaves from an Autobiography.* 1944.

Cardus, Neville. *Sir Thomas Beecham: A Memoir.* 1961.

Jefferson, Alan. *Sir Thomas Beecham: A Centenary Tribute.* 1979.

Reid, Charles. *Thomas Beecham: An Independent Biography.* 1971.

Beerbohm, Henry Maximilian "Max" (1872–1956)

A notorious wit and dandy while yet an Oxford undergraduate, Henry Maximilian Beerbohm (known as "Max") was one of the aesthetes of the 1890s who survived to a sedate old age. Writer of essays, reviews, and parodies, and caricaturist of political, literary, and dramatic celebrities, Beerbohm both witnessed and ironically interpreted Victorian and Edwardian elite culture. His meticulous prose style and his experiments in verbal and visual representation bear affinity to those of the more celebrated modernists.

Beerbohm established his reputation as a writer with the publication of the facetiously titled *Works* (1896), seven flamboyant essays (with a bibliography!), some of which had first appeared in the avant-garde periodical, *The Yellow Book.* Also published there was *The Happy Hypocrite* (1897), an extended fairy tale influenced by the manner of Oscar Wilde. Set in the time of the Regency and replete with footnotes, the tale unfolds with sophistication and artifice while celebrating the conversion of a wicked lord to a life of purity through the love of a good woman. Beerbohm's subsequent collections of essays are addenda to *Works*, albeit less flamboyant: *More* (1899), *Yet Again* (1909), *And Even Now* (1920), and *A Variety of Things* (1928).

He launched a career as a mordantly ironic caricaturist with *Caricatures of Twenty-Five Gentlemen* (1896), black-and-white portraits of contemporaries, followed by *The Poet's Corner* (1904), an irreverent reflection on the "greats." Thereafter, his albums, no longer restricted to reproductions of newspaper sketches, consisted of selections from gallery exhibitions. Their subjects range from contemporary life to allegory to fictional history. Significant among the last is *Rossetti and His Circle* (1922), a series of wholly invented scenes from the lives of the pre-Raphaelites.

In 1898 Beerbohm became drama critic for the *Saturday Review*, a post he held until 1910, when he renounced weekly deadlines and the social whirl of London by marrying Florence Kahn, an American actress, and retiring to the Italian Riviera, where he lived until his death, except for trips to England to arrange exhibitions and longer sojourns during the two World Wars. In Italy he completed his only novel, *Zuleika Dobson* (1911), his most famous work. Subtitled "An Oxford Love Story," it is a self-conscious fantasy, probing the myths of romantic love, the aristocratic ideal, the venerability of the university, and the conventions of narrative fiction. From Italy he also issued *A Christmas Garland* (1912), parodies of contemporary authors.

In retirement Beerbohm attained greater precision both as a draftsman and a writer, but he drew his inspiration more from memory than from immediate observation. *Seven Men* (1919), a series of pseudoautobiographical reminiscences of eccentric characters of the 1890s, no less than his albums of drawings in the 1920s, reflects this essentially retrospective tendency. Knighted in 1939, Beerbohm enjoyed a twilight reputation as a radio broadcaster, often gleaning his material from notebooks dating from before the First World War.

In choosing **Lytton Strachey** as the subject for his Rede Lecture at **Cambridge** in 1943, Beerbohm extended his ironic observation of earlier eras to commentary on the clash between Victorian and modernist values.

Ira Grushow

Bibliography

Cecil, Lord David. *Max: A Biography.* 1965.
Danson, Lawrence. *Max Beerbohm and the Act of Writing.* 1989.
Grushow, Ira. *The Imaginary Reminiscences of Sir Max Beerbohm.* 1984.

Bell, Vanessa Stephen (1879–1961)

The daughter of the critic Sir Leslie Stephen and the sister of **Virginia Woolf**, Vanessa Bell was brought up in a cultured environment (the photographer Julia Margaret Cameron was her great aunt, and Bell was an enthusiastic photographer for most of her life). She founded the Friday Club as an informal art society in 1905 after leaving the Royal Academy Schools. In promoting discussion through its meetings and as a social forum, it was modeled on the liter-ary gatherings organized by her brother Thoby. It was in the interchange between these meetings that the **Bloomsbury Group** gained its cast of characters. From 1910 the club became an exhibiting society based at the Alpine Club. In the same year she first met **Roger Fry**, who included four of her works in the second post-impressionist exhibition.

During this period, when she exhibited with the New English Art Club, her painting did not contradict the prevailing orthodoxy; however, the effects of Fry's Post-Impressionist exhibitions affected her deeply. The formal simplicity and bold use of color that she discovered in paintings by Gauguin and Matisse, along with the sense of structure that she had already perceived in Cézanne encouraged her to paint in 1911–13 a series of paintings—such as *Studland Beach* (1911–12, Tate Gallery, London)—that were confident and uncompromising in their sense of purpose and originality. During this period Vanessa Bell was painting her most extreme abstractions, even though she was also painting more traditional themes such as still lifes at the same time.

Her abstract paintings also sprang from her involvement with the Omega Workshops, of which she was a codirector from 1913 to 1919, and indeed her first solo exhibition was mounted by Omega in 1916. In the same year she moved to Charleston in Sussex with **Duncan Grant**, who as a **conscientious objector** worked on the land. There she continued her design work both privately, in creating with Grant the environment around Charleston, and publicly, designing decors for **ballet**, textiles, and pottery, while with Grant and her son Quentin she collaborated between 1940 and 1942 on the decorative scheme for Berwick Church.

In 1919 she and Grant joined the London Group, an exhibiting society of which they remained key figures until their deaths. The work of Matisse continued to exert an influence on her painting in terms of its color, simplicity, and unforced expressions of lyricism—all of which were emphasized especially in those paintings that she executed while traveling in France in the 1920s and 1930s when she regularly stayed in Cassis and that celebrated, as did Grant's paintings, the pleasure and sensuality of their life together. Such an outlook became less popular by the end of the 1940s, and her work (like Grant's) correspondingly fell from favor—her retrospective exhibitions being mounted post-humously. In her last twenty years her painting became tighter and less gesturally expressive although with an often high-keyed color.

Andrew Wilson

Bibliography
Bell, Quentin, and Angelica Garnett. *Vanessa Bell's Family Album.* 1981.
Spalding, Frances. *Vanessa Bell.* 1983.
Vanessa Bell: A Memorial Exhibition (catalog). 1964.

Bennett, (Enoch) Arnold (1867–1931)

Novelist, short-story writer, playwright, critic, journalist, prodigious letter writer, Arnold Bennett was a multifaceted celebrity in his day. At the height of his popularity, posters advertising his latest novel were plastered on London buses. He was offered and refused a knighthood. As he lay dying of typhoid, straw was spread around Chiltern Court to deaden traffic noise, a custom previously followed only for royalty. Since his centenary, some studies have begun to recognize Bennett's significance in the transition of the novel from realism to modernism. Of the thirty-six novels he wrote, the primary works are: *A Man From the North* (1898); *Anna of the Five Towns* (1902); *The Old Wives' Tale* (1908); *Buried Alive* (1908); *Clayhanger* (1910), *Hilda Lessways* (1911); *The Card* (1911); *These Twain* (1915); *Riceyman Steps* (1923); *Lord Raingo* (1926); and *Imperial Palace* (1930).

Bennett was born of potter's stock in Burslem, the Potteries, Staffordshire, although his father, Enoch, became a solicitor. Bennett inherited his father's driving ambition, but when he was twenty-one, he abandoned his father's dream of a legal career for him and went to London. There his friendship with Frederick Marriott, an art teacher, spurred him to a succession of literary efforts, culminating in his publishing the short story "A Letter Home" in the avant-garde periodical *The Yellow Book* and in his accepting the post of assistant editor of a penny paper called *Woman.*

Within six years of his association with *Woman,* Bennett established not only the direction of his concern for serious writing, but also the pattern of frenetic productivity that was to astound and dismay his friends throughout his life. By September 1900 he had, besides his daily work, begun one sensational novel; published his first serious novel, *A Man from the North;* begun his first initial success, *Anna of the Five Towns;* published *Journalism for Women;* published three one-act plays called *Polite Farces;* collaborated on another play with his friend Arthur Hooley; and helped dramatize Eden Philpotts' novel, *Children of the Mist.*

By 1903, after the death of his father, he moved to Paris, became fluent in the language, acquired a mistress, and became a close friend of the scholar, critic, and linguist Marcel Schwob, in whose circle Bennett met many Continental artists. But he longed for marriage. At thirty-nine, during the course of a stressful eighteen months, Bennett planned to marry a young American, Eleanor Green, but, rebuffed, married his older secretary, Marguerite Soulié, who had theatrical ambitions. The marriage proved disastrous for both. They were legally separated in 1921, but Marguerite would never give him a divorce and outlived him. Nevertheless, in relative married contentment he had begun the major work he had been considering for four years. So inspired was he that in ten months of 1907 he completed the 200,000-word *The Old Wives' Tale,* written in a special calligraphy on special paper. Within the same period he produced two shorter, farcical novels and a bewildering list of essays, short stories, dramatic writings, and popular philosophies.

His astounding fecundity was distinguished by its quality. *The Old Wives' Tale* won him the respect of discriminating critics and brought him requests for his work from prestigious literary journals, like **Ford Madox Ford**'s *English Review.* The novel captures the impression of the passing of every day for a lifetime in the awareness of two sisters, one of whom lives a conventional life at home, the other of whom elopes to France, where she survives the Franco-Prussian War and the Paris Commune.

Some months before the publication of this novel, Bennett had begun to write articles headed "Books and Persons" for *New Age,* another prestigious journal. His articles heralding the new Russian and French writers placed him unquestionably among the avant-garde and made him, at the midpoint of his career, a cultural leader for the aspiring young.

In 1909 he was exhilarated by the first full-scale production of *What the Public Wants,* starring Sir Charles Hawtrey and Ben Webster and praised by **Max Beerbohm**. He immediately wrote *The Honeymoon,* which in 1911 starred

Marie Tempest and was acclaimed for its humor. He also published the important first novel of the Clayhanger trilogy, a sensitive portrait of the growth of a loveable young man. Before he completed the second Clayhanger novel, he published *The Card* (in 1952 made into a movie starring Sir Alec Guinness) and wrote, with Edward Knoblock, the play *Milestones,* which ran for 600 performances in 1912.

Always restless, Bennett was persuaded in 1911 by his American publisher, George Doran, to visit the United States. He was acclaimed in New York, Washington, Chicago, Indianapolis, Philadelphia, Boston, and the universities of the New England states, and noted his experiences in *Those United States* (1912). His affluence enabled him to buy Comarques, a country estate in Essex, and a large yacht. He recorded his voyages at sea in *From the Log of the Velsa* (1914). But then the **First World War** broke out. Bennett, drawn back to London into close association with the newspaper magnate **Lord Beaverbrook**, found himself forced into political activity in Beaverbrook's Ministry of Information. He wrote a series of weekly war articles for the *Daily News,* became a director of the *New Statesman,* and toured the Western Front.

During the war years he completed the Clayhanger series, wrote five more minor novels, and completed three plays. By 1922 he had fallen in love with a young actress, Dorothy Cheston, who agreed to become his common-law wife and took his name by deed poll. He published *Riceyman Steps* (1923), a psychological study of miserliness that brought him the James Tait Black Memorial Prize for the best novel of that year. In 1926 his only child, Virginia, was born and he published *Lord Raingo,* his depiction of the War Cabinet in action and a powerful study of melancholia in a good man in decline.

Bennett's last years were burdened by his young wife's unsatisfied theatrical ambitions, his need for more money to maintain his expensive living, and poor health. His productivity included the dramatization of an earlier novel, *Mr. Prohack* (1922), which launched Charles Laughton's career. After travels in Germany and Russia with Beaverbrook, he began work upon his last completed novel, *Imperial Palace* (1930), a tour de force about the hotel world and a sympathetic portrait of the "new woman."

Bennett's accuracy in locating, in his best work, the forms, the courses, and the strains in personal relationships links him with earlier writers like Anthony Trollope and contemporaries like Henry James, and helped pave the way for the fine discriminations found in younger writers like **D.H. Lawrence** and **Virginia Woolf.** Woolf's attack on Bennett in 1924 began the derogation of his work that persists in academic circles.

Olga R.R. Broomfield

Bibliography

Broomfield, Olga R.R. *Arnold Bennett.* 1984.

Drabble, Margaret. *Arnold Bennett: A Biography.* 1974.

Hepburn, James. *Letters of Arnold Bennett.* 4 vols. 1966–86.

Lucas, John. *Arnold Bennett: A Study of His Fiction.* 1974.

Roby, Kilner E. *A Writer at War: Arnold Bennett.* 1972.

Bernal, J(ohn) D(esmond) (1901–1971)

J.D. Bernal is significant in the development of x-ray crystallography (a technique for determining the arrangement of atoms within crystalline materials) and in the social relations of science, which he approached from a deeply committed Marxist viewpoint. He was elected to the **Royal Society** in 1937, was awarded their Royal Medal in 1945, and received the Lenin Peace Prize (1953). He had four children, two by his wife, Eileen, whom he married in 1922.

Bernal was born in Nenagh, Tipperary, Ireland and attended school at Stonyhurst and Bedford before gaining a scholarship to Emmanuel College, **Cambridge**, where he studied mathematics, natural sciences, and **physics** (1919–23). From 1923 to 1927 he was employed at the **Royal Institution**, London, under Sir William Bragg, before returning to Cambridge, first as Lecturer, then as Assistant Director of Research, in structural crystallography. During the **Second World War** he worked for the Ministry of Home Security on the effects of air raids of different sizes. Thereafter he worked for **Lord Mountbatten** on preparations for the invasion of Europe, including studying ways of measuring the Normandy beaches and the construction of artificial harbors. In 1938 he became Professor of physics at Birkbeck College, London, where he was based for the rest of his career, from 1963 to 1968 as Professor of crystallography.

Bernal's major scientific contribution lies in x-ray crystallography, with which he developed a fascination while still an undergraduate. At the Royal Institution he worked on the structure of graphite and developed and applied novel crystallographic techniques. In this period he developed his interest in the structures of biological molecules, which laid the foundations for the development of **molecular biology**. At Cambridge, in what is widely considered his most creative period, he worked with various collaborators successively on the structures of sex hormones and other sterols, water, protein crystals, and the tobacco mosaic virus. After the war, at Birkbeck, his rebuilt department acted as an institute for the study of the structure of things continuing work on biological and inorganic materials.

He joined the **Communist Party of Great Britain** shortly after graduating, having become a committed Communist in his first year. As an active member of the Cambridge Scientists' Anti War Group, and the Association of Scientific Workers, Bernal was associated with **J.B.S. Haldane**, Joseph Needham, Hyman Levy, Lancelot Hogben, and other left-wing scientists active in the so-called "visible college" of the 1930s. In the post-war period his beliefs led him to take a key role in several international organizations that ran counter to Cold War conditions, including the World Peace Council and the World Federation of Scientific Workers.

Along with his scientific papers, and inspired by his Marxism, he produced a series of major theoretical and historical works on the social relations of science, including *The Social Function of Science* (1939), on the social usefulness of science and the importance of state planning to maximize its potential. The first part of *Science in History* (1954) is an attempt at a broad synthetic and Marxist account of its subject. The second is a study of the state of contemporary science, which Bernal constantly revised in different editions as his views of the Soviet Union changed.

Bernal was a major figure of the Left who held views about science and society that would now be difficult to sustain but have been hugely influential. This, along with his crystallographic work, makes him one of the most significant of twentieth-century British scientists.

T.M. Boon

Bibliography
Goldsmith, Maurice. *Sage: A Life of J.D. Bernal*. 1980.
Werskey, Gary. *The Visible College: A Collective Biography of British Scientists and Socialists of the 1930s*. 2nd ed. 1988.

Bevan, Aneurin "Nye" (1897–1960)

Aneurin "Nye" Bevan was a Labour MP and one of the key figures in **Clement Attlee**'s postwar Labour governments of 1945–51, being largely responsible for the formation of the free **National Health Service** (NHS) in Britain, which came into existence in July 1948. His protests against the attempt of **Herbert Morrison**, **Hugh Gaitskell**, and others in the government to impose prescription charges led him to resign from office in 1951 and to act as the center of a loose grouping of the socialist Left within the **Labour Party** that became known as the Bevanites, although he subsequently returned to the center of the party in the mid-1950s.

Bevan was born on 15 November 1897 in Tredegar, South Wales, was educated at elementary school and at Sunday school, and began work as a miner at the age of thirteen. He worked in the mines for nine years, during a turbulent period of industrial and syndicalist activity in South Wales, before winning a South Wales Miners' Federation scholarship to the Central Labour College, London, where he took courses on the history of socialism, Marxism, economics, and finance. On his return to Tredegar in 1921 Bevan became involved in the activities of the miners' union and was Chairman of the Tredegar Council of Action during the **General Strike** of 1926. Yet Bevan was mainly a political animal. He was returned as a member of his local District Council in April 1922 and was a member of the Monmouthshire County Council from 1928 to 1929 before becoming the miners' MP for Ebbw Vale. He represented that parliamentary constituency from 1929 until his death in 1960.

In Parliament Bevan campaigned fiercely for the interests of the working classes, tirelessly championed the cause of the unemployed, and strongly opposed **Fascism**. He briefly supported **Oswald Mosley**'s New Party moves in 1931 because Mosley seemed to offer policies to deal with the unemployed, but he quickly became disillusioned as Mosley moved in the direction of Fascism and never actually joined the party.

He opposed the Household **Means Test**, ranted against Fascism, and operated through the left-wing journal *Tribune* to attack a Labour Party that was increasingly dominated by **Ernest Bevin**, the trade union leader. It was in 1934 that he married Jennie Lee, who, in her own right, became an influential force within the British Labour Left. During the **Second World War** Bevan rejected the political truce agreed to by the major political parties and fought the war on two fronts—against the Fascists and against the Tory Party. Indeed, he was an unflinching critic of **Winston Churchill**. It was during these years that he gained a reputation for being an orator reminiscent of fellow Welshman **David Lloyd George**.

Yet Bevan's finest hour came when he became Minister of Health and Housing in the Attlee government of 1945. In that role he cajoled the private doctors and the British Medical Association, who referred to him as that "squalid nuisance," the "Minister of Disease," and a "Tito from Tonypandy," into working with the NHS, which was formed in 1948. His remark that his Tory opponents were "lower than vermin" caused great controversy at the time. The NHS transcended the wartime reforms that were considered and the Labour Party's policy by effectively nationalizing the hospitals, creating a public general-practitioner service, and making the treatment of illness and the provision of medical treatment entirely free. In his book *In Place of Fear* (1952) he explained that it was ludicrous to expect patients to await a vital operation because they lacked the requisite number of self-contributions. But the NHS proved expensive, and Morrison and other members of Attlee's government decided to attempt to limit the expenditure and to introduce the prescription charges. Bevan fought off these attempts until the 1950 general election, but then, on 17 January 1951, he was moved from Health to become Minister of Labour and National Service. The move coincided with the decision of Gaitskell, the Chancellor of the Exchequer, to impose health charges. Bevan's bitter row with Gaitskell led to his dramatic resignation from the government on 24 April 1951.

Between 1951 and 1955 Bevan became the figurehead of a loosely organized group of left-wing, Bevanite MPs, who advocated unilateral nuclear disarmament and challenged official policies. Indeed, it was Bevan's decision to oppose the Parliamentary Labour Party line

of supporting the manufacture of the hydrogen bomb, which almost got him expelled from the party in 1955. At that point, however, Bevan's position began to change. He lost to Gaitskell in the election for the post of party Treasurer in 1954 and lost again to Gaitskell in the leadership contest of December 1955. From that point onward he appears to have come to an understanding with Gaitskell, who made him Shadow Colonial Secretary. Bevan was positively patriotic over the **Suez crisis** of 1956 and rose in the party hierarchy by winning the post of Treasurer, which he held from 1956 to 1960. After his patriotic showing over the Suez and the Soviet invasion of Hungary, he was made Shadow Foreign Secretary. With his rapprochement with Gaitskell, Bevan soon became a spent force for the Left. He effectively divested himself of the title "leader of the Left" at the 1957 Labour Party conference by attacking unilateral disarmament and eventually rose to become deputy leader in 1959. In 1960 an abdominal operation revealed that he had a malignant cancer, from which he died on 6 July 1960.

Keith Laybourn

Bibliography

Bevan, Aneurin. *In Place of Fear*. 1952.
Campbell, John. *Nye Bevan and the Mirage of British Socialism*. 1987.
Foot, Michael. *Aneurin Bevan, 1897–1945*. 1962.
———. *Aneurin Bevan, 1945–1960*. 1973.
Lee, Jennie. *My Life with Nye*. 1980.

Beveridge, William Henry (1879–1963)

If any one individual can be singled out as the architect of Britain's **welfare state**, it must be William Henry Beveridge. He was born in 1879 into an upper-middle-class family stationed in India, and in his youth he trod the conventional path of public school (Charterhouse) and **Oxford**. However, Beveridge's youth was spent during years of social questioning in Britain, and while at Oxford he was influenced by the social reformist liberalism of Edward Caird, then Master of Balliol. On leaving Oxford, Beveridge worked as a leader-writer of the Conservative newspaper, the *Morning Post*, while living at the Toynbee Hall university **settlement** in East London.

Unemployment and casual labor were the scourges of Edwardian **London**, and Beveridge

B

believed that these problems could be remedied by limited state intervention to adjust the supply/demand malfunctionings of the labor market. As he saw it, the answer was a system of labor exchanges, and it was his passionate advocacy of these that brought him to public attention. In 1908 Beveridge became a part-time, temporary civil servant with the Board of Trade to work on the planning of labor exchanges.

Gradually, therefore, Beveridge was being drawn into the complex world he was to inhabit for the rest of his active life: journalism, research, social administration, and academia. In 1909 he published a major study, *Unemployment, a Problem of Industry*. He became convinced that state social insurance, as represented by the 1911 National Insurance Act, could be extended to cover all the social risks that befell workers over the course of the life cycle; simultaneously, the state could intervene at strategic points of economic activity and improve industrial efficiency.

During the **First World War**, Beveridge worked in the **Ministry of Munitions** and the Ministry of Food. In 1919 he was knighted and appointed Director of the **London School of Economics and Political Science** (LSE). Until he returned to Oxford in 1937 as Master of University College, much of his formidable energy was directed at the expansion of LSE into a social science institution of world standing. There were many forays into government-related work, notably as a member of the 1925–6 **Samuel** Commission on the Coal Industry and as Chairman of the Unemployment Insurance Statutory Committee (1934–44). The latter post confirmed his long-standing view—outlined, for example, in his pamphlet *Insurance for All and Everything* (1924)—that social insurance could form the basis for a much more comprehensive social security system.

Thus, by the time of the outbreak of the **Second World War**, Beveridge had amassed a wealth of experience and expertise in social questions that should have placed him immediately in a high position as a government adviser. That this did not happen was partly due to the lack of coordinated planning in the first year of war. But it also arose from Beveridge's rather difficult personality: immensely hardworking, widely read, and intelligent, he could be insensitive, vain, and rude to colleagues, especially when crossed. These personality traits partly explain why Beveridge did not have more influence in the world of politics. But, paradoxically,

they were indirectly to present him with the greatest opportunity of his career.

In 1940 Beveridge was placed in charge of a rather insignificant Ministry of Labour manpower survey. Anxious to be rid of a rather troublesome colleague, **Ernest Bevin** recommended that Beveridge be appointed Chairman of a proposed inquiry into the reorganization of social insurance and allied services that was to be part of the overall post-war reconstruction program set up in 1941. Accordingly, in June 1941 Beveridge was appointed Chairman of an interdepartmental committee of civil servants established "to undertake, with special reference to the inter-relation of the schemes, a survey of the existing national schemes of social insurance and allied services, including workmen's compensation, and to make recommendations."

The last four words of the committee's terms of reference were to prove vitally important, for Beveridge's liberal interpretation of them resulted in a report that went well beyond what the government had expected. Beveridge was easily able to dominate his committee: In December 1941, for example, he composed a memorandum containing all the broad recommendations that were to appear in the subsequent report. Thus, although there was considerable consultation and evidence-gathering from major organizations (such as the trade unions and the employers), the essence of the report was Beveridge's.

In summary, the report recommended that all of the disparate state income-maintenance services that had grown up piecemeal since 1911 be pulled together, made universally available and comprehensive in coverage, and funded by state social insurance. Hence, for the first time, unemployment benefit was to cover the whole population and was to be supplemented by national assistance. Sickness benefit was also universalized and raised to the same level as unemployment benefit. Workmen's compensation was to be reformed, and new benefits for maternity and death were proposed. An important change was that the two **old-age pension** systems (originating in 1908 and 1925, respectively) were amalgamated into one contributory scheme to which, for the first time, was attached a retirement condition. Three important assumptions underpinned the entire Beveridge plan: **Family allowances** would help alleviate child poverty, but more important to Beveridge was their role in preserving the gap between wages and benefit and, hence, work incentives; a comprehensive preventive and curative **National Health Service** would ensure that the social security system did not have to subsidize absence from work through illness; and full employment would both create a large enough tax base to fund the scheme and simultaneously prevent it going bankrupt through an excess of claims. Beveridge's emphasis on the importance of these three assumptions shows how confident he was that the relationship between social security and economic growth could be symbiotic and mutually reinforcing.

Historians are agreed that Beveridge's personal contribution to the report was enormous. To read the transcripts of oral evidence is to discover the extent of Beveridge's ability to persuade, cajole, or out-argue witnesses on highly complex questions. To read the report itself is to understand why contemporaries were uplifted by the nobility of its language and its optimism for a better world.

Yet, paradoxically, historians now recognize that many of the recommendations made by Beveridge were already "in the **civil service** pipeline" and that essentially his contribution was to rationalize these existing plans into one comprehensive whole. Family allowances had been considered by the Treasury at the start of the war (as an anti-inflationary, wage-control device, they would have protected the lowest-paid families from the full effects of a wage freeze), and had been the subject of a Treasury White Paper published in May 1942. Beveridge universalized unemployment benefit, but benefit levels were no higher—relative to wages—than they had been in the late 1930s. And in some respects his recommendations almost seemed to mark a backward step. Full subsistence pensions were to be attained only after a twenty-year transition period of slowly rising pension levels, and thus were to commence at a level out of line with the "subsistence principle" that was said to be central to the whole report. Again, Beveridge's emphasis on state social-insurance funding, with flat-rate benefits and flat-rate contributions (rather than a tax-funded, means-tested benefit system) meant that certain problems, such as varying expenditure on rent, were left unresolved.

However, these retrospective caveats cannot detract from the remarkable adulation the report received when it was published on 1 December 1942 from a public hungry for good news after three hard years of war. This was the first factor that made the report appear more radical than its contents actually merited. The second was the reluctance of **Winston Churchill**'s wartime coalition government to commit itself to implementing the report—a reluctance that led to a heated House of Commons debate on 16–18 February 1943, at the end of which there was a substantial **Conservative** back-bench rebellion. Because of these background events, the report was assured of a place in history.

Only in the very broadest sense did the Beveridge Report become the basis for the post-war welfare state. Beveridge's draft recommendations had been whittled down under Treasury pressure in the summer of 1942, and the report was less than he had originally hoped for. Further paring down took place when a committee of civil servants under Sir Thomas Sheepshanks shaped the proposals into legislation in 1943–5. The principal relevant statutes were: the 1945 Family Allowances Act; the 1946 National Health Service Act; the 1946 National Insurance Act; the 1948 National Assistance Act. Together with the **Education Act of 1944**, these founded what became known as the welfare state.

As author of a best-selling government report, Beveridge was showered with considerable public adulation for the rest of the war. All this he greatly enjoyed. He contributed to public debates about the post-war world, notably in *Full Employment in a Free Society* (1944), and was elected to Parliament as Liberal MP for Berwick-upon-Tweed in 1944. His political career was short-lived, however, for in the 1945 general election he lost his seat. Ever active, he accepted a peerage, continued his public career (for example, as Chairman of the Newton Aycliffe Development Corporation), and died in 1963.

John Macnicol

Bibliography

Beveridge, Lord. *Power and Influence*. 1953.
Harris, Jose. *William Beveridge*. 1977.
Social Insurance and Allied Services (Beveridge Report). Cmd. 6404. 1942.
Williams, Karel, and John Williams, eds. *A Beveridge Reader*. 1987.

Bevin, Ernest (1881–1951)

Shortly after the First World War, Ernest Bevin founded the **Transport and General Workers'**

B

Union, which for long was the largest trade union in Britain. He was, with **Trades Union Congress** General Secretary **Walter Citrine**, largely responsible for the direction the British trade union movement took after the **General Strike** of 1926. After the financial crisis of 1931 he played a significant role in the reshaping of the **Labour Party's** policy that became the basis of the program enacted by the 1945 Labour government. In 1940 he became Minister of Labour, overseeing the wartime government's labor policies and, in the process, contributing to the creation of the post-war **welfare state**. After the war Bevin served as Foreign Secretary in the Labour government, helping to shape the international order that prevailed for the next forty years.

Born in Winsford, Somerset, on 7 March 1881, the illegitimate child of an agricultural laborer, Bevin had a childhood marked by poverty and insecurity. His mother died when he was eight years old, forcing him to move to his half-sister in Devon. When his formal education ended at eleven, he went to work for neighboring farmers. After two years of hard work for sixpence a week plus room and board, he moved to Bristol to live with his half-brother, eventually settling down as a mineral-water deliveryman. As a young man he became active in the Baptist church, then abandoned membership in the church, though not his religious faith, and became involved in the Bristol Socialist Society. It was at this time that he married Florence Townley, with whom he had one child, Queenie, born in 1914.

Because of his work for the unemployed, Bevin was asked in 1910 to organize the carters for the Dock, Wharf, Riverside, and General Labourers' Union, known as the Dockers' Union. He did this so well that he was then invited to work full-time as a regional organizer for the Dockers' Union; four years later he was appointed as one of three national organizers. Bevin quickly concluded that increased organization provided the best defense for workers. He strongly supported the creation of a large general union, one that linked workers in different trades. During and immediately after the First World War the trend inside the trade union movement was toward greater concentration and organization. Using a plan suggested by Bevin, for example, the Trades Union Congress (TUC) in 1920 created a new General Council to provide more centralized direction to the trade union movement. In that same

year, after he had achieved national fame for his role in successfully presenting the dockers' case for a wage increase to an arbitration tribunal, the Shaw Committee, Bevin took advantage of his new prestige to help push for the creation of a new transport workers' organization. His energy and practical ability proved decisive in overcoming the difficulties that had prevented previous amalgamation attempts and creating the Transport and General Workers' Union out of fourteen different unions. It came into being on 1 January 1922, and Bevin was elected General Secretary, a lifetime appointment.

Although Bevin's central organizational goal as a trade unionist remained fixed, his strategies changed over time. Always angry at the exclusion of the working class from full membership in British society and at its failure to accept the trade union movement, he could often be belligerent and even at times flirt with direct action, the use of organized working-class power, to secure political changes. Most notably, he supported the Council of Action that in 1920 opposed British intervention in the Soviet-Polish War. Until the General Strike of 1926, he sometimes thought that organized trade union power could compel changes in the way management treated workers. Increasingly, however, his need to deal with "facts as they are" led him to conclude that what was later called corporatism—the cooperation of business, the unions, and the state—provided the most effective route for working-class advancement. Particularly after the failure of the General Strike, which he had supported and helped lead, convinced him that capitalism was not about to give way to socialism, he, along with Citrine, successfully steered the TUC along this path.

Because the trade union movement had been so weakened by the growth of **unemployment** and by the failure of the General Strike, Bevin concluded that trade unions had to work to change not just wages and working conditions but all social and economic policies that affected working people. Through his membership on the Economic Advisory Council and the Macmillan Committee, he tried, and failed, to influence the economic policy of the 1929 Labour government, which rejected his advice to do more to overcome unemployment. After Labour's disastrous electoral defeat in 1931, however, Bevin, particularly through his membership on the National Council of Labour,

Bevin Boys: an alternative to military service for conscripts after 1943.

which coordinated relations between the Labour Party and the Trades Union Congress, worked to reshape Labour's domestic and foreign policies. In part because of his influence, Labour developed a viable reformist program that endorsed **nationalization** of a limited range of industries and Keynesian policies to regulate the economy. Bevin played an even more important role in reshaping the Labour Party's approach to foreign affairs. Opposed to traditional balance-of-power politics and suspicious of the ruling **Conservative Party**, the Labour Party in the 1930s refused to support rearmament even in the face of a growing threat from Germany. In part once again because of Bevin's efforts, the Labour Party changed its position after 1937 and became a strong advocate of military opposition to **Fascism**, even though this involved support for a distrusted Conservative government.

Throughout the 1930s Bevin's corporatist trade union strategy had only partial success outside the confines of the Transport and General Workers' Union, signally failing to help unemployed workers or those who were not union members. At times, it also overrode rank-and-file activism and undercut the attempts of militants to expand trade union membership.

But in May 1940 Bevin became Minister of Labour in the coalition government created at the height of the wartime emergency. Appreciating that the Ministry of Labour would provide him a key position from which to shape domestic policy, Bevin viewed the war as an opportunity to create the kind of industrial order that he had been advocating for over a decade. Corporatism had been problematic because neither the state nor business would cooperate fully with the trade union movement. Now the war and his own position in the government ensured that cooperation. Bevin used this new partnership as the basis for the various measures he put in place to mobilize the entire country behind the war effort. He also took advantage of the moment to secure new institutional recognition for the trade union movement, which increased its membership by about a third. Believing that workers had a right to employment and security, Bevin converted the Ministry of Labour into a major policy-making department, greatly expanding its power to defend working-class conditions and **standard of living** and, in the process, helping to prepare the ground for the creation of the welfare state after 1945.

After Labour won a massive victory in the 1945 election, he was appointed Foreign Secretary. Now he saw himself defending not just the working class, but all of Britain. For Bevin, the best way to protect British national interests—its world position, the basis of Britain's economic well-being, and the perceived threat from the Soviet Union—was to draw closer to the United States and pull back from Europe. In these years he played an important role in supporting the **Marshall Plan**, the aid plan to Western Europe that helped to revive its still lagging economy, and in creating in 1949 the North Atlantic Treaty Organization, which established a stable balance of power on the European continent. From the **Foreign Office** point of view, Bevin's work in these years was an immense success, preserving Britain's great power status and helping to contain the alleged threat from the Soviet Union, a judgment many historians have endorsed. It might also be said, however, that Bevin's determination to preserve Britain's traditional world position may have unintentionally hastened Britain's decline by delaying its coming to terms with its reduced power, tying it to an expensive military posture that interfered with economic growth, and turning it away from the most effective available path to economic modernization, membership in the emerging European Community.

Bevin's legacy as Foreign Secretary remains a subject of debate. But his legacy as a trade union leader and Minister of Labour has endured and changed the institutional shape of Britain. Bevin created one of the largest unions in Britain, which continues to defend its members' interests in the ways he envisioned. His ideals of working-class rights to employment, adequate wages and working conditions, and social security were partially achieved by the 1945 Labour government. Even though they have been eroded since 1979, they remain a permanent achievement.

Peter Weiler

Bibliography

Bullock, Alan. *The Life and Times of Ernest Bevin.* 2 vols. 1960–67.
———. *Ernest Bevin: Foreign Secretary, 1945–1951.* 1983.
Coates, Ken, and Tony Topham. *The History of the Transport and General Workers' Union.* 1991.
Weiler, Peter. *Ernest Bevin.* 1993.

Big Bang

Big Bang is the highly evocative name given to the changes in the London Stock Exchange's system and ownership that took place on 27 October 1986 and led to one of the most important transformations in the **City of London**'s history. The origins of Big Bang are to be found in a combination of factors. The most immediate one was a court case by the Office of Fair Trading against the Stock Exchange's rule book, considered to contain restrictive practices. In an agreement between the Trade and Industry Secretary, Cecil Parkinson, and the Chairman of the Stock Exchange, Nicholas Goodison, in July 1983, the court case was dropped in return for the abolition of fixed commissions by the end of 1986. There were, however, other underlying causes, such as the increased competition from New York, where fixed commissions had been abandoned in May 1975, with the risk of international business bypassing London; and the growing concern about the adequacy of the capital of the partnerships of stockbrokers and jobbers in order to make the necessary investments and compete in a global market. It therefore quickly appeared that the dismantling of fixed commissions should be accompanied by the opening of the Stock Exchange to outside members and a switch from single to dual capacity—that is, the end of the separation, unique to the London Stock Exchange, of the functions of the broker who dealt on his client's behalf with the "wholesaler," the stockjobber, who traded from a book of stocks and shares. The result was the replacement of the Stock Exchange floor by an electronic system, the SEAQ (Stock Exchange automated quotations system), the purchase of most of the brokers and jobbers firms by **clearing banks, merchant banks**, and foreign banks, often at inflated prices, and huge investments in new information technology. Although a balance sheet remains premature, Big Bang has strengthened the position of the City of London as the leading financial center in Europe, and institutional investors have gained from the new system. With the increase of market capacity, however, many security firms incurred severe losses and had to pull out.

Youssef Cassis

Bibliography

Reid, Margaret. *All-Change in the City: The Revolution in Britain's Financial Sector.* 1988.

Birth Control

The 1877 trial of freethinkers Charles Bradlaugh and Annie Besant for publishing a purportedly obscene edition of an American pamphlet on family limitation did not, as was once thought, initiate widespread use of birth control; it did coincide, however, with a European-wide transition in family fertility. By the early years of this century anxiety about the "racial" and imperial consequences of the declining birth rate had combined with the social hygiene crusades to make sex and procreation topics of worried discussion in the public press and, more discreetly, the journals catering to the intellectual elite. Yet even educated middle-class British women had little knowledge of birth control, and most physicians considered it harmful and were ignorant of effective methods. Nevertheless, it was clear from their birth rates that the middle classes had been using birth control for several decades. The preventives most commonly employed—*coitus interruptus* (withdrawal), abstinence, and the condom—all required male cooperation.

For working-class women, whose birth rates remained high, informal networks existed to pass on information about preventing conception, and there was a host of—more or less unsavory—commercial sources. Improved rubber pessaries (diaphragms and cervical caps) had been added to the older homemade douches, vaginal sponges, soluble pessaries, and other female barrier methods. Yet even working-class women who knew of their existence would probably have found most methods repugnant and impossible to use in homes lacking sanitary facilities and privacy. Many, if not most working-class women seem to have relied on **abortion**—either self-induced or performed by midwives, female relatives, or disreputable professional abortionists—long after safer, preventive methods were better known.

After the First World War **Marie Stopes'** candid discussions of marital sex and birth control made her the most widely known figure working for women's access to safe, effective contraception. Her early writings carried a strongly feminist message of women's right to reproductive freedom and sexual pleasure within marriage. Moreover, Stopes argued that birth control would rescue the British "race" from biological degeneration and, by improving the health of mothers and babies through child spacing, replenish the population, not diminish it as opponents claimed.

In 1921 Stopes opened the Mothers' Clinic in North London to provide birth control to poor women and launched the Society for Constructive Birth Control and Racial Progress to pressure the Ministry of Health to offer birth control services at local maternal and infant welfare centers. In October of the same year the King's physician, Lord Dawson of Penn, strongly endorsed birth control in a speech to a lay church congress. In November the Malthusian League opened the Walworth Women's Welfare Center; three years later the Society for the Provision of Birth Control Clinics (SPBCC) took over Walworth to train doctors and nurses and began opening clinics in London and provincial cities. Stopes' clinic and those of the SPBCC and of Dr. Norman Haire, an Australian sex reformer, provided birth control—usually the diaphragm or cervical cap and spermacide—free or at cost.

Throughout the 1920s eugenists, clergymen, scientists, feminists, socialists, and literary and intellectual leaders explored the scientific significance of birth control and its implications for Britain's national future. As controversies about birth control raged in the press, women's groups affiliated with the **Labour Party** and the **Liberal Party** organized to influence the Ministry of Health, members of Parliament, and the party conferences to support government-run birth control. Arguing that contraception improved mothers' health and ability to rear healthy children and would increase the self-sufficiency of the working class, Conservative MP **Nancy Astor** and Ernest Thurtle, Labour MP for Shoreditch, introduced resolutions and private bills; they pointed urgently to evidence of the ill effects of too-frequent childbearing gathered in studies of maternal mortality and abortion.

In 1930, with the advent of a new Labour government, the birth controllers won a partial victory. The Ministry of Health quietly decided to allow local welfare centers, at their discretion, to dispense birth control devices to married women on strictly limited medical grounds. The same year the Lambeth Conference of Anglican bishops, long opposed to birth control, gave its limited blessing.

In the 1930s the voluntary birth control clinics, now federated as the National Birth Control Association (NBCA), concentrated on persuading the ministry to broaden its criteria to include social and economic factors and on convincing local authorities to provide birth control services at welfare centers. A number of local officials were actively supportive; where they refused to act, or interpreted the ministry's medical grounds too narrowly, the NBCA coordinated establishment of voluntary clinics. By 1939, 282 of 409 local authorities in England and Wales had made some arrangement to provide contraceptive services.

Although official medical opinion remained unfavorable, many individual doctors learned about birth control and began prescribing it for private patients. The findings of the clinical research initiated by Stopes, Haire, and (after 1927) the Birth Control Investigation Committee helped gain still more medical adherents.

In the mid-1930s, however, renewed fears of a dwindling population strengthened the always-vocal **Roman Catholic** opposition to government sanction of birth control. The birth rate of all classes continued to decline in the wake of Depression and high **unemployment**, and predictions of depopulation converged with uneasy awareness of the population-enhancement policies being pursued in Italy and Germany. The **Second World War** stripped the birth control movement of its momentum as doctors, nurses, and local and national volunteers found other vital assignments. By 1945 only about sixty clinics of the renamed Family Planning Association (FPA) were still operating.

The reproductive behavior of British couples, however, as documented by a post-war study, had moved toward a modern norm of deliberate family planning. Although relatively few women had actually visited a birth control clinic in the 1930s and 1940s, the 1949 report of the Royal Commission on Population showed that increasing numbers of couples of all classes wed during those decades used birth control—principally the condom and withdrawal.

While the acceptability of concerns about "racial" quality and imperial destiny receded after the war, the question of the ideal population for Britain continued to trouble political and social leaders. As it had after the First World War, the cultural climate encouraged married women to give up their jobs to returning veterans and devote themselves to bearing the children needed to ensure an adequate work force. The national birth rate, declining since the 1870s, rose steeply right after the war and stabilized slightly lower in the 1950s before slowly rising again throughout the 1960s.

FPA leaders, fearing that the renewed push for population growth would limit birth control to medical grounds within the new **National Health Service** (NHS), chose to continue running clinics on a voluntary basis. At no time during planning of the NHS did the Labour government contemplate providing complete contraceptive services, and FPA leaders made no attempt to persuade it to do so.

During the 1960s, however, perception of a world "population bomb," increased (nonwhite) **immigration**, and higher birth rates turned British attention to the environmental and "quality of life" problems attendant on overpopulation. Conservative and Labour MPs and pressure groups outside government began to see family planning services as essential to a responsible population policy.

In the meantime, the contraceptive pill had come into being and was in general use in Britain by 1961. Much more than other female methods, the pill effected a revolutionary change in contraceptive behavior. In spite of concerns about side effects in the 1960s, by 1970 oral contraceptives were second only to the condom in popularity among women of all ages.

In 1967, when national birth rates were high and the trend toward women's participation in the labor force was both well established and conceded to be economically necessary to families and the nation, Parliament passed the Family Planning Act (preceded by the Abortion Act). The legislation, still permissive rather than mandatory, authorized local officials to offer birth control, at cost, to married and single women under NHS auspices; but it left many loopholes for recalcitrant or timid local officials. Only in 1974, upon reorganization of the NHS, was a fully effective, comprehensive program of birth control free to British women of all ages, classes, and marital status included in the National Health Service. It had taken more than fifty years from the opening of Marie Stopes' first birth control clinic. Since then, birth control, like other NHS services, has been subject to cutbacks but has remained firmly rooted in Britain's health and population policy.

Roberta A. Clark

Bibliography

Leathard, Audrey. *The Fight for Family Planning: The Development of Family Planning Services in Britain, 1921–74.* 1980.

Lewis, Jane. *The Politics of Motherhood: Child and Maternal Welfare in England,*

1900–1939. 1980.

———. *Women in England, 1870–1950: Sexual Division and Social Change.* 1984.

Soloway, Richard Allen. *Birth Control and the Population Question in England, 1877–1930.* 1982.

Weeks, Jeffrey. *Sex, Politics and Society: The Regulation of Sexuality since 1800.* 2nd ed. 1989.

Black and Tans

The Black and Tans were police recruited in Great Britain and Northern Ireland to overcome a shortfall in the strength of the previously all-Irish Royal Irish Constabulary (RIC) due to resignations and falling enlistments caused by the Anglo-Irish War. Recruitment, begun in December 1919, mainly attracted unemployed ex-soldiers. Although Irish republicans claimed that many of the new police were criminals and hooligans, all had to meet RIC standards of physical fitness, character, and intelligence. Because of their motley outfits—dark green and khaki—necessitated by a shortage of regular RIC uniforms, they were nicknamed for a type of foxhound raised in County Limerick. Between 1919 and 1922 some 12,000 Black and Tans were recruited, for an average service of eight months. The Black and Tans in mid-1921 numbered about 7,000 out of a total RIC strength of 14,000.

The "Tans," as they soon became known to their republican foes, operated actively in Ireland from March 1920 to October 1921. The Black and Tans were distinct from the Auxiliaries ("Auxis"), a blue-uniformed, elite police unit—better paid than the "Tans"—recruited starting in July 1920 exclusively from former British officers and eventually numbering 1,500. Both "Tans" and "Auxis" were paramilitary mercenaries lacking army discipline, police training, and either knowledge of, or sympathy with, the Catholic Irish. The Black and Tans, especially, quickly acquired a reputation for drunkenness and disorderly conduct. The distinctive uniforms of the "Tans" and the "Auxis" made them easily identifiable targets for gunmen and, combined with their bad reputation, placed them in constant danger.

Sir Hamar Greenwood, Chief Secretary for Ireland from April 1920, consistently defended the terrorism practiced almost from their arrival in Ireland by the "Tans" and the "Auxis"—as did Prime Minister **David Lloyd George** less enthusiastically. Although many of their brutalities were unauthorized reprisals for Irish Republican Army (IRA) attacks on public offices, police barracks, and British personnel, some were premeditated. Notable Black and Tan atrocities were the sacking of the town of Balbriggan, County Dublin (20 September 1920), and the "Bloody Sunday" raid (21 November 1920) on a Gaelic football match in Dublin's Croke Park, in which twelve spectators were killed and sixty wounded. The "Tans" were also held responsible for the murder of leading republicans, including the mayors of Cork and Limerick; the shooting of IRA prisoners "attempting to escape"; the indiscriminate beating and whipping of civilians; and the burning of scores of cooperative creameries. The power of the paramilitary police auxiliaries was enhanced by the Restoration of Order Act of August 1920, which authorized secret courts-martial, suspension of coroner's inquests, and, by implication, the use of torture to extract information.

Terrorism by the auxiliary police in Ireland damaged Great Britain's image internationally and affronted public opinion domestically. **Liberal Party** and **Labour Party** politicians, churchmen, editors, journalists, and even King **George V** denounced the savagery and pressured the Lloyd George government to negotiate an Irish settlement. Police terrorism thus may have indirectly contributed to the military truce of July 1921 and the subsequent **Irish Treaty**.

Don M. Cregier

Bibliography
Bennett, Richard. *The Black and Tans.* 1959.
Duff, Douglas V. *Sword for Hire.* 1934.

Black People in Britain

In 1900, at the height of Britain's imperial power, the vast majority—366 million of Britain's 425 million subjects—were not white. Yet only a small number of Black people, perhaps several thousand, lived in the British Isles. In the course of the twentieth century British authorities and Black Britons themselves have included in the category "Black" or "coloured" an ethnically heterogeneous population, reflecting the geographical span of the Empire and the racial hierarchies it fostered. Among them were East and West Africans, West Indians of African as well as Asian descent, British Indians and "Cingalese" [Sinhalese], Burmese, Arabs, Adenese and Berbers, British Somalis, Egyptians, Goans, East Africans of Asian descent, French Algerians, Portuguese, Hondurans, and Maltese. Interracial marriage and racially mixed children have further complicated the composition of this population.

Black people have lived and worked in Britain for centuries. In the decades before the Second World War, black people in Britain comprised two major groups: students and other relative elites who came to Britain for education and often returned to the colonies; and working people who more often settled in Britain, forming families and communities.

Some of the more prominent Black figures in early twentieth-century Britain included Duse Mohamed Ali (1866?–1945), editor of the *African Times and Orient Review* (1912–1920); Dr. Harold Moody (1882–1947), founder and president of the League of Coloured Peoples; John Richard Archer (1863–1931), Mayor of Battersea in 1913 and Labour councilor for over twenty years; MPs Mancherjee Merwanjee Bhownagree (1851–1933), Conservative for Bethnal Green, 1895–1905; and Shapurji Saklatvala (1874–1936), Labour and later Communist for Battersea, 1922–9; cricketer Learie Constantine, Baron Constantine of Maraval and Nelson (1902–71); Satyendra Prasanno, Baron Sinha of Raipur (1864–1928); Indian Nationalist Vengalil Krishnan Krishna Menon (1896–1974); and a circle of Pan-Africanist intellectuals that included Cyril Lionel Robert (CLR) James (1901–89), George Padmore (1902?–59), and Eric Williams (1911–81), who became the first President of Trinidad and Tobago in 1961.

The London-based League of Coloured Peoples was Britain's major Black self-help organization in the 1930s and 1940s. Although at times incorporating Indians, including longtime league officer K.A. Chunchie, and actively soliciting white patrons such as Lady Kathleen Simon, the organization was largely dominated by West Indian students and professionals and to a lesser extent by West Africans. Another major organization was the West African Students' Union, who published the journal *Wasu*. Marcus Garvey (1887–1940) spent his last years in London and published the journal *The Black Man* in the 1930s.

Most Black people in Britain were not celebrities, however, but working people, part of a global and multiracial colonized work force whose labor was mobilized in service of the Empire. During both World Wars hundreds of thousands of colonial workers and soldiers served in Britain and Europe. But the most visible permanent settlements in the late nineteenth and early twentieth centuries were found in British seaports, shaped by the labor requirements of the British mercantile marine.

In the early twentieth century Britain's merchant shipping industry relied on the colonies for one-third of its work force and paid those workers at colonial wage levels. Many Black seamen chose to migrate from the colonies to British and European seaports seeking better wages and working and living conditions. Black seafarers who migrated to Britain, transgressing the geographical barriers between colony and metropole, took refuge in multiracial communities in working-class dockside neighborhoods. The largest Black settlement, numbering several thousand, was Bute Town in Cardiff, notorious worldwide as Tiger Bay, but substantial settlements, numbering in the hundreds, existed in several other ports. These included Toxteth in Liverpool; Mill Dam and Holborn in South Shields; Kingston-upon-Hull; Salford, the port of Manchester; several Bristol Channel ports, including Newport and Barry Dock; and, in **London**, Stepney, Poplar, and Limehouse in the East End. Black seamen were also found in dozens of other British ports.

Among Black seamen as well as white, seafaring was a kin- and community-based occupation. Like migrants the world over, Black settlers in Britain lived with, worked with, and relied upon networks of kin, co-villagers and compatriots to survive in Britain. In particular, many Black seamen relied on ethnic and kin networks for housing and maintenance between voyages. West Africans, Somalis, Arabs, and other Black settlers clustered in dockland enclaves linked or defined by kinship, culture, language, religion, and other common bonds. Here they had access to shops, cafes, social clubs, boarding houses, and religious institutions operated by fellow countrymen and by Black and white women. Women were active in this ethnic service sector, assisting in and managing cafes, acting as shills or informal agents for boarding houses, and operating brothels, market stalls, and other local businesses. Although such businesses provided some employment ashore, most Black workers in Britain remained seamen. Because of this, Black women were relatively scarce, and interracial marriage was common. Although some interracial children experienced upward mobility through the schools, most tended to remain within these communities to work and to marry.

Of necessity, Black people in inter-war Britain enjoyed a measure of integration and mutual toleration with the white working people among whom they lived, worked, and married. Although class, ethnic, and religious divisions and even conflicts existed within, as well as between, Black and white groups, conflict and violence were not everyday occurrences. Black people maintained social and religious organizations and amenities that served their own while integrating them into the wider working class through **marriage**, work, and other activities and institutions.

In spite of, or perhaps because of, official mistrust and hostility, embodied in measures such as the Coloured Alien Seamen Order (1925) these settlements maintained a surprising degree of geographical discreteness, longevity, and ethnic cohesiveness. Enumerations under the Coloured Alien Seamen Order suggest the relative size and proportion of different ethnic groups in the eighteen largest settlements remained relatively stable between 1925 and 1939. These settlements also sustained numerous religious, cultural, and social institutions, among them the Islamia Allawia Friendly Society of Cardiff, the National African Sailors and Firemen's Union of Liverpool, the Somali Association of Great Britain, the Islamic Association of Great Britain, and the Improved Benevolent and Protective Order of Elks, a "Negro Friendly Society" active in London's East End. But race discrimination affected them all, prompting organization among Black seafarers "irrespective of creed or religion." Such organizations included the Cardiff Coloured Seamen's Committee, formed to combat union race discrimination, and its successor, the Colonial Defence Association; and the Coloured Nationals Mutual Social Club of North Shields, formed to resist the British Shipping Assistance Act (1935), which effectively barred Black seamen from subsidized ships.

Thus, Black settlements in early twentieth-century Britain reflected the multiracial and global character of Britain's still expanding Empire and portended the Black immigration that accompanied the Empire's post-war implosion. They continued to exist on the eve of the Second World War, forming the nucleus of many post-war settlements.

During and after the **Second World War**, Britain's global work force was once again mobilized in aid of the mother country. Munitions workers, technicians, and other war workers were imported to Britain from India and elsewhere. The size and distribution of Black settlements in Britain altered as men from the colonies came to industrial centers to do war work or dispersed to the countryside like the "Honduranian" lumberjacks who harvested timber in Scotland. Thus began the post-war pattern of Black settlement in Britain's industrial cities as well as the ports. Yet, port communities remained and became social centers for African-American GIs, colonial troops, and other Black war personnel.

The war and **decolonization** produced a shift of focus among Black activists away from the metropole and toward the colonies, exemplified in the Pan-African Congress in Manchester in 1945. Yet the "Back to Africa" movement involved elites, while workers' migration from the colonies to Britain accelerated in the post-war period. After the war migration from the Caribbean and other colonized areas resumed, encouraged by the Nationality Act of 1948, which granted British citizenship to all imperial subjects. Frequently dated to the arrival in London of the Caribbean migrant ship *Empire Windrush* in 1948, the reconstitution and evolution of Britain's Black communities was actually an ongoing process. Since the Second World War the bulk of Black migrants have come from the West Indies, Pakistan, India, Bangladesh, and East Africa, but migration from other colonies and former colonies has continued. Large numbers of women as well as men have migrated, in particular from the Caribbean, to undertake medical training, or to work in **nursing** or as typists or **domestic servants**. In contrast to pre-war Black migrants who were usually seafarers, many Black migrants since 1945 arrived with technical or other occupational skills valuable to many British industries.

During post-war reconstruction, London Transport, British Rail and other industries recruited in the West Indies to fill jobs that white Britons rejected. Black migrants also came on their own, spurred by post-war depression in the colonized world and, in the case of the West Indies, the McCarran-Walter Act (1952), which barred West Indian British subjects from entry to the United States under Britain's immigration quota. The **National Health Service** absorbed nurses and other medical personnel who came from the colonies to train in Britain. Investigators in the early 1950s found many Black people were beginning to experience upward social mobility, and also found a wide range of experience and practice among different locales in Britain and among different ethnic groups.

By the late 1950s, after a decade of highly publicized migration, there were approximately 192,000 Black migrants in Britain, constituting less than half of 1 percent of Britain's population: 107,000 West Indians, 50,000 Indians and Pakistanis, 5,000 Nigerians, and 30,000 others. Yet their presence provoked disproportionate alarm. When the British economy slumped in the late 1950s, the government sought to curtail Black migration, spurred by a series of white attacks on Black residents of St. Anne's Well, Nottingham, and Notting Hill, London, in August 1958. The Commonwealth Immigrants Act of 1961, essentially a "work voucher" scheme, backfired, prompting a wave of migrants from the colonies hoping to beat further restrictions. Continuing efforts to restrict Black migration between 1968 and 1981 were accompanied by increasingly embittered public debate of a racially charged character and punctuated in the 1980s by inner-city rioting by Black and white unemployed youth, events widely misconstrued in purely racial terms. Because of their concentration in public-sector employment, Black Britons may also have been disproportionately affected by Conservative policies of privatization and cuts in state-supported services during the Thatcher years.

By the late twentieth century Black neighborhoods had formed in most of Britain's industrial centers, largely composed of Bengalis, Pakistanis, Indians, and West Indians, but also of Greek and Turkish Cypriots, Africans, and other formerly colonized people, including Asians expelled from Uganda, Kenya, Tanzania, and Malawi following unilateral declarations of independence in the 1970s. Notable Black settlements include Handsworth and Sparkbrook in Birmingham, which has the largest Black population outside of London, Moss Side in Manchester, Chapeltown in Leeds, and St. Paul's in Bristol. In London, Notting Hill has become a center of Trinidadian settlement, site of the famous Notting Hill Carnivals, while Southall has attracted Indians, and Brixton, Jamaicans. In the late 1980s there were approximately 2.5 million Black people in Britain, amounting to perhaps 5 percent of the country's population. Of these an estimated 45 percent were born in Britain, and perhaps three-quarters of a million were Islamic.

Ethnic institution building and cultural and religious practices continue, coexisting with varying degrees of cultural syncretism or assimilation, and of interracial and multicultural activity. Second- and third-generation Black Britons are coming of age, transforming British cultural life. Mosques now inhabit abandoned churches, while Rastafarianism, a millenarian but politicized variety of Pan-Africanism, has become widespread among youth of Jamaican descent. For the first time in decades, the 1987 elections returned four Black Members of Parliament, among them London activists Diane Abbott and Bernie Grant. They proceeded to form a parliamentary Black Caucus. The Islamic Party of Great Britain was formed in autumn 1989 and fielded candidates in the 1992 elections, most notably in Bradford.

The experiences of Chinese settlers in some ways resembled those of colonized Black people, but there were also significant differences. Before the Second World War most Chinese migrants to Britain came from Hong Kong and Kwangtung province in southern China, but since the war they have been joined by ethnic Chinese from Malaysia and the New Territories. Although many pre-war migrants were seafarers, Chinese businesses and communities were also well established ashore. Investigators have stressed Chinese settlers' maintenance of ties to China, including the remittance of wages abroad, the practice of importing brides from China to Britain as well as marital endogamy in Britain, and the training of British-born children in Chinese cultural practices. This, they argue, accounts for the persistence of distinctive Chinese communities in such places as the London docklands and Toxteth in Liverpool.

Laura Tabili

Bibliography

Collins, Sidney. *Coloured Minorities in Britain*. 1957.

Fryer, Peter. *Staying Power: The History of Black People in Britain*. 1984.

Little, Kenneth. *Negroes in Britain*. 1972.

Sivanandan, A. *A Different Hunger: Writings on Black Resistance*. 1983.

Visram, Rozina. *Ayahs, Lascars, and Princes: The History of Indians in Britain, 1700–1947.* 1986.

Blackett, P(atrick) M(aynard) S(tuart) (1897–1974)

P.M.S. Blackett, the son of a stockbroker, was destined for a career in the **Royal Navy**. He became a naval cadet at the age of thirteen and received an intensive scientific and technological training. He went to war in 1914 as a midshipman and ended as a lieutenant, having been in action several times. Resigning from the navy, he was sent to **Cambridge** to complete his interrupted studies. He graduated in physics in 1921 and remained in **Ernest Rutherford's Cavendish Laboratory** as a research student, Fellow of King's College, and University Lecturer until 1933, when he accepted a chair at Birkbeck College, London. In 1937 he moved to Manchester, where, except for war service, he remained until 1953. From 1953 to 1965 he was at Imperial College, London. At Manchester and Imperial College he presided over the rapid post-war expansion of two of the largest **physics** departments in the country. He won the Nobel Prize in 1948 for his work on cosmic rays; in the 1950s his research concentrated on terrestrial magnetism. Although one of Britain's leading experimental atomic physicists, Blackett never had anything other than a temporary advisory role in the development of **nuclear weapons**.

As a Professor of physics, a Fellow of the **Royal Society** (1933) and as a former naval officer, he became involved in the rearmament effort, serving as a member of the **Tizard** Committee on Air Defense and the Aeronautical Research Committee. In 1939 he became a scientific civil servant at the Air Ministry's Royal Aircraft Establishment, where he worked on bombsights. From the middle of 1940, however, he was concerned not with the design of equipment, but with the statistical analysis of the use of equipment in operations, first at the **army**'s Anti-Aircraft Command, from early 1941 at the **Royal Air Force**'s Coastal Command, and from early 1942 at the Admiralty. His major concern from 1941 to 1945 was anti**submarine warfare**, to which he and his team made major contributions. Blackett was associated from the 1920s with leftist bohemian circles and remained a lifelong socialist, deeply committed to the efficient use of existing science and technology. On the Maud committee he argued that Britain could not build an atomic bomb in wartime; at the Admiralty he became known as an opponent of strategic bombing, believing that better use could be made of bombers in the antisubmarine campaign. He was President of the left-wing Association of Scientific Workers (1943–6). After the war, as a member of the Advisory Committee on Atomic Energy, he opposed on political and strategic grounds the building of a British bomb. Unlike most British scientists he did not see the atomic bomb as a decisive weapon, but rather as an extension of strategic bombing. He took his objections to the Prime Minister and his senior colleagues and consequently was excluded from official military-scientific affairs for the rest of his life. A victim of the Cold War, he was barred from the United States for many years. Nevertheless, through a series of books, articles, and lectures between 1948 and the late 1950s he emerged as one of Britain's leading strategic thinkers. In the early 1960s Blackett's attentions turned to technology and British industrial performance, and he became a leading adviser to the **Labour Party**, playing a key role, in the early years of the Ministry of Technology. In his late sixties, and especially as President of the Royal Society (1965–70), he was very much the "archbishop of science." Blackett was one of the socialist scientists of the inter-war years who also made important intellectual contributions outside science; like many socialist intellectuals of the generation, he established close links with India and Africa.

David E.H. Edgerton

Bibliography

Lovell, Bernard. *P.M.S. Blackett: A Biographical Memoir.* 1976.
Zuckerman, Solly (Lord). *Six Men Out of the Ordinary.* 1992.

Blatchford, Robert Peel Glanville (1851–1943)

In the 1890s and early 1900s Robert Blatchford was one of the most widely read socialists in Britain. His major book, *Merrie England* (1893), sold more than 2 million copies, while the newspaper he edited, the *Clarion*, was for many years one of the most important socialist publications in the country. Blatchford was a popular journalist and crusader on behalf of the socialist cause, although he was certainly not an original thinker. Moreover, his popularity was ephemeral, and his increasing jingoism and opposition to organized religion alienated many of his followers.

Born in 1851, Blatchford was apprenticed in his early teens to a brush maker in Halifax before eventually joining the army, an experience that made him a devout patriot and imperialist. In the 1880s he began a career as a journalist and became the editorial writer for the radical *Sunday Chronicle* in Manchester. Writing about local slum conditions for the paper, Blatchford turned to socialism for a solution to the problems he encountered, influenced by the work of Henry George and William Morris. In 1918 he launched his own newspaper, the *Clarion*, a unique publication that explained the principles of socialism while entertaining its readers with a mixture of short stories, poems, and a healthy dose of humor. While it became the most widely read organ of the socialist movement, the *Clarion* supported no single party or faction; rather, it deployed popular literary idioms in an attempt to disseminate a general message of socialist fellowship.

Throughout the 1890s Blatchford devoted his energy to encouraging various Clarion clubs—educational, social, recreational, and political organizations aimed at educating the masses in socialist principles by demonstrating that socialism had as much to do with how one lived one's life as it did with abstract doctrine. In 1893 he published *Merrie England*, through which he attempted to explain socialism to the general reader. It was Blatchford's most successful book, an effective piece of propaganda that was responsible for the conversion of many individuals to the socialist cause.

During the Boer War Blatchford lost credibility because of his support of British war aims. His enthusiasm for British imperialism, combined with his intense dislike of industrial capitalism, was a unique position for a socialist to hold, and it repelled those with more pacifist leanings. Nevertheless, the success of *Britain for the British* (1902) demonstrated that Blatchford could still attract many loyal supporters. Following the Boer War, however, Blatchford alienated many of them when he formally repudiated organized Christianity, which he had come to view as a barrier to progress and which he attacked in *God and My Neighbour* (1903) and *Not Guilty: A Defence*

of the Bottom Dog (1905). During the early years of the new century Blatchford also wrote several novels, the most important of which were *Julie* (1900?), the story of a slum girl, and *The Sorcery Shop* (1907), a utopian novel that closely paralleled Morris' *News From Nowhere*.

In the early 1900s Blatchford campaigned for unity among various socialist organizations, as he had in the 1890s. Nevertheless, despite the electoral success of the newly formed Labour Party in 1906, he continued to attack the policies and personal style of Keir Hardie and remained suspicious of Labour's electoral ties to the Liberal Party. Furthermore, his increasing warnings about German militarism fell on deaf ears in the socialist movement. Hence, when Britain declared war on Germany in 1914 and Blatchford swung the *Clarion* behind the government, many of his supporters deserted him.

During and after the war Blatchford remained an active journalist. He also began his drift to the Right, eventually considering himself a Tory Democrat. He was opposed to women's suffrage and in the general election of 1924 voted for the Conservative Party. Following his wife's death in 1921, he became a spiritualist and retreated from public view, abandoned by many colleagues after he repudiated his earlier socialist convictions.

For more than a decade few socialists were as popular with the British working class as Blatchford. Although he played only a minor role in the formal electoral struggles waged by the Left, and although his jingoism and disdain of parliamentary politics lost him support, Blatchford was a passionate critic of the social evils of capitalism, and his vivid description of those evils appealed to many who shared his vision of what a transformed society might look like.

Chris Waters

Bibliography

Blatchford, Robert. *My Eighty Years*. 1931.
Thompson, Laurence. *Robert Blatchford: Portrait of an Englishman*. 1951.
Waters, Chris. *British Socialists and the Politics of Popular Culture, 1884–1914*. 1990.

Blitz and Battle of Britain

The phase of the Second World War known as the Blitz, from September 1940 to May 1941, followed directly upon the Battle of Britain beginning in July 1940. The Battle of Britain was a prolonged contest between the German air force (the Luftwaffe) and Fighter Command of the **Royal Air Force** (RAF). In this battle, Fighter Command frustrated Germany's plans for a seaborne invasion of England, a projected operation called Sea Lion by the Germans. The Blitz (German for lightning) refers to Germany's bombing of Britain, especially by night, from the climax of the Battle of Britain until the Luftwaffe had to turn its attention primarily to the Russian front in May 1941. The Blitz failed to achieve the destruction of Britain's economy or the collapse of public morale.

Adolf Hitler expected Britain to negotiate once the **army** had been driven from the Continent and France had surrendered in June 1940. **Winston Churchill**'s new government, however, vowed to fight on despite the weakness of Britain's post-evacuation army. Hitler therefore had to think of ways other than the existing **submarine** blockade to force Britain out of the war. A Luftwaffe bombing campaign might by itself, Hitler hoped, cause the British to give up. If not, the German army would have to cross the English Channel for an invasion of Britain. An immediate crossing in June or July was impractical, but Sea Lion might be possible by September. Although the British army would not present much of an obstacle to such an invasion, Hitler had to worry about Britain's awesomely superior navy. Still, if the Luftwaffe could gain control of the channel skies, then perhaps it could fend off the British fleet sufficiently for a crossing to be made. There was, however, a time limit on Sea Lion: The Luftwaffe had to win its battle with the RAF before autumnal gales would render the channel impassable to landing craft, and Hitler had already wasted weeks of summer weather while hoping for a negotiated peace, his mind on his projected racial and ideological crusade against the Soviet Union.

Preliminary Luftwaffe operations against channel shipping and naval forces began in July and continued into August with only partial success. **Royal Navy** destroyers had to give up their base in Dover but could still dominate the channel from other ports. Without a clear-cut victory over the Royal Navy, the Luftwaffe nevertheless shifted its attack inland against Fighter Command's bases and other facilities on 13 August.

The Luftwaffe seriously outnumbered Fighter Command, but the British enjoyed certain compensatory advantages. Hitler's bombers were extremely vulnerable to the RAF's Hurricane and Spitfire fighters; therefore, the contest boiled down to a struggle between Fighter Command's Hurricanes and Spitfires and the Luftwaffe's Messerschmitt 109s—the only fighter plane the Germans had that could protect their bombers. The 109 was better than the Hurricane and at least as good as the Spitfire, but its operations were hampered by a number of factors. Its limited fuel capacity prevented lengthy patrols over England—Germany had neglected drop-tank technology—and the 109s' pilots had to remain at least relatively close to the bombers they were supposed to protect, thereby restricting tactical flexibility. Furthermore, since most of the fighting took place over England, British pilots who had to bail out could rejoin their units, while Germans who had to jump became prisoners of war.

Most important, the British had a well-developed **radar** and battle-control system, enabling Air Chief Marshal Sir Hugh Dowding to utilize his limited resources to the fullest. The Germans did not entirely understand the British system and its importance and consequently did not make much of an effort to destroy it. This is usually regarded as a disastrous mistake on the part of Hermann Goering, Commander-in-Chief of the Luftwaffe; yet radar was hard to knock out in those days, and the British had several backup systems—mobile radar stations and their code and cipher breaking system, nicknamed ULTRA, for example—so a prolonged antiradar campaign might simply have wasted German resources and precious time before autumn.

Despite Britain's advantages, and the bravery of Dowding's pilots, the Germans appeared to be winning as of early September. True, German losses were high, but Fighter Command was running out of experienced and rested pilots. On 7 September, however, Germany shifted its attacks primarily to **London**, thereby giving Fighter Command bases a much-needed breather. Goering did this for two reasons. For one thing, his planes had accidentally bombed civilian areas of London in August, provoking British retaliatory raids on Berlin, much to Hitler's and Goering's embarrassment—hence the revenge bombing of London beginning on 7 September. In addition, the Luftwaffe was convinced that Dowding was saving his limited resources by refusing all-out battle—which was true, al-

B

ARP shelter: Aldwych Underground Station.

Bomb damage in London, near St. Paul's, during the Blitz.

though Fighter Command had not suffered as much as the Germans imagined; in any case, the Luftwaffe thought it could force Fighter Command into a final and fatal battle of attrition by attacking something Dowding would have to defend to the death, namely London. Yet, still Dowding would not take the bait.

Seeing Fighter Command's relative inactivity as evidence of its debilitation, Goering expected total victory when he launched a gigantic raid on 15 September. To their unpleasant surprise, the Germans found Fighter Command full of fight, and Luftwaffe losses correspondingly catastrophic; at this moment of supreme crisis, Dowding had at last thrown in all that he could of his carefully husbanded forces. Hitler, dismayed by Fighter Command's apparent new lease on life, and increasingly worried about the weather, postponed and eventually canceled Sea Lion.

Although speeches, books, and movies have ever since emphasized Britain's extreme peril in the summer of 1940, later reflection suggests that Sea Lion never had much of a chance. Even if the Luftwaffe had kept after Fighter Command bases, and even if that had led to Fighter Command's defeat, Dowding could and would have retreated beyond the Messerschmitt 109's range and saved his remaining assets for invasion day. The RAF's Bomber Command could have destroyed much of Sea Lion's shipping in its German-held ports at night—and in fact did so even though Sea Lion was never launched. Most important, the Royal Navy could have operated in the channel at night, safe from the Luftwaffe, tearing up Sea Lion's ports and convoys during the weeks it would have taken the German army to stage an adequate invasion, given the growing strength of Britain's army as of September. Thus, although Sea Lion was not merely a bluff, as some have thought, it seems unlikely that the Luftwaffe could ever have guaranteed its success even if it had reduced Fighter Command to a remnant; it is, therefore, unlikely that Hitler would ever have launched his projected invasion.

In this context, the Blitz must be seen as a poor substitute for Sea Lion. With invasion no longer possible after 15 September, the bombing of Britain lost most of its rationale. All that remained was the hope of crippling Britain's economy and/or terrorizing the British people into surrender. In retrospect, the Germans had little chance of achieving either objective. Air power enthusiasts before the Second World War had exaggerated the impact of bombing on both factories and morale. Moreover, the Luftwaffe's bombers did not carry bomb loads sufficient for an effective strategic bombing program. Besides, once Sea Lion was canceled, the Germans could no longer justify the extreme bomber losses they had experienced in daylight raids during the Battle of Britain; therefore, most of the Blitz was carried out at night, making it impossible to hit factories with any degree of accuracy.

Consequently, terror was the sole remaining purpose of the Blitz. Yet the British public did not panic and did not demand an end to the war. Instead, British civilians crowded in their underground and other bomb shelters at night and dug their cities out of the rubble by day, adding the story of their own bravery to that of Fighter Command, inspiring the admiration of the American public, helping to prepare Americans psychologically for their entry into the war on Britain's side. Frustrated, Hitler turned against Russia in June 1941, leaving an undefeated Britain at his rear.

Karl G. Larew

Bibliography
Collier, Basil. *The Battle of Britain.* 1962.
Fitzgibbon, Constantine. *The Blitz.* 1970.
Hough, Richard, and Denis Richards. *The Battle of Britain.* 1989.
Parkinson, Roger. *Dawn on Our Darkness: The Summer of 1940.* 1977.
Sansom, William. *The Blitz: Westminster at War.* 1947.

Bloomsbury Group
The Bloomsbury Group, a coterie of intellectuals and artists, has a secure place in the cultural history of twentieth-century Britain, including as it does a writer of genius in **Virginia Woolf** and the century's most important economist in **John Maynard Keynes.**

Bloomsbury, the name attached to the group, derived from the Bloomsbury section of **London,** near the **British Museum,** whose streets and squares were mostly designated with titles and family names associated with the Duke of Bedford, who owned much of the land. The area is respectable but unfashionable; it adjoins raffish Soho; and the two together might be taken to represent the combination of respectability with a touch of bohemianism that

Bloomsbury itself came to exemplify. The group had its beginnings foreshadowed when Sir Leslie Stephen died in 1904, and the Stephen children, Vanessa, Thoby, Virginia, and Adrian—orphaned but all in their twenties—moved away from the family house in upper-middle-class Kensington to live on their own at 46 Gordon Square, Bloomsbury. There they started to entertain on Thursday evenings, and out of these spirited informal gatherings the group emerged.

The origins of Bloomsbury go back to the early years of the nineteenth century: The group's essential seriousness, masked as it might be by wit and unconventionality, came from their Victorian forebears, even though they themselves were consciously in revolt against them. James Stephen, the great-grandfather of the Stephen children, was one of the most active members of the Clapham sect, a group of evangelical **Anglicans**, notable for their campaign against the slave trade. His son, also James, was a central figure in the administration of the British colonies, and his grandsons were Fitzjames, a famous judge and conservative Utilitarian, and Leslie, a prolific literary critic, the founder of the *Dictionary of National Biography*, and well known for his abandonment of the Christian faith. Less apparent was the importance of the feminine line. The Stephen children's mother, Julia Jackson, had the famous photographer Julia Margaret Cameron as an aunt. That generation was active in the upper-class artistic circles of late Victorian London.

The most immediate origins of the group go back to the young men who were friends of Thoby Stephen's at **Cambridge** at the turn of the century, among them John Maynard Keynes, **Lytton Strachey**, and **Leonard Woolf**. Keynes, Strachey, and Woolf were members of the secret Cambridge discussion society, the **Apostles**, at that time dominated by the philosophy of **G.E. Moore**. Moore believed, and led his disciples to believe, that, as he stated in the most famous sentence of his *Principia Ethica* (1903): "By far the most valuable things, which we know or can imagine, are certain states of consciousness, which may be roughly described as the pleasures of human intercourse and the enjoyment of beautiful objects." Two other crucial Cambridge contemporaries, not members of the Apostles, were Clive Bell and Thoby Stephen himself. Although Thoby would die of typhoid in 1906, he was the true maker of the group,

having introduced his sisters, Vanessa and Virginia Stephen, to his Cambridge friends. Clive Bell would marry Vanessa, and Leonard Woolf would marry Virginia. (Lytton Strachey's cousin, **Duncan Grant**, was also an early member of the group.)

Before the First World War these young people believed that rationality had triumphed and they would be able to create a new modern world. They endlessly discussed all sorts of issues in their weekly gatherings in Gordon Square. They also believed in attempting to live sexual lives free of guilt and Victorian hypocrisy; perhaps even more unusual for the time, they enjoyed free and frank sexual conversations in mixed company.

Bloomsbury functioned most cohesively as a group in the years before the First World War. Its fame would come later, after the war, when they were no longer so sure that reason would conquer all and their original optimism had dimmed. (Yet Keynes became dedicated to ways that **economics** could be used to improve gradually the human lot.)

They had become even stronger as a group in 1910 when they were joined by two Cambridge men, both Apostles and both of a somewhat older generation: **E.M. Forster** and **Roger Fry**. Fry was already a prominent art critic. That year he re-met Clive and **Vanessa Bell**, and, with the assistance of Clive and others, he selected the paintings for the Manet and the Post-Impressionists exhibition in London at the end of the year. In effect, it was the introduction of modern art to England. For Bloomsbury, its immediate influence was upon its painters, Vanessa Bell and Duncan Grant. Years later, Virginia Woolf, with the exhibition in mind, made her famous observation in "Mr. Bennett and Mrs. Brown" that "on or about December 1910, human character changed." By this she meant not only the new art in the exhibition, but also the emergence of modernism in literature, especially as it came to full flower in the next decade in the works of **James Joyce**, Forster, **D.H. Lawrence**, **T.S. Eliot**, and Woolf herself. She contrasted the modernists to the prevailing popular realism, singling out **H.G. Wells**, **Arnold Bennett**, and **John Galsworthy**, decrying their unwillingness to see beyond realism to less literal and more imaginative truths of human character.

In the artistic world, modernism was represented in the theories of Fry, and later by Clive Bell. Both emphasized the formal values of paintings, which in effect meant turning attention away from representation to the shapes on the canvas, a precursor to abstraction. In *Art* (1914) Clive Bell put forth the doctrine of "significant form": One should not look for representational or symbolic aspects in art. The painter whom Fry and Bell most revered was Paul Cézanne, and the Bloomsbury painters strove for something of his qualities in their work, particularly in the period 1910–18. Under Fry's leadership, Vanessa Bell, Grant, and other painters came together from 1913 to 1919 as the Omega Workshop, to apply their ideas of abstraction and what would now be recognized as modern design to objects of ordinary life, such as screens and chairs. Bell and Grant continued to design and paint throughout their long lives. Charleston in Sussex, the house where they lived together until she died in 1961 (Grant died in 1978) is now a monument to their art in the paintings on the walls and the decorations of the rooms.

The giants of the group—and it is striking that one group of close friends should have included so many eminent figures—were Keynes, Woolf, Strachey, Fry, and Forster, although he was not at the center of the circle. Those figures, along with Leonard Woolf, were so important that they have separate entries in this encyclopedia and so it is not necessary here to outline their careers and importance. There were some further literary figures—less significant—who were more or less members of what was never a formal organization, such as the novelist David Garnett, who was Duncan Grant's lover and later the husband of Bell and Grant's daughter, Angelica, indicating something of the sexual minuet that characterized their lives and that has emerged in the modern biographies of members of the group. There was also Desmond MacCarthy, the literary critic. Among others, such writers as T.S. Eliot and the younger John Lehmann became good friends.

After the First World War the members of the group became increasingly famous. They remained close friends, frequently meeting in London and at Charleston as well as vacationing in France, the country outside of England that had their strongest allegiance. But their gatherings were less frequent than they had been before the war. Ever at the very center of the group were the two sisters, Virginia Woolf and Vanessa Bell. Deaths diminished the group: Strachey in 1932, Fry in 1934, the tragedy of

the death of the Bells' son, Julian, in the **Spanish Civil War** in 1937, Virginia Woolf by suicide in 1941, Keynes in 1946. All through their lives and accomplishments, there was a commitment to fight against what they saw as Victorian pretense and humbug, to penetrate below the surface to what might violate ordinary standards of reality but would nevertheless be something "truer," to follow ideas bravely wherever they might lead, not to forgo their middle-class comforts, but to work for a better world economically and artistically for others. They were crucial shapers of modernism in this century.

Peter Stansky

Bibliography
Bell, Quentin. *Bloomsbury*. 1968.
Edel, Leon. *Bloomsbury: A House of Lions*. 1979.
Rosenbaum, S.P., ed. *The Bloomsbury Group*. 1975.
———. *Victorian Bloomsbury*. 1987.
Shone, Richard. *Bloomsbury Portraits*. 1976.
Palmer, Alan, and Veronica Palmer. *Who's Who in Bloomsbury*. 1987.
Richardson, Elizabeth P. *A Bloomsbury Iconography*. 1989.

Boer War (1899–1902)

The Anglo-Boer War ended the Victorian era and ushered in the twentieth century for Britain on a disquieting note. It demonstrated British diplomatic isolation in the days before the First World War and effectively dispelled the myth of British colonial invincibility. A preview of the war had occurred with a Boer victory in a skirmish in 1881 after which the British government was obliged to concede independent status to the Boer republics of Transvaal and Orange Free State. The uneasy tension that existed after 1881, however, exploded when gold and diamonds were discovered in the Boer territories in the latter part of the nineteenth century.

Gold and diamond discoveries were of little concern to the theocratic, agrarian Boer life-style. The Boers (farmers) were a dour Calvinistic people descended from seventeenth-century German and Dutch settlers; the *het Volk*, as they called themselves, were fundamentalists in life as in faith. One of their strongest beliefs was that the white man was to be forever superior to the black, who was scripturally ordained to be a permanent hewer of wood and drawer of water. One reason they had trekked north, away from the British Cape Colony in the 1830s, was that Britain abolished slavery in 1833. Their god-given right, they believed, ought not be tampered with. The increasing flow of *uitlanders* (Afrikaans for outsider, many of whom were British) scrambling into the Boer republics for the gold and diamonds was of growing concern to them, just as the harsh Boer treatment of *uitlanders* troubled the British.

Following the Jameson raid of 1895–6, that half-baked scheme for an *uitlander* revolt concocted by Cecil Rhodes, an escalating series of events and fruitless negotiations exacerbated relations between the Boers and Britain. There is creditable evidence that British Colonial Secretary Joseph Chamberlain and his representative in South Africa, Sir **Alfred Milner**, conspired to prevent any peaceful solution to the problem—both men probably influenced by the machinations of Rhodes. Milner in particular has been characterized as an intransigent obstacle to peace. Following a series of failed political negotiations, the Boers took the offensive, invading British Natal in October 1899.

Although superficially the war seemed a mismatch, in reality the Boers had several advantages. They were a hardy outdoors people, raised to horseback riding, hunting, and shooting. In addition, the Boers had used tax revenues they had raised from the hated gold and diamonds to purchase the latest armaments from German dealers; their weapons were, if anything, superior to the British. Furthermore, on the eve of the war the Boer forces comprised over 50,000 mounted soldiers, with rifles and ammunition for many more. In contrast, as late as September 1899, the British could muster no more than 14,750 men. Whitehall authorized a reinforcing contingent of 47,000, but not until 29 September.

In spite of this unreadied state, British public opinion ran high that this war would be no more than another of "Queen Victoria's little wars," quickly wrapped up once the fleet arrived bearing soldiers from the "thin red line." In truth, the only European foes the British **army** had faced since the Crimean War were the Boers themselves, who had in 1881 effortlessly trounced it at the battle of Majuba Hill. British confidence nonetheless was high when Sir Redvers Buller was sent out to command the forces.

Considering the Boer advantages, it is not surprising that in the early days of the invasion there were several Boer successes, leading the British press to dub the week of 9–15 December as "Black Week." General Lord Methuen was bested at Magersfontein, General William Gatacre was repulsed at Stormberg, and commanding General Buller, defeated at Colenso, was forced to abandon his drive to relieve the Boer siege of the British military depot at Ladysmith. The Boers were able to sustain a multifront campaign against the British and besiege, in addition to Ladysmith, the strategically significant towns of Kimberley and Mafeking. The scale of these disasters, as well as the inept defense he made of his actions, led to Buller's dismissal and replacement by General Frederick "Bobs" Roberts, Lord Roberts of Kandahar.

In time, the British reinforced their garrisons, and the weight of the full army turned the military tide. With their reinforced might, the British were able to relieve their forces, break the sieges of the three cities, go on the offensive, and capture Johannesburg and Pretoria by June 1900. The Boers refused to surrender, however, and fighting continued for two more years. By the time a British victory seemed certain, Lord Roberts was recalled for a hero's return to Britain, and General **Horatio Kitchener** was left to mop up the remaining Boer resistance. The British government under Lord Salisbury felt the time appropriate for elections and called what came to be known as the Khaki election in 1900. Pro-Boer **Liberals** such as **David Lloyd George** attacked government policy, while the **Conservative** administration wrapped itself in the flag, and the election was a victory for Tory war policy, maintaining their 130 seat majority and vindicating their war effort.

In the latter stages of the war the Boers abandoned full-scale encounters against the British and turned to guerrilla tactics conducted by small *kommando* units. Their defeat was a tedious process in spite of the overwhelming military strength of the British. Further, Britain proved to be friendless in Europe, jeered at by the European press for its inability to defeat an enemy it outnumbered twenty to one. After a century of enjoying "splendid isolation," the British found their diplomatic seclusion troubling and resolved after the war to shore up its diplomatic alliances. Finally, in a pique of anger over such untoward tactics as the *kommandos*, Lord Kitchener began a scorched earth policy, erecting miles of barbed wire quadrants with corner blockhouses, systematically sweeping for Boer units. In addition, Boer women and children were herded into concentration camps, where many died of malnutrition and disease. Britain was criticized internationally, and Liberal opposition leaders characterized government policy as "methods of barbarism."

By the spring of 1902 peace talks were begun, concerned in the main with the questions of Boer independence and white sovereignty. The peace of Vereeniging of May 1902 allowed the Boers a degree of political autonomy and complete racial supremacy. The final twenty months of guerrilla warfare had produced some strategic gains for the Boers, therefore. All British hopes for the Cape Colony color-blind voting policy applied to all South Africa were dashed. By the time of the peace negotiations the British public was so tired of the prolonged war that the government was ready to extricate itself by whatever circumstances. The Boers, in turn, fearing a Liberal victory in the next election, felt more comfortable negotiating with the Conservatives. The Boer republics were annexed and put under the direct rule of Alfred (now Lord) Milner. Britain also agreed to help repair damage to Boer territories by granting the Boers interest-free loans. British loss in lives was about 22,000, while Boer combat deaths exceeded 7,000. In addition, perhaps as many as 20,000 Boer women and children died in concentration camps. British performance was the subject of a Royal Commission investigation begun in September 1902. Chaired by the Earl of Elgin, the commission issued a harsh indictment of the current system in July 1903, and reforms in the military were initiated that had implications for British performance in the First World War.

In the end, however, the Boers, though vanquished on the battlefield, were more calculating in defeat than were the British in victory. They reasoned that through the union of four African states that developed after the war (the Union of South Africa was created in May 1910), they might achieve dominion not only over their former two republics, but of all **South Africa**, and especially with the prerogative to treat their black subjects just as the Old Testament seemed to suggest to them.

Their strategy prevailed. Many Boers became tacit supporters of the Empire; Boer generals were feted as heroes in London following the war. The Boer conviction proved in the long run more intractable than was the British: the *het Volk* survived Queen Victoria, and the Boers won the Boer War after all.

Newell D. Boyd

Bibliography

Farwell, Byron. *The Great Boer War.* 1976.
Kruger, Rayne. *Goodbye Dolly Gray: The Story of the Boer War.* 1959.
Pakenham, Thomas. *The Boer War.* 1979.
Warwick, Peter. *Black People and the South African War, 1899–1902.* 1983.
———, ed. *The South African War: The Anglo-Boer War, 1899–1902.* 1980.

B

Bomberg, David (1890–1957)

David Bomberg was one of the only twentieth-century British artists to emerge from Jewish ghetto life in the East End of London. After two years at the **Slade School of Art**, Bomberg began to show his paintings in mixed exhibits to critical acclaim. Like the Vorticists, with whom he was identified although he never became a member of the movement, he rejected naturalism in order to describe the dynamic new world of technology and urban life. In 1914, the year of his first solo exhibition, he visited Paris, and he joined the London Group of avant-garde artists in rebellion against the prevailing naturalistic traditions of British painting. His celebrated early work *The Mud Bath* (1914), based on several preliminary studies (1912–13), was inspired by Schevzik's Steam Baths in the East End of London. Its human figures of swimmers and divers were rendered in abstract, geometric form. Bomberg followed this work with the prismatic images of *Ju-Jitsu* (ca. 1913) and *In the Hold* (1913–14).

After two years in the armed forces, he was commissioned in 1917 to paint a large-scale work for the Canadian War Memorial Fund. Although he adopted a more representational style than in his pre-war work, the painting, *Sappers at Work* (1918–19), was initially rejected as being too radical and had to be repainted. This was the first of many occasions that Bomberg's work was rejected as unorthodox. After several unsuccessful exhibitions in London, Bomberg attempted to make his living by turkey farming and rabbit breeding. Living in the country helped deflect the urban orientation of his early work and arouse his interest in landscape painting. In 1923, using funds provided by artist Muirhead Bone, Bomberg went to Palestine as an unofficial artist for the Zionist Organization. He remained abroad for four years, painting landscapes in Palestine and in Spain in a more realistic style and using richer colors than he had hitherto employed. In the 1920s and 1930s, Bomberg developed an expressionistic approach to painting. He formulated a belief in the redemptive power of art in the face of the alienation and inhumanity of technology, rooting his work in nature and in a belief in the importance of the spiritual consciousness of the artist. During the Second World War, his only successful commission was *Bomb Store* (1942).

Although he was largely ignored by the art world, his influence began to spread through his radical teaching methods and theories of art. Between 1945 and 1953 Bomberg taught at the Borough Polytechnic, where he urged students to concentrate less on accuracy than on organic structure and on an existential expression of being. His students, who included Frank Auerbach (1931–), and Leon Kossoff (1926–), exhibited first as the Borough Group (1947–50) and later as the Borough Bottega (1953–7). Since a 1979 Whitechapel Gallery, London, exhibition of his later work, his expressionistic, figurative paintings have been critically revalued to balance his original reputation as an associate of English **Vorticism**.

Nannette Aldred

Bibliography

Arts Council of Great Britain. *David Bomberg, 1890–1957.* 1967.
Cork, Richard. *David Bomberg.* 1987.
———. *David Bomberg* (Tate Gallery). 1988.
Lipke, William. *David Bomberg: A Critical Study of His Life and Work.* 1967.
Whitechapel Art Gallery. *David Bomberg: The Later Years.* 1979.

Bonar Law, Andrew (1858–1923)

Although Andrew Bonar Law's tenure as Prime Minister lasted hardly more than six months, from 1922 into 1923, his career as a whole was of lasting significance. In particular, his accession to the **Conservative Party** leadership in November 1911 occurred at a critical time for his party, battered as it had been by internal dissension and three successive electoral defeats. That it recovered its nerve and revived its prospects was in no small part due to his aggressive

partisanship. During the **First World War**, however, Bonar Law assumed a more statesman-like role, collaborating successfully in a coalition with **David Lloyd George** in administering the war effort and overseeing the subsequent transition, first to peacetime **reconstruction** and then to party government once again in 1922.

In many ways he was an unlikely choice for a party whose upper reaches remained so English, Anglican, and patrician. Bonar Law was none of these; born in 1858 in Canada, the son of a melancholy Presbyterian minister, and educated in Scotland, he began a career in the Glasgow iron trade. That experience disclosed no particular ambition or aptitude for political life, except for an undeniable effectiveness in debate that stemmed from his diligent preparation and exceptional memory. Those capacities stood him in good stead in his first parliamentary contest, in the Khaki election of 1900, when he benefited from a surge of wartime patriotic sentiment and was elected for a Glaswegian seat he had not been expected to win. Making his mark, appropriately enough, as a Parliamentary Secretary to the Board of Trade, it was not long before Bonar Law adapted his dry but formidable debating style to the realities of the Commons. His growing concentration on politics was probably accentuated by the death in 1909 of his wife, to whom he had been deeply devoted.

By 1910, through diligent application and a direct, pugnacious style, he had earned a reputation within a Conservative Party shorn of much of its talent by the electoral debacle of 1906 and of much of its cohesiveness by the controversy over **tariff reform**. Bonar Law attracted further attention by his willingness to foresake his safe suburban London seat to contest an almost hopeless one in the free-trade citadel of Manchester. Though he lost the election, he gained in stature and returned to Parliament shortly thereafter in a by-election. Having earned high marks for his courage and selflessness, he was more than merely an idle spectator when the party met in November 1911 to choose a successor to **Arthur Balfour**, who had resigned as party leader. After a deadlock between the top two candidates, **Austen Chamberlain** and Walter Long, Bonar Law emerged as the compromise choice, prompting Lloyd George to remark that "the fools have stumbled on the right man by accident."

For the next three years, however, Bonar Law did more to earn himself a place in Liberal demonology than in the good graces of constitutional scholars. Sensing that the resurgence of the Irish Question afforded an opportunity to restore Conservative Party unity, he threw his weight against Home Rule and encouraged **Ulster** separatist militancy to the point that he appeared to be condoning, even inciting, a direct challenge to parliamentary sovereignty. Whether Bonar Law's vehement "new style" was merely a tactical device to arouse the electorate for the anticipated campaign, or whether it was a reckless strategy born of despair and Ulster bigotry, is still unclear. Irresponsible it certainly was, but whatever the verdict, Bonar Law had no doubt where his duty lay when the war broke out in August 1914.

Resignation in the face of duty dominated the remainder of his life. Bonar Law readily accepted the immediate suspension of partisan activity, and when **H.H. Asquith** broadened his government in 1915, he accepted without complaint a position (that of Colonial Secretary) beneath what his stature would have entitled him. With the further reconstruction of the government late in 1916, in which he was instrumental in forming a coalition with Lloyd George, he deferred again, accepting only the position of Chancellor of the Exchequer and leaving the prime ministership to his Welsh colleague. The strain of wartime administration, the onset of throat cancer, and the loss of two sons in battle all eventually prompted his retirement from politics, though it proved to be shortlived. His intervention in October 1922 brought the Lloyd George coalition to an end, but by then the ill and morose Bonar Law had little interest in doing more than returning public life to normal. In May 1923 he resigned as Prime Minister (being succeeded by **Stanley Baldwin**), having only five months left to live. When Bonar Law was laid to rest in Westminster Abbey, Asquith is reputed to have quipped that it was fitting to "have buried the Unknown Prime Minister by the side of the Unknown Soldier." Apocryphal or not, the comment evokes Bonar Law's remoteness and failure to elucidate a constructive program with which his name would be associated. But he did not conceive of his role as a Conservative politician in that way. If his career had reflected the growing weight of business interests within the party, he too, like the Unknown Soldier, might be regarded as a victim of the war, having sacrificed his health, ambition, and family. And yet, he might also be regarded as one of its victors,

having restored, and then preserved, the interests of his party.

Frans Coetzee

Bibliography
Blake, Robert. *The Unknown Prime Minister: The Life and Times of Andrew Bonar Law, 1858–1923.* 1955.
Ramsden, John. *The Age of Balfour and Baldwin, 1902–1940.* 1978.

Bondfield, Margaret (1873–1953)

Margaret Bondfield contributed much to the trade union movement and Labour politics. A former shop assistant, Bondfield began her political career when she moved to London in 1894. There she joined a series of leftist organizations and, building upon her work experience, embraced Marxism. Bondfield also joined the National Union of Shop Assistants, Warehousemen, and Clerks, where she rapidly rose to the position of Assistant Secretary. In 1899 she served as the only woman delegate to the **Trades Union Congress** (TUC). Despite her socialist convictions, Bondfield quickly became disenchanted with the Marxist concept of class struggle, preferring instead the ethical socialism of the **Independent Labour Party** (ILP) as well as the **Fabian** variant.

In 1896 Bondfield went undercover to investigate married **women's employment** in the textile trades. This experience radicalized her, making her a tireless champion of working women. Throughout the next decade Bondfield joined a welter of working women's organizations, which she served with energy and distinction, assuming leadership roles in all of them. Among them were the Women's Trade Union League, the Women's Cooperative Guild, the **Women's Labour League**, the National Federation of Women Workers, and the Standing Joint Committee of Women's Industrial Organisations.

Prior to the First World War Bondfield also took an active part in the **women's suffrage** battle, but her loyalties were first to her class. As such, she was unwilling to promote the limited franchise that women's suffragists found acceptable. As President of the Adult Suffrage Society, Bondfield crusaded for universal suffrage, a position that enraged the more radical suffragettes.

With the outbreak of hostilities, Bondfield, by then a national leader of the ILP, opposed the war. She concentrated her energies in National Federation of Women Workers and the War Emergency Workers' National Committee. As she solidified her own leadership positions, she allied more closely with the **Labour Party** leaders, moving with them further to the Right. In 1918 Bondfield was elected to the General Council of the TUC. She became its first woman chairman in 1923, the same year she was elected MP for Northampton. She served as the Parliamentary Secretary to the Ministry of Labour during the first Labour government, and in 1924 she became the Minister of Labour, thus making her the first woman **Cabinet** member and Privy Councilor in British history. Bondfield supported Prime Minister **Ramsay MacDonald** and the unpopular fiscal policies of **Philip Snowden** even in the formation of the National government. Her loyalty to the party leadership cost her the respect of the Left, her parliamentary seat, and, ultimately, her leadership position in the TUC. With her political career ended, Bondfield turned to public work. She remained active throughout the Second World War in such organizations as the YMCA and the National Council for Social Service.

Donna Price Paul

Bibliography

Bondfield, Margaret. *A Life's Work*. 1949.
Hamilton, Mary Agnes. *Margaret Bondfield*. 1924.

Bowen, Elizabeth Dorothea Cole (1899–1973)

Elizabeth Bowen's family came to Ireland in 1653 under Oliver Cromwell. Her early years were spent divided between Dublin and the family estate, Bowen's Court, in County Cork. After traveling in Europe, Bowen settled in London when she was in her early twenties and, under the tutelage of Rose Macaulay, began to write short stories. *Encounters*, her first volume of stories, appeared in 1923, the year of her marriage to Alan Cameron, an employee of the **British Broadcasting Corporation** (BBC). After stints in Northamptonshire and Oxford the couple settled into a Regent's Terrace house and became part of a circle that included Cyril Connolly, John and **Rosamond Lehmann**, William Plomer, **Stephen Spender**, and **Virginia Woolf**.

During the late 1920s and the 1930s Bowen's short stories and novels appeared al-

most yearly. Her first novel, *The Hotel* (1927), was followed in 1929 by *The Last September*, one of her best works, which details the romance of a young Anglo-Irish woman and a British soldier stationed in Ireland during 1920–1. After *Friends and Relations* (1931) and the more substantial *To the North* (1932), she published *The House in Paris* (1935) and *The Death of the Heart* (1938), novels that made her widely known. These works express her view of the world as a tenuous and dangerous place; her characters are inevitably subject to betrayals both by other persons and by their countries.

During the **Second World War** Bowen worked as an air raid warden in London and as an employee of the Ministry of Information. In this capacity she made frequent trips to neutral Ireland to assess the state of Irish opinion regarding Britain. Both these occupations (and the bombing of her own London house) diverted her from writing, but they made their way into her fiction in the short-story collections *Look at All Those Roses* (1941) and *Ivy Gripped the Steps* (1946) and her brilliant novel of wartime love and espionage in London and Ireland, *The Heat of the Day* (1949). In this era Bowen also published two autobiographies: *Bowen's Court* (1942), the history of her family's tenure in Ireland, and *Seven Winters* (1942), the story of her own childhood.

After the war Bowen and her husband took up full-time occupancy at Bowen's Court, which she was the first woman to inherit. During these years she favored nonfiction: a gathering of essays and reviews, *Collected Impressions* (1950), and an eponymous study of *The Shelbourne Hotel* in Dublin (1951). Following her husband's death in 1952, Bowen embarked upon a more restless existence, one marked by struggles to keep up the estate. Her post-war fiction, *A World of Love* (1955), reflects her absorption in the problems of decay for the Anglo-Irish gentry still inhabiting southern Ireland. She traveled ceaselessly (often to American universities) and wrote eclectic articles for such publications as *Mademoiselle*. By 1959 she could no longer afford Bowen's Court and sold it to a neighbor who demolished it. Nineteen sixty marked the publication of *A Time in Rome*, her observations of various trips to Italy. Bowen spent the last decade of her life based in England, traveling and writing fragments of autobiography. These appeared in the posthumous *Pictures and Conversations* (1975). Her bizarre last novel, *Eva Trout: or Changing*

Scenes (1968), reflects her difficult later years. She died of lung cancer in February 1973 and was buried in the family plot in Ireland.

Bowen embodied many paradoxes of this century: She followed in the English literary tradition but insisted on her membership in the Anglo-Irish "race"; she wrote as a woman but denied being a feminist in any political or social sense; she claimed not to be a historian, but she often discussed past events in fiction and essays. Certainly cognizant of the modernist tradition, she preferred a more traditional style, combining her love of Jane Austen, Henry James, and Anthony Trollope with the Irish fondness for the ghost story. While she has often been viewed only as a brittle recorder of tea party concerns, she must be understood in the larger social context of the brutal history through which she lived: the "Troubles" in Ireland, culminating in the Irish Civil War, and the two World Wars, which confirmed all that she detected to be wrong with the century she inhabited.

Heather Bryant Jordan

Bibliography
Bloom, Harold, ed. *Elizabeth Bowen.* 1987.
Gindin, James. *British Fiction in the 1930s: The Dispiriting Decade.* 1992.
Glendinning, Victoria. *Elizabeth Bowen: Portrait of a Writer.* 1977.
Jordan, Heather Bryant. *How Will the Heart Endure? Elizabeth Bowen and the Landscape of War.* 1992.
Lee, Hermione. *Elizabeth Bowen: An Estimation.* 1981.

Boxing

When William Hazlitt wrote his famous essay "The Fight" in 1821, boxing was already well established in Britain. It was in Britain that professional boxing originated in the eighteenth century, and since then Britain has produced some of the world's most famous boxers, especially at the lighter weights. Until the latter years of the nineteenth century most boxing took place in the open air between bare-knuckle opponents. The last great "prize fight" of this kind was the contest between the English champion Tom Sayers and the American J.C. Heenan at Farnborough in April 1860. Thereafter there was a gradual move indoors, to boxing with gloves according to regulations (Queensberry Rules), which laid down the size of the ring, the duration of rounds and intervals, the stipula-

tions for knockdowns, and the prohibition of wrestling holds. Weight divisions were clarified in 1909 by the National Sporting Club, London. Thus, a formerly brutal sport was made relatively civilized.

By this time two strands of boxing had become established. Amateur boxing was a popular recreational activity based on a host of clubs and a complex network of competitions throughout Britain. Governed by the Amateur Boxing Association (ABA), founded in 1880, it had become an essentially working-class sport by the early twentieth century. In the 1980s there were an estimated 25,000 participants. It increasingly developed into a feeder for the other strand, professional boxing. This too, in its participant and spectator forms, was working class, performed in a series of small halls and fairground booths across the country. Its heyday came between the 1920s and the 1950s, when a particular style of skillful, defensive boxing relying on quick footwork was much appreciated by the crowds. Still remembered from this era is Welshman Tommy Farr's heroic contest with Joe Louis for the world's heavyweight title in 1937 and the two fights between Randolph Turpin, the British middleweight, and Sugar Ray Robinson in 1951. Both captured the public's imagination and evoked strong feelings of patriotism. Ironically, though, Turpin was Black, and it was only in 1948 that **Black people** had been permitted to fight for British titles. Futhermore, professional boxing has owed much for its development to ethnic minorities, from the celebrated Jewish fighter Daniel Mendoza in the late eighteenth century through to the dominance of Black boxers like Frank Bruno, Lloyd Honeygan, and Dennis Andries.

Often regarded as a potentially dangerous sport, boxing has once again come under scrutiny following serious injury in the ring (Eubank v. Watson, 1991). Medical arguments concerning the likelihood of brain damage add weight to the demands for boxing's abolition. It may well be moral, rather than economic, pressures that determine the future of professional boxing in Britain.

Jeffrey Hill

Bibliography
Butler, Frank. *A History of Boxing in Britain.* 1972.
Shipley, Stan. "Boxing" in Tony Mason, ed. *Sport in Britain: A Social History.* 1989. pp. 78–115.

B

Brailsford, H(enry) N(oel) (1873–1958)

As an author, journalist, and editor, H.N. Brailsford wrote about politics and world affairs for nearly sixty years, establishing himself as one of the most eloquent and incisive socialist commentators of his generation.

Born in Yorkshire, the son of a **Methodist** clergyman, he grew up mainly in Scotland, attending the University of Glasgow, where he studied with **Gilbert Murray** and Edward Caird. After additional study at **Oxford** and the University of Berlin, he embarked on an academic career, which he soon abandoned for journalism. In 1897 he resigned a position as subeditor of the *Scots Pictorial* to enlist in the Philhellenic Legion, a volunteer force fighting alongside the Greeks in their struggles against the Ottoman Empire, an experience he recounted in his only novel, *The Broom of the War-God* (1898). He soon won the attention of **C.P. Scott**, who sent him to Crete as a *Manchester Guardian* correspondent, the start of a long, but intermittent, connection with that paper as an editorial writer and foreign correspondent. This was followed by stints as lead writer and commentator on foreign affairs with a succession of Liberal periodicals: the *Morning Leader*, the *Tribune*, the *Daily News*, and, especially, the *Nation* throughout **H.W. Massingham**'s editorship from 1907 to 1923.

During the first decade of the century Brailsford became involved with several groups agitating on behalf of liberal movements abroad and befriended Russian exiles living in London, like Prince Peter Kropotkin and Theodore Rothstein. Membership in the Balkan Committee and familiarity with the region made him a logical choice to lead a British relief mission to Macedonia in 1903–4 and later to serve on the international Carnegie Commission of Inquiry into the origins of the Balkan Wars. In 1906 he published his study *Macedonia*, which remained for many years the authoritative cultural and historical analysis.

Despite his professional and personal links with Liberal Nonconformity, Brailsford began to gravitate to the Left at the time of the **Boer War**, and in 1907 he joined the **Independent Labour Party** (ILP) in protest against the Liberal policy in Egypt. Liberal editors, like Massingham and **A.G. Gardiner** of the *Daily News*, did not attempt to curb his attacks on the Liberal government, readily publishing Brailsford's denunciations of the Anglo-Russian *entente* and his defense of Egyptian nationalism.

In 1909, largely at the instigation of his first wife, Jane Malloch Brailsford, Brailsford became involved in the **women's suffrage** campaign, later serving as Secretary of the ill-fated Conciliation Committee. In 1910 he was adopted as a women's suffrage parliamentary candidate for South Salford in opposition to Hilaire Belloc but withdrew in favor of a Liberal suffragist.

In much of his writing Brailsford sought to extend his friend and journalistic colleague **J.A. Hobson**'s economic analysis of imperialism to international diplomacy more generally. In his celebrated *The War of Steel and Gold*, published in June 1914, he deplored the covert relationship between finance and diplomacy that stimulated an armed competition between capitalist powers. Calling for more democratic control over foreign policy at home and concessions to Germany overseas to achieve a genuine concert of Europe, he inveighed against the imperialist conspiracy against the public interest in the hope of averting international conflict. During the war he called for a negotiated peace, refuting allegations of Germany's sole war guilt. In addition, he became the leading proponent of international government, pleading for an inclusive league of nations responsible for international trade and investment and empowered to enforce its decisions. His *A League of Nations* (1917) attracted attention among progressive internationalists, not only in England but in the United States.

After defeat in the 1918 general election, contesting Montrose for Labour, Brailsford traveled through Central Europe, reporting on the devastation in the aftermath of war. His graphic accounts, sympathetically depicting the plight of defeated peoples in Germany and Austria-Hungary, were published in the *Herald*, the *Manchester Guardian*, and the *New Republic* and later provided the material for two books, *Across the Blockade* (1919) and *After the Peace* (1920). In addition, he offered expert advice on Central Europe in several reports for the **Labour Party** Advisory Committee on International Questions. One of the first Western journalists to visit the Soviet Union, he returned from a 1920 trip impressed by the economic strides being made but critical of the suppression of dissent. He recorded his impressions in *The Russian Workers' Republic* (1921) and, after a second trip, in the more circumspect *How the Soviets Work* (1927).

In 1922 Brailsford was appointed editor of the *New Leader*, the restructured ILP weekly, which, over the next four years, he transformed into an internationally respected periodical. Mingling ideological exhortation with cultural enrichment, Brailsford offered a growing audience incisive analyses of world affairs and economic problems, as well as a literary section that included contributions by **E.M. Forster, Julian Huxley, H.W. Nevinson, Bertrand Russell,** and **H.G. Wells.** In his own *Socialism for Today* (1925) and in the *New Leader* Brailsford helped to propound the ILP Living Wage program, which sought to increase mass purchasing power by compelling industries to pay wages sufficient for a civilized standard of life. Formulated for the ILP by a committee consisting of Brailsford, Hobson, E.F. Wise, and Arthur Creech Jones, the Living Wage became the focus of its policy for coping with **unemployment** and a source of conflict with **Ramsay MacDonald.**

Dismissed as editor in 1926 by the dominant ILP Scottish contingent, Brailsford continued as a political columnist for the *New Leader* until he broke with the ILP in 1932, joining the dissident **Socialist League** within the Labour Party. In addition, he began to travel more extensively, to the United States and to India, to lecture abroad, and to write for the *Baltimore Sun, Reynolds' News,* and, most significantly, for the *New Statesman,* during **Kingsley Martin's** editorship. His books during these years, *Olives of Endless Age* (1928) and *Property or Peace?* (1934), recapitulated his views on internationalism and the links between capitalism and war, while *Rebel India* (1931) was an outspoken plea for Indian autonomy.

During the 1930s he continued to denounce the Versailles settlement and to call for disarmament, but after the outbreak of the **Spanish Civil War** he came to recognize the need for collective security and offered one of the strongest indictments of **Neville Chamberlain's** policy at **Munich** to appear in the British press. During the Spanish conflict he chaired the Labour-Spain Committee, raised money for Spanish relief, recruited volunteers, and assisted refugees. Early in the **Second World War** he began to broadcast in the **British Broadcasting Corporation** (BBC) **Overseas Service;** in the book *From England to America* (1940), he appealed for American entry. He continued to work for the cause of **Indian nationalism,** writing several pamphlets and his 1943 **Left Book Club** volume, *Subject India.* Late in the war he advocated the unpopular line of magnanimity toward Germany as a way of avoiding the pitfalls of Versailles. *Our Settlement with Germany* (1944) was widely attacked, notably by **Communist Party** functionaries.

After the war, in declining health, Brailsford undertook trips to India for *Reynolds* to cover the elections, to Germany in 1947, and to Yugoslavia in 1950. Among the very few honors he received in a long career was an honorary LL.D. from his own University of Glasgow in 1944. His last years were devoted to a long-contemplated history of the Leveller movement, published posthumously as *The Levellers and the English Revolution* (1961).

Brailsford belongs to a long tradition of radical writers and pamphleteers, his intellectual links as much to Thomas Paine and Shelley as to Marx and Hobson. He was, above all, a dissenter, not in the religious sense—he rejected his Methodist upbringing—but as a radical critic of dominant institutions and values. Moving from Liberalism to a quasi-revolutionary socialism, he remained committed nonetheless to the ideal of political democracy. He was an internationalist who abhorred xenophobia, a socialist whose loyalties could not be confined within national boundaries. More than a journalist, he was, during his long career as a man of letters, an exemplary voice of reason, never wavering in his quest for international conciliation, social justice, and the liberation of subject peoples.

F.M. Leventhal

Bibliography

Leventhal, F.M. *The Last Dissenter: H.N. Brailsford and His World.* 1985.
Martin, Kingsley. *Editor.* 1968.
Taylor, A.J.P. *The Trouble Makers.* 1958.

Brandt, Hermann Wilhelm "Bill" (1904–1983)

Bill Brandt, Britain's outstanding photographer, was born in Hamburg and brought up in Germany. At sixteen he developed **tuberculosis** and was sent to Davos, Switzerland; in 1927 he moved to Vienna to complete his treatment. In Vienna he entered the circle of the educationalist Dr. Eugenie Schwarzwald, who introduced him to Ezra Pound, through whom he met the artist and photographer Man

Ray in Paris. Brandt attended the Man Ray studio in 1929 and took pictures in Paris, Hungary, and Spain. Perhaps because of his English father, Brandt developed an antipathy to Germany and determined to settle in England, which he did in 1931–2. His first major publication was an illustrated book, *The English at Home* (1936), published by B.T. Batsford. He had worked for *Weekly Illustrated*, but the bulk of his photojournalism was for *Picture Post*, another weekly illustrated magazine established in October 1938. His art photography appeared in *Lilliput*, a monthly magazine of stories and pictures in the style of the German *Querschnitt*, to which he contributed between September 1937 and November 1949. His second notable publication was *A Night in London* in 1938, published by *Country Life*. In both of his books of the 1930s he relied, though not exclusively, on montage pairings, meant to draw attention to social extremes and to sexual encounters. Brandt's sources were German expressionist films of the 1920s, an influence later supplemented by the films of **Alfred Hitchcock**.

Brandt was at his busiest during the war years, when he became a kind of national landscapist for *Picture Post* and *Lilliput*. In 1940–1 he accomplished two major portrait series for the nation: one of blitzed Londoners sheltering in the underground system (Ministry of Information), and another of British statuary heroically staged in Canterbury Cathedral (National Buildings Record). In his more workaday war journalism he represented Britain as Arcady (Hyde Park and the Thames at Windsor). During 1944 he took portraits and fashion pictures for *Harper's Bazaar*, and developed a bleak manner that was influential in film and photography in the 1960s. He gradually ceased to work as a journalist, partly because he was unwilling to abandon a hieratic, indoor manner that he had developed during the 1930s. The reportage style of the new era was, by contrast, active and instantaneous. He worked sporadically at fashion photography during the later 1940s, but from around 1945 turned increasingly to the female nude, collected in *Perspective of Nudes*, his last great book, in 1961. His final works were seawreck montages, which addressed themselves to touch as much as to sight. In the 1960s and 1970s he reprinted many of his earlier pictures on a larger scale than ever and with more regard for sharp tonal contrasts, as if he wanted to sum up a dispar-

ate career in journalism in a few broadly stated symbolic images.

Ian Jeffrey

Bibliography

Mellor, David. *Bill Brandt: Behind the Camera*. 1985.
Jeffrey, Ian, ed. *Bill Brandt*. 1993.

Brass Bands

Brass bands are a type of instrumental music ensemble that is almost exclusively amateur and has a precise instrumental lineup: nine Bb and one Eb cornets, three Eb tenor horns, two baritones (in Bb), two euphoniums (in Bb), two tenor trombones, one bass trombone, two Eb basses and two Bb basses, and percussion. Though some European and Australasian countries have cloned this genre, it originated in Britain in the nineteenth century and has remained one of the important elements of its music culture. Brass bands are mainly concentrated in working-class urban areas.

By the beginning of the twentieth century brass bands had acquired all of their major, permanent characteristics. The best of them have technical virtuosity almost equal to that of professional groups, but the idiom and style of brass band players are distinctly different from those of orchestral brass players. The central focus for brass bands has been the contests that are held regularly and are organized into a number of classes or divisions so that bands of more or less equal competence compete against each other. The system allows for promotion between divisions. At contests, adjudicators are enclosed in cubicles to keep the identity of bands secret and ensure impartiality. Competing bands play either a set test piece or, in other cases, a test piece of their own selection. National contests are held every year for which bands have to qualify in preliminary regional competitions.

Most bands carry the name of industrial or commercial sponsors. The longest unbroken relationship between a band and an individual company is probably that enjoyed by the John Foster and Son Black Dyke (Textile) Mills Band, which has won the national contest many times. Other bands of long distinction have changed names more than once, reflecting the peaks and troughs of the industrial concerns around which they are based.

There has been strikingly little change in the brass band movement in the twentieth century. The repertoire is relatively conservative, but several important composers (including **Edward Elgar, Ralph Vaughan Williams, Gustav Holst**, Harrison Birtwhistle and Hans Werner Henze) have written for brass bands. There is no canon of works that makes the brass band repertoire important alongside that of mainstream art music. The bulk of the popular repertory has always been made up of transcriptions of art and **popular music**. Though the number of brass bands has declined in the late twentieth century, there are still, by some estimates, about 2,000 of them, and they continue to occupy an important place in the territory between British art and popular music culture.

Trevor Herbert

Bibliography

Herbert, Trevor, ed. *Bands: The Brass Band Movement in the Nineteenth and Twentieth Centuries.* 1991.
Taylor, A.R. *Brass Bands.* 1979.

British Broadcasting Corporation (BBC)

Founded in 1922 as a private monopoly regulated by the Post Office, the BBC became a public corporation in 1927 and rapidly established itself as a major institution of British national culture. **John Reith**, the extraordinary figure who became its first Director-General, enunciated a paternalistic vision of "public service" that sought to counter the growing influence in Britain of Americanized mass culture. He rejected the notion that the public ought to be given what it wanted. Reith viewed culture as a form of self-improvement, a means of personal and social discipline. Painfully aware that the new medium of radio lacked respectability and tradition, BBC programmers constructed a schedule that reflected the most treasured cultural aspirations of the middle and upper-middle classes. Symphony, **opera**, and chamber music occupied a privileged place on the broadcast schedule. Leading intellectuals provided "talks" on a variety of topics. Sunday was dominated by religious programs, followed by lengthy periods of silence. Announcers were expected to speak with a proper accent and wore full evening dress while broadcasting. During the 1920s Reith's ideal of public service uplifted the medium and the corporation as much as the vast audience it sought to improve.

Yet middle-class cultural paternalism, like its aristocratic antecedents, could never completely divorce itself from public criticism and accountability. Although the broadcast schedule clearly gave disproportionate weight to the tastes of highly cultivated minorities, the BBC offered enough concessions to popular taste to escape broadcasting into a void. From the beginning a tension existed within the BBC between giving the public "what it wanted" and "what it ought to have." This tension became exacerbated as the audience rapidly increased in size. Between 1929 and 1933, for example, the number of license holders doubled, and by 1935, 98 percent of the population had some access to wireless programs. This increase reflected in part the ability of the BBC to provide a strong regional system of broadcasting that offered alternatives to the national programs from **London**, but it also resulted in pressures on the organization, both external and internal, that exposed the contradictions of the Reithian ethos. The popular **press**, though committed to the notion of the BBC's monopoly, hired radio critics who often deplored the organization's cultural elitism. Commercial stations on the Continent, such as Radio Luxembourg, beamed a steady stream of **popular music** that captured a sizable British audience, especially on Sundays. As the BBC grew in size and moved to modern headquarters in Broadcasting House in 1932, corporation officials began to modify the assumptions that buttressed Reith's cultural mission.

During the 1930s the BBC proved itself more responsive to public demand than its official rhetoric sometimes indicated. The number of variety and light entertainment shows increased dramatically; even jazz, which Reith abhorred, found its place on the schedule. Educational programming diminished, and talks became more popularized. Gradually, the corporation began to abandon its Sabbatarianism; the controversial "silent periods" on Sunday disappeared. After long opposition from some quarters, the BBC accepted the notion of systematic listener research and hired an expert from **advertising** to discover what the public wanted. The BBC still launched expensive operatic productions and continued to finance experimental dramas, but these and similar decisions regarding resources could not involve a rationale that listener research flatly contradicted. Even a monopoly committed to sustaining the arts could not ignore completely the sometimes subtle, sometimes brutal, pressure of statistics. Listener research gradually became the box office of the BBC.

There were other important changes during the 1930s. Technology and reception improved enormously; like the cinema, gramophone, and newspaper, radio became fully integrated into the everyday life of British citizens. The *Radio Times* sold over 3 million copies a week, and the *Listener* enjoyed a circulation greater than both the *New Statesman* and the *Spectator* combined. Empire broadcasting began in 1932, vastly extending the range of the BBC; for the first time, British subjects around the world could hear the voice of the King, including, most dramatically, during the abdication crisis of 1936. Freed from a series of restrictions imposed during the 1920s, the BBC became an important source for news, gradually overcoming the justified complaint by trade unionists that the BBC had supported the government during the **General Strike**. In 1936 the Ullswater Committee issued its report recommending renewal of the BBC's charter formulated by the Crawford Committee a decade earlier. In 1938 John Reith resigned to become Chairman of Imperial Airways, a decision he soon and forever regretted.

The **Second World War** solidified the international reputation of the BBC, whose news and **overseas broadcasts** in a variety of languages became valuable sources of information. Although early in the war the corporation sustained heavy criticism for its unimaginative broadcasts, the adoption of a Forces Program especially designed for the troops became immensely popular among all segments of the population. During the **Blitz**, two broadcasters in particular captured public attention: **Winston Churchill** brought the cadences of eighteenth-century rhetoric to a twentieth-century medium; and the novelist **J.B. Priestley**, speaking in a distinctive Yorkshire accent once considered inappropriate for broadcasting, focused in his *Postscripts* on highly specific and concrete examples of the humane values that united the British. As the war progressed, the entertainment show *ITMA* included fictional characters whose catch phrases became part of everyday language, and, perhaps less predictably, *Brains Trust* transformed intellectuals such as **Julian Huxley** into national personalities. Behind the scenes, the staff of the corporation more than doubled, and the bureaucracy was reorganized to accommodate growth. F.W. Ogilvie, Reith's

ineffectual successor, was eased out in 1942, to be replaced for a short period by a joint leadership. Although the BBC continued to distrust controversial political broadcasts, the discussion of war aims received more attention than Churchill would have liked. Throughout the war, correspondents broadcast vivid reports from the front lines, including the beaches of Normandy.

From a background in the newspaper industry, William Haley became Director-General in 1944 and, until he resigned eight years later, committed himself to extending the Reithian ethos into the post-war era. In 1946, as part of a major reorganization, radio split into three distinct services. The Light Programme captured the vast majority of the audience; the Home Service, which emphasized the spoken word, proved a distant second; while the Third Programme, beloved by the cultivated elite, consumed one-third of the available airwaves to appease 1 percent of the listening public. In 1949 the **Beveridge** Committee convened to review the BBC's charter and, after sifting through prodigious testimony, recommended that the monopoly continue, thereby overriding the objections of some members who argued for greater competition because of the rise of **television**.

Experiments with television began before the First World War. Pioneer John Logie Baird, like Reith a Scot, began to cooperate with the BBC in 1929, but his mechanical scanning system, for all its cleverness of design, eventually succumbed to its electronic rivals. In 1936 the BBC began broadcasting as the first regular high-definition television service in the world. Audiences remained tiny, though appreciative, until 1939 when operations ceased for the duration of the war. In June 1946 service resumed in an environment of rapid technological development and decreasing unit costs that helped assure the success of the new medium. During the 1950s, television came into its own, accelerating the decline of both radio and cinema. The telecast of the coronation of Queen Elizabeth II in 1953 reached over half the British population.

In a society that prided itself on free speech, centralized control over two powerful media of mass communication became increasingly anomalous. In the early 1950s criticism of the BBC's monopoly became more insistent, not only from well-organized pressure groups, but also from within the ranks of the **Conservative**

Party, which returned to power in 1951. In 1955, after complex negotiations, the Independent Television Authority began the process of awarding franchises to commercial television companies for designated regions of the country. Though ITV proclaimed adherence to the ideals of public service and remained heavily regulated, few doubted that it offered the public "what it wanted" rather than "what it ought to have." ITV's high salaries lured away some of the BBC's best staff. Audience ratings assumed a new importance.

The 1960s marked an important turning point in the history of the BBC. Hugh Greene, the Director-General for virtually the entire decade, modernized the corporation to reflect the complicated social and cultural realities of a booming consumer economy. Greene welcomed more daring and controversial programming. The long-running Z Cars brought greater realism to the police show; the play Cathy Come Home exposed the problems of housing; Till Death Do Us Part discovered unlikely sources of amusement in cranky characters. In these and similar programs, television audiences encountered personalities and situations that earlier, more paternalistic broadcasting routinely excluded. The satirical That Was The Week That Was, first broadcast in 1962, became emblematic of the decade's more open programming, not least because of its unpredictability.

The allocation of a new television channel to the BBC in the early 1960s allowed the corporation to segment its programming according to audience, not unlike the division of radio into separate services after the Second World War. BBC 2, which began broadcasting in 1964, catered to a more cultivated viewer. Its dramatic programs, in particular, paid an unexpected dividend as the BBC entered the financially more troubled 1970s. The cost of licenses, a major source of income, failed to keep pace with the soaring prices of labor and new technologies such as color. For example, the license fee for color television, adjusted for inflation, did not increase between 1968 and 1985, even though from 1975 to 1983 the price of television soared 68 percent in real terms. Like their counterparts in the film industry, British television producers discovered that the international market, especially the United States, offered a lucrative market for certain types of programs. The Forsyte Saga, Civilization, The Six Wives of Henry VIII, and Elizabeth R, all produced by BBC 2 in the late 1960s and early 1970s, sold internationally at considerable profit. In the United States, public broadcasting and major oil companies eager to improve their tattered image during an era of rocketing prices especially welcomed prestige productions from the BBC.

Commercial competition also affected radio broadcasting. In 1964 Radio Caroline, a pirate station operating offshore, broadcast a steady diet of popular music that enraged BBC officials and captured the public imagination. Though government eventually cleared the sea of pirates, the BBC once again reorganized itself to accommodate its audience. Radio 1 devoted itself to popular musical programming; Radio 2 concentrated on more traditional light music; Radio 3 resembled the old Third Programme; and Radio 4 stressed current affairs and the spoken word. The introduction of commercial radio in Britain in the early 1970s terminated a half-century of BBC monopoly. Local broadcasting, in particular, expanded enormously both from the BBC and from various commercial franchises, not all of which proved financially successful. Listening habits also changed as the transistor and other technological changes such as the Walkman made radios more portable, especially for the young.

Broadcasting also transformed the nature of politics. The BBC had always played a major role in public affairs broadcasting, and during the 1950s it introduced a number of widely respected programs such as Panorama and Tonight. Beginning in the 1960s, however, politicians began to appreciate more fully the power of images on electoral opinion. Harold Wilson, for example, altered certain aspects of his appearance and speaking style to accommodate the viewing audience. In 1975 the House of Commons permitted its debates to be broadcast on radio; thirteen years later television entered the chamber. More and more, election campaigns revolved around television coverage, as commentators warned of the Americanization of British politics. During the 1980s Margaret Thatcher's confrontational style of leadership became obvious to millions not only in her response to aggressive interviewers such as Robin Day, but also in the vivid images emerging from the Falklands War and the miners' strike. Increasingly, television shaped the political agenda, and the BBC, like ITV, were no longer mere observers but became active participants in the electoral process. If by the 1990s the BBC no longer commanded the "brute force of mo-

B

nopoly" that Reith defended with pride, its ability to accommodate itself to changing audiences and technologies made it an integral part of twentieth-century British culture.

D.L. LeMahieu

Bibliography
Briggs, Asa. *The BBC: The First Fifty Years.* 1985.
——. *The History of Broadcasting in the United Kingdom.* 4 vols. 1961–79.
Reith, John. *Into the Wind.* 1949.
Scannell, Paddy, and David Cardiff. *A Social History of British Broadcasting.* vol. 1: *1922–1939.* 1991.
Seymour-Ure, Colin. *The British Press and Broadcasting since 1945.* 1991.

British Broadcasting Corporation (BBC) Overseas Broadcasting

Though it went by different names as it evolved historically, BBC Overseas Broadcasting always helped shape the image of Britain abroad. The Empire Service began in 1932 as one of **John Reith**'s many contributions to the medium. Innovations in the technology of transmission combined with quality programming helped make "This is London calling" a familiar phrase throughout the world. In 1938 the **British Broadcasting Corporation** started broadcasting in foreign languages, in part as a response to similar initiatives on the Continent. Unlike the Germans and Italians, however, the corporation eschewed more overt **propaganda** and often defined its public narrowly. In the Arabic Service, for example, the BBC sought an elite rather than a mass audience.

The **Second World War** magnified immeasurably the significance of external broadcasting. The Overseas Service expanded to fourteen languages in 1939 and to forty-five languages by 1944. As country after country fell to the Nazis, Britain became a major source of news and inspiration for the occupied populations. In 1941 the BBC initiated the V for Victory campaign, an effort at propaganda that began modestly enough but rapidly became so powerful an emblem of resistance in France, Belgium, and Holland that the Germans adopted the symbol for their own purposes, thereby eventually blunting the campaign. Throughout the war external broadcasting constantly encountered difficult political problems. The British govern-ment's Political Warfare Executive, for example, pressured the corporation to inject more propaganda into its international broadcasts, particularly the news. The BBC resisted these efforts by arguing that high standards of objectivity preserved the greatest asset of the Overseas Service, its credibility with foreign audiences. The Soviet Union permitted broadcasts in English to its territory but balked at programs in Russian. The complex sectarian disputes of governments in exile forced BBC officials to become nimble diplomats, especially with the French. German jamming undermined some efforts at propaganda, but it proved less effective when announcers especially selected for their low-pitched voices spoke in short, simple sentences. By the end of the war most commentators agreed that the BBC succeeded brilliantly in achieving superiority over the airwaves.

After the war external broadcasting suffered deep cutbacks in both staff and services. The government forced the BBC to surrender wavelengths, and the number of languages broadcast diminished considerably. The advent of the Cold War, however, once again provided overseas broadcasting with a mission. The BBC carried less propaganda than the Voice of America, though both services struggled to overcome sophisticated jamming techniques. During the 1950s and early 1960s government continued to reduce the budget of overseas broadcasting as the BBC, like Britain itself, withdrew from Empire. In 1965 external broadcasting became known as the World Service, and projecting the image of Britain abroad entered a new phase. Radio continued to serve BBC enthusiasts around the world, but the export of **television** programs became far more lucrative. BBC Enterprises, established in the 1970s, established complex cofinancing agreements and sold television programs to international buyers, especially in the United States. Commercial television and the introduction of new technologies of transmission and reproduction during the 1980s made the BBC only one of many British voices in the global culture of the late twentieth century.

D.L. LeMahieu

Bibliography
Briggs, Asa. *The BBC: The First Fifty Years.* 1985.
——. *The History of Broadcasting in the United Kingdom.* 4 vols. 1961–79.
Mansell, Gerard. *Let Truth Be Told.* 1982.

British Council

The British Council is the organization that promotes cultural relations between Britain and other countries. Since beginning in 1934 as the British Committee for Relations with Other Countries, it has expanded to over eighty countries. Its programs promote an appreciation of Britain's culture and knowledge of the English language overseas by fostering personal contacts in the professional, educational, scientific, and cultural fields. The council publishes and distributes literature, organizes classes, libraries, and exhibits, and provides technical assistance in fields such as health, agriculture, and literacy. Although the government supervises and funds the council, it is technically an unofficial body. When it started, the council sought to raise money from private contributions. The government granted it only £5000, hoping that companies involved in foreign trade would become substantial contributors. However, business leaders were slow to support it, and it soon became too big to depend on voluntary contributions. In effect, it functions as an arm of the British government conducting what could be called cultural **propaganda**. Partly because it might be resented as a propaganda agency, the council never established offices in the United States.

The council's history reflects the changing requirements placed on British foreign policy since 1934. In the years before the **Second World War**, when German and Italian propaganda was actively promoting **Fascism,** it was regarded as an indirect answer to this challenge, indirect because it avoided political attacks on Adolf Hitler and Benito Mussolini, concentrating on the less controversial areas of culture and language. This was in keeping with the **appeasement** policies of British governments. This same reluctance to inflame relations with the Fascist powers also explains why the council got little financial support. It was obliged to limit itself to a few modest programs in Europe and the Middle East.

The **Foreign Office** official who was the chief sponsor of the council, Rex Leeper, and George Lloyd, who became its chairman from 1937 to 1940, both pressed for a more activist program. When the war began, the council expanded rapidly. Despite the new Ministry of Information, which handled official press and propaganda programs, the council still assumed many new tasks. From making films on cultural subjects to sponsoring classes in neutral countries and programs for American soldiers stationed in Britain, the council showed its worth and prospered accordingly. By 1945 it was receiving over £2 million a year to support these activities.

When the war ended, the council initially faced some cutbacks and questions about its future. A new era brought different challenges: Britain's worldwide Empire was disintegrating and its status as a leading power was put in doubt by a crumbling economy. The council's work in the colonies expanded as a way to reinforce allegiance to the Crown and then to ease the peaceful transition from colonial status to membership in the British Commonwealth. Even as Britain's military and economic fortunes declined, investment in the council seemed to be a good way to enhance national prestige and promote exports. Although Eastern European Communist regimes impeded council activities, the British Council still had a role to play in the Cold War. It conducted whatever cultural exchanges it could behind the Iron Curtain and kept alive contacts with the people in these countries.

By the 1980s the council had become a vast organization with a budget of close to £300 million. Little known at home in Britain or in the United States, it still had an important presence around the world. Much of its work was under contract from host countries and supported by payments: Its English-teaching program in Hong Kong held classes for over 10,000 fee-paying students, for example. Technical-assistance work to developing countries has become an important task of the council in this era. Through this work, and its network of libraries and institutes, it has enhanced Britain's influence and visibility around the world.

Donald S. Birn

Bibliography

Donaldson, Frances. *The British Council.* 1984.
Taylor, Philip M. *The Projection of Britain: British Overseas Publicity and Propaganda, 1919–1939.* 1981.
White, A.J.S. *The British Council: The First Twenty-five Years.* 1965.

British Museum

The British Museum was the world's first secular public museum, based upon principles of universal knowledge derived from French Encyclopaedists. Its collections of antiquities contain 3 million to 4 million objects, and the derivative library numbers in excess of 15 million items. Established by Act of Parliament in 1759 as "a cabinet of curiosities," available to the public, both "studious and curious," it came into the twentieth century purged of all its scientific departments. The creation in South Kensington of the British Museum (Natural History) by 1883 left on Great Russell Street in Bloomsbury only antiquities and the several library departments. The present building dates from 1823–47, with galleries added in 1884, 1906–14, 1938, and 1978. Incendiary damage of 1941 encouraged extensive modernization and reorganization. The British Library, separated by Act of Parliament in 1973, was to move during the 1990s to new facilities at Somers Town west of St. Pancras Station.

The original British Museum consisted of three departments: Manuscripts, Printed Books, and "Natural History and Modern Curiosities." Before 1900 what began as "Modern Curiosities" was clearly distinguishable into Antiquities, still including ethnographical collections, plus Coins and Medals. Reorganizations have differentiated among Antiquities: Greek and Roman, Oriental, Egyptian, Western Asiatic, Prehistoric and Romano-British, Medieval, and Later. Ethnography's enlarged collections moved in 1970 to the Museum of Mankind in Burlington Gardens off Piccadilly. A Department of Scientific Research provides supportive laboratory facilities.

Until 1836 the collections of prints were held within Antiquities; thereafter a separate department came into being. Oriental Manuscripts were recognized as distinct from 1867. While a Reading Room existed from the outset, with a distinctive Superintendent from 1856, the creation of the British Library permitted the drawing together of the discrete elements of Printed Books and Manuscripts. The Patent Office Library was integrated with the National Library of Science and Invention in 1966. Materials that came from the original Royal collections were joined by not only the Oriental collections but also the records and library of the East India Company, custody of which was transferred in 1982. A National Sound Archive was added in 1983.

Clyde Curry Smith

Bibliography

Barker, Nicolas et al. *Treasures of the British Library.* 1989.
Caygill, Marjorie. *Treasures of the British Museum.* 1985.
Miller, Edward. *That Noble Cabinet: A History of the British Museum.* 1973.

Brittain, Vera Mary (1893–1970)

Vera Brittain is best known as author of the autobiographical memoir *Testament of Youth* (1933), which deals with the personal and political significance of the **First World War** from a woman's point of view. *Testament of Youth* is generally considered to be one of the major British literary productions concerned with the Great War and is certainly the best known by a woman author. It was a best-seller in Britain and North America when it first appeared and has enjoyed continued success ever since.

While her reputation as a major twentieth-century author rests on *Testament of Youth*, Brittain published more than twenty books and was a prolific journalist. The books include *Testament of Friendship* (1940), Brittain's memoir of her close friend and fellow writer Winifred Holtby; a second volume of autobiography, *Testament of Experience* (1957); nine novels; and several works of social commentary. In the inter-war decades her journalistic pieces appeared in a wide variety of publications, ranging from the feminist weekly *Time and Tide* to *Good Housekeeping*.

Brittain was politically active throughout her life as a **feminist** and in the cause of peace. The peak of her feminist activity was in the 1920s and early 1930s, when she worked with the Six Point Group and the Open Door Council, two important inter-war feminist organizations. Brittain had been involved in internationalist activities from the mid-1920s, when she was a frequent speaker for the **League of Nations Union**. Her preoccupation with questions of war and peace deepened as the political situation worsened in the 1930s. In 1936 she became involved with the Christian pacifist **Peace Pledge Union**. As she later wrote of her conversion to **pacifism**: "I had come to see the enemy . . . as war itself." During the **Second World War** her outspoken criticism of the evils of war brought her opprobrium at the time but earned her a place in the history of British peace activism.

Born on 29 December 1893, Brittain was the daughter of a successful Staffordshire paper manufacturer. She vividly describes her upbringing in *Testament of Youth*, explaining that her education was designed to fit her for "provincial young ladyhood," but that she rebelled against conventional upper-middle-class patterns for women and instead successfully fought to achieve admission to university. Brittain entered Somerville College, Oxford, in 1914 and completed her first year but then left Oxford for war service as a Voluntary Aid Detachment nurse. As the war was beginning, she had fallen in love with Roland Leighton, a school friend of her brother's, and in *Testament of Youth* she movingly recounts the story of their love, Leighton's death in action, and the subsequent deaths of her only brother and two other close friends.

Brittain returned to Oxford after the war, completing her studies in 1921 with a degree in history. After Oxford she and Holtby, her Somerville contemporary, set up house together in London. In 1925 Brittain married the political scientist G.E.G. Catlin, and from its beginning their marriage was consciously and deliberately feminist. Brittain kept her own name—a significant symbolic statement during this period—and never allowed the marriage to interfere with her career. For many years Catlin was a Professor at an American university, and the couple lived apart for extended periods in order to accommodate both careers. The marriage also accommodated the intimate friendship between Brittain and Holtby: From 1927 until her premature death in 1935, Holtby formed part of the Brittain-Catlin household.

From her early struggles to escape the fate of "provincial young ladyhood" to her later achievements as a writer and social activist, Brittain was representative of the group of educated middle-class women who brought to fruition the goals of Victorian bourgeois feminism in the years following the First World War. Throughout her adult life she was sustained by feminist convictions and driven by a fierce desire to achieve personal autonomy.

Deborah Gorham

Bibliography

Bailey, Agatha. *Vera Brittain.* 1987.
Berry, Paul, and Alan Bishop. *Testament of a Generation: The Journalism of Vera Brittain and Winifred Holtby.* 1985.
Bishop, Alan, ed. *Chronicle of Youth: Vera Brittain's War Diary, 1913–1917.* 1981.
Gorham, Deborah. *Vera Brittain: A Feminist Life.* 1996.

Britten, (Edward) Benjamin (1913–1976)

An English composer, pianist, and conductor, Benjamin Britten, together with **Michael Tippett**, led the generation of composers following that of **Ralph Vaughan Williams**. The first performance of Britten's opera *Peter Grimes* (7 June 1945), marked the revival of English opera, a revival sustained by Britten's subsequent eleven operas and those of Tippett. Britten's sympathy for the voice found further outlet in thirteen song cycles, roughly half of which were written for his lifelong companion, Peter Pears, and in his writing for boys' voices. *On Receiving the First Aspen Award* (1964) contains an important statement of Britten's artistic beliefs, which found particular expression in his music for amateurs, such as the children's opera *Noye's Fludde* (1957), and in the creation of the festival at Aldeburgh, where he lived from 1947. Among many official honors, Britten was awarded the Order of Merit (1965) and a life peerage (1976).

Born in Lowestoft, the son of a dentist, Britten enjoyed a musical upbringing. He began composing at the age of five, and such was his progress that Frank Bridge accepted the thirteen-year-old Britten as a pupil. Lessons with Bridge continued throughout Britten's school days, and both Bridge's professional instruction and Britten's formidable talent are well in evidence in the remarkable *Quatre Chansons Françaises* (1928). Britten's further development was somewhat frustrated by unsympathetic teaching during his period at the Royal College of Music in London (1930–3), although he gained more help from John Ireland's composition lessons than he was later to acknowledge. Despite opposition, he managed to secure a handful of prestigious performances while still at the college—his Op. 1, the *Sinfonietta* (dedicated to Bridge), was first performed at an Anne Macnaghten/Iris Lemaire concert (31 January 1933). A proposal to study composition further with Alban Berg was thwarted.

In 1935 Britten began writing incidental music for **documentary films** produced by the General Post Office (GPO), which led to further requests for incidental music from the Group and Left Theatres. Such work was highly beneficial. Britten developed a technique for writing music of expressive immediacy often for restricted forces, a technique that he exploited subsequently when he turned to opera. Another advantage was his meeting and friendship with **W.H. Auden**, with whom he collaborated on several projects (*Coal Face*, 1935, *Night Mail*, 1936, both GPO; and *The Ascent of F6*, 1937, Group Theatre with **Christopher Isherwood**). The bitter irony heard in the orchestral song cycle *Our Hunting Fathers* (Auden, 1936) and *Ballad for Heroes* for tenor, chorus and orchestra (Auden/Swingler, 1939) can be traced in part to Britten's developing political and social consciousness at the hands of Auden, although the latter's attempts to accelerate Britten's personal development met with little success. Auden's emigration to the United States in January 1939 was, however, an important factor in prompting Britten to follow suit the following April.

Britten's two-and-a-half-year residence in the United States (prefaced by a short visit to Canada) was a period of liberation. The grief occasioned by the deaths of his parents was objectified in the *Sinfonia da Requiem* (1940), dedicated to their memory, and Britten's commitment to Pears was consummated. Two song cycles, *Les Illuminations* (Rimbaud, 1939) and the *Seven Sonnets of Michelangelo* (1940), the latter Britten's first cycle written for Pears, mark the arrival of musical maturity, although the opera *Paul Bunyan* (Auden, 1941) was not a success. The chance reading of an article by **E.M. Forster** on Suffolk poet George Crabbe not only led Britten to realize how essential his native surroundings in Suffolk were to his well-being, but also provided him with the subject matter for *Peter Grimes*, the writing of which was facilitated by a $1,000 grant from the Koussevitzky Foundation. He returned to England in 1942, completing the *Hymn to St. Cecilia* (Auden) for unaccompanied chorus and *A Ceremony of Carols* en route. On arrival Britten registered as a **conscientious objector** and was subsequently exempted from military service on condition that he took part in concerts for the **Council for the Encouragement of Music and the Arts** (CEMA).

Following the success of *Peter Grimes* and the tragic chamber opera *The Rape of Lucretia* (Ronald Duncan, after André Obey, 1946), Britten, with **John Piper** and Eric Crozier, formed the English Opera Group (1947), which was subsequently responsible for the artistic direction of the Aldeburgh Festival (1948). The comic chamber opera *Albert Herring* (Crozier, after Maupassant, 1947) was succeeded by *Billy Budd* (Forster/Crozier, after Melville, 1951), with an all-male cast and, together with the chamber opera *The Turn of the Screw*

(Myfanwy Piper, after Henry James, 1954), continued to explore the theme, characteristic of many of his opera librettos, of innocence corrupted by evil. Sounds heard during a recital tour with Pears that included Java and Bali (1955), are re-created in the gamelan effects punctuating the ballet *The Prince of the Pagodas* (1956), and a performance of the Japanese *noh* play *Sumidagawa* influenced the ethos and spare dimensions of the church parable *Curlew River* (William Plomer, 1964), which heralds Britten's late style. Before this, however, both the full-scale opera *A Midsummer Night's Dream* (Britten/Pears, after Shakespeare, 1960), and the *War Requiem* (Wilfred Owen, 1962) testify on the one hand to the richness and diversity of Britten's musical thought, and on the other to its seriousness of purpose, the requiem being an impassioned indictment of war.

Much of Britten's instrumental and vocal music was composed for particular performers, and his friendship with Russian cellist and conductor Mstislav Rostropovich (begun in 1960) was celebrated in the Cello Sonata (1961), three Cello Suites (1964, 1967, 1971) and Britten's only major orchestral work to follow *The Young Person's Guide to the Orchestra* (1946), the Cello Symphony (1963). In 1967 the scope of the Aldeburgh Festival was enlarged with the building of the concert hall at the Maltings, Snape, and although Britten's penultimate opera, *Owen Wingrave* (M. Piper, after James, 1970), another pacifist work, was written for **British Broadcasting Corporation** (BBC) television, his final opera, *Death in Venice* (M. Piper, after Thomas Mann, 1973), was first performed there. Britten was unable to conduct, having earlier in the year undergone open-heart surgery from which he never recovered fully. Only small-scale works were possible thereafter, most significantly the Third String Quartet (1975), linked both thematically and psychologically to *Death in Venice*, Britten seemingly identifying himself in the quartet with the opera's hero, Gustav von Aschenbach.

Trevor Bray

Bibliography
Carpenter, Humphrey. *Benjamin Britten: A Biography*. 1992.
Evans, Peter. *The Music of Benjamin Britten*. rev. ed. 1989.
Kennedy, Michael. *Britten*. 1981.
Mitchell, Donald, and Philip Reed, eds. *Letters from a Life: The Selected Letters and*

Diaries of Benjamin Britten, 1913–1976.
2 vols. 1991.
Stansky, Peter, and William Abrahams.
*London's Burning: Life, Death, and Art
in the Second World War.* 1994.
White, Eric Walter. *Benjamin Britten: His
Life and Operas.* 2nd ed. 1983.

Brockway, (Archibald) Fenner
(1888–1988)

Fenner Brockway was born of a long line of
missionaries in India in 1888, a pedigree that was
to become evident in any number of the radical
causes to which this tireless campaigner gave
himself over a life and career that spanned most
of the century. Brockway was nothing if not an
evangelist or crusader, albeit of the secular variety. While shedding the theology that drove his
forebears' sense of mission, Brockway nevertheless retained a zeal and an appetite for conversion
that was the match of any late Victorian proselytizer, whether it was in the service of anti-
imperialism, socialism, or world disarmament.
Brockway's intellect and passions were formed
when he was a young journalist by his contact
with many of the leading radical figures of the
pre-**First World War** period. He claimed that it
had been **Keir Hardie** himself who had converted
him to socialism, the **Pankhursts** who had made
him a suffragette, and **George Bernard Shaw**
who had given him his inspiration with a personal charge to "find out what the life force is
making for and make for it too." Brockway
joined the **Independent Labour Party** (ILP) in
1907, an affiliation and a commitment to what
he believed to be a purer variant of British socialism and that was to endure for thirty-eight years.
He became editor of the ILP paper, the *Labour
Leader*, at the age of twenty-four and held the
post until immersion in antiwar activity forced
his departure in 1917. He had been one of the
founding members of the **No-Conscription Fellowship** in 1914 and became its Secretary the
following year. His stance as a **conscientious
objector** ultimately led to his imprisonment for
twenty-eight months under appalling conditions
and at times in solitary confinement. After his
release in 1919 Brockway resumed his socialist
crusade in earnest. Replacing **H.N. Brailsford** as
editor of the *New Leader* (sucessor to the *Labour
Leader*) from 1926 until 1929, he remained a
major force behind the paper for nearly two decades. Brockway served the ILP variously as its
Organizing Secretary (1923), General Secretary

(1928 and 1933–9), representative on the executive of the Socialist International (from 1925
until 1932), and Chairman (1931–3). In 1932 he
supported the ILP's break with the **Labour Party**,
a position that he was later to regret bitterly.
During the period 1929–31 he represented East
Leyton in the House of Commons. The 1930s
saw Brockway deeply involved in anti-Fascist
activity at home and abroad, particularly in the
struggle for democratic Spain. His eventual departure from the ILP after the **Second World War**
came over the disagreement between those (like
Brockway) who believed that the Labour victory
of 1945 signaled the beginning of the realization
of a socialist utopia in Britain and those who
dismissed the election to power as a false, reformist dawn. His shift to the ranks of the
Bevanite Left of the post-war Labour Party culminated in his return to the House of Commons
as MP for Slough in 1950, a seat held until his
defeat in the 1964 general election. In Parliament
Brockway lost no opportunity to campaign for
the dissolution of the British Empire. Together
with Tony Benn, he helped to found the **Movement for Colonial Freedom** in 1954, a vocal and
highly regarded pressure group that had a considerable impact on the independence debates of
the decade that followed. After his forced retirement from the House of Commons, Brockway
carried his crusades into the House of Lords
from 1964. Continuing concern for the developing world, opposition to the Vietnam War, and,
most especially, peace activism filled his later
years as a life peer. In 1979 he founded the World
Disarmament Campaign along with Philip Noel-
Baker and served as co-chairman of the organization until 1986. A familiar and much-loved
figure at antinuclear demonstrations to the very
end of his life, Brockway was perhaps the last of
a particular breed of twentieth-century British
radicals of the pre-First World War generation—
optimistic to a fault, utterly free from cynicism,
and an unshakable believer in the perfectability
of human society and its institutions.

Brian Phillips

Bibliography

Brockway, Fenner. *Inside the Left: Thirty
Years of Platform, Press, Prison, and
Parliament.* 1942.
———. *Ninety-eight Not Out.* 1986.
———. *Towards Tomorrow: The Autobiog-
raphy of Fenner Brockway.* 1977.
Kennedy, Thomas C. *The Hound of Con-
science: A History of the No-Conscrip-*

tion Fellowship, 1914–1919. 1981.
Moorhead, Caroline. Troublesome People:
Enemies of War, 1916–1986. 1987.

Brooke, Rupert Chawner (1887–1915)

The poet Rupert Brooke was born at Rugby on 3 August 1887, the second of four children, all of whom died at an early age. His father was William Parker Brooke, Rugby schoolmaster, distinguished classics scholar, and Fellow of King's College, **Cambridge**. Rupert's mother, the dominant figure of the family, was the former Mary Ruth Cotterill, a niece of the Bishop of Edinburgh.

After attending the local preparatory school, Hillbrow, Rupert moved on to Rugby at the age of fourteen, which placed him under the direct supervision of his father, the new housemaster of School Field. Rupert was a model student who also excelled at **cricket** and rugby, but he suffered emotional conflicts, especially with his puritanical mother, on account of his **homosexual** orientation. Rupert's first recorded sexual encounter in 1909 was with Denham Russell-Smith, whom he had known at Rugby.

In 1906 Brooke went to King's College on scholarship to read classics like his father. But from first to last Brooke was a vaguely rebellious, poor to mediocre student, known best for his charm and physical appearance. He joined the **Fabian Society**, but his socialism, which he combined with **anti-Semitism** and anti-**feminism**, mixed the aims and views of Edward Carpenter, Hilaire Belloc, William Morris, and **H.G. Wells**. He found the "Simple Life" socialism of Carpenter more appealing than the "scientific" socialism of **George Bernard Shaw** and **Beatrice and Sidney Webb**. It was through the Fabian Society that he met the most important young women in his life, Katharine "Ka" Cox and the daughters of Sir Sidney Olivier, Noel and Brynhild. In the fall of 1908 James Strachey sponsored Brooke's election to the Cambridge **Apostles**. Although he barely managed a second on his classics exam, Brooke held his own with the more intellectual Apostles, including **G.E. Moore**, James and **Lytton Strachey**, and **John Maynard Keynes**.

By the summer of 1908 Brooke had become the center of a new group of Cambridge "Simple Lifers," soon to be known as the neo-pagans. Philosophically, neo-paganism amounted to little more than a mild rebellion against Victorian conventions and parental authority. In practice it meant bohemian dress, nude bathing, vegetarianism, and camping out unchaperoned in the summer. In 1909 Brooke left Cambridge for a rustic life in nearby Grantchester, determined to become "a BLOODY poet," rather than a conventional academic. But a strain of repressed sexual puritanism in Brooke had always been at odds with his boisterous bohemianism. He suffered a nervous breakdown in 1912 after an unsuccessful love affair with fellow neo-pagan Ka Cox.

In late 1912 Brooke left Grantchester for London, where with literary patron Edward Marsh he launched the immensely popular *Georgian Poetry*. The "Georgian" poets were the subjects of considerable derision in the post-war years, but the five-volume series included works of **D.H. Lawrence, Robert Graves, Siegfried Sassoon**, Isaac Rosenberg, and Edmund Blunden. In the summer of 1913, Brooke toured North America and the South Pacific. A three-month idyll in Tahiti resulted in some of Brooke's most memorable poetry. He returned to England in June of 1914. When the **First World War** broke out, Marsh arranged for Brooke to be commissioned in **Winston Churchill**'s Royal Naval Division. He was never to see combat. Brooke died of blood poisoning on the eve of the **Gallipoli** campaign and was buried on St. George's Day 1915 on the Greek isle of Scyros.

Brooke's posthumous fame rests largely on the timing of his death. He died while the war was still thought to be a glorious adventure, before the grim horrors of trench warfare had been brought home to the volunteers and the general public. His romantic war poetry captured the mood of the early months of the Great War. Rupert Brooke became the symbol of the heroic self-sacrifice of his doomed generation and perhaps something more. With the passage of time, he has become known more as an image and a symbol of an era than either as a poet or a "neo-pagan."

Gordon B. Beadle

Bibliography
Delany, Paul. *The Neo-Pagans*. 1987.
Hassall, Christopher. *Rupert Brooke*. 1964.
Rogers, Timothy. *Rupert Brooke*. 1971.

Burgess (Wilson), (John) Anthony (1917–1993)

Widely regarded as one of the foremost contemporary fiction writers in English, Anthony Burgess began his long and prolific literary career while living in Malaya, where he served as an education officer with the British colonial service from 1954 until the coming of independence in 1957. In 1949 he had written a fictional account of his wartime experiences in Gibraltar, but this did not appear as *A Vision of Battlements* until 1965. He began writing fiction during his Malayan years "as a sort of gentlemanly hobby, because I knew there wasn't any money in it." *Time for a Tiger*, his first published novel, appeared in 1956 under his *nom de plume*, which consists of his confirmation name, Anthony, and his mother's maiden name.

The son of a bookkeeper and a music hall singer, he was left motherless at eighteen months as a result of the 1919 influenza epidemic. Abundantly reflected in Burgess' fiction is his Catholic background, which is part of an ancient regional and family heritage. Burgess attended the Xaverian College in Rusholme but renounced **Roman Catholicism** at about age sixteen. Although intellectually he was convinced that he could be a freethinker, emotionally he remained very much aware of hell and damnation.

His most persistent youthful ambition was to become a composer, and when he entered the University of Manchester he wanted to study music. However, lacking the science background required by the music department, he had to take English language and literature instead. While at Manchester, he met a Welsh girl, Llewela (Lynne) Isherwood Jones, a distant cousin of **Christopher Isherwood**. They were married in 1942, and the marriage, increasingly unhappy as she succumbed to alcoholism, lasted until her death in 1968.

In 1940, after taking his degree, Burgess joined the British **army** and was assigned to the Royal Army Medical Corps. He was then sent to join a small entertainment group as a pianist and arranger. In 1943, having been transferred to the Army Education Corps, he was sent to Gibraltar, where he remained until 1946. During his first year there his wife was hospitalized in London with severe injuries resulting from a beating at the hands of American GIs, deserters bent on robbery. In time Burgess overcame the consuming rage he felt against all American soldiers, but his horror of the action itself remained undiminished and was the inspiration for the most shocking scene in *A Clockwork Orange* (1962), the brutal assault on the writer

and his wife, as well as the woman-beating incidents in *The Right to an Answer* (1960).

After Burgess was discharged in 1946 his career oscillated between music and teaching. For a time he was a pianist with a jazz combo in London and did arrangements for Eddie Calvert, "the man with the golden trumpet." Then he became a civilian instructor at an army college of education, a lecturer in an emergency-training college for potential teachers, and, finally, like the hero of *The Worm and the Ring* (1961), an underpaid senior master in a grammar school in Banbury, Oxfordshire, where he remained for four years. Discouraged and desperate, he kept applying for jobs to better himself. Then one night in a drunken stupor, he "quite unconsciously" scrawled out an application for a teaching position in Malaya and was subsequently offered a post in Kuala Kangsar.

The Malayan Trilogy, which includes *Time for a Tiger* (1956), *The Enemy in the Blanket* (1958), and *Beds in the East* (1959), is based largely on Burgess' experiences. Subsequently published in one volume entitled *The Long Day Wanes*, it encompasses not only the passing of the British Raj a year before it occurred but some of the less-happy events that were to follow the birth of Malaysian independence.

With the coming of independence, Burgess and other erstwhile colonials were deported, but he soon found another teaching post in Brunei, Borneo. In Borneo, as in Malaya, he refused to join the British colonials in their isolation from the native community. He had a perfect command of Malay and mixed freely with the people, and, at the expense of antagonizing his fellow colonial officers, he won their trust and respect. His stay in Borneo ended when he collapsed in front of a class and was rushed back to England, where doctors diagnosed his ailment as a brain tumor.

When it was decided that the tumor was inoperable, Burgess was told that he would probably be dead within the year. Thanks to shrewd investments by his wife, the Burgesses had enough money to live through his "terminal year" (1959–60), and Burgess set to work writing novels, chiefly to secure posthumous royalties. The five novels he produced—*The Doctor Is Sick* (1960), *One Hand Clapping* (1961), *The Worm and the Ring* (1961), *The Wanting Seed* (1962), and *Inside Mr. Enderby* (1963)—include some of his best work, and they were not the only things he wrote. As the novels came out, his health improved steadily, and he began to take on various nonfiction writing chores as well—music critic, drama critic, television scriptwriter. Some months after his first wife died in 1968, he married Liliana Macellari, an Italian *contessa* and a philologist and translator.

Altogether Burgess produced twenty-nine novels. The best known is *A Clockwork Orange,* a seriously philosophical, picaresque tale narrated by a demonic young hoodlum who could be either Russian or English or both. Burgess and his first wife encountered some of his prototypes, called *stilyagi,* during a 1961 visit to Leningrad, and he was struck by their resemblance to the English teddy boys of the 1950s, whom they were indeed copying. His other major novels include *The Right to an Answer* (1960), *Nothing Like the Sun* (1964), *Tremor of Intent* (1966), *Enderby* (1968), *Napoleon Symphony* (1974), *Earthly Powers* (1980), *Any Old Iron* (1989), and his last novel, *A Dead Man in Deptford*, published several months before his death on 25 November 1993. His major nonfiction books include *Re Joyce* (1965), *The Novel Now* (1967), *Shakespeare* (1970), *Ernest Hemingway and His World* (1978), *Flame into Being: The Life and Work of D.H. Lawrence* (1985), and his two-volume autobiography, *Little Wilson and Big God* (1986) and *You've Had Your Time: Being the Second Part of the Confessions of Anthony Burgess* (1990).

Geoffrey Aggeler

Bibliography

Aggeler, Geoffrey. *Anthony Burgess: The Artist as Novelist.* 1979.

———, ed. *Critical Essays on Anthony Burgess.* 1986.

Bloom, Harold, ed. *Anthony Burgess.* 1987.

Boytinck, Paul. *Anthony Burgess: An Enumerative Bibliography with Selected Annotations.* 2nd ed. 1977.

Modern Fiction Studies (special Burgess issue), vol. 27 (1981).

Butler, R(ichard) A(usten) (1902–1982)

R.A. Butler, commonly known by the acronym "RAB," was a leading Conservative politician of the post-war period. As Minister of Education (1941–5), he created the post-war system in the **Education Act of 1944**. In opposition between 1945 and 1951 he played a key role in reshaping the **Conservative Party**. As Chancel-

lor of the Exchequer (1951–5), he became a symbol of the post-war economic and social consensus known as "Butskellism." He served as Lord Privy Seal (1955–9) and was a reforming Home Secretary (1957–62). Butler was Chairman of the Conservative Party (1959–61), leader of the House (1959–61) and Deputy Prime Minister (1962–3). He completed the trio of top **Cabinet** posts as Foreign Secretary (1963–4). In 1957 and 1963 he seemed to be on the point of becoming Prime Minister, but he was thwarted both times by **Harold Macmillan**. In 1965 he accepted a life peerage as Baron Butler of Saffron Walden and became Master of Trinity College, Cambridge, a post he held until 1978.

Butler came from a family connected with both the University of **Cambridge** and imperial service in India, where he was born. He was able to enter Parliament at the age of only twenty-seven through his marriage in 1926 to heiress Sydney Courtauld. In 1929 he was elected for the safe Conservative seat of Saffron Walden, for which he sat until retiring in 1965. As Undersecretary for India (1932–7) and for foreign affairs (1938–41) Butler was at the center of the major political struggles of the 1930s. As the Foreign Secretary, **Lord Halifax,** was in the **House of Lords**, Butler became the principal spokesman in the House of Commons during the crucial pre-war period. Although not able greatly to influence policy, his prominent role as a "man of **Munich**" did him immense damage in the post-war period and contributed to his failure to attain the premiership.

Butler's two major contributions to the shaping of post-war Britain occurred before his long service in high office in the 1950s. The measure with which his name will always be associated is the Education Act of 1944, which resolved the long-standing religious complexities and framed the system that has been in place ever since. As Minister of Education Butler worked in the background of the war effort, with little interest or support from the Prime Minister, **Winston Churchill**. During the opposition years of 1945–51 Butler, as Chairman of the Conservative Research Department, played a major part in the reformulation of the party's philosophy, attitudes, and policies. He chaired the group that drafted the Industrial Charter of 1947 and forced its adoption upon an unwilling Churchill. The charter committed the Conservative Party to the acceptance of Keynesian interventionism and the **welfare state**, and it symbolized the determination to break with the image of the dole queues of the 1930s.

In 1951 Butler became Chancellor of the Exchequer and presided over decontrol and the end of rationing. His successful tenure culminated in a tax-cutting budget before the 1955 election that was widely credited with helping the Conservatives increase their majority. However, a sterling crisis and a revised budget in the autumn of 1955 tarnished his reputation, and Anthony Eden moved him from the Treasury. His role in the 1956 Suez crisis was regarded as weak and indecisive, and when Eden resigned, Butler was found to have little support in the Cabinet. He had a difficult relationship with the new Prime Minister, Macmillan, who exploited his administrative skills and prestige but also left him exposed to humiliation. Butler was laden with a mixed bag of duties, which he adroitly juggled, and was shuffled from post to post. Even so, when Macmillan resigned in 1963 Butler was the favorite to succeed him. Macmillan promoted the candidacy of the Foreign Secretary, Lord Home, and Butler failed to press his claims, to the disgust of some of his supporters. An urbane and feline character, Butler was always more of an establishment mandarin than a partisan political combatant. He was the ideal second-in-command, but many concurred in Macmillan's verdict that "he lacked the last six inches of steel" necessary for leadership. He remains, together with Lord Curzon and Austen Chamberlain, the archetypal "best Prime Minister we never had," more fascinating in failure even than in success.

Stuart Ball

Bibliography

Butler, Lord. *The Art of the Possible.* 1971.

Cosgrave, Patrick. *R.A. Butler: An English Life.* 1981.

Howard, Anthony. *RAB: The Life of R.A. Butler.* 1987.

Thorpe, D.R. *The Uncrowned Prime Ministers.* 1980.

B

C

Cabinet, The

The modern Cabinet is the product of continuous historical development, shaped by the events of this century. No statute law governs its existence, although it has been several times mentioned in legislation. Thus it possesses no independent legal standing, although in political terms it may be succinctly characterized as the supreme coordinator of national policy, always provided it enjoys the confidence of a functioning majority in the House of Commons. In fact, a historical assessment of its role in the twentieth century involves the ways in which the various Cabinets have discharged that task of coordination, a responsibility collectively shared by the ministers who compose it; chosen by the Prime Minister, nearly all Cabinet ministers bear departmental assignments as well. Prior to 1900 the Prime Minister's standing among his Cabinet colleagues was universally accepted as *primus inter pares*—that is, "first among equals."

Whether any measure of equality has survived these nine decades is open to question, in the main as a result of the roles played by, and the powers accrued by, twentieth-century premiers, but also as a function of the heavier departmental responsibilities borne by his or her colleagues. Yet the Cabinet survives, at the very least, as an oft-consulted collective associate of the Prime Minister, and its individual members discharge essential tasks of government in executing the policies agreed to by the Cabinet and accepted by Parliament. The Cabinet retains a key role in contemporary political practice, although its role is subject to the style of the Prime Minister, who need not involve the Cabinet in the resolution of all policy matters, including matters of great importance. Collective responsibility, entailing free discussion among Cabinet colleagues until a decision is reached, but thereafter mandating acceptance and defense by all, whatever their personal view, dictated that a veil of secrecy be draped over Cabinet proceedings and provided one rationale for the Cabinet's refusal to maintain a record of its proceedings until late 1916.

Since the Second World War as few as sixteen to eighteen ministers were included in Cabinets led by **Clement Attlee** and **Winston Churchill**, although after 1955 numbers were added; a typical post-1955 Cabinet would include twenty-one or twenty-two, considerably exceeding what is widely thought to be an optimal size of twelve to sixteen. In 1992 Prime Minister John Major observed conventions, naming twenty-two in all: the Premier (owing office to his leadership of the largest parliamentary party), two Treasury ministers—the Chancellor of the Exchequer and the Chief Secretary—the Lord Chancellor, the leaders of the House of Commons and the House of Lords, and sixteen others, most of whom bear the title of Secretary of State—Foreign, Home, Environment, Defence, Education, Transport, Social Security, Agriculture, Employment, Trade and Industry, Health, Northern Ireland, Wales, Scotland, Citizen's Charter, and National Heritage. Because of the vast expansion of government business, both at the departmental and the Cabinet level, the twentieth century has witnessed the development of a far-reaching network of Cabinet committees, designed to ease ministerial burdens. In contemporary parlance, these committees reduce "overload" and enable the Cabinet to concentrate upon essentials. An inevitable result is that much business is settled without recourse to the Cabinet, nor is the "appeals" mechanism an easy one for dissenters from a particular Cabinet committee's decision.

Originally, the impetus for the committee system was the deadly business of war. In late 1916 **David Lloyd George** essentially created both a new Cabinet system, including committees, and innovative Cabinet procedures; during the Second World War, Churchill presided over a major expansion of the extant Cabinet committee system. Both war premiers replaced the peacetime Cabinet model with a War Cabinet, designed to free a handful of leading ministers from departmental tasks in order to focus on basic tasks; Churchill involved himself in military matters to a much greater degree than had Lloyd George. In the interim, Lloyd George's innovative committee system had been scaled back, although, contrary to what is often asserted, it survived his own political downfall in 1922, as did certain other innovations that stamp him as the major Cabinet reformer of the century—for example, his establishment of a Cabinet Secretariat charged with keeping Cabinet minutes and managing the flow of War Cabinet and government business. Indeed, S.S. Wilson has enumerated in excess of 850 Cabinet committees for the years 1922–39, although the vast majority were *ad hoc*, and some never met.

In 1945 Attlee left no doubt that the committee system was there to stay, even as he returned to the larger peacetime Cabinet model. Thus, Cabinet committees proved a permanent addition, although governments remain extraordinarily protective about their identity and functions. In 1983 **Margaret Thatcher** went further than her predecessors in acknowledging four major standing committees (that is, permanent for her regime)—namely, Home and Social Affairs; Legislation; Economic Strategy; and Overseas and Defence. The Prime Minister chaired the latter two; curiously, a subcommittee of the last functioned, in effect, as a War Cabinet during the **Falklands War** of 1982, although the full Cabinet continued to meet. Peter Hennessy reported that at least another 156 committees were in existence at this time; most were *ad hoc*, and apparently all were supported to some degree by the record-keeping mechanism housed within what is now known as the Cabinet Office.

Cabinet committees can be differentiated functionally by composition: Ministerial committees often include ministers outside the Cabinet as well as within; official committees are composed of civil servants, often working in tandem with ministerial committees but almost certainly in command of greater detail (they played hardly any role prior to 1939); mixed committees, drawing upon ministers and civil servants, are few in number. Taken together, Cabinet committee activities constitute a well-hidden portion of contemporary Cabinet practices, although their records, for the most part, are made available with Cabinet records after thirty years.

Indeed, their ability to formulate policy at the sub-Cabinet level—even if the Cabinet does not review their decisions, they are binding under the terms of collective responsibility—constitutes a major plank in the arguments of those who contend that the Cabinet no longer plays the role of "hyphen-buckle" assigned it by Walter Bagehot in *The English Constitution*. In broadest terms, they argue, Cabinet government has given way to what is characterized as "Prime Ministerial government," and the Cabinet itself has decayed into a "dignified" element of the English constitution. The "efficient" element is centered in the person of the premier, dominating his colleagues and supported by the administrative bureaucracy, specificially the senior civil servants—particularly the Cabinet Secretary, head of the Cabinet Office—who advise the Prime Minister and answer directly to him or her. Well before Thatcher's long tenure, Richard Crossman had all but single-handedly popularized the concept of "Prime Ministerial government." Subsequently, Crossman drew upon his own experiences in **Harold Wilson**'s Labour governments of 1964–70 to compile virtually a day-by-day account of how a much-weakened Cabinet functioned. Nonetheless, the concept of "Prime Ministerial government" stands independent of Crossman's account; the major scholarly work outlining its historical development, *The British Cabinet*, had already been published by John Mackintosh in 1962. It is fair to remark that scholarly treatment of the Cabinet over the past generation has embraced the notion that the dynamic between the Cabinet and the Prime Minister has altered—some say dramatically—toward the accretion of power in the latter's dealings with ministers, whether as individuals or collectively in the Cabinet.

Yet it is also incumbent to acknowledge that several "insiders"—Crossman's own colleagues, including Harold Wilson—reject the contention that the Cabinet has been shorn of

National Government in 1931: L–R (seated): Philip Snowden, Stanley Baldwin, Ramsay MacDonald, Herbert Samuel, Lord Sankey; L–R (standing): J.H. Thomas (second from left), Neville Chamberlain (second from right).

War Cabinet in 1941: L–R (seated): John Anderson, Winston Churchill, Clement Attlee, Anthony Eden; L–R (standing): Arthur Greenwood, Ernest Bevin, Lord Beaverbrook, Kingsley Wood.

effective power and operates only as Downing Street proposes. Where Crossman reduced the present-day place of collective responsibility to that of "collective obedience . . . to the will of the man at the apex of power," Patrick Gordon Walker joins Wilson in insisting that the Cabinet discusses nearly all significant matters; further, since the Cabinet can influence, resist, and, in some cases, alter policies initially formulated elsewhere, it remains a partner in government, collectively responsible for achievements and deficiencies. "Elsewhere" in this case is not only a reference to the work of Cabinet committees; it relates as well to the contentious work of both "partial Cabinets," charged with resolving matters that are conventionally not brought to the attention of the full Cabinet—nuclear weapons policy has been so handled since 1945, with only one exception—and "inner Cabinets," best understood as informal gatherings of the Prime Minister, a few favored Cabinet colleagues, and possibly even advisers or senior civil servants, whose agreement preempts the Cabinet's role. Such alternative decision-making mechanisms are all the more important in light of the fact that modern Cabinets rarely (and, in some regimes, never) take formal votes; rather, the Prime Minister sums up the sense of the discussion and the Cabinet's decision. Obviously, the question of the Cabinet's collective responsibility remains a vital one, as is evident in Michael Heseltine's angry resignation from Thatcher's Cabinet in 1985.

Changes in the nature of twentieth-century politics and the tasks of government were bound to tell upon the pre-1916 relationship between the Premier and the Cabinet; further, it is clear that the dynamic of that relationship has altered in favor of the former, whose power to command attention has become virtually "presidential." Finally, the disposition to command attention and to dominate proceedings is to a considerable degree a function of the personality and style of the Premier: Lloyd George and Thatcher, for example, in contrast to Attlee and Stanley Baldwin. Although the controversy over whether the Prime Minister remains "first among equals" or whether, instead, the office has evolved into one different in kind from that held by Cabinet colleagues may continue, the actual changes in their relationship are a part of the events of the past three-quarters of a century.

John F. Naylor

Bibliography

Crossman, R.H.S. *Inside View.* 1972.
Gordon Walker, Patrick. *The Cabinet: Political Authority in Britain.* 2nd ed. 1972.
Hennessy, Peter. *Cabinet.* 1986.
Mackintosh, John P. *The British Cabinet.* 3rd ed. 1977.
Naylor, John F. *A Man and an Institution: Sir Maurice Hankey, the Cabinet Secretariat, and the Custody of Cabinet Secrecy.* 1984.
Wilson, Harold. *The Governance of Britain.* 1976.
Wilson, S.S. *The Cabinet Office to 1945.* 1975.

Callaghan, (Leonard) James (1912–)

A pragmatic, temperamentally conservative man of shrewd populist instincts and great professional resilience, James Callaghan was Prime Minister from 1976 to 1979. He took over the leadership of the last Labour government before Thatcherism changed the political landscape; the middle ground, which had been his natural habitat, was already breaking up as he reached the peak of his career. Unusually, Callaghan also held each of the other major offices of state: Chancellor of the Exchequer (1964–7), Home Secretary (1967–70), and Foreign Secretary (1974–6). Also rare among twentieth-century British leaders were his working-class background and his lack of a university education. Callaghan was raised by his widowed mother in a poor and strongly Baptist home; his work as a tax clerk drew him into trade union activity, which in turn led to political ambitions. Elected to Parliament for Cardiff South in 1945, he held junior positions in the 1945–51 government. In the following decade he rose to prominence as a robust moderate, more at home with the party's grass roots than intellectually with its left wing or personally with the Labour revisionists led by Hugh Gaitskell.

Callaghan's career briefly seemed destroyed by his chancellorship. Although he did much for Britain's trade balance and currency reserves, and made several imaginative (if sometimes controversial) tax reforms, he was held responsible for the long, unsuccessful fight against devaluation and for the deflationary measures it required. He rebuilt his career at the Home Office. He addressed Northern Ireland's problems with compassion, showed less sensitivity to immigration issues, and otherwise was largely indifferent to 1960s liberal opinion. He also cemented his closeness to the unions, and hence his importance to the parliamentary party, as a key opponent of the government's unsuccessful attempt to radically reform industrial relations.

As Foreign Secretary after Labour's return to power in 1974, Callaghan placed a conventional emphasis on the "special relationship" with the United States, tried with little success to deal with problems in Rhodesia and **Cyprus**, and oversaw the largely cosmetic renegotiation of terms preceding the 1975 referendum on continuing British membership in the **European Community**. He succeeded **Harold Wilson** as Prime Minister in August 1975. Lacking a clear parliamentary majority, he faced a restless union movement, a divided party, and an inflationary economy too weak to sustain levels of public expenditure. His experience and tactical skills were severely tested. He is widely thought to have acquitted himself tolerably well in adverse circumstances, until the final months of an increasingly beleaguered three years. He maneuvered deftly to form a pact with the **Liberals** to secure a working parliamentary majority. He handled his **Cabinet** skillfully, not least in securing agreement to a loan from the International Monetary Fund. The episode, however, was to many an emblem of Britain's economic decline and fading status. Callaghan was personally popular; his avuncular solidity contrasted warmly with Wilson's style. However, neither this nor his links to the unions prevented a bitter series of **strikes** in the "winter of discontent" of 1978–9 that led to an election defeat in May.

Callaghan retired from the party leadership to the back benches in 1980 and was created a life peer (as Baron Callaghan of Cardiff) in 1987. He symbolized the passing of an era in party politics. His undoctrinaire Labourism was rooted in memories of the 1930s, a strong union movement, a mixed economy promising full employment, and an extensive **welfare state**. This political orientation was steadily eroded by economic and cultural changes, shifting intellectual currents, and a growing polarization of Left and Right, which accelerated after the fall of his own government.

Steven Reilly

Bibliography
Callaghan, James. *Time and Chance*. 1987.
Hennessy, Peter, and Anthony Seldon, eds. *Ruling Performance: British Government from Attlee to Thatcher*. 1987.
Kellner, Peter, and Christopher Hitchens. *Callaghan: The Road to Number Ten*. 1976.

Cambridge, University of

In the twentieth century the University of Cambridge has become one of the world centers for scientific research and has been distinguished for its work in the fields of **philosophy, literary criticism, economics, physics,** and biological sciences. Despite genuine efforts to make the colleges of Cambridge accessible to less-affluent students, the ancient university retains a measure of the ambience of social exclusivity and privilege that defined it in the years prior to 1918.

Before the First World War Cambridge was distinguished by the presence of philosophers **G.E. Moore, Alfred North Whitehead, Bertrand Russell,** and Russell's pupil Ludwig Wittgenstein. Russell was dismissed during the war for the publication of an allegedly seditious pamphlet, and Wittgenstein left Cambridge, though he returned in 1929. More than 2,100 Cambridge men were killed in the war, among them poet **Rupert Brooke,** and 2,900 were wounded. A disproportionate number of Cambridge men lost their lives, probably because they were commissioned as officers upon enlistment, and officers were more likely to perish than enlisted men.

The war was perceived as a turning point, after which Cambridge began to evolve into a modern, meritocratic research university. In 1919 three developments marked this evolution: The Ph.D. degree was introduced, Greek was abolished as an entrance requirement, and **Ernest Rutherford** was appointed Professor of experimental physics and Director of the **Cavendish Laboratory.** The new degree marked the emphasis on graduate studies and original research that has characterized twentieth-century Cambridge, while the abolition of Greek made it easier for students from state schools or with training in scientific subjects to gain admission. Rutherford presided over a series of landmarks in experimental physics between 1920 and 1938, including the discovery of the neutron by James Chadwick, the splitting of the atom, and advances in theoretical quantum mechanics by Paul Dirac.

In 1920 a combination of misogyny and fear of admitting **women** to university governance allowed a repetition of the 1897 vote denying women degrees. In addition, places for women at the university were limited to 500, so that a man had a 90 percent greater chance of gaining admission than a woman. After 1920, when the **University of Oxford** admitted women to degrees, Cambridge's position was widely viewed as reactionary, but it did not admit women to degrees until 1948.

In the immediate post-war period Oxford and Cambridge joined the other British universities in requesting state assistance to cover their financial losses during the war and the increased costs of instruction and research, especially in the sciences. A Royal Commission reporting on the colleges' finances in 1922 resulted in the modernization of university governance. Among other administrative reforms, pensions were created to allow the oldest members of the teaching staff to retire, and women became eligible for university teaching posts.

Between the wars the number of subjects proliferated, especially in the sciences, with new teaching posts in physics, metallurgy, mineralogy, zoology, entomology, geology and geophysics, physiology, and pharmacology, among others. In addition, the first Professor of political science was appointed in 1926, and the English tripos (or field) gained steadily in popularity. Classics flourished under Professor A.E. Houseman, and **history** turned from the purely political and diplomatic to the study of social change, under the direction of Regius Professor of Modern History **G.M. Trevelyan**. In 1921 geography became a recognized field, and the Scott Polar Institute for the exploration of the Antarctic was founded in the same year.

Throughout the 1920s student politics in Cambridge were largely conservative, and more than a quarter of the undergraduates served as volunteer strikebreakers during the **General Strike** of 1926. By contrast, student and staff politics veered to the Left in the 1930s, with the participation of a small but highly visible number of Cambridge students in the **Spanish Civil War**. A genuine concern for social justice resulted in an admiration for Communism and an atmosphere of greater seriousness in debate and student life.

In the 1930s **John Maynard Keynes** theorized the need for government to use public works to lessen **unemployment**, and the study of macroeconomics developed at Cambridge. In the English faculty **F.R. Leavis** began to

develop his school of literary criticism and founded the journal *Scrutiny*. During the **Second World War** Cambridge staff worked to break the German codes, and Cavendish physicists contributed to the development of **radar** and atomic energy.

After the war the university entered a period of rapid expansion. The number of students more than doubled between 1938 and 1984. New colleges were founded and existing colleges expanded: Fitzwilliam, Churchill, and Robinson were new conventional colleges; Wolfson College was created to give a college affiliation to the university staff; Darwin and Clare Hall were established as graduate colleges, catering to the numerous graduate students whose social and educational needs were poorly served by the undergraduate colleges.

The number of places for women continued to be inadequate, although two new women's colleges, New Hall and Lucy Cavendish College, were founded in the post-war period. Lucy Cavendish catered especially to mature women returning to university after an absence and, like Clare Hall, attempted to create a community of Fellows and students by abolishing artificial distinctions such as separate dining areas for staff and students. The numbers of women at Cambridge at last rose in the 1970s, when the men's colleges began to admit women. By the 1990s all of the men's colleges were mixed, but three of the women's colleges, New Hall, Newnham, and Lucy Cavendish, had chosen to remain single-sex.

Cambridge continued its tradition of excellence in scientific research after 1945: Frederick Sanger won the Nobel Prize for his work on insulin, **Francis Crick** and James Watson discovered the structure of DNA, and advances in radioastronomy resulted in the discovery of quasars and pulsars. The student revolts of the 1960s touched Cambridge but had little long-term effect apart from the establishment of the Student Union and increased student representation on committees. More important were the university's efforts to make access more democratic and student life more comfortable and informal. In 1966 Cambridge joined the Universities Central Council on Admissions (UCCA), which coordinated applications to all British universities and replaced Cambridge's complex admissions procedure. By the late twentieth century the university's efforts to admit the most-talented students irrespective of social origin seemed to be having an effect. In 1990 the university admitted approximately 45 percent of its students from state schools, a considerable gain over the small minority admitted before 1914. The increase reflected the widening of access to **primary** and **secondary education** as well as the universities' determination to recruit students on the basis of merit alone.

Despite its academic strength and its efforts to become more accessible, Cambridge has remained, in the public mind, the preserve of the privileged student. Together with other universities, it has come under pressure from government to operate at lower cost by raising the ratio of students to teachers, modifying or even abandoning the traditional small classes.

Elizabeth Morse

Bibliography

Brooke, Christopher. *A History of the University of Cambridge*. vol. 4: *1870–1990*. 1992.

Fowler, Laurence, and Helen Fowler, eds. *Cambridge Commemorated: An Anthology of University Life*. 1984.

Howarth, T.E.B. *Cambridge between Two Wars*. 1978.

McWilliams-Tullberg, Rita. *Women at Cambridge: A Men's University—Though of a Mixed Type*. 1975.

Camden Town Group (1911–1913)

The Camden Town Group (CTG) of artists working in **London** can be identified by their objective studies of everyday life fused with a knowledge of the theories and practice of Post-Impressionism. The group grew out of, and largely formed, its identity through the Fitzroy Street Group, which had been formed in 1907 to exhibit work and provide a meeting place of artists with similar concerns. The CTG was a formalized response to existing exhibiting opportunities, in particular to the New English Art Club (formed in 1886) and the Royal Academy. Its importance is greater than its comparatively brief existence would suggest and lies in its support for the development of the modern movement in British art.

Originally designed as an expansion area for the middle and upper classes, Camden Town, a region of northwest London, had declined since the arrival of the railways, and its large houses had been divided into lodgings for a predominantly working class population.

In 1905, returning from nearly seven years abroad, **W.R. Sickert** took lodgings and a studio in the neighborhood. Life in the domestic interiors, music halls, and urban spaces of Camden Town became the subject of his painting and that of several of his associates (for instance, Sickert's *The Camden Town Murder* series of 1909, exhibited in 1911; and Spencer Gore's paintings of Mornington Crescent).

Sickert had taken his motifs from similar subjects when he was in Europe, but by 1911 he had revised his earlier style of painting after contact with younger painters, especially Gore (1878–1914). After Gore's death, evidence of Sickert's use of his methods became more pronounced. The constructed design of the decorative surfaces and the reflected color that Sickert started to use to describe the shadows also showed the influence of Lucien Pissarro (1863–1944), who had joined the Fitzroy Street Group in 1907. Sickert was significant in helping the group achieve credibility, and the example of Gore and Harold Gilman (1876–1919) helped revive Sickert's practice.

The CTG included Sickert, Gore, Gilman, Charles Ginner (1878–1952), Malcolm Drummond (1880–1945), Robert Bevan (1865–1925), James Dickson Innes (1887–1914), **Augustus John**, Henry Lamb (1883–1960), **Wyndham Lewis**, and others. Most of the artists had also been members of the Fitzroy Group, but two women artists, Ethel Sands and Nan Hudson, were excluded from the CTG specifically on the grounds of their sex.

The group's main function was as an exhibiting organization and, in addition to the three Camden Town Group shows at the Carfax Gallery, in June and December 1911 and December 1912, four of the group—Lewis, Lamb, Gore, and **Duncan Grant**—showed in the English Group section (chosen by Clive Bell) of the second Post-Impressionist exhibition in 1912–13. Most also were in the *Post-Impressionists and Futurists* exhibition at the Dore Galleries in October 1913, and the *English Post-Impressionists, Cubists, and Others* exhibition in the Brighton Art Gallery in 1913–14. The group also achieved prominence as a number of its members had solo shows in 1912 and 1913. In 1913 it enlarged its membership to become the London Group, which achieved prominence as an exhibiting society.

Nannette Aldred

Bibliography
Baron, Wendy. *Camden Town Recalled.* 1976.
Baron, Wendy, and Malcolm Cormack. *The Camden Town Group.* 1979.
Compton, Susan, ed. *British Art in the Twentieth Century: The Modern Movement.* 1987.

Campaign for Nuclear Disarmament

Launched in February 1958 by a small group of mainly established public figures, the Campaign for Nuclear Disarmament (CND) quickly became a mass movement dedicated to ending British possession of **nuclear weapons**. The CND's first peak of activity occurred in its early years; its second came twenty years later when deteriorating East-West relations, changes in NATO (North Atlantic Treaty Organization) strategy, and the defense policies of the British and American governments stimulated a new wave of protest.

The movement began as a moral crusade. Many of the CND's founders believed that unilateral disarmament would serve as an example to the superpowers and allow Britain to find a new role in the aftermath of its humiliation in the **Suez crisis** in 1956, which had revealed the nation's declining international stature. Support for the CND often represented a fusion of morality and anxiety; the movement attracted thousands who were otherwise politically inactive. The CND's leaders largely envisaged a pressure group pursuing conventional lobbying methods, and to many the **Labour Party** was a more plausible target than the **Conservative** government of the day. The movement, however, rapidly grew into a more loosely structured, broadly based coalition. The CND absorbed other recently founded groups and inherited from the Direct Action Committee responsibility for a march from London to the Atomic Weapons Establishment at Aldermaston in 1958. Such annual marches, their direction reversed in later years, became a central unifying experience in the movement. Tensions were, however, often present. The founders of the CND had no real wish to democratize the growing movement. For two years it lacked formal machinery for electing leaders or deciding policy; although decisions of its annual conference became in principle binding, the leadership was adept at remaining relatively autonomous.

In the early 1960s the CND's annual marches and rallies attracted crowds of up to 150,000. Local groups and affiliated groups in trade unions and the professions flourished, and in 1960 the movement's influence was visible in the Labour Party's temporary conversion to unilateral disarmament. However, the CND's appeal diminished as Cold War tensions eased and unused nuclear arsenals became a less-considered aspect of life. By about 1964 the CND had passed its first peak: It continued to exist as an organization but faded as a popular movement.

Events from the later 1970s stimulated a remarkable revival. A peace movement spread unevenly but powerfully across much of Western Europe, and the CND had the experience, status, and organizational framework to play the leading role in its British manifestation. The causes were several. President Jimmy Carter's decision to develop the neutron bomb and to deploy Cruise and Pershing II missiles in Europe heightened fears that the United States envisaged fighting a "limited" nuclear war in Europe. The Soviet Union's invasion of Afghanistan in 1979 increased East-West tensions. The rhetoric and policies of President Ronald Reagan and Prime Minister **Margaret Thatcher**, described as the "CND's best recruiting sergeants," contrasted sharply with the vocabulary of detente. Thatcher, determined to replace Britain's aging Polaris system with the Trident class of nuclear-armed submarines, was seen by many critics as an aggressive, willing agent for American policy.

The CND's national membership had dwindled to about 3,000 by the mid-1970s; it rose dramatically to over 50,000 in 1982 and a peak of 100,000 in 1984, with perhaps as many as 200,000 people belonging to affiliated and local groups. As in the CND's first incarnation, membership was disproportionately from the educated middle class. Although the organization is officially nonpartisan, a majority leaned to the Left; the movement influenced the Labour Party's adoption of a unilateralist stance. Numerous protests and demonstrations attracted wide publicity, enhanced by advertising campaigns and the appeal of leaders such as Bruce Kent and Joan Ruddock. At Easter 1983 100,000 people formed a human chain between two nuclear weapons factories; in October 400,000 rallied in London's Hyde Park. The government was alarmed by changing opinion polls and allocated a budget of £1 million to counter the CND's arguments.

Campaign for Nuclear Disarmament march from Aldermaston, 1961.

However, the CND was unable to transform government policy. Although public opinion about nuclear weapons was aroused and anxious, polls suggested that while new generations of weapons and American intentions were distrusted, a substantial majority remained convinced that Britain should possess a nuclear arsenal. The CND had also to deal with complex relations with other more-or-less institutionalized groups, particularly the women who sustained a long protest at the U.S. base at Greenham Common, whose fundamentalist views and unflinching determination were often caricatured by opponents as "loony Leftism." Tensions rose to a point that prevented the CND organizing any large-scale demonstrations against the arrival of Cruise missiles in December 1983. By 1984 disputes over the way forward were dividing the CND; many local groups believed that protests against particular weapons diverted attention from a more comprehensive opposition to nuclear arms. This emphasis underlay the 1986 "Basic Case" campaign, combining heavy advertising with much decentralized local activity. By then, however,

the movement's impetus was fading. After the collapse of the Warsaw Pact and the Soviet Union, the CND sought ways to avoid the slide into relative obscurity that had occurred in the 1960s. It continued to advocate that Britain abandon nuclear weapons and leave both NATO and the **European Union**. The CND describes its ultimate hope as the achievement of "a world free of all weapons of mass destruction;" it consequently supports all attempts to achieve reductions in stockpiles of not only nuclear arms but also of chemical, biological, and "massively destructive" conventional weapons. The organization's national membership in 1992 was about 55,000. Although much of its activity is decentralized, it retains a firm structure and claims to be one of the largest peace organizations in the world.

Steven Reilly

Bibliography

Byrne, Paul. *The Campaign for Nuclear Disarmament*. 1988.

Driver, Christopher. *The Disarmers*. 1964.

Marsh, Catherine, and Colin Fraser, eds. *Pub-*

lic Opinion and Nuclear Weapons. 1989.

Parkin, Frank. *Middle Class Radicalism: The Social Bases of the British Campaign for Nuclear Disarament.* 1968.

Taylor, Richard K. *Against the Bomb: The British Peace Movement, 1958–1965.* 1988.

Taylor, Richard K., and Colin Pritchard. *The Protest Makers: The British Nuclear Disarmament Movement of 1958–1965: Twenty Years On.* 1980.

Campbell-Bannerman, Henry (1836–1908)

Sir Henry Campbell-Bannerman led the **Liberal Party** to its greatest electoral victory in January 1906. His brief premiership, lasting until April 1908, launched a critical phase of British constitutional and social reform.

The Glasgow-born Henry Campbell, educated at the Universities of Glasgow and **Cambridge**, had twelve years' experience in the family firm of warehousemen and drapers before entering the House of Commons in 1868. By 1871 he was a junior minister and had acquired a longer surname as the price of a substantial inheritance from an uncle.

C.B., as he preferred to be called, was an efficient and unspectacular administrator as Edward Cardwell's Financial Secretary at the War Office and at the Admiralty under Lord Northbrook (1882–4). Displaying an unexpectedly jaunty imperturbability, he further enhanced his reputation as Chief Secretary for Ireland and then as Secretary of State for War in successive Gladstone and Rosebery ministries.

C.B.'s great gift was his modest amiability. His radical political convictions were comfortably consistent with the post-Gladstonian Liberal agenda of Irish Home Rule, church disestablishment, and curbing of the **House of Lords**. Sociable and inclined to indolence, he looked no further than the speakership by 1895. He expected **H.H. Asquith** and others to be "fully ripe" for leadership by the turn of the century, and he emphatically preferred a calmer life to the fighting vanguard role for which Lord Rosebery and other colleagues determined he should be reserved.

After the fall of the Rosebery government in 1895, the leadership of the Liberal Party as a whole was in abeyance. Several years of discord and jockeying for the succession preceded Sir William Harcourt's retirement from the Commons leadership. With Asquith declining to take up the task, C.B. was a near-unanimous second choice for what most Liberals imagined was an interim leadership of the opposition. Lord Spencer, Asquith, and the ex-Premier Rosebery all had stronger desires and better prospects of being the next Liberal Prime Minister.

C.B. proved to be a remarkably effective leader of a deeply divided party. He survived electoral defeat in 1900 and the machinations of rival imperialist and radical factions during and after the bewilderingly protracted **Boer War**. When the **Conservative** government was plunged into turmoil over **tariff reform** and education policy, C.B. skillfully focused his own forces on the weakened enemy.

In office from December 1905, in spite of maneuvers by Asquith, **Sir Edward Grey**, and **R.B. Haldane**, to deny him the premiership, he harnessed a wide range of old and emerging talent. Determined to implement a program of liquor licensing and educational and electoral reform, he set the government on a course of conflict with the power of the House of Lords. His most acclaimed achievement was the magnanimous post-**Boer War** South African settlement.

No twentieth-century Prime Minister was more popular with either his colleagues or his opponents nor more trusted by the electorate.

Cameron Hazlehurst

Bibliography

Harris, Jose F., and Cameron Hazlehurst. "Henry Campbell-Bannerman" in John P. Mackintosh, ed. *British Prime Ministers in the Twentieth Century.* vol. 1: *Balfour to Chamberlain.* 1977. pp. 43–77.

Searle, G.R. *The Liberal Party: Triumph and Disintegration, 1886–1929.* 1992.

Wilson, John. *CB: A Life of Sir Henry Campbell-Bannerman.* 1973.

Canada

Britain's relationship with Canada in the twentieth century evolved from that of mother country to relatively insignificant North Atlantic Treaty Organization (NATO) ally and trading partner over ninety years. At the beginning of the century Canada was the senior self-governing Dominion of the British Empire, having been created in 1867, and its French-Canadian Prime Minister, Sir Wilfrid Laurier (1841–1919), was an imperial statesman. Except for the 30 percent of Canada's population who were of French descent (and spoke French as their first language), the country, its institutions, and government were overwhelmingly British. In an era of large-scale immigration, Protestants from Britain were given highest priority. About 85 percent of Canada's foreign investment was British, and through Canada's Governor-General (appointed by the monarch on the advice of the Canadian Prime Minister, and always a British peer), Britain continued to exert influence in Canadian affairs. Although internally self-governing, Canada depended on Britain for much of its external capital, as well as for the conduct of its foreign affairs. Although the Cardwell reforms of the 1860s had reduced the British garrison in Canada to a minimal level, bases in Halifax, Nova Scotia, and Esquimalt, British Columbia, continued to provide valuable anchorages for the **Royal Navy**, which remained Canada's primary instrument of defence.

At the Diamond Jubilee and Imperial Conference held in 1897, Laurier was pressed by Britain to agree to the creation of an imperial council, possibly leading to a federation of the white self-governing parts of the Empire. Laurier, throughout his tenure as Prime Minister (1896–1911), remained opposed to this because of the strong opposition of French Canada, and he led the way to the creation of a sense of Canadian nationalism that frustrated all proposals for imperial federation. When pressed by Britain to send Canadian troops to the **Boer War**, Laurier allowed volunteers from English Canada to go but refused to commit Canada to a policy of supporting British wars. English Canada was very pro-Empire and would support almost anything Britain did, whereas French Canada remained deeply suspicious of anything that was not in Canada's direct interest.

Although valuing Canada as part of the Empire, Britain's efforts to curry favor with the United States led to an agreement over the Alaska boundary in 1903 that was unpopular in Canada. Britain's negotiation of this treaty led to feelings in Canada that the country should take a greater role in its foreign affairs. While continuing to press the nationalist Laurier on matters of imperial federation, the Naval Scare of 1909 also resulted in a call to the

Dominions for assistance in keeping the Royal Navy on a par with that of Germany. Laurier, ever mindful of his French-Canadian constituency, decided instead to create a separate Royal Canadian Navy that would be available for use by the Royal Navy in wartime. Although derided by the pro-British opposition, this "tin-pot" navy was created with British assistance in 1910.

As a part of the Empire, Canada was committed to war by the British declaration of August 1914 but had the option of deciding to what degree it would prosecute a war effort. English Canada rallied eagerly to the flag, whereas French Canada remained either indifferent or even hostile to fighting a war on Britain's behalf on a distant continent. Ultimately, the Canadian contribution to the Allied forces on the Western Front was significant; the Canadian Corps of four divisions numbered 600,000 men, and many Canadians also served in the Royal Navy and Royal Flying Corps. Although Canadian units were under overall British command, the Canadian government ensured that they were kept together and not split up throughout the British Expeditionary Force. Over 60,000 Canadians died on the Western Front, and at battles such as Ypres (1915) and Vimy Ridge (1917), established a reputation for fearlessness and dogged determination second to none, and were reckoned better troops on the whole than their colleagues in the British **army**. Canada also contributed substantial material such as food and war supplies. This war record gave Canada, along with the other Dominions, a greater say in the British war effort, and their Prime Ministers were given seats on the Imperial War Cabinet in 1917. They also signed the Treaty of Versailles separately, but as part of the British Empire delegation. The experiences of participation in war and the succeeding peace contributed substantially to Canadian nationalism.

The Canadian Liberal government, led by W.L. Mackenzie King (1874–1950), continued the Laurier tradition of Canadian nationalism, as opposed to the more pro-British Conservative opposition. At the 1923 imperial conference, King argued that each dominion should pursue its own foreign policy and sign its own treaties (which Canada did, with the United States in 1923, over the issue of fisheries), with only the courtesy of consultation with Britain. Although opposed by imperial federationists

C

such as **Lord Curzon**, this was clearly the direction in which the emergent Commonwealth was moving. At the imperial conference of 1926, the **Balfour** report defined the relationship of the Dominions and Britain as "autonomous communities within the British Empire" equal to each other and owing common allegiance to the Crown. This was passed into law in the **Statute of Westminster** of 1931, which ended the right of the British government to intervene in Dominion affairs without their permission. Henceforward, all owed allegiance to the Crown separately, so that **George V** was King of Canada as distinct from King of the United Kingdom. Although to many this was but a minor legal distinction, it marked the true independence of Canada. The Governor-General was now a representative of the Crown alone, not the British government; High Commissioners were exchanged between London and Ottawa as the new channel of communications. Nevertheless, Canada's final court of appeal lay with the Judicial Committee of the Privy Council, and amendments to the British North America Act of 1867, which acted as Canada's primary constitutional document, still had to be made in Westminster at Canada's request.

Although the United States was rapidly becoming Canada's most important trading partner, Canada hosted the Imperial Economic Conference in Ottawa in 1932, which introduced a series of protective tariffs within the Empire. Canada remained closely tied to the imperial system during the Great Depression, in part because of American protectionism, and continued to rely on London financiers for much of its capital. In this period Canadians such as Max Aitken (**Lord Beaverbrook**) moved in London circles as magnates of considerable power. Canadians who aspired to the elite of their country or of Britain customarily went to **Oxford** or **Cambridge**.

As a fully self-governing Dominion of the Empire, Canada chose to declare war on Germany a week after Britain in September 1939. Although French Canada, as before, was largely indifferent to the war, Canadians served in large numbers in all three services. The Canadian army (which comprised the major home defense of Britain after the fall of **Dunkirk** in 1940) later served in Italy and Western Europe. The First Canadian Army in the invasion of Normandy had both British and Canadian corps. Forty-five squadrons of the Royal Canadian Air Force served in Britain, Europe, and the Far East, and the Royal Canadian Navy helped to keep the vital convoy routes to Britain open. As a producer of food and munitions and as the center of the Commonwealth Air Training Plan, Canada played a vital role in the Allied war effort, which has tended to go unrecognized by British and American historians. Canada collaborated with Britain and the United States in the development of the atomic bomb and continued to cooperate with Britain in nuclear technology after the United States pursued its own program after 1945.

The post-war period saw a rapid decline in the importance of Canadian trade with Britain, as Canada became more closely tied to the United States and Britain moved toward Europe. Although Canada enjoyed Commonwealth trade preferences until the 1970s, this had ceased to be a major Canadian concern. As founding members of the Commonwealth and NATO, Britain and Canada cooperated closely in many areas, but with the emergence of Canada as a predominantly North American state, the ties to Britain aside from cultural links became fewer. Events such as the appointment of the first Canadian-born Governor-General in 1952 and the proclamation of a new Canadian flag in 1965 were symbolic of Canada's moves to a less British-centered society. The proportion of Canada's population of British descent fell below 45 percent as post-war immigration tended to come from Southern Europe, the West Indies, and Asia. In 1981 Britain severed its last formal authority over Canada with the passing of the new Canadian Constitution Act; Westminster still had to pass constitutional acts as requested in 1931. With the proclamation of the new constitution by Queen Elizabeth II in April 1982, common allegiance to the Crown remained the sole formal link between Britain and Canada.

David R. Devereux

Bibliography

Cowan, Helen I. *British Emigration to British North America* 1961.

Marsh, James H., ed. *The Canadian Encyclopedia.* 1985.

McNaught, Kenneth. *The Pelican History of Canada.* 1982.

Pomfret, Richard. *The Economic Development of Canada.* 1981.

Wigley, Philip G. *Canada and the Transition to Commonwealth.* 1977.

Capital Punishment

Reduction to zero of the number of crimes punishable by the death penalty ended a long historical process that began in the early nineteenth century. In 1800 approximately 200 crimes (mainly against property) were capital offenses. At the beginning of the twentieth century the number of capital crimes had dropped to four: murder, treason, piracy, and sabotage. A death sentence was mandatory when an individual was convicted of murder; judges had no discretion in this matter. Clemency from the Home Secretary sometimes, but not always, commuted the death sentence into a prison term. From 1900 to 1949, 657 people were executed by hanging, or approximately half of those convicted of murder. Application of the death penalty depended upon many factors, including gender—only 10 percent of **women** convicted were actually executed—and victim—those found guilty of murdering a **police** officer had almost no possibility of reprieve.

The abolition of the death penalty in 1965 represents a case study in parliamentary lobbying, for, throughout the century, public opinion polls showed strong support for retention of capital punishment. In 1921 the Howard League for Penal Reform made abolition a principal objective. In 1925 the National Council for the Abolition of the Death Penalty was established to act as a coordinating body for those pressure groups dedicated to the cause. Many reformers pinned their hopes for success on the **Labour Party** as the vehicle for abolition. As a result, in the 1920s and 1930s the issue did not command a place among major public policy issues.

The advent of a Labour government in 1945 heartened those who believed that abolition was close. Debate about the issue rarely touched on the rationale of deterrence; it usually focused on the essential inhumanity of capital punishment as well as the possibility of error in its application. Although corporal punishment in prisons was abolished in 1948, the death penalty remained. Only in 1955 did the issue come to the forefront of British politics. Several notable cases resulted in questioning the wisdom of the death penalty. In December 1952 two youths, Christopher Craig and Derek Bentley, were surprised while breaking into a warehouse in Croydon, and Craig, age sixteen, shot and killed a policeman. Bentley had already been in police custody for fifteen minutes at the time of the fatal shots. Bentley, age nineteen, was convicted of murder under the felony murder rule and paid with his life. Craig, the killer, was too young for execution and was sentenced to life imprisonment. The most famous case, however, was that of John Christie, who in 1953 was found guilty of murdering six women, including his wife. The problem was that four years earlier a lodger at the same address named Timothy Evans had been convicted of murdering his own wife and child and executed. Many people came to believe that Christie, who had testified at Evans' trial, had committed all the murders and that Evans, an innocent man, had been wrongfully executed.

In 1955 a newly formed National Campaign for the Abolition of Capital Punishment used these cases to question the death penalty more strenuously than ever. As a result, the Homicide Act of 1957, while not abolishing the death penalty, created categories of capital and noncapital murder. In 1965 the Abolition of Capital Punishment Act suspended the death penalty completely for a period of five years; Parliament made this permanent in 1969. Attempts in 1979, 1983, and 1988 to reintroduce the death penalty for specific offenses have failed. The gallows, so fearsome a force in British society for so long, appears, for the moment at least, to have passed into history.

Richard A. Cosgrove

Bibliography

Blom-Cooper, Louis, ed. *The Hanging Question.* 1969.

Christoph, James B. *Capital Punishment and British Politics.* 1962.

Edwards, Ruth Dudley. *Victor Gollancz.* 1987.

Tuttle, Elizabeth Orman. *The Crusade against Capital Punishment in Great Britain.* 1961.

Caricature and Political Cartooning

Between 1890 and 1914 the incisive caricatures of **Max Beerbohm**, the Scot *Cynicus,* and Aubrey Beardsley, and the caustic satire by Australian Will Dyson heralded a twentieth-century revival of caricature and political cartooning.

Between the wars **David Low**, like Dyson from the Antipodes, brought a keen outsider's political sensibility and a dramatic style that dominated newspaper political cartooning for a generation. Newspapers and magazines actively sought out caricature and comic art. In the 1930s *Punch*'s editor EVOE (E.V. Knox) encouraged his art editors, George Morrow and Fougasse (Kenneth Bird), to turn an enervated comic weekly into a showcase for modern cartooning. After the **Second World War** political cartooning diverged in style and content. In the 1950s and 1960s the Berlin-born Vicky (Victor Weisz) continued the radical tradition that Low had reworked, while the acerbic Carl Giles used a set of stock characters to do political and social satire. At the same time Ronald Searle expanded the limits of caricature, influencing most pictorial satirists since then. In the 1960s *Private Eye* encouraged more barbed cartoons than the respectable media. In the 1970s and 1980s caricature and visual satire found a wider audience, from that of the *Economist* to **television**, where *Spitting Image* and *Monty Python's Flying Circus* flayed British political culture and society with great exuberance. In the early 1990s crudely drawn, deliberately vulgar cartoon magazines such as *Viz* and *Oz* flourished, while *Punch* foundered and died.

Until the 1890s British caricature was shaped largely by the formal, emblematic, slightly bizarre style of John Tenniel at *Punch*, the incisive line of Ape (Carlo Pellegrini), and the more sycophantic Spy (Leslie Ward), both in *Vanity Fair*. The deceptively simple caricatures by Max Beerbohm, a consummate insider, made him one of the most subtle social critics of the Edwardian era. As the century ended Aubrey Beardsley in the *Yellow Book* and E.T. Read in *Punch* produced unsettling visual satire with a sexual and zany tinge. In 1901 Tenniel was succeeded as *Punch*'s political cartoonist by the more inventive Lynley Sambourne, and ten years later by the pedantic illustrator Bernard Partridge. Outsiders such as *Cynicus*—Scotsman Martin Anderson—and the colonials who worked at the *Bulletin*, Sydney's radical weekly, brought their irreverence to political cartooning in Britain. The *Bulletin*'s "graduates" included Norman Lindsay, Australia's most celebrated caricaturist-illustrator, the self-taught Phil May, whose simplified line influenced most all modern cartoonists, and the moralist Dyson. His angry full-page images of the bloated capitalist and his sympathetic rendering of the suffering masses animated Labour's *Herald* before the First World War.

During the war Dyson, Dutchman Louis Raemaekers, and most other political cartoonists turned their talents to propaganda, stridently vilifying the Kaiser and "the Huns." The war and personal loss enervated Dyson, though he generated several haunting political cartoons before he died in 1938. Meanwhile, at the *Daily Mirror* and the *Evening News*, W.K. Haseldon gently lampooned English life and times, and Poy (Percy Fearon) artlessly created a number of popular comic symbols, especially Dilly and Dally, the Whitehall civil servants; Dora, the harridan of the **Defence of the Realm Act**; and John Citizen, to replace the obsolete John Bull.

In 1919 New Zealander David Low arrived from the *Bulletin*, and he swiftly became the leading Fleet Street cartoonist. At the Liberal *Star* and **Lord Beaverbrook**'s *Evening Standard*, Low's trenchant radical politics, his striking visual and verbal satire, sense of humor, and technical mastery enlivened editorial cartooning. His caricatures and characters—an impish Beaverbrook; a complacent pipe-smoking pig farmer, **Stanley Baldwin**; ostrich-like **Neville Chamberlain** with his umbrella; a jack-booted Adolf Hitler; a cheeky Benito Mussolini; the old gasbag, Colonel Blimp; the **Cliveden Set** appeasers; and the gentle, dumb **Trades Union Congress** (TUC) carthorse—still shape our view of those troubled years. At the same time, at Beaverbrook's mass-market *Daily Express*, Sidney "George" Strube flourished. His "Little Man"—the put-upon everyman of the inter-war years—reflected the public's escapist mood.

The radical Vicky (Victor Weisz) was the most compelling political cartoonist of the 1950s and 1960s. His jagged, sharp line influenced Nicholas Garland, the leading political cartoonist of the 1980s. Giles and Jak (Raymond Jackson) replaced Strube, doing situational political and social satire in the dailies. Leslie Illingworth and Michael Cummings, who were conservative politically, produced striking, memorable black-and-white cartoons of a Britain in decline.

Influenced by modern art and the movies, cartoonists employed caricature much more effectively. Before television, newspapers and periodicals such as the *Tatler*, the *Bystander*, the *Sketch*, the *Listener*, the **New Statesman**, the *Spectator*, *Harper's Bazaar*, and especially *Lilliput* used caricaturists regularly. H.M. Bateman in *Punch* and elsewhere brilliantly exploited the comic strip as well as other aspects of comic art. Pont (Graham Laidler), in his short career at *Punch*, 1932–40, captured the English coping with the slump, the looming war, and the **Blitz**. Our perceptions of the famous and notorious in this century have been shaped by Edmund Dulac's delicate lines, Tony Wysard's elegant distortions, Richard Winnington's deceptively simple images, R.S. Sheriff's heraldic abstractions, Bill Hewinson's reveries, John Jensen's flowing figures, and the perceptive eye of Trog (Wally Fawkes). Sir Osbert Lancaster made the satirical pocket cartoon his speciality, and he had a caustic disciple in Marc (Mark Boxer). After the war Ronald Searle's zany exaggerations of people, scenes, and situations grounded in the history of caricature and a feel for the humorously bizarre, stimulated a generation of caricaturists, especially Ralph Steadman and Gerald Scarfe.

By the late 1960s most constraints were gone from the upmarket media. *Private Eye* accepted barbed images by Nicholas Bentley, William Rushton, Timothy Birdsall, and Barry Fantoni. In the 1970s and 1980s caricaturists in the British media left few prominent individuals or groups unscathed. At the *Economist*, KAL—an American, Kevin Kallaugher—caricatured the power elite. In newspapers, magazines, and on television Peter Fluck and Roger Law animated their cruelly distorted puppets of the prominent for *Spitting Image*. The *Guardian*'s satirical comic strips included Steve Bell's bitingly caustic *Maggie's Farm*, and Posy Symonds' fluent satire of the politically correct Weber family and friends. Downmarket comics filled with crude political and social satire flourish. Caricature and political cartooning are alive and well in 1990s Britain.

Peter Mellini

Bibliography

Feaver, William, and Ann Gould, eds. *Masters of Caricature*. 1981.
Godfrey, Richard. *English Caricature: 1620 to the Present*. 1984.
Lambourne, Lionel, and Amanda-Jane Doran, eds. *The Art of Laughter: Cartoonists and Collectors Choice*. 1992.
Low, David. *British Cartoonists, Caricaturists, and Comic Artists*. 1942.
Russell, Leonard, and Nicholas Bentley, eds. *The English Comic Album*. 1948.

Caro, Anthony (1924–)

By the time Anthony Caro first visited the United States in 1959–60, his sculpture had been formed for a decade by a reaction to the achievement of **Henry Moore**, for whom he had worked as a part-time assistant 1951–3. A work like *Woman Waking Up* (1956, Arts Council, London), whose form was achieved by applying material to an armature, reveals how far his sculpture was in conception from Moore's. At the time Caro had moved from the influence of the expressionist sculpture of Pablo Picasso to an attachment to the paintings of **Francis Bacon**, Willem de Kooning, and Jean Dubuffet, as well as the related contemporary sculpture of William Turnbull and Eduardo Paolozzi. By 1959 he had started to move away from figuration, with a group of abstract plaster sculptures that he destroyed in 1960. Yet, it was his experience in the United States, under a Ford Foundation grant, that was to change his sculptural orientation.

He had already met Clement Greenberg in 1958, but during his year in the United States he also had contact with painters like Jules Olitski and Kenneth Noland, who made Caro realize the importance of color and of a planar frontality and flatness. Furthermore, of decisive impact was his discovery of the sculpture of David Smith and the tradition of bolted and welded steel, which Caro extended in his own work. The result of this conversion can be seen in *Twenty-Four Hours* (1960, Tate Gallery, London), which confidently asserts his new-found approach to sculpture that was part of the modern world, not only through its choice of material and fabrication but also spatially. By abolishing the plinth, the sculpture invaded the space of the viewer, creating a more direct relationship between it and the beholder.

Caro's example revitalized British sculpture in the mid-1960s. From 1953 to 1966 and again from 1968 to 1973 he taught sculpture part-time at St. Martin's School of Art, and his discoveries were imparted to a group of younger sculptors who also taught part-time at St. Martin's—the New Generation sculptors—who included David Annesley, Michael Bolus, Phillip King, Tim Scott, William Tucker, and Isaac Witkin. Their work is characterized by an openness of form, a high-keyed sense of color, and a use of a wide range of materials.

In 1967, following the death of David Smith, Caro bought from Kenneth Noland many tons of materials that Smith had amassed for use in his sculpture. By this time Caro's work, always lyrical through the 1960s, was displaying an increasing variety of formal invention. At the beginning of the 1970s his rate of production increased, he increasingly dispensed with the application of color and often exploited the weathered surface of his material. In this way the appearance of the sculptures became less impersonal and more human, a change underscored by the new scale articulated in his *Table Sculptures* executed during this period. Over the last decade Caro has increasingly used paintings as a source for his sculptures and a more figurative element has often appeared, for instance in his *Descent from the Cross (after Rubens)* (1987–8, Modern Art Museum, Fort Worth). Another recent development has been his construction of architectural sculpture, which he has called Sculpitecture. His first piece, *Child's Tower Room* (1984), was commissioned for an exhibition by the **Arts Council of Great Britain**. This work involves the whole body—again invading the space of the viewer—and in 1987 he collaborated with his wife, Sheila Girling, and American architect Frank Gehry to construct a *Sculptural Village.*

Andrew Wilson

Bibliography

Blume, Dieter. *Anthony Caro Catalogue Raisonné.* 5 vols. 1980–4.
Hilton, Tim. *Anthony Caro, Sculpture, 1969–1984.* 1984.
Rubin, William. *Anthony Caro.* 1975.
Waldman, Diane. *Anthony Caro.* 1982.
Whelan, Richard. *Anthony Caro.* 1974.

Carson, Edward Henry (1854–1935)

Edward Carson, barrister, **Cabinet** minister, judge, and **Ulster** Unionist leader, was born in Dublin on 9 February 1854. A Trinity College, Dublin, graduate, he was admitted to the Irish Bar in 1877 and the English Bar in 1893, becoming a Queen's Counsel in 1889. He was knighted in 1900. Carson served as a Conservative MP from 1892 to 1921 and as a minister in Conservative (1892, 1900–5) and coalition (1915, 1916–18) governments. From 1910 to 1921 he was leader of the Irish Unionist bloc of the **Conservative Party**. Carson was a Lord of Appeal from 1921 to 1929, with a life peerage (Baron Carson of Duncairn). He died at Cleve Court, Kent, on 22 October 1935.

Carson was an immediate success at the Bar as both prosecutor and defense counsel. As senior Crown prosecutor in Dublin (1889–92), he zealously enforced the Crimes Act of 1887. His devastating cross-examination of Oscar Wilde in the latter's libel suit against the Marquess of Queensberry (1895) led to Wilde's sod-omy conviction and confirmed Carson's towering reputation. Carson's famous defense, in the Archer-Shee case (1910), of a naval cadet accused of theft was the subject of **Terence Rattigan**'s play *The Winslow Boy* (1946).

Carson's skill as a prosecuting attorney in Dublin, which attracted the attention of **Arthur Balfour**, led to his appointment as Solicitor-General for Ireland in 1892, and for Great Britain from 1900 to 1905. After establishing his credentials as an uncompromising opponent of **Irish nationalism** and Home Rule, Carson in 1910 succeeded Walter Long as head of the Irish Unionist bloc in the House of Commons. Carson's certainty that Ireland's economy depended on Ulster's heavy industry, and that freedom from British tariffs guaranteed the latter's health, strengthened his anti-nationalist beliefs. After declining to stand for the Conservative Party leadership in 1911, Carson committed himself to fighting Home Rule.

The **Asquith** government's introduction of a Home Rule bill in 1912, after nullifying the **House of Lords'** veto by the Parliament Act of 1911, convinced Carson that only vigorous—and, if necessary, extralegal—measures would balk Home Rule. In addition to skillful obstructionism in the Commons, Carson took the lead in raising and training an 80,000-man armed force of Ulster Volunteers (consisting mostly of Protestants) to resist Home Rule forcibly if it became law. Along with his Ulster lieutenant, James Craig, he made plans for converting the Ulster Unionist Council into a provisional government in Belfast. Carson persuaded **Andrew Bonar Law**, the new Conservative leader, to pledge support of his party for the Ulster Unionists in 1913.

Although Carson and his followers illegally imported guns from Germany and made other preparations for armed resistance to a prospective Dublin government, the Asquith Cabinet did not seriously interfere with them. The government's offer to exclude the six mainly Protestant northeast counties of Ulster from Home Rule for six years was rejected as a "stay of execution." There was a serious prospect of civil strife in Ireland, and possibly Great Britain, when the **First World War** began in August 1914.

Carson's offer of the Ulster Volunteers to the British army as a division was promptly accepted, although the same privilege was not extended to the largely Catholic National Volunteers. The Home Rule bill became law in

1914, but its operation was suspended for the duration of the war. Carson joined Asquith's coalition Cabinet in 1915 as Attorney General but soon resigned in protest against military policy. Following the Easter Rebellion in 1916 **David Lloyd George** and Carson negotiated a plan for permanently excluding from Home Rule the six Protestant Ulster counties, but the scheme collapsed. Lloyd George included Carson in his coalition government formed in December 1916, initially as First Lord of the Admiralty until July 1917, subsequently as Minister without Portfolio in the War Cabinet until January 1918. At the Admiralty, Carson acted as spokesman for the naval professionals and disagreed with the Prime Minister over many issues, notably Lloyd George's decision to use warships to convoy merchant vessels threatened by German **submarine warfare**.

After the war Carson realized that some form of Irish self-government was inevitable and concentrated on maintaining a British connection for the "Six Counties." In 1920 he threw his support behind the Government of Ireland Act, which established a separate government within the United Kingdom for Northern Ireland—ironically, a form of Home Rule. Carson retired from politics in 1921 upon receiving his judicial appointment.

Carson was a magnetic personality whom even his political enemies liked. Although a painstaking lawyer, Carson was not a successful administrator in public office. Historians dispute whether he was an effective leader of the Ulster resistance movement or a figurehead for less prominent figures.

Don M. Cregier

Bibliography
Hyde, H. Montgomery. *Carson*. 1953.
Marjoribanks, Edward, and Ian Colvin. *The Life of Lord Carson*. 3 vols. 1932– 6.
Stewart, A.T.Q. *Edward Carson*. 1981.

Cary, (Arthur) Joyce Lunel (1888–1957)
Author of seventeen published novels, two of them posthumous, British writer Joyce Cary was born in Londonderry, Ireland, where he spent his earliest summers. From these he gleaned material for two novels of childhood, *Castle Corner* (1938) and *A House of Children* (1941). Cary attended **Oxford**, with a pass degree in 1912, his time there punctuated by a period in Paris, where he intended to become a writer. He later served with the Red Cross in the First Balkan War (1912–13) and as a colonial officer in Nigeria (1914–19). In Africa he seriously attempted to write prose fiction, but it was more than a decade after he departed to live in Oxford that his first three novels appeared. *Aissa Saved* (1932), *An American Visitor* (1933), and *The African Witch* (1936) were all set in Africa and demonstrated Cary's capacity to create memorable characters, both African and British. In 1939 Cary published his most successful novel of Africa, *Mister Johnson*, in which he engaged the theme that would pervade his later work: the relentless power of the personal human imagination for good or ill.

Cary was much interested in the politics of African colonialism. In *The Case for African Freedom* (1941, rev. 1944) and *Britain and West Africa* (1946, rev. 1947), he argued for an end to colonialism but warned against a pullout that would leave the former subjects without the economic and political resources to survive. These political tracts had been preceded by *Power in Men* (1939), written for the short-lived Liberal Book Club. Here he attempted to reach an adequate definition of human freedom. He disliked the old liberal notion of liberty as an absence of restraint and insisted on freedom as an imaginative creative power that it was the duty of government to enhance. Cary's books on politics and his *Art and Reality* (1956) can be read as paralleling the themes of his greatest works, the first and second trilogies. The first trilogy, composed of *Herself Surprised* (1941), *To Be a Pilgrim* (1942), and *The Horse's Mouth* (1944), studies the relation of the creative imagination in art to the world. Here, in the character Gulley Jimson, Cary's lifelong interest in the work of William Blake is especially evident.

The second trilogy is interested in the creative imagination in politics. Composed of *Prisoner of Grace* (1952), *Except the Lord* (1953), and *Not Honour More* (1955), it was the last work that Cary published and is most impressive in its scope and complexity. *The Captive and the Free* (1959), edited from his manuscripts after his death, is all that Cary could accomplish of a trilogy on the religious imagination, planned to round off his principal thematic concerns.

Cary's trilogies are notable for the creation of powerful, eccentric characters who in narrating reveal themselves. Both present three main characters, each narrating one story and appearing as a character in the other two. The result is a tripling of perspectives, each of which points two ways—outward to the world and inward to the narrator.

For some time Cary was neglected in Britain, probably because his politics were neither fashionably left nor right, though liberal according to his own views of human imagination and freedom. His independent position, though certainly engaged with the issues of the day, was perhaps too sensible and disruptive to political cant.

In America he was sometimes criticized for the moral indeterminacy that the technique of multiple perspectives in the trilogies was said to create, the judgmental voice of an independent narrator never being heard. Others argued that Cary's method was deeply concerned with an ethic of personal integrity and creativity centered in the notion of a freedom to which human beings are inevitably condemned. It was this paradox to which Cary continually returned in his novels.

Hazard Adams

Bibliography
Adams, Hazard. *Joyce Cary's Trilogies: Pursuit of the Particular Real.* 1983.
Bishop, Alan. *Gentleman Rider: A Biography of Joyce Cary.* 1988.
Foster, Malcolm. *Joyce Cary: A Biography.* 1968.
Mahood, M.M. *Joyce Cary's Africa.* 1964.

Catholicism
See ROMAN CATHOLICISM

Cavendish Laboratory
The Cavendish Laboratory houses the Department of Physics of the University of Cambridge. The site of some of the most consequential scientific work of the last hundred years—including the discovery of the electron (1897), the artificial splitting of the atom and the discovery of the neutron (1932), the elucidation of the struture of DNA (deoxyribonucleic acid) (1953), and the discovery of pulsars (1967)—the Cavendish Laboratory has been the training ground for more than twenty Nobel Prize winners in the course of the twentieth century. Perhaps because of popular writings like J.D. Watson's book *The Double Helix* (1968), the laboratory has enjoyed a significant cultural presence outside the boundaries of fundamental science—for example, in the domains of history and literature, where it has often been used as the institutional embodiment of scientific expertise.

Established in 1871 and opened in 1874, the Cavendish Laboratory was financed by the university's Chancellor, the seventh Duke of Devonshire (1808–91), who gave it his own family name. Under the first two Cavendish Professors of Experimental Physics, James Clerk Maxwell (1831–79, Cavendish Professor 1871–79) and John William Strutt, the third Baron Rayleigh (1842–1919, Cavendish Professor 1879–84), researchers at the laboratory worked on the determination of electrical standards. In the early years of the twentieth century, in the wake of the discoveries of x-rays (1895) and radioactivity (1896), Joseph John Thomson (1856–1940, Cavendish Professor 1884–1919) brought the laboratory international repute for his research into the constitution of electricity and matter. The laboratory also achieved recognition for its development of scientific instruments such as C.T.R. Wilson's (1869–1959) cloud chamber and F.W. Aston's (1877–1945) mass spectrograph.

While Thomson's pupil and successor, New Zealander **Ernest Rutherford** (1871–1937, Cavendish Professor 1919–37) devoted many of the laboratory's resources to his own specialist field of research, radioactivity and the study of the atomic nucleus, he also fostered the study of atmospheric physics under E.V. Appleton (1892–1965) and J.A. Ratcliffe (1902–89), research into low-temperature physics by P. Kapitza (1892–1982) for whom the Royal Society Mond Laboratory was opened in 1933, and x-ray crystallography. As a leading spokesman for British science, Rutherford did much to consolidate and strengthen the position and influence of Cavendish **physics** in the Empire. Many of his students—**P.M.S. Blackett**, J. Chadwick (1891–1974), and J.D. Cockcroft (1897–1967) among them—subsequently achieved distinction as physicists, scientific administrators, and policymakers.

After the Second World War, during which many Cavendish physicists contributed to the development of **radar** and **nuclear weapons**, William Lawrence Bragg (1890–1971, Cavendish Professor 1938–53) initiated and encouraged new lines of research at the laboratory, including molecular biology under M.F. Perutz (1914–) and J. Kendrew (1917–) and radioastronomy under M. Ryle (1918–84, Astronomer Royal 1972–82).

During the 1960s and 1970s, under the successive professorships of Nevill Mott (1905–, Cavendish Professor 1954–71) and Brian Pippard (1920–, Cavendish Professor 1971–82) the laboratory continued to expand and diversify in terms both of space and personnel, reflecting the importance attached to science in post-war culture. In 1974 the laboratory moved to a new site in West Cambridge to make room for further expansion. Under Sir Sam Edwards (1928–, Cavendish Professor 1984–), its research is concentrated in five fields: condensed-matter physics, radioastronomy, high-energy physics, laboratory astrophysics, and energy research.

A new Interdisciplinary Research Centre for the study of superconductivity was opened in 1991, indicating that at the end of the twentieth century, as at the beginning, the Cavendish Laboratory remains at the forefront of research in physics.

Jeffrey A. Hughes

Bibliography

Crowther, J.G. *The Cavendish Laboratory, 1874–1974.* 1974.

Cecil, Robert Gascoyne (1864–1958)

Lord Robert Cecil was a **Cabinet** minister and statesman and one of the architects of the **League of Nations**. His parliamentary career spanned fifty-two years (1906–58), and he served in three Cabinets, but Cecil is most notable for his involvement in the creation of the League of Nations at the Versailles Peace Conference (1919). He obtained a peerage in his own right as Viscount Cecil of Chelwood (1923) and was a recipient of the Nobel Peace Prize (1937).

Born to politics as the third son of the third Marquess of Salisbury, Britain's three-time Prime Minister (1885–1902), Cecil was educated at Eton and **Oxford**, where he was President of the Union (1885). He was called to the Bar (1897) and married Lady Eleanor Lambton, daughter of the Earl of Durham (1899). Cecil became a King's Counsel (1899) and practiced before the parliamentary Bar prior to entering the House of Commons as Unionist MP for East Marylebone (1906).

In the 1906–10 Parliament, Cecil led the Unionist Free Traders against **tariff reform**. Cecil's fidelity to free trade contributed to his defeats at the two elections of 1910, at Blackburn in January and at Wisbech in December. Politically ostracized, Cecil attempted to create an Independent Conservative Party to challenge a vacancy in South Kensington (1911). His rebellion prompted the **Conservative Party** to endorse his return to the Commons as its member for Hitchen (1911). In the 1906–14 Parliaments Cecil associated with the die-hard Conservatives who opposed Irish Home Rule, reform of the **House of Lords**, and disestablishment of the Welsh Church. Yet he also championed the progressive causes of **women's suffrage**, labor copartnership, and the independence of members from party pressure.

At the start of the **First World War** Cecil headed the British Red Cross Department of Wounded and Missing. He joined the government as Undersecretary for Foreign Affairs (1915) and became Minister of Blockade (1916–18). Cecil drafted and circulated to the Cabinet a memorandum advocating the establishment of a League of Nations (1916), later attending the Versailles Peace Conference as Chairman of the Supreme Allied Economic Council and Britain's chief delegate on the League of Nations Covenant Committee (1919). Cecil and President Woodrow Wilson worked together in writing the League of Nations Covenant and incorporating it into the Versailles treaty.

Cecil thereafter devoted his career to the League. He first served as a League delegate for the Dominion of South Africa (1919), and Prime Minister **Stanley Baldwin** appointed Cecil as minister in charge of League affairs (1923). He resigned from office over the failure of the Anglo-American Naval Disarmament Conference (1927), but **Arthur Henderson**, Foreign Secretary in the second Labour government, reappointed Cecil as delegate to the League in 1929. Cecil tirelessly promoted the League in Britain, Europe, and North America. At home he co-founded the **League of Nations Union** and organized the Union's famous and controversial **Peace Ballot** (1934–5), in which the vast majority of over 11 million respondents supported the League. He helped organize the International Peace Campaign (1936) and launched a "Save the League: Save the Peace" declaration in the British **press** (1937). Cecil also made several speaking tours to promote the League in Canada, the United States, Germany, and Italy.

Cecil's achievement as an international statesman overshadowed his long parliamentary career. He was a leading progressive Conservative in the Commons before 1914 and a respected independent Conservative in the Lords after 1923.

Gary M. Stearns

Bibliography
Cecil, Lord Robert. *All the Way.* 1949.
———. *A Great Experiment.* 1941.
Rose, Kenneth. *The Later Cecils.* 1975.

Censorship

Censorship in Britain in the twentieth century has been the obverse of **propaganda**. Propaganda is the art of inducing people to leap to conclusions without first examining the evidence; censorship, by denying access to certain kinds of information in the name of morality, national defense, or the public good, helps shape perceptions of reality that may or may not be accurate but continue or enhance a particular set of standards or values the propagandist and censor intend to impose upon the society generally. Censorship has involved principally the mass media—broadcasting (radio and **television**), film, and print (books, magazines, and newspapers)—although controversy has erupted from time to time in the arts. The 1960s musical *Hair* came in for much criticism on grounds of obscenity when it opened in London, for example. Pornography has always been the target of censorship of the arts, along with "obscene language" and "indecent exposure."

Parliamentary legislation affecting censorship has included the 1904 Wireless Telegraphy Act, which gave licensing power for broadcasting to the government; the 1908 (revised in 1953) Post Office Act aimed at curbing indecent or obscene matter; the **Defence of the Realm Act** (DORA) in 1914, designed to limit enemy access to vital wartime information; the 1917 **Venereal Disease** Act, which suppressed publications about such disease; the 1934 Contraceptives Act, which restricted the sale of contraceptives; the 1955 Harmful Publications Act, intended to protect children from obscene material; the 1968 Theatres Act, limiting what could be done on stage; and the 1968 Race Relations Act, prohibiting public notices or advertisements suggesting racial discrimination.

The **film industry** and broadcasting imposed self-censorship in order to promote certain values and standards. In the former instance, British filmmakers created the British Board of Film Censors (BBFC) in 1912 to restrict what could be depicted on film. These limits affected such subjects as religion, politics, the military, social standards, language, sex, crime, and violence, the Royal Family, Jesus Christ, and foreign heads of state—that is, Christ could not be portrayed on film, and statesmen could not be portrayed negatively. Films also were obliged to avoid using profanity, explicit **sexuality**, and political controversy.

Censorship of the **British Broadcasting Corporation** (BBC), a government-owned monopoly though independent of the government, was established by its first Director-General, Sir **John Reith**. He believed that the BBC should enhance public morality through programs that catered to conventional Christianity, paid homage to the Royal family, and avoided reference to atheism, spiritualism, Marxism, family planning, **homosexuality, abortion**, or drugs. Even in "public service" broadcasting, Reith's BBC ignored non-Christians or those whose views and/or life-styles were outside the mainstream of British society. These strictures remained on BBC broadcasting until the Independent Television Authority challenged the BBC monopoly and presented controversial topics in the 1960s. The corporation soon followed suit.

Censorship in peacetime concerned public morals. In wartime it dealt with public morale and safety and, at the same time, despite occasional grumbling, was generally more acceptable than in peacetime. In 1914 under DORA, which extended for censorship purposes of the Official Secrets Act of 1911, it was an indictable offense to publish information of value to the enemy. Censors examined items concerning the war and issued D (Defense) Notices if they did not pass scrutiny.

At first, journalists resented the limits imposed upon their right to present war news openly and freely. In time, however, the censors learned to work with journalists, granting limited but direct access to the front, the fleet, munitions factories, prisoner-of-war camps, and interviews with leading war personalities; in exchange the press refrained from publishing what the government deemed harmful while at the same time publishing "official" information. The British **press** became an accomplice to official propaganda, by censoring itself in line with official policy. Censorship could not disguise the harsh realities of **rationing** or military defeats, but, abetted by the press, it could foster a false impression of what the front was like, which weakened the appeal of **pacifists** and other dissenters. The censors also helped bring America into the war by controlling what passed between Britain and the United States through journalists and others. Britain had the only access from Europe to the transatlantic cable, which made the control relatively easy.

Censorship in the **Second World War** followed similar patterns. At first, to quote American journalist Quentin Reynolds, the censors were "petty, absurd, and tyrannical." Then after 1941 when Brenden Bracken became Minister of Information and censorship returned to ministry control, the press was treated with greater trust, and mutual respect between censor and journalist developed much as it had after 1915. Meanwhile, the censors also examined films and broadcasts—a censor sat in the BBC studio with a finger on the cut-off button—and all materials printed or otherwise leaving or entering the country, such as cables, letters, articles, and films, all with an eye toward protecting the British war effort.

Robert Cole

Bibliography

Aitken, Jonathan. *Officially Secret.* 1971.
Pronay, Nicholas, "The Political Censorship of Films in Britain between the Wars" in Nicholas Pronay, and D.W. Spring, eds. *Propaganda, Politics, and Film.* 1982.
St. John-Stevas, Norman. *Obscenity and the Law.* 1956.
Tribe, David. *Questions of Censorship.* 1973.
Whitehouse, Mary. *Cleaning Up TV: From Protest to Participation.* 1967.

Chamberlain, (Joseph) Austen (1863–1937)

Born on 16 October 1863, the eldest son of the prominent Birmingham politician Joseph Chamberlain, Austen Chamberlain was groomed from an early age for a career in politics. He entered Parliament in 1892 as the Unionist member for Worcestershire East and, after 1914, held his father's seat, as Conservative member for Birmingham West. Benefiting from his family connections, Chamberlain's political rise was rapid. He gained his first Cabinet seat in 1900 as Postmaster-General and went on to serve twice as Chancellor of the Exchequer (1903–5, 1919–21), Secretary of State for India (1915–17), Lord Privy Seal (1921–2), and First Lord of the Admiralty (1931). In a parliamentary career that spanned forty-five years, he came within reach of the premiership in the early 1920s but saw it slip out of his hands because of his support for continuation of **David Lloyd George's** coalition government. Chamberlain's most productive period was his tenure as Foreign Secretary (1925–9) in **Stanley Baldwin's** second government, during which he negotiated the **Locarno Pact** (1925). After 1931 he assumed the role of backbencher and elder statesman.

Chamberlain's political career was conducted in the shadow of his famous father, an influential and powerful force in British politics in the decades before the First World War. Expected to follow in his father's footsteps, educated at Rugby and **Cambridge**, Chamberlain entered Parliament in the early 1890s and, benefiting from the family name, found rapid advancement to a post in the **Cabinet**. He nearly gained the leadership of the **Conservative Party** in 1911 but gave way to **Andrew Bonar Law** in the interest of party unity. The outbreak of war brought a seat in Lloyd George's War Cabinet. After the war Bonar Law's ill health led to Chamberlain's leadership of the Conservative Party and the House of Commons. Dissatisfied with Lloyd George's government, Conservative backbenchers met at the Carlton Club (19 October 1922) to vote against continuing the coalition. Chamberlain's support for its continuation cost him the party leadership and his chance at the premiership.

The rift that separated Chamberlain from the party was mended when he was asked by Baldwin to serve as Foreign Secretary. Meeting with his French and German counterparts, Chamberlain played a central role in negotiating the Locarno Pact (1925). Britain and Italy guaranteed Germany's western frontiers with Belgium and France, while other nonaggression pacts were concluded between Czechoslovakia and Poland. Yet no similar guarantees were forthcoming for Germany's eastern frontiers. While pro-French in sentiment, Chamberlain was convinced of the need to bring Germany back into the community of nations. For his efforts, Chamberlain received a Nobel Peace Prize and a knighthood. Contrary to expectations, the Locarno Pact failed to have any lasting impact. The hopes of building a new concert in Europe were rapidly overtaken by the events of the 1930s.

The fall of Baldwin's government in 1929 marked the decline of Chamberlain's political fortunes. With the formation of the all-party National government, he was offered the Admiralty rather than the preferred **Foreign Office.** Chamberlain retired to the back benches after the 1931 general election in hopes of clearing a path for the advancement of his stepbrother (**Neville Chamberlain**) to the chancellorship. In the aftermath of the political debacle of the abortive **Hoare-Laval Pact** (1935), Baldwin offered Austen the Foreign Office, but he declined the invitation. He found consolation in the successful political career of his brother. Chamberlain's death on 16 March 1937 came just months before Neville succeeded Baldwin as Prime Minister.

Throughout his public life Chamberlain was dogged by unfavorable comparisons between himself and his father. While father and son bore a remarkable similarity in dress and outward manner, Chamberlain lacked his father's political ambition and skill. His aloofness and arrogance worked to prevent him from rising to the top. While Chamberlain was noted for his sense of duty and loyalty, these same characteristics cost him the premiership in 1922 when he supported Lloyd George against the rank and file of the Conservative Party. Prepared for greatness, Chamberlain never managed fully to live up to expectations.

Van Michael Leslie

Bibliography

Chamberlain, Austen. *Down the Years. 1934.*
————. *Politics from the Inside: An Epistolary Chronicle, 1906–1914.* 1936.
Dutton, David. *Austen Chamberlain: Gentleman in Politics.* 1985.
Petrie, Charles. *The Chamberlain Tradition.* 1938.
————. *The Life and Letters of the Right Hon. Sir Austen Chamberlain.* 2 vols. 1939–40.

Chamberlain, (Arthur) Neville (1868–1940)

A Conservative politician associated with the policy of **appeasement** in the 1930s, Neville Chamberlain was educated for a career in business, entering local politics in Birmingham prior to the First World War. He served as Lord Mayor of Birmingham (1915–16) until he resigned to become Director-General of National Service (1916–17) under **David Lloyd George.** After the war Chamberlain entered Parliament

and achieved a solid record as Postmaster-General (1922–3), Paymaster-General (1923), Minister of Health (1923–4, 1931), and Chancellor of the Exchequer (1931–7). After succeeding **Stanley Baldwin** as Prime Minister (1937–40), Chamberlain confronted a deteriorating international situation. His response was the adoption of a dual policy of negotiation and rearmament. With the outbreak of war on 1 September 1939, he continued as a much criticized wartime leader. The failure of the Norwegian campaign galvanized opposition to Chamberlain's conduct of the war and led to his resignation on 10 May 1940.

Chamberlain was the second son of the noted Birmingham politician Joseph Chamberlain. Throughout his public life Chamberlain was influenced by a family background that stressed politics and public service. While his older stepbrother (**Austen Chamberlain**) was groomed for politics, Chamberlain found himself sent instead into business. Educated at Rugby and Mason College, Birmingham, he began a career as an accountant, which was interrupted by his father's plan to recoup financial losses by growing sisal in the Bahamas. This scheme was doomed from the start by the poor soil of the islands and the low market value of sisal. Chamberlain's seven years as a planter on remote Andros Island reinforced his natural tendency toward aloofness.

On returning to England in 1897, Chamberlain took up the life of a successful businessman, managing a number of local companies in Birmingham. He served on the Birmingham City Council at the age of forty-two and was elected Lord Mayor four years later. Chamberlain's time in municipal politics earned him a reputation for innovation and reform. He made important contributions in the areas of health care and **town planning,** a record that led to his appointment in Lloyd George's government as Director-General of National Service in charge of mobilizing civilian manpower for industry. The ill-defined duties and powers of the post, combined with the personal hostility of the Prime Minister, led to his resignation and a lifelong animosity between Chamberlain and Lloyd George.

In 1918, nearing fifty, Chamberlain entered Parliament as the Conservative member for Ladywood, Birmingham. The fall of Lloyd George's coalition government in 1922 opened the way for rapid advancement under **Andrew Bonar Law** and Baldwin. In little more than a

A GREAT MEDIATOR

John Bull. "I've known many Prime Ministers in my time, Sir, but never one who worked so hard for security in the face of such terrible odds."

"A Great Mediator" (Bernard Partridge, *Punch*, 5 October 1938). This was published one week after the Munich Conference. *Punch* subsequently adopted a more anti-appeasement stance.

year Chamberlain served as Postmaster-General, Paymaster-General, Minister of Health, and Chancellor of the Exchequer. He gained a reputation as a man who could get things done. Chamberlain was responsible for the Housing Act (1923) and the Local Government Act (1929). He reorganized the Conservative Central Office and headed the Conservative Research Department. **Winston Churchill** referred to Chamberlain as the "packhorse" of the administration.

In the National government that took office in 1931 Chamberlain returned to the Treasury, where he dealt with a range of difficult economic issues, sponsoring the introduction of a 10 percent general tariff and welfare reform. His position as Chancellor also placed him in the forefront of the debate over rearmament and foreign policy. Chamberlain urged an appeal to the country in the 1935 general election on the issue of defense but was overruled by Baldwin. Arguing that rearmament must be selective and paced so as not to damage the recovery of the weak British economy, Chamberlain pressed for expansion of the **Royal Air Force**. His efficiency, energy, and willingness to take the lead on important policy matters marked him as the heir to Baldwin.

Once in office as Prime Minister, Chamberlain found his plans for economic recovery and social reform sidetracked by the need to deal with the growing threats to peace posed by the Fascist dictators and Japan. Chamberlain's appeasement policy stressed the removal of grievances through negotiation and the buildup of an effective deterrence through selective rearmament. He tried to renew good relations with Japan and worked to separate Benito Mussolini from Adolf Hitler. Faced with the need to defend a global empire with limited resources, Chamberlain viewed appeasement as a pragmatic policy in line with British interests.

The zenith of appeasement came during the crisis over the Sudetenland. After the absorption of Austria in early 1938, Hitler demanded self-determination for the German-speaking minority of the Sudetenland. Convinced that Britain was not prepared for war, Chamberlain made a series of sensational trips to Germany to attempt to end the crisis peacefully. Meeting with Hitler on 15 September 1938, and then again on 22 September, he sought to reach a negotiated settlement. After the discussions broke down due to Hitler's demands that Germany annex the Sudetenland without delay,

last-minute efforts by Mussolini led to the **Munich Conference**. The Munich agreement (30 September 1930) saved the peace by turning over the Sudetenland to Germany at the expense of Czechoslovakia. While Chamberlain was hailed as the savior of peace, hopes were shattered by Hitler's invasion of the rump Czech state (March 1939). Britain responded by issuing ill-considered unilateral guarantees to the nations of Central and Eastern Europe threatened by German aggression while attempting to negotiate an alliance with the Soviet Union.

With the advent of war, Chamberlain continued to serve as Prime Minister with limited success. His war ministry was hampered by the refusal of the **Liberal Party** and **Labour Party** to serve under him, although his harshest pre-war Conservative critics, **Anthony Eden** and Churchill, were taken into the government. Britain adopted a defensive strategy that called for the continuing buildup of the armed forces and the avoidance of offensive action based on the belief that, in a long war, superior Allied resources would prevail over Germany. Confident of victory, Chamberlain proclaimed in April 1940 that Hitler had "missed the bus." But rising public and political pressure forced the government to adopt a more active strategy that led to Allied efforts to block the flow of iron ore from Scandinavia to Germany. The subsequent German invasion of Norway and the failure of British forces to stop the Nazi conquest of Norway opened the way for the fall of Chamberlain's government. Labourites, Liberals, and dissident Conservatives came together to topple Chamberlain from power. After a series of heated debates, the government majority fell from 240 to 81. Chamberlain resigned on 10 May 1940, to make way for an all-party government under the leadership of Churchill. He continued in the government as Lord President of the Council and leader of the **Conservative Party** until failing health forced his resignation. Following a series of operations, Chamberlain died of cancer on 9 November 1940.

History has not treated Chamberlain kindly. Branding him as one of the "guilty men" of the 1930s, his critics have charged that he pursued an appeasement policy that only served to encourage aggression, led Britain into a war that it was unprepared to fight, and directed the war effort ineptly. While these charges all contain elements of the truth, Chamberlain's contributions to social reform, his role in building up the Royal Air Force, and the administrative efficiency shown in preparing Britain to wage total war, not to mention the successful transition from peacetime to wartime administration that laid the foundation for Churchill's success, mark Chamberlain as something less than the failure his critics have depicted him to be. In retrospect, his greatest failure was the inability to grasp fully the nature of the threat posed by Hitler. Not even Hitler, Chamberlain believed, could contemplate a massive war of destruction that might leave Europe and Germany in ruins. But if he had illusions about Hitler and the nature of the next war, his illusions were shared by the majority of the British people until the debacle of **Dunkirk** and the fall of France.

Van Michael Leslie

Bibliography

Charmley, John. *Chamberlain and the Lost Peace.* 1989.

Dilks, David. *Neville Chamberlain: Pioneering and Reform, 1868–1940.* vol. 1. 1984.

Feiling, Keith. *The Life of Neville Chamberlain.* 1946.

Macleod, Iain. *Neville Chamberlain.* 1961.

Parker, R.A.C. *Chamberlain and Appeasement: British Policy and the Coming of the Second World War.* 1993.

Chatham House

The Royal Institute of International Affairs, better known as Chatham House after its address in St. James' Square (the former London residence of the Earl of Chatham), was the first private organization set up in Britain to study comprehensively international relations. Though similar organizations later arose, Chatham House remains the most prestigious British forum for the impartial discussion and analysis of events and trends in world affairs.

The origins of Chatham House date to the Paris Peace Conference of 1919. Certain members of the British delegation, including Lionel Curtis, **Lord Robert Cecil**, Eyre Crowe, and J.W. Headlam-Morley, were anxious to perpetuate the stimulating exchange of views and ideas they were experiencing. Consequently, a meeting was held in May 1919 at the Hotel Majestic to consider forming a private organization for the ongoing study of international relations, and after a number of further meetings, the British Institute of International Affairs came into being in July 1920.

The founding members agreed that the organization should remain nonpartisan and avoid appearing as a lobby group, while still favoring international cooperation. The peace conference itself became the first subject of study for the new organization, a multivolume *History of the Peace Conference of Paris*, written by individuals with firsthand experience, being completed in 1924. In the same year Arnold Toynbee agreed to take on the task of writing detailed annual surveys of international affairs, studies that lasted, under various authors, into the 1960s. In 1926, through the influence of certain prominent members, Chatham House became the Royal Institute of International Affairs (RIIA).

Funded by subscription and private donations, the work of the RIIA in the inter-war years came to include most of the activities for which it is known today: the journal *International Affairs*; group and individual studies of regional problems or particular aspects of international relations; a comprehensive and current library and press cutting service; international conferences to encourage the exchange of information and ideas; and invitations to prominent figures in international affairs to come and give a talk at Chatham House. Frank and open discussion was sought by keeping these talks private: the **press** was excluded, and those present agreed not to make public anything that might be construed as sensitive information—the origin of the term "Chatham House rules."

In August 1939 Toynbee, then Director of Studies at Chatham House, persuaded a reluctant **Foreign Office** to enlist the expertise of the RIIA in the form of a Foreign Research and Press Service. Its influence, however, was minimal, and after the war the formal link with British foreign policy-making was severed. In the post-war decades Chatham House continued its wide range of activities and studies, its growing prestige enabling it to enlist many heads of state and other prominent figures as patrons and speakers. The scale of its current work and sponsorship can be gathered from the size of its annual budget—over £2 million in 1990.

S.P. MacKenzie

Bibliography

King-Hall, Stephen. *Chatham House: A Brief Account of the Origins, Purposes, and Methods of the Royal Institute of International Affairs.* 1937.

McNeill, William H. *Arnold J. Toynbee: A Life.* 1989.
RIIA Annual Reports, 1922–1990.

Chemistry

The history of chemistry in Britain in the early twentieth century, as in the world at large, was closely linked to the history of **physics**, and it would be difficult to classify some studies, such as those on radioactivity and atomic structure, as belonging solely to either domain. Nonetheless, British physicists and chemists have also had quite self-conscious professional identities, the chemists usually dating theirs to the founding of the Royal Institute of Chemistry in 1877. By 1900 several chairs of chemistry existed in British universities (the University of London B.Sc. in chemistry dates from 1858). University College London (UCL) and the universities of Glasgow and **Cambridge** have had a worldwide reputation for chemical research and teaching throughout the century. In the first decade of the century British chemistry in virtually every respect was much less formidable than its Continental, especially German, counterparts, most British chemists gaining their degrees at European universities. Since the Second World War British chemistry, both industrial and academic, has stood somewhat in the shadow of American chemistry as evidenced by the fact that two of the Nobel Prizes for chemistry awarded to British nationals since 1945 were given for work done in America, notably that on chemical structure that earned Geoffrey Wilkinson the prize in 1973. In the second half of the century much of the most acclaimed British chemical work has been inseparable from biochemistry and **medical research**. Frederick Sanger's 1958 Nobel Prize for Chemistry, for instance, was awarded for work on the structure of insulin.

The **First World War** quickly illuminated the deficiencies of the British chemical industry. Dyestuff production, for example, was almost entirely dependent on German chemistry. In response, the wartime government promoted research into, and manufacture of, the basic chemicals used in dying and explosives. After the war the still-shaky British industry witnessed a series of mergers, again in response to German developments (especially the creation of IG Farbenindustrie), of which the formation of Imperial Chemical Industries (ICI) in 1926 was by far the most significant. In 1927 **Alfred Mond** set up a research council at ICI to link research in the universities and the chemical industries. The British chemical industry in these years was the parent to several significant synthetic medical compounds. In the 1930s the English pharmaceutical company May and Baker synthesized several of the first effective sulphonamides, and in 1944 ICI produced *Paludrine*, an antimalarial. British chemists first established the formula of penicillin.

Radioactivity and atomic constitution were two areas before the Second World War that witnessed significant contributions by British chemists working in academic environments. William Ramsay, Professor of chemistry at UCL, received the Nobel Prize for his discovery of the inert gases in 1904, the same year that Lord Rayleigh received the prize for physics. Between 1904 and 1919 Frederick Soddy at the University of Glasgow, and then Aberdeen, was acknowledged as the world expert in radiochemical research. Soddy helped elucidate the nature of isotopes, work for which he received the Nobel Prize in 1921. The following year it was received by Francis William Ashton, who, while at Cambridge, isolated more than 200 natural isotopes. In 1913 at the University of Manchester H.G.J. Moseley, using x-rays, first determined atomic number in terms of excess positive charge on the nucleus. This fundamental work revealed gaps in the periodic table, leading to the discovery of new elements. At about the same time new ideas about atomic structure—the **Rutherford** atom—were employed in the development of new theories of chemical bonding. The electronic theory of valency was largely developed by N.V. Sidgwick at the **University of Oxford**. Also in the first two decades of the century the structure of chemical crystals was investigated by means of x-rays; a method developed by W.H. Bragg and extended by J.M. Robertson, Professor of physical chemistry at the University of Glasgow. Similar studies, but using electrons instead of x-rays, were developed in 1927 by G.P. Thomson, Professor of natural philosophy at the University of Aberdeen.

The inter-war years saw chemistry's expansion as an academic subject. Laboratory extensions were built and new buildings were erected at at least twelve universities, including Cambridge, King's College London, and Birmingham. British university chemists also made important contributions to organic chemistry in these years. The acknowledged systematizer of twentieth-century organic chemistry was Christopher Ingold. In the second decade of the century he worked with Jocelyn Field Thorpe at Imperial College; in 1924 he became Professor of chemistry at Leeds and then in 1930 at UCL. By 1961, when he retired, the Chemistry School at UCL was world famous.

The onset of the Second World War saw a British chemical profession five times the size it had been in 1914. A central register drawn up by various scientific societies at the start of the war recorded 6,000 persons working in pure or industrial chemistry. The chemical industry itself, at its peak of wartime expansion, employed nearly half a million people.

After the war, mainly because of developments in the petrochemical industry—the refining in the United Kingdom (UK) of Middle East crude oil—the British chemical industry expanded at nearly twice the rate of other manufacturing industries. These years saw expanding employment opportunities for qualified chemists even though U.K. research expenditure was less than 2 percent of turnover, compared with 5 percent in Germany and 4 percent in the United States. The 1960s and 1970s saw the results of this policy in pruning and mergers.

By 1970 a number of bodies represented the interests of British chemists, notably the British Chemical Society, the Royal Institute of Chemistry, the Society for Analytical Chemistry, and the Faraday Society. In 1980 the Royal Society of Chemistry was chartered incorporating all of these previous groups. Post-war British chemical research has been dominated by large-scale expensive collaborative operations, although individual British chemists have continued to distinguish themselves and gain Nobel Prizes. In 1964 the Nobel Prize for Chemistry went to Dorothy Hodgkin for her work at Cambridge on x-ray crystallography. For work on photochemistry, also at Cambridge, in the late 1940s, George Porter and Ronald Narrish received prizes in 1967. In 1969 it was given to Derek Barton for work on molecular structure. Barton was variously associated with Imperial College and Birkbeck College, London, and the University of Glasgow, although the work for which he received the prize was done at Harvard (1949–50).

Christopher Lawrence

Bibliography

Brock, William H. *The Fontana History of Chemistry.* 1992.
Findlay, Alexander. *A Hundred Years of Chemistry.* 3rd ed. rev. 1965.
Findlay, Alexander, and William Hobson Mills. *British Chemists.* 1947.
Russell, Colin A., ed. *Recent Developments in the History of Chemistry.* 1985.

C

Chesterton, G(ilbert) K(eith) (1874–1936)

G.K. Chesterton, a prolific and versatile man of letters, belonged to a circle of writers that included Hilaire Belloc, Maurice Baring, **George Bernard Shaw, H.G. Wells, C.F.G. Masterman**, and Ronald Knox. He was born in London into a prosperous middle-class family, Liberal in politics and Unitarian in religion. After attending St. Paul's School, he studied at the **Slade School of Art**, but did not take a degree, directing his energies instead into journalism. He was employed as a free-lance journalist for the *Speaker* and the *Daily News* and later wrote columns for *Illustrated London News* (1905–36) and his own *G.K.'s Weekly* (1925–36).

Growing out of his journalism, Chesterton's social criticism combated the **Boer War** and the political corruption behind the **Marconi scandal** and opposed cosmopolitanism and utopianism, whether in the form of **imperialism**, socialism, communism, **Fascism**, or industrial capitalism. He defended the importance of social organizations small enough to avoid the imposed uniformity of Empire but large enough to avoid rank individualism. As a professed liberal and democrat, Chesterton defended the "common man" against the collective state. He advocated, instead, a social model called "distributism," which maintained that the family was the fundamental unit of society and that the means of productive wealth, especially **land ownership**, should be widely distributed.

Between 1901 and 1936 Chesterton published over two-dozen volumes of collected essays. But his most enduring works have been his novels and literary criticism. Among his best fiction is *The Napoleon of Notting Hill* (1904), a futuristic battle over a London neighborhood; *The Club of Queer Trades* (1905); *The Man Who Was Thursday: A Nightmare* (1908), a proto-surrealist detective story; *The Ball and the Cross* (1909), a comical search by an atheist and a Christian for a place to duel; and the five volumes of Father Brown detective stories collected in 1951 as *The Father Brown Omnibus*. Among Chesterton's works of biographical and literary criticism, the most notable are *Robert Louis Stevenson* (1902), *Robert Browning* (1903), *Charles Dickens* (1906), *George Bernard Shaw* (1909), and *The Victorian Age in Literature* (1913). His poems range from the witty and whimsical to the religious, the best being, perhaps, *The Ballad of the White House* (1911), about King Alfred's successful struggle against Danish invaders. As a religious writer his most influential work is *Orthodoxy* (1908), written while he was an Anglican. This explanation of his own religious convictions followed upon *Heretics* (1905), a work that exposed the weaknesses in the reasoning of influential thinkers and movements of the day. Chesterton's important religious works after his conversion to **Roman Catholicism** in 1922 include a biography of *St. Francis of Assisi* (1923); *The Everlasting Man* (1925), a study of Christ; and *The Thing* (1929), a collection of essays.

Andrew Tadie

Bibliography

Chesterton, G.K. *Autobiography.* 1936.
Corrin, Jay P. *G.K. Chesterton and Hilaire Belloc: The Battle against Modernity.* 1981.
Sullivan, John. *G.K. Chesterton: A Bibliography.* 1958.
———. *Chesterton Continued: A Bibliographical Supplement.* 1968.
Ward, Maisie. *Gilbert Keith Chesterton.* 1943.
———. *Return to Chesterton.* 1952.

Child-Rearing

Practices of child-rearing have been eloquently described in oral history, personal diaries, letters, and autobiography, which indicate a wider variety of behavior and experience than manuals and professional trainings indicate. Legal practice, too, defines what is considered acceptable or tolerable treatment of a child rather than describing actual children's lives, or parental duties, since legal discourse only defines what is wrong, not what is right.

The Edwardian child was more likely to suffer corporal punishment at home and in school, and legal "reasonable" chastisement was permitted. In the 1930s there was intense public debate about whipping, after which the law, schools, and parents were discouraged from using negative methods of regulation and encouraged to see violence as an illegitimate means of child-rearing. This trend was in part a reflection of the development of a psychological explanation of behavior through which norms of development became part of the normative understanding of professionals and, by way of books and radio broadcasts by Cyril Burt, Susan Isaacs, and Donald Winnicott, of parents, too. Children were to be encouraged toward adjustment or normalcy, often in highly age-specific forms, rather than discouraged from wickedness and criminality.

If behavior was increasingly dominant as the main interest evoked in descriptions of development, the other strand remained the attention to the child's body. The health visitor was a specialized health professional whose role was to support the mother in correct upbringing for infants. This derived both from fears for the physical state of the population, supported by anthropometric study, and from medical discourse, which emphasized feeding as the key to national strength. The state was to assist inadequate mothers by providing cheap, clean milk, medical inspection and advice, and nutritionally adequate **diet** in the school meal system. New Zealand doctor Truby King was one contributor to this account by insisting that the child should be regulated through dietary restriction, fed by the clock, and discouraged from contact with other bodies but encouraged to move freely in the air. There is little indication that the British working class agreed with these notions, as commentators often disapprovingly noted. Upper- and middle-class children were more affected since they were often cared for by trained nursemaids.

Just before the Second World War psychiatrist John Bowlby outlined the theory of maternal deprivation, which was elaborated in *Child Care and the Growth of Love*. The experience of war brought questions of parental, particularly maternal, care to the fore through **evacuation**, when schoolchildren were removed from homes in port and industrial cities and billeted in the country, and through the notion of state responsibility for children. Post-war reforms such as the **family allowance**, free education for all from age five to fifteen, and a comprehensive health insurance scheme also called attention to children as the embodiment of the future. The Illingworths, pediatricians, summed this feeling up in their child-rearing manual, in which feeding and loving were cut loose from the restrictive timetable of Truby King and children's needs were to be met to some extent on demand. In the 1960s Dr. Benjamin Spock represented the most explicit statements of such attitudes in which the child was seen more as a self-regulating mechanism than the vessel for an imposed regimen. Psychodynamic thinking played a part in encouraging parents to recognize the role of unconscious desires and dreams, to reject repression as damaging, and to liberalize child care. This discouraged the rather distant child-rearing practices of the middle- and upper-class family, as did the **domestic servant** shortage. Attention was thus focused on the mother, and her emotional deficiencies or inadequacies became the problem for which professional care was the solution, rather than the physical or regulatory problems of the Edwardian mother. Attendance at clinics became general, and advice about child-rearing was freely offered by midwives, health visitors, nurses, and doctors. The British Medical Association provided all new parents with free pamphlets that reproduced many of the ideas of the more technical medical and psychological literature. Since the birthrate had begun to rise again, babies of 1945–57 were the most carefully fostered group of children in the century. Physical condition improved in this period, teeth and eyesight especially, with free care; advertisers redoubled their efforts to increase the market for diapers, cream, milk, and pap food.

Yet Britain remained a society in which children were confined in terms of public space, had low levels of specialized education for the under-fives and little presence in political debate. Mothers were seen as the key providers of correct child care, and, in practice, state intervention was limited to dealing with deviant groups. In the 1970s Sir Keith Joseph reproduced a nineteenth-century argument, "cycles of deprivation," arguing that child problems were reproduced by young single mothers. In 1984 **Margaret Thatcher** described the family as "the nursery of civic virtue" so that the privatization of child care was now to be rendered almost complete. School milk was withdrawn, meals were no longer regulated, maternity allowances were abolished, and family allowances were detached from inflation. Nursery schools, despite commitment, were not built. Yet government intervention to help rear children from "defective" families increased. Juvenile justice revived the "short, sharp shock"; parents were to be fined for child mis-

demeanors; **birth control** and sex education increased to prevent reproduction. The armory of advice literature and magazines multiplied, as did specialist child shops, especially Mothercare.

Children were affected by the long-term change in advice and government support. Social life for children was family-based, while families contracted as people moved around the country. **Divorce** replaced death as the most common disruption in parenting. Children were less violently treated and better physically cared for, and parents were increasingly well-informed about norms of child development. Mothers remained the main rearers of children. Dependency of children lengthened through **unemployment**, housing shortages, low wages, and school attendance, ending at eighteen.

Deborah Thom

Bibliography

Cooter, Roger, ed. *In the Name of the Child: Health and Welfare, 1880–1940.* 1992.

Finch, Janet. *Family Obligations and Social Change.* 1989.

Hardyment, Christina. *Dream Babies: Child Care from Locke to Spock.* 1983.

Humphries, Stephen. *Hooligans or Rebels? An Oral History of Working Class Childhood and Youth, 1889–1939.* 1981.

Lewis, Jane. *The Politics of Motherhood: Child and Maternal Welfare in England, 1900–1939.* 1980.

Riley, Denise. *War in the Nursery: Theories of the Child and Mother.* 1983.

Children's Literature

Historically considered as a substandard literary canon, children's literature is difficult to define. Crossing generic boundaries, it is the only literary field defined by its intended *audience*. Because children's literature is not generally written by children, it seems to reflect adult conceptions of childhood rather than the concerns of children themselves. Increased academic attention to children's literature, related to the prominence of literary theory, has focused on the representations of the child and childhood in children's books.

Despite scholarly disagreements over historian Philippe Aries' hypothesis that childhood is a modern "invention," few would disagree that the idea of a separate children's literature is largely a legacy of romanticism. If the golden age of children's literature—1860 to 1930—was predominantly British in character, the history of British children's literature throughout the twentieth century has become an increasingly complex story.

Critics like Jack Zipes and Alison Lurie point to the "subversive" nature of children's texts, speculating that they are quietly critical of the adult social order and that they reflect utopian aspirations. Other critics have seen the literature as formally and politically conservative, leading children to accept dominant Western and middle-class values. In most cases, however, the subversive and conservative element might be said to coexist, as the works of **Rudyard Kipling** and E(dith) Nesbit (1858–1924) suggest. Kipling, the imperialist, wrote many of his most complex and inventive works for or about children, including *Kim* (1901), *Just So Stories* (1902), *Puck of Pook's Hill* (1906), and *Rewards and Fairies* (1910); the content of these books does not clearly endorse the Empire. Nesbit, the **Fabian** socialist, revolutionized children's literature by eschewing both Victorian didacticism and manners; in her finest work, the Psammead stories—*Five Children and It* (1902), *The Phoenix and the Carpet* (1904), and *The Story of the Amulet* (1906)—she challenges Edwardian complacency; yet, her fictional children often seem to be middle-class youngsters on a fantastic holiday, visiting foreign cultures and times for an exotic thrill.

Drawing on a great Victorian legacy, fantasy seems the defining genre for British children's literature through much of the century, with nostalgic overtones. The impulse for adults who wrote for children before the First World War is often more regressive than it is exploratory, imagining childhood itself as the pastoral neverland of J.M. Barrie's (1860–1937) *Peter Pan* (1904) or Kenneth Grahame's (1859–1932) prepubescent male arcadia in *The Wind in the Willows* (1908). Perhaps only Beatrix Potter (1866–1943) might be said to have subverted the pastoral mode by means of her representations of aggression and violence in *The Tale of Peter Rabbit* (1901) and in her subsequent picture books for the very young.

The **First World War** and its aftermath appear to have brought an end to the explosion of children's books now considered classics. In contrast to the burgeoning institutional supports for children's literature in the United States, in Britain there was a general lack of interest in children's books. The notable achievements of the 1920s were the poetry and poetic stories of Walter de la Mare (1873–1956) and Eleanor Farejon (1881–1965) and the animated-toy stories of Margery Williams Bianco (1881–1944). A.A. Milne's (1882–1956) *Winnie-the-Pooh* (1926) and *The House at Pooh Corner* (1928) were not as sentimental as Bianco's work, but they recalled the prewar pastorals of Grahame and Barrie.

The arcadian impulse before the war seems significantly watered down in its postwar manifestations. Though the great Edwardian fantasies were undoubtedly escapist, the 1920s gave rise to escapism of a more overtly commercial sort, exemplified by the career of Enid Blyton (1897–1968), the best-selling British children's author of all time and also the author most vilified by children's literature critics. Blyton began to flood the market with works like *Sunny Stories for Little Folk* (1926) and by 1950 had an annual income in excess of £100,000. More problematic is the *Doctor Dolittle* series (1922 onward) by Hugh Lofting (1886–1947). Lofting's experience in the trenches of Flanders gives a radical edge to the stories, but they are marred by racism and a contempt for the masses.

The influence of the *Swallows and Amazons* series (1930–47) of Arthur Ransome (1884–1967) has been far greater in Britain than in the United States. The twelve novels resurrect the adventure stories popular at the turn of the century, but they are more domesticated and often set in the romantic landscape of the Lake District. Like earlier Edwardian fantasies, they take place in a world ostensibly without adults and evoke the idea of childhood as a holiday. But as Peter Hunt points out, there is a "subtle regulation" of the child's world by the adult world in Ransome's fantasies. Others have criticized the series' middle-class values. Still widely read in Britain, Ransome's novels anticipate the domestication of British children's fantasy in the 1940s and 1950s.

J.R.R. Tolkien (1892–1973), another veteran of the Flanders trenches, spent the major part of the 1930s writing *The Hobbit* (1937), widely regarded as the major work of fantasy between the wars. Tolkien's imaginary Middle-Earth undoubtedly influenced **C.S. Lewis**, who read the novel in manuscript. Lewis' *Chronicles of Narnia* (1951–6), an allegorical retelling of the Christian myth in seven novels, is more apparently didactic than Tolkien's novels. Tolkien's influence may be felt in the other major children's fantasy of the period, Mary Norton's (1903–) Borrowers series (1952–82), but with a distinctly post-war flavor. Miniaturized like the hobbits, Norton's Borrowers are depicted as a Victorian family attempting to escape the surveillance of the "human beans." Without the religious undercurrents to be found in Tolkien and Lewis, Norton creates a more social and political allegory in which her adolescent heroine, Arietty, negotiates postmodern dangers as well as crises of gender and sexuality. Norton's depiction of an old-fashioned domestic world under siege figures the enormous changes taking place in children's literature and the conception of childhood after the Second World War. In recent decades children's writers have continued to explore alternative worlds, in high fantasy and in historical fantasy such as L.M. Boston's (1892–) Green Knowe series (1954–64), and Phillipa Pearce's (1920–) highly acclaimed Tom's Midnight Garden (1958). Darker psychological elements and a further mixing of genres become apparent in the works of Alan Garner (1934–) and William Mayne (1928–). Garner's metafictional experiments in books like Red Shift (1973) and Mayne's virtuosic use of subgenres of children's literature challenge historically conservative conventions. However, the fiction of this period is not unrelievedly dark: The comic novels of Roald Dahl (1916–90), notably James and the Giant Peach (1961), Charlie and the Chocolate Factory (1964), The Witches (1983), and Matilda (1988), are very popular with children. Dahl was the best-selling children's writer living in Britain at the time of his death, despite adult objections to his works from both the Left and the Right. Perhaps such objections are not entirely disinterested, since adult hypocrisy is often the main target of Dahl's satire.

Though undoubtedly there are run-of-the-mill British "problem novels," the much touted "new realism" for children seems more of an American than a British phenomenon. The finest contemporary British children's texts are rooted in tradition, even as they test traditional generic boundaries as well as the boundaries between child and adult worlds. Innovators such as Joan Aiken (1924–), Nina Bawden (1925–), Leon Garfield (1921–), Jane Gardam (1928–), Aidan Chambers (1934), and David Rees (1936–) are not so easily pigeonholed. It should be noted that Britain has produced the

century's most innovative experiments in poetry written for children, in the work of Ted Hughes (1930–) and Charles Causley (1917–).

Richard Flynn

Bibliography

Carpenter, Humphrey, and Mari Prichard. *The Oxford Companion to Children's Literature.* 1984.
Hunt, Peter, ed. *Children's Literature: The Development of Criticism.* 1990.
Inglis. Fred. *The Promise of Happiness: Value and Meaning in Children's Fiction.* 1981.
Townsend, John Rowe. *Written For Children: An Outline of English Language Children's Literature.* 1983.

Christie, Agatha Miller (1890–1976)

Author of eighty-one novels, 149 short stories, thirteen plays, two autobiographical works (signed Agatha Christie Mallowan), some verse, and miscellaneous other writings, Agatha Christie may well prove the best-selling writer in English of the twentieth century. Although she wrote six "straight" novels under the name Mary Westmacott and nine romance thrillers and spy novels, and although several of her plays were successful, Christie's major achievement lies in her development of British detective fiction. The British detective form (as opposed to the American tough-guy detective form) follows a tradition set by Arthur Conan Doyle's Sherlock Holmes stories—that is, it underplays physical violence; it stresses cerebral riddle-solving; it preserves the tone of comedy of manners; and it affirms the existing social/moral order. The form is fundamentally Aristotelian in structure with a firm beginning, middle, and end. It engages readers by inviting them to compete with the detective in unraveling the mystery. It observes "fair play" rules that supply readers with clues they need in order to compete. Finally, it suggests that by means of intellectual apprehensions, productive social organization can be recovered and preserved. Christie wrote sixty-one novels in this highly formulaic genre, beginning with *The Mysterious Affair at Styles* (1920) and ending with *Elephants Can Remember* (1972). Her work is widely regarded as having set the standard against which other writers of whodunits must be measured.

No single Christie whodunit accounts for her special achievement. The sheer quantity of her writing is part of that accomplishment. So is the inventiveness with which she combined and recombined, mixed and remixed, elements of plot, characterization, setting, and ending to create a long list of fresh-seeming, if familiar, surprising, if predictable, narratives.

Though she experimented with several central characters, her most popular series detectives were the Belgian-born, mustachioed Hercule Poirot, who solved problems by exercising his "little grey cells"; and Miss Jane Marple, the English spinster who solved them by applying the knowledge of human character she had acquired through observation of the villagers of St. Mary Mead.

Christie's novels, widely reprinted, often with variant titles, have been translated into 103 languages. Many of her novels and her short stories have been adapted for the stage, for the movies, and for television production. During her lifetime, Christie tended to object to such adaptation, but several of her plays, including *Ten Little Indians* (1945), *The Mousetrap* (1952), (the longest-running play in British theatrical history), and *Witness for the Prosecution* (1953) were developed from her own earlier novels or short stories.

While some readers value her work primarily as one of the best sources of detail of British social history from the 1920s through the 1970s, she defined herself as merely "a tradesman in a good honest trade."

Mary Wagoner

Bibliography

Bargainnier, Earl F. *The Gentle Act of Murder: The Detective Fiction of Agatha Christie.* 1980.

Barnard, Robert. *A Talent to Deceive: An Appreciation of Agatha Christie.* 1980.

Christie, Agatha. *An Autobiography.* 1977.

Gill, Gillian. *Agatha Christie: The Woman and Her Mysteries.* 1990.

Morgan, Janet. *Agatha Christie: A Biography.* 1984.

Wagoner, Mary. *Agatha Christie.* 1986.

Church of England

The Church of England, or Anglican Church, is the legally established national church of England (not of Scotland, Wales, or Northern Ireland). As England is, in turn, the largest constituent part of the United Kingdom, comprising over 80 percent of its population, its national church has long held a central place in Britain's public life. But in the twentieth century it has experienced an erosion of its membership and some loss of its general influence and stature. Nevertheless, it remains a large and important cultural, social, and political institution.

Its modern history can be traced back to 1534 when, during a wider religious turbulence on the Continent, ties with Rome were severed by Henry VIII, immediately occasioned by his need of a divorce. The Church of England emerged as an ecclesiastical hybrid—Protestant in that it was no longer under papal jurisdiction (the Crown now assuming the title of Supreme Governor), but claiming a Catholic heritage in its retention of the historic episcopate. This dual character has given the Church a theologically broad and comprehensive character, embracing both "Protestant evangelicals" and "Anglo-Catholics." This combination is sometimes referred to as a *via media,* or middle way, between Western Christianity's two major camps.

The Church is divided into two provinces, Canterbury and York, each headed by a metropolitan archbishop. The southern province is the larger, comprising twenty-nine English dioceses, which include Canterbury itself and the ancient diocese of London. It also contains a new (1980) Diocese of Europe, which is the Anglican ecclesiastical presence on the mainland of Europe. The northern province is composed of fourteen dioceses, notably York and Durham. Most dioceses are, in turn, subdivided into archdeaconries (led by archdeacons), and thence into deaneries (led by rural deans).

The base organizational unit, covering the whole of England, is the parish, of which there are over 13,100. All have a parish church, some more than one. (In 1991 there were 16,500 churches). Most are served by a full-time priest paid a stipend out of national church funds. In 1989 these "incumbents" numbered (with assistants) 9,827, to which must be added 487 (1989) women deacons in full-time parish positions. Increasingly, such clergy serve more than one parish, especially in rural areas. In part this is a matter of necessity since inflation eroded financial resources. It also reflects a decline in church membership and clergy. Indeed, throughout the twentieth century clergy numbers have dropped to less than half their strength in 1901. Nevertheless, the Church's institutional and pastoral presence in every English village, town, and city throughout England ensures a continued marked contribution to English society.

Among that population, though, the link with the Church has eroded over the years. Church statistics show that in 1988 infant baptisms, at 288 per 1,000 live births, and Easter communicants, at 41 per 1,000 adults, were less than half the 1930 figures (699 and 85, respectively). Confirmations have fallen even more dramatically, from 227,000 in 1910 to 62,000 in 1989. This represents an undeniably substantial attrition, reflected also in a 1989 English church census that indicates a membership of only about 1.6 million, or about 3 to 4 percent of the English adult population. This is slightly higher, at 5 to 6 percent, in the rural countryside and suburbs but under 2 percent in the urban conurbations.

Nevertheless, recently the decline may have slowed. Church communicant rates, for example, are unchanged since at least 1976 (at 18–19 per 1,000 adults). In the same period, parish income has increased one-third. Furthermore, the Church of England has a large penumbra, perhaps 40 percent of the population, who retain a residual Anglican identity. This reflects its historic cultural status as the national church. But this penumbra, too, has shrunk over time.

Secularization also affects the Church's contribution at the national level, although the ties to the state, and its presence at state occasions, still give the Church of England visibility and a capacity to exercise some influence. State ceremonies include, for example, Remembrance Day ceremonies featuring the Bishop of London, and the coronation, which is an Anglican liturgical act in Westminster Abbey. Formal ties between Church and monarchy are also strong. Thus, the monarch, as the Church's Supreme Governor, has the formal right to make appointments to all bishoprics (and many other Church posts). Since Victorian times, however, this right has been exercised in practice by the Prime Minister through a Patronage Secretary. In 1977, as part of a wider process of granting the Church a greater degree of self-government, a Crown Appointments Commission was formed in which the Church was given a greater voice in composing a short list (of two names). But the Prime Minister still makes the final decision, including the possibility of asking for further names to be submitted.

The Church of England also has an official presence within the **House of Lords**. Twenty-six bishops serve as Lords Spiritual, with full voting and speaking rights. The Archbishops of Canterbury and York, and the Bishops of London, Winchester, and Durham always have seats. Twenty-one of the other diocesan bishops serve according to seniority defined by the date of their appointment as diocesans. The Bishop of Sodor and Man, however, has an equivalent seat instead in the Manx Parliament, and the Bishop of Gibraltar in Europe (Diocese of Europe) is not eligible.

From this position, the Church of England makes an official contribution to the legislative process and gains informal access to the corridors of power. In practice, bishops nowadays give their Lords membership a relatively low priority. Attendance, therefore, normally devolves on one bishop by rota, and a few others by choice, usually including the Bishop of London, whose office is adjacent to Parliament. On this limited basis, however, the bishops make a contribution as a respected Christian voice on a wide range of topics, briefed by an official from the Archbishop of Canterbury's staff at Lambeth Palace.

There is no equivalent presence within the more powerful House of Commons. Indeed, Anglican clergy remain barred from seeking election. Many members (predominantly Conservative) are active lay Anglicans, but they rarely speak or vote as Anglicans. When parliamentary business in the Commons arises concerning the Church of England, it is often handled by a member who also serves as one of the Church Commissioners. In addition, there is an Ecclesiastical Committee, with members from both Houses, which liaises with the Church when parliamentary action is required.

That flow of ecclesiastical legislation has diminished in recent years through the gradual creation of Church bodies with devolved powers. In 1919 an Enabling Act established a Church Assembly, which was, in turn, replaced in 1969 by a more powerful General Synod. The Synod is composed of a fifty-three member House of Bishops (all diocesans and nine elected suffragans), a House of Clergy (259 members elected from among archdeacons, cathedral deans, and other clergy), and a 258-member House of Laity (elected by active lay people from each diocese).

Although subjected to criticism as cumbersome, expensive, and bureaucratic, the General Synod has become the central policy-making body of the Church of England, to which important advisory committees and permanent commissions report. These include, for example, Boards of Education (BE) and Social Responsibility (BSR). The BE develops policy for the Church's substantial investment in elementary (grade) and secondary (high) schools, which, in turn, entails dialogue with the Department of Education and Science. Equivalent links exist between dioceses and local educational authorities, both of whom run schools directly. The BE also works closely with the National Society for Promoting Religious Education, one of many semi-independent organizations associated with the Church of England. The BSR develops reports on a wide range of social and international issues and publishes *Crucible*. Its range is indicated by its subdivision into Committees for Industrial and Economic Affairs, International and Development Affairs, Social Policy, and Race and Community Relations.

Ecumenical relations are handled by the Council for Christian Unity. These include links with **Roman Catholics**, the other major church in England, and with various ecumenical agencies such as the World Council of Churches, the Conference of European Churches, the Council of Churches for Britain and Ireland, and Churches Together in England. Financial affairs are handled by a Central Board of Finance (created in 1914), which in 1991 had a budget of nearly £12 million. Like the rest of the central bureaucracy, it is based at Church House, Westminster, which is headed by a Secretary-General. However, a separate and independent agency, the Church Commissioners, handles clergy salaries and pensions. In 1991 its expenditure totaled over £200 million.

Besides these synodical and bureaucratic agencies, the other major focus of national authority in the Church of England lies in the office of Archbishop of Canterbury and his support staff at Lambeth Palace, London. Though lacking the powers and claims of the Pope, the Archbishop is the senior bishop and *de facto* leader of the Church of England. Officially, the Archbishop is Primate of All England (the Archbishop of York being merely Primate of England) and chairs the House of Bishops, an important leadership group in an episcopally ordered Church. He is a well-known public figure, having access to the Prime Minister, the House of Lords, and the media.

The Archbishop is also the focus of symbolic unity for the Anglican Communion, a grouping of twenty-eight self-governing Anglican Churches in 164 countries with a combined membership of around 70 million. They include the Episcopal Church in the United States, the Anglican Church of Canada, and, within Britain, the Scottish Episcopal Church and the Church in Wales. Episcopal representatives of all the various churches have been brought together approximately every ten years since 1867 by the Archbishop of Canterbury at Lambeth Conferences. These have been supplemented in recent years by a London-based Anglican Consultative Council (1969) and a Primates' Meeting (1979), both also presided over by the Archbishop. The Archbishop has become an important international religious figure, dealing with the Pope and leaders of other churches on a personal basis.

The traditional influence of the Church was conservative, reflecting its association with the state and its strength among the more privileged and rural sectors of society. Indeed, politically, it became known as the "Tory Party at prayer," and its episcopal leaders were seen as part of a dominant sociopolitical establishment, having been predominantly nurtured in an ethos of elite public schools and **Oxford** and **Cambridge**. Some of this conservatism remains, not least among the Church's active laity, in regard to issues such as the monarch, Church establishment, and hostility toward trade unions. This group reflects the wider views of relatively privileged suburban sectors. However, some shifts toward more centrist, liberal outlooks can be discerned in recent decades, particularly with the Church's synodical and episcopal leadership. In part, this is the result of changed theological understandings; in part, a broader recruitment process. The result has been some notable conflicts over public policy, especially involving Church leaders such as David Jenkins (Bishop of Durham 1984–94) and Robert Runcie (Archbishop of Canterbury 1980–91), and the Conservative government of **Margaret Thatcher**. Issues included defense policy, discussed in the controversial Church report *The Church and the Bomb* (1982), and urban policy, scrutinized in *Faith in the City* (1985). Similar trends are found in Church reactions to the **Falklands War** (1982) and the Gulf War (1991). Yet there are limits to this shift. The Church of England remains a church of the more privileged, and its lay membership reflects this. Institutionally, its conservatism can be seen in its reluctance to approve the ordination of women to the priesthood, although this changed in 1992 (and threatened to provoke a minor schism). But in all its diversity, the

Church of England still embodies a uniquely English Christian heritage and thereby remains an influential institution throughout the land.

George Moyser

Bibliography

Brierley, Peter. *"Christian" England: What the 1989 English Church Census Reveals*. 1991.

Lloyd, Roger B. *The Church of England; 1900–1965*. 1966.

Medhurst, Kenneth, and George Moyser. *Church and Politics in a Secular Age*. 1988.

Norman, Edward R. *Church and Society in England; 1770–1970*. 1976.

Welsby, Paul A. *A History of the Church of England; 1945–1980*. 1984.

Churchill, Winston Spencer (1874–1965)

Winston Churchill's political career spanned the first six decades of the twentieth century, and during almost all this time he was one of the best known and most significant of public men. He changed his party allegiance twice and was always suspected of being an ambitious adventurer, a diagnosis apparently confirmed by the political and strategic blunders that marked his progress. Between 1908 and 1929 he served as a **Cabinet** minister for eight separate departments. The most important of these were his period at the Admiralty during the critical period of Anglo-German naval rivalry before 1914 and his less successful reign as Chancellor of the Exchequer in 1924–9. After a decade in the wilderness, he became the man of the hour in 1940, succeeding **Neville Chamberlain** first as Prime Minister and later as leader of the **Conservative Party**. He served two terms as Premier, in the first and most important seeing the nation through to victory in 1945. He returned to power from 1951 to 1955, when he also stepped down as party leader. In later life he declined a dukedom, but in 1953 he accepted a Knighthood of the Garter. Churchill was also an accomplished military historian and biographer, especially of his illustrious ancestor, the first Duke of Marlborough, and of his father, Lord Randolph Churchill.

The crucial influence upon Churchill's early life was the legend left by the meteoric rise and fall of his father, a controversial and rebellious Conservative politician who died after a debilitating illness when his eldest son was only twenty. Winston Churchill's first career was in the **army**, and he served in India and fought at the Battle of Omdurman (1898). Out of uniform as a newspaper correspondent during the **Boer War**, he was captured and then managed to escape. However, his military exploits and his journalism were only intended to be the prelude to a political career. After one unsuccessful by-election attempt (1899), he became Conservative MP for Oldham in 1900. He proved to be an awkward backbencher, more often a critic than a supporter of his own government. Relations were thus already strained before the bombshell of Joseph Chamberlain's campaign for **tariff reform** burst over the Conservative ranks in 1903. A strong commitment to free trade was to prove to be almost Churchill's only consistent principle for the next thirty years; in 1904 it led to his "crossing the floor" to join the **Liberal Party**. Churchill's pushiness had alienated many: After this apparently adroit quitting of a sinking ship, he became a figure of deep and lasting loathing for many Conservatives. Certainly, the rewards proved to be quick and great. After the Liberal landslide of 1906 Churchill was given a prominent junior ministerial post, and on **H.H. Asquith**'s succession to the premiership in 1908 he entered the Cabinet as President of the Board of Trade. In this office and then as Home Secretary from February 1910 to October 1911, he was one of the government's most energetic reformers, forging a close friendship and radical alliance with the Chancellor, **David Lloyd George**. Two incidents only marred his reputation: the use of troops to quell industrial disturbances in South Wales, which led to two deaths, and his risky presence at the scene of the Sidney Street siege (1911) by police against a gang of East European revolutionaries.

In 1911 Churchill's career changed course when he was transferred to the Admiralty. The period was dominated by the naval challenge from Germany and the growing antagonisms that were to lead to war. Churchill rapidly became a convinced navalist, clashing bitterly with Lloyd George for greater funding for warship building. This was a characteristic feature of Churchill's career: He was a political chameleon who took on the colors of whichever ministry he headed, regardless of consistency or of any wider vision. Thus he had fought against naval spending as a radical social reformer in 1908–9 and was later to refight the same battle as an economizing Chancellor of the Exchequer in the 1920s. The coming of war showed

C

Churchill at his best and at his worst. In the crisis of July 1914 he used his initiative to mobilize the fleet and avoid the risk of a sudden German coup, but he caused alarm by his reckless sending of naval troops to be captured at Antwerp. His constant interference in operational decisions led to strains with the professional head of the navy, **Lord John Arbuthnot Fisher**. This came to a head with the failure of the **Gallipoli** campaign (1915), a disaster that nearly broke Churchill and that hung over him like a pall for the next twenty-five years. When the first coalition was formed in May 1915, the Conservatives demanded Churchill's removal from the Admiralty, and after six unhappy months as Chancellor of the Duchy of Lancaster he quit Westminster to serve as a battalion commander on the Western Front.

When Churchill was recalled to office—over bitter Conservative protests—in July 1917, both the political situation and the internal health of the Liberal Party had been turned upside down by the fall of Asquith and Lloyd George's accession to the premiership. This fractured the Liberal Party into two warring factions, and during the next five years Churchill became Lloyd George's most important coalition Liberal supporter. He served as head of the **Ministry of Munitions** from July 1917 until January 1919, as Secretary for War and Air for the following two years, and then as Colonial Secretary from February 1921 until the fall of the coalition in October 1922. Together with his close friend F.E. Smith, now Earl of Birkenhead, and R.S. Horne, Churchill was in the inner circle of coalition leaders whose loose commitment to party ties and hedonistic social life were mistaken by many critics for lack of principle and even honesty. When Lloyd George fell, Churchill was cast into the darkness with him, even losing his seat at Dundee in the 1922 general election.

This defeat was to lead to his first spell in the wilderness. During the following two years Churchill completed a passage back to Conservatism that had begun after 1918. On both the domestic front and abroad he had placed increasing emphasis upon the danger of socialism, and even of Bolshevism, and had been an advocate of Allied intervention in Russia. After 1923 he shed his Liberal affiliation for the guise of "Constitutionalist." He was adopted by local Conservatives for the safe seat of Epping, which he represented for the next forty years. The prodigal son was welcomed back to the fold in

a manner that took many Conservatives' breath away when, following the 1924 victory, **Stanley Baldwin** appointed him Chancellor of the Exchequer. He remained at this post throughout the ministry, from November 1924 to June 1929. During this time, with some doubts, he restored Britain to the **gold standard** (1925) and also played a part both typically pugnacious and yet also generous in spirit in the **General Strike** and coal strike of 1926–7. Despite being Chancellor, he was never the second figure in the government, being still out of sympathy with his party over tariffs and constantly suspected of coquetting with Lloyd George.

Out of office after the Conservative defeat in 1929, he drifted out of touch with its Baldwinite leadership. In part, this marked the start of a dilettante period, which mixed foreign travel with journalism and biography. Churchill concentrated his attention upon his country house of Chartwell and sought to make his family financially secure and recoup money lost in the crash of 1929. He became an infrequent, and thus resented, attender at Westminster. His political crusades of the 1930s were in fact the product of deep convictions but only rendered his isolation all the greater. He appeared reactionary, in an uneasy alliance with the "diehard" Right, and was believed to be intriguing to bring down the National government. His opposition to Baldwin's bipartisan India policy had led to his resignation from the Shadow Cabinet in January 1931 and his omission from the National Cabinet in August; for the next four years he led the India "revolt." In 1936 his support for **Edward VIII** in the abdication crisis led to his being howled down in the House of Commons; his career seemed to be over.

This apparent lack of balance and judgment inevitably colored views of Churchill's other theme during these "wilderness years": the danger of Nazi Germany and the need for rearmament, especially in the air. This stand was less marked or consistent than he and others later made it seem but was strongly critical of the government all the same. After **Munich** he gained in credibility, forging an alliance with **Anthony Eden** and the younger antiappeasers. On the outbreak of war in September 1939 Neville Chamberlain was forced to offer him a key post, and he returned to the Admiralty. As the stock of Chamberlain and other ministers dropped, Churchill's rose. He came to personify the "bulldog spirit" and was the only credible replacement for Chamberlain when the latter fell. **Labour** agreed to serve under Churchill, and he combined the posts of Prime Minister and Minister of Defense from May 1940 until July 1945; he also succeeded Chamberlain as Conservative leader in October 1940. Churchill believed that all his life had been a preparation for this moment of supreme national danger and that he was "walking with destiny." His leadership was of vital importance after the fall of France, rallying the people behind the decision to fight on regardless. He was difficult to work with and for but was also inspirational and energetic, producing a stream of ideas that were then filtered through his immediate staff. He made a second vital contribution by forging a close relationship with the American President Franklin D. Roosevelt, which brought the United States almost into the war even before the attack on Pearl Harbor. The defeat of Adolf Hitler had absolute priority: After the German invasion of Russia (June 1941), Churchill welcomed the Soviet Union as an ally. However, he gave priority to the traditional British sphere in the Mediterranean theater, searching once again for the "soft underbelly" in order to avoid the costly frontal assault. This led to the Italian campaign

C

BIG BULLY! RATTLING THE SABRE AT US INNOCENT LITTLE ONES!

"Big Bully" (David Low, *Evening Standard*, 9 April 1940). This appeared a month before Churchill became Prime Minister. Although critical of Chamberlain, Low portrayed Churchill sympathetically.

after 1943 and the "percentages agreement" with Joseph Stalin on post-war influence in the Balkans (1944).

The Conservative Party had always been uneasy about its new leader and resented his inner circle of cronies, mainly political outsiders like Brendan Bracken, Robert Boothby, and Lords **Beaverbrook** and Cherwell. However, with Churchill's prestige at their head, neither they nor he anticipated the Labour victory in the general election of May 1945. Churchill ran an ill-judged and overconfident campaign, but he took the blow of rejection very hard. As leader of the opposition (1945–51), he tried to remain above domestic partisan politics. He was largely uninterested in the party's policy review but gave a general, if reluctant, endorsement. His main interest was in being a "world statesman." He opposed British withdrawal from Empire but also feared an American return to isolationism in the face of tightening Soviet control in Eastern Europe. At Fulton, Missouri, his "Iron Curtain" speech (5 March 1946) gave early warning of dangers of Communism and the onset of Cold War. In October 1951 the Conservatives returned to power, and Churchill served a second term as Prime Minister until April 1955. He attempted to reconstruct the closest thing possible to the wartime coalition, offering merger to the Liberals and including experts and other nonparty figures. Churchill deliberately set out to show moderation in social policy. The **nationalization** of iron and **steel** was reversed, but other Labour reforms were left untouched, and the **welfare state** was shown to be safe in Conservative hands. The affluence of the later 1950s was heralded by the removal of controls and **rationing**, although the appeasement of the unions stoked inflationary pressures. Churchill again gave most attention to his attempts at superpower diplomacy, being after 1953 the only one of the "Big Three" wartime leaders still in power. Believing that he alone could achieve a breakthrough with Russia, he constantly postponed his promised intention to hand over to his heir-apparent, Eden. He made a good recovery from a major stroke in July 1953, but his powers were clearly fading, and he was eventually almost forced to quit in 1955. During his final years he was still subject to his "black dog" of depression and suffered further physical decline. In 1964 he retired from a House of Commons that he had barely attended for several years.

Churchill's was a long but erratic career, full of false starts and remarkable achievements, of insights and reckless impulsiveness, of early promise and dashed hopes. It was founded upon his extraordinary character and abilities, reluctantly admitted by his enemies, but was also hampered by the distrust he continually aroused, at least until becoming war leader in 1940. If he had retired from politics in the late 1930s, his career would certainly have outshone that of his father, but otherwise would have deserved the verdict of biographer Robert Rhodes James: "a study in failure." His stubborn and eventually triumphant leadership in the **Second World War**, inextricably interweaving personal and national recovery, self-confidence, and success, was his greatest achievement. The "finest hour" in 1940–2, when total victory seemed to be almost within the grasp of Nazi Germany, determined the course not just of British but of world history. Much else in Churchill's career was bronze or even lead, but this was golden, and upon this alone rests his scarcely challenged claim to be the most significant individual in British history, and one of the dozen most significant figures in world history, since 1900.

Stuart Ball

Bibliography

Addison, Paul. *Trust the People: Winston Churchill in Home Affairs, 1900–1955.* 1992.

Blake, Robert, and William Roger Louis, eds. *Churchill.* 1993.

Churchill, Randolph. *Winston S. Churchill.* vols. 1–2. 1966–7.

Gilbert, Martin. *Winston S. Churchill.* vols. 3–8. 1971–88.

———. *Churchill: A Life.* 1991.

Pelling, Henry. *Winston Churchill.* 2nd. ed. 1989.

Citrine, Walter McLennan (1887–1983)

General Secretary of the **Trades Union Congress** (TUC) in the years 1926–46, Walter Citrine was an important force for moderation in the trade union movement. He went on to be a member of the National Coal Board before becoming Chairman of the British Electricity Authority (1947–57). He was created first Baron Citrine of Wembley in 1946.

Citrine, who grew up in the Liverpool area, was of Italian extraction. Both his father and grandfather had been British seamen. Physically weak, he endured an unhappy period of hard manual labor in a flour mill before finding work as an electrician. Though from a Conservative working-class family, he became a member of the **Independent Labour Party** around 1906. Joining the Electrical Trades Union (ETU) during the 1911 industrial unrest in Liverpool, he was elected the union's first full-time District Secretary in 1914. His eagerness for self-improvement included learning shorthand, a useful means of advancement in the world of trade union bureaucracy. His skills as an administrator took him to the Manchester headquarters of the ETU as Assistant General Secretary in 1920 and then in the same role to the TUC in 1924. Given the poor state of the health of his superior, Fred Bramley (1874–1925), he was soon taking additional responsibilities, and from October 1925 until September 1926, when he was appointed General Secretary, he was Acting General Secretary.

After the trauma of the **General Strike** (1926) Citrine worked hard to get the TUC and the trade union movement accepted as indispensable parts of British democratic society. He was a warm supporter of the talks between the TUC and influential industrialists—the Mond-Turner Talks—which took place in 1928 and which aroused strong criticism from both Communists and right-wing industrialists. He also worked closely with the machinery of government when opportunity arose, serving in the 1930s on the National Economic Council, the Consultative Committee of the Treasury, a Royal Commission that investigated economic and social conditions in the West Indies (1938–9), and, during the **Second World War**, in various important capacities.

In these endeavors his moderate and anti-Communist views were similar to those of other powerful British labor movement figures such as **Ernest Bevin** and **Arthur Henderson**, with whom he worked. His acceptance of a knighthood in 1935 aroused much controversy. In fact he had declined this honor in 1932 and a peerage in 1930. Citrine also was a major moderate figure in international trade union affairs, being President of the International Federation of Trade Unions (1928–45). Attending its meetings in Berlin he witnessed the rise of the Nazis. He was a founder of the World Anti-Nazi Council and, from its inception in 1936, was Chairman.

With **Clement Attlee**'s post-war government, Citrine took senior posts in newly **nation-**alized industries, accepting a peerage and leaving the TUC (1946). He served on the National Coal Board (1946–7), the Central Electricity Authority (1947–57), and (part-time) on the U.K. Atomic Energy Authority (1958–62). In retirement he wrote two volumes of autobiography, among the finest by any British trade unionist.

C.J. Wrigley

Bibliography

Citrine, Walter. *Men and Work: An Autobiography.* 1964.
———. *Two Careers.* 1967.
Lovell, John C., and B.C. Roberts. *A Short History of the TUC.* 1968.
Martin, Ross M. *TUC: The Growth of a Pressure Group, 1868–1976.* 1980.

City of London

The City of London has remained throughout the twentieth century the preeminent world's financial center. Unrivaled before 1914, in competition with New York in the inter-war years, the City reemerged at the top in the 1960s, overcoming the decline of the British economy. Along with New York and Tokyo, **London** is in the 1990s one of the three main financial centers in the world and the leading one in the European zone. The City has played a key role in the British economy: Its activities have been essential for the balance of payments and, more recently, its world role has enhanced Britain's international economic status.

The golden age of the City of London started in 1870, following the defeat of France in the Franco-Prussian War, which ended the free convertibility of Bank of France notes. Its unrivaled financial position meant, in the first place, that the bulk of world trade was financed through the medium of bills of exchange drawn on London. With over 40 percent of the total exported capital of the world in 1913 raised on its financial markets, London was the leading center for the issue of foreign loans and equities as well as the capital of international banking. There were more branches of foreign banks opened in the City—about thirty in 1913—and a larger number of multinational banks based in London—thirty-one overseas banks totaling 1,387 non-U.K. branches in 1913—than in any other city. The nominal values of the securities quoted on the London Stock Exchange—over £11 billion in 1913—was larger than that of the New York and Paris stock exchanges combined. Insurance, another British speciality, was spreading its activities all around the world, with the emergence of large composite companies with offices in several cities in North and South America, Australia, and other parts of the Empire. London's dominance in insurance was also due to the unique role played by Lloyd's, first and foremost in the field of marine insurance, but also, and increasingly from the early twentieth century, through its capacity to insure new risks. Many commodities were traded primarily, if not exclusively, in London, and markets such as the Baltic Exchange for the chartering of ships, or the London Metal Exchange had no equivalent elsewhere.

This financial supremacy was primarily due to Britain's dominant position in the world economy: its share of world trade—25 percent in 1870 and still around 14 percent in 1913, despite the emergence of its main rivals, Germany and the United States; Britain's Empire and position at the heart of the system of international payments centered on its deficit with industrialized countries and its net surplus with India; and the role of the pound sterling in the smooth functioning of the international **gold standard**. But this financial supremacy was also due to the development of the British financial institutions. The banking system was structured to manage the financing of world trade: The major London **clearing banks**, which by 1913 concentrated in their hands about two-thirds of the deposits of England and Wales, provided the necessary cash credit, while the **merchant banks'** accepting business was the basis of world trade finance. The Bank of England, despite its loss of touch with the market, had by the beginning of the twentieth century devised methods to control the outflow of gold. The London Stock Exchange was the cheapest in the world for dealing in highly marketable securities. The business opportunities offered in London also attracted many foreign entrepreneurs and speculators who launched new ventures and enchanced the dynamism of the City.

The **First World War** terminated this supremacy, although not the prominent role of the City. Britain had to sell about 15 percent of its overseas investments in order to finance the war effort, and, with the suspension of the pound's convertibility, the dollar started to replace sterling as the means of payment for international commerce, in particular American foreign trade. But if New York was ready to challenge London's ascendancy, the City was no less determined to recover its former position. The restoration of the gold standard in 1925 at its pre-war parity was a deliberate effort in this direction. The City retained some advantages, in particular its expertise and experience, but its main handicap in comparison to New York was its lack of capital. In the 1920s the City was able to regain much of its pre-war international role, in particular as the center for commercial credit and short-term funds, as well as in shipping and insurance, but in the foreign issues it was largely overtaken by New York. The disruption of international trade and the Great Depression of the 1930s, followed by the Second World War, undermined the City's overseas activities, which, as a result, reinforced its links with the domestic economy. For example, while in 1910 foreign securities comprised 60 percent of all securities listed in the London Stock Exchange, by 1938 this proportion had fallen to 30 percent.

The resurgence of the City of London after the Second World War, despite the comparatively poor general performance of the British economy, was primarily due to the opportunities it was able to seize in the 1960s and 1970s to become the center of new markets, in particular for Eurodollars and Eurobonds. The Eurodollar market developed out of dollars held outside the United States by banks, **multinational corporations,** and others and traded entirely outside the United States. From $1.5 billion at the end of 1959, it reached nearly $50 billion in 1970 and $600 billion in 1980. The Eurobond market grew out of the Eurodollar market to provide longer-term loans than was usual with Eurodollars, which were either lent short term, particularly in the inter-bank market, or as syndicated medium-term credits. The City was able to capture these markets because of its experience in international finance, the range of professional skills available, which had no equivalent in any other financial center, and the concentration of foreign banks in the square mile. But the City was also able to supplant New York at the time of the undisputed financial supremacy of the United States because of the various regulations imposed by the American government, in particular the ceiling on interest rates paid on time deposits (known as Regulation Q), which made it more attractive to deposit dollars abroad and, above all, in London.

In the 1970s and 1980s Britain had the highest share of international banking activity, holding 20 percent of the world's foreign assets in 1985; in the mid-1980s, London was also the principal market in foreign exchanges, with 30 percent of a turnover that reached $600 billion a day in 1989. Although London's equities market was substantially smaller in volume than that of New York and Tokyo, it was more international and remained the largest in Europe. The City also retained strong international positions in various commodity markets and in insurance, as well as in such services as accountancy, law, and funds management. The difference from the pre-1914 or the inter-war periods was that very few of these transactions were now dealt in sterling and that much of this activity was undertaken by the foreign banks represented in London; their number rose to 521 in 1989, or twice the number in any other center.

The City of London is one of the success stories of the British economy. Nevertheless, it is often criticized for neglecting the domestic industry and diverting capital abroad, thereby contributing to British economic decline. This is a matter of controversy since the City also has strong defenders. The clearing banks have been criticized for their reluctance to grant long-term credit to industry and for their lack of managerial role. The capital markets have been held responsible, particularly prior to 1914, for the huge volume of foreign investments—some £4 billion in 1913—which, critics argue, would have been better employed at home. More generally, the City has been accused of "short termism," from the company promoter of the early twentieth century, more interested in a fast buck than in the long-term prospects of the company introduced to the market, to the mechanism of the takeover bid, which prevents managers from taking a long-term view of the prospects of their company if this were to affect its immediate results. Finally, British monetary policy has been seen as systematically favoring the interests of the City to the detriment of industry, the most striking examples being the rejection of bimetallism in the late nineteenth century, the return of the pound to gold at its pre-war parity in 1925, and monetarism in the early 1980s. On the other hand, it has been argued that there was no demand from industry for long-term banking credit; that capital exports were the results of a rational behavior on the part of individual investors and ensured

an efficient allocation of funds; and that the City was always prepared to support worthwhile long-term projects while takeover bids ensured the replacement of poor management. As to the monetary options of the British government, there is no evidence that decisions were made in order to favor City interests.

Youssef Cassis

Bibliography
McRae, Hamish, and Frances Cairncross. *Capital City: London as a Financial Centre.* 2nd ed. 1991.
Michie, R.C. *The City of London: Continuity and Change since 1850.* 1992.
Van Helten, J.J., and Y. Cassis, eds. *Capitalism in a Mature Economy: Financial Institutions, Capital Exports, and British Industry, 1870–1939.* 1990.

Civic and Repertory Theater
Civic theater in Britain is funded by local authorities on the principle that there should be active civic support for the cultural life of the community. These theaters often house repertory companies that may be funded from a variety of sources, including the local authority, the **Arts Council of Great Britain**, and business or private sponsorship. Sometimes known as "regional theater" or "municipal theater," civic theater is essentially noncommercial (while still profiting from box office takings), distinct from the commercial **London** West End theater as well as from the two national companies that employ a repertory system, the **Royal National Theatre** and the **Royal Shakespeare Company**.

The repertory movement in Britain began in the early years of the century as a reaction to the tendency of actor-managers to reduce the number of new plays performed and to select plays according to their long-term marketability. The intention of the repertory movement was to present new productions for short runs on a regular basis, to offer a high quality and varied repertoire of plays, to secure civic or state patronage, to forge links between a theater and its community, to provide a forum for contemporary dramatists and a training ground for young actors, and to decentralize the theater away from London.

In 1904 Miss Annie Horniman (1860–1937) opened the Abbey Theatre in Dublin, the first repertory company in the British Isles. However, the idea of repertory theater was

C

brought to prominence by Harley Granville Barker (1877–1946) between 1904 and 1907 during seasons at the Royal Court. In 1907 Granville Barker and William Archer (1856–1924) published *A National Theatre: Schemes and Estimates*, in which the idea of repertory theater was promoted. In 1908 Miss Horniman bought the Gaiety Theatre, Manchester, and set up the first English repertory company. The repertory movement began to flourish in the provinces, in competition with the old touring companies. In 1909 the Glasgow Repertory Company was formed at the Royalty Theatre. In 1911 a trial season at Kelly's Theatre, Liverpool, led to the formation of the Liverpool Repertory Theatre, the first theater in the country run by a public board. Subsequently, a number of new repertory companies were founded, including the Birmingham Repertory Theatre (1913), Plymouth Repertory Company (1915), Sheffield Repertory Company (1919), Scottish National Players (1921), Oxford Repertory Company (1923), and the Hull Repertory Company (1923). In 1926 the Festival Theatre at Cambridge was opened. The Northampton Repertory Company was established at the Theatre Royal in 1927. In 1931 the **Old Vic** theater in London was given over exclusively to the repertory system. Further new repertory companies included the York Repertory Company (1935), Perth Repertory Company (1935), Windsor Repertory Company (1938), Oldham Repertory Company (1938), and the Dundee Repertory Company (1939).

In 1939 the **Council for the Encouragement of Music and the Arts** (CEMA) was formed with grants from the Treasury and the Pilgrim Trust. In 1944 the Conference of Repertory Theatres (later the Council of Repertory Theatres and Council of Regional Theatre) was founded. This period saw the restoration and reopening of the Theatre Royal, Bristol (1943), the opening of Glasgow Citizens' Theatre (1943), and the founding of the Salisbury Repertory Company (1945).

After the Arts Council of Great Britain was established in 1946, four new repertory companies were founded: the Bristol Old Vic Company, Guildford Repertory Company, Kidderminster Repertory Company, and the Midland Theatre Company. Subsequently, other new repertory companies were established, including the Library Theatre Company, Manchester (1947), Ipswich Repertory Company (1947), Nottingham Repertory Company (1948), Ches-

terfield Repertory Company (1949), Canterbury Repertory Company (1951), and the Lincoln Repertory Company (1955). In 1956 the English Stage Company was formed at the Royal Court, London. In 1958 the Belgrade Theatre, Coventry, opened—the first purpose-built repertory theater since the war.

The 1960s saw a wealth of new theater companies and buildings, including the Welsh National Theatre Company (1962), Chichester Festival Theatre (1962), Victoria Theatre, Stoke-on-Trent (1962), Phoenix Theatre, Leicester (1963), Nottingham Playhouse (1963), Everyman Theatre, Liverpool (1964), Crewe Theatre (1965), Watford Civic Theatre (1965), Edinburgh Civic Theatre (1965), Octagon Theatre, Bolton (1967), and the Northcott Theatre, Exeter (1967). The 1970s saw further expansion of the repertory movement with the opening of the Crucible Theatre, Sheffield (1971), formation of the Contact Theatre Company, Manchester (1973), reopening of the Haymarket Theatre, Leicester (1973), opening of the Royal Exchange Theatre, Manchester (1976), Salisbury Playhouse (1976), Stephen Joseph Theatre-in-the-Round, Scarborough (1976), reopening of the Oldham Coliseum (1977) and Liverpool Everyman (1977), and the opening of the Wolsey Theatre, Ipswich (1979).

From 1945 until the mid-1970s subsidy for the arts grew at an extraordinary rate. One negative aspect of subsidy was to create a ranking of civic theaters, with Bristol, Birmingham, and Nottingham standing higher than Dundee, Crewe, and Chesterfield. In 1977 the Arts Council grant was withdrawn from the Chesterfield Civic Theatre, which ended the repertory company. In 1981 the Arts Council withdrew grants to the Old Vic (Prospect) Company, Crewe Lyceum Theatre, and the Canterbury Marlowe Theatre, resulting in the demise of the companies. Generally, the arts in Britain did not fare well during the **Thatcher** years. Repertory companies were forced to compete on a more commercial basis, while many have been struggling to remain solvent. In spite of recent difficulties, repertory theater remains an essential part of contemporary British culture.

Brian Pearce

Bibliography
Elsom, John. *Theatre outside London.* 1971.
Rowell, G., and A. Jackson. *The Repertory Movement: A History of Regional Theatre in Britain.* 1984.

Civil Service

In England, as in other contemporary Western European states, the public sector employs approximately 30 percent of the work force. Those who work for the government departments directly accountable to Parliament, a useful definition of civil service, account for only about 10 percent of those paid out of public funds. At the beginning of the 1980s approximately 675,000 men and women held such positions. In 1960 the total stood at 719,000, a peak in civil service employment. Because of the difficulty posed by definition, statistics about the civil service should be treated with some caution. Nevertheless, until recent times the number of civil servants has generally followed an upward trend, except for a contraction during the years of Depression and fiscal crisis in the 1930s.

The civil service has undergone considerable alteration in its composition during the course of the century. The industrial staff, for example, represented a majority of civil servants prior to the Second World War, but accounted for less than a quarter of the whole by the 1980s. As the size of the industrial sector grew smaller, the number of nonindustrial civil servants increased, largely in response to the need to staff the expanding social services provided by the welfare state. As a consequence, many in the civil service work in local and regional offices throughout the country and serve the public directly. Only about one-quarter of civil servants carry out their duties in Greater London.

The 1853 Trevelyan-Northcote Report set the terms of the modern discussion about the civil service. In this crucial document Sir Charles Trevelyan (1807–86) and Sir Stafford Northcote (1818–87) called for recruitment by open, competitive examination to a unified civil service that distinguished sharply between those engaged in "intellectual" (policy-making) duties and those engaged in "mechanical" (managerial) duties. In replacing a system of patronage with a system of merit, Trevelyan and Northcote envisioned departments of state headed by politically responsible ministers advised by politically anonymous officials.

Such ideas, representing a radical departure from previous practice, gradually garnered widespread acceptance, and, after 1870, successive governments took steps to implement these recommendations. The Civil Service Commission, established in 1855 to oversee competitive examinations, developed these along the lines of the classical curriculum characteristic of the public schools and Oxford and Cambridge on the grounds that individuals of intelligence enhanced by the best "all-round" or "general" education would make the best civil servants. Consequently, men of high intellectual caliber but little or no training in particular areas of policy began to enter civil service careers. These developments took hold over a period of time. Not until 1919, with the appointment of Sir Warren Fisher (1879–1948) as Permanent Secretary to the Treasury and head of the civil service and the imposition of open-competition examination as virtually the only mode of entry into the higher ranks of the civil service did the so-called administrative class finally approach the unified, generalist elite proposed by Trevelyan and Northcote.

The large number of royal commissions and official government investigations dedicated to topics pertaining to the civil service since the Trevelyan-Northcote Report attest to the way in which the role of the civil service raises sensitive questions about good governance, social equity, and political access. Three issues in particular provoke debate. First, the disagreement about whether the generalist or the specialist expert makes the most efficient government official persists. Second, the class and gender biases that continue to mark civil service recruitment create a perennial source of grievance. Finally, the extent of official influence on policy-making generates worry and suspicion.

The champions of the generalist civil service, most notably Warren Fisher, seemingly achieved the upper hand after 1919. The alternative view, which stresses the effectiveness and vigor of the expert and considers generalist knowledge as necessarily superficial, always had support in business circles and has attracted renewed interest in recent years.

Although ostensibly based on merit, open competition in practice tended to operate in a class-biased way. The type of education privileged by the examinations set by the Civil Service Commission was enjoyed mainly by the able children of the middle and upper classes, and the administrative class consequently became increasingly dominated by the products of public schools and Oxford and Cambridge, especially Oxford. This trend, already visible at the turn of the century, became even more deeply entrenched after the First World War. The need to recruit more widely during the Second **World War** went some way to counter this pattern, but it reasserted itself after 1945, proving remarkably resilient even as recruitment procedures underwent considerable revision.

The composition of the civil service exhibits gender bias as well as class bias. The first **women** to enter the civil service found themselves relegated to clerical positions and to positions in the inspectorate pertaining to women's issues. In 1894 the Treasury imposed a **marriage** bar, requiring any female who married to resign her position, which remained in force until 1947. After the First World War, the Civil Service Commission allowed women to sit for open-competition examination, although they continued to be ineligible for positions in many departments, especially those dealing with foreign affairs and defense. Women also earned lower rates of pay than men, an inequity that successive governments refused to address until the 1950s. At the end of the century, women still dominate the clerical grades and rarely hold high-level positions.

The role of the civil service in governance has often come under harsh scrutiny by both Left and Right. The advice given by civil servants to inexperienced **Labour** ministers in 1924 and in 1929, for example, has been suggested as an explanation for Labour's failure to take radical measures to combat **unemployment** and economic Depression during this period. Since the 1980s Thatcherite Conservatives have pointed to a Left-Liberal consensus among civil servants schooled in a post-war welfare state ethos as a source of entrenched obstruction within the government opposed to the implementation of significant policy changes.

The issue at stake here, the nature of the relationship between minister and official advisers, has been candidly explored by Richard Crossman (1907–74) in his *The Diaries of a Cabinet Minister* (1975–77). Political appointees who come to their positions with little or no background or experience suffer under some obvious handicaps managing departments staffed by those who can call upon a long experience in government service. This particular point of friction has roots in the very nature of parliamentary government, which depends upon **Cabinet** ministers appointed to office for political reasons.

During most of the twentieth century the Whitley system of joint consultation governed civil service staff relations. Named for J.H. Whitley (1866–1935), who chaired the Committee on Industrial Relations during the First World War that developed the concept, Whitleyism posited a system of committees composed of representatives of labor and management empowered to resolve disputes without recourse to strike action. Although intended to transform industrial relations in all economic sectors, the system took hold only in the public sector, with the foundation of the Civil Service National **Whitley Council** in 1919. Whitleyism placed a genteel stamp on labor relations in the civil service for fifty years. The rise in trade union militancy after 1969 profoundly altered this system. An effort to preserve the **standard of living** of its membership in inflationary times led civil service unions to engage in a series of **strikes** during the 1970s. Although these achieved some measure of success at first, the 1981 confrontation between civil service unions and the **Thatcher** government ended with a government victory. This outcome upheld the constitutional authority of the government when the civil service carried its challenge to the point of undermining government policy.

Some developments in the character of the civil service since the Second World War have maintained the centralizing trajectory established under Fisher's leadership during the inter-war years. The merging of the executive and clerical grades in 1947 followed by the addition of the administrative classes in 1971 exemplify this trend. The 1968 creation of the Civil Service Department also expressed government preference for a unified, centrally-controlled civil service. Even more recently, however, countervailing tendencies have begun to develop. Since the 1960s individual departments have taken primary responsibility for recruiting new entrants to their ranks. The Thatcher government abolished the Civil Service Department in 1981 and introduced new management systems at the departmental level to control costs and to assure efficiency in administration. With such initiatives Conservatives sought to reduce the civil service in size, curb its power, and increase its efficiency. The lengthy tenure of the **Conservative Party** in office gave the government an opportunity to see to it that these changes left a permanent stamp on the civil service. But this development may not resolve the persistent political tensions that revolve around the civil service, since these often serve to express larger conflicts within the polity and the society at large.

Gail Savage

Bibliography

Chapman, Richard A. *The Higher Civil Service in Britain.* 1970.

Fry, Geoffrey K. *The Changing Civil Service.* 1985.

———. *Statesmen in Disguise: The Changing Role of the Administrative Class of the British Home Civil Service, 1853–1966.* 1969.

Kelsall, R.K. *Higher Civil Servants in Britain from 1870 to the Present Day.* 1955.

Martindale, Hilda. *Women Servants of the State.* 1938.

Clark, Kenneth Mackenzie (1903–1983)

From the late 1920s onward Kenneth Clark occupied a unique position in the world of the visual arts in Britain and exercised a major influence on wider cultural matters. His role is difficult to define because he belonged to no single category or profession. His primary importance is as a critic working in the tradition of Ruskin and Pater. His best works in this vein, *The Gothic Revival* (1928), *Landscape into Art* (1949), and *The Nude* (1956), may all be said to have transformed the attitudes of general readers toward their subjects. They are characterized by a lucid power of synthesis and a coolly idiomatic prose style that sometimes disguise the fact that Clark was also a formidable scholar. His *Catalogue* (1935) of Leonardo's drawings at Windsor laid the modern foundations of Leonardo scholarship, and was followed in 1939 by a monograph on the artist that has never been superseded. At the outset of his career Clark was apprenticed to Bernard Berenson and aspired, like his master, to a life of scholarly contemplation, but he was distracted by his appointment to a series of public posts: Keeper of Fine Art at the Ashmolean (1931–3), Director of the National Gallery (1934–46), Surveyor of the King's Pictures (1934–44), Slade Professor of Fine Art at Oxford (1946–50), Chairman of the Arts Council of Great Britain (1953–60), and Chairman of the Independent Television Authority (1954–7). He was also at various times a Trustee of the British Museum, member of the Advisory Council of the Victoria and Albert Museum, and Vice Chairman of the Royal Opera House and National Theatre. After his resignation from the ITA he embarked on a pioneering career as a television performer, culminating in the thirteen-part series *Civilisation*, first shown by the British Broadcasting Corporation (BBC) in 1969. Alongside these public achievements Clark assembled a fine, eclectic collection of works of art and was a key patron of modern British artists, including Victor Pasmore, Graham Sutherland, John Piper, and Henry Moore. He was knighted in 1938 and made a Companion of Honour in 1959. He received a life peerage in 1969 and the Order of Merit in 1976.

Clark came from a line of Scottish thread manufacturers who had amassed a considerable fortune. His parents moved between sporting estates in Suffolk and Argyll and the yachts, villas, and casinos of the Riviera. Clark's father was eccentric, ebullient, and very often drunk. His mother was Quakerish, intelligent, and reserved. This mixed heredity, artfully evoked in the first part of his autobiography, *Another Part of the Wood*, powerfully informed Clark's character in which an urgent desire to communicate enthusiasm mixed oddly with an aloofness that many found chilling.

Clark's neglected childhood offered one great consolation—the discovery of what he later described as "a freak aptitude" for responding to works of art. At Winchester he was neither happy nor distinguished, but his flair was spotted by an imaginative headmaster, Montague Rendall, who provided lantern lectures on the *quattrocento*. At Oxford Clark read history, but his real education took place in the Ashmolean, studying the drawings of Raphael and Michelangelo under the watchful eye of the Keeper, C.F. Bell, a connoisseur of the old school who also suggested the subject of his first book, *The Gothic Revival*, and took him to meet Berenson at I Tatti.

After Oxford Clark spent two years working with Berenson on a projected revision of *The Florentine Drawings*. The experiment was not an unqualified success—Clark was too independent to be a good apprentice—but it determined much of Clark's subsequent career, and the values of I Tatti, with its mixture of intellectual endeavor and Bloomsbury manners, were to shape Clark's life.

In 1927 Clark had married Jane Martin, an able and attractive undergraduate contemporary, who believed passionately in his talent. His career now underwent a meteoric succession of changes. He was invited to catalog the Leonardos at Windsor in 1928; he helped organize the great Italian exhibition of 1930 at Burlington House; and in 1931 he was appointed to C.F. Bell's post at the Ashmolean.

C

Both Clarks moved easily between officialdom and high bohemia. They were young, fashionable, and widely courted. In 1934 Clark became the youngest Director of the National Gallery.

Clark's directorship was widely perceived as a success. He improved beyond recognition the hanging, lighting, and decoration of the gallery, while also establishing a scientific department and making notable acquisitions, ranging from the seven Sassetta panels of St. Francis to Ingres' *Madame Moitessier*. His relations with his staff were less happy. His wealth, success, and confidence had attracted envy in the profession, and in 1937 he made a serious mistake, pushing through against strong curatorial opposition the purchase at a Giorgione price of four small panels that were subsequently attributed to Previtali. Clark's discomfiture was widely relished, and the episode dimmed his appetite, never very keen, for institutional life. The advent of war reinvigorated his sense of public responsibility: The entire collection was evacuated to the Manod caves in Wales, but one great picture was brought to London each month throughout the air raids to console a public who also crowded to hear the lunchtime concerts held in the empty galleries. Clark also worked in the film division of the Ministry of Information and was instrumental through the **War Artists'** scheme in helping to preserve the lives of most significant British artists, while at the same time commissioning at modest expense an invaluable record of the war.

Clark resigned from the gallery at the end of 1945 to devote himself to writing and lecturing. For the next thirty years he was always in demand, and many of his best pieces were written to order. The lecture was the form that best suited him and, with the exception of *Piero della Francesca* (1951), all of his best critical books grew from lecture series. Next to art he found his greatest enjoyment in the act of writing, and he developed a vivid, untheoretical style in which thought and feeling are closely and persuasively fused. His work is empirical and intuitive—he always proceeds by attempting to understand the individual genius of both artist and work of art. His achievement both in his writings and through **television** was to open the minds of ordinary people to the power of art, much as Ruskin had been able to do in the previous century. By a paradox of history, Clark attained his greatest fame and influence at a period—the 1960s—when his ideas and values

were most under threat. His point of view was uncompromisingly male, Western, and bourgeois. His long career represents an unusual link between a near-Victorian high culture and the world of mass communications. His success lay in communicating the idea of that culture to the widest possible audience without compromising either his beliefs or his material.

Fram Dinshaw

Bibliography

Clark, Kenneth. *Another Part of the Wood: A Self-Portrait*. 1974.
——. *The Other Half: A Self-Portrait*. 1977.
Secrest, Meryle. *Kenneth Clark: A Biography*. 1984.

Clause Four

Clause Four is the most controversial part of the **Labour Party**'s constitution, adopted in 1918. Largely written by **Sidney Webb**, the leading **Fabian** theorist, in collaboration with **Arthur Henderson**, the party's Secretary, the clause is the only specific reference in that constitution to Labour's domestic aims. Clause Four, Section Four, of the Party Objects (to give its full title) committed the Labour Party:

> To secure for the workers by hand or by brain the full fruits of their industry, and the most equitable distribution thereof that may be possible, upon the basis of the common ownership of the means of production, distribution and exchange and the best obtainable system of popular administration and control of each industry or service.

(At the 1929 Labour Party Conference the words "distribution and exchange" were added to the phrase "means of production" in the original statement.)

The chief significance of Clause Four in 1918 was that it marked an ideological shift away from the Labour Party's early social liberalism toward an overtly socialist commitment involving the common or public ownership of major parts of the British economy. Moreover, the clause offered the party a broad formula that served to unite what was then a loose and heterogeneous political grouping.

For the next forty years Clause Four continued to perform this unifying function for the party. In 1959, however, **Hugh Gaitskell**, then leader of the party, attempted to amend the clause on the grounds that it was a source of misunderstanding and electoral unpopularity. In the face of fierce opposition he was forced in 1960 to withdraw his proposal. Clause Four remained part of the constitution in spite of the acceptance by Labour since 1945 of a market-oriented mixed economy. In 1995 a special party conference voted to eliminate it.

Tudor Jones

Bibliography
Cole, G.D.H. *A History of the Labour Party from 1914.* 1948.
McKibbin, Ross. *The Evolution of the Labour Party, 1910–1924.* 1974.
Pelling, Henry. *A Short History of the Labour Party.* 10th ed. 1993.
Williams, Philip. *Hugh Gaitskell: A Political Biography.* 1979.

Clearing Banks

The clearing banks, also called joint-stock banks and High Street banks, are responsible for most of the commercial banking activity in the United Kingdom: They accept deposits, allow customers to use checks, grant credit in the form of loans and overdrafts, discount bills of exchange, and provide various other services for their customers. Founded mostly in the 1830s and numbering over a hundred in the mid-nineteenth century, they became dominated in 1918 by a small group of five giant banks, known as the "Big Five"—the "Big Four" since 1968: Barclays, National Westminster, Lloyds, and Midland.

The origins of the clearing banks date to the Bank Acts of 1826 and 1833, which put an end to the Bank of England's monopoly by authorizing the formation of joint-stock banks, the former outside a radius of 65 miles around London, the latter in the capital itself but without the right of issuing notes. The joint-stock form of ownership was at first considered, in particular by private bankers, as inadequate for the business of banking. However, the number of joint-stock banks increased rapidly: Their number reached 99 in 1850 and 122 in 1875. The London joint-stock banks gained full recognition with their admission to the London Clearing House in 1854. The amalgamation movement that started in the 1860s and intensified in the 1890s reduced their number to 41 in 1913; among them a dozen banks based in London, with a network of branches covering the whole country, controlled about two-thirds of the country's deposits. The apotheosis of this movement took place in 1918 with the almost simultaneous merger, two by two, of the ten leading banks, giving birth to the "Big Five": the Midland Bank, Lloyds Bank, Barclays Bank, the Westminster Bank, and the National Provincial Bank. They controlled 90 percent of the bank deposits of the country in 1938. The National Provincial Bank and the Westminster Bank merged in 1968 under the name of National Westminster Bank; and the Midland, the largest bank in the world in the inter-war years, was taken over by the Hong Kong and Shanghai Banking Corporation in 1992, while continuing to trade under its own name.

The origins of these banks are diverse. Three main streams can be identified. First, the London joint-stock bank tradition, with the National Provincial Bank, established in 1833, and the Westminster Bank, established in 1834 under the name of London and Westminster Bank. Second, the provincial banks: Lloyds Bank and the Midland Bank. Both came from Birmingham—Lloyds Bank was established as a private bank in 1765 and converted into a joint-stock bank in 1865; the Midland Bank was founded in 1836 under the name of Birmingham and Midland Bank—and were of a comparatively small size when they moved to the capital, respectively in 1884 and 1891. Through an aggressive amalgamation policy, they were to become the two largest banks in the country twenty years later. Third, the Quaker private banking tradition with Barclays Bank. Although its origins can be traced to a private bank run by John Fraeme in the City of London in the 1690s, the bank was founded in 1896 by the amalgamation of twenty private banks in London and the country, whose partners were all linked by family relationships and a former adherence to the **Society of Friends**.

Given the specialization of the English banking system, the role of the clearing banks has mostly consisted in accepting deposits and granting short-term credit in the form of discounts, loans, or overdrafts. In the pre-1914 period this role was perfectly adapted to the requirements of the London money market. The bulk of world trade was financed through the medium of bills of exchange drawn on London. These bills were accepted by the **merchant banks**—that is, they promised to pay them at maturity, usually three months; they were then discounted by the bill brokers—also known as discount houses—and sold to the clearing banks, which kept them as a self-liquidating investment. The clearing banks were therefore providing the cash credit that activated the entire system. These conditions were altered by the First World War as the national debt absorbed an increasing proportion of the resources of the clearing banks and international commerce was greatly disrupted during the Depression of the 1930s.

It has been questioned whether deposit banking as practiced by the English clearing banks was as well suited for the requirements of British industry. Several committees inquired into that matter, in particular the Committee on Finance and Industry, also known as the Macmillan Committee, which published its report in 1931 and whose main recommendation was that the "gap" in the supply of long- and medium-term finance for small business—known as the "Macmillan gap"—should be filled.

The clearing banks have been criticized for their apparent failure to supply manufacturing industry with long-term credit, whether in the form of long-term loans or direct ownership of securities, on the model of the German banks. This criticism corresponds to the official banking orthodoxy; actual banking practices, however, varied over time. In the first half of the nineteenth century local bankers were closely linked to industrialists, and permanent overdrafts and rolled-over short-term loans were, in fact, equivalent to long-term commitments. The intensification of the amalgamation movement in the 1880s and 1890s seems to have changed this attitude as general managers in London decided to put an end to what they considered overcommitments. There is, however, no evidence that there existed a demand for long-term credit from industry. The situation changed again in the inter-war period. During the 1919–20 boom, the clearing banks abandoned much of their prudence and granted large overdrafts, particularly to the heavy and textile industries, which, with the downturn of the 1920s, often had to be converted into frozen loans and nursed for the remainder of the period. Although it can be argued that this long-term commitment was forced upon them by the prevailing circumstances rather than deliberately chosen as a new policy, the clearing banks appear on the whole to have adopted a positive attitude toward industry: Their support was not exclusively dictated by security motives, and advances meeting the banks' lending criteria were seldom refused. The clearing banks have also been criticized for their lack of managerial role and, especially during the inter-war years, for not using their position as creditors to encourage the rationalization of the basic industries. It is true that the banks did not play that role, not only because they did not want to but also because they lacked expertise in industrial finance and were primarily concerned with maintaining their creditors' interests. However, if they were unable to induce industrial reorganization, they used their position as powerful creditors to discipline and reconstruct management.

Contrary to their European counterparts, the English clearing banks developed only slowly into banking groups. Before 1914 they were unable to take a controlling interest in another company because they worked with a very small capital. A first move took place at the end of the First World War with the "affiliation" of some of the Irish and Scottish banks to the major clearing banks. The first of its kind was the affiliation of the Belfast Bank to the Midland Bank in 1917, making the former a subsidiary of the latter. A second step was the control of overseas banks, most notably by Barclays Bank, which created in 1925 Barclays Bank D.C.O.—Dominion, Colonial, Overseas— after acquiring the capital of the Anglo-Egyptian Bank, the Colonial Bank, and the National Bank of South Africa. The first control over a merchant bank was not taken until 1967, when the Midland Bank took one-third share in Samuel Montagu. Since the 1970s, however, the number of subsidiaries of the clearing banks increased considerably.

The position of the clearing banks has been declining since the end of the First World War. The total amount of their deposits did increase, from £961 million in 1911–13 to £2.731 billion in 1936–8 at current value; at real value, however, they increased by only 60 percent. And although they rose from £6.4 billion in 1951 to £45.8 billion in 1979 at current value, they rose only by 12 percent in real terms. The clearing banks maintained a large share of banking deposits in the inter-war years, but they faced an increasingly strong competition from other financial institutions, in particular building societies whose proportion of bank deposits rose from 6 percent in 1923–5 to 23 percent in

1936–8. After the Second World War the share of bank deposits held by the clearing banks fell from just under 70 percent in 1951 to 54 percent in 1965 and just over 18 percent in 1979. This was due to a large extent to the competition of the foreign banks in London, in particular in the wholesale deposits—that is, deposits of large sums mainly by financial institutions and large corporations, including nonsterling deposits, on which the clearing banks have increasingly depended since the 1960s. The clearing banks have been partly responsible for this decline. Despite some innovations in their practices, they were content for decades to operate a price cartel and remain strictly within the frontiers of deposit banking. On the other hand, from the 1930s to the 1960s, the assets of the clearing banks were dominated by the government debt, which represented about two-thirds of their deposits in 1950, and they were, until the late 1970s, the main target of the financial authorities in their policy of credit control. The deregulation of the 1980s, the increased internationalization of financial services, and the revolution in information technology have presented the British clearing banks with new opportunities and at the same time forced changes upon them that have brought them closer to the "universal banking" model.

Youssef Cassis

Bibliography

Collins, Michael. *Money and Banking in the U.K.: A History.* 1988.

Holmes, A.R., and Edwin Green. *Midland: One Hundred Fifty Years of Banking Business.* 1986.

Nevin, Edward, and E.W. Davis. *The London Clearing Banks.* 1970.

Winton, J.R. *Lloyds Bank, 1918–1969.* 1982.

Cliveden Set

The Cliveden Set was a term that came to be applied in the 1930s to the group of friends of Waldorf, Viscount Astor and his wife, Nancy, who met at their Buckinghamshire country house, Cliveden. The term was coined by the Communist journalist and editor Claud Cockburn in 1937 and was meant to refer to a small and highly influential secret cabal of wealthy conservative power brokers who enjoyed great, but unofficial, influence over the government. The story of the political significance of Cliveden is really the story of the transplanted Virginian **Nancy Astor,** who inspired the political weekends at Cliveden and whose ideas set their agendas. With two active political careers in their Anglo-American family, Lord and Lady Astor turned their great estate of Cliveden into a regular meeting place for political discussion among public figures of many stripes of British public opinion. This interest in playing host to a cross section of politics was enhanced by the fact that Lord Astor owned the *Observer* newspaper and his brother controlled *The Times,* two of the most influential journals of the day.

By the mid-1930s the most important international question that confronted Britain was: How could war with the dictator powers, Germany, Italy and Japan, be prevented? In 1937 **Neville Chamberlain** had replaced **Stanley Baldwin** as Prime Minister and meant to seek a lasting peace through identifying the reasonable demands of the dictators and trying to meet them peacefully. This was the essence of the policy that came to be called **appeasement.** In this regard, **Lord Halifax,** Lord President of the Council and a close confidant of the Prime Minister, traveled to Germany in November 1937 to meet the Führer.

Cockburn, sole proprietor of a small journal called *The Week,* was violently opposed to appeasement. A Communist and brilliant satirist, Cockburn opposed the Halifax visit and published a story that purported to reveal that one of the major seedbeds of appeasement thinking was the Astor country house. He soon coined the term "Cliveden Set" and popularized the idea that government policy was being made not in Parliament but in the luxurious Thames-side house of an Anglo-American millionaire and his politically prominent wife.

It is true that the Astors supported the policy of appeasement and frequently entertained prominent appeasers such as Thomas Jones, **Geoffrey Dawson,** and Lord Lothian in their home. Cliveden also welcomed such anti-appeasers as **Anthony Eden,** Lord Cranborne, and **Harold Macmillan.** The Cliveden Set, as a political entity, was a myth created by a clever and disaffected opponent of what was certainly a disastrous policy. Neville Chamberlain, however, took no orders from Cliveden.

R.J.Q. Adams

Bibliography

Cockburn, Claud. *Cockburn Sums Up: An Autobiography.* 1981.

Gannon, Franklin Reid. *The British Press and Germany, 1936–1939.* 1971.

Grigg, John. *Nancy Astor: A Lady Un-ashamed.* 1980.

Koss, Stephen. *The Rise and Fall of the Political Press in Britain.* vol. 2: *The Twentieth Century.* 1984.

Clothing and Fashion

Clothing development is influenced by a complex web of social, cultural, and economic factors, none of which is unique to this century or to Britain. Indeed British clothing since 1900 has shared the same design influences as the rest of Europe and North America. The country has lost any notion of "Britishness" in its dress, although nonconformist street styles add a touch of independent styling within an otherwise international look.

A few national differences remain. Scotland retains its national dress based on the late eighteenth-century military kilt, coupled with early nineteenth-century romantic styles, but the kilt is now worn regularly only by a small minority. Most Scotsmen only don them for their weddings, hired from the clothing rental shops. Welsh national dress was never anything more than a nineteenth-century fiction. The black steeple hats and red flannel cloaks are now restricted to Eisteddfods and bogus tourist amusements.

Thus a study of male, and especially female, dress in twentieth-century Britain covers the same style trends as New York, Paris, Berlin, or Vienna. The befrilled S bend of the 1902–6 period gave way to the more upright slim line put forward in Paris by 1909. During the **First World War** hemlines shortened and became so flared that some mistakenly predicted the revival of the crinoline. However, following the dictates of Paris, British **women** took up the boyish *garçonne* look. Skirts were shortened to the knee by 1926, breasts were flattened with corselettes, and to be fat became a social disaster. By the mid-1930s feminine lines, heightened by long bias-cut skirts heralded a revival of womanly curves.

The restrictions of the **Second World War**, however, did mark a uniquely British type of dress, as the government assumed control of the quantity and quality of both textile and garment production through its utility clothing scheme. Women's styles remained virtually unchanged from 1940–6 with broad-shouldered and neatly tailored, knee-length suits and dresses. As soon as the long-skirted, corseted New Look was launched in Paris in 1947, British women once again adapted their styles to French lines. It was not until the mid-1960s, through the success of Mary Quant's generation of innovative young designers, that Britain regained any sort of fashion independence. This was retained thereafter through British youth subcult street styles, though these are only worn by a minority.

The clothing of British men is epitomized by British traditions of excellence in craft tailoring. Saville Row and far cheaper local independent tailors or factories made up suits for all social classes. Conventional styles of the dark striped city suit and country tweedy jackets change slowly, with some businessmen still wearing Edwardian-style overcoats with velvet collars. Bowler hats, however, disappear year by year. The mass of working-class men wore shabby suits, flannelette shirts, and cloth caps from 1900 through to the Second World War, saving their "best" for Sundays. Dramatic change came from the late 1960s with the mass adoption of American jeans, sneakers, jogging suits, bomber jackets, and sweatshirts.

Specific British influence on twentieth-century dress can be related to economic and social developments. The outstanding feature is the increasing diffusion of stylish clothes for women, trickling throughout British society, reaching to all levels by the mid-1950s. This is a reflection of the steady economic improvement in the lives of working-class families. In the period 1900–20 most working-class women wore simple jackets, long skirts, and blouses. At home the ubiquitous apron or overall covered shabby working dress.

By the 1930s there was an increasing demand for cheap but fashionable clothes, especially in the more prosperous south, fed by the development of a larger ready-to-wear industry. By the 1950s British teenagers became the newest fashion consumers. In the 1990s it is still possible to identify the really wealthy through their clothes, but it is also possible for the less affluent, but stylish, to be just as "fashionable."

Against this background of socially expanding consumerism came a related technological response from the British textile and clothing industries. Viscose-based rayon, developed in the United Kingdom mainly by the firm of Courtaulds from 1906, was at first much despised for its glittering sheen and poor shrinking and wrinkling qualities, but by the late

1930s it was being widely worn, particularly in various creped finishes. From 1940s onward the use of pure synthetic fabrics became widespread, starting with nylon in the United States and, by the 1950s, British polyesters—Terelene and Crimplene—together with acrylics—Courtelle. The British textile industry declined steadily under the weight of cheaper, rival imports. From the mid-1980s sports-influenced styles decreed blended and new synthetics—stretch Lycra, microfibers, Neoprene, and imitation rubbers—and there was also a move toward more-natural cottons, linens, and wools, a trend related to the fashionable "green" issues of the 1990s.

The technology of garment manufacture has changed less dramatically through the century. Men's wear has been manufactured on a highly mechanized production-line basis since the late nineteenth century, largely based in the Midlands. By the 1920s Burton's and John Colliers were producing thousands of "made to measure" suits a week in their factories. Women's wear, because the styling changes seasonally, has to be manufactured through more flexible processes—namely, in small factories. Chain stores like **Marks and Spencer** made fashionable clothing at popular prices more accessible, and the importation of clothes manufactured in the Third World has intensified competition among British retailers, styles changing with ever greater alacrity.

A major problem facing British fashion designers throughout the century has been the role of Paris as international arbiter of style. Thus wealthy British women bought their important clothes directly from Paris couturiers or from their **London** annexes, while the London couture trade, centred in the Mayfair district by 1900, was forced to copy Paris styling. Compared to Paris with over 100 couture houses, London had only a dozen or so, and most were badly financed, relying for their clientele only on the social elite, supplemented by a few actresses and film stars and sales to ready-to-wear companies for copying. Styles related to the etiquette of the Court and social season—presentation, ball, dinner, and silk day dresses for weddings—all of a certain elegant, albeit conventional, style.

Among these are two types of garments that can be identified as particularly British. First, from the 1930s the full-skirted, romantic evening/wedding dress, usually in pale colors, revived again in the 1980s by Diana, Princess of Wales. Well-known London fashion designers in the 1900–14 period included Lucile (Lady Duff Gordon); Mme. Hayward, Reville and Rossiter, who dressed Queen Mary; Kate Reilly, who trained Madelaine Vionnet; and Sarah Fullerton Monteith Young. The great London department stores of Jay's, Harrods, Marshall and Snelgrove, and Selfridges dressed the rich and middle classes and had counterparts in every major British city. From the 1930s to the 1950s British couture shone on the international scene through the work of a talented generation of designers such as Norman Hartnell, Victor Stiebel, Peter Russell, Charles James, Hardy Amies, John Cavanagh, Ronald Patterson, and Michael Sherrard.

The second British style of international fame was the tailored suit. By 1900 walking suits were worn by women not only in the country but also for town expeditions. The most famous tailoring houses, Creeds and Redfern, were joined in the late 1930s by Lachasse, Digby Morton, and Hardy Amies, and later by Vivienne Westwood and Paul Smith. In the mid-1930s top British tailoring ready-to-wear companies included Jaeger, Dorville, Dereta, Brenner Sports, and Windsmoor.

With these developments clients began to drift away from the couture houses. After the cancellation of the presentation of debutantes in 1958, the success of the British couture industry declined, retaining only an aging clientele, while the younger generation shifted to the new boutiques. By the 1960s many couture houses had closed, most, with the exception of Hardy Amies, failing to develop the lucrative ready-to-wear lines and perfume/accessory franchises that keep the international couture system afloat. Even the house of Hartnell, which survived his death in 1979, finally closed in 1992.

However, a new breed of designer was born out of the explosion of talent in London in the early 1960s, such as Mary Quant in Chelsea, John Bates, Barbara Hulanicki at Biba, Jane and Jane, Sally Tuffin, and Marion Foale, mostly graduates of London colleges of art and **design**. Their reasonably priced, boutique clothes, many sold in Soho for men as well as women, were ephemeral, young, and fun. Along with **popular music**, young London fashions took the international fashion world by storm. From this point on, young British designers and street/subcult styles exerted a dynamic influence on top designers the world over. Thus the old "trickle down" fashion-diffusion system was

C

finally broken, and mass-produced lines are now styled through a fusion of couture, *pret-a-porter*, street, and ethnic influences.

In a multicultural society many Britains of Asian descent dress in either traditional styles or modernized versions of them, shopping at specialist textile and fashion shops selling saris and Muslim dress. These, along with street dress and young Black British styles, are influencing mainstream fashion through the work of the new young generation of British designers, such as Helen Storey, Red or Dead, John Richmond, Rifat Ozbek, Workers for Freedom, Pam Hogg, John Galliano, and Body Map. It is within this strand of innovative design that a unique sense of "Britishness" in dress can still be found.

Lou Taylor

Bibliography

Arch, Nigel, and Joanna Marschner. *Splendour at Court: Dressing for Royal Occasions since 1700.* 1987.

Bell, Quentin. *On Human Finery.* 1976.

McDermott, Catherine. *Street Style: British Design in the Eighties.* 1987.

Wilson, Elizabeth, and Lou Taylor. *Through the Looking Glass: A History of Dress from 1860 to the Present Day.* 1989.

Clubs

Around 1900 the number of gentlemen's clubs in **London** peaked at about 200, most of which had been founded during the previous thirty years. By the 1980s there were forty left, the survivors tending to be the oldest clubs. These fell into two main categories. The eighteenth-century clubs, privately owned, exclusive, and aristocratic—the most notable being White's, Brooks', and Boodle's, still clustered together at the top of St. James' Street—provided congenial premises where gentlemen could carouse and game among themselves. By contrast, the great nineteenth-century clubs were economical in principle, member-owned ventures in low-cost communal luxury, founded essentially by and for middle-class professionals, though forming their own hierarchy of exclusivity. The grandest have survived best, snobbery being a principle highly resistant to change. The economical clubs have suffered most, especially the least exclusive. But along Pall Mall, once lined with clubs, a number still survive—most notably, the Athenaeum, Travellers', and Reform. One of

the most notable to succumb was the United Services, which closed its cavernous premises in 1976, unable to sustain its military identity and membership despite having absorbed two other defunct clubs, the Junior United Services and the civilian Union.

The last old-style London clubhouse to be built was the Royal Automobile Club's Louis XIV-style palace in Pall Mall, which opened in 1911, though with distinctively modern features such as a swimming pool. The **First World War** killed off many clubmen, actual and potential, though it produced a few new clubs of lucky survivors, such as Buck's, deservedly famous for Buck's Fizz— champagne and fresh orange juice. Another that captured the interwar mood was the Gargoyle, a socially mixed intellectual bohemian club owned by David Tennant where members as various as **Virginia Woolf**, **A.J. Ayer**, and Tallulah Bankhead dined, danced, and drank. The **Second World War** bombings destroyed several clubhouses, though a few, such as the **Conservative Party**'s Carlton, found new premises, or rebuilt, like the Naval and Military. A rare new post-war club has been the Groucho, favored by journalists and other "media types," and named, of course, after the man who said that he did not want to belong to any club that would have him as a member.

Surviving through the twentieth century has taxed the ingenuity of club managements. Rent, operating expenses, and wages have all risen dramatically: Between 1843 and 1977 these costs rose for the Reform Club by 772 percent, 1,331 percent, and 5,307 percent, respectively, with over half of the increase occurring in the inflationary 1970s. Good servants, so vital to a successful club, are harder to find and expensive to keep. Bars have become important sources of revenue, even at the dignified Athenaeum, which long held out against this lucrative vulgarity. Most clubs have relaxed rules regarding women guests; some have even offered them memberships. Standards of membership have also been relaxed, with businessmen increasingly being tolerated for their valuable expense-account entertaining habits. Some clubs have survived by accommodating others: the Naval and Military in Piccadilly houses the Ladies' Carlton, the Cowdray (ladies), the Canning, the Goat (naval officers), and Portland (a bridge club). The Oriental shrewdly capitalized on the value of its Hanover Square freehold during the 1970s property boom, erecting an office block and buying a more luxurious clubhouse with the profits. While few clubs have managed to maintain a waiting list for membership, one that has is the Garrick, which has successfully maintained its distinctive literary-theatrical ambience, helped by the considerable copyright income from *Winnie the Pooh*, bequeathed to it by A.A. Milne—evidence of the club's remarkable hold on its members' affections.

Christopher A. Kent

Bibliography

Cowell, F.R. *The Athenaeum: Club and Social Life in London, 1824–1974.* 1975.
Hough, Richard. *The Ace of Clubs: A History of the Garrick.* 1986.
Lejeune, Anthony, and Malcolm Lewis. *The Gentlemen's Clubs of London.* 1979.
Woodbridge, George, *The Reform Club, 1836–1978.* 1978.

Clydesiders

"Red Clydeside" has loomed large in the annals of the British Left. It gained its name between 1915 and the mid-1920s from the nature of industrial and political events in Glasgow and other industrial centers along the Clyde. In 1915–16 there was serious unrest in munitions factories and shipyards led by militant shop stewards, many of whom the government deported from the area, and also successful rent strikes. In early 1919 an engineering dispute escalated into a general strike in the area, during which the red flag was raised over Glasgow city hall and the government sent in tanks to overawe the inhabitants. In the 1922 general election Glasgow returned ten **Independent Labour Party** (ILP) MPs, while in the rest of western Scotland a further ten were elected.

As a result the area acquired a reputation for being the nearest British equivalent to the working-class revolutionary strongholds of St. Petersburg. John Maclean (1879–1923), a leading Marxist speaker in the area, was appointed an Honorary President of the First All Russian Congress of Soviets and also, in January 1918, Bolshevik Consul in Glasgow. Several leading shop stewards became founders and leading figures in the **Communist Party of Great Britain**, most notably William Gallacher (1881–1965), who was an MP from 1935–50. Gallacher later suggested that in 1919 there had been a revolutionary situation on the Clyde but no adequate leadership. However, most historians have doubted that Glasgow, let alone Britain, was near to revolution in 1919.

Nevertheless the Clydeside can be seen as an exceptionally militant area. John Foster, in making such a case, has pointed both to the continuing high levels of industrial unrest after the end of the **First World War** and to the link between high levels of support for Left candidates and the presence of large-scale shipbuilding, mining, and steel, as at Govan, Greenock, Kelvingrove, and Motherwell.

The Clydesider group of ILP MPs elected in 1922 were beneficiaries of this radical industrial and political background. They also benefited from Labour's crusades against the appalling Glasgow slum housing and from the party's ability to gain the Irish vote. They established a collective identity in British politics through being radical by Westminster's standards. This image was reinforced by **James Maxton** and others being involved in several parliamentary uproars and subsequently sometimes being suspended from the House of Commons. Maxton was a charismatic figure of the Left during the inter-war years, a guardian of the ILP socialist faith. **John Wheatley**, drawing on his experience in Glasgow municipal politics, was quick to take up Ministry of Health ideas on housing and became responsible for the greatest success of the first Labour government, the 1924 Housing Act. Emmanuel Shinwell (1884–1984) and Tom Johnston (1881–1965) were to hold office under **Ramsay MacDonald** and **Clement Attlee**, but their actions by then owed little to the earlier special politics of Clydeside.

C.J. Wrigley

Bibliography

Duncan, R., and A. McIvor, eds. *Labour and Class Conflict on the Clyde, 1900–1950.* 1992.
Foster, John. "Working-Class Mobilisation on the Clyde, 1917–20" in C.J. Wrigley, ed. *Challenges of Labour.* 1992. pp. 149–75.
McKinley, Alan, and R.J. Morris, eds. *The ILP on Clydeside, 1893–1932.* 1991.
McLean, Iain. *The Legend of Red Clydeside.* 1983.
Melling, Joseph. *Rent Strikes: Peoples' Struggle for Housing in West Scotland, 1890–1916.* 1983.
Middlemas, Robert Keith. *The Clydesiders.* 1965.

Coal Mining

Coal mining occupies a special position not only in Britain's economic history, but in its political development and the evolution of the role of the British state. In many ways its rise and decline represent crucial transitions in the the country's economic and political experience as an industrial power.

During the nineteenth century coal was central to Britain's industrialization, to the growth of its **railway** system, to its export earnings, and to ocean transport throughout the world. The major coalfields (in South Wales, the Midlands, the northeast, and in southern Scotland) had, in turn, become centers of heavy industries such as iron and **steel**, engineering, chemicals, and shipbuilding. The resulting boom in output, exports, and employment continued until the First World War, by which time there were more than 1,400 collieries and 3,000 individual firms, accounting for one-third of Britain's exports and employing 1 million men and boys—almost 10 percent of the male labor force.

By the twentieth century the statistical significance of the coal industry was also associated with powerful social and political forces. The dependence of society on the supply of fuel, the concentration and coherent solidarity of mining communities, the self-consciousness and militancy of miners, and the sensitivity of the rest of society to an occupation that appeared at once dangerous, exploited, and heroic—all gave coal mining a special place on the national scene. And this was reflected in state intervention (to regulate working methods, safety, hours of work, and minimum wages) at a time when governments were otherwise reluctant to intervene in business matters.

Ironically, the **First World War** both dramatized and eroded the importance and strength of the industry on the national scene. On the one hand, coal played a vital strategic role in what was the first great industrialized war. As a result, the miners were able to use their enhanced bargaining power to secure higher rates of pay and a direct role in wartime administration, while the government, with the aims of maximizing output, curbing profiteering, and avoiding industrial unrest, introduced controls over the finances, organization, and labor policy of the industry. On the other hand, however, the war led to a postponement of investment and modernization and a substantial increase in coal production in Britain's erstwhile export markets. After the war, and a temporary and artificial boom, the prosperity of the industry was undercut by high production costs, stagnating trade, increasing foreign competition, and economies in the use of fuel. The British coal industry now suffered from excess capacity, an unwieldy structure, antiquated equipment, and inflexible and high costs.

Given the history of poor labor relations and entrenched attitudes, the outcome was inevitable and uncomfortable. The mine owners pressed for the only form of cost-cutting—wage reductions—available in the short run; the miners accused the owners of exploitation and a failure to pursue the sort of reorganization that would make the industry more competitive; neutral observers became profoundly depressed at the sight of an industry in need of rationalization but incapable of attaining it; and the government was confronted with industrial unrest, widespread **unemployment**, devastation throughout whole communities, and demands for financial help and an interventionist policy (e.g., to enforce industrial reorganization) that it found ideologically impossible to offer.

These problems were the more compounded—especially in the 1920s—by Britain's commitment to an orthodox monetary policy, which established an exchange rate at which coal exports were even more uncompetitive. This was a point emphasized by **John Maynard Keynes** in 1925 when he opposed the return of the pound sterling to the **gold standard** at a high rate of exchange. Soon after his warning, in 1926, the coal industry experienced its worst inter-war crisis. Resisting the owners' proposal to reduce wages and increase hours of work, the miners went on strike and were joined temporarily by other unions in a **General Strike**. The General Strike collapsed after a few days, but the miners held out grimly for six months, ultimately accepting defeat and wage cuts. But the reduction in labor costs helped little: Economic dislocation continued for the rest of the 1920s, and from 1928 was aggravated by the worldwide Depression. Suffering in the coalfields in the course of the great slump of 1929–32 was extreme, unemployment rose to over 20 percent (with figures of 40–60 percent in some important districts), and the industry appeared to stagnate, even at the lower level of output it was forced to accept.

This prolonged and inevitable decline in one of Britain's erstwhile great staple industries was not, of course, steady. In the 1930s, along with the British economy generally, the coal industry experienced a recovery, which was accentuated by the needs of rearmament after 1936. After 1934, too, the government attempted to spur the rationalization of coal mining into bigger units under the aegis of a Coal Mines Reorganisation Commission. But neither industrial policies nor the forces of the market were able to revive the fortunes of coal to a significant extent.

The experience of coal mining during the **Second World War** was in many ways a rerun of that of the First, although in 1939–45 government intervention was even more elaborate and the political leverage of the miners even greater. By the end of the war the industry's productivity, welfare, and future had become much more overt matters of national concern, and the numerous plans to use public intervention to restructure it were capped in 1946 by the **Labour** government's surprisingly uncontentious move to nationalize coal mining with the device of a public corporation, the National Coal Board (NCB).

Over the next forty years or so the NCB had a checkered history (it was renamed British Coal in the 1980s). Massive investment and structural (administrative) changes streamlined the industry and enhanced its productivity. At the same time, however, the monolithic scale of the corporation made for unwieldiness and inefficiency. More important, cheap alternative fuels (particularly oil) and technical changes among industrial and domestic consumers (using gas and oil to run transport, heating systems, and machinery) diminished the scope for expansion. The industry therefore continued its decline, at least as measured in terms of output and employment. By the late 1980s the vast majority of coal produced was used to generate electricity—and even that market was threatened by alternative fuels (gas, oil, nuclear). Moreover, in spite of **nationalization**, the industry's instability continued—in large part owing to the centralization of labor bargaining, which increased the authority of the miners' union. And when there was a threatened shortage of oil, strike action for higher wages proved a powerful and disruptive weapon. This was the case, for example, in 1972 and 1974, when the miners gained large improvements in their wages (in 1974 their successful strike was even instrumental in bringing down the **Conservative** government).

These gains, however, proved ephemeral. At one level the long-run stagnation in the market for coal, and at another level the political apprehension at the power and instability of the miners' union, were to weaken the miners and the industry. It was little wonder that the Conservative government elected in 1979 was determined to reduce both the power of the union and the significance of the industry, which, it felt, was excessive in relation to the demand for coal. This now-familiar situation provided the context for the major and violent **miners' strike of 1984–5**, when the miners claimed that the government was intent on closing large numbers of mines—a claim denied by the government, although later events seemed to justify it. The miners experienced a crushing defeat, thanks to the stockpiling of coal, the government's determination and planning, the reduced

TABLE 1: OUTPUT, EXPORTS, AND EMPLOYMENT IN BRITISH COAL MINING, 1913–93

	Number of pits	Employment (in thousands)	Output (million tons)	Exports (million tons)
1913	3287	1118	287	98
1920	2851	1248	229	39
1929	2419	857	258	77
1938	2125	791	227	46
1947	958	705	195	5
1960	698	583	191	6
1975	241	245	125	2
1980–1	211	294	125	-2
1992–3*	50	44	80	-18

* A number of mines in 1992–3 were not producing coal, even though still "open." The major run-down of the industry, which accompanied the move toward privatization, came in 1993–4.

strategic significance of coal as an industrial fuel, and the fact that a large number of miners refused to join in the strike.

With the defeat of the National Union of Mineworkers in 1985, the stage was set for further radical changes. One change was a major spurt in labor productivity: By the end of the decade the number of miners had been reduced by 50 percent, but the output had stayed the same. Yet in spite of this increase in productivity the industry continued to face economic trouble as the demand for British coal continued to stagnate. A degree of protection was afforded by favorable long-run contracts (originally signed under government pressure) with the then-nationalized electricity generating plants. But by the early 1990s the latter had been privatized and made more responsive to market forces alone; the government was unwilling to extend any form of subsidy to coal mining; and both the state and large consumers of coal had clearly decided that the political instability created by the past history of a powerful mining union was to be avoided by running down the industry even further. By 1994 the once great industry had been reduced to a dozen or so mines and 10,000 miners and was on its way into private hands. Coal mining had become an entirely negligible activity, and, as far as this staple industry of the initial industrialization was concerned, the nineteenth century finally came to an end in the last decade of the twentieth century. The process of decline—from both economic supremacy and political centrality—had proved long, poignant, and painful. It had been strongly resisted, but the effort had been unavailing. Economic forces had, inevitably, triumphed. And in the process, coal mining, like Britain itself, had discovered that fundamental economic change cannot be divorced from political controversy, ideological debate, and social disruption.

Barry Supple

Bibliography
Ashworth, William. *The History of the British Coal Industry.* vol. 5: *1946–1982: The Nationalized Industry.* 1986.

Buxton, Neil K. *The Economic Development of the British Coal Industry from Industrial Revolution to the Present Day.* 1978.

Kirby, Maurice W. *The British Coalmining Industry, 1870–1946.* 1977.

Supple, Barry. *The History of the British Coal Industry.* vol. 4: *1913–1946: The Political Economy of Decline.* 1987.

Cole, G(eorge) D(ouglas) H(oward) (1889–1959)

Always known by his initials, G.D.H. Cole was a major intellectual figure on the British Left throughout the first half of the twentieth century. Along with such figures as R.H. Tawney and Harold Laski, he exercised an immense influence on the developing thought of the labor movement. His output was prodigious, including more than 100 books, and spanned a vast intellectual terrain. Associated first with the early-century development of the doctrines of Guild Socialism, a version of industrial self-government, he maintained this emphasis in his thought thereafter but also wrote and campaigned on many other fronts.

His background was an unlikely one for a socialist intellectual (his father, of appropriately Tory disposition, was in suburban real estate in London), but his conversion experience came at St. Paul's School when he encountered the work of William Morris. Henceforth he was a socialist, of an imaginative and uncompromising William Morris kind. From his Oxford base, first as student then as teacher, he organized an assault on the prevailing Webb version of administrative socialism and sought to substitute a more participatory model. In the decade that had the First World War as its center, Cole came to prominence as the major theorist of the new doctrine of Guild Socialism.

On one side he was influenced by the syndicalism and industrial unionism whose impact and meaning he interpreted in his first book, *The World of Labour* (1913); on another side, by the theoretical critique of state sovereignty by the political pluralists. When combined with his own understanding of the meaning of William Morris, this provided a basis for his embrace of the idea of National Guilds (as expounded in the pages of the *New Age* by A.R. Orage and S.G. Hobson) and his own development of this idea into the theory of Guild Socialism. Its root idea was industrial self-government by workers, but Cole broadened it into a general social theory. In a rapid succession of books (such as *Self-Government in Industry*, 1917, and *Guild Socialism Re-Stated*, 1920) he made and refined the Guild Socialist case, which became very influential for a time.

His prodigious industry also made him an indispensable figure in the developing institutions of the labor movement (including a period as the **Labour Party**'s Research Secretary following its 1918 reorganization). As interest in Guild Socialism declined with the economic slump in the 1920s, Cole turned his attention to wider matters and became a one-man think tank for Labour as the party negotiated the problems of the inter-war period. Having become a Reader in economics at Oxford in 1925, he was well placed to offer a steady flow of policy advice and was one of those who provided a bridge between **John Maynard Keynes** and the Left.

He was an active participant in the politics of the Left over a long period, from a perspective he liked to describe as "sensible extremism." At Oxford the "Cole Group" was a home for young left-wing intellectuals and a place of passage for many who later became Labour politicians (such as **Hugh Gaitskell**). In the 1930s his **Society for Socialist Inquiry and Propaganda** (SSIP) gave birth to the **Socialist League**, while he invented the **New Fabian Research Bureau** (NFRB) to provide Labour with an unofficial source of new policy ideas. He continued to produce an endless flow of books and pamphlets on a vast range of topics, including his series of weighty "Guidebooks for the Intelligent Man" on current issues, and threw himself into the campaign for a **Popular Front** against **Fascism**. In 1944 he became the first Chichele Professor of Social and Political Theory at Oxford, where he remained until retirement in 1957, producing his multivolume *History of Socialist Thought* (1953–60).

The influence of G.D.H. Cole is writ large over the whole landscape of the labor movement for half a century. All of its institutions—party, trade unions, **Fabian Society**, *New Statesman*, workers' education—were shaped by his work. Yet he always remained unorthodox and maverick, his restless energy and radical imagination rubbing uneasily against the conservative anti-intellectualism of much of the British labor movement. **Clement Attlee**'s description of him as a "permanent undergraduate" captures some of this, as does Christian socialist Maurice Reckitt's famous ditty: "with a Bolshevik soul in a Fabian muzzle; Mr. G.D.H. Cole is a bit of a puzzle."

Yet Cole remains a formidable and, in some respects, a surprisingly contemporary figure. If much of his vast work was necessarily bound by the time in which it was written, interesting only for the historian, there is also much that remains of more enduring interest. The breadth of his work is extraordinary, encompassing several disciplines (**history, economics**, literature, social and political theory) and providing a monument to, as well as an example of, impressive popular scholarship. Yet his distinctive legacy derives from his early engagement with Guild Socialism and his continuing sense that the Left had to devise a decentralized and participatory model of socialism, different from either welfare statism or Communism, if it was to find a future. That was an unfashionable view for much of Cole's life, but it may not be so unfashionable now.

Anthony Wright, MP

Bibliography

Carpenter, L.P. *G.D.H. Cole: An Intellectual Biography*. 1973.
Cole, G.D.H. *Self-Government in Industry*. 1917.
Cole, Margaret. *The Life of G.D.H. Cole*. 1971.
Wright, A.W. *G.D.H. Cole and Socialist Democracy*. 1979.

Committee of Imperial Defence (1902–1939)

From 1902 to 1914 and 1919 to 1939 the Committee of Imperial Defence (CID) was the British government's main advisory body on every aspect of home and overseas defense. It played a major role in formulating the underlying principles of defense policy and prepared plans to ensure that the armed services and their respective ministries would respond in a coordinated manner if war were declared. At the end of 1916 its permanent secretariat, which recorded proceedings and communicated decisions to the appropriate departments, was transformed into an organization that served the **Cabinet** as a whole and subsequently became the Cabinet Office. This was one of the key innovations in governmental machinery to result from the **First World War**.

The CID was established in December 1902 as Britain began to modernize its forces and overhaul the machinery for the higher direction of military and naval policy in light of the **Boer War** and the growing challenge of Germany. The old standing Defence Committee of the Cabinet was recast by **Arthur Balfour**, the Prime Minister, to include senior officers from the services as well as such Cabinet ministers as the Chancellor of the Exchequer, First Lord of the Admiralty, and Secretary of State for War. It was further remodeled in May 1904 along lines suggested by the influential Lord Esher (1852–1930), who saw it as the cornerstone of the structure supporting his proposed War Office reforms. The Prime Minister, previously an ordinary member, now became the chairman and, initially, the only permanent member, though Esher, too, was made a permanent member in 1905. The Prime Minister exercised absolute discretion in the choice of other members, thus giving the body greater flexibility and authority. Simultaneously, the CID's ability to tackle problems in detail was vastly strengthened by the creation of a full-time secretariat. The first Secretary was Sir George Clarke (1848–1933), followed by Sir Charles Ottley (1858–1932) in 1907 and Captain Maurice Hankey (1877–1963) in 1912. However, the CID had no executive functions, its recommendations being submitted to the Cabinet or the departments concerned for action.

After 1906 much of its work was delegated to subcommittees. One, the Committee on the Coordination of Departmental Action, produced the War Book, a comprehensive list of the steps to be taken in the event of hostilities. While some tasks were eased by the formation of a general staff for the **army** in 1906, the lack of a similar naval staff until 1912 hampered full integration of the policies of the army and the **Royal Navy** during this period and contributed to the Admiralty's poor performance at the crucial CID meeting on 23 August 1911, when the army's case triumphed and the shift toward future British involvement in a Continental land campaign consequently grew more pronounced.

With the coming of war in 1914, the CID fell into temporary abeyance, its work being absorbed by other bodies. Britain's smooth mobilization showed the value of the War Book, but the CID had failed to provide blueprints for the necessary expansion of the army, the conversion of industry to war purposes, or the additional reorganization of governmental machinery. A smaller body than the twenty-strong Cabinet was needed for swift response to the pressures of war so, in November 1914, Prime Minister **H.H. Asquith** set up the War Council, a special Cabinet committee to review war policy and strategy. Hankey and the CID staff acted as a secretariat to the War Council and its successors, the Dardanelles Committee (June 1915) and the War Committee (November 1915). When **David Lloyd George** replaced Asquith in December 1916, he combined the functions of the War Committee and the Cabinet by creating a five-man War Cabinet with its own secretariat under Hankey. Now, for the first time, a formal record was kept of Cabinet proceedings.

The CID was revived in 1919, with Hankey staying on as Secretary to both the Cabinet and the CID. Before the War Cabinet was dissolved, it instructed the service departments to assume that the British Empire would not be engaged in another major war for ten years, a policy endorsed periodically by the CID until 1932. Nevertheless, the CID continued to advise the Cabinet as to how Britain's defense organization could best meet the changing conditions of the post-war world. To facilitate close consultation between the army, navy, and air force, the Chiefs of Staff Subcommittee was established in 1923 and was soon the most important element in the CID. Subordinate to it were the Joint Planning Committee (1927), the Deputy Chiefs of Staff Committee (1932), and the Joint Intelligence Committee (1936).

Early in 1934 the CID recognized Germany as the potential enemy for the purposes of long-term planning. A significant rearmament program was introduced in March 1936, and, to remove some of the load of responsibility from the shoulders of **Stanley Baldwin**, then Prime Minister, Sir Thomas Inskip (1876–1947) was appointed Minister for the Coordination for Defence. In this new post, Inskip was to exercise, on the Prime Minister's behalf, the daily supervision of the CID, but he had no department and no executive authority.

In the years immediately before the Second World War the CID was instrumental in establishing and developing the Cabinet War Rooms, an underground headquarters in Whitehall where the Cabinet and Chiefs of Staff could be protected from air attacks. At the end of July 1938 Hankey retired, and **Neville Chamberlain** decided that Hankey's dual role had grown too large for one person. He therefore separated the two appointments. Edward Bridges (1892–1959) became Permanent Secretary to the Cabinet Office and Secretary to the Cabinet, while Colonel Hastings "Pug" Ismay (1887–1965) became Deputy Secretary (Military) to the Cabinet and Secretary of the CID.

On the outbreak of war Chamberlain formed a small War Cabinet on the 1916 model, and the secretariats of the Cabinet and the CID were merged into a single War Cabinet Secretariat. The Committee of Imperial Defence ceased to have a separate existence on 5 September 1939 and was never resurrected.

Peter Simkins

Bibliography

D' Ombrain, Nicholas. *War Machinery and High Policy: Defence Administration in Peacetime Britain, 1902–1914.* 1973.

Ehrmann, John. *Cabinet Government and War, 1890–1940.* 1958.

Ismay, General Lord. *Memoirs.* 1960.

Johnson, Franklyn A. *Defence by Committee: The British Committee of Imperial Defence, 1885–1959.* 1960.

Roskill, Stephen. *Hankey: Man of Secrets.* 3 vols. 1970–4.

Commonwealth Literature

The term Commonwealth literature acknowledges and celebrates the extraordinarily diverse literary productivity of the nations that emerged from the dissolution of the British Empire after the Second World War. The specific wealth held in common is the English language, and the currency of the term Commonwealth literature draws the attention of a worldwide Anglophone audience to this body of work, which already includes three Nobel Prize winners: Australian Patrick White (1973), Nigerian Wole Soyinka (1986), and Saint Lucian Derek Walcott (1992).

In retrospect, **William Butler Yeats**, Augusta Gregory, and John Millington Synge at the turn of the century were perhaps the first Commonwealth writers— the first to write out of the characteristically "Commonwealth" crossing of urgent nationalism and devotion to the tradition of the shared language (earlier Irish writers like Jonathan Swift, Oliver Goldsmith, and Oscar Wilde had been agreeably assimilated to British literature). But the notion of a Commonwealth developed only in the 1930s as a description for the British Isles along with what would now be called the settler colonies: **Canada, Australia, New Zealand,** and **South Africa**. It was novelists from these regions, many of whom had spent considerable time in England, that after the war first began to be regarded as comprising Commonwealth literature. Among them were Patrick White,

who had returned to Australia to write; **Doris Lessing**, who came to England from Rhodesia (now Zimbabwe) in 1949 and immediately published her first book, *The Grass Is Singing;* Nadine Gordimer of South Africa; and Margaret Atwood of Canada. Their work was observant and generally realistic, making their farflung landscapes seem vivid and accessible to British readers. Yet from the beginning some of these novels address themselves particularly to the intellectual forum of the Commonwealth (rather than to either a specifically local or a "universal" audience)—as, for example, when Alan Paton's *Cry the Beloved Country* (1948) presents urgent South African issues before the tribunal of the Commonwealth.

The breakup of Empire induced an unprecedented migration back to the metropolis between the end of the war and the restrictive legislation of the early 1960s. One consequence was the discovery of authors from the "New Commonwealth"—the Indian subcontinent, Anglophone Black Africa, the West Indies, and Malaysia. They were initially perceived as exotics; publishers responded to a taste for informative, almost ethnographic, novels by offering the sights and sounds of the tropics in books like R.K. Narayan's *The Financial Expert* (1952), Chinua Achebe's *Things Fall Apart* (1958), and the genial early novels of V.S. Naipaul. But soon novels of all sorts began to appear, along with brilliant accounts of what it was like to *be* a Commonwealth writer: George Lamming's *The Pleasures of Exile* (1960), Nirad Chaudhuri's *Autobiography of an Unknown Indian* (1963), and C.L.R. James' *Beyond a Boundary* (1963).

Though fiction was the most widely disseminated genre, immigrant theater was lively in London even in the 1950s; many plays were produced for radio and the stage, though they were only rarely published. Publishers favored playwrights engaged in active dialogue with the Western tradition: from Nigeria, Soyinka rather than Duro Ladipo; from South Africa, Athol Fugard rather than Gibson Kente. As for poetry, in addition to public readings in London the **British Broadcasting Corporation** (BBC) Colonial Service was an important medium. Several Commonwealth verse anthologies appeared during the 1960s, and in 1965 an extensive Commonwealth arts festival was mounted at the Royal Court Theatre in London, coinciding with first issue of the *Journal of Commonwealth Literature.* Other periodicals in the field soon appeared, especially *Kunapipi, Ariel,* and *WLWE.* Beginning in 1969 the Booker Prize has honored a succession of Commonwealth authors, including V.S. Naipaul, Ruth Prawer Jhabvala, J.M. Coetzee, Michael Ondaatje, Salman Rushdie, and the Japanese-born Kazuo Ishiguro.

The sense that Commonwealth writing in some way constitutes a unified body of literature is grounded on the shared language, the relation (however attenuated) to its literary tradition, and more mundanely on the economic value of metropolitan publication, and on the alluring electronic simultaneity of the "global village" in the late twentieth century. Yet three distinct sorts of Commonwealth literature can be identified: (1) new national literatures around the world; (2) new literatures of immigrant communities in England (for example, the novelist and screenwriter Hanif Kureishi was born in England and the playwright Mustapha Matura in Trinidad, but both write out of and for the communities of **Black people**); (3) writing in England (as well as Canada and the United States) by self-styled exiles or expatriates who seem to participate in neither of the above categories. Unlike Sam Selvon or Wilson Harris, who continue to write West Indian literature though they live in Canada and England, authors like Naipaul and Rushdie seem most comfortable addressing the Anglophone Commonwealth at large; behind them stand the examples of **Joseph Conrad** and **James Joyce.**

The growing national literatures in English are not always well served by the umbrella term "Commonwealth literature," which invites a wider audience but tends to discount a work's relation to its indigenous languages, literatures, and culture. Particularly in Africa, India, and parts of Asia, literatures in English are subdivisions of larger multilingual literatures, but in practice "Commonwealth literature" refers only to the part of a nation's literary production both *written* in English and addressed to readers of English— that is, to an audience for the most part external to the place, unfamiliar with local language and custom. Amos Tutuola's novel *The Palm-Wine Drinkard* (1952), for instance, was widely praised for its vividly fractured language, but Commonwealth readers were unaware of the novel's indebtedness to Yoruba narrative (e.g., the novels of Daniel Fagunwa). Even in 1991 Ben Okri's hallucinatory novel

The Famished Road, out of the same Yoruba tradition, was often characterized in terms of Latin American magical realism, a style from another hemisphere and another language that nevertheless has the advantage of being more familiar to Anglophone readers than Okri's own culture.

English is a global language, or a global family of languages, but accessibility to a wide readership seems an important criterion for any work's inclusion in "Commonwealth literature." So, for example, the extensive Onitsha market literature of Nigeria, pulp fiction written for a local audience in heavily creolized English, is not construed as Commonwealth, but neither is the impressive work of Jamaican "dub" poets like Linton Kwesi Johnson, even though they perform, record, and publish in London. In Britain itself, there is some danger that the designation "Commonwealth" serves as a code for minority literature; when, for example, Kazuo Ishiguro's *The Remains of the Day,* a novel by a longtime British resident about a very British butler, is classified as Commonwealth literature, the term seems primarily to signal the author's ethnicity.

Indeed, because of its political implications the specific term "Commonwealth literature" is disputed; some cultural critics regard the notion of Commonwealth literature as an example of how Britain still lays claim to the products of its former colonies. Such critics prefer to speak of "post-colonial literature(s) in English." Other critics, noting that in practice "Commonwealth literature" means "non-British, non-American literature in English," prefer to speak of world literature written in English.

Laurence A. Breiner

Bibliography

Adam, Ian, and Helen Tiffin, eds. *Past the Last Post: Theorizing Post-Colonialism and Post-Modernism.* 1990.

Ashcroft, Bill, Gareth Griffiths, and Helen Tiffin. *The Empire Writes Back: Theory and Practice in Post-Colonial Literature.* 1989.

King, Bruce. *The New English Literatures: Cultural Nationalism in a Changing World.* 1980.

McCrum, Robert. *The Story of English.* 1986.

Riemenschneider, Dieter, ed. *The History and Historiography of Commonwealth Literature.* 1983.

Communist Party of Great Britain

For the first time since the 1920s there were no official Communist candidates in the British general election of 1992. The Communist Party of Great Britain (CPGB) had changed its name a year before at its Forty-third Congress to the Democratic Left. It urged its few members (about 1,400) to support the candidates best able to defeat the **Conservatives,** whether Labour, Liberal Democrat, or Scottish National.

The fact that Karl Marx regarded Britain as a mature capitalist society ripe for revolution must have inspired some British workers and intellectuals to form a movement to realize his aims. A number of such organizations—among them the Social Democratic Federation, the British Socialist Party, and the **Independent Labour Party** (ILP)—came into existence toward the end of the nineteenth century. As elsewhere, the **First World War** and the Leninist seizure of power in Russia in 1917 led to splits. Eventually, in July 1920 a small group of radicals, believing themselves to be the true heirs of Marx, founded the CPGB. They considered themselves to be the advance guard of the proletarian revolution. Their tactic was to seek affiliation to the **Labour Party,** which by 1918 had became the main opposition party, but its reformist leaders steadfastly refused to allow the CPGB to affiliate.

Affiliated as it was to the Communist International, or Comintern, the CPGB was obliged to implement the policy decisions dictated by Moscow. As happened in other Communist Parties, it lost members with each dramatic shift in policy. Although high turnover in membership was regrettable, it made it easier for the leaders to retain control over a party composed of inexperienced members. Leninist principles of democratic centralism and against factions compounded that control.

The CPGB operated through the trade unions and the Labour Party and sought to get its own members elected to Parliament. For most of its existence it denounced Parliament as a capitalist conspiracy, but one useful as a forum for party propaganda. Several Communists were elected to Parliament in the inter-war period. In 1922 J.T. Walton Newbold won the Scottish constituency of Motherwell. In the same year Shapurji Saklatvala, a middle-class Indian, was elected at North Battersea (London) as a Labour MP although he was a member of the CPGB. Defeated in 1923, he was re-elected as a Communist in 1924. In that year the Labour Party decided that no member of the Communist Party (or any other competing party) could be an individual member of the Labour Party. In 1935 William Gallacher was elected for the Scottish mining constituency of West Fife, the first Communist to defeat a Labour candidate. The only other CPGB candidate to stand, Harry Pollitt, was defeated. The fact that only two Communists stood in 1935 was in keeping with the changed party line. In the elections of 1929 and 1931 the CPGB had fielded twenty-five and twenty-six candidates, respectively. In 1928, following Comintern instructions, the "class against class" line had been introduced, and this meant fighting Labour as the "second capitalist party" instead of seeking affiliation with it. By 1935 the line had changed again into one of unity in the fight against **Fascism** and war. Albert Inkpin, party Secretary since 1920, fell victim to the change of line in 1929 and was succeeded by Harry Pollitt, who remained as Secretary until 1956.

The CPGB directed its campaigns before 1939 against **unemployment**, colonialism, Fascism, and war and managed to extend its influence well beyond its ranks. **John Strachey** and, to a lesser extent, Emile Burns popularized Marxism during the 1930s when the attraction of Communism grew. Among the intellectuals identified closely with the CPGB were scientists **J.D. Bernal** and **J.B.S. Haldane** and philosopher John Lewis. Serious music was represented in the CPGB by Alan Bush, and the **film industry** by Ivor Montagu. Sean O'Casey was one of a number of writers supporting Communism. Two contributors to Marxist literary theory, Christopher Caudwell and Ralph Fox, were among the 526 British volunteers killed in the **Spanish Civil War** on the Republican side.

When the Hitler-Stalin Pact was announced on 23 August 1939, shock waves registered throughout the CPGB. In the mistakenly named *Labour Monthly,* its editor, CPGB theorist R. Palme Dutt, welcomed it as "logical." However, when war was declared on Germany, most CPGB members automatically assumed they would support it. The full implications of the Nazi-Soviet Pact had not yet sunk in. A pamphlet by Pollitt entitled *How To Win The War* stated, "The Communist Party supports the war, believing it to be a 'just war.'" After the Soviet invasion of Poland on 17 September, presented as an act of liberation, the CPGB was advised by its Comintern representative Dave Springhall that the war was imperialist and to be opposed. On 3 October this line prevailed in the Central Committee by twenty-one votes to three; Pollitt, Gallacher, and J.R. Campbell, editor of the *Daily Worker*, who remained unconvinced, were later persuaded to toe the party line.

Until the attack on the Soviet Union by Germany on 22 June 1941 the CPGB kept up its attack on the war. It lost some of its 18,000 members during this period but gained others from among the more militant trade unionists and some **pacifists**. Exploiting the genuine grievances of ordinary workers under wartime conditions and Labour complicity in government policies, it called for the replacement of the coalition by a "People's Government" that would bring peace. It attempted to win support for this objective through a "People's Convention" held in London in January 1941, an event attracting delegates from a host of Communist front organizations such as air raid shelter committees, tenants groups, peace groups, factory committees, and anticolonialist organizations. Although the government was authorized to intern individuals and ban publications deemed dangerous, it used its powers sparingly. It did arrest **Sir Oswald Mosley**, the Fascist leader, and more than 700 of his supporters. By contrast, hardly any Communists were taken into custody. The *Daily Worker* was banned on 21 January 1941, as was Claud Cockburn's *The Week*, but other Communist publications, such as *Labour Monthly*, were left untouched. The bans were lifted after the Nazi invasion of the Soviet Union.

Immediately after the attack on the Soviet Union Prime Minister **Winston Churchill** announced British support for the Soviets. The CPGB immediately swung round to supporting the war effort; it became super-patriotic, denounced **strikes**, and joined the political truce. This move meant that it did not field candidates in by-elections and resisted opportunities for criticism of government policies. It did, however, join with other groups to campaign for a Second Front. Admiration for the Soviet Union's war efforts was fostered by the popular media, which spurred a growth in party membership. At the time of the German defeat at Stalingrad membership rose to an all-time peak of around 100,000, but it then began to decline. Common Wealth, a respectably radical, new political group critical of government policy, probably attracted some who might otherwise have opted for the CPGB.

In the election of 1945 the CPGB, fighting on a program close to that of Labour, put up twenty-one candidates. Only two of them were successful: Gallacher at West Fife and Phil Piratin at Mile End (London). In addition, D.N. Pritt, who followed the CPGB line consistently, as he continued to do until his death, was reelected as a Labour independent. Once the Cold War started, the CPGB attempted to promote trade union militancy against the Labour government. It had gained support during the war mainly in the firemen's union, the Electrical Trades Union (ETU), the draughtsmen's union, the **National Union of Mineworkers**, the Amalgamated Engineering Union, scientific workers, and some others. As it supported the Soviet Union unwaveringly, it became less and less popular. In the 1950 election it nominated a record 100 candidates, all of whom were defeated, including Gallacher and Piratin. Pro-Communist fellow travelers, standing as independents after their expulsion from the Labour Party, were also unsuccessful. Nor have any Communists been elected to Parliament since then.

Joseph Stalin's attempt to destroy Tito (1948), the invasion of Hungary (1956), the exposure of Stalin at the Twentieth Congress of the Communist Party of the Soviet Union (CPSU) (1956), and the Soviet invasion of Czechoslovakia (1968) all contributed to the decline of British Communism. It also suffered from a ballot-rigging scandal by its members in the ETU. In 1951 the CPGB promoted a program labeled *The British Road to Socialism,* which, in fact, advocated an East European-type system. John Gollan, who replaced Pollitt in 1956, could do little to revive the party's fortunes. In the 1960s it supported the CPSU in its dispute with Chinese leader Mao Tse-Tung and exploited opposition to the Vietnam War and **nuclear weapons** and left-wing disappointment with **Harold Wilson**'s Labour government.

CPGB membership declined from about 34,000 in 1964 to under 20,000 in 1977. In that year it revised its program in a more reformist, Euro-Communist direction, provoking another split. The New Communist Party, led by Sid French with a membership of 1,000, was established to advocate a more-Stalinist approach. Meanwhile, Trotskyist organizations such as the Workers' Revolutionary Party (1959) and the Socialist Workers' Party (1976) were increasingly recruiting its potential clientele. In the 1980s **Militant** was the main standard bearer of this trend. The CPGB retained a residual influence in the 1980s, especially through its theoretical journal *Marxism Today* and, to a lesser extent, the daily *Morning Star* (formerly *Daily Worker*). It retained some prestige through one or two prominent trade unionists like Mick McGahey of the miners and Ken Gill of the engineers. On 9 December 1990 the CPGB decided to drop Marxism-Leninism in favor of democratic socialism. The collapse of Soviet Communism in 1991 led to the CPGB's decision to regroup under its new name of Democratic Left.

David Childs

Bibliography

Branson, Noreen. *History of the Communist Party of Great Britain, 1927–1941.* 1985.

Childs, David. "The Cold War and the 'British Road,' 1946–53," *Journal of Contemporary History*, vol. 23 (1988), pp. 551–71.

———. "The Communist Party and the War, 1939–41," *Journal of Contemporary History*, vol. 12 (1977), pp. 237–53.

Klugman, James. *History of the Communist Party.* 2 vols. 1968–9.

Macfarlane, L.J. *The British Communist Party: Its Origin and Development until 1929.* 1966.

Pelling, Henry. *The British Communist Party.* 1958.

Wood, Neal. *Communism and British Intellectuals.* 1969.

Composers and Music

Sir **Edward Elgar**'s assessment of *A Vision of Life* (1907) by Sir Hubert Parry (1848–1918) as "fine stuff" is indirect evidence of his own debt to the nobility and grandeur of Parry's music, qualities the latter continued to explore during the Indian summer of his career in his Fifth Symphony (1912), the symphonic poem *From Death to Life* (1914), and the *Songs of Farewell* (1918) for unaccompanied chorus. In contrast, Elgar's view of the music of Sir Charles Stanford (1852–1924) as "neither fish, flesh, fowl nor good red-herring!" ignores the restrained ardor of Stanford's Clarinet Concerto (1902), the manly vigor of the *Songs of the Sea* (1904) for baritone, male chorus, and orchestra, and the fiery passion that erupts intermittently in the Fifth Irish Rhapsody (1917).

However, despite the achievements of Parry and Stanford, neither composer could match Elgar; nor, indeed, could Sir Granville Bantock (1868–1946), although the novelty of the voluptuous harmonies and Straussian exuberance in his three-part cantata, *Omar Khayyam* (1906–9), and in *Sappho* (1906) for contralto and orchestra, led some of his contemporaries to think so. Bantock, close friend of Elgar and for a time of **Frederick Delius**, also supported Josef Holbrooke (1878–1958), like himself a pupil of Frederick Corder at the Royal Academy of Music, and the self-taught Havergal Brian (1876–1972). Each composer's large output is still being reassessed, but with Brian it is doubtful whether the centrality of his thirty-two symphonies, beginning with the immense *Gothic* (1919–27), will be displaced, or in the case of Holbrooke his Wagnerian operatic trilogy *The Cauldron of Annwyn* (1912, 1914, 1929). The greatest operatic success of this period was, in fact, the 216 consecutive performances of *The Immortal Hour* (1913) by Rutland Boughton (1878–1960), whose dissatisfaction with the London operatic scene prompted him to create at Glastonbury a center for opera performance supported by a commune of artists (1914–27).

Another prolific pupil of Corder, Sir Arnold Bax (1883–1953), self-confessed "brazen romantic" and Celtic enthusiast, established his reputation with a substantial collection of tone poems, including *In the Faery Hills* (1909) and *Tintagel* (1919). Subsequently he embarked on a series of seven symphonies, the First (1922), by turns aggressive and searingly elegiac, a bitter response to the events of the First World War and the Easter Rising of 1916. John Ireland (1879–1962), too, was deeply affected by the war, the Edwardian pleasantries of his Phantasie Piano Trio (1906) being displaced by the sour harmonies of the Second Piano Trio (1917), written, according to Ireland, with "the boys going over the top of the trenches" in mind. Also like Bax, Ireland was an accomplished pianist, and both developed an individual pianism—Bax, for instance, in his Second Piano Sonata (1919) and in *Winter Legends* for piano and orchestra (1930), Ireland in his Concerto (1930) and in *Sarnia* (1941), three pieces celebrating Guernsey, one of Ireland's spiritual homes.

In contrast to Ireland's stylistic evolution, that of Frank Bridge (1879–1941) paralleled radical trends on the Continent more closely. As a pupil of Stanford (as were Ireland and the vast majority of English composers of his generation), Bridge's initial idiom was conservative, although invigorated by thorough professionalism as in the First String Quartet (1906) and Phantasy Piano Quartet (1910). However, in response to an increasing awareness of musical developments abroad and a deepening consciousness accelerated by his reaction to the war—Bridge was a pacifist—his late style, heralded in the monumental and sometimes systematically bitonal Piano Sonata (1924), was brought to fruition in the highly chromatic, aggressively energetic Third String Quartet (1927). The latter work, dedicated to the American patron of chamber music, Mrs. Sprague Coolidge, who supported Bridge financially from 1923 onward, was succeeded by further chamber works in a similar style, including the spacious Piano Trio (1929), before a partial relaxation was achieved in the partly neo-classical Fourth String Quartet (1938). The centerpiece of these late works is the elegiac cello concerto, *Oration* (1930), a funeral address for the lost of the First World War and, by implication, a passionate indictment of all war.

For those intent on studying abroad rather than with Corder or Stanford, Iwan Knorr at the Hoch Conservatory, Frankfurt, became the preferred master, teaching Roger Quilter (1877–1953), Henry Balfour Gardiner (1877–1950), Cyril Scott (1879–1970), and the Australian Percy Grainger (1882–1961). Both Quilter and Balfour Gardiner were essentially Edwardian composers; their best works—in Quilter's case, songs; in Gardiner's, such orchestral pieces as *Overture to a Comedy* (1906) or *A Berkshire Idyll* (1913)—hardly transcend their period. By contrast, Scott, for a time, earned himself the reputation of a modernist. However, it was Grainger's openness to sounds, be they natural or man-made, heard in the music hall or produced by newly invented instruments, that was indicative of a more radical aesthetic. Unfortunately, interest in his serious works has been eclipsed by the popularity of the folksong settings *Molly on the Shore* (1907) and *Country Gardens* (1918).

Apart from Quilter, several other composers of his generation specialized in songwriting, including Ivor Gurney (1890–1937), whose considerable poetic talent was nurtured by an abiding love for English literature, particularly the Elizabethan and Georgian poets. Gerald Finzi (1901–56), too, could encapsulate the essence of the text he was setting in distinctive music, especially in response to Hardy's and Shakespeare's words, and in the ecstatic song cycle *Dies Natalis* (1926, 1939), for high voice and strings, a minor masterpiece. Finally, the songs of Peter Warlock (1894–1930) exhibit a wide range of feeling, from the rumbustious "Rutterkin," via the jolly, uncomplicated "Pretty Ring-Time" and quietly introspective "Sleep," to the bleak despair of "The Curlew."

E.J. Moeran (1894–1950), who lived with Warlock for a time and whose song collection *Seven Poems of James Joyce* (1929) is influenced by him, expanded his style and technique during the 1930s to include a Sibelian thematic growth in his G Minor Symphony (1934–7). The tough vigor of the Sinfonietta (1944) marks a further step toward modernism, although the outer movements of the Violin Concerto (1942), with their poetic dreaming, reveal the continuing strong influence of both Delius and **Ralph Vaughan Williams** on his style. Herbert Howells (1892–1983), too, was indebted to both composers, a ruminative pastoralism suffusing the String Quartet *In Gloucestershire* (1923), and a Delian sense of loss in the *a capella Requiem* (1936), subsequently expanded into *Hymnus Paradisi* (1938). Each new recording of the neglected music of John Foulds (1880–1939) helps fill out the incomplete picture of his achievement. His piano concerto, *Dynamic Triptych* (1929), can stand beside Vaughan Williams' concerto (1931) without loss of face as can his Ninth String Quartet, *Quartetto Intimo* (1932), beside Bridge's later quartets.

During his lifetime, Foulds' reputation was based on his light music, the *Keltic Lament* (1911) catching the public's ear. Other composers, Haydn Wood (1882–1959), Eric Coates (1886–1957), and Frederic Curzon (1899–1973), specialized in this area. Coates' belief that music should play a vital part in everyday life became fact with the advent of broadcasting, and the choice of his music for signature tunes—the march *Calling All Workers* (1940), introduced the radio program *Music While You Work*, while another march, *Knightsbridge* (1933), heralded the TV program *In Town Tonight*—introduced it to an enormous audience. The syncopated piano novelties of Billy Mayerl (1902–59), such as *Marigold* (1927) and the suite *Four Aces* (1933), also became immensely popular.

For many composers of Vaughan Williams' generation, the progress of modernism on the Continent meant little or nothing. Nonetheless, Lord (Gerald) Berners (1883–1950), blessed with a talent for mimicry, could imitate Satiesque wit and satire in his *Trois petites marches funèbres* for piano (1914) and, by contrast, approach an almost expressionist idiom in another group of piano pieces, the *Fragments psychologiques* (1921). Influenced by Busoni, Bernard van Dieren (1887–1936), likewise approached expressionism in his *Six Sketches* for piano (1911) and in parts of the Chinese Symphony (1914), although in his later music he withdrew from such an extreme position. With **William Walton's** generation, some involvement with modernism was *de rigueur*. Thus Sir Arthur Bliss (1891–1975) originally drew for inspiration on the music of Ravel, Stravinsky, and Les Six as well as ragtime in, for instance, *Rout* for soprano and chamber ensemble (1920), its Gallic carnival atmosphere punctuated by the singer's nonsense syllables. However, by the time of the expansive and richly scored *Music for Strings* (1935), an Elgarian romanticism held sway. Constant Lambert (1905–51) pursued a similar course initially, but with the ragtime influence more pervasive, particularly in *The Rio Grande* for piano, chorus, and orchestra (1927) and the Piano Sonata (1929). The astringent, world-weary Concerto for Piano and Nine Players (1931), which became a memorial to Warlock following his suicide, marked a new departure, although the balmy climate of *The Rio Grande* returned with syncopated rhythms and warm lyricism in the ballet *Horoscope* (1937). Alan Bush (1900–), like Bliss, changed course radically during his career, the dissonant counterpoint of his early String Quartet, *Dialectic* (1929), giving way to a simplified idiom that could be used, as in the Byron Symphony (1960), to communicate with a wider audience and thereby give expression to his Communist beliefs.

A more sustained commitment to modernism can be heard in the music of other composers of Walton's generation. Sir Lennox Berkeley (1903–89), a pupil of Nadia Boulanger in Paris and a lifelong friend of Poulenc, found Stravinsky's neo-classicism congenial. Unfortunately, Berkeley's reticence can sometimes lead to anonymity, but such works as the precision-crafted *Six Preludes* for piano (1945) and the grave, yet radiant, *Four Poems of St. Teresa of Avila* for contralto and string orchestra (1947)

reveal a successful balance between emotional statement and restraint. In her series of thirteen string quartets, Dame Elizabeth Maconchy (1907–) turned to Bartok rather than Stravinsky as a model—the five-movement design of her Seventh Quartet (1956) forms an obvious allusion to that of Bartok's Fourth—but for Elisabeth Lutyens (1906–83), Humphrey Searle (1915–82), and Benjamin Frankel (1906–73) it was the twelve-tone works of the Second Viennese School that proved influential. As early as 1939 in her Chamber Concerto No. 1, Lutyens began to explore her characteristic brand of serialism, which became fully developed in *O saisons, o chateaux!* (1946) and reached a new level of intensity in *Quincunx* (1960), both vocal works with orchestra. Searle's preference for Schoenberg's emotionalism coupled with his enthusiasm for Liszt, made possible his one-movement Piano Sonata (1951), closely modeled on Liszt's and employing Lisztian thematic transformation but within a twelve-tone context. Frankel's development of an individual twelve-tone style during the 1950s bore fruit in his eight symphonies composed between 1958 and 1971, although the richly somber Violin Concerto (1951), written "in memory of the 'Six Million'" contains some of his most eloquent music. Another composer to draw on serial processes, if not a systematic twelve-tone technique, during the later part of his career was Alan Rawsthorne (1905–71), who made an initial impact with his *Theme and Variations* for two violins (1937) and the orchestral *Symphonic Studies* (1938). In these works his music's rapidly shifting tonal centers, facilitated by inflecting major thirds to minor and vice-versa, created a distinctive idiom that he perfected in the Violin Sonata (1958). By introducing serial processes in his Quintet for piano and wind (1963) and Third Symphony (1964), Rawsthorne expanded the expressive scope of his style, adding to its variety and breadth.

During the 1930s British music benefited from the arrival of several emigrés intent on avoiding the horrors of **Fascism**. Egon Wellesz (1885–1974), Mátyás Seiber (1905–60), and Franz Reizenstein (1911–68), pupils of Schoenberg, Kodály, and Hindemith respectively, were all influential as teachers. Another Schoenberg pupil, Roberto Gerhard (1896–1970), was ignored for the first decade or so following his arrival, a time when he was consolidating his use of serialism; in the First String

Quartet (1950–5) he developed his own technique of applying serial principles to rhythm. Subsequently he relinquished thematicism, leaving the organization of timbre as the prime structural factor in, for instance, his Concerto for Orchestra (1965) and the three final chamber works, *Gemini* for violin and piano (1966), and *Libra* (1968) and *Leo* (1969), both for small ensembles of contrasting instruments.

Sir Andrzej Panufnik (1914–91), another emigré (arriving in 1954 from Poland), together with Wellesz and Gerhard, bequeathed a considerable symphonic legacy. So, too, did such native composers as Edmund Rubbra (1901–86) and William Alwyn (1905–85), while George Lloyd (1913–), Malcolm Arnold (1921–), and Robert Simpson (1921–) continued to do so. In contrast to the vibrantly colorful symphonies of the romantics Alwyn and Lloyd, those of Rubbra, propelled by contrapuntal thinking and muted in color, stand like ancient monuments, awesome in their totality, yet arising from very modest beginnings. A similar evolutionary process can be traced in Simpson's symphonies, although his model is not, as it was for Rubbra, sixteenth-century polyphony, but Beethoven, particularly for his dynamism and thematic development. While the symphonies of Arnold are outwardly more immediately attractive, the enigmatic juxtaposition of a popular, light entertainment tune within a nonpopular context raises important aesthetic questions about the nature of stylistic unity, questions that have been increasingly highlighted by the enthusiasm of more recent composers for drawing on widely divergent models on which to base their style. Another precursor of this development is Ronald Stevenson (1928–), whose *Passacaglia on DSCH* for piano (1962) has a "global" range of reference, including the music of the work's dedicatee, Shostakovich, African drumming, and a Scottish Pibroch.

The free atonal style developed by Peter Racine Fricker (1920–90) acted as an influential antidote to British insularity during the immediate post-Second World War years but was soon eclipsed by the avant-garde music of the "Manchester School," Alexander Goehr (1932–), Sir Peter Maxwell Davies (1934–), and Sir Harrison Birtwistle (1934–). Davies' earlier expressionist style, developed in such diverse theatrical works as the *Eight Songs for a Mad King* (1969), *Versalii Icones* for naked male dancer and instrumental ensemble (also

1969), and the opera *Taverner* (first produced in 1972), has been superceded by a calmer, more classically oriented idiom as revealed in the First Symphony (1976) and the series of Strathclyde Concertos, works completed following Davies' move to remote Hoy in the Orkneys. Birtwistle's development has been similar in certain ways, the portrayal of frequently gratuitous violence in his ritualistic opera, *Punch and Judy* (1967), giving way to a more approachable scenario, the quest for self-knowledge, in *Gawain* (1991). Among more conservative figures, the fluent and adaptable character of the music of Richard Rodney Bennett (1936–), ranging from film music in various pastiche styles, via jazz, to a melodious twelve-tone idiom, attracted several commissions early in his career, including three large-scale operas, beginning with *The Mines of Sulphur* (1963) for Sadler's Wells. And the warmth and richness Nicholas Maw (1935–) derives from a mixture of radical and traditional elements permitted him to produce a successful romantic comedy for Glyndebourne, the opera *The Ring of the Moon* (1970), and the expansive voyage of self-exploration for orchestra, *Odyssey* (1972–90).

For composers born during the 1930s, the range of styles a composer could adopt was wide; for those born during the next decade, the range was even wider. At one end of the spectrum, Brian Ferneyhough (1943–) has composed works like the Sonatas for String Quartet (1967) on the knife-edge of intelligibility and playability, providing a model for younger composers of "The New Complexity" such as James Dillon (1950–). In contrast, composers belonging to the "English experimental tradition," often owing allegiance to Cornelius Cardew (1936–1981), who himself was influenced by Satie and Cage, can take the simplest of tonal materials but arrange them so as to undermine tonal music's onward momentum, as in *Lento* (1991) for orchestra by Howard Skempton (1947–). Another possibility is the "neo-romanticism" of David Matthews (1943–), who has drawn on Mahler's alternately soaring and plunging lines (as well as **Michael Tippett's** metric flexibility) in his Third Symphony (1985). Finally, an individualist such as John Tavener (1943–) lies outside the current trends, being dragged into the limelight as fashion dictates. Following an early success with the dramatic cantata *The Whale* (1966) at a Proms performance in 1968, a period of relative neglect was succeeded by another Proms success, the ecstatic *Protecting Veil* (1987) for cello and strings, which has achieved something of a cult status.

Trevor Bray

Bibliography

Howes, Frank Stewart. *The English Musical Renaissance*. 1966.

Pirie, Peter J. *The English Musical Renaissance*. 1979.

Stradling, Robert, and Meirion Hughes. *The English Musical Renaissance, 1860–1940: Construction and Deconstruction*. 1993.

Trend, Michael J. *The Music Makers*. 1985.

Compton-Burnett, Ivy (1884–1969)

The author of twenty novels, Ivy Compton-Burnett was a technical innovator and a devastatingly witty critic of the Christianized, patriarchal morality perpetuated in the novel proper. After her first novel, *Dolores* (1911), an uneven parody of George Eliot, Compton-Burnett forged an original narrative technique in her subsequent nineteen works by writing the dialogue or dramatic novel, consisting primarily of conversation and of minimal commentary by a narrator. In 1925 *Pastors and Masters*, her first experiment in extended dialogue and her only novel set in contemporary times, was published to puzzled or awestruck reviews. After turning to the late Victorian and Edwardian country gentry as her chosen subject and setting, she brought to maturity her original voice and form in her third novel, *Brothers and Sisters* (1929), a tragicomedy of inadvertent incest. Although all of her novels after *Dolores* are remarkably consistent in quality, perhaps the novels of her middle period best exhibit the searingly acute rationality that she trains on family life and human relations, as in the profoundly disturbing *Elders and Betters* (1943), a family drama of inter-generational carnage in which the wicked appear to flourish, and in *Manservant and Maidservant* (1947), in which children, a wife, a younger brother, and a servant strive to outwit and overthrow a family tyrant. Her later novels, including *A Father and His Fate* (1957) and *A God and His Gifts* (1963) became even more astringently dialogic as she continued to pare away extraneous exposition. In 1967, near the end of her long life, she was named Dame Commander of the Order of the British Empire. *The Last and the First*, probably her most conventionally optimistic novel because of the triumph of a wise and benevolent heroine over a tyrannical stepmother, was left unfinished at her death, pieced together from notebooks, and published posthumously in 1971.

A troubled family history provided her with much of the material and motivation for her fiction. The daughter of a renowned but controversial homeopathic doctor and an imperious mother, Compton-Burnett was born in Pinner, Middlesex, and educated at home with her brothers in Greek and Latin, later receiving a degree in classics at Royal Holloway College in 1906. Her young womanhood was blighted by the **First World War** and a series of family tragedies—the death of her father, her two brothers, and her mother and the apparent double suicide of two younger sisters. After several years of emotional and physical prostration, Compton-Burnett emerged as a distinctive novelist with *Pastors and Masters*. By setting up a quiet, orderly, but sociable life with the furniture expert, Margaret Jourdain, her companion for several decades and a member of the declining gentry about which she wrote, Compton-Burnett was able to draw upon her turbulent early life and produce a novel almost every two years.

Earlier assessments of Compton-Burnett's novels, while frequently laudatory, have been limited by a cultural resistance to Compton-Burnett's perspective as a woman writer who relentlessly satirizes hierarchical mythmaking as institutionalized in the language that constructs religion, literature, the family, and society. Many readers have been daunted by the difficulty of her style, committed as it is almost exclusively to dialogue characterized by formal but simple diction and syntax and abundant clichés and aphorisms, but rendered complex by virtue of its unremittingly ironic tone. As suggested by her most clear-sighted characters, Compton-Burnett's novels propose the heretical views that God is "one of the best-drawn characters in fiction," that "the sight of duty does make one shiver . . . The actual doing of it would kill one, I think," that "there is horror in every heart, and a resolve never to be honest with anyone else," and that "we only oppress the weak." However, the novels also suggest that if we acknowledge sharing this flawed human nature, "to know all is to forgive all," and that through insight and intelligence, human beings can grow in tolerance and charity. Because Compton-Burnett's expansive moral perspective has been persistently misread as cynical, pessimistic, or deterministic, and because her dialogue technique has proven hard to imitate, her novels continue to be regarded as apart from the mainstream British novel. But Henry James' *The Awkward Age* (1899) is one of Compton-Burnett's predecessors; and **Ronald Firbank, Christopher Isherwood,** and **Muriel Spark** make similar exclusive use of dialogue in their notable novels.

Kathy Justice Gentile

Bibliography

Baldanza, Frank. *Ivy Compton-Burnett.* 1964.

Burkhart, Charles, ed. *The Art of I. Compton-Burnett: A Collection of Critical Essays.* 1972.

Gentile, Kathy Justice. *Ivy Compton-Burnett.* 1991.

Liddell, Robert. *The Novels of Ivy Compton-Burnett.* 1955.

Spurling, Hilary. *Ivy: The Life of I. Compton-Burnett.* 1984.

Conductors

Before the Second World War the only conductor able to approach **Sir Thomas Beecham** for the breadth and diversity of his services to British music was Sir Henry Wood (1869–1944). His indefatigable enthusiasm and support for the Promenade Concerts, begun in 1895 and involving the newly formed Queen's Hall Orchestra, turned them into a London institution. Neither the change in administration when the **British Broadcasting Corporation** (BBC) assumed control in 1927, nor the destruction of the Queen's Hall (the Proms' venue) in 1941, proved terminal, the Proms surviving to the present day and now expanded into a two-month summer music festival second to none. Wood was particularly keen to promote British music and, in addition, to introduce new music from abroad—he gave the world premiere of Schoenberg's Five Orchestral Pieces in 1912. As well as being indirectly responsible for creating the London Symphony Orchestra, he visited the provinces frequently, conducting the major choral societies and raising standards of orchestral playing.

In 1942 Sir Adrian Boult (1889–1983), renowned for his restrained, gentlemanly mien

while conducting, became the associate conductor of the Proms (until 1950), but his most important work was as the musical director and conductor of the BBC Symphony Orchestra (1930–50), molding it, soon after its inception, into a first-rate body of players. Like Wood, he was keen to introduce modern music from abroad, conducting concert performances of Berg's *Wozzeck* (1934) and Busoni's *Doktor Faust* (1937), as well as support British music. Many of his recordings of **Edward Elgar's** and **Ralph Vaughan Williams'** symphonies have become classics. Sir John Barbirolli (1899–1970) also excelled in this repertory—he conducted the first performances of Vaughan Williams' *Sinfonia antarctica* and Eighth Symphony—and in late romantics such as Bruckner, Mahler, Strauss, and **Frederick Delius.** Following a five-year term conducting the New York Philharmonic, Barbirolli became permanent conductor of the Hallé in 1943, rescuing it from the doldrums into which it had fallen after the brilliant years (1920–33) under Sir Hamilton Harty (1879–1941) and reviving its earlier excellence during an association that lasted twenty-seven years. A similar dedication to a provincial orchestra was shown by Sir Dan Godfrey (1868–1939), who formed the Bournemouth Municipal Orchestra, remaining its conductor for more than thirty years. One of his policies was to invite British composers to conduct their own works, and Hubert Parry, Charles Stanford, Granville Bantock, and Elgar, among others, accepted.

Following the Second World War the outstanding British choral conductor was Sir Malcolm Sargent (1895–1967), whose sense of occasion and unfailing panache won him great popularity. He conducted the Royal Choral Society for nearly twenty-five years and the Huddersfield Choral Society for even longer. As the principal conductor of the Proms from 1948 until his death, he could demonstrate his talents as a fluent speaker during his address to the Promenaders on the last night of the Proms each year. Another "Prom hero" was Sir Colin Davis (1927–), who, as conductor of the BBC Symphony Orchestra (1967–71), brought a freshness and dynamism to the music of, in particular, Berlioz, most of whose works he recorded, Stravinsky, and **Michael Tippett,** his performance of the latter's opera, *The Midsummer Marriage,* at Covent Garden in 1970, acting as a revelation. Two years earlier, David Atherton (1941–) became the youngest conductor to appear at that house, but his most influential work has been as a promotor of twentieth-century music, directing the London Sinfonietta in many first performances and premiere recordings, for instance, his recording of Tippett's opera, *The Ice Break* (1991). Sir Simon Rattle (1955–), too, has given considerable support to contemporary British music, while his association with the City of Birmingham Symphony Orchestra (principal conductor since 1979) has led to many recordings of the standard repertoire, in particular works by Mahler, Sibelius, and Stravinsky.

Other conductors have specialized in the British "late romantics." Sir Charles Groves (1915–92), following Beecham's death, took over his mantle as a champion of Delius' music, and, early in the Frank Bridge revival, Groves conducted an important recording of Bridge's orchestral works (1976). Bryden Thomson (1928–91) recorded all of Bax's symphonies, and Vernon Handley (1930–) has recorded all of Stanford's. Richard Hickox (1948–), at one time considered a baroque specialist, has of late produced several notable recordings of British twentieth-century choral music, in particular Elgar's *The Apostles* (1990) and **Benjamin Britten's** *War Requiem* (1991).

Trevor Bray

Bibliography

Jefferson, Alan. *Sir Thomas Beecham: A Centenary Tribute.* 1979.

Kennedy, Michael. *Adrian Boult.* 1987.

———. *Barbirolli: Conductor Laureate.* 1971.

Kenyon, Nicholas. *Simon Rattle.* 1987.

Pound, Reginald. *Sir Henry Wood: A Biography.* 1969.

Reid, Charles. *Malcolm Sargent: A Biography.* 1968.

Conrad, Joseph (1857–1924)

Although probably the major English novelist between the Victorian and high-modern periods, Joseph Conrad (Jozef Teodor Konrad Korzeniowski), because of his Polish origins, densely formal style, and idiosyncratic tragic sense, is also an anomaly in the English tradition. His work has an enormous range of geographical settings—Malaysia, London, the Congo, South America, Russia. His mixed style fuses semipopular romanticism, like that of Marryat's sea stories or **Rudyard Kipling's** colonial fiction, to political psychology, difficult syntax, deep moral skepticism, and intricate irony in the line of Flaubert, Turgenev, and James.

Conrad's father, Apollo Korzeniowski, was a gifted, volatile member of the Polish *szlachta* (or free gentry), whose literary work included translations from English (Shakespeare and Dickens), original plays, and political tracts. When he was arrested in 1862 for his political activism, his wife and four-year-old son went with him into forced exile in Russia. There Conrad's mother died of **tuberculosis**; his father died in Cracow when Conrad was eleven. The political-domestic themes, the scathingly ironic tone, and the even more caustic "sub-ironic"— Conrad's own term—bitterness in much of Conrad's storytelling may derive in part from these early deaths of his parents. He was, however, steered fussily and generously toward adulthood by his middle-class uncle Tadeusz Bobrowski.

For whatever reasons, the adolescent Conrad, no scholar, insisted on leaving Poland to become a sailor. Shipping out first from Marseilles and then England, he went to Malaysia, Borneo, Venezuela, and the Congo, among other places. As a twenty-eight-year-old foreigner he passed the English Master Mariner's examination in 1886—he later drew the scene of the examination in bold relief in *A Personal Record* (1912) as an instance of stern but benign bureaucracy. During this period his bilingual letters to Mme. Poradowska, a distant relative, express his pessimism and toy with mechanistic metaphors for the description of a brutal world. His "Up-river Book" (1890), kept while captain of the Congo steamer *Roi des Belges*, is a navigational notebook on the river and is nonliterary. Conrad had to overcome odds to gain British citizenship and status, among them the disapproval of those in Poland who regarded him as a deserter of his country.

In his late thirties, as a result of chronic illness from his Congo voyage and belated marriage, Conrad decided to leave the sea and risk a novelist's career in English, his third or even fourth language. The first years of the writing career and the last of the sea life dovetail. *Almayer's Folly* (1895) and *An Outcast of the Islands* (1896) study mediocrity, isolation, and failure abroad in miserable "outposts"; the early, deservedly famous sea tales insist on the tedious, domesticated, laborious work lives of sailors. With *The Nigger of the "Narcissus"*

(1897), partly a study of crowd pyschology, partly an analysis with Schopenhauerean and Nietzschean overtones of the limits of sympathy, Conrad broke through to a highly structured, formal, political-aesthetic style. That style owed something to collaborations on grandiloquent pulp novels with **Ford Madox Ford,** who accurately attributed to Conrad a supreme gift for the "architectonics" of fiction. Some of the ironic devices Conrad and Ford worked out together—delayed recognitions, sense impressions treated in stark isolation from each other, craftily scrambled time sequences, layered ironies of reported speech, studied nonanswering in dialogue—were to influence later writers like **Virginia Woolf** and William Faulkner.

In Conrad, however, direct drawing of material labor governs the entire narrative, from events down to syntax, much more than in Ford, or, for that matter, in any other high modernist. Persistent attention, for example, to the variety of breath sounds—laughter, snores, whispers, coughs, and grunts—of the *Narcissus'* sailors links their bodies to the fact that the sailing ship itself depends for movement on the air of the material physical world. In *Heart of Darkness* (1899) a collective obsession with ivory, and in *Nostromo* (1904) an obsession with the silver of the national mine, lead to similar highly complex social organization around one material sign treated as both real and symbolic.

Conradian characterization is often founded on paradox and self-deception. The Black man aboard the *Narcissus,* Jimmy Wait, believes himself to be a malingerer who is duping the rest of the ship by pretending to be ill, and turns out against his desperate denial to be, in fact, dying. This simple "knot"—pretending to oneself to pretend to others to be dying—is a typical structure of illusion in Conrad. By the end of the story, in addition, Wait also seems to stand not only for the fear of death but for the historically repressed memory of the slave trade, in process of being buried. This indefinite shadow of a political theme of slavery inside the inspired study of the sea, of the senses, and of a collective narcissistic fear of death is typical of the "problem" of Conrad: Is he only a conservative moral psychologist or also a radically political psychologist?

Heart of Darkness employed the device Russian critics call *skaz*: A narrator inevitably tells more about himself than his ostensible subject. The mass death of African laborers in the Belgian Congo is made a journalistically real memoir, at the same time as it is a study in prose chiaroscuro. It begins the drawing of racial murder in modern literature. The story has been both attacked as racist and defended for its critique of racism. The narrator, Marlow—also a narrator in *Lord Jim* (1900), another work on later colonialism's intersection with personal illusions—observes the contrast between degraded managerial bureaucracy in the Congo and the grandiose insane imperialism of the famous character Kurtz.

Conrad's middle period saw the production of three clearly political novels. *Nostromo,* Conrad's "largest canvas," engages the theme of political psychology amidst pathetic revolutionary politics in a composite South American country. *The Secret Agent* (1907), Conrad's most burlesque tragedy, centers on Winnie Verloc, a Londoner who unwittingly marries a triple agent to secure a safe home for her idiot brother. In the novel's crisis she learns that her pathetic brother has been blown to bits carrying explosives in a mission to blow up Greenwich Observatory—perhaps, in effect, to destroy Time itself. (This "outrageous" story was adapted by **Alfred Hitchcock** in the film *Saboteur.*) The last of the political novels, *Under Western Eyes* (1911), daringly rewrites *Crime and Punishment* in a more opportunistic, flat, and skeptical key and is a remarkable modern exercise in belligerent revision of a literary predecessor.

During the First World War the Conrads worried about their son Borys in the war, while Conrad's craft became more deftly perfunctory and more saleable. *Chance* (1913) and *Victory* (1915) were his first books to sell well. The war seemed to him to confirm warnings he had made in such pieces as "Autocracy and War" (1905) about German and Russian sociology as seen from his Polish-English perspective. In his political views, Conrad assimilates the liberal traditions of the Polish *szlachta* class and of English constitutionalism to a virtually Hobbesian temperamental belief in the presence everywhere, not least in language and dialogue, of direct force as well as of subtler forms of coercion.

Some biographers define Conrad as having had three lives: the Polish youth, the French-English sailor, the English novelist. Conrad said he saw an intentional unity in his life, a movement toward England and writing. The different Conrads pictured since his death include the sea writer; the existential modernist and deviser of limits of loneliness; the aesthetic-formalist-symbolist; the major ironist; the radical skeptic; the political novelist; the polyglot predicter of English's status now as a language inflected by nonnative speakers. His works have survived interpretive storms a bit in the manner of his own taciturn, rigid sea captains. His greatest work fuses aesthetic and political themes with extraordinary tragic force and precise prose craftsmanship.

Aaron Fogel

Bibliography

Fogel, Aaron. *Coercion to Speak: Conrad's Poetics of Dialogue.* 1985.

Karl, Frederick R. *Joseph Conrad: The Three Lives.* 1979.

Najder, Zdzislaw. *Joseph Conrad.* 1983.

Conscientious Objection

Historical examples abound, especially in the literature of certain Christian pacifist sects, of individuals refusing, even in the face of persecution, imprisonment, or death, to engage in military activities on the plea that conscience would not allow them to fight and kill fellow human beings. As a principle of British law, however, conscientious objection to military service is of recent derivation, initially recognized in a hastily drafted clause to the Military Service (No. 2) Act (1916), Britain's first comprehensive **conscription** measure. During the **First World War** confusion over the meaning of this so-called "conscience clause" and inadequate administrative machinery for its enforcement created serious difficulties for both individual conscientious objectors (COs) and for the government that had attempted to make provision for them. The fact that the injustices and abuses imposed upon COs during the First World War were evoked to prevent their repetition in the Second was one of the shining victories for civil liberties and common decency in twentieth-century Britain.

The first conscience clause incorporated into British statute law was not concerned with the refusal to participate in warfare but with religious and medical objections to compulsory vaccination. Provisions of the Vaccination Act (1898) allowed exemption if parents could convince two justices that they believed vaccination to be harmful to the health of their children. In 1907 the government amended this procedure to permit exemption by means of a statutory declaration under oath. But while conscientious objection had thus been established as a legal principle before the imposition of conscription, the original procedures for establishing the *bona fides* of objectors proved to be inadequate for a society at war.

When Prime Minister **H.H. Asquith** decided in late 1915 that both military and political necessity had made compulsory military service inevitable, several **Liberal** members of his coalition **Cabinet** expressed serious reservations about conscription; one of them, **Sir John Simon,** resigned in protest. Fearing that Simon might try to organize resistance in the House of Commons, Asquith hastily inserted a clause into the proposed military service bill that recognized the right of exemption from military service "on the ground of a conscientious objection to bearing arms." Whatever Asquith's original motives for the inclusion of a conscience clause, his refusal thereafter to limit the right of conscientious objection to members of certain religious bodies that had traditionally opposed war established an important legal precedent. Despite the argument of many **Conservative** politicians and most military officers that nonreligious exemption would open a Pandora's box of unpatriotic and even subversive political resistance, Asquith held fast to the position that moral or intellectual as well as religious objections could be acknowledged as legitimate. Thus broadly interpreted, the British conscience clause became a pioneering model whose generous provisions were not matched in most other countries, including the United States, for half a century. Still, this vaunted reputation was only established after a number of sincere conscientious objectors had suffered considerable injustice or abuse.

Most problems in implementing provisions for conscientious objection during the First World War arose from the ambiguity of wording in the conscience clause and from the deficiency of the administrative machinery created to enforce it. When the act was introduced, statements by government spokesmen seemed to imply that while COs would be exempt from combatant service, they would be required, and for the most part would be willing, to "do something"—civilian work of "national importance" at the very least—in support of the war effort. This was a serious miscalculation that would cause no end of trouble. The burden of dealing with the question first fell upon members of local tribunals who were asked to judge the worthiness of applications for exemption filed in their districts. Few of the local citizens sitting on these voluntary bodies had either administrative experience or judicial training. Yet they were asked to sit in judgment of all pleas for exemption, including ill health, serious economic hardship, and essential civilian occupation as well as conscientious objection, and to make the appropriate determination in each case. Their task was made doubly difficult by the murky directives from the Home Office and by the presence of a military representative who acted as a sort of devil's advocate on behalf of the **army**, questioning the authenticity of nearly every applicant, especially conscientious objectors.

Between early 1916 and the end of the war over 16,000 men applied for exemption on the basis of conscientious objection. Local tribunals were expected to determine whether a CO's objections were genuine and, if so, whether his exemption should be absolute, temporary, or conditional upon his engagement in some form of military or civilian alternative service. Most COs received an exemption that satisfied their objection, but around 6,000 either declined to recognize the tribunals, refused to accept the kind of exemption they were granted, or were judged "not genuine."

At first, nonexempted conscientious objectors who did not respond to call-up orders were arrested by the police and, after a local court appearance, handed over to the military authorities. Once in military hands, COs were generally court-martialed for refusing to obey orders and sentenced to confinement in military prisons, where they continued to be subject to the military discipline. After several sensational and highly publicized incidents in which COs were severely ill treated while under military control, the army, anxious to be rid of a vexatious problem, issued Order X, which provided that court-martialed COs be handed over to civil authorities for the execution of their sentences. The government, no less concerned than the army about filling the prisons with a new species of political prisoner, tried to accommodate objectors through the creation of the so-called Home Office scheme, which established work centers where COs were housed and given "civilian work under civilian control." Over 4,000 objectors availed themselves of this alternative to prison, but, in the end, the scheme

proved to be troublesome for the authorities, unsatisfactory for the COs, and unpopular with the public. Still, difficulties surrounding the Home Office scheme were nothing compared to the imbroglio created by 1,300 "absolutist" conscientious objectors who, as a result of their refusal to accept any compromise short of total exemption, were subjected to repeated sentences at hard labor for what was literally, although not technically, the same offense. Some of these individuals were stupidly or brutally treated, and a few died or became seriously ill as a result of their ordeal. Publicity arising from these exceptional cases, skillfully disseminated by war-resistance groups, especially the **No-Conscription Fellowship**, caused the government embarrassment and exasperation far out of proportion to the number of individuals involved.

Eventually, after the socially prominent Margaret Hobhouse had appealed to both Cabinet ministers and public opinion to secure the release of her absolutist son Stephen, a few seriously ill absolutists, including Stephen Hobhouse and **Clifford Allen**, Chairman of the No-Conscription Fellowship, were released from prison through a special dispensation, but critics claimed that the government was merely resurrecting the old "cat and mouse" ploy used against suffragettes. Most absolutists refused to cooperate with any scheme for the mitigation of their sentences and were released only after the war ended, many of them in a seriously debilitated condition.

The story of conscientious objectors was one of the most irksome and least edifying chapters in the history of the Great War, but it was not entirely futile. Even before the war ended, administrative changes had been introduced that took the military establishment entirely out of the recruiting process. These reforms did not affect the treatment of COs before 1918, but they were a direct response to the difficulties that had been encountered in handling cases of conscientious objection. When compulsory military service was reintroduced in 1939, other changes, enacted to ensure that the worst problems and abuses of the Great War were not repeated, brought efficacious results. For one thing, after 1939 local tribunals were appointed by the Ministry of Labour and National Service, and their membership included individuals with legal training and experience. Furthermore, these bodies, which dealt exclusively with conscientious objectors, were guided by clear and explicit directions allowing for various forms of exemption, including absolute exemption.

In practice, the choice for the nearly 60,000 COs who appeared before tribunals during the **Second World War** was between conditional exemption on agreement to take up work of national importance under civilian control or entrance into military service as a noncombatant. There were, inevitably, cases of injustice or ill treatment, but incidents of serious abuse were rare, and the ability of tribunals to provide a satisfactory exemption to most COs is clearly demonstrated by the fact that only 10 percent of Second World War objectors served any time in prison as compared with nearly one-third between 1914 and 1918. Improved machinery and sensible procedures were not the only reasons for the more efficient, and more humane, treatment of COs during the Second World War. Individuals on both sides of the issue made a significant difference. For the government, **Ernest Bevin**, Minister of Labour and National Service from 1940, showed sense and sensitivity in dealing with conscientious objectors, and the Central Board for Conscientious Objectors (CBCO), which acted on behalf of COs, generally cooperated with the state, unlike the resolutely hostile No-Conscription Fellowship during the Great War. An awareness of the worse problems and abuses of the First World War and a determination not to repeat them allowed Great Britain to set a standard for the treatment of conscientious objectors during the Second World War that has never been surpassed and rarely equaled.

Thomas C. Kennedy

Bibliography

Barker, Rachel. *Conscience, Government, and War: Conscientious Objection in Great Britain, 1939–45.* 1982.

Boulton, David. *Objection Overruled.* 1967.

Braithwaite, Constance. *Legal Problems of Conscientious Objection to Various Compulsions under British Law.* 1968.

Graham, John W. *Conscription and Conscience: A History, 1916–1919.* 1922.

Kennedy, Thomas C. "Public Opinion and the Conscientious Objector, 1914–1919," *Journal of British Studies,* vol. 12 (1973), pp. 105–19.

Rae, John. *Conscience and Politics: The British Government and the Conscientious Objector to Military Service, 1916–1919.* 1970.

Conscription

Mandatory service (conscription) to raise military forces was unused in Britain after the end of the wars against the French Revolution and Napoleon. In the century that followed, Britain relied upon a great fleet and a small professional volunteer army to police its worldwide Empire and protect its interests. The Crimean War, the **Boer War**, and numerous small imperial conflicts throughout the nineteenth century were all fought with volunteer forces. While by the early twentieth century there was a small pro-conscription movement in Britain—led by Field Marshal Lord Roberts, hero of the Boer War, and his National Service League—it never succeeded in convincing either Parliament or the nation of the need for mandatory service.

The **First World War**, a conflict of unexpected size and scope, changed the way in which Britain raised its armies. The nature of that conflict—trench warfare punctuated by massive frontal assaults—required huge numbers of troops, and virtually the entire high command of the British **army** and a growing number of politicians had by this time come to see compulsory military service as the only way to raise sufficient manpower for the Western Front once voluntary enlistments dropped off drastically after mid-1915. Conscription, however, was not popular among large elements of the public and many members of the **Liberal Party** who were supporters of the **Asquith** coalition government. As a stopgap measure either to gain the needed men or to prove the inadequacy of voluntarism, Asquith supported the so-called "Derby scheme" (named for the seventeenth Earl of Derby, who chaired the effort) in the autumn of 1915 to exhort men voluntarily to "attest" that they would serve when called. Inadequate numbers came forward, and Asquith, caught between his anti-compulsion Liberal supporters and the determined pro-compulsion Tories who were angered by the troop shortage, brought in Britain's first mandatory service bill in January 1916. The law (the "bachelor's bill") applied only to unmarried men between the ages of eighteen and forty-one, and continued inadequate intake of men forced, in May, a general conscription bill that included married men.

Asquith's government fell in December, to be replaced by another coalition under the more energetic **David Lloyd George**. The manpower problems of the British army on the Western Front were not overcome simply by the application of conscription, and, before the end of the war, further legislation was passed increasing the age of liability to conscription to fifty and applying mandatory service to previously exempted Ireland. The Easter Rising of 1916 made its enforcement in Ireland virtually impossible, but even consideration of the possibility demonstrates the desperation of the government.

Britain's experience with conscription in the First World War offered a valuable lesson: During the seventeen months in which unrestricted voluntarism raised Britain's first army of continental size, many men possessed of the skills needed for the production of necessary military and export goods were gratefully enlisted by the army. Therefore, if conscription were to prove useful, it would have to be implemented at the outset of any prolonged struggle in order to allow the state the power to discriminate among men of military age, based upon their usefulness to the national war effort.

Another point worth noting is this: Britain was a liberal democracy with no tradition of mandatory military service, and, as a result, there were sizable minorities in the population who objected on moral, religious, or political grounds to the implementation of such legislation. This created the need to deal with large numbers of **conscientious objectors**. Special regional tribunals had to be created throughout the nation with the power to exempt inductees from military service for reasons of conscience.

Mandatory military service in Britain ceased in April 1920, and the army was demobilized. Thereafter there was no thought of peacetime compulsion: The idea was unpopular among the electorate; there was a general perception in and outside of government circles that Britain had no enemies to fear for the immediate future; and, finally, the military costs could be better spent on other needs in a time of tight budgets.

During the 1920s Britain was the only European power to disarm as promised at the peace conference. By 1935, with war raging in Asia and with Germany rearming openly in defiance of the Treaty of Versailles, the British government announced modest steps toward

Military recruitment in Trafalgar Square during the First World War.

rearmament. With Nazi Germany seen as the greatest and closest threat, the issue of conscription was again raised, though the three successive Prime Ministers of the National government in the 1930s, **Ramsay MacDonald, Stanley Baldwin,** and **Neville Chamberlain,** all opposed its imposition.

By 1938, with Adolf Hitler threatening to annex the Sudetenland, Britain's French allies were pressuring Chamberlain to impose conscription. He opposed it, both for industrial and military purposes, as he felt it essentially inefficient and disruptive to labor-capital relations. The ultimate failure of the **Munich Conference** to satiate Hitler convinced many—if not the Prime Minister—that national organization of both industry and the military would be necessary for the war that was likely to come.

As the demand intensified for labor for munitions (especially aircraft) factories long understaffed during the years of disarmament and for volunteers for the increasing armed services, it became clear that voluntarism would once again be unable to supply the men—and ultimately women—needed. By April 1939 Chamberlain acquiesced and a modest conscription bill was introduced—the first peacetime law of its kind in modern times. It called only for only six months' service for young men between age twenty and twenty-one.

War came in September 1939, and the liability of men to military service was broadened. **Winston Churchill** and his all-party War Cabinet brought in even more precedent-shattering legislation: In June a bill was passed that made all persons and property liable for wartime service. In March 1941 the "Essential Work Order" issued under this legislation gave the Minister of Labour and National Service, **Ernest Bevin,** the power to regulate and retrain labor as it was needed for the war effort. By the end of 1941 more than 90 percent of males between the ages of fourteen and sixty-four were either in the military or working in industry, and more hands were needed. Hence, in December the government responded with legislation that subjected all persons, regardless of sex, between the ages of eighteen and fifty to some form of national service. At least in theory, the state had taken compulsory powers over the entire adult population.

In practice, industrial conscription was applied with great restraint and, in the main, was successful. In comparison to the First World War, trades disputes were fewer and less harmful to munitions production. By the close of the war Britain had almost 5 million men under arms, and its industrial establishments continued to be more productive than would have been predicted by even the greatest optimist in pre-war years. Conscientious objection continued throughout this war, too, though it attracted far less attention and drew less public support—and a number of the best known anti-conscriptionists of the 1914–18 conflict joined the war effort against Fascism.

Military conscription continued in Britain until 1962. Since then all British forces have been raised through voluntarism.

R.J.Q. Adams

Bibliography

Adams, R.J.Q., and Philip P. Poirier. *The Conscription Controversy in Great Britain, 1900–18.* 1987.

Dennis, Peter. *Decision by Default: Peacetime Conscription and British Defense, 1919–1939.* 1972.

Hayes, Denis. *Conscription Conflict.* 1949.

Kennedy, Thomas C. *The Hound of Conscience: A History of the No-Conscription Fellowship, 1914–1919.* 1981.

Conservative Party

(Known as the Unionist Party c. 1895–1925; often referred to as the Tory Party, a name deriving from its eighteenth-century origins.)

The Conservative Party has been the principal force on the right of center in British politics since it emerged in its modern form during the first half of the nineteenth century. Despite periodic crises and divisions, the party has remained remarkably cohesive. No space has been left for any potential rivals on the Right, a fact illustrated by the failure of both the British Union of Fascists in the 1930s and the **National Front** in the 1970s to draw off any significant amount of Conservative rank-and-file support. While rifts have occurred within the Conservative Party in Parliament and leaders have been overthrown, internal warfare has rarely been allowed to benefit opposing parties. In times of crisis the party instinctively draws together and rallies round the leader: a cliché of the period is that "loyalty is the Conservative Party's secret weapon." The foremost aim and function of the party is the winning of power, as much to prevent government falling into the hands of the Liberal or Labour Parties as to implement any specific Conservative program. In this the Conservatives have been spectacularly successful: Since the Home Rule crisis of 1886 they have governed, either alone or as the predominant partner in a coalition ministry, for all but thirty-two years.

The party's electoral strength rests upon two foundations. In the first place, it has had the support of almost the whole of the upper class and of a large majority of the middle class. Middle-class support for the Conservatives grew after 1867 and increased still further with each of the three major rifts in the **Liberal Party,** which until 1918 was its principal opponent. The first of these was the Liberal split over Ireland in 1886, which led to a Conservative alliance with the splinter group of Liberal Unionists. Liberal Unionist leaders served in the **Cabinet** from 1895 to 1905, and their group formally merged with the Conservatives in 1912: From this junction dates the present full official name of Conservative and Unionist Party. Second were the Liberal divisions during and after the **First World War**; and third, the Liberal splits after the crisis of 1931, which culminated in the absorption of the National Liberal followers of **Sir John Simon** in the Woolton-Teviot pact of 1948. Conservative middle-class support had been traditionally centered upon the **Church of England** but, as a result of these changes came to embrace many Nonconformists as well. However, even before the 1918 Reform Act this middle-class support would never have been enough on its own to win general elections.

The second factor on which Conservative electoral success has been based was the support of a large number of working-class voters. Indeed, until 1945 more working-class voters supported the Conservatives than the **Labour Party,** which from the early 1920s had displaced the Liberals as the alternative governing party on the Left. The reasons for this are not solely explicable in negative terms or by a simplistic concept of deference toward social superiors, though these factors may have played their part. The Conservative Party was always the party most sympathetic toward agriculture and the self-employed, whether artisan, craftsman, shopkeeper, or small businessman. In addition they had a less puritanical approach to working-class life-styles than Liberals and Labour on issues ranging from temperance reform at the beginning of the century to the sometimes unwelcome intrusions of the **welfare state** in the

1980s. Finally, the Conservatives were adept at exploiting national **patriotism** and pride, especially during Britain's period as an imperial and world power until the 1950s. Since then, accommodation to decline has produced a series of traumas for the party, from the fiasco of the **Suez crisis** in 1956 to the difficulties of membership of the **European Union,** only briefly enlivened by the success of the **Falklands War** of 1982. The success of the Conservative Party has often been partly attributed to the support it has attracted from women voters from all classes. Since 1918 **women** have provided a large proportion of the party's local membership and its most active voluntary workers, although the parliamentary party has remained a mainly male preserve, and also exclusively a middle- and upper-class one.

The strength of the party organization has contributed to both its cohesion and to its electoral success. The Conservative Party organization has always had a powerful reputation, although its financial resources and its efficiency have often been exaggerated, not least by its opponents. The party organization consists of two complementary elements. The National Union (founded 1867) is the representative body of the rank and file, with one recognized local association affiliated in each constituency. There is a regional tier, with England and Wales divided into twelve provincial areas, Scotland has its own separate structures. The National Union has an Executive that meets regularly, a Central Council (similar to, but smaller than, the Conference), and an Annual Conference. The National Union has influence but little formal power; policy is settled by the party leader, and the leader is selected by the parliamentary party. The second element in the organization are the professional salaried officials. At the national level these are located in the Conservative Central Office (founded 1870), which is responsible to, and directly controlled by, the leader. The Central Office provides a range of services to the leadership and MPs, but its primary role is to support the efforts of local associations to win elections. The Conservatives' greatest asset has always been their extensive network of full-time trained local agents, which are employed by the individual local parties and not by the Central Office. The doctrine of local autonomy is paramount and jealously protected: The Central Office influences but does not dictate to the local branches. The ideal of an agent in each constituency was never attained, but the Conservatives have always had many more such agents than their rivals. However, their number has declined from 506 in 1959 to 288 in 1988.

There have been three significant periods of reorganization since 1900, each responding either to defeat or to change in the electoral system. The first of these followed from the reverses of 1906 and 1910, which led to the establishment of the Unionist Organisation Committee in 1911. Under its recommendations the Chief Whip was relieved of the task of overseeing the party machinery outside Parliament, and a new position of Chairman of the Party Organization, to be appointed by the leader, was established. The first such Chairman, Sir Arthur Steel-Maitland (1876–1935), modernized the organization in the period 1911–14. The second period of change followed from the provisions of the Reform Act of 1918. J.C.C. Davidson (1889–1970), Party Chairman 1926–30, gave a high priority to the development of branches for women and for working-class trade unionist members. The third period of reassessment followed the decline of the party machine during the Second World War and the defeat of 1945. Between 1946 and 1951 the Central Office was reorganized and large sums were raised under the energetic chairmanship of Lord Woolton (1883–1964). At the same time the Maxwell-Fyfe Committee (1949) recommended reforms in the National Union, in particular limiting the payments that constituencies had formerly expected from their candidates. Since the 1950s organizational developments have been of a minor but continual nature. Throughout the century the Conservatives have been the pioneers in political organization and in campaigning techniques and have made innovative use of new media and technology, from cinema vans to computerization.

The history of the Conservative Party since 1900 can be divided into five phases. The first of these was the period of defeat and disunity from 1900 to 1914. Under the leadership of Lord Salisbury (1830–1903) the Unionist coalition won a second successive victory in 1900, but the party's fortunes swiftly declined after **Arthur Balfour** succeeded his uncle in 1902. The principal cause of the problems of the following decade was the policy of **tariff reform**, first raised in 1903 by the second-most-powerful figure in the ministry, Joseph Chamberlain (1836–1914). His proposals to draw the Brit-

ish Empire closer together through **imperial preference** captured the hearts and minds of the Conservative rank and file. However, tariff reform proved to be extremely divisive. It was opposed by a small group of free traders among the MPs and senior ministers. More seriously, it was a disastrous vote loser in urban areas, due to working-class fears that "food taxes" on cheap imported basics would raise the cost of living. Pragmatists in the party, therefore, sought to drop the commitment to full preference, leading to bitter conflicts with its "whole-hog" supporters. The internal divisions that resulted led to a Cabinet crisis in 1903 and largely contributed to three successive electoral defeats in 1906 and January and December 1910. The party was further divided over resistance to the Liberal government's Parliament Act (1911), and in 1911 Balfour resigned the leadership. His unexpected successor, **Andrew Bonar Law**, restored party morale with a series of vigorous attacks upon the government, especially in support of **Ulster**'s case during the passage of the Irish Home Rule bill in 1912–14.

The First World War transformed the position of the Conservative Party. As the "patriotic" party its advocacy of vigorous prosecution of the war led to increased popularity, and it also benefited from the splits and eventual decline of the Liberal Party. The Conservatives joined a coalition ministry under Liberal Prime Minister **H.H. Asquith** in May 1915. This proved to be an unhappy arrangement, and in the crisis of December 1916 Bonar Law gave Conservative backing to the claims of **David Lloyd George**. Although a Liberal, Lloyd George shared the Conservatives' priorities over the war effort, and his coalition of 1916–22 was a stronger and more cohesive government. When the war was won in 1918, Lloyd George was at the height of his popularity, and Bonar Law readily agreed that the coalition should be continued into peacetime to grapple with the problems of the **post-war reconstruction**. However, after economic depression and failures of policy in 1920–1 the continuation of the coalition became increasingly unpopular among Conservative MPs and local activists. In March 1921 Bonar Law resigned for reasons of health, to be replaced by **Austen Chamberlain**. Chamberlain was an inflexible and autocratic leader, thought by his followers too closely committed to Lloyd George. The revolt from below against the coalition culminated in defeat for Chamberlain at a meeting of Conservative MPs that he

C

convened at the Carlton Club on 19 October 1922. Bonar Law led the victorious rebels, and thus ousted both Chamberlain as party leader and Lloyd George as Prime Minister.

The fall of the coalition was the formative event in Conservative politics between the wars. It marked a decision to return to normal party politics, with Labour replacing the Liberals as the main opposition. The events of 1922 also brought to the fore a group of anticoalitionist junior ministers who were to dominate the leadership until 1940. The most important of these was **Stanley Baldwin**, who replaced the dying Bonar Law as leader and as Prime Minister in May 1923. Despite leading his party into an unnecessary defeat in the December 1923 election and a serious assault upon his position in 1929–31, Baldwin remained leader until 1937. Espousing a brand of moderate Conservatism and epitomizing traditional English virtues, he attracted widespread popular support. As a result of this and of the Liberal-Labour rivalry, the Conservative Party dominated the inter-war decades. Between 1918 and 1945 it was the largest party in the House of Commons for all but two-and-a-half years. In the crisis of August 1931 the Conservatives agreed to serve under **Ramsay MacDonald** in a National government in which they were by far the largest element. In 1935 Baldwin replaced MacDonald as Prime Minister, and in 1937 he handed on both the premiership and the Conservative leadership to **Neville Chamberlain**. Chamberlain's period as leader was dominated by controversy over foreign policy, and his policy of **appeasement** led to the resignation of the Foreign Secretary, **Anthony Eden**, and to clashes with the group of antiappeasers led by Eden and **Winston Churchill**. Chamberlain exerted a much closer grip on the party than Baldwin had done, and while his policy appeared successful his critics were almost dragooned out of the party in the winter of 1938. However, the outbreak of war left Chamberlain discredited. After a substantial rebellion by Conservative back-bench MPs in the Norway debate of 8–9 May 1940, he was forced to resign the premiership to Churchill. He remained party leader until declining health led to his resignation in October 1940, when Churchill was elected without opposition in his place. However, even the great war leader's prestige could not prevent the party receiving popular condemnation for the failures of the 1930s at home and abroad,

and thus its second decisive defeat during this century in the 1945 general election.

The period in opposition to the 1945–51 Labour government saw the Conservatives not only energetically reorganizing but also engaged in a fundamental reappraisal of philosophy and policy. As a result, between the late 1940s and the early 1970s the Conservatives accepted the three pillars of the post-war consensus: universal free benefits in the welfare state, a role for government intervention in economic matters founded upon Keynesian theories, and some form of partnership in industry between trade unions and employers. Although Churchill remained unenthusiastic, these policies enabled the Conservatives to regain power in 1951 and to remain in office continuously until 1964. The key figures in this period were Eden, who succeeded Churchill in April 1955 but retired after the Suez crisis in January 1957; **Harold Macmillan**, Prime Minister and Conservative leader from 1957 until November 1963; and **R.A. Butler**. Butler twice seemed on the brink of becoming Prime Minister, but in 1963 Macmillan maneuvred to block him on personal grounds and was instead succeeded by **Sir Alec Douglas-Home**. Macmillan's sudden resignation had actually been due to ill health, but since 1961 his ministry had been enmeshed in economic stagnation, public scandal, and diplomatic rebuffs, and by 1963 defeat seemed likely. Although his aristocratic lineage was an easy target for the meritocratic campaign of Labour, Douglas-Home managed to regain some lost ground, and the Conservatives lost the 1964 general election by only a narrow margin.

In August 1965 Douglas-Home stood down, and the first formal party leadership election by a ballot of MPs took place; it was also the first leadership selection while in opposition since that of 1911. The victor was **Edward Heath**, whose lower-middle-class background was thought more publicly acceptable than Macmillan's "Edwardian" style or Douglas-Home's "grouse moor" image. Heath survived the party's loss of further seats to Labour in the 1966 election, but he never secured the affection of either the public or his parliamentary followers. It was to general surprise that despite this and contrary to the opinion polls, he won the 1970 election and became Prime Minister. The failures of the Heath ministry of 1970–4 have been the catharsis of modern Conservatism. The reversals of policy, the failure to control inflation or contain the trade unions through legislation on industrial relations, and two defeats at the hands of the miners led first to the fall of Heath and second to the rise and development of **Thatcherism**. After losing the two elections of February and October 1974, Heath was forced to hold a ballot for the party leadership in February 1975 in which he was defeated by **Margaret Thatcher**. Thatcher and Sir Keith Joseph (1918–) had served in the Heath Cabinet but, since its defeat, had raised the standard of a Conservatism founded upon the free market, rolling back government intervention in the economic and social spheres and leaving as much as possible to individual initiative. This was the core of Thatcherism, although in the 1980s this also came to stand for a style of government: authoritarian, centralizing, and secretive. Public concern over national economic decline and the power of the trade unions, symbolized in the "winter of discontent" of 1978–9, was receptive to this rejection of the post-war consensus and led to Conservative victories in the 1979, 1983, and 1987 elections. Thatcher was the dominant personality in both the Conservative Party and national poli-

tics throughout the 1980s and had the fervent support of the rank and file. However, failures in economic policy, the "poll tax," and her divisive approach to Europe led to her failure to win the leadership ballot forced by Michael Heseltine (1933–) in November 1990 by the 15 percent margin necessary under the rules. In the second ballot, John Major (1943–) emerged as her successor.

Stuart Ball

Bibliography

Blake, Robert. *The Conservative Party from Peel to Thatcher.* 1985.

Fair, John D., and J.A. Hutcheson, "British Conservatism in the Twentieth Century," *Albion*, vol. 19 (1987), pp. 549–78.

Norton, Philip, and Arthur Aughey. *Conservatives and Conservatism.* 1981.

Pugh, Martin. "Popular Conservatism in Britain: Continuity and Change, 1880–1987," *Journal of British Studies*, vol. 27 (1988), pp. 254–82.

Ramsden, John. *A History of the Conservative Party.* vol. 3: *The Age of Balfour*

C

Conservative front bench, July 1970, including three Prime Ministers: Alec Douglas-Home (second from left), Edward Heath (fourth from left), and Margaret Thatcher (second from right). The photograph was taken several weeks before the death of Chancellor of the Exchequer Iain MacLeod (fifth from left).

and Baldwin, 1902–1940. 1978.

Seldon, Anthony, and Stuart Ball, eds. *Conservative Century: The Conservative Party since 1900.* 1994.

Constitutional Crisis (1909–1911)

The constitutional crisis of 1909–11 was rooted in the twin dilemmas the **Liberal Party** faced after 1906. On the one hand, despite its landslide victory in 1906 and consequent overwhelming majority in the House of Commons, the Liberal government could only watch with mounting impatience and seeming impotence as the Unionist-dominated **House of Lords** cut its legislative program to ribbons. Bills to reform education, plural voting, and liquor licensing—all issues dear to the Liberal constituency—were rejected by their Lordships. On the other hand, the Liberals were faced with unprecedented financial demands, having to fund simultaneously both increased naval construction and the recently introduced (1908) **old age pensions**, a problem their Unionist opponents claimed to be able to master through revenue raised by **tariff reform.**

By 1909 these challenges were acute, but the Liberal **Cabinet**, bound to free trade and an ambitious program of social reform, could hardly concede. Its response was to counterattack, employing budgetary policy to do so. Legend has it that the Liberal Chancellor of the Exchequer, **David Lloyd George**, deliberately concocted his provocative 1909 budget, with its provisions of sharply higher taxes on inheritance, automobiles, petrol, and land, as well as a "super tax" on very high incomes (those over £5,000), as a trap to bait unwary peers. Blinded by their fury at so transparently vindictive a budget, they would take the unconstitutional step of rejecting that budget and thereby fatally exposing themselves, as well as their Unionist colleagues in the Commons, to electoral demolition on the cry of "peers versus people." In fact, while Lloyd George was not blind to these rhetorical implications, he introduced the budget to raise additional revenue; that it provoked a crisis was due less to Liberal intentions than to constitutional ambiguities, especially the absence of a written constitution.

When the House of Lords rejected the budget on 30 November 1909, the Liberals invoked "recent" parliamentary custom to argue that the peers had no such right. Unionists responded that the budget's vindictiveness, not the peers' rejection, violated the unwritten constitution, and that the electorate was the logical final arbiter. But an appeal to the voters in the bitterly contested election of January 1910 failed to resolve the crisis. If anything, it aggravated the situation by leaving the two parties evenly matched, with the Liberals retaining power only by virtue of the continued support of the Irish Nationalists.

Although the Unionists, having lost the election, now acceded to the budget's resubmission and passage through the Lords, the Liberals were determined to introduce legislation to limit any further exercise of the peers' absolute veto. That commitment was also the price to be paid for Irish support, for they recognized that the Home Rule they desired could never be enacted with a hostile and powerful House of Lords. Efforts to curb the Lords' powers, to reform its composition, and, in the wake of **Edward VII**'s death in May 1910, to effect a compromise between the parties on the issue, all dominated most of 1910. When they failed, a second election to break the stalemate was inevitable. At first glance, the results of that election, held in December 1910, simply replicated those of the previous January, but there was one crucial difference. By securing a public mandate to retain power, the Liberals were able to extract a private pledge from the new king, **George V**, that he would be willing to create new peers in a number sufficient to swamp the upper chamber and ensure its acquiescence to the Liberal bill to eliminate its absolute veto.

As the conflict moved toward its climax in August 1911, political temperatures rivaled those of the concurrent record heat wave. The Liberals insisted that upsetting the historic, if illusory, balance of the constitution was the only way to preserve the sanctity of representative government; some Unionists were prepared to admit that a hereditary chamber with equal authority was now indefensible, but other Tories, the "diehards," maintained that principle dictated not submission but defiance. Everything the diehards held dear about their country—its traditions of a hereditary peerage, patrician government, and imperial authority—was now bound up in their defense of the House of Lords. Whether the crisis could be resolved peacefully, or whether it would require the Liberals to invoke the King's pledge, make a mockery of the constitutional process, and prompt civil disobedience (and perhaps civil war in Ireland) depended on whether the Diehards would be outvoted by the handful of Liberal peers and their more conciliatory Unionist brethren.

On 10 August 1911 these drastic prospects were avoided; the Diehards lost the vote, though by a narrow margin (131–114) with thirty-seven Unionist peers voting for the bill. The resulting Parliament Act eliminated the House of Lords' ability to interfere with finance bills and abolished its absolute veto. The most it could do would be to delay legislation, for any bill passed in the Commons during three successive sessions would become law regardless of the Lords' actions. While passage of the act marked a landmark in constitutional history, it did little to dampen the acrimonious tone of pre-war politics, for in one sense the Diehards' defiance simply spilled out of the upper chamber and into the press, the debating platforms, and the streets of Ulster.

Frans Coetzee

Bibliography

Blewett, Neal. *The Peers, the Parties, and the People: The General Elections of 1910.* 1972.

Dangerfield, George. *The Strange Death of Liberal England.* 1935.

Jenkins, Roy. *Mr. Balfour's Poodle.* 1954.

Murray, Bruce. *The People's Budget, 1909–1910.* 1980.

Phillips, Gregory. *The Diehards: Aristocratic Society and Politics in Edwardian England.* 1979.

Cooperative Movement

The Cooperative movement is a form of association for the purposes of trade, business, or agriculture, involving open membership, democratic control, dividends on purchases, and ownership by the members. The movement effectively began with the Rochdale Society of Equitable Pioneers in 1844 and enjoyed its greatest success in retailing and production. With 12.5 million members by the 1930s, the movement represents an important aspect of modern British economic and social history.

By the late nineteenth century a federal structure was in place, based on the Co-operative Union (formed 1869) in Manchester, whose annual congress provided policy-making and educational leadership. This task of developing and promoting cooperative enterprise was taken up in 1991 by the United Kingdom Co-operative Council, comprising twelve national institutions ranging from the Co-operative Wholesale Society (CWS) to the Co-operative Bank.

At its height, between the 1930s and 1950s, the movement owned 29,000 retail shops, hundreds of factories, a bank, a building society, an insurance company, its own internal newspaper, *Co-operative News*, and, from 1929, a weekly, *Reynolds' News*. From the early 1960s to the 1980s, however, there was an accelerating decline caused by factors including attempts to cater for nearly all consumer needs and tastes, the emergence of highly efficient and specialized commercial competitors, and a conservative management. By 1991 the number of societies had fallen to sixty-nine (from a maximum of 1,455 in 1903), with about 5,000 retail outlets. Trade volume stood at £7.333 billion, of which some 62 percent was in foodstuffs, but with significant activity in dairy production, pharmacy, motor trades, and funeral furnishing. Membership stood at 8.1 million. By this time there was clear evidence that the long-term decline had been stopped, following massive reorganization, and the introduction of a new chain of superstores in the 1980s.

In the areas of distribution, production, and services, the CWS (established 1863) was dominant, accounting for many of its own products. This had initially been in goods such as footwear and biscuits, but later included insurance (the Co-operative Insurance Society), banking (the Co-operative Bank), and agriculture. In 1991 the CWS accounted for 27 percent of the movement's trade. Apart from the CWS, cooperative production has been insignificant in Britain. The Co-operative Productive Federation was established in 1882 to provide support, and by 1914 there were seventy-three small copartnership enterprises, chiefly in the clothing, footwear, and printing trades. These declined to about thirty-five in the early 1970s, when there were several major attempts to promote worker cooperatives. Numerous worker takeovers followed the high level of business failures during and after the 1970s. The Industrial Common Ownership movement, as it was known, was concentrated in wholefoods, radical bookselling, and printing, although collectively it employed only about 8,500 workers.

The movement, led by the Co-operative Union, has always been active in the area of education—running, for example, correspondence courses in such subjects as bookkeeping and establishing the Co-operative College in 1922, based first in Manchester and, from 1946, at Stanford Hall in Loughborough. Education was also a prime concern of the guilds, the most significant of which was the Women's Co-operative Guild (WCG) founded in 1883. The WCG, an important pressure group, had 12,809 members in 1900, reached a peak of nearly 90,000 in the late 1930s, but declined to about 6,000 in the early 1990s.

While in theory the Cooperative movement is nonpolitical, the Co-operative Congress decided in 1917 to establish a political arm in an attempt to bring direct influence on government on behalf of the consumer. One Co-operative Party candidate, A.E. Waterson, was elected MP for Kettering in 1918, but he immediately allied himself with the **Labour Party**. The fortunes of the two parties have been linked ever since. A formal understanding was reached in 1927, allowing cooperatives to affiliate locally with Labour, and from 1946 sponsored individuals ran as Co-operative and Labour candidates. The number of MPs reached a peak of twenty-three (from thirty-four candidates) in 1945. The credibility of the party was not helped by the defection of four MPs to the Social Democrats in 1981, and in 1983 only eight MPs (out of seventeen sponsored) were elected. In the election of April 1992 fourteen were elected out of twenty-three.

Brian Dyson

Bibliography

Bonner, Arnold. *British Co-operation*. 2nd ed. 1970.
Carbery, Thomas F. *Consumers in Politics*. 1969.
Cole, G.D.H. *A Century of Cooperation*. 1945.
Flanagan, Desmond. *A Centenary Story of the Co-operative Union, 1869–1969*. 1969.
Richardson, William. *The CWS in War and Peace, 1938–1976*. 1977.

Council for the Encouragement of Music and the Arts (CEMA)

The Council for the Encouragement of Music and the Arts, or CEMA as it was generally known, was the first experiment in state sponsorship of the arts and was the immediate forerunner of the **Arts Council of Great Britain**.

Launched late in 1939 under the aegis of the Board of Education but with funds from the Pilgrim Trust, CEMA was a direct response to the threat to the arts posed by the coming of the **Second World War**. With theaters and concert halls closed in anticipation of bombing and with workers resettled in newly established industrial hostels, often isolated from urban amenities, access to entertainment was severely limited. In addition, the **conscription** of musicians and actors reduced the ranks of **orchestras** and theater companies, while restrictions on civilian transport, which made it difficult for groups to tour, eliminated employment opportunities for many artists. As early as September 1939 the Board of Education and the Treasury began to negotiate with a view to providing financial assistance to voluntary organizations involved in **adult education**. Officials recognized the need to preserve music, drama, and the arts during the emergency and to provide sufficient entertainment to sustain the morale of the civilian population. It was believed essential to show government concern about the cultural life of the country not only to reassure its own people, but for the sake of Britain's image abroad.

An ephemeral organization called the Art and Entertainment Emergency Council, including **Sir Kenneth Clark**, who had already initiated lunchtime concerts in the National Gallery and the **War Artists'** Advisory Committee to employ artists to record the war, appealed to the government to utilize professionals in the arts, but CEMA stemmed instead from negotiations between Thomas Jones, Secretary of the Pilgrim Trust, and Lord De La Warr, then President of the Board of Education, in December 1939. De La Warr envisaged a temporary expedient to aid beleaguered cultural pursuits during the emergency by encouraging amateur music and drama and by assisting unemployed performers. The Pilgrim Trust hoped to bolster the effort of voluntary agencies experienced in community arts by means of grants and by dispatching itinerant music and drama organizers to work with amateur groups. While CEMA's earliest policy formulations recognized the need to help unemployed professional artists, the initial orientation was toward amateur and educational activity of a distinctly populist sort, in which professionals might play an auxiliary role, but in which the emphasis would be on popular participation.

Yet even at the outset it was unclear whether the greater availability of culture would mean the provision of entertainment or the stimulation of amateur activity. Alongside the music travelers and drama organizers, CEMA funded concerts in canteens as well as orchestral performances, and by 1940 it began to sponsor tours by Old Vic troupes to Lancashire and South Wales. When the London Blitz began, CEMA began to dispatch "flying squads" of musicians to air raid shelters, rest centers for the homeless, and, more extensively, to munitions factories, generating a rivalry with the Entertainments National Service Association (ENSA). Generally, ENSA concerts featured a more popular genre of entertainment, while CEMA programs consisted mainly of classical music.

The Pilgrim Trust's initial grant of £25,000 was matched in the spring of 1940 by a Treasury grant, and for a time CEMA's funds derived equally from private and public sources. Eventually, however, it became wholly government funded, and the original private administrative committee was transformed into a larger council appointed by the Board of Education and under its direct supervision. As its structure began to change, so too did its mission, with a shift away from the encouragement of music making and playacting by the people themselves to maintaining the highest standards of the arts in wartime and rendering assistance to performing artists.

The shift in emphasis from amateur to professional activity accelerated once the Pilgrim Trust withdrew at the beginning of 1942, after increasing its contribution to £50,000, and John Maynard Keynes was appointed as Chairman by the activist President of the Board of Education, R.A. Butler. During the four years of Keynes' dynamic leadership, CEMA became less populist, concentrating on quality and professional standards, but equally emphasizing entertainment more than education. Keenly interested in appointments to the council and its panels, Keynes demanded a high level of financial accountability from sponsored bodies, like the Old Vic and the British Institute of Adult Education. While eager to diffuse the artistic life of the country, he kept a tight rein on CEMA affairs, even when his Treasury responsibilities required lengthy absences in Washington. Keynes reversed the antimetropolitan bias that dominated CEMA thinking during the Pilgrim Trust's more missionary phase by promoting a London Old Vic season and collaborating with a controversial, tax-exempt commercial company, Tennant Plays.

During Keynes' tenure the annual Treasury grant grew to more than £200,000, the administrative structure of CEMA was overhauled, with the appointment of regional officers in place of the music and drama travelers, and financial arrangements shifted from direct grants to guarantees as a way of encouraging local enterprise to become self-supporting. His aversion to bureaucratic red tape led him to streamline CEMA's often chaotic internal structure: Full-time paid directors of music, drama, and art were appointed, and advisory panels were constituted in each of the three areas. At Keynes' instigation CEMA took over the management of the Theatre Royal, Bristol, in 1942 and began the complicated negotiations to restore Covent Garden as the home for a national opera and ballet after the war. From 1943 on he and his colleagues were absorbed in transforming CEMA into a permanent peacetime organization that would supervise state patronage of the arts. With minor structural changes the renamed Arts Council received a Royal Charter and began to function in 1946 as an autonomous agency carrying forward the work CEMA had begun.

During its six years of existence CEMA had demonstrated that the receptivity of the public to the arts exceeded all expectations. By stimulating activity and providing entertainment, it had accomplished its initial goals of salvaging culture, raising morale, and providing employment for distressed professional artists. The Arts Council that replaced it at the end of the war bore the imprint of Keynes' conception of public patronage. His scheme was a compromise between private initiative and state control. Financially dependent on the Treasury, the Arts Council would determine how to appropriate its own funds, free from the intervention of Whitehall or the surveillance of Westminster.

F.M. Leventhal

Bibliography
Glasgow, Mary. "The Concept of the Arts Council" in Milo Keynes, ed. Essays on John Maynard Keynes. 1975. pp. 260–71.
Hutchison, Robert. The Politics of the Arts Council. 1982.
Leventhal, F.M. "'The Best for the Most': CEMA and State Sponsorship of the Arts in Wartime, 1939–1945," Twentieth Century British History, vol. 1 (1990), pp. 289–317.

White, Eric Walter. *The Arts Council of Great Britain.* 1975.

Council Housing

Immediately after the First World War the government obliged local authorities to survey their **housing** needs and to submit plans to address the problem of housing shortages. Exchequer subsidies were then made available to local authorities, who by 1939 had built 1 million homes, equivalent to 10 percent of the housing stock. In so doing, council provision of accommodation assumed a central position in the housing market, and this was extended successively until 1982 when it represented 32 percent of dwellings. Between 1919 and 1987 14.2 million houses were built in Britain, 43 percent by councils. Of many regional variations, the greatest reliance on council housebuilding was in Scotland, where councils were responsible for 71 percent of all dwellings built in the years 1919–87.

Explanations of the initial development of council housing vary. One view is that public housing was, like other areas of **Liberal** social welfare provision, a result of successful working-class agitation; another explanation is that state intervention was inevitable because of pre-1914 private-enterprise failures to provide suitable low-rental accommodation for workers; a third possibility is that disruptive wartime rental and building controls necessitated continuing public involvement in the housing sector after the war. And, though the "Homes Fit for Heroes" election pledge is often thought to have prompted council housing, recent research shows that few "Heroes" were housed in this way, and that council housing was in fact, in **David Lloyd George's** words, an "insurance premium" to placate a demobilized, disenchanted working class during the 1918–19 period of intense industrial strike action.

The initial legislation, the Housing and Town Planning Act (1919), was curtailed within months, once a degree of social stability was achieved and, in the face of rapidly escalating building costs, once the extent of the Treasury's financial commitment was realized. Housing subsidies were forthcoming from both **Conservatives** (1923) and the first **Labour** administration (1924), but there was an important philosophical difference in their approaches: The Conservatives accorded councils only a residual role where private enterprise was unwilling to

provide homes, whereas Labour viewed municipal housing as central to the growth of the overall housing stock. When returned to power, and confronted with a dearth of private rented housing, the Conservatives continued the framework established by Labour. However, by focusing on aggregate numbers of council houses built in the 1920s, little account was taken of either regional variations or the weekly rental levels fixed for council housing, which were frequently beyond the means of the low paid. So, although 625,000 council houses had been built by 1929, when policy shifted in 1930 and 1933 toward Treasury subsidies for **slum** clearance and "de-crowding" initiatives, the underlying problem of an insufficient supply of working-class housing remained.

Between 1945 and 1955 councils constructed 1.6 million new houses, 50 percent more than between the wars, reflecting the political urgency of the housing issue. As the Labour minister responsible, **Aneurin Bevan** proposed an emergency program of local-authority housebuilding, with the private construction sector limited to just 20 percent of total housebuilding. When in power between 1951 and 1964, and despite their ideological preference for private-sector provision, Conservative politicians conceded a central role to council housing, though the emphasis of policy changed with the ending of general housing subsidies in 1956 and a move to more specific financial support for the demolition of downtown slums and the relocation of families in council houses, frequently on the periphery of the cities.

Local authorities dominated new rental construction after the Second World War, and, by the early 1960s, the stock of council housing had overtaken the proportion in the private rental sector. Under Labour, returned to power in 1964, a national housing plan the following year proposed a further acceleration of council housebuilding. Output reached 180,000 in 1967, but public-expenditure cuts in response to the devaluation crisis in 1967 meant the central government reined in its financial commitment to local authorities. So 1968 was an important turning point: The age of mass council housebuilding, begun in 1945, was to come to an end in the early 1970s.

The housing shortage was much less by 1970 than formerly, and the political imperative for new housebuilding slackened accordingly. In addition, though high-rise building accounted for a relatively small proportion of local-authority housing, the image and reality of this type of dwelling contributed to a developing critique of council housebuilding and housing management. Changed housing priorities recognized "special needs,"—for example, in dwellings for the aged and infirm—and, together with an emerging awareness of urban environmental considerations, renovation and renewal meant that demand for council housing slackened and, conversely, the retention of private-sector housing was strengthened. In 1978, in a repeat of the foreign-exchange crisis of the 1960s, stringent public-expenditure controls were a condition attached to loans obtained from the International Monetary Fund, and capital projects such as housing were trimmed accordingly.

Since 1979 successive Conservative administrations have mounted a powerful critique of the public-housing sector. The principal tactic has been to tap a rich seam of public disquiet regarding council housing management, drawing on tenants' complaints and housing departments' administrative complacency. Conservative politicians claimed that municipal landlordism was itself the problem. Restrictive monetary targets for public expenditure were another device developed to contain councils' capital expenditure on housing in the early 1980s. The main focus of policy was directed, however, at tenants' "right to buy" the property they had rented from councils, normally on very favorable terms and at heavily discounted prices. This anticollectivist, or privatization, strategy was given further impetus after 1986 by boosting private landlords, either as individuals through tax and investment incentives or by means of encouraging housing associations as the builders and managers of rented accommodation. From 1988 existing council housing stock was de-municipalized by means of Housing Action Trusts and Tenants' Choice schemes whereby management and responsibility passed to local housing associations following ballot arrangements that have attracted considerable criticism. In one of the biggest transfers, almost 75,000 properties, the homes of more than a quarter of a million Scots, were removed from the public sector and transferred to a private agency called Scottish Homes in 1989 on the basis of a minority vote of the tenants involved.

The significance of council housing in Britain extends far beyond simple quantitative

Lansbury Estate, Poplar: Post-war council housing.

measures of additions to housing stocks. Developed on a mass-produced basis, often with experimental materials or methods, and concentrated on peripheral green-field sites with highly standardized designs and minimal landscaping, council housing has become associated with second-class tenure. Council residents have also been stigmatized as second-class citizens, since, unlike owner occupiers, tenants do not participate in the long-run appreciation of house values. Excluded from capital accumulation, council tenants have also endured low-quality health and education provisions. As a result, council housing has re-created the process of social segregation through the mechanism of residential segregation.

Richard Rodger

Bibliography

Daunton, Martin J., ed. *Councillors and Tenants: Local Authority Housing in English Cities, 1919–1939.* 1984.

Dunleavy, Patrick. *The Politics of Mass Housing, 1945–1975.* 1981.

Forrest, Ray, and Alan Murie. *Selling the Welfare State: The Privatisation of Council Housing.* 1987.

Lowe, Stuart, and David Hughes, eds. *A New Century of Social Housing.* 1991.

Merett, Stephen. *State Housing in Britain.* 1979.

Swenarton, Mark. *Homes Fit for Heroes: The Politics and Architecture of Early State Housing in Britain.* 1981.

Country Houses

The country house has enjoyed at least two dramatic reversals of fortune in the twentieth century. Traditionally the social and economic center of the great landed estate, it lost many of its former functions with the decline of agriculture from the 1870s onward, and particularly after the First World War when so many of the great estates were dismembered. By the 1930s many country houses appeared even to their owners as relics of a bygone age, fated to be demolished, sold off, even exported to America. Since the Second World War, however, they have benefited from a sudden aesthetic and cultural revaluation not only among connoisseurs but also among the general public, and owners have consequently reaped enhanced economic returns through government grants and the commercial exploitation of tourism.

Before the First World War most of rural Britain was parceled up into large agricultural estates, and most of these estates could claim a country house of some kind, ranging from the small manor houses of the parish gentry to great palaces like the Duke of Devonshire's Chatsworth. All of these houses would accommodate the owner's family and servants, when not in London for the "season," offer entertainment for parties of friends staying for weekends or longer, provide working space for the managers of the estate, and serve as physical symbols of the landlord's local status and power. Some would be opened on ceremonial occasions to the local public so that the interiors could be admired and/or envied. But public visitation of country houses had probably been declining since the early nineteenth century, as **railways** made many houses accessible to too large a public, and owners sought to shield their possessions from the democratic franchise and rising taxation.

From the 1910s taxation and agricultural decline combined to dismantle many great estates, and their associated houses lost their commercial and symbolic functions. Could the country house survive simply as a house? Owners were, on the whole, dubious and unsentimental. If pressed, they would sell or lease the house even before selling off the estate. Between the wars there was still a lively market for country houses, as the automobile made entertaining in the country more popular. Failing a sale, owners might demolish, perhaps to rebuild on a smaller scale; something up to 10 percent of the nation's country houses were destroyed before 1940. Although early twentieth-century taste valued the very oldest houses—medieval and Tudor—neither owners nor connoisseurs shed many tears over the loss of the run-of-the-mill country house built after 1660.

The **Second World War** triggered another wave of sales and demolitions. Wartime shortages of servants, fuel, and building materials and requisition by government for evacuated schools, military uses, and the like had driven many owners out of occupation. After the war few people—neither old owners nor new rich—wished any longer to live in large, draughty, unmodernized houses in remote parts of the country. Consequently, another 15 percent or so of the nation's country-house stock fell to the wrecking ball, and many more were gutted for institutional uses as schools, government offices, nursing homes, hotels, and the like. **Evelyn Waugh**'s *Brideshead Revisited* (1945) was a best-selling elegy to a country-house world that seemed dead and buried.

But in the late 1940s public interest in country houses had finally begun to stir, as sales of *Brideshead* suggest. Popular interest in **architecture** of all periods was booming, perhaps stimulated by the German bombing raids. A government inquiry into the fate of historic houses, chaired by Sir Ernest Gowers, reported in 1950 and focused its attention almost exclusively on the great country houses, recommending government subsidy to help preserve up to 2,000 of the best houses in private ownership. A limited grant system to help owners of historic buildings was in place by 1953.

Most important was the 1950s boom of motor tourism, both foreign and domestic. Already during the war, the **National Trust**, which had hitherto concentrated its efforts on the preservation of open space, had begun to acquire country houses with a view to opening them to the public. After the war, private owners began to contemplate commercial opening as well. The pioneers were the Marquess of Bath at Longleat (1949) and Lord Montagu at Beaulieu (1952). Hundreds followed their example. As early as 1954, 150 houses had opened on a semicommercial basis, drawing 2 million visitors; a decade later, 600 houses attracted over 10 million. Owners became tourism entrepeneurs, adorning their houses—now often "stately homes"—with safari parks, funfairs, motoring museums, garden centers, farming exhibitions, adventure playgrounds, whatever might give them the competitive edge.

In the 1970s the popularity of the country house broke through onto an even higher plateau. Economic downturn and cultural conservatism combined to generate a kind of mania for the preservation of these jewels of the national heritage. An exhibition about demolished country houses at the Victoria and Albert Museum in 1975 attracted much comment. Demolitions were halted entirely by firmer legislation. The **Labour** government was loudly berated, and not only by the right-wing press, for its failure in 1977 to buy and keep intact the Earl of Rosebery's house and collections at Mentmore. Books about country-house life, fashions, and architecture dotted the best-seller lists, notably Mark Girouard's series of sumptuous social histories and a raft of books pro-

duced under the aegis of the National Trust and *Country Life* magazine. There was even a spate of new country-house building in the once despised neo-classical style.

This mania showed no signs of abating in the 1990s. What had seemed a world dead and buried in 1945 was full of life a half-century later. Taking tax benefits into account as well as grants and tourist income, public opening kept hundreds of houses in private ownership and decent repair. Hundreds more had never had to open at all, still maintained largely by agriculture or cannier investments. Three-quarters of all country houses extant in 1880 remained standing in 1980, over half in private ownership, perhaps a third with some public access, more than a quarter retaining some of their original estate land. The country-house mystique remained buoyant and helped to sustain substantial fragments of the old country-house world for those among the titled and leisured rich who held on through lean years.

Peter Mandler

Bibliography

Clemenson, Heather A. *English Country Houses and Landed Estates.* 1982.
Cornforth, John. *The Inspiration of the Past: Country House Taste in the Twentieth Century.* 1985.
Robinson, J.M. *The Latest Country Houses.* 1984.
Strong, Roy, et al. *The Destruction of the Country House, 1875–1975.* 1975.

Coward, Noel Pierce (1899–1973)

Playwright, actor, director, composer, librettist, and fiction writer, instrumental in the development of the English **musical revue**, Noel Coward wrote and produced over fifty dramatic works and was knighted in 1970 for his varied contributions to British theater.

Born shortly before Christmas in 1899 in Teddington, Middlesex, Coward was encouraged early to pursue a life in the theater. As a child he appeared professionally in several children's "fantasies." His earliest experiments in writing were all directed to the stage and eventually toward his own performance. Coward served briefly in the **army** in 1918 but was discharged due to poor health. Years later he contributed to the war effort through active participation in the **Entertainments National Service Association** (ENSA).

Success came to Coward when he was still young. In the early 1920s he had four plays produced in both London and New York: *The Young Idea* (1923), *The Vortex* (1924), *Fallen Angels*, and *Hay Fever* (both 1925). Five Coward productions ran simultaneously in London in 1925, including *On with The Dance*, a musical revue commissioned by C.B. Cochran. Other contributions to revue included *Sirocco* (1927) and *This Year of Grace* (1928), which were a flop and a runaway success, respectively. Coward elicited extreme reactions from contemporary audiences for his liberal portrayals of the social and sexual mores, but he often masked controversial subjects in witty dialogue. *Design for Living* (1933), one of Coward's most controversial plays, also became one of the greatest successes of his career. Other memorable productions from this period were *Bitter Sweet* (1929), *Private Lives* (1930), in which Coward starred with Gertrude Lawrence and **Laurence Olivier**, *Cavalcade* (1931), *Words and Music* (1932), and *To-Night at Eight* (1936).

The musical play *Operette* (1938) was followed by the hugely popular *Blithe Spirit* (1941), which ran for a record-breaking 1,997 performances in London. Coward produced other lighthearted works, including *Present Laughter* (1943) and *Sigh No More* (1945), before striking out in a serious vein with *Peace in Our Time* (1947). Coward returned to comedy with *Relative Values* (1951) and *Quadrille* (1952). *Nude with Violin* starred John Gielgud in 1956, and in the same year Vivien Leigh appeared in *South Sea Bubble*. Late in his career Coward wrote an adaptation of a Feydeau play entitled *Look After Luke* (1959) and a retrospective on acting, *Waiting in the Wings* (1960). His last original musical, *Sail Away*, was produced in 1963, and his last stage appearance was in his own *Suite in Three Keys* (1966), which hinted at his **homosexuality**.

Coward also had a celebrated cinematic career, notably during the **Second World War**, when he provided scripts, usually based on his plays, for such memorable films as *In Which We Serve* (1942), *This Happy Breed* (1944), *Blithe Spirit* (1945), and *Brief Encounter* (1945), all of which, in very different ways, extolled English virtues. He achieved some notoriety as a film actor as well, especially in *In Which We Serve*, where his portrayal of Captain Kinross was modeled on the career of **Lord Mountbatten**, and in later films like *Our Man in Havana* (1959).

Coward performed leading roles in the plays written by others, including **George Bernard Shaw**'s *The Apple Cart* (1953), and achieved success in the United States performing his own clever songs on the stage, in nightclubs, and on **television**. Throughout his career Coward found pleasure in the pursuits of watercolor painting and fiction writing. He produced two collections of short fiction, *To Step Aside* (1939) and *Star Quality* (1951), as well as two volumes of autobiography, *Present Indicative* (1937) and *Future Indefinite* (1954). His impact on the British stage, often deprecated by later playwrights, continues to be felt through the frequent revivals of his plays.

Martha A. Schütz

Bibliography

Fisher, Clive. *Noel Coward*. 1992
Lahr, John. *Coward the Playwright*. 1982.
Lesley, Cole. *The Life of Noel Coward*. 1976.
Mander, Raymond, and Joe Mitchenson. *Theatrical Companion to Coward*. 1957.
Morley, Sheridan. *A Talent to Amuse: A Biography of Noel Coward*. 1969.
Morley, Sheridan, and Graham Payn, eds. *The Noel Coward Diaries*. 1982.

Crick, Francis (1916–)

One of several British physicists to move into biology after the Second World War, Francis Crick built his career on the belief that complex biological phenomena can be explained using the laws of **chemistry** and **physics**. His role in the biological revolution of the 1950s and 1960s was crucial, starting in 1953 with the double-helix structure for DNA (for which he shared the 1962 Nobel Prize for Medicine) and culminating in 1961 with the demonstration that the genetic code is read in triplets. Throughout this period Crick was a towering influence in molecular biology, formulating many of the basic ideas about how gene structure determines protein structure and coordinating an informal network of collaboration. More recently he has influenced fields as diverse as embryology and the structure of chromosomes. Since 1976 he has been interested in the workings of the brain and the problem of consciousness.

Crick entered biology in 1947, after spending the war in naval research, and two years later joined the **Medical Research Council** (MRC) unit in the **Cavendish Laboratory**,

Cambridge. In 1953 a collaboration with James Watson (1928–), a visiting American postdoctoral fellow, resulted in the double-helix model for the structure of DNA, an intellectual tour de force that combined information from x-ray crystallography and stereochemistry.

The double helix launched a decade of intense international activity in which the relationship between DNA structure and protein structure was worked out. The theoretical basis of this relationship was largely formulated by Crick: He proposed both the Sequence Hypothesis and the Central Dogma and deduced the necessity for adaptor molecules (transfer RNA) before any experimental evidence for their existence existed. It was the theoretical physicist George Gamow (1904–68) who suggested that the translation from DNA sequence to protein sequence could be treated as a formal coding problem, but it was Crick and his colleague Sydney Brenner (1927–) who established the rules by which hypothetical codes were tested against known protein sequences and showed, by an ingenious genetic experiment, that the code was read in nonoverlapping triplets.

In 1962 the MRC unit moved to a new research institute, the Laboratory for Molecular Biology, and Crick became head of the Molecular Genetics Division, a position he soon shared with Brenner. By the mid-1960s the genetic code had been broken, and Crick moved on to the problem of embryonic development and the role of the redundant DNA in multicellular organisms. In both areas his ideas have had a major influence on the direction of the field.

In 1976 Crick moved to the Salk Institute, California, and started working on the brain. The molecular biology that emerged in the 1950s resulted from the successful fusion of different traditions, and Crick is attempting to do the same thing to the neurosciences: bridging the gaps between neurophysiology, neuroanatomy, psychophysics, and computer modeling. He sees himself as a theoretical biologist, a role that is familiar to a physicist but rare in biology. There are many who would claim that he is the outstanding theoretical biologist of our age. Among many honors is the award of the Order of Merit in 1991.

Guil Winchester

Bibliography
Crick, Francis. *What Mad Pursuit: A Personal View of Scientific Discovery.* 1988.
Judson, Horace. *The Eighth Day of Creation: Makers of the Revolution in Biology.* 1979.
Olby, Robert. "Francis Crick, DNA, and the Central Dogma," *Daedalus,* no. 4 (1970), pp. 938–87.

C

Cricket

For more than 100 years cricket has been one of the most popular of British sports. Its capacity for uniting all social groups and virtually all regions of Britain resulted in its commonly being referred to at the end of the nineteenth century as "the national game," a title since claimed by soccer. Cricket's association with good sportsmanship and fair play gave rise to its being a symbol of civilized behavior. "It isn't cricket," in popular parlance, signified a lapse from the standards of decent conduct.

Though cricket is a game with a long history, its specifically "modern" form was developed during the second half of the nineteenth century. An essentially southern English sport, with strong roots in both villages and towns, it was disseminated to other parts of the country by middle-class men who had learned the game at public school. Its popularity was consolidated by the promotional activities of touring "circuses" of professional cricketers from the 1840s to the 1860s. By the following decade the predominant form of cricket was one sponsored by clubs based in the English counties. They had formed themselves into a competition (the County Championship) in 1864, the leading places being taken by Nottinghamshire, Yorkshire, Lancashire, Surrey, and Kent in the later years of the century. It was this branch of the game that came to be designated "First Class" and was governed by officials of the London club, Marylebone Cricket Club (MCC). But the existence of this level should not be allowed to mask the fact that much high-quality cricket was played by clubs not part of the county circuit. Of particular note was the "league" cricket played in the industrial towns of the Midlands and north, which developed its own style and ethos.

In common with other sports, county cricketers were frequently paid professionals. By the end of the century professionals dominated the playing staffs of the leading counties in numerical terms, though (unlike soccer) the "all-professional" team was unknown. The amateur concept remained strong, and many men from an upper-class social background considered it beneath their dignity to play for money. Several of the game's leading players have been from this group, especially in the "golden era" before 1914 when names such as A.C. MacLaren, G.L. Jessop, C.B. Fry, and F.S. Jackson often dominated proceedings. It was people of this social class who controlled the game both off and on the field of play. Few professionals became captains of county clubs before the 1960s, and no professional captained the England team between 1888 and 1952. Although eventually abolished in 1962, the distinction between amateur and professional carried immense social meaning, and until 1962 the most prestigious noninternational fixture in the cricket season was the Gentlemen v. Players match.

The leading cricketer from the 1860s until the turn of the century, the man whose name was synonymous with cricket, was W.G. Grace. Grace's importance was manifold. As a player his all-round achievements far outstripped those of his contemporaries. He thus helped to release some of the commerical potential of cricket, profiting from it himself (though, as a member of the country gentry, he played as an amateur, he nevertheless made far more money as a sportsman than he did from his profession in medicine). And he established techniques of both batting and bowling that became the norm for years to come.

Largely because of Grace's stature, cricket also became an exportable commodity, taken up predominantly in the British Empire. By the 1890s, regular competitions among England, **Australia,** and **South Africa** were taking place. In the inter-war period, the West Indies, India, and **New Zealand** joined this imperial club. Later additions were Pakistan (1952) and Sri Lanka (1988). The "Test Matches" among these countries represented the pinnacle of cricketing achievement, with those between England and Australia—the two oldest cricketing countries—producing especially keen contests. Australia had the better of these exchanges over the period (1920–53), when for much of this time they had the services of Don Bradman, a batsman whose achievements in consistently high scoring are unparalleled, even by the mighty Grace.

The duration of play in Test Matches gradually increased to five days by the 1950s, but otherwise the game underwent few changes in organization or technique until the 1960s and 1970s, when two important innovations were made to maximize the spectator and commercial appeal of the game. In 1963 a competition of one-day matches (initially sponsored by Gillette) was introduced into the English county circuit. Its immense popularity prompted similar departures from tradition in 1969 and 1972, enhancing cricket as a **television** spectacle and stimulating improvements in some aspects of play, notably the art of fielding. One-day cricket is now an essential part of the English game. The second innovation came in 1976 when the Australian media proprietor Kerry Packer launched World Series Cricket (WSC). This venture, aimed at bringing together a highly paid group of the world's top players to perform in matches that would attract a vast television audience, had major effects on the English game. In the short term, by enabling the star cricketers to play off their employers against WSC and thus push up their earnings, it broke the long-established hold of the MCC over English professionals and brought them better treatment. In the longer run, new methods of presenting cricket were adopted (mainly overseas), and the number of Test Matches—the game's biggest money-making feature—was greatly increased. Though undoubtedly more commercial than ever before in the aftermath of the "Packer Revolution," cricket nevertheless still retains a social cachet and aesthetic quality lacking in most other British sports. It is, significantly, one of only a few British sports capable of generating a literature of "poetic" proportions.

Jeffrey Hill

Bibliography

Brookes, Christopher. *English Cricket: The Game and Its Players through the Ages.* 1978.

Frindall, Bill, ed. *The Wisden Book of Test Cricket, 1877–1984.* 1985.

Lewis, Tony. *Double Century: The Story of MCC and Its Cricket.* 1987.

Midwinter, Eric. *WG Grace: His Life and Times.* 1981.

Sissons, Ric. *The Players: A Social History of the Professional Cricketer.* 1988.

Crime

Since it makes exciting copy, crime has been a popular subject with many sections of the British media throughout the twentieth century. However, from the mid-1950s general concern about crime became much sharper because of a steep and accelerating rise in crime statistics.

The judicial statistics, on which most assessments have been made, have as their basis crimes reported to the police. These statistics show that throughout the century the vast majority of serious crimes that could be prosecuted on indictment were offenses against property—in particular, different forms of theft and the handling of stolen goods. While property offenses consistently accounted for over 90 percent of recorded, indictable crime, those offenses that generated the most fear and the most publicity—namely, violent and sexual crimes—accounted for only about 5 percent of the annual total. The homicide rate constituted only a fraction of violent crimes. At the beginning of the century the national homicide rate was annually about 1 crime per 100,000 of the population; with some fluctuations this gradually fell to an all-time low of 0.3 per 100,000 in the early 1950s, after which it began to rise, just exceeding the rate of the beginning of the century in the mid-1980s. Serious crime as a whole remained constant between 1900 and 1914; thereafter it began a gradual rise, slackening in the decade following the Second World War but soaring from the mid-1950s. Allowing for the increase in population, the figures show an annual rate of 249 crimes per 100,000 of the population in 1901, 2,374 per 100,000 in 1965, and 6,674 per 100,000 in 1984. An interesting implication of the pattern of these statistics is that the mass **unemployment** of the inter-war years had little impact on criminal behavior; the sharpest increase in offending appears to coincide with growing affluence from the mid-1950s.

Yet while the official statistics continued to be used to justify political campaigns and policy-making, and while their annual publication was commonly seized on by the **press**, considerable debate developed over their value, particularly in the last third of the century. The problem of the "dark figure"—that is, the number of crimes committed but never reported—had been recognized by the Victorians, but other difficulties were increasingly highlighted. Were more crimes listed because of an improvement in **police** recording procedures, including an end to the Metropolitan Police habit in the first quarter of the century of recording some reports of thefts as reports of lost property? Were more thefts being reported because of a growth in the insurance business and the need for a victim to make a report to the police in order to file an insurance claim? Was the marked increase in rape during the 1980s attributable to the fact that there was less stigma attached to the victim, a greater public awareness, and more sympathetic police interviewing? Were more crimes of violence reported generally because of a decline in public tolerance for rough and violent behavior? In the attempt to get a better understanding of levels and patterns of criminality, victim surveys began to be conducted from the mid-1970s. The most comprehensive was *The British Crime Survey,* first conducted for 1981 and involving one person age sixteen years or above in each of 11,000 households in England and Wales and 5,000 households in Scotland. In many respects the findings of the survey underlined the conclusions to be drawn from the official statistics—namely, that violent and sexual offenses were few in number while much crime was extremely petty. However, the survey did suggest that the increase in burglary was only a fifth of that shown in the official statistics during the 1970s.

While the statistics suggest that most crime in twentieth-century Britain has been petty and nonviolent, such a conclusion would not be apparent from reading the popular press. The century has seen the creation of a succession of what, with reference to the portrayal of youth gangs during the 1960s, has been described as "folk devils." Indeed youth gangs often figured in this role: In the period before the First World War there was concern over the original "hooligans"; in the inter-war period it was the razor-gangs, notably in Glasgow; and with the growth of **youth culture** after the Second World War, there came, in succession, the Teddy Boys, the Mods and the Rockers, and the Skinheads. Offenders, given a generic name based on their *modus operandi*, were also popular with the press: The "motor bandit" and the "bag snatcher" of the inter-war years was replaced in the aftermath of the Second World War by the "cosh boy" and then by the "mugger." Individuals might also earn a new name signifying the horrendous nature of their crimes, furnishing the media with good copy and their readers or watchers with vicarious thrills: Peter Sutcliffe, even after his arrest and conviction, remained better known as "the Yorkshire Ripper."

Throughout the century most offenders were young males, often under twenty years old. Though in the popular imagination youth gangs were the most public manifestation of youth deviance, offenses by youths were not always committed in groups, and youth groups were by no means all criminal. Older offenders might come together in gangs to conduct armed robberies—notably, the Great Train Robbery of 1963—but organized gangs of what might be termed "professional criminals" were responsible for only a small percentage of crime. In the first half of the century organized criminal gangs were most commonly connected with the more dubious bookmakers; the clashes between the Darby Sabini gang and the Brummagen Boys, and the Sheffield gang wars of the 1920s, all involved racecourse rivalry between bookies. Organized gangs, notably the Messina brothers, established a hold over London vice from the early 1930s; they treated their rivals with appalling brutality, but they also managed to develop links with respectable society. The Messinas' mantle passed, in the 1950s, to Peter Rachman, who was as much involved with **slum** racketeering and gambling as vice, and who, shortly before his death in 1963, had a brief and unpleasant encounter with the most celebrated of the London gang leaders, the Kray twins. The Krays' business empire ran the gamut from vice to protection.

The majority of offenders processed by the courts during the Victorian period were from lower-class groups. This contributed markedly to the postivist tradition in criminology, which considered criminals to be members of an identifiable social group. From the 1920s the lower courts began to be clogged with individuals charged with contravening traffic legislation in motor vehicles; the popular notion remained that this was not "real" crime committed by "real" criminals, and positivist criminology, with its continuing interest in subcultures, underpinned the popular view. In the aftermath of the Second World War and the subsequent **immigration** of Afro-Caribbeans and Asians the positivist view of the criminal influenced the behavior of many rank-and-file police officers and, in some instances, also police orders and tactics. Young Afro-Caribbeans were seen, especially in the 1970s and 1980s, as particularly prone to street crime; the police response was often heavy-handed, and this was a significant element in provoking the **urban riots** of the 1980s.

But also since the end of the Second World War positivist criminology has been subjected to considerable criticism. "Labeling" theorists urged that criminality is not something inherent in an individual but a label applied by society,

and that it is therefore as important to study lawmakers, law-enforcers, and media campaigns as it is to study lawbreakers. This, in turn, has been criticized from a radical perspective for not explaining why individuals offend, particularly the large numbers involved in property crime, and for implying that offenders are the victims of official labels. For the radical criminologists the key requirement is an analysis of the economic system that creates laws, thereby criminality, as a means of maintaining itself and its social structure. They have stressed the contrast between the large number of lower-class property offenders prosecuted for the theft of goods of relatively little value, and the few white-collar offenders prosecuted for fraud and embezzlement involving hundreds of thousands of pounds. A series of scandals in the **City of London** during the 1980s—notably, the Guinness affair of 1989–90 that led to the imprisonment of four well-known, highly respected businessmen—added weight to the radicals' arguments, yet "white-collar" crime has remained a much underresearched area.

Clive Emsley

Bibliography

Gatrell, V.A.C. "Crime, Authority, and the Policeman-State" in F.M.L. Thompson, ed. *The Cambridge Social History of Britain, 1750–1950.* vol. 3. 1990, pp. 243–310.

Hough, Mike, and Pat Mayhew. *The British Crime Survey: First Report.* 1983.

McClintock, F.H., and N.H. Avison. *Crime in England and Wales.* 1968.

Pearson, Geoffrey. *Hooligan: A History of Respectable Fears.* 1983.

Taylor, Ian R. *The New Criminology.* 1973.

Cripps, (Richard) Stafford (1889–1952)

Stafford Cripps (Richard was never used) was a prominent Labour politician. He joined the **Labour Party** in 1928, and in 1930, while still without a parliamentary seat, he was appointed Solicitor-General on the sudden retirement of the incumbent. He was knighted as a customary dignity of his office and entered Parliament in January 1931. He led the Labour Left from 1932 until he was expelled from the Labour Party in January 1939. During the **Second World War** he served as ambassador to Moscow (1940–2); Lord Privy Seal and leader of the House of Commons (1942); and Minister of

Aircraft Production (1942–5). He was readmitted to the Labour Party in February 1945 and served in the post-war Labour **Cabinet** as President of the Board of Trade (1945–7); Minister of Economic Affairs, and Chancellor of the Exchequer (1947–50).

Educated at Winchester and at University College, London, Cripps began a promising career as a research chemist but soon decided to follow his father and grandfather into the **legal profession**, where both had been eminent. He became a barrister in 1913. His career was interrupted by war service and illness, but after he returned to the law in 1919 he quickly established a fine reputation and a lucrative practice, mainly in patent and compensation cases. He became Britain's youngest King's Counsel in 1927. His legal work for the London County Council impressed **Herbert Morrison**, who ultimately persuaded him to join the Labour Party. This decision was doubtless facilitated by the fact that Cripps' father, Alfred—a former Conservative MP—had, as Lord Parmoor, joined Labour in 1924, accepting **Ramsay MacDonald**'s invitation to be Lord President. Like Parmoor, Cripps was a deeply committed Christian all his life, and his political concerns evolved from his work in Christian peace organizations.

After the 1931 general election Cripps found himself one of only forty-six Labour MPs, and one of a tiny handful with real parliamentary ability. He therefore became one of the triumvirate that led the Parliamentary Labour Party through this difficult period. The political and economic crisis of 1931 convinced him that "gradualism" was dead, and his arguments that the next Labour government should assume emergency powers to deal with establishment opposition brought him opprobrium in the Conservative press and rebukes from an embarrassed Labour leadership. Cripps was the effective leader of the **Socialist League** (the formal organization of the Labour Left) from 1932 until its support for the **Unity Campaign** led to conflict with the Labour Party and the League's dissolution in 1937. In 1938–9 he again incurred the wrath of the Labour leaders by campaigning for the **Popular Front**, which resulted in his expulsion. During the 1930s Cripps displayed considerable political naivete and tactical ineptitude. Despite this, and despite a dull platform manner, his parliamentary talent and overwhelming sincerity continued to inspire great loyalty.

The outbreak of war found Cripps with no obvious role. In 1939–40 he undertook a tour of India, China, and the Soviet Union, acting as an unofficial government envoy. When Cripps returned, **Winston Churchill** appointed him ambassador to Moscow. The job was difficult and frustrating, particularly before the German invasion, and Cripps' independent approach caused some disquiet in the **Foreign Office**, but his mission was popularly regarded as a success. Assisted by his distance from the political parties, by the apparent vindication of his stance against **appeasement,** and by his identification with the Soviet alliance, Cripps returned home to enormous public acclaim and was widely regarded as an alternative Prime Minister. Churchill had little option but to appoint him to the War Cabinet.

In March 1942 he was dispatched to India to seek an accommodation with its nationalist leaders. They recognized his personal goodwill, but he was unable to offer acceptable terms and returned to Britain empty-handed. It has been argued that the India mission represented Churchill's attempt to discredit Cripps. If so, it was partly successful: His popular support declined, and after some disputes with Churchill and setbacks in the Commons he was moved out of the Cabinet to the important, if politically marginal, post of Minister for Aircraft Production, where his technical and administrative skills made him highly effective.

By the end of the war Cripps had become an ardent proponent of a planned, mixed economy rather than wholesale **nationalization.** His tenure in the key economic ministries was successful, although inevitably unpopular given the tremendous difficulties Britain faced. As President of the Board of Trade he had primary responsibility for **rationing,** which became more severe after the war. His lean frame, moralistic outlook, vegetarian diet, and simple life-style helped to identify him permanently in the public mind with the harsh austerity measures he and the government were obliged to introduce.

During the severe winter of 1947 the government's popularity waned and its economic planning lost direction. Cripps and others therefore attempted to replace the Prime Minister, **Clement Attlee,** with the Foreign Secretary, **Ernest Bevin.** Attlee met his difficulties by creating the Ministry of Economic Affairs under Cripps. Here Cripps displayed his usual efficiency, reinforcing his austere image with re-

C

peated exhortations to hard work. The new ministry could not really work effectively while separated from the Exchequer, and the forced resignation of the Chancellor, **Hugh Dalton**, provided the opportunity to combine the ministries, with Cripps in charge. Ironically, his three deflationary budgets of 1948–50 marked the beginning of Labour's attempts to reduce welfare expenditure.

Cripps' health had long been troublesome; the chronic overwork of the war and post-war years exacerbated the illness that led to his resignation in October 1950 and his death eighteen months later.

Cripps was a towering figure through two decades of British political history. Despite his inconsistencies he remained unswervingly devoted to the highest ideals of service. He served the Labour Party as its visionary conscience when it was at its lowest ebb and as a leading practical contributor in its years of greatest achievement.

D.P. Blaazer

Bibliography

Cooke, Colin. *The Life of Richard Stafford Cripps.* 1957.

Cripps, Sir Stafford. *The Struggle for Peace.* 1936.

Eatwell, Roger. *The 1945–1951 Labour Governments.* 1979.

Estorick, Eric. *Stafford Cripps.* 1949.

Morgan, Kenneth O. *Labour in Power, 1945–1951.* 1984.

———. *Labour People.* 1987.

Crosland, (Charles) Anthony "Tony" Raven (1918–1977)

Anthony "Tony" Crosland was one of the foremost British socialist thinkers in the post-1945 period. He was also a leading **Labour Party** politician, holding a series of ministerial posts, including that of Foreign Secretary, in the Labour governments of 1964–70 and 1974–9.

Born 29 August 1918 in Sussex, Crosland was educated at Trinity College, **Oxford**, where, after graduation, he took up the post of tutor and lecturer in **economics** in 1947. In 1950, however, he abandoned an academic career to become Labour MP for South Gloucestershire. He lost his seat in 1955 but exercised great influence within the party as a socialist thinker with the publication of his major work, *The Future of Socialism* (1956).

This was the most coherent statement of the "revisionist" position in the party debate on policy and strategy. From this point onward Crosland became the principal intellectual exponent of **Labour revisionism.**

In *The Future of Socialism* Crosland argued that Western capitalism had been transformed by important economic developments since 1945 and that socialism would therefore need to be reappraised. Like his friend and colleague **Hugh Gaitskell**, Crosland regarded socialist aims as essentially ethical; they sprang from such ideals as liberty, fellowship, social welfare, and equality. The pursuit of equality required, in his view, a redistribution of resources and wealth in society by means of social expenditure and progressive taxation. Such measures would, in turn, he stressed, depend on sustained economic growth. Crosland, like Gaitskell, offended Labour traditionalists by maintaining that public ownership should no longer be considered an indispensable part of socialist policy. Other methods—particularly educational reform and fiscal measures—were likely, he thought, to provide more effective means of attaining the ethical ends of socialism. He also invited the charge of doctrinal heresy by championing a mixed economy with a vigorous private sector.

By 1959 Crosland had returned to Parliament as Labour MP for Grimsby. During this period he strongly supported Gaitskell, the party leader, in his bitter struggles with the Labour Left over **Clause Four** and defense. When Labour returned to power in 1964, Crosland filled important ministerial posts, including those of Secretary of State for Education and Science (1965–7) and President of the Board of Trade (1967–9).

With Labour unexpectedly in power again in 1974, Crosland was appointed Secretary of State for the Environment in **Harold Wilson's** second administration. Despite a disappointing result in the party leadership contest that followed Wilson's resignation in 1976, Crosland was promoted in that year to the post of Foreign Secretary in **James Callaghan's** new government. He held that post until his sudden death on 19 February 1977.

Crosland's last months in office were marred by a deepening economic crisis that culminated in the Labour government seeking loans from the International Monetary Fund in return for cuts in its public-spending programs. That episode challenged a major assumption underlying his revisionist analysis—that redistribution could be achieved by high social expenditure financed by continuous economic growth.

Nevertheless, Crosland will be remembered as an effective **Cabinet** minister and, above all, as a major British socialist writer whose book *The Future of Socialism* must rank as one of the seminal expressions of democratic socialist thought in the twentieth century.

Tudor Jones

Bibliography

Crosland, C.A.R. *The Conservative Enemy.* 1962.
———. *The Future of Socialism.* 1956.
Crosland, Susan. *Tony Crosland.* 1982.
Lipsey, David, and Dick Leonard. *The Socialist Agenda: Crosland's Legacy.* 1981.

Curzon, George Nathaniel (1859–1925)

George Curzon, **Conservative** politician, began his political career as MP for Southport (1886–98). Serving as Undersecretary of State for India (1891–2), and Undersecretary of State for Foreign Affairs (1895–8), he showed considerable talent. Nevertheless, the official announcement in 1898 that he would succeed Lord Minto as Viceroy and Governor-General of India was greeted with public surprise. Curzon took over as Viceroy in 1899 and served until 1905 when he resigned. He was then out of office until May 1915 when he joined **H.H. Asquith**'s coalition War **Cabinet** as Lord Privy Seal. When **David Lloyd George** replaced Asquith, in December 1916, Curzon became Lord President of the Council. In January 1919 he was appointed Deputy Foreign Secretary, and in October he assumed full control of the **Foreign Office**. Curzon remained Foreign Secretary until January 1924, serving under three Prime Ministers. Returning to office after the defeat of the **Labour** government in November 1924, he was given the lesser post of Lord President of the Council. He died after a short illness in March 1925. On being appointed to the viceroyalty in 1898 he accepted an Irish peerage as Baron Curzon of Kedleston. He was an Irish representative peer in the **House of Lords** from 1908 to 1916 and leader in the Lords from 1916 to 1924. In 1911 Curzon received an Earldom; in 1916 he succeeded his father as Baron Scarsdale; and in 1921 he was elevated to a Marquisate.

At thirty-nine Curzon became the youngest Viceroy in history. The viceroyalty, possessing enormous powers, gave ample scope for his considerable administrative ability. Many of his policies, especially tax reductions and restoration programs for India's neglected monuments, earned favor with the people of India. More important, he rigorously upheld the principle of equality before the law for both Indians and Europeans. Curzon's viceroyalty is generally regarded as the apogee of British rule in India. However, the partition of Bengal, as part of an effort to promote greater administrative efficiency, created an outcry within India that lost him much domestic popularity. At the same time the Conservative government in Britain was concerned by Curzon's autocratic methods, especially in his prosecution of a forward policy in British India's relations with Tibet, Persia, and Afghanistan. Moreover, Curzon had been involved since 1904 in a series of clashes with **Lord Kitchener** over the administrative control of the Indian army. The row became increasingly acrimonious, and it was with a sense of relief that Curzon's resignation was accepted on 22 August 1905. He returned to England an embittered man.

On his return Curzon found himself without a seat in the House of Commons and, because his barony was in the Irish peerage, excluded from the House of Lords. He received no public honor for his viceroyalty. It was not until 1908 that he entered the House of Lords after securing election as an Irish representative peer. He played a key role in the **constitutional crisis** of 1911, leading the "hedger" Conservative peers, whose abstention allowed the passage of the Parliament bill to curb the veto power of the House of Lords.

The **First World War** brought a return to office for Curzon as a member of the War Cabinet of 1915. His concern about the prosecution of the war led him to participate in the conspiracy that toppled Asquith and brought Lloyd George to power in December 1916.

From January to October 1919 Curzon served as Deputy Foreign Secretary under **Arthur Balfour**, who was fully occupied with the Paris Peace Conference. In October Curzon succeeded as Foreign Secretary, but his tenure was clouded by conflicts with Lloyd George, who sought to manage foreign policy, consigning Curzon to a subordinate role. Members of

Lloyd George's personal Secretariat, along with the Cabinet Secretariat, exercised functions that would normally have been discharged by the Foreign Office. In 1922 the tension between the two men came to a head during the Chanak crisis when Lloyd George's support of Greek ambitions against Turkey almost led to an Anglo-Turkish war. Curzon wrote out his resignation, which remained undelivered when on 19 October Lloyd George resigned. Continuing as Foreign Secretary Curzon helped Lloyd George's successor, **Andrew Bonar Law,** form his administration, and when the latter resigned for ill health in May 1923, Curzon confidently expected to become Prime Minister. However, he was unpopular with many of his colleagues and as a peer could not represent the government in the Commons. **Stanley Baldwin** formed a new government in which Curzon, his ambition thwarted, agreed to serve, belatedly gaining public acclaim for his skillful settlement of the Turkish issue by the Treaty of Lausanne (1923). Under both Bonar Law and Baldwin the problem of German **reparations** dominated government policy. In January 1924 the Baldwin government fell, and when the Conservatives returned to power in November, Curzon became Lord President of the Council instead of returning to the Foreign Office.

Curzon was a major political figure in twentieth-century Britain. As Viceroy, in opposition, and finally in government for all but ten months between 1915 and March 1925 Curzon played a prominent role. Neither popular nor ideologically committed,he was intelligent and hard-working. He sought power for its own sake, while believing that the superiority of his abilities imposed the consequent public duty to serve his country and the British Empire.

G.H. Bennett

Bibliography

Dilks, David. *Curzon in India.* 2 vols. 1969–70.

Gilmour, David. *Curzon.* 1994.

Mosley, Leonard. *Curzon: The End of an Epoch.* 1960.

Nicolson, Harold. *Curzon: The Last Phase, 1919–1925.* 1934.

Ronaldshay, Lord. *The Life of Lord Curzon.* 3 vols. 1928.

Rose, Kenneth. *Superior Person.* 1968.

Cyprus

Britain occupied Cyprus in 1878 as a base to contain Russia and safeguard the Suez Canal. Greek Cypriots, who outnumbered their Turkish cohabitants four to one, soon demanded *enosis,* or reunion, with Greece. Britain gave limited autonomy to Cypriots but refused *enosis* as an extremist demand. Tension escalated when Britain declared Cyprus a possession (1914) and a colony (1925) and when Turkey defeated Greece militarily in 1922. Nationalistic violence exploded in 1931, and Britain imposed martial law. Talk of *enosis* waned during the **Second World War,** when British troops defended Cyprus and the Green government-in-exile residing in London.

Britain opposed *enosis* during the early Cold War because Cyprus offered strategic facilities and Communist revolution threatened Greece. In 1947 London offered Cypriots a legislature with a Greek majority to govern on domestic matters if they accepted a British governor to handle foreign and military affairs and permanently repudiated *enosis.* The Cypriot majority, backed by Athens, refused, vowing "no constitution without self-determination" and suggesting that *enosis* would enhance British security by mollifying the populace, but Britain remained unconvinced.

Conflict intensified in the early 1950s when two panhellenic nationalists coordinated their *enosis* campaigns. Michael Mouskos, a Greek Cypriot crowned Archbishop Makarios III in 1950, demanded British evacuation and appealed to Greece for support. Lt. Col. George Grivas, a Cypriot, Greek army veteran, and royalist, plotted violence to demoralize the British. Grivas established the National Organization of Cypriot Fighters (EOKA), terrorized British nationals, encouraged anti-British demonstrations, and conducted sabotage bombings beginning 1 April 1955.

British officials responded firmly to the Makarios-Grivas initiatives. Agreeing in 1954 to evacuate Egypt, they eyed Cyprus as their strategic cornerstone in the region and relocated troops there experienced in counterterrorism in Egypt. On 28 July 1954 Colonial Office Minister of State Henry Hopkinson declared that Cyprus "can never expect to be fully independent. . . . Nothing less than continued sovereignty over this island can enable Britain to carry out her strategic obligations." Greek Cypriots denounced this "Hopkinson never" policy, while Turkish Cypriots applauded it and advocated partition of Cyprus into ethnic regions if Britain ever departed. Britain also arranged to postpone substantive debate on Cyprus at the **United Nations.**

In 1955 Britain pursued, without success, diplomatic solutions to the Cyprus problem. A conference between London, Athens, and Ankara in August-September failed to reconcile Greece's demand for *enosis*, Turkey's opposition, and Britain's strategic needs. Prime Minister **Anthony Eden** then appointed as governor Field Marshal John Harding, who declared martial law, banned demonstrations and the bearing of weapons by civilians, detained dozens of suspects, and sent 36,000 troops against EOKA in the Troodos Mountains. Simultaneously, Harding opened negotiations with Makarios, offering limited autonomy and partial amnesty for EOKA members, and modifying the "Hopkinson never" by suggesting that Cyprus could enjoy self-determination in the future. But Makarios refused to denounce EOKA's violence or renounce *enosis*. In March 1956, following a wave of terrorism, Harding arrested Makarios and deported him to the Seychelles.

The **Suez crisis** in 1956 demonstrated Cyprus' limited strategic value and enabled EOKA to rebound. In early 1957 British strategists deemed it unwise to continue battling terrorists on an island of questionable importance and decided to defend their interests with nuclear deterrence and air-mobile forces. If airbases at Akrotiri and Dhekelia could be retained, they could surrender the remainder of Cyprus. Political considerations led to the same conclusion. EOKA's vitality and Makarios' enduring popularity demonstrated the appeal of *enosis* to Greek Cypriots.

In 1957 Prime Minister **Harold Macmillan** repudiated the "never" policy, released Makarios, and appointed a liberal, Hugh Foot, as governor. Meanwhile, ethnic warfare between Greek and Turkish Cypriots physically segregated the communities. Britain appealed to Greece and Turkey to formulate a settlement that would enable British withdrawal, curb the violence, and avoid a breach in the North Atlantic Treaty Organization (NATO).

Greece and Turkey opened talks on Cyprus in late 1958 and initialed a settlement in January 1959. Cyprus would become independent; executive, legislative, military, and judicial power would be divided proportionately between Greeks and Turks; *enosis* and partition would be proscribed; Greece and Turkey would gain military rights on the island under a tripartite alliance; and Britain would retain base rights at Akrotiri and Dhekelia. At the London conference of February 1959, Britain helped polish the plan and convinced Makarios to approve it. Negotiations ensued on technical matters, such as demarcation of the British bases. Cyprus became independent in August 1960. Makarios became President; Fazil Kutchuk, a Turk, became Vice President; and Grivas retired to Greece.

Independence ended Britain's role in Cyprus, but basic problems persisted. Sporadic violence between Greek and Turkish Cypriots flared immediately. British forces served as peacekeepers until a U.N. force replaced them in March 1964. Violence against Turks escalated in the early 1970s, and extremists deposed Makarios in July 1974, prompting Turkey to occupy northern Cyprus in a month-long war. In 1983 Turkish Cypriots declared the Turkish Republic of Northern Cyprus, a state that only Ankara has recognized.

Peter L. Hahn

Bibliography

Crawshaw, Nancy. *The Cyprus Revolt: An Account of the Struggle for Union with Greece.* 1978.

Kelling, George Horton. *Countdown to Rebellion: British Policy in Cyprus, 1939–1955.* 1990.

Stephens, Robert. *Cyprus, A Place of Arms: Power Politics and Ethnic Conflict in the Eastern Mediterranean.* 1966.

D

Dalton, (Edward) Hugh John Neale (1887–1962)

Hugh Dalton was a prominent **Labour Party** politician and intellectual, a member of the coalition government during the **Second World War**, and first Chancellor of the Exchequer in the post-war Labour government.

He was born near Neath in Glamorgan, the only son of an **Anglican** cleric and tutor to the sons of Queen Victoria. After attending Eton, Dalton was an undergraduate at King's College, **Cambridge**, studying economics under **John Maynard Keynes**. He became involved in the Cambridge **Fabian Society** in 1907, converting fully to socialism a year later. Upon taking his degree, Dalton briefly read for a law degree, but turned instead to postgraduate work at the **London School of Economics**, all the time committing himself further to socialist causes. In 1914 he married Ruth Fox.

During the **First World War** Dalton served initially with the Army Service Corps, then transferred to the Royal Artillery and fought in Italy between 1917 and the end of the war. He recounted these experiences in *With Guns in Italy*, published in 1919. At the end of the war, while a full-time lecturer in **economics** at the London School of Economics, he became involved in policy work for the Labour Party. His search for a parliamentary seat was unsuccessful until October 1924, when he was elected for Camberwell, Peckham, switching, in 1929, to the Durham mining seat of Bishop Auckland, which he held, except for 1931–5, until the end of his career in the Commons.

Dalton's expertise on economic affairs, cemented by studies on inequality, and his ease in foreign policy, quickly caught the eye of the Labour Party leadership, and he was perceived from an early date as a prospect for office. He also found a place on the National Executive Committee of the party as early as 1925. With the formation of the second Labour government in 1929, he was considered for Cabinet rank, but had to settle for the undersecretaryship at the **Foreign Office**, under **Arthur Henderson**. Dalton acquitted himself well and avoided being tainted in the government collapse in August 1931.

In the election of October 1931 Dalton lost his seat by a small margin, which damaged his chances for the party leadership. He was, however, able to use the period between 1931 and 1935 to build a power base within the party headquarters at Transport House. In particular, he dominated domestic and foreign policy-making. With **Herbert Morrison**, Dalton helped shape Labour's commitment to economic planning in the 1930s. Dalton's views on domestic reform, drawn from a Fabian perspective, academic training in economics, and the observation of experiments in the Soviet Union, were best articulated in his *Practical Socialism for Britain*, published in 1935. These views permeated the major party policy statements of the 1930s, *For Socialism and Peace* (1934) and *Labour's Immediate Programme* (1937), for which Dalton was largely responsible. He also helped turn Labour from a pacifist foreign policy to one that favored standing up to the European dictators through rearmament. With the help of **Ernest Bevin** and **Walter Citrine** of the **Trades Union Congress**, Dalton had, by 1937, with the party's adoption of *International Policy and Defence*, left his imprint on both foreign and domestic policy. In 1935 he returned to parliamentary politics, regaining the Bishop Auckland seat. Despite his ill-fated support of Morrison for the parliamentary leadership in 1935, he was successful as party Chairman. Throughout this period Dalton also served as a patron to a younger socialist intellectuals, like **Hugh Gaitskell, Evan Durbin**, and Douglas Jay.

By the beginning of the war Dalton was a prominent member of the Labour leadership. In May 1940, with the formation of the **Churchill** coalition, Dalton was made Minister of Economic Warfare, in charge, among other things, of the economic blockade and subversion of German-dominated Europe. He occupied this post until 1942, a period characterized by much intrigue over his running of the Special Operations Executive, Britain's secret arm, dedicated to "setting Europe ablaze" with anti-Nazi movements. In February 1942 he was moved to the Board of Trade, becoming its President. Here, Dalton displayed his characteristic energy and exuberance, tackling such questions as coal and clothes **rationing** and reconstruction. One of his greatest achievements was the Distribution of Industry Act (1945), which aimed at relocating industry in depressed areas, a concern of his since the 1930s.

After Labour's election victory of July 1945, Dalton expected to become Foreign Secretary, a post he had long coveted. **Clement Attlee**, had doubts, however, and instead made Dalton Chancellor of the Exchequer. In the desperate economic conditions facing Britain at the end of the war, this was a key post, and Dalton became an integral member of Labour's "Big Five": Attlee, Morrison, Bevin, and **Stafford Cripps**. His time at the Treasury was marked by achievement and crisis. His budgets were marked by a commitment to policies of "cheap money," inflating the economy, and to distinctively socialist planning through economic controls. He also nationalized the Bank of England, a central plank in Labour's platform. In this regard, Dalton was a successful Chancellor, a proponent of "socialist advance," who delighted his supporters in the Labour Party as much as he alienated his Conservative rivals. If Dalton was undone, it was by the weakness of the British economy. This began with the post-war American loan, which he had supported, continued through the arguments within the **Cabinet** about Britain's overstretched resources (Dalton demanding cutbacks in military expenditure), and ended with the crisis of sterling convertibility in the summer of 1947, demanded ac-

cording to the terms of the American loan. After weeks of economic crisis following convertibility, Dalton was forced in August 1947 to suspend it, thus signaling Britain's diminished economic standing.

In November 1947, minutes before officially introducing the budget to the House of Commons, Dalton casually revealed its contents to a journalist. He was forced to resign because of this indiscretion. He was never again to exercise the same level of direct power he had enjoyed within the party and the government before 1947. Dalton did return to the Cabinet, first in October 1948, as Chancellor of the Duchy of Lancaster (with responsibility for European affairs), then, between 1950 and 1951, as Minister of Town and Country Planning. He remained active in the work of the National Executive Committee.

After Labour's defeat in 1951 Dalton moved into the role of elder statesman. He lost his seat on the National Executive in 1952 in the wave of Bevanite left-wing success. Once off the Executive, he concentrated on promoting his protegés, such as Gaitskell and **Anthony Crosland**. After the election of 1955 he resigned from the Parliamentary Committee to clear the way for younger members.

Dalton's contribution to the Labour Party was enormous. He played a profound role in shaping the policy assumptions that were adopted, in both domestic and foreign affairs, in the 1930s and brought to power in 1945. He may have been, as well, the most "socialist" Chancellor of the Exchequer the party has ever had, a symbol of Labour achievement between 1945 and 1947. No less important, Dalton fostered a generation of younger politicians, many of whom came to office in the 1960s. Finally, Dalton began a trend of lively autobiography in the Labour Party; his memoirs and diary provide a fascinating and entertaining picture of the party between the 1930s and the 1950s.

Stephen Brooke

Bibliography
Dalton, Hugh. *Call Back Yesterday*. 1954.
———. *The Fateful Years*. 1957.
———. *High Tide and After*. 1962.
Pimlott, Ben. *Hugh Dalton*. 1985.
———, ed. *The Political Diary of Hugh Dalton*. 1986.
———, ed. *The Second World War Diary of Hugh Dalton*. 1986.

Dawson, Geoffrey (1874–1944)

Geoffrey Robinson (who changed his name to Dawson in 1917), one of Britain's most distinguished journalists in the twentieth century, was editor of *The Times* from 1912 to 1919 and from 1922 to 1941.

Dawson was educated at Eton and Magdalen College, Oxford, both institutions with which he maintained close links all of his life. He was also the owner of a large estate in Yorkshire and, as such, occupied a natural place in the center of British social and public affairs.

He received his early political and journalistic experience in South Africa, where he served as Private Secretary to the British High Commissioner, Lord Milner, and then became editor of the *Johannesberg Star*. He became one of a number of young acolytes of Milner, who on their return to England later went on to form the Round Table group, dedicated to the study of imperial and international affairs. Dawson returned to London in 1910 and in 1912 was chosen as editor of *The Times*, Britain's most influential newspaper, by the paper's proprietor, Lord Northcliffe. During his first period as editor of *The Times*, Dawson played a crucial role in the high politics of the First World War, particularly with his famous editorial of 4 December 1916, which precipitated the resignation of H.H. Asquith as Prime Minister and his replacement by David Lloyd George. However, in 1919 Dawson resigned as editor due to political disagreements with the highly opinionated Northcliffe, and from 1919 to 1923 he served as Estates Bursar of All Souls College, Oxford.

In 1923 Dawson returned to the editorial chair of *The Times,* which had been bought by J.J. Astor on the death of Northcliffe in 1922. Dawson's second period as editor proved to be more controversial than the first, as he had to steer the paper through the series of domestic and international crises in the 1930s. His shortcomings as an editor were highlighted by his involvement in the Chamberlain government's advocacy of appeasement from 1937 to 1939. Dawson enjoyed close friendship and political affinity with leading Conservative ministers of the inter-war years, notably Lord Halifax and Neville Chamberlain. This meant that under Dawson *The Times* was favored with a level of intelligence enjoyed by few members of the Cabinet, but also that *The Times* thus became enmeshed in the policies of the government of the day, surrendering some of its independence for an active role in Chamberlain's pursuit of accommodation with Nazi Germany. Dawson's celebrated editorial of 7 September 1938, for instance, presaged the dismemberment of Czechoslovakia at the Munich Conference.

During the first year of the Second World War *The Times* regained some of its old reputation with constructive criticism of the War Cabinet, but Dawson retired in 1941 with his reputation tarnished as one of the arch-appeasers of Nazi Germany.

Richard Cockett

Bibliography

Cockett, Richard. *Twilight of Truth: Chamberlain, Appeasement, and the Manipulation of the Press.* 1989.

The Official History of The Times. vols. 4: *1912–48*; and 5: *1939–66.* 1952–84.

Woods, Oliver, and James Bishop. *The Story of The Times.* 1983.

Wrench, John Evelyn. *Geoffrey Dawson and Our Times.* 1955.

Day Lewis, Cecil (1904–1972)

Cecil Day Lewis was born 27 April 1904 at Ballintubbert, Ireland. His mother died when he was four, so the boy was reared in London by his father, an Anglican curate, and a devoted aunt. After attending Sherborne, he entered Wadham College, Oxford in 1923. Sure of his poetic vocation from boyhood, he continued to write verse at college, where in his third year he met another undergraduate, W.H. Auden, whose sheer intellectual assurance tended to overwhelm and reprogram Day Lewis. He and Auden together edited *Oxford Poetry 1927.*

Day Lewis' first volumes, *Beechen Vigil* (1925) and *Country Comets* (1928), are neo-romantic and Georgian productions. In *Country Comets*, dedicated "To Her Whose Mind and Body Are a Poetry I Have Not Achieved," the chief tension is between philosophic universals and individual particulars. The poems ask if man is a monad (part of a system but without personal freedom) or a nomad (a free individual alienated from any coherent social system). *Transitional Poem* (1929) shows Auden's influence. The volume treats social problems and bristles with Audenesque images drawn especially from geology and other natural sciences. *From Feathers to Iron* (1931) makes symbolic use of the poet's wife's first pregnancy to urge the children of English privilege to develop cutting edges in an effort to become socially and politically useful.

Arising out of the many explorations of *Transitional Poem*, *The Magnetic Mountain* (1933) is a full-fledged work of prophetic urgency. The mountain is the new industrial revolution, drawing everyone into a workers' fellowship that alone is capable of building a new world. The fellowship is cast as a pilgrimage, a new Exodus from Egypt whereby the past must be abandoned so the future can be born. In 1935 Auden produced *Look, Stranger!* to force his generation to look analytically at the socioeconomic crisis of the age. So Day Lewis wrote *A Time to Dance*, rejoicing that the little son whose birth is looked forward to in *From Feathers to Iron* would grow up in a different world as a result of proletarian calls to arms. Day Lewis extended the previous three volumes in the form of a verse drama, *Noah and the Waters* (1936). Previously invited to march to a mountain, the world's magnitudes are now urged, with new fervor, to get aboard the Ark before the Flood rises. *A Hope for Poetry*, his first book of prose criticism (1934), also offered this advice.

Barely supporting a growing family on a teacher's salary, Day Lewis turned to writing **detective fiction** under the pseudonym Nicholas Blake. So remunerative was this new venture (he was eventually to write twenty volumes of such fiction, mostly centered on a detective named Nigel Strangeways) that he abandoned teaching and devoted his full time to writing and political activism. In 1936 he joined the **Communist Party of Great Britain** and helped establish the fledgling Gloucestershire party organization. His 1937 novel, *Starting Point*, expressed his political activism: ". . . all the comrades; in streets, in the country, in prison, in factories, in the little room above the tobacconist's shop and the May-Day Demonstration—they were with him and would be with him as long as he lived. . . . they were the spies [history] sent forward into a hostile country . . . whose promise perhaps they alone could fully realize."

But by 1938 he decided he must choose between political activism and poetry.

To make a clean break with the three previous years he moved to a thatched cottage outside Musbury in Devon. *Overtures to Death and Other Poems* (1938) lost the sure utopian vision of *The Magnetic Mountain*. The collection is about death: bombers with "iron embryos," laughing children slaughtered in the streets, and the drugged deaths of habitués of cinematic "dreamhouses." Living now in Thomas Hardy country, and making translations of Virgil's *Georgics* (1940), Day Lewis' *Word Over All* (1943) and *Poems: 1943–1947* exhibit his conclusion that the Ivory Tower of the secluded poet is superior to the Brazen Tower of Communist propagandist. As Auden had once influenced his poetic utterance, now echoes of Hardy sing out of "Birthday Poem for Thomas Hardy." But even in this flowering of his lyric gift he is troubled by irreconcilable choices and philosophic antinomies.

War brought Day Lewis first to a **Home Guard** platoon and then to London as an editor for the Ministry of Information (1941). It also produced emotional storms in the poet's previously quiet life. A passionate affair with the wife of a neighboring Musbury farmer produced a son, several poems, and—much later—the somewhat autobiographic Nicholas Blake story *The Private Wound* (1968). Day Lewis also developed a liaison with novelist **Rosamond Lehmann**. In 1949 he fell in love with the twenty-four-year-old actress, Jill Balcon, whom he married in 1951 after divorcing his first wife.

His first marriage to Constance Mary King left two sons (one of whom wrote his father's biography); the second produced a daughter and a son, the actor Daniel Day Lewis.

In 1951 Day Lewis' translation of Virgil's *Aeneid* was broadcast by the **British Broadcasting Corporation** (BBC) as part of the **Festival of Britain**. In the same year he was elected Professor of Poetry at Oxford. During the five-year period of incumbency, he became a public reader of his poetry, often in concert with Jill Balcon. He was awarded the C. Litt. honor from the Royal Society of Literature (1965) and in 1968 succeeded **John Masefield** as Poet Laureate, thereby becoming the first Irish-born laureate since Nahum Tate (1652–1715). But his final four volumes of verse, *Pegasus* (1957), *The Gate* (1962), *The Room* (1965), and *The Whispering Roots* (1970), received little critical attention for the work of an active Poet Laureate. The critical silence was all the more noticeable in that these volumes contained some of his best poems. After 1969 his formerly robust health declined. He died at Lemmons, Hadley Wood, Hertfordshire, the home of the novelists Elizabeth Jane Howard and Kingsley Amis, both bitter critics of the socialist welfare state for which Day Lewis once fought.

Elton Edward Smith

Bibliography

Cunningham, Valentine. *British Writers of the Thirties.* 1989.

Day Lewis, C. *The Buried Day.* 1960.

Hynes, Samuel. *The Auden Generation: Literature and Politics in England in the 1930s.* 1976.

Riddel, Joseph N. *C. Day Lewis.* 1971.

Smith, Elton Edward. *The Angry Young Men of the Thirties: Day Lewis, Spender, MacNeice, Auden.* 1975.

Decolonization

Within two decades of the end of the Second World War the British Empire was dismantled and transformed into the Commonwealth of Nations. This whole process of decolonization did not have much effect on domestic politics or cause any major domestic political controversies. However, many of the colonies, especially in Africa, contained diverse ethnic groups that had maintained independent and often rival or hostile social systems before and during British rule. In many cases the British had deliberately kept them apart in a policy of divide and rule. On the point of independence, they were suddenly expected to share a sense of nationhood and a willingness to cooperate in friendly rivalry in a competitive electoral system. This did not always happen, and many of them competed vigorously for office.

India was the most developed colony in the Empire both politically and economically, with British control beginning in the eighteenth century. The British introduced a series of reforms in 1909, 1919, and 1935 that gave greater responsibility for governing India to Indians while ultimately maintaining control. This was done in response to Indian pressure as well as the needs of the British to involve Indians in the running of the country. By 1939 **Indian nationalism** had become highly organized and had mobilized Indians throughout the subcontinent. It was led by Mohandas Gandhi and Jawaharlal Nehru for the Indian National Congress, founded in 1885 and overwhelmingly supported by Hindus; and Muhammad Ali Jinnah, who was mobilizing an increasingly large number of Muslims behind the All-India Muslim League, founded in 1906. By 1945 the Labour government was committed to independence for India; the Indian nationalists would accept nothing less. Gandhi and the Indian National Congress demanded that the government of India be turned over to its representatives at independence. This demand was rejected by Jinnah and the Muslim League, which, in 1940, passed a resolution calling for a separate country for Muslims. The Muslim League would not shift from its position, and Congress reluctantly agreed to the partition of India into states of India and Pakistan in August 1947. Freedom did not come without bloodshed in the northwest part of India when many Muslims migrated to Pakistan and Hindus to India. War was also to break out over the right to the state of Kashmir. In 1971 Pakistan was divided when East Pakistan seceded and became the new nation of Bangladesh.

With India independent, the argument for maintaining a number of other colonies lost its force. Ceylon (Sri Lanka), smaller and with a prosperous export economy of tea and rubber, had an even more developed political system with a wider franchise than India. In spite of the division between the minority Tamils and the majority Sinhalese, independence was achieved smoothly in 1948. Burma had received its independence a month earlier on 4 January 1948, and, in general elections held soon after war's end, Aung San received an overwhelming vote of support for his call for independence. He was assassinated in 1947, but Burma became independent under Thakin Nu.

Malaya, an exporter of rubber and tin, played an important role in the Sterling Area. Before independence could be granted the British had to deal with Communist guerrillas, mostly of Chinese extraction, who were soundly defeated. Tunku Abdul Rahman led the Federation of Malaya to independence in 1957. In 1963 Singapore, Sabah (the former British North Borneo), and Sarawak joined the federation, which then changed its name to Malaysia. Singapore, however, dropped out of the federation in 1965. The remnants of the British Empire in Asia were Brunei, which became independent in February 1984, and Hong Kong, which is scheduled for return to China in 1997.

While independence for India had long been conceded, the British had no plans for freeing their colonies in Africa, but within a decade of the Second World War they were also well on their way toward freedom. In West Africa independence began with the Gold Coast, which had a long history of protest but was an apparently model colony. In 1946 the British introduced a new constitution that would set the colony along the slow road to freedom. In protest, however, the United Gold Coast Convention was formed in 1947. Riots broke out the following year, and in 1949 Kwame Nkrumah founded the Convention People's Party. He instituted a policy of **strikes**, boycotts, and demonstrations—"positive action" as it was called—that dramatically increased opposition to British rule. The British held elections in 1951, which only confirmed Nkrumah's hold on the country. Accordingly, plans were drawn up for independence, which came in 1957, when Nkrumah led the country to freedom under the ancient name of Ghana.

Once the Gold Coast became independent it became impossible for Britain to retain its remaining African colonies. **Harold Macmillan** recognized this in February 1960 when he said that the "wind of change" was blowing through Africa and that the British had to take account of the "growth of national consciousness." Nigeria was one of those countries where the British thought independence would come later rather than sooner because of its ethnic diversity, with Yorubas in the western region, Ibos in the eastern region, and Muslim emirates in the north. The British introduced three different constitutions in the complicated political situation before conceding independence in 1960 under the newspaperman Nnamdi Azikiwe as Governor-General, Abubakar Tafawa Balewa as Prime Minister, and Chief Obafemi Awolowo as leader of the opposition.

The other British colonies in West Africa were Sierra Leone and The Gambia, Britain's oldest colony in West Africa and the smallest on the mainland. Sierra Leone was established in 1787 around Freetown as a settler colony for Blacks then living in England, and the hinterland was acquired during the late Victorian "scramble for Africa." Independence was granted in 1961, and internal tensions came to the surface in the 1967 army coup. The Gambia was pushed toward decolonization more by the British than by local politicians; elections outside the capital were not held until 1960. It became independent in 1965.

Of the nonsettler colonies in East Africa, Tanganyika became independent in 1961, Uganda in 1962, and Zanzibar in 1963. Tanganyika, brought under German control in 1884, was taken over by Britain as a **League of Nations** trust territory in 1919. Unlike many African colonies, a united nationalist party had risen in Tanganyika under Julius Nyerere, and the country experienced more than twenty years

of peaceful development under his leadership after independence. In 1964 it merged with Zanzibar—British territory from 1890 until independence—to become the United Republic of Tanzania.

Uganda was dominated by its largest kingdom, Buganda, which was opposed by the three smaller kingdoms of Bunyoro, Toro, and Ankole. As a result, no single nationalist party dominated the country. This has led to continuous political problems since independence with various coups, such as the 1971 one led by Idi Amin, who instituted a particularly bloody dictatorship, ended only by invasion from Tanzania in 1979.

The situation in Kenya was even more complicated because it was also settled by Europeans and Asians who hoped to maintain power after independence. Administered since 1888 by William Mackinnon's British East Africa Company and the British government, Kenya had the pastoral Masai people, the Kikuyu, and the Luo as the dominant groups. The Kikuyu Association was formed in 1920, and the next year the more assertive Young Kikuyu Association (later the Kikuyu Central Association) was established. Other organizations were also created before 1944, when the Kenya African Union was founded (mostly with the support of Kikuyus); in 1947 Jomo Kenyatta became its leader. A rival organization, the Kenya African Democratic Union, represented the Luo and smaller groups. The nationalist movement in Kenya turned violent from 1952 to 1956, when a group of Kikuyu, the Mau Mau, took to the bush to fight for "Land and Freedom." The Mau Mau were led by a group of ex-servicemen and peasants who acutely felt the economic and social deprivation that gave rise to the whole movement. The British suppressed the movement, but independence came in 1963 under Kenyatta, who dominated the country until his death in 1979.

Northern and Southern Rhodesia were created by Cecil Rhodes and the British South African Company. The company ruled the South until 1923 and the North until 1924, when they both became Crown colonies. In 1953 the prosperous Rhodesias and the poor Nyasaland were joined into a white-controlled Central African Federation. Opposing the Federation, Northern Rhodesia became dominated by Kenneth Kaunda, who led it to independence in 1964 under the name of Zambia. Kaunda created a one-party state in 1972 and ruled until 1991.

Nyasaland's experience paralleled Northern Rhodesia's: It was dominated by an individual, Hastings Banda, who took the nation, renamed Malawi, to independence in 1964 and became its president for life in 1971.

Southern Rhodesia presented a problem to the British government because of the European settlers. The African nationalist party, the African National Congress, founded by Joshua Nkomo, split in 1963 into the Zimbabwe African People's Union (ZAPU) and the more radical Zimbabwe African National Union (ZANU). The white response came in November 1965, when Ian Smith and his government issued a Unilateral Declaration of Independence and instituted white-minority rule. The British government, favoring majority rule, responded with economic sanctions, which proved ineffective. The struggle waged by ZANU and ZAPU finally led to the defeat of white Rhodesians, general elections, and independence in 1980, when the country, led by Robert Mugabe of ZANU, was renamed Zimbabwe.

In the Mediterranean the two islands of **Cyprus** and **Malta**, important as military bases, became independent in 1960 and 1964, respectively. In North Africa, Egypt became especially important after the opening of the Suez Canal in 1869. In 1882 it was conquered by the British, but it became a protectorate in 1914. This ended with independence in 1922, but the British maintained troops there until 1956. Sudan, taken over in 1898, also became sovereign in 1956. **Palestine** came under British control in 1919 as a League of Nations mandate. A homeland for the Jews had been promised in this area by the British in the 1917 **Balfour Declaration**. Pressure from immigrant Jews in Palestine and the American government led to the establishment of the Jewish national homeland of Israel in 1948.

In the Caribbean and the Americas, Jamaica, Trinidad, and Tobago became independent in 1962, and Barbados in 1966. In 1967 Anguilla, Antigua, Dominica, Grenada, Nevis, St. Kitts, St. Lucia, and St. Vincent were linked with Britain as "Associated States," but Grenada became independent in 1974, Dominica in 1978, St. Lucia and St. Vincent in 1979, Antigua in 1981, and St. Kitts-Nevis in 1983. The Bahamas became independent in 1973, while Bermuda has, since 1968, been a self-governing British dependency. On the mainland, British Guiana became independent as Guyana in 1966, and British Honduras (Belize) in 1981.

Most of the newly independent states remained in the Commonwealth of Nations, which meets formally every two years. Political decolonization is almost complete, with just a few territories around the world, such as Anguilla, Ascension Island, British Virgin Islands, Caymen Islands, Falkland Islands, Gibraltar, Hong Kong (scheduled for return to China in 1997), still ruled by Britain. Economic decolonization, however, is a burning question in many countries of the Commonwealth, raising talk of a "second independence."

Roger D. Long

Bibliography

Chamberlain, M.E. *Decolonization: The Fall of the European Empires.* 1985.

Darwin, John. *Britain and Decolonization: The Retreat from Empire in the Post-War World.* 1988.

Gifford, Prosser, and Wm. Roger Louis, eds. *The Transfer of Power in Africa: Decolonization, 1940–1960.* 2 vols. 1982.

Hargreaves, John D. *Decolonization in Africa.* 1988.

Mansergh, Nicholas. *The Commonwealth Experience.* vol. 2: *From British to Multiracial Commonwealth.* 2nd ed. 1982.

Defence of the Realm Act (DORA)

Legislation in the form of the Defence of the Realm Act empowered the government to make temporary regulations necessary "for securing the public safety and the defence of the realm" during the **First World War**. DORA was really several acts, the initial legislation passed on 8 August 1914 being amended and extended several times.

DORA gave birth to hundreds of regulations. The public readily understood some curbs on normal activities—for instance, the ban on showing lights at night in large cities like **London** and Birmingham in case this facilitated an airborne attack. They found others more puzzling: The authorities had to explain that shooting at pigeons must stop because someone might bring down an official "messenger." To prevent leaks of information useful to the enemy, the **press** and international mail were censored through DORA. Newspaper reports on military campaigns could only

Simple, plain, functional forms, with a modicum of decoration (frequently floral) were preferred over styles favored on the Continent, such as Art Deco or the more expressionistic variants of Art Nouveau.

Other organizations promoting the union of art and industry were formed in the 1920s, such as the government's British Institute of Industrial Art and the Federation of British Industries' Industrial Arts Committee. But these design-reform organizations had little practical effect. Many British industries, rendered complacent by sales within the Empire, continued to downplay the importance of design and also complained that artists were not properly trained to design for industry, a charge that had much validity and reflected the bias in British education that favored the liberal arts as opposed to vocational training. The course for industrial artists at the RCA, for example, emphasized training in the fine arts; artists were expected to acquire specialized knowledge of industrial techniques on the job. The other major training institution for industrial artists, London's Central School, had a more crafts-based curriculum, but neither school provided any training for design in the new light-metal industries that arose in the inter-war period. This situation remained true for nearly all British schools that offered courses in design (with the exception of Birmingham in the mid-1930s) until after the Second World War.

Design education in inter-war Britain thus remained oriented toward the crafts-based industries, such as furniture, clothing, jewelry, pottery, and textiles. Since it was possible for so-called "fine artists" to become designers for these industries without much technical training, many of the most prominent designers during the period were painters or sculptors like **Paul Nash, Duncan Grant, Vanessa Bell, Graham Sutherland,** and **Ben Nicholson.** This new association between "fine art" and "design" was given further emphasis during this period through **Roger Fry** and Clive Bell's aesthetic of "significant form," which they codified between 1910 and 1914. For Fry and Bell, art's most fundamental quality was its design rather than its content. By emphasizing that art was more concerned with abstract design than with mimetic representation, Fry and Bell made it easier for fine artists to take up a career in design, which had formerly been associated with artisans. Thus, although Ruskin and Morris' goal of integrating art and industry was not

accomplished in the 1920s and 1930s, one of their major objectives had been accomplished during this period: The hierarchical distinction between art and craft that had prevailed in the nineteenth century was essentially abolished through the widespread use of "design" as an inclusive term covering both art and craft. However, fine art and design were separated once again after 1945, when design became a more specialized, technical profession.

The Depression of the early 1930s brought renewed attention to the economic significance of design among government officials, educators, artists, and design reformers. The Boards of Trade and Education formed the Council for Art and Industry in 1934 under the direction of **Frank Pick**, a chief executive of the London Underground whose own devotion to the principles of Ruskin and Morris led him to commission modern artists and architects to create a unified design for the **London** transport system. Council members argued that design should become a specialized profession, but they continued to think of the designer as an artist rather than as a technician and to focus their inquiries on the training of designers for crafts-based industries. A similar understanding of the nascent design "profession" as the province of artists was advanced by many writers on the design question, such as **Herbert Read, Nikolaus Pevsner,** and John Gloag; the first professional society of designers, the Society of Industrial Artists, was formed in 1930 primarily by artists (its first President was the painter Paul Nash).

While design reformers did look abroad to see how British design could meet foreign competition, most continued to express a conservative, provincial aesthetic. Many reformers professed allegiance to traditional "English" styles of design that emphasized "plain and good," organic, and functional forms in conscious opposition to more avant-garde styles derived from French surrealism or American "streamlining." And most British industries remained indifferent to the whole question of product design.

It was not until the Second World War that the government and industries recognized that the United States would be their primary competitor for export markets after the war, and that, consequently, more attention would have to be given to design for the light-metal industries. The government decided that British designers ought to follow the American model, established in the 1920s, of the professional "industrial designer." This spelled the end of the arts and crafts conception of the designer as a broadly trained artist who needed little specialized knowledge to design for the crafts-based industries. Instead, the designer was redefined as a specialist versed in the technical requirements of a chosen industry.

The government established the Council of Industrial Design in 1944 to promote this new conception of the "industrial designer" as opposed to the "industrial artist." Similarly, design education at the RCA shifted from its inter-war emphasis on the union of the arts toward a more technologically oriented training for the demands of the light-metal industries when Robin Darwin was appointed Principal in 1949.

The austere, functional forms favored by design reformers in the inter-war period gave way in the later 1950s and 1960s to a wide variety of style influenced by Continental and American designs. In the 1960s British design attained international prominence, not only through the works of individual designers but also through the promotional efforts of contemporary design reformers such as Terence Conran, who gave the field notable visibility through his own designs, the chain of Habitat stores he established in the 1960s, and the Design Museum he opened in 1988. But the history of contemporary British design is as much one of continuity as it is of change: While design aesthetics and approaches changed after the war, many British industries continued to remain relatively indifferent to design. The **Thatcher** government attempted to promote a closer integration of design and industry through its "Design for Profit" campaign of 1982. In this respect, at least, the Thatcher government resembled many that had preceded it.

Michael Saler

Bibliography

Heskett, John. "Industrial Design" in Boris Ford, ed. *The Cambridge Cultural History.* vol. 9. 1992. pp. 288–318.

Naylor, Gillian. "Design and Industry" in Boris Ford, ed. *The Cambridge Guide to the Arts in Britain.* vol. 8. 1989. pp. 254–93.

Saler, Michael. *Medieval Modernism: The Legitimation and Social Function of Modern Art in England, 1910–1945.* Ph.D. dissertation, Stanford University, 1992.

Detective Fiction

The Anglo-American detective story typically displays three essential features: First, a serious crime, usually murder, must be committed early on; second, the identity of the criminal must not be revealed until the end; third, all clues, when finally assembled, must point to the criminal, and to no one else. There is considerable debate as to whether a detective story must include a detective figure, official or unofficial, but in Great Britain, as in America, the most important and lasting works in the genre have typically featured such a character. In addition, British detective stories, at least those written during the golden age of the 1920s and 1930s, generally take place within a relatively close and stable social milieu, usually rural or suburban, and seem to be concerned with restoring a prelapsarian societal innocence through the identification and scapegoating of the criminal.

At the beginning of the twentieth century British detective fiction was still dominated by the lean silhouette of Arthur Conan Doyle's (1859–1930) manic-depressive reasoning machine, Sherlock Holmes, who was given a new lease on life in 1901, in *The Hound of the Baskervilles*, after a hiatus of eight years and an (apparently) fatal plunge into the Reichenbach Falls. Conan Doyle would continue to write Holmes stories well into the 1920s, thereby sustaining the popularity of the short-story form during a period of declining magazine sales. One beneficiary of Conan Doyle's example was **G.K. Chesterton**, who launched his own decidedly un-Holmesian, but quite popular, continuing detective hero in the short-story collection, *The Innocence of Father Brown* (1911). Short, dumpy, clumsy, reticent, and intuitive, Father Brown took a fideistic and aleatory approach to the mysteries of crime that reflected Chesterton's own paradoxical, and Catholic, attitudes toward the mystery of life itself.

Detective novels were still being written during the first decade of the century, but not until the appearance of *Trent's Last Case* (1913), by E(dmund) C(lerihew) Bentley (1875–1956), did the detective novel regain a dominant market position. Like Chesterton, Bentley had set out to have some fun at the expense of the morose and coldly rational Holmes. His detective-hero, Philip Trent, an artist and occasional newspaper reporter with an avocational attraction to solving murder mysteries, owes more akin to Wilkie Collins' Franklin Blake

English style of dancing came to represent clarity of execution, lightness of attack, and sustained musicality.

Embraced as a national institution, the Sadler's Wells Ballet achieved international stature with its first visit to New York in 1949 and its frequent world tours during the 1950s. De Valois was made a Dame of the British Empire in 1951, and her achievement received its own accolade in 1956, when the two companies became the Royal Ballet. She retired as Director of the Royal Ballet in 1961 but continued to teach at its school, revive her own works, and serve the National Ballet of Turkey, which she founded in 1947. She was honored with the Order of Merit in 1992.

Universally known as Madam, de Valois has always claimed that "we shape no event as forcibly as events shape us." Yet in realizing her imaginative ambition, she herself shaped Britain's artistic life with sublime practicality and enduring wisdom.

Barbara Newman

Bibliography
de Valois, Ninette. *Come Dance with Me.* 1957.

Diet and Nutrition

The twentieth century has seen great improvements in diet and nutrition in Britain. The mass of the population now eats a much more varied and healthful diet than it did at the turn of the century, consuming more meat, milk, cheese, eggs, vegetables, and fresh fruit and fewer starches. Previously, only the wealthiest could afford a diet so rich in protein and protective foods. Over the years, too, people in the lower income brackets increased their calories while those at the upper end of the scale consumed fewer. Patterns of food consumption, once highly differentiated by class in Britain, have thus become more homogeneous. A concomitant of this has been the fading of physical differences that existed between the income groups at the start of the century because of unequal degrees of nutrition. Advances in nutritional science and food technology, the spread of public awareness, a rise in real incomes, and government policy all contributed to these developments.

The government began to pay serious attention to the nation's diet at the start of the century. Two reasons for this were the high percentage of working-class recruits rejected for military service in the **Boer War** because of poor **health**, and the falling proportion of the nation's children being born to the middle and upper classes. About 80 percent of the population were considered working class before the First World War. If this group was increasing, it meant the future vitality and defense of the nation would depend even more heavily on those with the highest incidence of physical deficiencies. Cases of rickets had more than doubled in the previous twenty years, and other disorders such as anemia, muscular weakness, and **tuberculosis** were rife. Working-class people also tended to be shorter and thinner: There was an average difference of two-and-a-half inches in height and sixteen pounds in weight between upper-class males and even the highest-paid workingmen. Investigations showed poverty and diet, not genes, to be at fault.

In all countries, food accounted for a much larger share of the household budget earlier in the century than it does today. In Britain before the First World War unskilled workers spent about two-thirds of their wages on food and still did not get enough calories or nutrients. Most working-class diets were deficient in protein, iron, calcium, and vitamins; fresh meat, milk, vegetables, and fruit were expensive and were bought only in small quantities. People depended mainly on foods providing the highest number of calories for the least cost: bread, potatoes, sugar, jam, bacon, and lard. In 1914 working-class adults ate an average of seven-and-a-half pounds of bread and three-and-a-half pounds of potatoes a week. In the typical family only the husband (the breadwinner) had meat more than once a week. Women and children subsisted largely on bread and jam consumed with strong, sweet tea. The fact that three-quarters of all Britons were city dwellers in 1900 added to the problem, since most did not have gardens and bought all of their food from retailers. Changes in food technology toward the end of the nineteenth century, moreover, had rendered some shop-bought items less nutritious, with vitamins in particular lost. New milling methods had produced a popular but depleted white flour in place of stone-ground flour that contained some of the husk; a new vegetable margarine now provided a cheap alternative to butter; and canned vegetables and condensed milk had become commonplace. Free school meals (authorized in 1906 for children in need) and maternity and infant welfare centers (which counseled mothers on nutrition, among other things) were two ways by which the government tried to improve the diet of the working classes in the years before 1914.

By the standards of the day the middle and upper classes enjoyed a more than adequate diet in the opening years of the century. The discovery of vitamins in 1912, however, led by the 1920s to a reassessment of what constituted good nutrition. Previously, diets were judged in terms of calories, protein, carbohydrates, and fat. Now, in addition to calories, nutritionists focused on the protective quality of the food. Fruits and vegetables (other than potatoes), once dismissed as low value because they provided few calories and no known other nutrients, were publicized as essential for health. By 1938 the nation was eating two-thirds more vegetables and twice the amount of fruit than in 1913. Consumption of meat, milk, eggs, and fats also rose. The problem was that it was primarily the middle and upper classes who were adapting their diets to the new teaching. Dietary surveys made in the 1930s disclosed that, although most people now got enough calories, food patterns among working-class families remained much the same as pre-war. Much of this was due to habit, but for at least 10 percent of the population, the prime reason was inadequate income—a factor hard to eradicate during the Great Depression.

Attempts by the government to raise the quality of the general diet met with mixed success in the 1930s. A campaign to increase milk consumption failed, and on the eve of the Second World War average intake of calcium in Britain was still only half what it should have been. Despite widespread publicity by a new Milk Marketing Board, few adults were convinced that they needed milk. The Milk Act of 1933 allowed elementary schools to sell subsidized milk, but only half of the children were enrolled in the program because families out of work still could not afford it. Advances in nutritional science offered the most satisfactory method of improving the national diet. By the early 1930s scientists could fortify commonly eaten foods to make them more nutritious; the government therefore ordered vitamins A and D to be added to milk and margarine, and calcium, iron, and vitamins to bread. Despite the continued monotony of many people's diets, the general standard of nutrition rose. In 1941 a study showed that children age fourteen to fif-

teen were more than two inches taller than their counterparts twenty years earlier. The **infant mortality** rate and the incidence of tuberculosis—also indicators of nutritional standards—had both fallen by 50 percent. This proved to be the beginning of a continuous improvement in national health associated with diet.

The war provided the opportunity for further change directed by the government and its scientific advisers. After January 1940 all foods except bread and vegetables were rationed, with equal shares of meat, dairy products, fats, and other foods allotted to each person. Children and expectant mothers received special supplies of milk, eggs, and juice, while factory workers and others in arduous occupations were provided with an extra, carefully planned, meal at the workplace. Subsidies and wage controls kept key foods within the purchasing power of everyone. Not only did health standards continue to rise, but the old unhealthful patterns of consumption finally began to give way. People were forced by food controls to draw more calories from milk and vegetables, and they became more knowledgeable about food values as the result of official publicity campaigns.

The **welfare state** established after 1945 ensured that wartime gains would be permanent. In 1948 all children became eligible for free milk at school. Infants were given orange juice and cod liver oil through clinics. **Family allowances**, paid to the mother, for each child after the first, were a method of increasing expenditure on food and other necessities for children. State **pensions** and social security benefits covering the entire population, meanwhile, served to strengthen purchasing power and hence the amount spent on food by groups with low incomes. A rise in real wages after 1950 brought benefits to the general population. By 1981 Britons were spending on average only 15 percent of their incomes on food. Few now suffered from deficiency disorders; cases of malnutrition were more likely to stem from overconsumption rather than underconsumption. Free school milk was ended in 1970. Since the mid-1970s there has been a rise in popularity of health foods and diet plans. The same period has also seen a great diversification of diet linked to the spread of supermarkets around the country, the **immigration** of large numbers of people from the British Commonwealth, Britain's entry into the **European Community**, and an unprecedented degree of **foreign travel** among ordinary people. Tastes and expecta-

Hollywood's dedication to escapism as a waste of a powerful new mass medium.

After the First World War Grierson had moved to the United States to study the mass media. He was particularly influenced by the ideas of Walter Lippmann, who argued that the new mass media, so significant during the recent war, needed to be controlled by a responsible information elite. On his return to the United Kingdom, Grierson created a cadre of public servants who were media professionals. Largely through his guidance, the British government and big business both turned to film sponsorship as a public information and public relations medium and as a form of artistic patronage. He intended to use films as public education and also challenge Hollywood, which often occupied more than 90 percent of British screen time. Beginning in 1927 Grierson produced both reports and films for the Empire Marketing Board (EMB), a branch of the Department of Overseas Trade, intended to promote the British Empire's products to the British public. Grierson made his first film, *Drifters* (1929), for the EMB. *Drifters*' portrayal of the workers who caught, packaged, and distributed Britain's fish harvest was a revelation. It was the first time that ordinary working people had appeared in a nondemeaning way in a British film. Like virtually all of Grierson's films, *Drifters* was seen primarily by nontheatrical audiences and was not shown widely in commercial release. Film societies, art theaters, and other elite venues were impressed, and Grierson quickly built a reputation and a following on the basis of this film. Over 300 documentary films were made in Britain in the 1930s, largely for the government and for big corporations such as Shell Oil and the public utility companies. A surprising number were socially critical and drew attention to a wide range of social welfare concerns such as poor housing, malnutrition, pollution, and inadequate education. Grierson convinced big business and government alike that they gained from drawing attention to problems, and his writings soon transformed his small following into a coherent group.

This movement experimented with a range of forms. The early films, including *Drifters*, were essentially low-budget versions of Russian-style silent film montage. Later films experimented with dramatic re-enactments, including the famous *Night Mail* (1936) and *North Sea* (1938). These films often employed sets and scripted dialogue, and everything that appeared in the final cut was carefully structured. Nevertheless, in their use of actuality-based drama and nonprofessional actors, they were innovative. At other times, Grierson's followers opted for a radical approach—to let ordinary people, speaking in their own words, address the camera lens directly and tell viewers about their everyday situations. This was particularly the case with *Housing Problems* (1935), which took viewers inside ordinary working people's homes in the East End of London. Other films adopted a minimal style, using a simple combination of charts, voice-over narration, and directly delivered testimony to let the facts speak for themselves. Films like *Enough to Eat* (1936), essentially illustrated lectures, were powerful indictments of social conditions.

First at the EMB and then, after 1933, at the General Post Office, Grierson surrounded himself with a group of young, mostly Oxbridge-educated men such as Basil Wright, Stewart Legg, Edgar Anstey, and Arthur Elton. There were other filmmakers, such as Paul Rotha, Harry Watt, and the Brazilian Alberto Cavalcanti, who were less directly aligned with Grierson, although they often collaborated with him. Grierson also attracted other artistic talents: **W.H. Auden, Dylan Thomas, Benjamin Britten**, and the painter William Coldstream all worked with him at some point.

Britain's documentary filmmakers came into their own during the **Second World War.** The Ministry of Information was a generous benefactor for documentary filmmakers, and some of their greatest films, such as *Target for Tonight* (1942) and *Fires Were Started* (1943), were made during this period. Many documentaries made during the war strongly resembled conventional fictional films. Their use of nonprofessional talent and their basis in real life events depicted in a nonheroic way foreshadow the style and content of Italian neo-realist films made later in the decade. The war also allowed documentary filmmakers to get their work shown widely in commercial venues for the first time. *Target for Tonight*, which stoically depicted the British at war, was a huge commercial success. Another, more subtle tradition was best exemplified in the work of **Humphrey Jennings**, whose image-poems are moving snapshots of Britain at war. *Listen to Britain* (1941) and *Words for Battle* (1941) conveyed in a sophisticated way the cultural effects of the war, and its impact upon dance, music, and poetry in Britain. *A Diary for Timothy* (1945) dramatized the ambiguity and uncertainty surrounding the return to peace for many British people.

After 1945 British documentary filmmaking went into a hiatus. Grierson returned from Canada to work for the Central Office of Information and UNESCO before ultimately settling down as producer and host of *This Wonderful World*, a documentary show produced by Scottish television. Several of Grierson's protegés, including Watt and Cavalcanti, gravitated toward the feature-**film industry**, while others, such as Anstey and Elton, produced successful scientific and documentary films for organizations like Shell Oil and the Transport Film Unit. Their films continued to be associated with a social conscience and artistic flair, but they received far less attention than during the war.

British Free Cinema was a new filmmaking approach that emerged in the early 1950s. Prominent figures in this group included Lindsay Anderson, Karel Reisz, and Tony Richardson. This younger generation of filmmakers owed relatively little to Grierson, and their technique was quite different. Free Cinema was an attempt to go out into the streets and to capture reality on film. Burdened by cumbersome equipment and nonsynchronous sound equipment, films like *Everyday Except Christmas* (1959) and *Momma Don't Allow* (1956) nevertheless managed to convey the sense of seeing the world for the first time. Many of their topics—Teddy Boys, jazz music, and coffee bars—show the transitions occurring in 1950s Britain. Free Cinema anticipated many of the ideas and methods of Cinema Verité and American direct cinema. Its films were structured around events as observed by the filmmakers, rather than previously written scripts. Voice-over narration disappeared, as did scripted dialogue and most staged action. Filmmakers tried to make people behave as if the film crew were not there, interfering as little as possible with their film subjects' lives. The notion of attempting to capture events on film as they happened, a common practice in combat cinematography, but practically unknown elsewhere, was innovative. The technology of the time was not up to the aspirations of these filmmakers: Film stock was not fast enough, cameras were not light enough to be held by hand and had to be mounted on a tripod, and, above all, filmmakers did not have lightweight synchronous sound equipment. Even so, their best work compares very favorably with that of their French New Wave contemporaries.

In the 1960s British filmmakers experimented with dramatic forms that blurred the line between documentary and fiction. Peter Watkins in *The War Game* (1965) and *Culloden* (1964) and Ken Loach in *Kes* (1969) used nonprofessional actors and dramatic settings to convey social realities that would simply not be possible for conventional documentary or fictional forms. Watkins' work was so controversial that *The War Game*, originally made for **BBC**-TV, which dramatized the aftermath of a nuclear attack, was never broadcast. **Television** has become the principal source of funding for documentary films in the United Kingdom, and documentary filmmakers such as Michael Apted and Roger Graef look to that medium for support.

Paul Swann

Bibliography

Barnouw, Erik. *Documentary: A History of the Non-Fiction Film*. 2nd ed. 1990.
Nichols, Bill. *Representing Reality*. 1992.
Swann, Paul. *The British Documentary Film Movement, 1926–1946*. 1989.

Dole, The

The dominant response to large-scale and persistent **unemployment** in inter-war Britain was to provide cash benefits to the out of work, pending a revival in the demand for labor. The legal and administrative apparatus deployed for the payment of unemployment benefits had its origins in the Edwardian period. Before 1911 there was no provision at the national level for meeting the immediate needs of the unemployed. But with growing evidence from the turn of the century that unemployment and poverty were not determined primarily by individual moral failing but by economic forces, pressure mounted for a more systematic means of dealing with the involuntarily unemployed. The resultant unemployment insurance scheme introduced in 1911 applied to only seven trades, with a work force of about 2.25 million men in a total male labor force of over 10 million. This limited scheme was never intended to cover all periods of unemployment. It was designed as a remedy for fluctuations in employment, not as a cure for longer-term unemployment. Nonetheless, it introduced the important principle that workers who made payments to an Unem-

D

friends or suitors. Such restrictions contrasted harshly with the freedom offered by day work. Financially, as well, domestic work compared unfavorably with alternative occupations. During the twentieth century domestic wages, once considered attractive by working-class women, quickly fell behind those offered in factories, shops, and offices. Servants, furthermore, were excluded from government regulation of hours and conditions and from the state-provided **unemployment** insurance that became an important feature of working-class life.

Such conditions made domestic work increasingly unpopular among young working-class people. As early as 1901 census-takers noted that the growth of domestic service had slowed and that prospective employers found servants increasingly difficult to find. The **First World War**, which vastly, albeit temporarily, expanded job opportunities for young women, halted the growth of the occupation completely and initiated an absolute decline in the supply of servants. Despite governmental attempts to encourage reform of household conditions and to channel unemployed women into domestic work, and despite numerous schemes designed to improve the status of domestic work through training, unionization, or reorganization, the decline continued through the inter-war years. Though the servant shortage affected small households earliest and most severely, by the middle of the century even the largest establishments found it difficult to attract staff. Massive social and economic changes brought by the **Second World War** and by the formation of the **welfare state** dealt the final blow to traditional domestic service by reducing demand as well as supply. Even the wealthiest families found it necessary to cut staff numbers, move into smaller quarters, and eliminate or curtail elaborate entertainment. Whereas in 1911 10 percent of British families had employed resident servants, by 1951 the proportion had dropped to 1 percent, and in 1981 to 0.1 percent. Clearly, and for the first time in British history, employment of domestic servants has become the exclusive province of the wealthiest families.

Increasingly, the servant culture of the Victorian and early twentieth-century periods is regarded with nostalgia and as a symbol of the vast changes Britain has experienced. The popular **television** series *Upstairs, Downstairs* (1973–5) is perhaps the best-known expression of historical and popular interest in domestic service. That interest has been affirmed as well by the publication of scholarly and popular studies of the servant system and of **country house** life, by the appearance of numerous former servants' autobiographies, and by the critical and popular success of novels featuring servants as central characters, such as Kazuo Ishiguro's *The Remains of the Day* (1989). While domestic servants no longer exist as a feature of everyday British life, their survival as symbols of the British past seems assured.

Julie S. Gibert

Bibliography

Dawes, Frank V. *Not in Front of the Servants: Domestic Service in England, 1850–1939.* 1973.

Horn, Pamela. *The Rise and Fall of the Victorian Servant.* 1975.

Huggett, Frank E. *Life Below Stairs: Domestic Servants in England from Victorian Times.* 1977.

McBride, Theresa M. *The Domestic Revolution: The Modernization of Household Service in England and France, 1820–1920.* 1976.

Drabble, Margaret (1939–)

Margaret Drabble's reputation as a socially significant writer was established in the 1960s when her bright and resilient protagonists became role models for women. But this popular appreciation led most critics to overlook her artful self-reflexive exhibition of the tales told by these engaging characters. These recent university graduates radiated the same promise as Drabble, the second daughter of a Sheffield judge, John Frederick Drabble and his wife, Kathleen. Following the path of her older sister, the noted novelist Antonia S. Byatt, Drabble read English literature at **Cambridge**, receiving double-first-class honors in 1960. In the same year she became an understudy to Vanessa Redgrave at the **Royal Shakespeare Company** and married actor Clive Swift. When her acting career was terminated by the birth of the first of their three children, she sought a creative outlet in writing novels about young women struggling to find a sense of purpose amid conflicting demands of career and family.

Drabble's early novels concerned literary young women seeking to gain understanding of their personal experiences by reshaping them as fiction. Her first novel, *A Summer Birdcage*

(1963), was a first-person account of the rivalry between two university graduate sisters. *The Garrick Year* (1964) drew on Drabble's brief theatrical experience and her own stormy marriage; *The Millstone* (1966) offered a portrait of a young academic unmarried mother. In the exposure of artistic choices by the young protagonists in these novels, Drabble revealed the essential paradox of narration: Subjective feelings distort the reporting of events, yet it is impossible for a writer to recount events without filtering them through a distorting medium.

In her fourth novel, *Jerusalem the Golden* (1967), Drabble experimented with third-person narration in the story of a young woman dazzled by the glitter of London life in contrast to her own bleak Midlands home. But despite the more objective narrative voice, as she explored her common background with that of the protagonist, Clara, Drabble began to realize the subjective power of landscape to influence a writer's perspective. She continued to develop this theme in *A Writer's Britain* (1979) and in books on *Wordsworth* (1966), *Arnold Bennett* (1974), and *The Genius of Thomas Hardy* (1976).

After the considerable success of her early novels Drabble extended her vision to include characters and situations more removed from her own circumstances: a wealthy heiress seeking virtue through voluntary poverty in *The Needle's Eye* (1972); a successful woman archaeologist in *The Realms of Gold* (1975); financial and property dealings in the pessimistic condition-of-England novel, *The Ice Age* (1977). With these novels and the more domestic *The Middle Ground* (1980) Drabble's focus gradually shifted from the career aspirations of youthful protagonists to broader social issues, while she continued to probe marital failure and the search for meaningful feminist identity. The preoccupations of characters in these middle novels are more representative than personal, and the novels function more as reflections on contemporary social concerns than as studies of individuals in search of aesthetic fulfillment. In *The Needle's Eye* and in *The Middle Ground* multicultural conflict and urban decay in London are brought into sharp focus, themes that intrude into her later books as well. The sense of disillusionment with Thatcherite Britain stretches even to the efficacy of language, as though the novel itself is no longer sufficient for comprehending individual character and social context.

Perhaps not surprisingly, Drabble stopped working on novels at this point and devoted five years to editing the fifth edition of *The Oxford Companion to English Literature* (1985). She remained active in the British literary scene with biographer Michael Holroyd, whom she married in 1982 following her divorce from Swift in 1975. She resumed writing fiction, with a trilogy of novels exploring anew the lives of Oxbridge women of her generation who had begun as idealists but had learned to survive disappointments and to live with paradox. In these later works, *The Radiant Way* (1987), *A Natural Curiosity* (1989), and *The Gates of Ivory* (1991), Drabble also returned to the problem of finding literary resolution, often deconstructing her own narratives and inviting readers to invent their own conclusions, while continuing to affirm the writer's "duty to seek to make sense of the world . . . to endeavor in the face of the impossible."

Brenda Keegan

Bibliography

Creighton, Joanne V. *Margaret Drabble.* 1985.
Hannay, John. *The Intertextuality of Fate: A Study of Margaret Drabble.* 1986.
Myer, Virginia C. *Margaret Drabble: Puritanism and Permissiveness.* 1974.
Rose, Ellen Cronan. *The Novels of Margaret Drabble.* 1980.

Drama

At the turn of the century the two most established dramatists were Arthur Wing Pinero (1855–1934) and Henry Arthur Jones (1851–1929), whose work looked back to French nineteenth-century conventions of the "well-made play," even though both were inspired by Ibsen. **George Bernard Shaw** was the new voice in the theater, an Irish Ibsenite, Wagnerian, and Marxist, championing a realism whereby character and dialogue were liberated from the conventional demands of plot. In Shaw's plays there is an emphasis on the discussion of ideas and social problems rather than action, leaving the audience with open questions: He describes *Major Barbara* (1905) as "A Discussion" and *Misalliance* (1910) as "A Debate in One Sitting." His plays debate and discuss politics (especially socialism and **feminism**), science, and **philosophy**. But while Shaw's aims are realistic, his plays are often fantastic, and his later work

The decade that followed saw the emergence of agitprop (agitation propaganda) theater groups, which engaged the talents of young dramatists like David Hare (1947–), Howard Brenton (1942–), David Edgar (1948–), and Howard Barker (1946–). The 7:84 Theatre Company of John McGrath (1935–) is possibly the best representative of the movement. These small counter-theater groups directly addressed working-class audiences, intending to mobilize them politically. Bond was a dominant figure during the 1970s and the early 1980s. His major plays, *Lear* (1971), *The Sea* (1973), *The Woman* (1978), and *Restoration* (1981), became increasingly radical and didactic. But agitprop soon lost its momentum. The dramatists, with the exception of McGrath, were beginning to work on more conventional stages, including the **Royal Shakespeare Company** and the **National Theatre**.

The three most popular dramatists of the 1970s and 1980s have been Michael Frayn (1933–), Simon Gray (1926–), and **Alan Ayckbourn**. Ayckbourn has been influenced by Stoppard. Trevor Griffiths (1935–) follows the example of Orton and Barnes in writing more politically directed comedy. Since the 1970s an important tradition of feminist theater has also emerged in the plays of Pam Gems (1925–) and Caryl Churchill (1938–).

Brian Pearce

Bibliography

Elsom, John. *Post-war British Theatre*. 2nd ed. 1979.

Innes, Christopher. *Modern British Drama, 1890–1990*. 1992.

Nicoll, Allardyce. *English Drama, 1900–1930: The Beginnings of the Modern Period*. 1973.

Taylor, John Russell. *Anger and After: A Guide to the New British Drama*. 2nd ed. 1977.

Worth, Katharine. *Revolutions in Modern English Drama*. 1973.

Dreadnought

HMS *Dreadnought* was the first modern battleship, whose development by Britain revolutionized naval warfare.

At the start of the twentieth century the mainstay of any navy was the battleship, a steel warship carrying a variety of guns of different sizes. However, as gunnery improved in range and precision, this diversity of armament became impractical. Battle ranges came to be determined by the largest-caliber guns, rendering the smaller armament redundant, and fire control at long range was difficult when a variety of shell splashes from different guns confused spotters.

The solution to this problem, concluded First Sea Lord **Sir John Fisher** in 1904, was to build a new type of battleship with a main armament all the same caliber. Such a new warship, however, posed a dilemma for the **Royal Navy**, in that as the leading naval power Britain had the most to lose from a technological revolution that rendered all existing battleships obsolete. Fisher argued that other navies already were studying the concept and would undoubtedly proceed on their own initiative if Britain did nothing. Moreover, Germany was engaged already in a warship race with Britain, and a technological revolution would force the Germans to start the race all over again.

Fisher's arguments won the day, and HMS *Dreadnought* was laid down in October 1905. Through the superhuman effort of the Royal Dockyard at Portsmouth, it was completed exactly a year later in October 1906. *Dreadnought* carried ten twelve-inch guns in five twin turrets, which were its sole armament other than a few dozen twelve-pounder guns for close-in defense against torpedo boats. The ship displaced 18,000 tons, and its revolutionary new steam-turbine propulsion produced a speed of twenty-one knots, much faster than pre-*Dreadnought* battleships.

The impact of *Dreadnought*'s development on the world's navies was dramatic. Every other navy was compelled to abandon its traditional battleship design and build ships of the new type, which soon became known generically as "dreadnoughts." By the **First World War** all of the world's battle fleets consisted mainly of dreadnoughts, with pre-*Dreadnought* battleships relegated to secondary roles.

HMS *Dreadnought* served in the Home Fleet until the outbreak of war in 1914, when it joined the newly formed Grand Fleet. In March 1915 it rammed and sank a German **submarine** while on its way to the Grand Fleet base in Scapa Flow. In May 1916 *Dreadnought* was transferred to second-line service guarding the Thames estuary as more-modern battleships took their place in the Grand Fleet and thus just missed the battle of Jutland, the great surface action for which it had been built. At the end of the war *Dreadnought* was decommissioned; it was sold for scrap in 1922.

David MacGregor

Bibliography

Hough, Richard. *Dreadnought: A History of the Modern Battleship.* 2nd ed. 1968.

Parkes, Oscar. *British Battleships.* 1970.

Sumida, Jon Tetsuro. *In Defence of Naval Supremacy: Finance, Technology, and British Naval Policy, 1889–1914.* 1989.

Drink

Alcohol consumption per capita peaked in Britain in the late 1870s and began to fall sharply in the following decades, a trend related to the growing availability of alternative recreations for the working class. The temperance movement, a significant force in late Victorian politics, was consequently losing impetus by the turn of the century. Convictions for drunkenness fell in England and Wales from 207,000 in 1905 to 152,000 in 1910. The working class continued to patronize pubs, however, which numbered over 100,000 in 1901. The middle classes tended to drink in hotels, clubs, and restaurants, or at home. Tastes were changing. Scotch whisky increased in popularity, particularly the lighter blends, which replaced the heavier malts, while brandy and rum declined. Champagne, hock, and port maintained their popularity among the better off. Governments became increasingly addicted to the habit of regular tax increases on alcohol, especially wine and spirits, with the 1908 budget.

The **First World War** saw dramatically increased taxes on alcohol, as well as restricted pub opening hours and the dilution of beer and spirits in the name of worker efficiency. The rise in drink expenditure from £164 million in 1913 to £390 million in 1919 was largely a reflection of inflation and taxation. After the war drink consumption continued to drop, from 0.68 proof gallons of spirits per capita in 1913 to 0.21 gallons in 1935. While beer remained overwhelmingly the working-class drink (four out of seven Bolton pubs did not even sell spirits in 1936), beer consumption fell between 1913 and 1935 from 27.5 to 12.8 gallons per capita. In Scotland, however, the working class were greater consumers of spirits. The American-inspired inter-war craze among the middle class for cocktails, reflected by the appearance in the Victoria Wine shops of forgotten drinks like Zip and Whoopee, did not affect the downward national trend.

The **Second World War** saw once again strict regulation of the drink trade. Beer was often in short supply, and its price rose, while quality fell, since oats and even potatoes were introduced into its manufacture, but it was left unrationed in the interests of sustaining morale. Spirits were soon scarce; distillers' operations were drastically curtailed by grain quotas, and existing stocks went abroad for precious foreign exchange. In April 1945 Prime Minister **Winston Churchill** personally ordered that distillers be allocated a supply of barley for whisky. Though a champagne and cognac drinker himself, Churchill recognized the vital contribution Scotch made to the maintenance of Britain's world position. An interesting aspect of wartime life was that members of the middle class, who before the war would never have entered a pub, began to be seen there, thus enhancing the mystique of the pub as a vital community institution. The war also brought women into pubs in growing numbers. Women had already become a distinctive market for the drink trade. The cheap Dutch liqueur Advocaat became popular with working-class women between the wars, especially in the north. Sherry and cider were also strongly supported by women drinkers. After the Second World War Babycham, a shrewdly named sparkling pear cider, developed a considerable following among women.

The most significant post-war development has been the rise in consumption of spirits and, even more, of wine. Increased spirits consumption, in the face of continued government tax increases, was a sign of renewed prosperity, and perhaps of increasing home consumption. Particularly popular were "white" spirits—gin, light rum, and, above all, vodka. Scotch consumption saw something of a comeback, especially from the 1960s, from the old single malts. Wine imports were prohibited during the war and even before that had borne a discriminatory tax burden in keeping with wine's perceived luxury status and the political clout of the brewing interest. Taxes on cheaper wines imported in wood were reduced in 1949. Thereafter wine became fashionable among the middle class, as a mark of sophistication and as part of the "good food" boom of the 1950s. The range of cheap, reasonable wines was greatly expanded not only by "Empire" wines—Australian and South African wines that were improving markedly in quality—but

D

Allies, Germany's tanks broke through the French Front in the Ardennes and split the Allied force in two, threatening the BEF and the French troops in Belgium with encirclement. The endangered Allied forces thereupon retreated to a perimeter around Dunkirk for evacuation. Germany's high command, fearful about wasting tanks in marshy coastal areas, called a halt to their advance, trusting the German air force (the Luftwaffe) to destroy the Dunkirk pocket.

It was a disastrous mistake. The Luftwaffe, drained from its previous battles, stationed far from the channel, and suffering bad weather as well as **Royal Air Force** harassment, could not prevent the evacuation; German planes were not equipped, nor their pilots trained to attack shipping in any case. By the time the German ground forces were allowed to move again, the perimeter was secure. The Luftwaffe and German artillery did force the **Royal Navy** to conduct most of the evacuation by night, but that was enough: 364,628 troops were removed, 224,686 of them British, the rest French plus some Belgians. The troops that escaped were disorganized and had been obliged to leave most of their equipment behind. Luckily, the Germans were not capable of launching a cross-channel attack for many weeks to come.

The vast armada of tiny, privately owned craft that assisted in the evacuation still symbolizes British self-sacrifice and pluck, although in truth most of the work was carried out by larger vessels. The legend has also obscured the fact that many British troops were evacuated later in June from other French ports. Nevertheless, the evacuation was a turning point in the **Second World War**. Without it, the British would have been hard-pressed to find manpower for the rest of the war, and it was also the first occasion when Germany's armed forces failed to achieve an important goal. While it is true that wars are not won by brilliant retreats, the British people—and others—soon drew upon the Dunkirk legend as a source of inspiration and hope during the new crises that followed the fall of France.

Karl G. Larew

Bibliography

Barker, A.J. *Dunkirk: The Great Escape.* 1977.

Gelb, Norman. *Dunkirk: The Complete Story of the First Step in the Defeat of Hitler.* 1989.

Horne, Alistair. *To Lose a Battle: France, 1940.* 1969.

Durbin, Evan Frank Mottram (1906–1948)

An intellectual, economist, and politician, Evan Durbin was a prominent member of the generation of young socialist thinkers that helped shape the policy and direction of the **Labour Party** from the 1930s on, a generation that included **Hugh Gaitskell** and Douglas Jay. He provided one of the clearest articulations of the democratic socialist case, in *The Politics of Democratic Socialism* (1940), a key text of twentieth-century British socialism.

Durbin, the son of a Baptist preacher, was educated at Taunton School, Devonshire, and then won a scholarship to **Oxford** in 1924, where he earned degrees in biology (1927) and politics, philosophy, and economics (1929). Leaving Oxford, Durbin became an academic economist at the **London School of Economics** until 1940. His family had been Liberal, but at secondary school he embraced Labour politics. At university he was active in the Oxford University Labour Club, and during the early 1930s he was a leading light of the **New Fabian Research Bureau**. His real contribution in this period was as an economic planner. Under the tutelage of **Hugh Dalton**, Durbin and others, such as Colin Clark, Gaitskell, and Jay, helped work out a credible socialist economic strategy for Labour based upon central economic planning and public ownership.

Throughout the 1930s Durbin had been concerned that socialist planning be infused with democratic methods and liberal tendencies. In part he was responding to the libertarian critiques of his London School of Economics colleagues Lionel Robbins and Friedrich von Hayek. The prevailing Marxist tone of socialist writing in the 1930s also disturbed him. In 1940 he brought these concerns together in *The Politics of Democratic Socialism*, one of the first "revisionist" texts in Labour's ideological discussions. His other writings, such as *Purchasing Power and Trade Depression* (1933), *The Problems of Credit Policy* (1935), *What Have We to Defend?* (1942), and numerous articles, collected in *Principles of Economic Planning* (1949), explored many of the same problems.

During the war he served as an economist with the **Cabinet** and then became an adviser to **Clement Attlee** on reconstruction policy. He helped write Labour's statement on economic strategy, *Full Employment and Financial Policy* (1944). Unlike others within this circle, he never completely embraced Keynesianism; at the time of his death in 1948, he still favored physical planning over demand management. An unsuccessful Labour candidate through the 1930s, Durbin was elected an MP for the North London constituency of Edmonton in 1945. He served as Parliamentary Private Secretary to Dalton until 1947 when he became Undersecretary to Charles Key at the Ministry of Works. On holiday in Cornwall in September 1948, he drowned while attempting to rescue two children.

Durbin's early death robbed Labour of a powerful right-of-center intellectual. His *Politics of Democratic Socialism* has served as a touchstone for a future generation of socialists and social democrats, including Gaitskell, Roy Jenkins, **Anthony Crosland**, Richard Crossman, Roy Hattersley, and David Marquand.

Stephen Brooke

Bibliography

Brooke, Stephen. *Labour's War*. 1992.

———. "Problems of 'Socialist Planning': Evan Durbin and the Labour Government of 1945," *Historical Journal*, vol. 34 (1991), pp. 687–702.

Durbin, Elizabeth. *New Jerusalems: The Labour Party and the Economics of Democratic Socialism*. 1985.

Durbin, Evan. *The Politics of Democratic Socialism*. 1940.

Phelps Brown, E.H. "Evan Durbin, 1906–48," *Economica*, vol. 18 (1951), pp. 91–5.

D

tries had long outpaced its rate of growth and productivity, and its shares of world manufacturing output (about 4 percent) and trade (about 9 percent) had shrunk to modest levels. The country had slipped down the international league table of economic performance, whether measured in terms of levels and growth rates of gross domestic product (the national output of goods and services), of the sophistication of its technology and economic organization, or of the average living standards of its citizens. This, however, is to apply relative measures in the context of the most advanced countries. In fact, the economy continued to grow throughout most of the century (even if its growth rate has been exceeded by an increasing number of other nations), levels of material welfare have continued to increase, and by the standards of the overwhelming majority of countries in the world, Britain remained an advanced, rich, and buoyant economy.

Table 1 makes clear the extent to which Britain's modern growth rate has lagged behind that of other leading industrial nations (a fact that has been intimately associated with its diminishing share of world manufacturing output and trade). On the other hand, it also shows that Britain's economic "decline" has not been a matter of retardation or even stagnation, but rather of other economies growing faster. Indeed, Britain's growth rate in the twentieth century has not shown a deterioration from that of the economy's halcyon days as the workshop of the world. Equally important, while latercomers undoubtedly overtook Britain, their growth rates have not continued to exceed Britain's by marked amounts. The contrast between Britain's economic achievement and that of other advanced countries is much less than that between the advanced countries as a group and poorer countries, which account for the bulk of the world's population.

A striking feature of Britain's economic history has been the extent of "structural change"—the relative decline (in terms of output and employment) of manufacturing and the growth of services. To a large extent this has been the inevitable consequence of economic development as wealthier consumers spend more on **health**, education, **leisure**, and services generally, and as technical efficiency enables physical output to be produced with proportionately less labor. At the same time, however, the recent rapid decline of old-established industries—especially the staple export industries of the nineteenth century, such as **coal**, textiles, iron and **steel**, and shipbuilding, and of formerly important twentieth-century industries such as electrical engineering and electronics and, until the influx of Japanese enterprise and capital, the **automobile industry** implies an unhealthy erosion of the country's manufacturing base. And this, in turn, has weakened Britain's trading position by narrowing the range of exports and making consumers more reliant on manufactured imports.

Many of these problems did not emerge until relatively late in the century. Even though there was some anxiety about industrial competition, especially from Germany and the United States, well before the First World War, manufacturing industries were still powerful and British trade and finance was still supreme. It was this strength that enabled Britain to endure the First World War so successfully, while its Empire was at its most extensive in the years immediately after 1918. Admittedly, the economic outlook became clouded in the post-war decade. On the one hand, the industries that had brought so much employment and buoyant activity to South Wales, Scotland, northern England, and the Midlands now appeared to have far too much capacity for the new conditions of world markets. Competition and the disruption of demand provoked crises, unprofitability, and widespread **unemployment** in coal, textiles, shipbuilding, engineering, and metallurgy. On the other hand, the new frailty

TABLE 1: ANNUAL GROWTH RATE OF GROSS DOMESTIC PRODUCT (%)

	1870–1913	1914–50	1951–73	1974–92
France	1.7	1.1	5.1	2.5
Germany	2.8	1.3	5.9	2.4
Japan	2.5	2.2	9.4	4.0
Netherlands	2.1	2.4	4.7	2.4
United Kingdom	1.9	1.3	3.0	1.9
Average	2.2	1.7	5.6	2.6
USA	4.2	2.8	3.7	2.4

of the export economy and, even more, the dislocation of the world's economy, trade, and finance helped erode the international strength of the pound sterling.

From many viewpoints, therefore, the 1920s were an unhappy decade, troubled by inadequate economic performance and intense labor disputes. And it was followed by the severest Depression of modern times (1929–32), during which Britain was forced to abandon both its traditional policy of free trade and the established value of the currency as sustained by the **gold standard**. But, as with overall economic performance as measured by growth rates, the situation was not unmitigatedly bad. In the 1930s Britain's recovery from the slump was more widespread and rapid than that in most other countries. And although unemployment continued at a high level and the reputation of the 1930s is not particularly admirable, through the inter-war period average living standards rose, many areas of the country (especially in the south) experienced a large measure of prosperity, and the economy proved resilient as new consumption patterns and industries (electrical engineering, retailing, motor vehicles, chemicals, and scientific instruments) flourished. As so often in British history, the benefits and costs of change were unevenly distributed geographically and socially.

The extent but also the limitations of Britain's continued position as an economic power were well exemplified in the **Second World War**. The economy was sufficiently efficient to sustain Britain's role as a major belligerent, but insufficiently large to allow it to survive the war without the help of such powerful allies as the United States and the Soviet Union. For a decade or so after the war, and in spite of apparent austerity, the economy recovered rapidly and was able to contend against competition from other countries that had been even more exhausted, or devastated, by war effort. But ultimately, and in spite of continued—even by its own standards, spectacular—growth, the British economy was outpaced by much of Western Europe and by the booming Japanese economy. Ever since the late 1950s therefore, the story has been a familiar, and occasionally contradictory, one: relative decline and a sense of unease and dissatisfaction, uncompetitive older industries and inadequate trade, disappointing productivity—but all joined with continuously rising living standards and a large measure of economic and social change as consumption patterns were modernized and new

sources of wealth and jobs (especially in the service sector, but also in North Sea Oil production) transformed the reality of British life. By the last decade of the twentieth century, and in spite of much disappointment, Britain was still among the richest 10 percent of the world's nations.

Arguably, Britain's economic performance has been adequate when measured in terms of the continued positive growth in output and living standards. But the fact remains that it has failed to rival its principal competitors and continued to frustrate the private and public aspirations of its citizens.

In principle, then, the economy could have grown faster and become stronger. The fact that it failed to do so has been variously attributed to conservative social and entrepreneurial attitudes, to inadequate and hidebound education and training, to bad industrial relations, to a neglect of capital investment, to a reluctance to accept the personal and social costs of change, and to neglectful or inappropriate government policies. There is evidence for each of these presumed "failings" over the last century—although it is not always certain that Britain is alone among developed nations in exemplifying them, or that they are consistent with the long-run economic record. Three things, however, do seem clear. First, each of these "explanations" exists as part of a complex national situation that is very difficult to change by any conscious action. Second, the interdependence of these characteristics, and their consequent resistance to manipulation, casts doubt on any "theory" that implies that there was a major and feasible alternative path to national prosperity. Third, in such a situation, economic performance and the attributes that determine it are the products of a long history: Britain's twentieth-century economy and growth record (including the attitudes, institutions, and behavior associated with it) are the products of its earlier development and its very success; and its recent experiences reflect as much maturity as failure. In this respect it is not at all clear that the economies whose achievements appear to have so easily outstripped Britain's will not themselves experience the same retardative forces as emerged from Britain's own economic maturity.

Barry Supple

Bibliography

Crafts, Nick F.R., and N.W.C. Woodward, eds. *The British Economy since 1945.* 1991.

E

ment in protest of the **Cabinet's** wish to "appease" Italy and for his prominent role in wartime diplomacy, symbolized by his attendance with the Americans and the Soviets at summit conferences at Tehran, Yalta, and Potsdam.

Every phase of Eden's career has provoked controversy among biographers and historians. So far as his period at the **Foreign Office** between 1931 and 1938 is concerned, the question is whether he should on the whole be regarded as an "appeaser" or an "antiappeaser." During his lifetime it suited him, and indeed the **Conservative Party** as a whole, to emphasize evidence that suggested that he had been a reasonably consistent opponent of the Fascist dictatorships and that his resignation in 1938 had been motivated by principled opposition to all that Chamberlain represented. In recent years, however, revisionist writers with access to relevant documents have pointed out that he was much less hostile to Germany than to Italy and that this found expression, in particular, in his unwillingness to support French calls for armed resistance to the remilitarization of the Rhineland in 1936. Again, doubts have been cast on the extent to which he was consistently hostile to Italy given that he acquiesced in the lifting of **League of Nations** sanctions in 1936 despite the fact that Abyssinia had been totally conquered. And even his resignation can be seen as motivated less by high principle than by personal pique at Chamberlain's interference in his running of foreign policy.

Whatever the merits of these various arguments, the fact is that he emerged in the 1940s as **Winston Churchill's** principal lieutenant, and it was widely assumed at the time that they had an almost father-and-son relationship of great harmony of view. Recent revelations suggest, however, that at times Churchill and Eden were bitter rivals and disagreed about much during the latter's second and third terms at the Foreign Office.

During Eden's second term, from 1940 to 1945, Churchill was at the height of his powers and almost invariably got his way when differences between the two men arose. But Eden robustly defended his opinions behind closed doors and may at times have been close to resignation. Above all, Eden was more willing than his chief to see the Soviets' point of view and to argue for concessions to them. For example, Eden is usually considered to have been more eager than Churchill to promote the controversial policy of enforced repatriation of prisoners

of war to the Soviet Union. These differences were further reflected in 1946 when Churchill, now leader of the opposition, gave a lead to the world in denouncing Soviet-style Communism in a speech in Fulton, Missouri. In private Eden made known his disapproval.

Increasingly, Eden's quarrels with Churchill became personalized, for the former believed that he should have been invited to take over as Conservative Party leader in the aftermath of the general election defeat of 1945. But Churchill refused to stand down either then or following another defeat in 1950. The upshot was that when Churchill formed his peacetime administration (1951–5) great hostility existed between him and the impatient Eden, who, as the coming man, was often able to defeat his chief in the Cabinet over major issues of foreign policy. It is, for example, not without irony that one of Eden's victories was to secure British withdrawal from the Suez Canal Zone in Egypt. Another strange twist arose when Churchill, hitherto so anti-Soviet, greeted Joseph Stalin's death in 1953 with the surprising claim that the new Soviet leaders were sufficiently different to justify the holding of a three-power summit. Eden, determined that his chief should not again be allowed to play the beau role on such an occasion, now conspired with the Americans to block Churchill's plan—though once Eden was himself Prime Minister he suddenly switched to supporting it, with the result that a summit was held in Geneva in July 1955.

Eden's final term at the Foreign Office was marked by two other major events that are usually held to reflect credit on him. First, he had a key role in a conference held at Geneva in 1954 to arrange a compromise settlement necessitated by the French decision to withdraw from Indochina. Second, he played a decisive part in persuading France to agree to West Germany being allowed to rearm under North Atlantic Treaty Organization (NATO) auspices.

Eden's premiership began auspiciously when he led the Conservatives to a general election victory in May 1955, and shortly thereafter he was able to bask in the world spotlight at the aforementioned Geneva summit. But soon storm clouds began to gather. First, economic problems (about which Eden was not particularly well-informed) multiplied, necessitating an emergency budget in October 1955. Then came increasing problems in the Middle East as Gamal Abdel Nasser led Egypt into an arms deal with Czechoslovakia followed by a sustained propaganda campaign against British influence in the region.

Eden's final months as Prime Minister were dominated by problems relating to Egypt, which brought matters to a head by nationalizing the Suez Canal—hitherto controlled by a company based in Paris. Though personally eager to take military steps to reverse this move, Eden in practice could not risk the hostility of the United States, the Commonwealth, the **United Nations**, the **Labour Party**, part of British public opinion, and even some of his own ministerial team. Hence by mid-October it appeared that a humiliating diplomatic compromise was the most likely outcome. But then French representatives proposed to Eden that Israel be secretly induced to attack Egypt, thereby providing a pretext for an Anglo-French armed intervention to separate the combatants and to protect the canal. The scenario was soon put into practice with catastrophic consequences. The United Nations, and the United States in particular, were not persuaded of the genuineness of Anglo-French proclaimed motives and brought overwhelming pressure to bear. The upshot was that the military operation was suspended, with Anglo-French forces in occupation of no more than a third of the canal. Eventually a humiliating withdrawal had to be accepted.

In the meantime Eden's health (weakened by a bile-duct operation that had gone wrong in 1953) was giving cause for concern. He accordingly resigned as Prime Minister and as a member of Parliament in January 1957. Whether health was the sole reason for his departure at this time may, of course, be doubted, though this was his story and he stuck to it. But then he also stuck to the story to the end of his days that he had had no foreknowledge of the Israeli attack on Egypt—something that no historian nowadays could possibly endorse.

Eden's overall significance was recognized in *The Times* obituary in 1977: "He was the last Prime Minister to believe Britain was a great power and the first to confront a crisis which proved she was not."

David Carlton

Bibliography

Carlton, David. *Anthony Eden: A Biography.* 1981.
Eden, Anthony. *The Eden Memoirs.* 3 vols. 1960–65.
James, Robert Rhodes. *Anthony Eden.* 1986.
Rothwell, Victor. *Anthony Eden: A Political Biography, 1931–1957.* 1992.

Education Act of 1944

The 1944 Education Act established a system of education that lasted until the 1990s. It represents the capacity of war both to produce social change and to ensure that the change is not as radical as reformers might have wished. Some of the act came from the 1938 report of the Spens Committee, which recommended that all children be divided at age eleven into groups capable of receiving a secondary education of some sort. Division at eleven and **secondary education** for all were already established practice in many Local Education Authorities by way of the selection through examination, the so-called "eleven plus," and a special-places scheme that meant that the only children who could have the differentiated, more academic curriculum of secondary schools had to pass through the sieve of examination. Reformers had argued that all children were capable of some sort of education beyond the restrictive curriculum of the contemporary form of primary schooling, the elementary school.

In 1942 Board of Education officials began to argue that educational reform was an essential component of reconstruction. **Winston Churchill**, who had experienced divisive effects of earlier reforms, was unenthusiastic, but **R.A. Butler** and Archbishop **William Temple** overcame some of his objections. Local authorities were already moving toward greater homogeneity of practice because **evacuation** and wartime mobility ensured some need for parity in the system. Bombing and alienation of buildings for military use meant that some improvement could be provided by replacement. All of these factors encouraged reform, as did the poor physical quality of aging schools.

The 1943 government White Paper that outlined the reforms established several key principles that went into the act virtually unchanged. These were that children should be allocated to secondary education by age, ability, and aptitude at eleven; Local Education Authorities should provide secondary education with parity between schools; primary schooling should start at five, and the school-leaving age should be raised as recommended in 1938 to fifteen. The contentious issue was the role of the churches in education. Eventually, the act left them with the voluntary-aided schools, supported by the local authority but administered by the church authorities. All local authorities were to provide development plans, which were both an audit of existing provision and a declaration of future plans.

The short-term outcome of the act set the pattern for the long-term effects. Selective schools, the grammar schools, continued to examine and select their pupils using the same examinations as before the act. Across the country 20 percent of eleven-year-olds received this kind of education, but local authorities provided it for a range of five percent to 32 percent. Few technical schools were provided for craft training, and few were built. Secondary modern schools, like the old higher elementary schools, provided for the majority of eleven-year-olds. The curriculum of the two main types of school was differentiated so that children left grammar schools and took the school-leaving certificate, the matriculation examination, which enabled access to higher education. The rest were discouraged from sitting for the examination and encouraged to have a more gender-specific education for adult life, with a slant toward manual jobs. Local authorities who wished to interpret the act by providing a differentiated education for all under one roof, in the multilateral school, were turned down by the Ministry of Education when they submitted their development plans. A hard-fought political battle finally raised the leaving age to fifteen in 1947.

The act confirmed the changes advanced by many local authorities before the war. Reform was limited by material deficiencies of long duration and consequent upon austerity. The curriculum was not centrally prescribed or much altered, and the segregation of the eleven-year-olds on academic lines was perpetuated. Historical debate has focused on the question of equality of opportunity and the secondary child; and the relative responsibilities of central and local government for innovation. Primary schooling and curricular content remain virtually unexamined.

Deborah Thom

Bibliography

Gosden, Peter H.J.H. *Education and the Second World War.* 1976.
Jeffreys, Kevin. "R.A. Butler, the Board of Education, and the 1944 Education Act," *History*, vol. 69 (1984), pp. 415–31.
Johnson, Richard et al. *Unpopular Education: Schooling and Social Democracy in England since 1944.* 1981.
Thom, Deborah. "The 1944 Education Act: The Art of the Possible?" in Harold Smith, ed. *War and Social Change.* 1986. pp. 101–28.

Edward VII (1841–1910)

The eldest son and second child of Queen Victoria and Prince Albert, Albert Edward was created Prince of Wales in 1841 and succeeded his mother in 1901. As future monarch, he was the object of the highest hopes of his parents, who hoped to create in him an ideal king—a moral and intellectual paragon. They were to be disappointed. Albert Edward, unlike his elder sister, the Princess Royal, the future Empress of Germany, or his younger sister, Princess Alice, the future Grand Duchess of Hesse, displayed no leanings toward anything intellectual. As for morality, his standards were those of the more rakish element of the upper class. The efforts of his parents were nonetheless unsparing and, in fact, may have had the opposite result of what they intended. He had the advantage, however, of extensive travel; the most notable success was a visit to Paris with his parents in 1855. As a result, he developed a lifelong love for France. He traveled as well to Canada and the United States, and extensively on the Continent. He studied briefly at **Oxford** and **Cambridge** and joined the Grenadier Guards. After his father's death in 1861, it was thought that an early marriage was desirable, and in 1863, after considerable negotiation, he married Princess Alexandra of Denmark, daughter of the future King Christian IX of Denmark; her sister Dagmar was later to marry Czar Alexander III of Russia, and her brother William was later to become King George I of Greece.

The Prince of Wales had a long apprenticeship. His mother, who mistrusted and disliked his style of life, would permit him virtually no role in her constitutional duties. As she suspected him of indiscretion, he was denied access to state papers until late in her reign. The Prince fulfilled a vast number of ceremonial functions, often with great success. He became, moreover, the center of much of England's social life; his London residence gave rise to the name of the Marlborough House set, admission to which was controlled by the Prince; for many persons he was the absolute arbiter of all things fashionable. He also became a frequent traveler, spreading goodwill for Britain in foreign courts. In 1871 he nearly died of typhoid on the tenth anniversary of his father's death. The Queen's dramatic rush to his bedside, and his seemingly miraculous recovery, restored the popularity of the monarchy, which had suffered greatly because of Victoria's seclusion since Prince Albert's death. Republicanism, which had become a considerable force, was crushed, and the Queen was well positioned to become the symbol and embodiment of a proud and imperial Britain.

The private life of the Prince was a source of worry to many persons, above all the Queen. It was thought by some that he might not be fit to ascend the throne, and he was, in fact, involved in several scandals, testifying in a widely publicized divorce proceeding and in a slander case and feuding with the members of the Churchill family. Respectable opinion, inspired by the **press**, believed that adverse publicity and the Prince's irregular sexual life far outweighed in the public mind his many public duties, such as his intermittent service on the Royal Commission on **housing**.

It is not surprising, therefore, that when he succeeded his mother in January 1901 his accession was greeted with apprehension. Yet he developed into an extraordinarily successful sovereign. He did not style himself Albert I, as his mother had hoped, and he immediately showed independence. He opened Parliament in state, something Queen Victoria had rarely done, and instituted a reign of considerable splendor and pagentry. The magnificence of his court pleased most Britons who found it reassuring in an age in which British power was increasingly challenged. Soon he became, even more than his mother, a comforting figure whose very presence on the throne seemed to assure continued British eminence. The state visit he and Queen Alexandra paid to Paris in 1903 was a triumph and paved the way for the Entente Cordiale between Great Britain and France. He came to be regarded as a kind of uncle to all of Europe and as one who could keep his difficult relatives in line, especially his nephew, the German Kaiser.

The result of his powerful personality was that his influence was exaggerated. He did not determine British foreign policy but rather acted as one who would smooth the way for policies determined by others. As he was not industrious, he probably never acquired the knowledge his mother did, but nevertheless his influence

was felt particularly in military, naval, and diplomatic matters. He established good relations with his ministers, especially with the **Liberal** Prime Minister, Sir **Henry Campbell-Bannerman**, with whom he shared gourmet tastes. The King also seemed in tune with the twentieth century because of the breadth of his friendships, but he never let anyone around him forget his position. From one point of view the high point of his reign came in 1909 when his horse Minoru won the Derby, to the wild enthusiasm of the crowd.

Most of his reign was marked by bitter political controversy, in which the King played a role, often revealing a strongly Conservative prejudice. When the struggle over the Parliament bill to limit the powers of the upper house intensified, he gave, but with great reluctance, an assurance that if the **House of Lords** did not pass the bill, he would create sufficient Liberal peers to get it through; and he did ask that an election be held in 1910. When the King died in May 1910 there were those who complained bitterly that he had been hounded to death by his government. But even those who did not hold such extreme views felt the loss of the King deeply, and the mourning was not only genuine but far more profound than had been the case in 1901. In a reign of just over nine years he had given his name to an era and had won the affection of his people. He had become a symbol of security in an increasingly dangerous world.

King Edward VII made a vital contribution to the evolution of the modern monarchy. If his mother had given the throne respectability, and if his father had played a vital role in distancing the monarchy from political controversy, King Edward gave it glamor and excitement. Much of the extravagance might have seemed inappropriate later, in an era of war and Depression, but the magnificence associated with the King's court was later blended by his descendants with Victorian domestic virtues. Queen Alexandra, moreover, beautiful even in old age, was the perfect wife for King Edward; with her understanding and her lack of interest in almost everything except her family, she was a model consort for her husband.

The King was survived by Queen Alexandra, who died in 1925, and by his second son, King **George V**. He was also survived by three daughters: Princess Louise, later Duchess of Fife; Princess Victoria; and Princess Maud, later Queen of Norway. His eldest son, Prince Albert

E

Victor, Duke of Clarence, died in 1892, and his youngest son, Prince John, died in 1871.

Arthur Mejia

Bibliography
Lee, Sir Sidney. *King Edward VII.* 1925–7.
Magnus, Philip. *King Edward the Seventh.* 1964.
St. Aubyn, Giles. *Edward VII: Prince and King.* 1979.

Edward VIII (1894–1972)

The eldest son of the future King **George V** and Queen Mary, Edward was created Prince of Wales (1910); succeeded his father as King (January 1936); abdicated (December 1936) and was succeeded by his brother, the Duke of York (King **George VI**); and was created Duke of Windsor (1937).

Prince Edward (or David, as he was known to his family) was raised in an atmosphere of discipline and order. His father and mother gave the young Prince little affection, at least by modern standards, and he was subjected to the severe regimes of his nurses and tutors. In 1907 he was sent to Osborne and in 1909 to Dartmouth, as his father was convinced that the **navy** would teach him everything he needed to know. Although this upbringing was often miserable, and although it marked the future King for life, it was little different from the upbringing of other upper-class British boys. The education to which he was exposed, both at home and in the navy, was undeniably narrow and strikingly nonintellectual. He was later exposed to a broader world at **Oxford**, and, under strict limitations, he was allowed to serve on the Western Front during the **First World War**.

It was after the war that he emerged as the center of attention for much of the world's press. His imperial tours, and his visits to the United States and elsewhere, made him a man who aroused passionate interest. His parents were often pleased by the goodwill he inspired, but they were just as often distressed by his casual and informal manner, which they thought inappropriate in the heir to the throne. They were also upset by his lack of interest in marriage and by his numerous affairs with unsuitable women. Generally these women were older and married, and with them the Prince lived a life that was basically self-indulgent and social; he showed little interest in affairs of state. During those years the adulation that surrounded the Prince led him to believe that he could always have his way, and his essentially frivolous life did not disabuse him.

The new King, although professing eagerness to reform the monarchy, soon reverted to his former style of life, which was interrupted by a serious complication. For several years he had had as his mistress Mrs. Ernest Simpson, née Wallis Warfield, of Baltimore, formerly married to Earl Spencer, an American naval officer from whom she was divorced in 1927. The King became determined to marry Mrs. Simpson, even though, by the time they would be able to marry, she would be twice divorced. As the King was the titular head of the **Church of England**, which did not recognize **divorce**, there was an obvious problem. Neither his Private Secretary, Alexander Hardinge, nor the Prime Minister, **Stanley Baldwin**, were able to dissuade him from his resolve to marry Mrs. Simpson.

The growing crisis was generally concealed from the British public by the self-censorship of the **press**, but early in December 1936 the storm broke. The political implications were clear, as enemies of Baldwin hoped to form a "King's Party" that, in a wave of royalist enthusiasm, would sweep Baldwin from office and bring to power a government that, among other things, would hasten rearmament. Among the leaders of this movement were **Lord Beaverbrook**, who cared little for the monarchy, and **Winston Churchill**, who most definitely did care. But Baldwin, who had far greater insight into the psychology of the British people, at least in peacetime, had come to the firm conclusion that the mass of the people would not accept as their Queen a twice-divorced woman whose background betrayed no sense of public duty. In this he was firmly supported by the **Labour Party** and by the Dominions. All halfway solutions failed to gain support, such as a morganatic marriage in which Mrs. Simpson would marry the King but not become Queen. When Churchill pleaded in the House of Commons that precipitate action should be avoided, he had an exceedingly hostile reception, for the country as a whole was clearly moving to the conclusion that the King must go. If Edward VIII had been willing to postpone his marriage to Mrs. Simpson for a year or two, or at least until after the coronation in May 1937, there might have been a very slight chance that he could have established himself so firmly on the throne that he could have had both Mrs.

Simpson and his kingdom. In any event, there was no possibility of marriage until Mrs. Simpson's divorce was final in April. But the King was impatient, and when he abdicated on 11 December, it was probably with considerable relief. He handed over the throne to his brother, the deeply distressed but far more suitable Duke of York, who became King George VI.

The King was not forced off his throne by a government embarrassed by his alleged concern with the unemployed, with whom he once expressed sympathy, or because of his supposed fondness for Nazism, based on an alleged statement to the German ambassador that as long as he was King there would never be another war between Germany and Britain. The King went, in part, because of a sense of his own inadequacy, but primarily because of the conservative (not in the political sense) nature of the British people. Although they were deeply loyal to the monarchy, that loyalty extended to the monarch only if he embodied that institution as it had been modeled by Queen Victoria and Prince Albert, and by Kings **Edward VII** and George V. King Edward VIII, however, most certainly did not represent the values of his family, as his mother, Queen Mary, who never forgave him, made clear. The damage to the monarchy was thought to be great; as it turned out, the new King and Queen, and their daughters, rapidly repaired the damage.

In 1937 the former King was created Duke of Windsor by his brother, with the provision that neither his wife, nor his children, could bear the designation "Royal Highness." This was seen by the new Duke, correctly, as a snub and was a principal reason why he and the Duchess, whom he married in June 1937, never lived again in England. The bitterness was compounded by financial problems, as the Duke negotiated with his brother over the sale of privately held royal assets and about the Duke's allowance. The subsequent life of the Windsors was social, as it had always been, although there were events with political overtones, such as their visit to Adolf Hitler in October 1937. In 1940 a difficult problem arose concerning the safety of the Duke and Duchess, who fled to Portugal in advance of the Nazi conquest. There were rumors, probably unfounded, that the Germans intended to restore the Duke to the throne as a puppet king after their planned conquest of Britain. In the midst of the **Blitz**, Churchill arranged for the Windsors, much to their displeasure, to go to the Bahamas. There

the Duke remained Governor until 1945, after which they settled in Paris and resumed their previous style of life. Only rarely, such as on the occasion of his mother's death, did he return to England. He died in Paris in May 1972, shortly after receiving a visit from Queen Elizabeth II. He was buried in the Royal burial ground at Frogmore. The duchess attended the funeral and was herself buried at Frogmore in 1986, still not a "Royal Highness."

Arthur Mejia

Bibliography
Donaldson, Frances. *Edward VIII.* 1974.
Windsor, Duke of. *A King's Story.* 1951.
Ziegler, Philip. *King Edward VIII: The Official Biography.* 1990.

El Alamein, Battle of

El Alamein is a town on the Mediterranean coast of Egypt, west of the Nile. Three **Second World War** battles were fought in this vicinity in the summer and fall of 1942, during which the German drive into Egypt was stopped and finally thrown back.

In the spring of 1942 General Erwin Rommel's Axis forces, German and Italian, launched a new phase of the desert war, sending Britain's Eighth Army reeling back into Egypt to a position near El Alamein. Here the front became very narrow, hemmed in by the sea on the north and the Qattara Depression on the south. Thus it was an ideal defensive position for the British, apart from the fact that they were near their great bases in Alexandria and Cairo, while Rommel's supply line now stretched many hundreds of miles back into Libya. Nevertheless, Rommel attacked again on 1 July. General Sir Claude J. Auchinleck, Commander-in-Chief, Middle East, took personal command of the Eighth Army and counterattacked the next day; after weeks of battle, the opposing forces settled down to a stalemate. Although Auchinleck had done well, receiving praise from Rommel himself, **Winston Churchill** believed that new commanders were needed for decisive victory. Therefore, Auchinleck was replaced by General Sir Harold R. Alexander and the Eighth Army was given to General Sir **Bernard L. Montgomery.**

In the summer and fall of 1942 German commitments to the Russian front, British attacks on Italian convoys supplying Rommel, and large shipments of materiel (including

American **Lend-Lease**) to Montgomery all made Rommel's position increasingly precarious. He attempted to throw Montgomery off balance by attacking Alam Halfa ridge on 31 August but failed to budge the heavily entrenched British. On 23 October Montgomery attacked with massive superiority in men and materiel, yet the narrow frontage now worked to Axis advantage, and it was not until 4 November that the enemy had been ground down enough by attrition to make their situation hopeless. Rommel, who had returned to Egypt on 25 October from sick leave in Germany, now defied Adolf Hitler's orders and began a skillful retreat back to Libya and ultimately Tunisia; Montgomery's pursuit was lackluster.

El Alamein was celebrated by the British as a great and decisive victory, and it catapulted Montgomery to lasting fame. Yet it had been costly, and perhaps unnecessarily so: The Axis cause in Egypt would have been doomed with or without Montgomery's offensive because of the Anglo-American landings in French Northwest Africa beginning on 8 November, which threatened Rommel's supply ports from the rear. Perhaps if Montgomery had waited until just before 8 November to attack, Rommel's resistance would have been far less stubborn; still, Britain needed a victory of its own at that point in the war.

Karl G. Larew

Bibliography

Barnett, Correlli. *The Desert Generals.* 1982.
Carver, Michael. *Dilemmas of the Desert War.* 1986.
Lucas, James. *War in the Desert: The Eighth Army at El Alamein.* 1982.

Electoral System

At the beginning of the century about 60 percent of men over age twenty-one had the right to vote. Most of them qualified under the householder franchise, which had given the franchise to adult male heads of households in boroughs in 1867 and in county constituencies in 1885. Because the older property qualifications still survived, plural voting by people who owned property in several places continued, though the lodger franchise did mean that some relatively prosperous nonhouseholders also had a right to vote. The redistribution of seats in the 1885 act had taken a step toward "one vote, one value," though attention was still paid to the old idea of communities on which the House of Commons had been based since the thirteenth century. In the early years of the twentieth century the electorate was a little over 7 million, and the House of Commons had 670 members.

Between 1906 and 1918 the only change in the national electoral system was that the 1911 Parliament Act required a general election every five years instead of every seven years. Women householders had gained the right to vote in municipal elections in 1869, and pressure for them to gain the right to vote in national elections attracted more attention and caused more disturbance than any other franchise issue before the war, though plural voting, the position of unenfranchised men, and the disparities in size among constituencies were all discussed. Wartime pressure for votes for soldiers and sailors, and more generally for democracy in the sense of universal suffrage, led to the 1918 Representation of the People Act. It dealt with all of these questions: It put men on the electoral register (to be drawn up twice a year, though retrenchment soon reduced this to once a year) at age twenty-one subject to a simple residence requirement; it put women on the register at age thirty subject to the slightly more complicated residence qualifications required for voting in municipal elections; it redrew the boundaries of seats in a way that recognized numerical equality as the basic principle for constituencies; and it provided for postal voting for men and women away from home in military service (and retained it for the universities).

Plural voting would have been greatly reduced by this residence-based system and by the new provision that all constituencies were to vote on the same day, but in any case no voter was allowed to vote in more than two constituencies; some people qualified for a vote for business premises, which produced about 250,000 additional votes, mainly for offices in the center of cities, and others received votes as university graduates, who numbered about 200,000 by 1945. To take account of the emergence of new universities, their total representation was increased from nine to fifteen (subsequently reduced to twelve as a result of the **Irish treaty**). Other changes in constituency boundaries recognized that the population was continuing to move from city centers and from the countryside into the suburbs. Limits on spending were reduced to a level that made it unlikely that candidates even in the largest constituencies could spend much more than £1,000, and the government relieved them from having to pay for the returning officers and other officials who ran the elections, though they had to put up a deposit of £150 (refunded if they obtained 12.5 percent of the votes cast) to reduce the risk of freak or frivolous candidacies. This act increased the electorate to 21 million and the seats in Parliament to 707, subsequently reduced to 615 by changes in Ireland. A separate act passed later in 1918 enabled women to stand for Parliament on the same terms as men, and the differences in the age and residence requirements, originally introduced to ensure that women should not become a majority of the electorate, were ended in 1928.

In 1944 it was recognized that further changes in the distribution of population once more meant that the outer districts of large cities were underrepresented. There was no time to do more before an election than create an additional twenty-five seats and set up a Boundary Commission to make changes for the future on a regular basis, within the limits of the representation given to the four countries in the United Kingdom by existing legislation, and with some regard for areas like Anglesey (as the present-day constituency of Ynys Mon was known), the Isle of Wight, Orkney and Shetland, and the Western Isles. Except for geographical areas like these, seats are not expected to have more than 25 percent more or 25 percent less than the average number of voters, and relatively few seats come close to so large a deviation from the average. At first it was thought that boundary changes could take place during the lifetime of each Parliament, but such frequent alterations would have been so great a strain on constituency organization that they were almost immediately based on the decennial census. The limits on spending were reduced once more and (in money terms) for the last time, though subsequent increases have not fully kept up with rises in prices. Campaigning in the second half of the century has focused more and more on the national activity of the central organizations and on newspaper and poster advertising before the election period has begun; neither of these developments was foreseen when limits were being placed on expenditures, and they are not subject to the constituency-based limits on spending that started in 1883. Parties are not able to buy broadcasting time for **advertising**, but as a public service free

time is allocated to them for the period between elections and—with rather more argument about the allocation of the time—during elections.

After the war the 1948 act abolished all plural voting and ended the university seats, and the House of Commons was reduced to 625 MP seats; it has remained close to that number in the decennial readjustments of seats. The act also provided for voting by mail for invalids and for those who had moved out of the constituency after the electoral register was published. In 1969 the reduction of the age of majority to eighteen led to a reduction of the age at which people received the right to vote.

In 1918 there was some discussion of changing the voting system to the "alternative vote," or the "single transferable vote," and the latter system was adopted for university seats. The question was considered by the government in 1929, when **Labour** was in office for the second time without any clear majority in Parliament or in the electorate, and the issue has been kept alive by subsequent elections in which minor parties like the **Liberals** have gained far fewer seats than their share of the popular vote suggests they might expect, but no steps have been taken along these lines in Britain. The United Kingdom has had eighty-one seats in the European Parliament since it joined the **European Community** in 1973. Elections have been held for these seats since 1979, using the same first-past-the-post voting system in Britain for them as for national elections, despite the general European reluctance to use that method.

Although it became less common for individuals to move from municipal office onto the national stage, municipal elections became more and more a branch of national party politics in the first half of the century, and by 1950 all municipalities of any size were run on party political lines after elections in which voting was determined by the popularity of parties at Westminster. The same readiness to vote in response to Westminster politics was visible in the first elections to the European Parliament. Voter turnout in municipal and in European elections has steadily been lower than in general elections, and in national elections it has never matched the polls of over 80 percent recorded in 1950 and 1951. Since then it has fluctuated around 75 percent, with some tendency for turnout to be lower in solidly held seats than in marginal seats; it is hard to tell whether this is the result of voter sophistication or of the parties' readiness to concentrate their full-time election agents in marginal seats. The main change in the electoral activity in the twentieth century is the increased importance of the political parties; the role of the national campaign by the party leader has become greater, broadcasting is conducted on lines laid down by discussions among the parties, and the polling of public opinion, which has become so important a tool for devising party strategy, is too complex and too expensive to be carried out on anything other than a party basis. Apart from a few changes like allowing candidates to list their party affiliation on the ballot paper, much of the advance of the parties to the center of the stage has proceeded without official recognition or restraint, and it is accepted much more fully than is sometimes pretended.

Trevor Lloyd

Bibliography

Butler, David. *The Electoral System in Britain since 1918.* 2nd ed. 1963.

Cook, Chris, and John Ramsden, eds. *By-Elections in British Politics.* 1973.

Craig, F.W.S. *British Electoral Facts, 1832–1980.* 1981.

———. *British Parliamentary Election Results, 1918–1949.* 2nd ed. 1977.

———. *British Parliamentary Election Results, 1950–1973.* 2nd ed. 1981.

———. *British Parliamentary Election Results, 1974–1983.* 1984.

Kinnear, Michael. *The British Voter.* 2nd ed. 1981.

Elgar, Edward William (1857–1934)

One of the most important English composers since Purcell, Edward Elgar made significant contributions to most musical genres, bringing the Victorian cantata and oratorio to fruition and establishing the British twentieth-century symphonic tradition. Elgar was capable of writing popular music of distinction, and the central tune from his first *Pomp and Circumstance March* (1901), when linked with Arthur Benson's patriotic words, "Land of hope and glory," became England's second national anthem. Born at Broadheath, near Worcester, the son of a tradesman, Elgar was gentlemanly by nature, and, with the help of his wife Alice, became a gentleman in fact, counting royalty among his friends. Following an honorary doctorate from **Cambridge** (1900), Elgar received

many official honors, including a knighthood (1904), the Order of Merit (1911), and a baronetcy (1931), and was appointed Master of the King's Music in 1924.

Although Elgar received some formal instrumental tuition including violin lessons from Adolf Pollitzer in London (1877–8), he was self-taught as a composer, absorbing what he needed from books and scores in his father's music shop at Worcester. He gained experience in performing and conducting in local music making, but his main livelihood was as a local violin teacher. Moving further afield, he joined W.C. Stockley's orchestra at Birmingham, which performed his *Sérénade mauresque* on 13 December 1883, and the following year *Sevillana* was given by August Manns at the Crystal Palace, London, a performance brought about by Pollitzer. Elgar's meeting with (Caroline) Alice Roberts, the daughter of a major-general, and his subsequent marriage to her (1889), brought him increased social status as well as confidence and spiritual support, but a move to London in 1889 to establish himself met with failure. The overture *Froissart* (1890), headed with an epigraph from Keats, "When chivalry lifted up her lance on high," was successfully performed in Worcester but not heard in London. Although Elgar, now in his mid-thirties, had to return to Worcestershire (Malvern) and to resume the modest career of a provincial music teacher, he did not abandon composition, testifying to his and his wife's strong belief in his latent genius. He wisely turned to the late Victorian market for festival cantatas and oratorios, and, returning to chivalry for his subject matter, composed *The Black Knight* (Uhland, trans. Longfellow, 1892), to be followed by the short oratorio *The Light of Life* (1896) and the cantatas *Scenes from the Saga of King Olaf* (Longfellow/H.A. Acworth, 1896) and *Caractacus* (Acworth, 1898), the latter set partly in the Malvern Hills and Severn valley. Drawing on his expanding knowledge of the nineteenth-century orchestral and operatic repertoire, gained at the Crystal Palace concerts when living in London and on visits to Bayreuth and Munich to hear Wagner's later operas (1892–3), Elgar reached an intensity in his developing style in *King Olaf* that heralds maturity, as it does in the slow movement of the Serenade for Strings (1892) and parts of the Organ Sonata (1895).

However, it was not until the orchestral Variations on an Original Theme ("Enigma")

(1899), dedicated to "My Friends Pictured Within," that Elgar reached musical maturity, significantly in the company of his wife (Variation 1) and friends (Variations 2–13), with Elgar himself as the final variation. More enigmatic than the variations (but not titled as such) was the sacred cantata *The Dream of Gerontius* (John Henry Newman, 1900), its Catholic text (Elgar was **Roman Catholic**) unsympathetic to some music lovers and especially to those members of the **Anglican** establishment who had the text's doctrinal infelicities expunged before performance in their cathedrals. Because of its difficulty and problems at rehearsal, the premiere at the Birmingham Triennial Festival (1900) was a failure, but a performance at the Lower Rhine Festival, Dusseldorf, in May 1902, conducted by Julius Buths, revealed the work's true stature. *Gerontius* was followed by the oratorio *The Apostles* (Elgar, after Bible, 1903), an advance on the former work in chromatic language and architectural grandeur, and *The Kingdom* (Elgar, after Bible, 1906), although the final oratorio in the planned trilogy was never completed. Elgar's faith wavered; his duties as the first Peyton Professor of Music at Birmingham University (1905–8) sapped his energy. Instead, building on his increasing mastery of purely instrumental music in the overtures *Cockaigne (In London Town)* (1901) and *In the South (Alassio)* (1904), and in the Introduction and Allegro for strings (1905), Elgar embarked upon two symphonies (A-flat Major, 1908; E-flat Major, 1911), the first of which was performed nearly 100 times during its first year. The opening theme, typically marked *Nobilmente*, and returning several times during the opening movement and finale, acts as a unifying agent, as does the idea of basing the third, slow movement on a melody that is a thematic transformation of the second, the scherzo. Between the two symphonies came the richly expressive Violin Concerto (1910), unusual for its accompanied cadenza and inspired possibly by a temporary romance.

In 1912 Elgar's move from Hereford, near where he had lived since 1904, to Hampstead in London, was marked by the completion of an ode for alto, chorus, and orchestra, *The Music Makers* (O'Shaughnessy, 1912), which forms, with its use of self-quotation, a retrospective of Elgar's achievements to date. More backward glances followed in *Falstaff* (1913), an extended "symphonic study," where a return to knightly virtues, but not vices, reveals an Elgarian quasi-

autobiographical interpretation of Shakespeare's character. The First World War, coming at a crucial moment in Elgar's creative development, stifled its impulse, although in *The Spirit of England* (Binyon, 1917), his last major work for soloists, chorus, and orchestra, the elegiac lament for the fallen is sustained with great compassion. A sudden efflorescence in 1918–19 produced three chamber works, the String Quartet, Violin Sonata, and Piano Quintet, all three also backward-looking to a certain extent, paying homage in part to Brahms. However, Elgar's late style is fully encapsulated in the Cello Concerto (1919), by turns poignantly elegiac, capricious, and passionate; in it, Elgar laments the passing of his own world. Following the death of his wife in 1920, Elgar completed no further works of substance, although a legacy of recordings of him conducting his own compositions was completed (1914–33). He returned to Worcester to live out his last years.

Trevor Bray

Bibliography

Kennedy, Michael. *Portrait of Elgar.* new ed. 1973.

Maine, Basil. *Elgar: His Life and Works.* 2 vols. 1933.

Moore, Jerrold Northrop. *Edward Elgar: A Creative Life.* 1984.

———, ed. *Edward Elgar: Letters of a Lifetime.* 1990.

Eliot, T(homas) S(tearns) (1888–1965)

Poet, essayist, playwright, critic, and "dictator" of literary taste, T.S. Eliot exerted an influence unequaled in Britain or the United States between the two world wars and after. Expatriated from the United States in his twenties, Eliot became a British citizen and embraced Anglo-Catholicism in 1927. His long poem *The Waste Land* (1922) seemed to mirror, if through a broken glass, the horror of post-war Europe. Its fragmentation and haunting musicality seemed apocalyptic in a world of shattered institutions and betrayed hopes.

A defender of tradition and orthodoxy, Eliot nevertheless led a poetic revolution. He denied the existence of *vers libre* but was responsible for some of the most radical innovations in verse form of the century. He was fastidious and socially conservative, and yet he was seen as a force for liberation by readers across the political spectrum.

Eliot's grandfather, a New Englander, chose a spiritual mission to the frontier: He established a Unitarian Church in St. Louis and in 1853 founded Washington University. Eliot's father was a successful businessman, a brick manufacturer, who was disappointed by his youngest son's choice of a literary vocation and did not live to see his success at it. His mother, a poet herself, nurtured his early literary interests.

Eliot entered Harvard University in 1906 and studied literature, **philosophy**, and **history** during what has been called Harvard's "glacial era" for its conservatism. He encountered there, among other luminaries, George Santayana, **Bertrand Russell**, Josiah Royce, and Irving Babbitt. The latter, whose lectures on the evils of romanticism complemented Eliot's own instinctive self-denial and rationalism, was especially influential. After a year in Paris (1910–11), Eliot began graduate work in philosophy at Harvard, eventually returning to Europe on a traveling fellowship in 1914. He completed his doctoral dissertation on the skeptical idealist philosopher F.H. Bradley in 1916 but never went back to claim the degree.

While at Harvard, Eliot studied Dante and Baudelaire intently and discovered, by reading Arthur Symons' *The Symbolist Movement in Literature*, the French poet Jules Laforgue. Eliot later described Laforgue as the poetic personality that had allowed him to find his own subject matter and voice—ironic, aloof, and disillusioned. "I learned," Eliot said, "that the sort of material I had, the sort of experience that an adolescent had had, in an industrial city in America, could be the material for poetry." The language, rhythms, and speech, he later wrote, of his immediate predecessors in the Anglo-American literary world were inadequate for the feelings of the poet writing of the "more sordid aspects of the modern metropolis."

The emotional expressiveness and power of Eliot's loosened verse form became clear in the poems collected in *Prufrock and Other Observations* (1917), a landmark of modernist writing. Eliot takes his reader into an urban phantasmagoria in these poems: Ghastly streets and strange surrealized drawing rooms reflect the states of the passionless, isolated souls of his poetic characters. In "The Love Song of J. Alfred Prufrock" (1915), the cityscape—the cat-like yellow fog, the "muttering retreats," and "sawdust restaurants"—seems responsible for the narrator's psychological malaise, his inability to "force the moment to its crisis."

Prufrock's problem is not just personal, but public and generational. This collection was followed by *Poems* (1920), with "Gerontion" (1920) as the leading item; and *Poems, 1909–1925*, which included "The Hollow Men" (1925).

Eliot's marriage to an Englishwoman, Vivien Haigh-Wood, in the summer of 1915 after a two-month acquaintance was a disaster for both parties. They were two temperaments at odds, incompatible in personal disposition and in background. Financial difficulties, compounded by Vivien's frequent physical and emotional illnesses and the disapproval of his family, led to a nervous breakdown for Eliot in 1921.

While recuperating in Lausanne, Switzerland, Eliot completed work on *The Waste Land*. The double crushing weight of a sense of personal loss and of cultural disintegration are felt in this echo chamber of historical significances. Disembodied voices are let loose like the furies on an "Unreal City," London as Dante's hell, doubling as every city in Europe. In this barren and dessicated land, sexuality has lost its fruitfulness. The poem is both a terrifying critique of a civilization and a passionate and lyrical cry of personal anguish. Lacking a single narrative center, the poem depends on fragmentation, a structural device that imitates the social deformations of the modern world. Eliot dedicated the poem to his friend Ezra Pound, whom he called "*il miglior fabbro*," the better craftsman, for his work editing the poem. The rediscovery of the manuscript of the poem in 1971 revealed that Pound had cut long narrative and dramatic sections and created the poem's montage effects of juxtaposition and contrast.

Eliot left Vivien Eliot in 1932 after years of acute mutual anguish. She died in a mental hospital in 1947. Eliot's second marriage in 1957, to Valerie Fletcher, his longtime secretary at the London **publishing** firm of Faber and Faber, brought him comfort and happiness during the final years of his life.

Eliot's powerful, polemical voice as essayist set the intellectual agenda for several generations of critics. He shaped and manipulated his own career through his criticism, even as he revised according to his tastes the history of poetry in English. Among his most striking essays from his early career are "Reflections on *vers libre*" (1917), "Tradition and the Individual Talent" (1919), "*Hamlet*" (1919), and "The Metaphysical Poets" (1921); from his late career, *Idea of a Christian Society* (1939), "The

Music of Poetry" (1942), and "From Poe to Valéry" (1948).

Eliot's social and political conservatism became increasingly pronounced in his critical writing dating from the mid-1920s. In 1933 he delivered at the University of Virginia his most notorious lecture series, later collected as *After Strange Gods: A Primer of Modern Heresy* (1934). In these talks, he made disparaging remarks about "foreign races" and "free-thinking Jews." He later refused to have the collection reprinted because of his embarrassment about its content.

Eliot's embrace of Anglo-Catholicism ultimately moderated the tone of his conservatism. His "Ariel Poems," published between 1927 and 1930, and his lyrical meditation *Ash Wednesday* (1930) work explicitly within the framework of Christian symbolism and contend with the problem of Incarnation. "Burnt Norton" (1936), the first of Eliot's *Four Quartets* (1943), is a meditation on temporality and on intimations of the eternal, tested against the fragile beauty of the natural world. The remaining three *Quartets*, "East Coker (1940)," "The Dry Salvages" (1941), and "Little Gidding" (1942), were written during the Second World War. Eliot takes his measure of the "topography of pain" in these religious poems, not through doctrinal claims, but through the ruggedness of experience.

Eliot devoted much of his creative energy in his late career to the writing of plays in verse. The lyricism of the voices of the chorus, the "poor women of Canterbury," in Eliot's poetic drama *Murder in the Cathedral* (1935), about the martyrdom of Thomas à Becket, represents the fulfillment of his ambitions to create a naturalistic theater in verse. *The Family Reunion*, a complex psychodrama about marital guilt, was first staged in 1939. After the war he produced three more plays, *The Cocktail Party* (1950), *The Confidential Clerk* (1954), and *The Elder Statesman* (1959). Eliot's verses for children, *Old Possum's Book of Practical Cats* (1939), achieved posthumous notoriety in the celebrated stage musical *Cats* in 1981.

Eliot was awarded the Nobel Prize for Literature and the Order of Merit in 1948. At midcentury, his preeminence seemed unshakable. Since then, he has come to seem more vulnerable—sometimes the subject of caricature—even as he still seems threatening. His star has fallen with, though not as far as, that of the "New Critics" he inspired. Eliot used avant-garde techniques for conservative ends. His politics were irrational and elitist. Yet he looked with unguarded eye at the "modern metropolis," and his social conscience dictated his decisions about poetic form. His monumental achievement can be measured not only in positive responses, but also in counterattacks: Many poets and critics alike, of his own generation and since, have honored him by defining their work against his strong influence. He captured the voices of a civilization in turmoil, and his taste defined an era. The pain and compassion of his poetry, and the strength of his critical imagination, remain compelling.

Elizabeth Muther

Bibliography

Behr, Caroline. *T.S. Eliot: A Chronology of His Life and Works.* 1983.
Bush, Ronald. *T.S. Eliot: A Study in Character and Style.* 1983.
Eliot, T.S. *The Letters of T.S. Eliot.* vol. 1: *1898–1922.* Valerie Eliot, ed. 1988.
Gordon, Lyndall. *Eliot's New Life.* 1988.
Moody, A.D. *Thomas Stearns Eliot, Poet.* 1979.
Ricks, Beatrice, comp. *T.S. Eliot: A Bibliography of Secondary Works.* 1980.

Ellis, (Henry) Havelock (1859–1939)

Havelock Ellis was Britain's foremost pioneer and popularizer of sexual **psychology**. Unlike his contemporary Sigmund Freud, he did not found a school of followers, nor did he ever organize his empirical studies into a firm theoretical framework; he also lacked Freud's clinical insight. Consequently, his work has not had the enduring influence of **psychoanalysis**. He did contribute to the sexual vocabulary such terms as "autoerotism," "narcissism," and "urolagnia," and he was one of the developers of the theory of erogenous zones.

The son of an often absent ship's captain and a strong-willed evangelical mother, Ellis, like many Victorian intellectuals, was diverted from a clerical career by religious doubts. He found inspiration in the works of George Drysdale and James Hinton (who both preached sexual freedom) and studied medicine at St. Thomas' Hospital.

Gifted with Jovian good looks, a feminine gentleness, and a sympathetic ear, Ellis was an attractive figure to emancipated women. He enjoyed long romances with Olive Schreiner and Margaret Sanger. His marriage to Edith Lees (1861–1916) was strained by her lesbianism, her violent temper, her lack of success as a writer, and his sexual inadequacy. After she died, he lived more happily with Françoise Delisle. Though Ellis advocated sexual freedom for women, his *Man and Woman* (1894) reflected Victorian assumptions about the sexes—that women were naturally passive and found fulfillment in childbearing, while intellectual genius and sexual aggression were usually limited to men.

In *Sexual Inversion* (1897) Ellis argued for toleration of **homosexuality**. Unfortunately, he gave the book to a shady publisher, and a bookseller was successfully prosecuted for selling it. It would be the first of seven volumes of *Studies in the Psychology of Sex* (1897–1928), published in the United States and translated into several languages. (No complete edition has ever been published in Britain.) Ellis was criticized for focusing on the exotic and the pathological, rather than on the everyday sex problems of married couples. Not until the sixth volume of *Studies* (1910) did he turn to such mundane issues as sex education, **marriage**, and mothering.

Ellis and Freud corresponded extensively and drew on each other's work, but at several points they diverged. Though they discovered dream analysis almost simultaneously, Ellis did not believe that dreams solely reflected wish fulfillment, and he thought Freud had overstressed sex as the prime mover behind human behavior. For Ellis, sexual psychology was shaped mainly by **genetics**; Freud looked more to environmental causes.

Ellis sometimes regretted that the general public knew him only as a writer on sex. He published more than fifty books on such topics as socialism, medicine, **philosophy**, religion, literature, travel, criminology, **eugenics**, and women's rights. He also edited the Mermaid series of Elizabethan dramatists, the Contemporary Science series of popular textbooks, and the first English editions of the plays of Ibsen.

Jonathan Rose

Bibliography

Brome, Vincent. *Havelock Ellis: Philosopher of Sex*. 1979.
Grosskurth, Phyllis. *Havelock Ellis: A Biography*. 1980.
Rowbotham, Sheila, and Jeffrey Weeks. *Socialism and the New Life: The Personal and Sexual Politics of Edward Carpenter and Havelock Ellis*. 1977.
Summers, Anne. "The Correspondents of Havelock Ellis," *History Workshop*, vol. 32 (1991), pp. 167–83.

Emigration

Emigration from the United Kingdom in the twentieth century initially consolidated the pioneering impact of previous generations of settlers upon the world's demographic, economic, political, and cultural geography. Since the principal destination of British emigrants also shifted early in this period from the United States to the white-settler societies of **Canada, Australia, New Zealand**, and to a lesser extent **South Africa**, emigration strengthened for a while the British character of these original heartlands of the Empire-Commonwealth. Such a shift largely reflected altering economic opportunities overseas, but it was also affected by changes in government policy. In the early twentieth-century, governments in Britain and the Commonwealth became more involved in determining the volume and character of migration—for example, through the provision of assisted passages, which the British government financed after the First World War and formally maintained long after the Second. Nevertheless, emigration became demographically, economically, and politically less welcome to the United Kingdom, and immigration ultimately less significant to the former settler societies of the Commonwealth, which increasingly recruited elsewhere such immigrants as they needed.

Long-term comparisons of the volume of emigration by U.K. citizens are complicated because only after 1913 were emigrants distinguished officially in the records from other passengers leaving the country. Nevertheless, assuming for the earlier period the same ratio between emigrants and other passengers as existed for the later, it is certain that emigration was high, even by nineteenth-century standards, in the decade 1901–10, probably amounting to over 1,816,000. In 1913 alone the recorded total reached a peak of 389,394. Figures after the war were never again so high, but they still totaled 1,811,553 between 1920 and 1929. True, in the Depression that followed, the total for 1930–8 was down to 334,467; indeed, for the first time net **immigration** was registered in that period. However, in the 1950s net emigration partly recovered to over 652,000 in the decade.

Compared with the population of the United Kingdom as a whole, emigrants were disproportionately young (mainly under forty-five) and included a more even balance of men and women and more young children than had been the case in the previous century (when single adult males had been more numerous). In-depth studies of the social and occupational backgrounds and regional origins of twentieth-century emigrants have scarcely begun, although it is known that most (though less so the Irish) came from urban roots and had commercial and industrial occupations. Certainly, most were destined for urban employment overseas, in spite of repeated attempts to settle them in rural areas. What is not known is the feature that distinguishes emigrants from those many more United Kingdom citizens of similar backgrounds who chose not to migrate. One distinguishing feature was probably the emigration of those with family or friends already overseas, so-called chain migration, a practice that would consolidate areas of existing British settlement. But such an explanation does little to account for the change in the direction of British emigration away from destinations in the United States toward the less densely settled societies of the British Empire, the Dominions.

In the 1880s and 1890s less than one-third of British emigrants sailed to Empire destinations, and most of the rest crossed to the United States. But nearly half embarked for the Dominions between 1901 and 1910, and as many as two-thirds in 1911 and 1912. In the 1920s over 65 percent chose homes in the Dominions; and nearly 47 percent did so in the 1930s even amid the difficulties of the Depression. After the Second World War opinion polls repeatedly showed a preference for Commonwealth instead of American destinations among those interested in emigration. The change largely reflected the expanding and more varied employment opportunities opening up in the Dominions as a result of economic diversification and urbanization, and the development of speedier, safer, and more comfortable sea, and later air, transport between the United Kingdom and Australasia, virtually eliminating the ordeal of earlier emigration voyages to those distant Empire destinations. In addition, ideological factors may have been involved: It is probable that imperial sentiment achieved a deeper penetration of British **popular culture** in the first half of the twentieth century, and this may have induced more British emigrants to settle among those commonly described as "kith and kin."

But such a shift was also encouraged early in the century by British and Dominions governments either to increase or certainly to deflect the existing flows of emigrants leaving the United Kingdom to British territories overseas. Some interest groups in the Dominions, such as labor organizations, Canadian nationalists, and the Afrikaners in South Africa, were often hostile toward the influx of yet more immigrants from Britain. But except in the last case or at times of local economic depression, they were normally unable to dent the prevailing popular and political sentiment that the immigrants needed for the further expansion of these British societies overseas should normally be drawn from the Mother Country. Certainly the governments of Canada, Australia, and New Zealand at various periods in the twentieth century, as earlier, attempted to attract selected immigrants from Britain, often with cheap sea passages or other inducements. It was, however, more remarkable when the British government first provided free passages to the Dominions for ex-servicemen and their families in 1919 and then passed the Empire Settlement Act in 1922. This legislation allowed for the expenditure of up to £3 million a year upon assisted passages for emigrants and overseas land settlement schemes, in financial cooperation with the Dominions. Imperial visionaries in the United Kingdom had been urging the British government to adopt such measures at least since the 1880s as a constructive response to the problems of poverty and social and political unrest at home and rising economic and political competition overseas: The redistribution of "surplus" British labor (including single women and orphaned or deprived children) in the underdeveloped territories of the Empire was popularly regarded as an important part of a process of imperial social and economic engineering. The onset of mass **unemployment** in Britain after the First World War was, however, the immediate trigger, and the imperial enthusiast Leo Amery (1873–1955), seizing his chance, was the principal ministerial architect.

Between 1922 and 1936 the Empire Settlement Act provided assisted passages for 405,230 people, about 36 percent of the total who emigrated to the Empire in these years: 186,524 went to Canada, 172,735 to Australia, and 44,745 to New Zealand (plus a mere

1,226 to South Africa). Substantial though these figures were in aggregate, they fell below the hopes of imperial visionaries. It is probable that the Empire Settlement Act increased the flow of emigration, encouraged the exodus of families, single females, and children (for whom special schemes were devised), and diverted some emigrants away from non-Commonwealth destinations. Symptomatically, however, the British government never managed to spend all the money allocated to the scheme. Although the act was renewed with less funding in 1937 (and again in 1952, 1957, 1962, and 1967 and only expired in 1972), doubts had grown by then about the merits of Empire migration that were never subsequently erased.

Demographic developments had made observers increasingly skeptical about mass migration. Birthrates were falling in Britain during the first half of the century, making the loss of young, fertile, and perhaps more enterprising citizens a hemorrhage the country could not apparently afford to encourage. The implications for the British economy and society of a declining and ageing work force were worrying. Moreover, given the larger populations of the Dominions, their own natural increases (the excess of births over deaths) were proportionately more vital to further growth than immigrants. True, the threat of Japanese invasion during the Second World War provoked a vigorous attempt subsequently to increase Australia's population through immigration, but by then the modestly growing size of the U.K. population finally required Australia (and other Commonwealth counties) to look outside the Mother Country and eventually even outside Europe for proportionately more of such stock as had to be imported. Commonwealth governments were also becoming more cautious about the immigrants they allowed in and assisted; increasingly, skilled workers only were required or those with capital or proven professional or entrepreneurial skills. These were, of course, also the personnel who in most cases could find attractive opportunities at home and whom the United Kingdom could least afford to lose.

In brief, since the Second World War the distinction between developed and developing economies, which earlier had encouraged mass migration from the United Kingdom to the United States and latterly to the Commonwealth, had largely eroded. At the same time, the self-interest the British government had

briefly seen in fostering imperial development by state-assisted settlement of "surplus" stock in the Dominions went into decline. A belief in the natural harmony among the parts of the Empire was giving way to increased competition for assets among the nations of the Commonwealth. Emigration, from a free society, could not be prevented, but it was no longer encouraged.

Stephen Constantine

Bibliography

Bean, Phillip, and Joy Melville. *Lost Children of the Empire.* 1989.

Carrier, N.H., and J.A. Jeffery. *External Migration, 1814–1950: A Study of the Available Statistics.* 1953.

Constantine, Stephen, ed. *Emigrants and Empire: British Settlement in the Dominions between the Wars.* 1990.

Monk, Una B. *New Horizons: A Hundred Years of Women's Migration.* 1963.

Plant, G.F. *Oversea Settlement: Migration from the United Kingdom to the Dominions.* 1951.

Entertainments National Service Association (ENSA)

One of the two largest civilian entertainment agencies ever organized (second only in size to the United Services Organization, or USO), ENSA was formed in 1938 to provide entertainment to the British and Allied armed forces at home and abroad. During the Second World War ENSA employed nearly 4,000 artists and supplied a full range of entertainment from soloists and stand-up comics to symphony orchestras and full-length plays.

In 1938, with the threat of war looming, Basil Dean, an established London theatrical director and producer, conceived of a voluntary organization to supply musical and theatrical entertainment wherever British troops were stationed. Failing to obtain the official sanction of the War Office, ENSA secured financial backing from the Navy, Army, and Air Force Institutes (NAAFI) in 1939. Among the talents ENSA attracted to its cause were the composers and conductors Sir Henry Wood, Arnold Bax, William Walton, and Sir Malcolm Sargent, who served on the advisory council of ENSA Music Division.

At the start of the war, blackout restrictions caused many of London's theaters to close, freeing large numbers of actors and performers to enlist with ENSA. Even so, the early days of the organization were characterized by the squabbling of agents, unions, and performers over the direction ENSA should take. Dust settled with the naming of the Theatre Royal, Drury Lane, as the official headquarters where shows were rehearsed and approved before being exported to the front. Actors and musicians traveled to the remotest outposts of the conflict—the Middle East, North Africa, and Singapore—to perform for the troops. When artists couldn't appear, films were shown. Seventy-four ENSA film units were continually in action giving up to 500 shows a week.

Inevitably, distance and excessive demand took a toll on the organization. ENSA was both affectionately and ambivalently referred to as "Every Night Something Awful" and "Every Night Same Act." In 1941 ENSA's four-year monopoly on army stages came to an end when the War Office instituted a dance band and concert party in each unit. But by 1946 ENSA had staged almost 3 million performances with an attendance exceeding 300 million. Many actors who had enjoyed only modest success on London's stages saw their careers flourish during the war. Terry Thomas was among those whose ascent to fame began in army uniform, and established entertainers, such as Gracie Fields, came out of retirement expressly to entertain the troops. Several servicemen discovered their true calling on the stages of ENSA and the RAF Gang Show. Tommy Cooper and Dick Emery owed their later careers as comedians to their wartime entertainment experience. Under the auspices of ENSA unprecedented numbers were exposed to the talents of such performers as Joyce Grenfell, John Gielgud, and Sir Adrian Boult, enlarging the demand and support for the arts in post-war Britain.

Martha A. Schütz

Bibliography

Dean, Basil. *The Theatre at War.* 1956.
Fawkes, Richard. *Fighting for a Laugh: Entertaining the British and American Armed Forces, 1939–1946.* 1978.
Hughes, John Graven. *The Greasepaint War: Show Business, 1939–45.* 1976.

Entrepreneurship

The identification of marketplace opportunities and their profitable exploitation have been important elements of Britain's economic performance throughout the twentieth century, the tariff protection of the 1930s and the **nationalized industries** of the post-1945 period notwithstanding. The economy's reliance on foreign materials and manufactures, the liberalization of international trade through the General Agreement on Tariffs and Trade (GATT), the European Free Trade Area (EFTA), and the **European Union,** and the pressure of overseas competition have ensured that living standards and employment have been closely bound up with the success of British owners and managers in organizing production and distribution efficiently. Over the course of the century, though, the requirements of the entrepreneurial task have been altered as the shape of the British economy and its constituent firms has changed.

Since 1900 production and distribution in Britain have been increasingly concentrated in large enterprises. The share of net manufacturing output produced by the 100 biggest industrial companies increased from 15 percent in 1909 to 45 percent in 1970, and the preponderance of substantial concerns may have been even more marked in the service sector. Small firms have declined in number and importance (the share of manufacturing output produced by companies employing 200 people or less fell from 35 percent in 1935 to 16 percent in 1963), and in most industries trade has become primarily the province of a small number of firms. Already by 1930 the five largest companies accounted for more than 65 percent of production in vehicles, chemicals, and food and tobacco, and for more than 50 percent in engineering, textiles, and clothing and footwear.

This shift from atomistic industries to oligarchic ones has transformed the nature of competition in the British economy. Marketplace success has become less a matter of efficient production and low costs and more a function of enterprise capability over a wide spectrum of activities: from the acquisition of raw materials, through the design of products and their physical production and distribution, to quality control, marketing, **advertising,** and financing. In order to ensure the efficient performance of these functions British companies have reduced their reliance on outside contractors, choosing instead to acquire the personnel and facilities to conduct them in-house. As they have built up these diverse capabilities, British firms have had to utilize them as fully as possible lest the cost of internalization prove prohibitive—hence their movement into new product lines and new geographical markets. By the 1970s the majority of Britain's leading companies had become highly diversified, **multinational corporations.**

The profitable operation of these complex businesses has required managerial expertise at three levels: the monitoring of the daily operations of individual plants, warehouses, and offices; the allocation of resources among these different units over the medium term; and long-term strategic planning for the enterprise as a whole. This combination of competencies has exceeded the abilities of even the most energetic and most gifted individuals, so the successful exploitation of commercial opportunities has demanded the elaboration of managerial hierarchies with clear chains of command and effective channels for the flow of information.

The organizational requirements of modern British businesses have not rendered the individual entrepreneur superfluous. Since bureaucracies do not build themselves, the capacity for organization has come to rank with a keen eye for products, techniques, and markets as an essential element of the entrepreneur's craft. Individuals who have excelled in this capacity have dominated British business in the twentieth century as surely as did the industrial patriarchs of preceding periods. **Alfred Mond** and Harry McGowan (1874–1961), who together centralized, simplified, and rationalized the decision-making apparatus at the chemicals giant ICI, and Francis D'Arcy Cooper (1882–1941) and Geoffrey Heyworth (1894–1974), who did the same for the soap and edible-fats concern Unilever, were no less important to their firms and the national economy than the Arkwrights, Wedgwoods, Chamberlains, and Cadburys before them.

ICI and Unilever, of course, were vast enterprises with assets that exceeded the resources of the wealthiest individuals and families. Their ownership, therefore, had to be spread over a large number of individuals and institutions. In the process, ownership and management tended to separate, and entrepreneurial responsibilities devolved upon professional managers with little or no stake in the ownership of the firms over which they presided. McGowan, Cooper, and Heyworth, for example, were essentially paid employees of the firms they organized.

Modern Britain has benefited from entrepreneurs who were quick to capitalize on new products, processes, and markets. The careers of men such as William Lever (1851–1925) and **William Morris,** Viscount Nuffield, testify to the enduring importance of traditional business acumen. In a world of multiunit, multifunction, multinational enterprises, however, this talent could reap its fullest reward only when it was allied with the capacity for corporate organization. The divergent fates of Morris Motors and Lever Brothers after their founders' passings confirm that administrative ability has become an essential entrepreneurial characteristic in twentieth-century Britain and that entrepreneurship, so defined, has borne heavily on the profitability of British enterprises and on the performance of the British economy.

Michael Dintenfass

Bibliography

Chandler, Alfred D. *Scale and Scope: The Dynamics of Industrial Capitalism.* 1990.

Hannah, Leslie. *The Rise of the Corporate Economy.* 2nd ed. 1983.

Reader, W.J. *Imperial Chemical Industries: A History.* 2 vols. 1970–75.

Wilson, Charles Henry. *The History of Unilever: A Study in Economic Growth and Social Change.* 3 vols. 1954–68.

Epstein, Jacob (1880–1959)

Jacob Epstein, Britain's most outstanding and innovative sculptor during the first half of the twentieth century, was born of Polish Jewish immigrants to America and brought up on New York City's Lower East Side. A mysterious childhood illness meant that even within his large family—he was the second son of eight surviving children—he was comparatively isolated and introverted, turning to reading and drawing. An art prize led him to the Art Students League, where he drew and painted, and he observed with great intensity the vivid life around him in the city. He also had a job in a bronze foundry. He came to Paris to study in 1902 and settled in London in 1905.

Henry Moore called him the father of modern British sculpture. With Henri Gaudier-Brzeska and **Eric Gill** in England, Modigliani and Brancusi in Paris, Epstein was one of the leaders of the resurgence of interest in direct carving. It was his visits to the Louvre during his period in Paris that first aroused his interest in primitive and enthographic sculpture, as well as in antiquities, an interest subsequently pursued at the **British Museum**. That interest was also expressed in two distinct fashions, both in his own sculpture and in a remarkably prescient collection he made of such work (exhibited as the Epstein Collection of Primitive and Exotic Art by the **Arts Council of Great Britain** in 1960). In much, if not all, of his monumental sculpture he was a carver and full of energy, occasionally crude; in his portrait sculpture he was an exceptionally sensitive modeler. For much of his career he was controversial, and he made public sculpture an issue of debate within Britain, coming to embody within cartoon, **caricature**, and even in music hall jokes the popular idea of the modern sculptor.

Critical opinion has come to appreciate in particular his monumental carvings—*Genesis* (1931), *Consummatum Est* (1936–7), *Adam* (1938–9), *Jacob and the Angel* (1940–2), of which the last great free-standing example is the bound figure of Lazarus, carved in Hoptonwood stone (1947), purchased in 1952 for the chapel of New College, Oxford, where it still resides. His lifelong themes were evocations of the life force, with an emphasis on symbols of fertility and maternity; and the spiritual, evoking specific religious imagery of both Old and New Testament and a more generalized paganism.

The controversy over much of his public sculpture may have forced a retreat and bound his imagination in much the way that Lazarus was bound. Public art in Britain suffered almost literally a monumental loss in the mutilation of the remarkable frieze of eighteen carved naked figures by Epstein commissioned in 1907 for the building of the British Medical Association in the Strand, London, by the architect Charles Holden (now the Embassy of Zimbabwe): the strength of feeling against these primal statues when the building became the High Commission for Southern Rhodesia led to the decay by neglect of the statues and their eventual semidestruction *in situ* by a deputation led by the architect, partly on the grounds of safety. The campaign for their retention was controversial and totally failed. Another lost masterpiece, the *Rock Drill*, exhibited at the London Group in 1915, combined a helmeted, armored, and menacing figure—an extraordinary amalgam of stylized warrior, bird, and insect—surmounting a real piece of machinery, a drill. Other publicly sited masterpieces remain, including the fan-

tastical and very affecting tomb for Oscar Wilde in the Père Lachaise cemetery in Paris, a sculpture in high relief of a winged demon angel, much affected by the absorption of Assyrian reliefs, particularly the Headed Bull in the British Museum. Here the dominant catalyst and influence was undoubtedly Eric Gill with his commitment to direct carving and truth to materials. Brancusi and Modigliani, both School of Paris artists and personal friends, were other readily assimilated influences, with their gift for simplification and understanding of ethnographic and antique art. Other lasting works include the highly energetic yet curiously charming monument to W.H. Hudson in Hyde Park, Rima (1925), also a carved relief, most strikingly influenced by the paintings of Gauguin; and the figures of *Night and Day* (Portland stone, 1928–9) on the facade of the headquarters of London Transport in St. James. Even with these stylized primitive figures Epstein had to bow to public opinion by diminishing the size of the penis on the boy's figure in *Day*.

A fundamental aspect of Epstein's practice was the modeling of portrait busts, to be cast in bronze, and he sculpted some of the best known of the day. Outstanding examples include his portraits of **Joseph Conrad**, Albert Einstein, **George Bernard Shaw**, and **Ralph Vaughan Williams**, who said he could not see his own likeness in the Epstein but could see his own father and grandfather.

From about 1911 portrait sculpture provided the main income for Epstein, always in need of funds for a grand life-style, a huge studio in Hyde Park Gate, and his zeal for collecting; in pursuit of income, he was to execute many banal likenesses. The intense, impressionistic realism of his portraits was explored in parallel to his primitive, sophisticated stylizations of mythical and symbolic figures, and in his early career in England he was associated with the avant-garde, particularly the **Vorticists**. He was also to make many portraits of children, including his own; the best are lively, unselfconscious, and totally unsentimental. A little-known aspect of his work is a series of vivid, brilliantly imaginative flower paintings.

His last years were marked by official honors and commissions. Epstein was given an Arts Council retrospective exhibition at the Tate Gallery in 1952 (the same year that his *Madonna and Child* was sited on the Convent of the Holy Child Jesus, Cavendish Square), received an honorary degree from the University of Oxford in 1953, and was knighted in 1954. In 1955 he was commissioned to create the major outside sculpture, *St. Michael and the Devil,* for the facade of the new Coventry Cathedral designed by Basil Spence.

Marina Vaizey

Bibliography

Buckle, Richard. *Jacob Epstein, Sculptor.* 1963.

Epstein, Jacob. *Let There Be Sculpture: Epstein: An Autobiography.* 2nd ed. 1963.

Gardiner, Stephen. *Jacob Epstein, Artist against the Establishment.* 1992.

Silber, Evelyn. *The Sculpture of Epstein with a Complete Catalogue.* 1986.

Equal-Pay Movement

Throughout most of the twentieth century British women have been employed at lower rates of pay than men even when doing the same job. The government's rationale for this inequality changed during the century. Prior to the First World War government officials claimed that women's output was less than men's, and that women were more expensive to employ because they were absent from work more often and had a higher turnover rate (partly due to the marriage bar). Later, as evidence emerged demonstrating that output was not linked to the gender of the worker, they relied on the family-wage argument—that is, male workers needed higher rates because they had families to support whereas women did not. But when reformers gathered data demonstrating that a significant minority of female employees were supporting dependents, usually elderly parents, whereas many male employees were bachelors supporting only themselves, opponents switched to a new argument.

The equal pay for equal work movement emerged in the civil service and in teaching first because these were the areas in which large numbers of women were doing equal work. Female employee organizations in both areas began lobbying before the First World War but had little success apart from the 1914 Royal Commission on the Civil Service report, which recommended equal pay for equal work. Although the House of Commons voted in 1936 to grant equal pay to female civil servants and in 1944 to extend it to teachers, in both in-

stances the government secured a reversal of the vote by threatening to resign. Fearing continued pressure for reform, Winston Churchill's wartime government appointed a Royal Commission on Equal Pay later in 1944 (with terms of reference forbidding it to make any policy recommendations) in order to prevent further action on the issue.

Following the war the feminist Equal Pay Campaign Committee and the trade union Coordinating Committee on Equal Pay conducted separate campaigns that culminated in the presentation of two lengthy equal-pay petitions to Parliament in March 1954. Shortly before this display of public and parliamentary support, the Chancellor of the Exchequer, R.A. Butler, had initiated a review of the government's policy; near the end of March he urged the Cabinet to introduce equal pay in the public services. In winning Cabinet approval Butler, noting that Labour had pledged to introduce equal pay at once if they were returned to office, suggested that the Conservatives should proceed in order to reap the electoral benefits at the forthcoming general election.

There was little progress toward equal pay for industrial women workers until the June 1968 women's strike at Ford's Dagenham plant. Claiming there would be continuing unrest unless the government acted, Barbara Castle, the Secretary of State for Employment, persuaded the Cabinet to allow her to introduce what became the 1970 Equal Pay Act. Since the act required equal pay only for women employed on "the same or broadly similar" work, it benefited a minority of female industrial workers.

The Equal Pay Act's limitations resulted in new pressure for legislation to provide equal pay for work of equal value in order to extend the law to those employed on sex-segregated jobs. British governments resisted this change until the European Court ruled in 1982 that Britain was not in compliance with the European Community equal-pay regulations. Under pressure from the court the Conservative government in 1983 reluctantly introduced regulations for equal pay for work of equal value, which broadened the scope of the law but did so in a manner that hampered efforts to use it effectively. While some important individual cases, such as *Hayward v. Cammell Laird* (1988), have been won under the 1983 regulations, equal-pay advocates have found them so inadequate as a means of eradicating pay discrimination that in the 1990s the

Equal Opportunities Commission was urging new equal-pay legislation.

Harold L. Smith

Bibliography

Meehan, Elizabeth M. *Women's Rights at Work: Campaigns and Policy in Britain and the United States.* 1985.

Rubenstein, Michael. *Equal Pay for Work of Equal Value.* 1984.

Smith, Harold L. "The Politics of Conservative Reform: The Equal Pay for Equal Work Issue, 1945–1955," *Historical Journal*, vol. 35 (1992), pp. 401–15.

———. "The Problem of 'Equal Pay for Equal Work' in Great Britain during World War II," *Journal of Modern History*, vol. 53 (1981), pp. 652–72.

Espionage

Although common in ancient times, spying probably did not become a part of statecraft until the emergence of modern diplomacy. Security structures, and their counterparts, espionage and treason, were enhanced by the processes of nation building in the nineteenth century. Wars in the twentieth century strengthened patriotic sentiment, while at the same time promoting espionage as an official part of the national effort under the rubric of intelligence gathering.

The celebrated cases of the "Cambridge spies," Anthony Blunt, Guy Burgess, John Cairncross, Donald Maclean, and Kim Philby, sent a *frisson* through British political circles in the 1950s and 1960s. Indeed, they continue to fascinate: Blunt, the aloof and snobbish aesthete who was the Surveyor of the Queen's Pictures; Burgess, the wicked, charming, and slovenly "monster of improbability," as Noel Annan has called him; Cairncross, lettered and intellectual; Maclean, the child of a great Liberal family; Philby, with a marvelous stutter, who seemed destined to rise to the top of the British security service. The frenzy to uncover the fourth, or even a fifth man, has been exceeded only by the panic of politicians, the **press**, and the public to find the reasons for the betrayal of these highly regarded members of the Establishment to the Stalin regime.

Some have regarded their treason as a matter of class. Sickened by the materialism of capitalism, they betrayed their class even more than their country by throwing in their lot with the social experiment and political alternative the Soviet Union represented. Others view the Cambridge spies as conflicted men, and their treason a function of their split personalities. Citing **E.M. Forster**'s famous dictum about preferring to betray one's country rather than one's friends, some have argued that their **homosexuality** drew them to political perversion because they were not governed by traditional family loyalties. Still others find the root of their political behavior in the society they kept. As members of the **Apostles**, the secret discussion society at **Cambridge**, they came from a university that, with its commitment to science and mathematics, was always different from **Oxford** and, from the sixteenth century onward, always more disloyal. In their misguided idealism, they made secrecy a habit.

These theories disintegrate under closer scrutiny. Blunt and Burgess were homosexual, but Philby was not, and Maclean's sexual propensities emerged under the influence of drink. While several of the spies were Apostles, not many Apostles were spies. The traitors of the 1930s were drawn to the Soviet Union, not because of its strength, but because of the widespread feeling that the Western democracies were weak. Marxism, made more attractive by the Comintern, was appealing because it had the appearance of internationalism. Moreover, the Soviet Union represented a new departure, unencumbered by the corruption that seemed to engulf France and Britain. In the wartime emergency, when the security services sought talent, they found it in the universities. Some university men went to Bletchley Park to break the German ciphers. The talented recruits included future spies, like Blunt, Burgess, Cairncross, Maclean, and Philby, enlisting in the national effort. Primed for betrayal, they relayed much of what they learned to their Soviet spymasters, in some cases even after the war.

In an age that has become fascinated by treason and espionage, it is not surprising that fiction should exploit these themes. The popularity of the **spy novel** goes back to the beginning of the century with Erskine Childers' *Riddle of the Sands* (1903) and the novels of John Buchan. Ian Fleming, **Graham Greene**, and John LeCarré have captured the more contemporary version of these ideas in invented characters like James Bond and George Smiley, who have extended the tradition of Buchan's Richard Hannay and **Somerset Maugham**'s Ashenden.

W.C. Lubenow

Bibliography

Andrew, Christopher. *The Making of the British Intelligence Community*. 1985.

Boyle, Andrew. *The Climate of Treason*. 1973.

Cecil, Robert. "The Cambridge Comintern" in Christopher Andrew, and David Dilks, eds. *The Missing Dimension*. 1984. pp. 169–98.

Glees, Anthony. *The Secrets of the Service: British Intelligence and Communist Subversion*. 1987.

McCormick, Donald. *The British Connection: Russia's Manipulation of British Individuals and Institutions*. 1979.

Thomas, Rosamund M. *Espionage and Secrecy: The Official Secrets Acts, 1911–1989*. 1991.

Ethical Societies

The British ethical societies emerged from the ferment of late nineteenth-century religious and social free thought. They were influenced by Unitarianism, Comtean positivism, the Hegelian idealism of the Oxford philosopher T.H. Green, secularism, and the American Ethical Culture movement. The societies and their members espoused views ranging from unorthodox Christianity to deism to militant secularism and humanism. Ethicism as a movement began in 1896 with the formation of the Union of Ethical Societies (renamed the Ethical Union in 1920) under the leadership of Dr. Stanton Coit (1857–1944) and reached its peak in 1900–14, when the societies formed an integral part of the progressive milieu and included many leading radicals, feminists, and socialists. It declined sharply during the First World War and fairly steadily thereafter. In 1963 the Ethical Union, together with the Rationalist Press Association—another moribund nineteenth-century movement—sponsored the formation of the British Humanist Association (BHA). The BHA prospered while its sponsors continued to decline, and in 1967 it absorbed the Ethical Union.

Much of the story of British ethicism can be told through Coit's biography. He was an American ethical culturalist who went to London in 1888 when appointed minister at South Place Chapel, which on his insistence became South Place Ethical Society. Coit's attempts to arm the society with a creed and social mission did not suit the members, whose aims were mainly self-educational, so Coit resigned in 1891. He then set about founding new ethical societies in Lon-

don, Belfast, Edinburgh, and provincial cities. In 1906 the Union of Ethical Societies reached its peak of forty-two affiliates representing between 3,000 and 4,000 members.

Coit's growing interest in ritualism led him in 1909 to persuade the West London Ethical Society to take over a disused church, which he decorated with representations of such figures as Buddha, Jesus, Florence Nightingale, George Bernard Shaw, and Socrates. Its mainly middle-class congregation attended a Sunday service whose forms increasingly resembled those of High Anglicanism. The society changed its name to the Ethical Church in 1914. Membership peaked at around 500, of whom nearly half left during the First World War due to Coit's ultrapatriotism. Coit retired in 1932 and was replaced by three assistant ministers. The most influential, H.J. Blackham, led the church slowly back into the mainstream of ethicism, a task made easier by a further slump in membership during the Second World War.

South Place evolved in a distinctive direction after Coit's departure and did not affiliate with the Ethical Union until 1950. Coit had dropped the title of minister; in 1897 the society dropped the position itself. In 1900 it appointed three lecturers: J.A. Hobson, a "New Liberal"; Herbert Burrows, a Marxist; and J.M. Robertson, a militant atheist and adherent of classical liberalism. This diversity continued in the society's later appointments. Its membership fell from close to 300 in 1910–14 to under 250 just after the First World War, but its fortunes revived after 1929 when it moved to the purpose-built Conway Hall in Holborn. By the mid-1930s there were more than 400 members, among them young campaigners for peace and social reform. Conway Hall rapidly became one of London's prime meeting venues for groups espousing minority opinions. The Second World War renewed the society's decline, and in 1967 it was dealt a heavy financial blow when it lost legal status as a religious and charitable organization.

D.P. Blaazer

Bibliography

Budd, Susan. *Varieties of Unbelief*. 1977.

MacKillop, I.D. *The British Ethical Societies*. 1986.

Eugenics

Eugenics is the science of effecting human betterment and social progress by altering the genetic "stock" of a population through selective breeding. It is usual to classify eugenic policies as either positive (encouraging births among the "most desirable" by selectively targeted, pro-natalist inducements, such as child allowances) or negative (restricting the procreation of the "least desirable" by policies such as segregation in institutions or sterilization of individuals). Not surprisingly, eugenics has been one of the most controversial reform strategies in the twentieth century.

Eugenics movements appeared in nearly all advanced industrial societies, but the British eugenics movement is conventionally seen as an outgrowth of the late nineteenth-century Social Darwinist movement. Research into family histories by eugenists Francis Galton and Karl Pearson seemed to provide evidence that the "leaders" in society (such as judges or peers) were dying out and that at the bottom of the social scale there was an ever-growing residuum of "degenerates."

In the early 1900s the British eugenics movement expanded in influence: The Eugenics Education Society (soon known as the Eugenics Society) was established in 1907, and a Chair of Eugenics was founded at University College, London; there was much lobbying of Parliament during the passage of the 1913 Mental Deficiency Act; and the *Eugenics Review* increasingly became a forum for eugenic proposals. In the late 1920s the British eugenics movement probably reached its peak of influence. Mass **unemployment** seemed proof of racial degeneration, and the rise of the **Labour Party** increased the appeal of eugenics to conservatives as an antisocialist reform strategy. Hence, the Wood Committee (an official committee under the joint auspices of the Board of Education and Board of Control) produced a report in 1929 that took a strongly eugenic line, arguing that mental deficiency was primarily inherited and that there was a growing "social problem group" at the bottom of society. The Eugenics Society initiated a number of studies designed to show that social qualities were primarily inherited, notably E.J. Lidbetter's *Heredity and the Social Problem Group* (1933). Based on the notion that Mendelian laws of inheritance could be used to prove that "defective germ plasm" (or inborn qualities) determined an individual's social position, these studies produced largely speculative and inconclusive results.

By the 1930s the influence of eugenics was waning. Membership of the Eugenics Society was always relatively small, despite its influence, and when the political climate of the 1930s became more hostile to eugenics, the society's weakness was revealed. Although an official *Report of the Departmental Committee on Sterilisation* (1934) gave a cautious endorsement of eugenics, the government remained wary. By the late 1930s the revelations of eugenics in practice in Nazi Germany were discrediting the British movement; there were increasing attacks on eugenics as naked class self-interest by left-wing scientists such as Lancelot Hogben and **J.B.S. Haldane**; and the role of inheritance in the causation of mental deficiency was being challenged by research such as L.S. Penrose's *Colchester Survey* (1938). Hence although the Eugenics Society and its dynamic General Secretary, Dr. C.P. Blacker, sustained a long campaign in the 1930s to achieve the legalization of voluntary sterilization, it was ultimately unsuccessful.

The Second World War did not mark the end of the British eugenics movement, for it did continue, albeit in a muted form (for example, in the "problem family" surveys of the late 1940s). The society remained active in the sponsorship of research into demography generally. But the establishment of a **welfare state** marked the victory of a liberal analysis of poverty and social problems that was so much at variance with eugenics as to marginalize it into ineffectiveness.

John Macnicol

Bibliography
Kevles, Daniel J. *In the Name of Eugenics: Genetics and the Uses of Human Heredity.* 1985.
Macnicol, John. "Eugenics and the Campaign for Voluntary Sterilisation in Britain between the Wars," *Social History of Medicine*, vol. 2 (1989), pp. 147–69.
Mazumdar, Pauline M.H. *Eugenics, Human Genetics, and Human Failings: The Eugenics Society, Its Source, and Its Critics in Britain.* 1991.
Soloway, Richard A. *Demography and Degeneration: Eugenics and the Declining Birthrate in Twentieth-Century Britain.* 1990.

European Community

See EUROPEAN UNION

European Union
(*formerly* European Community)

Britain joined the European Community in 1973 though membership was first sought in 1961. Accession came after a long period of controversy within Britain, between those who saw Britain's future in Europe and those who sought to stress the special relationship with the United States and a continuing independent global role; and within the Community, between the French government of Charles de Gaulle and the five other members (Germany, Italy, Belgium, Netherlands, and Luxembourg). De Gaulle resented Britain's connections with the United States and wanted to move the European Community to a position of independence from the United States, especially in its foreign and defense policy, but also with regard to American direct investment in Europe.

By the late 1960s, however, both of the main political parties—Labour and Conservative—had come to accept the need to seek membership, and with the departure of de Gaulle in 1969, the six member nations agreed to reopen the question of British membership at their summit meeting at The Hague in December 1969. Negotiations were successfully concluded between **Edward Heath**'s Conservative government and the six in the summer of 1971, the principle of membership was narrowly approved in the House of Commons in October 1971, with the **Labour Party** seriously split on the issue, and the Treaty of Accession was signed in January 1972.

Accession involved a commitment on the part of Britain to take part in what the founding Treaty of Rome (1957) referred to in its preamble as "an ever closer union of peoples," though there were disagreements about what precisely this meant. But Britain was unambiguously committed to the Common Agricultural Policy; to removing trade barriers with other members of the Community; to accepting a system whereby money to finance the common activities went to the Community as of right; to a common commercial policy in relations with nonmembers; and to a legal system under which British courts would apply legislation agreed in the Council of Ministers that had not been approved in the House of Commons. Some commentators believed that this represented a challenge to British sovereignty, though others denied this since the whole arrangement rested upon a treaty between sovereign states, which had been approved by Parliament, and from

which the British could withdraw without any constitutional or legal impediment.

In February 1974 the Heath government was defeated in a general election and replaced by a Labour administration under **Harold Wilson**, which had by now moved into a position of hostility toward the Community and decided to renegotiate the terms of accession. It remained cautious in its approach to Europe throughout its period of office, which ended with **Margaret Thatcher**'s electoral victory for the Conservatives in May 1979. Renegotiation, which had insignificant consequences, led to a referendum about membership in 1975 when around 60 percent of those who voted said "Yes." Despite this, the left wing of the Labour Party remained hostile: In opposition in the early 1980s, the party's official policy was to withdraw. Labour MPs did not take up their seats in the European Parliament until 1976, and the trade union movement was unenthusiastic.

It was not until the late 1980s that the Labour Party shifted toward a pro-membership stance. In the 1987 election the issue was fudged, but by 1992 Labour had become much more positive in its approach to Europe than Thatcher's Conservatives. It now supported more advanced forms of integration in the Community, such as the proposal for a European social charter, which would promote higher standards for workers, and membership in the monetary union, under which separate national currencies would be abandoned in favor of a single European currency by the late 1990s—called the European Currency Unit (ECU)—under the management of a European Central Bank.

The **Conservative Party**, in contrast, moved from a position of support for membership and a positive attitude toward involvement under Heath to a position of caution under Thatcher, with increasingly sharp divisions about the issue between the right and left wings of the party. Thatcher made her position clear in a speech to the College of Europe in Bruges in the fall of 1988, when she explained her dislike of the Brussels bureaucracy, of what she saw as excessive centralization, and of socialism at the European level. She projected a policy of sentimental nationalism toward Europe, criticized European federalism, and strongly supported protecting Britain's sovereignty, freedom in international society, and links with the United States. When Thatcher came to office, she inherited a situation in which, because of Britain's need to import significant quantities of food and the way in which the Community was financed—through the so-called own resources system—Britain had a significant excess of contributions to, over receipts from, the Community. This was thought to be unreasonable since Britain was by now not among the richer European states. The European Community was the context of Britain's continuing economic decline. As a result Thatcher was determined that Britain should contribute less, and this led to considerable acrimony between her and the other government leaders. It was not until June 1984 that this problem was settled, but the acrimony continued and became attached to other issues.

From the time of the settlement of the budgetary problem the Conservatives found themselves unwillingly taking part in an accelerating process of integration. The reasons for this were complex, but the main elements were the realization that unless concessions were made to the more supranational ambitions of the others, especially the French, Britain could be left behind on the margins of Europe and could miss out on the specific economic benefits resulting from the completion of the single market by the end of 1992. The main feature of the diplomacy between Britain and its partners after 1984 was, therefore, for Britain reluctantly to agree to increased powers for the common institutions, and increases in the level of regulation from Brussels, but to mitigate them as much as possible. Diplomacy leading to the agreement of the Single European Act in December 1985, which set out the procedures for completing the single market by the end of 1992 and gave greater powers to the European Parliament, showed clear signs of these tensions. A group of cautious states led by Britain, including Greece and Denmark, were forced to give ground to a group of more ambitious states, led by France.

The Maastricht Treaty (1991) also illustrated this tension, but for the British government there were other complicating factors. John Major, who succeeded Thatcher in 1991, was faced with the problem of negotiating the next stage in the development of the Community's arrangements, in particular those for monetary union, and for strengthening the Community's machinery for coordinating foreign and defense policies. It was probable that Major himself was more pro-European than his predecessor; he had, for instance, linked

sterling with the other currencies in the exchange-rate mechanism of the European monetary system when he was Chancellor of the Exchequer. But as Prime Minister, he now had the problem of keeping the right wing of his party in line. It was, therefore, necessary for him to appear to have fought fiercely against integration at Maastricht, the town in Holland where the negotiations took place. He won what he could claim was the important concession that Britain would not join the monetary union unless that was approved by Parliament and also succeeded in avoiding any commitment to the social charter. With the approval of the Maastricht Treaty by member nations, including Britain, in 1993, the European Community was transformed into the European Union, although disagreement over the extent of monetary and other forms of integration persists.

Paul Taylor

Bibliography

George, Stephen. *Awkward Partner: Britain in the European Community.* 1990.

Gregory, F.E.C. *Dilemmas of Government: Britain and the European Community.* 1983.

Kitzinger, Uwe. *Diplomacy by Persuasion: How Britain Joined the Common Market.* 1973.

Lodge, Juliet, ed. *The European Community and the Challenge of the Future.* 1989.

Taylor, Paul. "The European Community and the State: Assumptions, Theories, and Propositions," *Review of International Studies*, vol. 17 (1991), pp. 109–25.

Euston Road School

"A New School for a limited number of pupils of Drawing and Painting" was established at 12 Fitzroy Street in London under the direction of Claude Rogers (1907–79), Victor Pasmore, and William Coldstream (1908–87). In February 1938 it moved to larger premises at 314/316 Euston Road, where it became popularly known as the Euston Road School. Associated teachers were Vanessa Bell, Duncan Grant, Augustus John, and John Nash. The painter and critic Graham Bell (1910–43) was also closely connected with the group from its inception. Its students included such established abstract painters as Geoffrey Tibble and Rodrigo Moynihan and the writer Adrian Stokes. De-

E

spite small numbers and brief duration the school acquired a powerful reputation.

In its prospectus, paid for by Sir **Kenneth Clark**, then Director of the National Gallery, stress was placed on "direct contact with teachers who are themselves practising painters." Particular emphasis was "on training the observation," and the result was a scrupulously constructed naturalism that recalled Degas and the early work of **W.R. Sickert**. A reaction to the tyrannical influence of the formalism of the *Ecole de Paris* among young British artists in the 1930s, the school represented a return to order and to contemporary relevance. Coldstream and Graham Bell had been moving in this direction for some time and in 1937 had published *A Plan for Artists* in which they argued against abstract and decorative art and on behalf of "the exploration and expression in paint, by actual experience, of the material world." Since 1934 Coldstream had been employed by the General Post Office Films Department, which, under the supervision of John Grierson, had both a **documentary film** and an **advertising** function. Graham Bell, who had arrived in London from South Africa in 1931, wrote on art for the *New Statesman*, and from 1936 showed increasing sympathies for the radical Left. It was financial support from Clark and Samuel Courtauld that helped both Coldstream and Bell to leave films and journalism and to return to full-time painting and teaching in 1937. Clark was also responsible for the financial liberation of Pasmore, who had practiced as a Sunday painter while working in the Public Health Department of London County Council since 1927. Pasmore's radicalism in the late 1930s was signaled by a turn from Parisian near-abstraction to the social style of early Sickert. Rogers, the other principal in the venture, consistently took Sickert as an example after his graduation in 1928 from the **Slade School of Art**, where he was a contemporary of Coldstream.

The influence of the Euston Road School, especially in British art education, was considerable: Pasmore, Rogers, and Coldstream all taught at Camberwell School of Art in London; Coldstream became Professor at the Slade in 1949, Rogers became Professor of Fine Art at the University of Reading, and in the 1950s Pasmore, as Director of Painting at the University of Newcastle, introduced basic design into the teaching of painting and sculpture. They were remarkable for their vision and their pro-

gram, still confident that art could intervene meaningfully in society.

Ian Jeffrey

Bibliography
The Euston Road School and Others. 1948.
Laughton, Bruce. *The Euston Road School.* 1986.

Evacuation of Children in the Second World War

The evacuation of schoolchildren was one of the most important episodes in the social history of the **Second World War**. Prior to the outbreak of war the anticipation of widespread bombing casualties had resulted in considerable civil defense planning for the dispersal of vulnerable groups in the population (essentially, schoolchildren, mothers with preschool children, the elderly, the blind, and the handicapped) from potentially dangerous bomb-targeted inner cities to safe reception areas in the countryside.

The first wave of government-organized evacuation began on 1 September 1939, just before the outbreak of war, and continued subsequently at a slower rate. Roughly 1.5 million evacuees availed themselves of the scheme in the first few days; and over the course of the entire war the figure was an estimated 4 million. Almost immediately, there was a public outcry over the condition of evacuee children who had been billeted in the countryside. Much concern was expressed over their poverty, inadequate clothing, lack of domestic manners, uncleanliness, and medical condition (with many complaints about vermin, head lice, and impetigo).

It is impossible retrospectively to assess the accuracy of these allegations, because systematic medical inspection was not carried out during the first wave of evacuation. It is probable that they were highly exaggerated, being symbolic of rural/urban cultural differences, class hostility, or the somewhat nervous atmosphere of the first few weeks of war. Whatever their accuracy, they initiated a lively debate on the condition of evacuee children and, by implication, of inner-city working-class children generally.

The anticipated heavy bombing raids did not occur until the **Blitz** of September 1940, and thus many evacuee children and mothers drifted back home; by early 1940, something like 80 percent had returned to the potentially danger-

Children being evacuated in September 1939.

ous city centers. There were subsequent waves of government-organized evacuation (in late 1940 and during the V1 and V2 rocket attacks of 1944). In addition, many people made private evacuation arrangements, either to safe areas within Britain or abroad.

Evacuation is much more than just another episode in wartime social disruption, because it was held by commentators to be responsible for dispelling official resistance to social reform. Most notably, a central theme of **Richard Titmuss'** *Problems of Social Policy* (1950) was that the revelations of the evacuee children's condition paved the way for the implementation of education reform, the **National Health Service**, and such specific child-centered measures as the expansion of free milk and meals in schools. Recent research has cast doubt upon this inter-pretation, however, arguing that evacuation may, in fact, have revealed the intransigence of class differences rather than eroding them.

John Macnicol

Bibliography

Calder, Angus. *The People's War.* 1969.

Crosby, Travis L. *The Impact of Civilian Evacuation in the Second World War.* 1986.

Macnicol, John. "The Effect of the Evacuation of Schoolchildren on Official Attitudes to State Intervention" in Harold L. Smith, ed. *War and Social Change: British Society in the Second World War.* 1986. pp. 3–31.

Titmuss, Richard M. *Problems of Social Policy.* 1950.

F

Fabian Society

Britain's oldest surviving socialist organization, the Fabian Society, has been variously characterized as the world's first think tank and an intelligence corps without an army. Its members have been mainly middle-class London-based intellectuals and have included every Labour Prime Minister. The Fabian strategy has been to conduct research into social and economic problems and to convey its recommendations to governing elites, thus promoting a gradual, rational, well-mannered socialism.

The society was launched 4 January 1884 at the home of Edward Pease (1857–1955), who would serve as general secretary from 1890 to 1913. Frank Podmore (1855–1910) suggested the name as an allusian to the Roman general Quintus Fabius Cunctator, who supposedly defeated Hannibal through delaying tactics. The early Fabians included **George Bernard Shaw, Sidney Webb,** and **Graham Wallas.**

All members had to subscribe to the Fabian "basis," drafted in 1887, but it was vague enough to accommodate socialists of all stripes. *Fabian Essays in Socialism* (1889), edited by Shaw, introduced Fabian thinking to a wide audience. In 1892 six Fabians, including Webb, were elected to the London County Council on a platform of "municipal socialism"—that is, expanded social and educational services.

Although Fabians attended the founding conference of the **Independent Labour Party** (1893) and the **Labour Representation Committee** (1900), the society at first kept its distance from this emerging political force. Shaw and Webb preferred to "permeate" the **Liberal** and **Conservative** parties, persuading them to adopt socialistic measures one reform at a time.

The Fabian leadership had little faith in proletarian democracy, preferring government by altruistic "brain-workers" like themselves. To train such a corps of experts, Webb used Fabian money to found the **London School of Economics and Political Science** in 1895.

By 1906 many younger Fabians had grown dissatisfied with gradualism. **H.G. Wells** attempted to transform the society into a militant socialist party and might have succeeded but for his childish personal attacks on the Fabian leadership. To reenergize the society, the Fabian nursery (for members under twenty-eight) was begun in 1906, the Fabian Arts Group and the first Fabian summer school in 1907, and the Fabian Women's Group in 1908.

In 1912 **Beatrice Webb** set up the Fabian Research Department, headed by **G.D.H. Cole** and William Mellor (1888–1942), to investigate how socialist economic management might work in practical terms. Later that year the Webbs founded the *New Statesman*, a weekly edited by Clifford Sharp (1883–1935). It would publish the work of the Research Department, along with polemics by Shaw, poetry by **Rupert Brooke,** and fiction by **Leonard Woolf.** In 1915 the Webbs assigned Woolf to prepare for the Research Department a plan for diplomatic machinery to prevent future wars. The result was *International Government* (1916), which outlined proposals that would be incorporated into the **League of Nations.**

By 1918 **Arthur Henderson** looked to the guidance of Fabian intellectuals to transform Labour into a governing party. He and Sidney Webb drafted a new **Labour Party** constitution, which significantly appealed to "producers by hand or by brain." In 1919 the Fabian Society formally became "a constituent of the Labour

Party," but it left open its options to work with other political movements.

Fabians were well-represented in **Ramsay MacDonald's** two Labour governments (1924, 1929–31), but the society lost intellectual momentum in the inter-war years. Impatient at its failure to offer concrete solutions to the worsening Depression, G.D.H. Cole formed the **New Fabian Research Bureau** in 1931.

Fabian activity revived during the Second World War. In 1940 Rita Hinden (1909–71) and Arthur Creech Jones (1891–1964) set up the Fabian Colonial Bureau, which established a cordial advisory relationship with the Colonial Office. The bureau argued that Britain had an obligation to promote colonial economic development and gradual self-government for the benefit of native peoples. Its members included several future leaders of emerging African nations: Julius Nyerere, Kenneth Kaunda, Hastings Banda, Jomo Kenyatta, and Tom Mboya. The success of the Colonial Bureau inspired the formation (in 1941) of the Fabian International Bureau, headed by Leonard Woolf, to advise on post-war reconstruction.

A majority of the Labour MPs elected in 1945 were Fabians, as were thirty-seven ministers in the **Attlee** government. The Fabians may have exaggerated their role in inspiring the British **welfare state,** which was mainly the work of Liberals like **David Lloyd George** and **William Beveridge,** but Beveridge himself had been a Fabian back in the Edwardian years.

New Fabian Essays, edited by Richard Crossman (1907–74) in 1952, reflected a loss of intellectual direction: After six years in power, the authors could not agree on a coherent redefinition of socialism. **Hugh Gaitskell** had invigorated Fabianism with a dose of Keynesianism, but his battles with **Aneurin Bevan** inevitably spilled over into the society, which lost members steadily throughout the 1950s.

Fabians again dominated the Labour governments of 1964–70 and 1974–9. The 1960s brought an influx of younger members, but membership fell off in the 1970s, when the society offered few answers to Britain's economic decline and trade union militancy. Linked as they were to the Labour Party, the Fabians were divided by the formation of the Social Democratic Party (SDP) in 1981. The SDP's founders included Shirley Williams (1930–), chairman of the Fabian Society, and three other Fabian of-

ficers. A membership ballot affirmed that members of parties other than the Labour Party could only be associate members of the society. The Fabians soon lost nearly one out of six members, but they survived to celebrate their centenary, as well as the election of Fabian **Neil Kinnock** as leader of the Labour Party in 1983.

Jonathan Rose

Bibliography

Britain, Ian. *Fabianism and Culture.* 1982.
Cole, Margaret. *The Story of Fabian Socialism.* 1961.
MacKenzie, Norman, and Jeanne MacKenzie. *The First Fabians.* 1977.
———, eds. *The Diary of Beatrice Webb.* 4 vols. 1982–5.
McBriar, A.M. *Fabian Socialism and British Politics, 1884–1918.* 1962.
Pugh, Patricia. *Educate, Agitate, Organise: One Hundred Years of Fabian Socialism.* 1984.

Falklands War

The Falklands Islands and the Falklands Dependencies—South Georgia, the South Sandwiches, and the British Antarctic—were long disputed between Argentina and Britain and from 1966 to 1982 were the subject of ongoing negotiations. The Argentines made a *de jure* case for possession based on their inheritance of the sovereignty exercised over the Falkland (or Malvinas) Islands by Spain from 1767 to 1811; the British advanced a *de facto* claim based on continuous occupation in the nearly 150 years since the last Argentine had left, as well as upon the self-determination of the islands' population. Early in 1982 the Argentine government decided to mask internal problems of hyperinflation and political repression by seizing the islands.

The first phase of the war began with the raising of the Argentine flag on South Georgia Island on 19 March by civilians landed by a navy transport and the landing of more than 100 Argentine troops a week later. On 31 March Prime Minister **Margaret Thatcher** and her advisers were persuaded by First Sea Lord and Chief of Naval Staff Admiral Sir Henry Leach to begin assembling a large naval task force to counter Argentine moves. This force was in preparation when Argentines invaded the Falklands. Before dawn on 2 April, 120

Argentine commandos came ashore to seize Government House in Port Stanley and the Royal Marine barracks two miles away. That morning, 800 reinforcements were landed with more expected by air. On the following day the Argentines seized South Georgia.

The second phase of the war, a naval struggle in the waters around the Falklands, began on 5 April with the departure from Portsmouth of the first ships of a task force that would eventually comprise forty-four warships and twenty-two auxiliary craft under the command of Rear Admiral John F. Woodward. The British announced that as of 12 April a 200-mile maritime exclusion zone would be imposed around the Falklands. On 16 April an Argentine task force, including an aircraft carrier, the cruiser *General Belgrano*, two destroyers, and three submarines, put to sea. Nevertheless, the British task force was able to take position off the Falklands. South Georgia was retaken on 25 April, and on 1 May aircraft from Ascension Island and the task force attacked the Port Stanley airfield. On 2 May a British **submarine** torpedoed and sank the *General Belgrano* with a loss of 386 Argentine seamen. The debate over whether the *Belgrano* was inside the exclusion zone or not has almost obscured the fact that this sinking was the deciding event of the war. What might have been became evident on 4 May when an Exocet air-to-surface missile launched from an Argentine aircraft crippled a destroyer, HMS *Sheffield*, which later sank. Masters of the sea, the British on 9 May began naval bombardment of Port Stanley. Only on 12 May were the Argentines able to begin major attacks by land-based aircraft. Though the Argentines had up to 216 fixed-wing aircraft and 20 helicopters available as against British air units totaling a maximum of 55 fixed-wing craft and 154 helicopters, the Argentine air strikes had little success until the British entered the narrow strait between East and West Falkland.

The third phase of the conflict, the ground engagement on East Falkland Island, began early on 21 May with raids on Port Louis, Goose Green, and Fox Bay as prelude to the liberation of Port San Carlos. Despite air attacks on fleet units in the vicinity, the British were able to land artillery, armored vehicles, and surface-to-air missiles, but four British ships were damaged at a cost of sixteen Argentine fixed-wing aircraft and four helicopters. In the next four days three more British ships were sunk and three damaged at a cost of fifteen Argentine aircraft and one helicopter. None of this stopped the invasion. Between 28 May and 4 June the British established the southern portion of a pincers on Port Stanley by capturing Goose Green despite adverse odds of four to one, then moving in to Fitzroy and Bluff Cove on the south coast. On 29 and 30 May the northern pincer was formed by the occupation of Douglas, Teal Inlet, and Mount Kent. British forces on the island now numbered about 9,500 and confronted nearly 8,400 Argentine defenders. The attack on Port Stanley began on 11 June with successful British assaults on Mount Longdon, Mount Harriet, and Great Ridge, followed by the capture of Wireless Ridge, Tumbledown Mountain, Mount Williams, and Sapper Hill. With the capital completely exposed to British artillery, General Menendez surrendered. When the British unilaterally announced the end of the conflict on 12 July, their losses amounted to 256 killed, 777 wounded, and 80 captured, while the Argentines had lost 746 killed, 1,336 wounded, and 11,400 captured. The British had lost six ships, 10 aircraft, and 23 helicopters; the Argentines, three ships, 107 aircraft, and 10 helicopters.

Joseph M. McCarthy

Bibliography

Blakeway, Denys. *The Falklands War.* 1992.
Cordesman, Anthony H., and Abraham R. Wagner. *The Lessons of Modern War III: The Afghan and Falklands Conflicts.* 1990.
Hastings, Max, and Simon Jenkins. *The Battle for the Falklands.* 1983.
Middlebrook, Martin. *Task Force: The Falklands War, 1982.* rev. ed. 1987.
Woodward, Sandy (John F.). *One Hundred Days: The Memoirs of the Falklands Battle Group Commander.* 1992.

Family Allowances

A universal system of state-funded children's allowances was introduced in Britain through the passage of the Family Allowances Act (1945) by **Winston Churchill**'s wartime coalition. The measure received bipartisan support, which seemed at the time to indicate a wide acceptance of its importance. In fact, family allowances have remained somewhat peripheral to both party politics and the **welfare state** in

F

Britain and have often been neglected or come under threat. Although key to the prevention of child poverty, they remain an underfunded and much-misunderstood adjunct to a social insurance system organized primarily around the wage. Britain's family policies are among the least generous in the **European Union**.

State aid to families with young children first became a matter of public discussion in the years before the First World War as politicians, worried about the "efficiency" and **eugenic** quality of the British population, looked to programs like school meals to improve children's health. A few socialists and sex radicals like **H.G. Wells** proposed that the state "endow" mothers as a reward for their "national service" of bearing children; some **feminists** also hoped that "endowment" would free women from direct dependence on men. Only after the First World War, however, when many saw the positive effects on child and maternal health of the extensive payment of cash "separation allowances" to soldiers' wives, did a wider campaign for the "endowment of motherhood," and later for family allowances, develop. A group of feminists and social reformers, including **Eleanor Rathbone**, established the Family Endowment Committee in 1917, and in 1924 Rathbone published *The Disinherited Family*, the Bible of the movement, which combined a lucid exposition of the inadequacy of wages to meet family needs with a survey of family policies in other European and Commonwealth countries.

In the early twenties Rathbone and other advocates usually argued for family allowances on two grounds: as a measure of recognition to unwaged wives and as the only means of guaranteeing adequate support of children, given that wages were not based on family needs. Such arguments were attractive to some feminists, although others feared that allowances would only deepen the identification of women with purely domestic roles. They also aroused interest among Labour's Women's Sections, and within the **Independent Labour Party** (ILP), which included a proposal for children's allowances in its 1926 program, "The Living Wage." ILP enthusiasm did lead to a joint **Labour Party-Trades Union Congress** (TUC) inquiry into family allowances in 1928, but in 1930 the TUC rejected the measure, fearing that allowances might adversely affect wage rates.

After the failure of the Labour Party initiative, the campaign for allowances languished.

Rathbone and other advocates continued to argue for improved benefits for children (whether in cash or in kind) during the 1930s; some politicians also saw a case for children's allowances for working men when they realized that, for men with many children, **unemployment** allowances (based on family size) could exceed wage rates. Yet not until the **Second World War** did a comprehensive national measure receive serious consideration. Many factors contributed to this new interest: growing cross-party parliamentary pressure; concern about the declining birthrate; the fact that numerous children were already receiving allowances as the dependents of servicemen; government interest in avoiding an inflationary wage spiral; the TUC's reversal of its old opposition; and, finally, the endorsement of children's allowances by **Sir William Beveridge** in his famous report of 1942 entitled *Social Insurance and Allied Services*. The 1945 measure established children's allowances at the rate of 5 shillings per week for each child except the first. After a determined campaign by Rathbone and others, the initial plan to pay the allowance to the father was overturned by a Commons free vote in favor of payment to the mother.

Family allowances received little attention and declined in value during the next twenty years. In the mid-1960s, however, when the work of Peter Townsend and other social scientists demonstrated that full employment and the welfare state had not rid Britain of poverty (especially child poverty), family policy came back on the political agenda. For the next twenty-five years, the Child Poverty Action Group (CPAG), under the successive leadership of Tony Lynes, Frank Field, and Ruth Lister, kept the problem of child poverty in the public eye. Support for a more comprehensive and generous family policy grew during the 1970s, especially within the Labour Party, and in 1975 the **Wilson** government passed the Child Benefit Act, which envisaged replacing both the family allowance and the child income tax credit by Child Benefit, a new, universal, tax-free, non-means-tested cash benefit for all children, including the first. Yet the government, worried about the cost, refused to commit itself to a date for the commencement of the new scheme and increasingly seemed likely to shelve the plan indefinitely. Minutes leaked from the Cabinet Office, and made public by Frank Field of CPAG, showed that ministers feared that trade unionists would object to the proposal to fund Child

Benefit in part by abolishing child tax allowances disproportionately enjoyed by male wage-earners, and at least one section of the TUC did object to any transfer "from wallet to purse" even though aggregate family income would rise. The ensuing public scandal, CPAG's successful lobbying of some sympathetic trade unions and Labour organizations, and the persistence of Barbara Castle, then Secretary of State for Health and Social Security, forced the government to meet its commitment. Child Benefit became payable from 1977.

If Labour governments have sometimes exhibited more concern for working men than children, **Conservative** governments have been critical of the universal nature of Child Benefit altogether. The **Heath** and **Thatcher** administrations consistently let the value of Child Benefit decline, preferring to build up new "targeted" programs for the low-waged, such as Family Income Supplement, introduced in 1971, and replaced by Family Credit in 1988. Critics such as CPAG charge that such programs tend to create a "poverty trap," since benefits decline as pay rises, and Prime Minister John Major to some extent broke with this tradition by raising Child Benefit substantially in his first budget in 1991. Yet Child Benefit remains contested; the best efforts of an alliance of feminists and poverty campaigners has not been able to compensate for the lack of party and union enthusiasm and for a political tradition hostile to the identification of children as legitimate claimants on state resources.

Susan Pedersen

Bibliography

Macnicol, John. *The Movement for Family Allowances, 1918–1945: A Study in Social Policy Development.* 1980.

McCarthy, Michael. *Campaigning for the Poor: CPAG and the Politics of Welfare.* 1986.

Pedersen, Susan. *Family, Dependence, and the Origins of the Welfare State: Britain and France, 1914–1945.* 1993.

Rathbone, Eleanor F. *The Disinherited Family.* 1924.

Fascism

In Britain, as in other countries, the ideological seeds of Fascism were sown before the twentieth century. However, the first organization in Britain that possessed a distinctively Fascist title did not appear until the 1920s. The heyday of British Fascism occurred in the 1930s with the emergence of the British Union of Fascists (BUF) under the leadership of Sir **Oswald Mosley**. The identification of Fascism with Nazi Germany created difficulties for British Fascism during the **Second World War**, and subsequently it has made little political progress. However, Fascist and related racial nationalist groups have continued to operate in Britain.

The British Fascisti, associated particularly with Rotha Lintorn Orman and reflecting the influence of Italian Fascism, began life in 1923. It was through the British Fascisti that William Joyce, who subsequently achieved notoriety as Lord Haw-Haw, became involved, later joining other organizations before departing for Germany in 1939. The Imperial Fascist League (the IFL), linked with Arnold Spencer Leese, was formed in 1928. Leese had spent many years in Africa before joining the British Fascisti on his return to Britain. There is a danger in regarding the IFL as a one-man band, but Leese's racial conspiratorial **anti-Semitism** became strongly stamped on the group.

In the 1930s various small groups sympathetic to Fascism, such as the Nordic League which had an overt anti-Semitic nature, began to appear. This period saw the emergence of the BUF under the leadership of Mosley. The BUF, formed in 1932, was the vehicle through which Mosley hoped to fulfill his political ambitions. He had previously been a member of both the **Conservative** and **Labour** parties before launching his short-lived New Party in 1931. In the initial stages Mosley and the BUF garnered a fair measure of support for the Fascist cause. Men who had fought in the **First World War** and shared the comradeship of the trenches only to become disillusioned with post-war Britain, provided one important source of support. In addition, the BUF appealed to young people, even without military service, who wanted to sweep away "the old gang" as the dominant political force. It appealed also to some conservative elements anxious about a perceived decline in Britain's role as a world power. In the early heady days of the BUF, the movement could count on the support of the Rothermere press through the columns of the *Daily Mail*.

An important turning point occurred in June 1934, when a meeting at Olympia in London generated considerable public violence and support for the BUF ebbed. In these circumstances the BUF soon became increasingly embroiled in the politics of East London, where the tradition of anti-Semitism and housing and labor problems became issues that Mosley hoped to exploit. The East End campaign turned violent, and, in an attempt to control the paramilitary style of the BUF, the government passed the Public Order Act of 1936, which forbade the wearing of political uniforms (one hallmark of the BUF was the black shirt). By this time Mosley's organization was identified increasingly with Adolf Hitler's National Socialists, which limited the movement's appeal. Even so, on the eve of the Second World War the BUF remained active, and Mosley, a charismatic politician and superb orator, continued to attract large audiences.

There is some dispute about the size of the BUF and whether membership fell in the course of the late 1930s. There is a greater agreement on the claim that the war led to the demise of the BUF as an effective political organization. Some members joined the armed forces, while leading figures such as Mosley, Leese, Alexander Raven Thomson, the movement's leading ideologist, and Neil Francis Hawkins, its Director-General, were interned by the authorities for much of the war. Even so, certain fringe organizations sympathetic to Fascism continued to function.

By the end of the war Fascism had become associated with the excesses of Nazi Germany, and its post-war history in Britain was an anticlimax. Leese, retracting nothing, published a news sheet called *Gothic Ripples* but remained politically impotent. When Mosley revived his political activity and formed the Union movement, through which he campaigned for European unity based on racial criteria, he attempted simultaneously to distance himself from his earlier political career. However, election defeats at North Kensington in 1959 and Shoreditch and Finsbury in 1966 showed that Mosley was generally regarded as beyond the pale.

When Leese died in 1956, his mantle passed to Colin Jordan, but his National Socialist movement, active in the early 1960s, exercised a negligible influence. In 1967 Fascist and racial nationalist groups united to form the National Front (NF). Its embrace of an extreme nationalism, its anti-Semitism, its opposition to Blacks and Asians, and its involvement in violent street politics persuaded many commentators that it could be regarded as a Fascist organization. It seemed for a period in the 1970s that the NF might play a significant role in British politics, but its failure to achieve any success in the 1979 general election was followed by its collapse and eventual disintegration into a variety of warring factions. Such groups, small in number, still survive, and John Tyndall, the former leader of the NF, is one of the better-known activists.

Colin Holmes

Bibliography

Benewick, Robert J. *The Fascist Movement in Britain.* 1972.

Lewis, D.S. *Illusions of Grandeur: Mosley, Fascism, and British Society, 1931–81.* 1987.

Lunn, Kenneth, and Richard Thurlow, eds. *British Fascism: Essays on the Radical Right in Inter-War Britain.* 1980.

Skidelsky, Robert. *Oswald Mosley.* 2nd ed. 1981.

Thurlow, Richard. *Fascism in Britain: A History, 1918–1985.* 1987.

Fashion
See CLOTHING AND FASHION

Fawcett, Millicent Garrett (1847–1929)
Millicent Garrett Fawcett was the principal leader of the constitutional women's suffrage movement in Britain during the period of its greatest activity, the years before 1914. Continuing her activities in changed wartime conditions, she presided over the movement's first and greatest success: the granting of the parliamentary vote to most women over age thirty in 1918.

Born into a prosperous middle-class Suffolk family in 1847, Millicent Garrett entered political life in 1867 with her marriage to Henry Fawcett, the famous blind radical politician and Cambridge Professor of political economy. Almost immediately she became active in many feminist causes, including legal reforms, employment, education, and a variety of moral issues. It was women's suffrage, however, that was from the start her leading interest. By the mid-1880s she was already the most important figure in a movement with many supporters but no real power. It was a movement divided by party political allegiance and weakened by the activities of politicians, few of whom wanted to do more than offer vague benevolence in return for electoral assistance.

Fawcett was intrumental in its unification and in the formation of the National Union of Women's Suffrage Societies (NUWSS) in 1897. The NUWSS was in its early years a loose confederation of suffrage societies, without the strong central headquarters and executive created on its reorganization early in 1907, when Fawcett was elected its first (and only) President.

It was, however, the militant activities of the **Women's Social and Political Union** (WSPU) that pushed women's parliamentary suffrage into the forefront of political controversy. The WSPU was formed in 1903, but it was not until 1906 that its unprecedented style of campaigning, characterized by verbal militancy, became a prominent feature of suffrage methods. Fawcett was in the early years among those NUWSS members who believed that the activities of the WSPU were to the benefit of women's suffrage, a sentiment that did not survive the WSPU's transition from militancy to violence in 1908–9.

Fawcett's domination of the constitutional movement, whose members, affiliated societies, and activities were more numerous though less newsworthy than those of the WSPU suffragettes, was not based on personal dynamism or autocratic methods of organization. In contrast to **Emmeline Pankhurst**, the WSPU leader, her strengths lay in her writing and in personal contacts. The respect and loyalty with which she was held turned into veneration as the movement struggled to achieve its aims in the harsh pre-war political climate. Her role in these years was that of standard-bearer, manifesting optimism in the most adverse circumstances. To the interested public she was the most acceptable of suffragists, her personality making respectable a cause otherwise sullied by its connection with violence. It must be added, however, that if suffragette militancy failed to impress politicians, the constitutional methods of Fawcett and her friends equally failed to persuade them of the justice and good sense of granting votes to women.

The outbreak of war drastically changed the position of a woman almost universally respected among suffragists and known for her international suffrage links. Unlike the majority of her close colleagues, she expressed unqualified support for the conduct of the war, with a passion markedly at odds with the reasoned approach that had always characterized her advocacy of women's suffrage. After much uneasy private debate the NUWSS Executive Committee split openly at a special council of the union in June 1915. The majority of the more active committee members left their posts, and henceforward the NUWSS, at least nominally, supported the war as actively as its President.

In the context of a catastrophic war and the suspension of active suffrage work, the passage of the Representation of the People Act in 1918, giving the vote to millions of women over age thirty, was a somewhat hollow victory. It was, however, duly celebrated by the NUWSS and its allies, the evergreen Fawcett, still NUWSS president, taking the chair at a victory rally in March 1918. She was to live eleven years longer, during which period she continued her feminist activities on several fronts. One of the most important was the agitation to complete the suffrage victory by enacting equal suffrage between men and women, finally accomplished in 1928.

In Fawcett the personality was easily overshadowed by the cause. A woman of strong passions, as her support for the **First World War** (and earlier, the **Boer War**) had shown, she excelled as a conciliatory and unifying force. Unique among her contemporaries for the longevity of her suffrage work and her achievements as a knowledgeable and witty writer, she did her best to conceal her personality from her colleagues and the public. To a later age she remains the principal, unwearying leader of the only mass movement inspired by British **feminism** in the twentieth century.

David Rubinstein

Bibliography

Caine, Barbara. *Victorian Feminists*. 1992.
Fawcett, Millicent Garrett. *What I Remember*. 1924.
Rubinstein, David. *A Different World for Women: The Life of Millicent Garrett Fawcett*. 1991.
Strachey, Ray. *Millicent Garrett Fawcett*. 1931.

Feminism

Edwardian feminism was an influential if heterogeneous movement, one that encompassed a wide variety of organizations and made itself felt in many aspects of social life. Despite this variety, three principal aims can be detected. First, from the mid-Victorian period feminists had consistently worked to improve **women's education** and **employment** opportunities, in order both to enrich women's lives and to free them of a humiliating dependence on **marriage** and men. Second, and again drawing on Victorian campaigns for **divorce** reform and against the state regulation of **prostitution**, feminists sought to reform sexual and moral standards: to raise the age of consent, to increase the penalties for wife and child abuse, and to apply to men the higher standards of chastity demanded of women. Finally, feminists insisted that women be given a greater voice in political life. Tens of thousands of women participated in the Edwardian campaign for **women's suffrage**, especially through the militant **Women's Social and Political Union** (WSPU), led by **Emmeline Pankhurst** and **Christabel Pankhurst**, and the constitutionalist National Union of Women's Suffrage Societies (NUWSS), led by **Millicent Garrett Fawcett**. By 1914 the "woman question" had become a central issue in British social and political life.

The outbreak of the **First World War** dramatically altered this situation. The question of whether to support the war divided many feminist organizations and decoyed many activist women into either relief work or **pacifist** efforts. The WSPU disappeared during the war, and some members of the NUWSS' Executive left the organization to found the British Section of the Women's International League for Peace and Freedom. Indeed, many pre-war feminists, among them Kathleen Courtney (1878–1974), Helena Swanwick (1864–1939), Margery Corbett Ashby (1882–1981), and Emmeline Pethick Lawrence (1867–1954), as well as such later recruits as **Vera Brittain**, spent the interwar years concerned as much with peace and international cooperation as with sexual equality. The war also shattered the remnants of Victorianism, making way for a more explicitly modern sensibility, one in which the high-minded rhetoric of feminism, and especially its concern with sexual purity, was increasingly labeled ridiculous, outdated, or prudish. Finally, the war consolidated other political shifts that decisively weakened feminism's political position. The strength of the **Labour Party** lay not in those educational and philanthropic associations in which women had exercised such an important role, but rather in the trade unions, in which women played little part and which were committed to an ideal of a "family wage" deeply at odds with the goal of economic independence for women.

For all of these reasons the feminist movement emerged from the war in a weakened position. Yet the movement in the 1920s also suffered from serious internal conflicts. The extension of the franchise to women over age thirty through the Representation of the People Act (1918) merely exposed the extent of the disagreements. The NUWSS, now renamed the National Union of Societies for Equal Citizenship (NUSEC), split repeatedly over such issues as protective legislation, **birth control**, and **family allowances**. Although most feminists were agreed on (and would unite to lobby for) complete political equality, finally achieved with the Representation of the People (Equal Franchise) Act of 1928, there was little consensus in other areas. There were four main groups, each of which viewed the old goals of economic independence and sexual emancipation differently.

A first group exhibited the most consistency with pre-war feminist demands. These "egalitarians," working through the London Society for Women's Service, led by Ray Strachey (1887–1940) and Philippa Strachey (1872–1968), or the Six Point Group and the Open Door Council, both founded by Margaret Haig Thomas, Viscountess Rhondda (1883–1958), continued to insist on strict legal and economic equality between the sexes and to campaign in particular for improved economic opportunities for women, an end to the marriage bar, an end to special "protective" legislation, and a more stringent interpretation of the ineffective Sex Disqualification (Removal) Act of 1919—all with little success. Yet other feminists were skeptical that such employment-centered efforts would ever affect the lives of the majority of women, especially of unwaged wives. Such "new feminists," led by **Eleanor Rathbone**, who succeeded Millicent Fawcett as the President of the NUSEC in 1919, lobbied for such "special" women's programs as family allowances, arguing that such measures would lessen wives' dependence on their husbands and, by eroding men's claim for a "family wage," make equal pay possible. Third, a number of women, including Dora Russell (1894–1986) and **Marie Stopes**, denounced the old ideal of sexual purity as repressive and antifeminist and supported birth control as an essential ingredient of women's emancipation—although such arguments were opposed by feminists who feared that birth control would merely increase women's vulnerability to men. A final, moderate feminist presence can be detected within the women's organizations of the labor movement, which were concerned to improve the lives of housewives and mothers—if not to challenge the sexual division of labor itself. The Women's Co-operative Guild and women in the Labour Party and the **Independent Labour Party** thus campaigned vigorously in favor of family allowances, improved social services, and the provision of birth control information to married women by public health authorities, sometimes in the face of serious party opposition.

By the 1930s, however, feminist organizations were small, divided, and somewhat demoralized. The ideal of domesticity proved difficult to challenge during the Depression, and the periods of wartime and of post-war reconstruction. The principle of **equal pay** was rejected by the National, **Conservative**, and Labour governments in turn, and the **welfare state** set up after 1945 explicitly presumed a male breadwinner and nonworking wife. Although children's allowances payable to the mother were introduced with the Family Allowances Act (1945), they were derisory in amount. With the exception of the brief revival of feminist campaigns for equal pay and day-care provision during the **Second World War**, women's political activism during the middle decades of the century took place largely within civic organizations that were not openly feminist, such as the Women's Institutes (which counted almost 500,000 members by the 1950s) and the Townswomen's Guilds (250,000 members by 1945).

Feminism reemerged both as an important ideological force and as a political movement in the 1970s. Yet the reasons for its revival, and indeed the goals of the movement, were not in the first instance economic, although the growth in women's participation in the labor force and a new sympathy within the trade union movement for women workers' concerns helped create a favorable environment for feminism. Lobbying by the older liberal feminist societies (the Six Point Group, the Fawcett Society) and pressure from the labor movement and especially from Labour Minister Barbara Castle together contributed to the passage and subsequent strengthening of the Equal Pay Act (1970)—which was made binding in 1975 and

applied to comparable work in 1983—and of the Sex Discrimination Act (1975). Civil libertarian groups and the Fawcett Society also co-operated to ease passage of the Abortion Reform Act (1967), which legalized **abortion** during the first twenty-eight weeks of pregnancy. Yet the women's liberation movement, as it came to be called, grew less out of the union movement or the old feminist societies than out of the protest movements and identity politics of the 1960s. Women active in the peace, student, and anti-Vietnam movements became deeply disillusioned by the sexism and the organizational dominance of their male colleagues; they also discovered that the revolution in sexual mores and in contraceptive technology could be used not to "free" women but to pressure them into sexual activity. Feminists organized in small, woman-only, nonhierarchical groups and concentrated on revealing and attacking the existence of sexism in personal and sexual life. National conferences of the women's liberation movement held from 1970 until 1978 put forward a program of six demands—equal pay, twenty-four-hour nurseries, free contraception, abortion on demand, legal financial independence for women, and the right to self-defined sexuality—but in 1978 the conference broke up over the question of whether a single resolution against violence against women should replace all other demands. Despite a lack of central direction, feminism in the 1980s continued to bear fruit. Women's centers, battered-women's shelters, rape crisis centers, women's studies programs, and campaigns against pornography and against violence against women survive in large part because of the diffusion of feminist ideas and the mobilization of feminist energies.

Susan Pedersen

Bibliography

Banks, Olive. *Faces of Feminism: A Study of Feminism as a Social Movement.* 1981.

Dyhouse, Carol. *Feminism and the Family in England, 1880–1939.* 1989.

Harrison, Brian. *Prudent Revolutionaries: Portraits of British Feminists between the Wars.* 1987.

Jeffreys, Sheila. *The Spinster and Her Enemies: Feminism and Sexuality, 1880–1930.* 1985.

Smith, Harold L., ed. *British Feminism in the Twentieth Century.* 1990.

F

Vicinus, Martha. *Independent Women: Work and Community for Single Women, 1850–1920.* 1985.

Festival of Britain (1951)

Originally proposed as an international exhibition to commemorate the centenary of the Great Exhibition of 1851, the Festival of Britain was devised as a nationwide series of exhibits and events from May to September 1951. Although eager to demonstrate Britain's recovery from the **Second World War**, the **Labour** government in 1947, facing shortages and austerity, found itself unable to allocate sufficient resources for an international exhibition without making inordinate demands on scarce material and labor needed for reconstruction. Instead, **Herbert Morrison**, the Lord President of the Council, called for a more modest national display illustrating Britain's contribution to civilization in the arts, science and technology, and industrial design. In contrast to earlier expositions, like the British Empire Exhibition at Wembley in 1924, which were confined to a single site, the Festival of Britain was planned as a series of events that would encompass the entire country. Whereas earlier exhibitions had celebrated Britain's far-flung interests by involving other countries or at least the Empire, the 1951 festival made a virtue of Britain's reduced stature by restricting its focus to the nation and emphasizing the vitality of British traditions.

The festival was planned by a group of young architects and designers under the direction of Gerald Barry, former editor of the *News Chronicle*; its centerpiece was a large multipavilion exhibit on the South Bank in **London** organized around the theme of the land of Britain, the people of Britain, and British contributions to discovery. Rather than adopt the traditional formal geometrical pattern of great exhibitions, the festival planners designed an informal grouping of buildings on the twenty-nine acre site between County Hall and Waterloo Bridge, applying the ideas of the modern international architectural style to the temporary festival buildings, all of which were dismantled after the festival ended. The most dramatic of the structures were the Dome of Discovery, a vast aluminum saucer supported by forty-eight tubular steel struts, and the graceful, vertical Skylon, a 250-foot-high, elongated pod that appeared to

Dome of Discovery and Skylon, South Bank, London, built for the Festival of Britain, 1951.

be suspended in mid-air but was actually supported by cables.

The official exhibitions also included a science exhibit at an enlarged Science Museum in South Kensington; a live architecture exhibit in Poplar, where contemporary principles of town planning and modern building techniques were applied in the reconstruction of a badly blitzed slum neighborhood, renamed Lansbury; a book exhibit at the Victoria and Albert Museum; an exhibition of industrial power in Glasgow; and a farm and factory exhibit in Belfast. Scaled-down versions of the South Bank exhibits were transported to Leeds, Nottingham, Manchester, and Birmingham by the mobile Land Travelling Exhibition and to the principal seaports by the festival ship *Campania*. A large portion of Battersea Park was tranformed into a pleasure gardens and fun fair, where designers and artists created a fanciful imitation of the eighteenth-century gardens at Vauxhall and Ranelagh and a British version of Tivoli.

The **Arts Council of Great Britain** sponsored a two-month London Season of the Arts, which focused on British music, painting, and literature and featured 200 orchestral concerts, performances of newly commissioned **operas** and **ballets**, and an array of classic British plays. Moreover, the Arts Council provided encouragement and financial guarantees to twenty-three arts festivals, including not only more-established events at Stratford, Edinburgh, and Aldeburgh, but new ones in Liverpool, York, Norwich, Oxford, Cambridge, and other towns. Its commissioning of works specifically for the Festival of Britain acknowledged the importance of the artists in British culture and enhanced its own role as arbiter of taste and official patron of the arts.

In addition, 2,000 villages and towns organized festival events on their own initiative, ranging from concerts to floral displays, from refurbishing ancient buildings to providing recreational amenities, adding an unprecedented dimension of popular participation to the more-traditional exhibition format.

The Festival of Britain succeeded beyond the expectations of many of its planners, who had been skeptical about whether the project, dogged by **strikes**, budgetary cuts, and persistent inclement weather in the winter of 1950–1, would ever be finished. Supported by much of the **press**, by the government, the Royal Family, which lent its patronage, and by the cultural elite, the festival opened at the beginning of May in a blaze of publicity, with a service of dedication at St. Paul's and an inaugural concert at the new Royal Festival Hall. During the next five months the crowds at the South Bank continued to mount, attracted not only by the narrative exhibits themselves, but perhaps even more by the flowers, illuminations along the riverfront, fireworks, cafés, and nightly entertainment. Nearly 8.5 million people visited the South Bank and 8 million visited the Festival Pleasure Gardens, although attendance at other official exhibitions was considerably smaller.

The festival offered opportunities for younger architects, designers, and artists to experiment, providing the first occasion for a concentrated display of modern **architecture** in Britain. The exhibits, carefully controlled by a Presentation Panel, furnished evidence of British craftsmanship and good quality in industrial **design**, which may have helped to promote British exports. If it exaggerated the extent of British recovery from war, it did help to dispel some of the gloom and bleakness so pervasive in the late 1940s. The use of temporary structures reduced the demand on building materials, although the expenditure of £10 million still meant the diversion of resources that might have been used for housing or social amenities. Yet many felt that by injecting a note of gaiety and fun at a time of economic crisis and war in Korea, the festival played a vital role in restoring public morale and in demonstrating British resilience to the rest of the world. However modest its economic and aesthetic contribution, it did provide, in Gerald Barry's words, "a tonic to the nation."

F.M. Leventhal

Bibliography

Banham, Mary, and Bevis Hillier, eds. *A Tonic to the Nation: The Festival of Britain 1951*. 1976.

Barry, Sir Gerald. "The Festival of Britain 1951," *Journal of the Royal Society of Arts*, vol. 100 (1952), pp. 667–704.

Frayn, Michael, "Festival" in Michael Sissons, and Philip French, eds. *Age of Austerity, 1945–1951*. 1964. pp. 330–52.

Film Industry

Until the early 1950s Britain had a major film industry that made its money primarily from showing American films. British filmmakers, unable to produce enough films to fill British screen time, have always had to compete with the popularity of American films in the United Kingdom. British filmmaking seems to occur in alternate bursts of crisis and creative activity. There has also been a traditional split between popular movies and elite art film.

Despite a long tradition of filmmaking, Britain, more than any other country, has been vulnerable to imports from other English-speaking countries. Hollywood has traditionally taken the lion's share of the British film market, often luring away many of Britain's most talented filmmakers.

Filmmaking began in Britain at about the same time it began in the United States. William Friese-Greene is recognized as the founder of British motion picture technology, his invention celebrated in the 1951 film *The Magic Box* (by director John Boulting). British filmmaker Cecil Hepworth anticipated many of American D.W. Griffith's technical and dramatic innovations and in films such as *Rescued by Rover* (1903) demonstrated a sophisticated sense of film structure and narrative. The Brighton School constituted a lively indigenous fiction film tradition, but British filmmaking was disrupted by the First World War, and production went into a prolonged decline. In the 1920s British studios produced very few films, and the government attempted to legislate British cinema into existence by requiring exhibitors to show British films and offering tax incentives for producers to make films in the United Kingdom. These measures enabled a group of entrepreneurs and filmmakers, most of them, like Alexander Korda, foreign nationals, to revive British production, although most British accomplishments until the mid-1930s lay in the area of **documentary film**. By 1937 British filmmakers were once again very busy, making more films than in any other single year. Many were so-called "quota quickies," inexpensive films intended to fill the bottom half of a double bill, produced by American-owned companies attempting to obey the letter, if not the spirit, of the quota laws. The most commercially successful film in the 1930s was Korda's *The Private Life of Henry VIII* (1933), the first British film that found a substantial overseas market. The small British studio system nurtured several directors, the most prominent being Anthony Asquith, Walter Forde, and **Alfred Hitchcock**. Gracie Fields and George Formby, both stars

with a special appeal to working-class moviegoers, were the decade's most popular stars, and light and musical comedies were the most successful genres.

The **Second World War** was a wonderful time for British film, despite **conscription** of many performers and the scarcity of materials and studio space. For the first time the supply of American films was strictly regulated, and the United States even agreed to throw open its screens to British films. Films like *The Way Ahead* (Carol Reed, 1944), *Next of Kin* (Thorold Dickinson, 1942), and *In Which We Serve* (**Noel Coward**, 1942) dramatized the war for British cinema audiences in ways that Hollywood could not. Filmmakers like Coward and David Lean evolved a style that mixed stoicism and social realism to evoke a stirring image of the British at war. **Laurence Olivier** fought the war in allegories such as *Henry V* (1944), widely regarded as the definitive screen adaptation of Shakespeare. The Ministry of Information (MOI) as very active in commissioning films and shaping motion picture content. *The Life and Times of Colonel Blimp* (**Michael Powell** and Emeric Pressburger, 1943), one of the most expensive British films made during the war, clearly showed the influence of MOI policy, as did many feature films made during the war. Motion pictures were one of the few unrationed luxuries, and British theatergoers went to the cinema more often than ever before, despite the risks of aerial bombardment.

The war also enabled the Rank Organization to obtain a virtual monopoly within the industry. J. Arthur Rank, whose family fortune derived from flour milling, had moved into the film industry in the early 1930s. A devout **Methodist** who initially became interested in using films for religious and philanthropic ends, he soon became the major force in the British film industry. The Rank empire grew quickly and branched out into production and exhibition. By 1945 Rank had absorbed most of the country's studio capacity and first-run theaters, his empire becoming comparable in size to one of the American studios. The **Labour** government tolerated Rank's ambitions because he was felt to be the only real obstacle to American control of the British film industry. After 1945 American competition returned with a vengeance. Labour did not, as was widely feared, nationalize the industry, but it did provide financial support, anticipating that films would become a significant factor in international trade.

In the decade after the war British cinema acquired an international reputation for "literary" films, with David Lean's successful adaptations of novels by Dickens, beginning with *Great Expectations* (1946) and *Oliver Twist* (1947). Olivier continued to direct and star in screen versions of Shakespeare: *Hamlet* (1948) and *Richard III* (1955). Anthony Asquith directed several films adapted from stage plays, notably **Terence Rattigan**'s *The Winslow Boy* (1949) and *The Browning Version* (1951), as well as Oscar Wilde's *The Importance of Being Earnest* (1952). The partnership of Powell and Pressburger continued triumphantly with the widely acclaimed *The Red Shoes* (1948). Carol Reed's work ranged over several genres, including the Irish political drama *Odd Man Out* (1947), the domestic melodrama *The Fallen Idol* (1948), the popular Cold War thriller *The Third Man* (1949), and an adaptation of **Joseph Conrad**'s *Outcast of the Islands* (1951). This did not constitute the bulk of British cinema production after 1945, which still consisted primarily of popular mainstream films. Filmmakers who catered to these mainstream tastes included Roy and John Boulting in films like *Brighton Rock* (1947), and Michael Balcon, the producer in charge of Ealing Studios, a part of the Rank Organization. Each year this studio produced a handful of films, the majority of them comedies, such as *Passport to Pimlico* (Henry Cornelius, 1949), *Kind Hearts and Coronets* (Robert Hamer, 1949), and *The Lavender Hill Mob* (Charles Crichton, 1951). These films echoed the problems of post-war Britain: diminished expectations and **standard of living**, a lessened role in international affairs, and daily life encumbered by red tape.

In the 1960s British cinema moved toward social realism and away from the classics and cosmopolitan London. *Look Back in Anger* (Tony Richardson, 1959), the screen adaptation of **John Osborne**'s play, inaugurated a series of films with working-class themes and settings. Other films in this mode included *Room at the Top* (Jack Clayton, 1959), *Saturday Night and Sunday Morning* (Karel Reisz, 1960), *The Loneliness of the Long Distance Runner* (Tony Richardson, 1962), and *This Sporting Life* (Lindsay Anderson, 1963). These films, often referred to as British "New Cinema," resembled the style and spirit of the French New Wave. Most were taken from plays or novels by young writers, like Osborne or Alan Sillitoe, who had tried to capture the feelings of dislocation and disillusion common among young working-class people in post-war Britain. Graphic and explicit, the language and actions of the New Cinema's working-class antiheroes often shocked critics and audiences, but many of these films were critically and commercially successful. Other British filmmakers who emerged in the 1960s included John Schlesinger, whose films included *Billy Liar* (1962) and *Far from the Madding Crowd* (1967), and Richard Lester, whose **Beatles** films, *A Hard Day's Night* (1964) and *Help!* (1965), were a vibrant upbeat rebuttal of the somber pessimism of British social realism.

In the 1960s American financing became increasingly important for the industry. Many of the bigger films made in the 1950s and 1960s, such as *Lawrence of Arabia* (David Lean, 1961), were coproductions that merged British talent and American money. The James Bond series, beginning with *Dr. No* (1962), carried this process further. American producers were attracted by Britain's skilled and relatively inexpensive work force and the favorable tax incentives and subsidies available for British filmmaking. Ultimately, many American films such as the *Star Wars* series and most of the Bond films were made in Pinewood, not Hollywood, although American production fled Britain in the 1980s, when the financial climate ceased to be as attractive.

During the 1950s and 1960s, largely because of competition from **television**, Britons lost the habit of going to the movies. Theaters closed in large numbers, and box office receipts went into a decline only recently reversed. Without a substantial domestic market, British film production has always been precarious and is largely dependent today upon support from television. Since its inception in 1982, Channel Four, Britain's innovative second commercial television channel, has become the largest producer of independent features in Britain. This policy has led to a dramatic recovery of British filmmaking, with films like *My Beautiful Laundrette* (Stephen Frears, 1985) and *Letter to Brezhnev* (Chris Bernard, 1985) produced with Channel Four support. Britain also has a new generation of cerebral nonmainstream filmmakers, such as Derek Jarman (*Caravaggio*, 1986) and Peter Greenaway (*Prospero's Books*, 1992). Uncompromisingly intellectual, these filmmakers have international followings but inspire

F

only limited popular interest within the United Kingdom.

Paul Swann

Bibliography

Auty, Martyn, and Nick Roddick. *British Cinema Now.* 1985.

Barr, Charles, ed. *All Our Yesterdays: Ninety Years of British Cinema.* 1986.

Dickinson, Margaret, and Sarah Street. *Cinema and State: The Film Industry and the Government, 1927–84.* 1985.

Landy, Marcia. *British Genres: Cinema and Society, 1930–1960.* 1991.

Park, James. *British Cinema: The Lights That Failed.* 1990.

Perry, George. *The Great British Picture Show.* 2nd ed. 1985.

Firbank, (Arthur Annesley) Ronald (1886–1926)

For decades after the death in 1926 of the novelist Ronald Firbank his work was considered of interest only to a Firbank cult of readers. But "a cult is not recognition," as Brigid Brophy remarked in her *Prancing Novelist* (1973), a ground-breaking analysis of Firbank's work and life. By now it appears that both the content and the aesthetic experimentation in Firbank's novels—especially *Vainglory* (1915) and *The Flower beneath the Foot* (1923)—merit as high a rank and as wide a readership as the work of **James Joyce** and **Virginia Woolf.**

Firbank was the son of Thomas Firbank, a Unionist MP elected in 1895 and knighted in 1902; and was the grandson of Joseph Firbank, a collier who made himself into a wealthy contractor in the business of railroad construction. Guaranteed an independent living by money inherited from his father and grandfather, Firbank put aside ideas of being an art historian or a diplomat, left Trinity College, **Cambridge,** in 1909 without taking a degree, and dedicated himself to work on his novels. At his own expense he had published his first stories in 1905. Because of publishers' wariness concerning Firbank's subject matter and style, and in spite of shrinking family money after the First World War, Firbank continued to finance the publication of his works. Only *Prancing Nigger* (English title: *Sorrow in Sunlight*) was published (in 1924) at the publisher's expense.

For most of his life Firbank was in poor health; **tuberculosis** exempted him from army service and kept him on the move in search of warm climates. A frequent sojourner in Italy, he died in Rome.

At an early age Firbank seems to have dedicated his life and work to the memory of Oscar Wilde. He associated himself at Cambridge with Wilde's son, Vyvyan Holland, and he cultivated friendships with remaining members of Wilde's circle, including Wilde's former lover Lord Alfred Douglas. Firbank's writing seems projected as work Wilde might have produced had he lived into the twentieth century. Firbank's cult of Wilde may be partly responsible for the critical reduction of Firbank himself to a cult.

But it is also possible that Firbank's work was snubbed because his **homosexuality** and his transvestite impulses are essential to the content and style of his novels. The possibility looks odd, admittedly, in relation to the era that celebrated Andre Gide and Marcel Proust and that saw ideas about homosexuality and transvestism inspire Joyce's work and Woolf's *Orlando* (1928). Yet Firbank's evocation of unconventional sexualities is more immediate and firsthand than it is in Joyce and Woolf, whose characters daydream about transgression of heterosexual conventions, or in whom transvestism is more fantasy than lived practice. In contrast, Firbank's heroes and heroines routinely put into practice their unconventional desires.

Firbank's work does not make unconventional loves an all-compelling focus of attention, however. He treats the power, pathos, and comedy of unrecognized eros matter of factly as well as lyrically. His greatest interest is in the mutual relations among love (in all its varieties), art, and contemporary social life, especially insofar as social life constitutes a dense world of transitional connections and multicultural contrasts. The real history of modern global imperialism is a constant point of reference in Firbank, no matter how artificial and apparently self-contained are the milieus of his novels' worlds.

In *Vainglory* the fragmentation and the passing of historical and social empires provides the context for the heroine's attempt to make art a defense against ruin. Although the novel ultimately exhibits art, including Firbank's own, as no less vain or fragile than worldly power, it suggests art's fragility as itself a value that worldliness should heed.

A gloomier picture of art emerges from *Prancing Nigger*, the story of a Black Caribbean family caught up in imitating white metropolitan colonialists. The novel portrays the family and their locale in terms of an exquisite aesthetic primitivism. But it also self-consciously dramatizes its portrayal as a form of exploitation: Firbank projects himself into his book in the character of a nefarious composer who seductively betrays the native inspirers of his primitivist operas. The heroine of *Prancing Nigger* withdraws from the world into religious asceticism as a protest against both empire and art.

Such withdrawal, simultaneously depending on and detesting the political state and the social conventions of the modern world, is a tragicomic constant in Firbank. In *The Princess Zoubaroff* (1920), a play, a group of wives withdraws from the yoke of marriage and sets up a lesbian convent in which to live. *The Flower beneath the Foot* (1923) mimes an averse withdrawal from English imperialism, which treads down equally the novel's European heroine and her Middle East counterparts. In *Concerning the Eccentricities of Cardinal Pirelli* (1926), the bisexual and pedophile cardinal is called to Rome to justify his sins. As the cardinal tries to declare himself in self-justifying terms that are beyond good and evil, the narrative reminds the reader that his subjection to Western ecclesiastical empire complements his own cathedral's usurpation of a formerly Moslem religious site.

The once narrow circle of Firbank's readers has contained numerous novelists. Clear signs of his influence can be found in the style and content of work by **Wyndham Lewis, Ivy Compton-Burnett, Evelyn Waugh, Graham Greene, Henry Green, Muriel Spark,** and Brigid Brophy.

Robert L. Caserio

Bibliography
Benkovitz, Miriam J. *Ronald Firbank: A Biography*. 1969.
Brophy, Brigid. *Prancing Novelist*. 1973.

First World War: Homefront (1914–1918)

The extreme demands of the first total war spurred major changes in British society on the homefront that included expansion of state control and government bureaucracy; an overall improvement in the standard of health despite the toll and tensions of war, long working hours, and eventual **rationing**; and significant intervention by the state in industry and conditions of labor. Some changes were only for the duration, while others left a post-war legacy. The government assumed such responsibilities as the formal takeover of the **railways** by the Board of Trade; intervention in food production and distribution; and control of industries from munitions to shipbuilding to chemicals. In 1916 it adopted the unprecedented power of military **conscription**.

At first, government food policy urged restraint in the consumption of bread, meat, and sugar as a patriotic duty. Following the shipping losses caused by the German **submarine warfare**, however, rationing was introduced by late 1917, beginning with localized rationing of coal and sugar. Queues became a standard feature of wartime life on the homefront, with popular frustration over shortages erupting into scattered protests and instances of looting. At one point the country had only four days' supply of sugar. But in early 1918 the government introduced comprehensive food rationing, queues disappeared, and the public gratefully accepted a system of remarkably equitable food distribution. National kitchens were established to supply ready-cooked meals to civilians, but they were only in certain areas and had little effect. The government urged Britons to grow as much of their own vegetables as they could. Garden allotments were cultivated on all kinds of plots, even around the Albert Memorial in Hyde Park, and factories introduced allotments to grow vegetables for their canteens.

From August 1914 throughout the war the **Defence of the Realm Acts** (DORA) gave the government wide powers to regulate in the interests of public and national security. Initially designed to control the flow of information and to protect communications and transport, these laws subjected civilians to military law. Under DORA, government adopted food-control measures, air-raid precautions, and the special policing of women accused of soliciting soldiers. **Propaganda** and **censorship** were also undertaken within the powers of DORA. The British government used film, pamphlets, photographs, and posters as media of propaganda. Propaganda to inflame public opinion in Britain over atrocities supposedly committed by the Germans employed sexual imagery, particularly rape and the violent abuse of virgins; false

F

accounts of supposed German outrages were widely circulated. Poster images exhorted civilians to take up war work, economize on food, and buy war bonds. Government censorship filtered war news in multiple forms, including film footage, letters from the front, and newspaper reports.

The state also adopted unprecedented forms of intervention in the management and control of industry, labor, and conditions of work, and the provision of essential industrial supplies. As the major supplier of weapons and munitions to Allied countries as well as to its own forces, British industry produced 250,000 machine guns, 52,000 airplanes, nearly 3,000 tanks, 25,000 artillery pieces, and 170 million rounds of artillery shells. In March 1915 government representatives met with the principal union leaders, particularly from the Amalgamated Society of Engineers, and drew up the Treasury Agreement, in which the unions agreed to the "dilution" of the skilled work force (meaning substitution by unskilled and semiskilled workers) for the duration, provided that the pre-war status quo would be restored at the end of the war. In June 1915 the Ministry of Munitions was established, with David Lloyd George as its first minister. It oversaw a remarkable collaboration among government, industry, and unions, with government intervention that contravened all principles of *laissez-faire* economics. The Munitions of War Act of July 1915 declared strikes and lockouts illegal, quite ineffectively. It also introduced compulsory arbitration under a system of special munitions tribunals, and workers were restrained from leaving their jobs by a system of leaving certificates. The ministry adopted control of wages and working conditions, not only in government arsenals and factories but also in private companies, which became "controlled establishments." By 1917 what had started as *ad hoc* interventions had become a total war economy. But not all ran smoothly. Increased participation in government by union and labor leaders backfired by creating a rift between union leaders and their rank-and-file membership. Syndicalist and socialist beliefs among workers were exemplified by the shop stewards' movement, particularly on Clydeside, which organized strikes throughout the war.

From mid-1915 there was virtually full employment. The war led to higher than ever levels of union membership, especially among women workers. The massive economic disruption, caused by the armed forces' draining of the industrial work force simultaneously with the need for munitions, opened up employment opportunities particularly for women workers, who had been confined to sweat-shop jobs and low-paid domestic service before the war. From July 1914 to July 1918 the employment of nonprofessional women and girls in the United Kingdom increased by nearly 1.6 million, of whom 891,000 were employed in industrial occupations. The Great War produced a proportional leap in the employment of women—from 26 percent of all those employed in the United Kingdom in July 1914 to 36 percent in November 1918. While approximately a million women worked on all forms of munitions, women also took jobs in transport, as shop assistants, and in clerical work.

Despite shortages and food rationing, the higher average income among working-class families due to wartime employment and separation allowances for the families of servicemen meant that the average diet improved significantly. Although wartime inflation was high, the average increase in wages for working-class families maintained the spending power of most and increased that of some. Observers commented on the improved health of children in working-class areas, noting also that children were better shod.

A contributing factor to the improved diets of workers were the factory canteens that were a wartime innovation. Factories under government control as well as some private establishments instigated canteens with ovens for workers to heat their own food, or sold workers plain hot fare at reasonable prices, or both. Women workers were a particular target of this campaign to build the strength of the work force, through the ministrations of women welfare supervisors. The Health and Welfare Department of the Ministry of Munitions conducted nutrition research and recommended menus for factory canteens and workers' hostels. A principal motive behind government sponsorship of canteens was the desire to keep workers sober; the drastic reduction of public-house opening hours is a legacy of the war that contributed at the time to the decline in infant mortality rates by reducing parental drunkenness.

Due to the improvement in diet, especially among the poorest-paid, unskilled workers, the standard of public health on the homefront actually improved despite the difficulties and the toll of warfare. There were, however, some countervailing factors. There was an increase in respiratory diseases, due to the effects of overcrowding at work and the strain of long working hours. More dramatically, the influenza pandemic of 1918–19 ravaged both the military and the civilian populations, killing approximately 200,000 British people.

The war did come to the homefront, although it was nothing like the **Blitz** would be in the **Second World War**. Nevertheless, hundreds of civilians were killed and wounded by bombs in air raids by Zeppelins, Gothas, and Giants, particularly on the east coast and in the southeast. Other Britons lost their lives in industrial accidents of wartime production; explosions in munitions factories killed hundreds of workers, such as the 19 January 1917 explosion at a chemical works in Silvertown, London, that destroyed the factory and the neighborhood around it.

A strange new outgrowth of wartime life were the **army** camps that sprang up over the countryside, especially in the early stages of war as new recruits had to be drilled and trained. British, colonial, and Dominion soldiers were to be seen everywhere: in streets, pubs, trains, cinemas, and parks. The attraction that troops exerted on some young women, and intermingling of soldiers and women in public places, led to concern about sexual morality and **venereal disease**, as well as innovations in policing. While **police** forces expanded to meet special wartime needs, women were granted semiofficial status as members of the Women Police Service and the Women Patrols of the National Union of Women Workers. In this new capacity they patrolled streets, parks, and cinemas to prevent sexual liaisons and were employed by the Ministry of Munitions to control and discipline women workers. Fear of sexual promiscuity was fostered by changes in young women's clothing (shorter skirts and trousers at work), hair (shorter), and independent social behavior, such as dining alone in **restaurants** and smoking in public.

Within months of the outbreak of war the public presence of soldiers included the wounded, in wheelchairs, on crutches, bandaged, some missing limbs. Public buildings and large private houses were converted into **hospitals** and convalescent homes. Factory workers and other groups organized entertainment and outings for wounded soldiers. Flag sellers and other patriotic charity fund-raisers were a constant presence on the streets and in the foyers of public buildings; it was as though they had taken the streets over from the suffragettes, who had suspended their protests for the war but were partially victorious before it was over, when women over age thirty gained the vote under the Representation of the People Act (1918).

Angela Woollacott

Bibliography

Braybon, Gail. *Women Workers in the First World War: The British Experience.* 1981.
Marwick, Arthur. *The Deluge: British Society and the First World War.* 1965.
Rubin, Gerry R. *War, Law, and Labour: The Munitions Acts, State Regulation, and the Unions, 1915–1921.* 1987.
Turner, John. *British Politics and the Great War: Coalition and Conflict, 1915–1918.* 1992.
Wilson, Trevor. *The Myriad Faces of War: Britain and the Great War, 1914–1918.* 1986.
Winter, J.M. *The Great War and the British People.* 1985.

First World War: Military (1914–1918)

According to pre-war plans, Britain would play only a minor part in a Continental war. If forced into conflict with Germany, it would leave the land fighting to France and Russia. Britain would hold the seas, maintain exports, and so provide military material for its allies. This conception did not survive the onset of war. Britain's vital interests were too obviously in peril, its allies too fragile, the German onslaught too menacing. So Britain's authorities instantly set about raising a mass army, at first by voluntary means, but from 1916 by compulsion.

Until that army could be trained and equipped, Britain's military participation was largely confined to its small regular **army**. In accordance with pre-war arrangements—confirmed only after protracted discussions early in August 1914 among civilian ministers and their military advisers—five of the seven divisions of the Regular Army crossed the English Channel and took up position on the left of the French, who numbered seventy divisions. They were hardly expected to be in the thick of the fighting.

This proved a miscalculation. The German attack through Belgium traveled much farther west than anticipated before wheeling south so as to outflank and overwhelm the French left before descending on Paris. At Mons on 23 August, the German far right crashed into the British Expeditionary Force (BEF), who momentarily stayed the advance before falling back under weight of numbers. For thirteen days the Anglo-French left wing retreated, until it was over the Marne and within sight of Paris. There on 5 September General Joseph Joffre, the French commander, counterattacked and drove the Germans into retreat. The British and French kept up the pursuit as far as the Aisne, where (13–17 September) they were brought to a standstill by a combination of trenches, barbed wire, machine guns, and artillery.

The French and German forces each swung north, seeking to outflank the other. Meanwhile, the BEF, at the insistence of its commander, Sir John French, was plucked from central France and returned to the coast. French believed that in unoccupied Belgium he might maneuver his cavalry to effect. Instead, his forces were beset by another massive German offensive, supported by heavy artillery and eager young recruits. At the first Battle of Ypres (October-November 1914) the numerically inferior and underweaponed BEF held—if at heavy cost—this onslaught, a further demonstration of the defensive capacity of even rudimentary trenches.

By the end of 1914, the phenomenon of trench warfare was beginning to dominate perceptions of the Western Front. What signified was not the trenches alone but the combination of trenches with the advanced weaponry thrown up by industrialization. Barbed wire, rapid-firing rifles, mortars, high-explosive and shrapnel shells, and machine-gun bullets bestowed upon defenders under cover great stopping power against an attacking force crossing open ground. Life in a trench might be a lamentable experience, with its constant accompaniment of rain, mud, lice, rats, and dismembered bodies, and its perils from shells and snipers, but it offered a much greater chance of survival than life in the open.

Here was a conundrum. If "trench warfare" gave so prodigious an advantage to the defender, how were the British and the French to liberate Belgium and humble the German military machine? In one view, the answer lay in resolute attacks on the Western Front supported by sufficient firepower to batter down the opposing trenches. From this conviction sprang mighty offensives by the French in the spring and autumn of 1915, with supporting operations by the British at Neuve Chapelle, Aubers Ridge, and Loos.

That these endeavors were not based on entirely false premises is suggested by the partial success of the British at Neuve Chapelle on 10 March 1915. A considerable quantity of ammunition—in terms of the small length of trench being attacked—overwhelmed the defenders and enabled British forces to seize the German front line (but not to go beyond that). Subsequent Allied operations during 1915, however, proved unrewarding. The objectives proved too ambitious, the support in guns and ammunition less than adequate.

Even at the beginning of 1915 some thoughtful men in Britain were expressing alarm at the potential trench stalemate on the Western Front. They drew the conclusion (which did not follow) that Britain, employing its sea power and ignoring the sentiments of its French allies, could do better elsewhere. They favored concentration against Germany's allies: either Austria-Hungary, in a process that **David Lloyd George** quaintly described as knocking the props from under Germany; or Turkey, around which Sir Maurice Hankey vaguely hoped to "weave a web."

Little good came of these reflections. The Germans manifestly could send aid to Austria-Hungary, which they were propping up, faster than the Allies could mount an operation against it. And the projected demise of Turkey would hardly lessen Germany's potentiality for overrunning Western Europe. Anyway, Britain could not disregard the wishes of France, which commanded the only considerable army standing between Germany and the channel. And Britain did not possess a large surplus of warships or troops for major operations in distant parts.

Britain did in 1914–15 take some action outside the Western Front. Sensibly, it dispatched a force to southern Mesopotamia, which was then in Turkish hands, to safeguard oil supplies from Persia. Less sensibly, it then attempted to overrun all of Mesopotamia with an inadequate force. Again, late in 1915 the British, along with the French, landed troops in Salonika—in neutral Greek territory—in an attempt to rescue Serbia, but to no avail.

Best remembered of 1915's extraneous operations was the **Gallipoli** expedition. This did not originate in a decision to divert Britain's military effort from the Western Front. Only the **navy**, using obsolete ships, was to figure in the proposed penetration of the Dardanelles. (It was anticipated, without investigation, that a fleet bombarding Constantinople would cause all Turkey to surrender.) This "ships alone" scheme soon failed before the shore defenses of Gallipoli. So it was decided to land troops on the peninsula and so open the Dardanelles to the fleet. The military operation also failed. Landings on 25 April secured toeholds on the shore but none on the high ground. Subsequent endeavors to press inland, despite a mounting commitment of military resources, availed nothing. By the end of 1915 the abandonment of the undertaking was well advanced.

For 1916, therefore, the nature of Britain's military activities seemed settled. The Western Front, whatever its perils, was the only region where some worthwhile purpose might be accomplished. The volunteers who had come forward at the outset were now trained and in uniform. Britain seemed able at last to participate fully in the war on land. But the appearance was deceptive. Whatever the accomplishments of industry and the **Ministry of Munitions** (formed in April 1915), Britain had yet to produce weaponry in the quantities and of the quality to support ambitious undertakings.

Planning for 1916 culminated in the Battle of the **Somme**, a mighty Anglo-French (but predominantly British) offensive in central France. It began on 1 July and continued to 19 November. Its first day was an abysmal failure. The new British Commander-in-Chief, **Sir Douglas Haig**, hoped to rupture the German defenses at a stroke and pour his cavalry into open territory. Consequently, he spread his relatively meager supply of guns and ammunition over a wide area. This left the German defenses largely intact and brought on his forces terrible casualties for pitiful gains.

The ensuing months on the Somme were a melange of major attacks (such as 14 July, 15 September, and 25 September), many weeks of sporadic and uncoordinated assaults by small groups, and finally a six-week period of struggle against rain and mud without discernible purpose. All told, the rewards for four-and-a-half months of campaigning were meager. A ridge of elevated ground had been captured, the tank had been unleashed, artillery techniques had undergone important refinements, and many Germans had been killed. But there had been no breakthrough, the enemy still occupied secure defenses, and Allied losses exceeded those of their enemies.

This comparative failure helped bring to power late in 1916 a new Prime Minister. Lloyd George took a dim view of British operations on the Western Front and Haig's apparent carelessness with his soldiers' lives. He also nursed an exaggerated respect for French commanders and believed that offensives should be launched in areas, such as Italy, where British forces would not be much involved.

Had Joffre and Haig had their way, the Somme campaign would have continued in 1917. But Joffre was sacked, and Haig was confronted with both a German withdrawal to new and formidable defenses (the Hindenburg Line) and his own Prime Minister's disbelief in the Somme strategy. At conferences early in 1917, Lloyd George failed to convince anyone, least of all the Italians, of the merits of a primarily Italian offensive. So he switched his allegiance to the new French commander, General Robert Nivelle, who promised in short order to rupture the German lines in the French sector of the Western Front. The BEF would provide only subsidiary support, at Arras. So enamored was Lloyd George of this proposal that he sought to place the British army under French command.

Nivelle's offensive proved short-lived, as did his command of the forces of France and Britain). The French army, disillusioned by the absence of swift success, mutinied. The only noteworthy gain from his operations, ironically, occurred in the British sector. Haig's forces on the first day of the Battle of Arras (9 April), aided by enhanced artillery, captured Vimy Ridge. But exploitation proved difficult. The weather was abominable, artillery could not be got forward with dispatch, and the enemy brought in reserves and threw up fresh defenses. Although all potential had departed after forty-eight hours, the Battle of Arras continued for six weeks at heavy cost.

Nivelle's fall from grace, and the French army's lapse into mutiny, presented Lloyd George with a problem. He remained averse to predominantly British offensives on the Western Front. But France's forces were not at this stage capable of any great effort, the Italian option was unsaleable, and Lloyd George was strangely unresponsive to a strategy of set-piece, small objective offensives (like the capture of Vimy Ridge on 9 April and of Messines Ridge

F

on 7 June). That left him with only one choice (which he affected to dislike): Haig's scheme for a decidedly ambitious drive out of the Ypres salient and toward the Belgian coast.

This undertaking (the third Battle of Ypres, or **Passchendaele**) was the brainchild of the British command but could not have occurred without the consent of its civilian masters. Beginning on 31 July 1917 and continuing until 12 November, it remains notorious even among First World War operations as an exercise in futility. It was not as costly as the Somme, its first day yielded modest gains, and its middle month (September) witnessed three limited successes. But these positive aspects were overshadowed by Haig's repeated striving after distant objectives and by his persistence in attacking during months of abysmal weather when ground turned to swamp, guns could not shoot with accuracy, and infantry were rendered almost immobile. The image of soldiers struggling in a sea of mud against unsuppressed opponents has haunted the imagination, and blighted Haig's reputation, ever since.

The year 1917 was not redeemed by the last military episode of the year, the initially much-acclaimed Battle of Cambrai (20 November–7 December). For the first time the British used a mass of tanks over good terrain and, more important, fired a fully predicted—and, therefore, surprise—bombardment. These tactics enabled the infantry to make progress, but there was no breakthrough, and Haig's forces were left fairly exposed. A surprise German counterattack ten days later recovered as much ground as had been gained.

The sorry events from July to December 1917 laid Haig open to dismissal. Lloyd George denigrated him but did not remove him. Instead, disregarding the Nivelle incident, he sought to diminish Haig's authority by elevating another Frenchman, General Ferdinand Foch. In time, Foch would become Allied Commander-in-Chief, but he never exercised large powers of control.

Soldiers in a trench at Givenchy, January 1918.

Yet in practical terms, Haig would not in 1918 decide the fate of his army to the extent he had done previously. In the first half of that year, the actions of Britain's forces were mainly *ad hoc* responses to the initiative that the enemy briefly seized in the wake of Russia's collapse. In the second half of the year various elements throughout the British army responded creatively to the piecemeal but mounting opportunities offered in the aftermath of Germany's failure.

By 1918 Britain's home industry, financial resources, and transatlantic allies were providing the BEF with the weaponry to do battle effectively. And the British army, in many departments but mostly important in its artillery branch, now possessed the expertise to employ guns, shells, tanks, and airplanes to maximum effect. The consequence was noteworthy. By 1918 Britain, like its enemies, was scraping the barrel for infantrymen. Yet thanks to an abundance of weaponry and the ability to employ it effectively, the terrible supremacy that defense had so far enjoyed over attack was receding. No trench system could long withstand a well-conducted, amply munitioned assault.

The year 1918, in consequence, falls into two phases. Between 21 March and 29 April, the Germans flung themselves on parts of the British sector, capturing many prisoners and some (fairly unimportant) ground. Having ceased to make progress, they then turned against the French, again with some success. This gave the British time, first to recuperate, and then to organize a succession of stinging counterattacks. Beginning at Amiens on 8 August, the BEF, with increasing support by its allies, dealt unremitting blows upon its adversaries. By mid-September the Germans had been driven from all of their gains of earlier in the year and were back on the Hindenburg Line. Here they intended to stand for the winter, but events had passed beyond their control. In great set-piece attacks on 18 and 26 September, employing large amounts of high explosives with the utmost skill, the British army overran first the ridge protecting the Hindenburg Line and then the central Hindenburg system. After that, a German surrender was only a matter of time.

The British military experience in the First World War is not remembered with favor. The prevailing image is of martyred infantrymen sacrificed by stubborn, unimaginative commanders. That perception is not wholly misguided. The war is noteworthy for an absence of inspired generalship and for many wasteful and culpable operations (even though some of them were the brainchild less of benighted militarists than of "imaginative" civilians).

Yet the war's dreadful immobility was not the result of military stupidity. It sprang from a revolution in weaponry that bestowed great power on the defense. And just four years of mobilization, experimentation, and growing expertise enabled this situation to be transformed. Four years, it deserves to be recalled, was significantly less time than it took to defeat Napoleon Bonaparte or Adolf Hitler.

Robin Prior
Trevor Wilson

Bibliography

Cruttwell, C.R.M.F. *A History of the Great War, 1914–1918.* 2nd ed. 1936.

Prior, Robin, and Trevor Wilson. *Command on the Western Front: The Military Career of Sir Henry Rawlinson, 1914–1918.* 1992.

Wilson, Trevor. *The Myriad Faces of War: Britain and the Great War, 1914–1918.* 1986.

Woodward, Llewellyn. *Great Britain and the War of 1914–1918.* 1967.

Fisher, John Arbuthnot (1841–1920)

John Arbuthnot Fisher was the British admiral responsible for modernizing the **Royal Navy** as First Sea Lord (1904–10) before the **First World War** and served again as First Sea Lord (1914–15) for a crucial year of that war.

Fisher was born in 1841 and joined the Royal Navy in 1854. During the Crimean War he saw action with the Baltic Fleet, and as a captain in the Mediterranean Fleet in 1882 he participated in the British intervention in Egypt. He took command of the gunnery school HMS *Excellent* in 1883 and dramatically reformed British gunnery methods. After commanding the Mediterranean Fleet, the premier sea command in the navy, Fisher became Second Sea Lord in 1902. As Sea Lord responsible for naval personnel, he thoroughly reorganized naval training, particularly the officer cadet system.

In 1904 Fisher became First Sea Lord and began six years of the most extensive changes the Royal Navy had seen. He created a naval war council, which, while far from being a full-fledged naval staff, was an important beginning.

He concentrated the British Fleet nearer home waters, after a century on far-flung colonial stations, in order to be ready for a European war. His most important innovations, however, were two revolutionary new warships. While commanding the Mediterranean Fleet Fisher had conceived the idea of an all-big-gun battleship, which became HMS *Dreadnought* (1906), and a battle cruiser with battleship armament and cruiser speed, which became HMS *Invincible* (1908). As First Sea Lord Fisher pushed both programs forward rapidly, and the new types of warship formed the backbone of the British Fleet when he retired in 1910. He had become Baron Fisher of Kilverstone in 1909.

First Lord of the Admiralty **Winston Churchill** recalled Fisher to service in 1914 to replace Prince Louis of Battenberg as First Sea Lord. Together they conceived a daring but confused attack on Germany's Turkish ally to break the stalemate in France. The original plan called for a naval squadron to force the Dardanelles, attack Constantinople, and knock Turkey out of the war. The initial naval attack (1915) stalled, and a subsequent larger operation that included an amphibious landing in **Gallipoli** was a costly failure. Fisher quarreled bitterly with Churchill, and both left the Admiralty amid great controversy in May 1915, but Fisher continued to speak out forcefully on naval and military issues until his death in 1920.

David MacGregor

Bibliography

Bacon, Reginald. *The Life of Lord Fisher of Kilverstone*. 2 vols. 1929.

Hough, Richard. *First Sea Lord: An Authorised Biography of Admiral Lord Fisher*. 1969.

Mackay, Ruddock F. *Fisher of Kilverstone*. 1973.

Marder, Arthur J. *Fear God and Dread Nought: The Correspondence of Admiral of the Fleet Lord Fisher of Kilverstone*. 3 vols. 1952–9.

Sumida, Jon Tetsuro. *In Defence of Naval Supremacy: Finance, Technology, and British Naval Policy, 1889–1914*. 1989.

Fleming, Alexander (1881–1955)

Alexander Fleming, the discoverer of penicillin, was born in Scotland, the son of Ayrshire farmers. In 1901 he enrolled as a medical student at St. Mary's Hospital Medical School in London. Qualifying in 1906, he joined Sir Almroth Wright as an assistant in the Inoculation Department of the hospital, working initially on techniques for the diagnosis and treatment of syphilis. During the **First World War** Fleming turned to problems of wound infection, identifying infective organisms in battlefield casualties and their means of action. Most important, Fleming explored the reasons the antiseptic techniques employed by surgeons did not work in war wounds. He showed that antiseptics not only could not reach the crevices where many microbes lurked, but also were rapidly removed by the discharge of fluid and pus. He also found that antiseptics could destroy the patient's leukocytes—the body's defense against invading bacteria—while leaving the bacteria themselves unharmed.

After the war Fleming returned to St. Mary's and in 1921 made his first major discovery, that of a ferment (an enzyme in today's terminology) present in most body fluids that had the power to dissolve certain bacteria. Then in 1928 Fleming discovered penicillin almost by accident when a mold spore contaminated a plate in which he was growing staphylococci, a form of bacteria. What was different about this mold was that it appeared to dissolve the surrounding bacteria. More exciting still, when Fleming made subcultures of the mold he found that, while the culture fluid was strongly antibacterial, it was nontoxic to human leukocytes and to laboratory animals. But Fleming failed to extract or purify the active principle in the fluid and, after a few tentative trials, gave up using it as a therapeutic agent. The penicillin was too unstable and weak for treatment purposes. And there it might have remained, but for the work of Howard Florey and Ernst Chain in **Oxford**. In 1940 Chain and Florey prepared enough partially purified penicillin for clinical trials, which confirmed and extended Fleming's original findings. By the end of the Second World War the bulk of commercially produced penicillin came from the United States. In 1945 Fleming shared the Nobel Prize for Medicine with Florey and Chain for the discovery of penicillin.

Fleming is best remembered for his work on penicillin, and his name often unduly overshadows those of Florey and Chain. But penicillin was only a small part of his work. Most of his routine work was concerned with the production of vaccines, a lucrative project that made the Inoculation Department financially independent of St. Mary's, and on which Fleming relied for his salary. In 1921 Wright appointed Fleming to take charge of the production of vaccines. When Wright retired in 1946, Fleming took over the department, renamed the following year the Wright-Fleming Institute. Fleming resigned in 1955 and died later that year.

David Cantor

Bibliography
Macfarlane, Gwyn. *Alexander Fleming: The Man and the Myth*. 1985.

Folk Song and Dance

In England the collection and publication of folk songs and dances was late by Continental standards. Only during the last decade of the nineteenth century did publication begin in earnest, a development encouraged by the foundation of the Folk Song Society in 1898. While Cecil Sharp (1859–1924) was not the first collector, he became the most important, collecting nearly 5,000 tunes in all and publishing more than 1,000, beginning with the *Folk Songs of Somerset* (in five parts, 1904–9). His views on folk song as outlined in *English Folk-song: Some Conclusions* (1907) were influential: He regarded folk song as a living musical expression open to everyone and was particularly zealous at promoting it in schools. In 1911 Sharp formed the English Folk Dance Society, which in 1932 was amalgamated with the Folk Song Society to become the English Folk Dance and Song Society. All three societies published journals containing scholarly articles and transcriptions.

Oddly enough, when **Ralph Vaughan Williams** first met Sharp in 1900, folk song was not mentioned, but following the collection of his first folk song in 1903, Vaughan Williams became an avid collector (of more than 800 songs and variants), making arrangements of many and firing the enthusiasm of other composers, such as George Butterworth (who subsequently worked with Sharp) and **Gustav Holst**. It was Sharp who suggested that Holst compose an orchestral piece drawing on folk song; the result was *A Somerset Rhapsody* (1907), based on Holst's favorite traditional tune, "It's a rosebud in June." Percy Grainger, having left his native Australia and settled in London for a period, joined the Folk Song Society in 1905. The following year he introduced the use of the wax-cylinder phonograph for the collection of folk songs. His cycle of *British Folk-music Settings* features several of the 500 he collected. The discovery of this wealth of English tunes provided composers with a new melodic resource—a significant number were modal rather than in the major or minor keys—that could be used to combat the influence of Continental, particularly German, melodic styles and give rise to a nationalist music.

The systematic collection of Welsh folk music began in 1908, encouraged by the formation of the Welsh Folk Song Society (1906), which published its own journal edited initially by J. Lloyd Williams (1909–48). The creation of the Welsh Folk Museum at St. Fagan's, near Cardiff, provided further impetus, recordings of folk material made *in situ* beginning in 1963. A decade earlier, the School of Scottish Studies at Edinburgh University (established in 1951) led to a resurgence of interest in Scottish folk music, although in Scotland the publication of collections of folk songs and dances had continued throughout the nineteenth and twentieth centuries.

Trevor Bray

Bibliography
Howes, Frank. *Folk Music of Britain and Beyond*. 1969.
Lloyd, Albert Lancaster. *Folk Song in England*. 1967.
Sharp, Cecil James. *English Folk-Song: Some Conclusions*. 3rd ed. 1954.

Fonteyn, Margot (1919–1991)

Prima ballerina of England's Royal Ballet and the embodiment of its flowing, lyrical style, Margot Fonteyn was one of the greatest classical dancers of the twentieth century. Equally revered by the dancers she inspired and the public she enchanted, she endowed her dancing with elegant simplicity, seamless physical grace, and sensitive musicality, and her growth as an artist paralleled the growth of the company she led and crowned its many years of international success.

Fonteyn's career began in 1934, when she made her debut as a snowflake in *The Nutcracker*, and ended in 1986 with a guest appearance as the Queen in *The Sleeping Beauty*. Having made her mark quickly with the Vic-Wells Ballet (renamed the Sadler's Wells Ballet in 1940 and the Royal Ballet in 1956), she established herself as its brightest star in 1946, dancing Aurora in *The Sleeping Beauty* when it reopened the Royal Opera House after the Second World War. Aurora became her signature role, and when the company first toured America three years later, Fonteyn conquered the country with her joyous, radiant characterization and gentle, effortless expressivity.

A refined and subtle interpreter of the great nineteenth-century classics, like *Swan Lake*, *Giselle*, and *La Sylphide*, Fonteyn was also the constant muse of the English choreographer **Frederick Ashton**, who created nearly two dozen roles for her. She was his ideal *Cinderella* (1948), his *Ondine* (1958), his Queen of the Air in *Homage to the Queen* (1953), and the luminous central presence in his masterpiece, *Symphonic Variations* (1946). His choreography and her poised and passionate interpretation of it together defined the Royal Ballet's illustrious style.

Fonteyn appeared as a guest artist with over thirty companies and created new **ballets** by such varied choreographers as **Ninette de Valois**, Roland Petit, John Cranko, and Martha Graham. As the resident star of the Royal Ballet until the early 1970s, she was partnered at home and on the company's many world tours by its noblest cavaliers, notably Robert Helpmann and Michael Somes. When she was forty-two and considering retirement, a new partnership with a young Russian defector, Rudolf Nureyev, revived and transformed her career. Fonteyn and Nureyev became ballet's first international superstars; set against his explosive energy and exotic ardor, her exquisite purity and impeccable technique shone with fresh authority.

Awarded a CBE in 1951 and a DBE in 1956, Fonteyn was also President of the Royal Academy of Dancing (1954–91) and Chancellor of Durham University (1982–91). Since modesty and intelligence informed her character as completely as her dancing, no title or honor ever distracted her from her single-minded pursuit of artistic excellence. The greater her fame, the harder she worked to perfect her natural gifts, until finally every aspect of her life reflected her love of her art and her unbounded devotion to it.

Barbara Newman

Bibliography

Bland, Alexander. *The Royal Ballet: The First Fifty Years.* 1981.

Clarke, Mary. *The Sadler's Wells Ballet: A History and an Appreciation.* 1955.
Fonteyn, Margot. *Autobiography.* 1975.
Money, Keith. *The Art of Margot Fonteyn.* 1975.

Foot, Michael (1913–)

A member of a dynasty of religious dissenters and political radicals, Michael Foot had a career as journalist, author, campaigner, and, above all, as a **Labour Party** politician. A long journey, from back-bench maverick to left-wing spokesman, then responsible "insider," and, finally, party leader, ultimately did little good to his party. Foot was educated at a **Quaker** school and **Oxford,** and his youthful conversion from Liberalism to socialism led him to Parliament as MP for Plymouth Devonport in 1945. For ten years a rebellious figure apparently indifferent to the attractions of office, he lost his seat in 1955. Returned to the House of Commons for Ebbw Vale in 1960, Foot pursued his intense commitment to nuclear disarmament and otherwise often seemed content to mix the irresponsibilities of dissent with the world of letters. By 1970 he perhaps realized that at age fifty-seven he was too old to remain an *enfant terrible.* He was elected to the Shadow Cabinet and a year later unsuccessfully contested the party's deputy leadership. An increasingly prominent voice of the Left, he became Shadow leader of the House in 1972 and served as a more self-disciplined bridge between wings of the party. In 1976 his links to the Left and the trade unions assisted his appointment as Employment Secretary, a post in which he was arguably too compliant in his dealings with the powerful union movement.

In 1976 **Harold Wilson** resigned as Prime Minister. Foot survived as the final challenger to the victorious **James Callaghan** in the struggle for succession and became deputy leader of the party. He and Callaghan represented its old Right and Left, and they joined in an effort to stabilize it as divisions grew deeper. As leader of the House Foot was often more effective than critics had expected in steering legislation through the Commons; his skills reflected his deep affection for, and knowledge of, the parliamentary process. He also worked hard to protect Callaghan's left flank until the latter's resignation in the wake of Labour's 1979 election defeat. In 1980 Foot replaced him as party leader, combining some center and right-wing support with that of the ascendant Left.

Foot became leader at a difficult, perhaps impossible, time. The party's conflicts were intense, public, and bitter, its machinery archaic, its electoral base diminishing. He cannot be said to have been equal to the job. He began an attack on **Militant**, but his memory of anti-Bevanite purges in the 1950s would not allow him to carry it through. He was unable to head off the party's Left-dominated National Executive, which imposed policies repugnant to many moderate Labour voters. Above all, he could not persuade the electorate that he was a possible Prime Minister. His rhetorical style and frail, shabby appearance let him be caricatured as more a mad prophet than a contemporary politician; although a cultivated man, he was accused of knowing more about the eighteenth century than about his own. In 1983 he led the party through a shambles of a campaign based on an impossible manifesto and a willful indifference to modern electioneering techniques. When resigning, he passed to his protegé **Neil Kinnock** a poisoned chalice, made more toxic by his own limitations as a leader.

Steven Reilly

Bibliography

Foot, Michael. *Debts of Honour*. 1980.
Hoggart, Simon, and David Leigh. *Michael Foot: A Portrait*. 1981.
Jones, Mervyn. *Michael Foot*. 1994.
Morgan, Kenneth O. *Labour People: Leaders and Lieutenants*. 1987.

Football

During the twentieth century football (soccer) replaced **cricket** as Britain's national game. It has more players and spectators than any other. There are few parts of England, Scotland, or Wales where it is not the most popular sport. From September to April football is inseparable from Saturday afternoons; every town and village has its teams and leagues ranging from the most humble who play for fun to the semiprofessional and the elite of paid players who perform before a paying audience for a living. By the 1930s the weekly football pool competition meant that the names of the leading professional clubs were familiar to many men and women who had never been near a football

ground. Football had grown out of its regional origins in northern England, the Midlands, and central Scotland and become part of the British **popular culture**. When England won the World Cup in 1966 everyone, except the Scots, rejoiced.

It was the football club that was the heart, if not the soul, of the game. Both at the recreational and the spectator level it was a site of sociability and the focus of local loyalties and rivalries. The English Football League, emulating American baseball, had its first season in 1888–9. The Scottish League began in 1890–1. By 1921 there were four divisions in England containing eighty-six clubs and two divisions in Scotland, and the pattern has changed little since then. Promotion and relegation added to the excitement. Winning the First Division became the prerogative of the big-city clubs. In Scotland this meant the Glasgow "old firm" of Celtic and Rangers, who were so dominant that in only four years during 1900–50 did one or the other of them fail to win the championship. It was more open in England. Between 1900 and 1915 eight different clubs won the English First Division. All save Birmingham's Aston Villa were located in the north. By the 1930s Arsenal, from London, had become the dominant club, winning five championships and in part reflecting a shift in the economic strength of England from north to south. Arsenal remained a leading club, but Liverpool became the phenomenon of modern times, breaking all records with eleven titles since 1972.

The most popular domestic competition is the Football Association (FA) Cup. This is a straightforward knockout first competed for in 1872. The final is usually in London, since 1923 at Wembley Stadium. If few can win the League, all can dream of winning the Cup, and big clubs are often knocked out by small fry along the way. It remains rare to win both English Cup and League. Only Tottenham (1961), Arsenal (1971), and Liverpool (1986) have done so in the twentieth century.

The British not only invented modern football; they also persuaded most of the rest of the world to take it up. But there has always been a tension between British parochialism and internationalism. The British had their own international championship, which lasted 100 years from 1883–4 to 1983–4. They refused to join the Fédération Internationale de Football Associations (FIFA) when it was established in 1904. They changed their minds after the First World War but left in 1928 following disagreements about what constituted amateurism. The British rejoined in 1946, and England first appeared in the World Cup in 1950, somewhat inauspiciously, as they lost to the United States.

The English League similarly lacked enthusiasm when the European Champions Cup began in 1955–6 and refused to allow the English champions to take part. The Scots were more sensible, and their representative, Hibernian, reached the semifinals. The following season Manchester United ignored parochialism and also reached the semifinals. There was no British winner until Glasgow Celtic in 1967, but after that British clubs did well in what had become three European competitions. Aston Villa (1982), Manchester United (1968), Nottingham Forest (1979, 1980), and Liverpool (1977, 1978, 1981, 1984) all won the Champions Cup.

But this international success was marred by violence and hooliganism. English clubs were banned from European competition between 1986 and 1990 after crowd trouble at the 1985 European Cup finals in Brussels. Thirty-nine people, most of them Italian fans of Juventus, were crushed to death following a charge by a Liverpool section of the crowd. Violence by a small but nasty minority of young men had long disfigured the game in England. The main response was increased policing and supporter segregation.

Then came the Hillsborough disaster. Ninety-five Liverpool supporters died on the overcrowded terraces of Sheffield Wednesday before the 1989 Football Association Cup semifinal. The government set up an inquiry, chaired by Lord Justice Taylor, that highlighted the financial problems of the game as leisure patterns diversified. His report recommended all-seater stadiums (rather than standing room) for the leading clubs and was in tune with a growing tendency for football to become more commercialized. Clubs vigorously pursued sponsorship and a more affluent consumer. Large sums were obtained from television to screen live, mainly First Division, matches. In 1991–2 the leading twenty-two clubs broke away from the Football League to form the Premier League and to make an exclusive agreement with a satellite television company. A small group of leading Scottish clubs seemed set on a similar course.

Tony Mason

Bibliography
Fishwick, Nicholas. *English Football and Society, 1910–1950.* 1989.
Mason, Tony. *Association Football and English Society, 1863–1915.* 1980.
———. "Football" in Tony Mason, ed. *Sport in Britain: A Social History.* 1989. pp. 146–86.
Walvin, James. *The People's Game: A Social History of Football.* 1975.

Ford, Ford Madox (1873–1939)

Novelist, poet and editor, art, literary, and cultural critic, Ford Madox Ford (Ford Madox Hueffer until 1919) was the grandson of the painter Ford Madox Brown and, consequently, was reared on the rim of the pre-Raphaelite circle. He repudiated it and embraced impressionism during his years of collaboration with **Joseph Conrad**. Ford and Conrad believed that a story could be told realistically only by rendering impressions, not by narrating events. Together they wrote three novels, with *Romance* (1904) the best known. Ford founded the *English Review* in December 1908 and edited it until December 1909, publishing established writers like **John Galsworthy**, Thomas Hardy, W.H. Hudson, Henry James, **H.G. Wells**, and Conrad and giving voice to new writers like **D.H. Lawrence** and **Wyndham Lewis**, both of whom Ford discovered and was the first to publish.

During this time he was involved in a notorious affair with Violet Hunt, which she commemorated in *The Flurried Years* (1928); it ended in 1919 when he was mustered out of the army and moved to the English countryside with the Australian painter Stella Bowen.

Before joining the British Expeditionary Force to fight in Flanders and France, Ford wrote, among many other books, critical studies of Madox Brown (1896), Rossetti (1902), Holbein (1905), and the pre-Raphaelite Brotherhood (1907); a trilogy on English culture published in the United States as *England and the English* (1907); pastiches in the manner of Henry James, of which *A Call* (1910) is most satisfying; satires on socialism and utopian thinking, the best being *The Simple Life Limited* (1911); and the historical novels of *The Fifth Queen* trilogy (1906–8) centered on Catherine Howard and Henry VIII. Ford praised James in his critical study of him (1913) as "the greatest of living writers and, in consequence, for me, the greatest of living men" just before writing his first undisputed masterpiece, *The Good Soldier* (1915), which rivals James' fiction with its elegance of form and its indictment of society. This novel of manners explores the sexual life of two upper-class couples and represents the perfection of Ford's idea of a novel: "the rendering of an Affair: of one embroilment, one set of embarrassments, one human coil, one psychological progression."

Ford published seven volumes of poetry before establishing a place for himself as a war poet in *On Heaven and Poems Written on Active Service* (1918). It answered his demand for a poetry that was at least as good as the best prose, a poetry that is written the way one speaks, expressing one's thoughts in the language of the day. Ford's final collection of poems, *Buckshee* in *Collected Poems* (1936), realizes this program completely in its concluding poem "Coda," a meditation on time.

Ford settled in France, shuttling between Paris and Provence, in 1922. He founded the *Transatlantic Review*, which survived for twelve issues in 1924, publishing such avant-garde writers as e.e. cummings, Ernest Hemingway, **James Joyce**, Ezra Pound, Gertrude Stein, and William Carlos Williams. At this time Ford began writing *Parade's End* (1924–8), a tetralogy (some insist it is a trilogy) on the Great War, which is arguably the best novel to emerge from the **First World War**. In the tortured relationships of Christopher Tietjens with his wife and lover, Ford realizes fully his constant theme of the anguish of sexuality, drawing modern human beings into love as uneasy compensation for modern war's witness that "man is to man a wolf." The completion of *Parade's End* coincided with the end of his relationship with Stella Bowen and the beginning of his association with Janice Biala, a Polish-American painter, which lasted until his death.

Parade's End made Ford a celebrity in the United States, where he traveled extensively and tirelessly promoted the works of young American writers. He continued to publish books until they numbered eighty-one at the time of his death. He completed a series of autobiographical memoirs that began with *Ancient Lights* (1911), continued in *Thus to Revisit* (1921) and *Return to Yesterday* (1931), and ended with *It Was the Nightingale* (1933), all of which emphasize his literary, not his personal, life. Ford's last book was *The March of Literature from Confucius' Day to Our Own*

(1938), written while he was teaching at Olivet College in Michigan, "a refuge for good writers who are down on their end-bones." He died in Deauville, France, on 26 June 1939.

Joseph Wiesenfarth

Bibliography

Green, Robert. *Ford Madox Ford: Prose and Politics*. 1981.

Judd, Alan. *Ford Madox Ford*. 1991.

MacShane, Frank. *The Life and Work of Ford Madox Ford*. 1965.

Moser, Thomas C. *The Life in the Fiction of Ford Madox Ford*. 1980.

Contemporary Literature (special Ford issue), vol. 30 (1989).

Foreign Office and Foreign Service

Lord Salisbury, Foreign Secretary and Prime Minister at the end of the nineteenth century, once compared the nature of British foreign policy to drifting "lazily downstream, occasionally putting out a boat hook to avoid a collision." His Foreign Office represented a self-confident country, practicing "splendid isolation," at the height of its power. In the twentieth century, however, as Great Britain declined steadily as a world power, the Foreign Office and Foreign Service changed as a result of political and social pressures.

Before 1914 these two institutions were separate entities, both, however, aristocratic in makeup and tone. Salisbury's mock insouciance was typical of aristocratic attitudes, as a public school (particularly Etonian) and Oxbridge education was obligatory in both the Foreign Office establishment in Whitehall and the Foreign Service. By 1914 fewer than 176 men ran foreign policy from London and a further 450 were in diplomatic service overseas. Reforms in 1906 gave a larger role in the management of foreign policy to the permanent staff, which adopted an anti-German and pro-French stance. While the old Foreign Office played an important role in policy-making prior to 1914, the **Cabinet** alone made the decision to declare war against Germany.

The **First World War** changed the Foreign Office and Foreign Service irrevocably. The Left remained suspicious about the role the Foreign Secretary, Sir **Edward Grey**, and the "striped-pants" diplomats had played in the events of August 1914. Grey, to 1916, and later **Arthur**

Balfour provided weak leadership, as from 1917 **David Lloyd George**, as Prime Minister, and the War Cabinet usurped the role of traditional diplomacy. Yet the functions of the Foreign Office increased significantly in managing the economic war against the Central Powers. On another level, women replaced men as shorthand typists, only to be themselves displaced as the men returned from the war.

In the democratic tide following the end of the war, the government implemented reforms that the 1914 Royal Commission on the Civil Service had recommended. The Foreign Office and Foreign Service were combined, the old property qualification for entrance was abolished, attention was drawn to the inordinate number of Old Etonians in the service, but no reform in the system of recruitment came for another two decades. Thus the Foreign Office and diplomatic service remained firmly elitist even though they never regained their pre-war influence. By 1926, under **Austen Chamberlain**, the Foreign Office stood for European conciliation and the realization that peace had become Great Britain's chief interest in an era of national decline and appeasement.

The Foreign Office fared badly in the years preceding the Second World War. **Neville Chamberlain**, Prime Minister from May 1937, took charge of British foreign policy; for its part, the Foreign Office's permanent staff had little confidence in the Prime Minister. As a result, the formal diplomatic structure was deliberately bypassed in the betrayal of Czechoslovakia, which paved the way for a new war, although **Lord Halifax**, who had replaced **Anthony Eden** as Foreign Secretary in February 1938, and Nevile Henderson, the ambassador in Berlin, endorsed **appeasement**.

Like the First, the **Second World War** stimulated change at the Foreign Office. In 1943 the Eden-Bevin reforms amalgamated the diplomatic service with consular and commercial functions; women were admitted for the first time into the foreign civil service; and the "Old Boy" network, although it did not vanish, became an exception to the general rule for entry in time for heavy recruitment to the service after 1945. In policy matters, the Foreign Office played a major role in the origins of the Cold War. **Ernest Bevin**, Foreign Secretary in Clement Attlee's Labour government, adopted a hard line toward the Soviet Union fully supported by the Foreign Office establishment but attacked by the left wing of the **Labour Party** for allegedly turning Great Britain into a dependency of the United States.

The 1950s were an unsettling decade for the Foreign Office and for British foreign policy. In June 1951 the Foreign Office's credibility was dealt a crippling blow with the defection to the Soviet Union of Guy Burgess, a diplomat, and Donald Maclean, the head of the American Department. The ill-fated **Suez crisis** of 1956, in which the Foreign Office was bypassed, ended the career as Prime Minister of Anthony Eden, who had resigned in 1938 in defense of the Foreign Office's prerogatives.

Further changes in the Foreign Office and diplomatic service reflected Great Britain's weakness in the post-war world. The Plowden Report in 1964 advocated that economic and commercial work become the most important role of the Foreign Office. As the Empire dissolved, the Whitehall headquarters was renamed the Foreign and Commonwealth Office (FCO) in 1968. In 1973 Britain entered the **European Community**, and British diplomats finally accepted the fact of diminishing world power. They also have had to acknowledge that most power in policy-making has passed to the Cabinet Office as successive Prime Ministers have taken the initiative in foreign policy.

Aside from losing influence, the Foreign and Commonwealth Office has continued to grapple with its elitist past. Although Oxbridge-educated personnel still dominate the foreign civil service, the home **civil service** plays an increasing role in external affairs, since emphasis is now on economic matters requiring expertise. The number of people employed by the FCO has risen to nearly 5,000 in Whitehall and over 200 British posts overseas. As recently as 1974 the FCO employed 91.1 percent men to 8.9 percent women, although today it claims to be an equal opportunity employer. As Great Britain integrates with the European Union and seeks to deemphasize domestic class distinctions, the trends toward less influence for the foreign civil service and more-open employment policies should continue.

John McDermott

Bibliography
Moorhouse, Geoffrey. *The Diplomats: The Foreign Office Today.* 1977.
Steiner, Zara. *The Foreign Office and Foreign Policy, 1898–1914.* 1969.
Strang, William. *The Foreign Office.* 1955.

Wallace, William. *The Foreign Policy Process in Britain.* 1976.

Foreign Travel

Britons in the twentieth century began to enjoy the luxury of foreign travel in a manner never before available because of the rise in incomes and the gradual social democratization of society.

The Cook's tour offered the middle classes the deference and attention paid to the British upper classes in England at affordable prices and without the complications of independent travel. Egypt, Italy, and Switzerland were among the most popular destinations, although as early as 1905 the Balearic Islands began to appear in Cook's brochures. One appeal of such organized tours was that they made unchaperoned travel by women acceptable. Respectable ladies could venture forth to climb in the Swiss Alps or ride bicycles through France. They could also cross the ocean aboard luxurious liners, such as the *Mauretania*, *Lusitania*, or the *Aquitania*, where sociability between men and women was encouraged. The *P and O Vestris*, a steam yacht chartered by Cook's tours, traveled to Sicily, Naples, Greece, Syria, and the Holy Land. Tours were arranged with several price structures to allow Britons of all classes to self-select the social status of their traveling companions. In 1921 the first Cairo to the Cape tour was organized by Cook's with the explorer Sir Alfred Sharpe as guide. British travelers were accommodated on rail, motor coach, and riverboat in making the Cairo to the Cape adventure of seven weeks for which they paid £1,500 pounds. After the 1922 discovery of King Tut's tomb, Egypt held a special fascination.

British travelers were attracted to historical sites, religious centers, and, after the First World War, to battlefields and gravesites. In addition to the usual hotel accommodations and sight-seeing excursions, some opted for camping and cycling tours of the Continent and the Mediterranean, while others enjoyed stays in chalets. In 1919 the first flying tour aboard the *Handley Page*, a redesigned First World War bomber, was advertised. Imperial Airways Company, formed in 1924, flew Britons from London to Paris for £10, connecting with other European airways to fly passengers to Moscow and India. Britons could board the *Graf Zeppelin* and fly to North America and Brazil. By 1929 British tourists to France numbered 881,000, approximately 40 percent of all visitors to France; at the same time Britons comprised 133,000, or 20 percent, of tourists to Italy, 200,000, or about 15 percent, of tourists to Switzerland, and 110,000, or 10 percent, of tourists to Germany. In addition to Continental travel, Britons also ventured to the Caribbean, the Mediterranean, America, and all points within the British Empire, often assisted by the uniformed Cook's guide.

The expansion of budget air travel and cheap package tours revolutionized the travel industry after the Second World War, despite restrictions on the amount of currency that could be taken out of the country. The Creative Travel Agents' Conference was established to regulate the activities of the leading agents— Cook's, Poly, Frame, Workers' Travel Association, Henry Lunn, Pickfords, and Dean and Dawson. In 1954 the travel allowance was raised to £100 pounds for Britons going abroad, which stimulated tourism. In the decade between 1950 and 1960 special trains carried tourists to the French Riviera, to Spain, and to Austria and Switzerland. Spain as a tourist destination blossomed because of the relatively low prices and spectacular climate. Abandoning Blackpool and Margate, Britons began to frequent Mediterranean beaches in profusion, turning stretches of the Costa Brava and the Costa del Sol, not to mention Majorca and Portugal, into a sun-baked version of English resorts. The desire for accommodations with hygiene and comfort on a par with France and Switzerland spawned clusters of Spanish condominiums along the coast, largely rented, leased, or owned by British visitors. By 1988 spending by British tourists overseas was estimated at more than £8 million, although this was nearly balanced by foreign tourists, who spent more than £6 million in Britain.

Barbara Bennett Peterson

Bibliography

Fussell, Paul. *Abroad: British Literary Traveling between the Wars.* 1980.

Mulvey, Christopher. *Transatlantic Manners.* 1990.

Pimlott, J.A.R. *The Englishman's Holiday.* rev. ed. 1976.

Swinglehurst, Edmond. *Cook's Tours: The Story of Popular Travel.* 1982.

Unwin, Philip. *Traveling by Train in the Edwardian Age.* 1979.

F

Forster, E(dward) M(organ) (1879–1970)

E.M. Forster, known to his friends as Morgan, was a leading British novelist of the twentieth century, with his own special position, asserting his own point of view, more intensely English than those somewhat earlier residents, **Joseph Conrad** and Henry James, who came to live and write in England, less of a realist than his immediate predecessors, the Edwardian novelists **H.G. Wells** and **Arnold Bennett**, less passionate than **D.H. Lawrence**. He was more of a modernist than Wells or Bennett, but less of a one than **Virginia Woolf** or **James Joyce**. He is a novelist and essayist who has much to say to the general reader as well as to any student of literature and of modern Britain.

Forster was the son of an architect, Edward Morgan Forster, who was descended from the Clapham Sect, a group of early nineteenth-century evangelical **Anglicans** who were devout philanthropists, particularly concerned with fighting the slave trade. Although in a formal sense Forster abandoned their values, he maintained, in a modern version, and in a much more lighthearted way, a good deal of their moral seriousness. Marianne, a daughter of Henry Thornton of Clapham, regarded Edward Forster as her favorite nephew and encouraged his marriage in 1877 to her protégée, Lily Whichelo. Their first child died at birth; the second, born on New Year's Day 1879, was to be called Henry Morgan Forster but, at his christening, in a typical Forsterian confusion, his father provided his own first name by mistake. Edward Morgan he remained thereafter. His father died when Forster was twenty-two months old, and in his early years the boy was surrounded and doted on by women: his mother, her mother, and his great aunt Marianne. When she died in 1887, she left him a legacy of £8,000, which gave him financial security until he began to make a comfortable living from his writings. He published her biography, *Marianne Thornton*, in 1956, which concluded: "She and no one else made my career as a writer possible, and her love, in a most tangible sense, followed me beyond the grave." Hence, in his earliest life, the theme of *Howards End*, money's ability to confer freedom, had been introduced. He had a happy childhood, living from 1883 to 1893 at Rooksnest, at Stevenage in Hertfordshire, which served as the model for the house Howards End.

As was typical of literary members of the English middle class, happiness was much curtailed when Forster went to boarding school, at the age of eleven, at Kent House in Eastbourne, and then, an intensely unhappy eight years at Tonbridge, which he would pillory as Sawston in *The Longest Journey*. He then went to King's College, **Cambridge**, in 1897, where he was supremely happy. His academic career was not particularly distinguished, but he made great friends there, became a member of the secret discussion society, the **Apostles**, and was encouraged in his interests by two young dons, Goldsworthy Lowes Dickinson (whose biography he wrote in 1934) and Nathaniel Wedd.

Trips to Italy with his mother helped liberate his imagination, and his first published story, "The Story of a Panic" (1904), tells of the central character, Eustace's, encounter with Pan in Ravello near Naples. It was there in 1902 that Forster became convinced of his vocation as a writer. His first novel, *Where Angels Fear to Tread*, was published in 1905. As in the story, Italy stands for the excitement of liberation, and its dangers, and is counterpoised to the restricted emotions of the English and what Forster sees as their undeveloped hearts. Lila Herriton, a young widow, takes an extended trip to Italy, where she secretly marries Gino, a younger lower-middle-class Italian. Forster gives such characters vitality and fecundity—they have a son—but he does not make them perfect noble savages. Lila's brother-in-law, Philip, one of Forster's Englishmen who thinks he understands, but doesn't, whose emotions have been curdled by thought, makes two trips to Italy to interfere, once to prevent a marriage that has already taken place, and second to kidnap the son of the union, an adventure that ends with an overturned carriage and the death of the baby.

His second novel, *The Longest Journey* (1907), is a less polished performance and is more typical of a first novel, something of a *Bildungsroman*, appropriately dedicated to the Apostles. It tells of Rickie, whose lameness stands for his emotional limitations. He is an observer, but when Agnes Pembroke's fiancé, Gerald, dies, Rickie eventually marries her. The famous opening of the fifth chapter, "Gerald died that afternoon," demonstrates Forster's technique that **Christopher Isherwood** called "tea-tabling," a suggestion that violence can lurk beneath the decorum of English society. Like Gino in *Where Angels Fear to Tread*, Stephen Wonham, Rickie's illegitimate half-brother, stands for the more emotional side of life, uncontrolled and exciting. The novel ends with Rickie sacrificing his own life in order to save the drunken Stephen.

His third novel, *A Room with a View* (1908), made even better known through a very successful movie version (1986), tells a similar story but, unlike the two previous novels, ends happily. Lucy Honeychurch has her feelings liberated by a visit to Florence and being kissed in a field by George Emerson. Back in England, she attempts to turn away from her true feelings by becoming engaged to the prig Cecil Vyse, but with the proddings of George's father and the manipulations of her cousin, the apparently unsympathetic Charlotte, she realizes she must follow her true feelings and marry George.

These three novels, though charming and effective, might not have survived if Forster had not gone on to write his two major works, *Howards End* (1910) and *A Passage to India* (1924)—opinions are divided on which is the more important, with perhaps the latter having an edge. *Howards End* was a great success, established Forster's reputation as a major novelist, and was his first novel to be published in America. The story catches with uncanny and prophetic exactitude the growing conflict between the world of "telegrams and anger" and the idealism and vulnerability of the liberal tradition at the end of its tether. It preaches the message of the need to "only connect" the prose and the passion, which are embodied in the world of the Wilcoxes, those who make money, and the Schlegels, those who believe in the arts and the importance of personal relations. The details of the social novel, questions of property, the tolerated violations of conventions by men (Mr. Wilcox has had a mistress) and the not-tolerated violations by women (Helen has an illegitimate child) take a parallel course to more sweeping questions: the role of nature, permanence, abiding English qualities, and even a certain mysticism in the role of Mrs. Wilcox, her house, and the wych elm that shadows it. The novel ends happily—the baby, Margaret's nephew, will inherit the house—and unhappily—Margaret is not able to save Henry Wilcox and make him see connections. Having written four novels in five years, Forster did not publish another novel until fourteen year later, and it would prove to be his last, even though he lived until 1970.

Since 1906 he had known Syed Ross Masood, and in 1910 he declared his passion for him, which was gently rebuffed. They remained close friends; Masood guided him in India in 1912 and would be the dedicatee of *A Passage to India*. In 1910, too, Forster came closer to the **Bloomsbury Group** and saw its members with increasing frequency. He started a novel, *Artic Summer*, but abandoned it. Inspired by a visit to Edward Carpenter, the apostle of socialism and **homosexuality**, in 1913 he wrote a novel of happy homosexual love, *Maurice*, but it was not published until 1971. He published one collection of short stories, *The Celestial Omnibus*, in 1911, and another, *The Eternal Moment*, in 1928. Before the war he also started to write short stories with erotic themes for his own amusement. These, and later stories, were published posthumously in *The Life to Come* (1972).

Forster started to write his Indian novel before the war, partially inspired by his trip, and after the war by serving as a secretary to the eccentric Marajahah of Dewas in 1921, an experience commemorated in his book *The Hill of Devi* (1953). During the First World War he worked in the National Gallery and then for the Red Cross in Alexandria, which inspired in two publications, *Alexandria: A History and Guide* (1922) and *Pharos and Pharillon* (1923). He also had his first affair, with Mohammed el Adl, and from then on his personal life was much more fulfilled. For him, the war had represented the defeat of reason, and *A Passage to India* is a darker novel than his previous ones. Despite their efforts, the Indians and the English are not able to get along, life is reduced to the meaninglessness, and the possible transcendence, of the *ou-boum* of the Marabar caves where Adela Quested thought, and then thought not, that she had been molested by Dr. Aziz. Connections are even less possible than they were in the world of *Howards End*. The Indians elevate Mrs. Moore into a deity, and Fielding and Aziz mean to be friends. But nature—in the shape of the rocks that divide them on their horseback ride at the conclusion of the novel—will not permit it. In the novel the social and the visionary impulses are magically joined. Seldom has there been a more convincing portrait of decent men and women trapped in the impossibilities of the imperial situation. Seldom has there been a more haunting evocation of the irrationalism that underlies so much of human behavior.

He wrote as well a book of literary criticism, *Aspects of the Novel* (1927), and two gatherings of essays, *Abinger Harvest* (1936)

F

and *Two Cheers for Democracy* (1951), ("only Love the Beloved Republic deserves [three]"). In 1924 he inherited the house his father had built for his aunt Laura, and that was his main home until he moved to King's College in 1946. There he lived until 1970, though he died at Coventry at the home of his longtime lover Bob Buckingham and his wife. Forster used his authority against the suppression of literature, as when he defended *The Well of Loneliness* in 1928 and *Lady Chatterley's Lover* in 1960. He came to embody those virtues that are thought of as peculiarly English: a firm belief in liberty, in fairness, in standing up for individual values, in refusing to be pompous, hieratical, self-adulating. In an intensely personal way he was not so distant from his Thornton forebears. Through his novels, and his other writings, he aimed to give pleasure, fulfill his aesthetic values, and also, to a degree, to improve the world and help the causes of private and public liberation.

Peter Stansky

Bibliography

Beauman, Nicola. *Morgan: A Biography of E.M. Forster*. 1993.
Crews, Frederick C. *E.M. Forster: The Perils of Humanism*. 1962.
Furbank, P.N. *E.M. Forster: A Life*. 1977–8.
Kirkpatrick, B.J. *A Bibliography of E.M. Forster*. 2nd ed. 1985.
Lago, Mary, and P.N. Furbank, ed. *Selected Letters of E.M. Forster*. 2 vols. 1983–5.
Stone, Wilfred. *The Cave and the Mountain*. 1966.
Trilling, Lionel. *E.M. Forster*. 1943.

Freud, Lucian (1922–)

Lucian Freud is widely regarded as Britain's foremost painter in the expressive figurative tradition, at least since the death of his one-time mentor, **Francis Bacon**. With his psychologically charged, often theatrically posed, images of alienated naked figures in drab urban interiors, his moody, muted pallette, and "hard won" painterliness, Freud is an exemplary member of the "School of London," which also includes such painters as Frank Auerbach, Leon Kossoff, and the younger American-born painter **R.B. Kitaj**.

Born in Berlin in 1922, he was the son of architect Max Freud and grandson of Sigmund Freud, a lineage that has undoubtedly played a role in the exotic persona Freud has always managed to cultivate. He moved with his family to England in 1932 and was educated at progressive boarding schools. In 1939, the year he became a naturalized British subject, Freud enrolled briefly at the East Anglian School of Painting and Drawing, Dedham, his only formal training.

He first came to public attention with drawings published in the wartime literary journal *Horizon*. Early works demonstrate a tentative surrealism, with incongruous arrangements of objects such as a stuffed zebra's head, a battered chaise longue, and a cactus plant, but he was more closely associated with the neo-romantic group that thrived in London during and after the Second World War. Intense, bulbous eyes, for instance, a characteristic of his early portraits, relate to the work of other artists in this group, such as John Minton, whose portrait he painted.

Freud made his own mark with meticulously executed realist works with a pervasive mood of alienation. **Herbert Read** dubbed him "the Ingres of existentialism," a perceptive remark in the context of an image such as *Interior in Paddington* (1951, Walker Art Gallery, Liverpool), which places an archetypal "angry young man" in disheveled raincoat, cigarette in one hand, the other a fist clenched, in claustrophobic proximity to a meticulously executed man-sized potted plant in an anonymous interior space. Later poses with comparable theatrical props include a male nude holding a rat (1977–8) and a female nude staring at a hard boiled egg halved in a dish (1980–1).

By the late 1950s Freud lost interest in the meticulous, Ingres-like sheen. He began to describe the face and body in terms of shape and structure, in *Pregnant Girl* (1960–1, private collection, United States) for instance; and often in female nudes the brushstrokes help delineate shape. By the time of the monumental 1985 self-portrait (private collection) attention to tonal detail is so acute, however, that paint builds up in concentrations devoid of any compositional function.

A close relationship with sitters is said to be important for Freud and on occasion contributes to his mystique as an artist. His widowed mother sat for an extensive series in the early 1970s, while several of his daughters have modeled nude. Compositions in the 1980s and 1990s have been increasingly ambitious—in terms of both scale and complexity. The standard was set by *Large Interior, W11 (After Watteau)* (1981–3, private collection), which involves five sitters (family members and his then-mistress, the artist Celia Paul) arranged in homage to Watteau's *Pierrot Content* (1712).

A series of monumental male nudes from the early 1990s feature the transvestite performance artist Leigh Bowery. More "Establishment" sitters have included Sir Jacob Rothschild, Lord Goodman, and Baron Thyssen-Bornemisza. Although the human form dominates his output, Freud has also executed cityscapes (viewed from his studio window) and obsessively detailed nature studies like *Two Plants* (1977–80, Tate Gallery). These recall Stanley Spencer, who might also be considered a precursor for nudes where there is a macabre attention to blood vessels and veins. Freud's artistic reputation was confirmed when he was named a Companion of Honour (1983) and later awarded the Order of Merit (1993).

David Cohen

Bibliography

Freud, Lucian, Nicholas Penny, and Robert Flynn Johnson. *Lucian Freud: Works on Paper* (exhibition catalog, South Bank). 1988.

Gowing, Lawrence. *Lucian Freud.* 1982.

Hughes, Robert, *Lucian Freud: Paintings* (exhibition catalog, British Council). 1987.

Lampert, Catherine. *Lucian Freud: Recent Work.* 1993.

Russell, John. *Lucian Freud* (exhibition catalog, Hayward Gallery). 1974.

Friends, Society of (Quakers)

British Quakerism began the twentieth century in a state of considerable theological ferment. The evangelicalism of the Victorian era, which had to some extent disfigured the distinctive Quaker identity during the previous century and made it difficult to distinguish the Society of Friends from many of the other nonconformist denominations of the period, was gradually giving way to the intellectual liberation of the so-called "liberal theology" of the day. The first decades of the century indeed came to be regarded as a Quaker Renaissance, when the energies and talents of a hitherto somewhat introspective society were turned more firmly outward than ever before, and Quakers sought and attained for themselves an influential role in the public culture of the nation disproportionate to their relatively small numbers. Quakers were increasingly keen to realign their faith with contemporary biblical scholarship, simultaneously undermining the place of Scripture in their corporate religious life while renewing the reliance on those "experiential" truths that were seen to be the hallmark of their seventeenth-century forebears.

A new emphasis on social responsibility and Quaker witness in national and international affairs gave rise to a generation of British Friends committed to bringing the historic values and testimonies of the society more directly into public life. The work of Quaker thinkers and writers like Edward Grubb, John William Graham, and, especially, John Wilhelm Rowntree helped shape an ideal of Quaker civic virtue and enlightened imperial citizenship. Quaker MPs like J. Allen Baker, T. Edmund Harvey, and Arnold Rowntree represented the society's concerns about disarmament, international conciliation, and social justice in the House of Commons with eloquence and occasional distinction.

Educational endeavors assumed a heightened importance in the life of the society, particularly with the foundation of Woodbrooke College at Birmingham in 1903. This institution, made possible through the generosity and vision of the irrepressible Quaker industrialist and philanthropist George Cadbury, aimed to raise the intellectual standards of Quaker ministry and provided the society with sources of spiritual nourishment that continue to flourish today. Woodbrooke and the Summer School movement out of which it grew, and the leadership of masterful Quaker teachers like Rendel Harris and John Wilhelm Rowntree, became the inspiration and formative influence for many of the most significant British Friends of the twentieth century.

The **First World War** prompted a comprehensive and sometimes painful reexamination of the society's pacifist heritage. British Quakers were forced to reinterpret their historic Peace Testimony of 1661 for the new century, and a consensus on the appropriate response to the European conflict was often difficult to achieve. While some Friends were eager to hold to what might be called the purist line on Quaker pacifism—refusing to consider any form of service in the larger war effort on the grounds that even such noncombatant activity could be construed as participation in the mili-

F

tarist system—others felt that Friends had an obligation to commit themselves to some form of amelioration of the war's horrors. The Friends Ambulance Unit, started in 1914 by the young Philip Noel-Baker (later to be awarded the Nobel Peace Prize in 1959 for his lifelong commitment to disarmament), provided less-absolutist Quakers—including many **conscientious objectors** after the introduction of **conscription** in 1916—with a new opportunity for humanitarian intervention, which could also claim strong roots in Quaker tradition. However, other total objectors chose to demonstrate their convictions by enduring lengthy and harsh prison sentences for their refusal to perform either military or alternative service.

The defining fire of the First World War experience forged a new and more mature internationalism among British Quakers. This was exhibited in the work of the Friends War Victims Relief Committee and the Committee for International Service (founded in 1919 and subsequently absorbed into the Friends Service Council in 1927), both of which brought considerable distinction to the Society of Friends with their contribution to the European reconstruction effort. The eminent Quaker peace activist Carl Heath helped consolidate and expand this reputation with his proposal for the establishment of permanent Quaker Centers in a number of European capitals, several of which flourished throughout the 1920s and 1930s and played a notable role in efforts to defuse interwar tensions and to aid the victims of **Fascism**. With the founding of the Quaker Center at the **League of Nations** in Geneva in 1922 (now the Quaker United Nations Office), the society embarked on a venture in international conciliation and alternative diplomacy that was to develop in the post-war United Nations era into one of the most respected nongovernmental organizations working in the fields of disarmament, conflict resolution, and human rights. In 1947, after the close of the Second World War (during which both the Friends Ambulance Unit and the Friends War Victims Relief Committee had again made significant humanitarian contributions), the British Friends Service Council and its counterpart body, the American Friends Service Committee, were jointly awarded the Nobel Peace Prize for their work.

Since the Second World War British Quakerism has grown into a far more heterogeneous community than at any other period in its history. The distinctly "universalist" flavor of much late twentieth-century Quaker theology has made the society an active and much-welcomed participant in a wide range of inter-denominational and inter-faith activities, although the shift away from the Christocentric basis of traditional Quakerism has met with a measure of opposition from those who fear the distortion of the Quaker inheritance into a recipe for a kind of bland ecumenism. Internationalism and the embrace of widely divergent Quaker traditions within the British Society of Friends had received a major boost with the establishment of the Friends World Committee for Consultation in 1937, a London-based body that continues to foster vital links among Quakers worldwide. Since 1945 British Quakers have consistently provided leadership, financial resources, and inspiration to a host of domestic initiatives promoting **race relations**, civil rights, and social and economic justice. Among British religious communities, the society has made contributions to national debates about criminal justice, national security issues, education, and the rights of women and of homosexuals. In the last decade of the century the Society of Friends remains a vibrant and progressive spiritual forum, showing little sign of the decline that has stalked so many other British denominations in recent decades.

Brian Phillips

Bibliography

Kavanaugh, John, ed. *The Quaker Approach to Contemporary Problems.* 1953.

Kennedy, Thomas C. "The Quaker Renaissance and the Origins of the Modern British Peace Movement, 1895–1920," *Albion*, vol. 16 (1974), pp. 243–72.

Orr, E.W. *The Quakers in Peace and War, 1920–1967.* 1974.

Punshon, John. *Portrait in Grey: A Short History of the Quakers.* 1984.

Wilson, Roger C. *Quaker Relief.* 1952.

Yarrow, C.H. Mike. *Quaker Experiences in International Conciliation.* 1978.

Fringe and Noncommercial Theater

In 1891 J.T. Grein founded the Independent Theatre Society in London, inaugurating a series of productions of "the new drama" with the British premiere of Ibsen's *Ghosts*. This was the first in a series of noncommercial theaters that sought to emulate the success of

European art theaters like Antoine's Theatre Libre or Otto Brahms' Freie Buhne. **Lilian Baylis'** presentation of Shakespeare at the **Old Vic** from 1914 marked the establishment of the most significant noncommercial theater company in twentieth-century Britain. It remained the home of classical theater until the formation of the **National Theatre** Company at the Old Vic in 1963.

After the First World War various "little theaters" (the Everyman, the Barnes, the Mercury, the Arts, and the Gate) functioned as theater clubs, introducing experimental and avant-garde plays from France, Germany, the Soviet Union, and the United States. In the 1930s a number of left-wing political theater groups were prominent, notably Unity Theatre and the various branches of the Workers' Theatre Movement. The Group Theatre was an interesting company dedicated to exploring the integration of poetry, painting, music, and dance in drama that exploited forms of popular entertainment.

In 1953 Joan Littlewood established her Theatre Workshop Company in Stratford East, and George Devine set up the English Stage Company at the Royal Court. These two companies were responsible for initiating the British theater renaissance after the Second World War, introducing new plays and a vigorous, direct, and less genteel style of performance that was to characterize productions of the 1960s. In 1960 the Shakespeare Memorial Theatre Company became the **Royal Shakespeare Company** and began operating in both **London** and Stratford.

The term "fringe theater" was first used in 1968. Fired by the political events of 1968 a number of theater groups surfaced in London and other centers to answer the revolutionary demand from the Paris streets for "power to the imagination." By the early 1970s a number of new venues had opened in London with the aim of presenting innovative theater work. Some of the most prominent were the Oval House, the Open Space, the Bush Theatre, and the Theatre Upstairs at the Royal Court. Jim Haynes' Arts Lab was a prototype of a number of arts centers that mushroomed in other parts of the country. Fringe audiences were predominantly left wing, youthful, and university-educated. The technical proficiency and middle-class decorum of West End commercial theater were anathema, representing for the new audiences the decadence of "the society of the spectacle."

Minuscule budgets placed severe restrictions on fringe theater practitioners, reinforcing an aesthetics of "rough," or "minimalist," staging in rooms whose small size necessitated an intimate actor/audience relationship that might be either informal or confrontational.

By the mid-1970s two trends were clearly identifiable in fringe theater—left-wing political theater and "physical" theater. About fifteen socialist theater companies were committed to developing a range of theatrical forms from full-scale dialectical dramas to popular entertainments expressing the marginalized culture of working-class people. A smaller number of groups were producing different kinds of "physical" theater: These were committed to antiliterary performance techniques, exploiting a visual and kinetic approach. Groups often used a workshop method to devise their shows collectively.

The serious reduction in **Arts Council** funding of fringe theater in the 1980s caused the demise of the majority of explicitly socialist theater groups. However, as a result of successfully targeting loyal audiences, some of the feminist, gay, and ethnic theater companies—for example, Monstrous Regiment, Gay Sweatshop, and Black Theatre Co-Operative—have survived into the 1990s, managing to present challenging productions in a wide range of styles. Other fringe companies confine themselves chiefly to presenting shoestring productions of seldom-performed European classics.

Robert Gordon

Bibliography

Craig, Sandy. *Dreams and Deconstructions.* 1980.

Davies, Andrew. *Other Theatres.* 1987.

Hunt, Hugh, Kenneth Richards, and John Russell Taylor. *The Revels History of Drama in English.* vol 7. 1978.

Fry, Roger Eliot (1866–1934)

Roger Fry was, in Sir **Kenneth Clark's** view, "incomparably the greatest influence on taste in England since Ruskin." Fry was described by the **Arts Council of Great Britain** in 1952, on the occasion of an exhibition of his paintings, as a person of "legendary fame." He was a dedicated polymath, most anxious to achieve in just that area where he had, in the opinion of many, the least talent: as a creative artist, a painter. His paintings are relatively drab but are fascinating testimonials to his unceasing search for visual acuity and truth as he perceived it. His lasting legacy to the discipline of art history is the use of the term Post-Impressionist, in connection with the two major, revelatory exhibitions of Post-Impressionist French painting he curated in London at the Grafton Galleries in 1910 and 1912. The 1910 exhibition, called *Manet and the Post-Impressionists*, consisted of over 150 paintings, not only Manet, but focusing on Cézanne, Gauguin, and Van Gogh. Fry was savagely criticized for promoting such outrageous art, and he referred to the storm of protest as an "outbreak of militant philistinism." Matisse was prominently featured in the 1912 exhibition, as were the Russian avant-garde and younger English artists.

Fry was born in London to a distinguished **Quaker** family—his father, Sir Edward Fry, was a judge—and he studied science at King's College, **Cambridge**, where he took an outstanding degree (a "double first" in both parts of the natural sciences tripos examinations). At Cambridge Fry was elected a member of the **Apostles**, the secret society credited with wielding a striking intellectual influence on English life. He also came under the influence of Professor J.C. Middleton, the art historian, who encouraged an emergent interest in drawing and painting. Fry went on to study painting and art history in Italy and Paris. Back in London in the 1890s he also studied art with the leading painter and printmaker, **W.R. Sickert**. He not only began to paint with dedication but started a parallel career as a reviewer, critic, lecturer, and author. By 1901 he was the regular art critic for the *Athenaeum*. Fry was a lobbyist for the visual arts, involved in the foundation of the National Art Collections Fund (1903), which acquired works of fine and decorative arts for public collections in Britain; the *Burlington Magazine*, the preeminent periodical of art history, of which he was editor 1910–19; and the Contemporary Art Society in 1910. From the time he "discovered" Cézanne in 1906, he was aligned with Bloomsbury artists and writers, the critic Clive Bell and his wife, the painter **Vanessa Bell**, with whom he had a romantic liaison for several years—Fry was to have affairs with many women, including Lady Ottoline Morrell and the alcoholic but talented painter Nina Hamnett, before finally settling for nearly the last decade of his life with Helen

Anrep. Fry's wife, the artist Helen Coombe, who was incurably mentally ill, outlived Fry by three years. Both **Virginia Woolf** and Quentin Bell wrote posthumous appreciative biographical memoirs of Fry.

Roger Fry had an unhappy period commuting to America as the curator of paintings for the Metropolitan Museum of Art in New York (1905–10). He had been offered the directorship of the National Gallery, London, just after he accepted the offer of the Metropolitan and had felt morally bound to refuse, but his metier remained Europe. After difficulties with J.P. Morgan, the President of the Metropolitan, he left the museum; in 1911 he refused the directorship of the Tate Gallery. He founded, with others of the **Bloomsbury Group** and **Wyndham Lewis**, with whom he was to quarrel, the Omega Workshops (1913) for the creation of objects for domestic use, decorated furniture, textiles, pottery, and the like. The workshop had several purposes, among them to reform design in the applied arts and to offer opportunities to young artists.

In different ways Fry's activities have influenced the appreciation and understanding of art. His championing of the moderns—Cézanne, Van Gogh, Gauguin, the Fauves, Matisse, Picasso—brought their art to the attention of the British public. The breadth and depth of his interest, his passionate advocacy of Italian primitives as well as the most advanced art of his time, and his emphasis on the formal qualities of painting as more important than the ostensible subject all contributed mightily to new ways of approaching visual imagery. A volume of his lectures and reviews, gathered together in a collection called *Vision and Design* (1920), was one of the first Pelican Books to be published and helped, along with his other books, to make his influence felt far and wide.

Marina Vaizey

Bibliography

Arts Council of Great Britain. *Vision and Design: The Life, Work, and Influence of Roger Fry.* 1966.

Spalding, Frances. *Roger Fry: Art and Life.* 1980.

Sutton, Denys, ed. *Letters of Roger Fry.* 2 vols. 1972.

Woolf, Virginia. *Roger Fry: A Biography.* 1940.

G

Gaitskell, Hugh Todd Naylor (1906–1963)
Hugh Gaitskell was leader of the **Labour Party** from December 1955 until his death in January 1963. He was a Labour MP from 1945 to 1963 and served as Minister of Fuel and Power (1947–50) and Chancellor of the Exchequer (1950–1) in **Clement Attlee's** post-war government.

Born 9 April 1906, Gaitskell was educated at Winchester and New College, **Oxford**, where he was taught and influenced by the socialist theorist **G.D.H. Cole.** By the time of the **General Strike** in 1926 he had developed strong sympathies with the labor movement. After a brief but influential period as an **adult education** tutor in the Nottinghamshire coalfield, Gaitskell became an **economics** lecturer in 1928 at University College, London, where he remained until 1939. Throughout the 1930s he was part of a small group of mainly Oxford-educated and London-based socialist intellectuals—the other members included Douglas Jay and **Evan Durbin**—who were eager to introduce Keynesian ideas on economic management into the Labour Party.

During the **Second World War** Gaitskell, as a German-speaking economist, served with distinction as a temporary civil servant—first, in the Ministry of Economic Warfare and later at the Board of Trade as **Hugh Dalton's** personal assistant.

Elected to Parliament in 1945 as MP for Leeds South, Gaitskell was appointed Parliamentary Secretary and then Minister of Fuel and Power and efficiently supervised the **nationalization** of the gas industry. He also played a key role in persuading the party leadership to accept the need for devaluing the pound during a sterling crisis in the summer of 1949. His evident grasp of the economic issues involved in

that episode strengthened his claims to succeed **Sir Stafford Cripps** as Chancellor of the Exchequer. Appointed in 1950 at the age of forty-three, Gaitskell faced as Chancellor the central problem of how to finance a greatly increased rearmament program, which he favored, from early 1951 onward. By that time he had become a fervent supporter of the Anglo-American alliance.

Another major area of controversy during his term as Chancellor concerned his decision to impose selective charges for **National Health Service** patients. This led to the resignation from the government of **Aneurin Bevan**, the acknowledged leader of the Labour Left, and **Harold Wilson**. The subsequent struggle with Bevan and his supporters was the first of a succession of internal party conflicts in which Gaitskell was to be embroiled.

In December 1955 he succeeded Attlee as Labour Party leader, easily defeating his main rivals, **Herbert Morrison** and Aneurin Bevan. His period of leadership was marked by fierce disputes and deep divisions within the party. At first, however, reconciliation seemed to be a major concern, with Bevan coming to the new leader's aid by opposing unilateral nuclear disarmament at the 1957 Party Conference.

In the field of foreign policy Gaitskell proposed fresh initiatives for multilateral disarmament. He sympathized with the Rapacki Plan (1958) for a demilitarized zone, which would include the whole of Germany in Central Europe. He built, too, on Britain's pivotal role in the Commonwealth, forging new links with the Third World and with nonaligned states. In the **Suez crisis** of 1956 Gaitskell opposed the Anglo-French invasion of Egypt. His attitude was shaped by his preference for close collaboration with the United States as well as by his own moral commitment to the **United Nations**.

In domestic affairs Gaitskell soon became closely identified with the revisionist position in the Labour Party debate over public ownership and its place in socialist policy and strategy. He shared the view held by **Anthony Crosland** and others that the traditional identification of socialism with the public ownership of the means of production was no longer relevant in the post-1945 world. Instead, he favored a more ethical approach to socialism, which he viewed as "a collection of ideals towards which we hope to advance." Public ownership and nationalization, its most commonly practiced form, were to be regarded merely as useful means of furthering those socialist ideals, rather than as fundamental. The central pillar of his socialism was equality, to be pursued through high social expenditure financed by steady economic growth and by redistributive taxation.

Following Labour's third successive general election defeat in 1959, the party was convulsed by bitter and divisive controversies. These revolved around, first, the question of the party leadership, with Gaitskell an increasingly beleaguered figure; second, the future direction of Labour policy; and, third, fundamental aspects of socialist doctrine. More specifically, deep divisions appeared over the issues of public ownership, nuclear defense, and the **European Community**.

On the first of these Gaitskell raised the political temperature by attempting in 1959–60 to amend **Clause Four** of the party constitution. He believed that the clause was a source of misunderstanding and electoral unpopularity insofar as it implied a commitment by Labour to the public ownership of the whole—or at least the bulk—of the British economy. By 1959 Gaitskell had reached the conclusion that its amendment was necessary in order to remove that damaging misconception and to clarify, too, the party's broader socialist aims. However, his proposal, made largely without advice or encouragement from his friends, aroused deep suspicion and unease throughout the party. There was a widespread fear that his plans posed a grave threat to Labour's socialist identity and purpose.

Gaitskell's stance in this controversy was further undermined by the manner in which, throughout 1960, the Clause Four and nuclear defense issues converged. Most of the biggest trade unions, which had provided in the past vital support for Gaitskell, opposed his proposal to change the party constitution. Three of those unions—the Engineers, the **Transport and General Workers**, and the Railwaymen—at the same time declared their support for a unilateralist defense policy.

Faced by the hostility of the Left and by the indignation of the trade unionist center of the party, and caught up in a gathering onslaught against his defense policy, Gaitskell was eventually forced in 1960 to abandon any attempt to amend Clause Four.

In his simultaneous struggle with nuclear unilateralists in the party, Gaitskell was defeated at the 1960 Scarborough Conference where, in a celebrated speech, he displayed political courage in resolving to "fight and fight again." He did indeed fight back to overturn the 1960 unilateralist decision at the Blackpool Conference the following year.

On the European question Gaitskell broke with most of his closest supporters at the 1962 Party Conference by opposing British membership in the European Community. He succeeded, however, in what was to be the last great controversy of his political career, in uniting the bulk of the party on this issue.

By the end of 1962 it seemed to many that Gaitskell's leadership was unchallenged, with his public and party prestige at an unprecedented peak. He was then suddenly struck down by a rare collagen disease and died in London on 18 January 1963.

Gaitskell's premature and unexpected death, at the height of his powers, occurred at a time when Labour's electoral prospects seemed promising. Certainly his style of party leadership had been assertive and at times confrontational. His qualities—courage, determination, trustworthiness, and intellectual honesty—were widely recognized. Yet, in the eyes of his critics, these were offset by failings of stubbornness, intolerance, and inflexibility. His detractors claimed, too, that he lacked any real understanding of the labor movement.

Nevertheless, by the early 1960s Gaitskell appeared to his diverse admirers to be supremely well-equipped to serve as a distinguished British Prime Minister. Many have since concurred with Philip Williams' judgment that, had it not been for a cruel twist of fate, Gaitskell might indeed "have been the great peacetime leader that twentieth-century Britain has badly missed, and sadly failed to find."

Tudor Jones

G

Bibliography

McDermott, Geoffrey. *Leader Lost: A Biography of Hugh Gaitskell.* 1982.

Rodgers, W.T., ed. *Hugh Gaitskell, 1906–63.* 1964.

Williams, Philip M. *Hugh Gaitskell: A Political Biography.* 1979.

Gallipoli

The operations at the Dardanelles and on the Gallipoli Peninsula arose out of the desire of **Winston Churchill** as First Lord of the Admiralty to use the **Royal Navy** offensively and the willingness of the War Council to believe that seapower alone could exercise a decisive influence on the outcome of the **First World War.**

Turkey had announced its adherence to the Central Powers in October 1914, and Britain had declared war on Turkey on 5 November. Churchill's scheme involved eliminating the forts protecting the Dardanelles and passing a fleet through the straits to Constantinople. The Turks would then surrender, the Balkan States unite against the Central Powers, and a combined Balkan army under British leadership proceed up the Danube valley, attacking Austria and Germany from the rear and forcing their surrender. In the interim the straits would be open to Russia, enabling that state to sell its wheat on world markets to pay for military supplies channeled to it by the British and French.

Naval operations against the Dardanelles forts began on 19 February 1915. A British fleet of twelve battleships eliminated the outer forts and entered the straits to deal with those at the narrows. Here the operation stalled. The ships could not get close enough to the forts to bring decisive fire to bear because of a series of minefields laid in the straits by the Turks. These minefields could not be swept by the hastily improvised British minesweepers owing to heavy fire from mobile howitzers on the Gallipoli Peninsula. The howitzers could not be eliminated by the ships' guns. A major operation on 18 March by eighteen ships succeeded only in the sinking of three battleships and the crippling of three others.

Lord Kitchener, Secretary of State for War, decided that troops must be landed on the peninsula to capture the forts, thus allowing the fleet through. On hand was a contingent of Australian and New Zealand troops training in Egypt. To these were added the British Twenty-ninth Division, the Royal Naval Division, and a French division, making a total of 70,000 troops. Six weeks were required for the newly appointed Commander, Sir Ian Hamilton, to prepare this force, thus giving the Turks time to strengthen their defenses on the peninsula.

The first landings took place on 25 April. The Twenty-ninth Division landed on the toe of the peninsula around Cape Hellas, and a combined force of Australian and New Zealand troops (the ANZAC Corps) landed near Gaba Tepe opposite the narrows forts. Although successful lodgements were made in both areas, neither proved capable of much expansion. At Hellas British troops, reinforced later by the French, lacked the firepower in the form of heavy artillery to blow the Turkish defenders out of their entrenched positions. Three attempts to advance (first, second, and third Battles of Krithia) without such fire support were halted with great loss of life. In the ANZAC area the hilly and tortuous country, which as much as the Turkish defender had thwarted progress inland on 25 April, continued to prevent even the launching of coherent operations. Through the months of May, June, and July, a stalemate occurred, while sickness began to take its toll on the attackers.

During this time the War Council in London resolved on an operation to break the deadlock. A new corps, the Ninth, composed of Kitchener Divisions was sent out, along with various other reinforcements for the ANZAC troops. On 6 August a determined effort was made to outflank the Turkish positions facing the ANZAC perimeter and capture the Sari Bair Ridge that dominated the position. The plan proved too ambitious. Several small lodgements were made on the ridge, but the small numbers involved were easily driven off by Turkish counterattacks. A landing to the north of ANZAC by the Ninth Corps at Suvla Bay managed to secure some ground that could be used as a base but was largely irrelevant to the main operation.

Following the August failure Hamilton was sacked and a new Commander, General Sir Charles Monro, appointed. He recommended immediate evacuation. Kitchener refused to accept Monro's views but, after visiting the peninsula, came to the same conclusion. The ANZAC position was evacuated on 19 December and Hellas on 8 January. This facet of the operation was well-planned and there were no casualties, the Turks seemingly unaware that Allied troops were leaving the peninsula.

The Gallipoli operations cost the Allies 265,000 casualties (49,000 dead) and the Turks over 300,000 (90,000 dead). The strategic basis on which it was mounted was largely illusory. There is little evidence that the Turks would have surrendered to a British fleet off Constantinople, and less that the Balkan States would have sunk their ancient hatreds to combine against such a formidable foe as Germany. In any case their armies were little more than peasant levies—no match for the battle-hardened forces of the Central Powers. As for Russia, transportation difficulties to the ports and lack of shipping would have prevented the sale of wheat abroad. Nor did the Allies have any surplus munitions with which to supply their eastern ally. After Gallipoli the attention of the British returned to what was always the decisive question of the war—how to defeat the German army on the Western Front.

Robin Prior
Trevor Wilson

Bibliography

James, Robert Rhodes. *Gallipoli*. 1965.

Moorehead, Alan. *Gallipoli*. 1956.

Prior, Robin. *Churchill's World Crisis as History*. 1983.

Robertson, John. *ANZAC and Empire: The Tragedy and Glory of Gallipoli*. 1990.

Wilson, Trevor. *The Myriad Faces of War: Britain and the Great War, 1914–1918*. 1986.

Galsworthy, John (1867–1933)

In 1932, at the height of his fame, John Galsworthy was renowned the world over, a member of the Order of Merit, a founder and first president of PEN International, and a recipient of the Nobel Prize for Literature. Never out of print in Britain or America, and translated into innumerable languages, his *magnum opus*, *The Forsyte Saga*—a trilogy, including *A Man of Property* (1906), *In Chancery* (1920), *To Let* (1921), and two connecting stories—is the quintessential Edwardian work of fiction. In it, and in other novels and plays, Galsworthy captured and portrayed the values of British society of his time.

Galsworthy was born in Surrey, the son of a wealthy, property-owning solicitor and an unaffectionate mother twenty years her husband's junior. He attended Harrow and Oxford without distinction, interested only in clothes and horse racing, and learning to affect a monocle. At his father's insistence he studied law in London and was called to the Bar at Lincoln's Inn, but he never had a brief of his own. Instead, he collected rents from his father's slum properties. Galsworthy's interest in social reform stems from this activity.

In an attempt to motivate his son, the senior Galsworthy sent John on trips to different parts of the Empire. On one of them he met one of the two people who would influence him toward a career as a writer. Joseph Conrad was first mate of the clipper ship *Torrens*, and the sailor-writer and the dilettante lawyer became mutually influential and supportive lifelong friends. The other great influence on Galsworthy's literary career was Ada Cooper Galsworthy, unhappily married wife of John's cousin Arthur. Ada, the model for Irene Forsyte, the beautiful heroine of the *Saga*, and John became lovers in 1895 in Paris, and she urged him to do something with his life. He obeyed by beginning to write. Fearing Galsworthy's father would disinherit him if she divorced and they married, the lovers waited until his death in 1904 to pursue her divorce. They were able to marry the next year, when Galsworthy had three apprentice novels and two collections of stories in print. Literary fame came in 1906 with the publication of *A Man of Property*, whose eponymous philistine antagonist, Soames Forsyte, based on cousin Arthur, became the central male figure in Galsworthy's fiction.

Other trilogies, replete with Forsyte characters, followed *The Forsyte Saga*: *A Modern Comedy* (1929) and *End of the Chapter* (1934). The best non-Forsyte novel is *The Country House* (1907).

Galsworthy's successful career as a playwright began with *The Silver Box* in the same year as the publication of *A Man of Property*. At his best, Galsworthy was a dramatist of conscience and a committed reformer. Between the two World Wars he ranked second only to George Bernard Shaw, and on a par with J.M. Barrie, Somerset Maugham, and J.B. Priestley. His most notable plays are the Ibsen-like thesis plays, *Strife* (1909), *Justice* (1910), and *Loyalties* (1922).

Although Galsworthy's reputation diminished after his death, his humanitarian concerns, his story-telling ability, and his deft portrayal of his social milieu, have ensured a continuing readership throughout the English-speaking world. Critical and scholarly interest awaits a revival.

Sanford Sternlicht

Bibliography

Fréchet, Alec. *John Galsworthy: A Reassessment.* 1982.
Gindin, James. *John Galsworthy's Life and Art: An Alien's Fortress.* 1987.
Marrot, H.V. *The Life and Letters of John Galsworthy.* 1936.
Sternlicht, Sanford. *John Galsworthy.* 1987.

Garden Cities

Conceived by Sir Ebenezer Howard at the turn of the twentieth century, Garden Cities were inspired by currents of thought originating in the eighteenth century: One was concerned with the social basis of landowning and the economics of real-estate development, the other with the design of model settlements and decent working-class **housing**. Similarly, the Garden City movement fed corresponding, though divergent, streams of twentieth-century thought: One, concerned with land reform and the socialization of incremental land values, led nowhere; the other exercised great influence on housing design and **town and country planning**.

Howard saw land reform as the foundation of all reform, dividends from Garden City development were to be deliberately limited and surplus return on capital applied for the benefit of the tenant community, a principle applied when First Garden City Ltd. developed Letchworth from 1903.

The socializing of development profits was an old element of the radical program fitfully revived by the **Labour Party**. Though there was nothing inherently partisan in Howard's ideas, it was thus natural that the social and economic ideals behind Garden Cities should have appealed to the Left, and Letchworth became a refuge for **conscientious objectors** and others out of sympathy with national aims during the **First World War**. Just as nothing much came of Labour's efforts to tap development profits, so for many years neither Letchworth, nor Howard's second foundation, Welwyn Garden City (1920), made profits that could be socialized. Indeed, even the necessary capital was not attracted. At Welwyn, government loans, writing off capital, and an end to dividend limi-

tation were necessary between the wars, and in 1948 it was made a New Town to take **London** overspill. Nor, but for parliamentary legislation in 1962, could Letchworth have survived the assaults of those who, attracted by the profits to be made from redeveloping low-density housing in the 1950s, took over First Garden City Ltd. The act transferred Letchworth's assets to a public corporation, thus safeguarding, at a cost of more than £3 million, Howard's social and economic ideals.

Howard's work appeared when Britain was temporarily losing its lead in urban planning and design. **Sir Nikolaus Pevsner** concluded that Howard's Garden Cities were backward-looking, like the picturesque villages descended from New Houghton (1729) or Nuneham Courtenay (early 1760s) or the model industrial settlements and garden suburbs derived from New Lanark and Styal (1783–4). Circumstances disguise the novelty and fertility of Howard's ideas. One was the slow development of Letchworth and Welwyn, a consequence of Howard's unrealistic optimism concerning the economic "magnetism" of his land reforms. Slow development produced architectural failure in the Garden City centers, and low-density building produced a "cottagey" rather than an urban scene. The fact that Letchworth's architects, Parker and Unwin, also worked at Earswick and Hampstead Garden Suburb obscured the real differences between that type of development and the Garden City.

Howard's essential originality derives from the scale of his planning. Earlier model settlements were small, rarely exceeding a few hundred inhabitants; their inspiration was local paternalism or **philanthropy**. Howard, however, intended nothing less than a profound alteration of the national settlement pattern, stemming the tide of rural depopulation and reducing the conurbations by means of groups of new, planned Garden Cities of 32,000 inhabitants each, built around Central Social Cities.

Planning on such scale meant that those who carried on his work—organizations like the Town and Country Planning Association and influential town planners like Sir Raymond Unwin—had to work at theoretical questions of the first importance for post-war reconstruction planning in the 1940s. As far as ambitions on such a scale could ever have been carried out, they were realized in southeast England by Sir Patrick Abercrombie's Greater London Plan

(1944), and it was Abercrombie's use of green belts, developed from the work of Howard and Unwin, that helped reconcile the conservatively minded Council for the Protection of Rural England to the plan, which was keenly supported by the Town and Country Planning Association. Green belts became part of general government planning policy from 1955. Industrial dispersal was also implicit in the Garden City, although it became part of government policy through the 1940 Barlow Report, which also owed much to academic geographers. Finally, the New Towns program can be discerned in embryonic form in the Garden City. Social balance and economic self-sufficiency were essential characteristics of both, and both (despite the appearance of England's first highrise building at Harlow) were essentially low-density developments. The good, plain standards of early New Town housing may also be seen to derive from Garden Cities ideals and practice. Parker and Unwin, influenced by C.F.A. Voysey, designed and planned the best pre-1914 housing estates, eschewing the florid historical styles of Port Sunlight and Bournville; their early achievements at Letchworth and elsewhere were carried forward by Unwin's work with the Tudor Walters Committee in 1918 and with the Ministry of Health to exercise a profound influence on the planning and design of housing estates and on the work of the post-war modernists who undertook Harlow and other early New Towns.

George C. Baugh

Bibliography

Culpin, Ewart G. *The Garden City Movement Up-To-Date*. 1912.
MacFadyen, Dugald. *Sir Ebenezer Howard and the Town Planning Movement*. 1970.
Miller, Mervyn. *Raymond Unwin: Garden Cities and Town Planning*. 1992.
Pevsner, Nikolaus. *The Sources of Modern Architecture and Design*. 1968.
Darley, Gillian. *Villages of Vision*. 1975.

Gardens and Landscape Architecture

Two sometimes contradictory dimensions of nineteenth-century garden planning informed twentieth-century British garden taste. The first, focusing on garden layout and design, promoted a formality expressed in orderly, enclosed gardens, inspired by mid-Victorian Italianate gardens as well as by a late-century revived interest in traditional herb gardens, topiary, and medieval kitchen gardens. The second current involved the plantings themselves more than an overall governing design. Gardeners favored the "wild garden" encouraged by William Robinson, and a garden of clustered masses of grouped plantings and borders was popularized by Gertrude Jekyll. Such gardens featured old-fashioned plants, wildflowers, and sometimes exotic trees, grasses, and broad-leafed plants admired for their foliage and color. Jekyll's remarkable sense of color and texture, described in her books and manifested in the impressionistic tonal harmonies of her herbaceous borders, influenced both her own and following generations of planters, most especially Lawrence Johnston at Hidcote and Vita Sackville-West at Sissinghurst.

Hidcote (1908 on), the first garden acquisition by the **National Trust** (1948), represents a remarkable synthesis of these divergent approaches to design and was the most influential garden for the rest of the twentieth century. American-born Lawrence Johnston took about ten acres from a farm of 280 acres at Hidcote Bartrim at the northern tip of the Cotswolds to form, from scratch, a completely new garden. Hedges of yew, beech, or lime enclosed two main axes, forming a T, and other hedges of holm oak, box, hornbeam, various hollies, and copper beech form outdoor rooms. Some sections are more strongly architectural due to terracing, paving, patterned brickwork, and topiary, although never so much as **Edwin Lutyens** and Jekyll's Hestercombe of 1904–10. Other areas of Hidcote present informal glades and woodlands and reflect more of the "wild garden" character of the Robinson tradition.

This synthesis of organized garden rooms and luxuriant plantings inspired the romantic creation of Vita Sackville-West's garden at Sissinghurst (1930–62), like Hidcote a layout of about ten acres. Her husband, **Sir Harold Nicolson**, was responsible for the "strong lines" of the layout with its geometric ordering of the site's "obtuseness," but, except for the spring borders in the Lime Walk, most of the garden's "wild" plantings within the severe hedges and walls are Vita's, especially the Rondel Rose Garden where a juxtaposition of profuse foliage within the limited constraints of the clipped hedges presents the quintessential Sissinghurst.

Equally rooted to its countryside is the late masterpiece of the arts and crafts movement, the Cotswold house and garden at Rodmarton Manor. Built in phases between 1909 and 1929 principally by Ernest Barnsley, Rodmarton fronts on a simple green and combines a large walled kitchen garden with a series of garden rooms and walks. The plantings and initial layout are by a Gloucestershire local named William Scrubey, who served as first head gardener. Long borders follow the Jekyll tradition of clustered groupings spiked with holly hocks, lilies, and delphiniums, and the Leisure Garden, designed for less labor-intensive maintenance, incorporates pavings softened by plantings that, like the manor house itself, connect Rodmarton to the rural traditions of the Cotswolds.

A similar continuity informs fifteenth-century Great Dixter, acquired in 1910 by Nathaniel Lloyd and enlarged by Lutyens, who in 1911 imported and attached a sixteenth-century wing and laid out the gardens. Further development by Christopher Lloyd, noteworthy author on gardening, created one of the most exceptional picturesque ensembles of house and garden of the century. Although always linked to the house, each garden area at Great Dixter, in the Hidcote tradition, maintains a distinctive character and reflects both the continuing inspiration of Christopher's mother, Daisy Lloyd, and the influence of Jekyll.

The Jekyll-Hidcote-Sissinghurst tradition of "English Garden" taste was carried on throughout the century by a group of professional gardeners whose writings and practical advice on gardening, together with the example of their gardens, have helped popularize this most English of creative pastimes. Renaissance villa gardens in Italy provided a historic inspiration for more-formal British gardens enriched with architectural ornament, following the publication in 1904 of Edith Wharton's *Italian Villas and Their Gardens*. Italianate gardens in twentieth-century Britain are best represented by the Italian garden at Hever Castle, Kent; by Harold Peto's Wiltshire home, Iford Manor, with its changing levels and "architectural bric-a-brac"; and by Port Lympne, Kent, whose monumental Great Stair and Water Garden may be the closest England came to its Italian Renaissance models.

Oliver Hill, whose architecture includes traditional work as well as designs reflecting an early British modernism, provides the essential transition in England from Jekyll to modern garden design. This is evidenced at its earliest full development at Joldwynds (1932), where geometric shapes, pristine architectural frames, and a serene quietness established the essential ingredients of the modern garden. Christopher Tunnard turned to functionalism, modern art, and Japanese garden art to strip the modern garden of the 1930s and beyond to its barest essentials.

With Geoffrey Jellicoe this abstraction is reflected in the spatial and psychic embodiment of the subconscious in environmental art, in what has been called the "garden of the mind." His work sought to translate the spirit of Naum Gabo, **Ben Nicholson**, **Barbara Hepworth**, and **Henry Moore** into landscape. At his long canal at Wisley, Surrey, and his Kennedy Memorial at Runnymede he sought to create a serenity and spaciousness, a translation of idea to landscape. At Sutton Place, a sixteenth-century manor house, Jellicoe's work ranges from the Paradise Garden, planted in the Jekyll tradition, to the serpentine lake, a twentieth-century tribute to the English landscape tradition. The whole is an allegorical fantasy that climaxes in that embodiment of the quintessential and the infinite, the Nicholson Wall of Carrara marble. And just as Jellicoe's *The Landscape of Man* (1975, with Susan Jellicoe) represents his *magnum opus* of written garden history, so his landscape allegory of world garden history is projected to be built at the Moody Botanic Gardens on the coast near Galveston, Texas. Over eighty years of age, Jellicoe at Sutton Place and Moody Gardens looked both to the historic past and to the twenty-first century.

Robert M. Craig

Bibliography
Brown, Jane. *The English Garden in Our Time: From Gertrude Jekyll to Geoffrey Jellicoe*. 1986.
Plumptre, George. *The Latest Country Gardens*. 1988.
Thacker, Christopher. *England's Historic Gardens*. 1989.

Gardiner, A(lfred) G(eorge) (1865–1946)

Editor of the *Daily News* (1902–19), A.G. Gardiner was born in Chelmsford on 2 June 1865. He embarked on a career in journalism, first as a reporter in Bournemouth before moving to Blackburn where he joined the small *Northern Daily Telegraph*. As a skillful editorial writer, Gardiner was promoted to editor of the weekly edition of the paper in 1886. When the proprietor of the *Northern Daily Telegraph*, T.P. Ritzema, became manager of the London *Daily News*, he recommended Gardiner to its new owner, George Cadbury, as editor of the troubled newspaper. Gardiner assumed the position in February 1902 at a time when the *Daily News*' revenues and sales were at low ebb as a result of its stand against the **Boer War** and the fierce competition of the half-penny daily press. Gardiner, however, had an outstanding senior staff that included such able journalists as J.A. Spender and **H.W. Massingham** (until he left to edit the *Nation* in 1906), who helped the young editor resolve the paper's serious problems. He proved to be a highly effective editor who not only achieved the respect of his editorial team, but recruited such new talent as **G.K. Chesterton, C.F.G. Masterman,** and Robert Lynd (as literary editors), **J.L. Hammond,** H.W. Paul, **H.N. Brailsford,** and R.C.K. Ensor as editorial and special-feature writers. Following the **Liberal** election victory in 1906, Gardiner became a staunch supporter of **Sir Henry Campbell-Bannerman's** government and an ardent advocate of the reforms of **David Lloyd George** and **Winston Churchill.** Meanwhile, with his colleagues, Gardiner resuscitated the *Daily News* as an organ of the Radical Liberals and, equally important, as a paper interested in literature and the arts. He devoted much time to writing and achieved the respect of Fleet Street for his knowledge of the British political scene during the pre-First World War era and for his success in converting the *Daily News* to a half-penny paper.

Unlike his friend Massingham, Gardiner accorded full support to his favorite **Cabinet** minister, Lloyd George, and Prime Minister **H.H. Asquith** when Britain entered the war in 1914. But in 1916, when Lloyd George's intrigues ousted Asquith, Gardiner supported Asquith against Lloyd George. Like Massingham, he bitterly criticized Lloyd George's conduct of the war and even more so the Paris peace settlement that Lloyd George had negotiated. In fact, as a result of his relentless attacks against Lloyd George and his government and especially Gardiner's assertion that Lloyd George's Treaty of Versailles was a "blueprint" for the next war, the proprietor of the *Daily News*, Henry Cadbury, fearing that his editor's animus against the popular Prime Minister was inimical to the best interests of the paper, prevailed upon Gardiner to relinquish the editorship but to continue to contribute columns to the journal and other Cadbury papers. He was replaced in September 1919 by Stuart Hodgson. In spite of his renown as a highly effective editor and polemicist, Gardiner did not seek another post and henceforth devoted himself to free-lance journalism and serious writing.

Gardiner's keen character sketches of prominent personalities, published collectively in *Prophets, Priests, and Kings* (1908), *Pillars of Society* (1913), and *Pebbles on the Shore* (1916), and special essays often signed as "Alpha of the Plough" were highly regarded even before his departure from the *Daily News*. As a freelancer, he published competent biographies of Sir William Vernon Harcourt (1923) and George Cadbury (1923) and a fine study of *John Benn and the Progressive Movement* (1925) and always found a good market for his articles and essays in numerous newspapers and periodicals. Often urged to write his autobiography and memoirs, Gardiner resisted the temptation and, even to the time of his death on 3 March 1946, at the age of eighty, maintained that all that needed saying about his life had already been said.

J.O. Baylen

Bibliography

Koss, Stephen. *Fleet Street Radical: A.G. Gardiner and the Daily News.* 1973.

Garvin, J(ames) L(ouis) (1868–1947)

J.L. Garvin was a distinguished journalist and editor of the *Observer* from 1908 to 1942. He was largely responsible for inventing the modern formula of Sunday journalism, as well as for the modern reputation of the *Observer*.

Garvin was born into considerable poverty in Birkenhead in 1868, the son of an Irish laborer who was killed at sea in 1869. He was educated locally and did not attend a university; his rise to the top of his profession was thus all the more remarkable. He left school to work as a clerk but in 1891 began his journalistic career as a reporter on the *Newcastle Daily Chronicle*. In 1899, after a rigorous apprenticeship in Newcastle, he moved to the *Daily Telegraph* as an editorial writer. It was during his years on the *Daily Telegraph* that he became a devoted follower of Joseph Chamberlain and a partisan supporter of his **tariff reform** campaign. Chamberlain's brand of Liberal Imperialism was to become Garvin's political creed for much of his life, and he also wrote three volumes of a massive biography of Chamberlain, which were published in 1932–4. Garvin was briefly editor of the magazine *Outlook* (1904–6) before **Lord Northcliffe** appointed him editor of the *Observer* in 1908.

Northcliffe, the owner of a number of newspapers, had bought the *Observer* in 1905, when it was an ailing journal of little consequence. Garvin was brought in as editor to revitalize the paper, and he succeeded triumphantly. Particularly in his principled campaigns on political issues, such as naval rearmament against Germany from 1908 to 1911, he established the paper's reputation and influence and became probably the best-known journalist of his day. However, he clashed increasingly with Northcliffe, a man of equally strong views. Northcliffe declared his wish to sell the paper in 1911 but generously allowed Garvin three weeks to find a buyer for the paper himself. Garvin found William Waldorf Astor, who was willing to buy the paper, and the *Observer* remained in the Astor family until 1976.

However, it was William Waldorf's son, Waldorf Astor (husband of **Nancy Astor**), who took the principal interest in the paper from the start and under whose guiding hand that the Garvin *Observer* prospered, increasing its circulation to 200,000 by the early 1920s. Garvin probably reached the peak of his influence during the **First World War**, and his signed articles on the editorial page of the paper became the most famous feature of the *Observer* throughout his editorship, required reading for the political classes. Indeed, during these years, it can be said that Garvin largely invented the tradition of modern Sunday journalism, describing his own creation as "half a newspaper, half a magazine or serial."

During the late 1920s, however, Garvin's influence began to wane as he grew increasingly isolated from the new political generation and, furthermore, lived in relative physical isolation at his home in Beaconsfield, cut off from Westminster and the small *Observer* office in London. During the 1930s he became an earnest advocate of a renegotiation of the Versailles treaty, which he had always considered to be misconceived, and thus became labeled as an appeaser. To a certain extent this was true, but at least he came to these conclusions himself and refused to be used as a voice of government

policy like some of his fellow journalists at the time. It was over **appeasement** that Garvin had his first serious political disagreements with Astor: after the **Munich Conference** Garvin supported the Prime Minister, **Neville Chamberlain**, as a symbol of national unity rather than out of conviction, whereas Astor tried, unsuccessfully, to persuade Garvin to argue in the *Observer* for a change of government throughout 1939 and 1940. When Chamberlain did resign in May 1940, Garvin and Astor found themselves similarly divided over the merits of **Winston Churchill** as Prime Minister, whom Garvin supported unconditionally and Astor regarded with grave suspicions. This divergence of views reached a peak during the first two months of 1942, when Britain's military fortunes were at their lowest ebb, and Garvin's resignation was accepted by Astor after Garvin had written two articles in the *Observer* flatly contradicting Astor's known views on the higher conduct of the war.

Garvin's departure from the *Observer* left considerable bitterness on both sides, but he went on to enjoy a brief Indian summer as a columnist on the *Daily Telegraph* (1945–7), after having written with somewhat less success for the *Sunday Express* (1942–5). He died in 1947.

Garvin ranks as one of Britain's most important and influential newspaper editors of the century, both for the influence he wielded through his weekly signed articles in the *Observer* and for his development of the Sunday newspaper as a distinct journalistic entity.

Richard Cockett

Bibliography

Ayerst, David. *Garvin of the Observer*. 1985.
Cockett, Richard. *David Astor and the Observer*. 1991.
Garvin, Katherine. *J.L. Garvin*. 1948.
Gollin, A.M. *The Observer and J.L. Garvin, 1908–1914*. 1960.

General Strike (4–12 May 1926)

To many Conservatives and some Liberals the General Strike appeared to be a challenge to constitutional government. To others it was simply a massive sympathy strike. Its failure brought to an end a century of talk of a "general strike" to bring down the capitalist system. The General Strike was also the concluding militant incident in a period of often tumultuous industrial unrest between 1910 and 1921. After it, industrial relations were less stormy and calls for widespread militant strike action were generally discredited.

The General Strike was essentially a mining dispute that spilled over. The problems of the British coal industry became apparent once the post-First World War boom gave way to worsening conditions after 1920. The government, which had controlled the mines from 1915 to 1916, hastily decontrolled the industry on 31 March 1921. Resuming full responsibility for the industry at a time of tumbling international coal prices, the private owners demanded substantial wage cuts, the amount varying according to the profitability of the pits, thereby spelling an end to national wage agreements and to the minimum wage. The Miners Federation of Great Britain (MFGB) expected reductions but was unwilling to accept cuts of the magnitude proposed. The MFGB was also insistent that a miner's wages should reflect the work put in and not the economic viability of his pit; for the union, closing marginal pits was preferable to keeping them open by paying the miners less for their labor. Futhermore, the MFGB argued that, if it were in the nation's interest to keep unprofitable mines operating, the government, not the miners through low pay, should provide the subsidy. The Conservative-dominated governments of 1921–6 had no desire to subsidize industries, least of all coal, which often was very profitable. Nevertheless, in 1921 and 1925 governments did provide subsidies and thereby raised expectations in the labor movement in 1926 that Stanley Baldwin could be pressured into doing so again.

Conflict in the mining industry became more serious when the Trades Union Congress (TUC) supported the miners in 1925 and 1926. In 1925 the General Council of the TUC agreed to organize an embargo of the movement of coal when a coal dispute seemed imminent, following a fall in coal exports and a demand by the owners for an end to national collective bargaining, substantial wage cuts, and an additional hour (to eight) to the miners' working day. In July 1925 Baldwin's nine-month subsidy merely bought time.

During that time, the government made careful preparations to deal with a general strike, reactivating its emergency organization that had been ready to undermine strikes in 1919–21. The Cabinet, for both political and economic reasons, was determined not to provide further subsidy. Several on the Tory Right hoped for a showdown with organized labor, feeling it to be both necessary and electorally popular. While the miners, the Communist Party of Great Britain, and Walter Citrine, the Acting Secretary of the TUC, warned of a probable clash in May 1926, the trade union leadership generally was ill-prepared, probably hoping that something would turn up. Their best chance of a compromise settlement centered on the Royal Commission on the Coal Industry, appointed in September 1925 and chaired by Sir Herbert Samuel, which reported in March 1926. However, the owners were inflexible on the need for longer working hours, the MFGB was resolute behind the policy of "not a penny off the pay, not a minute on the day," and Baldwin refused to offer proposals, even about the reorganization of the industry.

The General Strike began at midnight on 3–4 May. At the start the TUC called out only certain key industries: railway, dock, and road transport workers; iron and steel; metals and heavy chemicals; the building trades; electricity and gas; and the printing trades. Engineers and shipbuilders, the "second line" of unions, were called out just before the strike was terminated on 12 May. Generally the strike was well supported. Across the country trades councils enthusiastically ran the strike in their areas, with growing efficiency as the days passed. They were dismayed when the TUC leadership unreservedly ended the dispute.

The government had wide powers under the Emergency Powers Act (1921). Furthermore, it could use a sizable body of volunteers. It also had its news bulletins and official announcements broadcast by the British Broadcasting Corporation, and its case was also put, in combative style, in the *British Gazette*, edited by Winston Churchill, which had access to far more newsprint than the TUC's news sheet, the *British Worker*.

Within the Conservative Party, the General Strike strengthened the hands of those on the Right who wished for tougher trade union legislation, and Baldwin, who earlier had successfully resisted this, now took action with the Trade Disputes Act (1927). Under the Boards of Guardians (Default) Act (1926), the government could put commissioners in place of elected Poor Law guardians where it deemed that too-generous relief was being given, a mat-

G

Armored cars escorting a food convoy during the General Strike, May 1926.

ter highlighted by the help given in some areas to miners' families.

The ending of the General Strike left the locked-out miners to struggle on alone. By late November they had been forced to return to work under whatever terms were locally available, leaving a residue of bitterness in mining industrial relations. Others also suffered, with many railwaymen, printers, engineers, and road haulage workers victimized by employers who ignored Baldwin's appeal after the strike that there should be no malice or vindictiveness. Trade unionism among miners and railwaymen fell by 26 and 22 percent, respectively, by the end of 1927, though it is possible that sympathy for the miners helped the **Labour Party** in some areas in municipal and parliamentary elections in the following years.

After the General Strike the labor movement indulged in fewer recriminations than it might have done as it reunited to oppose Baldwin's trade union legislation. Under its President, Ben Turner (1863–1942), the TUC, reverting to cooperation rather than confrontation in industrial politics, engaged in talks on a wide range of matters from January 1928 with a group of prominent industrialists led by Sir **Alfred Mond.** The General Strike has often been seen as a turning point in British labor's history, but perhaps it is better seen as accelerating trends already underway after the post-war economic boom and the failure then of more-militant trade unionism.

C.J. Wrigley

Bibliography

Clegg, Hugh Armstrong. *A History of British Trade Unions since 1889.* Vol. 2: *1911–1933.* 1985.

Laybourn, Keith. *The General Strike of 1926.* 1994.

Morris, Margaret. *The General Strike.* 1976.

Phillips, Gordon A. *The General Strike: The Politics of Industrial Conflict.* 1976.

Renshaw, Patrick. *The General Strike.* 1975.

Skelley, Jeffrey, ed. *The General Strike 1926.* 1976.

Genetics

The word "genetics" was coined in 1905 by the British biologist William Bateson (1861–1926) to describe the study of heredity and variation. Bateson, an enthusiastic supporter of the work of Gregor Mendel (1822–1884), founded a school of genetics in **Cambridge** that popularized and extended Mendel's work. During the First World War the center of genetic research shifted to the United States, but major contributions were made by **J.B.S. Haldane** and R.A. Fisher (1890–1962), who demonstrated independently that Mendelian genetics could provide the mechanism for Darwinian evolution. Haldane and Fisher dominated British genetics between the wars and pioneered the field of biochemical, biometrical, and ecological genetics. After the Second World War new schools of fungal and bacterial genetics were founded, and genetics established itself in the British university system. However, the most spectacular advances came from the new field of **molecular biology**, which established the chemical relationship between genes and proteins and transformed not only genetics, but the whole of the biological sciences. In recent decades British scientists have made notable contributions to human molecular genetics.

In 1900 Bateson became a vocal propagandist for Mendel's newly rediscovered work, seeing it as a vindication of his own belief in the importance of discontinuous variations in evolution. Together with his colleague Raymond Punnett (1875–1967) he discovered the phenomenon of linkage and established much of the terminology that is used today. In 1919 Bateson was appointed the first Director of the John Innis Horticultural Institution and moved to Merton, South London. The first chair of genetics, therefore, went to Punnett; created in 1912, it carried with it no departmental building, and genetics in Cambridge declined.

After Bateson's death in 1926, the Cambridge biochemist J.B.S. Haldane joined the John Innes as a genetics consultant and directed a path-breaking series of experiments into the genetics of flower color. The experiments combined separate genetic and chemical studies and established that genes act by controlling simple chemical processes and that these are conserved throughout the plant kingdom. The John Innes

also established a worldwide reputation for cytology through the work of Cyril Darlington (1903–81).

In 1933 Haldane was appointed to a chair of genetics at University College, London (UCL), and the mathematician R.A. Fisher was appointed Galton Professor of Eugenics, also at UCL. Fisher made lasting contributions to statistical theory and demonstrated mathematically (as did Haldane) that Darwinism and Mendelism are compatible; this reconciliation later became known as the evolutionary synthesis. He also collaborated with the **Oxford** zoologist E.B. Ford (1901–88), who tested Fisher's mathematical predictions by studying the effect of genetic mutations in wild populations. At Cambridge an influential school of genetics was established in the Botany Department by David Catcheside (1907–).

After the Second World War the institutional basis of genetics expanded. The number of genetics departments rose from two in 1945 to fourteen in 1972. Of these the most influential was Glasgow (created in 1946), where Guido Pontecorvo (1907–) founded a school of fungal genetics that seeded many of the later departments: Pontecorvo's group was the first to show that functional genes could be divided by recombination. The other major development was in Edinburgh, where Conrad Waddington (1905–75) built up the largest center for genetics in the country, attracting research funding from both the Agricultural Research Council and the **Medical Research Council**. Most of these post-war genetics departments have since disappeared in the move toward integrated schools of biological sciences. Independent departments of genetics survive only at Glasgow, Leeds, Nottingham, and Cambridge.

Outside the universities important research was funded by the Medical Research Council (MRC). William Hayes (1913–94) transformed the field of bacterial genetics by the discovery of two "sexes" in bacteria and launched an influential school that went on to colonize the new genetics departments. In 1965 the Hayes group moved from the Hammersmith Hospital, London, to Edinburgh, where they formed one-half of a newly created Department of Molecular Biology. This department made major contributions to the recombinant DNA revolution of the 1970s, pioneering the use of bacteriophage vectors.

In human genetics the MRC Blood Group at the Lister Institute (founded in 1946) and the

MRC Clinical and Population Cytogenetics Unit at the Western General Hospital, Edinburgh (founded in 1956), have acquired worldwide reputations. The Blood Group was associated with the UCL Galton Laboratory, which was transformed into a center for human genetics by Fisher's successor, Lionel Penrose (1898–1972). In recent years human molecular genetics has been led by the British cancer research organizations (notably the Imperial Cancer Research Fund) and the large teaching hospitals. In Oxford David Weatherall (1933–), Professor of clinical medicine, has pioneered the molecular characterization of genetic diseases caused by hemoglobin deficiencies.

Britain is playing an active part in the Human Genome Project, which aims first to map and then to sequence the human genetic material.

Guil Winchester

Bibliography

Box, Joan Fisher. *R.A. Fisher: The Life of a Scientist.* 1978.

Clark, Ronald W. *J.B.S.: The Life and Work of J.B.S. Haldane.* 1968.

Fincham, J.R.S. "Genetics in the United Kingdom: The Last Half-Century," *Heredity*, vol. 71 (1993), pp. 111–18.

Punnett, R.C. "Early Days of Genetics," *Heredity*, vol. 4 (1950), pp. 1–10.

Scott-Moncrieff, R. "The Classical Period in Chemical Genetics," *Notes and Records of the Royal Society*, vol. 36 (1978), pp. 307–51.

George V (1865–1936)

The second son of Albert Edward, Prince of Wales (later King **Edward VII**), and Princess Alexandra of Denmark (later Queen Alexandra), George became Duke of York (1892), Prince of Wales (1901), and succeeded his father as King (1910).

As a young man Prince George did not expect to become King, but the death of his elder brother, the weak and disreputable Duke of Clarence, in 1892 put him in the line of succession. Shortly thereafter he married his brother's fiancée, Princess Mary of Teck, and adopted a disciplined domestic life far more in line with the standards set by his grandmother, Queen Victoria, than those of his rakish father. Nevertheless, he always remained devoted to his parents. He was educated to be a naval officer,

and the traditions, values, and principles of the **Royal Navy** were foremost in his character. Protocol and sartorial correctness were immensely important to him. His sons were brought up in the manner of the British upper class: Stern regimens were imposed by parents, tutors, and nurses. The King found it difficult to treat his sons as adults until they married. In the case of the future **Edward VIII**, who was still unmarried at George's death, relations were never satisfactory.

George V was an exceedingly successful constitutional monarch. Although he fully understood that his basic prerogatives were limited, he did not hesitate, in private, to make his views known; his influence in several instances was marked. When he became King in May 1910, he was immediately faced with the crisis over the Parliament bill and, whatever his personal views may have been about the proposed limitations on the powers of the **House of Lords,** he supported the **Liberal** administration of **H.H. Asquith.** He did, however, request that a second general election be held in 1910, and he later showed resentment that the possibility of a Conservative government was kept from him in that year. But at the height of the crisis he did all he could to make it clear to the Tory majority in the Lords that he would indeed honor his pledge to Asquith to create sufficient new peers to get the bill passed. He was most relieved when the passage of the bill saved him from that most disagreeable duty. He also did his best to cool passions during the crisis over Irish Home Rule, 1912–14.

During the **First World War** he was an admirable symbol of the nation, although, as a first cousin of the Kaiser, he was faced with some embarrassments. Eventually, in 1917, he gave the English name of Windsor to his dynasty. He and Queen Mary achieved considerable popularity during the war; they were among the few who took the pledge to abstain from alcohol for the duration of the war and lived up to it, although the King was given a dispensation after a severe riding accident in 1915 during a visit to the front. In military matters, the King played a significant role in his support of his generals, particularly **Douglas Haig**; royal influence was important in blocking **David Lloyd George**'s attempts to purge the higher command, many of whom, like Haig, had close personal associations with the King. Above all, he was highly conscious of the revolutionary implications of the war; he had only

G

to look at the collapsed and collapsing monarchies of Eastern and Central Europe to see the potential danger to his throne, and he did all he could to distance the House of Windsor from many of his continental relatives. He played a key role, for example, in keeping his deposed cousins, the Czar and Czarina of Russia, out of England.

After the war the King continued to play his constitutional role with skill. In 1923 he made the important decision to deny the prime ministership to **Lord Curzon** and to give it to **Stanley Baldwin**. He carefully sounded out the leadership of the **Conservative Party**, but the decision was essentially his. He realized that a peer, isolated in the Lords, would be inappropriate with **Labour** as the opposition; after all, Labour was virtually unrepresented in the upper chamber. And in 1924 he accepted a Labour government with good grace; one of his major concerns was whether the Labour ministers would wear court dress; assured that they would, he was relieved. He established close relations with many members of his Labour governments, often appreciating their earthy humor. In 1931 he made his most controversial and dramatic political intervention when he persuaded **Ramsay MacDonald** not to leave office but to form a new National government of all parties to deal with the financial crisis.

In 1935 the King and Queen celebrated their silver jubilee, and the affection that greeted them on their progresses through London was impressive. The King seemed to have been genuinely surprised for he thought of himself as rather dull; in fact, the more fashionable elements of society so regarded him. But the warmth of the great majority of his people illustrated the enormous success and importance of his reign. King George, consciously or unconsciously, understood the role of monarchy in the modern world and how it personalized and humanized the extraordinary complexities of government and society in the twentieth century. The British people had come to see the King not only as a mystical figure representing the essence of the nation but also as the head of an actual family with whom they could identify. The King realized this and used modern technology to reach out to his people; his Christmas broadcasts, which started toward the end of his reign, were an enormous success and enhanced his role as a father figure.

King George was the synthesizer of the various factors that constitute the modern monarchy. He understood that political power was no longer available to the sovereign but that political influence, wielded behind the scenes, could be potent. This influence would stem to a great extent from prestige, which, in turn, would come from the monarch's position and family life. It would also stem from knowledge, for if the monarch was diligent in reading the state papers sent to him, he would accumulate a vast store of information that could be translated into influence. King George understood what his grandfather, Prince Albert, had tried to impress on Queen Victoria: that the sovereign, in public, must be above or beyond politics and thereby immune to political blame. He also understood what Queen Victoria so passionately believed: that the monarchy must be respectable. And he understood, as did his father, that the monarchy had to be exciting and splendid and glamorous. King George carefully maintained the pageantry that his father had revived, but, fortunately, in light of the horrors of the war and the miseries of the Depression, he clothed it in an aura of Victorian respectability, domesticity, order, and duty.

King George died on 20 January 1936. He was survived by Queen Mary, who died in 1953, and by four sons: King Edward VIII, later Duke of Windsor; Prince Albert, Duke of York, later King **George VI**; Prince Henry, Duke of Gloucester; and Prince George, Duke of Kent. His youngest son, Prince John, died in 1919. He was also survived by a daughter, Princess Mary, the Princess Royal, Countess of Harewood.

Arthur Mejia

Bibliography
Nicolson, Harold. *King George the Fifth.* 1952.
Rose, Kenneth. *King George V.* 1983.

George VI (1895–1952)

Second son of the Duke of York, later King **George V**, and of Princess Mary of Teck, later Queen Mary, he was created Duke of York (1920) and succeeded his brother as King (1936).

Like his father, King George VI did not expect to be King and throughout much of his life lived in the shadow of his immensely popular older brother, the Prince of Wales, the future King **Edward VIII**. Also, like his father, he was trained for the **Royal Navy**, which he joined as a midshipman in 1913; he served at the Battle of Jutland in 1916. Again, like his father, he was fortunate in his domestic life, marrying in 1923 Lady Elizabeth Bowes-Lyon, a daughter of the fourteenth Earl of Strathmore. In the 1920s he was most noted for his work with the Duke of York's camps, an idealistic effort, which continued until the war, to bring together boys of all classes in an informal setting and thereby to lessen class tensions. The theme of his life was basically domestic; to a great extent the lives of the Yorks revolved around their daughters, born in 1926 and 1930.

The failure of his elder brother to accept the principles embodied by King George V was a matter of concern to the entire Royal Family, and in 1936 the affair of the new King with Mrs. Ernest Simpson increasingly became a growing threat to the life of the Yorks, for the Duke was his brother's heir. By the fall of 1936, the determination of the King to marry Mrs. Simpson led to his abdication in December, and the Duke, to his and his wife's dismay, ascended the throne; the bitterness caused by the abdication never entirely ended, and the new Queen was unable to forgive her brother-in-law. However, the King immediately set about restoring the monarchy's prestige. In order to emphasize continuity with his father's reign he styled himself George VI, forgoing the use of his own Christian name of Albert. He continued traditions such as the Christmas broadcast, a great effort, as the King had struggled all his life against a stammer that often made public speaking difficult. Above all, he reestablished the Royal Family as the center of domestic tranquility and virtue while at the same time he continued the formality and pagentry of his father's court. He resolved the difficult financial problems caused by the abdication and created his brother the Duke of Windsor, pointedly denying to the future Duchess the right to the designation of "Royal Highness."

The King and Queen were notably successful in their new roles. State visits to France in 1938 and to the United States in 1939, both undertaken in the expectation of war, were considerable triumphs. Although the King played a smaller role in politics than his father, he continued the tradition of familiarizing himself with the activities and policies of his governments, and his influence was occasionally felt, particularly in matters affecting the military. He would have preferred **Lord Halifax** to succeed **Neville Chamberlain** in 1940 but neither exercised, nor tried to exercise, any influence over

the outcome. During the war the Royal Family, second only to **Winston Churchill**, became a symbol of Britain's resistance to the Nazis; the King's almost daily presence in London and Royal tours of the devastated regions brought him great popularity and respect. After the war the King accepted, as his father had done, a **Labour** government, and he may have played a role in the selection of **Ernest Bevin** as Foreign Secretary. From time to time he queried the policies of the government and asked for detailed explanations, but he never deviated from his constitutional role. He set an example in the acceptance of post-war austerity, although the splendid marriage in 1947 of his elder daughter, Princess Elizabeth, to her cousin, Philip Mountbatten, was an immensely popular antidote to the grim life of the period.

The King's health started to deteriorate in the late 1940s, and he was eventually found to have cancer, which necessitated the cancellation of a tour of Australia and New Zealand. The King died on 6 February 1952, and the mourning of the nation demonstrated the deep affection with which he was regarded.

Arthur Mejia

Bibliography
Bradford, Sarah. *King George VI.* 1989.
Wheeler-Bennett, John W. *King George VI.* 1958.

Gill, (Arthur) Eric Rowton (1882–1940)

An accomplished and celebrated sculptor, wood engraver, and designer of type faces, Eric Gill is best known for his most conspicuous commission: a series of stone reliefs placed over the principal doorways of the new headquarters of the **British Broadcasting Corporation** (BBC) at Broadcasting House, Portland Place, London (1929). His main typefaces were Perpetua and Gill Sans, produced in the early and mid-1920s for Stanley Morison, adviser to the Monotype Corporation. Many of his wood engravings, of which he produced more than 1,000, were published by St. Dominic's Press in Ditchling, Sussex, and in 1920 he was a founder member of the Society of Wood Engravers.

Gill was Britain's last thoroughly national artist, as well as a proselytizer and writer with firm views on the role of an artist in modern society. His views were made known through over 500 articles, some of which were published as *Art-Nonsense and Other Essays* in 1929.

Although his views of consensus values were mostly critical, this never stood in the way of official commissions and honors, of which he received a number in the 1930s: an Honorary Associateship of the Royal Institute of British Architects (RIBA) in 1935, for example, before being elected Associate of the Royal Academy in 1937. His national distinction was recognized in 1935 when he was commissioned by the British government to carve a large relief of *The Creation* for the League of Nations building in Geneva. **Henry Moore**, who would take his place as national sculptor in the 1940s and after, was one of his assistants in the 1920s. The artist and writer **David Jones** was also subject to his influence—at Gill's Ditchling Community in 1921.

Gill was brought up in a **Church of England** ambience, although he was received into the **Roman Catholic Church** in 1913. In 1914 he was commissioned to do a series of Stations of the Cross for Westminster Cathedral—his first major public work. He remained a religious artist, although his own definition of religion was broad, and he also associated his work with primitivism and with the barbarian.

Gill, who defined himself primarily as a stone carver, trained as an artist and then as an architect between 1900 and 1903. In his spare time he studied monumental masonry, and lettering and writing, and it was as a letter cutter that he established his independence in 1903. In all, 762 of his lettered inscriptions have been identified. An important early influence was Dr. Ananda Coomaraswamy, a botanist and geologist with an interest in the arts of India and Ceylon. Coomaraswamy helped him establish links between the true, the good, and the beautiful, which involved the infusion of eroticism into his largely religious subjects. Coomaraswamy also put him in touch with C.R. Ashbee's Guild of Handicraft, thus pointing to the importance of cooperation and community, and drew his attention to William Blake as a possible role model. In 1905 Gill joined both the Art Workers' Guild and the **Fabian Society**, from which he resigned in 1908, at the time of his meeting with Coomaraswamy. Although a founding member of the Artists' International Association in 1933, he had reservations about the constraints imposed by the systematic and the social. In his *Autobiography* (1940), written at a time when he was dying of lung cancer, he listed seven escapes: from art school, from the architec-

tural profession, scientific materialism, the arts and crafts movement, socialism, London, and the fine-art world. His constant problem was one of reconciling his independence with involvement in society. His preference was for small-scale communities: In 1907 he moved from London to Ditchling in Sussex, where he remained until moving to Capel-y-ffin in the Black Mountains in Wales in 1924; then in 1928 he moved again, to Pigotts, near High Wycombe in Buckinghamshire. The Ditchling and Welsh years were given over mainly to design and engraving. In 1924 he received a government invitation to design postage stamps and new silver coinage; the move to Pigotts brought an increase in sculpture commissions. In 1928 he was asked by the architect Charles Holden to carve three stone reliefs of *Winds* for the outside of the new London Underground Railway headquarters at 55 Broadway.

His career as a public sculptor was advanced by the need for war memorials stemming from the carnage of the **First World War**, in which he served briefly in the **Royal Air Force** Motor Transport Division. His major memorial, completed for the University of Leeds in 1923, was *Christ Driving out the Money Changers from the Temple.*

Although a moralist opposed to contemporary commercial culture, he was no ascetic. One principal piece of 1923 was of a naked female acrobat, *Splits*, and he often chose to depict scenes of love and coitus. The most tender of these love pieces is of the head and shoulders of *Tobias and Sara* (1926). His largest and most programmatic erotic tableau is of *Odysseus Welcomed from the Sea by Nausicaa*, completed for the Midland Hotel, Morecambe, in 1933. Originally considered as *High Jinks in Paradise*, it was finally described by Gill as a "holy picture," by which he seems to have meant that it epitomized Christian ideas of love as outlined in the Gospel according to St. Matthew. The women who welcome Odysseus give food, drink, clothing, and a helping hand. The same sort of conflationary process is evident in his *Prospero and Ariel*, one of his BBC pieces of 1931, where Prospero also takes the place of God the Father, and Ariel shows the stigmata on his hands.

Gill was an unusually powerful writer and expositor of ideas that validated his artistic practice. The importance of stone carving for him was that it represented a collaboration between the artist, who was partly responsible for the concept, and nature, which contributed its materials and resistance. The artist's work was thus justified by nature. Copying from preliminary models was bad because it broke the connection with nature and with the moment of apprehension. Gill extended this insight to society at large, deploring disjunctions of the sort that separated laborers from the totality of their work. He was the last major British artist to act on such a root-and-branch opposition to the culture at large.

Ian Jeffrey

Bibliography
Collins, Judith. *Eric Gill: Sculpture.* 1992.
MacCarthy, Fiona. *Eric Gill.* 1989.
Skelton, Christopher, ed. *Eric Gill: The Engravings.* 1990.
Speaight, Robert. *The Life of Eric Gill.* 1966.
Yorke, Malcolm. *Eric Gill: Man of Flesh and Spirit.* 1981.

Gold Standard

The gold standard was an exchange-rate system, and adherence to it was one of the pillars of British economic policy through the first three decades of the twentieth century. The gold standard combined the free convertibility of the pound sterling with a stable rate of exchange. Thus the pound traded within just a few cents of the official parity of £1=$4.86 from 1900 to 1914.

The gold standard's appeal to British policymakers and their economic advisers was both economic and political. By assuring traders and investors that any pound balances they accumulated could be converted to the currencies of their choice or to gold at predictable rates, the gold standard promised to promote the international trade so important to Britain's prosperity. By subordinating interest rates and the money supply to the maintenance of the official exchange rate, the gold standard seemed to insulate domestic economic management from political pressures.

The **First World War** disrupted international trade and capital flows, altered domestic monetary requirements, and, consequently, forced Britain and most other gold-standard countries to suspend free convertibility at the official exchange rates. Beginning with the 1918 report of the Cunliffe Committee on Currency and Foreign Exchanges after the War, successive official inquiries recommended that Britain re-

turn to the gold standard as soon as wartime dislocations had passed. In his budget speech of April 1925 the Chancellor of the Exchequer, **Winston Churchill**, suspended the embargo on the export of gold and restored the free convertibility of the pound at the pre-war parity of £1=$4.86. This decision, which Churchill later judged mistaken, was made in the face of opposition from **John Maynard Keynes**, who, along with a few dissidents in finance and industry, believed that this exchange rate overvalued the pound and that the downward adjustment of domestic prices that overvaluation necessitated would involve large-scale **unemployment**, industrial unrest, and a sharp rise in bankruptcies. Churchill and the many economists, bankers, and manufacturers who supported him acknowledged that the return to the gold standard would be painful but claimed the long-term benefits from an increase in international trade would ultimately outweigh the dislocations.

The Bank of England was able to maintain the official parity of the pound in the second half of the 1920s only by pegging the bank rate at levels higher than the sluggish state of the economy warranted. In the summer of 1931 the Depression, a banking crisis in Central Europe, and domestic fears about the size of the government's deficit combined to cause a run on the pound. In late August the **Labour** government collapsed when it failed to agree on expenditure cuts that might have restored confidence or secured foreign financial support for the official exchange rate. The National government that replaced it was unable to stem the tide, and on 21 September 1931 Britain abandoned the gold standard.

Since 1914 the gold standard had been more potent in Britain as a myth than as an instrument of economic policy. To its proponents, the gold standard symbolized the stability and prosperity of the pre-war years, and their concern to restore it rested on the belief that doing so would return Britain to that golden age. To Keynesian critics of the gold standard, the reestablishment of the pre-war parity represented the sacrifice of British industry to the financial interests of the **City of London**.

Both the enthusiasm for the gold standard in the 1920s and the scorn were misconceived. The smooth operation of the system before 1914 had been the effect, and not the cause, of the buoyancy of the British economy. In the absence of an environment favorable to international trade, the gold standard could only reflect economic strains and dislocations, not overcome them. On the other hand, Britain's export industries suffered between the wars from deep-seated managerial and organizational deficiencies and from structural changes in the world economy. Even if the return to the pre-war exchange rate in 1925 did overvalue the pound, this only exacerbated problems that were independently causing British trade to decline and unemployment to mount.

Michael Dintenfass

Bibliography

Clarke, Peter. *The Keynesian Revolution in the Making, 1924–36.* 1988.

Keynes, John Maynard. *Essays in Persuasion.* 1931.

Moggridge, D.E. *British Monetary Policy, 1924–1931.* 1972.

Pollard, Sidney, ed. *The Gold Standard and Employment Policies between the Wars.* 1970.

Golding, William (1911–1993)

William Golding's reputation rests largely upon his first novel, *Lord of the Flies* (1954), which has sold millions of copies, been filmed twice, and been studied by generations of students. While his critical reputation alternated between periods of disparagement and praise, he continued to write, publishing eleven volumes of fiction, as well as several books of essays, travel, and drama. In 1983 he received the Nobel Prize for Literature.

Golding was born in Cornwall, the son of a schoolmaster at the Marlborough School. Throughout his childhood he was an avid reader, particularly of the adventure novels so popular for boys' reading. At Brasenose College, **Oxford**, he studied science before specializing in Anglo-Saxon literature. After taking his degree in 1935 he began his career as a teacher at Bishop Wordsworth's School in Salisbury. During the **Second World War** he served in the **Royal Navy**, where he rose in rank from ordinary seaman to command of a rocket ship. Following the war he continued to teach until 1961, when his established reputation enabled him to write full-time.

It may be surprising that Golding, whose career stretched over thirty-five years, should be known best for his first novel. Yet *Lord of the Flies*' vivid narrative of marooned boys who try—and fail—to maintain the habits of civilization, along with the book's suggestive use of mythic symbolism, have made it an unforgettable experience for multitudes of readers both casual and academic. The novel adapts the shipwreck motif, reaching back through a long tradition including *Robinson Crusoe*, *The Swiss Family Robinson*, Jules Verne's *The Mysterious Island*, and Robert Michael Ballantyne's *The Coral Island* in order to reach conclusions more applicable to the ethos of the early Cold War. Whereas earlier shipwreck novels show civilization's consoling and enabling power, Golding's presents as an "inescapable recognition" the notion that "everything is a bad business."

The other novels of Golding's early career are variations on the themes proposed in his first. They examine characters in extreme situations in order to reveal the fragility of human existence. *The Inheritors* (1955), describing the life, struggles, and eventual destruction of a band of Neanderthals who come disastrously into contact with a band of primitive humans, points out how the qualitites that underlie technological advancement are not those of sensitivity or compassion. *Pincher Martin* (1956) shows how the spirit of technology fails an unscrupulous sailor who, washed overboard from his warship, creates a narrative of his own survival during the few moments before he drowns.

Golding's next pair of novels remains focused on individuals in distress and further explores the possibility of creative expression as a means of consolation. The narrator of *Free Fall* (1959) seeks redemption for his life as a user and abuser of others in the act of narration itself. In *The Spire* (1964), Golding's best novel, a work rich in historical detail and allegory alike, the dean of a medieval cathedral perseveres, in spite of obstacles both worldly and spiritual, to transform a mystic vision into the reality of stone.

After *The Spire* and through the 1970s Golding worked principally from earlier ideas, publishing *The Hot Gates* (1965), a book of essays; an unsuccessful novel of contemporary life, *The Pyramid* (1967); and a collection of shorter historical fictions, *The Scorpian God* (1971). During this period Golding's prestige declined substantially.

Darkness Visible (1979), an enigmatic fusion of allegory and contemporary issues that portrayed the forces of change and conservatism as equally incompetent, did much to re-store Golding to the public eye, as did the next year's *Rites of Passage* (1980), a densely histori-cal novel about a motley sea voyage to Austra-lia in the early nineteenth century, which won him the Booker Prize. Golding does not seem to have been able to sustain this resurgence, and later novels—*The Paper Men* (1984) and the sequels to *Rites of Passage, Close Quarters* (1987) and *Fire Down Below* (1989)—have been seen as flawed.

Golding's inability to sustain the success of his greatest work made him a controversial choice for the 1983 Nobel Prize in Literature. Nonetheless, the strength of his best writing, its blending of historical models, themes, and set-tings with modern ideas, its artful descriptions, and its mythic aspirations remain significant.

Warren Olin-Ammentorp

Bibliography

Biles, Jack I., and Robert O. Evans, eds. *Will-iam Golding: Some Critical Consider-ations.* 1978.
Crompton, Don. *A View from the Spire: Will-iam Golding's Later Novels.* 1985.
Dick, Bernard F. *William Golding.* 1987.
Oldsey, Bernard S., and Stanley Weintraub. *The Art of William Golding.* 1965.

Gollancz, Victor (1893–1967)

Publisher, political and social campaigner and writer, Victor Gollancz was founder (1928)—and until his death the driving force—of the highly successful publishing firm of Victor Gollancz Ltd. Passionately political, in 1936 Gollancz founded the **Left Book Club**. During the **Second World War** he supported the war ef-fort and helped victims of the Nazis. A **Jew**, he worked for post-war reconciliation with Ger-many and organized Jewish help for Arabs; he fought, too, against **capital punishment**, and for many charitable and progressive causes and pub-lished more than thirty books and pamphlets on moral issues, music, and himself. His awards included honorary doctorates from Trinity Col-lege, Dublin, and the University of Frankfurt, the Glorious Star of China, the Grand Cross of the Order of Merit of the Federal Republic of Ger-many, and a knighthood (1965).

Gollancz was born in London on 9 April 1893, the only son of Alexander and Helena (née Michaelson) Gollancz, a family of Polish origin with a long rabbinical heritage. Alex-

ander was a jeweler, two of whose brothers were knighted for academic achievements. Gol-lancz rebelled against his father's unquestioning Jewish orthodoxy and political conservatism. Educated at St. Paul's School, he then read clas-sics at New College, **Oxford**, in 1912–14. His army service included a period of secondment as a teacher to Repton School (1916–18), where he found his vocation as a political educator and was dismissed for fomenting political dis-sension among staff and pupils. In 1919 he married Ruth Lowy, with whom he had five daughters.

Gollancz entered publishing in 1921 with Benn Brothers Ltd. and in 1923 became man-aging director of a new general publishing com-pany, Ernest Benn Ltd. Personality clashes led to Gollancz's departure in 1927 to set up Vic-tor Gollancz Ltd. on a borrowed working capi-tal of only £12,000. Within a few years he was acknowledged to be the most exciting general publisher in London. He had remarkable drive, energy, and belief in his own judgment, and, a rebel by nature, he delighted in shocking the publishing establishment by his bold **advertis-ing** and his innovations (with Stanley Morison) in typography and jacket design. He made au-thors believe in his commitment to their work and in several instances transformed unknowns or the modestly successful into big sellers. By 1932 his best-selling authors included A.J. Cronin and **Dorothy L. Sayers**.

Success enabled Gollancz to begin the po-litical publishing that he saw as the chief *raison d'etre* of his firm. The Liberal of youth and early adulthood had become a socialist, and in 1936 he founded the Left Book Club. Run with Gol-lancz's usual energy and flair for improvisation, and subsidized by the firm, the Left Book Club (LBC) quickly became important in the move-ment for a **Popular Front** against **Fascism**. By April 1939 its membership was almost 60,000 and around 2 million books, half a million pam-phlets and 15 million leaflets had been distrib-uted under its auspices. Communists were vi-tally important in the organization of the LBC, and Gollancz, though instinctively antitotalitar-ian, was a fellow-traveler who later regretted his moral compromises over the political slant of the club's publications.

During the **Second World War** Gollancz's main energies were devoted to trying to unite the ranks of the Left behind the war effort, but he also worked with the National Campaign for Rescue from Nazi Terror to secure government help for victims of Nazi persecution. Once the war was over, he vociferously challenged the view that all Germans were guilty and launched Save Europe Now in 1945 to assist suffering Germans materially and fight against vengefulness. A convinced Judaeo-Christian (though a member of a no religious group), he gave much assistance to Christian Action; with the outbreak of hostilities between Israel and the Arabs, he founded the Jewish Society for Human Service to help Arabs suffering from the effects of war and to annoy the leaders of the Jewish community in Britain.

During the 1950s Gollancz's main crusade was as chairman of the National Campaign for the Abolition of Capital Punishment. He had become a convinced **pacifist**, who for the rest of his life continued to assist a wide range of charitable and progressive causes, including prison reform and nuclear disarmament. However, as he got older and increasingly disillusioned with politics, he spent more time on metaphysical and religious reading, reflection, and writing and on his lifelong passion for serious music. He died on 8 February 1967.

Although the depth of his commitment to moral crusades and his writing occasionally distracted him, he was his firm's effective, though increasingly erratic and old-fashioned, head until he suffered a stroke in the autumn of 1966. Highly egocentric, he was miserly with authors, his style was autocratic, his temper short and violent, and he could not take criticism. Yet his enthusiasm was infectious, his kindness and generosity to those in need legendary, and his flair and energy so apparent that those who could tolerate working with him often found him inspirational.

As a lifelong opponent of the principle of private profit, he bitterly resented being described as a capitalist or businessman, yet among the many contradictions of his life is the fact that his most permanent achievement was his firm. His major importance was as a publisher of genius, but he also had an important role in British political debate. His political publishing was a key anti-Fascist force in the 1930s and helped to bring **Labour** to power in 1945. Subsequent Gollancz campaigns, particularly those on behalf of postwar Germany and against capital punishment, had a powerful humanitarian effect on public opinion.

Ruth Dudley Edwards

Bibliography
Edwards, Ruth Dudley. *Victor Gollancz: A Biography.* 1987.
Gollancz, Victor. *More for Timothy.* 1953.
———. *My Dear Timothy.* 1952.
———. *Reminiscences of Affection.* 1968.
Hodges, Sheila. *Gollancz: The Story of a Publishing House, 1928–1978.* 1978.

Government of India Act (1935)

This act marked the final legislative attempt by a British Parliament to create a constitution for India. Although the act made important steps toward self-government for Indians, it proved to be a failure, largely because of antipathy to British measures on the part of important Indian political groups. At home, opposition was also strong on the part of Conservative backbenchers and imperially-minded segments of the British public. Only part of the act's provisions were ever implemented because of the onset of the Second World War.

The act emerged from the ruins of the **Round Table Conference,** which was an attempt to gain Indian cooperation in fashioning a new constitution. Unable to gain that cooperation, the National government pressed ahead with its own plans, which were presented in a White Paper of March 1933. The White Paper drew forth heated opposition from certain segments of the **Conservative Party,** led by **Winston Churchill,** who were greatly dismayed at what they saw as a retreat from Empire, which could only weaken Britain's power and influence in the changing, troubling world of the 1930s. In India, opposition on the part of most nationalist politicians was no less intense. Largely because of these pressures, especially on the homefront, passage of the act was delayed until August 1935.

The 1935 act had several important features. At the center, there was to be a complex federal structure, with representation for British interests, the princely states, and the remainder of India. The central government's power in provincial affairs was to be limited. Self-government would be established at the provincial level, where assemblies would be elected by the general population, with only emergency powers reserved to the British governors. Special safeguards were established for the Muslim community, including the creation of new Muslim-majority provinces, reserved appointments to government posts, separate electorates, and considerable autonomy for the provincial governments.

Indian opposition to the act remained strong. The princes objected to their diminished legal status under the terms of federation and insisted upon safeguards for their future sovereignty. The Indian National Congress had for years been demanding complete independence and therefore rejected the act as an imperialist smokescreen designed to prevent any real transfer of power to Indians. Under Jawaharlal Nehru's leadership the Congress decided in 1936 to contest the provincial elections scheduled for the following year, but then to refuse to form ministries, as a means of demonstrating both their popular support and their opposition to the new constitution.

Elections to the provincial assemblies were held in 1937. The results were an overwhelming victory for the Congress, which now claimed a mandate for rejecting the 1935 act. Nonetheless, the Congress was persuaded to form ministries in those provinces where it had majorities or near majorities. Once in power, the Congress governments aggressively pursued nationalist agendas, which alienated both the Muslim minority and the Indian princes. Because of pressure from these two groups, the British were unable to implement the federal scheme for the central government before war broke out in 1939. The Congress ministries resigned that autumn, after the British unilaterally declared India to be at war with Germany. During the duration of the war the constitution created by the 1935 act was held in abeyance, and India was ruled by the British authorities with little support, and much opposition, from most Indian nationalists. Only the Muslim political leadership gave support to the British, with the hope of getting a separate Muslim state after the war. Drastically altered circumstances in both Britain and India in the post-war period made impossible a return to the constitution created by the 1935 act.

The 1935 Government of India Act was the final legislative attempt by a British Parliament to impose a constitution upon a unified India. Upon conclusion of the Second World War, British power in Asia was so weakened that the **Labour** government could do little more in India than beat as orderly a retreat from Empire as possible. Communal divisions in the subcontinent had deepened as well, making any hopes for a unified, independent India impossible, even with a weak central government, as envisaged in the 1935 act. The tragedy of partition, which unfolded in 1947-8, was a stark monument to the inability of the British to legislate a constitution for an independent India that would be acceptable to most Indians.

Lynn Zastoupil

Bibliography

Moore, R.J. *The Crisis of Indian Unity, 1917–1940.* 1974.
Peele, Gillian. "Revolt over India" in Gillian Peele and Chris Cook, eds. *The Politics of Reappraisal, 1918–1939.* 1975, pp. 114–45.

G

Grant, Duncan James Corrowr (1885–1978)

Although Duncan Grant's reputation is tied up inextricably with that of the predominantly literary **Bloomsbury Group**—he is often regarded as its "court painter," having been welcomed into the group through his cousin **Lytton Strachey**—this has served to obscure his major contribution to the introduction of modernism in Britain. In 1907, after a period spent at Westminster School of Art, he attended Jacques-Emile Blanche's Academie La Palette. After returning to England the following year, he cemented his friendship with future **Bloomsbury Group** members, especially **John Maynard Keynes**. However, despite having visited Matisse, Picasso, and Gertrude, Michael, and Leo Stein in Paris by 1909, he continued to paint in a fairly conventional manner until 1910 when his painting began to change following **Roger Fry's** first Post-Impressionist exhibition (Grant exhibited six paintings in the second exhibition in 1912). However, even then the influences at work were as much the painters of the Sienese Trecento or the Florentine Quattrocento as Cézanne or even Maurice Denis, and this can be recognized in paintings from this period such as *The Dancers* (1910, Tate Gallery, London). Similarly, the mural panels executed in 1911 for the dining room at London's Borough Polytechnic—*Football* and *Bathing* (Tate Gallery, London)—reveal his adulation for Michelangelo as well as his fascination for Romanesque and Byzantine mosaic. Furthermore, paintings such as *The Tub* (1912) or *Head of Eve* (1913), both in the Tate Gallery, show the influence of work by Matisse and Picasso from 1906 and 1907 that he had seen in Paris in 1909.

What this emphasizes is the extent to which Grant's painting is formed not from doctrinaire belief in modernist theory or style but rather from a desire to fit the style to the purpose in hand. This open-minded attitude perfectly suited him for the demands of decorative projects, of which the commission from the Borough Polytechnic had been the first. In 1913 he was one of the founders of the Omega Workshops, under the direction of Roger Fry (Grant was a codirector until 1919), and this set the pattern that was to continue through his career for an interchange between his painting and his decorative projects that went both ways. His nonfigurative paintings of 1914 and 1915 all have their genesis in much of his work for Omega. However, the best expression of this relationship within his work is to be found in the environment he created with **Vanessa Bell** after 1916 at Charleston in Sussex.

His work following his first one-man exhibition in 1920 at the Carfax Gallery continued to reveal the polarities that formed his art: between modernist experimentation and the traditions of the Italian Renaissance, between the literary and visual arts, and between the fine and decorative arts. Within all of this, the life he made with Vanessa Bell at Charleston, London, and Cassis also came to be a major subject in his art. Not only did his paintings depict his surroundings and the many relationships among family and friends, they also—even when they are just still lifes—reflected the lifestyle he led; and this despite Bloomsbury's belief in the necessary distinction between art and life and his own belief in the significance of formal values over a painting's subject. This conflict is found not only in the decorations at Charleston but also more clearly in the various mural commissions he undertook of which the most complex and accomplished in these terms are those made with Vanessa Bell and Quentin Bell for Berwick Church in Sussex between 1940 and 1942 and those for the Russell Chantry at Lincoln Cathedral from 1956.

It is the problematic nature of this closeness between his way of life and his painting that provides one explanation for the progressive decline in his reputation since the middle-1930s (along with that, for different reasons, of many of his contemporaries). His work—along with its sensual depiction of his hedonist vision of life—was seen to be increasingly out of step with the times. Although he had shown at the British Pavilions for the Venice Biennale in 1926

and 1932, the thirty-three paintings he was to have shown in 1940 in Venice were only shown in London because of the war. However, during the period between his retrospective at the Tate Gallery in 1959 and his death in 1978 his achievement was gradually rediscovered, along with the reawakening of interest in the writing of the Bloomsbury Group, even though his significance extends far beyond their predominantly literary concerns.

Andrew Wilson

Bibliography

Mortimer, Raymond. *Duncan Grant.* 1944.
Shone, Richard. *Bloomsbury Portraits: Vanessa Bell, Duncan Grant, and Their Circle.* 1976.
Watney, Simon. *The Art of Duncan Grant.* 1990.

Graves, Robert von Ranke (1895–1985)

During his lifetime Robert Graves published more than 120 volumes of poetry, fiction, criticism, translations, and studies of myth. He was born 26 July 1895, the third of five children of Alfred Perceval Graves and his second wife, Amalie (Amy) Elizabeth Sophie von Ranke. The Graves family was Anglo-Irish, tracing its lineage from John Graves, who was Sheriff of Limerick in 1719. The family included a variety of professionals, as well as John Crosbie Graves, first Commissioner of Police, Dublin, whose daughter married the German historian Leopold von Ranke, grandfather to Amy von Ranke Graves.

Robert detested his public school, Charterhouse, but was much influenced by one of the masters, George Mallory, who introduced him to the writings of **George Bernard Shaw**, Samuel Butler, **Rupert Brooke**, and **John Masefield** and personally to Edward Marsh, the organizer of the Georgian movement. His entry to St. John's College, **Oxford**, was delayed because of the **First World War**. By joining a good regiment, the Royal Welch Fusiliers, he was doing what his birth and breeding required of him. His physical and psychological wounding during the war so affected him that he rejected the expectations of his class and ancestry, though he did receive his B.Litt. from St. John's. His first marriage, to Nancy Nicholson, daughter of the painter Sir William Nicholson, produced four children, some poems that subverted the paradigms of Georgian poetry, and one of the most turbulent scandals in modern literature: his alliance with Laura Riding. She would dominate his life, end his marriage, and lead him into close understanding of the women of power whom he would portray in the novels *I, Claudius* (1934) and *Claudius the God* (1934), among others. Prose, including the novels and his autobiography, *Goodbye To All That* (1929, rev. 1957), he described as "show dogs" he raised to support his "cat," poetry. Even his *Greek Myths* (1955), *Hebrew Myths* (1964), which he wrote with Raphael Patai, and his important Latin translations for Penguin were so termed. The exception among his prose writings was *The White Goddess* (1948, rev. 1952), in which he articulated his archetypal powerful woman, the goddess of the title, whose human expression is the muse, the inspiration and guide of every true poet.

Graves and Laura Riding had, at the suggestion of Gertrude Stein, moved to Deya, Mallorca, in 1927. Forced to leave by the **Spanish Civil War**, they finally settled in the United States in 1939, where they separated. Throughout the years of the Second World War Graves and Beryl Hodge, who would be his second wife, lived in England until they could return to Deya. He was with Beryl Graves when he wrote *The White Goddess* and the poems that celebrated her. The rest of his life and writing would probe his experience of this archetype. **T.S. Eliot** published *The White Goddess* at Faber, thereby continuing a friendship of years. (Originally, Eliot and Graves were to write the book that became *A Survey of Modernist Poetry* (1927), by Graves and Riding, a seminal text in New Criticism.)

Deya was Robert Graves' permanent address after 1950, and he lived there until his death. He and Beryl had four children, the last of whom, Juan, is addressed in the poem "To Juan at the Winter Solstice" (1945), in which Graves states that there is "one story and one story only/ That will prove worth your telling": the story of the poet and the goddess who loves and destroys him. Though living on his island, Graves traveled much, to give the Clark Lectures at **Cambridge** in 1954–5 and to succeed **W.H. Auden** as Oxford Professor of poetry in 1961–6.

Graves is often remembered for his refusal to compromise his moral or aesthetic sense in such controversies as his combat with **William Butler Yeats** over the exclusion of Laura Riding from the *Oxford Book of Modern Verse*, his

revisions of biblical history in *King Jesus* (1946) and *The Nazarene Gospel Restored* (1954), his portrayal of Milton in *The Story of Mary Powell: Wife to Mr. Milton* (1943), and his turning *The Rubaiyat of Omar Khayyam* (1967) into a Sufi text.

Frank Kersnowski

Bibliography

Graves, Richard Perceval. *Robert Graves: The Assault Heroic, 1895–1926.* 1986.
———. *Robert Graves: The Years with Laura, 1926–1940.* 1990.
Higginson, Fred H. *A Bibliography of the Writings of Robert Graves.* 1987.
Kersnowski, Frank, ed. *Conversations with Robert Graves.* 1989.

Green, Henry (1905–1973)

The nine novels of Henry Green have yet to gain the popular recognition and the academic attention they merit, but they have been a creative influence on important English novelists since the publication of Green's precocious and brilliant books, *Blindness* (1926) and *Living* (1929). The work of **Christopher Isherwood, Evelyn Waugh**, Brigid Brophy, and **Muriel Spark** typically exemplifies Green's impact, which shows itself as a characteristic lightening of the weighty artistic medium one finds in works by **James Joyce** or **Virginia Woolf**, but with no sacrifice of the elevated artistic rigor associated with the latter.

Henry Green was the pen name of Henry Vincent Yorke, son of a distinguished Gloucestershire family. Green attended Eton, where he began to write *Blindness*. He went to **Oxford** in 1924, but he did not like the study of Anglo-Saxon or his tutor, **C.S. Lewis**, and did not finish his degree. His family owned a foundry and heavy-engineering business in Birmingham—the Farringdon Works and H. Pontifex and Sons Ltd.—which Green joined. In 1927–8, as an apprenticeship to a managerial position, he worked in the foundry, earned a workman's wages, and lived in working-class quarters. *Living* emerged from the experience.

When he married in 1929, he transferred to the firm's London office. He apparently took with him an internalized sense of inhabiting both sides of class difference and conflict, for his social ties in **London** were divided between a smart set that included Aly Khan and a working-class set that included the writer James Hanley, whose

G

work Green promoted. The smart set was portrayed in Green's *Party-Going* (1939). Its publication by **Virginia** and **Leonard Woolf's** Hogarth Press was secured by John Lehmann, a loyal admirer of Green's work.

In 1938, hoping to evade service in the armed forces in the impending war, Green joined the Auxiliary Fire Service, for which he was to work throughout the **Blitz**. His next three novels, *Caught* (1943), *Loving* (1945), and *Back* (1946), capture the blackly humorous, near-hysterical life of civilian populations in wartime, more or less under fire, impressed into partisan service even if they prefer neutrality, and pushed to the brink of psychosis by the back-to-back sequence of two World Wars. Another trio of novels, the highly experimental and playfully melancholy *Concluding* (1948), and the two novels almost entirely in dialogue form, *Nothing* (1950) and *Doting* (1952), turned out to be Green's last fiction.

Although his writing had always been done apart from Pontifex, and although his pseudonym represented his intention to separate his novels from his business, it was the collapse of the foundry after the post-war boom that oddly put an end to his novels. Green, still an active executive (he had become chairman of the British Chemical Plant Manufacturers Association), became caught up in fruitless struggle with his father over Pontifex's future: Green wanted to avoid closing the works, out of loyalty to the workers with whom he had once lived, but he lost the fight and was forced to retire in 1959.

Although he completed two unproduced play scripts and was at work on a memoir of his time with the Auxiliary Fire Service, which was to have been a sequel to an earlier memoir, *Pack My Bag* (1939), he retreated into ever-intensifying privacy and silence. His ties with relatives long-attenuated (he did not once visit the Gloucestershire estate during his last twenty-five years), Green withdrew, behind growing deafness, into steady television-watching and occasional pub-crawling, although he may have maintained his old habit of reading eight books a week.

In Green's first novel, the hero thinks, "What was the use of his going blind if he did not write?" The thought in its context suggests not that writing is a substitute for seeing, but that it is instead a subtle abstract alternative to all conventional sensation—and to sense. Inspired by English modernism's tendency toward abstractness of content, meaning, and form in art, and influenced as well by the same tendency in Henry James and Gertrude Stein, Green makes his novelistic narrative and dialogue, even though their content is deeply realistic, a highly abstract inflection of what is actual. The result for the reader is an uncanny simultaneous sense of artifice and reality. Joyce's *Ulysses* produces the same sense. But Green's work, relative to Joyce's, makes more subtle the obviousness and pervasiveness of artifice in the production of the uncanny effect.

Green's successors may have found his work most remarkable for the breadth of sociological and historical analysis he amalgamated with the claims of artifice. Especially in *Living* and *Loving* the novelist's analytic tracing of the fineness of the web of social and economic relations, across class lines and within them, surpasses similar accomplishments in **Ford Madox Ford** and **D.H. Lawrence**. Moreover, the attention in Green's novels to the combined overdetermination and underdetermination of social forms by eroticism is also not surpassed. In *Caught*, *Loving*, and *Back*, eros no less than arms is shown to determine the array of global forces. In contrast, in *Nothing* and *Doting,* love's power is shown to decline under the Cold War era's domination of human possibilities.

Robert L. Caserio

Bibliography

Holmesland, Oddvar. *A Critical Introduction to Henry Green's Novels.* 1986.

Stokes, Edward. *The Novels of Henry Green.* 1959.

Yorke, Matthew, ed. *Surviving: The Uncollected Writings of Henry Green.* 1993.

Green Movement/Party

Environmental and ecological issues have acquired increasing significance in Britain since the early 1970s. Their growing prominence reflects international trends, greater scientific knowledge, increased media attention, and the efforts of campaigners and pressure groups. Although the Green movement of political activists has not had the impact of similar movements in several other developed countries, it has nevertheless raised public consciousness, fought many local and national campaigns, and had some effect on government policy, the agenda of the major parties, and the actions of major companies. The movement consists of numerous organizations and is characterized by extreme diversity of values, goals, and tactics. If defined broadly, it includes long-established pressure groups such as the **National Trust** and the Council for the Protection of Rural England, which are essentially conservationist in aim, cautious in method, and enjoy a degree of "insider" status in their attempts to influence government policy. At the opposite end of the spectrum are groups such as Friends of the Earth and Greenpeace; the latter in particular takes radical positions and uses dramatic nonviolent direct-action protests to publicize its causes. Many activists distinguish between a limited, politically reformist concern for the natural environment and a genuinely "green" philosophy, which comprehensively rejects the foundations of industrial society and believes that only a radical shift of values can avert ecological disorder. These "dark green" elements of the movement tend toward a global rather than national view of inequality, pacifist sentiments, and sometimes a variety of mystical and spiritual beliefs about humanity's relationship to nature.

The Green movement confronts a policy-making process that scatters among many departments and agencies decisions with environmental consequences. It is perhaps further handicapped by the marginal status of the Green Party, which, apart from a burst of growth and publicity surrounding its relatively strong showing (15 percent of votes cast) in the 1989 elections to the European Parliament, has not been a serious electoral force. Founded as "People" in 1973, renamed the Ecology Party in 1975, and relaunched as the Green Party in 1985, it takes positions on all major political issues, attempting to offer a radical vision that is neither of the conventional Right nor Left. It has suffered from internal conflicts between more- and less-radical factions, from an unwieldy structure stressing democratic rather than effective decision-making, and from Britain's "first-past-the-post" electoral system, which is a major obstacle to minor parties. Attempts to streamline the party's processes and redefine its outlook came to little at its annual conference in 1992, at which over half of its executives resigned. The party's membership had fallen to 8,000 from a 1990 peak of 20,000—itself a small figure relative to an estimated membership of all environmental groups of over 3.5 million. Most sizable groups, indeed, have preferred not to jeopardize their public image or access to political elites by associating with this small, often chaotic, party.

Steven Reilly

Bibliography

Dunleavy, Patrick, Andrew Gamble, and Gillian Peele, eds. *Developments in British Politics 3*. 1990.

Porritt, Jonathon. *Seeing Green: The Politics of Ecology Explained*. 1985.

Porritt, Jonathon, and David Winner. *The Coming of the Greens*. 1988.

Rudig, Wolfgang, ed. *Green Politics One*. 1990.

Greene, (Henry) Graham (1904–1991)

Novelist, playwright, essayist, and writer of short stories, Graham Greene was born in Berkhamstead, England. Educated at Berkhamstead School, where his father was headmaster, and Balliol College, **Oxford**, he was a staff member of *The Times* from 1926 to 1930. By 1930 three forces had begun to shape his career and would dominate it throughout: journalism, film, and **Roman Catholicism**. *Journey without Maps* (1936), the chronicle of Greene's walk across uncharted Liberia, and *Lawless Roads* (1939), a report on the condition of the Church in southern Mexico during the 1930s revolution, were joined by a constant stream of journalistic reports on trouble spots and political crises in Latin America, Africa, and Asia. Greene established a rhythm in his career whereby reportage would become background material for a novel. Journalism taught Greene much about accuracy and style. Film also played a significant role in his career. During the 1920s and 1930s, Greene reviewed several hundred films, demonstrating a keen interest in, and mastery of, the form; later he wrote at least nine film scripts, including those for his own *The Third Man* (1949), *Our Man in Havana* (1959), and *The Comedians* (1967). He even appeared in one film, in François Truffaut's *La Nuit américaine* (1973). The influence of film, whether in the form of parallel montage, establishing shots, changing camera angles, or focused dialogue, is everywhere felt in his novels and stories. The third influence, Catholicism, entered his life in 1926 when he converted and in the following year married Vivien Dayrell-Browning. His conversion, he has said, was primarily intellectual, and intellectual problems and puzzles largely established and define the thematic issues in his writings: the nature of evil, the paradoxical nature of love, whether sacred or profane, the functions of suffering, "social gospel," the redemptive powers of sin, and the concept of spiritual and physical fatherhood. Paradoxes brought both attention and censure: attention paid by national news magazines, especially in 1948; censure from Vatican offices demanding that he revise *The Power and the Glory* (1940), *The Heart of the Matter* (1948), and *The End of the Affair* (1951) to make their handling of matters of faith less paradoxical, particularly so that they would not seem to imply that fornication, drunkenness, suicide, and adultery could be paths to sainthood.

Greene's career began promisingly. *The Man Within* (1929), a historical thriller set in early nineteenth-century Sussex and peopled with smugglers, sold well enough to justify Heinemann's confident £600 advance, but the promise was quickly squelched with *The Name of Action* (1930) and *Rumour at Nightfall* (1931), two historical novels that Greene later refused to reprint, claiming they were written too much under the shadows of **Joseph Conrad**'s later novels. He did not return to historical topics until *Lord Rochester's Monkey* (1974) and *The Return of A.J. Raffles* (1975), nor did he consciously allow Conrad into his world again until *A Burnt-Out Case* (1961), whose Congo setting made Conrad's presence inevitable, and *The Human Factor* (1978).

History in terms of the past simply was not Greene's area, though the workings of history in the contemporary world became the topic, after religion, most characteristic of his novels. From *Stamboul Train* (1932) until *Getting to Know the General* (1985), Greene's novels occupied themselves with political struggles throughout the world, whether post-Depression Europe, colonialist struggles in Indochina, the workings of social gospel in South America, or the shadowy actions of Cold War **espionage**. For the latter, Greene had particular knowledge, since he worked for MI5 and knew Kim Philby well.

Greene divided the ten novels written between *Stamboul Train* (1932) and *The End of the Affair* (1951) into "entertainments" and "novels," but this classification has been of little use to readers and critics, and Greene himself dropped it later. It is more accurate to say that Greene was fusing mass culture (**detective fiction**, melodrama, and the thriller) with high culture (tragedy, the novel of ideas) in these

works. The thriller's concern with public and often violent action and the tragedy's concern with problematic human decisions and their consequences met in a complex but often weak human being, who is marooned in a modernist wasteland. Some critics have labeled this bleak world "Greeneland," causing Greene to rage against their failures to confront the realities of his descriptions, but the settings form rich metaphors of a fallen world as much as realistic depictions of topography, customs, and milieu. *It's a Battlefield* (1934) and *The Power and the Glory* (1940) are representative of this period in his career. The former interweaves four plot lines, crosscutting as in the film *Grand Hotel*, involving individuals caught up in the economic, intellectual, cultural, and moral wasteland of London. *The Power and the Glory*, which takes its title from the *Pater Noster*, confronts a nameless Mexican lieutenant who believes suffering can be eliminated from his world through destruction of certain institutions, with a nameless priest who learns that suffering defines the human condition. Hunter and prey pursue each other across the harsh landscape of southeastern Mexico before the inevitable ending when the priest is captured by the lieutenant, but not before being captured by God. The novel ingeniously uses its Lent and Easter time scheme to underline the religious themes of the novel, themes Greene pushed into the realm of sainthood and miracles in *The Heart of the Matter*, set in wartime Sierra Leone, and *The End of the Affair*, set in the wartime of the German V-1 rockets in London. Even in this period, though, there is another side to Greene, one often forgotten, which saw him writing children's books such as *The Bear Fell Free* (1935) and *The Little Steamroller* (1953).

The late 1940s and 1950s brought a serious mid-life crisis. Greene began to experiment with Dickensian first-person point of view, more consciously with Fordian time shifts, and to venture into other genres, particularly drama such as *The Living Room* (1953) and *The Potting Shed* (1957), further exploring the numinous world. He separated from his wife, though he would never divorce her, and moved to France, where he lived in Antibes for the rest of his life. In the novels of this period— *The Quiet American* (1955), Greene's warning to Americans and Europeans alike about attempts to reestablish colonial hegemony in southeast Asia, and *A Burnt-Out Case*, the tale of a famous architect, disillusioned with his work, who decides to visit a leper colony in the Congo—Greene meditated Hamlet-like over the superiority of detachment over involvement. Burnt out himself, he believed the story of Querry in *A Burnt-Out Case* would probably be his last novel.

Greene could not have known that he had almost three decades of creative life left, that he had seven more novels and two autobiographical volumes ahead of him. Much of his activity from the late 1950s on was retrospective in nature, especially the writing of the autobiographical volume *A Sort of Life* (1971). Also, in planning a collected edition of his works, Greene extensively revised earlier novels: *Brighton Rock* (1938) lost its **anti-Semitic** references; a chapter was restored to *The Heart of the Matter* in an attempt to distance the reader from Scobie early in the work; and *The End of the Affair* was so extensively revised that its affirmation of miracles became a statement of the problematical and coincidental. Tone also changed, and from *The Comedians* (1966) on, rich veins of intellectual and physical humor moved from the shadows in which they hid in the earlier works into the foreground, a process seen clearly in *Travels with My Aunt* (1969), *Monsignor Quixote* (1982), Greene's postmodern redaction of Cervantes, and *Doctor Fischer of Geneva; or, The Bomb Party* (1980), a witty fable concerning human greed. Greene died in 1991, fully recognized as one of the major novelists of his generation.

David Leon Higdon

Bibliography

Allain, Marie-Françoise. *The Other Man: Conversations with Graham Greene.* 1983.

DeVitis, A.A. *Graham Greene.* rev. ed. 1986.

Greene, Graham. *A Sort of Life.* 1971.

———. *Ways of Escape.* 1980.

Sherry, Norman. *The Life of Graham Greene.* 2 vols. 1989–94.

Wobbe, R.A. *Graham Greene: A Bibliography and Guide to Research.* 1979.

Grey, Edward (1862–1933)

Sir Edward Grey was a Liberal politician and statesman. The son of an army officer, he belonged to a distinguished family, his ancestors including the Whig Prime Minister Lord Grey. Educated at Winchester and Balliol College, Oxford, he was an undistinguished student and was expelled in 1884. This misfortune was really a stroke of luck, because under the influence of his parish rector, the church historian Mandell Creighton, Grey was inspired to give up rural pleasures for the responsibilities of a public life. In 1884 he became private secretary first to Evelyn Baring, the future Lord Cromer, and then to the Liberal Chancellor of the Exchequer H.C.E. Childers. Grey stood successfully as the Liberal candidate for Berwick-on-Tweed in 1885, retaining the seat until his elevation to the peerage as Viscount Grey of Fallodon in 1916. He served as a junior minister in the **Foreign Office** during the Liberal governments of W.E. Gladstone and Lord Rosebery (1892–5) and became Foreign Secretary in the last Liberal government and the first wartime coalition (1905–16). He was made Knight of the Garter in 1912.

It was Grey who declared in 1895 that the French advance in the Sudan was unwelcome, a policy that led eventually to the Anglo-French confrontation at Fashoda in 1898. In the disunion after the fall of the Liberal government in 1895, Grey followed Rosebery, becoming one of the leaders of the Liberal Imperialist faction of the party. He supported the **Conservative** government during the **Boer War** of 1899–1902, even though many other Liberals were highly critical of the conduct of the war and some even sympathized with the Boers. Similarly, Grey supported Lord Lansdowne's foreign policy, including the alliance with Japan in 1902 and the Entente Cordiale with France in 1904. A believer in the value of continuity in foreign policy, Grey was swayed very little by Radical Liberal calls for the reduction of military and naval expenditures and the avoidance of Continental entanglements.

When the Conservative government resigned in December 1905, Grey joined his fellow Liberal Imperialists **H.H.** Asquith and **R.B.** Haldane in an effort to dislodge the new Prime Minister, the Radical Liberal Sir **Henry Campbell-Bannerman**. This intrigue failed, but Grey joined the **Cabinet** nonetheless. He soon made his mark as the first Foreign Secretary to orient British policy clearly around the single dominating fact of Germany's emergence as an aggressive power. Grey sought a balance of power and thus was not interested merely in an understanding with Germany. In 1906 he was able to reach a settlement of the first Moroccan crisis between France and Germany after making it clear that Britain would not abandon the

Entente Cordiale. Unknown to most Cabinet members, this special Anglo-French relationship included secret discussions concerning a common military strategy. Grey recognized that Russia, weakened by defeat in its war with Japan (1904–5) and shaken by revolution, might exchange its alliance with France for one with Germany. Hence, he cemented the anti-German alliance of Britain, France, and Russia with the Anglo-Russian Convention of 1907. This arrangement involved more than an alignment against Germany, for Grey was also able to promote a relaxation of tensions between Britain and Russia over Afghanistan, Persia, and Tibet.

It would be a mistake, therefore, to see Grey's foreign policy as Liberal in any idealistic sense of the word. He was guided by Britain's security interests as a great power. As a result, he was the object of much criticism from Radicals and socialists opposed to normal relations with Russia and outraged by an international anarchy that seemed only to benefit the incipient military-industrial complexes of Europe. In domestic policy, Grey's stances were rather more liberal. He supported **women's suffrage**, land reform, and Irish Home Rule. He was prepared to go much further than many of his colleagues to accommodate the trade unions during the wave of labor unrest that swept over Britain and Ireland between 1910 and 1914.

Grey's claim to greatness rests on his struggle to maintain the peace of Europe before the outbreak of the **First World War** in 1914. Throughout these years Britain remained free of any formal treaty obligations to its French and Russian allies. In 1911 another German effort to strain the Anglo-French Entente Cordiale produced the second Moroccan crisis. Once again, the attempt failed. Significantly, Grey's policy had apparently gained such acceptance from his colleagues that none other than the Radical Chancellor of the Exchequer, **David Lloyd George**, delivered the clear warning in July that further German interference invited war with Britain, and not just with France. Liberal unity was as yet more apparent than real, for in the narrow escape from war the whole Cabinet learned for the first time of the secret discussions with the French. This revelation led to some dissent among ministers, but in the end Liberal illusions about splendid isolation gave way to realistic appraisals, and the Cabinet became even more committed to France. Unfor-

tunately, Grey was unable in the aftermath of the crisis to achieve an overall settlement of great-power rivalries. With German help he was successful, however, in containing the Balkan Wars of 1912–13.

The assassination of the Austrian Archduke Franz Ferdinand in Sarajevo in June 1914 transformed the prospects for peace in Europe. Grey was unable to use Britain's formal freedom of maneuver to persuade Austria-Hungary and Germany to pull back from war with Serbia, Russia, and France. His great speech in the House of Commons on the coming war was not a rousing call to arms but a heavy-hearted account of his efforts in the cause of peace.

Once Britain had entered the conflict, Grey's diplomacy became part and parcel of the larger military struggle. He maintained good relations with the United States and succeeded in bringing Italy over to the side of the Allies (1915). While he seemed to appreciate emotionally that the war would change everything, Grey did not foresee that secret agreements and understandings might become dead letters or worse in the post-war turmoil in Russia, Europe, and the colonial world. Fortunately for Grey, who suffered from steadily worsening eyesight, his wartime responsibilities ended in December 1916 when Lloyd George replaced Asquith as Prime Minister of a reconstructed coalition government. Grey devoted most of his subsequent public activity to the **League of Nations Union**, although he continued to play a role in the leadership of the **Liberal Party** and served as Chancellor of Oxford University (1928–33).

Grey resumed his country life, given up four decades earlier, especially his love of birds. Perhaps this return to a former life was a way of acknowledging that the basis for his foreign policy simply no longer existed, that the war had indeed turned the world upside down and left a man like him on unfamiliar ground.

Ian Christopher Fletcher

Bibliography

Grey of Fallodon, Viscount. *Twenty-Five Years, 1892–1916.* 2 vols. 1925.

Hinsley, F.H., ed. *British Foreign Policy under Sir Edward Grey.* 1977.

Robbins, Keith. *Sir Edward Grey: A Biography of Lord Grey of Fallodon.* 1971.

Trevelyan, George Macaulay. *Grey of Fallodon: The Life and Letters of Sir*

Edward Grey, afterwards Viscount Grey of Fallodon. 1937.

Guild Socialism

Guild Socialism was a political theory and movement that advocated workers' control of industry through a system of democratic "guilds" of producers. The idea was first elaborated in 1912 by S.G. Hobson and A.R. Orage in the monthly *New Age*. It was further developed by others, including A.J. Penty, M.B. Reckitt, William Mellor, and **G.D.H. Cole**, who became its leading spokesman. A National Guilds League was founded in 1915, immediately after the Guildsmen's near-successful attempt to "capture" the **Fabian Society**. Although its membership never exceeded 1,000, the league enjoyed influence among trade unionists, largely as a result of its control of the Fabian (later Labour) Research Department. A practical attempt to realize the guild idea in the building industry in the early 1920s collapsed after some initial success. The National Guilds League disbanded in 1924. Guild Socialism thus died as a movement, although there were subsequent attempts within the labor movement to rekindle interest in its ideas.

Guild Socialism was a reaction against the impersonality and alienation of industrial capitalism, and, more specifically, against the state socialism of the Fabian Society, which provided the theoretical basis of much of the labor movement's political thought. Guild Socialists believed that the greatest injustice was not that the workers were poor, but that they were—to use Hobson's term—"wage-slaves," a condition that state ownership and control of industry would do nothing to change. They believed also that the root of capitalist power lay not in the state but in the workshop, and therefore could not be fundamentally challenged by political means alone. The latter view was the basis of the Guild Socialists' ubiquitous slogan, "Economic Power Precedes Political Power."

Some Guild Socialists, informed by the medieval movement of the late nineteenth century, were opposed to industrial civilization itself and proposed a return to handicraft manufacture in a medieval guild system. Their case was first argued by Penty in *The Restoration of the Gild* [sic] *System* (1906). The majority, however, accepted both the permanence and desirability of industrialism, maintaining that

machine production, if justly organized, could reduce both drudgery and material want.

The modernist stream of Guild Socialism may be seen as an Anglicized and intellectualized version of the syndicalist ideas imported from France and the United States, which inspired many of the leaders of the strike waves of 1911–14. Syndicalism aimed, by means of an insurrectionary general strike, to replace the state with direct working-class power organized into "one big union." Unlike the syndicalists, most Guild Socialists argued that the state was necessary to represent people in those activities and interests that all had in common. Their view was deeply influenced by the pluralist theories of J.N. Figgis and F.W. Maitland, who had argued that the state was merely one of many forms of association into which the members of a given community might enter, and had no right to claim sovereignty over other associations such as churches or trade unions. In Cole's adaptation of pluralism, the guilds would represent the citizens in their capacity as producers on equal terms with the state, which would have the particular function of representing them as consumers. While most Guild Socialists broadly accepted Cole's view, others—most notably Hobson—held that an individual could not thus be in conflict with itself and saw the state as embodying the spiritual, rather than the economic, aspects of the citizens' personalities.

Guild Socialism's life as a political movement began within the **Oxford** University Fabian Society, in which Cole and Mellor were leaders. Although the attempt to capture the Fabian Society was conducted with the maximum possible abrasiveness, the core of the "Old Guard" Fabian leadership (**George Bernard Shaw** and **Sidney and Beatrice Webb**) tried hard to keep the insurgents within the fold. To this end, and in the hope that empirical research would cool their ardor, the Old Guard offered them a committee to investigate the rival proposed modes of social ownership. The strategy backfired: the committee almost immediately metamorphosized into the Fabian Research Department (FRD), which disseminated guild propaganda among trade union leaders while providing them with information to assist in the practical conduct of industrial disputes.

The FRD's activities laid much of the groundwork for the founding of industrial guilds. The building guilds, which originated in Manchester in 1920 under Hobson's leadership, were initially favored by a government-sponsored boom in post-war **housing** construction. Their collapse in 1923 was due to the end of government subsidies in the context of a general economic slump, the hostility of the building employers, and Hobson's financial mismanagement. Many Guild Socialist leaders had looked askance at the guilds from the beginning, arguing that they could not work on a piecemeal basis and that control of the state was necessary to facilitate wholesale change.

The National Guilds League was another victim of the slump, which forced trade unions into a defensive posture. Its demise was hastened by a split over attitudes to the Russian revolution, the participation of some members in the formation of the **Communist Party of Great Britain** (CPGB) in 1921, and the CPGB's takeover of the **Labour Research Department**.

In the early 1930s two discrete efforts were made to revive guild ideas. A group around Hobson established the House of Industry League, which advocated replacing the **House of Lords** with a chamber of functional representatives. A group around Cole and Mellor formulated a set of proposals for workers' control of socialized industry. Some of their proposals were formally adopted by the **Labour Party**, but they had no effect on the **nationalization** policies of the next Labour government. The libertarian upsurge within the Left in the late 1960s occasioned a further renewal of interest in Guild Socialism's hitherto neglected place in labor history.

D.P. Blaazer

Bibliography

Briggs, Asa, and John Saville. *Essays in Labour History, 1886–1923*. vol. 2. 1971.

Carpenter, Niles. *Guild Socialism*. 1922.

Cole, G.D.H. *Guild Socialism Restated*. 1920.

Glass, S.T. *The Responsible Society*. 1966.

Reckitt, M.B., and C.E. Bechhofer. *The Meaning of National Guilds*. rev. ed. 1920.

H

Haig, Douglas (1861–1928)

Promoted to Field Marshal in January 1917 and made an Earl in 1919, Douglas Haig was Commander-in-Chief of the British Expeditionary Force (BEF) in France and Belgium from December 1915 until the end of the **First World War**. His performance during that period remains among the most controversial aspects of the 1914–18 conflict.

Born in Edinburgh of a prominent Scotch whisky manufacturing family on 19 June 1861 and educated at Clifton and Brasenose College, **Oxford,** Haig entered Sandhurst in 1884, graduating first in order of merit. He was assigned to the Seventh Hussars in 1885 and served in India from 1886 to 1892. Taciturn and ambitious, Haig was nevertheless regarded as a capable administrator who emphasized the need for education and efficiency. The principles of war he absorbed at the Staff College in 1896–7 had a considerable influence on his conduct of operations in the First World War. Having won further recognition in the Sudan in 1898, Haig served with the Cavalry Division in the early stages of the **Boer War,** mostly as chief staff officer to Sir John French (1852–1925). The successful cavalry charge preceding the relief of Kimberley in February 1900 reaffirmed Haig's faith in the value of the mounted arm. In May 1901 he was given command of the Seventeenth Lancers, combining regimental duties with those of a column commander.

Haig's career flourished after the South African War. From 1903 to 1906 he was Inspector General of Cavalry in India. Then, at the War Office, first as Director of Military Training (1906–7) and then as Director of Staff Duties (1907–9), he helped shape and implement the **army** reforms of **R.B. Haldane,** including the transformation of the Militia, Volunteers, and Yeomanry into the Special Reserve and **Territorial** Force, as well as the creation of an Expeditionary Force and the Imperial General Staff. In 1909 Haig was appointed Chief of the General Staff in India, spending a frustrating two years trying, without total success, to prepare the Indian army for a wider role. However, in 1912 he took over the Aldershot Command, a post carrying with it the field command of I Corps when the BEF was mobilized for war against Germany.

On 25 August 1914, during the retreat from Mons, Haig's normally calm demeanor deserted him when German troops entered Landrecies, menacing his headquarters, but he quickly regained confidence, and on the Aisne in September his corps only narrowly missed seizing the Chemin des Dames ridge ahead of the Germans. At the First Battle of Ypres in October–November his resolute leadership of I Corps contributed to the blocking of German attempts to reach the English Channel ports, even though the old BEF was thereby largely destroyed. As the BEF was reorganized, Haig was elevated to the command of its First Army on 26 December. In 1915, like many others, he was unable to find a solution to the trench deadlock and misread the lessons of the attack at Neuve Chapelle in March, opting thereafter for lengthy artillery preparation rather than hurricane bombardments. His disillusionment with his superior, Sir John French, increased on 25–26 September at Loos, where the late arrival of reserves prevented the First Army from exploiting initial gains, an episode that precipitated French's replacement by Haig as Commander-in-Chief of the BEF on 19 December 1915.

With Britain still the junior partner in the alliance with France, Haig could not attack in Flanders, as he wished, in 1916, being obliged to participate in a joint offensive on the **Somme**. He envisaged a swift breakthrough, whereas Lieutenant-General Sir Henry Rawlinson (1864–1925), whose Fourth Army launched the attack, favored a more gradual "bite and hold" approach. Haig's failure to resolve such differences led to fatal ambiguities in the assault plan. Following the disastrous opening of the offensive on 1 July, Haig grew reconciled to a dour battle of attrition prior to another major assault at Flers-Courcelette on 15 September, when tanks made their operational debut. Haig has, perhaps, been unfairly blamed for using tanks prematurely, yet, a decisive breakthrough having once more eluded him, he undoubtedly prolonged the offensive unnecessarily until mid-November.

David Lloyd George, who succeeded **H.H. Asquith** as Prime Minister in December 1916, was highly critical of Haig. However, he stopped short of dismissing him, and Haig managed to resist a move in February 1917 to make him permanently subordinate to the new French Commander-in-Chief, General Robert Nivelle (1856–1924). Indeed, French army mutinies in 1917 caused the BEF to shoulder the main burden of Allied endeavors on the Western Front. While the BEF displayed marked tactical improvements in the assault phases of its battles at Arras (April), Messines (June) and Cambrai (November), Haig's performance in his offensive at Ypres from 31 July to 10 November was undistinguished, for he allowed the Fifth Army commander, General Sir Hubert Gough (1870–1963), to set unrealistic early objectives and again persisted with a costly battle too long in appalling conditions.

Recent studies suggest that Haig underestimated the threat to the Fifth Army in March 1918 and, at one stage of the German "Michael" offensive, was prepared to fall back on the channel ports, away from his French allies. Even so, he supported the establishment of a unified Allied command under General Ferdinand Foch (1851–1929), and, during the German Lys offensive, showed commendable tenacity, exemplified by his "backs to the wall" order of 11 April. Later, Haig was one of the first to sense that the German army could be defeated in 1918. Moreover, in the final "Hundred Days" campaign, starting at Amiens on 8 August, the BEF won the greatest series of victories in the British army's history, achievements often forgotten in assessments of Haig. He returned home in 1919 to be Commander-in-Chief, Home Forces, and retired in 1921. In his last years he immersed himself in the cause of ex-servicemen, inspiring the formation of the British Legion and becoming its President. He died on 29 January 1928.

Peter Simkins

Bibliography

Blake, Robert. *The Private Papers of Douglas Haig, 1914–1919.* 1952.

De Groot, Gerard J. *Douglas Haig, 1861–1928.* 1988.

Terraine, John. *Douglas Haig: The Educated Soldier.* 1963.

Winter, Dennis. *Haig's Command: A Reassessment.* 1991.

Woodward, David R. *Lloyd George and the Generals.* 1983.

Haldane, J(ohn) B(urdon) S(anderson) (1892–1964)

J.B.S. Haldane was one of the most distinguished biologists of his generation, remembered above all for his contribution to the uniting of Darwinian evolutionary theory and Mendelian genetics in a series of papers published from 1924. These were collected and systematized as *The Causes of Evolution* in 1932, the same year that he was elected a fellow of the **Royal Society**. Haldane was a significant public figure and author of popular scientific essays. A man of strong convictions, he was for years a major figure in the **Communist Party of Great Britain**. After a successful academic career at **Cambridge** and in London, in 1957 he moved to India to continue his work, becoming a citizen of that country in 1961. He was married twice and had no children.

J.B.S. was the only son of J.S. Haldane, a distinguished **Oxford** physiologist; his sister is the novelist Naomi Mitchison (1897–). The Haldane family was of lowland Scottish noble extraction and politically illustrious; his uncle, **R.B.** (later Viscount) **Haldane**, was a Liberal War Minister and Lord Chancellor. Haldane was educated at Lynam's School, Oxford, and Eton, winning a mathematics scholarship to New College, **Oxford**. He gained first-class honors not only in that subject, but also in classics and **philosophy** (1914). During the **First World War** he served as an officer in France and

Mesopotamia. From 1919 he worked in **genetics** and physiology at New College, Oxford, before joining Gowland Hopkins at Cambridge as Reader in Biochemistry in 1922. Parallel with this, he was put in charge of genetic investigations at the John Innes Horticultural Institution (1927–36). In 1933 he moved to University College, London (UCL), as Professor of genetics, then of biometry. He made three trips to fight in the **International Brigade** during the **Spanish Civil War**, gaining experience that led to his book *A.R.P.* (1938), a quantitative study of the likely bomb damage in the anticipated world war. He remained at UCL until he took up a post at the Biometry Research Unit of the Indian Statistical Institute in Calcutta, transferring in 1962 to the Laboratory of Genetics and Biometry at Bhubaneswar.

Much of his work involved the application of mathematics to biological problems. His genetic and evolutionary researches were usually achieved not by experiment, but by reanalyzing established data about plant and animal populations. Mathematics, Haldane believed, was essential to Darwinian theory, because it was necessary to prove not only that natural selection could explain that species change, but, crucially, that it could have caused change at a sufficient rate to explain the variation observed in nature.

Along with his genetic work he undertook several series of physiological experiments. In 1939 he investigated the cause of casualties after the submarine *Thetis* sank, by observing the effects on himself and three others of being enclosed in a sealed chamber simulating submarine conditions. Later in the war he undertook similar work for the Admiralty on the physiological effects of gases at high pressure.

His works aimed at a general audience demonstrated a marked willingness to extrapolate from scientific to social principles. *Daedalus* (1924), for example, is a meditation on the deliberate directing of human evolution to enable the colonization of other worlds. *Callinicus* (1925) contains a robust defense of chemical warfare. *My Friend Mr. Leakey*, a collection of children's stories, was published in 1937. He wrote more than 300 weekly columns for the *Daily Worker*.

Haldane will continue to be remembered as a biologist with equally strong convictions about society as about science and as one whose example inspired generations of students.

T.M. Boon

Bibliography

Clark, Ronald W. *J.B.S.: The Life and Work of J.B.S. Haldane.* 1968.
Dronamraju, Krishna R., ed. *Haldane and Modern Biology.* 1968.
———. *The Life and Work of J.B.S. Haldane with Special Reference to India.* 1985.
Werskey, Gary. *The Visible College: A Collective Biography of British Scientists and Socialists of the 1930s.* 2nd ed. 1988.

Haldane, R(ichard) B(urdon) (1856–1928)

R.B. Haldane was a Liberal politician, jurist, educator, and philosopher. The second son of Robert Haldane and Mary Burdon Sanderson, he was educated at Edinbugh Academy, the University of Edinburgh, and Goettingen University. He studied law at Lincoln's Inn, was called to the Bar in 1879, became a King's Counsel in 1890, and continued to practice in Chancery, the Privy Council, and the **House of Lords** until 1905. He stood successfully as a Liberal candidate for East Lothian in 1885 and held the seat until elevated to the peerage as Viscount Haldane of Cloan in 1911. His many honors included the Order of Merit (1915). He played a significant role in the last **Liberal** government, which enacted numerous social and constitutional reforms and confronted considerable domestic turbulence before leading Britain and the Empire into the First World War. Complicated and cerebral, he was capable of supporting such apparently divergent positions as military training for schoolboys and votes for women.

A Liberal Imperialist associated with Lord Rosebery, Haldane only entered the Liberal government with **H.H. Asquith** and Sir **Edward Grey** in December 1905 after they had failed to dislodge the new Prime Minister, the Radical Liberal Sir **Henry Campbell-Bannerman**. Haldane served as Secretary of State for War (1905–12) and Lord Chancellor (1912–15). As War Minister, he was responsible for crucial reforms that placed the **army** on a sound footing for war in Europe. They included the establishment of a General Staff, later enlarged to an Imperial General Staff in 1909, and the formation of an Expeditionary Force, complete with transport and supply arrangements. In the Territorial and Reserve Forces Act (1907) the forces available to the Regular Army upon mobilization were reconfigured by transforming the Militia into a Special Reserve and organizing the Volunteers into a **Territorial** Force. The reforms were debated in an atmosphere of growing anxiety over the German threat to British naval supremacy and even the danger of invasion. Their enactment and implementation represented a triumph for Haldane over, on the one hand, Radical economism and **pacifism** and, on the other hand, **Conservative** militarism and navalism.

Haldane was also responsible, in concert with the Home Secretaries Herbert Gladstone, **Winston Churchill,** and Reginald McKenna, for the deployment of troops to maintain public order in Britain and Ireland. Although the Liberal government generally showed restraint during the labor unrest of 1910–12, some lives were lost in collisions between strikers and soldiers, and worries were expressed about continued working-class adherence to Liberalism. In June 1912 Haldane became Lord Chancellor. He supported the cause of law reform, especially with regard to the law of real property and conveyancing. Although limited in what he could do by the overlapping jurisdictions of the Home Office and the Lord Chancellor's Office, he also supported legal-administrative reform. In line with his predecessor as Lord Chancellor, Lord Loreburn, Haldane tried to appoint and promote magistrates and judges on the basis of professional, not party-political, distinction. His greatest contribution lay in his efforts to improve the efficiency of the Judicial Committee of the Privy Council and the House of Lords, which handled important appeals from around the Empire.

Haldane's work for international peace and order included an unsuccessful mission to Berlin in 1912 for the purpose of seeking a reduction in the naval arms race and generally relaxing tensions between Britain and Germany. Haldane's admiration for German culture and philosophy became a liability during the **First World War.** He was forced to resign when Asquith formed the first coalition government in 1915.

A Hegelian who took a broad view of the state, Haldane did not allow his enemies to drive him from public life and administration. A lifelong educator and one of the cofounders of the **London School of Economics** in 1895, Haldane continued to take part in a wide variety of initiatives for the improvement of educational institutions and opportunities in both London and the provinces. He was President of Birkbeck College, University of London, from 1919 to 1928.

Haldane served once again as Lord Chancellor during the first Labour government in 1924. He subsequently led the Labour opposition in the House of Lords. He was probably the most distinguished Liberal leader to accept the **Labour Party** as the legitimate successor to Liberalism. His death in 1928, on the eve of the world Depression, spared him the disappointments of the second Labour government and the larger political changes that made Liberalism all but redundant in British and European politics.

Ian Christopher Fletcher

Bibliography
Haldane, Richard Burdon. *An Autobiography.* 1929.
Heuston, R.F.V. *Lives of the Lord Chancellors, 1885–1940.* 1964.
Koss, Stephen E. *Lord Haldane: Scapegoat for Liberalism.* 1969.
Maurice, Sir Frederick. *Haldane: The Life of Viscount Haldane of Cloan.* 2 vols. 1937–9.
Spiers, Edward M. *Haldane: An Army Reformer.* 1980.

Halifax, Earl of (Edward Frederick Lindley Wood) (1881–1959)

Edward Wood was born to wealth, privilege, and social status, and, upon the death of his father in 1934, he inherited the title of Viscount Halifax. He was educated at Eton and at Christ Church, **Oxford,** and was subsequently elected a Fellow of All Souls College, Oxford. A deeply religious Anglo-Catholic, he had considerable personal virtues, including an extraordinary ability to remain detached, objective, and fairminded about highly contentious issues. A lifelong **Conservative,** he sat for years in both Houses of Parliament and held a number of important political and diplomatic posts, but he is primarily remembered as an arch-**appeaser** who, as Foreign Secretary under **Neville Chamberlain,** yielded to Nazi threats and abandoned Czechoslovakia in the infamous **Munich** agreement of 1938.

After holding several lesser ministerial posts, he was, as Lord Irwin, appointed as Viceroy of India (1925–31), a curious selection in view of his minimal knowledge of the subcontinent. India was then in a state of turmoil and near chaos, with nationalists demanding extensive political concessions from Britain. By nature a conciliator, he responded with dignity, calm, and fairness, eliciting respect from all parties concerned. He acted firmly but not brutally in trying to maintain law and order, publicly stated that Dominion status for India was inevitable, and cut a deal with Mohandas Gandhi in 1931 that temporarily reduced the violence and agitation. He could do little personally to affect the course of constitutional development or mitigate the communal violence between Hindus and Muslims.

After his return to Britain, he served briefly as Secretary of State for War (1935), becoming painfully aware of the wretched state of Britain's defenses. He also held a number of other posts, including Lord Privy Seal (1935–7), Leader of the House of Lords (1935–8, 1940), and Lord President of the Council (1937–8). But it was his appointment as Foreign Secretary (1938–40) that proved so fateful. Here he gained his reputation as a bungling appeaser, who shamefully agreed to turn portions of Czechoslovakia over to Adolf Hitler. In some respects the oppobrium is justified. He initially misjudged the Nazis, admitting after a visit to Germany that he personally liked many of their leaders and believed Hitler was sincere in not wanting war. He loyally supported Chamberlain during the Czech crisis, allowing the authority of the **Foreign Office** to be circumvented and usurped by some of the Prime Minister's personal advisers. Incredibly, he did not personally attend the three critical meetings that Chamberlain had with Hitler at Berchtesgaden, Godesberg, and Munich to settle the Czech crisis.

However, more recent scholarship has partially rehabilitated his reputation. Unlike Chamberlain, Halifax saw Munich as a "horrible and wretched business," done out of dire necessity because of British military weakness, French indecisiveness, and the geographical isolation of Czechoslovakia. After Munich, Halifax encouraged Chamberlain to take a firmer line against Germany, pressed for more vigorous rearmament, gave military guarantees to Poland, Rumania, and Greece, and also attempted to negotiate an alliance with the Soviet Union, though with little enthusiasm and conviction.

Halifax was seriously considered as likely Prime Minister when Chamberlain resigned in May 1940, but he wisely recognized his unsuitability and deferred to **Winston Churchill**. In December, Churchill asked Halifax to become ambassador to the United States (1941–6), a crucial posting since Britain desperately needed American economic and military assistance even though the United States was technically at peace and isolationist in tendency. Initially unenthusiastic, Halifax accepted out of a sense of duty and had what could be labeled a successful term. He got along well with President Franklin D. Roosevelt, committed no serious blunders, ran the large British Embassy staff with tact and efficiency, and educated the American public to Britain's dire peril and military needs.

Upon his return to Britain in 1946, he retired from politics and enjoyed playing the role of the country gentleman on his Yorkshire estate. He received numerous honors and took time to write his disappointing memoirs, *Fullness of Days*. Despite his intelligence and integrity, his deep sense of **patriotism** and religious piety, and his unquestionable accomplishments, he will undoubtedly be primarily remembered as an "appeaser," although perhaps one less culpable than several of his colleagues.

David C. Lukowitz

Bibliography

Birkenhead, Frederick, Earl of. *Halifax: The Life of Lord Halifax*. 1965.
Charmley, John. *Chamberlain and the Lost Peace*. 1989.
Colvin, Ian. *The Chamberlain Cabinet*. 1971.
Halifax, Lord. *Fullness of Days*. 1957.
Roberts, Andrew. *The Holy Fox: A Life of Lord Halifax*. 1991.

Hamilton, Richard (1922–)

Richard Hamilton is regarded as the father of pop art in England, given his central role as a founding member of the **Independent Group** at London's **Institute of Contemporary Arts** in 1952. His contribution to the ground-breaking exhibition *This Is Tomorrow* at the Whitechapel Art Gallery in 1956 stands as an index of the concerns of those pop artists of the 1960s. Pop art for Hamilton at this time was a matter of using as subject matter that which was popular, produced for a mass audience, and inscribed by the sleek character of American **advertising**, American science fact or fiction, and American styling and design, especially of cars. Those members of the Independent Group to whom Hamilton was closest—such as Reyner Banham, Lawrence Alloway, and John McHale—proselytized for a media- and consumer-based aesthetic of all-inclusiveness and persuasive nowness foreshadowing the concerns of later pop artists. This was underlined by his collage-catalog of consumerist fantasy: *Just what is it that makes today's homes so different, so appealing?* (1956, Kunsthalle Tubingen, Prof. Dr. Georg Zundel Collection).

Hamilton's contribution to *This Is Tomorrow* was one of five environmental presentations executed by him between 1951 and 1958. These various works emphasize the extent to which Hamilton's investigation of a popular aesthetic was approached with an almost scientific zeal. Important in the formation of this approach and of central significance to Hamilton's development had been D'Arcy Wentworth Thompson's book *Growth and Form* (1917), which focuses on biological structural processes. His period as an art teacher also helped to crystallize in his mind a continually questioning manner of working. In 1952–3 he taught ideas developed from *Growth and Form* at the Central School of Arts and Crafts in London, where his fellow teachers included **Victor Pasmore**. From 1953 to 1966 he taught at the University of Durham, where his first-year design course was merged in 1958 with Pasmore's basic studies course, which had a formative influence on his students such as Bryan Ferry, Mark Lancaster, Stephen Buckley, Tim Head, and Noel Forster.

However, at the core of his work is the debt he owes to Marcel Duchamp and Francis Picabia, especially their use of a man-machine metaphor. This debt to Duchamp permeates much of Hamilton's output but can be most clearly displayed in his typographic version of Duchamp's *Green Box* (1957–60) and his reconstruction of Duchamp's *Large Glass* (1965–6, Tate Gallery Collection, London). Duchamp provided probably the most significant precedent for Hamilton by providing him with a model of practice for his exploration of the language and visual conventions of art within the context of the everyday. Similarly Hamilton's work concerned with mass culture as a subject matter is presented very much as fine art within a sophisticated, urbane, but frequently ironic range of reference.

After his exhibition at the Hanover Gallery in 1964, which brought together much of his output of the previous ten years, Hamilton increasingly diversified, not only with regard to the object of his scrutiny (perspective and the Guggenheim Museum, fashion photography and the still life, Irish politics and the self-portrait), but also the means of representation (computer and hi-fi amplifier fabrication, various conjunctions of paint and photograph, installations and holograms). This stands as a testimony to his inquiring vision and underlines that he is not involved with contemporary gimmickry for its own sake, but as a means of extending and revitalizing artistic traditions of past centuries.

Andrew Wilson

Bibliography

Hamilton, Richard. *Collected Words, 1953–1982*. 1982.
Morphet, Richard. *Richard Hamilton*. 1970.
———. *Richard Hamilton*. 1992.

Hammond, John Lawrence Le Breton (1872–1949) and Lucy Barbara (1873–1961)

The Hammonds were pioneer social historians who are remembered especially for their trilogy: *The Village Labourer* (1911), *The Town Labourer* (1917), and *The Skilled Labourer* (1919). They gave an account of the condition of the English working class during the period of the Industrial Revolution that became a classic statement of the "pessimistic" case in a long-running debate over the **standard of living**. John Lawrence Le Breton Hammond (known as Lawrence) married Lucy Barbara Bradby (known as Barbara) in 1901; they had no children. Their historical partnership developed in later years as their increasingly precarious health (hers tubercular, his mainly coronary) led to a steady withdrawal from an active participation in public affairs in London and the establishment of an even-paced life of authorship in the country.

Both of the Hammonds received a classical education, on which their literary work drew. They were as adept at painting the contrast between ancient Athens and modern Manchester as at elucidating the Homeric references in the discourse of Mr. Gladstone. Both came from professional families infused with moral and intellectual earnestness; his father was a clergyman of the **Church of England**; hers, the headmaster of a boarding school (Haileybury) that notoriously recruited **civil servants** for the British Raj. The Hammonds gave this heritage a radical twist. Barbara made a striking impression in her youth as an early **feminist** and became active in social work in London at the turn of the century. Lawrence began a career as a journalist associated with journals on the Liberal Left like the *Nation* and, increasingly in later years, the *Manchester Guardian*. He was prominently associated with the "**New Liberalism**," which took shape in the social reforms of the Edwardian period, until his appointment as as Secretary of the Civil Service Commission (1907–13). This meant that he had to renounce overtly partisan polemics—an initial impetus toward writing history instead.

With their first book, *The Village Labourer* (1911), the Hammonds established their reputation. Technically their work was founded upon Barbara's scrupulous research, especially in the public records, expounded in Lawrence's supple prose. Their account of how agricultural laborers fared during the enclosure of open fields in the period 1760–1830 opened up a far-reaching debate. They did not deny the economic rationality of the process, but they pointed to the way that its costs were borne by the rural poor. The book culminates in an account of the laborers' revolt of 1830, which they took as the response to an injustice that could only have been perpetrated while the landed interest governed England untrammeled. This was indeed a study of class exploitation; but the Hammonds were neither Marxists nor determinists, but liberals who looked to the advent of representative government for effective remedy. Their work acquired immediate political overtones with the inception of **David Lloyd George**'s Land Campaign in 1913, which made the land the pivot of Liberal social policy.

In turning their attention next to the urban working class, the Hammonds reinforced the left-wing image of their *oeuvre*. *The Town Labourer* (1917) did not disparage industrialization as such but again asked the awkward question: Who had paid for it? They regarded the Industrial Revolution as an exercise in exploitation that fit the ideologies of an age that took social inequality for granted. Published at the end of the First World War, with revolution on the streets abroad and reconstruction in the air at home, their findings once more fed into current political debate. Their trilogy was completed with *The Skilled Labourer* (1919), which analyzed the impact of technological change in making skilled craftsmen redundant in the early nineteenth century. It presented the Luddite movement in an unwontedly sympathetic light, suggesting that it constituted not only an understandable response by the inarticulate in defense of their livelihood, but also an excuse for repression by a reactionary government.

Other books followed, notably the study of the Chartist era that Penguin Books later published in an abridged—and best-selling—edition as *The Bleak Age* (1947). But the Hammonds' view of the Industrial Revolution remained their claim to attention—not all of it favorable. In the 1920s their interpretation was contested by J.H. Clapham, with all of his authority as Professor of economic history at **Cambridge**. He mounted an "optimistic" case on the standard of living by constructing a real wage index that showed substantial gains by industrial workers. Though the Hammonds publicly bowed on this point in face of the apparent weight of new statistical evidence, subsequent research was to show that Clapham himself had depended on a flawed price index.

Lawrence's own historical research in old age was devoted to the great Liberal statesman who had been the hero of his youth. In *Gladstone and the Irish Nation* (1938) he made brilliant use of the privileged access he had been given to Gladstone's diaries to render his Irish policy comprehensible in historical context. Again this is a book in which passion and elegance are counterpoised in giving form to a mass of arcane and rebarbative detail. The resulting portrait of Gladstone succeeds in conveying a sense of the man on which all subsequent scholarship has built. This was Hammond's last major contribution to historical scholarship. During the **Second World War** he returned to his old job of editorial writer on the *Manchester Guardian*, but it was a valetudinarian life for the Hammonds thereafter.

The Hammonds have often been identified as socialist, yet their outlook throughout their joint career remained true to the nostrums of liberal reformism. Insofar as the Hammonds rested their interpretation of the Industrial Revolution upon a quantitative assessment, it was by no means overturned; and its main thrust, in fact, was qualitative in its concern for the impact of economic change on ordinary people's lives. While they depicted the bleak age of early industrialization, they also pointed to the civilizing process that urban life underwent from the middle of the nineteenth century. Though their work came to serve as a straw man, to be knocked down in a dismissive way by a new generation of professional economic historians,

H

its scholarly credentials have survived with remarkable resilience.

Peter Clarke

Bibliography

Clarke, Peter. *Liberals and Social Democrats.* 1978.

Thomis, Malcolm I. *The Town Labourer and the Industrial Revolution.* 1974.

Winkler, Henry R. "J.L. Hammond" in Hans A. Schmitt, ed. *Historians of Modern Germany.* 1971. pp. 95–119.

Hardie, (James) Keir (1856–1915)

Keir Hardie's career symbolized the emergence of independent Labour politics. He was born in Legbrannock, Lanarkshire, on 15 August 1856, the illegitimate son of a Scottish farm servant. Childhood poverty and underground employment in **coal mining** from the age of ten were formative experiences. His early involvement in trade union activities led to his effective exclusion from the industry in his mid-twenties. Alongside his agitational and rebellious tendencies he had a zealous devotion to self-improvement. After moving to Cumnock in Ayrshire in the early 1880s, he developed his journalistic talents, made an ambivalent compromise with middle-class radicalism, and keenly supported the **Liberal Party**.

Industrial and political pressures broke this allegiance. Hardie's outlook was radicalized in 1886–7 by another failed attempt to develop effective Scottish mining trade unionism. In January 1887 he established a newspaper, *The Miner*, and made links with socialists. Sixteen months later, in April 1888, he fought a by-election at Mid-Lanark as an Independent Labour candidate. In retrospect, this may seem a significant shift, although the extent of his ideological break with Liberalism remains controversial. His vote was 617, only 8.2 percent of the total in a three-cornered contest. Later that year he played a major part in the formation of the Scottish Labour Party, an alliance of radicals, land reformers, and trade unionists. This party's character illuminated the complexities of Hardie's own politics—assertions of independence, but a heavy legacy from his earlier Liberalism.

A symbolic moment came in July 1892 with his election to Parliament as the Independent Labour member for West Ham South. Unlike two contemporaries and despite some local Liberal support, he retained his indepen-

dence, attacking the subsequent Liberal government on labor questions, especially unemployment, and attracting criticism for his outspoken republicanism. Another crucial development came in 1893 when Hardie chaired much of the foundation conference of the **Independent Labour Party** (ILP). From the following year he and the new party became almost synonymous. With the *Labour Leader*, his successor to the *Miner*, moving to weekly publication in March 1894, Hardie was emerging as a dominant figure in the socialist movement.

Yet the late 1890s proved difficult years. He lost his parliamentary seat in 1895, and the ILP's early optimism faded. Together with other ILP leaders he defeated attempts to fuse the ILP and the Marxist Social Democratic Federation into a United Socialist Party. Instead he favored a broad labor alliance of trade unions and socialist groups. This strategy was consummated in February 1900, with the foundation conference of the **Labour Representation Committee** (LRC), an achievement that owed much to Hardie's vision.

Alongside this organizational pragmatism, Hardie demonstrated principle and courage in his outspoken opposition to the British military campaign in **South Africa**. His outrage, although expressed frequently in the language of socialism, was fueled more by Liberal antimilitarism. Despite the widespread British support for the **Boer War**, Hardie won a parliamentary seat in the election of 1900. His return as one of the two MPs for Merthyr Boroughs owed much to quarrels among the Liberals, who dominated this South Wales industrial seat. His victory meant that the LRC had one thoroughly loyal spokesman in the new Parliament. Alongside his robust assertions of independence, however, Hardie was flexible in his attitude toward electoral deals with the Liberals. This reflected his situation in Merthyr and also his blend of non-Marxian socialism and Liberal radicalism. The Liberal electoral landslide of 1906 brought thirty victories for Labour candidates, mostly the results of a secret pact with the Liberals. The LRC became the **Labour Party**, and Hardie became Chairman of the Parliamentary Labour Party.

Hardie's year and a half in this post attracted considerable criticism. Initially he led a parliamentary group that seemed to make a significant impact—for example, securing the reversal of the **Taff Vale judgment** on trade union liability. Over time, the limitations of the

Labour position became more apparent, and frustration tended to focus on Hardie's leadership. Moreover, he always faced a major problem in reconciling his awareness of organizational limitations with his agitational and propagandist instincts.

From his resignation of the Parliamentary Labour Party chairmanship to the outbreak of the First World War, Hardie acted almost as an elder statesman with radical proclivities. He vigorously defended the Labour Party against critics from the Left who claimed that the compact with the unions was damaging to socialist prospects, but he often felt unhappy about the caution of many Labour politicians. He had deep reservations about syndicalism, but he reacted to the industrial struggles from 1910 with bitter indictments of Liberal government policy. On the **women's suffrage** question, his consistent and passionate advocacy of a liberal case for sexual equality led to tensions with many less-committed colleagues. On all domestic issues in Edwardian Britain Hardie continued to work within the confines of Labour politics, often his attitudes were still informed by Liberal values, but he articulated forcefully the emotions of the dispossessed and the disadvantaged.

The splendor and the tragedy of Hardie's career lay in his internationalism. An Empire tour in 1907–8 found him ambiguous on the White **Australia** policy, but he evoked a storm by his denunciations of British rule in India. His brief visit to South Africa brought riotous scenes as he condemned racial discrimination, including the practices of white trade unions. Above all, Hardie became preoccupied with the threat of militarism within Europe and placed increasing hope in the Second International as a means of averting catastrophe. The collapse of such hopes in August 1914 culminated for him in a bruising meeting in his constituency, cut short by patriotic disorder. The destruction of Hardie's political hopes was essentially the end of his career. Effectively a casualty of the war, he died on 26 September 1915.

An internationalist who was a thorough Scot, a pragmatist who was a romantic and a visionary, Hardie came for many to symbolize a radical political change. Yet he always remained an outsider, a loner through whose personality were reflected the achievements and the tragedies of the British Left.

David Howell

Bibliography
Benn, Caroline. *Keir Hardie*. 1992.
Hughes, Emrys, ed. *Keir Hardie's Speeches and Writings*. 1928.
McLean, Iain. *Keir Hardie*. 1975.
Morgan, Kenneth. *Keir Hardie: Radical and Socialist*. 1975.
Stewart, William. *J. Keir Hardie*. 1921.

Health of the Population

The change in the incidence and distribution of disease and death among the British people in the twentieth century has been of such a colossal nature that it makes all other previous changes of this sort seem insignificant. The first half of the century saw a massive decline in morbidity and mortality from infectious diseases, especially among children. The second half witnessed a rising incidence of degenerative diseases in an increasingly **ageing** population. Most, but not all, statistics point to the increasing health of the population. Statistics, however, are only pointers, not definitive signs, since nearly all numbers used to indicate health are measures of the absence of disease, not measures of positive well-being.

At the beginning of the century, qualitatively speaking, the poor, and especially the children of the poor, suffered chronic, low-grade ill health punctuated by episodes of severe, sometimes fatal, illness. Infectious diseases and nutritional disorders such as diphtheria, scarlet fever, osteomyelitis, and rickets were common. Undernourishment was the norm among the poor. In 1910 the report of the government's Chief Medical Officer on the health of schoolchildren found 10 percent with serious defects of vision, 40 percent with bad teeth, and 40 percent with "unclean heads or bodies." It also noted that children were victims of a host of other complaints such as ringworm, enlarged tonsils, and adenoidal disorders. Crippling, if not fatal, diseases such as mastoid infection were common. In 1917 Professor Arthur Keith (1866–1955) found 70 percent of a sample of University of **Cambridge** students to be above "full stature" (defined as 5 ft. 8 ins.). However, Medical Boards examining working-class recruits at almost exactly the same time, 1917–18, found only 36 percent were in this category. In contrast to this grim picture, by the year 2000, if current trends continue, the overall portrait of the nation's health will show a well-nourished population relatively free of sickness in its younger age groups but containing a large proportion of elderly folk suffering from chronic degenerative disorders (mainly arteriosclerotic diseases) and cancer. The point where the early pattern turns into the late one is roughly situated at mid-century.

The decline in mortality that was occurring in the late nineteenth century accelerated in the first half of the twentieth. In 1901 the crude annual death rate in Britain was about 18 per 1,000; by 1960 it had fallen to 11.5. Thirty years later, in 1990, the figure had declined only slightly, to 11.2. Correspondingly, over the same period, life expectancy increased. In 1901 a man could expect to live just over forty-five years, and a woman nearly fifty. By 1960 these figures had jumped to roughly sixty-eight and seventy-four, respectively. By 1990 a further five years had been gained by both sexes. Scottish death rates, perhaps because of the comparatively late urbanization of central Scotland, have remained consistently higher than those of England. In general during the century regional differences in mortality have diminished. In the decade 1901–10 death rates in nonindustrial areas were 25 percent lower than those in industrial areas in England and Wales. But by 1950 urban areas were offering definite advantages over the rural.

All of these crude figures, impressive as they are, simply disguise the site at which the greatest changes in twentieth-century mortality occurred. Practically every gain was made among children, and almost entirely among children born during the first half-century. Of 1,000 children born in 1900, 230, nearly a quarter, failed to reach the age of fifteen. By 1950 the figure had declined to 40 per 1,000. Even these figures disguise where the most significant changes took place. The fall in death rates occurred preponderantly among children under age four, most notably among infants under one year. In this latter group mortality fell from around 160 per 1,000 in 1900 to under 30 in the 1950s. The relation of these variations in mortality to occupation and class is an area of controversy. Nevertheless, it is indisputable that mortality, although it has fallen in all classes, has remained higher, at all ages, among the unskilled than among the professional classes.

These remarkable changes in mortality have been accompanied by a spectacular change in the pattern of disease. Between 1901 and 1971, 73 percent of the fall in mortality can be attributed to a decline in deaths from infectious diseases. Children were the principal beneficiaries of this reduction. Diphtheria, measles, whooping cough, scarlet fever, and infantile diarrhea nearly all disappeared as causes of **infant** and child **mortality**. In the population as a whole deaths from **tuberculosis** have shown the most notable decline. In the last decade of the nineteenth century nearly 1,500 people of every 1 million in the population would die, every year, of respiratory tuberculosis. In 1971, 13 people in every million died of the same cause. Corresponding to the decline in mortality from infectious disorders has been a decline in the morbidity caused by these and other diseases. Again, children have been the beneficiaries. The chronic disabling diseases of childhood, notably crippling infections of bones and joints, have become far less common. But even among the non-aged adult population the incidence of severe infectious diseases, such as lobar pneumonia, has declined considerably.

Many factors have played a part in the pattern of decline. Better **housing** and better sanitation have continued to contribute substantially to the change, just as they did from the mid-nineteenth century onward. Much prominence was given in the past to specific medical measures, such as inoculation and antibiotics. However, it is clear that although in most instances these technologies did make a small difference, they actually arrived late on the scene, when curves were already making spectacular falls. The exact effect of medical intervention is thus problematical. Nonspecific medical intervention, such as the provision of milk depots, district midwifery, and **nursing** services have, presumably, been highly significant, but again their effect is hard to measure. The crucial factor seems to have been better **diet and nutrition**. The benefits of a larger and more varied diet began to have an effect in the late nineteenth century, and these benefits accrued in the twentieth century as the quantity and quality of food intake per capita gradually increased. Better nutrition made it possible for people to resist and recover from the diseases of childhood. Evidence of better nutrition is to be found in the trend toward earlier physical maturation and in the increase in heights and weights of schoolchildren. Such changes correlate extremely well with increases in the per-capita national income. Besides increasing, this latter has also shown some reduction in inequality in the twentieth century. Nonetheless, throughout the century, the poor have remained smaller in stature than the rich.

The height of the poor was already increasing before the First World War, and the interwar years showed continuing gains. The **Second World War** itself had beneficial effects; food distribution was more equitable, and some groups were the beneficiaries of positive discrimination. By the end of the war 40 percent of schoolchildren had school dinners and 70 percent had school milk. By the mid-1950s less than 2 percent of schoolchildren were in what medical officials considered an unsatisfactory condition. By the 1960s the slow increase in height, which had been going on since the nineteenth century, may have come to an end. Around this time doctors first began to comment on undesirable obesity in schoolchildren.

Such comments mark the turning point between the two parts of the century. Whereas childhood is the predominant theme in discussing the first half of the century, age and its diseases dominate the second. Between 1950 and 1990 the population of the elderly (over sixty-five years of age) grew by 3.7 million to 8.9 million, to represent 15.6 percent of British residents. But, just as crude figures for the early century disguise drastic changes among infants, so these later figures hide the rapid expansion in the population over seventy-five years old. In 1948 at the start of the **National Health Service** these folk numbered 1.7 million (3.4 percent of the population); by 1990 they accounted for 4 million (6.9 percent). This age shift and the disappearance of the childhood infectious disorders has been reflected in the causes of death. Of the total number of deaths registered in 1990 about 46 percent were related to the circulatory system, 25 percent to cancers (notably breast and lung cancer), and 10 percent to the respiratory system. Many of the people dying from these conditions were, of course, chronically sick before death. In fact, expectation of life without disability has risen very little in the second part of the century. In 1988 expectation of life with "chronic disability" was fourteen years in males and seventeen years in females. The geriatric hospital, it might be said, has replaced the sanatorium as a symbol of sickness in the adult population. Looking at specific disorders, ischemic heart disease predominates as the main cause of death, even though the actual incidence has fallen since the 1970s. During the 1980s it claimed, on average, 459 lives a day. Stroke is the second-largest killer, followed by lung cancer. Scotland tops the age-specific mortality lists for the whole of Europe in all of these categories.

Measures of morbidity are much more difficult to achieve than measures of mortality, especially if the sickness does not come to the attention of a doctor. In a survey of sickness carried out between 1943 and 1952, two out of three people reported awareness of ill health in the month prior to interview, with females complaining of more ill health than males. In spite of this high level of complaint, only one in four had seen a doctor, and only one in eight had lost time from work or been confined to the house. Similar surveys forty years later produced similar results. Although masses of statistics have been available since the advent of the National Health Service, measuring morbidity is fraught with problems. It seems certain, however, that inpatient **hospital** treatment has increased. Despite fewer beds, 9.1 million people were treated as hospital inpatients in 1990–1, compared to 3.8 million in 1951. This surely does not indicate the deteriorating health of the people but, in part, greater public willingness to present for medical treatment. But how far curative medicine has improved the lives of the British people in the twentieth century is a moot point. Arguably the greatest medical benefits have not been in the most spectacular conditions—heart attack, kidney failure, and cancer—which have been the source of some fairly spectacular but contentious therapies. For most people the great benefits of medicine have been at a much simpler level, in the use of drugs or surgery for disorders such as asthma, skin disease, hernias, varicose veins, and a whole range of other complaints that, while not life-threatening, are sufficiently intrusive to make normal life unpleasant or even impossible.

Immigration has also made a difference to the pattern of British health. In general, ethnic minorities have poorer health than the rest of the population. For example, in the early 1990s death from heart disease was 46 percent higher among Asian women, and strokes killed 76 percent more Afro-Caribbean men, than the average. Poverty, although significant, is not the only cause of the difference. As yet undetectable cultural factors also play a part. Schizophrenia is three times more common among Afro-Caribbeans living in England than among those in Jamaica. Tuberculosis is 25 percent more common among Asians than the white population.

Although, therefore, there are many indications that in general the health of the British people is better at the end of the century than it was at the beginning, there is still a problematic relation between health and the absence of disease. This is indicated, for example, by the increasing suicide rate among young men in the 1980s. The curve of **drug addiction** has also continued to rise, as has that of AIDS and HIV infection.

Christopher Lawrence

Bibliography

Barker, Theo, and Michael Drake, eds. *Population and Society in Britain, 1850–1980*. 1982.

Department of Health and Social Security. *On the State of the Public Health: The Annual Report of the Chief Medical Officer*. 1991.

Floud, Roderick, Anabel Gregory, and Kenneth Wachter. *Height, Health, and History: Nutritional Status in the United Kingdom, 1750–1980*. 1990.

McKeown, Thomas. *The Role of Medicine: Dream, Mirage, or Nemesis?* 1979.

Heath, Edward Richard George (1916–)

Prime Minister from 1970 to 1974, Edward Heath led a **Conservative** government initially determined to depart from many of the principles and policies of its recent predecessors. It foundered, however, on economic difficulties and a crisis in industrial relations. Heath's long career is also noteworthy for a strong commitment to the **European Community** (EC) and for vehement criticism of **Margaret Thatcher's** policies and manner after her 1979 election victory.

Unusually for a Conservative leader, Heath came from a lower-middle-class family with no history of political involvement. More conventionally, he took a degree at **Oxford**, where he was President of the Union, and served with distinction in the **Second World War**. In 1950 he was elected to Parliament for Bexley, one of several promising newcomers who broadened the social and intellectual base of the party. Heath was not by nature an ideologue, a rebel, or a favorite with the party's grass roots. His rise to prominence was as an insider: He joined the Whips' Office when the party gained power in 1951, became Deputy Chief Whip the following year, and was promoted to Chief Whip in 1955. Despite his reputedly brusque manner,

often later a disadvantage in his dealings with back-bench MPs, he emerged with some credit from the difficult task of managing party opinion during the 1956 **Suez crisis**. From 1959 to 1964 he held several government posts: As Lord Privy Seal he was widely praised for his handling of Britain's vetoed application for EC membership, and at the Board of Trade he showed an undoctrinaire approach to industrial policy.

Heath replaced Sir **Alec Douglas-Home** as party leader and leader of the opposition in 1965. Although he often fared poorly in parliamentary exchanges with Prime Minister **Harold Wilson** and showed little flair for the more combative demands of his role, in some respects he became a commanding figure. He pursued a comprehensive review of party policy that formed the basis of the 1970 election manifesto and reflected his own vision of a modernized, flexible, more efficient economy as the nation's greatest need. The 1970 government broke with aspects of the "post-war consensus" which the major parties had embraced for a generation. The "Heathites" put more faith in market mechanisms, less in state intervention in the economy. They disdained incomes policies and public funding of weak companies or industries, dismantled some interventionist agencies, and pursued cuts in personal and corporate taxes to stimulate investment. Increased charges for some social services reflected unease at the growth of the **welfare state**. Heath's generally pragmatic search for efficiency, which often made him appear more comfortable with civil servants than with fellow politicians, extended to reorganizing parts of central and local government and the **National Health Service**.

Also crucial to Heath's agenda was the reform of industrial relations by the creation of a tighter framework of labor law. The 1971 Industrial Relations Act, however, turned into a shambles. Effectively crippled by trade union opposition, it greatly impeded government-union relations at a time of mounting industrial unrest. The government, indeed, ran into trouble on several fronts. Inflation drove it to adopt a statutory prices-and-incomes policy; it moved to support failing companies; it passed the 1972 Industry Act to create extensive new powers of state intervention. The phrase "U-turn" became a cliché of the day: Heath seemed to have lurched toward a rough-and-ready form of corporatism, in which government sought the cooperation of business and organized labor in an uncomfortable triangle. In 1973 a mismanaged confrontation with the miners' union led to the imposition of a three-day work week to save power supplies. In an atmosphere of crisis Heath called an election for February 1974. He was unable to secure a renewed mandate, and a minority Labour government was formed and won a slender majority in an October election. Heath had lost three of four elections; although reluctant to resign as party leader, he was replaced by Margaret Thatcher in February 1975.

The Heath government left a legacy of high inflation, a large spending deficit, and a weak balance of trade. Many of its noneconomic initiatives proved short-lived, dismantled by successive Labour and Conservative administrations. Given Heath's abiding commitment, it is apt that at least his success in bringing Britain into the European Community survived. His decision to suspend the Northern Ireland Parliament and impose direct rule from London also set a course difficult to alter.

Assessments of Heath's career inevitably vary. His years as Prime Minister were marked by numerous failures, but at a time of acute difficulties. To many observers his essentially moderate and pragmatic approach, and the decency and humanity that underlay his famous reference to the "unacceptable face of capitalism," contrasts starkly with the tenor of the Thatcher era. The years after 1979 saw Heath as something of an exile in his own party, often highly regarded abroad for his internationalist, pro-European outlook but shunned by the ascendant Thatcherites.

Steven Reilly

Bibliography

Campbell, John. *Edward Heath: A Biography*. 1993.

Hennessy, Peter, and Anthony Seldon, eds. *Ruling Performance: British Governments from Attlee to Thatcher*. 1987.

Holmes, Martin. *Political Pressure and Economic Policy: British Government, 1970–1974*. 1982.

Laing, Margaret. *Edward Heath: Prime Minister*. 1972.

Henderson, Arthur (1863–1935)

Familiarly known as "Uncle Arthur," Henderson was one of the three most important figures in the early history of the **Labour Party**, along with **Keir Hardie** and **Ramsay MacDonald**. Party Secretary for twenty-three years, intermittent leader of the Parliamentary Labour Party, and **Cabinet** minister in four governments, he made a major contribution to party structure and doctrine both before and after the crisis of 1931 that ended the second Labour government.

Born into poverty in Glasgow 13 September 1863, Henderson was the son of a laborer and sometime cotton spinner who died when his son was nine, reducing the family to penury. Henderson left school shortly thereafter, working first in a photographer's shop. Although he resumed schooling when his stepfather moved the family to Newcastle, his formal education was limited, and at the age of twelve he was apprenticed as an iron molder. It was also during his early Newcastle years that he converted to **Methodism**, the formative moral and intellectual influence on his development, a faith he retained throughout his life. Like Keir Hardie, **Philip Snowden**, and **George Lansbury**, Henderson was to build his political doctrine on a strong foundation of religious conviction.

After Henderson qualified as a journeyman iron founder in 1883, he became active in his local union, later becoming district organizer for Northumberland, Durham, and Lancashire. By 1892 his life as a manual worker had ended, and for the next eleven years trade union activity was the focus of his energy. Thus, in addition to lay preaching and temperance reform activity, Henderson established contacts within trade unionism and the labor movement more generally, eventually becoming national organizer for the Friendly Society of Ironfounders, known for its conciliatory industrial policy.

What is notable about Henderson's politics in the 1890s is his unflagging Liberalism, a key factor in his appointment as agent to the **Liberal** MP for Barnard Castle and his election to the Darlington Town Council. Despite his identification with local Liberalism, he was selected in 1903 by the **Labour Representation Committee** to contest Barnard Castle in the by-election precipitated by the retirement of Sir Joseph Pease and won the seat with the support of many Liberals who favored a Labour representative with orthodox Liberal principles. One of the initial band of five independent Labour MPs, Henderson remained suspect in the eyes of **Independent Labour Party** (ILP) militants. Yet the fact that Henderson appeared ideologically indistinguishable from the Lib-Labs in the

House of Commons in no way vitiated his allegiance to the fledgling Labour group.

During the next years he collaborated with MacDonald on a handbook for election agents, and by 1904 he was chosen as Treasurer of the Labour Representation Committee, succeeding David Shackleton as its Chairman in 1905–6 and subsequently assuming the role again from 1908 to 1910. Ineffective at first in the Commons, he played a vital role in organizing constituencies in anticipation of the 1906 election, later serving as Chief Whip to the Labour contingent in the House. In 1911 he yielded the chairmanship to MacDonald to became Secretary, a position he held with consummate skill until 1934, exercising a domination over Labour Party machinery unmatched in its history. Admitting MacDonald's superior endowments, he recognized that his talents were organizational, not inspirational, gifts that complemented MacDonald's. Even though Labour did not improve its parliamentary position before the war, Henderson's efforts helped to transform it from a sectional pressure group to a national party.

In August 1914, when MacDonald resigned the chairmanship over Labour's decision to support war credits, Henderson was elected leader. Although he had been Secretary to the British section of the Second International, he abandoned his initial espousal of neutrality and endorsed British involvement in the **First World War**, situating himself in the mainstream of Labour opinion. His principal aims were to preserve party unity and to ensure that Labour cooperated in the national effort. More than anyone else, he was responsible for ensuring that the Labour Party, in contrast to European socialist parties, did not split. This implicated him in the government's recruitment efforts and led to a key role in the 1915 Treasury Conference to secure an industrial truce.

In May 1915 Henderson was invited to join the **Asquith** coalition as Labour's representative in the **Cabinet**, nominally as President of the Board of Education, but effectively as adviser on labor matters. As the first Labour Cabinet minister, he enhanced his prestige in the movement, temporarily outdistancing MacDonald in reputation, while reinforcing his indispensability as **David Lloyd George**'s industrial conciliator, a task that sometimes incurred trade union enmity. He remained in the government when Lloyd George became Prime Minister, this time as part of the five-man War Cabi-

net, but was forced out in August 1917 when his colleagues disavowed Labour participation in a projected international socialist conference in Stockholm.

Abandoning the chairmanship of the Parliamentary Labour Party, he devoted himself to party reorganization with a view to extending membership, strengthening local parties, and devising a new post-war program. If he ceased to be Labour's most visible representative, a burden shouldered through the war, he relished his role as Uncle Arthur, expert wire-puller and reconciler of disputing factions. It was his control over the electoral machinery, deriving from close links with the unions and constituency activists, that made his authority unassailable. He was the principal architect of the new constitution, the mastermind of that precarious balance between a democratic, constituency-based mass organization, with individual membership, and a union-financed oligarchic structure.

Having abandoned Barnard Castle after fifteen years, Henderson was beaten at East Ham South in the 1918 election, reentering the House for Widnes in 1919, but enduring prolonged absences from the Commons as a result of recurrent election defeats in the next few years. He represented Newcastle East in 1923, Burnley (1924–31), and Clay Cross (1933–5), but for most of that period his crucial activity was as party manager, supervising the selection of candidates, touring the country, setting up the advisory committees, and reorganizing the party into regions. He retained the secretaryship when he entered the first Labour government in 1924 as Home Secretary, a ministry MacDonald grudgingly conceded to him, despite Henderson's self-sacrificing efforts to secure MacDonald's return to the leadership two years earlier.

His brief tenure at the Home Office was unremarkable, but he served as a member of the British delegation to the 1924 London Conference on the Dawes Plan to schedule the payment of **reparations** and later to the **League of Nations**, where he was one of the main proponents of the Geneva Protocol to institutionalize the peaceful resolution of disputes. After Labour left office, he continued to champion the cause of the League of Nations, while recognizing the need for effective sanctions as a guarantee of security, a stance initially abhorrent to much of Labour's **pacifist** opinion. In addition, he used his office as President of the

Labour and Socialist International to enlist European working-class movements in the effort to secure peaceful settlement of disputes through the League of Nations.

In 1929 Henderson managed to wrest the Foreign Office from MacDonald, who had served as his own Foreign Secretary in 1924. The Prime Minister continued to keep exclusive control over **Anglo-American relations**, circumvent Henderson's authority, and barely conceal his growing suspicion of his longtime colleague. As the architect of a more responsible and realistic Labour policy, formulated in *Labour and the Nation* in 1928, Henderson was determined to implement specific goals, assisted by his able Foreign Office team—**Hugh Dalton, Lord Robert Cecil**, and Philip Noel-Baker. At his urging, Britain signed the Optional Clause of the League of Nations Covenant, prescribing compulsory arbitration for all justiciable disputes, as well as the General Act, extending arbitration and eliminating a nation's right to judge its own case. At the Hague Conference in 1929 he sought to reconcile French and German differences over reparations, and at League sessions in Geneva he was instrumental in preparing the way for a general Disarmament Conference, which he was nominated to chair. Finally, in talks with the Soviets he made significant progress toward the normalization of relations, including the exchange of diplomatic representatives and Soviet pledges to refrain from propaganda. In overcoming the resistance of the service chiefs and the defenders of national sovereignty to measures such as the Optional Clause and the General Act, he did more than any other figure in the party to foster the idea of collective security as the only way to make the League an effective agency for peace.

In the August 1931 financial crisis that brought down the second Labour government Henderson opposed MacDonald's efforts to impose cuts in **unemployment** benefits, although he had originally accepted the need for projected economies. Once he realized the depth of opposition in the **Trades Union Congress** (TUC) to reductions, Henderson, always responsive to consensus, decided that the unity of the labor movement took precedence over the need to balance the budget. His resistance was crucial to swaying the majority of the Cabinet to his position, leading to an irreparable breach with MacDonald. Elected leader of the Parliamentary Labour Party in opposition, he lost his seat in the 1931 electoral de-

bacle and did not return to the Commons for two years.

He retained the presidency of the international Disarmament Conference, which opened in February 1932, although he was now only a private citizen rather than Foreign Secretary. His credibility deliberately undermined by the National government, Henderson refused to be deflected from the pursuit of multilateral concessions. If his single-mindedness prevented disruption in the proceedings, it was insufficient to galvanize competing powers into an accord, especially under the shadow of the Manchurian conflict. After months of laborious negotiations delegates conceded the principle of weapons reduction but refused to stipulate precise levels or to grant equality to Germany. Henderson's efforts at personal diplomacy in European capitals was equally abortive, and, once Adolf Hitler withdrew from the conference, its failure was complete.

In 1933 Henderson was awarded the Wateler Peace Prize; the following year he became only the third Englishman to receive the Nobel Peace Prize. Despite worsening health and disappointment over the collapse of the Disarmament Conference, he was reluctant to retire from politics, clinging to the party secretaryship until 1934, only a year before he died.

Never as charismatic as Keir Hardie or MacDonald, Henderson is too easily overlooked in the search for heroes of the labor movement. Leader only briefly and never Prime Minister, he devoted himself primarily to the party structure, which was largely his creation. More than any other figure he epitomized the alliance between trade unions and party that remained Labour's bedrock. His socialist ideology was a practical trade unionist view of incremental gains through parliamentary democracy, couched in laborist terms palatable to all elements. Transforming himself from an insular union official into a leader of European socialism and world statesman, he became the most prominent internationalist in the party during the 1920s, largely responsible for reorienting Labour's foreign policy to an increasing reliance on the League of Nations. An unflagging advocate of disarmament, he came closer to a conception of collective security than any British politician in those years, recognizing that only through the enforcement of peace, by military sanctions if necessary, could aggression be curbed. Architect of the modern Labour Party, he became by 1931 the tribune of peace for ordinary people throughout the world, eager to end the competitive armaments struggle.

F.M. Leventhal

Bibliography

Hamilton, Mary Agnes. *Arthur Henderson.* 1938.

Leventhal, F.M. *Arthur Henderson.* 1989.

McKibbin, Ross. *The Evolution of the Labour Party, 1910–1924.* 1974.

Winkler, Henry R. *Paths Not Taken: British Labour and International Policy in the 1920s.* 1994.

Wrigley, Chris. *Arthur Henderson.* 1990.

Hepworth, Barbara (1903–1975)

Barbara Hepworth, one of the leading British sculptors of the modern movement, was celebrated in her day as an exemplary female achiever. She was made a Dame of the British Empire and received numerous other honors. Born in Wakefield in 1903, Hepworth was a native of Yorkshire, a distinction she shares with **Henry Moore**, her senior by several years, as well as the critic and supporter of both sculptors, **Herbert Read**. Hepworth's and Moore's careers overlapped in several instances. They studied together at the Leeds School of Art and then at the Royal College in London, and they belonged to the same avant-garde groups in the 1930s before going on to establish international reputations in the post-war period. Arguably, Hepworth has been unduly eclipsed by Moore, with his phenomenal institutional success, even though she anticipated Moore in certain formal respects, such as the piercing of holes through the sculpture.

From the start of her career Hepworth was devoted to the tenets of modernism, subscribing to the doctrine of "truth to materials" and direct carving. Her early torsos reveal an awareness of Maillol's simplified arcadian vision, while her animals and birds are indebted to Henri Gaudier-Brzeska, the pioneering modernist sculptor and **Vorticist** killed in the First World War. Another influence in these pieces is that of her first husband, John Skeaping, an animal carver. **Eric Gill** and **Jacob Epstein** were also mentors, the influence of the latter clearly felt in her uncharacteristically primitive-looking *Figure of a Woman* (1929–30), with its bulky limbs and clasped hands.

Hepworth was crucially involved in the development of abstraction in British art from the time she moved to Hampstead in the 1930s with **Ben Nicholson**, who became her second husband. She participated in such groups as Unit One, which set out in 1934 to represent "the expression of a truly contemporary spirit," and the international group, Abstraction Creation, and regularly visited Paris, where she befriended Brancusi, Mondrian, Miro, Arp, and Calder. Hepworth also contributed to the book *Circle* (1937), an international survey of Constructivism edited by Nicholson, Naum Gabo, and the architect J.L. Martin. In clean-cut, sparse, sometimes minimal sculptural compositions Hepworth pursued simple geometric shapes such as the cone and the cylinder. However, in 1939, with the onset of war and the birth of triplets, Hepworth moved to St. Ives, where she, Nicholson, and Gabo formed the nucleus of an art colony that would span several generations and have a profound influence on the course of British art. Hepworth was deeply affected by the dramatic scenery of Cornwall, with the sounds of the sea and the glowing light for which St. Ives is legendary. The response was felt in her work as form became more complex and organic, retaining nonetheless a simple, compact, rhythmic force. The scooped-out inner sections began to be differentiated from the smooth outer forms either by rougher, more robust carving or by the introduction of color, often blue to signify sea and sky.

In a foreword to one of Hepworth's exhibition catalogs in the 1930s the scientist **J.D. Bernal** compared Hepworth's abstraction to megalithic art, whose break from neolithic naturalism, over many thousands of years, resembled the modern movement's break with Renaissance pictorialism. This foreward would prove prophetic in relation to Hepworth's carving. On an iconographical level, the prehistoric metaphor would intensify as Hepworth's reputation grew and she was able to place works in more commanding and dramatic locations. Sculptures were actually titled "menhirs," and the late work, *Family of Man* (1970), consisting of nine bronze "figures"—comprising stacked geometric forms—is a Stonehenge-like arrangement. Bernal's foreword also anticipated a dynamic relationship between Hepworth and architecture that culminated in what is undoubtedly her best-known piece, the megalithic twenty-one-foot-high pierced sculpture, *Single Form* (1964), installed in front of the United Nations building in New York as a memorial to the late Secretary-General, Dag Hammerskjöld, who originally commissioned it. Although, like Moore, success encouraged Hepworth to engage assistants and cast enlarged pieces in bronze, carving remained more central to her aesthetic preoccupations.

Hepworth continued to live and work in St. Ives until her death in a studio fire at the age of seventy-two. The Trewyn studio and garden now serve as a Barbara Hepworth museum, in accord with her wishes.

David Cohen

Bibliography
Bowness, Alan. *The Complete Sculpture of Barbara Hepworth, 1960–69.* 1971.
Gardiner, Margaret. *Barbara Hepworth: A Memoir.* 1982.
Hammacher, Abraham M. *Barbara Hepworth.* rev. ed. 1981.
Hepworth, Barbara. *A Pictorial Autobiography.* 1970.
Hodin, J.P. *Barbara Hepworth.* 1961.

Heron, Patrick (1920–)

Patrick Heron is one of the leading figures of post-war abstract painting in Britain and the central artist in the Middle Generation of artists that also included Roger Hilton, Bryan Wynter, and Terry Frost. As a figurative painter until 1956, he was much influenced by Henri Matisse, George Braque, and Pierre Bonnard and was one of a very small handful of artists in Britain who engaged with this tradition of French painting. A leading London art critic from 1946 until 1950 (especially for the *New English Weekly* and the *New Statesman*), he supported artists who worked within this tradition, and as a formalist—both as critic and artist—followed the lead given earlier by **Roger Fry.**

His move to abstraction from 1955 has been attributed to the impact of the American abstract expressionist painters who had shown at the Tate Gallery in 1956 as part of the touring exhibition *Modern Art in the United States.* Although the rapidity of the change can be explained in this way, the underlying nature of the work cannot. A formalist in approach, Heron regarded the mythic dimension found in the work of the Americans as anathema. Furthermore, his position within a specific European tradition was fundamental to his development; his paintings of this period derive more from Monet, Bonnard, and Matisse than the work of Mark Rothko or Robert Motherwell. Indeed, his critical writing as London correspondent for *Arts (New York)* between 1955 and 1958 bears this distinction out; praise for the dramatic achievement of the Americans is tempered by criticism for their formal laxness of approach. His uncompromising stance is echoed in his stripe paintings of 1957 in which, variously, horizontal bands of color are applied to vertical canvases and vertical bands to horizontal canvases.

Heron's means of expression has always been centered on color even though the formal appearance of his work has undergone many changes over the last thirty years, a process that he has himself described as a successive complication or simplification of the picture surface. The return to under-drawing in the mid-1960s encouraged a tightening of compositional structure that led in the 1970s to what have been termed his "wobbly hard-edge" paintings. Since the early 1980s he has abandoned this process for a more gestural approach and a more open composition. His work was the subject of retrospectives in 1952 (in Wakefield), 1967 (Edinburgh and Oslo), 1968 (Oxford), and 1985 (London), and has shown widely in England and abroad. In 1959 he was awarded the Grand Prize (International Jury) in the Second John Moores Liverpool Exhibition and in 1965 the Silver Medal at the VIII Bienal de Sao Paulo. He was named a CBE in 1977.

Andrew Wilson

Bibliography
Heron, Patrick. *The Changing Forms of Art.* 1955.
———. *The Colour of Colour.* 1979.
Knight, Vivien. *Patrick Heron.* 1988.
Knight, Vivien, and John Hoole, eds. *Patrick Heron.* 1985.

Historic Preservation

Compared to its Continental neighbors, Britain was slow to develop a popular interest in the preservation of historic buildings and slower still to legislate effective protections for them. Practically until the 1960s it was possible to demolish or alter a privately owned building without permission, whatever its historic value. Popular consciousness and eventually legislative protection made great strides after the Second World War, in tandem with a growing apprecia-

H

tion of the financial value of the architectural heritage, especially as a tourist attraction.

An influential minority, connected to the arts and crafts movement, did organize to promote the cause of historic architecture as early as 1877, when the Society for the Protection of Ancient Buildings (SPAB) was formed. But the SPAB soon developed a fusty, antiquarian reputation and restricted its interests mostly to medieval and ancient monuments. Legislation in 1882, 1900, and 1913 gave government only limited powers to acquire (normally with their owners' consent) a handful of these older, usually ruined, buildings. On the whole, the public remained suspicious of compulsory powers over private property and scornful of aesthetes' claims that older buildings gained in beauty what they lost in utility.

After the First World War, when state intervention in economy and society extended, the arts remained largely untouched, and architecture—"the Cinderella of the arts," its lonely advocates complained—entirely. Rapid suburbanization, road development, and electrification effected a holocaust of historic buildings in the 1920s and 1930s. Public concern continued to focus on the oldest structures, such as Stonehenge and Hadrian's Wall. Local authorities were given compulsory-purchase powers to protect historic buildings in 1932, but no money for the purpose, so the powers went unused. Huge chunks of Georgian townscape were pulled down, including John Nash's Regent Street in London. That led to the formation in 1937 of the Georgian Group, originally as an offshoot of the SPAB, small but well-connected, with a genteel and aesthetic, rather than scholarly, tone.

The Second World War wrought a great change. Patriotic feeling attached itself more clearly to the physical environment, built as well as unbuilt. The "national heritage" in buildings and landscape was coming into focus. Historic preservation also became part of the lively contemporary debate on the post-war reconstruction of cities and the development of town and country planning. A remarkably large audience suddenly appeared to interest itself in scholarly architectural topics. Not only popularizing enthusiasts like John Betjeman and Osbert Lancaster, but even architectural historians like John Summerson, J.M. Richards, and Nikolaus Pevsner became fixtures of the Sunday newspapers and British Broadcasting Corporation (BBC) radio and television. Pevsner's Buildings of England series began to appear in 1951, sold well in Penguin paperback, and became instant authorities. Their catholic taste and high level of scholarship represented an amazing leap over the Methuen Little Guides that had served as the standard county guides since late Victorian times. The Georgian Group began to score preservationist victories—Nash's Regent's Park was saved after the war—and already in 1958 there existed a Victorian Society, indicating how rapidly the public appetite for some historic buildings was spreading to encompass them all. Hundreds of community preservation groups popped up to protect less-spectacular buildings and districts of local value, and they found a national mouthpiece in the Civic Trust, founded in 1957 at the instigation of Conservative Minister Duncan Sandys. This mounting public awareness meant that the post-Second World War burst of state intervention would extend to historic preservation. Even in the midst of war (1944) the government had undertaken the epic task of classifying all of the best historic buildings of Britain into Grades One and Two. From 1947 owners of these "listed" buildings were required to notify their local authority of intention to alter or demolish. After the Gowers Report on Historic Houses in 1950, Historic Buildings Councils for England, Wales, and Scotland were established (1953) to help private owners with grants for maintenance and repair. Yet government action lagged behind public opinion. Urban local authorities, in particular, were unwilling to forgo the higher rateable values offered by redevelopment of their crumbling historic districts. At the center, Conservative governments after 1951 were reluctant to use the powers or spend the money intended by their Labour predecessors for historic preservation. Most of the available funds were expended in the 1950s on a small number of country houses; cities were left to fend for themselves. Urban renewal schemes of the 1950s and early 1960s accounted for even more destruction, possibly, than the unplanned development of the 1920s and 1930s.

The consequence was a spectacular uprising of public opinion that began in the mid-1960s and continued into the 1990s. Local preservationist groups grew increasingly militant, and the central government was gradually forced to match rhetoric with action. Conservation areas, offering protection for whole districts, were created by legislation in 1967. Listed-building demolition became practically impossible in 1968. The Historic Buildings Council for England had its budget, virtually at a standstill since 1953, increased from £575,000 to £11 million in the course of the 1970s, with a growing proportion specifically allocated to urban sites. An old argument for preservation was now heard more widely: that Britain's bricks-and-mortar endowment was its most valuable national asset, uniquely able in the postindustrial world to draw dollars, marks, and yen from abroad.

In this atmosphere it was not surprising that political conservatism after 1979 manifested itself also in **architecture**. Popular affection for historic buildings built now not only on the buildings' own merits, but also on a negative anti-modernism. These feelings were stoked up both by Thatcherites, who approved of the "heritage industry" for economic reasons, and by more traditional conservatives (including the Prince of Wales), who had nostalgic and communitarian motives. Against these forces it proved impossible in the 1980s to replace the least-distinguished Victorian building with the most-distinguished modern design. By the late 1980s some cultural critics of the Left were worrying that the triumph of the "heritage industry" was symptomatic of a culture in terminal decline, though even they may secretly have preferred historic buildings to the **postmodern architecture** of their own day.

Peter Mandler

Bibliography

Fawcett, Jane, ed. *The Future of the Past: Attitudes to Conservation, 1147–1974.* 1976.

Hewison, Robert. *The Heritage Industry: Britain in a Climate of Decline.* 1987.

Lowenthal, David, and Marcus Binney, eds. *Our Past before Us: Why Do We Save It?* 1981.

Watkin, David. *The Rise of Architectural History.* 1980.

Wright, Patrick. *On Living in an Old Country: The National Past in Contemporary Britain.* 1985.

History

In the twentieth century the discipline of history has been characterized by growth and diversification. The majority of those who profess the discipline are employed by institutions of postsecondary education. As such institutions have increased in number and size for most of the century so has the discipline of history grown. Not only has the number of professional historians grown but so have the resources available to them through archives, research institutes, and modern techniques of retrieval and duplication of materials. Additionally, the published product of historical study has expanded as the numbers of commercial and academic publishers and historical journals have increased.

If the growth of the discipline is essentially self-evident, the process of diversification has been far more complex. While it would be inaccurate to assert that a consensus ever existed producing a uniform British history, in the early twentieth century there was a preponderance of political history, much of it written in narrative form and from a Whiggish point of view. The most significant dissenting element in the pre-First World War era was made up of **Fabian** historians with wider-ranging interest in the economic and social aspects of the past than the traditional Whigs and reflecting a more critical view of modern capitalist society.

As was true of many facets of British society, the discipline of history, if not fragmented, was, at very least, reshaped in the post-First World War era, and that process continued beyond the Second World War into the second half of the twentieth century. Yet reference to a singular process is essentially misleading. Rather, a number of major influences for change have come to bear upon, and significantly transform, the discipline.

The first such influence has, in fact, served to raise the question of whether one can still talk of a single discipline. Partly as a result of the adoption of some of the approaches and techniques of emerging social sciences and also because of increasing specialization within history itself, a wide range of subdisciplines has developed. As each such subdiscipline has generated its particular methodology and identified its particular areas of interpretative disputation, so it has tended to become less accessible to the nonspecialist.

A partial list of prominent subdisciplines would have to begin with the emergence of a distinctive economic history in the 1920s and could continue with the post-Second World War development of demographic history, provoked in part by Peter Laslett's *World We Have Lost* (1965) and the "new" social history, for which the model was **E.P. Thompson**'s *Making of the*

English Working Class (1963). Urban history, business history, the history of **popular culture**, and other specializations should be added to this list. Perhaps the extent of departure from traditional political history is most graphically measured, certainly in terms of popular perception, by the growth of the field of sports history, even generating its own specialized journals. Obversely, even within the realm of political history, specializations have developed in areas such as government finance and administration.

Considerable time might be spent contesting whether such developments have produced mere specializations within the discipline or have more clearly defined subdisciplines. However, when the distinctions are not just those of particular subject matter but also involved discrete methodologies, then the term subdiscipline does appear warranted. For example, when work in economic and demographic history not only rests heavily on statistical evidence about the past but also involves sophisticated statistical analysis of past society incomprehensible to nonspecialists, then it can reasonably be argued to have formed a subdiscipline. Though in a very different way, the "new" social history, in seeking to comprehend the ideas and actions of large numbers of people left out of many traditional histories, has reached well beyond the documentary record as a source of information about the past. In the use of folklore, political doggerel, and the like as sources and a broadly imaginative interpretation of them, a subdivision has effectively emerged.

Next to methodology, ideology has exerted the most potent force for diversification, or even fragmentation, within the discipline. Pre-First World War Whig orthodoxy involved a belief in the progressive quality of British political history characterized by the steady advance of orderly parliamentary democracy under responsible leadership. After the upheaval of the First World War, this orthodoxy came under attack from both the Left and the Right as the optimism on which it had rested evaporated in the face of experience. Marxist and non-Marxist critiques of capitalism were matched on the Right by less-idealistic assessments of parliamentary history such as those embodied in the work of Sir **Lewis Namier** on eighteenth-century politics. Historians' claims to a scientific objectivity notwithstanding, ideological differences have continued to mark historical writing in the twentieth century. The hardening of positions during the Cold War and the fragmentation on the Left, often bitter in tone, that surfaced markedly after 1956 were the most obvious influences in sustaining diversity. The emergence of a rigorous conservatism in the 1980s generated a parallel trend in historical scholarship led most notably by J.C.D. Clark with his work on seventeenth- and eighteenth-century English society and politics, which insists on the strength of traditionalism and questions notions of inevitable progress.

Ideological and methodological divergence have been clearly displayed in one of the most controversial topics in British history, the "standard of living debate." Here the issue has been whether the first half century of industrialization served to benefit the majority of English people. As discussion of this issue involves fundamental judgments on industrial capitalism as an economic and social system, most historians bring to it predispositions. Methodological differences, which may or may not overlap with those arising from ideology, also become involved as opinions diverge on how improvement or deterioration might be assessed; are material conditions the primary indicators or do contemporaries' responses to their situation carry equal or greater weight in an overall judgment?

While arguably the most prominent debate centers on industrialization, it is by no means the only topic in British history to have become a focal point, or battleground, for the work of historians of differing opinions, ideologies and methodologies. The timing, pace, and implications of the decline of feudalism, the causes and significance of the English Civil War, the political activity of George III in the 1760s and 1770s, the primary influences on the growth of government in nineteenth-century Britain, the motives for late nineteenth-century imperial expansion, and issues derived from the varied problems of the British economy from the 1870s onward provide a mere sampling of the topics over which British historians have differed.

Increasing specialization, differences over ideology or methodology, and awareness of variations of regional experience have all served to make works of broad synthesis more difficult to develop. Many broad generalizations, once confidently stated, have become victims of the maturation and often increasing complication of the historical discipline. Efforts to bring together the disparate aspects of the history of a particular era tend to do just that, assembling essays on a wide range of topics within an anthology. Single works of wide-ranging synthesis, such as Harold Perkin's *Origins of Modern English Society* (1969) or J.C.D. Clark's *English Society, 1688–1832* (1986), have become relatively rare.

Norman Baker

Bibliography

Cannadine, David. "British History: Past, Present—and Future?" *Past and Present*, no. 116 (1987), pp. 169–91.

Elton, Geoffrey. *Modern Historians on British History, 1485–1945.* 1970.

Kenyon, J.P. *The History Men: The Historical Profession in England since the Renaissance.* 1983.

Kitson Clark, G. "A Hundred Years of the Teaching of History at Cambridge, 1873–1973," *Historical Journal*, vol. 16 (1973), pp. 535–53.

Knowles, M.D. "Academic History," *History*, vol. 47 (1962), pp. 222–32.

Hitchcock, Alfred (1899–1980)

Alfred Hitchcock was Britain's leading film director at the time he moved to the United States on the eve of the Second World War. He briefly returned to Britain in 1944 to help with the war effort by making two short films for the Ministry of Information, and later to make *Under Capricorn* (1949) and *Stage Fright* (1949), to shoot locations for a remake of *The Man Who Knew Too Much* (1955), and for his penultimate film, *Frenzy* (1972). A master craftsman, who preplanned every detail of his films, he spent most of his long career frightening his audiences with a series of suspense thrillers.

Born in London to Roman Catholic parents, he began working for the British branch of Famous Players-Lasky in 1919, initially designing title cards for their films. He then served successively as scriptwriter, set designer, assistant director, and finally director. In 1924 Michael Balcon's Gainsborough Pictures sent him to Germany, where he made his first two features, *The Pleasure Garden* and *Mountain Eagle* (1926), at Emelka Studios-Munich, much influenced by German expressionism and by *Kammerspielfilme*, or street realism.

Upon his return to England, the young Hitchcock gained a reputation as England's preeminent fiction director in a series of six silent suspense films, including *The Lodger* (1926). He made Britain's first talkie, *Blackmail* (1929), originally shot as a silent film, but then reshot with sound. Hitchcock proved adept with the new sound medium. *Blackmail* uses sound motifs—the word "knife" is used rhythmically to haunt a young woman who is being blackmailed for having killed a would-be rapist. The film features a justly celebrated chase across the dome of the **British Museum**. As an employee of British International Pictures he directed adaptations of **John Galsworthy** and Sean O'Casey, the revue *Elstree Calling* (1930), and the sardonic *Rich and Strange* (1931), which portrays two young London suburbanites discovering life on a world cruise.

During these years Hitchcock was still finding his metier, but he subsequently signed a contract to make five films for the Gaumont-British Picture Corporation, which included several of the thrillers that established his reputation. *The Man Who Knew Too Much* (1934) and the adaptation of John Buchan's *The 39 Steps* (1935) are his best films from this period. Both feature the elaborate chase sequences that became his hallmark. The fast-paced *The 39 Steps*, which depicts Richard Hannay's attempts to elude Nazi pursuers, is structured around a series of escapes and chases. In contrast, the two subsequent films, *Secret Agent* (1936) and *Sabotage* (1936), ambiguous, narratively complex, and full of black humor, were less successful with audiences. Following the lightweight *Young and Innocent* (1937), Hitchcock made *The Lady Vanishes* (1938), which returned to the theme of the Nazi menace and celebrated British amateur heroics. He made one more film in Britain, *Jamaica Inn* (1939), for Charles Laughton's Mayfair Pictures before moving to the United States, where he signed a seven-year contract with David O. Selznick.

Attracted to America by the availability of money and resources, Hitchcock promptly demonstrated his adaptability by winning two Academy Awards with his first American film, *Rebecca* (1940), admittedly derived from a British novel. Working in the United States throughout the 1940s, he soon emerged as one of Hollywood's most skillful filmmakers, with bizarre thrillers like *Shadow of a Doubt* (1942) and *Strangers on a Train* (1951), both of which featured aberrant personalities in quintessentially American characters. He returned briefly to Britain to make *Under Capricorn* in 1949, a critical and commercial failure set in nineteenth-century Australia. His next film *Stage Fright*, made for Warner Brothers in London, was also poorly received. Back in the United States, Hitchcock made a series of commercially successful films, employing popular male Hollywood stars, like Cary Grant and James Stewart. His choice of actresses, from Madeleine Carroll and Margaret Lockwood to Grace Kelly and Eva Marie Saint, reveals a preference for clever, but elusive, women, frequently blonde, whose sexuality was never blatant. The justifiably famous films of these years included *Rear Window* (1954), *To Catch a Thief* (1954), the remake of *The Man Who Knew Too Much* (1955), *Vertigo* (1957), *North By Northwest* (1959), and *Psycho* (1960). Hitchcock's powers seemed to wane during the 1960s with a succession of critical and commercial failures, although *Frenzy* confirmed that he was still a brilliant exponent of the psychological thriller. Hitchcock, who became a U.S. citizen in 1955, was a familiar figure to American audiences, hosting his own television series from 1955 to 1965. He died in 1980 while working on a film about George Blake, the British double agent.

The leading studio filmmaker of his day, Hitchcock retained more creative control over his movies than any of his contemporaries. He had a sustained, often pessimistic, artistic vision, perhaps derived from his **Roman Catholicism**, which infused his work and moved his audience in a powerful way, and a technical mastery that raised the psychological thriller to cinematic art.

Paul Swann

Bibliography
Kapsis, Robert E. *Hitchcock: The Making of a Reputation.* 1992.
Ryall, Tom. *Alfred Hitchcock and the British Cinema.* 1986.
Spoto, Donald. *The Art of Alfred Hitchcock.* 2nd ed. 1992.
————. *The Dark Side of Genius: The Life of Alfred Hitchcock.* 1983.

Hoare-Laval Pact (1935)
The Hoare-Laval Pact of 1935 was an abortive effort by Britain and France to satisfy Italian territorial ambitions in **Abyssinia**. While Italian interest in the region went back to the 1890s, the Fascist dictator Benito Mussolini used a minor border incident at Walwal as a pretext for conquest. Abyssinia turned to the **League of Nations** for protection under the League's Covenant. Anxious not to alienate Italy as a possible ally against Adolf Hitler's Germany, Britain and France preferred a policy of territorial concessions over one of collective security.

In December 1935 British Foreign Secretary Sir **Samuel Hoare** and his French counterpart, Pierre Laval, concluded an agreement that sought to turn over half of Abyssinia to Italy in the vain hope of appeasing Mussolini. The details of the plan, however, were leaked to the French press. Coming on the heels of an election pledge by **Stanley Baldwin**'s National government to uphold the League and collective security, the public outcry against the agreement forced the **Cabinet** to repudiate the deal and to demand Hoare's resignation. The League moved ahead with sanctions against Italy but excluded oil. Britain's decision not to close the Suez Canal to Italian shipping made the defeat of Abyssinia inevitable.

The failure to deal successfully with the Italian invasion of Abyssinia discredited the League as an effective instrument of peace and encouraged further aggression by the Fascist dictators, making the Hoare-Laval Pact an important milestone on the road to the **Second World War**.

Van Michael Leslie

Bibliography
Braddick, Henderson B. "The Hoare-Laval Plan: A Study in International Diplomacy" in Hans W. Gatzke, ed. *European Diplomacy between Two Wars, 1919–1939.* 1972. pp. 151–71.
Hardie, Frank M. *The Abyssinian Crisis.* 1974.
Parker, R.A.C. "Great Britain, France, and the Ethiopian Crisis," *English Historical Review,* vol. 89 (1974), pp. 293–332.
Templewood, Viscount. *Nine Troubled Years.* 1954.
Waley, Daniel. *British Public Opinion and the Abyssinian War, 1935–6.* 1975.

Hoare, Samuel John Gurney (1880–1959)
A **Conservative** politician, Sir Samuel Hoare is remembered for his role in the controversial **Hoare-Laval Pact** (1935) and strong association with the policy of **appeasement** before the Second World War. Educated at Harrow and **Oxford**, serving as MP for Chelsea (1910–44), Hoare held several ministerial offices between

the wars: Secretary of State for Air (1922–9, 1940), Secretary of State for India (1931–5), Foreign Secretary (1935), First Lord of the Admiralty (1936–7), Home Secretary (1937–9), and Lord Privy Seal (1939–40). His most notable achievement was the drafting of the Government of India Act (1935). After the fall of Neville Chamberlain's government in May 1940, Hoare became ambassador to Spain (1940–4). He was elevated to the peerage as Viscount Templewood in 1944.

As Foreign Secretary under Stanley Baldwin, Hoare negotiated the 1935 Anglo-German Naval Treaty that permanently fixed German naval strength at 35 percent of the level of British naval forces while allowing Germany parity in submarines. Coming only two months after Adolf Hitler's announcement of an expanded German army and reactivated air force, the naval treaty represented a bilateral revision of the naval clauses of the Versailles treaty that appeared to sanction German rearmament. Hoare later participated in the abortive Hoare-Laval Pact (1935) that called for the partition of Abyssinia in the face of Italian aggression. The news of the agreement came on the heels of an election-year promise by the British government to uphold the League of Nations and collective security. Negative public reaction to the plan led the Cabinet to repudiate the pact and to ask for Hoare's resignation. The failure to deal forcefully with the Italian invasion of Abyssinia discredited the League and helped pave the way for war by encouraging further aggression by the Fascist dictators.

Prior to the Second World War Hoare was an influential member of Chamberlain's inner circle of pro-appeasement advisers with his membership on the powerful Committee of Imperial Defence. While Home Secretary, he took a constructive role in prison reform by insisting on more humane conditions and limiting the imposition of capital punishment. Hoare continued after the outbreak of war as a key member of Chamberlain's War Cabinet, but after Winston Churchill's accession to power, he found himself exiled to purportedly neutral Spain until 1944.

Although Hoare was a man of ability and intelligence, his reputation for political intrigue, complicity in the Hoare-Laval Pact, and embrace of appeasement earned him disapprobation as one of the "guilty men" of the 1930s responsible for the disastrous course of British foreign policy. His political memoir of this pe-

riod, *Nine Troubled Years* (1954), nevertheless stands as a cogent defense of Chamberlain and appeasement.

Van Michael Leslie

Bibliography

Cross, J.A. *Sir Samuel Hoare: A Political Biography*. 1977.
Templewood, Viscount. *Nine Troubled Years*. 1954.

Hobson, J(ohn) A(tkinson) (1858–1940)

J.A. Hobson was a leading Liberal social theorist and economist whose ideas were disseminated mainly through his work as a radical author, journalist, and lecturer. He contributed importantly to the formation of British welfare thinking, his reputation resting on his writings in three main areas: an unorthodox economic theory of underconsumption, a major reformulation of liberal thought, and a trenchant critique of imperialism.

Hobson was born in Derby, where his father edited a local Liberal newspaper. After reading Classical Greats from 1876 to 1880 at Oxford, he worked as a school teacher and university extension lecturer but inherited sufficient wealth to be able to choose a career of independent writing. His "heretical" economic views, originally developed in conjunction with A.F. Mummery in *The Physiology of Industry* (1889), brought him to public attention but occasioned dismissive criticism by the leading economists of the day. His consequent rejection by the academic world never ceased to rankle. From the 1890s onward Hobson's radicalism was further developed through his activities as a journalist in leading Liberal forums, such as the *Nation* and the *Manchester Guardian*, which brought him into contact with other radicals such as L.T. Hobhouse, and through his editorial work on the *Ethical World* and the *Progressive Review*. In 1894 he became a founding member of the Rainbow Circle, a political and intellectual discussion group that included Ramsay MacDonald and Herbert Samuel, and he lectured regularly for the South Place Ethical Society for forty years. Hobson served as an expert adviser or witness for a number of committees and commissions of inquiry. During the First World War he was active in the peace-seeking Union of Democratic Control, and in 1918 he stood unsuccessfully for Parliament as an independent. After the war

Hobson moved closer to the **Labour Party** and counseled on the formulation of their policies, while remaining a left-Liberal at heart and fostering the growth of a political middle ground. He published over fifty books and pamphlets and hundreds of articles.

Hobson's underconsumptionism, which received belated if qualified recognition by **John Maynard Keynes** in the 1930s, was both an economic and an ethical theory. It sought to explain the crises of capitalism and the prevalence of poverty and **unemployment** as the result of insufficient spending power. Initially, Hobson believed this to be the consequence of oversaving by the rich; later, he expanded his views and located the cause of underconsumption also in a general maldistribution of wealth. In his earlier writings on poverty, unemployment, and the development of capitalism, he particularly condemned low wages for depriving large segments of society of the ability and will to consume. In *The Economics of Distribution* (1900) and especially in *The Industrial System* (1909) Hobson distinguished between a productive and an unproductive surplus, the former reflecting the cooperative contribution to production above legitimate costs and profits, and to which a society had a claim; the latter—unearned "improperty"—the reflection of the monopolistic and wasteful distortion of sectional and egoistic interests. The solution was an ambitious program of social reform, which entailed the redistribution of wealth, encouraged and directed by the state, including graduated taxation on incomes and inheritance and a system of state **old-age pensions**, a minimum wage, the regulation of the labor market, and social insurance. Though these ideas were not exclusive to Hobson, he played a significant part in including them in the new Liberal platform, through which they influenced the legislation of the 1906–14 Liberal administrations. Hobson has been criticized for failing to distinguish between saving and investment, but he nevertheless exercised influence on welfare economics. In particular, he repudiated the fairness of free, uncontrolled markets. He attempted to inject qualitative considerations into the narrowly quantitative "dismal science" of **economics** and to associate wealth with human flourishing in a manner inspired by the writings of John Ruskin. In the inter-war period he preached the virtues of rational economic planning as the democratic response to the ris-

ing dictatorships and as a policy that would maximize the efficient utilization of resources and humanize both producers and consumers.

It is as part of his larger opus, however, that Hobson's economic theories must be interpreted. He was, above all, a humanist and rationalist, a holistic thinker whose aim was to draw together the discrete fields of economics, **political thought**, social theory, international relations, and even **psychology**. Hobson's organic perspective suggested not only the interdependence of these areas but, in conjunction with Hobhouse, a view of society as an entity subject to evolutionary laws of development toward increasing rationality and self-regulation. As expounded in *The Social Problem* (1901), society was perceived as having needs and interests of its own that were not identical to those of its members. This allowed Hobson to posit a sophisticated theory of rights that identified both the individual and society as entitled to the property necessary to their coordinated development. Despite the potential authoritarian and conservative implications of an organic perspective, Hobson preserved a liberal outlook by insisting that the health of a society depended on allowing the free development of its members and by arguing that human diversity, when tempered by a consideration of the social nature of individuals, contributed both to individual and social utility. At the same time, he sometimes strayed into illiberal territory, exhibiting paternalistic tendencies, dallying with a mild form of **eugenics**, and falling prey for a while to **anti-Semitic** prejudices.

Hobson's organicism provides the key to his seminal modifications of liberal theory, best illustrated in his *The Crisis of Liberalism* (1909). He regarded the relationship between individual and society as one of mutual sustenance and raised the ideal of welfare to coequal status with that of liberty. Hobson abandoned the atomism and *laissez-faire* implicit in earlier liberalism, adopted a view of liberty as the unimpeded development of human potential, replaced the notion of competition with that of cooperation, and sought to break down sectional boundaries in an attempt to offer the underprivileged the full benefits of citizenship. He advocated a benevolent and impartial state, which would attain humanist social ends and act as the democratically accountable agent of a rational social organism when individual action alone could not secure civilized standards. Communitarian and collectivist ideas combined with a respect for individual development to locate Hobson at the heart of turn-of-the-century **New Liberalism**. The outcome was an ideology that laid the foundations for the British **welfare state** and increasingly attempted to marry the liberal respect for diversity with an insistence on greater equality and mutual obligation. During the First World War Hobson expressed disquiet at the growing state restrictions on civil and political rights, which he regarded as spreading the spirit of "Prussianism" into Britain. This led him to become more concerned with the irresponsible use of the power of existing states and attenuated his enthusiasm for too-extensive state intervention, though he never abandoned his belief in collectivism.

Hobson's famous *Imperialism: A Study* (1902) was an application of his social and economic thought, later to be praised by Lenin. He saw imperialism not primarily as the wielding of political control over colonies, but as a product of sectional financial and business interests. Because underconsumption limited effective demand, those interests faced saturated home consumption and needed to find new markets for their surplus capital. In conjunction with aggressive antisocial military interests, they exploited subject peoples, perpetuated the domestically harmful social and political structure of the Mother Country, and fanned irrational jingoistic support for imperialism. Hobson's views were strengthened by his 1899 experiences as a reporter on the South African **Boer War**, which led to *The War in South Africa* (1900) and *The Psychology of Jingoism* (1901). His solutions were to eliminate nefarious sectionalism, subject dangerous monopolies of economic power to social control, and appeal to the application of reason to public affairs.

In international relations Hobson combined an early regard for a Cobdenite breaking down of global barriers through free trade with an appreciation of the need for an international federalism and some form of international government. He wished to link the centralized supranational regulation of the conduct of existing states with a respect for self-determination and diversity that allowed for the existence of national units—views he detailed in *Problems of a New World* (1921) and *Democracy and a Changing Civilisation* (1934). By the time of his death in 1940 Hobson had exercised an indirect but subtle impact on twentieth-century British politics, in shaping both progressive social thought and expectations of public policy. Since then, he has come to be recognized as one of the most versatile and creative British social thinkers of his time.

Michael Freeden

Bibliography
Allett, John. *New Liberalism: The Political Economy of J.A. Hobson.* 1981.
Freeden, Michael, ed. *J.A. Hobson: A Reader.* 1988.
————. *Reappraising J.A. Hobson: Humanism and Welfare.* 1990.
Hobson, J.A. *Confessions of an Economic Heretic.* 1938.
Townshend, Jules. *J.A. Hobson.* 1991.

Hockney, David (1937–)

Within the iconography of the "Swinging Sixties" in London the image of David Hockney held a special position. Walking down the street, dressed in a gold lamé jacket, with a shopping bag to match and with dyed golden blond hair, Hockney came to personify the image of the artist as celebrity. At the Royal College of Art, which he attended 1959–62 (and where he won the Gold Medal), he was at the center of a generation of students who are often associated with the emergence of pop art in Britain, including **R.B. Kitaj**, Peter Phillips, Derek Boshier, Allen Jones, and Patrick Caulfield.

Despite the clear evidence of the influences on Hockney's painting during this early period—from the work of Pablo Picasso, Alan Davie, **Francis Bacon**, or Jean Dubuffet—the strongest motivation was his desire to create a painting that would have a literary basis, be figurative in expression, and whose subject matter would be personally oriented to his interests and obsessions. Although the work of Peter Blake (who had left the Royal College in 1956) would have provided one example of such an approach, it was the work of R.B. Kitaj—with whom he formed a close friendship—that encouraged him to embark on painting that had an overtly autobiographical dimension or dealt with the issues raised in his mind by his own **homosexuality**. His suite of etchings *The Rake's Progress* (1961–3), executed after returning from a visit to New York in 1961, (at which point he also dyed his hair blond) provide an indication of the extent to which he took Kitaj's encouragement seriously and underline the extent to which his labeling as a pop artist was misapplied.

After his first solo exhibition at Kasmin's Gallery in 1963 he made a visit to Egypt following a commission from the *Sunday Times* and then moved to Los Angeles until 1967. He was stunned by the quality of light and bright color that he found there, and that, coupled with clear architecture, manicured lawns, swimming pools, and roads, formed both subject and backdrop for his paintings of this period. Painted in acrylic rather than oil, Hockney's paintings started to assume first a flatter and then an increasingly photo-realist surface. His drawings similarly changed toward the use of a more detached and purely linear approach. This was especially apparent in his etchings. A comparison of *The Rake's Progress* with his *Illustrations for Fourteen Poems for C.P. Cavafy* (1966) emphasizes his evolution toward an unadorned clarity of line. What this later project also stressed was the importance that poetry held for Hockney as a source of inspiration. While at the Royal College he had discovered Walt Whitman as a model for his autobiographical approach to painting (*We Two Boys Together Clinging*, 1961, Arts Council of Great Britain, refers directly to Whitman's *Leaves of Grass*). Ten years after turning to Cavafy he made a suite of etchings inspired by Wallace Stevens' *The Man with the Blue Guitar*.

In 1975, the year before he returned to Los Angeles after a period spent living in London and France, Hockney designed the Glyndebourne Festival Opera production of Igor Stravinsky's *The Rake's Progress*. This was the first of many such commissions—following his designs for Jarry's *Ubu Roi* in 1966—which recall, by virtue of their unified vision, Serge Diaghilev's achievement in persuading artists like Picasso to design for the ballet more than fifty years earlier. Such commissions also give an indication of Hockney's inquiring mind, which has led him to create works with Xerox and fax machines as well as Polaroid and other forms of photograph, in the same way as he has always sought out and investigated new and different forms of printmaking, often with startling results.

An understanding of theatrical artifice and a sense of spatial organization—demanded by the brief for his designs for the opera—have worked their way into his paintings. In a move away from the naturalism that had been found in his drawings and etchings, these new paintings, like *A Visit with Christopher and Don, Santa Monica Canyon, 1984* (1984, the artist), have also been formed within the context of his continued fascination with the work of Picasso and his strongly held belief in the continuing vitality of a Cubist tradition.

Andrew Wilson

Bibliography

Glazebrook, Mark. *David Hockney: Paintings, Prints, and Drawings, 1960–1970.* 1970.

Livingstone, Marco. *David Hockney.* rev. ed. 1987.

Stangos, Nikos, and Henry Geldzahler. *David Hockney by David Hockney.* 1976.

Tuchman, Maurice, and Stephanie Barron, ed. *David Hockney: A Retrospective.* 1988.

Webb, Peter. *Portrait of David Hockney.* 1988.

Holiday Travel

By 1900 the British annual holiday was no longer viewed as a luxury and had spread from the upper and middle classes to better-paid manual workers. The rise in real income and the greater ease of transport, either by coach, train, or automobile, facilitated travel, especially for working-class families seeking a respite from the constraints of urban life. Interest in travel was prompted by an increase in advertising by travel agencies, the **railways**, and tourist centers, all of which proclaimed the pleasures and restorative benefits of recreational travel. In 1911 the **Trades Union Congress** adopted a resolution calling for paid annual holidays for all workers. Although legislative efforts to provide compulsory paid holidays proved abortive, by 1925 1.5 million manual laborers had, through collective bargaining agreements, secured paid holidays, and by 1937 the number had risen to 4 million. In 1938 Parliament passed the Holidays with Pay Act authorizing voluntary collective agreements that included paid holidays to be negotiated by the Ministry of Labour. By 1939 11 million Britons earning under £250 were entitled to paid vacations. Holiday savings clubs proliferated, and some vacations were subsidized by charitable agencies like Holiday Fellowship or noncommercial agencies like the Workers Travel Association.

The most popular holiday venues were seaside resorts, especially Blackpool, Brighton,

Southend, Hastings, Bournemouth, Southport, and Ramsgate. The seaside resort offered attractions of promenades (a seven-mile promenade at Blackpool), public gardens, bandstands, illuminations (fireworks), piers, concert halls, sports facilities, bathing pools, theaters and restaurants, and beach cottages.

During the **Second World War** restrictions on travel and the exigencies of coastal security impeded the progress of holiday travel in Britain. The government encouraged a "holidays at home" scheme and also sponsored work camps as an alternative to traditional vacations. By 1945 80 percent of Britain's work force had become entitled to paid holidays, but due to the immediate shortages in accommodations, these holidays were initially staggered over several months between June and October.

In addition to seaside travel and the emergence of cultural festivals designed to attract domestic and foreign vacationers, camping and caravanning became popular in the inter-war period, especially given the British fondness for walking, bird-watching, and other rural pursuits. In 1938 the Camping Club of Great Britain tabulated 500,000 Britons on camping excursions of more than three days. By 1939 there were 80,000 members of the Youth Hostels Association, which had been founded ten years earlier. The Cyclists' Touring Club and the National Cyclists' Union claimed 60,000 members and 3,500 clubs by 1938. In 1939 the Commons, Open Spaces, and Footpaths Preservation Society successfully promoted an Access to Mountains bill and secured vast additional lands to be placed under the **National Trust**.

In 1946 the Ministry of Labour announced that paid holidays were in force in nearly all British industries where collective bargaining agreements existed, normally providing the worker with twelve days' vacation in addition to public holidays. Since the 1950s vacation time has increased, but more and more of it, for Britons of all classes, has been spent abroad, despite the continued popularity of holiday camps, seaside resorts, and **country houses**.

Barbara Bennett Peterson

Bibliography

Brunner, Elizabeth. *Holiday Making and the Holiday Trades.* 1945.
Hamilton, Ronald. *Now I Remember: A Holiday History of Britain.* 2nd ed. 1983.
Pimlott, J.A.R. *The Englishman's Holiday.* rev. ed. 1976.
Walton, John K. *The Blackpool Landlady: A Social History.* 1978.
Walvin, James. *Beside the Seaside: A Social History of the Popular Seaside Holiday.* 1978.

Holst, Gustavus Theodore von (1874–1934)

An English composer and teacher of Scandinavian descent, Gustav Holst was a contemporary and close friend of **Ralph Vaughan Williams**, whom he met in 1895. They shared many enthusiasms in common, including one for folksong, and on "field days" discussed each other's works in progress. Like Vaughan Williams, Holst took an active part in amateur music making and directed annual informal festivals at Thaxted, Essex, from 1916. Retiring by nature, he was bewildered by the success of *The Planets* and *The Hymn of Jesus*, and during the 1920s he developed a more astringent style in pursuit of his ideal of "tender austerity," best exemplified in the *Lyric Movement* for violin and chamber orchestra (1933), his penultimate work. He refused all official honors except the Howland Memorial Prize, for distinction in the arts, from Yale University (1924) and the Gold Medal of the Royal Philharmonic Society (1930).

Born in Cheltenham, the son of a piano and harp teacher, Holst received little encouragement to become a composer. Even at the Royal College of Music, London (1893–8), he found composition lessons with Charles Villiers Stanford (1852–1924) unsatisfactory, although he welcomed his teacher's advice to develop self-criticism. While a student, he conducted the Hammersmith Socialist Choir, and in 1901 he married the choir's youngest soprano, Isobel Harrison. On leaving the college, Holst earned his living as a trombonist before turning to teaching in 1903. In 1905 he became the Director of Music at St. Paul's School, Hammersmith, an appointment he held for the rest of his life, and he served as Director of Music at Morley College (from 1907). He undertook additional teaching activities at the Royal College of Music and the University of Reading (both 1919), and was invited to become the Visiting Lecturer in Composition at Harvard in 1932.

An early, sustained addiction to Wagnerian chromaticism was finally cured by the discovery of English folksong, its integration into Holst's style clearly evident in *A Somerset Rhapsody* (1907). An interest in Hindu literature and philosophy, enlivened through learning Sanskrit, provided a different input, manifest in the economy and restraint of the opera *Savitri* (from the *Mahabharata*, trans. Holst, 1908). This harbinger of his later style was overshadowed by the more conventional suites for military band (No. 1, 1909; No. 2, 1911) and especially Holst's masterpiece, the highly colorful orchestral suite *The Planets* (1916), the war music of *Mars* acting as a model for countless film scores, and the sturdy, wholesome tune of *Jupiter* subsequently (and regrettably) linked to a patriotic hymn text. The expressive content of *The Hymn of Jesus* (Apocryphal Acts of St. John, trans. Holst, 1917), an unusual combination of wild dance and mystic contemplation, draws on the best elements of both *Savitri* and *The Planets*, but having created a successful alternative to Wagnerian opera in *Savitri*, it seemed regressive for Holst to resort to Wagnerian parody in his next opera, *The Perfect Fool* (Holst, 1922), the opening ballet of which acts as a summary of much of its most attractive music. Following the bracingly exuberant *Fugal Overture* (1922), the *Fugal Concerto* (1923), a rather bland neo-classical study in diatonic counterpoint, marks a new departure, more persuasively essayed in the *Terzetto* (1925) for flute, oboe, and viola, which is polytonal according to the different key signatures for each instrumental part but in reality sounds at most only occasionally bitonal. The masterpieces of this new style, the bleak landscapes of the orchestral *Egdon Heath* (1927), a homage to Thomas Hardy, and *Betelgeuse* from *Twelve Songs* (H. Wolfe, 1929), numb the spirit. However, a return to human warmth in *Hammersmith* (1930) for military band and the *Scherzo* (1934) of a projected symphony suggest a final stylistic synthesis, but one that Holst was unfortunately unable to pursue further.

Trevor Bray

Bibliography

Holst, Imogen. *The Music of Gustav Holst.* rev. ed. 1986.

Short, Michael. *Gustav Holst: The Man and His Music.* 1990.

Home, Alec Douglas- (1903-)

Sir Alec Douglas-Home (later Lord Home of the Hirsel) had four main roles. As Prime Minister (1963–4) he oversaw a marked recovery in Conservative fortunes. As **Conservative Party** leader (1963–5) he devised the present mechanism for electing party leaders. As Foreign Secretary (1960–3, 1970–4) he held office during Britain's two attempts to join the **European Community** (EC). As a retired party leader he was the most influential elder statesman since **Arthur Balfour**.

Until 1960 he was unknown outside Scotland. Coming from a landed, nonpolitical Scottish family, he was educated at Eton and Christ Church, **Oxford**, where his interests were nonpolitical. As Lord Dunglass he was MP for Lanark (1931–45, 1950–1), with social issues his main concern. As **Neville Chamberlain**'s parliamentary Private Secretary (1936–40) he was briefly at the center of things.

Because of serious illness (1940–3) and electoral defeat, Home was largely outside national politics from 1940 to 1955. Even as a junior Scottish minister (1951–5), he was based in Edinburgh. In 1955, at age fifty-one, he joined the **Cabinet** in the inconspicuous role of Commonwealth Secretary (1955–60). As such, he displayed quiet flair, but it was becoming leader of the **House of Lords** (1957–60) on the unexpected resignation of Lord Salisbury that moved him toward the Conservative inner circle.

His appointment as Foreign Secretary caused great surprise, which soon abated. Home's main task was to contain Soviet aggression, with crises in Berlin, Laos, and Cuba. Of all post-war Foreign Secretaries save **Ernest Bevin**, Home was the most ready to answer Soviet threats in language they understood. Elsewhere, Home played little visible part in the EC negotiations (1961–3), but the outcome, putting defense before economics, and Atlanticism before anti-American Gaullism, was in accord with his long-held principles.

Home's premiership was less controversial than the way he was chosen. After disasters in 1962–3, **Harold Macmillan** fell ill and resigned suddenly. The obvious successors, **R.A. Butler**, Lord Hailsham, and perhaps Reginald Maudling, canceled out. After more systematic soundings of party opinion than ever before or since, Home emerged as the most generally acceptable figure, though no voting figures have ever been published. Of Cabinet colleagues, only **Iain**

Macleod and Enoch Powell refused to serve under him.

The public, the party, and Home himself had not considered Home as a possible candidate until the week in which he took office. The Peerage Act (June 1963) allowed him to disclaim his hereditary earldom (1951–63) and enter the House of Commons, as Sir Alec Douglas-Home, at a by-election, sitting as MP for Kinross and West Perthshire (1963–74). These constitutional intricacies, his uncertain command of **television** and **economics**, and **Harold Wilson**'s adroitness in public relations all told against him. His strength in foreign policy, shown in effective handling of crises in East Africa and **Cyprus**, made little impact. The fashions of the day were against him, and he against them; yet the policy of his government emphasized liberal Conservatism, rapid economic growth, and an expensive social program.

On 9 April 1964 Home announced an autumn election, a quietly prosperous summer ensuing, though Labour remained well ahead. By 29 September a poll put the Conservatives 2.9 percentage points ahead, Wilson however remaining much more popular than Home. In a neck-and-neck finish, Home lost by four seats, having been an estimated 100 seats behind on taking office.

In 1964–5, faced with the novel experience of opposition, he made an unconvincing parliamentary gladiator. Murmurings began in his own party, and **Edward Heath**'s star was rising fast. On 22 July 1965, unwilling to fight for position, Home resigned.

Unprecedentedly, he remained at the top, first as Shadow Foreign Secretary (1965–70) and then as Foreign Secretary (1970–4). In this period his reputation and popularity grew markedly. His policies, except toward the Soviets, were not inflexible. He supported EC entry, and on Rhodesia he tried to steer a middle course. He chaired the party committee whose report *Scotland's Government* (March 1970) called for an elected Scottish Convention with limited powers. A firm Christian, he attacked the permissive society but supported Wilson's abortive plan (1969) for reducing the House of Lords to 250 nominated peers.

His second Foreign Secretaryship was on predictable lines, combining firmness with reconciliation. He normalized relations with China and visited Peking. He increased British involvement in defense east of Suez, reversing Labour policies. He tried, and failed, to reach agreement on Rhodesian independence. Most strikingly, he expelled 105 Soviet spies, with only short-lived repercussions.

Home was more successful as Foreign Secretary, elder statesman, and symbol of integrity in public life than as premier. Taking office at a period when aristocracy was fashionably linked with British decline, he was more unlucky than other post-war premiers in the timing of his premiership. In fact, in fourteen years in high office, he rarely put a foot wrong. In addition, as author of three books, a thinking Christian, a learned naturalist, and one who reflected deeply on the fundamentals of international relations, he now appears as much of an intellectual as his former critics. Despite this, his premiership matters most as the last occasion, probably, on which a leader drawn from the old aristocracy will ever come to the fore.

Note on nomenclature

Alexander Frederick Douglas-Home (1903–18) became, on his grandfather's death, Lord Dunglass (1918–51), a courtesy title held by him as a commoner. On his father's death, he became the fourteenth Earl of Home (1951–63), then disclaimed his hereditary peerages for life, being known as Sir Alec Douglas-Home (1963–74). In December 1974, he returned to the House of Lords as a life peer, under the new title of Baron Home of the Hirsel.

John Vincent

Bibliography

Churchill, Randolph S. *The Fight for the Tory Leadership.* 1964.
Dickie, John. *The Uncommon Commoner: A Study of Sir Alec Douglas-Home.* 1964.
Home, Lord. *The Way the Wind Blows.* 1976.
James, Robert Rhodes. *Ambitions and Realities: British Politics, 1964–70.* 1972.
Young, Kenneth. *Sir Alec Douglas-Home.* 1970.

Home Guard

Reviving a proposal made by **Winston Churchill** in October 1939, **Anthony Eden** proposed to the **Cabinet** on 13 May 1940 the creation of a Local Defence Volunteers Force. He announced the project in a radio broadcast the following day. The first volunteers were trickling in to police stations before his speech concluded; 250,000 volunteered in the next twenty-four hours, 1.5 million by the end of June. Operational control of the force was vested in the Commander-in-Chief, Home Forces (General Sir Edmund Ironside), but selection of leaders proceeded locally on a democratic basis without formal ranks. On 23 July its name was changed to Home Guard by Churchill, who felt it would devour an invading army. In August the Home Guard units were affiliated to country regiments.

Volunteers had to improvise meeting places, uniforms, weapons, and training procedures. In a given local group wearing business suits, coveralls, and bits of First World War uniforms, and bearing clubs, hunting rifles, and homemade pikes, the only concession to uniformity was often a common armband with the initials "HG." The first shipment of 300 American rifles (eventually to total half a million) arrived in July, the first uniforms in the autumn. Training was remarkably various, from rudimentary close-order drill to sophisticated programs of instruction in assassination and sabotage. One school, at Osterly Park in Middlesex, headed by Tom Wintringham, a veteran of the **Spanish Civil War**, was so successful that it was taken over as War Office School (No. 1) for the Home Guard. Eventually there were four official schools.

By February 1941 ranks and commissions had been introduced and the age limit lowered to permit use of the Home Guard as a training ground for seventeen- and eighteen-year-olds prior to their armed forces call-up. Professionalization continued in December with the National Service (No. 2) Act, which introduced **conscription** and compulsion. Those who had volunteered prior to the act were free to leave, while those who remained or were subsequently conscripted could be compelled to forty-eight hours of service per month. By the summer of 1943 there were 1.75 million Home Guards organized into 1,100 battalions. Their average age was just under thirty, and only 7 percent were ex-service personnel. Heavily involved in civil defense activites in cities, elsewhere they were still oriented to local defense against sea or air invasion. From 1942 onward many of them were assigned to antiaircraft defenses, with 140,000 in that role by September 1944.

Some historians, mocking the military abilities of Home Guards, have held that an invading German force would have made short work of them. Whether or not this was true, the Home Guard was of enormous significance in shaping and expressing civilian commitment to the war. In addition, it vastly extended the manpower of the armed forces by assuming ever greater responsibility for coast watching, guarding factories, landing fields and bridges, manning roadblocks, taking on antiaircraft duties, and assisting in civil defense, all of which freed regular military personnel for other tasks, especially in the months preceding the Allied invasion of the Continent in June 1944. The success of that invasion and subsequent campaign eliminated the need for the Home Guard, and it was officially disbanded on 31 December 1944.

Joseph M. McCarthy

Bibliography
Brophy, John. *Home Guard: A Handbook for the Local Defense Volunteers.* 1940.
Calder, Angus. *The People's War: Britain, 1939–1945.* 1969.
Graves, Charles. *The Home Guard of Britain.* 1943.
Lampe, David. *The Last Ditch.* 1968.
MacKenzie, S.P. *The Home Guard: A Political and Military History.* 1995.
Street, A.G. *From Dusk till Dawn.* 1947.

Homosexuality

In the late nineteenth and early twentieth centuries recognizably modern homosexual identities emerged in Britain. As these identities were slowly consolidated, the ground was prepared for the growth of a movement that would challenge popular prejudices and work for a change in the laws that prohibited sexual activity between men. While the 1950s and 1960s were dominated by cautious lobbying for legal reform, the 1970s and 1980s witnessed the development of a more radical gay and lesbian movement and the rapid growth of a gay urban subculture.

Although an underground homosexual subculture can be traced back several centuries, little was known about it in Victorian Britain. In the 1890s, however, following the passage of the Labouchere Amendment to the 1885 Criminal Law Amendment Act (which made male homosexual acts illegal), it was brought to the attention of the public through a series of scandals. Culminating in the trials of Oscar Wilde, they consolidated a public image of the homosexual and offered moral lessons about the dangers of deviant sexual behavior.

It was amid this "moral panic" about homosexuality that the first generation of sexologists began their work. In the face of older notions of homosexuality as a sin, they argued that homosexuality was an innate condition of certain individuals that could not be avoided and hence should not be persecuted. Edward Carpenter's study, *The Intermediate Sex* (1908), was central to the new thinking, as was the work of **Havelock Ellis**, whose *Sexual Inversion* was the first volume of his massive *Studies in the Psychology of Sex* (1897–1928). When the British Society for the Study of Sex Psychology was established in 1914, with Carpenter as its president, its work was inspired by Ellis. While it attracted a number of progressive intellectuals in the 1920s, the society had little impact, either on attitudes or government policy.

Although no documented lesbian subculture existed in Victorian Britain, passionate, homoerotic friendships between women were common. Moreover, some women managed to "pass" as men in the public sphere. Both phenomena lasted into the new century, a period in which some women attempted to define themselves through the new language of sexology— an attempt that could backfire, given that the work of sexologists also served to render intense friendships between women suspect. Although Parliament tried to bring lesbianism within the scope of the criminal law in 1921, it remained immune from the penalties applied to male homosexuals. Radclyffe Hall's novel, *The Well of Loneliness* (1928), drew heavily on Ellis' notions of "congenital inversion" and had for many women as great an impact as the Wilde trials had for men. For many years it offered the best available, and most often cited, defense of lesbianism.

During the 1930s and 1940s a cautious sex-reform movement emerged. Under the leadership of Liberals like Norman Haire, it pressed for legal change in the status of male homosexuals. After the Second World War the number of men indicted for homosexual offenses grew rapidly, further fueling the demand for a change in the laws. This led the government to appoint a committee to examine those laws, chaired by Sir John Wolfenden. In the **Wolfenden Report** (1957), the committee called for the decriminalization of homosexuality. Although the Homosexual Law Reform Society was created in 1958 to press for the implementation of the report's recommendations, law reform only came about in the changed moral climate of the 1960s with

the passage of the Sexual Offences Act in 1967, which decriminalized private homosexual acts between men over the age of twenty-one in England and Wales. (Parliament lowered the legal limit to eighteen in 1994.) Lobbying by the Scottish Minorities Group, founded in 1969, in part led to the extension of the act to Scotland in 1980. The act was extended to Northern Ireland in 1982.

Many support groups for homosexuals emerged in the 1960s, including the Minorities Research Group (1963) for lesbians. The Campaign for Homosexual Equality (CHE) was established later by those who believed that education and reform were still necessary following the passage of the 1967 act. By the early 1970s, a period in which the values of consumer culture penetrated an increasingly vibrant gay subculture, it was the largest gay organization in Britain. While women were initially active in the organization, the rapid growth of the women's liberation movement attracted women who believed that the CHE was not an adequate vehicle for the promotion of lesbian issues.

The 1970s marked a turning point in the evolution of homosexual consciousness in Britain. When the Gay Liberation Front was established in 1970, it spearheaded a much larger movement that stressed "coming out," openness, pride, and self-assertion. Arguing that homosexuals needed to play a more active role in their own liberation, radical lesbians, inspired by the women's liberation movement, along with members of the new gay movement, called for profound changes in hegemonic sex roles and a rejection of prevailing images of homosexuality. By the early 1980s many of the newer gay groups, including those established by members of ethnic minorities, were funded by local **Labour** councils. This led to a **Conservative** backlash, evident in Section 28 of the Local Government bill (1988), which prohibited the "promotion" of homosexuality as an acceptable life-style by the councils. The 1980s also witnessed the emergence of new organizations to deal with the devastating consequences of the AIDS crisis, most notably the Terrence Higgins Trust, named after the first Briton known to have died of AIDS.

Throughout the twentieth century gay men have fought to change the laws that made them criminals. Lesbians and gay men have also worked to create supportive communities and struggle against prevailing homophobic attitudes. But it has only been since the 1960s that those struggles have led to significant changes in the status of homosexuality in British society.

Chris Waters

Bibliography

Cant, Bob, and Susan Hemmings, eds. *Radical Records: Thirty Years of Lesbian and Gay History, 1957–1987.* 1988.

Jeffery-Poulter, Stephen. *Peers, Queers, and Commoners: The Struggle for Gay Law Reform from 1950 to the Present.* 1991.

Lesbian History Group, ed. *Not a Passing Phase: Reclaiming Lesbians in History, 1840–1985.* 1989.

Weeks, Jeffrey. *Coming Out: Homosexual Politics in Britain from the Nineteenth Century to the Present.* rev. ed. 1990.

Horse Racing

Horse racing, a sport that has traditionally brought together the aristocratic and plebeian elements of British society, is composed of two main branches: flat racing (under Jockey Club rules) and jumping (governed by National Hunt rules). The latter is further subdivided into steeplechasing and hurdling. Races are arranged according to the ages of horses, which are officially "handicapped" by weight on the basis of their performances. A complex range of races therefore operates. The best known are the "classics"—flat racing events for three-year-olds at Newmarket (1,000 and 2,000 Guineas), Epsom (the Derby and the Oaks) and Doncaster (St. Ledger); and the premier steeplechasing event, the Grand National, first run in 1839, held in the spring at the Aintree course (Liverpool), notorious for its difficult fences.

Race crowds have always been socially mixed, and in the nineteenth century at holiday times often had a festive atmosphere. The attraction of certain meetings—notably Royal Ascot—for the upper classes is a reminder that racing also fulfils a purpose in the social hierarchy. To be seen in the Royal Enclosure at Ascot is an important mark of status.

Since the eighteenth century horse racing has been a highly organized and scientific business of rearing and racing thoroughbreds. Vast amounts of capital have been required to participate—hence the sport's association with the landed classes and royalty. More recently, the costs involved have prompted the emergence of syndicates of owners, frequently non-British. For the general public, however, interest in racing is, and always has been, largely confined to betting. It was betting that accounted for the popularity of racing as a spectator sport from the late nineteenth century to the 1950s. During this period most racecourses were enclosed, admission fees were charged, and the more disreputable elements associated with race-going were controlled. The immense popularity of betting drew large crowds to the racecourses, though the proceeds of their transactions benefited racing itself hardly at all. This parasitic feature did not escape the attention of the sport's organizers. After several efforts to rectify the problem, a solution was tried in 1929 in the form of the Totalisator ("Tote"), a system of centralized on-course betting in which a proportion of the total pool of bets placed was redirected into the further development of the sport itself. The principle was sound, though early practice marred its effectiveness, and in the 1930s the amounts of money accruing to racing were small. Subsequent modifications to the Tote system, together with legislation to channel some of the proceeds of private bookmakers into racing through the Horse Race Betting Levy Board, have ensured a healthier return. The flow of funds into racing has been further enhanced by extensive **television** coverage since the 1960s, which has induced companies to sponsor events. By the mid-1980s, 20 percent of all prize money derived from this source. Television, however, has been a factor in reducing the crowds at racecourses, as has the legalization in 1961 of ready-money betting. The opening of betting shops meant that people could place their bets and watch a televised race without having to journey to the nearest racecourse. In this new climate of falling attendance some courses found it hard to meet the cost of upkeep and were forced to close. Nevertheless, there are still many courses operating up and down the country, and the race-goer is assured of a rich variety of meetings on most days of the week.

Jeffrey Hill

Bibliography

Arlott, John, ed. *The Oxford Companion to Sports and Games.* 1975.

Vamplew, Wray. *The Turf: A Social and Economic History of Horse Racing.* 1976.

Hospitals

During the twentieth century the role of hospitals within the British medical care system changed substantially. In 1900 hospitals constituted one of several treatment alternatives for the sick; by the 1990s they had become the central focus of the national medical system. This development was associated with the gradual transition from a private to a publicly funded medical service; with the expansion of medical technology, medical teaching, and **medical research**, which were located in hospitals; and with the professional ambitions of the hospital consultants, whose status and influence were increasingly enhanced by the expansion of the biomedical sciences. By the 1990s all major cities and country towns contained at least one district hospital, offering accident, emergency, and maternity services, as well as a range of more-specialized treatments. These hospitals are mostly funded and administered within the **National Health Service**. Admissions, except for accident and emergency cases, are by referral from the family doctor (general practitioner). The general hospitals are complemented by special hospitals treating selected types of cases, such as the Hospital for Sick Children and the Brompton Hospital for Diseases of the Chest. Except in the relatively small number of private hospitals, treatment is free under the National Health Service provision.

In the early twentieth century there were three major types of hospitals in Britain: the old, established voluntary hospitals, dating mainly from the eighteenth century and financed by endowments and voluntary contributions, where patient admission was an act of charity (some of these were the specialist hospitals, nineteenth-century foundations, which delivered care to selected categories of patients, most of whom paid for their treatment); the Poor Law infirmaries, financed by local taxation and providing care for the poor and needy; and municipal hospitals, including locally funded isolation hospitals for infectious disease cases. There were also cottage hospitals run by provincial general practioners for their own patients.

Each of these types of hospital performed a somewhat different function. The voluntary hospitals were the largest sector and the closest to modern general hospitals. Their staffing was important to the career structure of the medical profession, and it was in them that the elite consultant physicians and surgeons had their

hospital practice. Many, notably the **London** foundations, had associated medical schools, and they increasingly became centers of medical research. The great London hospitals dominated this sector, but voluntary hospitals were also found in the major provincial cities.

In the early nineteenth century hospitals in general had been resorted to reluctantly by ordinary people, who considered them to be tainted by the stigma of charity. This perception, changing by 1900, had disappeared completely by 1950. In the second half of the twentieth century hospital treatment has come to be considered as a rightful benefit by the British people.

The National Insurance Act of 1911 was a major step in this progression. Although the hospitals were not directly involved in this legislation, it had profound consequences for the hospital system. Previously, outpatient departments had functioned as alternative doctors' surgeries, but, under the act, free medical benefits could be obtained only through general practitioners. Fears of financial insolvency led the hospitals to introduce pay-beds and to revise their admissions policies. Outpatient services were increasingly restricted and came to provide a specialist consultative service, complementing that of the general practitioner. The referral system, in which patients are passed on to hospitals for surgery, or specialist diagnosis or treatment by general practitioners, became an established feature of this new order.

Following the First World War the financial position of the voluntary hospitals became increasingly acute, and the policy of charging patients more widespread. Between 1891 and 1938 hospital revenue derived from gifts and investments fell from 88 percent to 33 percent, while that derived from patient charges rose from 11 to 59 percent of total revenue. Changing social and political circumstances also brought change to other parts of the hospital sector. Under the Local Government Act of 1929 hospitals administered by the Poor Law authorities (the infirmaries and the infectious disease hospitals) were transferred to local authority responsibility. The lingering deterrent effect of Poor Law application was thus finally removed from this sector.

During the **Second World War** some of the hospitals were placed under government control for the first time. At the outbreak of war the government set up the Emergency Medical Services (EMS) to deal with expected heavy civilian air raid casualties. The Ministry of Health took charge, at the national level, of part of the voluntary and municipal hospital sector, which was regionally and locally administrated. A regional blood transfusion service, and national pathology and public health laboratory services, were established. This wartime experience encouraged a positive attitude toward the reorganization of the hospital services among the medical profession and demonstrated also that such reorganization was possible.

The foundation of the National Health Service (NHS) in 1948 saw the complete transformation of hospital administration in Britain. Most of the hospitals were nationalized, although hospital consultants retained the right to treat private patients in NHS hospitals (pay-beds). The nationalized hospitals came under the overall control of the Ministry of Health (later the Department of Health and Social Security). England and Wales were divided into thirteen regions, on the principle that each region should contain a university with a medical school. Regional Hospital Boards were to plan for the hospital and specialist services, while day-to-day management was in the hands of 388 Hospital Management Councils, each responsible for one large hospital or a group of hospitals. The thirty-six teaching hospitals (ten in Scotland, twenty-six in England and Wales) were independently administered. They retained their own boards of governors and had separate funding; thus they continued to have a privileged status within the NHS.

From the beginning the hospital sector took the major share of NHS spending. In 1950 hospitals accounted for 54.9 percent of the total NHS budget; by 1987–8 this had risen (with some fluctuations) to 66.2 percent.

Although the British government quickly realized that NHS expenditure would have to be carefully regulated, there was little attempt to plan or rationalize the hospital system during the 1950s. In this decade hospitals competed to acquire specialist consultants and new medical technology. Government constraints meant that there was little capital expenditure, however. Further, the NHS had left the old unequal distribution of hospital facilities among the different regions of the country unchanged. While London and the southeast generally were almost overprovided with hospitals, large areas of the north and northeast were relatively poorly served.

In 1962 the government responded to this situation by introducing a Hospitals Programme, which aimed to secure a better distribution of hospital beds by building new hospitals, and to improve efficiency and cut costs by reducing the average length of stay in a hospital. The plan proposed ninety new hospitals and the modernization of others. It was believed that larger hospitals would mean significant economies of scale, and the plan promoted a movement toward district general hospitals with 600–800 beds serving a population of 100,000–150,000 and providing treatment and diagnostic facilities for both inpatients and outpatients in all of the common specialties, including geriatrics and mental illness.

The 1960s were a decade of expansion; the 1970s brought economic uncertainty, and the rising price of fuel brought a new dimension of crisis into the funding and management of the hospital service. The continuing rapid expansion of expensive medical technology and the realities of an ageing population both contributed to ever-increasing pressure on the hospital service. From the early 1970s British governments were engaged in a continuous search for improved management and reduced, or at least controlled, spending in the hospital sector. This trend resulted in a series of crises within the service, including repeated major industrial action by doctors, nurses, and ancillary staff in the later 1970s and 1980s. Until 1989, however, government policy was remarkable for its continuity, focusing on issues of management and the reallocation of resources, despite much-publicized arguments about minor issues such as the abolition of pay-beds in hospitals.

In 1989 the Conservative government introduced proposals that marked a radical departure from established policy in the NHS. The White Paper *Working for Patients* proposed changes in the organization of the delivery of services, rather than changes in the level or sources of finance. Since April 1991 hospitals may choose to opt out of local authority control and to establish their own self-governing hospital trusts. A number of big hospitals, including Guy's Hospital in London, have chosen to manage their own resources in this way, and many others have indicated that they intend to follow suit. Under this new system, district health authorities are obliged to contract with the independent hospital for services and may also contract with other health authorities for services unavailable (or unsatisfactory) within their own districts.

Since 1950 financial constraints and scientific and professional developments have combined to change the role of the British hospital. Whereas at mid-century hospitals were essentially treatment centers, for inpatient care, they now function increasingly as diagnostic centers, with a large outpatient constituency seen after referral. Length of stay for inpatients has been substantially reduced, while the number of inpatients treated has greatly increased. The care of the elderly and of the mentally ill is increasingly short-term and directed toward rehabilitation and community care. In the 1990s British hospitals provide a technical support service within a framework of community care, but they supply the latest technology and specialist medical treatment, continue to train medical students and pursue medical research, and provide a recognized professional career structure for large numbers of medically qualified persons.

Anne Hardy

Bibliography

Abel-Smith, Brian. *The Hospitals, 1800–1948: A Study in Social Administration in England and Wales.* 1964.

Allsop, Judith. *Health Policy and the National Health Service.* 1984.

Rivett, Geoffrey. *The Development of the London Hospital System, 1823–1982.* 1986.

Watkin, Brian. *The National Health Service: The First Phase, 1948–1974, and After.* 1978.

Webster, Charles. *The Health Services since the War.* Vol. 1: *Problems of Health Care: The National Health Service before 1957.* 1988.

Hotels

London before the First World War saw the heyday of the grand hotel, many recently built during the speculative building boom encouraged by the two Jubilees of 1887 and 1897. The most opulent were Claridge's in Brook Street, favored by visiting royalty; the huge Savoy in the Strand, built by Richard D'Oyly Carte; and the Carlton in Piccadilly, built by César Ritz, who came to England to manage the Savoy but decided to build his own hotel, taking for it the Savoy's great chef, Auguste Escoffier, whose

organizational genius made possible the à la carte menu. There were numerous other large hotels, including the Victoria near Trafalgar Square, owned by the Gordon Hotels chain, the world's largest, founded by the forgotten Victorian entrepreneur Frederick Gordon. With 500 rooms, the Victoria had only four bathrooms, no running water in the rooms, no elevators and no central heating. Chamberpots and shallow tin baths kept under the bed were still the order of the day here and in most hotels. Hotels were largely managed and staffed by Continental **immigrants** and **refugees**, though the myth that only a foreign male could be a great chef and hotelier was punctured at Rosa Lewis' small, ultra-exclusive Cavendish Hotel, patronized by **Edward VII**. Two hotels particularly favored by American visitors were the large and bustling Langham in Portland Place, and the small, discreet Brown's in Dover Street, where Franklin and Eleanor Roosevelt honeymooned in 1905.

In major provincial cities the main hotels were usually owned by **railway** companies. These generally had excellent **restaurants**, as indeed at least until 1939 it was a point of pride for a major hotel to have a top-class restaurant and wine cellar. A significant development outside London was the growth of the Trust House chain, founded by Earl Grey, to take over small rural inns and wean them from excessive dependence on the **drink** trade by providing reasonably priced accommodation and meals to travelers, especially touring cyclists, and later motorists. The seaside hotel trade continued to expand with the new development of the all-inclusive holiday camp and hotel offering constant programmed activities, an idea pioneered by the Canadian Billy Butlin.

London saw some inter-war hotel building, particularly on the former sites of the great ducal townhouses, the Dorchester in Park Lane being the best known. But the stock of hotel accommodation suffered heavily from requisition, neglect, and bombing during the **Second World War**. This created opportunities for postwar property speculation, and men like Max Joseph, Charles Forte, and Charles Clore made great fortunes in the hotel business, which boomed as overseas tourists created great demand for hotel rooms. New hotels were built with government grants to encourage tourism, some of them assaulting the London skyline, like the high-rise Hilton in Park Lane. Meanwhile, the practice of converting private hous-

Piccadilly Hotel (R. Norman Shaw, completed 1908).

ing to hotel use, common since the mid-Victorian era in Bloomsbury, extended outward to Pimlico, Kensington, and beyond.

Christopher A. Kent

Bibliography

Borer, Mary C. *The British Hotel through the Ages.* 1972.

Fielding, Daphne. *The Duchess of Jermyn Street: The Life and Good Times of Rosa Lewis of the Cavendish Hotel.* 1964.

Taylor, Derek. *Fortune, Fame, and Folly: British Hotels and Catering from 1878 to 1978.* 1977.

Hours of Work

In 1900 the normal working week for male manual workers in Britain was fifty-four hours, a figure that had fallen to thirty-nine hours by the mid-1980s. This significant shortening of the working week has been matched by a shortening of the working year as holidays with pay have been introduced, and with a shortening of the working life-span as more education has delayed entry into the labor force for the young and as increased retirement provision has accelerated withdrawal from the work force at older ages. Within these overall trends, white-collar workers have consistently enjoyed shorter working hours than blue-collar workers, and **women** have worked for fewer hours per week than men.

At the beginning of the century most British men worked a nine-hour day and a six-day week. Average hours of work tended to be higher in agriculture and the service sector and marginally lower in the heavily unionized construction, **coal mining**, and printing trades. Trade unions had campaigned vigorously for an eight-hour day (forty-eight-hour week) since the 1890s, but success in achieving this goal was patchy and often temporary. In 1919 and 1920, however, most employers, with the encouragement of the government, adopted the forty-seven- or forty-eight-hour week. This was partly to recompense the work force for the sacrifices of the war years, partly to mollify the trade unions and aid post-war industrial recovery. There was little change to this normal working week until the end of the Second World War when, between 1945 and 1947, a forty-four-hour working week became established as the norm. This new norm survived for fifteen years, but it fell to forty hours between 1960 and 1966, and it edged down further, to thirty-nine hours, in the early 1980s. Since the Second World War the actual hours worked by male manual workers have been three to four hours per week above the contractual norm because of regular overtime work. Full-time female manual workers have worked about four hours per week less than men, and white-collar workers have typically worked one hour a week less than manual workers.

Holidays with pay were exceptional before the First World War, but by 1938 unions had negotiated a week's paid leave for over 4 million manual workers. Holiday entitlements have grown considerably since 1945 and by the mid-1980s stood at an average of thirty-three days per year, eight of which were public holidays. In consequence, the average annual working time of a fully employed British male manual worker has fallen from around 2,760 hours in 1900 to 1,770 hours by the mid-1980s. The average number of years worked by men has also fallen as the minimum school-leaving age has risen to sixteen and as average retirement ages have fallen. For women, however, the trend in years worked is upward, because of the pronounced rise in married women's participation in the labor force since the Second World War.

Paul Johnson

Bibliography

Bienefeld, M.A. *Working Hours in British Industry*. 1972.

Cross, Gary. *A Quest for Time: The Reduction of Work in Britain and France, 1840–1940*. 1989.

House of Lords

In 1900 the House of Lords was a legislative body of just under 600 members, all of whom (except for twenty-six Church of England bishops and half-a-dozen judges, appointed to enable the House to continue in its ancient role as a supreme court of appeal in judicial matters decorously and without any claim to intervene by the lay majority) held hereditary titles. They stood at the head of a wider aristocracy of titled men, some of whom held noble titles that did not give them a right to sit in the Lords, some hereditary holders of the title of knighthood (baronet), and a larger number of men who had won the honor of knighthood with the title Sir before their names but had not gained the right to pass it down to their sons. While its membership was mainly English, it contained sixteen of the old (pre-1707) Scottish peers and twenty-eight of the old (pre-1801) Irish peers chosen from among themselves by those who had not yet gained U.K. titles. This titled aristocracy was itself only the most visible part of a land-owning elite of several thousand people who lived mainly on their rental incomes and—at least in the countryside—enjoyed considerable political influence as a direct consequence of **landownership**.

The families of the landowning elite dominated the upper ranks of politics—in 1900 members of the House of Lords had held the premiership for seventeen of the past twenty-five years and the Foreign Secretary post for forty-three of the past fifty years—and of activities like the Church of England and the **army** that were closely linked to politics. There was a constitutional convention that the House of Lords did not intervene in financial matters, but its capacity to affect other legislative matters had been shown by its destruction of the **Liberals'** Home Rule bill in 1893.

The power of the landowning elite had been declining for some time, directly because of the agricultural depression of the last quarter of the nineteenth century, and less directly because the owners of the commercial and industrial wealth that had grown up in the nineteenth century and, to a far lesser extent, the industrial working class wanted more political power. The most publicly visible step in the reduction of the power of the position of the House of Lords was the Parliament Act of 1911, but it continued to resist Liberal legislation in the years before 1914.

Its prestige suffered considerably from the activities of **David Lloyd George**, who increased the membership, which had risen to about 650 by 1914, by over a hundred peers in the six years of his premiership; some of these creations were the traditional recognition for services in the **First World War** and some were an acknowledgement of the role of industrialists in the economy and the war effort, but some were given to newspaper owners for their support, or to less easily defined allies for services that clearly included cash contributions to Lloyd

George's political machine. The diminished position of the House of Lords was symbolized by the decision not to give the premiership to the distinguished Conservative peer **Lord Curzon** in 1923; Curzon had other shortcomings, but it was widely believed that the decisive point was that parliamentary business would now be mainly a matter for the House of Commons, partly on general democratic grounds and partly because the **Labour Party**, by this time the official opposition, had virtually no supporters in the Lords. The respectability of the Lords was rebuilt between the wars, and its membership increased very little in the second quarter of the century. The post-war Labour government further diminished its powers by reducing its right to reject legislation from two sessions to one.

Two substantial changes were made in the premiership of **Harold Macmillan**. In 1958 he brought forward legislation that provided for men and women to be made life peers, and this change allowed governments to offer, and recipients to accept, membership in the House of Lords without having to worry about the social and financial difficulties that might face heirs to the title. In 1963, under pressure from Anthony Wedgwood Benn, who was determined not to leave the House of Commons despite the death of his father, Lord Stansgate, Macmillan's government brought forward a Peerage Act that allowed people to renounce titles upon succeeding to them; the immediate effect, apart from allowing Benn to stay in the House of Commons, was to let **Lord Home** and Lord Hailsham leave the House of Lords to stand for the leadership of the **Conservative Party** when Macmillan retired. About a dozen people renounced peerages early in the lifetime of this act, but the right of renunciation has been used very little since 1975. The act allowed all remaining Scottish peers to sit in the Lords—no new Irish peers had been selected for the Lords since 1922, and none benefited in 1963—and it also allowed "peeresses in their own right" (heiresses to peerages whose grant allowed women to call themselves by the title) to sit in the Lords, which had not previously been permitted.

Partly because of this act, but to a much greater extent because of the 1958 act, the membership of the House of Lords has increased to about 1,150, of whom about a third are life peers under the 1958 act, and the remaining two-thirds are the surviving peers by

hereditary succession. As only six new hereditary titles have been created since 1964, three of them for members of the Royal Family, the hereditary membership will presumably diminish by the failure of heirs. The House of Lords continues to act as a revising body for the details of legislation passed in the Commons, and it has gained greater respect for this role by moving from acceptance of legislation produced by Conservative governments, and guarded hostility to Labour legislation, to a more detached attitude. Future changes in the Lords will probably be governed more by constitutional developments caused by relations with the European Union than by any reawakening of the Peers versus the People struggles of the early years of the century.

Trevor Lloyd

Bibliography

Bromhead, Peter A. *The House of Lords and Contemporary Politics, 1911–1957.* 1958.
Cannadine, David. *The Decline and Fall of the British Aristocracy.* 1990.

Housing

During the twentieth century the provision and built form of British housing has been transformed. In aggregate terms the overall housing stock has tripled since 1900, and the spatial implications of such quantitative additions on the formerly compact nineteenth-century cities have been considerable. Of greater significance has been a transition in housing tenure. Owner occupancy has replaced rented accommodation as the predominant form of tenure. Before the First World War approximately 10–20 percent of occupants owned their own home; by 1938 this figure had risen to 32 percent, and by 1983 to 62 percent. The decline in privately rented accommodation was also accompanied by a growth in **council** (or public) **housing**, rising from approximately 1 percent of the housing stock in 1914 to 10 percent in 1938 and 32 percent in 1980. As public authorities and mortgage companies replaced private landlords in the finance and management of the housing market, so social relationships, community organizations, and landlord-tenant relations have altered. Though both quantitatively and qualitatively British housing experienced significant changes during the twentieth century, this has taken place against a background of considerable geographical variations, as in Scotland where council housing represents about 70 percent of the housing stock. Also, dwellings built before the twentieth century still constitute locally up to 20 percent of the national housing stock, thus providing a measure of visual and residential continuity to the urban landscape.

The simultaneous development of council housing and owner occupancy, both at the expense of private-sector rented accommodation, gathered pace after the First World War. Historians have sought to interpret these developments with reference to the pre-1914 housing market, and four explanations are customarily advanced. One interpretive strand emphasizes the emerging intervention by municipal authorities in the late nineteenth and early twentieth centuries to regulate construction standards, **town planning**, and unsanitary housing. Council housing after 1919 is explained as a logical consequence of the failures of unregulated private enterprise, specifically the activities of the building industry, and the limited achievements of philanthropic housing associations; twentieth-century housing policy is analyzed in terms of the gradual and inevitable acceptance of state intervention as the replacement for market-based housing provisions. A second interpretive framework has been offered by **Marxist historians**, who explain the provision of council housing as a response to the long-run decline of landlords', builders', and investors' profits, though this does not accord with the buoyancy of owner occupancy after 1920. A third explanation is also ideologically based. Historians have viewed the **Conservative Party**'s encouragement to home ownership as a tactic to counter the sustained early twentieth-century **Liberal** attack on landowners' and property interests. Whether this "ramparts strategy" was a consciously manipulative policy remains unclear, however, though tax advantages to private homeowners, introduced between the wars, remain a totem of the Conservative Party.

A fourth approach claims not that the crisis in the housing market prompted state intervention, but that state intervention prompted a crisis in the housing sector from which council housing resulted. More specifically, a virtual ban on wartime building and a restriction on rental increases in response to intense political pressure to contain wartime inflation so distorted the market that it could not return to normal after the war. The rents of 85 percent of the housing stock of 8 million homes were re-stricted under government legislation passed in 1915, and since the shortage of houses was estimated at almost 1 million in 1919, rising to 2.8 million in 1931, this disequilibrium between housing supply and demand could not be addressed by abandoning rent controls and using the price mechanism. Rent restrictions continued to apply to 70 percent of accommodation throughout the 1920s, and this restraint on builders' and landlords' profits caused housing finance to be rerouted through building societies. The decline of landlordism was initiated; the rise of mortgage finance for owner occupancy assured.

The transformation in the housing sector was accentuated by broader national trends. For those in work, disposable incomes rose significantly; real earnings, though largely unchanged in the early and mid-1920s, rose by about 20 percent during the inter-war years, with real net national income rising by almost 40 percent. Savings mirrored these trends, with a sevenfold increase in the value of building society deposits. As a result, and with the single exception of 1932, mortgage advances were higher in each successive year from 1921 until the threat of war reined in private investment from 1937. Between 1928 and 1938 the number of private individuals who turned to mortgage companies for housing finance increased from 500,000 to 1.5 million, largely because the cost of borrowing to homeowners declined sharply from its 6 percent interest rate level in the 1920s to 4.5 percent in the mid-1930s once Britain abandoned the **gold standard** in 1931, and because the amount of housing finance required fell as building costs lurched downward between 1921 and 1937. Many national economic indicators reinforced characteristics within the housing sector so as to produce a strong trend toward both a rising owner occupancy and a consequential structural shift away from privately rented accommodation.

The spatial implications of inter-war housing developments have had long-standing effects for British society. Since council housing was undertaken on green-field sites, in projects involving the simultaneous construction of hundreds of dwelling units and planned, financed, and administered by an emerging bureaucracy of experts in housing and town planning departments, homogeneity remains its most striking and durable feature. Designs and costings were submitted for approval to a central government department in London where prevailing **Garden Cities** principles were strongly influenced by Raymond Unwin (1863–1940). As the leading architect of the Garden City movement before the First World War, Unwin had been heavily involved in projects at Letchworth (1903) and Hampstead Garden Suburb (begun in 1906). It was Unwin's contribution to the Tudor Walters Report (1918), a path-breaking treatise on housing standards and designs for the working class, which determined street layout, internal designs, and building materials to be incorporated in council housing projects. The initial standards were generous in land, materials, and internal space, but in a period of financial austerity the proposals were successively scaled down to produce the architectural monotony of council housing still apparent in most British cities and rural areas today.

Private housing developments were also undertaken mainly on the periphery of British cities. Together with the financial considerations noted earlier and inner-city housing demolition programs, a halving in the average price of automobiles between 1924 and 1936, and a proliferation of new household goods combined to encourage an exodus to semidetached villas (duplexes) in new suburbs and commuting zones. This was most marked in **London**, the southeast counties, and in the Midlands during the 1930s, where the service sector and the emergence of new manufacturing industries provided more-stable employment for an expanding middle class and the upper strata of the working class.

Two distinctive housing types—the council house and the private semidetached villa—developed in the inter-war years. These replaced the geometrically laid out streets of terraced houses for those with low incomes, and the Victorian villas organized on the presumption of cheap servant labor. Minimum standards of space, decency, and amenity governed both new forms of housing, though the two/three bedrooms, one/two public rooms, kitchen, WC and bathroom, and small garden plot of council housing developments was meaner in dimensions and detailing than for private housing. The most important long-term consequence was to perpetuate the class dimension of British housing. Crudely, residential segregation in the form of **slums** and suburbs characterized social segregation in the nineteenth-century city; council housing and "three bedroom semis" reproduced this separation of the working and middle classes in the twentieth century.

Wartime enemy action accounted for the loss of about 500,000 houses, or about 4 percent of the housing stock, and together with the suspension to housebuilding during the Second World War, the combined housing shortage in 1945 was estimated at 1.25 million houses. Because of new household formation in the intervening period before such housing could be completed, the real shortage of housing was estimated at 3 million houses—equivalent to about 24 percent of the pre-war housing stock. An annual program of 300,000 houses—not far short of the record 366,000 built in 1936—was planned in 1946 by the **Labour** administration. In six years, 1945–51, housebuilding for private owners never approached the levels achieved in a single year from 1933 to 1939. Rent restrictions froze private rentals at 1939 levels. Faced with such shortages, the political consensus accorded council housing the highest priority, yet despite the construction of 1.2 million houses between 1945 and 1951, the shortage, still estimated at 1 million to 2 million houses in 1951, dominated housing policy for the ensuing two decades.

Housing in the 1950s was dominated by "general needs"—that is, by the urgency of adding significant numbers to the housing stock. This was achieved by continuing provision of central government finance to local councils, and, in the course of the 1950s, 2.45 million new houses were built, two-thirds of them by councils. To a considerable degree this was a replication of the approach adopted in the 1920s, and, as in the inter-war years, a subsequent, developing strand of housing policy was based on slum clearances. This gathered pace in the 1950s and continued throughout the 1960s and 1970s, so that councils demolished 1.4 million older houses, displacing more than 3 million individuals in the process, often to new multistory block flats on the periphery of cities. The social dislocation that resulted, together with media coverage hostile to the provision of high-rise housing for family dwelling, proved instrumental in restricting the extent of tower-block housebuilding.

As private-sector housing provision resumed its quantitative ascendancy in the 1960s, public priorities, though never abandoning the general provision of housing for low-income families, increasingly recognized the aged, disabled, single-parent, and problem families as having discrete housing requirements. By the 1970s public housing provision was more carefully targeted, an approach also adopted with respect to a program of housing renovation undertaken partly as a reaction to the soulless image of council housing estates and the dilapidation of private rented housing, but also in response to central government funding in the wake of **urban riots**. A system of improvement grants was expanded in the 1970s to provide many households with exclusive rather than shared access to baths, WCs, kitchens and sinks, as well as electrical rewiring, insulation, and structural repairs. The combined effect of postwar new building and improvement programs has meant that whereas in 1950 approximately half of the British population shared either washing or cooking facilities, only 5 percent did so in the 1980s.

While local and central government officials grappled with the quantity and quality of the post-war housing stock, private builders simultaneously responded to new supply opportunities. The framework of integrated town and regional planning that developed after 1947 identified areas for housing expansion. This, the consolidation of firms within the building industry, and other factors such as the mushrooming of mortgage finance, contributed to significant inflation in land values, which was translated into increased house prices. Aside from the tax advantages available to mortgage holders, the rising capital value of houses penalized those who did not participate in homeownership. Again, housing became an agent of social polarization, particularly in the house price booms of 1972, 1979, and the late 1980s.

A different housing phase developed with the election of the Conservatives in 1979. Based on an ideological critique of council housing, the **Thatcher** administration presented the housing problem as the very existence of municipal landlordism. Two overlapping phases of policy resulted. One, from 1979 to 1986, pursued a policy of reluctant collectivism, with the public sector providing only for special-needs housing where private enterprise was unable to meet it. Consequently, central government restrictions on local-authority capital expenditure greatly reduced the volume of new council housebuilding. Coupled with it was a "right to buy," a tenant's right to acquire, at heavily discounted prices, the council house he or she occupied. With sales exceeding completions in 1982, the council housing stock began to decrease for the first time in its history. The sec-

ond phase, announced in 1987, and given legislative force in 1988–9, signaled another anticollectivist approach to housing provision. Though the promotion of homeownership remained a priority, Conservative attention was aimed at extending privatization to the rented-housing sector. Diverse strategies were employed: investment and tax incentives for privately rented accommodation, deregulation of new lettings, and the creation of umbrella organizations such as Housing Action Trusts and Tenants' Choice schemes, designed to de-municipalize the housing stock by enabling tenants to opt for private housing association status to address their housing concerns. Such initiatives are designed to break down the social and residential segregation that has become more pronounced in British society in almost every decade of the twentieth century.

Richard Rodger

Bibliography

Ball, Michael. *Housing Policy and Economic Power: The Political Economy of Owner Occupation.* 1983.

Bowley, Marian. *Housing and the State, 1919–1944.* 1945.

Burnett, John. *A Social History of Housing, 1815–1985.* 2nd ed. 1986.

Daunton, Martin J. *A Property Owning Democracy? Housing in Britain.* 1987.

Dunleavy, Patrick. *The Politics of Mass Housing in Britain, 1945–1975.* 1981.

Rodger, Richard. *Scottish Housing in the Twentieth Century.* 1989.

Huxley, Aldous Leonard (1894–1963)

Aldous Huxley, novelist, essayist, poet, biographer, and mystic, is most famed for three of his novels: *Point Counter Point* (1928), an innovatively structured account of upper-class and bohemian London life on the eve of Fascism's rise; *Brave New World* (1932), a dystopian forecast of life in the year A.F. (after Ford) 600; and *Island*, a utopian account of a present-day paradise in which persons achieve individual integrity, freedom from the fear of death, and fine attunement to reality by means of mysticism and discriminating use of drugs.

Huxley was the grandson of the Victorian scientist and proponent of Darwinism T.H. Huxley and the great-nephew of the Victorian literary critic and poet Matthew Arnold. Three intense encounters with mortality marked Huxley's early years: his beloved mother's death in 1908; a disease of the cornea in 1910, which blinded him for more than a year; and the suicide of his elder brother in the opening days of the First World War. In spite of these troubles, Huxley achieved distinction as an **Oxford** undergraduate and published his first book of poems in 1917. He participated in the brilliant circle of writers, thinkers, and politicians at Lady Ottoline Morrell's Garsington Manor, where he befriended the novelist **D.H. Lawrence** and met Maria Nys, a Belgian refugee, whom he married in 1919.

Huxley's first novels, *Crome Yellow* (1921), *Antic Hay* (1923), and *Those Barren Leaves* (1925), are influenced by Thomas Love Peacock's novels from a century earlier, as well as by *South Wind* (1917) by Norman Douglas (1868–1952). The novels represent clever young men adrift in the post-war world who are surprised to discover that amorality in general, and sexual promiscuity in particular, do not free them from unhappiness and self-division. Personal self-division becomes in *Point Counter Point* a "human fugue" of social fragmentation and incoherence, which is replicated in the fragmented, counterpointed structure of the novel's narrative. But a pair of redeemers from incompleteness also appears in the novel in the figures of Mark and Mary Rampion, characters based on D.H. Lawrence and his wife. Huxley's adherence to Lawrence (he edited the first posthumous edition of Lawrence's letters in 1932), combined with the impact on Huxley of Buddhism and Gandhian pacifism during a Far Eastern tour in 1925, intensified his already strong didactic bent.

This didacticism dominates *Brave New World* and shapes the rest of Huxley's career, in an impressively unabated manner, even during the moments of Huxley's further aesthetic experiments with narrative form (after *Point Counter Point*) in *Eyeless in Gaza* (1936) and *Time Must Have a Stop* (1944). The primary tenets of Huxley's teaching are a nondogmatic belief in personal immediate experiences of eternity, which transcend time and the world yet nevertheless enlighten and guide mundane actions; and a quasi-anarchist advocacy of international **pacifism**, urging nonattachment to politics (albeit not detachment from them altogether). These tenets, however much they seemed sensible to the young of the post-war generation, appealed less to the young men and

women of the 1930s, whose anti-Fascist Leftism and sympathy with the republicans of Spain prided itself on political engagement. Fighting a losing battle on behalf of pacifism, Huxley migrated in 1937–8, with his wife and a fellow mystic, Gerald Heard (1889–1971)—who also influenced the novelist **Christopher Isherwood**—to Los Angeles. He undertook film work, writing scripts for MGM, Fox, Disney, and Universal; his novels *After Many a Summer Dies the Swan* (1939) and *Ape and Essence* (1948) are in part satiric visions of Hollywood.

Huxley undertook to become an American citizen in 1954. His application was rejected because he could not claim that his pacifist objection to the right to bear arms was a religious conviction rather than a purely philosophical one. But this disclaimer of religious inspiration did not mean a lessening of the mysticism Huxley had summed up at the end of the Second World War in *The Perennial Philosophy* (1945). As an experiment in mysticism, in 1954 Huxley asked Humphrey Osmond, an English psychiatrist researching the effect of mescaline on schizophrenia, to supervise Huxley's taking of the drug in order for him to explore the possibilities of expanded consciousness. The blissful results are described in *The Doors of Perception* (1954) and are elaborated in *Island*, which presents a program for averting both the dystopia of *Brave New World* and the post-nuclear age horror of *Ape and Essence*.

It now appears that Huxley's work includes a forecast of literary criticism's recent castigations of modernist art for its alleged irresponsibly disinterested relation to the world's political state. Although the modernist artistic forms of Huxley's work are at one with those of **James Joyce, Virginia Woolf**, and **Wyndham Lewis** (and are more like theirs than like Lawrence's), Huxley appears more up-to-date than they in his didactic contention that art and aesthetics, no matter how avant-garde, are of secondary importance in comparison with clear-eyed historical consciousness and with historical well-being. Equally up-to-date, Huxley's mixture of novelistic and documentary modes in his two remarkable biographies of seventeenth-century French clergy, *Grey Eminence* (1941) and *The Devils of Loudon* (1952), instance the mixed modes of "new historicism." Nevertheless, the contemporary interest in Huxley is probably mitigated by his contention, especially in the biographies, that politics damnably betrays mysticism, as well as by the datedness (however full of charm) and the irony (however produced by chance) of *Island*'s embodiment of the ways of living and the values of California's 1960s "counterculture."

Robert L. Caserio

Bibliography
Bedford, Sybille. *Aldous Huxley: A Biography*. 1974.
Nance, Guinevera A. *Aldous Huxley*. 1988.
Woodcock, George. *Dawn and the Darkest Hour: A Study of Aldous Huxley*. 1972.

Huxley, Julian Sorell (1887–1975)

Although by profession a biologist, publishing his most significant work, *Evolution, the Modern Synthesis* in 1942, it is perhaps as a popularizer and statesman of science that Julian Huxley made his greatest impact. He was elected a Fellow of the Royal Society in 1938 and knighted in 1958. His grandfather was T.H. Huxley, the scientist and evolutionist, and his brother the novelist Aldous Huxley. After Eton and a first-class degree in natural science (zoology) from Oxford (1909), his career was characterized by a large number of comparatively short appointments, including chairs in biology at Rice Institute in Texas (1913) and zoology at King's College, London (1925). He was Secretary of the Zoological Society of London (1935–42) and first Director-General of UNESCO (1946–8).

His scientific work was equally varied. His 1914 paper on the ritualization of behavior in the courtship of the great crested grebe is considered a landmark in the scientific study of animal behavior. His early laboratory research into ontogeny (the study of the development of individual organisms) included work on the metamorphosis of amphibians on an experimental diet of ox thyroid gland (1920). His *Problems of Relative Growth* (1932) investigated the relative development of different parts of animals, challenging some of the assumptions of animal taxonomists. From 1935 he took a close interest in evolution, publishing on "clines," the "gradations in measurable characteristics" within species.

Evolution, the Modern Synthesis combined some of his own findings with those of other scientists in field studies, genetics, and mathematical studies of inheritance. Together with Ernst Mayr's synthetic account published in the same year, this book was an important landmark in evolutionary studies. Huxley continued to theorize about the nature of evolutionary change, publishing further editions of his book in 1963 and 1974.

Huxley extended science into the public sphere in two main ways. He published widely in magazines essays that were later collected in volumes such as *Essays of a Biologist* (1923) and *On Living in a Revolution* (1944). Several themes, including his notion of "scientific humanism" and man's place in evolution, recur in these works. *The Science of Life*, with G.P. and H.G. Wells (1929–30), is an influential textbook aimed at the general reader. Huxley was awarded the Kalinga Prize for popularization of science in 1953. As a public advocate of science, and believer in rational, scientistic solutions to human problems, he personified the socially concerned scientist. He was an important reforming influence within the British Eugenics Society and was active in several 1930s "middle opinion" organizations such as Political and Economic Planning. Similarly, he appeared in socially reforming documentary films, including *Enough to Eat?* (1936), in which he presented the arguments of scientists and doctors on working-class malnutrition. Later, he was a regular panel member for the radio program *Brains Trust*. His term at UNESCO provided the opportunity for him to develop on a global scale his views of the importance of science.

It has been said that Huxley was one of the best-known figures of his day. It is perhaps, therefore, as a communicator of science, both to specialist academic audiences and to the general public, that he may best be remembered.

T.M. Boon

Bibliography
Baker, J.R. *Julian Huxley: Scientist and World Citizen: A Biographical Memoir*. 1978.
Huxley, Julian. *Memories*. 2 vols. 1970–2.

Hyndman, Henry Mayers (1842–1921)

Henry Mayers Hyndman was the founder and longtime authoritarian leader of the Social Democratic Federation (SDF), known until 1883 as the Democratic Federation, the first important Marxist socialist society in Britain. The SDF and other socialist organizations founded in the 1880s and 1890s helped lay the foundation for the Labour Party.

Hyndman seemed a most unlikely candidate for the role of advocate of the disadvantaged. Born 7 March 1842, the eldest son of John Beckles Hyndman and Caroline Seyliard Mayers, he was the scion of a wealthy family of entrepreneurs. An 1861 graduate of Trinity College, Cambridge, the affluent Hyndman was a Tory stalwart prior to his conversion to socialism in 1880, after which he devoted his life to the socialist cause.

A determined agitator and a vigorous debater, Hyndman made his major contribution to socialism through his writing. His books and pamphlets include *England for All: The Textbook of Democracy*, published for distribution to those attending the Democratic Federation's inaugural conference in 1881; *The Historical Basis of Socialism in England* (1883); *The Economics of Socialism* (1896); and *Marx Made Easy* (1921). His autobiography, *The Record of an Adventurous Life* (1911) and *Further Reminiscences* (1912), is also an important socialist record. Finally, Hyndman financed the SDF's weekly newspaper, *Justice*, which was launched in 1884 and ceased publication in 1925, thus becoming the longest-running socialist publication in Britain. After 1925, *Justice* was published as *Social Democracy* until its termination in 1933.

The best-known political Marxist in Britain, Hyndman eventually eschewed violence, opting for parliamentary action to achieve the social revolution. Hyndman stood for Parliament five times: as an Independent in Marylebone in 1880; and as a Social Democrat in Burnley in 1896, 1906, and twice in 1910. As a political activist, he agitated on behalf of the unemployed in the 1880s—he was tried and acquitted for his part in the West End riots of February 1886, opposed the **Boer War**, advocated Indian self-government, and supported Britain's participation in the **First World War**. Hyndman also rendered valuable service to British **feminism**. From the outset, the SDF espoused adult rather than manhood suffrage and welcomed women as full members of the federation.

Although riven by factionalism, the SDF achieved a considerable membership by the early 1890s. After the formation of the **Independent Labour Party** in 1893, the SDF's influence waned because of Hyndman's refusal to affiliate the SDF with the emerging Labour Party. In 1911 the SDF became the British Socialist Party (BSP), but when the BSP refused to support the war effort, Hyndman, in spite of his loyalty to the Second International, broke with the BSP and in 1916 formed the National Socialist Party (NSP). After the war (during which Hyndman served on the War Emergency Workers' National Committee) the NSP reverted to its earlier name and finally affiliated with the rising Labour Party.

Joan B. Huffman

Bibliography

Hyndman, H.M. *The Record of an Adventurous Life*. 1911.

Pelling, Henry. *The Origins of the Labour Party, 1880–1900*. 2nd. ed. 1965.

Pierson, Stanley. *Marxism and the Origins of British Socialism*. 1973.

Tsuzuki, Chushichi. *H.M. Hyndman and British Socialism*. 1961.

I

Immigration

During the twentieth century Britain has been a net exporter of people, and at all times immigrant groups have represented a small percentage of the total population. Even so, immigration has been a persistent phenomenon. Although emphasis has been placed on the immigration since 1945 of **Black people** (Afro-Caribbean peoples) and Asians (groups originating on the Indian subcontinent), the earlier arrival of these groups captured less interest. Furthermore, the immigration of Europeans and other groups, whether before or after 1945, has usually been largely ignored.

Blacks and Asians were present in Britain before 1914, but the arrival of military personnel and workers increased their numbers during the **First World War**. The inter-war Depression inhibited migration but not the arrival of Black and Asian students, many of whom were later to become prominent in their own countries. The **Second World War**, like the earlier world conflict, increased the demand for labor, bringing a number of Black workers to Britain from the Caribbean. The cumulative effect of such developments was that by 1945 small Black and Asian populations, spatially concentrated in **London**, a few ports, and university towns, were already in evidence.

The immigration of Afro-Caribbean and Asian groups has increased since the end of the Second World War. The shakiness of immigration records and a number of lacunae in census returns make it difficult to be precise about the quantitative flow of immigration during this period. However, recent Labour Force Survey figures, which update the 1981 census data, suggest an Afro-Caribbean immigrant population of 318,000; the size of the Asian immigrant population is estimated at 739,000, the majority of whom would have arrived after 1945.

This immigration produced a concentration of Black and Asian groups in the conurbations of Britain. Brixton, in South London, an old haunt of music hall artists, witnessed the growth of a Black population. Bradford, in the north of England, attracted various communities whose origins can be traced to the Indian subcontinent. Many of the immigrants, whether Black or Asian, found public-sector employment, on the buses, on the London Underground, with British Rail, and also in the **National Health Service**. Mixed in with these immigrants were a number of middle-class professionals (some of whom became "de-skilled" in Britain). In general, Black and Asian groups have remained predominantly working class.

It has, however, been the **Irish** who have constituted the largest single immigrant minority in Britain. In 1981 the number of Irish from the Republic was estimated at 606,851. Since 1922 there has been a continual flow of immigrants into Britain from the southern counties, a process that continued even during the Second World War when Eire was a neutral country. In the late 1940s and 1950s Irish immigration reached levels last attained in the nineteenth century. These workers figured prominently in the building trade, helping Britain overcome the shattering impact of the war and modernize its infrastructure. In the post-war years an increasing number of middle-class professional Irish people also crossed the water to Britain. Still, the Irish immigrant community remained essentially working class. Moreover, although less visible spatially than some other immigrant groups, in certain cities it possessed notable geographical concentration, especially London, a traditional magnet for all immigrants; Birmingham; and Lancashire, where Liverpool remains the most Irish of English cities.

In the early part of the twentieth century the arrival of Russian Polish Jews fleeing westward provoked heated debate. An indeterminate number, estimated at 100,000, came to Britain. The East End of London, particularly Whitechapel and Stepney, drew in a large number of the newcomers, as did Leeds and Manchester. In Scotland Russian Poles settled in Glasgow, especially in the Gorbals area of the city. This immigration from Russian Poland was effectively halted by the outbreak of the First World War, although restrictions had been effective since the aliens legislation of 1905. The next important phase of Jewish immigration occurred in the 1930s when approximately 50,000 Jewish **refugees** arrived from Austria and Germany. Following the Second World War much smaller Jewish immigrations have occurred. The granting of independence to India led to the arrival of a small number of the so-called Baghdadi Jews. The **Suez crisis** in 1956 and the resulting expulsion of Jews from Egypt resulted in a further small influx. Finally, although immigration from Eastern Europe since 1945 has so far been slight, there were a number of Jews among the 21,000 Hungarians who came in 1956–7 in response to the Soviet invasion.

Blacks, Asians, Irish, and **Jews** have attracted the most attention, but there are other immigrants and refugees who have remained largely invisible. In the early twentieth century a number of Germans settled in England and Wales where, according to the 1911 census, they numbered 53,324. They were a mixed community that included German-Jewish financiers at the social apex. In the middle were German clerks who worked in the business houses of Manchester and London. Below these groups were German workers, such as those who toiled in the Cheshire saltworks and women who served as governesses. In the years leading to the First World War Germans came increasingly under hostile scrutiny; after the outbreak of war in 1914 they were subjected to violence in a number of British cities. The strength of public hostility led to the internment or deportation of Germans remaining in Britain. In effect, therefore, the First World War helped destroy an important immigrant community. It took the arrival of refugees in the 1930s to reconstitute the German community, but whereas the pre-war community was reli-giously diverse, the refugees of the 1930s were primarily of Jewish origin.

Among other immigrant groups who have added to the texture of British life are the Italians. During the Second World War they, along with people of Austrian and German nationality, were interned and deported as enemy aliens. Following the war, however, the British government actively recruited workers from Europe to help rebuild the nation, and Italian workers were featured among these recruits. In addition, Latvians, Estonians, and Poles were brought to Britain from displaced-persons camps in Europe. In the case of Poles, these newcomers added to a Polish population already living in Britain, consisting of former military personnel and their dependents who had resisted a return to Poland. Mainly as a result of such developments the 1951 census counted 161,020 residents in Britain born in Poland. In the early post-war years the government also recruited approximately 8,000 Ukrainians from a prisoner-of-war camp at Rimini rather than allow them to be returned against their will to the Soviet Union.

However important it is to recognize this European dimension to immigration, it should not result in the neglect of those groups who, in common with Blacks and the various peoples from the Indian subcontinent, came to Britain from "beyond the oceans." A small Chinese presence can be detected before the First World War, but since 1945 the Chinese population has undergone a substantial increase, principally as a consequence of immigration from Hong Kong. Whereas before 1914 the small Chinese population congregated in a specific part of London (the Pennyfields area), as well as in Liverpool and Cardiff, there is today scarcely a town in Britain that does not have a small Chinese population. Furthermore, in contrast to their role earlier in the century when they worked mainly in merchant shipping and laundries, the Chinese since 1945 have become heavily involved in the food trade, especially as owners of take-away restaurants. When to this mosaic of immigration is added other groups that have come to Britain—for example, from West Africa, East Africa, **Cyprus**, and indeed the United States—it can be readily understood why perceptive observers have described the British as "among the most ethnically composite of the Europeans."

Immigration into Britain has not proceeded without legislative controls. Until the

1905 Aliens Act no restrictions were imposed on the entry of aliens, but agitation over immigration from Russian Poland produced the first serious breach in the long-standing open door policy. Further legislation in 1914, 1919, and 1971 guaranteed that the Home Office maintained strict control over the entry of alien immigrants and refugees.

For much of the twentieth century the entry of Commonwealth subjects remained unhindered. The Commonwealth Immigrants Act of 1962 marked the onset of a more restrictive process. Further controls were imposed in 1965 and 1968. Then in 1971 the Immigration Act tidied up the entire legislative apparatus of immigration controls affecting both aliens and Commonwealth subjects. Henceforth anyone who could not establish a patrial link with the United Kingdom through having parents or grandparents born there was denied automatic entry as an immigrant. Additional controls since 1971 have reaffirmed that principle, making it more difficult for immigrants and refugees to enter Britain in the 1990s than at the beginning of the century.

Colin Holmes

Bibliography

Colpi, Terri. *The Italian Factor: The Italian Community in Great Britain.* 1991.

Fryer, Peter. *Staying Power: The History of Black People in Britain.* 1984.

Holmes, Colin. *John Bull's Island: Immigration and British Society, 1871–1971.* 1988.

Tannahill, John Allan. *European Volunteer Workers in Britain.* 1958.

Visram, Rozina. *Ayahs, Lascars, and Princes: Indians in Britain, 1700–1947.* 1986.

Walvin, James. *Passage to Britain.* 1984.

Imperial Preference

Schemes of imperial preference were first advocated in the late nineteenth century by British and Dominion advocates of federation of the Empire. In the late 1840s as Britain moved into the heyday of free trade, the colonies lost all tariff privileges in the Mother Country's market with the abolition of the Corn Laws in 1846 and then by the Navigation Acts in 1849. All late-Victorian advocates of preference believed its revival would bring two benefits. They agreed with the resolution of the Ottawa Conference of 1894, which stated that a customs agreement between Britain and the self-governing colonies would place trade within the Empire on a more favorable basis than that carried out with foreign countries; and, second, they were confident that such economic links would strengthen imperial sentiment in the face of growing challenges from rising powers, notably Germany and the United States.

Joseph Chamberlain gave imperial preference its most powerful impetus when in 1895 he became Colonial Secretary in Lord Salisbury's Unionist coalition. Passionately committed to the ideal of closer imperial ties and concerned about Britain's relative decline in the face of new empires, Chamberlain envisaged a grand scheme of imperial federation modeled on the earlier German Zollverein. He was encouraged to proceed with his large vision because, just before the 1897 Diamond Jubilee, **Canada**, the senior Dominion upon which his main hopes hinged, had granted a preference on British goods of 25 percent, which was raised to $33^1/_3$ percent in 1900. Indeed, virtually the entire debate over the question revolved around the self-governing Dominions, with the other British colonies excluded.

During the meetings with the Dominion Premiers, both in 1897 and at the Colonial Conference of 1902, Chamberlain's hopes for imperial federation through a combination of political union, shared imperial defense, and commercial union had foundered on the rock of increasing Dominion nationalism, especially in Canada. His vaulting aim failed even though the Canadian Premier, Sir Wilfrid Laurier, had urged Britain to implement the policy of reciprocal preference. By 1902 Chamberlain was prompted to advance boldly on preference because of what he perceived as the heightening of imperial sentiment by the Dominion military contributions during the **Boer War**. In addition, Britain now had something to offer the Dominions, since in 1902 the Chancellor of the Exchequer revived an old Corn Duty on grain and flour to help defray costs from the war. Chamberlain then visited **South Africa** in the late winter of 1903, convinced that the **Cabinet** had agreed to an abatement of the duty in favor of the colonies. Upon his return, however, Chamberlain found that the Cabinet had caved in to free traders within their ranks and withdrawn the preference.

In a dramatic speech, Chamberlain on 15 May 1903 at Birmingham appealed over the heads of the Cabinet for a reappraisal of the country's fiscal system, including the introduction of imperial preference. Since free-trade sentiment was so strong in Britain and so many industries were prospering under the system, Chamberlain's call split his own coalition, alienated the new Prime Minister, **Arthur Balfour**, helped reunite the **Liberal Party**, and antagonized much of the electorate, fearful that preference would mean "dear food."

At a stroke, Chamberlain had catapulted fiscal issues into the center of British political debate. But so strong were free-trade beliefs that **tariff reform**, as Chamberlain's program was called, led the Unionists to three successive electoral defeats—1906 and twice in 1910. In 1913 **Andrew Bonar Law** dropped preference from the Unionist platform. Although preference remained a strong element in the Unionist Party thereafter, nothing was done until after the First World War. In 1919 Britain, which had imposed tariffs during the conflict, lowered duties by one-third for goods of imperial origin only. It was not until the advent of the Great Depression and the formation of the National government late in 1931 that widespread preferences became feasible. At the Imperial Economic Conference in Ottawa in the summer of 1932, **Neville Chamberlain**, the Chancellor of the Exchequer, negotiated a wide range of preferential agreements between the Dominions and Britain.

In the wake of Britain's severe economic difficulties following the end of the Second World War, especially the cessation of American **Lend-Lease** in late August 1945, the new **Labour** government was forced to seek a large loan from the Truman administration. This loan of $3.75 billion was only approved on the condition that Great Britain accept policies of increasing multilateral trade through adhering to the General Agreement on Tariffs and Trade (GATT) whereby the United States sought to dominate the world economy. Thereafter, although Britain retained imperial preference and while for some years after 1945 the Commonwealth remained Britain's major export market, U.K. entrepreneurs became increasingly focused on multinational enterprises outside the area of the former Empire. In 1973 Britain was finally admitted to the **European Community** on terms whereby it disavowed imperial preference, much to the chagrin of a number of old-fashioned Tories and Commonwealth countries such as **New Zealand** and Canada, which lost important economic benefits. In retrospect, the

aspirations of Chamberlain and his followers to develop imperial preference to reassert British power appear chimerical.

Richard A. Rempel

Bibliography

Garvin, J.L., and Julian Amery. *The Life of Joseph Chamberlain*. vols. 3–6. 1934–69.

Hancock, W.K. *Survey of Commonwealth Affairs*. vol. 2. 1942.

Porter, A.N., and A.J. Stockwell. *British Imperial Policy and Decolonization, 1938–64*. vol. 2. 1989.

Sykes, Alan. *Tariff Reform in British Politics, 1903–1913*. 1979.

Imperialism

In 1901 Queen Victoria died still Empress of India. In 1947 King **George VI** became the last Emperor of India. In the course of these years Britain had moved from being the paramount imperial power to first a junior partner of the United States, and then after 1947 to a European partner with only fading memories of imperial glory. The granting of Indian independence opened the door to the final demise of the British Empire.

The century began with the British **army's** unimpressive performance in the **Boer War**, the longest, most costly, and most humiliating war that Britain fought between 1815 and 1914. Reeling from its effects, the mood of the British public toward the Empire moved from a Victorian optimism to an Edwardian pessimism. The **First World War** accelerated this loss of confidence, although the British Empire actually expanded by the acquisitions of mandates over former German colonies and Turkish possessions in Africa, the Pacific, and the Middle East. The principle of self-determination for European nationalities proclaimed at the end of the war encouraged the development of nationalism in the Empire and the demand for more autonomy by the so-called white Dominions.

The British Empire during the years 1919–39 existed in what might be termed a "twilight zone." Britain could still project imperial power, ranging from sending battleships to impress the locals to waging serious antiterrorist campaigns in Ireland and Palestine. The old and the new methods of colonial domination were juxtaposed during these years. The last regimental cavalry charge of the British army took place in

July 1919 in a small battle against the Turks. The first use of aircraft for counterinsurgency purpose occurred in 1916 in the Sudan. In the 1920s the airplane was increasingly seen as a way to control uprisings cheaply without using ground forces. Given the limited funding and the antiwar attitude of the British people, the projection of power—showing the flag, with minimum use of force—was the basis of imperial defense.

After 1918 **Canada, South Africa, Australia**, and the Irish Free State all pursued more-independent policies. At a 1926 Imperial Conference the doctrine of a British Commonwealth of Nations, later codified in the **Statue of Westminster** in 1931, was first promulgated. It defined Britain and the Dominions as "autonomous communities within the British Empire, equal in status, in no way subordinate one to another in any aspect of their domestic or external affairs, though united by a common allegiance to the Crown and freely associated as members of the British Commonwealth of Nations." Between the two World Wars, demands for self-government and independence were building in India, led by Mohandas Gandhi and the Indian National Congress. The question of Indian independence deeply divided the British public, although the 1935 **Government of India Act** conceded a measure of self-government to India. In spite of the efforts of **Winston Churchill** to preserve imperial power, the Second World War accelerated the decline of British influence, the transformation of the Empire into a Commonwealth, and eventual independence for India. Churchill's stunning defeat in 1945 dramatically revealed that his postwar imperial agenda did not match that of the British people, who looked forward to the promise of a **welfare state**, not imperial glory. Following the war, Britain found it difficult to restore the old colonial relationships. With the arrival in India of **Lord Mountbatten** as Viceroy in 1947, the British government announced its intention to retire from the subcontinent. Over the next twenty years the "winds of change" that **Harold Macmillan** recognized produced rapid **decolonization** in Asia and Africa and the end of Empire.

Richard A. Voeltz

Bibliography

Barnett, Correlli. *The Collapse of British Power.* 1972.
Beloff, Max. *Imperial Sunset.* 2 vols. 1970–89.
Clayton, Anthony. *The British Empire as a Superpower, 1919–1939.* 1986.
Gupta, P.S. *Imperialism and the British Labour Movement, 1914–1964.* 1975.
Lapping, Brian. *End of Empire.* 1985.
Louis, William Roger. *Imperialism at Bay: The United States and the Decolonization of the British Empire, 1941–1945.* 1978.

Independent Labour Party

Formed at a conference held in Bradford in January 1893, the Independent Labour Party (ILP) played a major part in the creation of the alliance between socialists and trade unionists that became the **Labour Party**. About 120 delegates representing a variety of local socialist and labor groups created a national organization with a Labour title and a socialist objective. The inaugural meeting was chaired by **Keir Hardie**, an Independent Labour MP who came to symbolize the style of the ILP.

The new party faced some fundamental strategic problems. Several of its leading figures, advocated an ethical approach to politics, sometimes characterized as the "religion of socialism," although this ethical commitment gradually became more a matter of style and rhetoric. Its prospects were measured increasingly in electoral terms, despite an often disappointing performance. In the 1895 election none of its twenty-eight candidates were successful. The only compensation came with the establishment of a small bridgehead in municipal authorities.

Electoral and financial weaknesses forced the ILP to consider a wider alliance. A small but significant section of the British working class was organized industrially often in trade unions with Liberal leaderships. The initial ILP position was critical of such leaders, but by the late 1890s it had become much more accommodating. In part this reflected the emergence of a party leadership known as "the Big Four"—Hardie, **Ramsay MacDonald, Philip Snowden,** and Bruce Glasier—who played a vital role in defeating moves for a combination between the ILP and the Marxist Social Democratic Federation. Instead, the ILP leaders worked for an alliance between socialist groups and trade unions. Backed by ILP members and sympathizers in some major unions, the result in February 1900 was the creation of the **Labour Representation Committee** (LRC) renamed six years later the Labour Party. Although the unions had the voting strength within this alliance and provided much of the money, the ILP was well represented in the leadership. MacDonald became the LRC's Secretary, and in the election of 1900 Hardie was one of its two successful candidates.

Hardie's victory was surprising since the election was held when popular support for the **Boer War** was at its peak. The ILP's position was strongly antiwar, and in 1901 its membership reached a low of just over 5,000. Yet the war helped open a new strategic option for the party. Shared sentiments and the common experience of hostility from jingoistic crowds brought ILPers and some antiwar Liberals together. Many ideological continuities remained, and some ILPers believed that a splintering of the **Liberal Party** could perhaps produce a realignment on the Left. It was in this context that MacDonald in 1903 negotiated a secret electoral deal with the Liberals to give a small number of LRC candidates (including ILPers) a free run against the **Conservatives**.

The result was that in the 1906 general election twenty-nine LRC candidates were successful, along with one other who joined the Labour group. Most of these had no Liberal opponent, several were ILP members, and seven were financed by the ILP, including Hardie, MacDonald, and Snowden. The ILP strategy of accommodation publicly with the unions and privately with the Liberals had been successful.

Yet within the ILP there were soon recriminations. Critics began to show impatience about the cautious implications of the alliance with the unions and to complain that the post-1906 Liberal dominance of the Commons made Labour's cautious parliamentary style an irrelevance. One symbol was provided by a 1907 by-election gain by the young and flamboyant Victor Grayson, a critic of parliamentary conventions. Volatile and unstable, he was a member of the ILP whose candidacy had not been endorsed by the Labour Party. He served as a focus for growing discontent with the ILP's strategy. Grayson's defeat in the January 1910 election marginalized one focus for critics, but hostilities did not really decline until many dissidents quit the ILP in 1911 to join the new British Socialist Party.

In 1914 the ILP reacted critically to British support for the war. Its opposition incorporated a variety of sentiments—**pacifism**, social-ist internationalism, often a broad opposition to militarism and secret diplomacy. MacDonald's own position was characteristically tortuous, but he became the symbol of the ILP's resistance to militarism. Links developed with antiwar Liberals especially through cooperation in the **Union of Democratic Control**. Many ILPers resisted **conscription** and went to prison. This antiwar stance strained the ILP's relationship with the patriotic trade unions. When the Labour Party was reconstructed in 1917–18, the trade unions strengthened their control over the organization, and the reforms threatened the ILP's position. Hitherto the Labour Party had no national scheme of individual membership. Any attachment had to be through a constituent body, normally the ILP. The 1918 reforms included a scheme for individual Labour Party membership that challenged the ILP's *raison d'etre*.

The election of 1918 removed all critics of the war from the Commons, but in 1922 they made a triumphant return. MacDonald became leader, and some of the ex-Liberals who had joined the ILP became Labour MPs. The ILP presence in Parliament also included a new element. On Clydeside during the war the local ILP had played a leading role in housing agitations and gained a dominant position in the local labor movement. In 1922 Labour made substantial gains in Glasgow; some of the new men, most notably **James Maxton** and **John Wheatley**, stood on the Left.

The ILP's parliamentary revival was paralleled by apparent success in discovering a new role. Under the chairmanship of **Clifford Allen**, a wartime **conscientious objector**, the party seemed set to become a "think tank" for the labor movement. Study groups were established, one of which produced in 1926, as an alternative to fiscal orthodoxy, the celebrated "Living Wage" doctrine. The party paper, renamed the *New Leader* became, under **H.N. Brailsford**'s editorship, perhaps the best journal ever produced by the British Left. But in 1925 Allen resigned, weary of attacks from the Left, and in 1926 Brailsford's editorship ended. The **Clydesiders**, effectively Maxton and Wheatley, became the ILP leadership.

Their attempt to use the ILP as an instrument for Left policies failed. ILP strength in the unions was limited: Most trade union leaders had a general hostility to the Left, which they saw as Communist-dominated. In fact from 1928 Communists in their "Class Against

Class" phase were bitterly hostile to the ILP. Squeezed from Left and Right, the ILP leadership could not count on committed support from the party's rank and file or from several of the ILP MPs. Even with the disappointing record of the 1929 Labour government, only a few MPs backed the radical criticisms of the ILP.

The sight of a small group of parliamentary critics legitimizing their behavior by reference to ILP policy produced a crisis. **Arthur Henderson** indicted the ILP rebels as a "party within a party." The collapse of the second Labour government in August 1931 did not resolve the conflict. Eleven months later a special ILP conference voted to break away from the Labour Party. The decision proved disastrous. Many erstwhile ILPers stayed with Labour, while the ILP under Maxton's leadership found itself overshadowed on the Left by a **Communist Party of Great Britain** entering into its **Popular Front** phase. Yet even in its declining years its anti-Stalinist position on the **Spanish Civil War** inspired **George Orwell** briefly to become a member. During the Second World War the party was marginalized by its antiwar stance, and its parliamentary presence effectively ended with Maxton's death in 1946. A dwindling membership lingered until 1975 when the party reformed as Independent Labour Publications and rejoined the Labour Party.

The ILP's trajectory illuminates much about the character of the socialist movement in Britain—the strategic debates, the compromises with pragmatic trade unionists, and the attempts to build a socialist constituency that was neither orthodox Communist nor cautiously reformist.

David Howell

Bibliography

Dowse, Robert E. *Left in the Centre: The Independent Labour Party, 1893–1940.* 1966.

Howell, David. *British Workers and the Independent Labour Party, 1888–1906.* 1983.

James, David, Tony Jowitt, and Keith Laybourn, eds. *The Centennial History of the Independent Labour Party.* 1992.

McKinlay, Alan, and R.J. Morris, ed. *The Independent Labour Party on Clydeside, 1893–1932: From Foundation to Disintegration.* 1991.

Morgan, Kenneth O. *Keir Hardie: Radical and Socialist.* 1975.

India, Partition of

The Second World War changed the Indian situation dramatically. With a **Labour** government under **Clement Attlee** in power in England in 1945, it was not a question of whether India would be granted independence but when, and to whom power would be handed. The situation had also changed dramatically regarding the relative power of the Indian National Congress, led by Mohandas Gandhi and Jawaharlal Nehru, and the All-India Muslim League, headed by Muhammad Ali Jinnah. Before the war the Congress was the dominant party in the country. During the war the leaders of the Congress party languished in prison and the organization was left without dynamic leadership or an effective organization. The Muslim League, however, was free to organize and it flourished, gaining strength as never before. On 23 March 1940 it passed its "Pakistan Resolution," officially demanding a separate homeland for the Muslims of India. League leaders believed that only in a homeland of their own could Muslims protect their interests and way of life; they could not do this as a Muslim minority in a Hindu-dominated nation.

The Viceroy of India, **Lord Wavell**, tried through a series of meetings and conferences to reach an agreement between the Congress and the League on a constitution for an independent India but was ultimately unsuccessful. On 19 February 1946 Prime Minister Attlee informed the House of Commons that a three-man **Cabinet** mission, composed of Lord Pethick-Lawrence, Sir **Stafford Cripps**, and A.V. Alexander, would be sent out to India to meet with Indian politicians in another attempt to solve the constitutional problem. By the end of April they had come up with a plan for a three-tier federal structure of province, group, and union that would give the League a measure of the power it was demanding. This plan would be discussed at the second Simla conference that followed.

The Cabinet mission agreed that the Muslims should be given the power to ensure the well-being of their religious, cultural, and economic interests, but it rejected League demands for control of the six provinces that would comprise Pakistan. It also rejected the idea of partitioning Bengal and the Punjab since non-Muslims would be left on the Muslim side. Furthermore, the mission argued, the new Pakistan would not be a viable sovereign state. What the mission proposed was a union, with the powers of the central government limited to defense, communication, finances, and foreign affairs. An executive and legislature would govern the center, and any major communal issue would require the approval of both the Muslims and the Hindus. All other issues would be decided by the provinces, which would form groups A, B, and C. Group B was in the western part of India (Baluchistan, the Northwest Frontier Province, the Punjab, and Sind); group C in the east (Assam and Bengal), and group A the center (the rest of India). A constituent assembly would be formed to work out the exact details of the plan, but in the meantime an interim government made up of Indians would be created to carry on the business of governing the country. The League accepted the plan as it might lead to the creation of Pakistan. The Congress met and on 6 July reluctantly approved the plan. After so many years of discussions, maneuvers, and disagreements, it looked as if the two parties might cooperate. Then, at a press conference on 9 July, Nehru stated that the Congress was in no way bound by the agreements reached at Simla. He also said that the groups might never occur, and that, even if they did, the powers of the central government was sure to grow. This was a startling statement that negated all of the understandings that had come about as a result of years of informal discussions and hundreds of hours of formal negotiations.

For the League it was the last straw, demonstrating conclusively that Muslim interests would not be respected if the Congress came to power in an independent India. When Wavell appointed the members of his interim Executive Council, he appointed six Congress members rather than the agreed-upon five. The League felt betrayed all around. On 27 July Jinnah denounced both the acts of the government and the attitude of the Congress. He called for 16 August to be declared Direct Action Day, a day when the League would demonstrate its strength in the streets. These demonstrations turned violent, especially in Calcutta where after a week of violence several thousand lay dead, more than 20,000 were injured, and more than 100,000 became homeless. The violence then spread across India.

The government went ahead with its plan for an interim government on 2 September. At first the League refused to appoint members to the new Cabinet headed by Nehru. This decision gave the advantage to the Congress, and by October Jinnah changed his mind, allowing Liaquat Ali Khan and four other League members to join the Cabinet while remaining aloof himself. As Finance Minister, Liaquat was able to block all Congress proposals and plans. Amid acrimony and accusations on both sides, the League demonstrated that a united government was impossible. With the League in a stronger position, the British made one more attempt to reach an agreement by inviting the leaders of the Congress and the League to London in December for more discussions, but these negotiations proved futile.

Following the failure of the negotiations, Attlee announced on 20 February 1947 that the British would transfer power by June 1948 to a government capable of maintaining peace. In addition, Lord Wavell would be replaced by **Lord Mountbatten**. Arriving on 22 March, Mountbatten decided within two weeks that India would be partitioned. Gandhi, however, never accepted what he believed to be the vivisection of India, but, while he was widely revered, he had been effectively supplanted by the politicians. The British government announced that India would be granted independence on 14 August 1947. In July Mountbatten informed the princes that upon independence they should accede to either India or Pakistan as British paramountcy would cease and sovereignty would be assumed by India and Pakistan only. By 14 August most of them had done so except for the large states of Hyderabad and Kashmir and the tiny state of Junagadh. Kashmir acceded to India on 26 October amid a great deal of fighting and bloodshed between Hindus and Muslims, but Junagadh and Hyderabad were invaded by India, thus becoming part of India as well. All three states had a majority population of Muslims.

The newly created Pakistan included West Pakistan, comprising the states of the Punjab, the Northwest Frontier Province, Sind, Baluchistan, and parts of Kashmir, and East Pakistan, comprising Bengal. Both the Punjab and Bengal were partitioned. The rest of the country became India. Mountbatten remained as the Governor-General of India with Jawaharlal Nehru as Prime Minister, and Muhammad Ali Jinnah became Governor-General of Pakistan and appointed Liaquat Ali Khan as Prime Minister. Independence was accompanied by large numbers of Hindus migrating to India and Muslims to Pakistan. In the Punjab this led to widespread violence between Muslims, Hindus, and Sikhs to the extent that law and order broke down completely in large areas of the state. Independence had come about amid the violence and anarchy that the British had feared. Gandhi remained aloof from the independence celebrations, touring Bengal in a successful attempt to keep the peace.

The virtual civil war between the communities caused Gandhi a great deal of anguish. He blamed the Congress leaders for the Hindu persecution of Muslims in Delhi and for withholding funds that should have been given to Pakistan. On 12 January 1948 he announced a fast to quicken people's conscience. Fearful of his death, Congress leaders quickly agreed to transfer Pakistan's funds, and Gandhi's fast lasted just a week. He earned the gratitude of Muslims in Delhi but antagonized members of the paramilitary Hindu communal group, the Rashtriya Svayamsevak Sangh, who accused him of being too partial to Muslims. It was a member of this group who assassinated him on 30 January. Gandhi's death achieved what his life could not, and peace was gradually restored throughout India.

Pakistan also faced the task of dealing with millions of refugees, a task that absorbed all of the resources and time of the government, especially Prime Minister Liaquat Ali Khan. Jinnah, amid an enormous workload of his own, was slowly succumbing to the cancer he had been battling for a decade and died on 1 September 1948.

The last British troops, those of the Somerset Light Infantry, left India on 28 February. Mountbatten continued as Governor-General of India until 21 June 1948. British rule in India ended in a way British officials had tried so hard to avoid: partition.

Roger D. Long

Bibliography

Brown, Judith M. *Gandhi: Prisoner of Hope.* 1989.

Gopal, Sarvepalli. *Jawaharlal Nehru: A Biography.* Vol. 1: *1889–1947.* 1976.

Menon, V.P. *The Transfer of Power in India.* 1957.

Wolpert, Stanley. *Jinnah of Pakistan.* 1984.

Ziegler, Philip. *Mountbatten.* 1985.

Indian Nationalism

The nationalist movement in India underwent radical changes in the twentieth century. Although it was dominated at first by those who shared the political ideals of British liberals, more radical voices soon came to the fore. Respect for British political institutions was replaced by demands for a political system reflecting Indian traditions, and the desire for greater participation in the imperial system was overtaken by the cry for independence. The two World Wars were crucial, greatly altering the political situation in India. Complicating matters was the growth of a separate Muslim nationalism, which culminated in the **partition of India** in 1947.

In 1900 Indian nationalism was dominated by the Indian National Congress, led by moderates such as G.K. Gokhale (1866–1915), who wished to use constitutional means to persuade the imperial government to open up greater political opportunities for Indians. A stiff challenge to this method emerged among extremists such as B.G. Tilak (1856–1920), who appealed to the Hindu masses with politicized religious revivals and who condoned the growing violence directed at British officials. This split intensified after 1905, when the British partitioned Bengal despite strong dissent from all leading Indian nationalists. Intense political unrest resulted, as extremists engineered a noisy, popular campaign to overturn the partition decision. The imperial government responded with harsh repression, thereby further weakening the moderate position, which depended on the goodwill of British liberals. The moderates managed to remain in control of the Congress, but only by expelling the extremists in a bitter contest in 1907. Liberal measures, such as the **Morley-Minto reforms** of 1909 and the reunification of Bengal in 1911, were insufficient to repair the damage done to the moderates.

The **First World War** significantly changed the nationalist movement. Most Indian politicians initially supported the war effort, believing that the reward for loyalty would be greater self-determination. Some radicals argued otherwise, and, in the Punjab, revolutionaries prodded by German promises of aid plotted an abortive uprising in 1915. About the same time Home Rule leagues were founded in Madras by Annie Besant (1847–1933), and in Pune by Tilak; both organizations were instrumental in revitalizing the nationalist movement. Muslim political consciousness rose dramatically during the war, too, since India was now at war with the Ottoman Empire, home of the Caliphate. By 1916 a pact had been reached between the Congress and the All-India Muslim League (founded in 1906) regarding a unified list of demands for greater political participation by Indians in both the central and provincial governments. The next year **Edwin Montagu**, Secretary of State for India, announced in Parliament that the British goal for India was eventual self-government within the Empire.

But Montagu's promise proved to be a hollow one. Once the war was over, British officialdom dragged its feet on the matter of constitutional reforms. Furthermore, the Rowlatt Acts were passed in 1919, extending some of the government's wartime emergency powers to meet the threat of sedition in the Punjab and elsewhere. Indian nationalists were outraged at this reward for their loyalty, and violent protests erupted throughout the land. Mohandas Gandhi (1869–1948) organized his first national demonstration, a successful general strike. In the Punjab matters came to a head in 1919 when British-commanded troops opened fire on a crowd of peaceful demonstrators in **Amritsar**, killing over four hundred. Indian nationalists were additionally appalled when the imperial government treated the officials in charge with leniency.

Gandhi emerged from the war as the dominant figure in Indian nationalist politics. He forged an alliance with Muslims, by joining the Khilafat movement, which was protesting the lack of imperial attention to Muslim interests, especially the perceived threat to Islam in the treaty ending the war with the Ottomans. Gandhi also gained control of the Congress leadership in 1920, fundamentally altering the style and content of Indian nationalism. A new constitution for the Congress was established, creating an effective grass-roots organization capable of reaching out to nearly every village in India. Furthermore, *swaraj*, or self-government, was now the proclaimed goal of the Congress, and a campaign of noncooperation was planned, involving resignations from governmental and educational posts, surrender of honorary titles and lucrative legal practices, nonpayment of taxes, and other measures directed against the imperial government. Gandhi's message, with its emphasis on Indian self-reliance, fired the imagination of a rising generation of young nationalists, led by S.C. Bose (1897–1945) and Jawaharlal Nehru (1889–1964). But

Gandhi disappointed his fiery disciples in 1922, when he called off the noncooperation campaign because of an isolated incident of violence by protesters.

The 1920s were a relatively quiet period for Indian nationalism. The Khilafat movement collapsed in 1924, after the Turkish government abolished the Caliphate. The abrupt end to noncooperation left the Congress listless, with debate confined to the question of participation in the moderate reform measures implemented in 1923–4. Gandhi was arrested for political agitation, spent two years in prison and afterward retreated to his ashram, concentrating on village improvement. Radicalism languished until 1927, when the **Conservative** government sent a commission to India to investigate the matter of further constitutional reforms. Angry at the lack of Indian representation on the commission, both the Congress and the Muslim League, now headed by Muhammad Ali Jinnah (c.1875–1948), boycotted its proceedings and appointed their own bodies, which made separate recommendations for a new Indian constitution. Nehru and Bose, meanwhile, began a socialist league in 1928, and made *purna swaraj*, or complete independence, their demand. In 1929 the Congress, with Nehru presiding, adopted the *purna swaraj* resolution, unfurled the flag of India, and proclaimed 26 January 1930 as independence day.

Gandhi reemerged in 1930 to lead a new campaign of civil disobedience. A dramatic march to the sea was organized, drawing worldwide attention to Gandhi's unique tactics and Indian nationalism. Soon most of the Congress leadership was in prison, and in the coming year many thousands more would join them as the campaign of civil disobedience gained momentum. The British government responded with a series of **Round Table conferences**, designed to gain Indian cooperation in fashioning a new constitution for India. The talks failed, and the British government created a constitution on its own, in the form of the 1935 **Government of India Act**. Gandhi and other nationalists were rearrested during this period, as Indian opposition to British measures remained steadfast. When elections to provincial assemblies were held in 1937, Congress won an overwhelming victory and proceeded to implement its nationalist agenda in those provinces where it controlled the majority of seats. Muslim fears of persecution at the hands of the Hindu majority escalated after 1937, and Jinnah successfully exploited the issue, rejuvenating the Muslim League with the charge of Hindu tyranny in those provinces governed by Congress administrations.

In 1939 the British government unilaterally declared India to be at war with Germany. The Congress provincial ministries resigned in protest, but the Muslim League seized the moment to declare its loyalty to the British, thereby gaining the support of the imperial government for most Muslim political demands, which after 1940 centered on a separate Muslim state. In the fall of 1940 Gandhi initiated a new protest campaign, involving individual acts of civil disobedience. In 1942, after rapid Japanese advances in Asia, the British government dispatched **Stafford Cripps** to India, in a vain effort to gain Congress cooperation for the duration of the war. Congress rejected Cripps' offer of Dominion status after the war, Gandhi deriding it as a postdated check on a failing bank. Soon Gandhi launched the Quit India campaign, which involved mass civil disobedience, large protests, violent acts of sabotage and assassination, and other measures, planned and unplanned. Gandhi and the bulk of the Congress leadership were arrested and spent most of the remaining war years in prison. Meanwhile, Bose, who was in exile, organized an army, composed of Indians captured by the Japanese in **Singapore**, and invaded India in 1944. His forces were quickly in retreat, and Bose later died on a plane flight to Japan in 1945.

In June 1945 Congress and Muslim League officials were invited to Simla for talks on effecting a transition to self-government. Attempts to create a unified, independent India failed, largely because the Congress and Muslim League leaders could not agree on a formula for creating a central government with safeguards for Muslim minority rights. Escalating communal violence in 1946 exacerbated the situation, and by early 1947 the Viceroy, **Lord Mountbatten**, decided to grant independence in August 1947 and to create two nations, India and Pakistan. Congress leaders, such as Nehru and Gandhi, agreed to partition with the greatest of reluctance, while Jinnah and the Muslim League were pleased at the decision, but not at the proposed boundaries. The decision to divide the subcontinent unleashed a fury of communal violence, which neither Indian nor Pakistani officials, let alone the British, could control.

Lynn Zastoupil

Bibliography
Brecher, Michael. *Nehru: A Political Biography*. 1959.
Brown, Judith M. *Gandhi's Rise to Power: Indian Politics, 1915–1922*. 1972.
Hardy, P. *The Muslims of British India*. 1972.
Hutchins, Francis. *India's Revolution: Gandhi and the Quit India Movement*. 1973.
Wolpert, Stanley. *Tilak and Gokhale: Revolution and Reform in the Making of Modern India*. 1962.

Infant Mortality

Despite the remarkable fall in other forms of mortality from 1870, infant mortality in Britain, like other Western countries, took longer to decline and remained high until the early twentieth century, the hot summers of these years resulting in epidemic diarrhea, which pushed up the deaths. Indeed, infant mortality rates in England and Wales increased dramatically in the late 1890s, causing much anxiety among politicians, social campaigners, and medical professionals.

Much of the concern over infant mortality rates stemmed from a wider apprehension about the diminishing birthrate and the perceived racial and social deterioration of the nation's population. What was at stake was Britain's future military and economic strength. Fears were heightened by the poor health of the working class as revealed during **army** recruitment for the **Boer War** and later the sheer loss of life of the **First World War**. Added to this were the predictions of a **population** decline in the inter-war years. Together, these factors gave the survival and **health** of infants an enhanced profile within state policy. Measures taken to prevent infant mortality included the state registration of midwives in 1902, as well as the introduction of municipal and voluntary health visiting, the creation of infant welfare centers and milk depots, and improvements in maternity services.

Rates of infant mortality in England and Wales varied greatly not only between rural and urban areas but also according to social class. Despite these differences, however, the overall rate of infant mortality declined substantially from the early twentieth century onward. Between 1900 and 1939 the infant mortality rate in England and Wales dropped from 154 to 51, and in 1981 had fallen to 11.9 per 1,000 live births. The reasons for this fall have been the subject of much historical debate, but its determinants can be divided into two groups: neonatal mortality (deaths within the first twenty-eight days of life) and postneonatal mortality (deaths after twenty-eight days of life and before one year of age). Postneonatal mortality is strongly influenced by breast-feeding customs and environmental and sanitary conditions, and is sensitive to social and environmental deprivation. In the early twentieth century the most common causes of postneonatal death were gastrointestinal and respiratory infections. The historical determinants of neonatal mortality are more difficult to discern, but they are primarily linked to events during **pregnancy and childbirth**, the most common causes of death being prematurity, congenital malformation, and birth injury.

Much of the decline in infant mortality in England and Wales during the twentieth century was due to the fall in postneonatal deaths, which accounted for the largest proportion of infant deaths at the beginning of the century. Such a reduction was largely due to the fall in deaths from infectious disease (especially diarrhea) among infants. Many historians have ascribed this change to general improvement in the **standard of living**, especially **diet and nutrition**. By contrast, neonatal mortality took much longer to decline, particularly those deaths occurring in the early neonatal period. As postneonatal mortality fell, so neonatal deaths increasingly accounted for the larger proportion of infant mortality. By the 1950s most infant deaths occurred close to the time of birth, and these cases have continued to form the larger proportion of infant deaths.

Lara Marks

Bibliography

Dwork, Deborah. *War is Good For Babies and Other Young Children: A History of the Infant and Child Welfare Movement in England, 1898–1918.* 1987.

Lee, C.H. "Regional Inequalities in Infant Mortality in Britain, 1861–1971," *Population Studies*, vol. 45 (1991), pp. 55–65.

Loudon, Irvine. "On Maternal and Infant Mortality, 1900–1960," *Social History of Medicine*, vol. 4 (1991), pp. 29–75.

Woods, R.I., P.A. Watterson, and J. Woodward. "The Causes of Rapid Infant Mortality Decline in England and Wales, 1861–1921," *Population Studies*, vol. 42 (1988), pp. 343–66; vol. 43 (1989), pp. 113–32.

Institute of Contemporary Arts (ICA) and the Independent Group (IG)

The ICA, a gallery, cinema, bookshop, and meeting place in central **London**, aims to provide new work in a critical environment that also encourages discussion of contemporary cultural theory and philosophy. The IG was an informal grouping of cultural workers who met at the ICA in 1952–5 and who were seriously engaged with the images and products of mass-produced urban culture. Individuals associated with the movement were involved in a number of significant exhibitions at the ICA and elsewhere. Until recently they have been chiefly considered in relation to the emergence of British pop art, but that reading of their work seriously omits many other facets of their collective and individual interests.

The ICA was established in 1948 by **Herbert Read** and Roland Penrose (1900–1984), who had made their reputations before the Second World War; they had been instrumental in the international surrealist exhibition (London, 1936), which was the inspiration for the new organization. The ICA's declared aims were to encourage cooperation among painters, writers, and the people of the theater, film, and radio; original members reflected this cross-range of interests, including the choreographer **Frederick Ashton**, critics Alex Comfort and Geoffrey Grigson, and art patron Peter Watson. The ICA aimed to show noncommercial experimental work and be a commissioning agent with its own library and archives. Concerned with cultural experience in its broadest sense, it encouraged experimentation in those media whose significance primarily lay in **popular culture**, like film and radio. In its first premises in Dover Street (1950–67) the program included a 1951 **Humphrey Jennings** memorial exhibition. Jennings was significant in the link between the surrealist founding group and the IG through his involvement with **Mass-Observation**, the **documentary** film movement, and his use of popular culture.

The year 1951 marked the first exhibition curated by **Richard Hamilton** for the ICA. Entitled *Growth and Form*, it showed the new landscape of natural form and scientific material and led to a publication, *Aspects of Form*, that explored the crossover between art, science, and technology.

Formed within (but "independent" from) the ICA, the IG aimed to develop an aesthetic for contemporary life that took into account new technologies and mass media. The IG did not constitute a school or movement but had a pluralist agenda that attracted a range of contemporary cultural workers including artists Eduardo Paolozzi, Hamilton, William Turnbull, Magda Cordell, Nigel Henderson, and John McHale; critics Toni del Renzio, Lawrence Alloway, and Rayner Banham; and architects Alison and Peter Smithson, James Stirling, Colin St. John Wilson, and Theo Crosby who, as the coeditor of *Architectural Design* and organizer of the influential *This Is Tomorrow* exhibition (1956), was important in disseminating the ideas of the IG.

The 1953 *Parallel of Art and Life* exhibition epitomized one aspect of the IG; it included work by the late nineteenth-century photographer E.J. Marey, x-ray, high-speed photography, children's art, and anthropological material. The random nonhierarchical imagery became a maze of visual experience. Organized by Paolozzi, Henderson, and the Smithsons, it included Henderson's photographs of graffiti and detritus and the Smithsons' images of modern people from home and glamour magazines. *Man, Machine, and Motion* (1955), a thematic exhibition that Hamilton organized, drew on a wide range of visual material displayed in grids of uniform-sized sheets of formica suspended from free-standing steel frames.

Parallel to the proto-pop aspects was "New Brutalism" within the IG. Never a homogeneous organization, the ideas of its members on art and architecture have continued to be significant, going some way to achieving the original aims of the ICA.

Nannette Aldred

Bibliography

Alloway, Lawrence. "The Development of English Pop" in Lucy Lippard, ed. *Pop Art*. 1966. pp. 27–69.

Hamilton, Richard. *Collected Words, 1953–1982*. 1982.

Robbins, David, ed. *The Independent Group: Postwar Britain and the Aesthetics of Plenty*. 1990.

Russell, John, and Suzi Gablik. *Pop Art Redefined*. 1969.

This Is Tomorrow Today: The Independent Group and British Pop Art. 1987.

International Brigade

Since it ended over fifty years ago, one of most enduring legacies of the Spanish Civil War (1936–9) has been the dramatic story of the approximately 59,380 international volunteers from fifty-three countries who went to Spain to serve in the International Brigades (IB) of the Republican army. During the course of the war between 2,000 and 4,000 British men and women joined this "anti-Fascist" crusade, primarily because they were convinced that, if Francisco Franco, Adolf Hitler, and Benito Mussolini were defeated in Spain, democracy would emerge triumphant and another world war could be averted.

The idea of using organized groups of foreign volunteers to fight for the Republican side first materialized in late July 1936 in Paris. With the backing of the Soviet Union, the Comintern launched in September a formal campaign to recruit an international corps of volunteers. In the following weeks thousands of prospective candidates were interviewed by Communist Party officials, and those selected were funneled through the Comintern's international network.

For many years the true composition of the volunteer units was obscured by the publicity surrounding the famous artists, poets, and writers identified with the conflict. This was especially true in Great Britain, where events in Spain attracted the attention of a number of eminent public figures. Even though only a handful of these celebrities actually went to Spain, their reputations overshadowed the fact that they constituted only a fraction of the overall number of individuals who took a stand on the war. Apart from a handful of middle-class professionals (mostly clerks and **army** veterans), the vast majority of British volunteers serving in the IBs were of working-class extraction. A large number of them were sailors, shipyard workers, industrial laborers, and miners.

There is insufficient evidence to establish a precise profile of the political affiliations of most English volunteers, but it is reasonable to assume that well over half of the volunteers were either Communist or sympathetic to the official **Communist Party** line. A small number of British participants on the Republican side, such as the novelist **George Orwell**, regarded themselves as left wing but anti-Communist.

In any event, it became immediately apparent to the newly inducted volunteers that their individual political beliefs were of secondary importance. This is because the Communists played a central role in determining the fate of all of those serving in the International Brigades. Not only was the party in charge of recruitment but, through its network of advisers and military strategists, it exercised considerable control over the operations of the Brigade units. For example, the greater part of the Political Commissariat system—the organizational framework of the International Brigades—was dominated by Communists like the Englishman Bill Alexander, who served as Political Commissar of the Anti-Tank Battery and, later in the war, as Commander of the British Battalion.

Since the war, scholars and IB veterans alike have debated the Communists' commanding role in the International Brigades. Some have argued that the strict discipline and military strategy imposed by the Communists was a necessary "evil" in the context of war. Others have condemned Communist practices, pointing to the fact that there were men and women who left Spain disillusioned by their experiences in the International Brigades.

Although a few English volunteers were among the first IB units serving in Spain—the Cambridge student and poet John Cornford and the artist Felicia Browne had been there since August—most British recruits arrived after October 1936. On arriving at Albacete, the base camp for the International Brigades, the British and other recruits underwent an intensive period of military induction and political indoctrination. The British troops were then sent to Madrigueras, where a training depot had been established. From this point, they were dispatched to the front lines.

Not everyone in the brigades was sent into battle. A small but significant number of men and women served in noncombatant roles, mostly as medical assistants (nurses), cooks, and ambulance and truck drivers. Fresh recruits were assigned to a unit in one of the five permanent International Brigades (XI–XV), which were themselves divided along linguistic lines. Nearly all of the English-speaking volunteers belonged to the XV Brigade, which was formed on 8 February 1937. This was composed of the 600-man British Battalion as well as members of the Dimitrov Battalion (mostly Czech, Polish, and Slavic volunteers). The XV Brigade later included Commonwealth and North American volunteers.

British volunteers saw some of the heaviest fighting of the war. They were used as shock troops at the Battle of Jarama (February 1937) and the Battle of Brunete (July 1937). Because the XV Brigade suffered heavy casualties in these engagements, it was reorganized to incorporate other groups. Thus, following Jarama, the British Battalion was restructured, comprising the **Clement Attlee** company as well as a battalion of Spanish regulars.

Like most of the foreigners who participated in the war, the English volunteers enjoyed good relations with the Spanish soldiers and civilians. This was amply demonstrated in November 1938, when the greatly reduced number of International Brigaders were asked to withdraw from Spain. They departed with the well wishes of thousands of Spaniards whose cheers made it clear that they would never forget the International Brigaders' contribution to the Republican war effort.

George Esenwein

Bibliography

Alexander, Bill. *British Volunteers for Liberty*. 1982.

Gurney, Jason. *Crusade in Spain*. 1974.

Johnston, Verle B. *Legions of Babel: The International Brigades in the Spanish Civil War*. 1967.

Richardson, R. Dan. *Comintern Army: The International Brigades and the Spanish Civil War*. 1982.

Internment of Enemy Aliens

Though lacking in precedent, the internment of enemy aliens—those nationals of enemy states either residing or traveling in Britain when war broke out—became a controversial feature of British security policy in both World Wars. In each case a growing fear that enemy aliens were engaging in espionage or sabotage was the motive for internment schemes.

Already primed by a spate of pre-war novels and plays dealing with the prospect of a German invasion made possible by agents carefully disguised as waiters and other innocuous figures, the **press** and the public, as soon as the war broke out in August 1914, began to call for the preemptive rounding up of German and Austrian nationals. Known spies were arrested at once, but internment was at first very limited in nature. In the autumn of 1914, however, growing public outrage over largely fictitious stories of German atrocities in Belgium, coupled with a widespread belief that military and naval reverses in the early weeks of fighting were the work of enemy spies, led to a progressive widening in the scope of internment. By the end of October 1914 the Home Office, responding to public and War Office pressure, had issued orders for the arrest of all male enemy aliens of military age. By November 1914 over 10,000 aliens were incarcerated in a variety of temporary locations, their final destination a makeshift camp on the Isle of Man.

The internment camps hurriedly set up often lacked adequate facilities, and living conditions for the internees on the Isle of Man were so substandard that a revolt occurred in which five internees were killed. This led to the release of 2,700 internees in December 1914. Hatred for the "Huns," however, continued to mount, public hysteria reaching a new peak after the sinking of the *Lusitania*. Aware of the popular mood of retribution and spy mania, Prime Minister **H.H. Asquith** announced on 13 May 1915 that "all enemy aliens of fighting age" were to be placed behind barbed wire. In all, nearly 30,000 German, Austrian, and other male aliens of lesser Central Powers were interned for the duration under less than ideal conditions on the Isle of Man and elsewhere.

On the outbreak of the **Second World War**, the Home Office, under Sir John Anderson, adopted a more discerning internment policy. Enemy aliens were examined by special tribunals and divided into three categories. Class "C" were judged harmless and were allowed to go free; class "B" consisted of those Germans whom it was considered safe to leave at large for the time being; and class "A" were those enemy aliens who were considered a security threat and were interned. As most German nationals living in Britain in 1939 were **Jews** and other anti-Nazi **refugees**, it is not surprising that of 73,800 cases reviewed, 64,200 were judged class "C" and only 600 men were interned.

In the spring of 1940, however, a new wave of hysteria over the "threat from within" arose as German forces struck at Norway and then the Low Countries. The success of the German assaults was widely, though erroneously, believed to be the work of traitors, and fears grew that Britain, too, had its Fifth Column—not least among German refugees. Spurred on by the new Prime Minister, **Winston Churchill**, the civil and military authorities, with the help of MI5, progressively extended the scope of internment. By June 1940 over 27,000 men and women, most of them hostile to Adolf Hitler, were confined under armed guard.

Again problems arose. Living conditions in the hastily prepared internment camps were often bad, and a plan advocated by Churchill to ship enemy aliens to **Canada** and **Australia** began to unravel after the ocean liner *Arandora Star*, carrying a mixed bag of internees and POWs to Canada, was sunk by a U-boat at the cost of over 650 lives. In July 1940 the internment process was halted and shipment overseas abandoned. As the invasion panic ebbed and public sympathy for the refugees increased, the Home Office began to release class "C" internees (by early 1941 at the rate of 1,000 a month). The same applied to those already transported to Canada and Australia, and by the end of 1942 virtually all but the class "A" internees had been released. Most of those who remained were repatriated in exchanges arranged by the International Red Cross in 1943 and 1944.

S.P. MacKenzie

Bibliography

Gillman, Peter, and Leni Gillman. *"Collar the Lot!" How Britain Interned and Expelled Its Wartime Refugees.* 1980.

Lafitte, Francois. *The Internment of Aliens.* rev. ed. 1990.

Speed, Richard B. *Prisoners, Diplomats, and the Great War: A Study in the Diplomacy of Captivity.* 1990.

Irish in Britain

Irish immigrants constitute the largest ethnic minority group in Britain and have done so since records began with the 1841 census. During the late nineteenth and early twentieth centuries the majority of Irish immigrants had gone to the United States, but this pattern changed with the introduction of immigrant quotas in 1921. While only 8 percent of Irish immigrants came to Britain between 1876 and 1921, the proportion rose to 90 percent from the mid-1930s. Between 1891 and 1926 there was a net emigration from Ireland of 1.1 million people. For the Republic of Ireland, which had a population of 3 million in 1926, the net loss by emigration in the years up to 1971 was a further 1.2 million. During the post-war economic boom in Britain the net average emigration to Britain rose to over 40,000 during the last half of the 1950s. The attraction of foreign investment and Ireland's entry into the **European Community** resulted in a small increase in the number of jobs and a net in-migration of 104,000 during the period 1971–81. However, with rapidly rising **unemployment** in the 1980s emigration began again so that by 1989 it had reached the levels of the 1950s.

Both push and pull factors have been operating throughout the period of emigration in the twentieth century. The agricultural economy of Ireland was unable to provide the employment opportunities available in the more industrialized British economy. Although much of the Irish **immigration** to Britain occurred at a time of full employment in Britain, Irish immigrants did meet the need for skilled workers at a time when there was a recognized skill shortage.

In the nineteenth century Irish immigrants were concentrated in all of the major industrial cities in Britain. However, Irish immigrants in the twentieth century increasingly located in the Midlands and the southeast of England where industrial expansion was greatest in the postwar era. More than 50 percent of the Irish immigrants born in the first half of the twentieth century left school by the age of fourteen with no qualifications. With the expansion of **secondary education** in Ireland, more than 70 percent of the Irish immigrants born in the second half of the century had second-level qualifications and stayed at school until the termination leaving age of 17–18. Each successive generation of Irish immigrants in the twentieth century became better qualified, so that by the 1980s Irish-born immigrants had higher rates of university-level qualifications than the British-born population. Irish immigrants throughout the century have been strongly concentrated in a number of occupation groups. Irish men have been concentrated in the building industry either as laborers, foremen, or contractors. Part of the attraction of this industry is that it has been relatively well paid. Irish men have also been prominent in the semi- and unskilled occupations. Irish women's occupations are equally concentrated in a few groups, including **nursing** and teaching, although they are more heavily represented in the semi- and unskilled occupations. However, throughout the course of the twentieth century Irish immigrants, both men and women, have become increasingly represented in service occupations.

By the beginning of the century studies of Irish communities had noted clear evidence of upward social mobility—that is, movement into a social class regarded as superior to that of the parents' generation. It has been shown that first-generation Irish immigrants experienced much greater downward mobility—that is, an inferior social class to that of their fathers—than did the British-born population. Second-generation Irish immigrants—that is, the British-born children of Irish parents—experienced greater levels of upward mobility. These levels of upward mobility were higher among women than men.

Successive generations of Irish immigrants, both men and women, have increasingly intermarried with the British-born population. There is evidence to suggest, however, that marriages that were mixed by birthplace were not mixed by religion. It is estimated that more than 90 percent of the Irish immigrants are **Roman Catholic**, and more than 70 percent of Irish immigrant marriages were to Roman Catholics. The importance of religion in the choice of marriage partner is also evident in the second generation.

Analysis of the fertility rates of Irish-born mothers has shown that there was a convergence of their fertility rates with the national British rates in the 1970s. Irish-born women by this period had also overwhelmingly adopted **birth control** practices not approved by the Catholic Church. Thus, by the end of the 1970s the contraceptive practices of Irish-born women were no different from those of the national population.

Overall, evidence about the integration of the Irish in Britain is contradictory. There has been a large-scale movement from agricultural occupations into industrial employment. However, Irish immigrants have not been able to attain the same levels of occupational achievement as those of the British-born population, with the same educational qualifications, at least in the first generation. There are signs of high rates of intermarriage as well as some cultural assimilation in terms of the fertility rates and contraceptive practices and religious beliefs and practices of Irish Catholics.

Dorren McMahon

Bibliography
Holmes, Colin. *John Bull's Island: Immigration and British Society, 1871–1971.* 1988.
Hornsby-Smith, Michael. *Roman Catholics in England: Studies in Social Structure since the Second World War.* 1987.

Hornsby-Smith, Michael, and Angela Dale. "The Assimilation of Irish Immigrants in England," *British Journal of Sociology*, vol. 39 (1988), pp. 519–43.

Jackson, John Archer. *The Irish in Britain*. 1963.

McMahon, Dorren. *The Assimilation of Irish Immigrants in Britain*. D.Phil. Thesis, University of Oxford, 1992.

Irish Land Purchase Act (1903)

Between 1885 and 1903 **Conservative** governments enacted a succession of Irish land acts directed at "killing Home Rule with kindness." This policy assumed that the agitation for Home Rule derived mainly from rural discontent, and that if tenant farmers became owners, discontent would fade away. Although the land policy failed in its political objective, it succeeded in creating a large class of small landowners. In 1885 fewer than 5 percent of Irish farmers owned their land, but by 1921 about 70 percent did.

The various land purchase acts, beginning with Lord Ashbourne's Act in 1885, enabled tenants wanting to purchase their holdings to borrow the full amount from a government fund on generous terms. Until 1891, however, the loan fund was small, and between 1891 and 1903—although the fund was substantially increased—procedures were so complex that prospective purchasers were discouraged. Moreover, many landlords were reluctant to dismantle their estates.

A breakthrough came in 1903 with the passage of the bill that became known as the Wyndham Act, after Chief Secretary George Wyndham, who introduced it. The 1903 act implemented recommendations of the Irish Land Conference of 1902 chaired by the Earl of Dunraven. The main differences from previous land acts were bonuses to landlords to sell their entire estates, and assurances to tenants that repayment rates would not exceed their rents. The repayment period was also extended from 49 years to 68.5 years.

The Wyndham Act was attacked by leaders of the Irish Nationalist Party—many of whom demanded compulsory sale by landlords—but it accelerated the breaking up of the great estates into family-owned farms. Between 1903 and 1910 about 270,000 of the remaining 500,000 Irish tenants became owners.

Don M. Cregier

Bibliography

Pomfret, John E. *The Struggle for Land in Ireland, 1800–1923*. 1930.

Winstanley, Michael J. *Ireland and the Land Question, 1800–1922*. 1984.

Irish Literature

The twentieth century has been marked by the establishment of Irish literature as a fully separate body of writing aimed at Irish publishers and theaters and enjoyed by an expanding readership within the most literate country in the world. However, this occurred only after centuries during which Irish writing in English seemed largely controlled by the need to appeal to English publishers, readers, and theaters. The radically different nature of the Irish past is underscored by remembering that early writing in English about Ireland tended to be dominated by imperialist English accounts and Irish reactions to them—such as the work of Jonathan Swift, the first major Irish writer in English.

While writing in Irish Gaelic enjoyed an impressive tradition of its own since the time of the ancient epic the *Táin Bó Cuailnge* (Cattle Raid of Cooley), most of the best known pre-twentieth-century Irish writers in English achieved what they did by living and writing in England or by writing works aimed largely at English audiences—in drama (Congreve, Sheridan), poetry (Goldsmith), and fiction (Sterne, Edgeworth). At the end of the nineteenth century two Dubliners, Oscar Wilde (1854–1900) and **George Bernard Shaw**, capitalized on their perspectives as outsiders in writing their extremely successful London satiric comedies. While Wilde was tragically destroyed by English society because of his **homosexuality**, Shaw fulfilled his stated ambition, since "England had conquered Ireland," to "come over and conquer England." Shaw always turned English rationalism an extra twist or two in his plays, thus "beating the English at their own game" and becoming the most successful and persistent dramatist of the twentieth century. Shaw's only play set in Ireland, *John Bull's Other Island* (1904), was staged in London after it was rejected by the Abbey Theatre in Dublin. His English satire *The Shewing-Up of Blanco Posnet* (1909) was suppressed in England and staged at the Abbey.

The nineteenth century saw the creation of Irish periodicals such as the *Nation* and the

Dublin University Magazine, but the establishment of Irish literature as independent came only at the beginning of the twentieth century in the form of the Irish theater movement founded by **William Butler Yeats** and his colleagues. Yet it is worth noting that Yeats spent formative years in London as well as Dublin and Sligo, that he was much influenced by English writers, and that several of the key early events of his Irish movement occurred in London: the foundation of the Irish Literary Society in 1891, for example, and the staging of his play *The Land of Heart's Desire* on a double bill with Shaw's sharply different *Arms and the Man* in 1894. This production was funded by Annie Horniman, a rich Englishwoman who was opposed to **Irish nationalism** but interested in **drama** and in Yeats personally. Ironically, the pioneering Irish nationalist theater, the Abbey, was housed in a building bought by Horniman in 1904. This curious relationship continued until 1910, when Lady Augusta Gregory (1859–1932) and Lennox Robinson (1886–1958) failed to close the theater on the occasion of King **Edward VII**'s death; as a result, Horniman withdrew her support, and Yeats and his colleagues were obliged to turn to Irish sources for funds.

Beginning his movement in London, depending on an English patron, illiterate in the Irish language and much better schooled in Blake and Shelley, Yeats nonetheless gave the impression that he and his movement came straight out of the Irish tradition of bards and rebels. He was championed by the Fenian rebel John O'Leary (1830–1907), and Yeats' nationalist heroines in *The Countess Cathleen* (1892) and *Cathleen ni Hoolihan* (1902) were played by Maud Gonne (1866–1953), a leader in the Irish nationalist movement and the woman who inspired many of his poems and plays. Less often remarked but very crucial were Yeats' critical activities in creating an Irish literary canon, including his editing of the anthology *Representative Irish Tales* (1891), his promulgation of lists of the "Best Irish Writers," and his many essays on Irish literature, which have colored critical views of Irish literature ever since. More than anyone else, Yeats succeeded in creating an audience for a distinctively new Irish literature, not only in Ireland and England, but internationally.

Interrelated with Yeats and his movement was the revolution in Irish politics and society. Indeed, future Irish rebels such as Pádraic Pearse (1879–1916), the leader of the 1916 Easter Rising, were inspired by Yeats' Poor Old Woman, who convinces a young man to lay down his life for Ireland. Pearse was driven by a messianic sense of mission that culminated in the Rising, which he led even though he knew it would fail in the short term. Of course, more than provoking historical events, Yeats and his movement reacted to them. While nineteenth-century Irish leaders and writers were largely Protestant and upper class, the Catholic middle class came to dominate the Republic of Ireland, as reflected in its leaders and writers. Yeats' movement was as much the romanticized swan song of the Ascendancy as it was the provocateur of the revolution.

The great works of Yeats and his close colleagues included his poetry volumes *The Rose* (1893), *The Wind among the Reeds* (1899), *The Green Helmet* (1910), *The Wild Swans at Coole* (1919), *The Tower* (1928), and others; his plays such as *On Baile's Strand* (1904), *The Only Jealousy of Emer* (1919), *The Words upon the Window-Pane* (1930), and *The Death of Cuchulain* (1939); John Millington Synge's (1871–1909) "peasant" plays, including *Riders to the Sea* (1904) and *The Playboy of the Western World* (1907); Lady Gregory's *Spreading the News* (1904), *The Rising of the Moon* (1907), and other plays; and Sean O'Casey's (1880–1964) Dublin trilogy of plays, *The Shadow of the Gunman* (1923), *Juno and the Paycock* (1924), and *The Plough and the Stars* (1926). Inspired by the translations of Douglas Hyde (1860–1947), Gregory and Synge invented a new Irish-English rural idiom that captured the distinctive features of English spoken in Ireland (influenced by its two major sources, the Irish language and archaic forms of English preserved in Ireland). Their works were more Irish than writing in English had ever been before, while resisting nineteenth-century stereotypes and futile attempts to capture Irish pronunciations in deliberate misspellings. O'Casey wrote similarly artful Dublin dialogue. Yet Yeats rejected O'Casey's experimental play set in London, *The Silver Tassie* (1928). Thereafter, the Abbey Theatre and Irish society in general began a conservative phase marked by **censorship** and less risk-taking.

The greatest master of Dublin writing, of course, was **James Joyce**. From the time of his 1901 pamphlet attacking Yeats' movement, *The Day of the Rabblement*, Joyce initiated a countermovement in Irish literature that was critical of Irish society and determined to become fully European, not just Irish. His four books of fiction are masterpieces of modernism and postmodernism: *Dubliners* (1914), *A Portrait of the Artist as a Young Man* (1916), *Ulysses* (1922), and *Finnegans Wake* (1939). Perhaps the most representative and influential writer after Yeats was Sean O'Faoláin (1900–1991), who grew up with the century, reacting to and helping shape many of its major events. He fought in the Irish Republican Army in the 1920s but became disillusioned by the conservative Irish state, establishing himself as one of its major critics in his prolific fictional and nonfictional prose. Especially as editor of the journal *The Bell* during the period 1940–6, O'Faoláin was a crucial conscience and the mentor of many younger Irish writers. Perhaps his closest successors today are the writers of the Field Day movement: the playwright Brian Friel (1929–), author of *Translations* (1980) and *Dancing at Lughnasa* (1990); Seamus Heaney (1939–), the leading contemporary poet, influenced by Yeats but not overcome by him as were other twentieth-century Irish poets; and Seamus Deane (1940–), the most influential critic writing in Ireland today and editor of the ambitious (and controversial) *Field Day Anthology of Irish Writing* (1991).

The riches of Irish literature can be suggested by listing other great writers: **Samuel Beckett**, Austin Clarke (1896–1974), Patrick Kavanagh (1904–1967), George Moore (1852–1933), Flann O'Brien (1911–1966), Kate O'Brien (1907–74), Máirtín O Cadhain (1907–1970), Pádraic O Conaire (1883–1928), Frank O'Connor (1903–1966), Liam O'Flaherty (1896–1984), Æ (George Russell, 1879–1916), Somerville and Ross (Edith Somerville [1858–1949] and Violet Martin [1862–1915]), and James Stephens (1882–1950).

James M. Cahalan

Bibliography

Cahalan, James M. *The Irish Novel: A Critical History.* 1988.

———. *Modern Irish Literature and Culture: A Chronology.* 1993.

Deane, Seamus, ed. *The Field Day Anthology of Irish Writing.* 3 vols. 1991.

Maxwell, D.E.S. *A Critical History of Modern Irish Drama, 1891–1980.* 1984.

Welch, Robert, ed. *The Oxford Companion to Irish Literature.* 1993.

Irish Nationalism

The phrase "Irish nationalism" was not used before the 1840s. However, the goal of an independent Irish nation-state dates to the 1770s, when Henry Grattan and others tried to establish an Irish parliament free of British control. The Rising of 1798, influenced by the French Revolution and aiming toward an Irish republic, was another important milestone. From these two sources derived the competing forces of constitutional and revolutionary nationalism, both active throughout the nineteenth century. Constitutional nationalism, associated with Daniel O'Connell, Isaac Butt, and Charles Stewart Parnell, sought Irish political autonomy within a British imperial framework. Revolutionary nationalism, associated with the United Irishmen, Young Ireland, the Fenians, and the Irish Republican Brotherhood, wanted an independent republic wholly separated from Great Britain. The former worked openly through political parties represented in the British Parliament, the latter secretively through conspiratorial networks.

Irish constitutional nationalism reached its apex between 1910 and 1916. The Irish Nationalist Party, led by John Redmond, acquired great political weight in the two 1910 parliamentary elections, for without the support of its more than seventy MP's Prime Minister **H.H. Asquith**'s **Liberal** government would have fallen. Under Irish Nationalist pressure the Liberals, after ending the legislative veto of the **House of Lords**, proceeded to enact an Irish Home Rule bill. This bill—decreeing an autonomous legislature in Dublin—became law in 1914 but was suspended for the duration of the **First World War**. The resistance of the **Ulster** Unionists to Home Rule had threatened to nullify the new legislation and might have precipitated an Irish civil war.

At the turn of the century the principal Irish separatist movement was the Irish Republican Brotherhood (IRB), descended from—and still popularly known as—the Fenians. Less important was the semi-legal party calling itself Sinn Fein (Gaelic for "Ourselves Alone"), led by journalist Arthur Griffith. Both organizations condemned the Nationalist Party for subservience to the British, a charge strengthened by John Redmond's outspoken support for the British cause in the First World War. In April 1916 the IRB launched the militarily hopeless Easter Rising against British rule. Although at first unpopular in Ireland, the Easter Rising gained widespread public sympathy due to the execution of its leaders—Pádraic Pearse, Thomas J. Clarke, James Connolly, and others—following military trials. An abrupt decline in the Nationalist Party's reputation was shown in parliamentary by-elections won by separatists in 1917 and 1918.

In 1917 the IRB took control of Griffith's Sinn Fein Party, and thereafter used it as its political front. Sinn Fein elected 73 MPs in the 1918 British parliamentary election, eclipsing the Nationalists, who won only six seats. The Sinn Fein MPs boycotted the House of Commons, instead constituting themselves as Dail Eireann, the constituent assembly of the Irish Republic. The Dublin-based Dail, in turn, established a *de facto* government and the Irish Republican Army (IRA), which successfully fought the Irish War of Independence against Great Britain between 1919 and 1921.

The IRB, IRA, and Sinn Fein split over approval of the **Irish Treaty** of 1921 with Britain, with the majority of each body supporting the treaty giving the Irish Free State—excluding six northern counties—Dominion status within the Empire. Two years before, the six Unionist-majority counties had acquired the very "Home Rule" the Unionists had rejected for all Ireland before the war. Irish nationalist politics was now recast. Most former constitutional nationalists in the south threw in their lot with William T. Cosgrave's pro-treaty Cumann na Gaedheal Party, a breakaway from Sinn Fein. (In the north, the Nationalists remained a significant party through the 1960s.) The anti-treaty forces—appropriating the Sinn Fein and IRA labels—under Eamon de Valera continued the revolutionary, separatist tradition by fighting, and losing, the Civil War of 1922–3 against the Free State.

Following the Civil War, de Valera broke with the hard-line separatists and organized the Fianna Fail Party, committed to achieving Irish independence through constitutional means. Defeating Cosgrave in elections in 1932, de Valera gradually, and peacefully, enlarged the Free State's powers. During the **Second World War**, the Free State (now known as Eire) remained neutral, and in 1949 it officially became the independent Republic of Ireland.

The goals of the republican separatists were thus achieved for southern Ireland, after 1922 using methods that constitutional nationalists could approve.

Nevertheless Ireland remained partitioned, the six northern counties still under British sovereignty. Ending partition perpetuated a mission for revolutionary nationalism. Sinn Fein and the IRA, after de Valera's departure, rejected first the Free State, then Eire, and in 1949 the Republic because they did not include all Ireland. The IRA went underground in the 1930s after de Valera outlawed it, initiating decades of resistance to British rule in the north. Its tactics embarrassed successive Free State and Republic governments whose nationalism was hardening into official patriotism. After 1970, the Northern Ireland ("Provisional") wing of the IRA raised the level of violence to the point where London in 1972 had to replace Home Rule with direct rule. Revolutionary Irish nationalism, represented mainly by the Provisional IRA, enjoyed a resurgence and attracted financial support or sympathy from Irish expatriates overseas—although remarkably little in the Irish Republic. It also became integrated into the transnational complex of nationalistic, revolutionary, and **terrorist** movements active from the 1970s onward.

The IRA ceasefire in September 1994 brought to an end twenty-five years of violence and raised hopes of a solution to the seemingly intractable Northern Ireland problem.

Don M. Cregier

Bibliography

Boyce, D. George. *Nationalism in Ireland.* 1982.
Cronin, Sean. *Irish Nationalism: A History of Its Roots and Ideology.* 1981.
Garvin, Tom. *Nationalist Revolutionaries in Ireland, 1858–1928.* 1987.
Rumpf, Erhard, and Anthony C. Hepburn. *Nationalism and Socialism in Twentieth-Century Ireland.* 1977.

Irish Treaty (1921)

The conflict known to the British as the Anglo-Irish War, and to the citizens of the Irish Republic as the War of Independence, was a brutal guerrilla war. Neither the Irish Republican Army (IRA) nor the British occupying forces had clean hands. Between January 1919 and July 1921 the people of southern Ireland were spectators, and often victims, of continuous violence and **terrorism**.

It was clear by the spring of 1921 that neither side was winning. The war was embarrassing to the British government, while the rebels knew that it was damaging the Irish economy and disrupting Irish society. The rebel leaders—Michael Collins, Eamon de Valera, and Arthur Griffith—feared that the IRA was losing public support. After unofficial contacts beginning in April 1921, Prime Minister **David Lloyd George** offered peace talks to Dublin's Dail Eireann regime. In July, de Valera traveled to London under a safe conduct to converse with Lloyd George. In the meantime both sides agreed to a military truce.

The Lloyd George-de Valera talks were unsuccessful. The latter insisted that there must be an independent Irish republic controlling its own trade, defense, and foreign policy, and that **Ulster** must abandon its Home Rule government and rejoin the rest of Ireland. De Valera was prepared for Ireland to remain "associated" with the Empire and to recognize the British King as its nominal head. Lloyd George rejected this, offering instead a modified version of Dominion self-government.

Although these preliminary talks failed, both sides were anxious to continue both the negotiations and the truce. An Irish negotiating team headed by Collins and Griffith was sent to London in October 1921. De Valera, wishing to distance himself from further talks, remained in Dublin. Both Collins and Griffith were convinced that they must accept reasonable British terms.

The unification issue was resolved by Lloyd George's offer of a boundary commission to delimit—and perhaps eliminate—Northern Ireland. The independence issue was thornier, as the British could not accept de Valera's association proposal and the Irish republicans insisted on their sovereignty. Finally a formula was hammered out under which the term "free state" would replace "republic," and there would be a special "oath of fidelity" rather than one of "allegiance" to the British monarch. Otherwise the British conceded Dominion self-government to the Irish, on the model of **Canada**, although they retained control over harbors and dockyards in three "treaty ports" (which were relinquished in 1938).

Signed in London on 6 December 1921, the treaty was immediately approved in the Dail's Cabinet by four votes to three, with de Valera voting against. De Valera and other opponents argued that without absolute sovereignty, Ireland would still be under British hegemony. On 7 January 1922 the Dail itself, after a heated debate, voted 64 to 57 in favor of the treaty. De Valera and most of those voting negatively refused to obey the new Free State government and fought against it in the Civil War of 1922–3. Although de Valera was eventually reconciled to the Free State, for decades the major cleavage in Irish politics was between those who had supported and those who had rejected the treaty of 1921.

Don M. Cregier

Bibliography

Curran, Joseph M. *The Birth of the Irish Free State, 1921–1923.* 1980.
Pakenham, Frank. *Peace by Ordeal.* 1935.

Isherwood, Christopher William Bradshaw (1904–1986)

Christopher Isherwood's reputation as a novelist was established with the publication of his third novel, *The Last of Mr. Norris* (1935). His fourth, *Goodbye to Berlin* (1939), later the subject of two movies, *I Am A Camera* and *Cabaret*, became his best-known work. Praised by **E.M. Forster** and closely associated with **W.H. Auden, Stephen Spender**, and John Lehmann, Isherwood and his finely written prose won worldwide attention. His late works include several distinguished autobiographies as well as critically acclaimed novels.

Isherwood, born in Cheshire, England, on 26 August 1904, was a descendant of Judge John Bradshaw, who had signed King Charles I's death warrant. His first and strongly autobiographical novel, *All the Conspirators*, was published in 1928. *The Memorial*, which received more-favorable critical reviews, followed in 1932 and featured a strong-willed female character similar to his mother, Kathleen. From 1930 to 1933, having dropped out of **history** studies at **Cambridge** and quit medical studies at King's College, London, Isherwood moved to Berlin where he wrote and worked as a tutor. His third novel, *The Last of Mr. Norris*, was first published by Hogarth Press and titled *Mr. Norris Changes Trains*. This work and his next, *Goodbye to Berlin*, drew heavily from his prewar experience in Germany. Both novels have an open-eyed narrator whose involvement with the world around him brings the reader swiftly into the manners and morals of the times, revealing many dimensions of the Nazi threat.

In 1939 Isherwood and Auden, having had three jointly-written plays produced in London

(*The Dog Beneath the Skin*, 1936; *The Ascent of F6*, 1937; *On the Frontier*, 1938) moved to New York. Isherwood subsequently relocated to Los Angeles, where he wrote film scripts and joined an active intellectual community that included **Aldous Huxley**, Thomas Mann, and Igor Stravinsky. Isherwood converted to Vedanta and began to edit and translate works with Swami Prabhavananda. His next novel was *Prater Violet* (1945), one of his wittiest and most popular. The book drew on experiences Isherwood had in London in 1933 when he wrote the screenplay for *Little Friend*, directed by Berthold Viertel. After a lapse of nine years, many of which were devoted to Vedanta and to writing screenplays, Isherwood published his least-successful novel, *The World in the Evening*. Meanwhile, in 1959 Isherwood began to teach in college, first at California State College, Los Angeles, an experience that would be valuable to his writing later.

Down There on a Visit, his seventh novel, is an episodic book narrated by Isherwood the author in 1962 and describes Isherwood the person as he was during certain periods of his past, beginning in 1928. *A Single Man* (1964) was considered by Isherwood to be his finest novel. Tracing the events of a single day in the life of George, a British expatriate and homosexual professor living in Los Angeles, the novel reveals George's alienation from the world around him. Isherwood's last novel, *A Meeting by the River* (1967), draws heavily on his Vedanta beliefs and his visit to the Ramakrishna Institute in Calcutta. This novel, about two brothers, one of whom decides to become a Hindu monk, was adapted into an unsuccessful Broadway play (1979).

Isherwood's accomplishment as a prose stylist is characteristic of his writing and the reason that **Somerset Maugham** said "that young man holds the future of the English novel in his hands." Typically witty, Isherwood's style possesses an immediate clarity and vivid psychological detail. His books frequently have an articulate narrator, who is occasionally called Christopher Isherwood. His grand subject and theme, however, have often been ignored. Almost everything Isherwood wrote from his first novel, *All the Conspirators* (1928), on is autobiographical—nine novels, four nonfiction memoirs and his journal, thousands of pages in length, still unpublished.

Isherwood's reputation has had to overcome the unpopularity of his personal convictions. After he and Auden emigrated to the United States, both refused to return to England during the Second World War. Many British intellectuals reacted in print with hostility. Meanwhile, critics in the United States generally have continued to consider Isherwood a British writer, despite his American citizenship. His conversion to Vedanta and his early espousal of **homosexual** causes adversely affected the critical attention he has received in the United States.

In 1965 Isherwood published *Ramakrishna and His Disciples*, a biography. *My Guru and His Disciple* (1980), his last and one of Isherwood's most powerful works, describes his spiritual development and gives remarkable insight into the author and his convictions, as does the earlier memoir, *Christopher and His Kind* (1976).

Miscellaneous works by Isherwood include two travel books. *Journey to a War* (1936), written with Auden and reporting on the Sino-Japanese War, is structured by alternating sections of Isherwood's diary entries and Auden's poetry. The book gives the reporters' reactions to an unorganized, dangerous situation. *The Condor and the Cows* (1949), composed during a trip to South America, contains some of Isherwood's most entertaining prose.

Isherwood's reputation as one of the leaders of the 1930s intellectual movement in England and as a writer of successful autobiographical novels and memoirs will be reevaluated upon the publication of his long private journal. His books generally should be considered as a continuous narrative about his life.

James White

Bibliography

Finney, Brian. *Christopher Isherwood: A Critical Biography*. 1979.
Fryer, Jonathan. *Eye of the Camera: A Life of Christopher Isherwood*. 1977.
Funk, Robert W. *Christopher Isherwood: A Reference Guide*. 1979.
Summers, Claude J. *Christopher Isherwood*. 1980.

J

Jarrow

The name Jarrow is synonymous with the horrendous levels of **unemployment** of the 1930s. It was made famous by the Jarrow March, or Crusade, of 1936, which symbolized to a generation the failures of the British economy during the inter-war years.

Jarrow was a relatively prosperous shipbuilding town in northeast England until the end of the First World War. From the mid-nineteenth century it had been dominated by Palmer's shipyard and was often referred to as "Palmerstown." However, shipbuilding began to decline after the First World War in the face of increasing overseas competition. As a result the large shipbuilding interests came together in 1930s to form the National Shipbuilders' Security (NSS) Ltd. The main purpose of the NSS was to reduce the capacity within the industry by buying up redundant or obsolete yards, and in this process Palmer's yard was bought up and closed in early 1934. At that time about three-quarters of the workers who paid into the state insurance scheme were unemployed. Indeed, the recorded percentage of unemployment in Jarrow was 72.9 percent in September 1935.

Out of this grim situation emerged the demand for work for Jarrow. Toward the end of 1934 it seemed possible the Palmer site would be used by a new steel syndicate, and the "Jarrow scheme" for an integrated steelworks was even discussed in the House of Commons in December 1935. But the Iron and Steel Federation objected, and the scheme was strangled at birth in July 1936. At this point it was decided to organize the Jarrow March. The inspiration came from "Red Ellen," Ellen Wilkinson, who had become the **Labour** MP for Jarrow in

Unemployed workers march from Jarrow to London, October 1936.

1935. She and many others had come to believe in the need to petition Parliament for a new steelworks, but it was not until July 1936, with all-party support, that a March Committee was formed to organize 200 men to march to London. Its purpose was to present to Parliament a petition from the citizens of Jarrow demanding work and to draw the attention of the British public to the plight of Jarrow and depressed areas. The march, which began on Sunday, 4 October 1936, was joined on many occasions by Ellen Wilkinson and was greeted in London, at Hyde Park and Memorial Hall, on 31 October, coinciding with the opening of Parliament. The marchers presented two petitions to the House of Commons, one from 12,000 people in Jarrow and the other from about 70,000 citizens on Tyneside, and then returned home by train to a hero's welcome.

Although the Jarrow March did not bear immediate fruits, by 1939 the Jarrow steelworks, much smaller than the integrated steelworks that had been projected, was built on the site of Palmer's shipyard. The "Crusade" had been partly successful; the image of Jarrow haunted many wartime and post-war economists, and politicians worked to avoid mass unemployment in the future.

Keith Laybourn

Bibliography
Kingsford, Peter. *The Hunger Marchers in Britain, 1920–1939.* 1982.
Vernon, Betty D. *Ellen Wilkinson.* 1982.
Wilkinson, Ellen. *The Town That Was Murdered.* 1939.

Jellicoe, John Rushworth (1859–1935)
John Rushworth Jellicoe was Commander-in-Chief of the Grand Fleet (1914–16) and First Sea Lord (1916–17) during the **First World War** and led the British fleet at the Battle of Jutland (1916).

Jellicoe was born in 1859, the son of a steamship captain, and entered the **Royal Navy** in 1872. As a junior officer he participated in the British intervention in Egypt in 1882. As Admiral Sir Edward Seymour's Flag Captain during the Boxer Rebellion of 1900, Jellicoe was severely wounded in the ill-fated expedition to relieve the besieged Peking legations.

A gunnery specialist known for his technical brilliance, Jellicoe was closely involved in Sir **John Fisher**'s naval reforms in the early 1900s. On the eve of war in 1914 First Lord of the Admiralty **Winston Churchill** appointed him Commander-in-Chief of the Grand Fleet. Jellicoe's rigid organization and cautious strategy contributed to the Royal Navy's failure to force a decisive action with the German fleet in the first two years of war.

Jellicoe's opportunity finally came at the Battle of Jutland on 31 May 1916. His skillful handling of the Grand Fleet enabled it to inflict heavy damage on the German fleet, convincing the Germans they could never hope to win naval supremacy by surface action. However, his highly centralized command structure and refusal to expose his battleships to unnecessary risk contributed to the German fleet's escape from total destruction. His tactics produced a heated controversy inside and outside the navy that endured for decades.

In December 1916 a general shake-up at the Admiralty brought Jellicoe to the office of First Sea Lord, at the head of the navy. There his reluctance to delegate was even more damaging than it had been in the Grand Fleet, but his quiet steadiness maintained morale in a time of great difficulty. As the **submarine** peril reached its peak in 1917, Jellicoe's conservatism delayed the adoption of convoys, with costly results. But once he was satisfied a convoy strategy was practical, he implemented it with the organizational skill that was one of his greatest strengths. Nonetheless, his civilian leaders' impatience with his cautious approach led to his dismissal as First Sea Lord in December 1917, after the submarine battle largely was won. He became Viscount Jellicoe of Scapa in 1918 and an Admiral of the Fleet in 1919.

After the war Jellicoe toured the overseas Dominions to assess future defense requirements. He recommended a strong, coordinated imperial defense policy, which political and budgetary constraints forestalled, but he also predicted the Japanese onslaught of 1941–2 with remarkable prescience. He served as Governor-General of **New Zealand** during the years 1920–4 and was created Earl Jellicoe in 1925. He devoted his remaining years to writing and to numerous civic organizations and died in 1935.

David MacGregor

Bibliography
Bacon, Reginald. *The Life of John Rushworth, Earl Jellicoe.* 1936.
Jellicoe, John R. *The Grand Fleet, 1914–16: Its Creation, Development, and Work.* 1919.
Patterson, A. Temple. *Jellicoe: A Biography.* 1969.
———. *The Jellicoe Papers.* 2 vols. 1966–8.
Winton, John. *Jellicoe.* 1981.

Jennings, Humphrey (1907–1950)
Humphrey Jennings may be the most important British documentary filmmaker of the twentieth century. John Grierson (1898–1972) was the founder of the movement, and there were others who were extremely important and made more films than Jennings. But his may have the most lasting value.

Jennings came to making films in his late twenties, but their quality was much enriched by his previous experiences. He was born in

Suffolk of middle-class parents and went to the Perse School in Cambridge. He remained in **Cambridge** as an undergraduate at Pembroke College and spent some years as a research student, studying Thomas Gray, but did not go on into academic life. Instead, he devoted some time to discovering his true metier. He was fascinated by the Industrial Revolution as both a creative and a destructive force and was continually amassing quotations about it. A much abbreviated version of this collection, *Pandemonium*, was finally published in 1985. He was a painter and a poet and regarded himself as a surrealist. He was also centrally involved in organizing—and exhibiting in—the famous surrealist exhibition in London in 1936. The following year he was one of the founders of **Mass-Observation**, dedicated to using anthropological techniques to find out about the natives of the British Isles.

Under Grierson's supervision, he started making films in 1934 with the General Post Office group. With the outbreak of the **Second World War**, the group began to work for the Ministry of Information as the Crown Film Unit. It was not until 1940 that Jennings came into his own, with a group of masterly films that were artistically strong as well as effective propaganda. In a characteristically understated way, British virtues and strengths were put forward while the enemy was not directly attacked. The first of his major films was the ten-minute *London Can Take It*, made for the United States, in 1940. Similarly effective short films, *Heart of Britain* and *Words for Battle*, were made in 1941, and the longer (twenty minutes) *Listen to Britain* in 1942. These plotless films were presentations of images (and his surrealist and Mass-Observation experiences helped shape his instinct for the telling image) that conveyed the essence of Britain. His masterpiece, *Fires Were Started*, was made in 1943. It was a "docudrama," recreating the **Blitz** of two years before but using real firemen in order to recount twenty-four hours in their lives: training a new member of the group, fighting a fire at a warehouse and hence protecting a freighter, and experiencing the death of one of their colleagues. In its unobtrusive way, it is a film about heroism and civilized values. He made seven more films before his early death, his most notable being *A Diary for Timothy* of 1944–5, in which the commentary, written by **E.M. Forster** and read by Michael Redgrave, suggested the new world that would emerge for the infant Timothy in Britain after the war. Film is very much a cooperative venture, but in these films Jennings was the controlling intelligence. His tough-minded lyricism raised the **documentary film** to new heights.

Peter Stansky

Bibliography
Hodgkinson, Anthony W., and Rodney E. Sheratsky. *Humphrey Jennings: More Than a Maker of Films.* 1982.
Jennings, Mary-Lou, ed. *Humphrey Jennings: Film-Maker, Painter, Poet.* 1982.
Stansky, Peter, and William Abrahams. *London's Burning: Life, Death, and Art in the Second World War.* 1994.
Sussex, Elizabeth. *The Rise and Fall of British Documentary.* 1975.
Swann, Paul. *The British Documentary Film Movement, 1926–1946.* 1989.

Jews

The Jewish community in Britain, never more than 1 percent of the total population, has played a disproportionately prominent role in the political, cultural, and economic life of the nation in the twentieth century. Over the period British Jews have become highly integrated into the nation and progressively assimilated to the general culture and society.

Until the 1880s a small Jewish community, numbering no more than 60,000, consisted primarily of descendants of immigrants from Holland and Germany. Three new waves of **immigration** after 1881 created the contemporary community. The first and largest, between 1881 and 1914, consisted mainly of **refugees** from economic hardship and **anti-Semitic** persecution in Russia. This wave increased the size of the community to about 250,000 by 1914. The second, composed of refugees from Nazism, arrived from Germany, Austria, and Czechoslovakia between 1933 and 1939 and numbered at least 50,000. The third and smallest wave entered after 1945 and included survivors of European Jewry as well as a trickle of Jews from former British-ruled territories such as Iraq, Egypt, Aden, and **South Africa**.

The Jewish population of Britain probably reached its highest point in the 1950s when it numbered 450,000. At that time 280,000 Jews lived in **London**, 30,000 in Manchester, 25,000 in Leeds, and 15,000 in Glasgow. Since then several demographic factors have produced a decline: **Emigration** (including a small but significant flow to Israel) has exceeded immigration; Jewish outmarriage has greatly increased; many persons of Jewish origin have chosen not to identify with the community; Jewish marriages have occurred at a later age; and families have grown smaller. By the 1970s the number of Jewish deaths each year greatly exceeded the number of births. The estimated Jewish population in 1992 was barely 300,000. The decline has been most striking in the provincial communities (other than Manchester). For example, by 1992 Glasgow had only about 7,000 Jews.

Before 1914 immigrant Jews concentrated in the East End of London, the Gorbals in Glasgow, the Leylands in Leeds, and Cheetham Hill in Manchester. In these so-called "ghettos" Yiddish-speaking Jews developed a distinctive subculture with their own synagogues, newspapers, trade unions, and friendly societies. The immigrants worked long hours in small workshops, especially in the clothing industry. Housing conditions were abominable, working conditions primitive, and overcrowding acute.

In the inter-war period the social composition of the community changed. The immigrants of the 1930s tended to be from the professional and business classes, while many of the second-generation of Russian-origin Jews, too, made their way in the business world or acquired educational qualifications that facilitated entry to the professions. Accompanying this upward social mobility was a change in residential patterns. The old Jewish East End declined as London Jews moved to areas in the northwest such as Golders Green. In Leeds Jews moved to Chapeltown. There were similar movements elsewhere.

These trends accelerated after 1945. London Jews moved farther out to districts such as Ilford, Finchley, Edgware, and Stanmore, in Glasgow to Giffnock, in Leeds to Moortown. By the 1990s yet further dispersion had occurred, taking substantial Jewish populations to the fringes of the great metropolitan areas.

The Jewish community had become overwhelmingly middle and upper middle class. Old wealth in the great banking patriciate of the nineteenth century, the so-called "Cousinhood" (Rothschilds, Montagus, Samuels, Cohens, and other interrelated families), had now been overtaken by the new plutocracy of commercial and real-estate millionaires represented by figures such as Sir Isaac Wolfson (creator of Great Universal Stores), the Marks, Sacher, and Sieff families (of **Marks and Spencer**), and Jack Cotton and Charles Clore (both real-estate tycoons). By the 1990s self-made men such as the tycoon David Young (later Lord Young), the bookmaker Cyril Stein, or the hairdresser Vidal Sassoon (who, however, moved to the United States) or self-made women such as the **television** personality Esther Rantzen were more characteristic of the community than the worthies of old.

British Jewry was unique in the diaspora in enjoying exceptionally strong centralized communal institutions. The most important religious figure was the Chief Rabbi. J.H. Hertz, Chief Rabbi from 1913 to 1946, was the most significant holder of the office. His religious authority extended over the United Synagogue. This umbrella group of orthodox congregations in London and associated synagogues in the provinces (and elsewhere in the Empire/Commonwealth), commanded the loyalty of the majority of practicing Jews.

The President of the main representative body, the Board of Deputies of British Jews, was recognized by the government as the chief spokesman for the community in secular matters. The Jewish Board of Guardians (later known as the Jewish Welfare Board) was the foremost charitable body. And the Joint Palestine Appeal (later Joint Israel Appeal) raised large sums each year for Zionist causes. The *Jewish Chronicle*, with a circulation in the postwar decades of around 50,000, dominated the Jewish **press** and drove out most competitors.

A general movement toward secularization and weakening of religious orthodoxy gathered pace after the 1950s. The number of kosher butchers declined and in most smaller provincial communities disappeared altogether. Synagogue attendance, other than on the High Holy Days (the New Year and the Day of Atonement), diminished. The proportion of Jews married in civil ceremonies increased. Sabbath observance deteriorated: Many orthodox synagogues could be found with large numbers of cars parked nearby on the Sabbath—denoting Sabbath-breaking even by congregants attending services.

Membership of Reform and Liberal congregations grew steadily. Overall these sections grew from around 10 percent to nearly a quarter of the community between 1950 and 1990. Over the same period the strict ultra-orthodox, living particularly in the Stamford Hill area of

London, grew significantly, mainly because of their high rate of natural increase.

Pressure from right and left tended to diminish the authority of the "centrist" orthodox United Synagogue. It was further weakened in the early 1960s by a controversy between the Chief Rabbi, Sir Israel Brodie, and Rabbi Louis Jacobs. The latter questioned some "fundamentalist" beliefs, such as the literal truth of the biblical description of the revelation. Jacobs led his congregation out of the United Synagogue. Although no other congregation seceded, by the early 1990s several other *masorti* (traditionalist) congregations were established. Their outlook was similar to that of American Conservative Judaism. There was never any real "Jewish question" in British politics, although Jewish issues occasionally bubbled to the surface of public debate. In the early years of the century resentment of Jewish immigration led to the Aliens Acts of 1905 and 1913, which limited the influx. The **Marconi scandal** in 1912–13 brought anti-Semitic sentiment into political discourse. During the **First World War** Jews were often the victims of anti-German feeling and later of anti-Bolshevik agitation. In the 1930s the British Union of **Fascists**, headed by **Sir Oswald Mosley**, conducted provocative marches through Jewish areas, leading to violence.

In the period 1945–8 Zionist terrorism in **Palestine** provided the pretext for anti-Semitic incidents in Liverpool and elsewhere in England and led to accusations of "double loyalty." But since the 1960s, perhaps because xenophobia has focused on Black and Asian immigrants from the Commonwealth, Jews encountered little hostility except from fringe elements.

Jews have played a significant role, as individuals rather than as a group, in British political life. A number of Jews rose to prominence in the **Liberal Party** in the first third of the century, notably **Herbert Samuel, Edwin Montagu,** and **Lord Reading,** all of whom held **Cabinet** office. The **Labour** landslide in the 1945 election brought a large cohort of Jews into the House of Commons. By 1969 there were thirty-nine Jewish MPs, of whom all but two were Labour members. Subsequently the number of Jewish **Conservative** MPs increased. In 1986 there were five Jews in **Margaret Thatcher's** twenty-two-member Cabinet.

Only rarely did a "Jewish vote" manifest itself. In the early years of the century Jews voted heavily for the **Liberals**; between 1918 and the 1960s most voted for Labour; thereafter, the Conservatives and Liberals appeared to gain Jewish support. Jewish voters were heavily concentrated in only a few constituencies but they rarely voted as a bloc and were seldom swayed primarily by Jewish issues. In Whitechapel in the early decades of the century, and later in districts such as Hendon and Finchley (Thatcher's constituency), they may have made an electoral difference, but these cases were the exception, not the rule.

By the early 1990s British Jewry was affluent, demographically declining, heavily concentrated in the outer suburbs of London and Manchester, inclining toward secularization (except on the ultra-orthodox fringe), and worried about its collective future. Major efforts in Jewish education, notably the expansion of Jewish day schools, offered one of the few signs of vitality in what was otherwise a community that, in spite of the successes of its individual members, appeared to be in danger of gradually dwindling away.

Bernard Wasserstein

Bibliography
Alderman, Geoffrey. *Modern British Jewry.* 1992.
Bermant, Chaim. *Troubled Eden: An Anatomy of British Jewry.* 1969.
Freedman, Maurice, ed. *A Minority in Britain: Social Studies of the Anglo-Jewish Community.* 1955.
Gartner, Lloyd P. *The Jewish Immigrant in England, 1870–1914.* 1960.
Krausz, Ernest. *Leeds Jewry: Its History and Social Structure.* 1963.
Lipman, V.D. *A History of the Jews in Britain since 1858.* 1990.

John, Augustus Edwin (1878–1961)

Most accounts of Augustus John, even when sympathetic, dwell on his relative failure as an artist. He began spectacularly and on graduation in 1898 won first prize for the Summer Composition at the **Slade School of Art** with *Moses and the Brazen Serpent.* In 1904 **Roger Fry** recognized him as the most remarkable member of the mildly anti-Establishment New English Art Club, and in 1907 **William Butler Yeats** wrote: "The students consider him the greatest living draughtsman, the only modern who draws like an old master." Yet in 1952 when John Rothenstein summed up his career in *Modern English Painters* it was that of "a forgotten man," an artist who had lacked "all those qualities that go to make a great organizer."

He did undertake some major projects, the first of which was the large *Lyric Fantasy* (Tate Gallery), which he began in 1911 and abandoned in 1915 unfinished. In 1916 the Arts and Crafts Society commissioned him to undertake a large study of folk life in Galway, but that too was not completed. Nor was the huge frieze, *Canadians at Lievin Castle*, which he proposed in 1918 when employed as a **war artist** with the Canadian forces. The problem was that, although he was an old master born out of his time, his gifts were for draughtsmanship and, more importantly, for publicity.

Rothenstein's judgment in 1952 was premature, for in 1974–5 John was the subject of an engrossing two-volume biography by Michael Holroyd that dealt largely with John the personality, the King of Bohemia. The legend transcended the artist, and it is as a legend that he is primarily remembered. He seemed to touch the imagination of all who met him. He accrued fables, the earliest of which was that his genius stemmed from a diving accident in the sea near to Tenby, his hometown, in 1897. Clearly handsome, as his photographs show, he was also charismatic and was rumored, by the end of his days, to have fathered more than 100 children. He epitomized the idea of a life lived to the prompting of the instincts. In 1906 **Wyndham Lewis**, a friend, wrote that John would "end by building a city and being worshipped as sole man therein—the deity of masculinity." That was apropos of John's Parisian *ménage à trois* with Ida Nettleship and Dorelia (Dorothy McNeil), to which the painter hoped shortly to add Alick Schepeler and Frieda Bloch. These women, and their children, appear in many of his idylls of that period, and it was a picture of Dorelia as a Gypsy Gioconda, *The Smiling Woman*, that finally made his name in 1909. The Gypsy element entered John's art in 1901 when he was employed at the Liverpool Art School, where he was influenced by John Sampson, a librarian and Romany specialist.

John's relative failure as a painter, despite his genius, may have been due to the number of influences to which he was exposed as a gifted student. He was an early devotee of El Greco, well before the El Greco craze of 1902, and he was an admirer of Rembrandt, Daumier, and Puvis de Chavannes. He was impressed by Gauguin and by Picasso, whom he met in 1907—although he thought Fry's Manet and the Post-Impressionists of 1910 "a bloody show." Then in 1907 he returned to London from Paris and came into close contact with the painter Dickson Innes, who lived in Fitzroy Street but painted mainly in Merionethshire in North Wales. John worked intermittently with Innes in the Mt. Arenig area until Innes' death from consumption in 1914, and in his company produced his finest work. In 1908 John had met Lady Ottoline Morrell in 1908, who introduced him to high society, within which he found a new milieu and source of energy. He became a portraitist to the talented and well-placed, painting Lord Leverhulme, "His Margarine Majesty," in 1920 and Thomas Hardy in 1923. After the Gypsy caravanning that had preoccupied him during the first decade of the century, he began to feature prominently in the café life of London, at Madame Strindberg's Cave of the Golden Calf in Soho, at the Crab-tree in Greek Street, the Cavendish Hotel in Jermyn Street, and at the Eiffel Tower in Percy Street. His café friends included the poet **Dylan Thomas**, to whom he introduced Caitlin Macnamara, Thomas' future wife, in 1936. Although he painted King Faisal of Iraq in 1919 and Tallulah Bankhead in 1930, his portrait years are best remembered for drawings of **T.E. Lawrence** in 1919 and **James Joyce** in 1930. Elected an Associate of the Royal Academy in 1921, he became a Royal Academician in 1928. In 1952 his *Chiaroscuro: Fragments of an Autobiography: First Series* was published.

Ian Jeffrey

Bibliography

Easton, Malcolm, and Michael Holroyd. *The Art of Augustus John*. 1974.
Holroyd, Michael. *Augustus John: A Biography*. 2 vols. 1974–5.

Jones, David (1895–1974)

Two strands run through David Jones' work as a poet, artist, and essayist: **Welsh nationalism** and **Roman Catholicism**. Both were borrowed enthusiasms. Jones was born and educated in England, but because his father was Welsh, he pursued a lifelong interest in Celtic lore and languages. He was born a Protestant but became a Catholic convert in 1921 and adopted the view that art was a form of religious expression.

The central experience of his life was his service as a private in the **First World War**. It became the subject of his first work, *In Parenthesis*, and influenced much of his art and writing. After studying at the Camberwell School of Art for five years, Jones enlisted in the Royal Welsh Fusiliers in 1915, was wounded in France, and returned to serve until nearly the end of the war. A few years later, after his conversion, he entered **Eric Gill's** religious community of Catholic artists and craftsmen at Ditchling. During his long association with Gill, Jones learned engraving and produced illustrations for a number of books, notably the Golden Cockerel Press edition of *The Ancient Mariner*. His paintings, watercolors, drawings, and engravings earned him considerable recognition and were frequently exhibited. His work is varied, but its best-known examples often contain flowers or animals, make use of allusions, and exhibit a sensitive and intricate artistic style.

Until 1937 Jones' reputation was that of a graphic artist. In that year, however, he published *In Parenthesis*, a book of mingled prose and verse narrating the experiences of soldiers at the front in the First World War. This work, which Jones had been writing since 1928, reflected the stylistic innovations of the period, especially those of **James Joyce** and **T.S. Eliot**. Its publication was enthusiastically supported by Eliot, who wrote an introduction for it, and it won Jones the Hawthornden Prize for 1938. Jones continued working as an artist, but his writing began to occupy him more, and in 1952 he published *The Anathemata*, an experimental and admittedly fragmentary work narrating the cultural history of Western Europe, with emphasis on British and Christian themes. In 1954 *The Anathemata* won an award from the American Institute of Arts and Letters.

In 1959 Jones' essays on art and other topics were published in a volume entitled *Epoch and Artist*. Its major theme is the striking contention that all things made by human beings, especially those without function, or "gratuitous," are inherently sacramental. Most of Jones' later writings are parts of a longer work that was never assembled and treat the life of Christ and Roman scenes connected with it.

Jones never married and up to 1947 lived with his parents or friends and in the community led by Gill. He suffered mental breakdowns twice and had to be hospitalized for them. After the second breakdown he lived in rooms in Harrow, near the hospital in which he had been treated until a stroke and physical injuries forced him to move to a nursing home, where he stayed until his death. Jones never sought notoriety or wealth—he generally refused to sell his paintings—but in spite of his modesty and his isolated way of life, his genius was recognized by many of his famous contemporaries.

Jones is often compared with William Blake not only because he worked in both art and literature, but also because his writing, thoroughly modern in its techniques, expresses intense religious conviction. It is a blend of cultural atavism and sophisticatedly experimental literary methods.

Jacob Korg

Bibliography

Blamires, David. *David Jones, Artist and Writer.* 1971.
Dilworth, Thomas. *The Shape of Meaning in the Poetry of David Jones.* 1991.
Rees, Samuel. *David Jones.* 1978.
Ward, Elizabeth. *David Jones, Mythmaker.* 1983.

Joyce, James Augustine Aloysius (1882–1941)

On the strength of a book of short stories (*Dubliners*, 1914) and three longer works of fiction that perplex the meaning of the word "novel" (*A Portrait of the Artist as a Young Man*, 1916; *Ulysses*, 1922; *Finnegans Wake*, 1939), Irish-born James Joyce stands as one of the most inventive and influential novelists to write in English in the twentieth century. To call him a "British" writer, however, would be a politically fraught misnomer. He spent most of his working life on the Continent, drew his inspiration mainly from European models, and had undiluted scorn for both English and **Irish nationalism**. But his subject was invariably "Dear Dirty Dublin" and the powerful influence of that "gallant, venal city" on its inhabitants. Ireland, where his books were banned for decades, now claims him as its own.

Most of the fifteen *Dubliners* stories were written in Trieste around 1905 but only published after a decade of struggle with skittish publishers and printers. These uneventful slices of Dublin life reveal a general paralysis of will, an inherited inability on the part of the central characters to free themselves from a moribund

Roman Catholic Church, as well as stifling family traditions, an ossified politics of nostalgia, ubiquitous alcoholism, empty routines of work, repressed sexuality, and the tyranny of the dead over the living. In "Eveline" a young woman offered an escape from the purgatory of life with her widowed father goes catatonic at dockside, unable to board the ship that will take her to a new life in Argentina. In "Counterparts" a man humiliated then sacked at work comes home drunk and beats his son, passing on that gift for impotent violence that Joyce saw as a central curse of Irish life. In "The Dead" a man realizes that his wife is more in love with the memory of a young man, now dead, who had loved her years ago, than she is with her husband here and now. It was in composing these stories that Joyce borrowed from the Church the term "epiphany," which has entered common parlance as a synonym for "any revelation," but which in Joyce's hands means some fragment of speech, thought, or gesture that momentarily lifts the veil to reveal (most typically) a character's spiritual deficiency.

A Portrait of the Artist as a Young Man is Joyce's semiautobiographical *Kunstlerroman*— a saga of the artist's early education. Stephen Dedalus, like Joyce, is shaped by a rigorous, sometimes violent, Jesuit pedagogy. As he moves from childhood to young manhood, Stephen grows into knowledge of himself, his five wayward senses, his family, Ireland, the Church, and the mysteries of Woman. He undergoes a series of archtypal experiences that awaken within him permanent appetites and ineradicable revulsions. Unjustly punished by a patriarchal Church that requires submission and the subordination of self to group, he is drawn toward the verbally rich and sensuous balm of Mariolatry. Even when Stephen begins to frequent brothels, the Virgin Mary does not "humiliate the sinner who approached her." When asked if he wishes to become a priest himself, he is tempted; but a deep-rooted instinct of rebellion makes him refuse. His spirit begins to distance itself from the Church, yet despite his apparent apostasy, the forms and language of worship he learned in Mary's Church stick with him. He does not avoid a sense of vocation and devotion; he only shifts its focus from the ecclesiastical to the secular world. He will become "a priest of the eternal imagination." His enemies will be whatever would hamper the soul from its free expression: repressive parochialisms of language, nationality, religion,

family. The book ends with his triumphant self-exile from the island prison of Ireland.

Ulysses breaks new ground both structurally and stylistically. The episodes of this Day in the Life of a City (16 June 1904) roughly parallel the episodes of Homer's *Odyssey*. But Leopold Bloom is no Ulysses; he is a wandering Jew in Christian Dublin, a pacifist, a sensual, compassionate cuckold, a humble servant of his languid wife, Molly, a man in search of a son to fill the void left by the death of his own son, Rudy. The surrogate son Joyce offers is none other than Stephen Dedalus, back in town after his Parisian exile is aborted by the terminal illness of his mother. Bloom and Stephen keep crossing paths during the day; late that night, after both visit the same brothel, Bloom takes bruised and drunken Stephen home for a tenuous communion over cocoa and biscuits.

What makes this comic epic so formidable to the average reader is the richness and variety of stylistic devices Joyce deploys, from highly allusive banter and parody, to "stream of consciousness" in which the unedited flow of a character's thoughts either complements or usurps the traditional third-person voice of the narrator, to Molly's great "interior monologue" that ends the book, forty-odd pages of unpunctuated (and uncensored) thoughts. *Finnegans Wake* (which began as a series of modernist exercises under the title *Work in Progress*) builds on the more hallucinatory experiments in *Ulysses*. The book is written in a hybrid, pan-European dream-language rich in "verbivoco-visual" effects that left Joyce's admirers scratching their heads. The nuclear family here— H.C. Earwigger ("Hear Comes Everybody"); his wife, the alluvial Anna Livia Plurabelle; their twins, Shem the "Gracehopper" artist and Shaun the bourgeois "Ondt"; and loony daughter, Isobel—is in fact all families, and their story is All Our Stories. The book is a densely textured challenge, but it can appeal to the mumbling dreamer we all have buried in our collective unconscious.

Minor works include a play, *Exiles* (1918), and *Collected Poems* (1936).

David Gullette

Bibliography

Ellmann, Richard. *James Joyce.* 1959.
Henke, Suzette. *James Joyce and the Politics of Desire.* 1990.
Kenner, Hugh. *Dublin's Joyce.* 1956.
Levin, Harry. *James Joyce.* 1941.

Judicial System

As a result of reforms undertaken in the late nineteenth century the British judicial system has enjoyed a period of unparalleled respect in the twentieth century. Rapidity of procedure, access to the courts, and efficient administration, as well as essential fairness, have made British courts an object of admiration by many other legal systems. No judicial system escapes criticism completely, and debates about British justice, usually with respect to the Diplock courts (nonjury trials) in Irish affairs, have called into question the reputation that British courts have otherwise earned.

The judicial system in the twentieth century has changed repeatedly as the courts have attempted to make themselves responsive to the complex demands of modern society. The most important principles for reform have relied upon simplified procedure and a timely appeals process. Any legal system represents an impenetrable maze to the layperson, but the British system has built upon the advantages of unitary jurisdiction.

The High Court of Justice has been the central institution of the judicial system since 1873. It is divided into three divisions, with the Queen's Bench Division exercising the jurisdiction formerly held by the historic common-law courts of King's Bench, Common Pleas, and Exchequer. The Queen's Bench Division possesses the basic civil and criminal authority in the country. The second division is that of Chancery, replacing the old Court of Chancery that had originated in the Middle Ages as a court of equity. Most actions in the Chancery Division deal with property, and the principles of equity prevail when in direct conflict with those of the common law. Since 1971 the third division has been called the Family Division because it handles legal matters with respect to matrimony, **divorce**, and adoption. Appeals from decisions in these courts go to the Court of Appeal, civil or criminal division as appropriate. The final court of appeal in each case is the Judicial Committee of the **House of Lords**.

Most citizens in Britain never become involved with this part of the judicial system. For ordinary purposes the courts are either the County Courts, Crown Courts, or Magistrates' Courts. Most minor civil litigation is heard in a County Court, and appeals go to the Court of Appeal and then to the House of Lords. Appeals in the British legal system are relatively rare, and appeals to the House of Lords are permitted only when a substantial point of law is at issue. Major criminal cases are heard in the Crown Court with a jury and presided over by a High Court judge. Minor criminal offenses are tried before a panel of Justices of the Peace. These justices are ordinary citizens without specific legal training who have a solicitor in court to instruct them on points of law that might arise. Justices of the Peace may imprison for up to six months or levy a fine of up to £2000. This latter court represents the sinews of the judicial system.

Another fundamental aspect of the judicial structure is the judges themselves. For the most part the upper echelon of the judiciary has sought anonymity. Public opinion throughout the century has generally held the judiciary in high regard. Criticism of the judiciary, when it occurs, usually focuses on two points: class bias and judicial legislation. The first complaint is based partly on the procedure by which judges are chosen from the ranks of practicing barristers. Surveys of the social backgrounds of the judiciary have shown a strong similarity based on public school education, attendance at **Oxford** or **Cambridge**, and middle-class social origins. The English Bar itself represents an elite even within the **legal profession**. Such a class of judges, unconsciously or otherwise, could hardly fail to reflect the experiences of a lifetime. Yet, in many instances, judges have earned a reputation as "liberal" or "conservative" where the social background is almost identical. Throughout the twentieth century a debate has ensued about the extent to which a judge should, if ever, allow personal policy preferences to affect the process of rendering a decision. In theory judges do not make the law but rather take the extant law and apply the appropriate set of facts to arrive at a correct decision. This mechanical model fails on historical grounds because the common law until the nineteenth century was essentially a judge-made body of law. If taken literally, it would mean that judges possessed no discretion to alter the course of law in response to changing social circumstances. A decision not to change the law represents a policy preference just as clear as an attempt to create new law. The judge, beyond semantic quibbling, always engages in policy decisions of one sort or the other.

This enduring dilemma has become more important in the latter part of the twentieth century because the courts have had to address issues that reflect the changing nature of British society. On race relations, for example, the courts have had to interpret various statutes, including the first Race Relations Act (1965). The attempt to remove color discrimination has tested the limits of judicial ability to modify basic social attitudes. Additional legislation has tried to close the loopholes left by various statutes, but the power of the judiciary is limited. Within the constitutional framework of Great Britain, for example, there are restraints on the doctrine of judicial review. No court has the authority to rule an Act of Parliament unconstitutional; a court may only decide whether actions taken under the language of the statute have exceeded the parliamentary grant of those powers. It is to Parliament, not the courts, that the British citizen looks for redress of grievances.

Finally, some important practical elements of the law now exist outside the formal judicial structure. The most obvious example in this regard is plea bargaining, by which an accused person negotiates a lesser charge rather than face a trial that might entail more severe punishment in return for which the prosecution does not bear the expense and hazards of a trial. Mediation arrangements for conflict resolution outside the purview of the courts is another example of a nonlegal part of the judicial system. Despite some infamous examples of judicial complacency (the Birmingham Six, 1974–91, wrongly accused of an IRA bombing), the judicial system of Great Britain has on the whole continued to serve the country well.

Richard A. Cosgrove

Bibliography

Lee, Simon. *Judging Judges*. 1988.
Paterson, Alan. *The Law Lords*. 1982.
Roshier, Bob, and Harvey Teff. *Law and Society in England*. 1980.
Stevens, Robert B. *Law and Politics: The House of Lords as a Judicial Body, 1800–1976*. 1978.

Juvenile Delinquency

The law provides one way of defining juvenile delinquency: In England and Wales criminal responsibility begins at the age of ten. (Before 1964 it was eight.) A child of this age is considered to be capable of deliberate criminal intent and liable to legal punishment. Up to the age of eighteen, however, he or she is dealt with by special "youth courts." (Before the 1991 Criminal Justice Act, the cut-off point for juveniles was the seventeenth birthday, and they were tried in "juvenile courts.") Juveniles contribute substantially to the official statistics of crime. In 1984, for example, males aged ten to sixteen accounted for only 12 percent of the male population of England and Wales but for well over one-third of all males cautioned or successfully prosecuted for burglaries, thefts, and criminal damage ("vandalism"). There is a similar overrepresentation of juveniles among female offenders. The year-groups most prone to delinquency are those aged fifteen and sixteen who have left school or are close to doing so. Only the young-adult age group (aged seventeen to twenty) makes a more disproportionate contribution, especially to the graver offenses: It accounted for 8 percent of the male population in 1984, but for one-third of all males cautioned or successfully prosecuted for robberies, and close to one-third of those dealt with for personal violence.

To this catalog of juvenile delinquency, however, four telling annotations should be appended. The first is that self-report studies indicate that the great majority of young people commit delinquent acts at some time, but only a minority of these acts result in a court appearance. The second annotation is that the increase in recorded juvenile crime is due, in part, to the massive increase since the 1960s in the use of police caution (administered to both parents and juveniles at the police station). Intended as a way of diverting children from the juvenile courts, the caution has had the effect of bringing into the legal net a wider range of delinquent behavior. The police have cautioned youngsters whom previously they would have treated informally. Third, despite the belief that delinquents are destined to a life of crime, delinquency constitutes a "passing phase." Most delinquents cease to appear in court once they enter their twenties, due perhaps to the influence of marriage and parenthood, or of involvement in lawful occupations and recreations. And, finally, official statistics suggest that offending by juveniles, in relation to their numbers, is decreasing, due possibly to an even greater incidence of cautions relative to prosecutions (and thus greater diversion from the juvenile court), and to more diversion from custody in young-offender institutions.

It is a staple of contemporary political discourse that delinquency is the product of moral decline brought about by the permissive society.

The historian is hard pressed, however, to discover a time when delinquency was not a cause of public anxiety. Today's soccer hooligans were anticipated by Mods and Rockers disturbing the Bank Holiday calm at seaside resorts in the mid-1960s; or by Teddy Boys destroying cinema seats to the sound of "Rock around the Clock" in the early 1950s. Between the wars chief constables and magistrates laid the blame for an increase in recorded delinquency on parental neglect, "Americanized" entertainment, and over-lenient juvenile courts. In the Edwardian years it was gangs of "hooligans," city-bred youth employed in "dead-end" jobs, that aroused public anxiety. Thus, crime fears or "moral panics" have frequently punctuated the history of delinquency, created by different anxieties, from fear over national decline in the Edwardian era to the financial and cultural independence of post-war youth.

Proportional to the anxiety delinquents have caused is the volume of literature attempting to explain the rise in delinquency, especially since the mid-1950s. Leslie Wilkins, one of the first to explore the phenomenon of rising crime in *Delinquent Generations* (1960), argued that the generation of children growing up during the Second World War, when fathers were abroad, mothers working, and the school system disrupted, had a greater tendency to commit offenses. The main flaw in the argument is that the cohorts of children born after the war were even more delinquent. The most dominant explanation of delinquency, however, has been that of the so-called "reformists" (sociologists, psychologists, and makers of social policy), who claim that youngsters who live in areas of urban decay or on vast housing estates, victims of poverty, broken homes and bad **housing**, will almost invariably become involved in delinquent activities. This interpretation of delinquency, moreover, inspired the legislation of 1933 and 1969, which made the young offender's welfare the prime consideration of juvenile justice.

A more down-to-earth explanation of the rise in delinquency has been advanced in recent years, one that links it to increased opportunities: a huge increase in the number of motor vehicles; an enormous expansion of self-service shops. Since the 1970s, however, the criminologists' focus has shifted from the origins of delinquency to the social and legal processes by which some individuals get "labeled" as delinquent. Their argument is that the reactions of the **police** and the juvenile courts, at times exacerbated by **press** and public fears, confirm and amplify an offender's deviance. As such, delinquency is not an inherent property of an individual but a property conferred by society.

Victor Bailey

Bibliography

Bailey, Victor. *Delinquency and Citizenship: Reclaiming the Young Offender, 1914–1948.* 1987.

Burt, Cyril. *The Young Delinquent.* 1925.

Cohen, Stanley. *Moral Panics and Folk Devils: The Creation of the Mods and Rockers.* 1972.

Pearson, Geoffrey. *Hooligan: A History of Respectable Fears.* 1983.

Rutter, Michael, and Henri Giller. *Juvenile Delinquency: Trends and Perspectives.* 1983.

J

K

Keynes, John Maynard (1883–1946)

John Maynard Keynes influenced twentieth-century Britain on three levels. First, as a publicist, he presented the classic critique of the Versailles peace settlement and later emerged as a spokesman for radical changes in British economic policy between the wars. Second, as a public servant, he exercised influence on British government policy from the time of his attachment to the Treasury during the First World War, and during the Second World War had an official responsibility for restructuring international financial relations. He was created Baron Keynes of Tilton in 1942. Third, as an academic economist, he wrote *The General Theory of Employment, Interest, and Money* (1936), which challenged the theoretical assumption that the economy was, in principle, self-correcting. All three roles helped establish "Keynesianism" as a doctrine of demand management by the state, aimed at maintaining full employment.

Keynes was born into an intellectual aristocracy clustered around the **University of Cambridge**. At King's College, Cambridge, he gained a first-class degree in mathematics in 1905—twelfth in the rank order of his class—a good but not brilliant result. As an undergraduate he was President of both the Liberal Club and the students' debating society (the Cambridge Union), with a well-formed aptitude for political controversy, especially on the side of free trade. He was also a member of the select society known as the **Apostles**, several of whom became the core of the **Bloomsbury Group**. Keynes' close friendship with such figures as the writer **Lytton Strachey** and the painter **Duncan Grant** was reinforced by their **homosexuality**.

It was as a protegé of Alfred Marshall that Keynes became an economist. His strictly academic research was initially in the field of probability. The full significance of his work here has only recently been appreciated, not least in providing a ground for knowledge that fell short of certainty yet was still rational. Such concepts resurfaced in the economic theories of his mature years. Keynes' attitude toward **economics** was somewhat ambivalent. He never held a university chair of economics, and no one was less content to leave economics to the economists.

With Marshall's backing, Keynes became editor of the prestigious *Economic Journal* in 1911 as a young university teacher still under thirty. This was to be an important thread of professional continuity in an otherwise extraordinarily diverse career. Keynes had started work as a civil servant in the India Office in 1906 but returned to Cambridge two years later to teach economics. Already in 1913 he was combining his academic expertise with his administrative experience in sitting as a member of the Royal Commission on Indian Finance and Currency.

During the **First World War** he entered the Treasury and was soon entrusted with wide responsibility for the external finance of the war. His ability to handle these problems prepared him to assume a later role as an expert adviser, an insider who really understood the system. The paradox was that he provided the sinews of a war in which he did not fully believe and, in denouncing its aftermath, made an even bigger name for himself as an outsider and a critic.

Sent to the Versailles peace conference as the official representative of the Treasury, Keynes resigned in June 1919, dismayed by the heavy scale of **reparations** demanded from Germany. He was determined to expose the treaty's shortcomings. In *The Economic Consequences of the Peace* (1919), Keynes fused high moral passion with hard economic analysis and revealed, moreover, his striking distinction as a writer. The nub of his case was that reparations implied a transfer of wealth from poverty-stricken Germany in the form of real resources, which Germany could only generate by establishing an economic domination over the rest of Europe for which no one was prepared. The fulsome reception accorded to the book, which made its author a household name in educated circles on both sides of the Atlantic, gave Keynes a platform of which he made full use thereafter.

Though keeping his fellowship at King's, Keynes did not revert to full-time academic teaching and research after the war but divided his time between Cambridge and his house in Bloomsbury, where the cultural and business life of London, as well as politics, were open to him. He became a rich man through speculation, worth half a million pounds at the peak in 1936. He married the ballerina Lydia Lopokova in 1925, and they appear to have had a happy if childless marriage, sustained by a common interest in the arts, of which Keynes was a great patron. Indeed, he was later to play a vital role in enlisting government support for the arts through the formation of the **Arts Council of Great Britain**.

Although he was called on periodically by the government for expert advice over economic policy, Keynes found his view overruled in 1925 when he argued against an imminent return to the **gold standard** at the traditional parity of $4.86. The Chancellor of the Exchequer, **Winston Churchill**, bore the brunt of Keynes' public criticisms for doing "such a silly thing." Keynes maintained that, with an inappropriately high parity for sterling, the monetary mechanism would not, in fact, work smoothly to deflate domestic prices but would provoke **unemployment**. At this stage, however, Keynes did not doubt the (Marshallian) postulate that a market-clearing equilibrium would be established in the long run.

Keynes' most famous dictum—"In the long run we are all dead"—is customarily cited to show his irresponsibility. What Keynes meant when he proclaimed this in the 1920s was not that the future could be treated with feckless disregard, but that it was irresponsible for policymakers to close their eyes to the immediate impact of their actions. He wanted them to appreciate the consequences of big decisions, not to ignore them.

Keynes had already become actively involved in **Liberal Party** politics. From 1923 he was chairman of the weekly paper the *Nation* (later amalgamated with the *New Statesman*), which, under the editorship of Cambridge economist Hubert Henderson, pressed for a more radical policy stance. This brought Keynes into close cooperation with **David Lloyd George**, a man of dynamic and optimistic temperament like himself. Little wonder that he later endorsed the New Deal policies of Franklin D. Roosevelt, with his message to the American people that they had nothing to fear but fear itself. Keynes was the quintessential exponent of "can-do" economics.

When the Liberal Party entered the 1929 general election with a pledge to cut the high level of unemployment to "normal" proportions, Keynes was thus identified as a prominent partisan opponent of **Stanley Baldwin's Conservative** government and of the "Treasury view" that it espoused. There were certainly other arguments against public works on the grounds of feasibility, but in 1929 the Treasury view that public expenditure necessarily diverted resources from more productive uses by private enterprise was crucial. To counter it, Keynes and Henderson produced their famous pamphlet *Can Lloyd George Do It?* Public works, it suggested, notably a loan-financed scheme of road building, could stimulate a cumulative process of economic recovery. Essentially this was a plea for a bold state-led initiative, in the confident hope that, with spare capacity available, such a program would succeed in mobilizing idle resources.

The inconclusive election results, however, suggested that Keynes had failed to persuade "outside opinion" of the merits of the Liberal proposals, and a minority **Labour** government took office from 1929 to 1931. Keynes was now given a chance to influence "inside opinion" through his concurrent membership of the (Macmillan) Committee on Finance and Industry and the newly instituted Economic Advisory Council (especially its committee of economists, of which Keynes was Chairman). There is a well-known jibe, in circulation from as early as 1931, that among five economists you would find six opinions, two of them held by Keynes. His interventions in policy debates over the previous couple of years may have fostered this impression of inconsistency. After all, he had advocated public works in 1929 in his pamphlet *Can Lloyd George Do It?* Yet he published an academic book, *A Treatise on Money* (1930), in which he stated that cheap money was the real solution. Then again, he outlined no less than seven remedies for unemployment, including both public works and cheap money, in testimony to the Macmillan Committee at the beginning of 1930. And later that year he moved toward the option of tariffs. But all of these different remedies were congruent and, in fact, were based upon a common analysis of the *Treatise*.

The novelty of *A Treatise on Money* was to repudiate the identity of investment and saving. Instead, it talked of enterprise and thrift as different processes controlled by different people—albeit in theory brought into equilibrium by the adjusting mechanism of the interest rate. With cheap money, enterprise could be relied upon to do the trick. But, he contended, cheap money was not on offer so long as the bank rate had to be kept up in order to protect the high parity of sterling fixed under the gold standard. Thus, given these rigidities in the real world, Keynes was ready to outline the case for a number of unorthodox policy expedients and joined forces with others who were prepared to consider appropriate action.

He supported the proposals put forward by Sir **Oswald Mosley**, then a minister in the Labour government, for state development programs. By 1931, however, such proposals were marginalized, as the government became caught in a mounting financial and political crisis that threatened the pound sterling on the foreign exchanges. Only when the position seemed untenable did Keynes opt for devaluation, though he was relieved when the new National government found itself forced off gold in September 1931.

After 1931 Keynes severed many of his direct political connections and, with an unaccustomed single-mindedness, devoted his energies to economic theory. Within a surprisingly short time he had stepped outside the analytical framework of the *Treatise* and was arguing his new theory of effective demand. He was crucially stimulated at this point by the "Circus" of younger economists at Cambridge, especially the ideas of R.F. Kahn and J.E. Meade, suggesting a fresh approach to the problem of saving and investment. Instead of investment

depending upon prior saving—the orthodox assumption—savings were seen as being generated by an initial act of investment through a process that multiplied income, output, and employment.

Thus, saving and investment were brought into equality by the equilibrating mechanism of changes in income or output. It followed that equilibrium might be reached while output was still below full capacity or full employment. It followed, too, that changes in output were now assigned the equilibrating task that was fulfilled under orthodox theory (including the *Treatise*) by changes in the interest rate. What role, then, did interest play? Keynes proceeded to explain interest in terms of "liquidity preference"—the premium that wealth-holders exacted for tying up their resources in ways that sacrificed the liquid advantages of holding cash.

The *General Theory* thus gave a wholly new account of how the economy worked—or failed to work. No longer did Keynes point to particular rigidities in the real world as the crucial reason why prices were prevented from making efficacious adjustments that would clear the market. He argued now that reductions in wages or interest rates, even if forthcoming, might simply be incapable of restoring full employment, which was a function of effective demand—that is, of prospective consumption plus investment.

Keynes claimed that his theory would "revolutionise the way the world thinks about economic problems"; but he acknowledged that it would necessarily be infused with political considerations in the process. The *General Theory* itself was largely silent on policy. Keynes, moreover, was fairly tentative in his subsequent practical recommendations, well aware that bottlenecks in production constrained the full use of resources and reluctant to advance a practicable target for "full employment" above a level of 95 percent.

It was only with the **Second World War** that Keynes' ideas gained widespread acceptance. In 1940 he was invited back into the Treasury, where he served as a top-level adviser for the rest of his life. A macroeconomic approach—designed to contain inflation by restraining demand for finite resources rather than simply to raise revenue—became the basis of the 1941 budget in Britain. Conversely, the feasibility of maintaining full employment after the war was proclaimed in the government's White Paper of 1944. But Keynes' own attention was increasingly consumed by planning for the post-war international economy, seeking new means of discharging the functions of the historic gold standard.

Keynes played a large part at the Bretton Woods conference (1944), which helped set up the International Monetary Fund and the World Bank. In contrast to his advocacy of tariffs in the conditions of the 1930s, he now reverted to fundamentally Liberal trade policies. His abilities as a negotiator were put to a supreme test at the end of the war when American support for Britain under the **Lend-Lease** agreement was abruptly terminated. Keynes was largely responsible for securing a large dollar loan from the United States and **Canada** to tide Britain over the transition to peace. It was an arrangement that he recognized as at once imperfect and necessary—a case he made with telling effect in the **House of Lords** in December 1945. There can be little doubt that these wearisome transatlantic negotiations taxed Keynes' strength—he had suffered a major heart attack in 1937—and he died suddenly at Easter 1946, just before the Order of Merit, Britain's highest honor, could be conferred.

The thirty-year boom in the world economy after his death boosted Keynes' own stock to dizzy heights; conversely, the subsequent rise of **Thatcherism** in Britain and of "Reaganomics" in the United States represented the explicit repudiation of a Keynesian approach to economic problems. Yet his own theoretical insights, which continue to fascinate scholars around the world, can hardly be dismissed as ephemeral. The *General Theory* may not offer an infallible way to conquer unemployment, still less inflation, but it remains the central pillar of Keynes' reputation as the most influential economist of the twentieth century.

Peter Clarke

Bibliography

Clarke, Peter. *The Keynesian Revolution in the Making, 1924–36.* 1988.

Harrod, R.F. *The Life of John Maynard Keynes.* 1951.

Hession, Charles H. *John Maynard Keynes.* 1984.

Moggridge, D.E. *Maynard Keynes: An Economist's Biography.* 1992.

Skidelsky, Robert. *John Maynard Keynes: Hopes Betrayed, 1883–1920.* 1983.

———. *John Maynard Keynes: The Economist as Saviour, 1920–1937.* 1992.

Kinnock, Neil Gordon (1942–)

Born into a working-class family in the largely pro-Labour community of Tredegar, South Wales, Neil Kinnock was leader of the **Labour Party** and of the opposition from 1983 to 1992. He was educated at University College, Cardiff, where his academic record was undistinguished, his political passion and ambition evident. There he met his future wife, Glenys Parry, who held strong left-wing views and became a substantial, sustaining influence. His career has been entirely within the Labour Party; he was elected MP for Bedwellty in 1970 and held the seat until 1994 when he was named a European Commissioner. A combative but often popular figure, Kinnock rebelled against the party leadership on many occasions but disassociated himself from the "hard Left." He was elected to the party's National Executive Committee in 1978 and became its education spokes-man in 1979. His rapid rise to the party leadership owed something to the patronage of **Michael Foot**, its leader from 1980, and much to the agility with which he picked his way through the minefield of bitter party conflicts at a time when Labour was both polarized and dispirited.

Kinnock succeeded Foot after Labour's disastrous 1983 election campaign. The party was at a low ebb: Institutionally archaic and cumbersome, it was challenged from within by a growing left wing that alarmed many voters, from without by the rise of the **Social Democratic Party/Liberal** alliance and by the need to adapt to demographic, economic, and social changes that had eroded its traditional working-class base. Its savage internal struggles at times suggested the death throes of a party committing political suicide. Kinnock attempted to unify and modernize the party, with energy, nerve, and some degree of skill and success. Before the 1987 election he launched a strong attack on the Trotskyist **Militant** group, which was burrowing into the party. Organizational reforms proceeded, if unevenly, and the 1987 election campaign saw greatly improved logistics and use of the media. It did not, however, bring victory. Kinnock launched a comprehensive policy review. While critics accused him of excessive flexibility, supporters admired his determination to rehabilitate Labour as a convincing alternative party of government. Under his leadership the party abandoned earlier unpopular positions, preferring managed market capitalism to extensive public ownership, stressing growth more than redistribution, accepting membership in the **European Community**, rejecting unilateral nuclear disarmament, and attempting to see voters as citizens and consumers rather than as foot soldiers in a class struggle.

Although Kinnock dragged the party back from the precipice of 1983, he was unable to overcome popular distrust of his own capacities. Hampered by his inexperience of government, he also suffered from a largely hostile **press**; most of the tabloid newspapers caricatured him as a verbose lightweight who had disguised rather than adapted his socialist views. After the 1992 election returned a fourth consecutive **Conservative** government, Kinnock resigned the Labour leadership. It is ironic that while his handling of the party's flaws and divisions was vital to its survival, he was too clearly associated with its most troubled times to escape their shadow.

Steven Reilly

Bibliography

Harris, Robert. *The Making of Neil Kinnock*. 1984.
Hughes, Colin, and Patrick Wintour. *Labour Rebuilt: The New Model Party*. 1990.
Morgan, Kenneth O. *Labour People: Leaders and Lieutenants*. 1987.

Kipling, (Joseph) Rudyard (1865–1936)

Rudyard Kipling, British poet, short-story writer, and novelist, born in India, is still known primarily as the poet of the British Empire, the author of "The White Man's Burden" (1899), as well as of *The Jungle Book* (1894), *Stalky and Company* (1899), *Kim* (1901), and *Departmental Ditties* (1886) and *Barrack Room Ballads* (1892). Kipling is also identified with a nostalgia for the Anglo-India of his young manhood, brought to the screen through Hollywood film adaptations of *Gunga Din* (1939), *Wee Willie Winkie* (1937), *Kim* (1950), and *The Man Who Would Be King* (1975). In addition to his literary significance, acknowledged in the award of the Nobel Prize for Literature in 1907, Kipling's vigorous **imperialism** and antidemocratic propaganda made him an important figure in twentieth-century British social and political history.

As with many British children born in India, he was sent to England to attend boarding school, where bullying and brutality, vividly described in *Stalky and Company*, made his childhood one of unhappy memories. Returning to India in 1882, Kipling became a journalist for the *Civil and Military Gazette*, a Lahore newspaper, and later for the more-prestigious *Allahabad Pioneer*, where he could indulge his passion for short-story writing. In *Plain Tales from the Hills* (1888) Kipling combined insights into Anglo-Indian society with fascinated appreciation for the cultured diversity of Indian life. Kipling's light, vernacular, and slangy verses from this period describe and celebrate the pathos of the ordinary British soldier doing his duty for Queen, country, and British civilization. "*Gunga Din,*" "*Fuzzy Wuzzy,*" "*Tommy,*" "*Danny Deever,*" and "*Mandalay*" are all poems in this celebratory mode. Kipling became increasingly popular after 1890, notwithstanding personal travails. The novel *The Light That Failed* (1890) was regarded as a failure, partly because readers objected to its English setting and to its pessimism about the success of Empire. In 1892, while on honeymoon with his new American wife, the former Caroline Balestier, in Japan, Kipling was ruined financially by a bank collapse. He then decided to live in his wife's home at Brattleboro, Vermont, until he could recoup his losses. While in Vermont Kipling produced the two popular *Jungle Books* (1894–5) that have made him famous with children to this day. Kipling continued to produce copious distinguished stories after 1900, but he increasingly became identified with an aggressive, muscular brand of imperialism. He also developed close relationships with Cecil Rhodes, the South African diamond tycoon and advocate of British expansion, and with Theodore Roosevelt, the energetic champion of the "strenuous life" and of American expansion overseas. The poem "The White Man's Burden" was written to encourage the United States to assume a colonizing destiny in the Philippines. The United States finally disillusioned Kipling, who viewed Americans as strangers to the British imperial ethos.

Just before the First World War, Kipling's extreme imperialist and conservative views marginalized him as a British man of letters. During the war, as before, Kipling was virulently anti-German, spurred by the loss of his son in combat. Thereafter he remained an unreconstructed believer in the British Empire, incapable of adjusting to Commonwealth notions that had begun to emerge. But from the start of his writing career Kipling had always

K

mixed criticism of British society and imperialism alongside of his advocacy. His later stories, such as *Debits and Credits* (1926), show considerable ideological and political complexity. Moreover, the mature Kipling's artistry does not falter. His stories brilliantly experiment with forms of ambiguity, ellipsis, and condensation in a way characteristic of modernist literary art—irrespective of the political persuasions of the artist.

Richard A. Voeltz

Bibliography

Carrington, Charles. *Rudyard Kipling*. 1955.
Mason, Philip. *Kipling: The Glass, The Shadow, and the Fire*. 1975.
Moore-Gilbert, B.J. *Kipling and "Orientalism."* 1986.
Wilson, Angus. *The Strange Ride of Rudyard Kipling*. 1977.

Kitaj, R(onald) B(rooks) (1932–)

R.B. Kitaj's central position in the British art world is due as much to the intellectual force of his often polemical stances as to the considerable originality of his work. It is as a champion of narrative content and high seriousness of subject matter in painting that he is held in special regard, but he is also credited with a central role in the resurgence of figuration and life drawing in recent British art.

Born Ronald Brooks in 1932 in Cleveland, Ohio, he took his stepfather's name when in 1941 his mother remarried a Viennese refugee, Dr. Walter Kitaj. Prophetically, he gained a family link with the dislocated **Jewish** intelligentsia whose broken lives would come to haunt his pictures. In the 1950s he traveled the world as a merchant seaman and serviceman, studying art in Vienna and France before enrolling at the Ruskin School, **Oxford**.

At the Royal College of Art in London he became the leader of a remarkable group of students that included **David Hockney**, Allen Jones, Patrick Caulfield, and other important figures in British pop art. Kitaj was soon compared to **T.S. Eliot** and Ezra Pound, sharing as he did these fellow expatriates' ability to mobilize artists around causes and styles. His own allegiance to pop was marginal, however, as his interests in collage and appropriation had more to do with surrealist collage and political art. Kitaj has a great love of quotation, fragmentation, and playful obscurantism, particularly of

learned and "highbrow" sources, another disqualifying factor in relation to pop art. His works often related to Continental literature or left-wing politics, prompting a formalist critic to describe his pictures as "littered with ideas." He felt a special identification with the German-Jewish literary critic Walter Benjamin, whom he adopted as a painterly alter ego in his seminal picture, *The Autumn of Central Paris (After Walter Benjamin)* (1972–74).

But just as Kitaj was a scourge of formal abstraction in the 1960s, in the next decade he pitted his reputation against excessive conceptualism, becoming a strong advocate of life drawing when this activity was held in widespread derision by avant-garde artists. A personal crisis—the suicide of his first wife in 1969—prompted a period of spiritual and artistic introspection. He was first able to take up work again through life drawing, encouraged to make a remarkable group of pastels by his new wife, the American realist painter Sandra Fisher. Soon he adopted drawing as a crusading cause, issuing a "call to order" in the form of a drawings exhibition curated for the **Arts Council of Great Britain**, *The Human Clay* (1976), held at the Hayward Gallery. It was in the catalog of this exhibition that Kitaj identified "a School of London," a term that would be taken up to refer to expressive figurative artists such as **Francis Bacon**, Frank Auerbach, Leon Kossoff, and **Lucian Freud**, a group with which Kitaj himself came to be identified.

At the same time of his new interest in drawing, he underwent a "return" to his Jewish roots, which would inform the central subjects of his mature pictures. The Holocaust theme dominated his solo exhibition in 1985, which he entitled *A Passion*, incorporating a chimney motif in lieu of a cross as the emblem of a Jewish passion. Typically for Kitaj, earlier pictures were hung in such a way as to make new sense in the context of the later development of his art: *If Not, Not* (1975–6), a painting originally commissioned for the new British Library and based on Eliot's *The Waste Land*, also relates to the Holocaust theme, with the gates of Buchenwald depicted in one corner. In 1989 he published the highly idiosyncratic *First Diasporist Manifesto*, in which he sought to define his Jewish preoccupations and painterly interests, a text in every way as obtuse and forbidding as the paintings it set out to illuminate. Few new works since 1984 have been exhibited, being saved, instead, for a major museum retrospective tour in London, New York, and Los Angeles in 1994–5.

David Cohen

Bibliography

Ashbery, John, et al. *Kitaj: Paintings, Drawings, Pastels*. 1983.

Livingstone, Marco. *R.B. Kitaj*. 1985.

Morphet, Richard, ed. *R.B. Kitaj: A Retrospective*. 1994.

Kitchener, Horatio Herbert (1850–1916)

Promoted to Field Marshal in 1909 and given an earldom in 1914 after serving as Commander-in-Chief in South Africa (1900–2) and India (1902–9), Horatio Herbert Kitchener was Secretary of State for War from 5 August 1914 until his death on 5 June 1916. In this capacity he expanded the existing military forces into a mass citizen **army**—the biggest in the country's history—enabling Britain to play an increasingly weighty part in the land campaigns of the **First World War**, particularly on the Western Front.

Born near Listowel in County Kerry on 24 January 1850, Kitchener passed out of the Royal Military Academy, Woolwich, in December 1870. He was then commissioned into the Royal Engineers, spending much of his early service in the Middle East and taking up a post in the Egyptian army in 1882. Apart from a period as Governor-General of the Eastern Sudan (1886–8), he remained with the Egyptian army for most of the next sixteen years, being appointed its Adjutant-General in 1888 and *Sirdar*, or Commander-in-Chief, in 1892. This phase of his military career reached its peak in the reconquest of the Sudan and the victory at Omdurman in 1898, achievements that established Kitchener as a national hero.

In December 1899, following British reverses in the **Boer War**, Kitchener was sent to **South Africa** as chief of staff to Lord Roberts (1832–1914), succeeding the latter as Commander-in-Chief in November 1900. His reply to Boer guerilla tactics was to set up lines of blockhouses from which drives by mounted troops were launched, and if, as in the Sudan, his success owed more to his organizational ability than battlefield flair, Kitchener's attrition policy eventually wore down Boer resistance. He provoked considerable outrage by introducing civilian concentration camps, but he adopted a conciliatory stance in the peace settlement of May 1902. From 1902 to 1909 Kitchener held the coveted post of Commander-in-Chief, India. He was soon involved in a prolonged dispute with the Viceroy, **Lord Curzon**, over the system of dual control whereby the military member of the Viceroy's Council exerted an influence that rivaled that of the Commander-in-Chief. Curzon's resignation in 1905 both reaffirmed the authority of the Commander-in-Chief and further enhanced Kitchener's personal prestige. Kitchener also began to reform the Indian army in several other respects, modernizing training, founding a staff college, improving mobilization machinery and instituting standardized corps and divisions to deal mainly with external threats rather than internal security problems. On his departure from India, Kitchener toured the Far East, Australasia, and the United States, advising the **Australian** and **New Zealand** governments on defense matters, before returning to Egypt, in 1911, as British Agent and Consul General. His benevolent yet autocratic rule there in the ensuing three years stifled political progress, but he developed Egypt's economic infrastructure and pushed through various social reforms protecting peasants against vested interest groups.

Home on leave at the outbreak of the First World War, a reluctant Kitchener was persuaded by the Prime Minister, **H.H. Asquith**, to accept the post of Secretary of State for War. Despite his ignorance of domestic conditions, Kitchener, like **Douglas Haig**, was one of the few leading British soldiers or statesmen to foresee that the war would be long and costly. Aiming to build an army large enough for Britain to assume a major role at the decisive stage of the war, he raised nearly 2.5 million recruits by voluntary methods in less than seventeen months, making it possible for Britain to place more than seventy divisions in the field during the conflict. In the absence of a government plan for the corresponding mobilization of manufacturing resources, Kitchener's achievements in expanding munitions output in the early months were also impressive. However, indiscriminate recruiting removed many skilled workers from the factories, and this, coupled with Kitchener's hostility to outside inference in War Office affairs, hindered the efforts of industry to respond quickly and fully to the new demands. Thus, while he undoubtedly laid the foundations for the spectacular production figures of later years, he was savagely attacked in May 1915 for the shell shortages afflicting the

British Expeditionary Force in France. With the creation of the **Ministry of Munitions** under **David Lloyd George**, the War Office, by the end of 1915, was shorn of most of its powers in this sphere save those of fixing the army's needs in munitions and overseeing their distribution, since control of the Royal Ordnance Factories and of research and development had been transferred to the new ministry.

As Secretary of State for War Kitchener did not pioneer alternative strategic policies, retaining his belief in the primacy of the Western Front. He also understood the realities of coalition warfare, stressing the importance of arms supplies to Russia. Though he generally supported the idea of operations in the Dardanelles, he displayed irresolution throughout the actual campaign on **Gallipoli** in 1915. Similarly, as voluntary recruiting steadily declined in 1915, he failed to give a clear lead on the **conscription** issue, making it harder for the government to prepare adequate machinery for the systematic use of available manpower. Inarticulate and uncomfortable in **Cabinet** and political debate, Kitchener saw his influence in government circles wane further after military setbacks in France and the Dardanelles in the second half of 1915. In December of that year Lieutenant-General Sir William Robertson (1860–1933) took office as Chief of the Imperial General Staff (CIGS) on condition that the CIGS would henceforth be the principal source of advice to the Cabinet on military operations. Kitchener remained popular with the public but, by 1916, his authority was effectively limited to areas of War Office administration, supply, and recruiting. He drowned on 5 June 1916 when the HMS *Hampshire*, taking him on a mission to Russia, struck a mine off the Orkneys and sank. Nevertheless, the mass army Kitchener bequeathed to the nation contributed significantly to the ultimate Allied victory.

Peter Simkins

Bibliography

Arthur, George. *Life of Lord Kitchener*. 3 vols. 1920.

Cassar, George H. *Kitchener: Architect of Victory*. 1977.

Magnus, Philip. *Kitchener: Portrait of an Imperialist*. 1958.

Royle, Trevor. *The Kitchener Enigma*. 1985.

Simkins, Peter. *Kitchener's Army: The Raising of the New Armies, 1914–16*. 1988.

L

Labour Party

The Labour Party has experienced a rapid, if troubled, political ascendancy in the twentieth century. In 1924, after only eighteen years of formal existence, Labour formed its first minority government, replacing the **Liberal Party** as the main rival to the **Conservatives**. Labour has formed governments in 1924, 1929–31, 1945–51, 1964–70, and 1974–9. The third Labour government, which took power under **Clement Attlee** after the Second World War, is regarded as the single most important reforming ministry of the twentieth century, laying down the foundations of the post-war **welfare state** and the "mixed" economy. Despite these achievements, Labour has been plagued by internal tension throughout the century, which undermined its claim to power.

After the election of 1906 the **Labour Representation Committee** formally adopted the name Labour Party, electing **Keir Hardie** as its parliamentary Chairman. Initially, Labour proved an effective pressure group, but after 1907, the party seemed content to follow Liberal initiatives. By-elections between 1910 and 1914 do not show that Labour was gaining substantial ground against the Liberals among working-class voters. Trade unions were, however, affiliating in increasing numbers, lending the party financial security.

Though the party was divided over support for Britain's war effort in 1914, the **First World War** strengthened Labour's position. In May 1915 the party leader, **Arthur Henderson**, joined the **Cabinet** as President of the Board of Education, giving Labour its first taste of office. When **David Lloyd George** became Prime Minister in 1916, he confirmed Labour's place in government by including Henderson in a smaller War Cabinet and giving two other MPs ministerial posts. Henderson left the government in 1917 and, out of office, turned his energies toward the framing of a new constitution for Labour in close consultation with the major unions and with **Sidney Webb**. The new constitution—adopted formally in 1918—replaced a loose federal structure with a more centralized framework. The annual conference became the sole determinant of National Executive Committee (NEC) membership, a development that effectively shifted power to the unions. This was offset somewhat by the adoption of a socialist imperative in **Clause Four** of the party's objects, which committed the party to realize the "common ownership of the means of production." The socialist commitment was underlined by the adoption of Webb's *Labour and the New Social Order* (1918), a statement that laid down the future avenues of policy, including the establishment of a national minimum standard of living, the control of industry, educational reform, and the redistribution of wealth through taxation.

The 1918 constitution was Labour's declaration of independence from the Liberal Party, ideologically and structurally. The party, fighting the 1918 "Coupon Election"—the first under complete manhood suffrage—without any electoral pacts, saw limited gains in the number of seats won, but real growth in total votes, 2.3 million, an increase of almost 2 million. In the election of 1922 Labour increased its parliamentary strength markedly to 142 seats and improved its total poll to 4.2 million votes. The new party leader was **Ramsay MacDonald**, a charismatic figure intent upon broadening Labour's appeal to all classes. This search for respectability paid off in the election of December 1923, which left Labour with the second-highest number of seats in the Commons. When the Conservatives were defeated over the question of **tariff reform** in January 1924, Labour formed its first minority government. Its aim was simply to cope, having neither the power in Parliament nor a developed vision of a socialist program. There were modest successes in foreign policy and in **housing**, but, otherwise, Labour concentrated upon governing without undue humiliation. Though it lost the election of 1924, it had, by its experience of government, further discredited the Liberal Party as a viable political alternative.

The election of May 1929 saw Labour returned to power, again with a minority government. It won 288 seats and 8.3 million votes, 39.3 percent of the votes cast. The major problem for the new government was its lack of an alternative economic policy in the face of deepening crisis. Like the Conservatives, Labour remained committed to financial orthodoxy, based upon balanced budgets, the **gold standard**, and *laissez-faire*. Within the party, there was much disquiet at the lack of socialist direction in the government. The Depression of 1931 forced the question. At the prompting of American banks and the all-party May committee of inquiry, MacDonald and his Chancellor of the Exchequer, **Philip Snowden**, recommended a reduction in government expenditure in the summer of 1931, including a 10 percent decrease in the rate of **unemployment** benefits. The unions and many of the Cabinet balked at supporting such proposals. Faced with irreconcilable divisions, MacDonald formed a National government with the Conservatives and Liberals in August 1931. Snowden, **J.H. Thomas**, and a handful of lesser Labour politicians joined MacDonald as the National Labour contingent in the government. Criticized by both their traditional opponents and their former leaders, and facing a powerful cry for national unity, Labour suffered a catastrophic defeat in the election of October 1931, with its parliamentary strength reduced to fifty-two seats and its more prominent leaders losing their seats.

Following the 1931 debacle much closer cooperation between the party and the trade union movement was established, formalized in a reinvigorated National Council of Labour. There was also greater emphasis upon devising a distinctive socialist approach to the economy. Under the aegis of **Hugh Dalton** and **Herbert Morrison**, proponents of planning put together a credible program of economic action based upon centralized economic planning and **nationalization**, an approach best expressed in the statements *For Socialism and Peace* (1934) and *Labour's Immediate Programme* (1937). The 1930s also saw a major shift in Labour's international policy, which moved from pacifist internationalism to support for rearmament by the late 1930s. The 1935 election marked a slight improvement in Labour's fortunes: It increased its parliamentary ranks to 154, and Attlee succeeded to the leadership.

The **Second World War** proved to be a turning point for Labour. The party, which played a major role in the downfall of **Neville Chamberlain** in May 1940, joined the coalition of **Winston Churchill**. Despite its relatively small numbers in the Commons, Labour was given a disproportionate number of places in the government. Attlee, Arthur Greenwood (1880–1954), Morrison, and the trade unionist **Ernest Bevin** were Cabinet members for all or part of the war.

War also encouraged a movement to the Left in public opinion. By 1943, opinion polls were pointing toward a substantial Labour lead over the Conservatives. The election of 26 July 1945 represents the zenith of Labour's fortunes. It captured 393 seats, a majority of 146 over all other parties, on a total poll of 11.9 million votes.

The 1945–50 Labour government was certainly one of the strongest of the century, including Attlee as Prime Minister, Bevin at the Foreign Office, Morrison as Lord President, **Stafford Cripps** at the Board of Trade, Dalton as Chancellor of the Exchequer, and **Aneurin Bevan** at the Ministry of Health. The problems facing the new government were enormous, both at home and abroad, but despite such constraints, Attlee and his ministers enjoyed much initial success, particularly in domestic policy. Between 1945 and 1948 the pillars of the welfare state and the mixed economy were erected. The National Insurance, National Assistance, and **National Health Service** (NHS) Acts were passed in 1946, the first two realizing many of the aims of the **Beveridge** Report, the last promising free and universal health care. In addition, a substantial program of nationalization was enacted: the Bank of England (1946), **coal** (1946), civil aviation (1946), cable and wireless (1946), inland transport (1948), gas (1948), and iron and **steel** (1949). By the end of the decade fully 20 percent of the economy was in the public sector.

The government stumbled in 1947 into a series of economic crises, beginning with a coal shortage that contributed to export and currency crises just at the time sterling was scheduled to become convertible according to the terms of the American loan of 1946. The economic crises undermined government confidence and unity. On the international front, Bevin was at first unsuccessful in his attempts to involve the United States in an alliance against the Soviet Union, although by 1947 the American leaders had become convinced of the Soviet threat. Due in large part to Bevin, the North Atlantic Treaty Organization was established in 1949. Britain's atomic relationship with America was less successful, prompting the Labour government to proceed with the manufacture of a British bomb at great cost. Within the Empire, significant strides were made toward **decolonization**, beginning with the concession of independence to India in August 1947.

In February 1950 Labour was returned with a majority of only six seats in the general election. By this time Attlee, Cripps, and Bevin were all in failing health. The government was also sapped by internal divisions within the leadership and the Parliamentary Labour Party. The most serious split was between the new Chancellor of the Exchequer, **Hugh Gaitskell**, and Bevan over budget proposals to impose charges in the NHS, in part to cover rising defense expenditure. In January 1951 Bevan, **Harold Wilson**, and John Freeman resigned over this issue. In the October election Labour polled the highest total vote in political history (13.9 million votes), but the Tories were returned with a majority of sixteen seats.

The party's spell in opposition was to last thirteen years. In the 1950s Labour was plagued by further divisions over strategy, foreign policy, ideology, and leadership. The first splits emerged in the Parliamentary Labour Party, where the "Bevanite" wing became increasingly fractious especially over foreign policy issues. Bevanism gained considerable influence on the National Executive Committee and in the constituencies, while at the same time the right wing of the party was beginning to coalesce around the parliamentary leadership of Attlee, Gaitskell, and Morrison, and around such new thinkers as **Anthony Crosland**. Party disunity did not help Labour's electoral fortunes. In May 1955 an election was called, at which Labour's parliamentary strength fell from 295 to 277. After Attlee retired in December 1955, Gaitskell scored a first ballot victory over Bevan and Morrison to become leader.

Despite a rapprochement between Gaitskell and Bevan, lack of political success persisted into the late 1950s. The question of **nuclear weapons** opened up further divisions between a pro-nuclear leadership and a large activist movement within the party centered on the **Campaign for Nuclear Disarmament**. There was also a growing breach between the Left and the Right over domestic policy, focusing in particular on the question of nationalization. The 1959 election was another blow; the party lost further ground to the Conservatives, generating discussion about decline in Labour support not only from middle-class supporters, but also from its traditional working-class base. Desperate to modernize the party's image and reinvigorate its popular appeal, Gaitskell attempted to eliminate the commitment to public ownership from the constitution, an initiative that was defeated at the 1959 party conference. A year later, the leader was defeated again, this time over nuclear weapons, when the conference endorsed unilateral disarmament. By 1961 Gaitskell was, however, able to secure the reversal of the unilateralist decision at the party conference.

Success for Labour came only as the British economy faltered in the early 1960s. In January 1963 Gaitskell, who died of a rare viral infection, was succeeded by Harold Wilson. The election of October 1964 gave Labour a slim majority of four seats over the Conservatives and the Liberals. The Labour Cabinet of 1964 started out with determination, abolishing prescription charges in the National Health Service, moving toward industrial reform with the National Board for Prices and Incomes, and shoring up Britain's economic health with a five-year plan committed to 25 percent growth in the gross national product (GNP) by the end of the decade. Wilson's call for an election for March 1966 resulted in a resounding personal triumph. Labour won 363 seats, with 48.7 percent of the vote.

Despite its substantial parliamentary majority, the 1966–70 government faced disunity and declining popularity, largely as a result of economic problems. Wilson's ministry dithered over the balance-of-payments problems, aban-

Labour Party Annual Conference in Brighton in 1971. Harold Wilson is second from left; James Callaghan, second from right.

doning any pretense of long-term planning. Confronted with inflationary wage pressures and growing union militancy, it failed to find a credible industrial policy, yielding instead to union demands. In the foreign sphere, it was unable to prevent the accession to power of a racist white-minority government in Rhodesia in 1966 and muted its criticism of American policy in Viet Nam. Yet, Britain became a more liberal society through the reforms of Home Secretary Roy Jenkins (1920–); education and the arts were vastly expanded with the advent of **new universities** and the expansion of comprehensive schools; and housing was increased significantly. By 1969–70 the government was regaining popularity. With favorable opinion polls, Wilson called an election in June 1970, but the Conservatives were elected with a thirty-seat majority.

During the period of opposition between 1970 and 1974 there was some rebuilding of links within the party, such as the establishment of the Trades Union Congress (TUC)-Labour Party Liaison Committee and its promised "social contract" between any future Labour government and the unions. But other issues of the early 1970s simply widened divisions for Labour. Britain's entry into the **European Community** proved divisive. The NEC, the Left, and the unions opposed entry, while a significant proportion of the Parliamentary Party, mostly centrists and right-wingers, were in favor. Within the party there was a burgeoning movement for constituency control over the election manifesto, the election of the leader, and the de-selection of local MPs, organized by the Campaign for Labour Party Democracy.

The two elections of 1974 returned Labour to power, first with a minority government, then, in October, with a small majority. The impression was again one of division and failure. The Cabinet was generally drawn from the Right, while the party outside Westminster was dominated by the Left. Even within the Parliamentary Party, there were organized factions, the Tribune group of the Left and the Manifesto group of the Right, which were divided over foreign and domestic issues. In March 1976 Wilson resigned unexpectedly and was succeeded by **James Callaghan**. Through 1976 and 1977 the party was further weakened. The $3 billion International Monetary Fund loan of 1976 raised the specter of 1931 and provoked much opposition. By 1977 the party had declined in parliamentary strength and was forced to adopt the expedient of a more formal Lib-Lab pact, based on a Liberal-Labour Consultative Committee. The "winter of discontent," characterized by wide-ranging public-sector strikes, brought the government down in March 1979.

In opposition, Labour's long-simmering tensions boiled over. In October 1979 the Left succeeded in vesting control of the manifesto with the National Executive Committee and in making re-selection of sitting MPs mandatory. The following year the annual conference overturned the decision on the manifesto but decided that the election for the leadership would be made the responsibility of the party conference, not simply the Parliamentary Party. Callaghan resigned as leader following the conference and was succeeded by the veteran left-winger **Michael Foot**. In January 1981 a special conference set out the details of a new "electoral college" to elect the party leader: The unions would get 40 percent of the vote, the constituencies and Parliamentary Party 30 percent each. This was the last straw for some right-wing MPs, provoking the most serious split in the party since 1931. A group of prominent right-wingers broke from Labour and, later in the year, established the **Social Democratic Party**. In June 1983 Labour fought a disastrous general election, gaining only 28 percent of the vote, the worst result since the early 1920s. After the election Foot was replaced by **Neil Kinnock**, under whose leadership, Labour slowly, and often painfully, healed many of its divisions. Relations with the unions improved, despite the **miners' strike** of 1984–5, and Kinnock succeeded in both reducing the power of the Left within the party and in revitalizing policy. In 1987 and 1992 he ran effective, though unsuccessful, election campaigns. After the unexpected defeat of April 1992 Kinnock resigned immediately after the election, and John Smith (1938–94) was elected leader. He was succeeded in 1994 by Tony Blair (1953–). Since the demise of the Liberals, Labour has been the progressive alternative in British politics, but its ability to regain power is questioned.

Stephen Brooke

Bibliography

Cole, G.D.H. *A History of the Labour Party from 1914*. 1948.

Foote, Geoffrey. *The Labour Party's Political Thought*. 1985.

McKibbin, Ross. *The Evolution of the Labour Party, 1910–1924*. 1974.

Morgan, Kenneth O. *Labour People: Leaders and Lieutenants*. 1987.

Pelling, Henry. *A Short History of the Labour Party*. 10th ed. 1993.

Tanner, Duncan. *Political Change and the Labour Party, 1900–1918*. 1990.

Labour Representation Committee (1900–1906)

Established in London in February 1900 by a conference of trade unions, cooperative societies, and socialist groups, the Labour Representation Committee (LRC) resolved to work for a distinct labor group in Parliament with its own whips and policy, but ready to cooperate with any other party to promote legislation in the direct interests of labor. It was thus a triumph for the principle of independent labor representation in Parliament.

For some years endorsement of this principle had been urged on the **Trade Union Congress** (TUC) by socialists, notably those in the **Independent Labour Party** (ILP). In general the trade union leaders were **Liberal** in their political sympathies, and often antisocialist, but by 1899 there was widespread concern among trade unionists about the threat to their legal rights. Thus at the 1899 Congress a resolution was passed that paved the way for the conference at which the LRC was born; representatives of about one-quarter of the total trade union membership attended. Of those that affiliated to the LRC most were of the "New Unionism" variety; many of the older craft unions, and the large mining, engineering, and cotton workers' unions, remained aloof.

The LRC was formed as an exercise in political pragmatism. Its stated aims were designed not to alienate "Lib-Lab" trade union opinion. This implied no commitment to socialism; the Marxist Social Democratic Federation (SDF) failed to get its "class-war" message endorsed at the conference. The role of the ILP, by contrast, has been viewed as decisive by labor historians. The ILP leader, **Keir Hardie**, dominated the founding conference and was the main parliamentary spokesman after the general election of 1900; Hardie was returned with one other LRC candidate. **Ramsay Mac-Donald**, LRC secretary and ILPer, envisaged the LRC as a progressive development from radical Liberalism that bolstered the cause of social reconstruction, not as a mere pressure group.

In the LRC's short history before it was renamed the **Labour Party** in 1906, two developments were of particular historic significance. The first was the **Taff Vale judgment** of 1901, which rendered trade unions financially liable for damages caused through strike action, a decision that resulted in waves of union affiliations to the LRC. By 1905 the **Miners Federation of Great Britain** was the only significant body still outside it. In 1903 MacDonald entered into talks with the Liberal Chief Whip, Herbert Gladstone, about an electoral arrangement between the parties. This produced a "pact" that operated with remarkable success in the general election of 1906: In the Liberal landslide, 29 LRC candidates were returned.

The LRC has to be placed in the context of the debate on the emergence of class as the main determinant of political allegiance in British politics. It was an important manifestation of this development, although those historians who caution against the notion of an inevitable eclipse of the Liberals by Labour as the progressive class-based party would stress that its significance was limited.

Graham Walker

Bibliography
Bealey, Frank, and Henry Pelling. *Labour and Politics, 1900–1906: A History of the Labour Representation Committee.* 1958.
Poirier, Philip P. *The Advent of the Labour Party.* 1958.

Labour Research Department
The Labour Research Department (LRD) was, for a brief period of time, the major advisory, research, and information body to the **Labour Party** and the trade union movement in the years immediately following the First World War. However, its activities became redundant once the Labour Party and the **Trades Union Congress** (TUC) developed their own research structures.

The LRD was formed in 1918 out of the desire of both the Labour Party, led by **Arthur Henderson**, and some of the **Fabians**, led by **Sidney and Beatrice Webb**, to establish an information and research section for the Labour Party and the wider Labour cause. The Labour Party decided to provide the Fabian Research Department (FRD) with accommodation in its new party headquarters and provided it with £150 per annum for the issuing of a daily Labour news service. In return the FRD placed its documents and information at the disposal of the party, to assist its advisory committees with their work and to publish the annual Labour directories. The new LRD that emerged had a constitution that allowed individuals and institutions to be members and was organized into four sections: the trade union survey, the cooperative section, the trades councils and local Labour Party section, and the general section. The LRD captured substantial trade union support between 1918 and 1921. It issued the *Monthly Circular*, a diary of Labour events, a magazine, and a variety of publications, such as the Webbs' *History of Trade Unionism*. But the LRD was always in financial difficulties and was not always popular with trade unionists, who saw the various trade union schemes put forward by **G.D.H. Cole** and R. Page Arnot, who became a prominent Communist activist, as a potential challenge to their authority. In addition, the Trades Union Congress was set along a course of changing its structure. In the immediate post-war years **Ernest Bevin** proposed that there should be a general council with its own administrative department and a group of joint departments (research, legal, and publicity) shared with the Labour Party and the **Cooperative movement**. A special congress in December 1919 approved these recommendations and authorized the formation of a Trade Union Coordination Committee. Henderson and the Labour Party quickly adopted these ideas for joint committees and eventually formed the National Joint Council with the TUC on 12 July 1921. The decision of the LRD to accept £6,000 per year from Russia to finance an inquiry into the nature of capitalist industry appalled the Labour and trade union leaders. The uneasy relationship between the LRD and the Labour Party and trade union movement was at an end. By 1924 the LRD, due to its financial difficulties and the power of the trade unions within it, had been reorganized. With its independence gone, its leading socialist spirits left.

Keith Laybourn

Bibliography
McKibbin, Ross. *The Evolution of the Labour Party, 1910–1924.* 1974.

Labour Revisionism

Labour revisionism was an ideological tendency within the **Labour Party** that prevailed during the 1950s and early 1960s. Its principal aim was to reformulate socialist principles and to revise Labour policies through a new analysis of the changed social and economic conditions of post-1945 British society. First outlined in *New Fabian Essays* (1952), Labour revisionism was most thoroughly and coherently expressed in **Anthony Crosland**'s major work, *The Future of Socialism* (1956). The period from 1956 onward, following **Hugh Gaitskell**'s accession to the party leadership, witnessed its increasing prominence as a major ideological influence within the Labour Party. During those years revisionist ideas—particularly on public ownership and economic strategy—were widely propagated and incorporated into official party policy statements such as *Industry and Society* (1957).

Labour revisionism can be examined most clearly in the ideas and writings of two distinct but connected groups—first, the parliamentary friends and supporters of Hugh Gaitskell (who included Crosland, Douglas Jay, and Roy Jenkins); and second, the organization Socialist Union and its related periodical, *Socialist Commentary*. Revisionism conspicuously became a "Gaitskellite" position from 1956 to 1963, since the party leader was strongly committed to revisionist ideas. It was, however, Crosland rather than Gaitskell who provided the main intellectual thrust behind this new political movement.

The emergence of Labour revisionism in the early 1950s was an intellectual response to the completion of the **Attlee**-led Labour government's program in 1951 and to the party's subsequent election defeat. The body of ideas that gradually took shape during the 1950s involved two major deviations from accepted Labour orthodoxies. First, revisionism repudiated the traditional view that socialism could be adequately defined as, or at least identified with, the public ownership of the means of production. It thereby questioned the established Labour commitment to extensive public ownership as a precondition for achieving all major socialist objectives. Second, revisionism presented a distinctive ethical restatement of socialism—in terms of such values as personal liberty, social welfare, and equality. Particular emphasis was placed on the pursuit of equality, which revisionists argued, would involve a variety of fiscal and social policy measures, including redistributive taxation, educational reform, and expanded social services (to be financed through economic growth). Public ownership and **nationalization** were to be regarded merely as useful means for promoting socialist ends. Moreover, revisionists challenged traditional Labour opinion by insisting that such ends could be attained within the framework of a market-oriented mixed economy.

The intellectual justification for this demotion of public ownership was provided by Crosland's analysis, refined in *The Future of Socialism*, of changes within post-1945 capitalism. Crosland maintained that during that period capitalism had been transformed as a result of a threefold transfer of economic power—toward the state, organized labor, and salaried managers in private industry. In the post-capitalist society that had emerged from this process public ownership had become, in Crosland's view, a matter of declining importance.

Revisionists sharpened differences within the party over its identity, direction, and purpose. Ultimately, they even appeared to threaten the foundations of party unity—most perilously during Gaitskell's ill-fated attempt to amend **Clause Four** of the party constitution in 1959–60. Its effect was to provoke a confrontation with both the fundamentalists of the party's Left and the traditionalists of its Right and Center. The damaging consequences of this were contained only by a subtle compromise that involved, from the early 1960s, a partial reinstatement of public ownership in party policy and rhetoric.

By the time of Gaitskell's death in January 1963 revisionist positions—a more instrumental view of public ownership, support for egalitarian fiscal and social policies, and acceptance of the mixed economy—were firmly entrenched. But Labour revisionism continued to be embraced by a relatively small group of Gaitskellite MPs and trade union leaders and London-based party intellectuals. The movement never really captured the hearts and minds of the bulk of Labour activists.

Harold Wilson's succession to the leadership in 1963 combined traditional socialist rhetoric with pragmatic policy-making. Yet in reality it was an unsatisfactory settlement, concealing deep differences over the nature and purpose of public ownership and over the future direction of democratic socialism—differences Labour revisionism had never sought to evade.

Tudor Jones

Bibliography

Bogdanor, Vernon. "The Labour Party in Opposition, 1951–1964" in Vernon Bogdanor, and Robert Skidelsky, eds. *The Age of Affluence*. 1970, pp. 78–116.

Crosland, C.A.R. *The Future of Socialism*. rev. ed. 1964.

Crossman, R.H.S., ed. *New Fabian Essays*. 1952.

Haseler, Stephen. *The Gaitskellites*. 1969.

Jay, Douglas. *Socialism in the New Society*. 1962.

Landownership

The transfer of land from the hands of the few into the hands of the many commenced in Britain after the First World War. In 1880 one-quarter of the rural land of England was in the hands of 363 landowners, who held estates of 10,000 acres or more. Another third was in the hands of 3,000 owners, who held estates of between 1,000 and 10,000 acres. There were 10,000 owners of estates of between 300 and 1,000 acres. In 1873 fifty-four landowners owned estates of 20,000 acres or more. In 1973 thirty-three of these families still lived on their estates. In 1979 6 million acres in England and Wales, compared with 12 million acres in 1873, were held in private hands in estates of 5,000 acres. At the end of the twentieth century 90 percent of land is privately owned, the rest being held by the Forestry Commission, government departments, local authorities, county councils, **nationalized industries**, Crown Estates, the **National Trust**, Church Commissioners, and **Oxford** and **Cambridge** colleges. Members of the aristocracy are still Britain's biggest individual landowners. The changes in landownership patterns were the result of taxation and agricultural policy.

The death knell of large estates began to toll in 1894 when Sir William Harcourt, the Liberal Chancellor of the Exchequer, introduced a levy on estates passing at death, referred to as death duties. In 1909 there occurred another attack on landowners under the aegis of another Chancellor of the Exchequer, **David Lloyd George,** who introduced four new taxes in 1909, all equally complex to implement. The cost of the valuation for the land taxes outweighed the revenue that would have been collected, and in 1920 the taxes were repealed.

It is often thought that the First World War caused the breakup of estates in Britain, when heirs to estates were killed, but younger sons and close male relations inherited both land and title. Under the Corn Production Act of 1917 landlords were prevented from raising agricultural rents, and powers were given to agricultural departments to enforce cultivation. Tenants, particularly in arable areas, were benefiting from the high corn prices, and, with such profits, tenant farmers were keen to purchase their farms. Between 1919 and 1921 one-quarter of the rural land of England changed hands. Owners of large tracts of land in counties throughout Great Britain sold distantly located parts of their estates in a calculated and businesslike way, divesting themselves of the burdens of landownership.

In 1921, in the midst of falling world prices, farmers were no longer guaranteed government support. The post-war boom in land sales came to an end. Between the two wars rural England suffered the worst depression in farming since that of the late nineteenth century. During those years the relationship between landlord and tenant was never more important, as agreements were made to lower rents and to keep estates maintained in a minimum working condition.

The Agricultural Act of 1947 was in many respects a continuation of the food campaign of the Second World War. In 1949 landowners were offered substantial government grants for improvements to water supplies and land drainage, the building of farm cottages, and the rehabilitation of hill farms. The landowner had become a professional with a highly complicated job to learn and perform. Land had become an attractive form of investment, thanks to the fiscal support given to landowners by the post-war socialist government. But land that had been in the possession of some families since the Middle Ages was among the large acreages put on the market in the 1950s in order to pay death duties. Death duties could be avoided, however, if the owner handed over all he owned to his successor three years before death, which was extended to five years in 1946.

The **Labour** governments of 1964–70 continued the attack on the landed interest initiated by their socialist predecessors in 1945 with the attempt once again to reap for the state the unearned increment in land values and the extension of the five-year rule to seven years to avoid death duties. The return of a **Conservative** government in 1970 coincided with a boom in the economy. For landowners there was the anticipated prosperity of farming when Britain would finally join the **European Community** in 1973. During this time, many **City of London** institutions entered the land market. The oil crisis of 1973 was followed by the return of a Labour government in 1974. Estate duty payable at death was abolished, and in its place was created capital-transfer tax. Any transfer of wealth, except between husband and wife, was subject to tax.

The year 1992 saw the fourth Conservative government elected since 1979 and the dismantling of the Common Agricultural Policy of the European Community, which had supported farmers in Britain for nearly twenty years. The continued pledge by the Conservatives to reduce the inheritance tax has encouraged landowners in their age-old quest for continuity in the countryside.

Madeleine Beard

Bibliography

Beard, Madeleine. *Acres and Heirlooms: The Survival of Britain's Historic Estates.* 1989.

Cannadine, David. *The Decline and Fall of the British Aristocracy.* 1990.

Lane, Allen (Williams) (1902–1970)

Allen Lane founded Penguin Books in 1935, transforming the publishing industry: Lane and Penguin inaugurated the paperback revolution and significantly altered the methods of producing and marketing books.

Allen Lane (born Allen Williams) changed his name when he entered the publishing business of his uncle, John Lane (1854–1925), whose company, The Bodley Head, had become prominent in the 1890s. By 1930 Lane, who had risen to Chairman of the Board, found himself at odds with conservative members over plans to publish **James Joyce**'s *Ulysses*. Lane won that battle but realized that he would need to form his own company in order to be able to strike out in new directions.

The idea for Penguin Books came to him in 1934, when he became convinced that there was a market for cheap but good-quality books. He soon devised a scheme to buy up the reprint rights to the sort of books he would have liked to find at a railway station, to put them in attractive covers, and to sell them for a uniform price of sixpence. There were paperback books during this period, but they tended to be of low quality, both in content and format. Lane wanted to combine high-quality books with low prices and mass marketing. He carefully selected a list of ten titles calculated to appeal to educated but middlebrow tastes, including titles by **Dorothy L. Sayers** and **Agatha Christie** along with Ernest Hemingway's *A Farewell to Arms* and Andre Maurois' biography of Shelley, *Ariel*. In 1936 Lane and his two brothers, Richard and John, began trying to solicit orders for the new series in Britain and Europe but met with only limited success until the Woolworth's chain of stores ordered 63,000 books, providing wide exposure and profitability.

In 1937 Lane met William Emrys Williams, who proposed a more directly educational role for Penguin Books: Williams' vision complemented Lane's, and the two envisaged the company as performing a vital public service. They soon launched a new line called Pelicans, nonfiction titles (the first was **George Bernard Shaw**'s *The Intelligent Woman's Guide to Socialism*), all also in uniform attractive paper covers and priced at sixpence. Pelicans also quickly became hugely successful. As war with Germany grew closer, Lane published a number of books called Penguin Specials, aiming to educate the public on the political crisis. Penguin also launched a children's series, Puffin Books, in 1940; originally intended to be purely educational—with early titles like *War on Land* and *War at Sea*—Puffins continued to thrive well into the 1990s with a list primarily made up of **children's literature**.

During the **Second World War** Penguin grew when many publishers faced paper shortages and economic hard times. Lane convinced the British government to create an Armed Forces Book Club in 1942, mailing out parcels of books to soldiers and, eventually, to prisoners of war all over the world.

Penguin Classics, one of the firm's most successful series, was launched in 1946. The Classics were the brainchild of E.V. Rieu, who also translated Homer for the series; his

Odyssey, the first Penguin Classic, went on to sell well over a million copies.

Penguins were not restricted to noncontroversial titles. In 1960 Lane determined to print an edition of **D.H.** Lawrence's *Lady Chatterley's Lover*. The book was immediately seized and prosecuted under a new obscenity statute, but Penguin mounted a successful defense; the highly publicized trial earned Lane and his company considerable goodwill.

After Lane's death in 1970 the firm underwent several difficult years, but in 1975 it merged with the American firm of Viking as Viking Penguin, reinvigorating its paperback publishing. Although the company now publishes hardbacks as well as paperbacks, Penguin remains synonymous with quality paperback publishing and has greatly surpassed Lane's original conception.

Raymond N. MacKenzie

Bibliography

Joicey, Nicholas. "A Paperback Guide to Progress: Penguin Books, 1935–c. 1951," *Twentieth Century British History*, vol. 4 (1993), pp. 25–56.

Morpurgo, J.E. *Allen Lane, King Penguin: A Biography.* 1979.

Williams, William Emrys. *Allen Lane: A Personal Portrait.* 1973.

Lang, Cosmo Gordon (1864–1945)

Cosmo Gordon Lang was a major leader of the **Church of England** throughout the first part of the twentieth century, beginning with his appointment as Bishop of Stepney in 1901. He was promoted successively to the archbishoprics of York in 1908 and of Canterbury in 1928, remaining as Primate until his retirement in 1942. He died in 1945.

Lang played an important role both within the Church of England and outside. He helped develop the Church of England's Mens Society (from 1901) and was active in the National Mission of Repentance and Hope during the First World War. He also was involved in forming a Commission on Church and State (1913) that led to the creation of a Church Assembly. In 1929 he had a brief role in the ill-fated revision of the Book of Common Prayer.

Within the Anglican Communion he was involved in the Lambeth Conference of 1920 and chaired its successor in 1930. He also made an important contribution to ecumenical relations—for example, in the 1920 Lambeth Conference's Appeal to all Christian People. This led to improved relations with the Orthodox and Swedish Lutheran Churches, and, in 1932, to inter-communion with the Old Catholics.

He also played a significant, if not central, part in affairs of state. He entered the **House of Lords** in 1909, contributing to debates surrounding the **constitutional crisis** of 1911. He remained a member until his death, having been made a peer as Baron Lang of Lambeth in 1942. Outside Parliament he served as a member of the Royal Commission on **Divorce** and Matrimonial Causes (1909) and the Joint Committee upon the Indian Constitution (1933).

He also achieved prominence through his extensive relations with the Royal Family, including, most notably, the period of the abdication crisis. As Archbishop of Canterbury at the time of **George V**'s death, he became embroiled in the controversy surrounding **Edward VIII**'s intention to marry an American divorcee. Given the Church's **marriage** laws, Lang saw grave difficulties in participating in the coronation planned for 1937. When the crisis came to a head in November-December 1936, Edward abdicated, but mainly because of political rather than ecclesiastical pressures.

Lang's career represented a shift toward recruitment from professional rather than aristocratic groups (his father was a senior clergyman in the Church of Scotland and Principal of Aberdeen University). But he followed the traditional leadership path of an Oxbridge education, attending Balliol College, **Oxford**, and becoming a Fellow of All Souls College.

His lasting significance is questionable. He was immensely industrious, an exceptional administrator, and was well-connected to leading politicians and aristocrats. But his accomplishments as Archbishop of Canterbury were modest.

George Moyser

Bibliography

Lockhart, J.G. *Cosmo Gordon Lang.* 1949.

Also see **Prayer Book Revision**

Lansbury, George (1859–1940)

Born on 22 February 1859, George Lansbury became active in **Liberal** politics in East London during the mid-1880s and converted to socialism by 1892. A prominent figure in East End politics thereafter, he finally entered Parliament in December 1910, as Labour member for Bow and Bromley, but he relinquished his seat in 1912 to force a by-election over **women's suffrage**, which he lost. The previous year, however, he had helped to found and had become principal editor of the *Daily Herald*, which developed into the liveliest newspaper the British Left possessed, so that, even outside Parliament, he retained a significant voice. He opposed the **First World War** on grounds of **pacifism**, and by 1918 his popularity among Labour supporters was unrivaled. Returned to Parliament in 1922, again for Bow and Bromley, he held the seat until he died. In 1924 he refused a minor position in the first Labour government but in 1929 accepted appointment as First Commissioner of Works. He alone of **Ramsay MacDonald's Cabinet** survived Labour's 1931 electoral defeat, becoming leader of the much-reduced Parliamentary Party. He resigned this position in 1935 and thereafter devoted himself to the peace movement, meeting with Adolf Hitler, Benito Mussolini, Franklin D. Roosevelt, and French Socialist Premier Leon Blum in a vain attempt to avert the coming war. He died on 7 May 1940.

Lansbury's achievements were many. Early on, as a socialist member of the Poplar Board of Guardians, he led the campaign to humanize treatment of indigents under the old Poor Law. He helped establish the Laindon and Hollesley Bay farm colonies where Poplar's unemployed might be sent to work. In 1921, as Poplar's mayor, he led the borough council in passive resistance to taxes called "precepts," payable to the London County Council, until poor rates were equalized. Lansbury maintained that the current policy unfairly penalized boroughs, like his own, where **unemployment** was high. The government imprisoned Poplar's councilors for contempt, Lansbury among them, but they all held firm. Eventually, Prime Minister **David Lloyd George** relented. The rates were equalized, and the councilors were freed, although they refused to purge their contempt.

This may have been Lansbury's greatest triumph. He suffered two grave defeats during his lifetime. The first occurred in 1912 when he resigned his parliamentary seat to compel a by-election on the issue of women's suffrage. He wanted the **Labour Party** to refuse to support **H.H. Asquith's** Liberal government until it had enfranchised women, even if this brought the **Conservatives** to power. Lansbury sought to force the hands of the Labour hierarchy by this strategy, but **Keir Hardie** was the only party leader who agreed. Other "rebels," some of whom were associated with the *Daily Herald*, also rallied to the cause, as did the **feminist** movement, including, most prominently, the **Pankhursts**.

Lansbury was a great resigner. He never hesitated to face the political wilderness, and he was too much of an individualist to acquiesce in policies with which he disagreed. He quit the **Liberals** in 1892 and the Marxist Socialist Democratic Party early in the twentieth century. He quit the Labour Party in 1912, although he rejoined shortly after the First World War. In 1935 he resigned the leadership of the Labour Party when it would not support his pacifist program in a world menaced by **Fascism**. This resignation represents his greatest political defeat.

He had inherited the leadership almost by default. After MacDonald's apostasy in 1931, there were no other senior Labour figures left. Lansbury led the 46 Labour MPs with verve and skill, but everything was overshadowed by the terrible denouement. Always opposed to war, he had become an out-and-out pacifist during the First World War. Repelled by crass materialism, he had returned, early in the century, to Christianity (which he had briefly abandoned during his Marxist phase). Now as leader of the Labour Party and also as a Christian socialist, he wanted a world conference to appease the "have not" powers, especially Germany. At the conference Britain and other wealthy nations would divest themselves of colonies and other material advantages and disarm to the level permitted Germany by the Versailles settlement. In fact, Lansbury believed that only if Britain disarmed completely and unilaterally would it be possible to avert another war.

This plan combined Labour's traditional anti-imperialist, internationalist, and pacifist aims and rhetoric, but, after 1933, unilateral renunciation of any British advantage over Germany seemed foolish to most people, including most of the Labour Party. For two years the party leader held views unacceptable to the vast majority of party members and supporters. In 1935 **Ernest Bevin**, leader of the **Transport and General Workers' Union**, made a brutal and somewhat unfair speech at the party conference attacking Lansbury. Although Bevin was nearly

L

shouted down for his unkindness, he secured a majority of the votes. Lansbury resigned as leader in order to campaign unequivocally for the world conference and pacifism. At the age of seventy-six, he accepted the presidency of the **Peace Pledge Union**. He had audiences with all of the major world leaders except Joseph Stalin, spending his energy in a vain effort to head off the conflagration he could see coming. He welcomed the **Munich** settlement and **Neville Chamberlain**'s own last-ditch efforts to save Britain from war with Germany.

Lansbury was a talented politician, speaker, and organizer. What made him remarkable was the stubbornness with which he clung to his principles. This explains why he quit so many organizations and positions and why he must have been a difficult colleague, but paradoxically it also helps explain why he became one of the best-loved and most-respected figures in the labor movement.

Lansbury's legacy has been the adamantine insistence among an element within the Labour Party that Britain must stand for moral principle, must set the world a moral example. Concretely this has meant demanding the total abolition of capitalism and unilateral disarmament, policies that Labour's leaders have usually thought utopian or worse.

Jonathan Schneer

Bibliography
Holman, Bob. *Good Old George: The Life of George Lansbury*. 1990.
Postgate, Raymond. *The Life of George Lansbury*. 1951.
Schneer, Jonathan. *George Lansbury*. 1990.

Larkin, Philip Arthur (1922–1985)
Philip Larkin, one of the best-loved poets of his generation, is known for his wryly ironic verse, which bypasses modernist literary experimentation and returns to more traditional poetic structure, modes of scansion, and rhyme. Larkin writes about England, solitude, and mortality in a way that mixes traditional forms with colloquial language; his work is lucid, clear, and accessible to a wide range of readers, even as its apparent simplicity—and the ordinary and even meager life it pictures—is matched with complex art and emotional intensity. His poetic subjects range from celebrations of provincial English mores to expressions of impatience with middle-class domesticity. At times the poetry

embraces solitude to the point of bitter reclusiveness, thereby conveying the tones of a nineteenth-century moralist who has lived on alone in the increasingly chaotic twentieth century. The poignant expression of this sense of alienation, mixed with yearning for alternatives, has won him his wide audience.

Born in Coventry on 9 August 1922, Larkin attended Henry VIII Grammar School and went to **Oxford** in 1940 to attend St. John's College. There he became acquainted with fellow writers and jazz enthusiasts Kingsley Amis and Bruce Montgomery (writer of detective novels under the name of Edmund Crispin). While Larkin was at Oxford, some of his verse was chosen to be included in the anthology *Poetry from Oxford in Wartime* (1944). In 1943 he was awarded first-class honors in English, and later the same year he took up the post of librarian at a small library in Wellington, Shropshire. He published two novels in succession, *Jill* (1946) and *A Girl in Winter* (1947). His failed attempt to write a third novel led eventually to his turning exclusively to **poetry**, though he claimed never to have relinquished his disappointment at abandoning the dream of writing novels full-time. Larkin's first book of poems, *The North Ship* (1945), was heavily influenced by **William Butler Yeats**. He had little luck in publishing until *The Less Deceived* (1955), the volume of poetry that established his reputation.

Larkin's career as a librarian continued through moves to the University College of Leicester, then to Queen's University, Belfast, and finally to the University of Hull in 1955, where he remained until his death in 1985. During his tenure the university underwent a rapid expansion, and Larkin personally oversaw the construction of the new Brynmor Jones Library.

Larkin's volume of poetry *The Whitsun Weddings* (1964) garnered him the Queen's Gold Medal for Poetry and was followed a decade later by *High Windows* (1974). During 1970–1 Larkin was a Visiting Fellow at All Souls College, Oxford, in connection with which he edited *The Oxford Book of Twentieth-Century English Verse* (1973).

Larkin expressed his keen interest in jazz by writing record reviews for the *Daily Telegraph*, subsequently collected under the title *All What Jazz* (1970; revised edition 1985). The expressiveness of jazz provided a counterpoint to the tight control and reserve of his poetry, although his reviews also contain a sense of alienated disappointment. He loathed the development of jazz after the 1930s and 1940s, and he supplements his contempt for Pablo Picasso and Ezra Pound with denunciations of Charlie Parker in his introduction to the volume.

Larkin vaunted himself as a self-proclaimed philistine, adopting the pose of the common man who does not know art but knows what he likes. At the same time his literary judgments are sophisticated as well as shrewd. Though he seldom wrote book reviews, their acute insights and vivid style reveal him to be a formidable critic. Several of these essays were issued in the volume *Required Writing: Miscellaneous Pieces, 1955–1982* (1983).

Larkin's attempt to align his art with common persons and experiences is not as straightforward as it appears to be. Dissociating himself from modernism—for example, he claimed to have disowned Yeats' influence in favor of Thomas Hardy's—Larkin nevertheless courted for himself the elite authority he criticized in the modernist masters. And in taking sides with ordinary, even mediocre, democratic life, he seemed to become an apologist (especially in *High Windows*) for antidemocratic political conservatism and reaction.

Janice Rossen

Bibliography

Bloomfield, Barry Cambray. *Philip Larkin: A Bibliography, 1933–1976.* 1979.

Booth, James. *Philip Larkin: Writer.* 1992.

Motion, Andrew. *Philip Larkin: A Writer's Life.* 1993.

Rossen, Janice. *Philip Larkin: His Life's Work.* 1989.

Thwaite, Anthony, ed. *Selected Letters of Philip Larkin, 1940–1985.* 1993.

Whalen, Terry. *Philip Larkin and English Poetry.* 1986.

Laski, Harold Joseph (1893–1950)

During his life Harold Laski was a major influence as a theorist and political activist in socialist and progressive circles in both Britain and the outside world. He was elected to the constituency section of the National Executive Committee (NEC) of the **Labour Party** every year from 1937 to 1949—an unprecedented achievement for someone who was never an MP. He was almost equally well-known in the United States, and he secured a substantial following in India as a prominent supporter of **Indian nationalism**. However, he was always a controversial figure and was discredited in the West during the Cold War era.

His earliest major writings—*Studies in the Problem of Sovereignty* (1917) and *Authority in the Modern State* (1919)—were completed during a six-year period as a lecturer in North America (he was at Harvard Law School from 1916 to 1920) and quickly established his reputation as a major pluralist critic of the sovereign state. However, his scholarly tone masked a burning political commitment, and Laski soon upset the Boston elite by supporting the 1919 police strike. This effectively ended his academic career in the United States, and he returned to Britain as a lecturer at the **London School of Economics** (subsequently promoted to a professorship at the age of thirty-three), where he was to remain as an inspiring teacher for generations of political science students.

During the early 1920s his pluralist belief in decentralized participation was tempered by a growing conviction that firm state action was necessary to bring about radical change, and he became active in the Labour Party and the **Fabian Society**. He tried to attain a synthesis between the pluralist and Fabian outlooks in *A Grammar of Politics* (1925), an encyclopedic work that outlined a socialist approach to political theory, constitutional practice, economic organization, and national sovereignty. However, in the latter part of the decade he began to fear that socialism would not be established by peaceful means, a feeling reinforced by the failure of the Labour government of 1929–31 to deal with the economic crisis. The establishment of a Conservative-dominated National government by **Ramsay MacDonald**, followed by the rise of **Fascism** in Europe, led Laski to despair about the continuation of democractic government in capitalist societies. *Democracy in Crisis* (1933) was a passionate critique of the contemporary situation that urged political leaders to make progressive reforms to save constitutional government. However, the triumph of Adolf Hitler in Germany seemed to undermine any remaining optimism that he had felt about the resilience of parliamentary democracy. He now turned to a personal form of Marxism, which he used analytically in *The State in Theory and Practice* (1935) and historically in *The Rise of European Liberalism* (1936). However, he retained a deep commitment to liberal values and hated the thought of violence. His position was therefore never Marxist in any conventional sense; his real message was that it was imperative for capitalism to accept socialist reform so that liberal civilization could be preserved. *Parliamentary Government in England* (1938) epitomized these contradictions, for the book simultaneously revered constitutional democracy and argued that it was impossible to implement in practice in an unequal society.

Because he was searching for a viable theoretical stance that would combine potentially incompatible goals, his political activity was often also tortuous. His pessimism about the West led him to perceive virtues in Stalinist Russia, and in 1936 he became one of the founders of the **Left Book Club**, which often promoted pro-Soviet propaganda in an attempt to bring about a **Popular Front** against Fascism. However, his continuing commitment to liberalism meant that he could never fully accept any dictatorship. His real enthusiasm in this period was therefore for the New Deal, and he hoped that Franklin D. Roosevelt's reinvigoration of capitalist democracy would triumph and be emulated in Europe.

In September 1939 he had no doubt that the war against Nazi Germany was justified and, until Hitler's attack on the Soviet Union in June 1941, he played a major role in countering Communist propaganda within the Labour Party. But he remained convinced that both Fascism and war stemmed from capitalism, and that it was vital to use the emergency situation to begin the process of a "revolution by consent." Now at the height of his influence with the Labour rank and file, he constantly urged the leaders of his own party and the American administration to institute fundamental domestic reform and to maintain unity with the Soviet Union. Such arguments alienated the political Establishment on both sides of the Atlantic, including **Clement Attlee**, the Labour leader.

In June 1945, as Chairman of the Labour Party NEC, Laski publicly announced that Attlee should not be bound by any agreements made by **Winston Churchill** at Potsdam and should attend the conference only as an "observer." Attlee immediately rejected this demand, and Laski served as the *bete noire* for the Conservatives throughout the election campaign. Although he continued to be prominent after the Labour victory, his position was substantially weakened, and his isolation was reinforced when he lost a notorious libel case at the

end of 1946. In this case his writings were used to sustain a claim that he had advocated violent revolution—a bitter blow for a man whose life's work had been to bring about peaceful change. In his last years he was thus a rather tragic figure whose influence had waned. He became increasingly disillusioned with both the United States and the Soviet Union, while condemning the Labour Party for its pro-American stance and for its anti-Zionist policy.

Convinced that the problems of his time were too urgent for leisurely academic reflection, Laski wrote too much, overestimated his influence, and sometimes failed to distinguish between analysis and polemic. But he was a serious thinker and a charismatic personality whose views have been distorted because he refused to accept Cold War orthodoxies.

Michael Newman

Bibliography

Deane, Herbert A. *The Political Ideas of Harold J. Laski.* 1955.

Kramnick, Isaac, and Barry Sheerman. *Harold Laski: A Life on the Left.* 1993.

Martin, Kingsley. *Harold Laski, 1893–1950: A Biographical Memoir.* 1953.

Newman, Michael. *Harold Laski: A Political Biography.* 1993.

Zylstra, Bernard. *From Pluralism to Collectivism: The Development of Harold Laski's Political Thought.* 1968.

Lawrence, D(avid) H(erbert) (1885–1930)

D.H. Lawrence, best known as the author of *Sons and Lovers* (1913), *The Rainbow* (1915), *Women in Love* (1920), and *Lady Chatterley's Lover* (1928), is ranked by many, along with **James Joyce** and **Virginia Woolf**, as one of the greatest British novelists of the twentieth century.

Born in Eastwood, a small Nottinghamshire town, Lawrence had humble beginnings. His mother, the former Lydia Beardsall, was a cultured, ambitious former schoolteacher whose family had declined socially; his father, Arthur John Lawrence, was an illiterate collier who worked underground for more than fifty years. Lawrence attended Nottingham High School between 1898 and 1901 and, in 1906, enrolled at University College, Nottingham, to study for a teacher's certificate. Disillusioned with university life, Lawrence wrote the first draft of a novel, "Laetitia" and in 1908 took a job at the Davidson Road School in Croydon where he excelled as an art teacher. Teaching discouraged him, however, so he left Croydon in 1912 and, for the rest of his life, concentrated on writing.

Lawrence first appeared in print after Jessie Chambers, his childhood sweetheart and the model for Miriam in *Sons and Lovers*, sent four of his poems to the editor of the prestigious *English Review*, Ford Madox Hueffer (later Ford Madox Ford). Ford published the poems in 1909 and in 1911 published the short story "Odor of the Chrysanthemums." Meanwhile, Lawrence revised "Laetitia," which was published as *The White Peacock* (1911) and was dedicated to his mother, who had died of cancer in December 1910.

Lydia Lawrence was a dominant force in her son's life. He claimed that she breathed him "like an atmosphere" and had his soul. He loved her, however, and was so badly shaken by her death that he was ill during much of what he called "the sick year" (1911). But he continued to write. Setting aside the manuscript of *Sons and Lovers* (begun in 1910 as "Paul Morel"), he wrote *The Trespasser* (1912), based on an episode in the life of his friend Helen Corke and her music teacher, who killed himself. Then, in a conscious effort to purge himself of his mother's influence, Lawrence completed *Sons and Lovers*, his novel about a young man inordinately attracted to his mother and hostile toward his father.

Long before *Sons and Lovers* was published, Lawrence broke his six-year engagement to Jessie Chambers. In 1912 he met Frieda Weekley, the wife of his French professor and a member of the illustrious German von Richthofen family. They married in 1914 after an elopement to Germany and began a nomadic existence, which continued for much of their life together, tempestuous, passionate, and marked by lack of money. During the tumultuous period that preceded the marriage, Lawrence worked energetically on a novel called "The Sisters," the story of three generations of Brangwens. Focusing on Ursula Brangwen, a young woman who decides to go to college, to have a career, and to remain unmarried, "The Sisters" was divided, late in 1914, into two volumes, *The Rainbow* and *Women in Love*. When *The Rainbow* was published just weeks after Great Britain declared war on Germany, critics and general readers alike were hostile. They objected to the novel's frank accounts of passion and were offended by the opposition of Lawrence's heroine to war and nationalism. Bowing to pressure, the publisher, Methuen, suppressed the novel.

Lawrence completed *Women in Love* in 1916; this novel, which many critics regard as his best, did not appear in print until 1920 in America and 1921 in Great Britain, because of the reaction to *The Rainbow*. In fact, Lawrence published no novels between 1915 and 1920. He did, however, publish four volumes of poetry and a travel book, *Twilight in Italy* (1916). He also completed *The Lost Girl* (1920); wrote his novella about lesbianism, *The Fox* (1922); and published *Studies in Classic American Literature* (1923). In addition, he began *Aaron's Rod* (1922), the first of three "leadership" novels that explore the connection between politics and personal relationships.

Partly because of the treatment of *The Rainbow*, Lawrence left England in 1919 and returned only for brief visits. Continuing the series of leadership novels, he wrote *Kangaroo* (1923) in Australia and *The Plumed Serpent* (1926), the novel he regarded as his most important, in Mexico. He also produced two more travel books, *Sea and Sardinia* (1921) and *Mornings in Mexico* (1927), and the novella *St. Mawr* (1925), which records his response to the American Southwest.

Lawrence's last years, like his first, were clouded by illness. Living in Italy, he wrote *Lady Chatterley's Lover* (two earlier versions of which have been published posthumously). More infamous than *The Rainbow*, the story of a love affair between Lady Chatterley and a gamekeeper was widely condemned for its sexual frankness and violation of social mores, and it had to be smuggled into Great Britain. Exulting this time over the furor his fiction produced, Lawrence continued to write even as he was dying. He produced more short stories, a number of essays, a travel book called *Etruscan Places* (1932), and *The Man Who Died* (1929), a novella about Jesus' sexuality originally called *The Escaped Cock*.

During his lifetime Lawrence received only one literary award, the James Tait Black Memorial Award for *The Lost Girl*. His stories about male-female relationships, his criticism of abstractions and idealisms, his insistence that sex is an all-formative mystery, his advocacy of amoral intuitive life "blood-knowledge" and at the same time of civilized order and values, and his experiments with traditional novelistic narrative continue to attract controversy.

Duane Edwards

Bibliography

Leavis, F.R. *D.H. Lawrence, Novelist*. 1955.

Moore, Harry T. *The Priest of Love: A Life of D.H. Lawrence*. 1974.

Schneider, Daniel J. *The Consciousness of D.H. Lawrence: An Intellectual Biography*. 1986.

Worthen, John. *D.H. Lawrence: The Early Years, 1885–1912*. 1991.

Lawrence, T(homas) E(dward) (1888–1935)

Lawrence of Arabia was a young Oxford archaeologist who became during the **First World War** an intelligence officer in Cairo and a liaison officer with the Arabs revolting against the Turks. His post-war notoriety was partly the result of publicity from the slide lectures presented in London by Lowell Thomas, an American journalist. Fame helped Lawrence influence aspects of the Middle East settlement, but he soon sought to evade media attention through anonymity in the ranks of the **Royal Air Force** and the **army** while pursuing literary interests. His death on a motorcycle in 1935 added to the romance surrounding the man who remains a popular historical figure, especially after David Lean's 1962 film, *Lawrence of Arabia*.

Lawrence's father, who came from an Anglo-Irish landowning family, married and had four daughters but separated from his wife when the family's Scottish governess became pregnant. He and the former governess never married but had five sons, of whom T.E., born in 1888, was the second. His illegitimacy affected him personally, but his childhood, lived mostly in France and Oxford, was economically secure and otherwise conventional. He studied languages and **history** at **Oxford**, receiving first-class honors in 1910. His Oxford mentor, David George Hogarth, introduced Lawrence to excavations in Syria and surveys in Sinai and, after the British declared war on the Ottoman Empire in 1914, secured his appointment to the Arab Bureau in Cairo.

Lawrence's pre-war exposure to Arabic language, people, and lands and familiarity with British intelligence were helpful in 1916, when he was posted to the Hejaz, along the Arabian coast of the Red Sea. While Cairo subsidized and supplied Sharif Husayn, who unilaterally declared an Arab revolt against the Turks, Lawrence worked more closely with Husayn's sons, Abdullah and Faisal, and their largely Bedouin followers to defeat Turkish garrisons in the northwestern Arabian peninsula and to blow up the Turkish-operated Hejaz Railway. Further operations led by Lawrence complemented the successful British liberation of **Palestine** in 1917 and of Syria in 1918 by General Edmund Allenby. While the military role of the Arab forces led by Lawrence was not decisive, the value to the British of Husayn and his sons was important as a counterweight to French territorial claims in Lebanon and Syria. Lawrence's partisanship on behalf of Faisal and his Arab following in Syria would not have been as significant had Thomas not publicized Lawrence's feats extensively to a London public hungry for colorful exploits after the horrors of the Western Front.

In 1919 Lawrence dramatically accompanied Faisal to the Versailles conference, where both were disabused of their illusion that the Allies might gratify the demands of Arab nationalism, especially if it meant the sacrifice of continued British influence in the region. In 1920, when Syrians ousted Faisal and the French occupied Lebanon and Syria, Lawrence wrote letters of protest to London daily newspapers. Then, in 1921, **Winston Churchill** took over the Colonial Office and called on Lawrence to help him organize a new Middle East Department to reduce the huge costs of maintaining the British position in Egypt, Palestine, and Iraq after the war. Lawrence supported Churchill's handling of the Cairo Conference and worked to secure Abdullah's position in Trans-Jordan and Faisal's in Iraq. Tired of public life, particularly his relentless pursuit by the media, Lawrence turned to revising his account of the Arab revolt, written immediately after the war as a Fellow of All Souls College. An aesthete and bibliophile, he published an expensive edition limited to subscribers, entitled *Seven Pillars of Wisdom* (1926), and an abridgement called *Revolt in the Desert* (1926). Joining the military ranks gave him enough anonymity and security to translate Homer's *Odyssey* and a French novel, as well to write his account of the Royal Air Force, *The Mint* (1929).

Roger Adelson

Bibliography

Knightley, Philip, and Colin Simpson. *The Secret Lives of Lawrence of Arabia*. 1969.

Mack, John E. *A Prince of Our Disorder: The Life of T.E. Lawrence*. 1976.

Wilson, Jeremy. *Lawrence of Arabia: The Authorized Biography of T.E. Lawrence*. 1989.

League of Nations

Britain played a major role in the creation and operation of the League of Nations. No other country left so great an imprint on this organization; certainly no other gave the League so much public support. Its appeal went across party lines, but the League still became an issue in British politics.

In Britain, as in the United States and elsewhere, the outbreak of the **First World War** led to discussions among intellectuals and politicians as to why the war had erupted and what could be done to prevent future wars. The suggestions of a **Cambridge** scholar, G. Lowes Dickinson, sparked the creation of one such group and had great influence on planning for the post-war world. Dickinson explained the war as the product of an anarchic world system and urged the creation of a "peace league" to end this anarchy.

As the war progressed, many other suggestions emerged, and two groups were established to promote post-war planning for an international organization: the League of Nations Society and the League of Free Nations Association. **Lord Robert Cecil**, a minister in the **Foreign Office**, drafted a memorandum in September 1916 that was placed before the **Cabinet** and helped shape official British attitudes on the creation of collective machinery to ensure peace. Cecil played a principal role in drafting the final version of the Covenant at the Paris Peace Conference.

Cecil also accepted the chairmanship of the **League of Nations Union** (LNU), which had unified the two rival groups of League supporters. Under his leadership, the LNU became the chief bulwark of the international League movement and a force in British politics. It attracted over 1 million members over the course of the inter-war period and helped shape support for the League.

The appeal of the League ideal in Britain was based on the widespread sentiment that the sacrifices of the war must be justified by the emergence of a better world. The League became for many the symbol of that better world, and they desperately wanted it to succeed.

It was assigned the tasks of settling international disputes, of furthering disarmament, and a range of other functions. Some hoped that it would also pave the way for a future world government. All of the optimism about the League's future could not conceal its obvious shortcomings. Its members were sovereign states who could not be transformed overnight into dedicated world citizens.

It became commonplace in Britain in the 1920s for politicians of all parties to heap praise on the League. In fact, few were anxious to have the League assume greater responsibility in world affairs, as Cecil, **Gilbert Murray**, and other leaders of the LNU wished. **Labour Party** leaders were suspicious of the way the Covenant had been grafted onto the peace treaty. They often said that the peace settlement would have to be revised and the new world body made over so that it was less of a "League of Victors" before they could give it their full support. **Conservative** leaders had their own objections to the League, which many perceived as a threat to national sovereignty. They generally favored it as an extension of conventional diplomacy but objected to its more far-reaching objectives.

In the 1920s, when no clear challenge to the peace arose, support for the League was a high-minded but rather abstract goal, based on the hope that any future dispute could be resolved by peaceful means. League supporters and politicians rarely mentioned publicly that peaceful restraints might fail, and that aggression might again provoke war.

When challenges to the League began to emerge in the 1930s, the difficulties of this limited view of collective security became apparent. Japanese action in Manchuria in 1931 was not regarded in Britain as a clear case of aggression. No one in Britain was sure of what was happening or what the rights and wrongs of it all were. When the League sent a **commission** headed by a British Conservative, Lord **Lytton**, to investigate the situation, its inconclusive report neither labeled Japan an aggressor nor raised the issue of sanctions against Japan.

Only when Italy invaded **Abyssinia** did League supporters face a challenge they could not ignore. The **Peace Ballot**, which the LNU supervised in 1934–5, provided an impressive demonstration of how widespread public suport for the League was in Britain. With responses from about half of the electorate, more than 11 million participants, the ballot demonstrated support for sanctions, even military sanctions, against an aggressor.

The National government went along with a limited policy of sanctions, which the League imposed, but these sanctions failed to deter Italy. Cecil and other LNU leaders tried to lead British opinion into accepting rearmament, so the League would be able to back up its sanctions policy. They even joined forces with old rivals like **Winston Churchill** in an "Arms and the Covenant" campaign to meet the challenge of **Fascism**. The League had to be given a real trial, so that other potential aggressors would see that aggression did not pay. Instead the League backed off from a reliance on sanctions, and public confidence in the League waned after 1936. The League of Nations Union lost many of its members, some to dynamic new **pacifist** groups such as the **Peace Pledge Union**. The central beliefs of British League supporters were hard to maintain in the late 1930s. They had hoped that public opinion was capable of creating a new world order by influencing the British government, which in turn could lead the League of Nations and the world. But the illusion was dispelled when the government, despite the encouragement of the Peace Ballot, refused to pursue a full sanctions policy against Italy.

Internationalists continued to oppose the **appeasement** policies of **Neville Chamberlain's** government and to press for collective security in the last years before the outbreak of the Second World War. However the League was no longer viable and their struggle had been lost. Their hope had been to support the League in order to put foreign policy on a new basis, to build a world regulated by law and not force.

Donald S. Birn

Bibliography

Birn, Donald. *The League of Nations Union.* 1981.

Cecil, Viscount. *A Great Experiment.* 1941.

Walters, F.P. *A History of the League of Nations.* 1952.

Winkler, Henry R. *The League of Nations Movement in Britain, 1914–1919.* 1952.

League of Nations Union

The League of Nations Union (LNU) was the largest and most influential organization in the British peace movement in the period between the two World Wars. Founded in 1918 with the merger of two groups of League supporters, the League of Nations Society and the League of Free Nations Association, the LNU was to attract over 1 million members during its twenty-seven-year existence. Its aim was to support and strengthen the **League of Nations** by encouraging an enlightened public opinion in Britain, which would in turn lead British governments toward pro-League policies. It worked as a pressure group, sending out questionnaires to parliamentary candidates before election and endorsing some of them. The Union also sponsored many educational programs that stressed to students the interdependence of nations and the importance of the League.

The LNU promoted a far-reaching vision of the League that appealed more to the Left than to **Conservatives**. Yet it still attracted some Conservatives who would never have considered joining any other peace society. As proof of the power of public opinion behind a strong League, it tried to build up its membership as rapidly as possible. This meant submerging differences in viewpoints among members and trying to please everybody. While the League itself remained a safe nonpartisan cause—that is, until the mid-1930s—the LNU maintained its membership and at least some influence. But when support for the League meant enforcing sanctions and perhaps dragging Britain into war, members resigned and the LNU declined.

The LNU was headed by two leaders: the Conservative politician **Lord Robert Cecil** and the Liberal Professor of Greek at **Oxford, Gilbert Murray**. Cecil had been a minister in the wartime government in 1916 when he urged the creation of a world body to prevent future war. He dominated debates of the Paris Peace Conference Commission on the League and won support for the Covenant. Murray had been active in developing support for the League idea and headed the League's Committee for Intellectual Cooperation.

The **Peace Ballot** of 1934–5 marked the high point of the LNU's influence. This poll of the public on whether it supported the League and sanctions against aggressors helped to push the British government into supporting sanctions against Italy for its invasion of **Abyssinia**. When this sanctions policy failed, the League cause began to fade.

The LNU remained active, although with relatively few members and little influence, throughout the Second World War. It conducted discussions on the post-war world and the need for a new **United Nations** organization. It also provided an important forum for the leaders of the many governments that were in exile in London, the London International Assembly. Only in October 1945, when the United Nations Association was founded, did the LNU finally expire.

Donald S. Birn

Bibliography
Birn, Donald S. *The League of Nations Union.* 1981.
Winkler, Henry R. *The League of Nations Movement in Great Britain, 1914–1919.* 1952.

Leavis, F(rank) R(aymond) (1895–1978)

An influential and controversial figure, F.R. Leavis helped establish **literary criticism** as a major force in British culture. His method of analyzing texts deeply influenced a generation of intellectuals that included **Raymond Williams** and Richard Hoggart. Leavis' critique of modern culture, which daringly encompassed the privileged literary elites of London, attracted disciples from across the political spectrum and reinforced the academic standing of literary studies in the major universities.

Leavis was born in Cambridge in 1895, the son of a shopowner who sold musical instruments. Educated at the Perse School, he served in the **First World War** with a medical unit on the Western Front. After the armistice he gained a scholarship to Emmanuel College, **Cambridge**, where he graduated with first-class honors in English in 1921. Three years later he received his Ph.D. from Cambridge for a dissertation on "The Relationship of Journalism to Literature," a topic that, like the field of English literature itself, was not in high repute. Leavis then embarked on his long, frustrating struggle for a permanent academic position at Cambridge, a quest that deeply embittered him. In 1929 he married Queenie Dorothy Roth, whose *Fiction and the Reading Public*, published in 1932, became a central text in his pessimistic critique of modernity. Borrowing heavily from contemporary figures such as **I.A. Richards** and **Wyndham Lewis**, as well as the crowd psychologists of the late nineteenth century, Leavis argued that the organic community of preindustrial England had gradually succumbed to a debilitating commercialism, most obvious in **advertising** and other forms of Americanized culture, but infecting influential novelists and reviewers as well. Only an intense program of education in English literature, involving the close, discriminating reading of texts, might preserve an authentic culture among a new, revitalized minority. Literary criticism would help re-create the "common reader" that industrialism destroyed.

In 1932 Leavis launched *Scrutiny*, a journal of literary and cultural criticism that, until its last issue in 1953, became the major medium of exchange for Leavis and his disciples. Many of his most influential books consisted of articles written for *Scrutiny*, including *The Great Tradition* (1948), about George Eliot, Henry James, and **Joseph Conrad**. An impassioned defender of "critical standards," Leavis evaluated the relative merits of the central figures of English literature. Among modernists, Conrad, James, **T.S. Eliot**, and **William Butler Yeats** stood high in his literary canon, but it was Charles Dickens and especially **D.H. Lawrence** whom Leavis most vigorously championed. In a series of penetrating essays, he argued that Lawrence remained "our last great writer." Critics complained that Leavis never really defined his "standards" and that his "revaluations" too often consisted of arbitrary judgments.

Leavis' influence as a teacher at Cambridge reached its peak in the decade following the Second World War. Many students found it easy to identify sympathetically with a social and cultural rebel whose opinions defied the intellectual elitism and privilege of **Bloomsbury** intellectuals and whose literary criticism involved a deep seriousness of purpose not always evident in academic study. Cambridge finally made him a University Reader in 1959. Leavis reaffirmed his controversial status in 1962 in a stinging, often *ad hominem* polemic against C.P. Snow and his ideas about the cultural superiority of science. After retirement from Cambridge, Leavis accepted a number of visiting appointments and honorary degrees. He continued to publish extensively during his last years, but his influence waned considerably as other schools of criticism—Marxist and deconstructionist, especially—gained favor.

D.L. LeMahieu

Bibliography
Bell, Michael. *F.R. Leavis.* 1988.
Billan, R.P. *The Literary Criticism of F.R. Leavis.* 1979.

Hayman, Ronald. *Leavis*. 1976.
Samson, Anne. *F.R. Leavis*. 1992.

Left Book Club

Established by the publisher **Victor Gollancz** in May 1936, the Left Book Club (LBC) was to become a highly influential force. At its peak in April 1939 it had 57,000 members, who received a book and the journal *Left News* every month. However, the aim of the LBC was always political, for it was designed to create an anti-Fascist **Popular Front** movement. It was based on local study groups, of which there were 1,500 in 1939, and these were buttressed by social and cultural activities. It campaigned for such causes as the Spanish Republic, Chinese resistance to Japan, and the establishment of an alliance with the Soviet Union, and its rallies were often far larger than those of the **Labour Party**. However, the LBC was deeply divided by the Nazi-Soviet Pact and the war. It continued until October 1948, but never regained its vitality, and had dwindled to 7,000 members by the time that Gollancz finally closed it down.

The LBC was created soon after the **Communist Party of Great Britain** (CPGB) had adopted its United Front policy against **Fascism**, and its success owed much to this fact. The CPGB now wanted to create a broad alliance and Gollancz was prepared to collaborate with them to this end. He had two major associates: **John Strachey**, who was effectively a Communist at the time, and **Harold Laski**, who was in the left wing of the Labour Party. Gollancz and Strachey ensured that the overwhelming majority of the Club's books were acceptable to the CPGB, and Communists played the leading role in its central organization. Laski was not informed of the extent of the collaboration between the CPGB and the LBC and, although he occasionally took an independent line, he generally played a less-active role in its affairs than his co-selectors.

By 1938 the LBC had published many of the most influential left-wing works of the era—above all, those by Strachey himself. However, by the autumn of that year, Gollancz was becoming increasingly worried by Communist domination of the LBC and began to assert a greater degree of independence. Laski was now highly critical of the CPGB, and in August 1939 he threatened to resign from the Club unless it distanced itself from the Nazi-Soviet Pact.

Gollancz managed to maintain unity when the CPGB appeared to support the war the next month, but the division in the LBC became evident when the Communists changed their stance. In the December 1939 issue of *Left News* Strachey argued that the war should be opposed, while Laski urged total support for it. Gollancz agreed with Laski, and in April 1940 Strachey also endorsed their position. Communists were now purged from the LBC's headquarters, and Gollancz used the Club to rally support for the war.

Between 1936 and 1939 the LBC had provided hope for thousands of people who were seeking a solution to the burning moral issues of the era. Despite its pro-Communist line, the Club's socialist propaganda and education probably ultimately strengthened the Labour Party and contributed to its victory in the post-war election.

Michael Newman

Bibliography

Dudley Edwards, Ruth. *Victor Gollancz: A Biography*. 1987.
Lewis, John. *The Left Book Club*. 1970.

Legal Profession

After centuries of public disdain and criticism the greatest change in the legal profession in twentieth-century Britain has been the extraordinary increase in prestige and status by both barristers and solicitors. The historic differences between the two branches of the profession have narrowed considerably. The prominence of the barrister has given way to a new respect earned by solicitors. The sharp demarcation between the two groups has blurred because legal responsibilities are now discharged more in common, and the financial rewards of legal practice are more evenly distributed. The traditional distinction that only barristers may plead in court while solicitors handle other legal affairs no longer holds. Solicitors may now act as advocates in County Courts, Magistrates' Courts, and in certain actions in Crown Court; barristers still hold a monopoly on appearances in the High Court, the Court of Appeal, and before the Judicial Committee of the **House of Lords**. In 1990 the number of barristers in England was approximately 3,600 and the number of solicitors was about 40,000. Despite some demands for fusion into one legal profession as in the United

States, this prospect does not seem likely in the near future.

Both segments of the legal profession have completed the process of professionalization in the twentieth century, whereby educational requirements have been strengthened and internal disciplinary control has won greater confidence from the public. Education for the Bar remains vested in the four Inns of Court in **London**: Inner Temple, Middle Temple, Lincoln's Inn, and Gray's Inn. Where once qualification for the Bar depended upon attendance at a set number of dinners, competitive examinations have replaced the earlier system. With respect to solicitors the older system of vocational education through apprenticeship has given way to a more sophisticated process that combines **university education** with clinical practice. This has reduced greatly the public perception of the profession as unethical and self-seeking.

Barristers have retained some of their customary privileges. In Britain, for example, judges are chosen only from the ranks of barristers and, more particularly, from the elite group of Queen's Counsels (QCs). Barristers remain independent contractors who share chambers (offices) with others, with whom they may sometimes find themselves on opposite sides in a particular case. The barrister may not deal directly with a client nor solicit litigation. The barrister instead takes instructions through the services of a solicitor. Success at the Bar still depends to some extent on the ability of the barrister to win the attention of solicitors who provide briefs (cases). The barrister is entitled to a specific fee, win or lose, and does not render services on a contingency basis. The limited number of barristers hones the advocacy skills of practitioners, so trials are usually legal battles between qualified adversaries.

In terms of public esteem the solicitors have made even greater advances. In 1900 the work of solicitors was restricted primarily to the conveyancing (drawing of deeds, or, more simply, doing the paperwork) of landed property. The increased complexity of business transactions made the role of the solicitor more crucial. Another source of greater public contact came in the business caused by the Legal Aid and Advice Act (1949). Although some provision for legal services for those who could not afford them had existed previously, the scope of this aid was narrow. This statute not only brought access to the legal system for many who otherwise could not have afforded it, but it also gave both an increase and stability to solicitors' incomes. Where too many lawyers had been a constant refrain, by the 1960s more solicitors were required to handle legal matters effectively. By the 1990s an equilibrium had been reached after a dramatic increase in numbers between 1960 and 1985.

Additional evidence for the improvement in the image of the legal profession occurred in its fictional portrayal. Where the attorney had previously served as an object of ridicule or contempt, the profession now gained a more favorable depiction. Perhaps the most famous barrister in this genre was the irascible Horace Rumpole, who was all too human and yet usually got it right in the end. Rumpole was the creation of John Mortimer (1923–), himself a practicing barrister before turning to literature as a career. If nothing else, the Rumpole sagas dispelled the myth of the barrister as removed from problems of daily life.

As public confidence in the legal profession grew, its place as confidant and adviser grew proportionately. Both branches have opened their ranks to **women**, making them somewhat more representative of society at large. Female membership in the profession hovers at about 10 percent, so the process of full integration is certainly not complete. The growing intellectual demands of the law have helped recruit individuals of wider outlook, and even greater specialization has not prevented this trend. The legal profession has prospered because its role in litigation and other legal procedures has demonstrated the broad range of benefits that competent counsel might provide.

Richard A. Cosgrove

Bibliography

Abel, Richard L. *The Legal Profession in England and Wales.* 1988.
Abel-Smith, Brian, and Robert B. Stevens. *Lawyers and the Courts: A Sociological Study of the English Legal System.* 1968.
Kirk, Harry. *Portrait of a Profession.* 1976.

Lehmann, Rosamond Nina (1901–1990)

While overshadowed today by **Virginia Woolf** and **Elizabeth Bowen**, Rosamond Lehmann was considered their equal by contemporary readers. Writing with grace and insight about the lives of girls and women—about their joys and desires and about the obstacles that often led them to disillusionment—Lehmann is one of the inter-war period's most distinctive and authentic writers of fiction about **women**.

Lehmann was born in 1901 at Bourne End, Buckinghamshire. Her father, Rudolph Chambers Lehmann, was well known, both as the editor of *Punch* and as an MP. The family provided a stimulating and supportive environment. Lehmann's younger sister Beatrix became an accomplished actress, while her brother John became a prominent writer, critic, and publisher, first at the Woolfs' Hogarth Press and then for his own magazine, *New Writing*. Rosamond Lehmann received a private education at home before attending Girton College, **Cambridge**, from 1919 to 1922, where she studied modern languages. She was twice married and twice divorced, first to Leslie Runciman, 1924–7, and then to Wogan Philipps (later Lord Milford), 1928–42.

The greater part of Lehmann's work was published between 1927 and 1944. Her fiction is concerned largely with women whose early expectations conflict with their experiences of life. *Dusty Answer* (1927), *Invitation to the Waltz* (1932), and *The Ballad and the Source* (1944) follow young girls as they move from the hopes of childhood into the trials of adolescence and a recognition of the difficulties of adulthood. In *A Note in Music* (1930), *The Weather in the Streets* (1936), and *The Echoing Grove* (1953), Lehmann shows the same or similar characters as adults, caught between memories of previous hope and the long disillusionment of middle age.

Critics of Lehmann's writing often praise her beautiful prose and her sensitive portrayals of inner life, but see her as lacking moral and historical vision, and have therefore assigned her a second rank. Such critics miss, however, what James Gindin has noted: that Lehmann's writing shows a clear social and historical awareness. In fact, her novels probe a wide range of difficult social and historical issues, including college-age lesbianism, adultery, **divorce**, illegal **abortion**, and the impact of war on twentieth-century women. Lehmann's writing handles such issues with a quiet but staunch refusal to settle for categorical answers. In *The Echoing Grove*—a work that stands comparison with **Ford Madox Ford**'s *The Good Soldier* (1915) and Rebecca West's *The Return of the Soldier* (1918)—two sisters at war for the love of the same man eventually put aside their jealousy and claim their solidarity in accepting "a new attitude towards sex: that a new sex may

be evolving—psychically new—a sort of hybrid" of genders.

After her daughter died of polio in 1958 Lehmann published only one more work of fiction, the short novel *A Sea-Grape Tree* (1976). This book and her memoir, *The Swan in the Evening* (1967), reflect spiritualist beliefs that Lehmann adopted as her personal answer to the problems of life. That critics like V.S. Pritchett found this faith embarrassing did much to keep her stock low. But readers today will find her novels sensitive, moving, and sociologically and psychologically compelling contributions to the representations of modern women in English fiction.

Warren Olin-Ammentorp

Bibliography

Gindin, James. "Rosamond Lehmann: A Revaluation," *Contemporary Literature*, vol. 15 (1974), pp. 203–11.

LeStourgeon, Diana E. *Rosamond Lehmann*. 1965.

Tindall, Gillian. *Rosamond Lehmann: An Appreciation*. 1985.

Leisure

Over the century as a whole there has been an increase of about twelve hours a week in leisure time for most of the employed population. The first major reduction in **hours of work** came in 1919–20 when the normal working week for manual workers in the better-organized trades was reduced from fifty-four to forty-eight hours. There was a further substantial reduction in 1946–9, with normal weekly working hours falling to 44.6 by 1950. In the second half of the century there was another reduction of normal hours to under forty by the 1980s. Already at the beginning of the century the Saturday half-holiday was well-established, but it was only after the Second World War that large groups of workers began to achieve a whole holiday on Saturdays.

A select group of workers had negotiated annual paid holidays before the beginning of the century, but the numbers became significant only in a series of staged advances from the end of the **First World War**. By 1945 10 million workers were covered by paid-holiday agreements, most of them for two weeks. Since then the time available for holidays has increased to the point where, in 1988, 99 percent of full-time manual employees were entitled to four or more weeks. In addition there were Bank Holidays, the most famous being the Monday August Bank Holiday, and established holidays at Christmas or New Year and at Easter and Whitsuntide.

Over the life cycle, constrained as it is by family commitments, the early working years tended, throughout the century, to provide most opportunities for leisure; **youth culture** can be discerned in more than embryo from its beginning. **Marriage** reduced, for both men and women but particularly for the latter, the time and opportunity for leisure, and it was not until the second half of the century that consistent patterns of retirement (at age sixty for women and sixty-five for men) and increasing longevity produced a new age of leisure for those who came to be called "senior citizens."

In terms of leisure activities the century in many ways may be described as a spectator society. The chief forms of spectating have been two: cinema in the first half of the century (annual admissions peaked at 1.6 billion in 1946), and **television** thereafter. Whereas in 1955 every resident in the United Kingdom made on average twenty-three visits to the cinema, in 1988 the equivalent figure was only 1.5; but by the latter date people were on average watching television for twenty-five hours each week. Watching sports live came a poor third to these two dominant forms of spectating.

Spectating, however, has not prevented more-active participation in leisure activities; indeed, it may have encouraged it, with the stars of sport, for example, offering role models for others less talented. Some sports, like golf, middle class in its origins, have grown from small beginnings to become major participant leisure activities. Others, like fishing, may be seen as part of the growth of hobbies in the twentieth century.

Spectating has also not prevented the continuation of leisure activities more deeply rooted in the past. Of these the most important are those associated with **drink** and the pub, the location for the biggest expenditure of money in leisure time over most of the century. Only in 1987 did expenditure on holidays, at 7.17 percent of total expenditure, take the lead from alcohol consumed away from home. The pub has had an ability to adapt to social changes and has facilitated a culture of participant competitiveness—in darts, for example—which has been sustained throughout the century.

But if the sociability of the pub has been one theme of leisure, the privacy of leisure within home and family has been another. Technology has facilitated this: The home has become more comfortable, and first radio (effectively universal by the late 1940s) and then television have provided forms of leisure enjoyable within the home. The automobile has similarly, outside the home, tended to make the family the organizing unit for leisure time; in the "family saloon" families could visit the seaside or parts of the national heritage of architectural and natural beauty.

The universality of spectating has helped create a national leisure calendar, dominated by sporting events (the Grand National, the Derby, the **Football** Cup Final, Wimbledon) but including also the celebration of Guy Fawkes night and Christmas. This national pattern suggests that, in leisure, distinctions of class, nation, gender, and race dissolve; everyone can place a bet on the Grand National and take an interest in its outcome. Undoubtedly over the century the more extreme forms of exclusiveness in leisure, represented by **London** society or by sporting and other **clubs** barring certain types of people, have diminished, but leisure activities tend to reflect rather than break down the divisions in society. Perhaps the most important of these is gender, for **women**, and particularly mothers, have rarely established for themselves any clearly demarcated time for leisure. Even those women in full-time employment enjoyed in 1991 ten hours less free time per week than men.

Leisure has often seemed to individuals to be properly free time, free not only from work, but from other constraints. Governments have not taken so relaxed a view. For them, leisure is potentially a problem; it can lead to the disorder of **football** crowds, or to drunkenness, or to damage to the environment, or simply to indulgence in entertainment perceived to be of low quality. Governments have, therefore, been concerned to control leisure activities, through licensing of pubs and of all places of public entertainment, through **censorship**, and through establishing a partially independent agency such as the **British Broadcasting Corporation** (1927) to provide a particular service. Governments have also been a major supplier of leisure activities of which they approve, including libraries, parks, museums, and swimming pools. And they have, particularly in the period after the Second World War, subsidized cultural activity through the **Arts Council of Great Britain** (1946).

Until the latter part of the century governments have often seen themselves in opposition, as suppliers of leisure, to the leisure industries. The commercial supply of leisure was well-established and large-scale at the beginning of the century—for example, in music hall or **horse racing**—but it has grown in scale at both the national and the international level. Most leisure throughout the century has been supplied through the market, but despite some striking examples of commercial supply and near monopolization of forms of leisure activity—for example, in the production of literature—there are also many ways in which leisure is organized without direct reference to the market. Voluntary organizations remain key suppliers: The churches were leaders in this in the first half of the century, and their role remains important; organized child and youth movements, like the Boy **Scouts** (1908) and the Girl Guides (1910), recruit large numbers of young people; community organizations, increasingly subsidized by the state, are also major suppliers, as are national organizations such as the Youth Hostels' Association (1930).

There is some evidence that, just as the supply of leisure has become of increasing importance in the economy over the century, so also leisure has become a more important part of people's lives. Certainly leisure has come to occupy a greater proportion of people's time; that, in turn, may mean that it has begun to become more important than work in the formation of individual identities, as a basis for sociability, and as the means by which people relate to their locality, nation, age group, class, race, and gender.

Hugh Cunningham

Bibliography

Clarke, John, and Charles Critcher. *The Devil Makes Work: Leisure in Capitalist Britain.* 1985.

Cunningham, Hugh. "Leisure and Culture" in F.M.L. Thompson, ed. *The Cambridge Social History of Britain, 1750–1950.* vol 2. 1990. pp. 279–339.

Halsey, A.H., ed. *Trends in British Society since 1900: A Guide to the Changing Social Structure of Britain.* 1972.

Jones, Stephen G. *Workers at Play: A Social and Economic History of Leisure, 1918–1939.* 1986.

Lend-Lease

American military assistance to countries that fought Germany in the **Second World War**, Lend-Lease helped Britain defeat Axis forces and committed the United States to enter the war as Britain's ally.

Franklin D. Roosevelt conceived of Lend-Lease to assist Britain, whose resources for purchasing military supplies became depleted soon after Germany occupied Paris. "The moment approaches," **Winston Churchill** warned Roosevelt in December 1940, "when we shall no longer be able to pay cash for shipping and other supplies" needed to defeat Berlin. Roosevelt realized the strategic necessity of supplying Britain, but his hands were tied by the 1934 Johnson Act, banning government loans to foreign states, and the 1939 Neutrality Act, preventing foreign sale of war materials on any terms but cash.

In late 1940 Roosevelt publicly declared that the United States would become "the great arsenal of democracy" and proposed Lend-Lease legislation. He used his famous analogy of loaning a garden hose to a neighbor whose house was on fire to justify Lend-Lease as a measure to defend the United States by enabling Britain to douse the conflagration in Europe.

Congress approved the first Lend-Lease law in March 1941, authorizing the President to "sell, transfer title to, exchange, lease, lend, or otherwise dispose of . . . any defense article . . . [to] any country whose defense the President deems vital to the defense of the United States." By 1945 the United States provided $50 billion in assistance to its allies, including $27 billion to Britain. Lend-Lease supplies were vital to the defeat of the Axis in all theaters.

Lend-Lease also proved significant in the United States' entry into war as Britain's ally. To protect Lend-Lease supply lines, Roosevelt in 1941 authorized repair of British ships in American yards, declared a protectorate over Greenland and the Azores, occupied Iceland, authorized navy convoys to sail midway to Britain and track German **submarines**, and convinced Congress to allow merchant ships to deploy deck guns and sail into war zones. By November 1941 three American navy ships had been damaged and more than 100 sailors killed safeguarding Lend-Lease material. A virtual Anglo-American naval alliance existed months before the December 1941 attack on Pearl Harbor.

Lend-Lease encompassed the best and worst of the Anglo-American wartime partnership. Churchill praised Roosevelt's "most unsordid act," and Roosevelt allowed British officials to participate in planning deliveries to European powers. On the other hand, many American officials saw Lend-Lease as a lever to reduce British trade barriers. At the second Quebec Conference (1944), Roosevelt committed Lend-Lease funds to restore Britain's industrial capacity after the war, but Harry S. Truman later reneged on Roosevelt's pledge, terminated Lend-Lease when the war against Japan suddenly ended, and used the American loan of November 1945 to elicit free-trade pledges from London. Though grateful for Lend-Lease assistance, British officials chafed at Truman's policy.

Peter L. Hahn

Bibliography

Dobson, Alan P. *U.S. Wartime Aid to Britain, 1940–1946.* 1986.
Kimball, Warren F. *The Most Unsordid Act: Lend-Lease, 1939–1941.* 1969.
Stettinius, Edward R. *Lend-Lease: Weapons for Victory.* 1944.

Lessing, Doris May Tayler (1919–)

As a chronicler of the century, writer Doris Lessing sits securely at the center of twentieth-century British literature, her fiction having documented directly the experience of living in post-war Britain from the shabby 1940s to the ethic of greed in the 1990s. With over thirty-five books, among them twenty novels, a parade of short stories, plays, poetry, essays, memoirs, and fables, Lessing provides a glimpse into a particular historical period by way of her intelligent depiction of that time. Hers has been a long-standing narrative critique of a nation responding to cultural, economic, political, psychological, sexual, and intellectual change, having set for herself the task of giving fictional shape to large social questions and the individual's experience of them as new and unpredictable.

A prolix, and sometimes ponderous, writer, Lessing has nevertheless drawn from her readers passionate commitment to those contemporary subjects she has been excavating. Feminism and sexual imbroglios are as much themes in her work as religious zealotry, schizophrenia, racial animosity, left-wing politics, terrorism, the death

of planets and parents. Thus her most important novel, *The Golden Notebook* (1962)—in which the conjoining of a particular historical and political moment permitted the creation of a remarkable tract for the times—stands as the paradigmatic example of Lessing's ability to reward the common reader, the feminist scholar, and the informed intellectual. In the novel's protagonist, Anna Freeman Wulf, Lessing comes close to realizing her vision of creating a twentieth-century Anna Karenina and of becoming herself an English Tolstoy.

Born in Persia to British parents, she was raised on a farm in southern Rhodesia, where her father had settled in the 1920s on subsidized land offered to British citizens willing to farm in then-colonial Africa. Thus, from early on, Lessing's first interrogations—sexual as well as racial—were percolated through the marginality of a colony that still perceived itself to be central to the British Empire. Married twice and involved in radical politics, she moved to England in 1949 with the manuscript of her first published novel, *The Grass Is Singing* (1950). Questions about long-standing assumptions among British colonialists in Africa regarding the certainty of their imperial role inform many of Lessing's African stories as well as the first four of her five-volume series, *Children of Violence* (1952–69), a quintet whose *Bildungsroman* form traces Martha Quest from childhood in Rhodesia through post-war Britain to an apocalyptic ending, the year 2000 marking both the century's and the series' end.

Her transition from the realistic to the fabular found itself modulated through three works: *Briefing for a Descent into Hell* (1971), *The Summer before the Dark* (1973), and *The Memoirs of a Survivor* (1974). Forming a kind of secular triptych, each novel concerns itself with its protagonist's mid-life crisis, a symptomatic fragmentation expressive of personal, gender, and societal malaise. While *The Summer before the Dark* represents the novel most connected to Lessing's earlier concerns, its forty-five-year-old heroine so typical of woman's estate as to seem almost a flattened Anna Wulf, *The Memoirs of a Survivor* becomes the work most connected to Lessing's later concerns. Its landscape—a London without name in the death throes of scavenging survival—prefigures those wastelands imagined in such novels as *The Good Terrorist* (1985) and *The Fifth Child* (1988), while its austere voice forecasts that of the chronicler in the series *Canopus in Argos* (1979–83).

The speculative fantasy and mysticism of Lessing's second series, *Canopus in Argos*, mark remarkable invention; in five volumes a set of galactic empires are engaged in rivalries and battles while a mythical and benevolent force manipulates, relocates, eradicates, and massages other empires in service of notions of commonweal and commonwealth. In retrospect, Lessing's aesthetic and political aversion to the England she had adopted in coming to London is evident here. Then and for some years it was a place where she could join others in the political debates represented by the **New Statesman**, the *Reasoner*, the **Campaign for Nuclear Disarmament** (CND), and the **Communist Party of Great Britain**, from which she resigned in 1956 following the invasion of Hungary and revelations about Stalinism. By the 1980s she proclaimed that political dogma was neither more nor less than religious bigotry. In *Prisons We Choose to Live Inside* (1987), for example, she describes her short-lived commitment to Communism as a sudden, total conversion to both a system of faith and a structure of belief, while *Shikasta* (*Canopus in Argos'* first volume, 1979) has a chronicle section devoted to the fictive biographical mappings of individuals inspired by late twentieth-century secular and national fanaticisms to systematic acts of terrorism.

Fictionalizations of the violent partisan passions inculcated by political orthodoxies may have propelled Lessing away from galactic fables and back to realism. Three novels, *The Diaries of Jane Somers* (1984), *The Good Terrorist*, and *The Fifth Child*, as well as a collection of short stories about, and sketches of, London in the 1990s titled *The Real Thing* (1992), describe a country in perilous social malaise. Its ironic title underscoring the matter, *The Good Terrorist* asks whether Britain in the last decades of the twentieth century will be piloted forward through storms of class division, civil disaffection, vandalism, racial discord, **unemployment**, intransigent governments and trade unions alike, and fanatical secular and religious orthodoxies. Panoramic in sweep and civilizing in intent, Doris Lessing's work chronicles the moral climate of late twentieth-century Britain, remaining true to the goal she announced so early on in "The Small Personal Voice" (1957):

In registering the intellectual and moral climate it is imperative for the writer to create dispassionately a world fed by social and philosophic urgencies.

Virginia Tiger

Bibliography
Draine, Betsy. *Substance under Pressure: Artistic Coherence and Evolving Form in the Novels of Doris Lessing.* 1983.
Knapp, Mona. *Doris Lessing.* 1984.
Seligman, Dee. *Doris Lessing: An Annotated Bibliography of Criticism.* 1981.
Sprague, Claire, ed. *In Pursuit of Doris Lessing: Nine Nations Reading.* 1990.
Thorpe, Michael. *Doris Lessing.* 1973.

Lewis, C(live) S(taples) (1898–1963)

C.S. Lewis, novelist, essayist, and critic, was born near Belfast, Northern Ireland on 29 November 1898. He attended the **University** of **Oxford** and was elected a Fellow of Magdalen College in 1925, where he taught until 1955, when he became Professor of medieval and Renaissance literature at **Cambridge**. His late marriage to American Joy Davidman became the subject of a successful play and film, *Shadowlands*, by William Nicholson.

The more than forty volumes Lewis wrote represent a remarkable range of interests. Those interested in defenses of orthodox Christianity are familiar with his *Mere Christianity* (1952). Readers of science fiction know his three interplanetary space novels, *Out of the Silent Planet* (1938), *Perelandra* (1945), and *That Hideous Strength* (1945). For children he created *The Chronicles of Narnia* (1950–6). Lewis first attracted attention outside of Oxford in 1936 with *The Allegory of Love: A Study in Medieval Literature*, still recognized as a classic work of literary criticism.

Lewis became a celebrity only after he began the publication of his books on religion, the first of which was *The Screwtape Letters* (1942). The **British Broadcasting Corporation** (BBC) secured him for three series of broadcasts, which were an enormous success and subsequently published as *The Case for Christianity* (1943), *Christian Behavior* (1943), and *Beyond Personality* (1945). These were later collected as *Mere Christianity*. In 1955 Lewis published an autobiography of his religious experiences to the age of thirty-one, under the title *Surprised by Joy*. The book is primarily an account of how Lewis passed, almost against his will, from atheism to Christianity.

While at Oxford, Lewis and a group of his friends (known as the Inklings) met regularly in Lewis' rooms to discuss literary matters and to read aloud the latest installments of work in progress. Among the regulars were Lewis (known as Jack to friends), his brother W.H. "Warnie" Lewis (1895–1973), Owen Barfield (1898–), J.R.R. Tolkien (1892–1971), and Charles Williams (1886–1945).

Lewis' most purely philosophical volume is *The Abolition of Man* (1943). He was an avid defender of objective values, of the idea that certain attitudes and beliefs are really true, and others really false. Lewis concluded that until quite modern times teachers (and almost everyone else) believed that the universe was such that objects did not merely receive, but could merit, our reverence or our contempt. Moreover, he maintains, this traditional morality is neither Christian nor pagan, neither Eastern nor Western, neither ancient nor modern, but general. Among other values Lewis defends in his works are freedom and the infinite significance of persons; the cardinal virtues (prudence, temperance, justice, and fortitude); and the theological virtues (faith, hope, and charity).

Because Lewis was by profession a literary scholar, he was able to relate theological and philosophical questions to myth and the imagination. Parallels in pagan mythology to the Christian story are for him not disconcerting similarities but significant signs of the truth of the Christian message. He concluded that myth puts us in touch with reality.

Michael H. Macdonald

Bibliography

Carpenter, Humphrey. *The Inklings: C.S. Lewis, J.R.R. Tolkien, Charles Williams, and Their Friends.* 1979.

Green, Roger Lancelyn, and Walter Hooper. *C.S. Lewis: A Biography.* 1974.

Howard, Thomas. *The Achievement of C.S. Lewis.* 1980.

Sayer, George. *Jack: C.S. Lewis and His Times.* 1988.

Wilson, A.N. *C.S. Lewis: A Biography.* 1990.

Lewis, (Percy) Wyndham (1882–1957)

Artist, writer, and critic, Wyndham Lewis was the founder of the only indigenous British avant-garde movement of the century, Vorticism. Acknowledged by **T.S. Eliot** as "the most fascinating personality of our time" and as "one of the few men of letters in my generation whom I should call, without qualification, men of genius," Lewis was a catalyst for the ideas of European cultural modernism in Britain. Though best known for his work as a painter, Lewis was also a prolific writer and the author of more than fifty books (including novels and works of philosophy or cultural criticism) and 360 essays and pamphlets.

Lewis was born off Nova Scotia of Canadian and American parentage. Unlike both Ezra Pound and Eliot, however—the other North American cultural expatriates with whom he associated—Lewis was raised and educated in Britain and Europe. Traveling extensively in pre-First World War Europe, he was exposed not only to the work of the European avant-garde, but also to the philosophical writings of Bergson, Nietzsche, and Sorel. Though Lewis constantly reinvented himself by casting off all previous influences, the elitist and antidemocratic strain of these early aesthetic, philosophical, and political influences were to remain important throughout his career, imbuing him with a dislike of compromised liberal democracy.

Lewis' irascible nature as well as his abstract and energetic aesthetic program alienated him from the clannish circle of early British modernists represented by **Roger Fry**, and his feud with this circle stood in the way of any substantial commercial success in either his literary or his artistic endeavors. For Lewis, Fry and the **Bloomsbury Group**—with their subtle cultural influence-peddling—epitomized the hopelessly anachronistic embroilment of British cultural life in the established privileges of wealth and status.

As a platform for his own theories, Lewis founded the short-lived Rebel Art Centre (1914) from which Vorticism developed as a movement in literature and the plastic arts. The major Vorticist exhibition was held at the Doré Galleries in June 1915. Though the literary monuments to this movement—*Blast I* (June 1914) and *Blast II* (July 1915)—marked a collaboration with the leading avant-garde figures such as Pound, Lewis would claim at the end of his life—and not without reason—that "Vorticism, in fact, was what I, personally, did, and said, at a certain period."

Lewis published his first great novel, *Tarr*, in 1918 and mounted his first one-man show in

1919, but his lack of popular success in publishing and exhibiting subsequently served to spur his eccentric movement outside the cultural mainstream. This movement took a more decidedly political turn in the 1920s, when Lewis turned his attention to the task of cultural criticism. His aesthetic estrangement from the British mainstream was compounded by his interest in right-wing and reactionary politics, which he expressed in a series of books such as *The Art of Being Ruled* (1926), *Paleface* (1929), and *Left Wings over Europe* (1936). Certainly, Lewis was not alone in this interest, but for him it was central to the inspirational impetus of his work.

In 1931 he published a work that was to prove disastrous to his career and that has marred his critical reception ever since. This work—*Hitler*—stands as one of the most important texts for the understanding of the interaction of **Fascism** and the avant-garde in the inter-war years, and though subsequently (and belatedly) recanted in two works of 1939 (*The Jews, Are They Human?* and *The Hitler Cult*), the mixture of casual **anti-Semitism** and authoritarianism in all three works has stood in the way of an adequate assessment of Lewis' role in European modernism.

In the war years Lewis was practically obliged to exile himself to **Canada** and the United States, and the experience of those years is distilled in what some consider his greatest work, *Self Condemned* (1954). If the period of exile in the Second World War fed Lewis' literary work, however, it was less productive for the visual artist. Painting portraits for money, Lewis also began to notice a deterioration in his vision, and in 1951 he became completely blind and ceased painting. On his return to Britain, he turned his last years of darkness to profit by concentrating on his writing. In these prolific last years he completed *Rotting Hill* (1951), a satirical work on the decay of contemporary Britain, as well as *Self Condemned*. Most notably, he completed the monumental metaphysical trilogy *The Human Age*—begun in 1928 with the publication of *The Childermass*—publishing two volumes, *Monstre Gai* and *Malign Fiesta*, in 1955.

The enigma of Lewis' biography consists in his apparent lack of any lasting influence on the subsequent development of British arts and letters. Of the "men of 1914"—Pound, Eliot, **James Joyce**, and Lewis—he is the only one not to have established an unassailable place in the critical canon. His implacable opposition to any and every other strain of British modernism and his political views go some way to explaining this anomaly, but it is also necessary to take note—as Lewis himself did in works such as *Time and Western Man* (1927), *The Apes of God* (1930), and *Men without Art* (1934)—of his idiosyncratic notion of aesthetic modernism. Eschewing the modernist fragmentation of individual experience, Lewis consistently favored an aesthetics of individualism in which the possibility for historically decisive action has not been lost.

Andrew Hewitt

Bibliography

Bridson, D.G. *The Filibuster: A Study of the Political Ideas of Wyndham Lewis.* 1972.

Jameson, Fredric. *Fables of Aggression: Wyndham Lewis, the Modernist as Fascist.* 1979.

Lewis, Wyndham. *Rude Assignment: An Intellectual Autobiography.* 1984.

Meyers, Jeffrey. *The Enemy: A Biography of Wyndham Lewis.* 1980.

Normand, Tom. *Wyndham Lewis, the Artist: Holding the Mirror Up to Politics.* 1993.

Liberal Party

The Liberal Party was one of two alternative British parties of national government between 1832 and 1924, vying with the **Conservative Party**. During this period, it governed the country for forty-five years, participated in governing coalitions for thirteen, and was in opposition for thirty-four. It was also within this period a major force in local governnment. Between 1924 and 1945, the Liberals—having lost their party of government status to **Labour**—nevertheless remained an important national political party, taking office in governing coalitions or keeping a minority government in office during nine of the twenty-one years. Their significance in local government, however, faded rapidly during these years. After experiencing near-extinction between 1945 and 1958, the Liberal Party—known from 1988 as the Liberal Democratic Party—achieved a modest revival. Although it has an insignificant parliamentary representation and only modest success on the local scene, the party draws millions of votes in parliamentary elections and holds the balance of power in scores of constituencies.

After its mid-Victorian electoral triumphs Liberal Party fortunes declined after 1886, when a large section of Liberal Unionists—including a radical reformist group led by Joseph Chamberlain—seceded in reaction to Gladstone's support for Irish self-government. The Liberals were also weakened in the 1880s and 1890s by dissension over foreign affairs between "Little Englanders" and "Liberal Imperialists," a tepid interest in social reform, unpopular policies such as temperance, and—after Gladstone's long-postponed retirement—a destructive leadership struggle.

The new century found the Liberal Party debilitated and—as shown in the 1895 and 1900 general elections—losing ground within the electorate. The **Boer War** dangerously sharpened the imperialist-isolationist division, threatening another party split. At this juncture the Conservative government came to its opponents' aid by passing the controversial Education Act of 1902, which infuriated Nonconformists by providing tax support for **Anglican** and **Roman Catholic** schools. In 1903 Joseph Chamberlain—who had split the Liberals in 1886—almost did the same for the Conservatives with his protectionist schemes. Although only a few Conservatives (including young **Winston Churchill**) abandoned their party to fight with the Liberals for free trade, a good many Liberal Unionists returned to their old party over the education issue.

Education and free trade, the main issues in the 1906 general election, enabled the reunited, resurgent Liberals to elect 400 out of 670 MPs and garner almost 53 percent of the contested vote. Under its successive Prime Ministers, Sir **Henry Campbell-Bannerman** (1905–8) and **H.H. Asquith** (1908–15), the Liberal Party veered leftward. Inspired by the collectivist ideas of the **New Liberalism**, progressive ministers like Churchill, **C.F.G. Masterman**, **Herbert Samuel**, and especially **David Lloyd George** sponsored welfare reforms—including **old-age pensions**, health insurance, and school meals—abhorrent to Gladstonians. The Parliament Act of 1911 stripped the Conservative-controlled **House of Lords** of its veto, and only the coming of the First World War prevented the Liberal government from implementing Gladstone's goal of Irish Home Rule. Although the Liberals lost their absolute majority in the two parliamentary elections of 1910, they were able to continue in office with the backing of Labour and Irish Nationalist MPs. Shaken by the **Marconi scandal** of 1912–13, which implicated several ministers, and by labor, feminist, and Irish agitation from 1911 onward, the Liberals were searching for a winning election issue when the war burst upon them in August 1914.

The Liberal Party reluctantly supported the government's decision to fight Germany, except for a few pacifists who gravitated to the antiwar **Union of Democratic Control** and eventually into the Labour camp. But the war soon inflicted shocks upon the Liberals from which they never recovered. While Liberal Imperialists like Asquith, Sir **Edward Grey**, and **R.B. Haldane**, as well as pragmatists like Lloyd George, took the conflict in stride, many party members were alienated by its devastating effect upon Liberal principles.

For several months the Asquith government advocated a business-as-usual policy, although a faction within the Parliamentary Party—later called the Liberal War Committee—stood behind Lloyd George's efforts to mobilize the country for all-out war. In May 1915 Asquith bowed to pressures within and outside the party and became head of a multiparty coalition. Lloyd George, as Minister of Munitions, acquired unprecedented power to regiment industry and labor in the national interest. The War Committee mobilized backbench Liberal votes for compulsory military service in January 1916, but **conscription** was a deadly blow to the party's voluntarist tradition. Many disillusioned Liberals thereafter became critical of government policies or apathetic.

The heaviest blow to the Liberal Party was the schism caused by Lloyd George's resignation from the Asquith government in December 1916 and his formation of a new coalition administration. As many as 175 Liberal MPs stood behind him, but the Asquith Liberals went into opposition and most of Lloyd George's ministers were Conservatives. The Liberal Party, in Parliament and outside, was now in disarray, with the organizational machinery still in Asquithian hands but most Liberals supporting Lloyd George's more vigorous war leadership. In May 1918 the Asquithians' failure to defeat Lloyd George in a confidence vote resulted in their proscription when the Prime Minister went to the country in the first post-war election the following December. Only thirty-six "Free Liberal" MPs were returned, while 127 Liberal recipients of Lloyd George's "coupon" were successful.

Lloyd George's attempts to transform his coalition into a progressive center party were rejected by his Conservative allies, who dumped him as Prime Minister in October 1922. Asquith and Lloyd George agreed to reunite their Liberal factions in 1923 in order to fight Conservative Prime Minister **Stanley Baldwin**'s call for protectionism. In the crucial general election of 1923 the Liberals and Labour each won about 30 percent of the vote, but Labour elected more MPs and was asked to form a minority government when Baldwin resigned. The decision of the Liberal leaders to admit Labour to office unconditionally was criticized, then and later, as politically suicidal. No longer seen as a party of government and weakened by internal bickering, the Liberals elected a mere forty MPs in the October 1924 election.

More ominous, perhaps, than electoral defeats was the Liberals' steady decline in municipal council seats throughout Britain in the 1920s. This trend, which had begun before the war, reached disastrous proportions by the end of the decade and resulted in the almost total collapse of the party's local leadership cadres. The endless feuding of the chiefs over money, policies, and personalities incurred public contempt and ridicule. By the time Lloyd George succeeded to the party leadership in 1926, the Liberals were probably beyond salvation as a governing party. Lloyd George made a valiant effort in the 1929 general election to revive the party on a platform of "conquering **unemployment**," but only fifty-nine Liberal MPs were returned.

During the second Labour government Lloyd George attempted with little success to promote constructive economic policies. He failed to persuade Labour to enact proportional representation or the alternative vote in order to give the Liberals a chance to elect MPs proportionate to their share of the electorate. Bad luck dogged the Liberal leader. Early in 1931 Sir **John Simon** and about a third of the Parliamentary Party rejected his whip, and in July he fell seriously ill. Hospitalized when the August 1931 economic crisis occurred, Lloyd George watched helplessly as his deputy, Sir Herbert Samuel, took the party into **Ramsay MacDonald**'s National government, and—against his advice—agreed to its fighting an election against Labour.

Although seventy-four Liberals were returned in the October 1931 election, as a party they were divided ineffectually among "Simonites," "Samuelites," and Lloyd George's tiny family group. These factions never reunited. The Simonites, or Liberal Nationals, in existence organizationally as late as 1966, like the Liberal Unionists before them gradually were absorbed into the Conservative Party. The Samuelites retained the official Liberal machine but not access to the National Liberal Fund that Lloyd George had acquired during his coalition days. Lloyd George took a conspicuous part in the 1935 election, distinct from the official Liberals, but afterward was semi-retired. All three Liberal factions contributed ministers to the successive National and coalition governments of the 1930s and 1940s, and included many articulate backbenchers and peers, but electorally the Liberals were insignificant until the 1960s. The number of official Liberal MPs fell from thirty-three in 1931 to six in 1951, while its share of the parliamentary vote dropped to a low of 3 percent in 1951 and 1955.

As the Conservatives and Labour had, over the years, appropriated so many of its ideological positions, the shrunken party had difficulty proving its right to life. Had Clement Davies, the Liberal leader in 1951, accepted Churchill's offer of a ministry in the new Conservative government, the party might well have gone the way of the Liberal Nationals. The decision to soldier on independently bore fruit in 1958, when the Liberals won their first by-election since 1929. By then, a new leader, Jo Grimond, had begun to restate Liberal principles of human rights and freedoms in contemporary terms. As British enthusiasm for collectivism waned, the Liberals' "middle way" became attractive to educated, middle-class suburbanites. Grimond's public image as a trendy **television** performer did his party no harm with its new constituency. In 1962 a Liberal won a spectacular by-election victory at Orpington, a commuter suburb, leaving the Labour candidate with a forfeited deposit. At about the same time, the Liberals fleetingly led the other two parties in popularity in a national opinion poll. The 1964 general election increased the Liberal MPs only to nine, but their share of the total vote rose to over 11 percent.

During the 1970s the Liberals enjoyed a degree of rejuvenation on the local level, elected hundreds of councilors, and in a number of communities rebuilt the leadership cadres that had disappeared forty or fifty years earlier. Reconstruction of local parties and identification with grass-roots causes was encouraged by Grimond's successor as leader, Jeremy Thorpe (1967–76). Thorpe's strategy paid off in the February 1974 general election, in which the Liberal vote exceeded 6 million—the largest in the party's history and close to 20 percent of the total vote—although electing only a disappointing fourteen MPs. Thorpe was criticized for turning down a coalition offer by Conservative Prime Minister **Edward Heath**, which would have brought Liberals into a government for the first time in a generation.

The next Liberal leader, David Steel (1976–88), was more Machiavellian, first negotiating a pact to keep a minority Labour government in office (1977–9), then contracting an electoral Alliance (1981) with the **Social Democratic Party**, a breakaway from Labour. The Alliance drew an impressive 25 percent of the vote in the 1983 general election, and 23 percent in 1987, but managed to elect only twenty-three and twenty-two MPs, respectively—seventeen of them Liberals. In 1988 Steel used what many Liberals and Social Democrats viewed as strong-arm tactics to effect a merger of the Alliance parties. Known now as the Liberal Democrats, and with Liberal Paddy Ashdown as leader following Steel's retirement, the enlarged party performed impressively in several by-elections, reaping the benefits of disillusionment with Tory rule. But with the Labour Party moving toward the political center, there seemed to be little immediate prospect of a Liberal Democratic breakthrough.

Don M. Cregier

Bibliography

Cregier, Don M. *Chiefs without Indians: The British Liberals, 1918–1935.* 1982.

Cyr, Arthur. *Liberal Party Politics in Britain.* 1977.

Douglas, Roy. *The History of the Liberal Party, 1895–1970.* 1971.

Morgan, Kenneth O. *The Age of Lloyd George: The Liberal Party and British Politics, 1890–1929.* 1971.

Searle, G.R. *The Liberal Party: Triumph and Disintegration, 1886–1929.* 1992.

Wilson, Trevor. *The Downfall of the Liberal Party, 1914–1935.* 1966.

Literary Criticism

L

Reflecting its epoch, twentieth-century criticism in Great Britain is best characterized by its radical diversity. If it has embraced an ideological militancy from time to time, it has also shown a fertility of invention, a willingness to combine with other fields, and a capacity to renew itself.

Around 1900 the university study of literature was dominated by philology and historical criticism, both strongly indebted to German and French models and evolutionism. While historical criticism had professionalized the discipline, it tended to lose the work of art in a background of origins and causes. Philology waned by the 1930s; historical criticism, which includes literary biography, remained the road most traveled by twentieth-century scholars.

The attempt to wrest the work of art from the control of other disciplines began toward the end of the Victorian period with a revolt against historicism, part of the larger idealist reaction to science and materialism. In Britain this was initiated by aestheticism, then taken up and carried much further by the early modernists. Aestheticism, which had proponents both in and beyond the academy, and which often ran under such names as impressionism, symbolism, or decadence, had its roots in the Pre-Raphaelites, A.C. Swinburne, and Walter Pater, reached its zenith in the 1890s, and lingered well into the Edwardian period. Its themes and values included skepticism and relativism; a subjectivizing tendency; aesthetic autonomy and the divorce between nature (or science) and art; formalism and craftsmanship; flight from the drab and an emphasis on novelty, the remote, and the irrational; a blurring of the line between criticism and creation; the spurning of social concerns and defiance of bourgeois morality and taste; faith in art; and hedonism.

The greatest single movement in twentieth-century criticism is modernism, which in the form given it by Ezra Pound and **T.S. Eliot** maintained its supremacy in Anglo-American high culture from the First World War to the early 1940s. Even afterward, movements were often refinements, narrowings, or reactions to modernism, to the point where some could divide the century between two broad periods, modernism and postmodernism. In a series of articles dating from 1910 T.E. Hulme protested the naturalism, subjectivism, and sentimental emotionality of Victorian writing and demanded a type of poetry that was concrete, accurate, and sophisticated.

An American, Pound arrived in London in 1908, was the motive force behind imagism, edited the anthology *Des Imagistes* (1914), and supported **Wyndham Lewis' Vorticism** (a vortex was a symbol of patterned energy and concentration). Arguing that poetry should be as well-written as prose, Pound urged the "direct treatment of *the thing*" as the basis of his objectivist aesthetics. The work of art should result from conscientious craftsmanship rather than from the spontaneous expression of private feeling.

An American who was trained in philosophy at Harvard, Eliot, like Pound, wrote criticism in partial justification of his poetics. *The Sacred Wood* (1920), which contains "Tradition and the Individual Talent," his essays on the metaphysical poets and Elizabethan dramatists, and his journal *Criterion* (1922–39), reestablished the canon of literature and articulated modernist principles. These principles include linguistic precision, complexity, irony and ambiguity, self-referentiality, impersonality by means of the creation of a narrator and masks, oblique as opposed to direct statements, and myth as a structural principle. Three of Eliot's main themes are his idea of tradition, the "dissociation of sensibility," and the "objective correlative." By tradition Eliot did not mean history per se, but the knowledge of the truly significant works, each of which altered the entire previous tradition. By dissociation of sensibility, Eliot called attention to the fragmentation of the self in modernity and pointed to a time when thought and feeling were integrated and mutually informing—that is, before the mid-seventeenth century and the rise of science and modernity. The objective correlative, a distancing strategy that derived ultimately from romantic aesthetics, means the events, symbols, or situations that are the objective equivalent for the poet's emotions.

Modernism entered the academy in the 1920s and 1930s through the pioneering effort of **I.A. Richards**, whose *Principles of Literary Criticism* (1924) set forth concepts of psychological value, communication, attitude and belief, internal equilibrium, and irony. His *Practical Criticism* (1929) came at the end of the decade in which many of the high-modernist masterpieces appeared and was designed to enable readers to come to terms with some of the most difficult and experimental literature ever written in the West. In this book Richards commented on students' misreadings of thirteen poems, categorized them by type of errors, and outlined a corrective method of "close reading," also known as contextualism. The method became part of the first-level teaching of literature in the English-speaking classroom (and eventually elsewhere) for half a century.

In Britain Richards exerted a potent influence on William Empson (who was his student at Cambridge) and **F.R. Leavis**, two of the principal critics of their generation. Empson's *Seven Types of Ambiguity* (1930) gave close reading its first "practical" masterpiece; its kernel idea combines contextualism with the notion that ambiguities of poetic language can be plotted in "stages of advancing logical disorder." *The Structure of Complex Words* (1950) carried the theme of ambiguity and lexical analysis to the micrological level. His later criticism takes up history and biography in an often polemical mode. Leavis' *Mass Civilization and Minority Culture* (1930) engages such themes as the neutralization of nature, cultural leveling, and the commercialization of taste through the power of the media. The cultured minority was a saving remnant in the machine age. He was the major force behind the journal *Scrutiny* (1932–1953) to which D.W. Harding, L.C. Knights, and Derek Traversi contributed.

New Criticism, so named from a book by the American John Crowe Ransom (1941), occupied the theoretical high ground in the academic study and teaching of literature from the 1940s to the 1960s. High-modernist aesthetics furnished its poetic canon and main premises, while Richards, who is the acknowledged father of New Criticism, and Empson provided central components of its method: the poem as object, self-reflexivity, polysemy, complexity, antididacticism, impersonality, craft and technique, and antihistoricism. New Critics proposed a highly formalistic approach to the work of art and rejected history and biography; their readings are characterized by a focus on irony, ambiguity, a tension of opposites, and equilibrium or closure. While the New Critics produced brilliant readings of texts, by the mid-1950s the movement was in decline, and readings became frequently repetitive and monotonous. Moreover, works were found to be so ambiguous that the value of formal closure was being seriously undermined. New Criticism had its principal success in America, but it was influential in Great Britain as well. While no New Critic,

Christopher Ricks shows its influence in his close readings.

In the 1950s and 1960s myth-and-symbol criticism flourished, living in part on New Critical premises (antihistoricism, objectivism, formalism, tension of opposites, and a quasi-religious quest for totality). The chief representative of this school is the Canadian Northrop Frye, whose *Anatomy of Criticism* appeared in 1957. What autonomy the New Critics invested in the poem, Frye extended to the entire world of literature, which operates along lines capable of being interpreted by a gigantic seasonal myth, a system mapped and managed by the genres.

Unlike the New Critics and myth-and-symbol critics, the Welsh Marxist Raymond Williams refused to exclude history. His analysis of cultural context embraces **sociology, economics,** and politics, but his application of Marxist and other theories shows that he is neither controlled nor captured by them. His works include *Culture and Society, 1780–1950* (1958), *The Long Revolution* (1961), and *The Country and the City* (1973). At **Cambridge** Williams' influence (along with allied inspirations from Richard Hoggart and the Institute for Contemporary Cultural Studies at the University of Birmingham) replaced that of Leavis. Williams' students include the **Oxford** Marxist cultural critic Terry Eagleton.

Although existentialism had made some inroads into Anglo-American criticism, it was not until the 1960s that European, mainly French and German, schools began to have a larger impact with (among others) T.W. Adorno, Michel Foucault, and Jacques Derrida. Inspired by Derrida, deconstruction takes linguistic ambiguity to the furthest limits into a radical undecidability of the text. The boundary of closure is dissolved, and the author, even as a fiction, is effaced. Where New Criticism values formal closure and the beautiful, deconstruction prefers the infinity of significations and the sublime. Deconstructive or postmodernist criticism (a label that includes deconstruction but also a number of other movements) valorizes plurality, indeterminacy, chance, novelty, antirationality, parody, rewriting, mixing genres, open form, multiple models, and *pietas* (a reverence for the local scene and private life, which relates to the increasing privatization of life).

During the 1980s the response to deconstruction has come from many quarters: New Historicism, **feminist** criticism, and cultural studies. Late twentieth-century criticism attempts to historicize the work of art, though the limits of the historical context vary considerably with individual critics. By returning to history, however, criticism has come full circle. At the outset of the century the work of art was lost among its causes; it was rescued, defended from external disciplines, and explored internally until its meanings were shown to be so superabundant that closure gave way to undecidability. Finally, in order to explain this semantic richness, history returned, and the work of art is again in danger of being lost in its backgrounds. One notes even a repetition of the aesthetic practice of dissolving the border between art and criticism in the so-called absence of textual boundaries (between life and art, from text to text) as well as in the tendency of postmodern critical readings to be performances.

This is not to say that the end merely repeats the beginning, because in its century-long journey criticism has been informed by intense study and refinement of its theory and practice.

John Paul Russo

Bibliography

Fekete, John. *The Critical Twilight: Explorations in the Ideology of Anglo-American Literary Theory from Eliot to McLuhan.* 1977.

Mulhern, Francis. *The Moment of Scrutiny.* 1981.

Norris, Christopher. *Deconstruction: Theory and Practice.* 1982.

Robinson, Alan. *Symbol to Vortex: Poetry, Painting and Ideas, 1885–1914.* 1985.

Wellek, René. *History of Modern Criticism.* vols. 5–6. 1986.

Lloyd George, David (1863–1945)

David Lloyd George, the most prominent Welsh politician of the century, was born in Manchester on 17 January 1863. He was a Liberal MP (1890–1945), Cabinet minister (1905–16), Prime Minister (1916–22), and leader of the **Liberal Party** (1926–31). Raised to the peerage as the first Earl Lloyd-George of Dwyfor in January 1945, he died of cancer in Llanystumdwy, North Wales, on 26 March 1945.

Although born in England, Lloyd George was of Welsh parentage and bilingual. When his father, a teacher named William George, died in 1864, David was adopted by his uncle, Richard Lloyd, a master shoemaker and Baptist lay preacher. Raised as a son by "Uncle Lloyd," David always used the double surname. In later life, Lloyd George recalled an impoverished childhood, but by contemporary local standards his family was middle class.

Richard Lloyd's family—including David's mother, sister, and younger brother—moved to the nearby, larger town of Criccieth in 1880. Meanwhile, Lloyd George attended an Anglican elementary school and was apprenticed as clerk to a law firm in neighboring Portmadoc. After experience in free-lance journalism and Liberal Party electioneering, Lloyd George was licensed as a solicitor in 1884.

Concealing his lack of religious commitment, Lloyd George exploited—both professionally and politically—the acrimony between North Wales' Nonconformist Welsh peasantry and its Anglican gentry. Married in 1888 to the wealthy Margaret Owen of Criccieth, in 1890 Lloyd George was elected Liberal MP for the Carnarvon Boroughs, a seat he held for fifty-five years. An intelligent woman with considerable political acumen, Margaret Lloyd George disliked London and chose to raise her family in Criccieth, living apart from her husband much of the time. His notoriety as the most philandering politician of his day, as well as Margaret's Nonconformist piety, explain why the couple's fondness increased with distance. Nevertheless, their marriage ended only with Margaret's death in 1941. Two of their five children—Gwilym and Megan Lloyd George—followed their father into politics, the former becoming a Cabinet minister.

While his sober brother, William George, managed their North Wales law practice, the youthful MP lost no time establishing a colorful political reputation, based largely on boldness and rhetoric. Parliamentary fights on behalf of Welsh (Anglican) Church disestablishment, local-option drink prohibition, and Welsh home rule produced newspaper stories (some written by Lloyd George) in London as well as North Wales. Outside Parliament Lloyd George was in demand as a platform orator and stump speaker before Nonconformist and temperance audiences, who were not informed of his occasional tippling.

Although gradually abandoning purely Welsh issues, Lloyd George was slow to become known as more than a back-bench gadfly. He

sat in Parliament for almost a decade before his unpopular opposition to the **Boer War** brought him nationwide publicity—at some risk to his personal safety. Lloyd George was drawn into an influential circle of Radical Liberals, including the party leader, Sir **Henry Campbell-Bannerman**, who deplored the war as imperialistic and costly.

Lloyd George strengthened his Liberal Party credentials after the war by his leadership of the turbulent struggle against the **Conservative** government's Education Act of 1902, which favored **Anglican** and **Roman Catholic** schools. Detested by Nonconformists, this law contributed to the Liberal electoral landslide of 1906. By then Lloyd George had become President of the Board of Trade in the **Cabinet** formed by Campbell-Bannerman late in 1905. At the trade ministry Lloyd George modified his radical image by promoting legislation useful to British business. He also achieved success as a labor negotiator, and—in conjunction with his friend and Cabinet colleague, **Winston Churchill**—began to develop an interest in social reforms.

The accession as Prime Minister of **H.H. Asquith** in 1908 resulted in Lloyd George's promotion to Chancellor of the Exchequer. He drastically changed the thrust of this office, usually occupied by fiscal moderates. In the celebrated "People's Budget" of 1909, Lloyd George appropriated funds not only for greatly enhanced defense spending—in response to German naval competition—and for the expensive new **Old-Age Pension** Act of 1908, but also for an ongoing "war on poverty." The use of a money bill to initiate policies—including a development fund to improve roads and agriculture—as well as to levy heavy new taxes brought about a showdown with the Conservative-dominated **House of Lords**. The year 1911 featured both a Parliament Act stripping the Lords of their legislative veto and a pioneering National Insurance Act in which Lloyd George introduced contributory health and **unemployment** benefits.

His anxiety to minimize defense costs to save funds for social programs gave the misleading impression that Lloyd George was a pacifist. He was, on the contrary, becoming ever more worried by German aggressiveness. During the dangerous Agadir crisis of 1911, he acted as the Cabinet's spokesman to warn Germany of the risk of war. Henceforth Lloyd George paid close attention to foreign affairs,

RICH FARE.

The Giant Lloyd-Gorgibuster: "FEE, FI, FO, FAT,
I SMELL THE BLOOD OF A PLUTOCRAT;
BE HE ALIVE OR BE HE DEAD,
I'LL GRIND HIS BONES TO MAKE MY BREAD."

"Rich Fare" (Bernard Partridge, *Punch*, 28 April 1909). The reference is to Lloyd George's 1909 People's Budget.

simultaneously urging peaceful accommodation with Germany and defense preparedness. As early as 1910, in suggesting an all-party coalition to solve national problems, he had recommended compulsory military training.

Lloyd George's political career was nearly terminated in 1912–13 by the **Marconi scandal**, in which he was accused of speculation and corruption and forced to apologize publicly. An ambitious rural land reform campaign, which Lloyd George launched in 1913 to revive flagging Liberal popularity, proved of marginal interest to the heavily urbanized electorate.

After helping Asquith carry a largely united Liberal Party into the **First World War**, Lloyd George quickly emerged as one of the most bellicose ministers. His sharp criticisms of the Liberal government's business-as-usual policy led to its fall in May 1915 and replacement by a coalition, still headed by Asquith. Appointed to a new **Ministry of Munitions**, Lloyd George ruthlessly thrust aside obstacles to increased production, especially restrictive trade union practices, and pressed successfully for military conscription. His complaints against the **army**'s static Western Front policy were unavailing, and the **Gallipoli** and Salonika campaigns of 1915, which he endorsed, were fiascos.

The rift between Lloyd George and Asquith widened as the latter failed to master such crises as the war's battle casualties and the ominous loss of British ships to German **submarines**. A movement for a negotiated peace, following the costly Battle of the **Somme** in 1916, elicited from Lloyd George a demand for a "knockout blow" against the enemy. He joined Conservatives, dissident Liberals, and powerful newspaper publishers in a conspiracy that toppled Asquith in December 1916 and also split the Liberal Party.

Innovations such as a small War Cabinet, an Imperial War Conference, a Cabinet Secretariat, and the appointment of "push-and-go" businessmen to critical jobs were among Lloyd George's contributions to an invigorated war effort. He also used the convoy system in 1917 to reduce shipping wastage, and in 1918 forced unity of Allied command upon distrustful British generals, but ultimately it was American entry on the Allied side that brought victory over Germany. Skillful manipulation of Parliament, the **press**, and public opinion enabled Lloyd George to ride out numerous attacks on his wartime leadership. As "the man who won the war," he led his coalition to a stunning electoral victory after the November 1918 armistice. But as a renegade Liberal, whose old party had been decimated by the voters, Lloyd George was a prisoner of the Conservative parliamentary majority.

Although Lloyd George had electioneered for tough peace terms for Germany, at the Paris Peace Conference of 1919 he took a moderate, constructive middle stance between American idealism and French vengefulness. More concerned now to stop the spread of Russian Bolshevism than to punish Germany, Lloyd George wanted to restore pre-war economic normality as far as possible. While acceding to severe arms limitations for the former enemy, the Prime Minister fought successfully to minimize Germany's war **reparations** and preserve its territory and industrial base. He accepted Wilson's peacekeeping **League of Nations**, although he preferred to trust British diplomacy and seapower.

As the Versailles treaty left much undone, Lloyd George during 1920–2 shuttled between London and various European cities to attend a succession of international conferences on European recovery. He failed to restore Germany and Russia to full European community membership, but he succeeded in ending military intervention against Moscow's Communist regime and in reestablishing Anglo-Russian trade. Lloyd George's government also integrated several former Arab provinces of Turkey (a wartime enemy) into Britain's sphere of influence and established a Jewish "national home" in **Palestine**.

At home, one of Lloyd George's earliest endeavors, Welsh Church disestablishment, was finally accomplished (1920), but another prewar bugbear—Irish self-government—still defied easy solutions. Two years of guerrilla war (1919–21) by Irish republicans forced the coalition government to concede Dominion status to Catholic southern Ireland, while according Protestant-majority Northern Ireland more-limited home rule. The **Irish Treaty** of 1921 alienated many Conservatives. Others were infuriated by the touting of peerages and other honors by Lloyd George's whips to raise money for his National Liberal Party. The Prime Minister's ambitious plans to allay the post-war economic slump, restructure the failing **coal** industry, construct "homes fit for heroes," and extend social services foundered on Conservative demands for fiscal restraint. After failing to organize a new, progressive center party, Lloyd

George tried various expedients to keep the coalition alive—and himself in power. The end came suddenly in October 1922, following a revolt of junior ministers fearful that the Prime Minister's bellicosity toward the new Turkish Republic might ignite a new war.

The 1920s were frustrating to the still-dynamic Lloyd George. Liberal Party reunion (1923) was halfhearted. Many followers of former Prime Minister Asquith still accused Lloyd George of apostasy and disloyalty. One source of intra-party discord was the the huge National Liberal Fund garnered during the coalition, which Lloyd George employed to run a London newspaper, the *Daily Chronicle*, and to finance policy studies of the coal industry, agriculture, and industrial reconstruction. Succession to the *de facto* Liberal leadership, following Asquith's retirement in 1926, came too late for Lloyd George. He made a final, failing effort to revivify the Liberal Party in the 1929 general election by a dramatic pledge to "conquer unemployment." In the midst of a serious illness in 1931, he abandoned the Liberal leadership.

Partially retired during the 1930s, the famous Welshman kept busy writing his memoirs, managing a model farm in Surrey (celebrated for its raspberries), and making occasional histrionic forays into politics. In 1935 he launched a "new deal" program inspired by the American example and organized a Council of Action to fight for it—with little success—in that year's general election. In high-paid articles for British and American newspapers, he stumped for rearmament, cooperation with the Soviet Union, and jettisoning of the Conservative government's **appeasement** policy. Lloyd George's curious admiration for Adolf Hitler, whom he visited in 1936, was balanced by outspoken support for the Republicans during the **Spanish Civil War**.

When the Second World War began in September 1939, he viewed British preparation as hopelessly inadequate and recommended a negotiated peace with Germany. Mainly to nullify Lloyd George's defeatism, Churchill in 1940 offered him first a Cabinet seat and then the Washington embassy. Possibly expecting a recall to power, he declined these posts but kept in close touch with the war and politics until poor health slowed him down in 1943. In that year Lloyd George married as his second wife, Frances Stevenson (1888–1972), his longtime secretary and mistress.

David Lloyd George has been controversial since death as in life. His commanding, charismatic personality attracted dedicated followers, some of whom were dropped unceremoniously after serving their purpose. His caustic repartee made bitter enemies, some of whom he later brought around to his side. The consensus of biographers and historians is that Lloyd George was a constructive politician, despite such personality flaws as egocentrism, amorality, and opportunism. His pre-war public career, with its contributions to the British **welfare state**, is rated more favorably than what followed. Lloyd George's achievements during the First World War, while important, were exaggerated by contemporaries to the detriment of less-spectacular figures. The post-war years brought him more failures than successes, but his peacemaking efforts in 1919–22 deserve marks for effort if not accomplishment. Bad luck dogged him after 1922. With a few thousand more Liberal votes in the right constituencies in the critical 1923 election, and good health during the 1931 political crisis, he might have returned to the corridors of power—where he was needed. Although Lloyd George has been portrayed as the consummate politician, his political skills were inferior to those of less imaginative and enterprising rivals. His private life, scandalous enough in the early twentieth century, raises few eyebrows today.

Don M. Cregier

Bibliography

Cregier, Don M. *Bounder from Wales: Lloyd George's Career before the First World War.* 1976.

Gilbert, Bentley Brinkerhoff. *David Lloyd George, A Political Life: The Architect of Change, 1863–1912.* 1987.

———. *David Lloyd George, A Political Life: Organizer of Victory, 1912–1916.* 1992.

Grigg, John. *The Young Lloyd George.* 1973.

———. *Lloyd George: The People's Champion, 1902–1911.* 1978.

———. *Lloyd George: From Peace to War, 1912–1916.* 1985.

Rowland, Peter. *David Lloyd George: A Biography.* 1975.

Lloyd Webber, Andrew (1948–)

Born in London into a musical family, Andrew Lloyd Webber, knighted in 1992, is the foremost living English composer of musicals for the theater. Lloyd Webber, whose father, William (1914–82), was the Director of the London College of Music (from 1964) and whose brother Julian is one of the leading British cellists, was educated at Westminster School, London. At the age of seventeen he won a scholarship to read history at Oxford, although he left after only a term. In 1965 his meeting with the lyricist Tim Rice (1944–) led to collaboration on several pop songs but, more important, the pop oratorio *Joseph and the Amazing Technicolor Dreamcoat* (1968, revised and staged in 1972) and the rock opera *Jesus Christ Superstar* (1971). Scores for the films *Gumshoe* (1971) and *The Odessa File* (1974) followed, succeeded by the musical *Evita* (Rice, 1978), based on the controversial life of the Argentine popular heroine Eva Peron. In the following years further musicals such as *Cats* (1981), *Starlight Express* (1984), *The Phantom of the Opera* (1986), *Aspects of Love* (1989), and *Sunset Boulevard (1993)* have added to Lloyd Webber's reputation, transforming him into a multimillionaire, his shows sold out months in advance. His other compositions include Variations for Cello and Rock Band (1977, orchestrated by David Cullen, 1985) for his brother, and the Requiem (1984), dedicated to his father. Both works reveal an eclectic idiom drawing on both popular and classical styles. An interest in art, particularly the pre-Raphaelites, has led him to form a foundation for buying works of art for the nation, and in 1992 he made a gift of a £10 million Canaletto to the Tate Gallery.

Trevor Bray

Bibliography
Günzl, Kurt. *British Musical Theatre*. vol. 2: *1945–1984*. 1986.

Locarno Pact (1925)

The international conference at Locarno, Switzerland (5–16 October, 1925), was the venue for the conclusion of a series of interlocking bilateral and multilateral agreements among Britain, France, Germany, Italy, and Belgium to create the Locarno Pact. Primarily designed to alleviate fears of future German aggression, the pact guaranteed the status quo of Germany's western border, together with the Rhineland demilitarized zone, while rejecting the use of force to secure territorial alterations. For Britain the importance of Locarno lay in the resulting improvement in European relations, particularly between France and Germany. The achievement of this goal had been a major aim of British foreign policy since 1919. Indeed, Locarno owed much to the efforts of the British Foreign Secretary, **Austen Chamberlain**.

Five years of recurrent Franco-German tension had culminated in a Franco-Belgian occupation of the Ruhr in January 1923. Efforts to allay French fears of future German aggression through some form of direct British guarantee of French security had repeatedly stalled. Chamberlain strongly believed that French and Belgian security was the key to bringing about a fundamental improvement in European relations. Immediately on entering office in November 1924, he was faced with having to reach a decision on the Geneva Protocol, an ambitious security scheme developed at the **League of Nations** in September. Compulsory arbitration in the event of dispute and mutual disarmament constituted the twin elements of the Protocol, which was designed to bolster the League Covenant. Chamberlain and the **Cabinet** viewed the scheme as unacceptable, if only because the French regarded it as an inadequate assurance of their security. Rejection was unavoidable, yet Chamberlain did not wish to act without being able to develop an alternative. On 20 January 1925 one was proffered by Gustav Stresemann, the German Foreign Minister, who suggested the conclusion of a Western European security pact. Nevertheless, it was only with considerable difficulty that Chamberlain persuaded the Cabinet to allow him to negotiate on the German proposals. On 12 March Chamberlain rejected the Geneva Protocol, but within a week he had reached outline agreement with the French government to negotiate a pact, together with German entry into the League. Negotiations between the different Foreign Offices proceeded to give substance to the sketch agreed between the British and French governments. In these negotiations Chamberlain, to appease Cabinet and Dominion concerns at the extent of any possible undertaking, stressed that the British guarantee would be strictly limited to Germany's western border. The Locarno agreements had substantially been made final before October, and the formal conference did little more than add finishing touches.

The Locarno Pact brought about a remarkable transformation in European relations that ushered in a new spirit of hope and conciliation.

Franco-German tension decreased significantly, and Germany was treated more as an equal than a defeated enemy. However, the security provided by Locarno was illusory. When German troops entered the demilitarized Rhineland on 7 March 1936, in breach of Locarno, the powers preferred to protest rather than uphold their obligations by declaring war.

G.H. Bennett

Bibliography

Dutton, David. *Austen Chamberlain: Gentleman in Politics*. 1985.

Johnson, Douglas. "The Locarno Treaties" in Neville Waites, ed. *Troubled Neighbors: Franco-British Relations in the Twentieth Century*. 1971. pp. 100–24.

Orde, Anne. *Great Britain and International Security, 1920–1926*. 1978.

Logical Positivism

The logical positivists were a group of mainly German and Austrian philosophers who met in the late 1920s and early 1930s to form the "Vienna Circle." The group was visited by the English philosopher **A.J. Ayer** and the American philosopher and logician W.V. Quine. Through Ayer's *Language, Truth, and Logic* (1936) it had a wide influence over English-speaking **philosophy**, especially from the aftermath of the Second World War until the early 1960s.

The program of logical positivism was the abolition of the central kind of philosophy called "metaphysics" to facilitate its replacement by science. The exponents of this philosophical school attempted to eliminate the putative claims of metaphysics as meaningless or literally nonsensical—by advocating a criterion to distinguish meaningful from meaningless sentences, called the "verification principle." This was the thesis that a sentence is literally significant if and only if the proposition it expresses is either empirical and contingent or a priori and necessary. This implies that a proposition is either decidable by observation and, if true, then could have been false, or decidable intellectually and, if true, then could not have been false. The propositions of science and common sense fall into the first category, those of mathematics and logic into the second. The sentences of metaphysics, disastrously, fell into neither category and hence did not even have the merit of being false: They were meaningless.

Stephen Priest

Bibliography

Ayer, A.J. *Language, Truth, and Logic*. 1976.
Priest, Stephen. *The British Empiricists*. 1990.

L

London

London in 1900 was the world's largest and most prosperous city. The metropolis accounted for a fifth of the population and a third of the income tax receipts of England and Wales. The financial institutions of the ancient **City of London** serviced the international economy, and the West End remained the metropolitan home of Britain's aristocratic elite. Yet late-Victorian Londoners were as fascinated by the city's poverty as by its wealth. Charles Booth's social survey, published between 1889 and 1902, described a metropolis in which one in three lived in poverty, one in eleven in "chronic want." Residential densities of up to 180 persons per acre existed in parts of the East End, where 1 million people crowded into five of London's poorest boroughs, tied to casual or sweated labor, particularly in the London docks. A city wealthy enough to support Britain's earliest department stores—Whiteley's in 1872, the more socially exclusive Harrods in 1884, Selfridges in 1909—and ninety cinemas even before 1914 was also, for the only time in its history, the **unemployment** capital of Great Britain, struggling to cope with waves of **refugees** from agrarian depression in the English shires and **anti-Semitic** persecution in Russia and Poland. The 2,000 men sleeping rough on the Thames Embankment and the 500 successful and 700 attempted suicides per year in the early 1900s provide grim indices of urban anomie.

The service sector had been the most dynamic component of the economy of late-Victorian London; heavy industry had been deterred by the capital's high rents and labor costs. The growth of services accounted for much of London's wealth, the absence of large-scale industry for its failure to dispel mass poverty. The **First World War** began the process of resolving this paradox. The war touched London only lightly, though bombs dropped by German Zeppelins from May 1915 killed 670 and injured 2,000. Many of London's buses disappeared from the streets, conscripted to carry troops on the Western Front, but, overall, total war inflicted few of its horrors upon the capital and brought a substantial benefit in the establishment of government munitions factories in the western suburbs. In peacetime these became the basis of London's inter-war industrial renaissance, resting largely upon new industries, particularly the **automobile industry** and electronics. London now benefited from its limited role in the first wave of British industrialization, largely escaping the problems of obsolescence and failing markets afflicting the older industrial areas in the Depression years. With the development of the national electricity grid in the 1920s, industry was free to gravitate to Britain's most buoyant market, and London became an attractive location for new consumer-goods industries. Industry of all kinds was drawn by the proximity of the financial services of the City and of central government, and by London's position at the center of national and international transport networks. After Britain's adoption of **imperial preference** in 1932, American firms were particularly tempted by the chance to operate from within the imperial tariff wall: Hoover and Gillette came to London in 1933 and 1937. More than half of the new firms founded in inter-war Britain were established in London and the southeast.

The *New Survey of London*, the sequel to Booth's work, though published at the height of the British Depression in the early 1930s, conveys an optimism contrasting strongly with the earlier survey. Booth's central problem of structural poverty had greatly diminished over the intervening years: The real wages of the unskilled worker had improved by 30 percent, and casual labor had virtually disappeared. Indeed, the London of these years emerges generally as a less nightmarish place than Booth's city. A drop of 40 percent in per-capita beer consumption, and the substitution of light for heavy ales had dispelled much of the drunkenness endemic in Victorian London and the violent crime that had accompanied it. The Londoner was now at greater risk of injury from the automobile than from his fellow man. A fall in levels of squalor and overcrowding had matched the drop in poverty levels, facilitated by the suburban extensions of the Underground Railway system and the electrification of the Southern Railway's suburban network in the 1920s. "Metroland"—the suburban hinterland of the Metropolitan Railway, sprawling into Buckinghamshire—epitomized the middle-class residential development of the period, unplanned and often architecturally unimaginative, but comfortable and well built. Private working-class house-building never recovered from the First World War, but municipal building filled

much of the gap, accounting for more than a third of all new houses built during the 1920s. Much of the old inner city remained visibly poor in the 1930s, but by all measurable indices of income, overcrowding, and **diet and nutrition**, the problem of poverty in London had improved substantially since Booth's day. The unemployment rate, nearly twice the national average in 1913, had fallen to half the national figure by 1929. Inter-war London was, by and large, an optimistic city.

This optimism was threatened during the 1930s less by the fear of internal decline than by the deterioration of the international position and the knowledge of London's vulnerability to aerial bombing. The **Committee of Imperial Defence** estimated in 1938 that 175,000 Londoners would die in the first twenty-four hours of war. Air raid precautions began at the time of the 1938 **Munich** crisis, with the digging of trench shelters in London's parks and squares and the free issue of 1.5 million metal "Anderson" shelters, but at the same time public swimming baths were being covertly requisitioned for the mass storage of papier-mâché coffins. To protect London's next generation nearly 1 million schoolchildren and 200,000 mothers were evacuated into the shires, an operation conducted with exemplary efficiency by the local authorities but nullified almost from the outbreak of war as homesick evacuees drifted back. In the event, the **Blitz** failed to justify more-pessimistic predictions. Inevitably London suffered far more severely than in 1914–18; 30,000 civilians were killed and 50,000 seriously injured by enemy action between 1939 and 1945 (around half of them in the Blitz proper between September 1940 and May 1941) and only one building in ten in the entire administrative county escaped damage, but London did not suffer as Hamburg, Dresden, Hiroshima, or Nagasaki suffered. Civilian morale fluctuated but never collapsed. Londoners endured some very low moments, notably in 1944 with the resumption of aerial bombing in the "little Blitz" of January, the arrival of the V2 rockets in the autumn, and the passing of the year without victory, but the traditional image of Cockney resilience was not baseless. Communal shelter in the deep-level tube stations—Piccadilly Circus accommodated 4,000 people—generated its own camaraderie, while the "blackout" and other air raid precautions produced their own consoling rituals.

The return of peace saw the resumption of many of the pre-war trends in London's

Barbican Centre (1981).

Docklands: Canary Wharf (1991).

development. The capital's economy became still more strongly focused upon the Commonwealth, the up-river docks and their ancillary industries enjoying an Indian summer of prosperity as, by 1950, a third of all Commonwealth trade passed through the Port of London. Once again war stimulated peacetime industrial growth, as outer London became a center of aircraft production in the 1950s.

The pressure of population in the inner city diminished further as the drift to the suburbs continued. The planning vogue of wartime had instilled the urge to control this centrifugal movement: Patrick Abercrombie's County of London Plan of 1944 envisaged the regulated movement of 1 million people from the central area in ten years, with around half of them to be accommodated in ten projected satellite **new towns**. Stevenage in Hertfordshire was designated the first new town of November 1946, and after the failure of its residents' legal challenge to the proposal to swamp their village with metropolitan refugees, another six new towns were created within thirty miles of London. The ordered decentralization policy of the post-war years succeeded in curbing London's inter-war sprawl and in protecting the "greenbelt" around the built-up area, at the cost of advancing the emaciation of much of the inner city.

The growing distinction between core and periphery was emphasized further, in many areas, by the arrival of new Commonwealth immigrants in the 1950s, drawn by labor shortages in the booming London economy and by the relaxation of **immigration** controls in the 1948 British Nationality Act. By the end of the decade 20,000 West Indians were settling in London annually, a figure that rose to 66,000 in 1961, along with 48,000 Asians, in anticipation of the controls introduced in the following year. By 1981 a sixth of London's population would be West Indian or Asian by birth or descent. For **Black people** in London, the price of a relative prosperity, compared to home circumstances, was prejudice, "ghettoization," and social tension, first manifested on a large scale in the Notting Hill race riots of 1958. For many, moreover, the transformation of the London economy in the 1960s would limit even their relative prosperity.

Britain's rapid retreat from Empire in the early 1960s destroyed the Commonwealth-oriented economy of the up-river docks and precipitated their closure from 1967. Riverside industry declined with them, and the collapse of other London industries followed. The 45 percent fall in manufacturing employment in Lambeth in the 1970s was mirrored in other inner London boroughs: By the mid-1980s only one in seven of the London work force worked in manufacturing industry. For the metropolitan economy as a whole these were symptoms of structural transformation rather than collapse, as Britain changed its economic orientation from Empire to Europe. The period from the mid-1950s saw an explosion of the business sector that led the central government to control new office building in central London from 1964. With occasional exceptions such as Seifert's Centre Point (1967), office building brought aesthetic disaster to much of the central business district, but it generated 100,000 jobs in ten years. The commercial office boom was followed by the expansion of financial services, as the overseas earnings of the City of London climbed from £200 million in 1965 to a peak of £9.3 billion in 1986. In the meantime London had prospered as a tourist center, receiving 8.4 million visitors a year by the mid-1980s.

These developments compensated the metropolis as a whole for the decline of its manufacturing sector, but they did not provide new jobs for the displaced manufacturing work force. London's unemployed numbered nearly 1 million, from a total population of 7.6 million, in the recession of 1980–1, and still stood at around 500,000 in the mid-1980s. Worst affected were London's young Black people, with a 40 percent unemployment rate, a statistic that exacerbated endemic tension between host and immigrant communities. This tension exploded into rioting in Brixton, Southall, Battersea, and elsewhere as part of the national wave of **urban riots** in the summer of 1981. These events provided the most conspicuous symptoms of the steady erosion of social cohesion in the inner city. Other symptoms included, by the early 1980s, the 25 percent of schoolchildren under the Inner London Education Authority (ILEA) coming from single-parent families, the 50,000 ILEA children who did not speak English as their mother tongue, and, above all, the increase in inner-city **crime** rates (the number of robberies in Brixton rose by 138 percent between 1976 and 1980). This loss of social cohesion was matched by the physical decay of the inner city, with 31 percent of inner-London dwellings classified as unsatisfactory by the Greater London Council in 1981. A new manifestation of metropolitan poverty appeared in 1988 with the abolition of the housing benefit for those under age eighteen, creating "cardboard cities" of youths sleeping rough on the South Bank, in Covent Garden, and elsewhere in the West End. A century of metropolitan development has changed much of Charles Booth's London, but the reemerging juxtaposition of wealth and deep poverty has produced a pattern with which Booth would have been familiar.

John H. Davis

Bibliography

Elliott, Michael. *Heartbeak London.* 1986.

Humphries, Steve, and John Taylor. *The Making of Modern London, 1945–1985.* 1986.

Jackson, Alan Arthur. *Semi-Detached London: Suburban Development, Life, and Transport.* 1973.

Mack, Joanna, and Steve Humphries. *London at War: The Making of Modern London, 1939–1945.* 1985.

Michie, R.C. *The City of London: Continuity and Change since 1850.* 1992.

Sansom, William. *Westminster at War.* 1947.

Weightman, Gavin, and Steve Humphries. *The Making of Modern London, 1914–1939.* 1984.

London Government since 1900

Victorian London had struggled to solve the problems of governing a conurbation too large for unitary government, a city whose government needed to reflect both the metropolitan and the parochial allegiances of its inhabitants. The model completed by the 1900 London Government Act comprised two tiers, with a central London County Council (LCC), created in 1888, handling metropolitan functions, and twenty-nine Metropolitan Boroughs exercising local powers. The apparent simplicity of this arrangement was marred, however, by various anomalies reflecting earlier *ad hoc* treatment of London's municipal needs. In London's central business district the City Corporation was a wealthy and powerful relic, exercising municipal authority—including **police** control—within the square mile of London's original medieval settlement. The boundaries of the administrative county of London, first defined in the 1850s, now failed to reflect the extent of the built-up area: By 1901 more than 30 percent of Londoners lived outside the county. Several standard municipal powers were denied London's authorities: water, gas and electricity supply, and the docks remained in private hands, while the Metropolitan Police force had been controlled by the central government since its creation in 1829.

The scope for a "municipal revolution" in London akin to that in Victorian provincial towns was, therefore, limited. The LCC, with its superior resources and its ability to promote metropolitan rather than parochial policies, possessed the greater potential, and it was this potential that the Progressive Party, mostly radical **Liberals** with a **Labour** fringe, sought to realize during their control of the council down to 1907. They promoted London's first large-scale **housing** schemes, purchased and operated its tramway network, and attempted to alleviate the capital's poverty, but their ambitious policies aroused local opposition in a city where metropolitan identity remained limited. They were defeated by the reaction to high-spending municipal government in an inflationary period, emanating from the highly assessed West End and from the Conservative suburbs. Between 1907 and 1934 control of the council passed to the **Conservatives** or "Municipal Reformers."

Municipal reform did not imply municipal nihilism. Progressive totems such as the direct labor Works Department and the loss-making Thames steamboat services were sacrificed, and the council failed to support proposals to extend the administrative county put before Viscount Ullswater's Royal Commission on London Government of 1921–3, but circumstances ensured that the LCC remained active. In 1904 it had inherited 500 schools on the demise of the London School Board; by the 1930s it was responsible for the education of 750,000 children. After the First World War it became the principal agent in London of the central government's housing drive; the inter-war period saw the building of both "cottage" estates and block dwellings on a far greater scale than before 1914, and the council was landlord to almost 100,000 households by 1939. With the reform of the Poor Law in 1929, it inherited responsibility for public assistance and for Poor Law medical services, including 140 **hospitals** and the London ambulance service. As education authority, housing authority, health authority and, before 1933, tramways authority, the inter-war council approached the ideal of the omnicompetent metropolitan body. Though the **Second World War** curtailed the council's normal activity, it increased its prominence as it supervised evacuation, civil defense, and the Rescue Service, which saved 25,000 lives during the conflict.

The council reached its zenith in the 1930s and 1940s; the subsequent development of the **welfare state** limited the scope for municipal enterprise. In 1948 the LCC's health services passed to the new **National Health Service**. Following the loss of the council's tramways to the nationalized London Passenger Transport Board in 1933, Whitehall was emerging as the top tier of London's administrative system. With local powers already in the hands of the boroughs, and London's water supply, docks, and electricity managed (from 1902, 1908, and 1925, respectively) by joint boards on which the LCC had only minority representation, the council's future role became doubtful. Political friction between the LCC, under Labour control since 1934, and the Conservative central government reinforced these doubts in the 1950s. In 1957 another Royal Commission on metropolitan government was appointed under Sir Edwin Herbert. It prompted legislation in 1963 creating an enlarged Greater London Council (GLC) governing almost the entire built-up area, but at the same time reshaping the second tier with the creation of thirty-two enlarged London Boroughs, envisaged as principal authorities in the new system. The GLC, at its inception in 1965, was assigned a "strategic" London-wide role, and given control of London's buses and underground railways in the only significant devolution of power from the central government in the entire period, but it was not entrusted with the education services already run by the outer boroughs, and it saw its own education service transferred to a new Inner London Education Authority on which its representatives shared power with those of the inner-London boroughs. From the start the Greater London Council was, therefore, a body with a large budget but a limited *raison d'etre*, making it vulnerable to politically inspired dismemberment in the 1980s. The election of a Labour Council in 1981, under the controversial Ken Livingstone, brought conflict with the **Thatcher** government over the council's proposals for industrial regeneration, aid to voluntary groups, and cheap public transport. Thatcher's reelection in 1983 led to the end of a century of democratic metropolitan government with the council's abolition in 1986. Its replacements include the unimaginatively titled London Residuary Body, charged with winding up its affairs and obligations, a number of *ad hoc* metropolitan agencies such as London Regional Transport and the London Fire and Civil Defence Authority, and various joint committees of the boroughs. Some powers have devolved to the boroughs and the City Corporation, while substantial reserve powers have passed to the central government. In 1995 London was the only European capital without a citywide municipal authority.

John H. Davis

Bibliography

Davis, John. *Reforming London: The London Government Problem, 1835–1900.* 1988.

Gibbon, Gwilym, and Reginald W. Bell. *History of the London County Council, 1889–1939.* 1939.

Hebbert, Michael, and Tony Travers, eds. *The London Government Handbook.* 1988.

Saint, Andrew, ed. *Politics and the People of London: The London County Council, 1889–1965.* 1989.

Young, Ken, and Patricia Garside. *Metropolitan London.* 1982.

London School of Economics and Political Science

The London School of Economics and Political Science (LSE) was founded in 1895, when **Sidney and Beatrice Webb** used a **Fabian Society** bequest to found a college devoted to the social sciences. The LSE was intended to demonstrate their belief that the objective study of social facts would ineluctably establish the case for state control of social and economic life.

The socialist reputation of the school was later reinforced by the presence of such future **Labour Party** leaders as **Clement Attlee** and **Hugh Dalton**. In the inter-war years the main symbol of LSE socialism was the Government Department under **Harold Laski**, whose transition by the 1930s to a sort of Marxism attracted an international-nationalist audience. During and after the Second World War **Richard Titmuss** and Brian Abel-Smith identified the

Social Administration Department with the Labour government-led **welfare state**.

However, the Webbs were collectivists in general before they were socialists in particular: State regulation was to become the creed of all parties, not just Labour. It was appropriate, therefore, that the school's first Director, W.A.S. Hewins, was a Conservative protectionist imperialist, and that another Director, **William Beveridge**, was a Liberal who in 1942 founded a welfare state whose aim was to make socialism unnecessary.

The open nature of the Webbs' legacy licensed other developments that made the school something very different from "a school for socialists." The emphasis on objective enquiry (the school's motto is *Rerum Cognescere Causas*) could easily generate research inconsistent with or irrelevant to collectivism. The school's title—"Economics and Political Science"—was clearly intended to be heuristic rather than mandatory; its subjects came to include **anthropology, history**, geography, **sociology, psychology**, linguistics, and **philosophy** (a department which, revived by Karl Popper, was as interested in natural as in social science). There is, oddly, no department of political science; politics is taught in the Department of Government.

In the Economics Department of the 1930s, following the earlier example of Edwin Cannan, Lionel Robbins, Arnold Plant, and Friedrich von Hayek were combatting not only socialism and collectivism, but also **John Maynard Keynes**—and this at a time when the trend of public policy in Britain was moving in the opposite direction. Anthropologists such as Bronislaw Malinowski, Raymond Firth, and Maurice Friedman, historians such as William Medlicott, and sociologists such as Morris Ginsberg were not primarily (or at all) exercised by questions of the practical relevance of their work. Robbins, an economist always deeply involved in public life, never lost his philosophical interest in questions of methodology, and this latter concern led him to emphasize the importance of mathematics to economics. His efforts here helped to create an Economics Department whose "pure" mathematical and econometric character came to replace its earlier "applied" concerns.

Most revealing of all was the succession, in 1951, of Michael Oakeshott to Laski's chair of political science. Oakeshott established himself as a "conservative" thinker of international repute, and his controversial inaugural (*On Political Education*) argued for the utter irrelevance of academic inquiry to practical politics and announced his view of the university as concerned solely with the former. Oakeshott's arrival exemplifies two important aspects of the school. First, it confirms that indifference to practical relevance is as strong an element in its tradition as is engagement. Second, it shows that, nonetheless, the question of the relationship between theory and practice has been a perennial theme in the school's academic life. Oakeshott himself was best known, before his arrival, for his published hostility to post-war British socialism.

What the Webbs had bequeathed was not a school for socialists or collectivists, still less a school where uncommitted scholarship had a subordinate place. The inheritance was, rather, a school solely concerned with social science (and the intellectual implications of that concern) and, therefore, with the relationship between academic inquiry and "practical" public policy. This core concern explains both the status of its library as the preeminent social science collection in Europe, and the attractions of its Graduate School, which has come to constitute more than half of its 5,000 students. These students come from almost every country; more than half are from outside Britain.

But the collective identity of the LSE does not reside only in this intellectual core; there is, in addition, the underlying question of how the school is governed. In the formal, teaching sense, the collective social science focus was given concrete form in the B.Sc.(Econ.) degree. This (the school's major degree) sought to expose undergraduates both to the variety and scope of the social sciences and to later specialized study in one particular field. It attempted to avoid the incommensurate and atomistic world of university institutions based on a variety of single-subject degrees. Academic specialization has inevitably imposed strains on these inter-departmental/inter-disciplinary collaborations, but there have always been compensating pressures. There has been a productive tension between successive directors (and the bureaucracy of which they are in nominal charge) and the academics. The autocratic ambitions of Beveridge were an important stimulus to this process, but the participatory values of the school probably owe more to the nature of social science inquiry itself—another unintended legacy of the Webbs. Since the 1970s, the strength of this collective identity has enabled the school to face numerous external pressures with a significant degree of self-confidence. It has so far weathered public-expenditure cuts by moving rapidly to a self-financing position, attempts by successive British governments to dictate its future, and the oscillations of British educational policy in general.

Alan Beattie

Bibliography

Beveridge, Janet. *An Epic of Clare Market.* 1960.

Caine, Sir Sydney. *The History of the Foundation of the London School of Economics and Political Science.* 1963.

Dahrendorf, Ralf. *LSE: A History of the London School of Economics and Political Science, 1895–1995.* 1995.

Robbins, Lord. *Autobiography of an Economist.* 1971.

Low, David (1891–1963)

David Low, the most influential political cartoonist of his era, was born in **New Zealand.** His Scots-Irish parents fostered his independence, as did the Antipodean radical tradition. As a child, he was attracted to **caricature** by English halfpenny comics, such as *Chips, Comic Cuts, Larks,* and *Big Budget.* A self-taught artist, Low was stimulated to refine his style by his discovery in *Punch* of Charles Keene, Linley Sambourne, and especially Phil May. At sixteen he joined the *Sketcher,* whose proprietor, Fred Rayner, taught him to draw from life. Low systematically sent his work abroad, and in 1911 the Sydney *Bulletin* lured him to its Melbourne office. At the *Bulletin,* a nursery for cartoonists and radical journalists, Low refined his techniques and style, stimulated by cartoonists such as Alf Vincent, Will Dyson, and Norman Lindsay. Low's best-selling *Billy Book* (1918)—a cartoon anthology mocking Prime Minister "Billy" Hughes—provoked Arnold Bennett to bring Low to the Cadbury newspapers' attention.

ON THE HOME FRONT

"On the Home Front" (David Low, *Evening Standard,* 6 February 1940). Low's celebrated Colonel Blimp is labeled "Tradition"; Neville Chamberlain is the figure in the center.

Low came to London in 1919 and swiftly became the leading Fleet Street cartoonist, first at the Liberal *Star*, then from 1927 to 1950 at **Lord Beaverbrook**'s *Evening Standard*. He launched a widely copied weekly cartoon series on **London** life and institutions. Anthologies of his cartoons at the *Star* and the *Standard* sold well. A series of perceptive caricatures for the *New Statesman* appeared as *Lions and Lambs* (1928) with "Lynx" (Rebecca West).

It was for the *Evening Standard* that Low produced his most famous and influential cartoons. His cast of characters: The diehard Colonel Blimp; the impish Beaverbrook; the flapper Joan Bull; the pipe-puffing pig farmer, **Stanley Baldwin**; the little dog Musso; Hit and Muss and Muzzler (Mussolini and Hitler); the Shiver Sisters; **Neville Chamberlain** and his umbrella; and the gentle TUC Carthorse delighted and informed a troubled generation. Low's Saturday "Topical Budget" filled an entire page with a panorama of the week's events and personalities. In 1934 Low introduced Blimp to the public as part of a one-man campaign against the tragic muddle of those locust years. In 1938 and again in 1940 the Foreign Office asked Beaverbrook to tone Low down. Both demurred. His cartoons reflected the public's horror at Hitler and Mussolini's aggression, and Low's annoyance and distress at the groveling, misguided appeasers.

In 1942 Low allowed Emeric Pressburger and **Michael Powell** to produce *The Life and Death of Colonel Blimp*. Unable to forestall this affectionate satire, **Winston Churchill** personally insisted that the Ministry of Information censor the film to conform to his mystical vision of the war effort and the British officer corps. Low's anthologies, *Low's Political Parade* (1936), *Low Again* (1938), and *Years of Wrath* (1949), were influential best-sellers. His caricatures, especially those in *The Modern "Rakes Progress"* (1934), enliven many of the prominent figures of this era.

After the war Low, feeling stale, left the *Standard* in 1950 for a short, unhappy stay with the *Daily Herald*. His final years, 1953–63, were spent with the *Manchester Guardian*. His clear moral and political viewpoint, visual and verbal satire, and technical mastery enlivened British editorial cartooning. Low was a lifelong self-educator, a quick study, and a hard worker; his cartoons and caricatures shape our view of his era. He finally received a knighthood for his work in 1962.

Peter Mellini

Bibliography

Bryant, Mark, ed. *The Complete Colonel Blimp*. 1991.
Low, David. *Low's Autobiography*. 1956.
Mellini, Peter. "Colonel Blimp's England," *History Today*, vol. 34 (1984), pp. 30–7.
Seymour-Ure, Colin, and Jim Schoff. *David Low*. 1985.

Lugard, Frederick John Dealtry (1858–1945)

Frederick Lugard was a British soldier and colonial administrator whose most notable contribution to the history of colonialism was his policy of indirect rule through local tribal chiefs. That policy and his name were especially linked with Nigeria, where he served as High Commissioner Northern Nigeria (1900–6) and as Governor and Governor-General of all Nigeria (1912–19). He received a knighthood in 1901 and entered the peerage as Baron Lugard of Abinger in 1928.

Born of missionary parents in Madras, India, in 1858, Lugard grew up in Britain, where he briefly attended Sandhurst. In 1878 he embarked upon a military career with the Norfolk Regiment. While in British India he had fallen in love with a woman who later left him for a circle of fast-living friends in London. Emotionally distraught, contemplating suicide, he abandoned his successful military career at age twenty-nine and set sail for Africa, where he hoped to find danger, or even death. Lugard finally calmed down enough in 1888 to enter the service of the African Lakes Company in eastern Africa, where he seemed to find his purpose in life—working for the greater glory of the British Empire.

Lugard put in years of dedicated service to that Empire in Nyasaland fighting slave traders; in Uganda, where he facilitated its creation as a protectorate in 1894; and in Nigeria, where he developed the concept of indirect rule. His system consisted of leaving intact the native states and chiefdomships in Nigeria, thereby controlling the colony through local, native rulers and tribal customs. Lugard's system of indirect rule had a enormous impact on colonial administration, soon becoming the norm in British West Africa. In 1902 he married Flora Shaw, correspondent for *The Times*, a colonial expert and an inveterate traveler in her own right. She could not stand the climate of West Africa, so in 1907 Lugard accepted the governorship of Hong Kong, where he helped found the University of Hong Kong. Lugard later returned to Nigeria to oversee the unification of the Northern and Southern protectorates. In 1919 he retired, but he remained active in colonial affairs, frequently speaking out on the subject in the **House of Lords**. He published *The Dual Mandate in British Tropical Africa* in 1922, and it quickly became the classic text on the subject of indirect rule. He died in England on 11 April 1945.

Richard A. Voeltz

Bibliography

Lugard, Frederick. *The Dual Mandate in British Tropical Affairs*. 5th ed. 1965.

Nicholson, I.F. *The Administration of Nigeria, 1900–1960*. 1969.

Perham, Margery. *Lugard: The Years of Adventure, 1858–1898*. 1956.

———. *Lugard: The Years of Authority, 1898–1945*. 1960.

Perham, Margery, and M. Bull, eds. *The Diaries of Lord Lugard*. 4 vols. 1959–63.

Lutyens, Edwin Landseer (1869–1944)

The **architecture** of Edwin Lutyens was grounded in the venerable associations of the English village, sustained by an Arts and Crafts sensitivity to materials and traditional building techniques, and invigorated by a spatial ingenuity that contributed to the creation of some of the most accomplished work of his generation in England. During an era of "pioneer modernism" it was the traditionalist Lutyens who established a position of preeminence in twentieth-century British architectural history unmatched since Christopher Wren.

Lutyens was born in the Surrey village of Thursley, and it was here amidst rambling country lanes, dense woodland copses, and hoary village structures that he formed his earliest architectural aesthetic. His first major work to embody this Lutyenesque domestic style was Crooksbury (1889–91), a rambling Surrey house whose added east brick wing of 1898 (since altered) would also introduce his restrained classical aesthetic wittily dubbed "Wrenaissance." It was also here that Lutyens met Gertrude Jekyll, whose plantings would join Lutyens' house designs and garden layouts to create an Edwardian tradition of comfortable cottages and old-fashioned **gardens**.

Lutyens' country houses of the 1890s and early twentieth century especially give evidence of this traditionalism. Munstead Wood (1894), Jekyll's home and garden laboratory, was a small estate of huts, cottages, and seasonal gardens. Munstead Wood house itself was a stone cottage, accented by oak casement windows, tall brick chimneys, and sheltering expanses of plain tile roofs that nestled the domestic forms close to the land and Jekyll's plantings. High Hascombe (1896), Fulbrook (1897), Orchards (1898), and Tigbourne Court (1899)—all in Surrey—continued to establish Lutyens' reputation, advanced significantly by the frequent publication of his houses in *Country Life*. Indeed, in 1904 Lutyens designed for *Country Life* its London headquarters, the architect's first office building and another exercise in the "Wrenaissance style." Moreover, it was for *Country Life* editor Edward Hudson that Lutyens built his most published house, the Deanery Garden (1901), and that he made habitable the ruined Lindisfarne Castle on Holy Island, Northumberland (1903), and altered Plumpton Place, Sussex (1928). These varied yet related architectural manipulations of history, traditional form, and contextualism help define the essential ingredients of Lutyens' vernacular aesthetic.

Deanery Garden lies unobtrusively behind ancient garden walls in the heart of the village of Sonning, Berkshire, the house less than 100 years old yet capturing the timeless spirit of the village setting. Folly Farm (also 1901 and in Berkshire) joins an existing aged farmhouse to a classical "seventeenth-century Dutch" wing by Lutyens (1906) and further to a 1912 vernacular wing, whose southwest corner suggests forms approaching the American Henry Hobson Richardson in his translations of the English Queen Anne traditions of Richard Norman Shaw. Little Thakeham (1902) in West Sussex offers ironic declarations and denials of axis and symmetry in its garden elevation and Elizabethan hall plan. Tigbourne Court is also remarkable in its architectural contradictions, juxtaposing a picturesque garden front, traditional building techniques, and unexpected classical references.

Homewood (1901) in Hertfordshire provides Lutyens' ultimate synthesis of these vernacular and classical themes; on Homewood's garden elevation a classical villa sprouts forth from the flanking and nestling farmhouse roof. Almost metaphorically, Lutyens declared here the birth of his classical persuasions from the womb of native vernacular traditions; as his

Deanery Garden, Sonning, Berkshire (Edwin Lutyens, 1901): A masterpiece of residential architecture built for Edward Hudson, editor of *Country Life*.

twentieth-century work evolved, classicism for individual projects would become dominant and explicit.

Nashdom (1905–9) monumentalized eighteenth-century Georgian facades, defined wholly by fenestration, axis, and projecting bays. His compact Georgian house in Kent, The Salutation (1911), with its red brick construction in two main stories and five bays with quoins, its central door, and its hipped roof with tall chimneys and three dormers created the model for the twentieth-century neo-Georgian suburban detached house. At Marsh Court (1901) artisan-mannerist details provide classical detail within a Haddon Hall inspired Tudor shell. And in Yorkshire Lutyens produced his most playful exercise in the "high game of architecture." Heathcote (which Lutyens called Sanmichele; 1906), was a mannerist pile of transmogrified classicism that more than vaguely referenced the mannerist decorative overlays of sixteenth-century Italy, the sculptural richness and scale manipulations of Nicholas Hawksmoor, and the composition of such Anglo-Palladians as Colen Campbell.

It is certainly at New Delhi (1912–29) that Lutyens both rationalizes and monumentalizes British classicism in the most "elemental" and memorable way. While his orderly layout at Hampstead Garden Suburb (1908–9), balancing The Institute with his Free Church and St. Jude's Church, looks forward to his classical planning at the Indian capital, the monumentality of his city plan of New Delhi and the masterful handling of climax, scale, and detail at his domed Viceroy's House is unsurpassed in his *oeuvre*. Only his Thiepval Memorial Arch (1924) and Liverpool Cathedral project (1929–43) would approach this classical grandeur and monumentality in their free composition of triumphal arch motifs. The elemental, abstract simplicity of Lutyens' Cenotaph in Whitehall (1919) distilled and conveyed the essential message of war's desolation. In a similar way at New Delhi, Lutyens masterfully embodied the final glories of imperial Britain; the focal climax of his plan, the Viceroy's House, is architecturally localized by Moghul details in a subtle and comfortable symbiosis with classical motifs, and humanized, especially by its gardens, by retaining the scale and spirit of an English country house. From his roots in the English vernacular, Lutyens crowned his career in India with a demonstration that he was a master of Western architecture's oldest established language: classicism.

Among his other major commissions were the Midland Bank in the City and the British Embassy in Washington. Lutyens was knighted in 1918, served as President of the Royal Academy, 1938–44, and received the Order of Merit in 1942.

Robert M. Craig

Bibliography

Brown, Jane. *Gardens of a Golden Afternoon: The Story of a Partnership, Edwin Lutyens and Gertrude Jekyll*. 1982.

Butler, A.S.G., with George Stewart, and Christopher Hussey. *The Architecture of Sir Edwin Lutyens*. 1950.

Gradidge, Roderick. *Edwin Lutyens: Architect Laureate*. 1981.

Inskip, Peter. *Lutyens*. 1979.

O'Neill, Daniel. *Sir Edwin Lutyens: Country Houses*. 1980.

Lytton Commission (1931–1932)

Named after its British chairman, Victor, Second Earl of Lytton (1876–1947), the commission was set up in December 1931 by the **League of Nations** in response to an appeal by China concerning the violation of its sovereignty by Japan. The Lytton Commission was to study and report on the circumstances surrounding Japanese military action following the Mukden incident of September 1931. Japanese troops of the Kwantung army had staged a mock bandit attack on the Japanese-controlled South Manchuria Railway near Mukden, and were using this as a pretext to take over Manchuria. The final report of the commission and how it was perceived highlighted the extent to which Great Britain and the other European powers were anxious to avoid a confrontation with Japan in the early 1930s.

The **Foreign Office**, under Sir **John Simon**, saw no vital interest at stake in Manchuria, an attitude shared by the other powers. It was accepted that Japan had acted with an unnecessary measure of force, but with the partial exception of the United States (which, at the instigation of Secretary of State Henry Stimson, adopted a policy of nonrecognition toward the new puppet state of Manchukuo), there was a fair degree of sympathy and understanding among the powers concerning the need to intervene in order to protect economic interests when the local Chinese authorities appeared unable to maintain order.

Given that its members were mostly representatives of the European powers, the Lytton Commission tended to reflect this mentality. A sympathetic point of view, however, was counterbalanced by the undeniable evidence that all control over Manchurian affairs had been forcibly taken out of Chinese hands. In drafting the commission's final report after many months of travel, Lord Lytton felt compelled to state that while no clear-cut violation of sovereignty had taken place in view of the inability of the Chinese government to keep the peace in Manchuria (and the right of the Japanese to defend their lives and property), the new status quo was unacceptable. He proposed that limited Chinese sovereignty be reestablished, with adequate safeguards for Japanese interests in the region and strict limitations on the number of Japanese and Chinese troops in the region.

The British government hoped that the evenhandedness of the final report would allow room to negotiate a face-saving formula that would avert a confrontation between the leading members of the League of Nations and Japan. Overt action by the League, it was feared, would drive Japan toward further aggression and might even provoke military action against the naval base at **Singapore** at a time when Britain was fully occupied with the political and economic consequences of the Depression. However, despite lack of action by Britain and the other powers in response to the report—the possibility of an arms embargo was raised and swiftly abandoned in **Cabinet**—when the League Assembly voted overwhelmingly in favor of the solution proposed by Lytton on 24 February 1933, the Japanese delegation walked out and announced that Japan would be leaving the League the following month.

S.P. MacKenzie

Bibliography

Bassett, R. *Democracy and Foreign Policy*. 1952.

Louis, William Roger. *British Strategy in the Far East, 1919–1939*. 1971.

Northedge, F.S. *The League of Nations: Its Life and Times*. 1986.

Thorne, Christopher. *The Limits of Foreign Policy: The West, the League, and the Far Eastern Crisis of 1931–1933*. 1972.

M

MacDiarmid, Hugh (Christopher Murray Grieve) (1892–1978)

Hugh MacDiarmid—poet, critic, nationalist, Marxist, polemicist—was the key figure in the literary and cultural movement called the Scottish Renaissance. As an editor, publisher, and essayist he defined and promoted it; as a poet he produced its finest work. Throughout his life, moreover, he sustained a public commitment to **Scottish nationalism** and the Scots language that has profoundly influenced the development of twentieth-century **Scottish literature** and language. His early poetry, written in Scots, appeared in *Sangschaw* (1925); *Penny Wheep* (1926); his book-length masterpiece, *A Drunk Man Looks at the Thistle* (1926); and *To Circumjack Cencrastus* (1930). Both an activist and a writer, MacDiarmid founded the Scottish Centre of PEN, helped found the National Party of Scotland, and was active in the **Communist Party of Great Britain**. Both his Marxism and his nationalism were part of a life-long resistance to English cultural, political, and literary dominance in Great Britain.

In the 1920s MacDiarmid launched the Scottish Renaissance by publishing a three-volume series, *Northern Numbers*, to introduce new Scottish poets. In 1922 he started *The Scottish Chapbook*, a journal of Scottish literature and cultural criticism aimed at redefining the national scene. His own Scots lyrics first appeared there, along with regular editorials on Scots as a literary medium that could be recuperated as a distinctive national language; his motto was "Not Burns, Dunbar." The *Scottish Chapbook* (August 1922–November/ December 1923) was succeeded by the *Scottish Nation* (May 1923–December 1923) and the *Northern Review* (May 1924–August 1924). In 1926 he wrote a series of articles in the *Scottish Educational Journal*. In every venue he argued for Scotland's culture, literature, and distinctive languages (Scots and Gaelic).

MacDiarmid's early lyrics were, in part, linguistic experimentation. Written in "Synthetic Scots"—a composite of words from any region or historic period—they were intended to assimilate the full range of Scottish life into literature and to demonstrate that modern intellectual poetry could be written in the Scots vernacular. His poetry was intended to instance a new, modern aesthetic as well as a vehicle for transforming Scottish national culture.

In *A Drunk Man Looks at the Thistle* (1926) MacDiarmid moved from lyrics to the long poem, a form he increasingly championed as a way of "opening out" and incorporating the complexity of modern life. Also written in Scots, it includes translations of poems from Russian and European writers as well as references to a wide range of literatures. Using quotation and allusion, MacDiarmid draws on alternative traditions to create a highly complex modernist text deliberately countering the canonized European tradition. *To Circumjack Cencrastus*, MacDiarmid's last long poem in Scots, reflects his increasing interest in Gaelic literature and history as Scotland's most distinctive tradition.

In the 1930s MacDiarmid shifted from writing lyrics in Scots, strongly based in the sounds and rhythms of the vernacular, to long poems in "Synthetic English" that experimented with both technique and theme. Several poems, notably "On a Raised Beach," use obscure, technical English vocabulary or minute examinations of physical detail in stones, plants, water, or landscapes to create a poetry that joins "aesthetic effects" with what MacDiarmid called "the work of prose." He wished to push English to express more complex possibilities of meaning and, in the process, to continue to challenge the English-based tradition. Many of his later poems explore Gaelic values and cultural forms such as bagpipe music and the Celtic myth. His most radical break with poetic tradition was the late "poetry of fact," including *The Kind of Poetry I Want* (1961) and *In Memoriam James Joyce* (1955), both containing extensive quotations, long lists of obscure words and references, commentaries on world language, and extended images. Little understood at the time, this poetry is postmodern in its move toward multiculturalism, linguistic play, and the dissolving of genre boundaries.

In his poetry, prose, political activity, and cultural analysis, Hugh MacDiarmid challenged the dominance of English language, values, and ideas in Britain. He called instead for a mutually complementary interchange of distinctive contributions from all of the countries that make up Britain. His major importance is as a leading proponent of Scots as a distinct language and as the foremost Scottish poet in the twentieth century.

Nancy K. Gish

Bibliography
Gish, Nancy, ed. *Hugh MacDiarmid: Man and Poet.* 1992.
MacDiarmid, Hugh. *The Letters of Hugh MacDiarmid.* 1984.
———. *Lucky Poet: A Self-Study in Literature and Political Ideas, Being the Autobiography of Hugh MacDiarmid (Christopher Murray Grieve).* 1943.

MacDonald, (James) Ramsay (1866–1937)
No twentieth-century British political leader has been more reviled than Ramsay MacDonald, Britain's first Labour Prime Minister in 1924 and 1929–31. His decision to offer the resignation of the second Labour government and to accept the King's commission to form a National government during the financial crisis of August 1931 provoked much animus among his supporters and sustained the view that he had planned to ditch the Labour government. It has long been an axiom of the **Labour Party** that his actions in 1931 marked him as a traitor, and MP William Lawther remarked that MacDonald was "bereft of any public decency." To many of his former supporters, the man who had created the Labour Party had also helped to undermine it in the 1930s.

MacDonald was born at Lossiemouth in Scotland on 12 October 1866, the illegitimate son of Anne Ramsay and, possibly, John MacDonald, a ploughman. Despite his social disadvantage he was a bright child, became a pupil teacher, and appeared destined for a career in teaching. However, in the summer of 1885 he took an administrative post in Bristol, and in 1886 he went to London, where he took a number of clerical positions until he became private secretary in 1888 to Thomas Lough, a Liberal Radical politician. He left Lough's employment in 1892 to pursue a career in politics and journalism.

MacDonald acquired wide political experience between 1885 and 1892. He joined the Social Democratic Federation, a quasi-Marxist organization, while in Bristol. His employment with Lough also put him in contact with many leading Liberal Radicals. Indeed, he continued to move within Liberal, Radical, and socialist circles throughout the 1890s. Initially he had ambitions of becoming a Liberal MP and was selected as the Liberal candidate for the Dover constituency shortly after the 1892 general election, but he was thwarted in his attempt to become a Liberal candidate for Southampton in 1894. Thereafter, he cultivated his socialist connections more assiduously, campaigning for the **Independent Labour Party** (ILP) candidate in the Sheffield Attercliffe parliamentary by-election in June 1894, joining the ILP in July 1894, and becoming the ILP and Labour Electoral Association candidate for Southampton in 1894, on whose behalf he was thoroughly trounced in the 1895 general election.

During the early 1890s MacDonald was introduced to **Sidney Webb** and joined the **Fabian Society**. He acted as a Fabian lecturer in 1892, touring South Wales, the Midlands, and the northeast, speaking on topics such as "Why are the many poor?" In 1896 and 1897 he was also a member of the Rainbow Circle, which first met in the Rainbow Tavern in Fleet Street and brought together some collectivist Liberals, such as **Herbert Samuel**, who believed that the old **Liberal Party** was about to disintegrate. This group published papers and, briefly, the *Progressive Review* in the hope of encouraging the formation of a new center party in British politics. This desire, as well as an interest in foreign policy, were to be two of the abiding passions MacDonald pursued throughout the rest of his political career.

Marriage to Margaret Gladstone in November 1896 provided MacDonald with the financial security that enabled him to develop his political career. The marriage settlement provided the MacDonalds with £160 rising to £300 per year, a considerable income for the time, in addition to his own earnings. The couple moved to 3 Lincoln Inn Fields, London, which was later to be the base for the **Labour Representation Committee** in its formative years. Margaret died on 8 September 1911, but in their brief marriage they had six children: Alister, born 1898; Malcolm in 1901; Ishbel in 1903; David in 1904; Joan in 1908; and Sheila in 1910. Margaret played an active part in Ramsay's early political career and was a partner whose loss he never overcame. MacDonald's political career had begun to blossom in the mid-1890s. He was elected to the executive of the Fabian Society in the spring of 1894, although the various conflicts within the body led him to move his energies to the ILP. He had joined the party in 1894 and its National Administrative Council in 1896, and he remained a leading figure in it, often acting as either its Chairman or Secretary, until the **First World War**. Thereafter he drifted away from the ILP and formally resigned from it in May 1930. MacDonald's work for the ILP alone would fill most lifetimes, but his real claim to fame arose from the fact that he, more than others, was responsible for the formation and early development of the British Labour Party.

The Labour Representation Committee (LRC) was formed in February 1900 and changed its name to the Labour Party in 1906. MacDonald was its leader, acting as Secretary, until he resigned over the decision of the Labour Party to support the British war effort in 1914. From the start he attempted to obtain trade union support, an endeavor that was greatly helped by the attack upon trade union funds that was leveled by the **Taff Vale judgment** in 1901. Although trade union support did flow into the LRC, MacDonald quickly realized that the infant organization needed to improve its parliamentary position in the short term. Only two of its candidates had been returned in the autumn 1900 general election, and MacDonald had been badly defeated in his Leicester contest. As a result, he held at least eight secret meetings with Jesse Herbert, confidential secretary to Herbert Gladstone, the chief Liberal Whip, to arrange the infamous "Lib-Lab" pact of 1903 whereby the Labour Party would be allowed a straight run against the **Conservatives** in about thirty seats in return for a similar arrangement for the Liberals. Despite denying that the pact existed, MacDonald operated it in the general election of December 1905 and January 1906. The LRC put fifty candidates into the field and had twenty-nine returned, of whom only five had faced Liberal opposition.

The 1906 general election was something of a personal triumph for MacDonald for he had built up the organization of the party, an enormous task in its own right but even more so when set against his ILP and other political activities. From the start, the LRC was an alliance of socialists and trade unionists rather than a socialist organization as such. Its main purpose was to attract trade union support. This exigent need qualified MacDonald's own ambition to create a party that would attract support from all the political classes, an ambition that was always thwarted by the increasing trade union domination of the LRC/Labour Party. Nevertheless, he helped shape the new party in its gradualist approach to social change through his creation of the Socialist Library, to which he contributed his own books, including *Socialism and Society* (1905), *Socialism and Government* (1909), and *The Socialist Movement* (1911). The dominating theme of his work was that a form of Social Darwinism ensured that private organizations would get bigger, that the state would need to intervene, and that socialism would emerge from the success, not the failure, of capitalism. Because of the influence of MacDonald and of the Webbs during the First World War, these essentially Fabian views became the defining factor in the socialism the Labour Party eventually espoused in 1918.

Following his successes in 1906, MacDonald dominated the Labour Party, rising to be leader of the Parliamentary Labour Party. He was also considered to be an effective MP for Leicester, the two-member constituency he represented from 1906 to 1918. But the price of his success was support for the Liberal governments of the pre-war years to such an extent that he was strongly criticized for creating a Labour "tail to the Liberal Party." His reputation for radicalism was restored, briefly, by his opposition to the First World War, which ultimately lost him his seat for Leicester in the 1918

RAMSAY THE UNRUDDY.

Sir Despard Murgatroyd—Mr. MacDonald.   *Mad Margaret—Socialism.*

D. M. "I ONCE WAS A VERY ABANDONED PERSON——"
M. M.   "MAKING THE MOST OF EVIL CHANCES."
D. M. "NOBODY COULD CONCEIVE A WORSE 'UN . . . ."   [*Dance.*
M. M.   "THAT IS ONE OF OUR BLAMELESS DANCES."—*Ruddigore*, Act II.

"Ramsay the Unruddy" (Bernard Partridge, *Punch,* 20 February 1924). MacDonald, the first Labour Prime Minister, had been in office less than a month when this cartoon appeared.

general election and earned him the appellation "traitor."

In the immediate post-war years, relieved of his parliamentary duties, he concentrated his efforts upon building up the propaganda machine of the Labour Party. However, in 1922 he was returned to Parliament for Aberavon, and shortly afterward he became leader of the Parliamentary Labour Party. When the Conservatives failed to win a majority for their protectionist policies in December 1923 MacDonald, at the beginning of 1924, was asked to form a minority Labour government, with Liberal support. It lasted less than ten months, achieved little, and was replaced by the Conservatives after the 1924 general election. For the next five years, he led a Labour Party to which, according to **Philip Snowden**, he was becoming a stranger. He was criticized for his inactivity in the 1926 **General Strike** and retreated into his concern for peace in international relations. Yet his fortunes improved greatly when he was returned for Seaham, a safer seat than Aberavon, and when the Labour Party won the general election of May 1929, although once again it was a minority government propped up by Liberal support.

The fortunes of the Labour government rose as the economy prospered and improved throughout 1929, but the Wall Street crash in the autumn of 1929 changed all that. As a result of the world recession, **unemployment** in Britain rose from about 1 million to 3 million in two years, the Labour government grossly overspent its budget and precipitated the financial crisis of August 1931, in which the **Cabinet** attempted to find the spending cuts demanded by the opposition parties, the May Committee, and the international community. The Cabinet split on the decision to cut unemployment benefits by 10 percent. MacDonald offered the resignation of his government to the King but returned with a mandate to form a National government, which would include Conservative and Liberal parties as well as any Labour support he could muster. These events led many within Labour ranks to suggest that MacDonald had schemed to ditch the second Labour government, although the recent work of David Marquand has refuted such an idea.

During the years 1931–5 MacDonald was Prime Minister of a National government, which won an overwhelming victory in the 1931 general election. During this period his power depended upon the Conservatives, who encouraged a move toward protectionism. MacDonald indulged himself in foreign policy and was very much involved in two conferences in 1932—the Geneva Disarmament Conference and the Lausanne Conference, which was concerned with German reparations. Thereafter, his political career declined. He found himself attacked by former colleagues, most notably Snowden, went into physical and mental decline, and was forced to resign as Prime Minister on 7 June 1935. He stayed on in government but had lost any real power. Indeed, his political decline was further evident when, in the general election of November 1935, he lost his seat at Seaham to Emanuel Shinwell, the man who had put him forward as Parliamentary Labour Party leader in 1922. MacDonald subsequently found a seat for Scottish Universities but thereafter played a diminishing part in the activities of the National government. He died of heart failure on 9 November 1937 while cruising in the Caribbean on the *Reina del Pacifico*. His body was returned to Britain and cremated on 26 November 1937, and his ashes were interred in the Spynie graveyard, near Lossiemouth, next to those of his wife.

Keith Laybourn

Bibliography

Barker, Bernard, ed. *Ramsay MacDonald's Political Writings.* 1972.

Laybourn, Keith. *The Rise of Labour.* 1988.

Marquand, David. *Ramsay MacDonald.* 1977.

Ward, Stephen R. *James Ramsay MacDonald: Low Born among the High Brows.* 1990.

Weir, L. MacNeill. *The Tragedy of Ramsay MacDonald.* 1938.

Mackenzie, (Edward Morgan) Compton (1883–1972)

Compton Mackenzie might have been expected to follow his actor father, Edward Compton, and actress mother, Virginia Bateman, onto the stage: He inherited from them an excellent voice, stage presence, and mimetic ability. After studying classics at St. Paul's School in London and **history** at Magdalen College, **Oxford**, however, he entered on a literary career. In his long life, he was to write more than 100 books, half of which were fiction. The others were varied—four books dealing with his life in the Royal Marines and British intelligence, in Greece and the Aegean, in the First World War; several on the history of Scotland; a history of the Indian army in the Second World War; several books on music; several on cats; and, among others, an autobiography that ran to ten volumes.

His third novel, *Sinister Street* (2 vols., 1913–14), brought him a considerable reputation. In a famous *Times Literary Supplement* article on "The Younger Generation," Henry James linked him in 1914 with Gilbert Cannan and Hugh Walpole as the hope for the future of the English novel, with **D.H. Lawrence** "hanging in the dusty rear." Mackenzie took his central character, Michael Fane, through a childhood and youth akin to his own, in a search for a pattern of conduct in a confusing world. **Ford Madox Ford** praised *Sinister Street* for recording "the history of a whole class, a whole region, during a whole period of life." In the early 1920s reviewers began wondering what had happened to Mackenzie's talent. To support an extravagant life, books poured out of his pen, flawed by being written at high speed; in the twelve-year period between 1923 and 1935, he wrote twenty-three books. Yet some of them were worth more than passing mention, including the first of many comic novels, *Poor Relations* (1919), two dealing with vacationers on Capri in the manner of novelist Norman Douglas, *Vestal Fire* (1927), and *Extraordinary Women* (1928), a novel about lesbianism. During and after the Second World War, he wrote a number of novels set in Scotland, some of which—such as *The Monarch of the Glen* (1941) and *Whisky Galore* (1947)—are gems of humor. *Water on the Brain* (1933) and *The Red Tapeworm* (1941) illustrate his talent for satire.

His most ambitious later work, *The Four Winds of Love*, a panoramic survey of the first four decades of the twentieth century, appeared in six volumes between 1937 and 1945. He interrupted writing it to come to the defense of the Duke of Windsor in *The Windsor Tapestry* (1938), and after that *The Four Winds* lost its focus.

Though he was knighted for his services to literature in 1954, critical acclaim still eluded him. Andro Linklater refers to his habit of dramatizing everything, including himself; his voice and personality made him a great success on radio and **television**. On the whole he preferred to stay on the surface in depicting character; he did not deal with the person within. Yet his astonishing memory gave him a Proustian ability to recall the very mood and temper of a time gone by.

D.J. Dooley

Bibliography
Dooley, D.J. *Compton Mackenzie*. 1974.
Linklater, Andro. *Compton Mackenzie: A Life*. 1987.
Robertson, Leo. *Compton Mackenzie: An Appraisal of His Literary Work*. 1954.
Young, Kenneth. *Compton Mackenzie*. 1968.

Macleod, Iain Norman (1913–1970)

Of Conservative leaders between **Winston Churchill** and **Margaret Thatcher**, Iain Macleod was one of the most distinctive. He set the British tropical Empire on the road to swift **decolonization**, purveyed a soundly progressive form of Conservatism, and by his example showed that middle-class men could succeed in a socially exclusive party. To many in the 1960s he was the best proof that the **Conservative Party** was neither stupid nor illiberal.

Macleod was born on 11 November 1913 at Skipton, Yorkshire, where his father, a Liberal, practiced medicine. Both of his parents were from the Hebrides, and Macleod went to a Scottish school, Fettes, before reading **history** at **Cambridge**. Between graduation in 1935 and 1945, his ambitions centered on bridge, a major source of income until 1952, and on which he wrote extensively. Until 1945, when he was thirty-two, he appears to have been nonpolitical, although in that year he unsuccessfully contested his home constituency of the Western Isles.

After **army** service during the Second World War, he joined a brilliant group of future ministers in the Conservative Research Department, where his mentor was **R.A. Butler**, and concentrated on the modernization of Conservative social policy. In 1950 he became MP for the London suburban seat of Enfield, which he held until his death.

In Parliament he specialized in health, making his reputation by demolishing **Aneurin Bevan** (27 March 1952), founder of the **National Health Service**, and becoming, at thirty-eight, Minister of Health (1952–5) under **Winston Churchill**, a post then outside the Cabinet. As Minister of Labour (1955–9) under **Anthony Eden** and **Harold Macmillan**, he handled the trade unions tactfully but on occasion firmly. Neither post gave him much scope.

As Macmillan's Colonial Secretary (1959–61), Macleod was an enthusiastic decolonizer. His achievement was that, without bloodshed, Britain left Africa, its tropical Empire becoming a Commonwealth of independent states. Though Macleod did not complete his task, his policies were never reversed. He treated the interests of white settlers as secondary, released imprisoned African leaders, and stood for a "deliberate speeding-up" of independence. Any other policies, he said, "would have led to terrible bloodshed in Africa."

The episode did him irreparable damage, and Lord Salisbury branded him "too clever by half," a phrase that stuck. An unsuccessful period as party Chairman and leader of the House (1961–3) did not help matters, and Macleod was unable to contest the leadership in 1963 or 1965, when he supported Butler and **Edward Heath**, respectively.

He retired from office in 1963, disagreeing with the choice of **Lord Home** as leader, and became editor of the *Spectator*, rejoining the Shadow Cabinet after the 1964 defeat. He became Chancellor of the Exchequer (20 June–20 July 1970) under Heath and died in office.

Convivial, an effective speaker, endowed with a photographic memory, debating skills, and courage, he had the talents and ambition to lead his party, though not the health; in the last twenty years of his life, he was in constant pain from severe arthritis and war wounds. Often called the "wordsmith" of his party, he was not original, but he vividly expressed the ideas of his time and as such was the least-dull "Tory" (as he always called himself) of his era.

John Vincent

Bibliography

Darwin, John. *The End of the British Empire.* 1991.
Fisher, Nigel. *Iain Macleod.* 1973.
Goldsworthy, David. *Colonial Issues in British Politics, 1945–1961.* 1971.

Macmillan, (Maurice) Harold (1894–1986)
As Prime Minister from January 1957 to October 1963, Harold Macmillan was the most prominent representative among **Conservative** Prime Ministers of the British post-war consensus. Like **Harold Wilson**, he was the first Prime Minister of his party to recognize, while failing to halt, British decline. The remarkable success of the first part of his premiership was followed by a second half marked by exceptional setbacks and scandals. Economically, he set Britain on a mildly inflationary path. Externally, he will be remembered for initiating, if not completing, the final **decolonization** of the British Empire, chiefly in Africa.

Harold Macmillan was the son of an American-born mother, Helen Hill, *née* Belles, by Maurice Macmillan, the son of the Scottish founder of Macmillan and Company, booksellers and publishers. He retained a lifelong connection with the firm, becoming Chairman on retirement from politics in 1964. Despite the relatively recent arrival of his family on the scene, Macmillan took readily to the part of aristocrat.

Intellectually as well as socially, Macmillan was from his youth part of the British intellectual and social elite. At Eton, he was one of that select intellectual minority, the scholars; at Balliol College, **Oxford**, then the leading academic college, he won an exhibition or minor award, and a first-class degree in classics in 1919, despite having been wounded three times, once severely, in the First World War. At Oxford, he moved in a brilliant circle around Monsignor Ronald Knox, the Catholic wit and scholar, and nearly became a Catholic.

Instead, he became aide-de-camp (1919–20) to the ninth Duke of Devonshire, then Governor-General of Canada, marrying in 1920 his daughter, Lady Dorothy Cavendish (d. 1966). Despite final reconciliation, the marriage was unhappy, and for most of his public career Macmillan, not through his own fault, was separated, a fact of which the general public was then unaware.

He was MP for the marginal seat of Stockton in 1924–9, and again in 1929–45, despite defeats in 1923, 1929, and in the 1945 landslide. His constituency perhaps shaped his outlook, as he always claimed. It was a northern industrial town in an area of high **unemployment**, and it focused Macmillan's mind on the need to defeat **Labour** on its own terms.

In the 1930s Macmillan was seen as distinctly in the left wing of his party and as an ineffectual figure unlikely to hold office. For a time in the mid-1930s he renounced the party whip, and in 1938–9 opposed **Neville Chamberlain**'s foreign policy. As a very minor member of the **Churchill** group, he voted against Chamberlain (May 1940), thus helping to put Churchill in power. His numerous books on social topics made little impact except as marking his dissatisfaction with pre-war Conservatism.

Under Churchill, however, he became, none too quickly, one of the premier's rising stars, holding very junior office in 1940–2 and minor office, briefly, in 1942. The fortunes of war then led him to be Minister Resident at Allied Headquarters in Northwest Africa (1942–5). There, under a succession of changing titles, he was the British minister immediately responsible for the whole Mediterranean theater. In this post he showed infinite sagacity, but in his old age his achievement was blurred by controversy over the British repatriation of Soviet nationals and others to death at the hands of the Soviet Union and Yugoslavia. His undoubted success established him as a serious political figure, and he was briefly Air Minister in Churchill's "caretaker" government of May–July 1945.

Despite defeat in the 1945 general election, Macmillan soon (November 1945) won a safe London suburban seat, holding it easily until retirement (October 1964). He took a vigorous part in the conduct of the Conservative opposition in 1945–51. When his party regained power in 1951, his appointment as Minister of Housing and Local Government (1951–4) placed him in the limelight.

Faced with an acute **housing** shortage, the Conservatives had rashly pledged themselves to build 300,000 dwellings annually, a seemingly impossible target. Using business advisers and methods, and reducing quality somewhat, Macmillan achieved an increase, taking public and private dwellings together, from 172,400 in Labour's last full year, to 309,000 in 1954, taking figures for England and Wales alone. This fact reflected real ability as well as a general rise in prosperity, and it was Macmillan's most unqualified personal achievement. Since this was a quiet period in education and health, Macmillan's success in housing was the most prominent element in Conservative social policy in the 1950s.

Macmillan was the only Prime Minister to reach sixty without having held one of the great offices of state. Even after that age, he had scant experience in senior posts, serving as **Anthony Eden**'s Foreign Secretary in 1955 for only eight months, and as his Chancellor of the Exchequer for thirteen months (December 1955–January 1957), in neither case making any particular mark. His one budget attracted attention only by introducing premium bonds, a form of state lottery.

It was the 1956 **Suez crisis** rather than ministerial achievement that made Macmillan Prime Minister, an office that at age sixty-two he could hardly have expected. It was Suez, too, that destroyed **R.A. Butler**, Macmillan's main rival and a consistent skeptic about the Suez invasion. Macmillan initially was all for war, not just to regain international control of the Suez Canal, but to conquer Egypt and overthrow Colonel Gamal Abdel Nasser. He ignored Treasury warnings that sterling would collapse; when it did so, because of American displeasure at the war, he

more than anyone insisted on stopping the campaign when victory seemed in sight. As Harold Wilson said, "he was first in and first out." When an ill and discredited Eden resigned (9 January 1957), Macmillan was the inevitable successor, having overwhelming **Cabinet** backing, and probably general party approval despite the absence of any formal election.

As Prime Minister, Macmillan achieved much. He reunited a divided party. In his only general election (8 October 1959) as Prime Minister, his party won for a third time and with an increased majority. He restored Anglo-American relations, at a low ebb because of Suez, and supposedly achieved an almost paternal relationship with President John F. Kennedy. He initiated, and partly carried through, a second and final phase of decolonization in Africa. Unlike Labour's decolonization of India, this was bloodless.

In defense he abolished **conscription**, placing his reliance on a professional **army** and the British independent nuclear deterrent, a footing that successive governments have followed. In foreign affairs he announced the Nuclear Test Ban Treaty (1963) and gradually persuaded his party to apply to join the **European Community** (July 1961). These policies can be seen as an attempt to restore British fortunes after the loss of Empire.

After a subdued year in 1957, Macmillan in 1958 set about adapting the ideas of **John Maynard Keynes** to a mildly inflationary environment and to his electoral needs. The result was the boom of 1958–60, a surge not seen since the war, with the stock market doubling. The loss of his entire Treasury team in January 1958 over what they considered excessive expenditure, though dismissed by Macmillan as "a little local difficulty" and ostensibly involving only a modest sum, marked deep differences over his connivance at mild inflation.

Macmillan's phrase, "You've never had it so good," though taken out of context and meant as a warning, was widely held to embody his outlook. Similarly, the use of the epithet "Supermac" by the cartoonist Vicky reflected the confidence Macmillan inspired in 1959. In the 1959 general election, helped by the poor electioneering of **Hugh Gaitskell**, Macmillan swept home on a tide of prosperity.

An African tour in January–February 1960 revealed attitudes not evident before the general election. Speaking in **South Africa**, he said, "A wind of change is blowing through the

THE ENTERTAINER

"The Entertainer" (Vicky, *Evening Standard,* 11 December 1958). John Osborne's play *The Entertainer,* about a faded music hall performer, was one of the highlights of the 1957 season.

continent," and his appointment of the liberal **Iain Macleod** as Colonial Secretary confirmed his new-found commitment to decolonization. Thereafter Macmillan's star waned. The economy required deflation, including a wage freeze, which caused not only resentment, but much debate about Britain's "stop-go" economy. Only the policy of entry into Europe heralded a new departure.

When French President Charles de Gaulle finally vetoed British entry (14 January 1963), he denied Macmillan greatness and left him without a policy. Macmillan paid a heavy price for his good relations with the United States, one of his main claims to fame but also the main obstacle to his European ambitions.

At home, a newly volatile public opinion temporarily made the hitherto insignificant **Liberals** the leading party. A sensational Liberal by-election gain at Orpington (14 March 1962), followed by the Vassall spy case (September 1962), a severe winter in 1962–3 with unemployment rising to the then supposedly unacceptable level of 4 percent, did not improve matters.

Against this background, the Profumo scandal (June 1963), though essentially unimportant, brought to light much seediness, raised lurid expectations, and generated an obsessive excitement that was damaging to the government. Nothing like it had occurred since the war.

Macmillan's main reaction was to move toward "liberal conservatism," chiefly by dismissing seven Cabinet ministers in the "night of the long knives" (13 July 1963), bringing in able new men, returning to inflationary policies, and laying the foundations of the fairly successful progressive politics of 1963–4.

After some hesitation, Macmillan finally decided in the summer of 1963 to continue as Premier. He then fell victim to prostate trouble, resigning on 9 October 1963, though playing a large, and controversial, part while still in the hospital in the choice of his successor. He then tactfully disappeared from active politics. Macmillan succumbed to a poor economic climate, to a chapter of newsworthy accidents, to an overserious estimate of his medical condition, to a shift in public mood associated both with loss of deference toward public figures, and a new sense that Britain was the "Sick Man of Europe."

Macmillan, after 1984 Earl of Stockton, died at age 92, the longest-lived of British Prime Ministers, and was buried beside his wife at Horsted Keynes, West Sussex. In his later years, spent in conditions of frugality bordering on hardship, he made much of his role as Chancellor of the University of Oxford, both in its ceremonial capacity and informally, talking late into the night to students, who were often startled by his radical views. Politically, he made known his disquiet over aspects of **Thatcherism**, such as privatization ("selling off the family silver") and the handling of the **miners' strike** of 1984–5, and over the social background of the Cabinet ("more Estonians than Etonians").

He presented himself as a patrician, as the last Edwardian, as a Whig (in the tradition of his wife's family), as a romantic Tory, as an intellectual, as a man shaped by the comradeship of the trenches and by the slump of the 1930s, as a shrewd man of business of bourgeois Scottish stock, and as a venerable elder statesman at home with modern youth. There was something in all of these views, which he did little to discourage, and which commanded public respect into the early 1960s. Whether he was ever a mainstream Conservative, rather than a skillful exponent of the post-war consensus, is more doubtful.

During his lifetime Macmillan wrote copiously. Of his social and economic books *Reconstruction: A Plea for a National Policy* (1933) and *The Middle Way* (1938) were the best known, but he also wrote his memoirs in six volumes published 1966–73, as well as war diaries that appeared in 1984. His own writings form the main primary source for his life.

John Vincent

Bibliography

Evans, Harold. *Downing Street Diary: The Macmillan Years, 1957–1963*. 1981.

Horne, Alistair. *Macmillan: The Official Biography*. 2 vols. 1988–9.

Hutchinson, George. *The Last Edwardian at No. Ten: An Impression of Harold Macmillan*. 1980.

Sampson, Anthony. *Macmillan: A Study in Ambiguity*. 1967.

Turner, John. *Macmillan*. 1994.

MacMillan, Kenneth (1929–1992)

The first and greatest choreographer to emerge from the ranks of the Sadler's Wells Ballet (the Royal Ballet after 1956), Kenneth MacMillan decisively redefined the language of classical **ballet** in Britain by applying it to contemporary subjects and probing studies of emotion and psychology. In contrast to **Frederick Ashton**, who provided British ballet with sunny, romantic works and serene visions of pure classicism, MacMillan created narratives of profound dramatic intensity and abstract works that echoed the texts and textures of their scores with remarkable sensitivity.

Born in Scotland and trained as a dancer, MacMillan choreographed several apprentice pieces while still a member of the Sadler's Wells Theatre Ballet; following the premiere of his first professional work, the astringent *Danses Concertantes* (1955), he abandoned dancing entirely and became the company's resident choreographer. Equally at ease working on a grand or intimate scale, he began exploring the themes of isolation, despair, and sexual fervor that would frequently engage him over the years. He also discovered his most important and inspiring interpreter, Lynn Seymour, who became for him the lonely adolescent in *The Burrow* (1958), the blithe young maiden in *Le Baiser de la Fée* (1960), and the shattered victim of a graphically portrayed rape in *The Invitation* (1960). MacMillan drew his most passionate and memorable dance portraits for Seymour, including the title roles of his full-evening *Romeo and Juliet* (1965)—now a staple of repertories around the world—and of the one-act (1967) and three-act (1971) versions of *Anastasia*.

By reshaping the classical vocabulary in striking, expressionistic terms, MacMillan invested his plotless ballets with a sharply dramatic focus. From the primitive barbarism of *The Rite of Spring* (1962) to the haunting austerity of *Song of the Earth* (1965), *Requiem* (1976), and *Gloria* (1980), they depicted both personal and universal emotion through visual imagery that distilled the subtlest nuances of text and music.

As director of the Berlin Opera Ballet (1966–9) and of the Royal Ballet (1970–7), MacMillan used the full resources of his companies to express his devotion to the nineteenth-century classics, mounting new productions of *The Sleeping Beauty* and *Swan Lake*. While leading the Royal Ballet, he expanded its repertory with the work of George Balanchine, Jerome Robbins, and Glen Tetley.

At the same time, he continued to adapt the classical steps and conventions to startling dramatic purposes, choreographing three-act narrative works in which *pas de deux* of exceptional intricacy and sensuality alternated with sweeping crowd scenes and solos fashioned as perceptive character sketches. These massive epics included *Manon* (1974); *Mayerling* (1978), the story of a doomed love affair between Crown Prince Rudolf of Austria and Maria Vetsera; *Isadora* (1981), a lavish rendering of the tragic life of Isadora Duncan; and the fairy-tale *The Prince of the Pagodas* (1989), set to music by **Benjamin Britten**.

In 1979 MacMillan received the Queen Elizabeth II Coronation Award from the Royal Academy of Dancing, and he was awarded a knighthood for his services to British ballet in 1983. He died suddenly backstage of a heart attack during a revival of his most ambitious ballet, *Mayerling*.

Barbara Newman

Bibliography
Thorpe, Edward. *Kenneth MacMillan: The Man and the Ballets*. 1985.

MacNeice, Louis (1907–1963)

Louis MacNeice, a poet and junior member of the **W.H. Auden-Christopher Isherwood-Stephen Spender** "literary axis," was born 12 September 1907 in Belfast of Irish parents. His father, John Frederick MacNeice, was the Anglican Bishop of Down, Connor, and Dromore, Ireland. After attending Sherbourne Preparatory School for Boys, Dorset, (described in his poems "The Kingdom" and *Autumn Sequel*, XXII), he went to Marlborough College (described in his *Autumn Journal*, XIII), where his close friends included Bernard Spencer, John Betjeman, Graham Shepard, John Hilton, and Anthony Blunt. During the years 1926–30 he studied at Merton College, **Oxford**, reading classics and **philosophy**, taking a double first in Honour Moderations and "Greats." While still an undergraduate, he edited *Oxford Poetry: 1929* with Stephen Spender. He published his first collection of personal poetry, *Blind Fireworks*, in 1929; was appointed Lecturer in classics at the University of Birmingham in 1930; and published *Poems* in 1935, during which year he visited both Spain and Iceland. In 1936 he was appointed Lecturer in Greek at Bedford College, University of London. His translation of Aeschylus' *Agamemnon*, with music by **Benjamin Britten**, was produced in November 1936 at the Westminster Theatre, London. He returned to Iceland with Auden in 1937; their joint travel diary in prose and poetry was subsequently published as *Letters from Iceland*. In December 1937 his two-act play, *Out of the Picture*, was produced by the Group Theatre.

MacNeice's visit to Barcelona in December 1938–January 1939 blossomed into *Autumn Journal: A Poem*, a poetic commentary on national and international affairs. The collection is the last expression of his identification with left-wing politics and with the discussion of momentous political issues in verse inspired by music hall rhymes and rhythms. The Nonaggression Pact between Germany and the Soviet Union shattered MacNeice's poetic group, which had pledged allegiance to Soviet Communism as the only political force disciplined enough to counter the menace of Nazism. MacNeice's next collection, *Plant and Phantom* (1941), abandoned politics and returned to the philosophic and moral interests he had exhibited as an Oxford undergraduate, although he continued to be hostile to capitalism.

When war came, MacNeice volunteered for the **Royal Navy** but was rejected because of poor eyesight. As a patriotic alternative, he served as a London firewatcher in the **Home Guard**. The impact of war also led him to join the **British Broadcasting Corporation** (BBC) as scriptwriter and producer, where he remained until 1954, aside from an eighteen-month stint as Director of the British Institute in Athens (1950–1). His second critical study, *The Poetry of W.B. Yeats*, appeared in 1941.

In 1942 he memorialized his school friend Graham Shepard, drowned in action on the Atlantic, in "The Kingdom," "The Casualty (in memoriam G.H.S.)," and *Autumn Sequel*, II. His poetry continued its more philosophic mood in *Springboards: Poems, 1941–1944* and *Holes in the Sky: Poems, 1944–1947*. A visit to India in 1947 was reflected in "The Crash Landing" and "Mahabalipuram."

MacNeice published a translation of *Faust* in 1951. What some critics and the poet himself considered his best work, *Ten Burnt Offerings*, appeared in 1952. In 1954 MacNeice received the Premio Italiano Award, in 1957 a D.Litt. degree from the University of Belfast, and in 1958 a CBE. His last three poetic works were *Visitations: Poems* (1957); *Solstices: Po-*

M

ems (1959); and *The Burning Perch: Poems* (1963). He died of pneumonia in London on 3 September 1963.

Elton Edward Smith

Bibliography
Coulton, Barbara. *Louis MacNeice in the BBC.* 1980.
Heberer, Adolphe. *Louis MacNeice, 1907–1963: L'homme et la poésie.* 1986.
MacNeice, Louis. *The Strings Are False: An Unfinished Autobiography.* 1966.
Smith, Elton Edward. *Louis MacNeice.* 1970.

Malta

To protect supply lines to India, Britain occupied Malta in 1802 and formally annexed it twelve years later. Predominantly Roman Catholic and European, many Maltese welcomed British rule. During the nineteenth century Britain imposed various constitutions that recognized Maltese domestic authority but reserved control of military and foreign matters. In 1849 London established the Council of Government, a legislature with a Maltese minority and an official majority. Maltese nationalists became critical of this arrangement in the 1880s, when the British governor decided to elevate English over Italian in official matters. London addressed the problem in 1887 by augmenting Maltese authority, but in 1903 it reclaimed substantial powers.

International developments of the interwar years generated tension between Britain and Malta. Political frustration and wartime economic dislocation provoked anti-British demonstrations in 1919–21. Britain established a Maltese legislature in 1921 to govern on domestic affairs, but the Nationalist Party demanded union with Italy, which Benito Mussolini welcomed. Britain postponed an election in 1930 after the Vatican endorsed the Nationalists, and when the Nationalists won elections in 1932 and promoted the Italian language, London suspended the government, suppressed Italian, and ruled by executive decree. The approach of war compelled London to restore a liberal, although interim, charter in 1939.

The **Second World War** underscored the strategic importance of Malta. Valetta had harbored the Mediterranean fleet since the 1920s. Between 1940 and 1943 Axis forces besieged the island and subjected it to 3,000 aerial attacks. British and Maltese units defended the islands as a base for **submarine** and aerial operations against enemy supply lines. Among the Maltese, the war dashed pro-Italian sentiment and fostered Anglophilia.

In September 1947 Britain granted Malta a legislature and Cabinet to govern domestic affairs. Meanwhile, the Nationalist Party advocated independence, while the Maltese Labour Party urged integration in the United Kingdom, to gain representation in Parliament and a greater share of British wealth. In December 1955 a British inter-party conference, citing Malta's importance to the North Atlantic Treaty Organization (NATO), deemed integration "practicable and reasonable." In a February 1956 referendum, 74 percent of Maltese voters endorsed integration, and the next month **Anthony Eden** declared he would implement integration and provide economic aid.

This movement toward integration quickly collapsed. Opposition parties in Malta criticized the referendum, which 40 percent of voters boycotted, as a distorted indicator. Clergymen warned that integration would encourage statutory anti-Catholicism, and Labour Party leaders realized the British aid would be paltry. British officials observed Maltese vacillation, remembered the bitterness generated by Irish integration, and reconsidered the wisdom of providing a potential balance of power in the Commons to Maltese representatives. In early 1958 the Maltese Labour Party demanded independence, and London again suspended the Maltese constitution. Integration was dead.

In 1962 Britain restored constitutional government to Malta, and the Nationalist Party won elections and opened negotiations with London aimed at independence and membership in the **Commonwealth** that was granted on 21 September 1964. Britain retained base rights in Malta for ten years in exchange for financial and military aid. The economy-minded government of **Harold Wilson**, over Maltese protests, soon withdrew from the base and curtailed aid, ending the British presence in Malta.

Peter L. Hahn

Bibliography
Austin, Dennis. *Malta and the End of Empire.* 1971.
Bradford, Ernle. *Siege: Malta, 1940–1943.* 1985.

Dobie, Edith. *Malta's Road to Independence.* 1967.

Manchester *Guardian*

Since its founding in 1821, the *Manchester Guardian* has evolved from a regional newspaper to a national one. Launched shortly after the 1819 Peterloo massacre, the paper has maintained a liberal stance down to the present time, though it has always been too determinedly independent to be in any sense a party newspaper.

C.P. Scott, its editor from 1872 to 1929, came out firmly against British conduct and policy in the Boer War. This criticism was so unpopular that police protection was required for his home, and *Guardian* reporters at times had to sneak into the building to avoid attack. But although the incident temporarily hurt the paper's circulation, in the longer term it confirmed Scott's and his paper's integrity and increased his influence. He worked behind the scenes for the Zionist cause and was influential in urging the 1917 Balfour Declaration of British support for the idea of a Jewish homeland in Palestine. The *Guardian* under Scott also strongly disputed the official pronouncements about the Irish uprisings of 1916 and 1919. Telling unpopular truths at the risk of being perceived as unpatriotic became something of a *Guardian* trademark, further enchancing its reputation for journalistic integrity. Contributors to the paper during the first few decades of the century included such distinguished journalists as J.B. Atkins, H.N. Brailsford, J.L. Hammond, H.W. Massingham, Kingsley Martin, C.E. Montague, Malcolm Muggeridge, and Arthur Ransome.

American President Woodrow Wilson sought *Guardian* support for his policies, as did British leaders. Critical of Allied treatment of the defeated Germany, the paper was widely read in the Weimar Republic. But it was from the start wary of Adolf Hitler and as early as 1932 warned its readers of Nazi anti-Semitism, its respected foreign correspondents, F.A. Voight and Alexander Werth, reporting the situation more accurately than most other papers of the 1930s. Its wartime editor, W.P. Crozier, met frequently with Winston Churchill and staunchly supported his policies. The paper shortages of the 1940s reduced the *Guardian* to about one-third its pre-war length, but its circulation increased, and it emerged from the war even less regional both in scope and readership.

The post-war decades saw the paper expand and improve its international coverage. Among its best-known correspondents during that era were Alistair Cooke from America, Darsie Gillie from France, and Sylvia Sprigge from Italy. The paper went national in the 1950s, finally removing the regional advertisements that had for so long covered its front page and replacing them with news stories—and, in 1959, removing the word "Manchester" from the title. In 1960 it began publishing in London.

Even though the *Guardian* supported the Conservative Party in 1950s elections, it continued to adhere to liberal philosophy and to maintain its independence from the official government line on the news. It firmly opposed the Suez campaign in 1956, and it was called unpatriotic during the 1982 Falklands War, when, unlike most papers, it steadfastly referred to "the British" rather than to "us." It was strongly critical of government policies during the Thatcher years and has leaned toward Labour in recent general elections, unlike the other "quality" papers. In 1986 its editor, Peter Preston, led a reform movement to print attributions for information handed out in Downing Street briefings, an attempt to break up the comfortable anonymity the press corps had for so long allowed the government.

After some hard financial times in the recession of the 1960s, the *Guardian* strengthened its circulation and advertising revenue base while maintaining its journalistic reputation for quality reporting and perceptive analysis by commentators like Norman Shrapnel, Ian Aitken, Peter Jenkins (who later defected to the *Independent*), and Hugo Young. In the mid-1980s it launched a number of successful initiatives to appeal to younger readers, and in 1993 it acquired control of the Sunday *Observer*.

Raymond N. MacKenzie

Bibliography

Ayerst, David. *Guardian: Biography of a Newspaper.* 1971.

Hennessy, Peter, and David Walker. "The Lobby" in Jean Seaton, and Ben Pimlott, eds. *The Media and British Politics.* 1987. pp. 110–30.

Koss, Stephen. *The Rise and Fall of the Political Press in Britain.* vol. 2: *The Twentieth Century.* 1984.

Mills, William Haslam. *The Manchester Guardian: A Century of History.* 1921.

Mansfield (Beauchamp), Katherine (1888–1923)

Famed for her short stories, Kathleen Mansfield Beauchamp (who later took the pen name of Katherine Mansfield) was born 14 October 1888, in Wellington, **New Zealand**, to Annie (Dyer) and Harold Beauchamp. The third daughter in a family of four girls and one boy, she had a comfortable, privileged childhood. Her father was a powerful figure in Wellington, a self-made man who left school at fourteen and eventually became the Director of the Bank of New Zealand. In 1903, she and her two older sisters were sent to London to attend Queen's College, where they studied for three years. After returning to New Zealand, Mansfield began to write prose poems and sketches. She returned to London in 1908, with a small allowance from her father, to try to establish herself as a writer. After a turbulent period of experimentation and upheaval, Mansfield began a long relationship with the critic John Middleton Murry. They started living together in 1912 but did not marry until 1918. Mansfield and Murry established a close friendship with **D.H.** and Frieda **Lawrence** and became acquainted with Lady Ottoline Morrell, **Bertrand Russell**, and various members of the **Bloomsbury Group**, in particular, **Leonard** and **Virginia Woolf**. Mansfield's relationship with Murry was intense and filled with conflict. She spent long periods apart from him, especially in the last years of her life when she went in search of a climate that would not exacerbate her advancing **tuberculosis**. Those same years produced some of her best stories, "The Garden Party," "The Doll's House," and "The Daughters of the Late Colonel." She died of tuberculosis in 1923, when she was only thirty-four years old.

Although standard critical opinion about literary influences on Mansfield have emphasized the impact of Anton Chekhov, it now appears that a greater influence was the aestheticism of the 1890s, especially the work of Oscar Wilde and the symbolists. Mansfield identified herself with Wilde's sexual and social rebelliousness, and her letters and notebooks provide impressive evidence that as early as 1906 she was experimenting with aesthete-influenced modernist techniques that would provide the basis for her own style as a writer of short fiction. In later years Mansfield was also influenced by the writings of Beatrice Hastings, a feminist whose work appeared in the journal *New Age*, edited by A.R. Orage.

Mansfield's first publications after moving to London appeared in the *New Age*. Some of these were collected in her first book of stories, *In a German Pension* (1911). She published only two other collections during her lifetime: *Bliss and Other Stories* (1920) and *The Garden Party and Other Stories* (1922). After her death John Middleton Murry edited several volumes of her writing, including previously unpublished stories and unfinished work, her letters, the *Journal of Katherine Mansfield* (1927), and *Novels and Novelists* (1930), a compilation of her book reviews. In 1937 he published a collected edition, *The Short Stories of Katherine Mansfield*.

Beginning in 1915, during the course of writing a longer, more complex story than her earlier efforts, Mansfield began to discover what she called, years later, "the *Prelude* method—it just unfolds and opens." *Prelude*, published in 1918 as one of the earliest efforts of the Hogarth Press, is based on Mansfield's memories of childhood in New Zealand. It is a new kind of story, a multilevel, spatially ordered narrative. She would continue to produce innovative and technically sophisticated stories throughout her career. "Bliss" (1918), "Je Ne Parle Pas Français" (1920), "Life of Ma Parker" (1920), and "At the Bay" (1921) demonstrate the diversity of her subject matter, which ranges from the conflicts of family life among the privileged to the suffering of lonely, impoverished individuals. Mansfield's contribution to the development of modernist short fiction has influenced the shape of the genre throughout the twentieth century.

Sydney Janet Kaplan

Bibliography

Alpers, Antony. *The Life of Katherine Mansfield.* 1980.

Hanson, Clare, ed. *The Critical Writings of Katherine Mansfield.* 1987.

Kaplan, Sydney Janet. *Katherine Mansfield and the Origins of Modernist Fiction.* 1991.

O'Sullivan, Vincent, and Margaret Scott, eds. *The Collected Letters of Katherine Mansfield.* 2 vols. 1984.

Tomalin, Claire. *Katherine Mansfield: A Secret Life.* 1987.

Marconi Scandal (1912–1913)

The Marconi scandal arose from a tender agreed in March 1912 between the Post Office and the

Marconi Wireless Telegraphy Company for the construction of an Imperial wireless network. It was rumored that the Marconi Company had benefited from inside connections to the Liberal government and that Liberal ministers had profited from advance knowledge of the deal. The scandal was exacerbated by **anti-Semitism** and compounded by the lack of candor of the accused ministers. Although they were eventually cleared of any wrongdoing, the Marconi scandal exemplified the worsening party strife in British politics before the First World War.

Those accused were the Postmaster General, **Herbert Samuel**; the Attorney General, Sir Rufus Isaacs; the Chancellor of the Exchequer, **David Lloyd George**; and the Liberal Chief Whip and Patronage Secretary to the Treasury, the Master of Elibank. Isaacs' brother Godfrey was the managing director of the English Marconi Company. Samuel and the Isaacs brothers were Jewish and became the targets of anti-Semitic attacks. The Welshman Lloyd George was vilified, of course, in aristocratic and Conservative circles for his Radicalism. When the scandal was ventilated in the Liberal-dominated House of Commons in October 1912, Samuel, Lloyd George, and Isaacs denied the allegations. (Elibank had resigned in August 1912 and was subsequently elevated to the peerage as Baron Murray of Elibank.) Although Samuel had clearly done nothing wrong in either a personal or public capacity, his colleagues remained under suspicion. A Select Committee was organized, but its inquiries were overshadowed by disclosures elsewhere. In March 1913 a successful libel suit brought by Isaacs and Samuel against a French newspaper revealed that Isaacs had purchased shares in the American Marconi Company and sold some of them to Lloyd George and Elibank. In June another libel suit brought by Godfrey Isaacs ended in the conviction of the journalist Cecil Chesterton, who had charged that behind the Marconi scandal lay a Jewish-Radical conspiracy, but a separate bankruptcy case revealed that Elibank had purchased more American Marconi shares as an investment of **Liberal Party** funds. Unable to agree, the Select Committee presented the Commons with majority and minority reports. Isaacs and Lloyd George offered their apologies, and the Commons passed a resolution accepting them. Elibank, upon his return from overseas, was the subject of a similar inquiry in the Conservative-dominated **House of Lords** in March 1914.

The Marconi scandal had unfolded in the context of bitter fights over such issues as Irish Home Rule and British land reform. Coming amid nebulous charges traded by Liberals and Conservatives about the evils of aristocracy and protectionism, on the one hand, and of plutocracy and socialism, on the other hand, the scandal only served to deepen public disillusionment with pre-war party politics.

Ian Christopher Fletcher

Bibliography

Donaldson, Frances. *The Marconi Scandal.* 1962.

Searle, Geoffrey. *Corruption in British Politics, 1895–1930.* 1987.

Marks and Spencer

"Goods and services once regarded as luxuries have become conventional comforts and are now almost decreed necessities. A fundamental change in people's habits has been brought about." Thus Simon Marks explained how Marks and Spencer contributed to improving the national **standard of living**. This was all the more impressive because what became Britain's largest and most successful retail firm had a beginning so modest as to seem mythical. In 1884 Michael Marks, a Russian Jewish immigrant who came to England to escape persecution, opened a stall in Leeds market. Soon after, the poor peddler hit upon a clever way to compensate for his inability to speak English while also drawing attention to his varied wares. "Don't ask the price, it's a penny," was the slogan he used to attract working men and women. His simple, straightforward approach was sufficiently successful that when he formed a partnership in 1894 with Yorkshireman Tom Spencer, a Gentile cashier in a local business, there were "original penny bazaars" in a number of towns, notably Manchester, which became his center of operations.

It was Simon Marks, Michael's son, and Israel Sieff, a close friend since Manchester Grammar School days, who reshaped the business during the inter-war era. They were responsible for establishing Marks and Spencer branches throughout English high streets and expanding turnover from £550,000 in 1919 to £23.4 million in 1939. Long after Marks and Spencer became a public company in 1924, it retained some of the character of the family business, not least because of the continuing presence of the Sieff clan. Fundamental to its success was the joint pursuit of business efficiency and worker welfare, a humane, intelligent approach also shared by Cadburys. During the 1930s M and S focused on foods and textiles; in so doing, it helped break down the social barriers dividing class and the masses by offering appealing garments at affordable prices. Determined to adapt advanced business methods that he saw at work during visits to America, Simon Marks used attractive premises, stock control, product testing, and rational administration methods to provide the highest quality at the lowest price under St. Michael's label. M and S pioneered cooperative relations with suppliers, turning competitors into allies by helping them improve production methods and ensuring a long-term association. "Close, personal, and friendly relations" was an ideal that applied not only to suppliers. In 1934 Flora Solomon, a Russian Jewish refugee, became the head of the newly formed Personnel Department of M and S. Under her direction, it pursued a policy of "management without tears," adopting welfare schemes to improve the well-being of workers and instituting training schemes to improve individual opportunity while strengthening teamwork.

The story of Marks and Spencer suggests that the work ethic did not die at the end of the nineteenth century, that the entrepreneurial failure all too common in heavy industry did not apply to retailing, and that social reform and competitive success are not necessarily adversaries.

Charles Dellheim

Bibliography
Briggs, Asa. *Marks and Spencer, 1884–1984.* 1984.
Rees, Goronwy. *St. Michael: A History of Marks and Spencer.* 1969.
Sieff, Israel. *Memoirs of Israel Sieff.* 1970.

Marriage

Marriage is often given serious consideration only when it breaks down, which means that anxiety about its stability as an institution has increased in the late twentieth century and that unfavorable comparisons have been drawn with the apparently more settled relationships of the early 1900s. As with so many aspects of human behavior, the reality is more complicated and contradictory.

Marriage has always been part of the typical experience of adult men and women throughout the century, but the proportion of women reaching their late forties who were (or had been) married fell during the first three decades of the century (from 87 percent in 1891 to 83 percent in 1931). Many women never married, in large part because of the imbalance in the sex ratio, which increased steadily from 1871 to 1911 and dramatically as a result of the **First World War**. But since the Second World War marriage has become increasingly popular. Indeed, contrary to the popular view of the 1960s as a decade of sexual license, during that time marriages mushroomed, rising to a high of 357,000 in 1971 (compared to 307,000 in 1931 and 254,000 in 1986). The proportion of marriages that were remarriages for one or both partners rose steadily from 11 percent in 1931 to 20 percent in 1971 and 35 percent in 1986, in large part a result of the even more dramatic rise in the **divorce** rate. In addition, the age at marriage for previously unmarried men and women dropped substantially from 26.8 for men and 24.6 for women in 1951 to 24.6 for men and 22.6 for women in 1971. In the late 1970s it began to climb again (to 25.1 for men and 23.1 for women in 1986). Thus, despite the publicity accorded the political activities of both the student movement and **feminists**, there was no rebellion by young people against the institution of marriage in the 1960s.

For **women**, to remain unmarried continued to carry the idea of failure until well after the Second World War. Marriage was also their main avenue for financial well-being. Job opportunities remained limited for women in the early part of the century, and it did not become common for middle-class women to work outside of the home, even before marriage, until after the First World War. The professions (including teaching) imposed a "marriage bar" on women during the inter-war years which remained until the **Second World War**. During the early part of the century marriage was, as Cicely Hamilton, a prominent feminist, put it grimly in 1909, the main "trade" for women.

The married couple was considered by most early twentieth-century social commentators to be the fundamental unit of society and the key to social order. The dominant model of marriage was based on the assumption of the male breadwinner and dependent wife and children, which was believed by social investigators, **philanthropists,** and policymakers to provide the best hope of ensuring work discipline on the part of working-class men. The reality was somewhat different. While middle-class married women did not go out to work, large numbers of working-class women engaged in part-time or casual work to make ends meet. Working men and women broadly agreed that a "good" husband meant one who brought home a regular wage and showed some regard for women's anxiety regarding the possibility of frequent **pregnancy and childbirth.** A "good" wife was above all a good household manager.

As Ellen Ross has convincingly demonstrated, the meaning of marriage for working men and women rested less on romantic love or verbal and sexual intimacy and more on an understanding of financial obligations, services, and activities that were gender specific. However, if either partner failed to keep his or her side of the bargain, separation was considered reasonable. This departed from the injunctions of middle-class commentators who insisted on the importance of marital stability as well as on gendered responsibilities within marriage. The 1912 Royal Commission on Divorce recommended relaxation of the strict laws on divorce, not so much out of a commitment to liberalization as a desire to make it possible for the large numbers of working people living "in sin" to remarry. Its recommendations were not followed. Views such as those of Mary (Mrs. Humphry) Ward, philanthropist and novelist, who wrote a passionate denunciation of divorce in 1909, prevailed. Ward saw marriage as a discipline and an order. The institution imposed rational bonds on irrational (sexual) urges, something many in the late Victorian and Edwardian eras regarded as a threat to civilized codes of behavior. In addition, if differences could not be worked out between husband and wife, then there was felt to be little hope for the wider society. The fact remained that in the early decades of the century separation followed by cohabitation was most common among working people. In contrast, by the third quarter of the twentieth century it was more likely that working people would indulge in all of the rituals of the white wedding and that the middle class would engage in at least a period of cohabitation before or between marriages.

Prescriptive ideas regarding marriage underwent considerable change during the century. By the inter-war years members of the legal profession and policymakers were beginning to conceptualize marriage as "companionate." **William Beveridge,** for example, whose 1942 blueprint laid the foundations for post-war social policy, insisted on the equal-but-different contributions of men and women within marriage. This changed little the prevailing notions about the proper division of labor within marriage (Beveridge himself believed that women's most important job in the post-war world would be to ensure "the adequate continuance of the British race"), or the extent to which social policies such as national insurance assumed married women to be completely financially dependent on their husbands. Nevertheless, it promoted a view of marriage as a partnership rather than the patriarchal relationship beloved of the Victorian paterfamilias.

In addition, beginning in the 1920s, a growing number of moral philosophers, churchmen, and professionals had come to question the restrictive divorce laws that were designed to preserve the stability of marriage as an institution. Attention began to focus more on marriage as a relationship, and the morality of keeping "dead shell" marriages intact was increasingly questioned. Truly moral behavior, it was suggested, first by people like Herbert Gray, a Methodist minister and a founder of the marriage guidance movement, and later in the 1960s by many within the **Church of England** Establishment, could only come from within the individual and could not be imposed by external regulation. This new-found emphasis on the importance of a privately grounded sexual morality was an important influence promoting the relaxation of the divorce law in 1969. However, once the priority accorded marital stability was abandoned in favor of securing better personal relationships, there was little left by way of defense against sexual relationships outside marriage as long as they were based on love and mutual respect.

In the 1968 House of Commons debates on divorce law reform, as in the recommendations of the 1912 Royal Commission, easier divorce was justified in terms of strengthening the institution of marriage. Divorce rates increased fourfold after 1969, but remarriage rates also doubled. In addition, the British Social Attitude Survey continues to show a surprising conservatism regarding expectations of marriage, moral values, and social roles within marriage; for example, while the idea of a "working mother" is now accepted by men and women, the vast majority of domestic labor continues to be performed by women. But behavior indicates that marriage is no longer regarded as the only acceptable place for sexual activity. Premarital cohabitation became virtually a majority practice in the 1980s. The extramarital birthrate doubled in the 1980s, from 12 to 25 percent, although more and more children born outside marriage are being registered by two parents.

Thus, marriage in the sense of a lifelong, legally constituted relationship is no longer as common as it was in the early part of the century, but the reasons for this are far from clear. Post-war income-maintenance systems and increased job opportunities have made it possible for women to support children independently of men, albeit with extreme difficulty. But the shift in values informing personal life has probably been more significant and is certainly more complicated. There is no slackening in the search for a meaningful personal relationship, but both the prescriptions regarding its form and the social reality are much more fluid now than in 1900.

Jane Lewis

Bibliography

Gillis, John. *For Better, For Worse. British Marriages, 1600 to the Present.* 1985.

Kiernan, Kathleen, and M. Wicks. *Family Change and Future Policy.* 1990.

Lewis, Jane. *Women in Britain since 1945.* 1991.

———. *Women in England, 1870–1950.* 1984.

Ross, Ellen. *Love and Toil: Motherhood in Outcast London, 1870–1918.* 1993.

Marshall Plan (1948–1951)

The American government, convinced that the fate of Western democratic society was at stake and that Europe must be rendered safe from Soviet Communism, initiated the Marshall Plan in 1948 to provide assistance for the economic recovery of war-torn Western Europe following the end of the Second World War. The nation that received the largest amount of aid was Britain, which had suffered considerable damage from aerial bombardment.

At the end of the war Britain desperately needed capital to revive its economy and to carry out extensive reconstruction. The nation had lost approximately one-third of its **housing** as a result of German bombing raids, and its merchant fleet was reduced to two-thirds of its pre-war level. British industry suffered both from the bombing and a five-year lag in repairs and replacements. To help finance the war, Britain had been forced to sell revenue-producing assets overseas, thus reducing its investment income by more than half. Between the destruction on land and sea and its internal and external disinvestment, Britain lost approximately one-fourth, or £7.3 billion, of its estimated total capital wealth as a result of its involvement in the war.

But money was needed for more than rebuilding. Britain also had to pay for social reforms in the areas of health and education and to keep adequate capital reserves to safeguard its role as the banker for the sterling area. There were also military commitments throughout the world, especially in Germany during the postwar period. Finally, Britain had to maintain a high volume of exports to help defray the cost of much-needed imports. However, in 1945 the volume of exports was less than half of the pre-war level. Industrial production rose in the postwar era, but not to the level necessary to keep the British economy in balance. Hence, Britain had an adverse balance-of-payments problem, especially with the dollar area, which also threatened British recovery.

Thus, when Secretary of State George C. Marshall announced in an address at Harvard University in June 1947 that the United States was willing to provide assistance to the war-ravaged nations of Europe, **Ernest Bevin**, the Foreign Secretary, was the first to respond to the American offer. However, the United States did not propose merely to dispense financial and material aid; it requested that each recipient nation determine what it required and what it could contribute to the total recovery of Europe. Britain's efforts after 1948 were so successful that it was able to dispense with Marshall Plan aid by 1 January 1951, eighteen months before the program was scheduled to be terminated. In all, Britain received a total of $2.696 billion in assistance. Approximately 40 percent of the funds received were expended on food, fertilizer, and tobacco imports; 40 percent on raw materials, mainly cotton, copper, and aluminum; 12 percent on petroleum products; and 7 percent on machinery and equipment. By 1950 Britain's industrial production was half as much again as it had been in 1938, and the deficit between income and expenditures was virtually eliminated by the end of 1950, although Britain's dollar-deficit problem was solved mainly by the devaluation of the pound from $4.03 to $2.80 in September 1949. Overall, the volume of intra-European trade was increased by more than 100 percent between 1947 and 1950.

With the inauguration of the Marshall Plan, the United States did more than just help rebuild Europe; it also accepted the leadership of the Western world, a role that Britain was constrained to relinquish after the Second World War.

Joan B. Huffman

Bibliography

Bullock, Alan. *Ernest Bevin, Foreign Secretary, 1945–1951.* 1983.

Burk, Kathleen. "Britain and the Marshall Plan" in Chris Wrigley, ed. *Warfare, Diplomacy, and Politics.* 1986. pp. 210–30.

Hogan, Michael J. *The Marshall Plan: America, Britain, and the Reconstruction of Western Europe, 1947–1952.* 1987.

Pelling, Henry. *Britain and the Marshall Plan.* 1988.

Martin, (Basil) Kingsley (1897–1969)

Between January 1931 and 1960 Kingsley Martin established the *New Statesman and Nation* as a widely read and internationally respected outlet for all shades of progressive thought. A scholar who never entirely turned his back on his academic roots, Martin acquired his first newspaper experience at the *Manchester Guardian* in the late 1920s—a period when he also helped establish, and then briefly edit, the *Political Quarterly.* An inveterate dissenter and a relentless polemicist, Martin was both writer and activist, witness his commitment to the **Campaign for Nuclear Disarmament** in the 1950s, the National Council for Civil Liberties a generation earlier, and, as a young man, the **Union of Democratic Control.** His views rarely reflected those of the **Labour Party** leadership, but he was without doubt a pivotal figure on the Left in mid-century Britain.

Martin's radicalism was the legacy of his Nonconformist upbringing, in particular the family values of tolerance, nonviolence, and cooperation. A pacifist, like his father, Martin registered as a **conscientious objector** on leaving school and served as an orderly in the Friends' Ambulance Unit during the final two years of the First World War. The Western Front served only to strengthen his **pacifism**, and, like so many socialists in the late 1930s, accepting the necessity of fighting **Fascism** was to prove a painful emotional experience. In the early 1920s Martin enjoyed academic success at both **Cambridge** and Princeton, culminating in tenure at the **London School of Economics.**

At the LSE **Harold Laski** quickly became a close friend and influence, introducing Martin to leading figures in the **Fabian Society** and the Labour Party. In 1927, following a series of clashes with the LSE's Director, **William (later Lord) Beveridge,** Martin left to become an editorial writer at the *Manchester Guardian.* Martin enjoyed a stormy relationship with his editor, the legendary **C.P. Scott.** Editorials espousing the need for democratic socialism were unlikely to meet with Scott's approval, and by 1930 Martin was lobbying hard to secure a new post—editor of the sickly Fabian weekly, the *New Statesman,* which was about to merge with its **Liberal** counterpart, the *Nation.* **Arnold Bennett** and **John Maynard** (later Lord) **Keynes,** Chairmen of the respective boards, gambled on a virtual unknown to make their new venture a commercial and critical success. The gamble more than paid off, as Martin took a circulation of 14,000 and added another 100,000 subscribers in the course of the next thirty years. Leaving a succession of outstanding literary editors, most notably Raymond Mortimer and V.S. Pritchett, to establish a stylish and influential review in the back half, Martin promoted undiluted English radicalism in the front half. For the editor, if not always his directors, the "Staggers and Naggers" was the socialist conscience of the British labor movement, an assumption unlikely to endear Martin to trade unionists such as **Ernest Bevin.** Despite the presence of Keynes—a Liberal—as Chairman, sales figures ensured editorial integrity.

In the 1930s and 1940s the *New Statesman and Nation* voiced first the concerns and then the aspirations of progressive middle-class opinion in Britain. Succeeding years saw the paper extending its influence to leaders of African and Asian independence movements, most notably in India where Martin was a regular and welcome guest in his later years. Admirers such as Jawaharlal Nehru recognized that Martin could on occasion be guilty of appalling misjudgments—most evidently over the 1938 **Munich** agreement and more contentiously over his refusal to publish **George Orwell**'s dispatches from Spain—but that the generosity, the idealism, and the sheer brilliance of his journalism more than counterbalanced a naivete and inconsistency that would have destroyed any lesser editor.

Adrian Smith

Bibliography

Howe, Stephen, ed. *Lines of Dissent: Writing from the* New Statesman, *1913 to 1988.* 1988.

Hyams, Edward. The New Statesman: *The History of the First Fifty Years.* 1963.

Martin, Kingsley. *Father Figures.* 1966.

———. *Editor.* 1968.

Rolph, C.H. *Kingsley: The Life, Letters, and Diaries of Kingsley Martin.* 1973.

Marxist Historians

The British Marxist historians are a generation of scholars who since the late 1930s have made critical contributions to their respective fields of historical inquiry and have significantly shaped not only the development of the historical discipline, especially the writing of social history, but also Marxist thought and democratic and socialist historical consciousness. This "generation" includes the more senior figures of Cambridge economist Maurice Dobb (1900–76) and journalists and writers Dona Torr (1883–1956) and Leslie Morton (1903–87), but its central figures have been the relatively younger historians Rodney Hilton (1916–), Christopher Hill (1912–), Eric Hobsbawm (1917–), George Rudé (1910–93), **E.P. Thompson**, and Victor Kiernan (1913–).

The intellectual and political formation of this generation began in the 1930s in the shadows of the world Depression, the triumph of Nazism and **Fascism** in Central Europe and Spain, and the ever-increasing likelihood of a Second World War. Convinced that the Soviet Union represented a progressive alternative model of economic development and the foremost antagonist to the further expansion of Fascism, and that the **Labour Party** was inadequate to the challenge of the contemporary crisis and the making of socialism, these older and younger historians (the latter were students at **Cambridge** or Oxford in this period) joined the **Communist Party of Great Britain** (CPGB),

believing they might contribute to the advance of working-class struggle through their scholarly labors. Thus, following the war and the return to civilian life they organized themselves into the Communist Party Historians' Group in order to elaborate and propagate the Marxist interpretation of British history.

The heyday of the Historians' Group was 1946–56; however, in 1956–7, in the wake of Soviet leader Nikita Khrushchev's speech on Stalinism to the Twentieth Congress of the Communist Party of the Soviet Union, the Soviet invasion of Hungary, and the failure of the CPGB to oppose the invasion and democratize itself, the group all but collapsed as many of its members resigned from the party in protest.

The several initiatives of the Historians' Group had met with limited success beyond Communist and Marxist circles; although one particular endeavor, the journal *Past and Present*, though not formally a group project nor intended to be merely a journal of Marxist historical studies, was founded in 1952 by several of its central figures and later became the premier English-language journal in the field of social history. Nevertheless, it is now recognized that the intellectual and political exchanges and comradeship that membership in the group afforded were both crucial to the historians' later individual and collective accomplishments and fundamental to the emergence of a distinctly British Marxist historical tradition.

Dobb, Morton, and Torr were crucial influences on the formation of the tradition. It was Dobb's *Studies in the Development of Capitalism* (1946) addressing the question of the transition from feudalism to capitalism, along with the debates to which it gave rise—collected in R. Hilton, ed. *The Transition from Feudalism to Capitalism* (1976)—that established the framework not only for the group's deliberations but also for the historians' continuing efforts in favor of the development of a Marxist synthesis, or "grand narrative," of British history. Morton's and Torr's influence can be seen in the historians' commitment to the writing of that narrative as "people's history"—that is, a history not limited to the lives and actions of rulers, but encompassing as well those of "the common people." Indeed, Morton's *A People's History of England* (1938) was a pioneering text in the historians' campaign to "democratize" the past both in extending the bounds of *who* was to be included in the essential historical record and in making it available and accessible to a popular and working-class audience.

Shaped by the experience and aspirations of the Historians' Group, the younger British Marxist historians produced their major scholarly writings in the decades following the mid-1950s, effectively recasting their respective fields of study in the process: Hilton, medieval and peasant studies; Hill, sixteenth- and seventeenth-century studies and the English Revolution; Rudé, Hobsbawm, and Thompson, late eighteenth- and early nineteenth-century social history and the study of labor and popular movements; and Kiernan and Hobsbawm, European history and **imperialism**.

Yet beyond their outstanding individual accomplishments there have been four paramount contributions that the British Marxist historians have made as a "collective." The first has been the development of "class-struggle analysis." Thus, the medieval world was not harmoniously organized into three estates but was an order of struggle between lords and peasants; the conflicts of the seventeenth century were not a mere civil war but a "bourgeois revolution" driven by struggles of the lower orders as well; the eighteenth century was not conflict-free but shot through with antagonisms between, in Thompson's worlds, "patricians and plebeians"; and the Industrial Revolution entailed not only economic and social changes but, in the course of the conflicts between "capital and labor," a dramatic process of class formation determined in great part by the agency of workers themselves.

The second contribution, linked to people's history, has been the pursuit and development of "history from the bottom up." The British Marxist historians have sought to redeem, or reappropriate, both the experience and the agency of the lower orders—peasants, artisans, and workers.

The third contribution has been the recovery and assemblage of a "radical democratic tradition." Alongside the Magna Carta we are offered the Peasant Rising of 1381 (Hilton, *Bond Men Made Free*, 1973); outside of Parliament in the seventeenth century we encounter Levellers, Diggers, and Ranters (Hill, *The World Turned Upside Down*, 1972); in the eighteenth century we hear not only the elites but also the crowds of London asserting the "rights of the freeborn Englishman" (Rudé, *Wilkes and Liberty,* 1962); and in the Age of Revolution we are reminded that within the "exceptionalism" of English political life there were Jacobins, Luddites, and Chartists (Hobsbawm and Rudé, *Captain Swing,* 1969; and Thompson, *The Making of the English Working Class,* 1963). This tradition also has its outstanding voices and intellectuals, including John Milton, Gerrard Winstanley, John Wilkes, Tom Paine, William Blake, William Cobbett, and William Morris.

Finally, another contribution of primary importance is that the historians have effectively helped to undermine the great "grand narratives" of both Right and Left. Their writings directly challenged the Whig version of history in which the development of English life and freedoms are comprehended as a continuous evolutionary and progressive success. And they also helped to clear away the (supposedly) Marxist presentation of history in which historical development is conceived of in unilinear, mechanical, and economistic terms. The narrative which they themselves have been developing may not have become the schoolbook version of past and present, but it has definitively shaped and informed radical-democratic and socialist historical consciousness in Britain.

Harvey J. Kaye

Bibliography

Cornforth, Maurice, ed. *Rebels and Their Causes.* 1978.

Kaye, Harvey J. *The British Marxist Historians.* 1984.

———. *The Education of Desire: Marxists and the Writing of History.* 1992.

Saville, John, ed. *Democracy and the Labour Movement.* 1954.

Masefield, John Edward (1878–1967)

John Masefield, Poet Laureate from 1930 to his death, was a versatile writer: lyric poet, narrative poet, playwright, novelist, autobiographer (four books), essayist, historian, children's writer, and critic. He was trained as an officer in the British merchant marine but jumped ship in New York City and worked in a carpet factory in Yonkers, New York, before illness and depression brought him back to England. After his return, for four years in London he struggled to put his nautical experiences into verse. In 1900 his work was discovered by **William Butler Yeats**. He was first successful with *Salt Water Ballads* (1902) and is still considered Britain's greatest sea poet despite the fact that he spent only two years at sea.

Masefield adopted and rejuvenated the British narrative-verse tradition that goes back to Chaucer. Five long verse narratives led to the laureateship. The first, *The Everlasting Mercy* (1911), the tale of a reformed drunkard, shocked the reading public with its explicit street language and its raw energy. *The Widow in the Bye Street* (1912), *Dauber* (1913), *The Daffodil Fields* (1913), and *Reynard the Fox* (1919) sustained his popularity, but subsequent narratives seemed strained, and critics and the public lost interest in the form. Unfortunately, the loss of interest especially obscures the distinction of *Dauber*, a story about a failed sailor-artist, and of *Reynard the Fox*, a story that evokes the community of sensations between animal and human life during a hunt.

Since Masefield always considered himself a storyteller, it was natural for him to gravitate toward the novel. Of his sixteen adult novels, two continue to be read, both tales of the sea: *The Bird of Dawning* (1933) and *Victorious Troy* (1935). One novel for young people, *Jim Davis* (1911), a tale of a boy caught up with smugglers during the Napoleonic Wars, and reminiscent of Robert Louis Stevenson, remains popular and in print.

During the First World War, Masefield served with the British Red Cross in France. He commanded an evacuation boat for the wounded of the battle for the Dardanelles, leading to his writing one of the finest campaign histories to come out of the conflict: *Gallipoli* (1916).

From 1904 to 1914 Masefield strove for success as a playwright but failed in his attempt to create an audience for the kind of poetic folk dramas that his friends Yeats and John Millington Synge had introduced in Ireland. In 1903 Masefield married an Anglo-Irish woman, Constance de la Cherois-Crommelin, with whom he lived happily until her death in 1960.

Masefield was awarded the Order of Merit in 1935 but outlived his literary reputation. He was buried in Westminster Abbey, ignored by contemporary critics; nevertheless, **Muriel Spark**'s distinguished study of him in 1953 shows Masefield's ability to influence contemporary writing.

Sanford Sternlicht

Bibliography

Drew, Fraser B. *John Masefield's England: A Study of National Themes in His Work*. 1973.
Smith, Constance Babington. *John Masefield: A Life*. 1978.
Spark, Muriel. *John Masefield*. 1953.
Sternlicht, Sanford. *John Masefield*. 1978.

Massingham, H(enry) W(illiam) (1860–1924)

Editor of the *Nation* (1907–23), H.W. Massingham was born on 25 May 1860 near Norwich. Following an education at the King Edward VI School, he was employed as a reporter by the *Eastern Daily Press*. In London, after a few years of work as a writer and editor for the national Press Agency, Massingham joined T.P. O'Connor's sensationalist paper, the *Star*, in 1888, serving briefly as assistant editor during 1889–90. He moved from the *Star* to the editorial chair of the *Labour World* in 1891 and a year later to the *Daily Chronicle*, where he worked as editorial writer, literary editor, parliamentary correspondent, and assistant editor until his appointment as managing editor in 1895. Massingham was also an active member of the **Fabian Society** and, until his resignation from the society in 1894, assisted in the publication of the *Fabian News* and the *Fabian Tracts*.

As managing editor of the *Daily Chronicle*, Massingham made the paper a major voice of advanced Liberalism and a highly respected medium of **literary criticism**. But in November 1899 he was compelled to resign because of his uncompromising condemnation of the **Boer War**. During the following eight years he worked as a free-lance writer contributing special articles and reports to the **Manchester Guardian** and the *Daily News*.

In early 1907 the Rowntree Social Service Trust employed Massingham to establish the weekly **Nation**, of which he became editor in March 1907. Under Massingham, the *Nation* became one of the most significant weeklies and, although not an uncritical mouthpiece of the **Liberals** and Labourites, was welcomed by both parties. With an innovative staff, Massingham increased the circulation of the *Nation* and made it a "jewel in the crown" of the journals owned by the Rowntree Trust. As his friend and colleague, H.W. Nevinson, later wrote, Massingham's journalism was "an expression of his ardent and impatient spirit" and reflected his "eager appreciation of literature, drama, and the pictoral arts." Indeed, he made the *Nation* a cultural as well as a political force in the British **press** firmament.

In his politics Massingham was basically an independent radical and something of a "troublemaker." Hence, in his criticism of the **Asquith** government, Massingham opposed large armament expenditures, supported the demands of the trade union movement, and was especially vocal in his advocacy of peace, **women's suffrage**, social reform, and Irish Home Rule and in his condemnation of jingoism, anti-German prejudice, and the *entente* with Czarist Russia. Above all, Massingham championed freedom of the press and its right of "fair criticism" and objective reporting during wartime.

Massingham opposed Britain's entry into the war in 1914, the establishment of an authoritarian wartime coalition government, and **conscription**, and he turned against his prewar heroes **David Lloyd George** and **Winston Churchill**. As the war became a bloody stalemate by 1916, Massingham urged a negotiated peace, so irritating the new Prime Minister, Lloyd George, that he requested the Rowntree Trust to restrain its "unpatriotic" editor. Unable to sway Massingham's employers, Lloyd George interdicted the overseas circulation of the *Nation*, but even this punitive device failed to silence Massingham's criticism. Throughout 1917 and 1918 Massingham continued to insist that Lloyd George must be forced out of office. Despairing of ousting the wily Prime Minister, following his victory in the "coupon" election of 1918, Massingham offered to resign as editor but was dissuaded by the Rowntree Trust. However, his hopes for a sensible lasting peace were buoyed by American President Woodrow Wilson's Fourteen Points and the prospects of a **League of Nations**. But, as his animus against Lloyd George and the continuation of the coalition government intensified, Massingham turned to the **Labour Party** and its "pragmatic socialism" as the only hope for the nation. Here, too, he was soon disappointed as the Labour Party leadership seemed to compromise its principles for short-term gains.

After the war Massingham assailed the post-war policies of the Lloyd George administration and Allied intervention in Russia and urged diplomatic recognition of the Soviet regime and the establishment of "responsible" government in Ireland, India, and Egypt. But his health declined, often necessitating long absences from the *Nation*'s office. This situation and disagreements with the Rowntree Trust over the weekly's parlous financial situation constrained Massingham to resign as editor in April 1923. A year and a half later he died, on 23 August 1924.

J.O. Baylen

Bibliography

Havighurst, Alfred F. *Radical Journalist: H.W. Massingham, 1860–1924.* 1974.

Mass-Observation (1937–1949)

Mass-Observation (M-O) was an organization founded in 1937 by Tom Harrisson, an anthropologist; Charles Madge, a journalist and later a sociologist; and **Humphrey Jennings**, a documentary filmmaker. Their purpose was political as well as academic. They believed that ordinary people's consciousness was stifled or distorted in the 1930s by those with political, commercial, and media power, and that establishing "a democratic social science" devoted to revealing what ordinary people did and said would lead to social change. Ironically, in 1949 the organization was handed over to market research and became a limited company. In the meantime the enterprise amassed a huge amount of data, and the deposits of M-O material at the University of Sussex represent a major archive for the study of British social history in the period 1937–49.

M-O began with a study of the everyday life of "Worktown" in Lancashire from 1937 to 1940. A group led by Harrisson investigated Bolton's social and political life, using the method they called "scientific observation." The Mass-Observers recorded people's conversations and behavior in places like pubs and churches, and on holiday in Blackpool, usually without the subjects knowing they were being observed.

The methods used remained central to M-O's research. Meanwhile, Madge developed another technique, the "day survey." He recruited volunteers to write a personal diary on the twelfth of each month. The project lasted from February 1937 to February 1938, by which time over 500 volunteers had participated. The dates included the day of the coronation of **George VI**, and M-O's first publication was based on the 12 May 1937 day surveys. Subsequently, Mass-Observation used its panel of volunteers to describe other special days, like Armistice Day, and to report on particular topics such as reading, drinking habits, and the political crisis of 1938.

From January 1939 to 1949 Mass-Observation sent out short questionnaires ("directives") to panelists each month to which detailed, candid, personal answers were expected. After the outbreak of the **Second World War** the directives focused on the way civilians were adapting to the war. The panel was asked about such things as **rationing, evacuation**, air raids, **conscription**, war work, reactions to the political situation, and post-war aspirations. In addition, panelists were asked to send in diaries covering not just one day but the entire month.

During the period 1937–45 a total of 2,847 individuals replied to at least one directive, though in any one month the number of replies received never exceeded 500. About the same number kept wartime diaries, though they did not all contribute every month. The panelists were mainly in lower-middle-class occupations such as clerks and schoolteachers. A minority of the men were industrial manual workers. Many of the women classified themselves as housewives, though few were mothers with small children. Most felt undereducated, and many were politically left-wing. Approximately equal numbers of men and women kept M-O diaries, though women's contributions were more sustained. Mass-Observation may have appealed particularly to **women** because it gave them a sense of being listened to at a time when they were still largely deprived of a voice in politics, trade unions, and the media.

Mass-Observation's work was commissioned by various agencies. For example, from early 1940 to the end of 1941 the Home Intelligence Department of the Ministry of Information paid for regular Mass-Observation reports on civilian morale. In 1942–3 M-O undertook on behalf of the management an investigation of attitudes toward work in a factory producing **radar** equipment. The Advertising Service Guild, an association of eight **advertising** agents, funded at least seven M-O studies. In addition, the organization's own small team of observers investigated topics such as family planning and reactions to the **Beveridge** Report, which formed the substance of newspaper articles and broadcasts, the income from which helped fund other M-O activities. Mass-Observation material was disseminated in over twenty books between 1937 and 1950.

Since 1949 there have been three attempts to reuse M-O's original techniques. In 1959 Harrisson returned to Bolton to assess the changes since the Worktown study. In 1977 a survey of attitudes to royalty was undertaken. And in the 1980s a panel of volunteers was re-cruited to send in directive replies and diaries in a direct revival of the original project.

Penny Summerfield

Bibliography

Calder, Angus. "Mass-Observation, 1937–1949" in Martin Bulmer, ed. *Essays on the History of British Sociological Research*. 1985. pp. 121–36.

Calder, Angus, and Dorothy Sheridan. *Speak for Yourself: A Mass-Observation Anthology, 1937–49*. 1984.

Summerfield, Penny. "Mass-Observation: Social Research or Social Movement?" *Journal of Contemporary History*, vol. 20 (1985), pp. 439–52.

Masterman, C(harles) F(rederick) G(urney) (1874–1927)

C.F.G. Masterman was a quintessential **New Liberal** politician, man of letters, and journalist imbued with an abiding Christian socialist commitment to social welfare. A trusted lieutenant and partner of **David Lloyd George** and **Winston Churchill** in many of their landmark social welfare schemes, including the National Insurance Act of 1911, Masterman remains a ubiquitous but marginal figure in the history of early twentieth-century Britain. His successes as a young man—his stellar career at Christ's College, **Cambridge**, followed by his literary and journalistic triumphs in London and swift rise to **H.H. Asquith's Cabinet** in 1914 as Chancellor of the Duchy of Lancaster—coupled with his perennial difficulties in finding a parliamentary constituency, have led contemporaries and historians since to view his life as a tragedy of unfulfilled expectations. He is remembered mostly for his lyrical jeremiads on social questions (*From the Abyss*, 1902; *The Heart of the Empire*, 1901; *The Condition of England*, 1909) and for his futile attempt to offer his party a coherent and "invigorating" vision of its future (*The New Liberalism*, 1920).

The title of Masterman's collection of biographical studies, *In Peril of Change* (1905), captures his ambivalent championship of radical change as the cure for the woes of his party and the nation. On the one hand, he chastised his peers for their dangerously anachronistic attachment to Victorian ideas and institutions. Masterman proposed a wide-ranging program intended to secure the economic liberty of citizens: labor exchanges; wage boards; land colonies for unskilled, unemployed men; medical inspection; and free meals for school children. He believed nineteenth-century philanthropic ventures such as the **settlement movement** were sentimental vestiges, wholly inadequate to the challenges posed by the segregation and aggregation of the poor in the modern city. Oddly enough, at the time he launched this attack in *The Heart of the Empire*, he was himself working closely with Cambridge House, the **Anglican** university settlement in South London.

On the other hand, a radical rupture with the British past was anathema to Masterman on both intellectual and political grounds. Intellectually, he remained attracted to the rhetoric, idealism, and spirituality of the high-Victorian sages, foremost among them Arnold, Carlyle, Maurice, Ruskin, and Tennyson, whose influence is palpable in his writings. Politically, he distrusted the coercive power of the state and, in particular, those brands of socialism that called for the overthrow of capitalism. Masterman imaginatively deployed what he called "the poetry of fact" in his struggle to transcend and recast the polarities of individualism and collectivism, faith and secularism, pastoral escapism and urban realism.

Masterman's political career was marked by painful ironies. While the support of John Burns, the leader of the 1889 Dock Strike, had helped Masterman secure his first parliamentary victory in West Ham (North) in 1906, only three years later Masterman had come to loathe his former patron's "impossibilities" and growing conservatism while serving as Burns' Undersecretary at the Local Government Board. Similarly, he vitriolically denounced Lloyd George for betraying Liberalism by forming the coalition government of 1918–22, during his own extended exile from Parliament (1915–23). Masterman's greatest political triumph, his appointment to a Cabinet-level post in 1915 as government spokesman on national insurance, was also the occasion of his greatest humiliation. Successive defeats, standing for South West Bethnal Green and then Ipswich, forced him to resign his office, and he was not reelected to Parliament until 1923. Masterman was not entirely a victim of circumstances. His lifelong battle with severe mood swings and the general fragility of his mental health exacerbated contemporaries' perceptions of his cynical detachment and inconveniently principled, perhaps even self-righteous, vision of politics.

Seth Koven

Bibliography
David, Edward. "The New Liberalism of C.F.G. Masterman" in Kenneth D. Brown, ed. *Essays in Anti-Labour History*. 1974. pp. 25–41.
Masterman, Lucy. *C.F.G. Masterman*. 1939.

Maugham, (William) Somerset (1874–1965)

Somerset Maugham was the most popular literary entertainer of the first half of the twentieth century, but when he died his realism and naturalism were no longer appreciated, and his direct, unadorned, subtle, ironic style no longer fashionable. A skilled observer and chronicler of the British character at home and abroad, he is now regarded as Britain's first short-story writer, while his novels and plays are generally given short shrift.

Maugham's father was a lawyer attached to the British Embassy in Paris in 1874, and Maugham was born in the Embassy to ensure his British citizenship. His mother was an Englishwoman brought up in France. Orphaned at ten, he was taken to England for the first time to live with a clergyman uncle. But he remained an outside observer, spending much of his life abroad. After education at the King's School, Canterbury, he studied in Germany and then qualified as a physician at St. Thomas' medical school in 1897. He used his medical experiences in his early writing about the **slums** of London, as in his first novel, *Liza of Lambeth* (1897). Its success encouraged him to abandon medicine for a literary career.

The work that made Maugham famous is the autobiographical *Of Human Bondage* (1915), the story of a young, club-footed artist-physician enslaved by his love for an unworthy woman. It is generally believed, today, that the protagonist's handicap is code for Maugham's **homosexuality**. His other major works of fiction include *The Moon and Sixpence* (1919), a sardonic representation of the life and career of the French painter Gauguin; *Cakes and Ale* (1930), a satire on **London** literary life; *Ashenden: or, the British Agent* (1928), detective stories based on Maugham's First World War experience as a secret agent; and *The Razor's Edge* (1944), the story of an American protagonist who tries to escape his war experiences by seeking serenity in Indian philosophy.

Maugham was an extremely successful playwright in the inter-war period because of his gift for dialogue and his ability to portray the social scene in dramatic form. His most popular drama, *The Circle* (1921), still frequently performed, illustrates the author's cynical view of marriage. Other plays include *Our Betters* (1917), *The Constant Wife* (1926), and *For Services Rendered* (1932).

Maugham's **First World War** service included driving ambulances on the Western Front. In 1915 he married Syrie Barnardo Wellcome, a marriage of convenience that produced one child and divorce in 1927. In 1926 Maugham bought a villa on Cape Ferrat in the south of France and lived there for the rest of his life except for a Second World War exile in the United States. In 1954 Maugham was made a Companion of Honour.

Maugham's themes in fiction and drama include the difficulty young men face in trying to find purpose and place in life; the impermanence of love and the frailty of marriage; the hypocrisy implicit in conventional morals, especially those rooted in Victorian values and practices; and the pomposity and pretentiousness of many, if not most, writers and other artists. Most important, perhaps, Maugham's stories retain interest for their depiction of British colonialists during the decay of Empire. Whereas in **Joseph Conrad**'s stories the agents of Empire retain close ties with home, in Maugham's stories the imperialists are adrift, seeming not to know whose interests they serve. They are outsiders both to England and to the native cultures surrounding them. All of Maugham's themes are conveyed, for the most part, through conventional, often slackly managed, narrative forms. The Ashenden stories are an exception and make metafictional play out of the similarities between novelists and spies.

Sanford Sternlicht

Bibliography
Barnes, R.E. *The Dramatic Comedy of Somerset Maugham.* 1968.
Calder, Robert L. *Willie: The Life of W. Somerset Maugham.* 1989.
Cordell, Richard Albert. *Somerset Maugham: A Writer for All Seasons.* 2nd ed. 1969.
Curtis, Anthony. *Somerset Maugham.* 1977.
Morgan, Ted. *Somerset Maugham.* 1980.

Maxton, James (1885–1946)

James Maxton was one of the most charismatic Labour politicians in British public life. His parliamentary career spanned the years from 1922 until his death in 1946. Essentially a Scottish radical, and often portrayed as a revolutionary wildman, he nonetheless became a highly respected and popular figure at Westminster among politicans of all parties. He never attained a position of ministerial power, and his parliamentary achievements were limited to back-bench influence on pieces of social legislation. However, his impact on the public as an orator, a propagandist, and a protester have ensured scholarly attention to his career and the celebration of his memory in left-wing circles.

Maxton was born into a comfortable middle-class home near Glasgow and took advantage of educational opportunities to become a schoolteacher. In 1904 he joined the **Independent Labour Party** (ILP), having cast off a youthful allegiance to Conservatism. His political motivation sprang practically from his experience working in school in working-class areas of Glasgow. He was outraged by both the poverty of many of the children and the repressiveness of aspects of the educational system.

Maxton took a high-profile stance against the First World War and endured a prison sentence for sedition. His reputation as an agitator and a rebel was never to fade. In the 1922 general election he was returned as Labour MP for Bridgeton, a Glasgow constituency that was a byword for social deprivation. More than anyone else, with his declamatory oratory and his long-haired bohemian physical appearance, he typified what the English **press** were disposed to find alarming about the new Scottish Labour intake to Parliament.

In the House of Commons Maxton did create a stir: In 1923 he labeled as "murderers" **Conservatives** who supported a government motion to cut health grants to local authorities. This resulted in suspension from the House, but it was not long before Maxton won the affection of political foes as well as friends. **Winston Churchill** became perhaps his greatest admirer. Maxton's humanitarianism disarmed potential critics.

The folksy legend that surrounded him has led many historians to dismiss him as a political thinker and strategist. Certainly, Maxton's strengths lay in popularizing ideas rather than patenting them. On the other hand, he knew clearly where he wanted Labour politics to go; in the 1920s, along with his ideological mentor and fellow Scot **John**

Wheatley, he set out to supplant the gradualism of **Labour Party** policy. He pursued this goal through the medium of the affiliated ILP, which had developed into a rallying point for left-wing critics of the Labour Party under **Ramsay MacDonald**. In 1926 Maxton, now Chairman of the ILP, led a campaign for the party program "Socialism in Our Time," a critical analysis of **unemployment** and poverty much influenced by the underconsumptionist economics of **J.A. Hobson**. The gulf between Maxton and the moderate Labour leadership widened in 1928 with the publication of the Cook-Maxton Manifesto, a declaration of class war that took the ILP closer to the **Communist** politics of A.J. Cook (1883–1931), the miners' leader. During the minority Labour government's tenure in 1929–31 Maxton was one of its fiercest critics, and his behavior raised questions about relations between the Labour Party and the ILP that came to a head after the fall of the government. In 1932 the ILP and Maxton opted for disaffiliation. Most historians, in the light of the ILP's subsequent decline, have viewed this as a calamitous error of judgment; some left-wing commentators have applauded it as principled opposition to gradualism.

After disaffiliation, Maxton drifted into the world of the marginalized extreme Left, although his command of his Bridgeton constituency never weakened. He remained a **pacifist** despite the worsening international situation, and when war finally came in 1939, he opposed it.

Maxton was essentially a figure of propagandist significance: He inspired, uplifted, and evangelized. He was the legend of "Red Clydeside" personified.

Graham Walker

Bibliography

Brown, Gordon. *Maxton*. 1986.
Knox, William. *James Maxton*. 1987.
McKinlay, Alan, and R.J. Morris, eds. *The ILP on Clydeside, 1893–1932: From Foundation to Disintegration*. 1991.

Means Test

The means test achieved notoriety in the early 1930s following the budgetary and financial crisis of 1930–1. Having witnessed the mounting insolvency of the Unemployment Insurance Fund, the National government decided in 1931 to divide those out of work into two distinct groups, imposing upon the long-term unemployed a means test as a qualification for state assistance. Henceforth there was to be no agreed schedule of payments to those who had exhausted their legal entitlement to **unemployment** insurance. Such persons were now to receive payments according to need. The exercise was initially carried out by local government officials, but widespread variations arose in the severity with which the test was administered. Some authorities regarded such payments as an extension of insurance and, therefore, a matter of right; others adopted very different standards as to what constituted an individual's available resources.

The political and financial wrangling to which this gave rise prompted the National government in 1934 to bring the determination of means-tested unemployment payments under the aegis of a national body called the Unemployment Assistance Board. Insurance was now a matter of rights, and assistance a matter of needs, as efforts continued to secure greater financial solvency.

W.R. Garside

Bibliography

Garside, W.R. *British Unemployment, 1919–1939: A Study in Public Policy*. 1990.
Deacon, Alan, and Jonathan Bradshaw. *Reserved for the Poor: The Means Test in British Social Policy*. 1983.

Medawar, Peter (1915–1987)

The British transplantation biologist and immunologist Peter Medawar was born in Brazil, the son of an English mother and a Lebanese businessman. Educated at Marlborough College, he went to **Oxford**, where he took a first-class degree in zoology, began research on embryo growth at Howard Florey's School of Pathology, and married his fiancé, Jean. During the Second World War Medawar turned to the problem of the rejection of skin grafts in burn victims, such as wounded airmen, and sought to find out how the body recognized foreign (non-self) tissue. He showed that there was a latent period, characteristic of an immune response, before the rejection of foreign grafts occurred, that subsequent grafts were rejected more quickly than earlier ones, and that a state of heightened resistance to subsequent grafts applied not just at the site of the original graft but all over the body. Medawar also described a massive invasion of the grafts by lymphocytes, paving the way for the later discovery that these lymphocytes were responsible for destroying the graft.

Medawar continued his work on skin grafts when he moved to Birmingham in 1947 and University College, London, in 1951. He showed that the immune system was not pre-programmed to distinguish between self and non-self, but learned to do so as a result of exposure to self-molecules during early development. For example, Medawar demonstrated that if fetal mice were injected with foreign tissue, they could accept it as self, and immunological tolerance to that tissue could be established. This principle was invaluable to biomedical scientists studying autoimmune diseases and how the immune system was shaped. His work on immunological tolerance during this period led to the award of the 1960 Nobel Prize for Physiology and Medicine jointly with the Australian Frank MacFarlane Burnet.

In 1962 Medawar became the Director of the National Institute for Medical Research (NIMR), the central laboratory of the state-funded **Medical Research Council** (MRC). There he continued his work on transplantation tolerance and immunosuppression, for example developing an anti-lymphocyte serum to prevent graft rejection. In 1969 a severe stroke left him partially paralyzed, and in 1971 he resigned the directorship of the NIMR. His final research at the MRC's Clinical Research Centre (where he worked from 1971 to 1986) was on problems of tumor immunity.

Medawar also wrote on a number of more-general science topics. Among his better-known books are *The Art of the Soluble* (1967), *Advice to a Young Scientist* (1979), and *The Limits of Science* (1984). He was the recipient of numerous awards, elected a fellow of the **Royal Society** (1949), knighted (1965), and appointed a Companion of Honour (1972) and a member of the Order of Merit (1982). His autobiography was published in 1986, the year before his death.

David Cantor

Bibliography

Medawar, Jean. *A Very Decided Preference: Life with Peter Medawar*. 1990.
Medawar, Peter. *Memoir of a Thinking Radish: An Autobiography*. 1986.

Medical Education

Nineteenth-century reforms in medical education, including the concentration of clinical training in the teaching **hospitals** and the development of the preclinical science curriculum, served primarily to demarcate the emerging medical profession from a host of other irregular healers. By contrast, twentieth-century developments were less concerned with defining the boundaries of medical orthodoxy than with redefining the division of labor within the profession.

With the establishment of National Health Insurance in 1911 and the Ministry of Health in 1919, the government targeted improvements in personal health services as the most effective way of combating the persistent burden of chronic illness and low-level disability. The general practitioner (GP), in particular, now came to be seen as a key figure in the pursuit of national **health** and efficiency. At the same time some began to question whether existing forms of clinical education provided an appropriate preparation for this kind of practice. The sorts of cases most frequently seen by GPs rarely found their way onto the wards of the teaching hospitals and so were largely ignored by clinical teachers. This point was made with particular force by Sir George Newman (1870–1948), Chief Medical Officer to the Board of Education from 1907, and subsequently to the Ministry of Health. Newman argued that clinical training should be reorganized to emphasize the diagnosis and treatment of common and chronic ailments, especially the early stages of disease rather than the advanced or acute cases that tended to dominate hospital practice. Embodied in a series of official reports by Newman and by the Education Committee of the General Medical Council, this view dominated discussion of the reform of medical education during the inter-war years.

The chief obstacle to such reforms was seen to lie in the entrenched interests of hospital consultants. A post in a teaching hospital served to advertise a doctor's skill in treating difficult or unusual cases, and was of considerable value in building up a lucrative private practice outside the hospital. Consequently, consultants were reluctant to fill their wards with the kind of routine and undramatic cases that reformers argued should be central to the clinical education of a GP. Nor was there any effective pressure from educational bodies to change the style or content of clinical teaching. So long as the market for medical qualifications was dominated by the Conjoint Board of the Royal Colleges of Physicians and Surgeons, examinations tended to be based on precisely the kind of hospital practice favored by the consultants that those bodies represented.

Consequently, Newman and his colleagues at the Board of Education sought to weaken the power of elite private practitioners over clinical teaching, and especially over qualifying examinations. The growth of the civic universities between 1900 and 1920 provided the necessary leverage. From 1908 the Board of Education began pressing for greater university involvement in the educational work of teaching hospitals throughout England. In particular, the appointment in 1909 of the **Haldane** Commission on the University of London created an opportunity to bring the great metropolitan teaching hospitals under academic control. These plans were seriously disrupted by the First World War and the recession that followed. Nevertheless, immediately following the war, Newman was able to secure the establishment of full-time university professorships in medicine, surgery, and gynecology in several London teaching hospitals. This policy was reiterated in the 1944 Report of the Interdepartmental Committee of Medical Schools (the Goodenough Report), and by 1950 full-time clinical chairs had been established in teaching hospitals throughout Britain.

This gradual extension of academic influence effectively broke the control of the Royal Colleges over basic medical training and certification, and by the 1960s medicine in Britain was almost exclusively a graduate profession. On the other hand, it is not clear that this led to the desired shift in emphasis in the clinical education of the GP. On the contrary, it was argued in some quarters that the replacement of consultants by full-time academics in the teaching hospitals led not to an emphasis on the practical needs of the GP, but to the introduction of even more esoteric material into an already overloaded curriculum. In 1968 the Royal Commission on Medical Education, chaired by Lord Todd, conceded that the undergraduate curriculum no longer provided an adequate preparation for general practice, and recommended that GPs should now undergo further training at the postgraduate level. Responsibility for setting up appropriate postgraduate training schemes passed to the Royal College of General Practitioners, initially established in 1952 to promote research in general practice. A number of such schemes were established in teaching hospitals during the 1970s and are generally regarded as operating very successfully.

Attempts to establish new forms of training in the more-specialized areas of hospital practice have been less successful. Shortly after the First World War the London teaching hospitals organized their own scheme of postgraduate education for would-be consultants. In 1921 a committee of the Ministry of Health chaired by Lord Athlone recommended the establishment of what became, in 1935, the British (later Royal) Postgraduate Medical School at the Hammersmith Hospital. It was the reorganization of the hospital system under the **National Health Service** (NHS) in 1948, however, that offered the opportunity for the most comprehensive reforms of postgraduate medical education. State control of the hospitals made it possible to link postgraduate training to the career structure and the expected needs of the hospital service, by creating a layer of hospital training appointments below the level of consultant. The 1948 *Report of the Inter-Departmental Committee on the Remuneration of Consultants and Specialists* (the Spens Report) and the 1968 Todd Report both devoted considerable space to discussing how these training posts ought best to be accommodated within the staffing structure of the NHS.

In fact, no such harmonious accommodation was to be achieved. While hospital services have expanded considerably under the NHS, consultants have sought to ensure that their privileges—in particular, the freedom to see private patients—should not be diluted. They have been successful in limiting the expansion of their own ranks, with the result that most of the growth in the hospital services since 1948 has taken place in the junior grades. In consequence, the main burden of routine hospital work now falls on junior doctors. Since the 1960s a number of official reports—most notably, the 1981 *Fourth Report of the Social Services Committee*—have argued that this undermines the training function of junior posts. But in a climate of financial stringency and political conservatism, little action has been taken to establish a more appropriate division of labor between junior doctors and consultants.

Steven W. Sturdy

M

Bibliography

Cooke, Alexander M. *A History of the Royal College of Physicians of London.* vol. 3. 1972.

Fourth Report from the Social Services Committee. 1981.

Fry, John, Lord Hunt of Fawley, and R.J.F.H. Pinsent, eds. *A History of the Royal College of General Practitioners: The First Twenty-five Years.* 1983.

Report of the Inter-Departmental Committee on Medical Schools (Goodenough Report). 1944.

Medical Profession

Medicine in twentieth-century Britain, as in most Western nations, has seen the growth of specialization. This has been the basis of an increasing gap between general practitioners (GPs) and hospital-based practitioners or consultants, a division that extends an older distinction that was founded, to some degree, on social class. Repeated state intervention in the provision of care has helped preserve the world's largest body of GPs but has also encouraged a referral system that ensured a noncompetitive flow of patients between GPs and consultants. To some extent it was the maneuvering of consultants that led to GPs being excluded from the hospital world where consultants developed "firms" of aspiring young specialists.

As the century opened, the profession was beset with problems. Most medical men worked in general practice. Some had full- or part-time appointments at Poor Law or municipal hospitals. A very few had prestigious positions at voluntary hospitals. Most of the men who held them were general physicians or surgeons, not specialists; they were unpaid and gave their services for a few hours each week. Such men, most of whom were Fellows of the Royal Colleges, usually had large, lucrative private practices. In England two colleges existed: The oldest, covering physicians, was probably more elitist than the one embracing surgeons. There were similar colleges in Edinburgh, Glasgow, and Dublin. Surgeons were referred to as "Mr." rather than "Dr.," usages that still apply. Some members of these colleges practiced in specialized fields, but there were no specialist qualifications. Not until 1929 was a third college formed—for obstetricians and gynecologists—and the qualifications it awarded were not formally recognized until 1950. Since then, other

Royal Colleges have been created for psychiatrists, pathologists, and radiologists, as well as one for GPs.

Around 1900 most of the profession, numbering over 20,000, served mainly as GPs. Many of these practitioners would treat complex conditions in the provincial towns and smaller hospitals of the nation. All doctors owed their right to call themselves members of a medical profession to the 1858 Medical Act, which established a General Medical Council to register and oversee them, but neither it nor the qualifications offered by the Royal Colleges and universities provided unique rights to practice. GPs were free to offer specialist care, and many unqualified people practiced healing. Aside from public appointments as medical officers of health, the only field reserved for medical men under the 1858 act was so-called club practice. This had been started in the 1820s by groups of workers who had formed self-help organizations called "friendly societies," and it was there that many of the profession's troubles began.

Club work undertaken by GPs was always poorly paid, but doctors accepted it as a way of securing income until they could attract a sufficient number of individual fee-paying patients. By the end of the nineteenth century club practice covered one-third of the work force—5 million out of 15 million wage earners (nonworking women and children generally being excluded). Half of the GPs were thought to be involved, and for one-quarter—4,000 to 5,000 doctors—the work bulked so large as to be crucial for their existence.

Between 1895 and 1910, in a conflict called the "battle of the clubs," the doctors formed trade unions in an attempt to improve their conditions but were frustrated by divisions within their own ranks. The profession was overcrowded, and whenever local doctors boycotted a club post, the friendly societies found a practitioner elsewhere to fill it. Consultants also failed to cooperate since the narrow sphere of club work tended to protect them from GP competition, the holding of club posts being enough to bar a doctor from hospital appointments. Between 1902 and 1910 consultants and others holding leading offices in the British Medical Association resisted the efforts of club doctors to transform that organization into one capable of reforming club practice.

State intervention broke friendly society control in the form of the National Insurance Act (1911), which provided medical care for insured workers. Doctors were free to build up a "panel" of such patients. Though the doctors resisted the act at first, they soon found the panel system led to a stable income. The system of GPs referring patients to consultants grew out of the 1911 act and was steadily strengthened as more and more patients and practitioners were drawn into panel practice. By 1938 40 percent of the population in England and Wales was covered by National Health Insurance, and 90 percent of GPs participated, drawing over one-third of their income from the work.

Still, the panel did not cover nonworking wives, children, the self-employed, or those earning above a certain income. Nor did the system offer hospital or specialist care. As time-honored charities offering free or low-cost care to the working class, voluntary hospitals expected consultants to give their services free, only small payments occasionally being offered. Municipal and Poor Law hospitals employed doctors on a salaried basis. The main source of consultant income came from private referrals, with nursing homes used for inpatient care. As the Depression deepened, many fee-paying clients disappeared. Young doctors found it easier to join the panel and use the income it provided to build a viable general practice. If they wanted to specialize, they could find places in the provincial and cottage hospitals. By the 1920s it was claimed that GPs formed the majority of voluntary hospital staffs, despite the fact that such hospitals operated on the closed-staff principle.

By the time the Second World War began, consultant leaders were determined to act; specialization seemed rampant, but there were no specialty boards to certify or restrict practice. Two-and-a-half million operations were performed by GPs in 1938–9, and too much of the paid work was thought to be going to GP-specialists. Led by Lord Moran, President of the Royal College of Physicians, consultants after 1948 made use of the new **National Health Service** to replace "consultoids" (as the GP-specialists were called) with fully qualified men. By 1991 there were 18,000 consultants, compared with 5,300 in 1949, with 40,000 juniors to aid them.

Still, in 1948, more than 20,000 GPs remained, and their number in 1991 exceeded 30,000. Like hospital doctors, they were spread more evenly throughout the country owing to the administration of the Health Service. By removing the last vestige of control by the friendly societies in 1948, state intervention also gave the profession more freedom than it had enjoyed since club practice began in the 1820s. But a sharp division had been created in British medicine: Consultants and their juniors worked almost entirely in hospitals, while GPs worked in the community, and only rarely did they meet.

In the aftermath of 1948 many GPs were demoralized by the split, and to raise their status, a College of General Practitioners was formed in 1952, securing the title of Royal College in 1967. It strove to make an independent specialty of work in the community, focusing GP interest on the social and psychological aspects of treatment rather than on the more heroic forms of clinical care.

Not until 1990 did a different movement begin, stimulated by a government determined to make doctors more accountable for services performed. Through the introduction of an internal market, cost consciousness in the Health Service has forced hospitals and consultants to forge closer ties with GPs to attract the patients they need. GPs, on their part, find it profitable to widen the care they offer, extending even to minor surgery. Though the internal market may falter for other reasons, it promises to narrow the division within the profession, producing a partnership that may promote the integration of British medicine.

Frank Honigsbaum

Bibliography

Honigsbaum, Frank. *The Division in British Medicine: A History of the Separation of General Practice from Hospital Care, 1911–1968.* 1979.

——. *Health, Happiness, and Security: The Creation of the National Health Service.* 1989.

Stevens, Rosemary. *Medical Practice in Modern England: The Impact of Specialization and State Medicine.* 1966.

Medical Research

Medical research, in the sense of an organized and institutionally based program of inquiry into the phenomena of health and illness, is almost exclusively a twentieth-century enterprise in Britain. That is not to ignore the important developments in medical science that occurred during the nineteenth century. Statistical and occasional experimental investigations, for instance, were employed in various nineteenth-century inquiries into public health. Likewise, research was encouraged by the expansion of the university system, where medical professionalization intersected with a new middle-class culture of technical expertise. But such developments were very modest when compared with the enormous expansion of research that has occurred since the start of the twentieth century as a result of the growing interest of the state and industry alike in health care.

In the industrial sector British pharmaceutical companies began to establish their own research laboratories in the closing years of the nineteenth century, emulating developments in the research-intensive German fine-chemicals industry and in American marketing techniques. Research played a dual role in the development of the British pharmaceutical industry. In the first place, the publication of scientific data on chemical composition and pharmacological activity provided a way for companies to distinguish their products, including a variety of new vaccines and antitoxins, from the unstandardized herbal preparations and secret remedies that had previously made up the bulk of the market. This strategy, aimed primarily at doctors rather than the lay public, enabled such companies to corner the growing market in prescribed drugs. Secondly, research supported a strategy of product innovation and especially of patenting, which introduced a new kind of competition into the industry. As a result, the British industry has been increasingly dominated by research-based companies like Burroughs Wellcome, Glaxo, Boots, and ICI. Such companies fund an enormous range of medical research in their efforts to maintain a footing in this highly competitive market.

Government support for medical research in Britain developed at much the same time as pharmaceutical research, though initially inspired by rather different interests. Growing concern at the poor **health of the** working **population** in the early decades of the twentieth century prompted considerable expansion of state involvement in **public health** administration. As nineteenth-century efforts to promote sanitary reform and other forms of environmental control were augmented, with the establishment of National Health Insurance in 1911 and the **National Health Service** in 1948, by state-spon-

sored schemes intended to provide improved medical care for all sectors of the population, so medical research gained support as a means of promoting efficiency and economy in the development and implementation of policy. Statistical research into the incidence of various forms of environmental causes and biological processes implicated in such illness offered a way of identifying the least costly and most appropriate means of prevention and treatment. At the same time, the evident success of the science-based pharmaceutical companies, particularly in standardizing doctors' prescribing habits, encouraged government to undertake its own research into experimental therapeutics and allied sciences. These preventive and therapeutic interests came together in the establishment, in 1913, of the Medical Research Committee (reconstituted in 1920 as the **Medical Research Council**), which remains the main channel through which the government funds medical research in Britain.

The same concern with efficient welfare provision lay behind the growth of medical research charities. Through the nineteenth century medical philanthropy had aimed primarily at providing general medical care, chiefly through voluntary **hospitals** and dispensaries. By the late nineteenth century, however, benefactors had begun to take a growing interest in the development of new medical knowledge, and medical research increasingly displaced hospitals as the favored object of private and public **philanthropy**. Single-disease organizations like the Imperial Cancer Research Fund (established 1902), the British Empire Cancer Campaign (1923), the Asthma Research Council (1928), and the Empire Rheumatism Council (1936) proved particularly successful in attracting private gifts. More-diversified programs of funding, closer to the program pursued by the Medical Research Council (MRC), were adopted by industry-based research foundations—notably, the Rockefeller Foundation, which spent copiously on medical research in British universities and research institutes between the wars; the Wellcome Trust, established in 1936 with profits from the Wellcome drug company; and the Nuffield Foundation, which funded both biomedical research and policy research into hospital provision.

Funding in each of these three sectors has shown roughly the same pattern of increase since 1900. From around £50,000 per year during the First World War, MRC funding increased slowly to £195,000 in 1937–8, but grew with increasing speed in the post-war years to reach £97 million in 1981–2 and £146 million in 1988–9. Total charity funding for medical research reached £128 million in 1987–8. But both of these are considerably outweighed by the British pharmaceutical industry's spending on research and development, which came to £871 million in 1989.

These diverse sources of funding have fostered a variety of approaches to medical research. At one extreme lies much of the in-house research conducted by drug companies, which routinely test large numbers of natural and synthetic chemicals for possible biological or chemical effects. At the other extreme lie the more speculative programs of research into what are taken to be the fundamental phenomena of life. Several British scientists have received the Nobel Prize for Medicine for their work on such projects: A.V. Hill (1922) for his studies of the chemistry of muscle activity; C.S. Sherrington and E.D. Adrian (1932) for their work on the nervous coordination of muscular function; Hans Krebs (1953) for his research into the chemistry of cell metabolism; and J.C. Eccles, A.L. Hodgkin, and Andrew Huxley (1963) for their investigations into the mechanism of nerve conduction.

Most research has fallen between these extremes, however, and reveals a continuing dialogue between the pursuit of fundamental biological principles and the search for specific medical applications. This combination of interests is apparent in several other Nobel Prize-winning research projects. For instance, Henry Dale's fundamental study of the chemical mechanism of communication between nerve cells (1936) grew out of a long-standing program of research into the pharmacological properties of various naturally occurring chemicals. The work of Frederick Gowland Hopkins on vitamins (1929) combined an interest in the basic chemistry of nutrition with an immediate concern to address problems of public health. The development of penicillin, for which **Alexander Fleming**, Howard Florey, and Ernst Chain were awarded the Nobel Prize in 1945, likewise straddled the divide between purely academic work on the chemistry of immunity and the commercial exploitation of new drugs, while the work of Frank MacFarlane Burnet and **Peter Medawar** on the nature of the immune response (1960) was stimulated by developments in organ and tissue transplant techniques. Per-

haps most spectacularly, the program of research into the chemical structure of the genetic code, which earned the Nobel Prize for **Francis Crick**, James Watson, and Maurice Wilkins in 1962, has since grown into the burgeoning biotechnology industry.

This tendency to combine fundamental and applied research, often within the same program of investigation, has been actively supported by all three sectors—industry, state, and charity. Indeed, though different organizations have frequently disagreed over the details of research policy, and notably over the issue of medical versus scientific or bureaucratic control of research, there has nevertheless been a remarkable degree of collaboration in promoting what has become in many respects a common enterprise. This is particularly clear in the case of university science, which has attracted support from the whole spectrum of funding agencies, at least in part because of the perceived independence of academic and especially fundamental research from particular sectional interests.

Such collaboration indicates basic agreement on the aims of medical research. In particular, the persistently close collaboration between the MRC and the large industrial foundations has resulted from a shared commitment to medical research as a means of promoting industrial and national efficiency. Much twentieth-century medical research, in this respect, has been motivated by a corporate philosophy of welfare, which identifies a healthy population as an important ingredient of a healthy industrial economy. Whether sponsored by industry, charity, or the state, medical research has been dominated by a search for new technology and especially pharmaceutical solutions to the problems of ill health, while politically contentious environmental and low-technology responses have been relegated to second place. This link between medical and industrial policy is particularly clear in the increasingly close collaboration between the MRC and the pharmaceutical industry during the inter-war years, which it was hoped would not only yield new forms of treatment, but would also help boost British trade figures.

Overall, then, this research agenda reflects the dominance of industrial priorities in British medical science. It also reveals the important service role that university-based research has played in providing the scientific raw materials for commercial developments and, more generally, in maintaining links between government-, industry-, and charity-funded research.

Steven W. Sturdy

Bibliography

Austoker, Joan. *A History of the Imperial Cancer Research Fund, 1902–1986.* 1988.

Austoker, Joan, and Linda Bryder, eds. *Historical Perspectives on the Role of the MRC.* 1989.

Hall, A. Rupert, and B.A. Bembridge. *Physic and Philanthropy: A History of the Wellcome Trust, 1936–1986.* 1986.

Tweedale, Geoffrey. *At the Sign of the Plough: Allen and Hanbury's and the Pharmaceutical Industry, 1715–1990.* 1990.

Medical Research Council

The Medical Research Committee, founded in 1913, was incorporated by Royal Charter as the Medical Research Council (MRC) in 1920. It has conducted and financed research over a wide spectrum of medically related subjects, although its emphasis has been on "pure" biomedical rather than applied research.

The Medical Research Committee was established with a fund provided by the government under the 1911 National Insurance Act. The money for **medical research** was included in the clauses of the act relating to **tuberculosis**, and it was assumed that attention would be initially devoted to researching this particular health problem.

In 1914 Sir Walter Morley Fletcher was appointed as the first Secretary, remaining in the post until 1933 and exercising much influence over the direction of research of the committee/council. Subsequent Secretaries included Sir Edward Mellanby (1933–49), Sir Harold Himsworth (1949–68), Sir John Gray (1968–77), Sir James Gowans (1977–87), and D.A. Rees (1987–).

During the **First World War** the work of the committee played an important part in reducing deaths from infections in the battlefield, and following the war Fletcher claimed that it had played a crucial part in securing victory. Fletcher was largely responsible for having the committee taken out of the hands of the Insurance Commissioners in 1920 and placed directly under the Privy Council as the Medical Research Council.

Public health research enjoyed a low priority in the following years. Research into infectious diseases—a prime concern during the war—was held in abeyance until the **Second World War**, when the MRC set up the Emergency Public Health Laboratory. This proved so successful that it remained as a permanent fixture after the war, although it separated from the MRC in 1960.

A third of the original research funds were earmarked to finance a central research institute, which was set up in London in 1914 and became known as the National Institute for Medical Research in 1920. The institute, under the leadership of Sir Henry Dale, 1928–42, became a world-renowned center. The balance of the MRC funds went to finance research at other centers and at the universities, where a great deal of important work was carried out.

While the MRC has been a very influential medical research body in twentieth-century Britain, it has not always appeared to be aware of the practical application or implications of that research. For example, the MRC's nutritional work attracted scientific acclaim in the 1920s and 1930s. Yet historians have argued that in practice it tended to reinforce traditional prejudices about working-class ignorance of food values. Historians studying the MRC's tropical health research have shown how MRC workers remained preoccupied at least until the 1950s with laboratory research, largely unaware of the broader social ramifications of the medical problems they were investigating.

Since the Second World War the council has become increasingly prominent in promoting, funding, and integrating research within the **National Health Service** and the universities. Numerous small research units (some of them short-lived) have been set up at **hospitals** and medical schools throughout the country. Besides the basic scientific research of a traditional kind the council has also sponsored research in areas such as social medicine. A string of Nobel Prize winners have been members of the scientific staff of the MRC, including Sir Hans Krebs, **Francis Crick**, and Sir **Peter Medawar** who, in the 1960s, was Director of the council's National Institute at Mill Hill. Clinical research has figured large in the council's program, and in the 1970s it established its own clinical research center in the new Northwick Park Hospital in North London. Constitutionally, the most important change in the MRC occurred in the 1960s when it was transferred from the auspices of the Privy Council to those of the Secretary of State for Education and Science.

Linda Bryder

Bibliography
Austoker, Joan, and Linda Bryder, eds. *Historical Perspectives on the Role of the MRC.* 1989.
Landsborough Thomson, A. *Half a Century of Medical Research.* 2 vols. 1973–5.

Merchant Banks

The merchant banks, also known as Accepting Houses, owe their name to their early role of financing international trade by accepting bills of exchange, which reached its peak in the period 1880–1914. The merchant banks, however, were able to survive the decline in the use of the bill of exchange, particularly after the Second World War, by specializing in new financial activities, such as corporate finance or funds management. The most successful merchant banks have enjoyed exceptional longevity, from the early nineteenth century to the present day, and include some of the most famous names in the City of London, such as Rothschild, Baring, Morgan Grenfell, Warburg, Schroeder, Kleinwort, and Hambro.

Identifying a merchant bank before 1914 remains a problem. Their two main activities consisted of accepting bills of exchange and issuing foreign loans and securities. Most merchant banks, in any case those established in the City before 1860, started as merchants before gradually abandoning trade and concentrating on its finance. Since 1914, however, merchant banks can be identified through the membership of the Accepting Houses Committee, which was formed at the outbreak of the First World War. Of the twenty-one firms that joined the Accepting Houses Committee on its foundation, ten were still members in the 1980s.

With the exception of Baring Brothers and Company, founded in 1763, the oldest merchant banks were established during the Napoleonic Wars: N.M. Rothschild and Sons and J.H. Schroeder in 1804, Wm. Brandt in 1805, Fredk. Huth in 1808, and Frühling and Goschen in 1814 were all of German origin; Brown Shipley, established in 1810, came from America; and only Antony Gibbs and Sons, dating from 1810, was of English origin. Two major merchant banks appeared a generation later: Morgan Grenfell, founded in 1838 by

American George Peabody and Company; and C.J. Hambro, who came from Denmark and opened a London house in 1840. A third wave of foundations took place twenty years later, with Kleinwort, Sons and Company in 1858, who came from Hamburg via Cuba, Seligman Brothers in 1864, and Lazard Brothers in 1870, respectively of German and French origins with American connections. Very few firms founded after that date were to play a major role in merchant banking; they started in the issuing rather than in the acceptance business. One such firm was founded by Philip Hill, who began as an estate agent and established the issuing house Philip Hill and Partners in 1932, which merged in 1965 with the old City firm M. Samuel and Company (the founder of Shell) under the name Hill Samuel and Company. Another is S.G. Warburg, founded in 1946 by Siegmund Warburg, scion of an old Hamburg banking dynasty who had emigrated to Britain in 1934. Warburg was to prove the most innovative bank of the post-1945 era by organizing the first hostile takeover bid and launching the first Eurobond issue.

The merchant banks have been able to survive because the specialization of the English banking system allowed them to concentrate on what would today be called "niches." The clearing banks did not really compete with the merchant banks for the accepting and issuing businesses; despite some competition from the foreign banks based in London, over 70 percent of the £140 million acceptances in 1913 were taken by the merchant banks, and between 1860 and 1904 Barings and Rothschilds issued 250 loans worth £1.9 billion. The volume of acceptances and of new issues fell after the First World War. The decline in world trade in the 1930s hit the merchant banks' accepting business by reducing the demand for trade finance; even in the 1920s the volume of acceptances never went beyond 80 percent of its pre-war level. Foreign issues in London also fell in the 1920s as a result of a series of embargoes to protect the pound and of competition from New York and Paris and further declined in the 1930s. Some old established firms such as Fredk. Huth and Goschen and Cunliffe had to be liquidated during the 1930s, but on the whole the major merchant banks were able to survive. They were able to compensate for the decline of foreign issues by arranging domestic issues, as more companies were formed in the 1920s, in particular large companies that could

M

use the services of a merchant bank. Morgan Grenfell and Lazard's arranged issues for a number of electrical companies, and Baring's and Rothschild's were involved in several of **Montagu Norman**'s schemes to rationalize declining sectors of the British industry, while new investment banks such as Charterhouse Investment Trust and Philip Hill handled smaller issues. After the Second World War merchant banks continued to raise funds for British industry and local authorities, but they increasingly tended to specialize in the more lucrative business of advising on takeover bids. In 1986 Morgan Grenfell's Mergers and Acquisitions Department handled 111 deals worth £15.2 billion and generating 32 percent of the firm's revenues. They also took up funds management on behalf of pension funds and other investment institutions such as unit trusts, as well as for individual customers. However, in the Eurocurrencies business, which has been at the heart of the rebirth of the City of London as a major international financial center, the merchant banks had to abandon the lion's share to foreign banks, especially American banks, based in London.

Despite being dwarfed by the clearing banks, the merchant banks have retained a kind of mystique in the English banking system. The scale of their operations; the persistence well into the twentieth century—for some, to this day—of family ownership; the wealth of their partners, unequaled in any other segment of the business community; their massive representation on the Court of Directors of the Bank of England as well as on the boards of innumerable City companies; their early integration into the upper classes—all of these reasons have contributed to the position of merchant bankers at the heart of the City aristocracy.

Youssef Cassis

Bibliography

Burk, Kathleen. *Morgan Grenfell, 1838–1988: The Biography of a Merchant Bank*. 1989.

Chapman, Stanley D. *The Rise of Merchant Banking*. 1984.

Kellett, Richard. *The Merchant Banking Arena*. 1967.

Methodism

John Wesley saw the Methodist Societies as a movement within the Church of England whose vocation was to spread scriptural holiness throughout Britain. By his death in 1791 there were 70,000 Methodists. Separation from the Church of England followed soon after his demise. The next hundred years saw rapid growth, despite schism and the formation of a number of separate Methodist churches. By 1900 Methodism was the largest strand of Nonconformity; its churches were full; and its spiritual earnestness and concern for the social welfare of the people were impressive. Much of this vitality has been maintained throughout the twentieth century, and the Methodist Church remains the biggest of the Free Churches. Nevertheless, the numerical decline has been severe, and Methodist influence in an increasingly secularized society has diminished.

The Wesleyan Methodist Church was marked by liberal evangelicalism, a social witness basically individualist though claiming to be collectivist, and the encouragement of cultural interests around the church. It had stronger emphasis on church, sacraments, and ministry than other branches of Methodism and appealed principally to the business and professional middle and aspiring lower-middle classes.

Nearer to the proletarian groups was the Primitive Methodist Church. Its success was greatest in the larger villages of the Midlands and the north of England. The laity had a greater role in this church, which was not without a hint of anticlericalism. Worship was free in style, and a Free Church orientation was more noticeable than in Wesleyanism.

The first steps toward the reuniting of the Methodist people were taken in 1907 with the union of the Methodist New Connexion, the Bible Christians, and the United Methodist Free Churches to form the United Methodist Church. Churchmanship here was similar to that of Primitive Methodism.

All three branches declined in membership before and after the First World War, despite some revival in Wesleyan Methodism during the 1920s. Union among all three had been mooted as early as 1913, and strong leadership in this direction was exercised by Arthur Samuel Peake (1865–1929) and John Scott Lidgett (1854–1953), the most able and influential Methodist of the century. It eventually came about in 1932 when the Methodist Church was formed. The Wesleyans at this stage had 517,551 members, the Primitive Methodists 222,021, and the United Methodists 179,527. Wesleyan influence was strongest in the new church. The other two united churches granted a major concession with the establishment of a Pastoral Session of Conference consisting solely of ordained ministers, hardly compensated for by the setting up of the office of lay Vice President.

Methodism after the Second World War was marked by energetic evangelism in Christian Commando campaigns, a World Methodism Year of Evangelism (1953), and special calls to evangelism (1971 and 1976) but without significant success. More impressive were progressive youth activity in the Methodist Association of Youth Clubs and university Methodist Societies, liturgical reform with the publication of the *Methodist Service Book* (1975), and greater social awareness. Long-standing concern over temperance and gambling had given the church's social witness a too negative and individualistic flavor, but the imbalance was corrected by greater stress on such issues as **race relations**, world development, peace and war, and matters related to **marriage**, the family, and human **sexuality**.

In 1946 the Archbishop of Canterbury called upon the Free Churches to establish inter-communion with the **Church of England** by "taking episcopacy into their system." The only church to respond was the Methodist Church, and in 1955 the two churches appointed teams to begin conversations to that end. Inter-communion was quickly seen as insufficient, and the report produced in 1963 proposed a two-stage process leading to organic union. The first stage was to include a service of reconciliation by which the ministries of both churches would be mutually accepted, the consecration of some Methodist ministers as bishops, and agreement that all future Methodist ordinations would be episcopal. The second stage would be organic union. Protracted discussion and voting was not completed until 1972 when the Methodist Conference agreed to go forward, but the General Synod of the Church of England failed to achieve the 75 percent majority required. A later attempt to bring the mainstream churches in England into a covenant giving recognition to each others' members and ministries and full inter-communion, together with a commitment to seeking further ways of expressing visible unity, also came to nothing. Failure to achieve union at this level did not dampen enthusiasm for local action, and many Methodist churches became involved in local ecumenical ventures.

A significant step was taken in 1974 when the first **women** were ordained to the Methodist ministry. The conference of 1939 had declared that there were no theological objections to such a move, but the practical difficulties and fear that it would delay union with the Church of England hindered progress.

Signs of renewal marked the late 1980s and early 1990s in increased numbers of candidates for the ministry and for local preaching, a new awareness of the variety of ministry with the development of ministers in sectors and in local appointment and of lay workers, and the renewal of the Methodist Diaconal Order. Concern for streamlining the organization of the church to enable greater effectiveness in policy-making was evident. In 1989 there were 431,549 members. Nevertheless, continuing numerical decline did not lead to introvertedness or defensiveness, and the Methodist Church remains a vital part of the British scene.

T. Mervyn Willshaw

Bibliography
Brake, George Thompson. *Policy and Politics in British Methodism, 1932–1982.* 1984.
Davies, Rupert. *Methodism.* 1976.
———, ed. *The Testing of the Churches, 1932–1982: A Symposium.* 1982.
Davies, Rupert, A. Raymond George, and E. Gordon Rupp, eds. *A History of the Methodist Church in Great Britain.* vol. 3. 1983.

Middle East Policy

The direct influence of British policy in the Middle East expanded militarily, politically, and economically throughout the nineteenth and in the first decades of the twentieth century. British policymakers used the strategic defense of all sea, land, and air routes to India as their justification for maintaining British paramountcy in the Middle East. The large British subsidies to friendly rulers and the increasing deployment of troops to protect their bases were reinforced in 1875 by the government's purchase of the largest block of shares in the Suez Canal Company, followed by the British military occupation of **Cyprus** in 1878, all of Egypt in 1882, and the Sudan in the 1890s. After the Second World War the indirect influence of British policy persisted through collaborative Middle Eastern regimes and British ties to several oil- and capital-rich countries of the Middle East. This British domination of a southern belt determined the course of British policy throughout the rest of the Middle East, despite diplomatic costs in Europe and the United States and the sacrifice of reputation in the Islamic world. The oil-rich regions became a preoccupation of British policy from the late 1940s, when the British Isles started to import more oil from the Middle East than from the United States, to the early 1970s, when the British exploited North Sea oil.

From 1902 to 1914 British policy focused on maintaining the Persian Gulf as a British lake by deploying the British **navy** and by forming alliances with various coastal rulers. During these years the **Foreign Office** held anti-British nationalists in Persia, Turkey, and Egypt at bay and shared in the division of the region into European spheres of interest. With Russia's army dominant in central Asia and northern Persia and with French colonists entrenched in North Africa, the British were paramount in the rest of the lands loosely tied to the Ottoman Empire. Just before the crisis at Sarajevo in 1914, the British government also secured control of the Anglo-Persian Oil Company to guarantee sufficient fuel for its navy. From 1914 to 1918 London initiated various policies in waging war against the Turkish Empire: building up a presence in the Persian Gulf and Suez, annexing Cyprus and Egypt, attacking the Dardanelles and **Gallipoli**, courting anti-Turkish Arab leaders, and mounting military campaigns in Sinai, **Palestine**, Syria, Mesopotamia, Persia, and the Trans-Caucasus and Caspian. Despite the view that the Middle East was peripheral to the principal military operations, policymakers persisted in British campaigns that led to the occupation of virtually the entire region at war's end.

At Versailles the British managed to frustrate Arab, Egyptian, and Persian nationalists but aroused the suspicions of the French, Italians, and Americans. They had sufficient troops in the Middle East to crush revolts in Egypt, Syria, Iraq, and Palestine, although the anarchy in Persia was beyond British control. The **League of Nations** mandates provided a convenient way of reducing British military costs, without sacrificing strategic predominance, by backing traditional Middle Eastern leaders willing to collaborate with the British. London agreed to French mandatory control of Syria, while retaining mandates in Palestine and Iraq.

The British declared Egypt "independent" but still controlled its foreign affairs, reserved the right to send in troops, and occupied Suez and the Sudan. The Arabian peninsula was encircled by the British, with puppet rulers throughout. Persia refused to toe the line, so the British had to acknowledge the Russian-trained military commander who founded the Pahlevi dynasty. More humiliating for the British, their wartime partitioning of Anatolia into French, Italian, and Greek zones turned into a nightmare as the Turkish army reconstituted itself and drove the Allies into the sea. London's last-ditch attempt at saving Chanak found support neither at home nor in the Dominions, still outraged by what their troops had endured at Gallipoli.

From 1923 to 1939 economic problems compelled the British to keep a low profile while protecting their interests in the Middle East. Most military forces, as well as advisers and equipment, were paid for by Middle Eastern taxpayers, as had been the practice in India and Egypt. The independence of Egypt in 1922 and Iraq in 1930 were more apparent than real, as the upper classes supported rulers closer to the British than to the masses. The British repressed their opponents by bombing raids in the countryside and by using informers in cities to capture anti-British nationalists, who were exiled or sent to prison. Palestine in the 1920s did not pose serious problems, although the agricultural development of land by Zionists was at the expense of Palestinian rural workers. In the 1930s the big influx of Zionists, especially into the cities, created more tension for the mandatory power. The British crushed the Arab revolt in Palestine during the late 1930s and then, unable to devise a partition scheme acceptable to Arabs, restricted further Jewish immigration in the White Paper of 1939.

During the **Second World War** Britain maintained a large military presence throughout the Middle East, eliminated pro-Axis leaders in Iran, Iraq, and Palestine, backed the Free French in Lebanon and Syria, expelled Axis armies from Libya, helped American military campaigns in North Africa and the Mediterranean, and coordinated the region's economy by means of the British-run Middle East Supply Center. The rulers and upper classes in the Middle East benefited economically from Allied demands for their goods and services, while the masses fell into worse misery.

From 1945 to 1967 the British military retreat from the Middle East was largely determined by the hatred of the British that became widespread throughout the area, nationalists having bitter memories of being let down by the British after the First World War and recognizing that Britain was now diplomatically vulnerable. The inability of the British to hold on in Palestine in the late 1940s was replicated in Egypt, Sudan, Jordan, and Iraq in the 1950s, and in the Arabian Peninsula during the 1960s. The British removed their last troops from Aden in 1967. The Cold War delayed the departure of the British by transforming much of the Middle East into an Anglo-American zone for containing the spread of Communism. This cooperation did help in 1953 to put the Shah of Iran back on his throne after he was forced out by Mohammed Mossadegh, who nationalized the Anglo-Iranian Oil Company. In return the Shah agreed to compensate the Anglo-Iranian Oil Company, which became British Petroleum. However, when Egyptian President Gamal Abdel Nasser nationalized the Suez Canal in 1956, **Anthony Eden** involved Britain in the ill-fated **Suez** campaign, in alliance with France and Israel, in order to uphold British predominance in the region and rebuff Nasser's unilateral action. However, as Nasser's pan-Arab nationalism expanded into Syria, Jordan, and especially the Arabian peninsula, the United States, hostile to the British initiative at Suez, reverted to a pro-British stance, sponsoring the Baghdad Pact of Turkey, Iraq, and Iran, an Anglo-American alliance that cracked with the Iraqi Revolution of 1958. British intelligence seems to have played a significant role in American efforts to contain the further spread of Soviet influence in the Middle East. After the 1960s the United States increasingly filled the gap left by British departure from the Persian Gulf, encouraging a buildup by the Shah and the Arab Gulf Cooperation Council. The rise in oil prices of the 1970s, led by the Organization of Petroleum Exporting Countries, hit Western motorists, while the fall of the Shah and the holding of American hostages in 1979–80 led Washington to take a hostile line regarding the spread of Arab and Islamic terrorism against the West. During this period London continued to put its financial resources at the disposal of the oil-rich regimes of the Middle East, as U.S. and Israeli forces replaced British military dominance in the region.

Roger Adelson

Bibliography

Adelson, Roger. *London and the Invention of the Middle East: Money, Power, and War, 1902–1922*. 1995.

Fitzsimons, Matthew A. *Empire by Treaty: Britain and the Middle East in the Twentieth Century*. 1964.

Fromkin, David. *A Peace to End All Peace: Creating the Modern Middle East, 1914–1922*. 1989.

Kedourie, Elie. *England and the Middle East: The Destruction of the Ottoman Empire, 1914–1921*. 1956.

Louis, William Roger. *The British Empire in the Middle East, 1945–1951*. 1985.

Monroe, Elizabeth. *Britain's Moment in the Middle East, 1914–1971*. 2nd ed. 1981.

Sykes, Christopher. *Crossroads to Israel: Balfour to Bevin*. 1965.

Militant

Essentially a party within a party until largely expunged by the Labour leadership, Militant (also commonly but incorrectly known as the Militant Tendency) is a Trotskyite organization that from the mid-1970s was a damaging presence in a **Labour Party** beset with problems. The group's name derives from its weekly newspaper, *Militant*, which since 1964 has been the main organ of the Revolutionary Socialist League, formed in 1955 as one of many small and schismatic British Trotskyite factions. The newspaper became a cover for the League's shadowy existence and came to provide its working name. Militant has maintained a rigid, anachronistic ideology, structure, and strategy. It holds fundamentalist Marxist-Leninist beliefs in the inevitable failure of capitalism and prospects for revolution. Organized on democratic centralist principles, in its mid-1980s heyday Militant had approximately 8,000 members and 300 full-time organizers. It followed a strategy advocated in the 1930s by Trotsky; dissatisfied with Western Communist movements, he recommended "entrism" into mainstream labour and social democratic parties. The "entrists" task is to prepare for revolution by educating the masses and positioning themselves to play a vanguard role in the final crisis. Militant follows a version of Trotsky's 1938 "transitional program," broadcasting extreme demands such as the nationalizing of Britain's 200 largest companies.

By 1970 Militant had gained control of the recently formed Labour Party Young Socialists and had firm footholds in several parliamentary constituencies. Its growth was aided in 1973 by the abolition of Labour's proscribed list of banned organizations and by the vulnerability of many decaying urban parties. In 1975 a report to Labour's National Executive Committee (NEC) exposed Militant's existence but drew little response from a Left-dominated NEC with firm memories of earlier party "purges." By 1981, however, the NEC was more finely balanced, the party's future was threatened by the creation of the **Social Democratic Party**, and media attention demanded a stronger response. Another inquiry again produced damaging evidence, but a mixture of party constitutional problems, leader **Michael Foot**'s tentativeness, and Militant's adroit maneuvers produced only five symbolic expulsions. Foot's successor, **Neil Kinnock**, abhorred Militant but did not feel free to act decisively until 1985. The provocative behavior of Militants who effectively controlled the Liverpool City Council provided the pretext for a vigorous attack. Although initially impeded by unforeseen legal problems, the attempt to root out Militant gathered force throughout the rest of the decade. The party's youth section was reclaimed, and mass expulsions occurred from constituency organizations. By the end of 1991 Militant was driven to abandon entrism and establish a clear identity outside the Labour Party.

Militant's real impact within the Labour Party is easily overstated. Only three Militants were elected to Parliament, and the group was never a major influence on national party policy. Nor was it the only "hard Left" faction essentially alien to Labour's gradualist, non-Marxist traditions. However, it did threaten to achieve influence in numerous, mainly inner-city, constituencies and served as an emblem of the party's struggles to unify and sustain itself. Much of the **press** delighted in exposing Militant's revolutionary goals and unscrupulous methods. In an era in which Labour was struggling with other internecine conflicts, a diminishing electoral base, and the challenge of **Thatcherism**, Militant damaged its image and sapped its energies.

Steven Reilly

Bibliography

Crick, Michael. *The March of Militant*. 2nd ed. 1986.

Shaw, Eric. *Discipline and Discord in the Labour Party, 1951–87*. 1988.

Milner, Alfred (1854–1925)

Alfred Milner was a statesman and diplomat whose career straddled the nineteenth and twentieth centuries, known especially for his imperial activities in **South Africa** during the **Boer War** (1899–1902). He served as a member of **David Lloyd George**'s War Cabinet (without Portfolio) (1916–18), as Secretary of State for War (1918–19), and as Colonial Secretary (1919–21). Knighted in 1895 and elevated to the peerage in 1901, he became Viscount Milner in 1902 and a Knight of the Garter in 1921.

The son of a British physician, he was born and lived for several childhood years in Germany. After three years at a Tübingen gymnasium, he received a traditional British education at King's College, London, and Balliol College, **Oxford**. Although called to the Bar by the Inner Temple in 1881, he was drawn to a life of public usefulness. For several years he attempted a journalist's career, working under John Morley and W.T. Stead on the *Pall Mall Gazette*, but he ultimately became disenchanted with what he considered the crassness of the profession.

In 1884 Milner launched his public career as personal secretary to Viscount Goschen, a Liberal Unionist politician, who was able, in 1890, to procure for Milner the director-generalship of accounts in Egypt, where he served under Imperial Consul Sir Evelyn Baring. From this experience Milner derived some notoriety with his publication in 1892 of *England in Egypt*. The turning point in his career, however, was his appointment in 1897 as High Commissioner for South Africa, after he had come to the attention of Colonial Secretary Joseph Chamberlain.

When Milner arrived in South Africa, tensions over rights in the Boer gold and diamond mines were already high between Britain and the Boer republics of the Orange Free State and the Transvaal. Although he arrived with an open mind he eventually concluded that the political problems between the British and the Boers could be resolved only by reform in Transvaal or by war. Scholars have concluded that Milner's intransigence at negotiations with the Boers helped to provoke war.

After 1902 Milner set about the repatriation of Boer farmers and organized a system of education that established English as the language of instruction. He encouraged settlement by British farmers and was partially responsible for the importation of Chinese laborers into the Rand, a policy that aroused a storm of opposition in England and helped defeat the **Conservative** government in the 1906 general election. Milner also cultivated what became known as his "kindergarten," a group of young men, including L.S. Amery, Philip Kerr (Lord Lothian), and Lionel Curtis, whose involvement in imperial affairs was to continue beyond the Second World War. Milner's efforts, however, were directed, ultimately, toward the unification of all South African colonies. By the time of his departure in 1905, steps had been taken toward the eventual creation of the Union of South Africa.

On his return to Britain Milner received a mixed response. His arrival coincided with a change in government and in attitudes toward jingoistic imperial adventures. The Liberal **Campbell-Bannerman** ministry was cool toward Milner's South African endeavors, one MP going so far as to introduce a motion of censure against him. Although unsuccessful, it did cause Milner to withdraw from the political limelight, devoting himself instead to the movements for national service and **tariff reform**, to the Rhodes Trust, and to discussions with his "kindergarten" that evolved into the political review *The Round Table*. Milner opposed Lloyd George's "People's Budget" of 1909, the subsequent Parliament Act of 1911, and the prospect of Irish Home Rule. In 1913 he published a volume of his speeches entitled *The Nation and the Empire*, and he planned to collaborate with Amery on a biography of Joseph Chamberlain, but the project was sidetracked by the outbreak of the **First World War**.

Despite their earlier disagreements, Lloyd George appointed Milner to his War Cabinet in 1916, with responsibility for such matters as the allocation of shipping tonnage between competing government departments. He also worked to strengthen the imperial relationship between the **Cabinet** and the Dominion Prime Ministers. In April 1918 he accepted the position of Secretary of State for War, assuming responsibility for the decision to enforce unity of Allied command. A hard-liner in his attitudes toward the German army and General Staff, he was moderate in statements regarding the treatment of the defeated German nation.

At the time the peace conference convened, he changed portfolios from the War Office to the Colonial Office. At Versailles his was not one of the more influential voices, and his tenure at the Colonial Office was relatively brief.

In February 1921 he retired from public service and, at this advanced age, married for the first time a widowed daughter of his old friend Admiral Frederick Maxse. Another volume of essays appeared in 1923, and in the fall of 1924 he and Lady Milner visited South Africa. After viewing some of the fruits of his labor he returned home, having contracted sleeping sickness, and he died on 13 May 1925. An influential public servant for three decades, Milner was a visionary exponent of imperial unity at a time when **imperialism** was beginning to be called into question. His reputation exceeded his achievements: Office and honors were heaped upon him despite his lack of identification with either major political party. At the time of his death he had been chosen Chancellor-elect of the University of Oxford.

Newell D. Boyd

Bibliography

Crankshaw, Edward. *The Forsaken Idea: A Study of Viscount Milner.* 1952.
Gollin, A.M. *Proconsul in Politics: A Study of Lord Milner in Opposition and Power.* 1964.
Marlowe, John. *Milner: Apostle of Empire.* 1976,
Wrench, John Evelyn. *Alfred Lord Milner: The Man of No Illusions, 1854–1925.* 1958.

Milton Keynes

Milton Keynes is a **New Town**, designated in 1967, named after a village on its eastern edge, and including the railway towns of Bletchley and Wolverton and the smaller town of Stony Stratford. Styled "city" from the beginning (though never chartered), it was intended to take London overspill and become a regional economic growth point.

Bestriding the principal rail and highway links between London (45 miles away) and Birmingham, the city is in that central belt of England most favorable to urban growth. Between 1967 and 1991 population increased by 109,000, jobs by 66,000. Three-quarters of the £3 billion invested was private capital, and in the 1980s the city's many new businesses grew strongly. Derek Walker's strong team of architects agonized over housing standards and design, but from the 1980s houses were built for sale rather than rent and Milton Keynes became relentlessly suburban.

Lord Llewelyn-Davies' master plan fixed a grid of primary roads to avoid the traffic congestion risked by centralized communications. To some it presaged Los Angeles, but architectural historian S.E. Rasmussen saw it, and the internal parklands, as a perfection of the pattern of London's seventeenth- and eighteenth-century growth. No other British town accommodates traffic as efficiently and elegantly as central Milton Keynes on its windy ridge, with its huge rectangular glass buildings, great domed church of Christ the Cornerstone (1990–1), glazed shopping malls, and Wren-like grid of spacious squares and boulevards. The **Open University** made its headquarters in Milton Keynes in 1969.

G.C. Baugh

Bibliography

Bendixson, Terence, and John Platt. *Milton Keynes: Image and Reality.* 1992.
Walker, Derek. *The Architecture and Planning of Milton Keynes.* 1982.

Miners Federation of Great Britain

The Miners Federation of Great Britain (MFGB) was founded at a conference held in Newport, Monmouthshire, in November 1889. Its constituents were existing district unions in the coalfields, and much power remained at the district level. The original members came from coalfields producing primarily for the domestic market, most significantly Yorkshire, Lancashire, Derbyshire, Nottinghamshire, and other Midlands districts. The Scottish miners joined in 1894, and South Wales in 1899. By 1900 the MFGB claimed a membership of 363,000. The federation's coverage was completed in 1908 with the entry of the Durham and Northumberland miners' organizations. At the outbreak of the First World War the membership had climbed to 761,000, a testimony to the prime place of coal mining in the British economy and to the federation's credibility.

Diverse conditions of production and contrasting market situations meant that there were always potential conflicts of interest within the federation. Its leaders were conscious of the difficulty in constructing any cohesive national strategy. Nevertheless, the MFGB made a successful defense of existing wage levels in a fifteen-week lockout in 1893 and moved toward a more aggressive strategy in the years before 1914. Conflicts in South Wales centered around the desire of employers to cut costs by attacking traditional practices, not least the financial compensation often paid to mineface workers, who endured difficult conditions. The pressures became generalized in the MFGB demand for a national minimum wage leading to the first national coal strike in March 1912, a stoppage lasting six weeks. The **Liberal** government responded with legislation that acknowledged the principle of the minimum wage but left its level to be settled by district negotiation.

Initially, the MFGB's politics were predominantly Liberal. The federation's first President, Ben Pickard, was a Yorkshire Liberal MP from 1885 until his death in 1904. In some constituencies miners dominated the electorate and could ensure that the Liberal nominee was a miner. Nevertheless, most Scottish miners' leaders were socialists, and in 1903 the Lancashire miners joined the **Labour Representation Committee**. Within the wider MFGB the political balance shifted. Respected Liberal officials died; Liberal Associations showed reluctance to endorse more miners' candidates; some coalfields experienced intensified demands by mine owners. From 1906 the **Labour Party** with its 30 MPs, including three miners, seemed a viable option. The MFGB held ballots on political allegiance in 1906 and in 1908. At the second attempt the supporters of the Labour Party won the vote by 213,000 to 168,000. After the January 1910 election almost all Miners Federation MPs sat as Labour Party supporters. In July 1912, the Scotsman Robert Smillie became the federation's first socialist President. The miners moved relatively slowly to Labour politics, but once made, the attachment, cemented by work experience, community ethos, and union solidarity, proved durable. By the 1920s the coalfields were Labour citadels and also included most of the communities where the **Communist Party of Great Britain** had a credible presence.

Miners' officials and many miners were strong supporters of British involvement in the **First World War**, though Smillie with his thorough **Independent Labour Party** (ILP) background was an exception to the rule. He maintained a sharp demarcation between his industrial and his political work, presiding over a union that made significant wartime gains. Gradually the industry became state controlled, a shift that had a buoyant effect on the aspirations of miners. The MFGB achieved a long-standing objective, wage increases on a national rather than a district basis, and had some slight involvement in the management of the industry. Experience of state control strengthened demands for public ownership, but initial post-war militancy was blunted in 1919 by the appointment of the **Sankey Commission** to explore the future of the mining industry. In the autumn of 1920 the miners staged a brief wage strike, but within months any ground for optimism had been destroyed.

The winter of 1920–1 saw the collapse of many export markets for British coal. The **Lloyd George** coalition decided on a precipitate return of the industry to uncontrolled private ownership. Predictably, mine owners in several coalfields demanded major wage cuts as of 1 April 1921. The MFGB's resistance was undermined by the refusal of its "Triple Alliance" partners—the Railwaymen and the Transport Workers—to engage in sympathetic strike action. The date of this climb-down, 15 April 1921, became known as "Black Friday" and marked the virtual end of post-war labor militancy.

The MFGB resisted for three months but were defeated. For the next two decades it had to operate in an industry where lack of international competitiveness and depressed domestic demand meant surplus capacity and downward pressure on wages. The French occupation of the Ruhr meant a transitory revival in British coal exports, but by 1925 the mine owners were demanding more wage cuts. The MFGB was now led by Herbert Smith, the President, a brusque Yorkshireman, and A.J. Cook, the Secretary, who was strongly identified with the Left and a passionate yet pragmatic advocate. Initially the **Baldwin** government retreated before the miners' resistance, backed by threats of sympathetic action. The crisis was simply delayed. At the end of April 1926 a seven-month lockout began, backed for just nine days by a **General Strike**. It ended in disaster for the miners with heavy wage cuts, mass **unemployment** and short-time working, victimization, and nonunionism. In Nottinghamshire a breakaway, the "Spencer Union," achieved recognition from the employers. Membership of the federation had peaked at 945,000 in 1920; at the start of the 1926 lockout it was 783,000, but in some years in the early 1930s it fell below half a million.

The beleaguered MFGB sought help from the 1929 Labour government, but little was achieved due to the government's minority status and its thorough economic orthodoxy. The federation spent the 1930s patiently rebuilding its organization. Leadership had passed to two Labour pragmatists, Joseph Jones and Ebby Edwards, while in South Wales and later in Scotland Communists played significant roles. Progress was slow, but in 1935 the MFGB felt strong enough to run a forceful wage campaign, while drawing back from any general stoppage. Similarly, in 1937 breakaway unionism was virtually eliminated, although on terms that involved the negotiated reabsorption rather than the destruction of the Spencer Union.

With the outbreak of the **Second World War** the MFGB's position was transformed. The industry ceased to be dominated by the question of excess capacity and became preoccupied with the maximization of output. The legacy of decades of decline became apparent as miners battled to meet production targets in pits that were often obsolete. Predictably the coalfields were the scene of much unofficial strike action. The political complexities of the **Churchill** coalition meant that the development of state control stopped decisively short of public ownership for the industry. Nevertheless, the MFGB achieved significant objectives: a national minimum wage in 1942 and a national conciliation system a year later. Such developments helped encourage the federation's transformation in 1945 into the **National Union of Mineworkers**.

The MFGB acquired heroic status in the labor movement. Its pitched political battles and the physically demanding character of much mining work ensured preeminence. Yet the real achievements often came at the local level, where the presence of mining unionism was a testimonial to working-class creativity, a vital resource in the battle to make mining communities islands of decency among the rigors of coalfield capitalism.

David Howell

Bibliography

Arnot, R. Page. *The Miners.* 3 vols. 1949–61.
Francis, Hywel, and David Smith. *The Fed: A History of the South Wales Miners in the Twentieth Century.* 1980.
Gregory, Roy. *The Miners in British Politics, 1906–14.* 1968.
Kirby, Maurice W. *The British Coalmining Industry, 1870–1946: A Political and Economic History.* 1977.
Supple, Barry. *The History of the British Coal Industry, 1913–46: The Political Economy of Decline.* 1987.

M

Miners' Strike (1984–1985)

The confrontation between the **Conservative** government and the **National Union of Mineworkers** (NUM) during Prime Minister **Margaret Thatcher**'s second term of office was the most dramatic, costly, and significant industrial dispute since the **General Strike** of 1926. It developed in March 1984 as the NUM, led by its radical President, Arthur Scargill, resisted a program of rapid pit closures planned by the National Coal Board (NCB) under the belligerent chairmanship of Ian MacGregor, a Thatcher appointee with little liking for public ownership or trade unions. The strike, lasting a year, was a showdown between a historically strong union and a government eager to show that its authority could not be resisted by industrial militancy. The NUM had undermined an earlier Conservative administration in 1972 and 1974 and forced Thatcher into a retreat in 1981; she and her **Cabinet** were determined not to be defeated.

In retrospect the strike appears to have been doomed to failure from the outset. Arguments continue as to whether the government, seeking revenge for past humiliations and pursuing a symbolic victory over the "crack troops" of the labor movement, actively provoked the strike. At the very least it anticipated and prepared for a prolonged dispute, ensuring that coal stocks were high and that **police** communications, equipment, and mobility were adequate to confront mass picketing and possible violence. Thatcher showed characteristic resilience and will, but little apparent sympathy for miners' families or understanding of the unique culture of mining communities, whose history of solidarity and interdependence contrasted starkly with the individualist tenor of **Thatcherism**. None of the other major actors emerged with great credit. MacGregor and Scargill seemed temperamentally and ideologically incapable of fruitful negotiation. Scargill saw the strike as part of a wider class struggle; believing that a ballot of all NUM members would probably fail, he maneuvered the union into a battle that lacked the legitimating force of a national vote. He was unwilling to condemn picket-line violence—to which police tactics often contributed—and in July 1984 refused a compromise that many would have considered a tactical victory. The **Labour Party** leader **Neil Kinnock** was trapped between conflicting segments of opinion, unable to influence Scargill, unwilling

fully to endorse his methods, yet equivocal in condemning violence.

In essence the strike was a war of attrition, in which heavy policing protected both a gradual drift back to work by disillusioned or desperate miners and a crucial refusal to strike in the productive Nottinghamshire coalfield. Despite the declarations of other union leaders, the importing of coal and movement of domestic output continued: solidarity was enhanced neither by the strike's undemocratic beginnings nor by Scargill's intransigent manner. Public opinion was influenced also by the government's strategy of remaining apparently detached from the NCB while vigorously condemning the miners' leadership, although in the strike's final weeks the government was more widely seen to be refusing opportunities of a settlement. When the strike eventually collapsed in March 1985, it was in some sense unclear who could claim victory. But in the longer term, the episode gravely weakened the NUM and demonstrated—not least to international opinion—the government's determination to subdue challenges to its authority by organized labor.

Steven Reilly

Bibliography

Adeney, Martin, and John Lloyd. *The Miners' Strike: Loss without Limit.* 1986.
Crick, Michael. *Scargill and the Miners.* 1985
Goodman, Geoffrey. *The Miners' Strike.* 1985.

Ministry of Munitions

In May 1915, in the midst of the **First World War**, the government created a new **Cabinet**-level department, the Ministry of Munitions, to improve the inadequate supply of military stores to the **army**. In charge was **David Lloyd George**, previously Chancellor of the Exchequer, who created a ministry that, in power and scope, was unlike any other seen in modern history.

Lloyd George had taken up the pursuit of the war with customary enthusiasm, and reports of an insufficient supply of munitions at the front inspired him to make that his cause. He pressed for the appointment of several government committees to hasten armaments deliveries, but the War Secretary, **Lord Kitchener**, who distrusted Lloyd George and his proposed innovations, proved uncooperative.

In May 1915, in response to evidence that the war was not being won as expected—the press reporting insufficient supplies of munitions at the front—the Prime Minister, **H.H. Asquith**, struck a bargain with the frustrated and rebellious Lloyd George and the Tory leader, **Andrew Bonar Law**, and agreed to a coalition government. Part of the cost of political peace was the creation of a Ministry of Munitions with full responsibility for the supply of war materiel. The passage soon after of a Munitions of War Act gave the new department almost total control over workers, management, and capital in order to improve munitions supply. It was an unprecedented gamble on the philosophy of state control by a liberal democracy.

Lloyd George's hostility to the War Office had made him an enemy of established **civil service** practice in wartime. He assembled at the ministry a senior staff made up of civil servants and politicians, but also of businessmen, academics, and other "outsiders," dubbed by the press "the men of push and go." Their sole qualification was their ability to get things done.

By the time the department was disbanded after the war, officials had built hundreds of state-owned factories and had exercised authority over hundreds more privately owned contractors. In each factory were posted rules of factory discipline which workers were required to obey. Trade union rules were suspended. The ministry controlled the supply of skilled labor and limited the rights of workers to leave the employ of a government contractor. Equally remarkable was the introduction onto the shop floor of thousands of young women workers ("dilutees") to replace the increasingly scarce men of military age who were called into uniform.

The ministry also controlled profits of contractors. Manufacturers were permitted to make only goods required by the ministry, and prices were set by the ministry on a "cost plus" basis. Factories were compelled to provide canteens, hot meals, sanitary facilities, and other amenities far beyond what had been typical practice.

The Ministry of Munitions was a success in transforming Britain's woefully inadequate facilities to develop and manufacture military stores. By the end of the conflict Britain's industrial capacity was better organized for the purpose than that of any other country. Lloyd George and the Ministry of Munitions—and the thousands of men and women who worked so untiringly under their leadership—proved that Britain achieved victory because of effective organization rather than military success.

R.J.Q. Adams

Bibliography

Adams, R.J.Q. *Arms and the Wizard: Lloyd George and the Ministry of Munitions.* 1978.
Bourne, J.M. *Britain and the Great War, 1914–1918.* 1989.
Gilbert, Bentley Brinkerhoff. *David Lloyd George, a Political Life: Organizer of Victory, 1912–1916.* 1992.
Grigg, John. *Lloyd George: From Peace to War, 1912–1916.* 1985.
The History of the Ministry of Munitions. 1922.

Molecular Biology

Any discussion of molecular biology is complicated by the fact that it has at least three definitions. In Britain it was first used in the 1930s to describe the three-dimensional structure of biological macromolecules. This is an area Britain pioneered: The field of x-ray crystallography was created by W.H. Bragg (1862–1942) and his son Lawrence Bragg (1890–1971), who were jointly awarded the 1915 Nobel Prize for **Physics**. In the 1960s British x-ray crystallography collected three Nobel Prizes for the structure of important macromolecules, the most influential being the double helix structure of DNA. This was published in 1953 and launched a fast-moving inter-disciplinary field also calling itself molecular biology, but with its intellectual roots shared with **genetics** and biochemistry. The new molecular biology had strong links with **Cambridge**: Key figures were **Francis Crick**, one of the codiscoverers of the double helix, and Frederick Sanger (1918–), the only scientist to have been awarded the Nobel Prize for **Chemistry** twice. More recently, molecular biology has been used to describe the study of any biological process at the molecular level. In this sense it covers much of current biology but has far less professional identity. Here Britain holds its own, with two Nobel Prizes in the 1980s. Both went to scientists working at the Laboratory of Molecular Biology in Cambridge, which remains the institutional center of the field.

The study of organic compounds by x-ray crystallography was pioneered by the elder Bragg, who founded a British school that flourished in the 1930s and 1940s. Originally based at the **Royal Institution**, London, it spread to Leeds, where William Astbury (1898–1961) worked on biological fibers such as keratin, and Cambridge, where **J.D. Bernal** pioneered the analysis of amino acids.

After the Second World War there was an influx of physicists into the biological sciences, largely funded by the **Medical Research Council** (MRC). In 1946 the MRC established a Biophysics Unit at King's College, London, directed by John Randall (1905–84), and a year later it set up a Unit for the Study of the Molecular Structure of Biological Systems at the **Cavendish Laboratory**, Cambridge, directed by Max Perutz (1914–). The Cambridge unit went on to become the center of the new molecular biology and in 1962 moved to the Laboratory of Molecular Biology (LMB), a purpose-built research institute on the outskirts of Cambridge.

In the same year the achievements of the Cambridge unit were recognized by two Nobel Prizes. Perutz and John Kendrew (1917–) shared the chemistry prize for the structure of the respiratory proteins hemoglobin and myoglobin; Crick, James Watson (1928–), and Maurice Wilkins (1916–) shared the 1962 prize for medicine for the structure of DNA. This is the famous double helix, which not only revealed the way in which the hereditary material is replicated but also implied that genetic information is carried in the one-dimensional sequence of the nucleotides. The DNA structure was influenced by data obtained at the King's College unit, and this is recognized by the inclusion of Wilkins in the prize. Two years later the 1964 chemistry prize went to Dorothy Hodgkin (1910–) for the structure of penicillin and vitamin B12. Hodgkin had been Bernal's research assistant in the 1930s and then moved to **Oxford**.

The LMB merged the Cambridge unit with Sanger's research group, previously based at the Biochemistry Department, Cambridge. Sanger's contribution to the new molecular biology was crucial since it was his sequence of the insulin molecule that first demonstrated that the order of the amino acids in protein molecules is fixed. This was rewarded by the 1958 Nobel Prize for Chemistry. Sanger also shared the 1980 prize for chemistry for devising a technique for sequencing DNA.

By the mid-1960s the genetic code linking DNA structure and protein structure had been cracked, and molecular biologists were moving on to new areas. The LMB pioneered the molecular study of cellular sciences and has been awarded two further Nobel Prizes: Aaron Klug (1926–) was awarded the 1982 prize for chemistry partly for his work on the structure of chromosomes, and Cesar Milstein (1927–) shared the 1984 prize for medicine for the construction of monoclonal antibodies.

Outside the LMB molecular biology flourishes in several biochemistry departments, notably at the University of Dundee, and at the Imperial Cancer Research Fund. There are no departments of molecular biology in British universities; the sole exception (at the University of Edinburgh) has become a research institute.

Guil Winchester

Bibliography

Abir-Am, Pnina. "The Politics of Macromolecules: Molecular Biologists, Biochemists, and Rhetoric," *Osiris*, vol. 7 (1992), pp. 164–91.

Olby, Robert. *The Path to the Double Helix.* 1974.

Perutz, Max. "The Birth of Molecular Biology," *New Scientist*, vol. 114 (21 May 1987), pp. 38–41.

Watson, James. D. *The Double Helix: A Personal Account of the Discovery of the Structure of DNA.* Gunther S. Stent, ed. 1981.

Mond, Alfred Moritz (1868–1930)

Alfred Mond was a prominent politician, businessman, and industrial statesman. The son of Ludwig Mond (1839–1909), cofounder of Brunner, Mond, Britain's principal alkali manufacturer and one of its largest enterprises, Mond took up law in preparation for a political career. His legal expertise, however, brought him into the chemicals business before he could secure a parliamentary seat. By the time he was elevated to the peerage as the first Lord Melchett of Landford in 1928, Mond had left his mark on the political and on the industrial life of his country.

Elected to the Commons for Chester as a **Liberal** in 1906, Mond gained a safe seat at Swansea in 1910 and was made a baronet. In 1913 he was made a Privy Councilor. An ardent proponent of an all-out war effort, Mond actively backed **David Lloyd George** to replace **H.H. Asquith** as Prime Minister, and in 1916 he was rewarded with the post of First Commissioner of Works. In 1921 he moved to head the Ministry of Health. Lloyd George's fall ended Mond's ministerial career, though he retained his Swansea seat until 1923 and represented Carmarthen from 1924 to 1928.

Following his exit from office, Mond emerged as a forceful advocate of business reorganization and the reformulation of British economic policy. He was particularly active in the movement to rationalize industry, the attempt to establish cooperation as the governing principle of industrial relations, and the campaign to strengthen imperial economic ties. In each sphere Mond's political activity in the private sector sustained his statesmanship on the national stage.

As an entrepreneur and manager, Mond endeavored to build businesses that would be large enough to reap economies of scale and to affect the organization of their industries internationally. In 1923 he presided over the formation of the Amalgamated Anthracite Collieries, a combine that would in five years control 85 percent of the Welsh anthracite industry. He also merged Mond Nickel with the International Nickel Company of New Jersey and was instrumental in the creation of the Finance Corporation of Great Britain and America Ltd. The crowning glory of Mond's rationalizing efforts was the creation, with Sir Harry McGowan (1874–1961), of Imperial Chemical Industries Ltd. (ICI) in 1926. Formed from Britain's largest chemical companies—Brunner, Mond, Nobel Industries, British Dyestuffs, and United Alkali—ICI was the largest manufacturing merger in inter-war Britain, and the company has remained one of the country's leading industrial enterprises. Mond also championed amalgamation and concentration as general principles of economic development, and in 1928 he won the agreement of the **Trades Union Congress** (TUC) to a resolution recommending the further reorganization of British industry.

Mond recognized that industrial restructuring threatened workers and that its success required their support. At ICI he tried to conciliate the labor force by establishing works councils, a profit-sharing plan, a workers' shareholding scheme, and a staff grade system. At the national level Mond organized an unofficial delegation of businessmen to meet with representatives of the TUC in the late 1920s after the Federation of British Industries and the National Confederation of Employers' Organisations had responded coolly to TUC overtures. Their talks (the Mond-Turner talks, 1927–8) produced a series of resolutions that included, in addition to their joint endorsement of rationalization, the industrialists' recognition of the TUC and its constituent unions, the employers' renunciation of the victimization of trade union activists, a plan for a standing National Industrial Council and conciliation machinery for the resolution of industrial disputes, and a joint statement of concern about Britain's adherence to the **gold standard**.

The First World War converted Mond from a Liberal free trader to a proponent of imperial economic unity. He supported **Stanley Baldwin**'s protectionist proposals, took part in **Lord Beaverbrook**'s Empire Free Trade campaign, chaired the Empire Economic Union, and toured **South Africa** on behalf of the cause. The same impulse animated Mond's stewardship of ICI, from the deliberate inclusion of "Imperial" in the company's title to the support the firm gave to the development of chemical industries in **Australia**, **Canada**, and **South Africa**.

Mond was the preeminent business spokesman for industrial and economic change in inter-war Britain. He was an early champion of corporate capitalism, and he established a singular example of the enduring benefits of integration, consolidation, and centralization in ICI. Mond also helped turn the business community toward protection and to define a consensual alternative in industrial relations after the 1926 **General Strike**.

Michael Dintenfass

Bibliography

Goodman, Jean. *The Mond Legacy: A Family Saga*. 1982.

McDonald, G.W., and Howard F. Gospel. "The Mond-Turner Talks, 1927–1933: A Study in Industrial Co-Operation," *Historical Journal*, vol. 16 (1973), pp. 807–29.

Reader, W.J. *Imperial Chemical Industries: A History*. 2 vols. 1970–5.

Montagu, Edwin Samuel (1879–1924)

Edwin Montagu was a Liberal politician and statesman. The second son of the banker Samuel Montagu, Lord Swaythling, he was educated at Clifton School, the City of London School, and Trinity College, **Cambridge**. After graduation in 1902, he soon translated the promise he had shown as President of the Union into the Liberal candidacy for West Cambridgeshire. He was elected to Parliament from that constituency in the Liberal landslide of 1906 and held the seat until defeated in the general election of 1922. He served in the last Liberal government and the wartime and post-war coalition governments. In 1915 Montagu married **H.H. Asquith**'s beloved correspondent, Venetia Stanley, daughter of Lord Sheffield. Montagu was one of the talented politicians who made their mark in the Edwardian **Liberal Party** but whose careers were subsequently damaged or wasted after the party's split in 1916.

With his cousin **Herbert Samuel**, Montagu was one of several **Jewish** Liberals who gained ministerial posts under Asquith. After serving as Asquith's Private Secretary, Montagu was a junior minister at the India Office (1910–14) and the Treasury (1914–15), the Chancellor of the Duchy of Lancaster (1915–16), the second Minister of Munitions (1916), and Secretary of State for India (1917–22). The target of **anti-Semitic** attacks, he was particularly embarrassed in 1912 by completely unfounded charges of corruption when the Indian government commissioned Samuel Montagu and Company, his family's financial house, to purchase silver for Indian currency.

In 1916 he resigned rather than remain in office after **David Lloyd George**'s overthrow of Asquith. In 1917, however, he returned to the **Cabinet** as Indian Secretary and soon declared Britain's intention of eventually permitting responsible government in India. An opponent of Zionism, he fought a losing battle against adoption of the **Balfour Declaration** (1917) on the formation of a Jewish state in **Palestine**. Montagu's main efforts were devoted to the cause of Indian reform. On the basis of the Montagu-Chelmsford Report (1918), he introduced legislation that established a degree of representative and responsible government at the provincial level but reserved certain key powers and functions for the British authorities. In the eyes of many Indians, the Government of India Act (1919) fell far short of meeting the demands for home rule or independence. It was Montagu's misfortune, moreover, that such bloody events as the **Amritsar Massacre** (1919) occurred during his tenure.

In 1922 Montagu was forced to resign when he permitted the publication of the Indian government's protest against the policy of Lloyd George's coalition government toward Turkey. Defeated in the general election of 1922, Montagu spent the last two years of his life as a political outsider. His premature death occurred soon after the general election of 1924, which confirmed the succession of **Labour** as the natural party of opposition during the **Conservative**-dominated inter-war decades.

Ian Christopher Fletcher

Bibliography

Levine, Naomi B. *Politics, Religion, and Love: The Story of H.H. Asquith, Venetia Stanley, and Edwin Montagu.* 1991.

Waley, David. *Edwin Montagu.* 1964.

Montgomery, Bernard Law (1887–1976)

Bernard Law Montgomery was the most famous—and most controversial—British general of the **Second World War**, noted especially for his victory at **El Alamein**, Egypt. He became a Field Marshal in 1944 and was named Viscount Montgomery of Alamein in 1946.

Son of an **Anglican** bishop, Montgomery was commissioned in 1908 from Sandhurst and fought in France during the **First World War**. In the peacetime **army** he became known for his dedication to professional excellence, yet he often rubbed people the wrong way. His marriage to Mrs. Betty Hobart Carver in 1927 was a happy one, but her death in 1937 caused his personality to turn inward again.

Montgomery served with distinction as a division commander in France in 1940 and then in England until August 1942, when he went to North Africa to lead the Eighth Army against General Erwin Rommel's forces. His task was to turn stalemate into victory; this he accomplished in the Battle of El Alamein (23 October– 4 November 1942) by virtue of a growing superiority in manpower and materiel and his own genius at organization and training. It had been an expensive victory, and his pursuit of Rommel afterward was uninspired; yet Montgomery became an instant hero, achieving a knighthood as well.

After campaigns in Italy, Montgomery took command of Allied ground forces during the invasion of Normandy in June–July 1944. This campaign caused friction between Montgomery and Supreme Commander Dwight D. Eisenhower, who regarded him as promising much but delivering too slowly. When Eisenhower assumed personal control of the ground forces, Montgomery resented being relegated to commanding only the northern wing of the line. He demanded the lion's share of supplies and troops, including many Americans, for a "narrow" thrust into Germany, but Eisenhower refused, preferring a "broad" front better suited to logistical realities—and to American pride. Montgomery's failed attempt to cross the Rhine in September 1944, along with his arrogant disregard of American sensibilities during the Battle of the Bulge (December 1944–January 1945) exacerbated tensions among the generals.

In 1946 Montgomery became Chief of the Imperial General Staff. From 1948 to 1951 he served as Chairman of the Commanders-in-Chief Committee of the Brussels Treaty Powers, and in 1951 he became Deputy Supreme Commander of the North Atlantic Treaty Organization—ironically, under Eisenhower again in 1951–2. He retired in 1958.

Montgomery was certainly egotistical and cantankerous, and that may have colored some of the criticism he has received. Slow he may have been, yet no one doubted his basic competence.

Karl G. Larew

Bibliography

Hamilton, Nigel. *Monty*. 3 vols. 1981–6.
Lewin, Ronald. *Montgomery as Military Commander*. 1971.
Montgomery, Bernard Law. *The Memoirs of Field Marshal the Viscount Montgomery of Alamein, K.G.* 1958.

Moore, G(eorge) E(dward) (1873–1958)

Of English-speaking philosophers in the twentieth century none enjoyed greater esteem and affection than G.E. Moore. An almost stereotypical **Cambridge** don, Moore lived a busy and happy life of great moment within the English intellectual community but of little notice outside that narrow universe. His enduring reputation rests on the originality of his work on epistemology and ethics, on the memory of his remarkable personality, on the appropriation of some of his ideas by the **Bloomsbury Group**, and on his role—in conjunction with **Bertrand Russell**—in redirecting the course of contempo-

rary British **philosophy** from idealism to realism.

G.E. Moore was born in the London suburb of Upper Norwood on 4 November 1873 and was a younger brother of the distinguished poet Thomas Sturge Moore. Educated at Dulwich College and precociously adept in classical languages and literature, Moore went to Trinity College, Cambridge, in October 1892 intending a career teaching in a public school. At Cambridge Moore excelled both intellectually and socially. Not only did he place in the first class in Part 1 of the classical tripos examination in 1894 and win the Craven Scholarship in 1895, he also was elected to the celebrated undergraduate discussion society, the **Apostles**, in 1894. It was in the company of the latter—younger dons and fellow undergraduates such as **Alfred North Whitehead**, J.M.E. McTaggart, and Bertrand Russell—that Moore's interest in philosophy was first piqued and then nurtured. Encouraged by his apostolic brethren, Moore devoted his fourth year to reading for the second part of the moral science tripos, in which he placed first in 1896. In 1898 he was elected to a prestigious Prize Fellowship at Trinity College where, but for a brief interruption, he remained for the rest of his life—as Lecturer in moral science (1911–25) as Professor of philosophy (1925–39), and editor of the preeminent British philosophy journal, *Mind* (1921–47).

Moore came to the study of philosophy, as he repeatedly confessed, not from a passion to understand "the world or the sciences" but from a bewilderment at the "things which other philosophers have said about the world or the sciences." In particular, it was the curious statements that his Cambridge teachers and friends—McTaggart, Russell, James Ward, G.F. Stout, and Henry Sidgwick—made about the world that provoked his interest. Denying the ultimate reality of time and space, affirming the transcendental existence of good and immortality, and urging the study of Kant, Hegel, and their contemporary Continental interpreters, the British neo-Hegelians at once redirected British philosophy off its traditional empiricist tracks, convinced their students of the transcendent importance of philosophical study, and produced arguments—such as McTaggart's celebrated "view that Time is unreal"—that Moore, at least, judged to be "perfectly monstrous."

This brief neo-Hegelian novitiate provided Moore with both his characteristic intellectual method and his abiding philosophical legacy: a revulsion against idealism and a defense of common sense, an insistence on clarity of expression, and a preoccupation with questions of epistemology and ethics. Beginning with early papers on "The Nature of Judgment" (1899), "Necessity" (1900), and "The Refutation of Idealism" (1903) and culminating in "The Defence of Common Sense" (1925), Moore, complemented by Russell, offered a critique of the prevailing idealist orthodoxy so compelling as to reorient the course of twentieth-century Anglo-Saxon philosophy back toward its traditional realist ambitions.

Nearly all of Moore's finest papers were directly prompted by the writings—and by what he judged to be the errors—of other thinkers, and he soon developed an argumentative strategy that at once clarified problems, fit his own temperament, and served as a model for others. Most striking and insistent was Moore's preoccupation with precision of meaning and argumentation. Fully two generations of British philosophers heard—in seminars, conferences, lectures, and conversations—Moore's incessant plea: "What *precisely* do you mean?" and this relentless quest for clarity helped in its turn to promote the development of linguistic philosophy in the two decades before and after the First World War. So, too, did Moore's own writings. Never a fluent writer nor a winning stylist, Moore wrote relatively little and always slowly, although he did produce one masterpiece, *Principia Ethica* (1903), one pot-boiler, *Ethics* (1912), and two sober volumes of papers and lectures, *Philosophical Studies* (1922) and *Some Main Problems of Philosophy* (1953).

Moore's life was quintessentially academic—rooted in the Cambridge routine of lectures, supervisions, committee meetings, editing, and writing to which he devoted himself single-mindedly from 1898 until his retirement in 1939. Blessedly for him, his family, and his friends, Moore seemed to possess a self-renewing source of youth and happiness that made him a splendid teacher and delightful friend. Above all else, Moore was a good man—of transparent and genuine simplicity, modesty, integrity, and kindliness. Never known to have spoken a cross word or to have stood upon his dignity, Moore was that rarity in academic life—a scholar wholly lacking in self-importance. And it was this beauty and sweetness of character, combined as it was with his earnestness of style and quality of work, that won him the affection and admiration of his many friends and colleagues.

Kirk Willis

Bibliography

Ayer, A.J. *Russell and Moore: The Analytical Heritage.* 1971.

Baldwin, Thomas. *G.E. Moore.* 1990.

Levy, Paul. *Moore: G.E. Moore and the Cambridge Apostles.* 1979.

Regan, Tom. *Bloomsbury's Prophet: G.E. Moore and the Development of His Moral Philosophy.* 1986.

Schilpp, Paul Arthur. *The Philosophy of G.E. Moore.* 2nd ed. 1952.

Moore, Henry Spencer (1898–1986)

Henry Moore is widely regarded as Britain's foremost visual artist of the twentieth century and as a major force in modern sculpture. His work is dominated by two themes: the mother-child relationship and the reclining female figure. An innovative and radical artist, closely allied with the modern movement in British art, Moore took liberties with form but never completely abandoned its human, figurative inspiration. Instead, his work actively synthesizes forms from different periods of art and various sources in nature. Much of the psychological power of his work and the popular response it elicits is believed to derive from this binding together of influences and associations.

Moore was born to a family of coal miners in the northern industrial town of Castleford. Like his great advocate, the critic and poet **Herbert Read**, and his fellow sculptor **Barbara Hepworth**, he was a Yorkshireman. After active military service in the **First World War**, where he was gassed at Cambrai, Moore studied at Leeds, where a sculpture department was set up especially to accommodate him, its only student. Afterward he won a scholarship to the Royal College of Art, London, where he subsequently taught for several years. As a student he already sensed a conflict between the conventional tuition he received and a burgeoning interest in avant-garde experiments. He was particularly drawn to the non-Western traditions in sculpture he was able to study at the **British Museum**; his interest in African carving dated back to Leeds where he was influenced by **Roger Fry's** *Vision and Design* (1920). **Jacob Epstein** was an early mentor and patron of Moore's, encouraging the Warren Gallery to give the young sculptor his first solo exhibition. Moore infused his work with the look of primitive art and carved "directly" from the block, in the spirit of a "truth to materials" advocated by Epstein and others. His *Reclining Figure* (1929, Leeds City Art Gallery) was inspired by a Mexican Chac Mool river deity encountered in reproduction in a magazine. It was also one of his first reclining female figures, which was to prove his most distinctive sculptural form. Such avant-garde attitudes met with disapproval in some quarters of the Royal College, and Moore was encouraged to move to the Chelsea School of Art in 1932, becoming its first head of sculpture.

In the 1930s Moore forged relations with other experimental artists when he and his Russian emigré wife, Irina Radetsky, acquired a studio in Hampstead, where his neighbors included Read, Hepworth, **Ben Nicholson, Paul Nash**, Roland Penrose, and Adrian Stokes. During this period Moore was involved in various group activities, such as Unit One, the short-lived alliance in 1934 of leading figures in the future abstract and surrealist camps, and the anti-Fascist Artists International Association. Moore was unable to accept the doctrinaire opposition between the surrealists (he sat on the organizing committee of the International Surrealist Exhibition held in London in 1936) and abstract artists such as Nicholson, whose group of constructivist artists and architects, Circle, he also joined. Typically for an artist who believed in synthesis and creative oppositions, Moore argued that "all good art has contained both abstract and surrealist elements, just as it has contained both classical and romantic elements." The synthesis at which he arrived attracted the label "biomorphism" to denote the general sense of growth and metamorphosis, a term that was soon used in relation to other artists. Despite his continued protestation that "vitalism" was the motivating force in his work, Moore's output of the 1930s represents the most cerebral and refined work of his career, as the primitive-looking and robust carvings of his early period gave way to more-extreme experiments in abstraction. The most momentous "breakthrough" of the 1930s was quite literally that, his pierced forms, in which he carved his legendary holes through the block to achieve a heightened sense of three-dimensionality—or "sculpture in the round," as he liked to call it—and to extend the metaphor of woman as landscape implicit in all of his reclining figures.

Recumbent Figure (1938, Tate Gallery), the first stone figure in which he pierced a hole right through, was commissioned for the terrace of modernist architect Serge Chermayeff's home on the Sussex Downs. Moore described it as mediating between the stark horizontals of the modern architecture and the undulating hills in the background. The idea of sculpture in the open air, with nature and the sky as ideal background, was crucial to Moore's aesthetic.

A desire to experiment more liberally with pierced forms led him to work in metals for the first time, as a way of avoiding the risks involved in using stone or even wood. Besides bronzes, he worked in lead, which complemented his sense of biomorphic fluidity. The outbreak of war in 1939 also had an impact on his methods. Restrictions in materials and an unwillingness to embark on long-term projects in such uncertain times led him to store ideas in plaster maquettes for later realization. When the time came, the growing demand for his work made it necessary to produce works more rapidly and in editions. Thus, bronze casting took over from direct carving as the principal means of expression for an artist who had insisted—and continued to insist—that he was a carver, not a modeler. However, his techniques of creating hard plaster finishes that had to be chiseled back, or later of taking the mold from polystyrene cutouts, were indeed more oriented toward carving than modeling.

Moore's response to the **Second World War** laid the foundation of his post-war popularity, transforming him into a "public artist" and an institution. He was commissioned by his friend and patron **Kenneth Clark** as an official **war artist** and, as such, recorded the experience of **Blitz** victims sleeping in the Underground stations and bomb shelters in his series of shelter drawings. These were exhibited in the National Gallery, its treasures removed for safe keeping. Moore then attempted to repeat his success with a series of drawings of "Britain's underground army," the coal miners of his native Yorkshire. In 1942 he was commissioned to carve a *Madonna and Child* for the Church of St. Matthew's, Northampton, by its rector, Walter Hussey, a major ecclesiastical patron of the arts. This consoling, almost neo-classical image, although greeted with bafflement by local people, represented a new degree of accessibility and humanism on Moore's part, a reflection of his sense of the needs of the times.

M

Moore's post-war sculpture represents a sometimes uneasy combination of civic humanism and the continuation of the experimentation of the 1930s. *Family Group* (1948–9, Moore Foundation) was made by a school and could almost serve as an icon of the emergent welfare state. By the time of the Festival of Britain in 1951, however, Moore was evidently more confident in reconciling public work with freedom of sculptural expression. His *Festival Reclining Figure* is a skeletal, completely opened-out, angular figure with a bold use of incised lines recalling the jigsaw-like marks on his drawings.

By the 1960s Moore enjoyed a phenomenal international reputation and was frequently called upon to produce monumental sculptures for prestigious architectural projects. His mammoth two- and three-piece bronze reclining figures extended the metaphor of woman as landscape by actually depicting limbs as eroded cliffs and craggy rock formations (even borrowing from paintings such as Monet's *Cliffs at Etretat* or Seurat's *Le Bec du Hoc* to reinforce the point). One of these bronzes was destined for Lincoln Center in New York. Other commissions included city squares, the forecourts of skyscapers, parliament buildings, and museum wings around the world, to the point where Moore sculpture in a city center became almost ubiquitous. Certainly among younger artists Moore's reputation suffered as a result of his popularity and success. A crowning moment for him, however, was the retrospective organized by the City of Florence at the Belvedere Fort where his sculptures vied with Brunelleschi's Duomo and his achievements were, implicitly, compared with Michelangelo, his artistic hero.

David Cohen

Bibliography
Berthoud, Roger. *The Life of Henry Moore.* 1987.
Moore, Henry, and John Hedgecoe. *Henry Moore.* 1986.
Read, Herbert. *Henry Moore: A Study of His Life and Work.* 1965.
Read, Herbert, and Alan Bowness, eds. *Henry Moore: Sculpture and Drawings.* 6 vols. 1944–88.
Russell, John. *Henry Moore.* 1968.
Stansky, Peter, and William Abrahams. *London's Burning: Life, Death, and Art in the Second World War.* 1994.

Morel, E(dmund) D(ene) (1873–1924)

Born Georges Edmund Morel de Ville in Paris, the son of a minor French official and his English Quaker wife, E.D. Morel was educated in English schools until the age of fifteen. Settling permanently in England at the age of seventeen, he began his career as a clerk in a Liverpool shipping firm. He soon became a journalist specializing in West African affairs and adopted his pen name, "E.D. Morel," for use in private life as well. Utilizing his expertise in African affairs, he wrote numerous exposés of the harsh system of exploitation imposed on Congo natives by King Leopold of Belgium. He became the organizer, leader, and chief propagandist, first of the Congo Reform Association and subsequently, during the First World War, of the Union of Democratic Control (UDC), a group critical of Britain's pre-war diplomacy. Alienated from his previous Liberalism, he entered the Independent Labour Party (ILP) in 1919, served as a Labour MP from 1922 to 1924, and became a crucial influence in formulating the Labour Party's post-war foreign policy.

Most of Morel's career was devoted to fomenting and organizing public pressure to bring about changes in British foreign policy. His Congo campaign, undertaken with Roger Casement, then a consular official, as silent partner, was a successful effort to force the British government to use its diplomatic weight to insist that Belgium eliminate the system of forced labor in the Congo. In the course of that crusade Morel became distrustful of Foreign Office officials and an opponent of the Anglo-French *entente*, which he felt had posed an obstacle to Congo reform. These anti-Foreign Office and anti-French views were fully developed before the outbreak of the First World War, and they account for his opposition to Britain's entrance into the war on the side of France. Concluding that the cause of the war had been the system of secret diplomacy, rather than Germany's perfidy, he joined with like-minded Liberals and Labourites in the UDC to agitate for parliamentary control of foreign policy as well as the establishment of an international organization to replace the system of alliances based on the balance of power.

Morel paid a heavy price for his unpopular wartime dissent. He lost his position as a prospective Liberal parliamentary candidate for Birkenhead. In a politically inspired trial he was convicted and sentenced to six months' imprisonment for a minor breach of wartime regulations in sending a copy of his widely read *Truth and the War* (1916) to a neutral country.

Emerging from prison in 1918, Morel discovered that the Labour Party, having recaptured much of its pre-war internationalism, had embraced much of his program for the post-war world. Though supremely indifferent to its domestic program, he entered the socialist ILP, judging that the working class would be the group most receptive to his foreign policy views. In the election of 1922 he stood successfully as a Labour candidate for Dundee, handily defeating **Winston Churchill** in a lively contest.

Morel's final crusade was his effort to gain revision of the Treaty of Versailles. While initially a supporter of Wilsonian views on the post-war world, he became convinced that the American President had betrayed his own principles in acquiescing in a settlement that was undeservedly harsh in its treatment of defeated Germany. The **reparations** imposed on that nation, the war guilt clause, and the transfer of German colonies to the victors were all the constant objects of Morel's denunciations in *Foreign Affairs*, the journal he edited, and elsewhere. Other critics of the treaty, such as **John Maynard Keynes**, may have been more influential on public opinion in general, but Morel, who targeted his writings on the Labour Party, played an important role in creating sympathy for Germany on the Left. By the time of his death in 1924 the Labour Party had been fully persuaded of the iniquity of the Treaty of Versailles.

As an organizer of public protest on matters of foreign policy Morel was a transitional figure linking nineteenth-century humanitarian crusades such as the anti-slave-trade movement and the campaign against Bulgarian atrocities with more broadly based mid-twentieth-century phenomena such as the **Campaign for Nuclear Disarmament**. While he, like his predecessors, relied heavily on the churches and the middle class for support during the Congo campaign, the UDC recruited members from women's groups and working-class organizations newly arrived on the political scene. The legacy of these efforts was mixed. The elimination of the harsh methods of rubber production in the Congo can only be judged an unqualified benefit to African natives. His depiction of Germany as a nation cruelly treated by the peacemakers in 1919 helped, however, to undermine support for the peace settlement and thus to pave the way for the **appeasement** policy of the 1930s.

Catherine Ann Cline

Bibliography

Cline, Catherine Ann. *E.D. Morel, 1873–1924: The Strategies of Protest*. 1981.

Louis, William Roger, and Jean Stengers, eds. *E.D. Morel's History of the Congo Reform Movement*. 1968.

Swartz, Marvin. *The Union of Democratic Control in British Politics during the First World War*. 1971.

Taylor, A.J.P. *The Troublemakers*. 1958.

Morley-Minto Reforms (1909)

In 1909 the British Parliament passed a reform bill that significantly expanded the opportunities for Indian participation in the Indian government. John Morley (1838–1923), Secretary of State for India, was chiefly responsible for these reforms, although Lord Minto (1845–1914), Viceroy of India, has often been given equal credit for the initiative.

The reforms were largely a response to the rise of militant **Indian nationalism**. Angry at the lack of opportunities for control of their political destiny, some Indian nationalists began to support extreme, sometimes violent, measures to attain desired ends. Morley believed that the tide of extremism could be stopped, and the forces of moderation in the Indian National Congress strengthened, by a timely measure of significant constitutional reform. The ideal of gradually transferring the British constitutional system to India was close to Morley's heart, and he consulted with G.K. Gokhale (1866–1915), a leading moderate nationalist who shared this vision of Empire. The result was the Indian Councils Act of 1909, which attempted to remedy the lack of political participation for Indians by introducing the elective principle into the Indian government, greatly increasing the number of Indians serving on the legislative councils in India and allowing greater opportunity for Indian council members to question budgetary matters. Morley also took nonlegislative steps in this direction, appointing Indians to his own council in London and inducing Minto to do likewise in India, thereby giving Indians executive responsibilities for the first time in the history of the British Raj.

Morley's reforms also included separate electorates for Muslims, who were a minority not nearly as politically advanced as some segments of the majority Hindu population of India. The initiative here came from Minto, who was responsive to the growing worries of Indian Muslims about militant Hindu elements in the nationalist movement. Morley at first balked at this departure from the standard principles of representative government, but soon conceded the need for special political privileges for the Muslim minority. While Indian nationalists, then and now, have seen this as an imperial strategy of divide and rule, more-neutral scholarship suggests that Morley and Minto were responding to pressure from a Muslim community that was beginning to express legitimate political fears and aspirations.

The Morley-Minto reforms would prove to be the last act of nineteenth-century constitutional reform in India. The First World War altered the situation drastically in India, and Morley's hopes for slowly and gradually increasing the amount of self-government in India would be dashed, largely because Indian nationalists no longer considered this to be the acceptable route to independence. Although further measures of constitutional reform would be passed by various British administrations, the idea that British liberals and Indian moderate nationalists could cooperate to fashion gradually a constitutional transition to self-government would become increasingly an unrealistic one in twentieth-century British India.

Lynn Zastoupil

Bibliography

Das, Manmath N. *India under Morley and Minto: Politics behind Revolution, Repression, and Reforms.* 1964.

Koss, Stephen E. *John Morley at the India Office, 1905–1910.* 1969.

Moore, R.J. *Liberalism and Indian Politics, 1872–1922.* 1966.

Wolpert, Stanley A. *Morley and India, 1906–1910.* 1967.

Morris, William (1877–1963)

William Morris, founder of Morris Motors Ltd., an important British motor vehicle firm, and benefactor of numerous organizations including the Nuffield Foundation, was a major figure in twentieth-century British economic history. Born in 1877, Morris began his business career selling, repairing, and later manufacturing bicycles in Oxford. In 1913 he manufactured his first motor vehicle, and by 1929 he was the leading British producer, supplying nearly half of the British market. Unlike most of his competitors in the British motor vehicle industry, Morris entered the industry with the intention of mass producing an affordable vehicle and competing head on with American automaker Henry Ford and the Model T. Adopting a strategy of buying major components from external parts suppliers, Morris was essentially an assembler at first. During the 1920s he was forced to increase the level of manufacture, usually through the purchase of major suppliers, such as Hotchkiss, who supplied engines but was reluctant to produce the volume of components needed.

Morris' early success was due mainly to effective product design, such as the famous Morris Cowley (1915), which was suited to the special needs of the British market. Major breakthroughs in manufacturing techniques were less significant. Morris was slow to move toward mechanized assembly, although he did experiment, albeit unsuccessfully, with automation in his Coventry engine shops in the 1920s. Morris ruled his work force as a benevolent autocrat, firmly antiunion but willing to grant higher wages and, for the period, progressive benefits such as holidays with pay. He was also influential as a critic of state intervention in the economy, preferring a more *laissez-faire* environment. He was one of the major financiers of **Oswald Mosley**'s New Party in the early 1930s and became the President of the League of Industry in 1932, set up by the National Council of Industry and Commerce to advocate a free-enterprise economy.

Morris' domination of the British **automobile industry** was relatively short-lived. Increasing competition after 1945 from the American firms of Ford and General Motors and questionable reinvestment policies led to a merger between Morris and the other leading British firm, Austin, in 1952. The newly formed British Motor Corporation was unable to rationalize the British sector of the industry, and American, European, and eventually Japanese firms continued to absorb market share. Further mergers brought nearly all of the major British vehicle manufacturers under the control of British Leyland Ltd. This move was no more successful, and, in an ironic twist of fate, the state was forced to bail out British Leyland in the early 1970s as British market share continued to fall to less than 20 percent. In July 1988 the firm was returned to private hands through a controversial purchase by British Aerospace, but it was sold to the German firm BMW in 1994.

Morris was well known as a philanthropist, giving over £30 million to various charities. He used his wealth to promote his own vision of society, one in which a voluntary welfare system would replace state organized relief. Major donations included the endowment of a number of chairs at Oxford and the creation of the Nuffield Foundation in 1943.

Wayne Lewchuk

Bibliography

Adeney, Martin. *Nuffield: A Biography.* 1993.

Andrews, P.W.S., and Elizabeth Brunner. *The Life of Lord Nuffield: A Study in Enterprise and Benevolence.* 1955.

Overy, R.J. *William Morris, Viscount Nuffield.* 1976.

Whiting, R.C. *The View from Cowley: The Impact of Industrialisation upon Oxford, 1918–1939.* 1983.

Morrison, Herbert Stanley (1888–1965)
Alongside **Clement Attlee** and **Ernest Bevin**, Herbert Morrison was one of the three most powerful political figures in the Labour governments of 1945 to 1951. His real importance to Labour was as the organizer of the victory of 1945 and of the **welfare state** that emerged. He was also Attlee's deputy and is considered to be the finest administrator the **Labour Party** has ever produced.

Morrison was born in London on 3 January 1888 into a middling working-class family. He received an elementary education and then held a variety of shop-assistant jobs. Deeply interested in politics, he joined the Westminster branch of the quasi-Marxist Social Democratic Federation in 1907. That was not to be his brand of socialism, and, in 1910, he switched to the Brixton branch of the **Independent Labour Party** (ILP), quickly becoming its Chairman and developing contacts with many socialist leaders. Indeed, by the end of 1910 Morrison was appointed the Secretary of the South-West London Federation of the ILP and stood, unsuccessfully, as ILP candidate for the Vauxhall ward of the London County Council in 1912. Between 1910 and 1913 he was active as Chairman of the Brixton branch of the National Union of Clerks. His involvement in Labour politics led him to be appointed as circulation agent for the *Daily Citizen*, the new Labour daily paper. During these years he developed a clear socialist perspective, advocating public works to deal with **unemployment**, and supported the **women's suffrage** movement.

During the **First World War** he assumed an antiwar stance and became even more closely involved with the ILP and the Labour movement, becoming part-time Secretary to W.C. Anderson, the ILP MP, a part-time agent for the National Labour Press, and Secretary of the London Labour Party. He received his call-up papers in 1916, and though his blind right eye exempted him from military service, he attended the Military Service Tribunal and agreed to work on the land.

From 1920 onward Morrison rose quickly in Labour circles. He became a member of the Hackney Borough Council, acting as Mayor in 1920 and 1921, and was member of the London County Council from 1922 to 1945, becoming its leader in 1939–40. At the same time he was also prominent in the Labour Party: He joined the National Executive in 1920 and was MP for South Hackney in 1923–4, 1929–31, and 1935–45, for East Lewisham in 1945–50, and for South Lewisham in 1950–9. He was also Minister of Transport in the Labour government of 1929–31 and was Minister of Supply for a few months in 1940 before becoming Home Secretary and Minister for Home Security from 1940 until 1945 and a member of the War **Cabinet** from 1942. Yet Morrison's finest hour came when he became the Lord President of the Council, leader of the House of Commons, and Deputy Prime Minister in Attlee's Labour governments of 1945–51. In 1951 he became Foreign Secretary, and, following Labour's defeat, he continued to act as deputy leader of the Labour Party from 1951 to 1955.

By any standards, Morrison's political career was impressive. He was a supreme organizer and administrator, whether organizing the London Passenger Transport Board in the early 1930s, imposing air raid precautions during the **Second World War**, or promoting the **Festival of Britain** in 1951. A skillful parliamentarian, he pushed through more than 70 bills in the first session of Attlee's post-war Labour government as leader of the House, including **nationalization** of **coal mining**, the **railways**, and other industries. He was largely responsible for the formulation of Labour's nationalization program, and his book *Socialization and Transport* (1933) committed Labour to the idea of a corporate public body as the model for state control. He was, above all, the supreme party organizer keeping the Labour backbenchers happy by creating subject committee groups among them. In the end, his epitaph must be that he gave cohesion to the Labour Party and Attlee's post-war Labour governments.

Nevertheless, there were many personal and political failures in his life. His first marriage was never happy, and he appears to have had several flirtations, including one with **Ellen Wilkinson**. Margaret, his first wife, died of cancer in 1953, and he married Edith Meadowcroft in 1955. Politically, his main setbacks occurred at the hands of Attlee, who defeated him for the Labour Party leadership in 1935, thwarted him in an attempt to assume the party leadership in 1939 and 1945, and delayed his own retirement sufficiently long enough to enable **Hugh Gaitskell** to become leader in 1955. Morrison's other major political failing was at the **Foreign Office** in 1951, where he was considered to be out of his depth.

He stood down as MP in 1959 and was elevated to the **House of Lords** as Lord Morrison of Lambeth. In 1960 he became President of the Board of Film Censors, a post he held until shortly before his death on 6 March 1965.

Keith Laybourn

Bibliography
Donoughue, Bernard, and G.W. Jones.
  Herbert Morrison: Portrait of a Politician. 1973.
Morgan, Kenneth O. *Labour People.* 1987.
Morrison, Herbert. *An Autobiography.* 1960.

Mosley, Oswald Ernald (1896–1980)

Sir Oswald Mosley is best remembered as the founder and leader of the British Union of Fascists, an organization he formed in 1932. Before that development Mosley had been an MP, affiliated initially with the **Conservative Party** and, following his alienation, with the **Labour Party**. He also formed the short-lived New Party in 1931. Fierce in his ambitions, even to the point of recklessness, Mosley failed to break the mold of British politics. A political exile for many years, he died in France in 1980.

Mosley was born in London on 16 November 1896, the eldest of three sons of Sir Oswald Mosley (who succeeded to the baronetcy in 1915) and Katherine Maud Mosley (*née* Edwards-Heathcote). When Oswald Mosley was five years of age, his mother separated from his father and took her young children to live in Shropshire, near her father's house.

In 1909 Mosley entered Winchester College where he developed proficiency in both boxing and fencing. He left Winchester in 1912 for Sandhurst in January 1914 but was expelled after some months. In October 1914, shortly after the outbreak of war, Mosley was commissioned in the Sixteenth Lancers. He applied subsequently to join the Royal Flying Corps, serving as an observer between December 1914 and April 1915. While attempting to secure his pilot's licence, he crashed his plane and broke his ankle, later returning to the front with the Sixteenth Lancers. However, the condition of his ankle deteriorated, and in March 1916 he was invalided out of the armed forces. By then he had gained sufficient wartime experience to savor the camaraderie of the trenches, a feeling that remained with him and later assumed a political significance.

Mosley spent the remainder of the war in the **Ministry of Munitions** and the **Foreign Office** but nurtured political ambitions. His first political step came in December 1918, when he won the Harrow division of Middlesex for the Tories with a majority of 10,943 out of a total vote of 16,957. Then, in May 1920, he married Cynthia Blanche, the second daughter of **Lord Curzon** of Kedleston, former Viceroy of India and Foreign Secretary in **David Lloyd George's** Cabinet, a marriage that could do no harm to his political ambitions. The Mosleys' personal wealth and social connections provided them with a glittering base from which to operate. But his discontent surfaced in public late in 1920 when he crossed the floor in protest against the government's policy on Ireland. At first Mosley retained the confidence of his local Conservative organization, but in 1922 he stood at Harrow as an Independent and retained the seat.

In the 1923 election Mosley held Harrow with a reduced majority, and in March 1924, two months after **Ramsay MacDonald** had formed the first Labour government, Mosley joined the **Independent Labour Party**. In the 1924 election he stood against **Neville Chamberlain** at Birmingham Ladywood and went down to a narrow defeat by 77 votes. However, in December 1926 he was returned to Parliament after winning a by-election at Smethwick

Oswald Mosley takes the salute from women members of the British Union of Fascists, October 1936.

with a large majority. The period between 1924 and 1926 was not wasted. In collaboration with **John Strachey**, he devised a program influenced by the economic theory of **John Maynard Keynes**. Furthermore, Mosley's active support of the miners in the 1926 **General Strike** created a fund of goodwill in the Labour ranks. Indeed, at this juncture Mosley was regarded in some quarters as a potential leader of the Labour Party.

In the 1929 election Mosley (who had succeeded to the baronetcy in 1928) was returned for Smethwick. Cynthia, his wife, entered Parliament as Labour MP for Stoke-on-Trent. With the Labour election victory in 1929 Mosley assumed the office of Chancellor of the Duchy of Lancaster outside the **Cabinet**. But the rebellious, impatient streak in his personality became evident as friction developed between Mosley and **J.H. Thomas**, the Lord Privy Seal, over how to cure the increasing **unemployment** problem. In making his stand Mosley also challenged **Philip Snowden**, the Chancellor of the Exchequer, who shared the orthodox economic views Thomas represented. Things came to a head with the Mosley memorandum of 1930, which

made radical recommendations for economic recovery, involving state intervention and a public works program. When it was rejected by the Cabinet, Mosley resigned on 20 May 1930.

When his proposals were defeated at the Labour Party conference in October 1930, he began to plan the foundation of the New Party, launched on 28 February 1931. During its brief life the party attracted such figures as **Aneurin Bevan, Harold Nicolson**, the philosopher Cyril Joad, and John Strachey. The New Party's results in the election of 1931 can only be described as disastrous: All twenty-four candidates suffered defeat.

In 1932 Mosley visited Italy to observe the Fascist experiment of Benito Mussolini, the visit spurring the formation of a British **Fascist** movement. Impatient with the slow grinding wheels of parliamentary democracy, Mosley envisioned a decisive role for himself in a dictatorial system, which, he believed, could solve pressing problems. On 1 October 1932 Mosley launched his new political movement, the British Union of Fascists (BUF).

The first two years of the BUF were successful and, according to some commentators, comparatively respectable. This image changed after a fiery, violent meeting at Olympia in London on 7 June 1934. Mosley's organization became increasingly associated with political violence and extremism, and public opinion began to harden against the movement.

Once the BUF began to espouse **anti-Semitism** more openly, members devoted a good deal of energy to street politics in East London. The BUF itself was increasingly influenced by developments in Germany and in 1936 changed its name to the British Union of Fascists and National Socialists. Mosley's Keynesian economic policies were abandoned in favor of a mixture of corporatism, totalitarianism, **patriotism**, and racism. The initially sympathetic Rothermere press withdrew its support. The government, disturbed by the increasing paramilitary style of the BUF, passed the Public Order Act in 1936, which forbade the wearing of political uniforms. The act did not prevent disorder or stop Fascist political activity, but it did exercise a degree of control over the movement, limiting the BUF's provocative marches through the East End.

In the midst of this political change, Lady Cynthia, who had always shared Mosley's political ambitions, died of peritonitis. It was three years before Mosley re-married, this time to Diana Mitford Guinness, the third daughter of the second Baron Redesdale and one of the celebrated Mitford sisters.

Increasingly in the late 1930s the BUF argued that if hostilities were to break out between England and Germany, it would result from a conspiracy organized by Jewish interests. When hostilities began in the autumn of 1939, some members of the BUF entered the ranks of the armed services. But in May 1940 Mosley and his wife were arrested and detained under Regulation 18B, which allowed the imprisonment without trial of anyone believed likely to endanger the safety of the realm. The Mosleys were released from prison in November 1943 on humanitarian grounds, Mosley suffering at this time from phlebitis.

After the war Mosley attempted to justify his pre-war attitudes in such publications as *My Answer* (1946) and *My Life* (1968). He channeled his political energies between 1944 and 1966 into the Union Movement with an emphasis on European unity based on racial criteria. Much of Mosley's activity was conducted in exile from his home at Orsay, just outside Paris,

but he did fight parliamentary contests on two occasions, at North Kensington in 1959 and Shoreditch in 1966. The former occurred in the aftermath of racial violence in Notting Hill in 1958, from which he hoped to derive political benefit. In both elections he polled few votes and lost his deposit. Nevertheless, to the end Mosley nurtured the belief that he had a European role to play when the great social crisis finally broke. The anticipated role never materialized. Mosley died at Orsay on 3 December 1980.

Colin Holmes

Bibliography

Lewis, D.S. *Illusions of Grandeur: Mosley, Fascism, and British Society, 1931–1981.* 1987.

Mosley, Nicholas. *Rules of the Game: Sir Oswald and Lady Cynthia Mosley, 1896–1933.* 1982.

———. *Beyond the Pale: Sir Oswald Mosley, 1933–80.* 1983.

Mosley, Oswald. *My Life.* 1968.

Skidelsky, Robert. *Oswald Mosley.* 2nd ed. 1981.

Thurlow, Richard. *Fascism in Britain: A History, 1918–1985.* 1987.

Mountaineering

Mount Everest, the world's highest mountain, was first climbed on 29 May 1953 by Edmund Hillary (1919–), a beekeeper from **New Zealand**, and Tenzing Norgay (1914–86), a Sherpa living in India. News of the ascent was published on 2 June, the day of Queen Elizabeth II's coronation, and the ascent was celebrated as the crowning achievement of the new reign and of the fledgling Commonwealth. The ascent of Everest symbolized British power during a period of imperial decline.

The Alpine Club and the Royal Geographical Society jointly sponsored nine expeditions to Everest between 1921 and 1953. Expeditions to climb Everest from Tibet in the 1920s ended in tragedy. Twelve porters or climbers died in the first three attempts, including schoolmaster George Mallory (1886–1924) and Oxford student Andrew Irvine (1902–24), who disappeared together climbing toward the summit. Attempts on Everest during the 1930s ended in frustration. Leading Everest climbers in the 1930s included former Air Force officer Frank Smythe (1900–49) and two farmers in Kenya,

Eric Shipton (1907–77) and Bill Tilman (1898–1978), each of whom wrote popular books about their ascents of Kamet, Nanda Devi, and other adventures.

The post-war era created a new political context for the ascent of Everest. Indian independence in 1947 and the Chinese invasion of Tibet in 1950 ended the British monopoly on Everest and forced climbers to approach the mountain through Nepal. A group of British climbers explored the southern slopes of Everest in 1951. The following year Tenzing nearly reached the summit in a Swiss expedition. In the last chance a British party would have to climb the peak for several years, Hillary and Tenzing reached the summit in a well-organized expedition led by an army officer, John Hunt (1910–). The ascent was greeted with acclaim, Hillary and Hunt receiving knighthoods.

After the 1950s British mountaineering grew in popularity at home and abroad. Rock climbing in Britain attracted more female and working-class climbers, transforming what had been a predominantly upper-middle-class male sport. Many women, such as the journalist Dorothy Pilley Richards (1893–1986), began climbing frequently during the inter-war years. Commercial sponsorship also expanded the number of professional climbers. Chris Bonington (1934–) left the ranks of the army and corporate management to pursue climbing and photojournalism. Large-scale expeditions continued to obtain funding and publicity by wrapping themselves in the flag. Bonington, for example, led several British expeditions during the 1970s, including the ascent of the southwest face of Everest in 1975. International expeditions have become more common; Bonington climbed Everest in a Norwegian expedition in 1985. While many climbers at the end of the twentieth century disavow the suggestion that their mountaineering contributes to national glory, broader public perceptions have been slow to change after having been so deeply engraved by the attempts to climb Everest in the first half of the century.

Peter H. Hansen

Bibliography
Bonington, Chris. *The Everest Years.* 1986.
Clark, Ronald W., and Edward C. Pyatt.
    Mountaineering in Britain. 1957.
Hunt, H.J.C. *The Ascent of Everest.* 1953.
Unsworth, Walt. *Everest.* 1981.

Mountbatten, Louis Francis Albert Victor Nicholas (1900–1979)

Lord Mountbatten was the last Viceroy of India. He also commanded Allied forces in Southeast Asia during and after the Second World War. In these two positions he had an important influence over the withdrawal of Britain from its Empire in Asia.

Born on 24 June 1900 as Prince Louis of Battenberg, Mountbatten was the son of Prince Louis Alexander of Battenberg (later Louis Mountbatten, Marquess of Milford Haven) and Princess Victoria Alberta Elizabeth Irene, the daughter of Louis IV of Hesse-Darmstadt. Mountbatten's father was the brother-in-law of Princess Beatrice (Princess Henry of Battenberg), and his mother was the granddaughter of Queen Victoria. Mountbatten was, therefore, closely related to several branches of European royalty, and he spent much of his childhood visiting them in Britain, Germany, and Russia. He attended Locker's Park School in Hertfordshire and the naval colleges at Osborne, Dartmouth, and Devonport. Mountbatten graduated in 1916 at the height of the First World War and soon saw action as a midshipman aboard the HMS *Lion.* His family's ties to Germany, however, overshadowed much of his war service. Anti-German hysteria forced his father to resign his position as First Sea Lord in 1914 and to change the family's name from Battenberg to Mountbatten in 1917. Nevertheless, these crises did not sever the young Mountbatten's connections to the rich and powerful. In 1921 he married Edwina Cynthia Annette Ashley, heiress to three sizable estates and to £2.3 million. He also befriended his cousin, the Prince of Wales, and accompanied him on his tours of the globe. Between the wars Mountbatten acquired the reputation of a playboy, but his service from 1925 to 1932 as a signals officer earned him the respect of the Royal Navy top brass.

Mountbatten's connections, courage, and inventiveness all accounted for a remarkably rapid series of promotions during the Second World War. He served courageously as captain of the destroyer *Kelly.* In March 1940 he returned the *Kelly* to port under tow during three days of almost constant enemy bombardment. He survived the sinking of his ship in May 1941 only by swimming out from under it after it capsized. Mountbatten's exploits caught the attention of the British public and became the subject of Noel Coward's war film, *In Which*

We Serve (1942). His daring also won the attention of Prime Minister **Winston Churchill**, who supported his promotion to command the aircraft carrier *Illustrious*. In April 1942, however, before the *Illustrious* was ready, Mountbatten was reassigned to Combined Operations in London, promoted simultaneously to the ranks of Vice Admiral, Lieutenant-General and Air Marshal, with a *de facto* membership of the Chiefs of Staff Committee. In this new position Mountbatten shared responsibility for the controversial and costly landing at Dieppe in August 1942 and the early preparations for the invasion of Normandy. In autumn 1943 Mountbatten received the rank of Admiral and the supreme command of Allied forces in Southeast Asia. He presided over the successful reconquest of Burma and prepared for an arduous campaign through the rest of Malaya and Indochina, but the atom bomb transformed this invasion into a series of unopposed landings.

After the war Mountbatten became directly involved with the most important result of Japan's brief dominion over Southeast Asia, the rise of nationalism. As Supreme Commander of Allied forces in the region, he faced the onerous task of restoring British, French, and Dutch colonial governments to territories that had recently been under the local administration of indigenous leaders. Mountbatten's liberal leanings went back at least as far as a brief period of study at **Cambridge** during 1919–20. He put these convictions into practice through efforts to accommodate the nationalist aspirations of Southeast Asian leaders. Given the demands of the European governments involved, however, he could do little to prevent rebellion in the East Indies and decades of war in Indochina. He resigned his command in the summer of 1946, was created Viscount Mountbatten of Burma in December, and Earl Mountbatten of Burma in 1947.

Mountbatten's experience in the Far East, his liberal political leanings, and his sympathy toward Asian national movements made him an obvious choice to supervise the **Labour** government's transfer of power in India. The government's previous failures to reconcile the differences between the Indian National Congress and the Muslim League made the task so daunting that he agreed to serve as India's last Viceroy only on the condition that the **Cabinet** would set June 1948 as the deadline for Britain's withdrawal. He arrived in Delhi in March 1947 determined to transfer power to a united India

that would remain a member of the Commonwealth. Congress, however, rejected his proposal for a loose federation of Hindus and Muslim states, and the Muslim League's refusal to accept a more powerful central government forced him to agree to a partition of the subcontinent between India and Pakistan.

The most controversial aspect of the agreement, which Mountbatten announced on 3 June 1947, was that independence would arrive on 15 August 1947 rather than in June 1948. The advanced date was the result of Mountbatten's hasty compromise with the Congress that ensured India's membership in the Commonwealth until it drafted a new constitution. He hoped that this membership would keep India and Pakistan at peace with each other and allied to Britain. But the speed of Britain's withdrawal left much of the partition incomplete by the appointed day and did not adequately account for the status of the princely states after the end of British rule. The failure to resolve these issues brought India and Pakistan to the brink of a general war during the months immediately following independence. As India's first post-independence Governor-General, Mountbatten contended with communal massacres and war in Kashmir. Even after his departure from the post in June 1948, he influenced the Commonwealth's decision to maintain India's membership once it became a republic.

Mountbatten returned to the navy in 1948 as a Rear Admiral, and in 1953 he became Second Sea Lord and Commander of North Atlantic Treaty Organization (NATO) fleets in the Mediterranean. The following year he became First Sea Lord. In spite of his opposition 6to Britain's role in the 1956 **Suez crisis**, Mountbatten became Admiral of the Fleet in 1956 and Chief of the Defense Staff in 1959. Even after he retired in 1965, he continued to serve the government, first in its attempt to forestall Rhodesia's declaration of independence the same year, then in its inquiry into prison reform in 1966. But his continued public activities and his connection with the Royal Family made him a target for the Irish Republican Army, which assassinated him on 27 August 1979 in a bomb explosion while he was fishing in Mullaghmoor Harbor in Ireland. The manner of his death aroused great public indignation, and he received a funeral in Westminster Abbey.

Lord Mountbatten embodied many contradictions. He was an aristocrat who was related to the Royal Family. Yet he supported many of the policies of the Labour government. He often appeared egotistical. Yet he tolerated and even welcomed criticism. He devoted much of his career to preserving the Commonwealth as the British Empire disappeared. Yet some of his most significant decisions may have made the Commonwealth less effective than he intended. Nevertheless, he was perfectly suited for his most important role as India's last Viceroy. His combination of courage, imagination, and charm allowed Britain to part with India on surprisingly cordial terms.

A. Martin Wainwright

Bibliography
Mountbatten of Burma, Louis, Earl. *From Shore to Shore: The Tour Diaries of Earl Mountbatten of Burma, 1953–1979.* Philip Ziegler, ed. 1989.
———. *Reflections on the Transfer of Power and Jawaharlal Nehru.* 1968.
Ziegler, Philip. *Mountbatten.* 1985.

Movement for Colonial Freedom

One of the more successful and influential left-wing pressure groups in the post-war era of British political life, the Movement for Colonial Freedom was founded in 1954. Although largely the brainchild of a group of radical Labour MPs, most notably **Fenner Brockway** and Tony Benn, the Movement was not formally affiliated with any political party and sought as diverse a membership as possible. Its aim was to mobilize a popular constituency for independence movements in British colonies and to bring together in a single coordinating body the various interest groups and committees devoted to separate issues that had sprung up in anti-imperialist circles. Activism and egalitarian participation were emphasized over research and the direction of experts—a feature that distinguished the Movement from its predecessor and erstwhile rival, the Fabian Colonial Bureau. The Movement also sought to represent the voices and views of the nationalist and independence movements themselves to British politicians and to the general public and was insistent in its call for the transition to full democracy in former colonies without delay. Although it encouraged membership and participation from all sectors of British society, the Movement was perhaps inevitably dominated by left-wing politicians, academics, religious activists, and artists, and its ideological program was sufficiently flavored with the rhetoric of socialism and liberation to prompt the occasional disquiet of the more mainstream members of the **Labour Party** leadership during its heyday in the late 1950s.

Brian Phillips

Bibliography
Brockway, Fenner. *The Colonial Revolution.* 1973.
———. *Towards Tomorrow: The Autobiography of Fenner Brockway.* 1977.
Goldsworthy, David. *Colonial Issues in British Politics, 1945–1961.* 1971.

Multinational Corporations

Twentieth-century Britain has been one of the world's most important sources of multinational investment. Before the Second World War British-owned multinational enterprise was more extensive than that of any other country. Subsequently, and up to the present day, it has remained the second most important source of foreign direct investment. At the beginning of the 1990s British multinationals were the largest foreign investors in the United States, with investments almost twice as large as those of Japanese corporations. Multinational corporations have been, therefore, highly significant for the British economy.

By the first decade of the twentieth century many British enterprises had extensive international operations. Britain has long been known to have been the world's largest capital-exporting nation before the First World War, but this has been traditionally regarded as mostly portfolio in nature—that is, not involving managerial control. Recent research has dramatically altered that view. By the most reliable estimates, Britain owned 45 percent of the world's stock of foreign direct investment in 1914, which amounted to $14.3 million.

British corporations were active abroad in virtually all economic sectors. There was extensive investment, for example, in extractive and natural resource industries in search of precious minerals, ores, and petroleum. The Shell Group, which since 1907 has been Anglo-Dutch, originated in part as a British company shipping oil from Russia to Asia in the late nineteenth century, and then found oil fields in Indonesia. British Petroleum originated as a British company that discovered oil in Iran in 1908, marking the birth of the Middle Eastern oil industry. British companies were equally active in tin and copper mining and in tea plantations.

British companies were also active abroad in the service sector. Before 1914 British accounting, engineering, and construction firms had extensive foreign operations, as did insurance companies. In 1913 over 40 British insurance companies were active in the United States alone, and they played a significant role in meeting the costs of the San Francisco earthquake in 1906. Britain was also the world's leading multinational banker. From the 1830s British banks had established overseas branches, first in colonial settlements in Australia and Canada, and later in Asia, Latin America, and Africa. By 1914 approximately 30 British banks owned and operated almost 1,400 branches outside the United Kingdom.

In terms of overall value, British multinational corporations had fewer investments in foreign manufacturing before the First World War, although Britain, together with the United States and Germany, was an active participant in this first stage of multinational manufacturing. Pioneer British companies included Dunlop, which owned tire factories in France, Germany, and Japan; and Lever Brothers and J. and P. Coats, manufacturers of soap and cotton thread respectively, with factories in the United States, Canada, South Africa, Australia, Russia, Switzerland, France, and Germany by 1914.

A number of factors prompted these British manufacturers to erect factories abroad. The spread of protectionism gave British companies the stark choice of losing their markets or surmounting tariff barriers by erecting factories behind them. The early British multinationals also found that they could service the needs of foreign markets better by producing in them. Different markets often had different requirements and tastes, and a local factory could help a British firm respond more effectively.

Although the First World War interrupted the growth of multinational enterprise, and led to British companies being stripped of their factories in enemy territory, the 1920s saw further foreign expansion by British multinational corporations. A new generation of manufacturing firms invested abroad in the inter-war years. The **Quaker** chocolate firms of Cadbury and Rowntree, for example, established factories in Australia, Canada, **New Zealand**, Ireland, and

South Africa in these years. It was not war, but Depression, that slowed the foreign growth of multinational enterprise. In the 1930s, as economic nationalism and exchange controls proliferated, and as political extremism and instability spread from country to country, many British firms preferred to participate in international market-sharing agreements, or cartels, rather than run the risks of owning assets abroad.

The Second World War seems to have inflicted more damage on British multinational enterprise than its predecessor did. There were spectacular losses, such as the forced sale of Courtaulds' American subsidiary to the Americans in return for assistance during the war. In the late 1940s and 1950s the granting of independence to former colonies in Asia and Africa was often followed by reductions in British direct investment, especially in the extractive and agricultural-related sectors. By 1960 Britain accounted for only 16 percent of the total stock of world foreign direct investment, while the United States accounted for 48 percent.

British multinational corporations showed some signs of stagnation, or at least lack of dynamism, in the post-war period. Between 1945 and 1960 about 80 percent of new British direct investment went to the Commonwealth, especially **Australia, Canada**, and **South Africa**. British firms were locked into small, slow-growing economies and invested comparatively little in the dynamic markets of Western Europe, the United States, and Japan. British multinationals were clustered in such traditional sectors as food, **drink**, and tobacco, and weak in more technologically intensive sectors. British multinational banking remained prolific—with almost 4,000 overseas banks owned in the 1960s—but branches and assets were concentrated in Asia and the Southern Hemisphere, with practically no presence in the United States or Continental Europe.

From the 1960s there was an accelerating change in the structure of British multinational investment. By 1981 food, drink, and tobacco was no longer the dominant sector of British multinationals, its place assumed by chemicals. There was also a geographical reorientation to Western Europe and the United States. From the late 1970s British multinational investment grew very rapidly, increasing fivefold between 1979 and 1986. For the 1980–9 period the United Kindgom was the world's largest home economy for outflows of foreign direct investment, with average annual outflows of $17 billion, or 20 percent of world outflows. Around three-fifths of this investment went to the United States. By the mid-1980s the value of British-owned assets in the United States exceeded those of American corporations in the United Kingdom.

Much of the huge flow of British direct investment abroad since 1980, especially in the United States, has taken the form of acquisitions of existing foreign firms. Unlike Japanese or Continental European firms, British corporations, used to mergers, acquisitions, and hostile takeovers at home, found it easy to finance foreign acquisitions on the well-developed British capital markets. Finally, few British corporations had the kind of technological or managerial advantage that they could exploit by new "greenfield" investment. They were, in fact, seeking to escape from their own small and slow-growth market into a more dynamic one.

This strategy was by no means always successful. During the late 1970s and early 1980s, for example, British banks made a series of major acquisitions of California banks, but most of these ventures proved unsuccessful, and by the end of the 1980s the British banks had all divested from California. The most spectacular failure was that of the Midland Bank, whose ill-fated purchase of Crocker National in 1980 led to losses of around £1 billion in the following six years before Midland withdrew from California. Many British manufacturing companies also experienced difficulties with their American acquisitions.

The only systematic attempt to study the costs and benefits of British foreign direct investment has been the Reddaway Report on British direct investment abroad, published in 1968, which suggested a favorable impact on the balance of payments, though on the basis of certain questionable assumptions. The gains from inward investment into Britain by foreign firms can be more readily gauged than those from outward investment. In the first half of the century American firms, and since the 1970s Japanese firms, have created employment, introduced and improved managerial practices, and transferred technologies into Britain. But it is certainly evident that Britain's ownership of some of the world's largest multinational corporations has failed to prevent its relative economic decline throughout the century.

Geoffrey Jones

Bibliography

Jones, Geoffrey. *British Multinational Banking, 1830–1990.* 1993.

——, ed. *British Multinationals: Origins, Management, and Performance.* 1986.

Stopford, John M., and Louis Turner. *Britain and the Multinationals.* 1985.

Munich Conference

On 29 September 1938 the British Prime Minister, **Neville Chamberlain**, met with the French, German, and Italian premiers in Munich to resolve the dispute between Germany and Czechoslovakia over the Czech western border region, the Sudetenland, which contained 3 million ethnic Germans. The leaders agreed to transfer the territory to the German Reich, and war was averted.

The Munich conference was a by-product of the foreign policy of **appeasement** of the prewar Chamberlain government (1937–40). British **Cabinets**, since the end of the First World War, had generally followed a policy of accommodation among the European powers. Chamberlain, however, took a more proactive approach and strove to seek out what he deemed were the reasonable grievances of the dissatisfied nations and resolve them through generous compromise. British opinion seemed to agree. Many wished, at all costs, to avoid another war; others thought that Germany had been treated too harshly by the Treaty of Versailles. Some felt that accommodation with the admittedly unappealing **Fascist** powers was the only alternative to a war that would leave Europe at the mercy of the Soviet Union.

The Sudetenland, formerly part of the Austro-Hungarian Empire, had been incorporated into the succession state of Czechoslovakia after the First World War. Leadership of much of the Sudeten German minority had come by the mid-1930s into the hands of Konrad Henlein and his Sudeten German Party, who, under the guise of seeking autonomy, were secretly working under German orders for unification with the Reich. By March 1938, in the hope of causing a crisis, Adolf Hitler instructed Henlein to press for demands that the Czech state could never grant.

Britain did not want war with Germany over distant Czechoslovakia; neither, despite their protestations, did France or the Soviet Union (both of whom had mutual defense treaties with Prague). In May 1938 rumors spread throughout the capitals of Europe that Hitler had lost his patience with the Czechs and meant to invade the Sudetenland. The British, to Hitler's surprise, warned him off, and there was no invasion. In fact, Hitler held his hand not because of the British warning but because he was not ready. Since 1937 German military commanders had been preparing their plans ("Operation Green"), but the army would not be prepared until October 1938. Hitler was certain that under no circumstances would the British and French fight to keep the Sudetenlanders within Czechoslovakia.

By the end of August German-Czech violence flared in the Sudetenland, and German propaganda filled the airwaves and the **press** with further threats. Chamberlain's attempt to negotiate a settlement to the quarrel through an independent British mediator, Lord Runciman, had also failed. Fearing that war was imminent, he took matters into his own hands and conceived his "Plan Z": to fly unannounced to Germany and confront Hitler directly to save the peace. It was quixotic, typical of the abrupt style of the Prime Minister; he had faith, ultimately, in no one but himself and believed only he could prevent war. Though the Czech government had agreed to Sudeten autonomy by this point, this was rejected by Henlein and his Nazi masters. By mid-September the British and French governments had decided that the Czechs must yield the Sudetenland to the Reich if the worst were to be prevented.

Chamberlain obtained an invitation to Hitler's Berchtesgaden retreat (a seven-hour airplane flight followed by a three-hour railway journey for the sixty-nine-year-old Prime Minister). They met on 15 September, and he came away feeling that he and Hitler were in agreement that the areas of 80 percent German population in the Sudetenland would be peacefully transferred to Germany. A second meeting followed in Bad Godesberg one week later, but this time Hitler raised the stakes, demanding that the transfer of the entire Sudetenland be completed by 1 October and that the issue of Polish and Hungarian minorities in eastern Czechoslovakia be dealt with at the same time. The two met the following day and remained deadlocked; as the Czech army was mobilized, even the optimistic Chamberlain thought war could not be avoided.

Chamberlain appealed to Benito Mussolini to use his influence with Hitler to break the deadlock; the Duce (fearful of war himself) did so, convincing Hitler that he would have his way without war. Hitler then invited the leaders to Munich—the Czechs were allowed to come, but they were kept under house arrest in their hotel while the conference was in session—and the result was essentially as Hitler had planned. The Reich received the whole Sudetenland, and Chamberlain dared to believe that he had gained "peace for our time." Czechoslovakia was dismembered as Hitler affirmed that he had no more territorial demands in Europe. Privately he was annoyed that he was denied his war to crush the Czechs.

The following March Hitler violated the Munich agreement by seizing the rest of Czechoslovakia and turned his attention to Poland. The democracies, shocked to reality, abandoned appeasement and reluctantly prepared to stop Hitler. Guarantees were issued by Britain to Poland and the Balkan States, but Hitler refused to believe that Britain and France might actually fight to prevent his plans. He was wrong, as September 1939 proved, but it is understandable that he felt as he did, given the tragedy of Munich.

R.J.Q. Adams

Bibliography

Adams, R.J.Q. *British Politics and Foreign Policy in the Age of Appeasement, 1935–39.* 1992.

Charmley, John. *Chamberlain and the Lost Peace.* 1989.

Gilbert, Martin, and Richard Gott. *The Appeasers.* 1963.

Rock, William R. *British Appeasement in the 1930s.* 1977.

Wheeler-Bennett, John W. *Munich: Prologue to Tragedy.* 1948.

Murdoch, Iris (1919–)

Iris Murdoch, prolific novelist, was born in Dublin of Anglo-Irish parents in 1919. After graduating from the Badminton School in Bristol, she read classics at Somerville College, **Oxford**. During the Second World War she was an Assistant Principal at the Treasury; immediately afterward she did relief work for the **United Nations** in London, Belgium, and Austria. In Brussels, she read Sartre and the French existentialists, and when she returned to England in 1947 she studied philosophy at **Cambridge**. The following year she became a Fellow of St. Anne's College, Oxford, where she remained until 1963. Though Murdoch is best known as a novelist, she has published five philosophical books, ranging from *Sartre: Romantic Rationalist* (1953) to *Metaphysics as a Guide to Morals* (1993). Between 1954 and 1993 she published twenty-five novels; *The Sea, The Sea* won the Booker Prize in 1978; she was awarded the CBE in 1976 and made a DBE in 1987.

The popularity of Murdoch's novels is remarkable because she is a twentieth-century rarity, a philosophical novelist. Although Murdoch says that bad art collaborates with our fantasy mechanisms, offering consolation instead of truth, she sees good art as a model for selfless contemplation of the actual world (*The Fire and the Sun: Why Plato Banished the Artists*, 1977). Her novels reflect the view that the study of literature is "an education in how to picture and understand human situations" (*The Sovereignty of Good*, 1970). They raise issues familiar to moral philosophy: the nature of justice, love, evil, social responsibility; the place of suffering; the possibility of believing in God; the question of how one decides to risk one's life, or sacrifice one's pleasures, for the Good. Indeed, a Platonic vision of the Good as the necessarily fundamental philosophical category dominates her later works. Murdoch's fiction shows us the practical consequences, the human significance, of ideas. Her characters frequently embody a philosophical stance or more loosely conceived set of attitudes; thus Palmer Anderson in *A Severed Head* (1961) not only is a psychoanalyst but shockingly acts out the implications of an uninhibited belief in psychoanalysis. Although Murdoch sometimes illustrates her own beliefs in her fiction, she also tests and even modifies them. In *The Sacred and Profane Love Machine* (1974), for example, she demonstrates the psychological truth of the idea that suffering will not make us virtuous, but she also shows that people who lead happy, comfortable lives can remain children.

In "Against Dryness" (1961) Murdoch praises the nineteenth-century novel, with its broad social scope, its multiple plots and detailed descriptions, partly because it shows the world as offering resistance to the ego, replicating the financial arrangements, emotional entanglements, and sheer accidents that pressure the lives of real people. In contrast, she argued, many twentieth-century novels appear "crystalline," depicting a hero agonizing over radical decisions, apparently free to control his destiny.

As she went on to develop the argument elsewhere, the moral life ought not to consist of such moments of decision, but of attention: By attending to other people, and to the Good, we become humbler, we learn that other people are real, we discover that many choices no longer need to be made, for we are "compelled almost automatically by what we can see."

Murdoch's preference for some of the features of the nineteenth-century novel—though reflected in her own multiple plots, in her occasional didacticism, even in her detailed evocations of, say, a marvelous *cassoulet* in *A Fairly Honourable Defeat* (1970) or the squalid bedroom in which the eponymous hero of *Bruno's Dream* (1969) lies dying—should not blind us to the experimental side of her fiction. Her plots are really parodies of plots, playing with the marriage plot (*A Severed Head*), the Gothic (*The Unicorn*, 1963), the mystery (*The Black Prince*, 1973). In the early books the parody of plot is connected with the way Murdoch's characters engage in a bewildering number of sexual liaisons, both heterosexual and homosexual and occasionally incestuous. In *A Severed Head*, Antonia, a married woman, sleeps with a psychoanalyst who sleeps with his sister, who ends up with Antonia's husband after she has eloped with his brother, the psychiatrist having eloped with Antonia's husband's mistress. Such relationships, and the innumerable accidents and coincidences that always characterize Murdoch's plots, make her realism not a matter of reproducing what is statistically probable, but of reproducing the variety, the unexpectedness, of human experience. Since the late 1970s Murdoch's novels have grown longer, even less firmly anchored in social reality. Reviewers have complained that they need more editing, center too much on the painful love affairs of the upper classes, are too allegorical, and even (surprisingly, since Murdoch continues to reject such traditional religious conceptions as belief in a personal God) too Christian; many women object to her avoidance of female protagonists and narrators who, in Murdoch's view, mark a book as a "woman's novel." Yet many of the characteristic themes and devices remain. In *The Message to the Planet* (1989), as in her first novel, the plot is driven by the protagonist's intense, quasi-romantic admiration for a philosopher whose ideas he pursues even as their author abandons them. Her heroes still share her embattled faith in words and ideas, still look for answers and messages. In the later books, however, the quest is more distinctly metaphysical. Although both *Nuns and Soldiers* (1980) and *The Message to the Planet* offer the familiar Murdoch picture of the contemporary sensualist, comfortably wreaking havoc in other private lives, they also meditate at length on the Holocaust as it is experienced, after the fact and in England, by the son of a Polish emigrant and a contemporary Jewish intellectual. Murdoch continues to present readers with an austere morality and a vision of the human personality so bleak as to recall original sin. Readers who want to see what a brilliant mind, contemplating objects as diverse as Plato's cave and the suitcases at Auschwitz, still makes of the English novel can find no better living writer.

Margaret Scanlan

Bibliography

Bove, Cheryl K. *Understanding Iris Murdoch.* 1993
Byatt, A.S. *Degrees of Freedom: The Novels of Iris Murdoch.* 1965.
Conradi, Peter J. *Iris Murdoch: The Saint and the Artist.* 1986.
Dipple, Elizabeth. *Iris Murdoch: Work for the Spirit.* 1982.
Ramanathan, Suguna. *Iris Murdoch: Figures of Good.* 1990.
Todd, Richard. *Iris Murdoch.* 1984.

Murray, (George) Gilbert (Aimé) (1866–1957)

Gilbert Murray was an eminent scholar and leader of the British internationalist movement. The best-known classicist of his generation, Murray was renowned for verse translations from Greek that were popular on the stage and in books. From the time of the First World War he became deeply committed to the cause of peace and began another highly public career that eventually made him leader of the **League of Nations Union** (LNU) and Chairman of the Committee of Intellectual Cooperation of the **League of Nations**.

Born in **Australia**, the son of a Catholic landowner who died when Murray was seven years old, he was brought to England at the age of eleven. He distinguished himself as a student at **Oxford** for his command of the classics and was appointed Professor of Greek at the University of Glasgow at the age of twenty-

three. Murray married Lady Mary Howard, the daughter of the Earl of Carlisle, in 1889 and went on to become the Regius Professor of Greek at Oxford (1908–36). A celebrity who tried his hand at writing for the stage, he was close to other celebrated figures, including **George Bernard Shaw**, who based characters in *Major Barbara* on Murray and his wife, Mary.

A supporter of British involvement in the **First World War**, he still pressed for reform of the international system to reduce armaments and secure the peace once the war ended. Murray warmly welcomed the creation of the League of Nations, and he served on two League commissions, one on minorities and the other on intellectual cooperation. He represented **South Africa** as a delegate to the Assembly in Geneva, 1921–3. When the League established the Committee of Intellectual Cooperation in 1922 to provide books and periodicals to libraries, Murray became involved. In 1928 he was elected Chairman of this body, a position he held for eight years.

Murray's other contribution to the internationalist cause was his leadership of the League of Nations Union (as Chairman of the Executive Committee, 1923–38, and joint President, 1939–45). The LNU attracted over 1 million members during the inter-war period and exerted influence on foreign policy. It was the main sponsor of the **Peace Ballot** in 1934–5, which polled 11.6 million people on disarmament and resistance to aggression and provided impressive evidence of British public support for the League of Nations.

The outbreak of war in 1939 did not cause Murray to lose faith in internationalism, and in 1945 he became a President of the United Nations Association, a position he held until his death in 1957.

Donald S. Birn

Bibliography

Smith, Jean, and Arnold Toynbee, eds. *Gilbert Murray: An Unfinished Autobiography.* 1960.
Wilson, Duncan. *Gilbert Murray O.M., 1866–1957.* 1987.

Musical Revues

A form of popular theatrical entertainment that consisted of a series of songs, skits, and dances performed by a single company and often revolving around a central theme, the English revue, first devised in the late nineteenth century, came to supplant the music hall tradition in the twentieth.

At the beginning of the century vaudeville and variety shows were well-established forms of popular theatrical entertainment in Europe and the United States. The future of the genre was threatened, however, by the development of film and the widespread introduction of the cinema. By the end of the 1920s when the "talkie" boom was in full swing, there were fewer than a hundred music halls throughout Britain. But as the music halls and variety acts learned to adapt to changing demands, their numbers increased again.

Among the new theatrical developments was the rise of the revue. American follies, a creation of Florenz Ziegfeld, inspired a British version called the "spectacular revue." These elaborate and colorful musical productions were staged at large theaters equipped for their grandeur. At the same time, a new brand of entertainment—the "intimate revue"—established itself in the smaller London theaters. The earliest impresarios of this form of revue were C.B. Cochran and André Charlot, who established regular venues for the genre at the London Pavilion from 1918 to 1931 and the Alhambra Theatre during the same period.

The intimate revue distinguished itself from the spectacular by offering the "intimacies" of revue: a combination of witty words, a variety of moods, quick-fire song and dance, and the popularity of a particular actor or actress. Another key to the intimate revue was a continuity of ideas and the use of a central theme. Herbert Farjeon's *Nine Sharp* used the device of a man fiddling with a radio dial to present a series of theatrical jibes at the **British Broadcasting Corporation** (BBC). Farjeon's revues at the Little Theatre set the standard for intimate revues in the late 1930s. Unlike the manager of the typical vaudeville house whose job was to patch performers' acts together, Farjeon approached the revue as a unified piece of writing—a talent that he shared with his contemporaries Ivor Novello and **Noel Coward**.

Coward's career as the creator of revues began in the early 1920s and reached popular prominence by the end of the decade. The contributions of entertainers like Coward and Joyce Grenfell to the **Entertainments National Service Association** (ENSA) during the Second World War ensured the survival of the English revue into the post-war era. Several intimate revues by Alan Melville offered vehicles for the actresses Hermione Baddeley and Dora Bryan in the early 1950s. Maggie Smith made her London debut in revues of the late 1950s.

In 1961 *Beyond the Fringe*, a satirical revue and product of the Cambridge Footlights Club, met with success on both sides of the Atlantic. Since the 1960s live revue has largely given way to **television** satire, with the exception of occasional stage revues devoted to the lives of specific artists such as Jacques Brel, Noel Coward, and Stephen Sondheim.

Martha A. Schütz

Bibliography

Grenfell, Joyce. *Joyce Grenfell Requests the Pleasure*. 1976.

Hartnoll, Phyllis, ed. *The Oxford Companion to the Theatre*. 1983.

Short, Ernest. *Sixty Years of Theatre*. 1951.

M

Namier, Lewis Bernstein (1888–1960)

Lewis Namier was one of Britain's most renowned historians—a highly creative scholar who gave his name to a school of historians and to a unique research methodology (Namierism), and whose contributions to historical studies have been of lasting consequence.

Born into a **Jewish** family in Polish Russia, Namier was educated privately and, after brief stints at Lvov and Lausanne universities, came to England in 1908 where he spent a year at the **London School of Economics** and subsequently entered Balliol College, **Oxford**. He achieved first-class honors in modern **history** and was co-winner of the Beit Prize in 1913. Offered an appointment by one of his father's business associates, Namier went to the United States in 1913. During the First World War Namier served briefly in the Twentieth Royal Fusiliers and was then transferred to the **Foreign Office** where he worked from 1915 to 1920, first in the **propaganda**, then the political intelligence sectors.

After the war Namier sought financial and professional security in various occupations, ranging from a temporary lectureship at Balliol (1920–1) and work for a Manchester cotton firm to a brief period as a correspondent for the *Manchester Guardian*. Supported ultimately by earnings from journalism, the generosity of friends, and several grants, Namier devoted himself from 1924 to 1929 to full-time historical research, the results of which appeared in two distinguished works, *The Structure of Politics at the Accession of George III* (1929) and its sequel, *England in the Age of the American Revolution* (1930).

Immediately establishing him in the forefront of British historians, these works marked a new stage in the study of eighteenth-century politics, Namier demolishing the long fashionable Whig interpretation of George III as would-be tyrant, denying the reality of two-party conflict by mid-century, playing down the extent of political corruption at the time, and emphasizing the importance of personal ambitions and vested interests in determining men's political actions. Even more influential than his conclusions was Namier's particular historical method: the procedure of structural analysis, a detailed investigation of the inner workings of eighteenth-century government, supported in turn by the technique of prosopography or collective biography. By collecting evidence about the life, career, connections, and behavior of each parliamentary figure, Namier was able to identify and test empirically the factors motivating the political actions of an individual or group. Although he was not as insensitive to the role of principles and ideas as some critics have implied—Namier was well aware of the complex forces influencing men's actions—his reliance on Freudian psychology, combined with a cynical view of human nature, caused him to regard all professions of principle as mere rationalizations of self-interest, thus oversimplifying the complex problem of political motivation.

Although rejecting Judaism early in life, Namier had always been a Jewish nationalist, and his commitment to Zionism intensified during the post-war decade. In 1929 he became Political Secretary to the Jewish Agency for Palestine, a post he quit in 1931 to take up the chair of modern history at the University of Manchester. He held this position until his retirement in 1953. As a professor, Namier was popular and successful, though much of his attention was absorbed during the 1930s in assisting Jewish refugees from Germany fleeing Nazi oppression. In 1939 he was selected as adviser to Chaim Weizmann at the Palestine conference, and during the years 1940–5 he was involved once again with the Jewish Agency. The wartime years intensified his interest in European history, and in 1946 he published *1848: The Revolution of the Intellectuals*, a modified version of his Raleigh Lecture delivered to the British Academy in 1944, the year he was elected a Fellow. It was followed by other writings dealing with the recent world conflict: *Diplomatic Prelude* (1948), based on the notes and recollections of contemporary statesmen, and two volumes of essays on pre-war diplomatic developments—*Europe in Decay* (1950) and *In the Nazi Era* (1952). Like so much of his work, these books were intended as preliminary to a larger enterprise—a full-scale history of modern Europe—which was never completed. In 1951 Namier returned to his primary field of interest—British parliamentary history—devoting the last ten years of his life to editing, with other scholars, three volumes in *The History of Parliament* series, a massive compendium of parliamentary biographies to which he contributed hundreds of entries. He also began a life of Charles Townshend, a work completed by a collaborator and published posthumously in 1964. Namier was knighted in 1952 and became an honorary D.Litt. of Durham (1952), Oxford (1955), and Rome (1956), honorary Litt.D. of Cambridge (1957), and honorary D.C.L. of Oxford (1960).

Few historians have been as influential as Namier in making the historical discipline what it is today. In no case is a knowledge of the historian's life more essential to the understanding of his work than it is in Namier's. The paradoxes of the man parallel a life that began with a childhood ordeal and never strayed far from the brink of mental disorder. Registered at birth as a Jew, only to be shielded from any knowledge of his cultural background until the age of ten, the future historian became an Anglican. The scholar who, denying the role of abstract ideas in history, removed mind from the historical universe, himself reflected many of the intellectual tendencies of his time. A convinced skeptic, he routinely leaned on the dubious science of graphology to analyze the handwriting of long-dead members of Parliament. Often perceived as idolizing the leisured gentry, he had become a Fabian socialist as early as 1916. Often deplored as a practitioner of the narrow-

est kind of history, he anticipated econometric historiography, as well as later interest in such topics as patronage. Neurotic and abrasive, plagued by insomnia and recurrent ill health, Namier inspired more respect than affection, and his scholarly reputation, which peaked during his lifetime, has not survived the vagaries of historical fashion untarnished.

Karl W. Schweizer
Charles Krantz

Bibliography

Colley, Linda. *Namier*. 1989.
Namier, Julia. *Lewis Namier: A Biography*. 1971.
Rose, Norman. *Lewis Namier and Zionism*. 1980.

Nash, Paul (1889–1946)

As one of the outstanding landscape painters in twentieth-century Britain, Paul Nash fulfilled a pivotal role in the history of English art during the 1930s and 1940s. His work embodies a characteristic "Englishness" in its almost exclusive insistence on depicting favorite sites in the southern counties, while at the same time it assimilated influences from the contemporary avant-garde from across the channel.

Nash's earliest sketches established a set of fundamental themes and strategies that were to nourish his output for the rest of his career. His drawings of childhood haunts already typify an approach in which crisp, dry strokes delineate wooded settings that seem to secrete an unnamed emotionality and create an effect of preternatural clarity.

Nash came to public notice with the startling pictures produced during his brief assignment as an official war artist at the Western Front in 1917. While the large oil painting *The Menin Road* (1918–19)—completed after the armistice and housed in the Imperial War Museum in London—shows infantrymen stumbling across a landscape of dead trees, mud, and shell craters, the bulk of Nash's war scenes are empty of human presence, the spectacle of nature grotesquely ravaged serving as a sufficient metaphor for the dehumanizing horror of modern warfare.

Back in England, Nash suffered a collapse, in part due to the strains of his frontline experience, and spent months recuperating at Dymchurch in Kent. Here he developed a most austere style, expelling all allusion to human figures and accentuating the symmetries of sea-wall, breakwaters, and skyline. One master-piece from this period (begun in 1925, though completed only in 1937) is *Winter Sea*, the all but monochrome depiction of stylized waves folding within an icy darkness onto a frozen shore. The bleakness of the image is redolent of psychic trauma but also reflects Nash's conscious interest in the geometric or non-organic aspects of the Constructivist style that his friends **Ben Nicholson**, the painter, and **Barbara Hepworth**, the sculptor, had already adopted. Nash's affinity with this clean-cut and essentially abstract aesthetic inspired him to set up an artistic circle called Unit One, which lasted just long enough to give rise to a group show and a collective album edited by **Herbert Read** in 1934.

Using a camera his wife had given him just before they left on a 1931 trip to the United States, Nash had begun experimenting with photography, characteristically avoiding his shipboard companions in favor of carefully framed shots of masts, rails, and life belts, elements congruent with the orderly aesthetic of Constructivism. In subsequent years Nash would use his photos both as blueprints for paintings and as a documentary resource—for instance, the *Dorset Shell Guide* (1936), Nash's act of homage to a beloved county, is illustrated with several photos of his favorite places.

Just when Nash's style was veering toward abstraction, he was intrigued and seduced by a very different impulse in Continental art, that of surrealism. Though reluctant to voice whole-hearted allegiance, Nash was an impressive participant at the International Surreal-ist Exhibition that Read and Roland Penrose mounted in London in 1936; that such canvases as *Harbour and Room* (1936) held their own alongside the provocative imagery of Continen-tal practitioners like Giorgio de Chirico and René Magritte explains Nash's international standing within surrealism—though this did not prevent him sharing a show in 1943 with Hepworth, an unashamed partisan of pure form. Essentially, Nash's style arose from the confluence of two major currents of avant-garde innovation during the inter-war years.

Yet if Nash enjoyed toying with abstrac-tions and dreams of foreign derivation, he could never finally bring himself to abandon explicit reference to the natural shapes of the places he loved. What makes his paintings so memorable is the controlled disposition across the canvas of such motifs as fences, hills, and copses, seem-ingly commonplace features of the actual coun-tryside that, through poetic suggestion, become compelling emblems of the visionary and point-ers to a kind of metaphysical order. A major instance of Nash's deepening interest in the in-visible resonances of landscape is the oil *Land-scape from a Dream* (1936–8), which persuades the viewer that an identifiable tract of the Dor-set coast might quite reasonably become the site of a magical ritual wherein a dark, brooding hawk—arguably a symbol of the artist as one who seeks to possess the earth from an aerial vantage-point—contemplates its own image in a mirror in whose unreal depths are discerned the reflections of a soaring bird and a sinking scarlet sun—allusions that bring together inti-mations of death and transcendence.

In 1940 Nash was able once again to ne-gotiate an appointment as official war artist and this time visited airfields and a wreckage dump near Oxford with camera and sketchpad; his tabulations of flying bombers and monstrous wrecks led to such masterpieces as the huge *Battle of Britain* (1941), which celebrates the victory of the **Royal Air Force** over the Luftwaffe in a breathtaking skyscape full of convoluted trails of white smoke, and the hor-rifying *Totes Meer (Dead Sea)* (1940–1), in which crashed aircraft lie inert beneath a spec-tral moon, as in some otherworldly graveyard for slaughtered birds.

Some of Nash's most hypnotic images emerged in the last few years of his life when, as an invalid slowly succumbing to chronic asthma, he spent hours sketching from inside a motorcar at favorite sites like the Avebury Circles or from a hotel balcony with a view to the Malvern Hills. The majestic climax of his career is a cycle of late oil paintings based on the view from a friend's garden near Oxford from that he could just make out the distant Wittenham Clumps, those wooded hilltops that had been almost his first outdoor subject. Steeped in cultural and personal associations as both the site of archaic burial rites and in a sense the locale of Nash's own artistic birth, the Clumps, as evoked in such a late and poignant oil as *Landscape of the Vernal Equinox* (1944), became a magnetic focal point for the viewer, whose eye grazes across the surfaces of wood-land forms transmuted by the soft hues and graceful lighting of a master of atmospheric effect. These panoramas set the seal on Nash's achievement as an illustrator and transformer of the English landscape, being images both of an actual view and of a transfigured or surreal version thereof, one that secretes a lifetime's fund of meditations upon the poetry of places.

Roger Cardinal

Bibliography

Bertram, Anthony. *Paul Nash: The Portrait of an Artist*. 1955.

Cardinal, Roger. *The Landscape Vision of Paul Nash*. 1989.

Causey, Andrew. *Paul Nash*. 1980.

Colvin, Clare. *Paul Nash. Places*. 1989.

Nash, Paul. *Outline: An Autobiography and Other Writings*. 1949.

Nation (1907–1931)

After purchasing the faltering *Speaker* in 1906, the Rowntree Social Service Trust employed the advanced Liberal journalist **H.W. Massingham** as editor to transform the weekly into the *Nation*, which was launched on 1 March 1907. Comprehensive, innovative, and lively, the *Nation* was produced by Massingham and a small brilliant staff that included **J.L. Hammond**, L.T. Hobhouse, F.W. Hirst, **Lytton Strachey**, Desmond McCarthy, Holbrook Jackson, **H.N. Brailsford**, H.W. Nevinson, **Arnold Bennett**, and **George Bernard Shaw**. Indeed, under Massingham, the *Nation* became an important medium for many British men of letters during the first third of the twentieth century. Nevertheless, although the circulation of the paper rose to 5,000 by 1909, its financial condition remained precarious, and it was kept afloat only by subsidies from the Rowntree Trust. Massingham's independence, advanced views, and role as an impartial critic of the major political parties (especially on foreign policy and naval expansion before 1914) merited great respect but prejudiced the *Nation*'s circulation and revenues. The paper also extolled peace initiatives, condemned jingoism, opposed large armament expenditures, supported **women's suffrage**, and urged social reform on the **Liberal Party**.

During the **First World War**, the *Nation* advocated the right of the press to "fair criticism" of the government and endeavored to provide objective reporting of the news. Inevitably, the paper ran foul of the government by opposing **conscription** and by criticizing the authoritarianism of **David Lloyd George** and the War **Cabinet**. And, as the war became a bloody stalemate, the *Nation* called for a negotiated peace. After failing to persuade the Rowntree Trust to restrain the paper, Lloyd George attempted to silence the *Nation* in March 1917 by prohibiting its foreign circulation on the grounds that it was providing **propaganda** for the enemy. But the ban provoked an uproar in Parliament that constrained Lloyd George to rescind it in mid-October. A major result of the *Nation*'s uncompromising independence, role as a forum of dissent, and demands for ending the war was a temporary surge in its circulation to approximately 11,000. What also increased the popularity of the paper was its enthusiastic advocacy of President Woodrow Wilson's Fourteen Points and a **League of Nations** as "the future safeguard of civilisation." However, after the war, the *Nation* continued its vendetta against Lloyd George and the coalition government and, despairing of the fractured Liberal Party, shifted its loyalties to the rising **Labour Party**.

During the immediate post-war years, the quality of the *Nation*'s staff was enhanced by the work of such able assistant editors as H.M. Tomlinson, Gertrude M. Cross, and **Leonard Woolf**, and the paper was enriched by the literary talents of Edmund Blunden, J. Middleton Murry, Frank Swinnerton, **Aldous Huxley**, Osbert Sitwell, **Bertrand Russell**, **Harold Laski**, and **G.D.H. Cole**. In early 1922 the Rowntree Trust merged the venerable *Atheneum* with the *Nation* and supported the paper's unrelenting criticism of British intervention in Russia and its advocacy of recognition of the Soviet regime, Irish independence, home rule for India, and the **nationalization** of the **coal industry**.

Worn out by hard work and the persistent financial troubles plaguing the paper, as a result of its declining circulation and advertising revenues and mounting costs of production, Massingham resigned as editor in April 1923. He had implemented the Rowntree Trust's drastic economies, but the paper continued to lose ground and, when the Trust rejected his proposals to increase the *Nation*'s popular appeal, Massingham gave up, most of the staff leaving with him. He continued to contribute articles to the paper until his death in August 1924.

Massingham's successor, H.D. Henderson, ably edited the *Nation and Atheneum* from 1923 to 1930, when he was succeeded by its last editor, the less able Harold Wright. Neither Henderson nor Wright could resuscitate the paper, which continued to decline until it was merged with the *New Statesman* in 1931. It was the demise of an outstanding weekly journal that had outlived its usefulness.

J.O. Baylen

Bibliography

Havighurst, Alfred F. *Radical Journalist: H.W. Massingham, 1860–1924.* 1974.

Koss, Stephen. *The Rise and Fall of the Political Press in Britain.* vol. 2: *The Twentieth Century.* 1984.

National Front

Dating from before the **Second World War**, there have been two principal traditions within the British extreme Right, identified by continuities both of ideology and of some personnel. One tradition derives from the Imperial Fascist League (IFL) of Arnold Leese (1878–1956), and the other from the British Union of Fascists (BUF) of Sir **Oswald Mosley** (1896–1980). Although the latter was the more important during the 1930s, the former tradition has dominated extreme Right politics in Great Britain during most of the period since 1945. The National Front (NF), brought together in late 1966 and early 1967 as an amalgamation of several earlier extreme Right and racist organizations, was a political party in the tradition of the IFL, especially when later in 1967 John Tyndall (1934–) and Martin Webster (1943–) managed to insinuate themselves into the leadership after moving from a self-avowedly neo-Nazi group despite the intentions of the NF's original founders to exclude them. By 1972, as the NF entered its most significant period, Tyndall was its Chairman and Webster, as National Activities Organizer, his deputy.

The NF was able to take advantage of the increasing public hostility during the 1960s to the presence of Afro-Caribbean and Asian immigrant settlers from the former British Empire, hostility that was also articulated by mainstream politicians such as the Conservative MP Enoch Powell. The NF's halcyon period, however, was from 1972 to 1977. Because of the first-past-the-post electoral system, it never came close to winning a seat in the House of Commons, but it was seen as a significant force especially in parts of **London** (most noticeably the East End, where there has been an intermittent tradition of extreme Right support throughout the twentieth century), the West Midlands, the city of Leicester and its environs, some of the northern textile towns in Lancashire and Yorkshire (such as Preston, Blackburn, and Bradford), and some of the **New Towns** around London inhabited largely by former Londoners. Although the NF made no electoral gains, it was securing sufficient votes in local elections in these places during the mid-1970s to trouble the major political parties.

It retained among its politicized and activist elite the conventional **anti-Semitism** of the extreme Right, but its more populist appeal was based on hostility to immigrants and on a demand for the repatriation of them and their descendants to their country of origin. Its emphasis on **immigration** set a political agenda that the **Conservative Party** was able to accept, albeit in a less extreme form.

In the mid-1970s the party survived a major split that produced the short-lived National Party, which did manage briefly to have two councilors on the District Council of Blackburn in Lancashire. The NF's unexpectedly poor performance in the 1978 local elections, especially those for the London borough councils (for which it had extended candidate coverage, particularly in the east and northeast London boroughs) showed that support had declined from a peak in 1976 and early 1977. Harassed by critical publicity about its leadership, increasingly the object of the attentions of an active anti-Fascist movement from late 1977, and with its principal policy issue taken over (albeit in a muted version) by the Conservative Party, the NF's decline accelerated. In the May 1979 general election it managed to run 303 candidates, but they averaged only 1.3 percent of votes cast in their contests.

After this major setback the NF experienced considerable internal turmoil. Several splinter groups broke away but in most cases were short-lived. Principal figures in the 1970s leadership, notably Webster and Tyndall, were marginalized or felt obliged to resign. Tyndall left the party in June 1980 and in April 1982 founded a British National Party (BNP), the fourth extreme Right party to bear this name. For several years it survived only in the political wilderness, but it has seen some slight local revivals since 1990, partly in light of the extreme Right resurgence across much of Western Europe. Throughout the late 1970s and 1980s, the NF was symbolically attractive to certain sections of urban white working-class male youth; for example, the party particularly focused upon mobilizing support among selected groups of **football** supporters, and certain clubs became notorious for their supporters' racist chanting at **Black** players.

In the 1983 general election the NF managed only 1.0 percent of votes cast in sixty seats fought. This setback was the occasion for a further split. One group to emerge from this became increasingly exclusive, rejected electoral participation, and flirted with ideological positions borrowed from Italian neo-Fascist terrorism; in 1991 it disbanded as a claimant to the NF name and formed a self-consciously exclusive grouping from a small number of dedicated activists. The other product of the mid-1980s split has had a checkered existence since then. It was able to offer only a single candidate in the 1987 election; in 1992 it fought fourteen constituencies, averaging merely 0.7 percent of votes cast.

The NF has been the most important component of post-war extreme Right politics in Great Britain. However, by the 1990s, associated with individuals having no public credibility or recognition, it seems most unlikely to be able to participate in any revival of the extreme Right, despite the political resonance on its name. The vanguard role in the extreme Right movement, such as it is, has passed to other groupings, especially the BNP.

Christopher T. Husbands

Bibliography

Husbands, Christopher T. "Extreme Right-wing Politics in Great Britain: The Recent Marginalisation of the National Front," *West European Politics*, vol. 11 (1988), pp. 65–79.

———. *Racial Exclusionism and the City: The Urban Support of the National Front.* 1983.

Taylor, Stan. *The National Front in English Politics.* 1982.

Thurlow, Richard. *Fascism in Britain: A History, 1918–1985.* 1987.

National Health Service

The National Health Service (NHS), established on 5 July 1948, made available to the entire population a comprehensive system of health care, free at time of use and funded overwhelmingly out of taxation.

Prior to the NHS, health care in Britain had been provided by a rather confused patchwork of services that had grown up in a piecemeal and uncoordinated fashion. **Public health** legislation had been put in place over the course of the nineteenth century, with the 1875 Public Health Act the zenith of the "environmental sanitation" movement. At the beginning of the twentieth century there were three major kinds of hospital: the voluntary (supported by a combination of public donations, income from endowments, and charges to patients), those run by the Poor Law (which were generally lower in quality), and municipal hospitals run by local authorities. Doctors tended to be either general practitioners (GPs) or consultants. The former served local communities and worked in Poor Law hospitals and received their income from fees to patients; the latter worked part of their time in the teaching hospitals and earned large incomes from treating wealthy patients in their private practices.

The British health care system of the early twentieth century was thus a highly market-oriented one. Collectivist provision existed only in the Poor Law medical service (for the destitute), in trade union medical benefit societies, friendly societies (which covered only the skilled minority of workers), and in a few company medical schemes. Two problems were particularly evident: the geographical maldistribution of doctors and **hospitals** (both of which tended to gravitate toward wealthy areas), and marked differentials in health status between social classes. Wide extremes existed within the medical profession: Even in the 1930s, a low-paid doctor might earn £600 per annum, while a Harley Street specialist could charge 100 guineas (£105) for one operation. These differences in income symbolized marked differences in quality of care offered.

In the early 1900s there were increasingly clamorous demands from socialists for a state medical service. Some interest was also shown by the British Medical Association, in its *Report on Contract Practice* (1905). An important early milestone was the 1911 National Insurance Act, which introduced National Health Insurance (NHI) coverage for 14 million men and women wage earners between sixteen and seventy years of age. In return for small weekly contributions from employee, employer, and the state, those earning less than £160 per annum (raised to £250 per annum in 1920) were provided with the free services of a GP, sickness benefit (followed, if necessary, by disability benefit), treatment for **tuberculosis**, and maternity benefit. The scheme was very limited, and indeed was seen by its originator, **David Lloyd George**, as no more than an "ambulance wagon." It had two major defects: the lack of coverage for the dependents of an insured person (which left working-class wives and children outside the scheme), and failure to provide access to specialist treatment (which left many life-threatening diseases untreated). Nonetheless, the 1911 health insurance scheme was a significant incursion by the state into the provision of health care.

In the 1920s and 1930s there was a steadily developing consensus, to which many sections of the political spectrum subscribed, on the need for some sort of state medical service. In 1919 the Ministry of Health was established. The 1926 report of the Royal Commission on National Health Insurance suggested that the ultimate solution should be a health care system funded principally by taxation rather than by extensions of NHI. In 1930 the British Medical Association published its report on *A General Medical Service for the Nation*, which suggested a service based on the extension of NHI coverage to wives and dependents and others of similar income status (such as the self-employed). However, within this apparent consensus, there were marked divisions over precisely what form a state medical service should take. A few radicals (represented, for example, by the Socialist Medical Association) wished to see the total abolition of private medicine, with complete hospital nationalization and all doctors employed by the state; at the other end of the political spectrum, Conservative opinion favored as large a private sector as possible, and any future state service limited in coverage. The GPs wanted a service based upon the extension of NHI and some access to specialist treatment; above all, they feared the prospect of becoming a "salaried service" in which they would have to work under the direction of central planners. The Poor Law hospitals had been taken over by the local authorities in 1929 and were thus vulnerable to **nationalization**; but, being of inferior status, they would have provided an inadequate basis for a fully comprehensive health service. The voluntary hospitals were in a stronger bargaining position, but their financial basis was weak. Lastly, no state health service would have been able to operate effectively without the full participation of the consultants. The irony was, therefore, that this most conservative group within the **medical profession** knew that they possessed considerable bargaining power in any

negotiations and thus were less afraid of state medicine than were many GPs. Substantial differences of viewpoint existed over such key questions as the role of private medicine, the extent of hospital nationalization, the degree of state control over doctors' clinical freedom, and the basis upon which any new service would be funded.

In effect, the logjam of disagreement in the late 1930s was broken by the **Second World War**. First, the Emergency Medical Service, set up in 1938 and implemented at the start of the war, achieved at a stroke the nationalization of hospitals and the coordination of other sectors. Second, the temporary radicalism of the early war years led to demands for a post-war **welfare state**, the centerpiece of which would be a National Health Service. Third, the peculiar political circumstances of wartime produced a landslide victory for the **Labour Party** in the 1945 general election. While it is likely that a post-war Conservative government would have introduced some kind of NHS, Labour's victory (and the appointment of **Aneurin Bevan** as Minister of Health) made it certain that the service would be universal, comprehensive, and tax-funded. These principles were embodied in the 1946 National Health Service Act, and—after some rather tortuous negotiations with the doctors—the NHS was launched two years later.

The new NHS was based on a tripartite administrative structure: hospitals; primary health care (for example, GPs and dentists); and the local authority services (such as the school medical service). Private medicine continued for those who wished to pay for it: This was part of Bevan's "deal" to win the support of the consultants and was seen by many as a right. In no way did planners of the new National Health Service imagine that its introduction would usher in a revolution in medicine. Essentially, its aims were threefold: to remove the barrier of cost at time of treatment; to open up access to comprehensive and specialist treatment for those hitherto excluded (notably, working-class women and children); and to enable rational planning under democratic control.

The progress of the NHS in its first twenty years was relatively tranquil. The main area of controversy was over its funding. Very soon after its establishment, there was concern that the overall cost was rising too rapidly; from certain quarters came the argument that a "free-at-time-of-use" health care system encouraged consumer irresponsibility. It was in partial response to these concerns, plus overall budgetary constraints, that the Labour government introduced the first round of NHS charges in 1951. These concerns also led to the appointment of the Guillebaud Committee on the cost of the NHS, which reported in 1956 and showed that, first, expenditure on the NHS was not rising as a proportion of GNP, and, second, that abuse by the public was not a major problem. Instead, it found, the NHS was having to deal with wage and salary claims, the rising cost of goods and services, and increased demands consequent upon the **ageing** of the population.

Nevertheless, the question of how demands should be fairly and efficiently rationed in a state service like the NHS was one that came under considerable scrutiny in the 1970s. Health economists began to examine all of the economic and behavioral variables that could affect clinical judgments: the decision whether to treat a patient in the hospital was the most important factor determining the level of health expenditure. Through rationing devices at micro-level, such as "clinical budgeting," attempts were made to improve the prioritizing of scarce resources.

Another related problem discussed in the 1970s was the geographical maldistribution of health care resources. This had been a feature of the pre-NHS system, and by the 1970s little seemed to have changed. Regions that had been poorly endowed with hospital resources in the late 1930s were in an identical relative position in the 1970s. To address this problem, a Resource Allocation Working Party was set up. Its 1976 report recommended a slow reallocation of hospital resources from rich to poor regions, and this was implemented.

The election of a Conservative government in 1979 seemed to portend a large-scale privatization of the NHS, but this did not happen. Health expenditure was constrained, as part of tight controls on overall public spending, but the NHS survived intact, although private medicine continued to grow steadily. In 1955 a mere 585,000 people had been covered by private medical insurance; by 1984 this figure had risen to 5.1 million. By the 1990s, however, major changes in health policy were underway. The 1990 National Health Service and Community Care Act introduced three major reforms. First, NHS hospitals were to be allowed to "opt out" of direct NHS control and enjoy quasi-autonomous status as "trust hospitals";

they were to take on a new role as providers of health care, negotiating competitive contracts for patient treatment with health authorities. By introducing an "internal market" discipline into the NHS and infusing health care providers with more of a business ethos, the government hoped to improve efficiency. Second, GPs were to manage their budgets more independently, becoming "fund-holding" practices. The third was perhaps the least-controversial change, since it represented the culmination of a series of efforts in this direction since the 1970s: Clinical audit was to be applied to more areas of health care provision, in order to monitor the unit cost of such services. Taken together, all of these reforms were controversial: Their supporters argued that they would, at long last, bring the discipline of the market into a state monopoly; their critics argued that they were designed to achieve the eventual privatization of the NHS. Thus as the NHS moved into the 1990s, it was the center of more controversy than at any time in its history.

John Macnicol

Bibliography

Allsop, Judith. *Health Policy and the National Health Service.* 1984.

Klein, Rudolf. *The Politics of the National Health Service.* 2nd ed. 1989.

Navarro, Vincente. *Class Struggle, the State, and Medicine.* 1978.

Pater, John E. *The Making of the National Health Service.* 1981.

Webster, Charles. *The Health Services since the War.* vol. 1: *Problems of Health Care: The National Health Service before 1957.* 1988.

National Theatre

The (Royal) National Theatre is a London-based institutional theater company, first proposed by the eighteenth-century actor David Garrick, championed in the nineteenth century by Henry Irving, and fruitlessly promoted during a campaign initiated in 1904 by the critic William Archer and the dramatist Harley Granville-Barker. There followed the laying of foundation stones on two separate sites in 1938 and 1951 (at the time of the **Festival of Britain**), but it was not until 1963 that a company was created. It moved into the **Old Vic** (in many ways its progenitor) as a temporary home while a permanent, purpose-built National Theatre was erected on yet a third site, on the South Bank of the Thames.

The first directorial team, under the actor-management of Sir **Laurence Olivier**, was largely recruited from the innovative Royal Court Theatre, with the addition of the critic Kenneth Tynan, whose presence as "dramaturg" proved a useful irritant and creative catalyst. That the **Royal Shakespeare Company** (RSC) already existed as a nationally subsidized institution with primary responsibility for the Shakespearean repertoire enabled the National Theatre (NT) to draw from the first on a wider range of plays, and the company's early years at the Old Vic proved a vintage period.

In their choice of new plays the directors avoided poaching from the commercial sector by preferring to stage works that required elaborate technical and casting resources, such as Peter Shaffer's ambitious epic *The Royal Hunt of the Sun*, or to take risks on then-unknown writers, as with **Tom Stoppard's** *Rosencrantz and Guildenstern Are Dead*—in both cases winning the extended loyalty of the dramatists concerned. Performances by Olivier ranged from a controversial Othello and Shylock, to Restoration comedy, Strindberg, and his final role as the aging Trotskyite in Trevor Griffiths' *The Party*. The company also helped develop younger acting talent, including, among others, Frank Finlay, Anthony Hopkins, Derek Jacobi, Maggie Smith, and Robert Stephens.

In 1973 the artistic directorship passed from Olivier to Peter Hall. In 1976 the company moved to the new National Theatre, designed by Denys Lasdun to offer three contrasting stage options—a traditional proscenium-arched Lyttelton, a fan-shaped openstage Olivier, and the smaller, but flexible, rectangular box of the Cottesloe—all housed within an interconnecting outer shell of foyers, restaurants, bookstalls, and advanced backstage facilities.

Hall's directorial tenure was dogged by controversy, with his own former company, the RSC, seeming to produce better work on a tighter budget. Despite the defection of Jonathan Miller and **Harold Pinter** from his team, Hall did succeed in breaking in theater spaces that had at first seemed technologically forbidding to actors and somewhat unyielding to audiences. He also continued to cultivate new and experimental writers, such as Howard Brenton and David Hare, and to take on the challenge of larger spaces and of audiences drawn from a mixture of genuine enthusiasts, school parties, foreign tourists, and businesspeople dispensing cultural hospitality.

Among other directors of this period, Bill Bryden inaugurated a series of "promenade" productions at the Cottesloe, while Peter Gill encouraged a wide range of young writers with studio productions based at the Old Vic. The larger stages at this time usually operated with their own companies under their own directors, who included Ian McKellen and Mike Alfreds. Successes included some spectacular revivals from the neglected Jacobean repertoire and productions of American plays by writers as far apart in age and temperament as Arthur Miller, Tennessee Williams, and David Mamet. Commercially viable productions often transferred to the West End, as financial considerations predominated over imaginative repertory building.

In 1986 Richard Eyre was named as Hall's successor, and one of his most promising appointments was of a director with special responsibility for receiving leading foreign companies. Generally, Eyre has kept a looser rein on a company now settling into middle age, made enforcedly "safer" in its choices by continuing economic constraints, although this has not silenced complaints that the NT remains better endowed relative to its output than most.

Simon Trussler

Bibliography
Elsom, John, and Nicholas Tomalin. *The History of the National Theatre.* 1978.
Whitworth, Geoffrey. *The Making of a National Theatre.* 1951.

National Trust
The National Trust for Places of Historic Interest or Natural Beauty is a private charity dedicated to the preservation of buildings and landscape of special aesthetic or historic interest. Its ambit covers England and Wales only; there is a separate, much smaller Trust for Scotland. Though not a branch of government, the National Trust was from its early days recognized as the principal repository for land that government was not able or willing to acquire for itself. For this reason, Parliament endowed the Trust with tax exemptions, statutory powers, and special responsibilities that helped it grow over the course of the century into the largest nongovernmental landowner and the largest membership organization in the country.

NATIONAL TRUST 555

The Trust was founded in 1895 by a quartet of liberal philanthropists: the great land-owning first Duke of Westminster, the social reformer Octavia Hill, Sir Robert Hunter, a lawyer with a longstanding interest in the preservation of open spaces, and Canon H.D. Rawnsley, a crusading Lake District clergyman. All had long histories of concern for the deteriorating spiritual as well as material condition of the urban masses and a conviction that exposure to natural beauty could serve as an antidote to both. The respectability of its founders and the careful distance it kept from party politics earned the Trust many bequests of land and money. By 1924 it had acquired over a hundred properties, especially in the Lake District and parts of Surrey threatened by **London**'s expansion.

Though historic buildings figured in the Trust's founding charter, only a few were acquired in these early years, mostly medieval relics recommended by the associated Society for the Protection of Ancient Buildings. But in the 1930s the more aristocratic section of the Trust's membership began to look to the Trust to take over some of the great **country houses** whose survival was threatened by agricultural decline after the First World War. Lords Zetland, Esher, and Lothian masterminded the establishment of a country-houses scheme in 1936. With the way smoothed by parliamentary legislation in 1937 and 1939, the Trust was able to acquire many of the greatest houses, especially after the Second World War when owners were under financial pressure. Many of these acquisitions were secured by James Lees-Milne, the scheme's Secretary until 1951.

Although the Trust's holdings of open space continued to grow unabated, the country-houses scheme wrought considerable changes. The Trust acquired with its houses much agricultural land meant to be worked commercially: 85,000 acres by 1958. It sought to become a model landlord as well as a nature conserver and countryside advocate. Its leadership became more aristocratic. Somewhat paradoxically, its membership also began to grow more quickly, as country-house tourism took off in the 1950s and the Trust subscription (giving free entrance to all properties) looked a bargain. Before the war the Trust had been the property of a small handful; by 1960 it had 100,000 members. This growth, coupled with the enhanced environmental consciousness of the decade, stirred up division over the Trust's iden-

tity in the 1960s. Agriculture, conservation, and tourism made uneasy bedfellows. The Trust's properties had also expanded to include everything from palaces to canals, gardens to working mills. A major appeal was made from 1963 to fund purchases of unspoiled coastline threatened by development ("Enterprise Neptune"). A feeling that the Trust's oligarchic leadership was not well-suited to managing this diverse national collection in a modern, accessible way culminated in an Extraordinary General Meeting in 1967. The leadership resisted this challenge but gradually reformed itself and paved the way for a rapid professionalization of the Trust's publicity and management. The new corporate style ushered in a period of spectacular membership growth, from 250,000 in 1971 to 2 million in 1990. Commercial activities swelled the Trust's coffers further: Center-city boutiques sold crafts and interior decorations, and publishing ventures catered to the country-house craze. Properties amounted to over half a million acres, including one-third of the coastline designated of "heritage" value by the government. Visitors to houses and **gardens** alone topped 10 million a year. Schoolchildren and community groups were offered educational and cultural services. Having fended off the charge of snobbery and exclusiveness in the 1960s, the Trust found itself in the 1980s still considered too "heritage"-minded by critics of the Left, but now also too socialist and bureaucratic by critics of the Right.

Peter Mandler

Bibliography
Gaze, John. *Figures in a Landscape: A History of the National Trust.* 1988.

Hewison, Robert. *The Heritage Industry: Britain in a Climate of Decline.* 1987.

National Union of Mineworkers (NUM)

The NUM dates from January 1945, succeeding the earlier **Miners Federation of Great Britain** (MFGB), formed in 1889. At its peak the MFGB had organized over a million miners, but the subsequent decline of the industry combined with shattering defeats in 1921 and 1926 to reduce membership substantially.

The federal structure of the older organization left its mark on the NUM. The new union represented a compromise between advocates of a genuinely national union and those who felt the need to protect local interests. The constituent unions of the MFGB became Areas of the NUM but retained much of their old power. Most of the NUM's full-time officials were employed in the Areas; often their bureaucracies and financial resources were extensive. The NUM had just two full-time national officials—a President and a General Secretary.

For several years this potentially divisive structure maintained its cohesion. The NUM was controlled by a right-wing **Labour** faction based on the coalfields of northeastern England, Yorkshire, Nottinghamshire, and Lancashire. A left-wing, frequently **Communist**, minority was centered in Scotland and South Wales. The majority faction's control was strengthened by the miners' post-war experiences. The Labour government brought the mines into public ownership as of 1 January 1947. The longstanding hostilities between union and mine owners ended; the NUM's status was enhanced, and buoyant demand for coal protected employment.

This security began to disintegrate in the late 1950s, when cheap oil supplies and changed energy demand meant widespread pit closures, especially in Scotland, South Wales, the northeast, and Lancashire. Miners' wages showed a relative decline, and the hope that a Labour government would reverse the trend proved illusory after 1964. The old NUM leadership became discredited, and a more militant response began to develop.

Even at the height of the Cold War, the Left had had some strength in the NUM. Successive Communists had been elected to the General Secretary post in 1946 and in 1959 and had worked harmoniously with the dominant faction. In the late 1960s and early 1970s the Left expanded its influence, eventually gaining control of the large Yorkshire coalfield. In 1972 the NUM embarked on its first national stoppage since 1926. A mid-winter strike revealed the vulnerability of the electricity industry to any withholding of coal supplies. A heavy blow was inflicted on the credibility of the **Heath** government. Two years later the battle was repeated; this time the **Conservative** government called an election but lost very narrowly. The myth that the NUM had brought down a government was born.

The stoppages were over wages. Mechanization had led in 1966 to the negotiation of the National Power Loading Agreement (NPLA). This aimed to gradually equalize wages for mineface workers, whose earnings had hitherto varied between coalfields. The result was to generalize discontent and to provide a solid basis for national **strikes**. These industrial victories were claimed by the Left as demonstrating the value of a more militant strategy. Yet from 1971 the NUM President was Joe Gormley, a man of the Right who successfully rode the tide of militancy.

From 1974 Gormley used his machiavellian skills to avoid embarrassing a Labour government tenuously clinging to office and facing economic difficulties. His efforts culminated late in 1977 in the destruction of the NPLA; its replacement by local productivity schemes ended one basis for national action. Relationships between Left and Right became increasingly bitter with accusations of procedural malpractice.

The ballot for Gormley's successor late in 1981 produced an easy victory for the Left's standard-bearer, Arthur Scargill. The central figure in the Left's advance in Yorkshire, he secured over 70 percent of the vote. With the once-dominant Right faction thoroughly demoralized, the Left effectively controlled the NUM. But the **Thatcher** government was unsympathetic to the public sector and hostile to the unions; more symbolically there was perhaps a need to reverse union successes in 1972 and 1974. A sizable contraction of the industry was signaled by the appointment of Ian MacGregor as Chairman of the National Coal Board in the summer of 1983.

NUM members in the early 1980s proved repeatedly unwilling to vote for strike action on either wages or closures. There were clear divergences of interest between more and less profitable Areas. Eventually the Left leadership endorsed the so-called domino strategy to avoid holding a national strike ballot. Each Area would call a strike and cumulatively there would be a stoppage. The tactic was employed in March 1984 and met with mixed success. Coalfields with fears of redundancies or strong Left leaderships struck; a minority of miners, especially in the Midlands, were reluctant or hostile. Among strikers, there was principled, solid, often moving commitment to the NUM. The government and the police responded with authoritarian measures; much of the media were hostile to the NUM and especially to Scargill. Some unions gave sympathetic support; others proved unable or unwilling.

The strikers' resistance was heroic but eventually unavailing. From November 1984 increasing numbers returned to work, and in March 1985, after almost a year, the stoppage ended without an agreement. The consequences for the NUM have been disastrous. A breakaway Union of Democratic Mineworkers emerged based largely in Nottinghamshire, the stronghold of the anti-strikers. The industry has seen mass closures; prior to the dispute the industry had around 200,000 employees; by 1991 it had fewer than 60,000. The Conservative victory in the 1992 general election led to further pit closures in anticipation of legislation to privatize the coal industry.

Debate about this decline has often been conducted in terms of a personalized argument over Scargill's industrial strategy. The President has become a highly controversial figure even within the NUM Left. Yet such a diagnosis can all too easily ignore the wider context. The vicissitudes of the NUM must be located within the changing fortunes of the post-war labor movement of the coal industry.

David Howell

Bibliography

Adeney, Martin, and John Lloyd. *The Miners Strike of 1984–85: Loss without Limit.* 1986.

Arnot, R. Page. *The Miners in Crisis and War.* 1961.

Howell, David. *The Politics of the NUM: A Lancashire View.* 1989.

Taylor, Andrew. *The Politics of the Yorkshire Miners.* 1984.

Nationalization and Nationalized Industries

The story of the nationalized industries provides one of the more curious episodes in Britain's contemporary history. Between the late 1940s and the late 1970s a considerable part of British business was nationalized and taken into state ownership. In 1979 the nationalized industries employed almost 2 million people and accounted for 10 percent of British output. However, the following decade saw the return of much of this industry to the private sector in the privatization program of Prime Minister **Margaret Thatcher**. By the early 1990s only a few economic activities remained in state ownership. Both nationalization in the 1940s and privatization in the 1980s were politically popular at the time, both sought in part to address the intractable problems of the British economy, and both achieved ambiguous results.

The era of nationalization is conventionally dated to the Labour government of 1945–51, but there was a prehistory of state investment in business, even though British governments had traditionally been strong advocates of *laissez-faire* policies. In 1914 the British government subscribed £2 million of capital, or over half the equity, to the Anglo-Persian Oil Company (later known as British Petroleum) in an attempt to secure an adequate supply of fuel oil for the **Royal Navy**. During the inter-war years a number of public corporations were established as a solution to market failure. These corporations were designed to ensure that the industries concerned were freed from day-to-day political interference in their affairs. The most important public corporations were the Central Electricity Board, established in 1926 to supervise the generation of electricity and to construct a national grid; the **British Broadcasting Corporation**; and the London Passenger Transport Board. The public corporation became the standard administrative model for the real wave of nationalization after 1945.

The Labour government that came to power in 1945 implemented an extensive nationalization program. The principal nationalizations measures, in chronological order, were the Bank of England (1946); civil **aviation** (1946); coal (1947); inland transport, notably the **railways** (1947); electricity (1948); gas (1948); and iron and **steel** (1949).

There was no single motivation in this sweeping legislation. The **Labour Party** had been committed, at least since its 1918 constitution, to take the basic activities of the economy under state control, and the aim of widespread nationalization was the basis of the policy manifesto, *Let Us Face the Future*, on which Labour fought the 1945 election. Labour believed that publicly owned industry could serve the public interest better than the private sector, and that the nationalized sector could assist in the implementation of government policies. It also argued that the private ownership of industries had involved wasteful competition, which had led in turn to failures to invest in modern equipment.

There was very little change to the structure of the nationalized industries in the 1950s and 1960s, despite the return of a Conservative government in 1951. The new government privatized the iron and steel industry and the goods side of road transport, but otherwise it left the nationalized sector in place. There were some minor extensions of state ownership under the Labour governments of 1964–70. In 1968, for example, the National Bus Company combined the already state-owned bus sector with most of the remaining private sector to create a large passenger transport corporation. However, a new wave of nationalization occurred in the 1970s. The continuing decay of British industry, rather than socialist ideology, was the driving force. The Conservative government of 1970–4 nationalized the aero-engine business of Rolls-Royce after the firm went bankrupt. In 1975 British Leyland, the last British-owned volume car manufacturer, was nationalized after a financial crisis following a long period of declining market share. In 1977 the shipbuilding and ship repairing industry, which had long been in a financially disastrous condition, was taken under state control, and in the same year Britain's aircraft manufacturing industry was nationalized to form British Aerospace.

The performance of the nationalized industries has aroused considerable controversy, in part because it is so difficult to judge. An initial point is that many of the nationalized industries began their public-sector lives as industries with considerable and long-standing problems. The National Coal Board created in 1947 acquired 800 firms that ran 1,470 collieries, with a notorious reputation for underinvestment and bad industrial relations. The Gas Council created in 1948 took over 1,000 separate gas undertakings of all shapes and sizes, the largest of which made one-eighth of all British gas output, and the smallest of which had just 132 customers. The shipbuilding and vehicle companies nationalized in the 1970s had been brought to the brink of disaster by incompetent private-sector management.

The performance of the sector after nationalization was mixed. Between the late 1940s and the late 1950s financial performance was generally poor. Between 1959 and 1967 the rates of return were generally much higher and compared well with the private sector. From the late 1960s to the late 1970s the financial performance of the sector deteriorated again. There were, however, considerable differences between industries in their financial performances, and the figures are hard to interpret because of industry differences. The financial performance of the **coal mining** industry, for example, was

poor, but it faced a contracting market, and its performance was in some respects superior to other Western European coal industries. There was also a great diversity in terms of productivity growth, both in different industries and in different time periods. The growth of labor productivity in the nationalized airlines, which were eventually merged into British Airways, was much higher than for manufacturing as a whole throughout the period 1948–85, while labor productivity growth in the National Bus Company was always much lower.

Critics claimed that the mere fact of public ownership produced inefficient managements, which contributed to the poor productivity of some industries, but the historical evidence would qualify such an image. The 1960s saw a form of managerial revolution in the public sector, which in some ways outpaced the private sector in developing investment appraisal techniques and new methods of corporate planning. These innovations were often associated with particular strong Chairmen, such as Alfred Robens in coal, **Walter Citrine** in electricity, and Richard Beeching in rail. It remains unclear whether the poor productivity performances in industries such as coal, rail, and steel can be ascribed to management failings or to more general problems in securing productivity increases in capital-intensive industries in difficult economic conditions.

Many of the difficulties of the nationalized industries stemmed not from managerial performance or motivation, but from the behavior of their single shareholder—the British government. The government did not, especially in the first decades of nationalization, specify what it wanted the nationalized industries to do. Each was told to provide an efficient, reliable, and economical service, and was expected to be financially self-supporting, "taking one year with another," a vague phase that offered little guidance to managers. There was no effective instruction as to how prices were to be set or what rates of return were expected until 1967, when the government ruled that prices should reflect long-run marginal costs. Later still, in 1978, a required rate of return was set for each industry's investment program. Governments regularly interfered with the investment, pricing, and employment strategies of the nationalized industries.

During the 1970s there was growing dissatisfaction with the nationalized industries. In 1974–5 the government had to supply £2.75

billion of financial assistance to them, although much of this money was spent on keeping prices low at the government's request, or keeping uneconomic railway lines in operating, again at the government's request. The nationalization of failed companies in the 1970s reinforced the sector's association with failure. The stage was set for the complete reversal of policy following the return of the **Conservative Party** to power in 1979.

The Thatcher government's program included a commitment both to reduce the public sector and to improve the efficiency of what remained in it. Privatization began slowly in 1981, when Cable and Wireless and part of British Aerospace were sold. After 1983 the program accelerated. British Airways, British Gas, British Leyland, British Shipbuilders, British Steel, British Telecom, the National Bus Company, and the water and electricity industries had been privatized by 1990. A nationalized sector continued into the 1990s, but as a shrunken residual of its former self, comprised of industries such as coal, railways, and nuclear power for which it was exceptionally hard to find buyers in the private sector.

The initial attraction of privatization was as an *ad hoc* means of raising funds. Asset sales were written off against public spending, and this cut the public-sector borrowing requirement of the government. As time passed, the Thatcher government developed broader justifications. It was argued that wider share ownership in general was economically beneficial, and the government encouraged individual investors to buy shares in privatization issues, often by underpricing assets so as to provide a give-away element in the flotation price. The government also argued that private-sector ownership would enhance economic efficiency as market forces exercised discipline on managers.

The performance of several firms, such as British Airways, appeared to improve dramatically with privatization, though often the most remarkable gains were made in the period immediately before privatization as managers prepared for the upheaval. In retrospect, however, the privatization program has been judged as a rather unsatisfactory exercise. Few efficiency gains have been identified, and studies have indicated that the principal gainers were the senior managers of the privatized companies, who awarded themselves large salary increases as they caught up with the level of the private sector.

A particular problem was that large corporations such as British Telecom were privatized as large and weakly regulated near-monopolies, reflecting the greater priority awarded to raising money from asset sales than to promoting competition. The subsequent predatory behavior of British Telecom, British Gas, and other privatized monopolies caused considerable concern and pressure for more satisfactory regulatory regimes. Passenger transport was one of the few sectors where competition was vigorously promoted. The National Bus Company was split and privatized in 1988 as over fifty separate companies. However, new entrants were not attracted to the industry, fares rose, and Britain's bus manufacturing industry collapsed because of a lack of orders. In addition, bus passengers continued to fall as many rural services were abandoned. Within a few years most of the privatized companies had been acquired by a few large groups.

Nationalization and, later, privatization were both attempts to deal with the problems of low competitiveness and poor productivity that beset so much of twentieth-century British industry. The British placed their faith largely in private ownership before 1945, in public ownership between the 1940s and the 1970s, and then in private ownership again in the 1980s. The results were in all cases ambiguous.

Geoffrey Jones

Bibliography

Ashworth, William, *The History of the British Coal Industry*. vol. 5: *1946–1982: The Nationalized Industry* (1986).
——. *The State in Business, 1945 to the mid-1980s*. 1991.
Chester, D.N. *Nationalization of British Industry*. 1975.
Gourvish, Terry. *British Railways, 1948–73*. 1986.
Kay, John, Colin Mayer, and David Thompson, eds. *Privatisation and Regulation: The U.K. Experience*. 1986.
Pryke, Richard. *The Nationalised Industries: Policies and Performance since 1968*. 1981.

Navy, Royal

British imperial, naval, and maritime dominance was a fact of global life during the nineteenth century. Such hegemony was maintained by the Royal Navy, the largest naval fleet in the world during the century after 1815. It provided security for the largest merchant marine force and for the financial, banking, insurance, and shipping services controlled from London. At this time the Royal Navy was the "senior service" of the British armed forces in addition to being the premier international naval force. It was overseen by the Board of the Admiralty, whose responsibilities encompassed the operating fleets, dozens of supporting bases, and several major dockyards at home and abroad.

The fleets consisted of a wide variety of warships. Most important during the early decades were the battleships, the replacements for the sailing Ships-of-the-Line that had dominated naval warfare earlier. Important modifications in battleship features, many initiated by the British, resulted in the *Dreadnought* revolution and in an innovative design called the battle cruiser, both introduced about 1905. The supporting warships of the early decades were cruisers and destroyers, the fast scouting and security forces responsible for maintaining international lines of communication and trade routes. Improvements in torpedo design and capabilities caused corresponding changes in destroyer tactics and use. The submarine as a viable and lethal warship originated during this early part of the century.

The American naval writer A.T. Mahan's influential "blue water" paradigm, touted as the strategic model that determined the British emphasis on imperial and maritime rather than Continental land factors, called for a major confrontation between opposing battle fleets. More-perceptive maritime and naval observers abandoned Mahanian concepts and recognized Sir Julian Corbett (1854–1922) as the most influential articulator of British maritime strategy. Corbett stressed continuous control of routes of communication and alternative uses of naval forces.

The occasion providing the most potential for a Trafalgar-type naval confrontation was the **First World War** Battle of Jutland fought in the North Sea on 31 May–1 June 1916, when the Grand Fleet under Admiral Sir **John Jellicoe** challenged the High Seas Fleet under Admiral Reinhard Scheer. The British-German figures were, respectively, 37 capital ships vs. 27; 149 warships vs. 99. Losses amounted to fourteen British ships and 6,100 killed; eleven German ships and 2,550 killed. The Germans immediately declared a victory, but the battle was indecisive; nothing changed and the Germans re-

mained blockaded for the duration of the war. Perhaps the most telling result was that the Grand Fleet was prepared for action immediately upon returning to its bases while the High Seas Fleet was not ready for several months.

During the inter-war period economic, political, and strategic commitments stretched British resources. This precipitated internal budgetary competition whereby the government was forced to set priorities among demands from the **Royal Air Force**, now an independent agency, the Royal Navy, once deemed dominant, and the **army**. Naval air forces remained dangerously deficient, resulting in serious gaps in reconnaissance capabilities against German U-boats.

Significant combat action during the **Second World War** included a British naval aviation attack against the Italian naval base at Taranto, immobilizing major units of the Italian fleet; a British squadron defeating an Italian squadron in the Mediterranean at Matapan; the contest between the British battleship *Prince of Wales* and battle cruiser *Hood* and the German battleship *Bismarck* and cruiser *Prinz Eugen*, in which the *Hood* was lost and hundreds of British warships converged in the North Atlantic to sink the *Bismarck*; and the later loss of the *Prince of Wales* and the *Repulse* off Indochina, victims of Japanese land-based aircraft. All of these occurred between September 1939 and December 1941.

The critical aspects of naval warfare for the British during both World Wars were the German U-boat campaigns against merchant shipping. In the First World War Germany immediately declared unrestricted **submarine warfare**, later canceled it, but then resumed it on 1 February 1917. The critical stage of sinkings of Allied shipping was in the spring of 1917 following American entry into the war. Implementation of a convoy system, the influx of American warships, and improved detection and weapons of antisubmarine warfare slowly tipped the balance in favor of the Allies. Similarly in the Second World War sinkings were spectacular up to the spring of 1943 when various countermeasures, use of small aircraft carriers for reconnaissance to protect convoys, and an increasing ability to read German secret codes contributed to the final defeat.

The fall of **Singapore** in 1942 signaled the end of British hegemony as a Pacific power; the **Suez crisis** of 1956 meant the virtual demise of influence in the **Middle East**; and the **Falklands**

War demonstrated only a temporary military revival. The Falklands campaign in the spring of 1982 when British forces, mostly naval, expelled about 12,000 Argentine invaders from the South Atlantic islands of South Georgia and the Falklands, was the primary operation of British naval and marine forces after Suez. The volunteer basis of the British forces, the highly professional manner with which the campaign was conducted, and the capability to overcome complicated logistical problems with no British base within thousands of miles were factors repeatedly praised. The naval forces were supplemented by "STUFT," ships-taken-up-from-trade, a total of fifty commercial ships including two major liners, *Queen Elizabeth II* and *Canberra*, tankers, a super-ferry, and specialized cargo ships. The British lost six warships, some to Exocet missiles.

Personnel of the naval forces consisted of officers, enlisted members including men and women, the shore establishment, and the Royal Marines, officers and enlisted. During wartime the merchant marine came under naval control. Naval officers were symbolically placed on the quarterdeck, enlisted persons on the lower deck. During the first two decades of the century Lionel Yexley (real name James Woods, 1862–1933), an advocate and journalist, led an important reform and representation movement. During the 1920s, pay, morale, and conditions on the lower deck deteriorated, culminating in a serious disturbance aboard a dozen battleships at Invergordon in northern Scotland in September 1931. The government conceded most of the demands and refrained from punitive measures. After the Second World War the volunteer character of the navy necessitated the improvement of conditions and pay and the associated professional status.

The leaders most identified with the Royal Navy during the twentieth century have been **Winston Churchill**, First Lord of the Admiralty, the civilian head, during the early years of both World Wars; Admiral Sir **John Fisher**, First Sea Lord, the professional head, 1904–10 and 1914–15; Admiral Sir Andrew Cunningham (1883–1963), a fleet commander and First Sea Lord during the Second World War; and Admiral **Earl Mountbatten**, First Sea Lord after the Second World War. Fisher was instrumental in the *Dreadnought* and battle cruiser innovations and other lower-deck and strategic reforms. Cunningham came closest to the "Nelson touch" of aggressive offensive operations.

Mountbatten guided the Royal Navy through the post-war transition.

In 1964 the armed forces of Great Britain were consolidated and unified under the Ministry of Defence, with Lord Mountbatten as the first unified Chief of Staff. An important strategic role, first for the RAF, and later for the Royal Navy, has been the independent nuclear capability for Great Britain. The naval vehicles for deployment of intercontinental ballistic missiles have been, first, Polaris missile submarines and, subsequently, Trident missile submarines. In each case a submarine carried sixteen missiles, later ones containing multiple nuclear warheads. The plan for the 1990s is four ballistic missile submarines. The program is closely tied to, and dependent upon, American strategic weapons systems.

Consistent reductions in the size of the forces of the Royal Navy have been achieved through a series of defense White Papers and retrenchment plans in 1957, 1968, 1981, and 1985. In 1968 the British naval forces shifted from an independent to a dependent status linked to the North Atlantic Treaty Organization (NATO).

Eugene L. Rasor

Bibliography
Carew, Anthony. *The Lower Deck of the Royal Navy, 1900–1939: The Invergordon Mutiny in Perspective.* 1981.
Kennedy, Paul M. *The Rise and Fall of British Naval Mastery.* 4th ed. 1991.
Marder, Arthur J. *From Dreadnought to Scapa Flow: The Royal Navy in the Fisher Era, 1904–19.* 5 vols. 1961–70.
Roskill, Stephen W. *Naval Policy between the Wars, 1919–1939.* 2 vols. 1969–76.

Nevinson, C(hristopher) R(ichard) W(ynne) (1889–1946)
The son of the noted journalist and author Henry W. Nevinson, C.R.W. Nevinson was educated at Uppingham and the **Slade School of Art**, which he attended from 1908 to 1912. He then moved to Paris for a year, where he worked at the Cercle Russe and the Académie Julian, mixing with the Italian Futurists who had just exhibited in Paris and with the French avant-garde and sharing a studio with Modigliani. Returning to London in 1913, he altered the character of his painting from atmospheric

post-impressionism to Futurism and was included in the 1913 exhibition of post-impressionists and Futurists at the Doré Gallery in London. There he showed *The Departure of the Train de Luxe from the Gare St. Lazare* (1913, present whereabouts unknown), which displayed a mixture of Cubist and Futurist technique. For the exhibition Nevinson arranged for the Italian poet Marinetti to lecture in London, and a banquet organized by Nevinson and **Wyndham Lewis** was held in his honor.

Although Nevinson participated in Wyndham Lewis' Rebel Art Centre, which saw the birth of **Vorticism**, his allegiances were with Marinetti and the Futurists. In 1914 this was stressed unequivocally when he co-signed and published with Marinetti *Vital English Art: Futurist Manifesto*. By this time Lewis, defining the Vorticist aesthetic as being in opposition to Futurism, was doubly annoyed to find his name and those of his colleagues at the Rebel Art Centre appended without their knowledge to the *Manifesto*.

By 1914 Nevinson' manipulation of Futurist imagery—which always owed a lot to the work of Gino Severini—was becoming more accomplished. However, with the outbreak of the **First World War** he joined the Royal Army Medical Corps as an ambulance driver. He was quickly horrified by the impersonally wrought carnage of modern warfare, which the Italian Futurists in 1915 declared to be "the only hygiene of the world." Despite exhibiting as a Futurist at the 1915 Vorticist exhibition at the Doré Gallery, and contributing to the second issue of the magazine *Blast*, Nevinson's painting was becoming increasingly figurative, less indebted to Futurist preoccupations and their pictorial conventions.

Discharged from the **army** on health grounds, Nevinson held a successful exhibition of his war paintings at the Leicester Galleries in 1916 and the following year was appointed as an official **war artist**. His paintings and prints of this period, such as *The Road from Arras to Bapaume* (1917, Imperial War Museum, London), *The Cursed Wood* (1918), and *After a Push* (1917, Imperial War Museum, London) highlight the way in which he allied their structured compositions to a strongly evocative expression of the horror and alienation of war. Critically, these works were among the most successful British war paintings.

In 1919 and 1920 Nevinson visited New York, whose architecture he was inspired to portray as symbolic of an optimistic New Age in prints such as *Metropolis* (1920–2) and *The Temples of New York* (1920). These were exhibited at the Leicester Galleries in 1921. Through the 1920s and 1930s he executed many contemplative landscape paintings, turning his back on his past. The 1930s also saw him conceive a number of ambitious and large-scale contemporary history paintings of urban life, such as *Amongst the Nerves of the World* (1928–30, The Museum of London) and *The Twentieth Century* (1932–5, Laing Art Gallery, Newcastle-upon-Tyne). In the public's eye he was understood to be an epitome of the modern artist as a result of his skill at manipulating the **press** to report his activities as an artist, all of which contributed to making his art more accessible and making a celebrity out of himself. Like his more famous contemporary, **Paul Nash**, he was one of the few to serve as an official artist in both World Wars.

Andrew Wilson

Bibliography

Knowles, Elizabeth, ed. *C.R.W. Nevinson.* 1988.

Konody, P.G. *Modern War: Paintings by C.R.W. Nevinson.* 1917.

Nevinson, C.R.W. *Paint and Prejudice.* 1937.

New Fabian Research Bureau

The New Fabian Research Bureau was a policy think-tank for the **Labour Party** in the 1930s. Like its sister organization, the **Society for Socialist Inquiry and Propaganda** (SSIP), the New Fabian Research Bureau (NFRB) grew out of an intellectual vacuum in the late 1920s. From 1918 the **Fabian Society**, losing membership and momentum, was no longer either a center of policy-making for the Labour Party or a focus for young socialists. The interests of **Beatrice and Sidney Webb** had settled on other horizons. Wishing to resurrect the Fabian tradition of research and discussion into issues of interest to socialists, **G.D.H.** and Margaret **Cole, Clement Attlee,** and **Stafford Cripps** established the New Fabian Research Bureau in March 1931. Cole gathered about him a group of young intellectuals, mining the rich vein of **Oxford, Cambridge,** and London Labour Party societies. This group included such figures as **Evan Durbin,** Colin Clark, **Hugh Gaitskell,** and John Parker, who became General Secretary of the NFRB in 1933. In 1932 most of this circle shunned the fledgling **Socialist League** and set about instead to create what one member called a "live pigeon hole" of ideas for Labour to draw upon. Quantitatively, this resulted in a significant number of publications, forty-two research pamphlets, and seven books over eight years. These included works on financial and economic policy and an early study of the Soviet Union. The bureau also published a periodical, the *NFRB Quarterly*, from 1938 onward. This prolific output came despite a small membership, 130 in 1933 rising to only about 800 in 1938. Where the SSIP and the Socialist League failed in stimulating socialist thought, the NFRB succeeded, albeit in a much quieter fashion. Its greatest influence was undoubtedly in economic policy, a sphere much neglected by the Labour Party until 1931. **Hugh Dalton** used the members of this group and the XYZ Club to formulate a credible economic policy for Labour through the 1930s. By the end of the decade, NFRB members, like Durbin and Gaitskell, were being co-opted onto the powerful Finance and Trade Subcommittee of the Labour Party. In 1938 it was suggested that the NFRB join the Fabian Society, a relatively amicable process that was effected late in 1938 and gave new life to the Fabian Society.

Stephen Brooke

Bibliography

Cole, Margaret. *The Story of Fabian Socialism*. 1961.

Durbin, Elizabeth. *New Jerusalems: The Labour Party and the Economics of Democratic Socialism*. 1985.

Pimlott, Ben. *Labour and the Left in the 1930s*. 1977.

New Liberalism

The term New Liberalism describes the change both in Liberal ideology and in the **Liberal Party** that occurred in the two decades before the First World War. In general, it marked a shift toward acceptance in both theory and practice of collectivism, the use of the state to overcome the shortcomings of an unregulated market economy.

Liberalism as an ideology had developed in the nineteenth century as a defense of the individual against both the state and society. Seeing the individual as rational, able to develop his personality and talents if freed of political and social restraints, Liberalism embraced *laissez-faire*, the idea that government should interfere as little as possible with the economy and with private property. It optimistically assumed that if individuals were free to follow their own self-interest, society would be self-regulating. The outcome would be progress—a gradual enrichment of the entire community and eradication of remaining social problems. In the last quarter of the nineteenth century Liberal assumptions and Liberal politics were subjected to severe strain. The long downturn in the economy that began in the early 1870s called into question the belief that the capitalist market economy, if freed of restraints, would result in continuous economic progress.

After the 1884 Franchise Reform Act the Liberal Party had to concern itself more with attracting support from the large number of new working-class voters who were being courted by the **Conservative Party** and, after 1900, by the new **Labour Party**. Disappointed by the 1892 Gladstone government, which had focused on such traditional Liberal causes as Irish Home Rule and disestablishment of the Anglican Church in Wales, and convinced that the Conservative electoral victory of 1895 demonstrated the need for an updated Liberalism, the New Liberals worked in the late 1890s to revise traditional political and social theory to justify a more active social reformism, one that might also make the Liberal Party more electorally attractive. The active propagators of a New Liberalism, as it was called at the time, were never a coherent group; they consisted of disparate journalists, academics, politicians, and Liberal activists. Most New Liberals rejected **imperialism** and saw their support for national self-determination and opposition to militarism as an important link to the Gladstonian insistence that the same moral principles applied abroad as at home.

At the beginning of the twentieth century men like the sociologist L.T. Hobhouse, the economist **J.A. Hobson**, and the journalist **H.W. Massingham** worked out a new version of Liberalism that justified collectivism, though understood in terms derived from an individualist Liberalism. Recognizing that an unregulated market economy failed to provide the means for many people to take care of themselves, they advocated reforms that addressed such problems while preserving the market economy on the grounds that state action actually made possible the fulfillment of a traditional Liberal ideal of freedom. Most radically, on the grounds that wealth was socially created, they extended the distinction between earned and unearned income from land to all forms of wealth. Claiming that all high incomes had unearned elements, they defended progressive taxation as an attack on unearned income, not a deterrent to enterprise or initiative. They thereby provided theoretical justification for the taxes necessary to support a more socially reformist state.

Responding to the growth of the new Labour Party and to the perception that it had to develop a new reformist program to retain working-class support, the new Liberal government introduced the first **old-age pensions** in 1908. Although recognizing that many aged working people had never earned enough money to be able to save for their old age, the Pensions Act reflected older Liberal concerns for character. It disqualified anyone who had previously applied for poor relief and provided a pension that was too small to live on in order to encourage thrift. In the next years, however, led by **David Lloyd George** and **Winston Churchill**, the Liberal government passed a budget in 1909 that applied the idea of taxing unearned income more highly than earned income and a National Insurance Act in 1911 that for the first time acknowledged officially that an unregulated market economy made it impossible for many workers to provide for themselves no matter how diligent they were.

Although still partially informed by older Liberal concerns for character, self-reliance, and the capitalist market, this legislation nevertheless marked a significant shift in Liberal approaches to the state and social reform, approaches that later governments would slowly expand and that would grow into the **welfare state** after the **Second World War**. What was new in these reforms was the underlying assumption that the state could be a positive force, that the measure of individual freedom, as T.H. Green, the Oxford philosopher whose work inspired many New Liberals, had said, was not how much the state left people alone but whether it gave them the capacity to fulfill themselves as individuals. Implicit in the reforms as well, and in the theoretical justification of them, was an expanded notion of community. The New Liberalism recognized that Gladstonian Liberalism had proven inadequate because its ideal of the public good was based on a narrow individualism that failed to recognize human interdependence.

Certainly, New Liberalism had serious shortcomings. Its view of human nature was simplistic, with no allowance for the irrational. It was naively optimistic about the possibility of overcoming all social problems. It failed to understand the rootedness of social and class conflict. And it overestimated the ability of the Liberal Party to represent, not just the middle class, but the public good. It was not responsible, however, for the collapse of Liberalism as an organized political force. The reasons for that have to be sought in the growth of class consciousness among the enlarged post-war electorate, in the changing allegiances of the growing trade union movement, and in the parochialism of the Liberal Party at a local level, not in the ability of Liberalism to respond to the problems of an urban, industrial society.

Peter Weiler

Bibliography

Allett, John. *New Liberalism: The Political Economy of J.A. Hobson.* 1981.
Clarke, Peter. *Lancashire and the New Liberalism.* 1971.
———. *Liberals and Social Democrats.* 1978.
Collini, Stefan. *Liberalism and Sociology: L.T. Hobhouse and Political Argument in England, 1880–1914.* 1979.
Freeden, Michael. *The New Liberalism: An Ideology of Social Reform.* 1978.
Weiler, Peter. *The New Liberalism: Liberal Social Theory in Great Britain, 1889–1914.* 1982.

New Statesman (1913–)

Since April 1913 the *New Statesman* has been the weekly voice of progressive opinion in the United Kingdom. Having absorbed the social science review *New Society* in 1989, it is presently entitled *New Statesman and Society.* However, in its most influential period, the three decades following merger with the Liberal *Nation* in 1931, it was the *New Statesman and Nation,* affectionately nicknamed the "Staggers and Naggers."

Inadequate capital and poor sales thwarted the early ambitions of the magazine's Fabian founders, **Sidney and Beatrice Webb,** and their chief asset, **George Bernard Shaw.** That their journal survived and thrived is attributable to the professionalism of Clifford Sharp and his deputy, J.C. (Jack, later Sir John) Squire. Although after wartime service its editor became a slave to both alcohol and, more puzzlingly, **H.H. Asquith,** the *New Statesman*'s early success reflected that of **Ramsay MacDonald**'s Labour Party; modest circulation belied accumulative influence in the corridors of power. The boorish Sharp, although burnt out by the late 1920s, had laid the foundations for the internationally renowned voice of the British Left edited between 1931 and 1961 by **Kingsley Martin.**

The mid-century golden age of the *New Statesman* has been eclipsed by the magazine's mixed fortunes since the disastrous editorial appointment in 1970 of former Cabinet minister and one-time deputy Richard Crossman. The ailing and inadequate Crossman, and the competent but uninspiring Anthony Howard, failed to stem a decline in sales initiated a decade earlier when the Sunday broadsheets usurped the weeklies' predominance in opinion and review. The 1970s and 1980s saw the problems of high overheads and low circulation exacerbated by declining **advertising** revenue. Financial instability fueled disharmony between directors and their editorial and administrative staff.

The absence of a firm commercial footing, and the succession of policy U-turns, mirrored **Labour Party** fortunes in the 1980s. Bruce Page brought headline-grabbing but costly investigative journalism from the *Sunday Times.* Hugh Stephenson, another highly regarded Fleet Street newsman, failed to adapt to weekly journalism. For veteran readers the *New Statesman*, however worthy the exposés, was now dull and too often poorly written—an insistence on political correctness maintained at the expense of stylish contributors and mainstream Labour supporters. A painful process of recovery, initiated by John Lloyd prior to an early return to the *Financial Times*, was maintained in the face of boardroom upheaval by Stuart Weir and, following his stormy departure, Steve Platt. While Labour after 1987 reconstructed itself as a credible alternative party of government, the *New Statesman* also edged toward the center as a qualified supporter of the "Kinnockite" social democracy.

Defeat in April 1992 saw the paper provide an important forum for debate on Labour's future strategy. Although the preceding thirty years had seen sales slump from around 100,000 to nearer 20,000, *New Statesman and Society* in the early 1990s seemed to have weathered the storm. Spurred on by the success of Charter 88, the magazine's high-profile campaign for constitutional reform, it celebrated its eightieth anniversary with qualified optimism.

Adrian Smith

Bibliography

Howe, Stephen, ed. *Lines of Dissent: Writing from the New Statesman, 1913 to 1988.* 1988.

Hyams, Edward. *The New Statesman: The History of the First Fifty Years.* 1963.

Rolph, C.H. *Kingsley: The Life, Letters, and Diaries of Kingsley Martin.* 1973.

New Towns

Created in the United Kingdom from 1946, New Towns were derived partly from the **Garden Cities** movement's practical idealism and partly from post-war reconstruction plans (including Sir Patrick Abercrombie's Greater London, Clydeside, and other schemes) for new **housing** and employment away from the congested, damaged urban and metropolitan areas. Lewis Silkin, Minister of **Town and Country Planning** (1945–50) in the **Labour** government, secured the passage of the 1946 New Town Act. Within three-and-a-half years Silkin designated nine New Towns to take Greater London overspill (one—Corby—had also to house the labor force of a large steelworks) and three more to reverse economic decline in South Wales and County Durham. In 1947–8 two Scottish New Towns were designated to take Glasgow overspill and compensate for the decline of Lanarkshire **coal mining.**

Conservatives, save for the redoubtable Lord Hinchingbrooke, had not opposed the 1946 act in principle, but particular proposed designations did not always pass easily through the **Cabinet,** and some early ones were fiercely contested at public inquiries and through the courts.

Hinchingbrooke's fear of totalitarianism, though unrealized, was not quite groundless. Each New Town development corporation would inevitably become the largest landlord in its area, and under the 1946 act all of its assets would pass to the local authority when development ceased. The prospect of a dozen or more borough councils with unprecedented and unparalleled concentrations of economic and social power was, however, averted in 1959 by a Conservative act providing for a Commission for the New Towns to take over each development corporation's assets when its work was done. Created in 1961, the commission acquired the assets of the first completed New Towns (Crawley and Hemel Hempstead) in 1962.

By then new designations had ceased. Corby's (1950) was the last for eleven years, apart from Cumbernauld's (to take Glasgow overspill) in 1955, for the Conservatives chose instead to work through the 1952 Town Development Act. Its results, however, were small, and in the early 1960s the Conservatives designated a second generation of New Towns: two to take Merseyside overspill, two to take Birmingham and Black Country overspill, and one to revive the Tyneside-Wearside economy. The Labour government elected in 1964 consolidated New Towns legislation in 1965 and undertook a third generation of New Towns. Successive generations were planned on ever larger scales, and third-generation New Towns were really expansions of existing large towns—Peterborough, Northampton, Warrington, and, most notably, Preston, which with neighboring towns formed the enormous Central Lancashire New Town (1970). Even **Milton Keynes** (1967), essentially a green-fields development, included Bletchley and two smaller towns.

The Commission for the New Towns was initially seen as permanent, managing assets in perpetuity. Cheaper houses were not sold so as to keep up the rented housing stock and simplify management, though long leases of better-quality houses were sold. That, however, did not accord with widening aspirations to home ownership (reflected in the 1968 Cullingworth Report), and the commission's policies were profoundly affected by the 1967 Leasehold Reform Act and the 1976 New Towns (Amendment) Act—Labour legislation giving tenants of leasehold houses the right to buy their freeholds and providing for the transfer of New Town housing to local authorities. In 1979 **Margaret Thatcher's** Conservative government ordered the commission to prepare an open-ended program of commercial and industrial asset sales that would eventually make the commission redundant when the New Towns program ended.

The end was foreseeable by the mid-1970s when the Labour government formulated new national planning policies: Physical and social problems accumulating in old town and city centers were to take priority, a change symbolized by the abandonment of Stonehouse New Town in 1976 to divert resources to Glasgow's regeneration. Milton Keynes development corporation, wound up in 1992, was the last in England.

The New Towns' contribution to the postwar housing program was quantitatively small, but those New Towns with strong design teams—for example, Harlow, Cumbernauld, and Milton Keynes—greatly enhanced Britain's reputation for urban **architecture**.

G.C. Baugh

Bibliography

Aldridge, Meryl. *British New Towns: A Programme without a Policy.* 1979.
Cullingworth, John Barry. *Environmental Planning, 1939–69. Vol. 3: New Towns Policy.* 1980.
Hall, Peter, H. Gracey, R. Drewett, and R. Thomas. *The Containment of Urban England.* 2 vols. 1973.
Schaffer, Frank. *The New Town Story.* 1972.

New Zealand

New Zealand became a British colony by the Treaty of Waitangi of 1840. From that date many immigrants settled in New Zealand, mainly from the British Isles. Most of New Zealand's 3 million non-indigenous population are of British descent. Extremely loyal to the "Mother Country," New Zealand supported Britain in times of war and conducted most of its trade with Britain. From 1907, when New Zealand was granted Dominion status, it began to see itself increasingly not as a British outpost, but as part of a South Pacific community.

In the **Boer War** New Zealand boasted that it was the first colony to send troops to the aid of Britain. New Zealand looked to Britain not only for its cultural heritage, but also for defense and trade. The British **navy** dominated the waters around New Zealand, and Britain provided the most significant overseas market for New Zealand's produce. British investors supplied most of the overseas capital borrowed by government or private concerns.

New Zealand contributed to the imperial forces in the **First World War** enthusiastically, fighting for "Crown and Empire" in a war that involved no immediate threat to its own security. Introducing compulsory military service in 1916, it emerged from the war with a casualty rate higher than any other Allied nation apart from Russia. Its unwavering commitment, stemming partly from loyalty to Britain, also acknowledged the conviction that the British navy was integral to New Zealand's own security.

After the war New Zealand, like the other British Dominions, signed the Versailles treaty independently and became a member of the **League of Nations** in its own right. This represented a significant move away from imperial subordination, despite enduring links. New Zealand contributed to the building of Britain's naval base in **Singapore** in the 1920s, identifying its own security as synonymous with that of the Empire. In the 1920s **Canada, South Africa,** and Ireland (Eire) urged Britain to recognize the independent status that they believed had been achieved by the Dominions as a result of the war. This was given legal recognition in the **Statute of Westminster** of 1931, which New Zealand delayed ratifying until 1947.

The 1935 election of the first Labour government ushered in a new departure in imperial relations, as the government aimed to "insulate" New Zealand from the world and make it more self-reliant. This resulted from the realization during the Depression of the 1930s that Britain, though still the dominant market for New Zealand exports, was not "bottomless." In foreign policy, too, the Labour government distanced itself from Britain by its more ardent support for the League of Nations, to the point of open disagreement during the **Spanish Civil War**. New Zealand favored enforcing sanctions against Fascist aggressors, while Britain pursued **appeasement**. However, as the League faltered, New Zealand again looked to the Commonwealth for its defense, the 1937 imperial conference marking the turning point.

When the **Second World War** broke out the Labour Prime Minister, Michael Joseph Savage, immediately expressed New Zealand's allegiance to the Mother Country. **Conscription** was introduced in 1940. New Zealand also supported the British war effort from late 1943 by introducing more extensive rationing of butter, meat, and other commodities that were in short supply in Britain. The major change was the emergence of the United States as New Zealand's principal ally, especially after the collapse of the Singapore naval base in January 1942. Attention shifted from security of the Empire to the Pacific where Britain, it was now realized, would no longer play a dominant role.

In 1943 New Zealand set up its own Department of Foreign Affairs. In 1951, for the first time, New Zealand entered into an alliance without Britain—a mutual defense pact among the United States, **Australia,** and New Zealand (ANZUS). In 1954 a second important treaty was signed—the South East Asian Treaty Organization (SEATO), giving New Zealand southeast Asian allies. By 1955 New Zealand's chief treaties and defense arrangements were firmly based in the Pacific and Southeast Asian regions.

Britain remained New Zealand's main export market until Britain joined the **European Community** (EC) in 1972, after which New Zealand could no longer rely exclusively on Britain for trade. In Europe New Zealand now had to negotiate not only with Britain, but also with other members of the EC, and increasingly sought markets elsewhere. Britain absorbed 80 percent of New Zealand's exports in 1935, but only 9 percent by 1985. In its antinuclear stance of the 1980s New Zealand alienated not only the United States (and effectively destroyed ANZUS), but also Britain. Pursuing an independent foreign policy, New Zealanders ceased to regard Britain as "home." The South Pacific was "home," and New Zealand was no longer the "Britain of the South" that it had been at the beginning of the century.

Linda Bryder

Bibliography

Kennaway, Richard. *New Zealand Foreign Policy, 1951–1971.* 1972.

Sinclair, Keith. *A Destiny Apart: New Zealand's Search for National Identity.* 1986.

———, ed. *The Oxford Illustrated History of New Zealand.* 1990.

Nicholson, Ben (1894–1982)

Ben Nicholson grew up in an artistic home where the urbanity of his artist father, Sir William Nicholson, and the down-to-earth nature of his mother, Mabel Pryde, are reflected in both the elegance and the uncompromising and primitive nature of his contribution to modernist painting in Britain. Despite a short period spent at the **Slade School of Art** in 1910–11, where be became friendly with **Paul Nash,** he was not formally trained, and he traveled abroad a great deal in Europe and America between 1912 and 1918.

It was only following his marriage in 1920 to the painter Winifred Dacre that he threw himself into his painting and specifically into the English avant-garde, partly as a reaction against the reputation that his father held both as a painter and, in collaboration with his uncle James Pryde (as the Beggarstaff Brothers), as a poster artist and illustrator. During this period he spent much time in Paris where he came into direct contact with Cubism and saw works by Pablo Picasso and Georges Braque. Following this experience he painted his first abstract paintings in 1924.

These were, however, an isolated experiment. Through the 1920s he painted landscape or still-life subject matter in a primitive and naive manner. This approach was taken up by other painters in England, especially those belonging to the Seven and Five Society, an exhibiting group of which Nicholson had been a member since 1924 and its dominating force from 1926 until its last, all abstract, exhibition in 1935. Although Nicholson found that this primitive approach was confirmed in 1928 when he and Christopher Wood discovered the naive artist Alfred Wallis during a visit to St. Ives, many of the other painters in the society painted in a naive style, while Nicholson's adopted a Cubist concern with flatness, an application in paint of the sculptor's tenets of truth to materials.

It is not then surprising that Nicholson should gradually move toward non-objective abstraction in the 1930s. In 1932 he and his second wife, the sculptor **Barbara Hepworth**, visited Paris where they met Picasso, Braque, Jean Arp, and Constantin Brancusi. They participated with the group Abstraction-Creation as well as the short-lived Unit One in London, and by 1934 he was making his first all-white abstract relief carvings and rectilinear abstract paintings. In the same year he visited in Paris with Piet Mondrian, who between 1938 and 1940 lived in London close to Nicholson and a like-minded group of artists that included Cecil Stephenson and **Henry Moore**, writers such as **Herbert Read**, and émigres such as Naum Gabo, Marcel Breuer and László Moholy-Nagy—all of which led to a number of exhibitions of modernist art in Britain that included Nicholson as the major British contributor. In 1937 he and Naum Gabo co-edited the book *Circle*, a statement of faith for these Hampstead modernists.

In 1940 Nicholson and Hepworth moved to St. Ives, which shortly became the center for continued modernist activity in Britain. During this time and after the war Nicholson moved between abstraction and figuration, predominantly through the carved and painted shallow relief. His international reputation grew as he won prizes at the Carnegie International in 1952 and the São Paulo Bienal in 1957; in 1954 he had a retrospective mounted at the 1954 Venice Biennale. In 1958 he left England to live in Switzerland, returning in 1972. He was awarded the Order of Merit in 1968, the same year in which he had a major retrospective at the Tate Gallery.

Andrew Wilson

Bibliography

Harrison, Charles. *Ben Nicholson*. 1969.
Lewison, Jeremy. *Ben Nicholson: The Years of Experiment, 1919–1939*. 1982.
———. *Ben Nicholson*. 1991.
Read, Herbert. *Ben Nicholson: Paintings, Reliefs, Drawings*. 1948.
Russell, John. *Ben Nicholson: Drawings, Paintings, and Reliefs, 1911–1968*. 1968.

Nicolson, Harold George (1886–1968)

Diplomat, novelist, biographer, broadcaster, critic, journalist, garden designer, MP, and ubiquitous committee man, Harold Nicolson (Sir Harold from 1952) will unfortunately be remembered by posterity for his marriage to writer Vita Sackville-West, an unusual early example of an "open" marriage punctuated regularly by **homosexual** affairs on both sides. This relationship has been endlessly celebrated, first, in the memoirs of friends and relations, later by feminist and gay writers seeking precursors, and finally fossilized by the immense academic output relating to the **Bloomsbury Group** (to which Nicolson and Sackville-West were only peripheral).

Socially and politically, Nicolson was far closer to the mainstream of the British Establishment than to the self-conscious bohemians of Bloomsbury. Son of a Scottish baronet of ancient (but now landless) family, he followed his father into the diplomatic service and enjoyed there a successful twenty-year career. His aesthetic sensibilities were not in the end compatible with a top-flight **Foreign Office** post, and he left the service in 1929. The catalyst was publication of his best-known book, *Some People* (1927), nine pen sketches of thinly fictionalized characters in Nicolson's life that were too frank and penetrating for certain Foreign Office higher-ups.

At first uncertain about his place in the modern world, he suffered through two unhappy episodes, as a popular journalist writing a gossip column for **Lord Beaverbrook's** *Evening Standard* and as a political journalist editing the paper of **Oswald Mosley's** short-lived New Party (breaking with Mosley over the latter's **Fascism**). By the mid-1930s, however, he had established himself as one of the leading and most prolific critics and essayists of his day. He wrote the official, best-selling biography of **George V** (1952), for which he received his knighthood, novels of no great importance, influential tracts on diplomatic theory, a highbrow column for the *Spectator* and middlebrow reviews for the *Daily Telegraph* and *Observer*. He also served as a National Labour MP for West Leicester (1935–45), was a governor of the **British Broadcasting Corporation** (BBC) and for many years Vice Chairman of the **National Trust**, and still found time to spend with Sackville-West at their Kent retreat of Sissinghurst Castle, where he designed the initial layout for her famous **garden**. His biographer has estimated that in a sample year (1938–9) Nicolson wrote 4,000 letters, 101 articles (including 52 book reviews), and one book, gave 120 talks (mostly on radio) and delivered 23 lectures, served on 27 committees, and traveled 77,281 miles (including 25 visits to his constituency).

Nicolson's style is charming and confiding, but his ideas are rarely profound. He was an essentially Edwardian character who found it hard to compete with the more arresting style of younger contemporaries like **Evelyn Waugh** or Cyril Connolly. He was too literary for the Foreign Office, but too Foreign Office for the literary set. Nicolson's lasting importance must be as a communicator between the highbrow world and the general public, a task for which his respectability served him well. His incessant lecturing and broadcasting, including on **television** as early as 1937, made him a familiar voice and face in millions of households. His old-fashioned public service ethic persuaded him of the importance of diffusing "civilization" downward to the masses, to whom he tried (perhaps unsuccessfully) not to condescend, and he got into trouble with the BBC's **Lord Reith** for lecturing on **James Joyce's** *Ulysses*. Like a kind of upper-class **J.B. Priestley**, he undoubtedly contributed to the better understanding between the classes that prevailed after the **Second World War**. In the 1950s he came to seem increasingly like a leftover from a bygone age, but his fame revived in quite a different context after his death in 1968, with the publication of his candid diaries.

Peter Mandler

Bibliography
Lees-Milne, James. *Harold Nicolson: A Biography*. 2 vols. 1980–1.
Nicolson, Nigel, ed. *Harold Nicolson: Diaries and Letters, 1930–1962*. 3 vols. 1966–8.
——. *Portrait of a Marriage*. 1973.
——. *Vita and Harold: The Letters of Vita Sackville-West and Harold Nicolson*. 1992.

1922 Committee, The

The 1922 Committee of **Conservative** backbenchers in the House of Commons, reputed to possess decisive power within the party, has become the best-known parliamentary organization in British politics. It was not created for this purpose, however, and has only become important since 1945. The committee evolved from a group of MPs who first entered Parliament in the general election of November 1922. The date in the name derives from this fact, and not from any connection with the fall of **David Lloyd George** in October 1922: None of its founders played any part in those events. The 1922 Committee was formed on 18 April 1923 with the simple aim of helping these new MPs find their parliamentary feet. For most of the inter-war period it functioned more as a lecture club than as a pressure group. Unlike other similar unofficial groups, the 1922 committee did not fade away. This was due to two factors. First, the Committee resolved in December 1925 to open its doors to all Conservative backbenchers, thus continually renewing the membership. Second, the 1922 Committee had no factional purpose and was loyal to the leadership: The party whips found it useful and took it under their wing. Although originally unofficial, since the mid-1920s the committee has become closely integrated into the formal party structures. Since 1965 the 1922 Committee has acquired administrative functions in leadership elections due to the fact that the leader has always been chosen by the parliamentary party. The influence of the committee grew during the **Churchill** coalition ministry of 1940–5 and was further extended during the thirty years after 1945. It provides a unique sounding board of opinion within the party. The leadership can be swiftly and often sharply alerted to matters causing concern among both MPs and the constituency rank and file. However, the belief that it ensures that unpopular policies are not adopted requires reassessment after the public repudiation of the poll tax during 1987–90.

Stuart Ball

Bibliography

Ball, Stuart. "The 1922 Committee: The Formative Years, 1922–1945," *Parliamentary History*, vol. 9 (1990), pp. 129–57.

Goodhart, Philip. *The 1922.* 1973.

Norton, Philip. "The Parliamentary Party and Party Committees" in Anthony Seldon and Stuart Ball, eds. *Conservative Century: The Conservative Party since 1900.* 1994. pp. 97–144.

No-Conscription Fellowship (1914–1919)

The No-Conscription Fellowship (NCF) was formed late in 1914 by young socialist/pacifists, including Fenner Brockway, editor of the Independent Labour Party's *Labour Leader*, and Clifford Allen, a Cambridge graduate active in socialist politics and journalism. Initially founded with the modest aim of providing a focus for the antiwar sentiments of men of military age who had vowed to resist the imposition of enforced military service during the First World War, the NCF eventually became the largest and most effective antiwar movement in modern British history, providing its 15,000 members with aid, comfort, and camaraderie while simultaneously testing the limits of dissent in a modern liberal society at war.

Until January 1916 the NCF, in conjunction with allied Christian pacifist bodies, especially the Society of Friends, developed an elaborate and efficient national organization while conducting a broad-based propaganda campaign against the threatened imposition of conscription. After compulsory military service was imposed, the NCF announced its intention to resist the implementation of conscription and, even though the 1916 Military Service Act included provisions for conscientious objection, to accept only absolute exemption from all forms of enforced wartime service. The fellowship's determination not to cooperate with any designs of the warrior state, adopted in April 1916 at an emotionally charged national convention, not only brought on a confrontation with the government but also threatened to alienate the majority of its members who were willing to accept something less than absolute exemption as an alternative to combatant military service. Faced with the possible dissolution of their organization, NCF leaders subsequently reversed their position and resolved to support all members whatever the level of their resistance. This decision reflects the moderating influence of older men and women, who took control of the fellowship after most of its younger "absolutist" leaders, including Allen and Brockway, had been imprisoned. Most important in this respect were Catherine E. Marshall, who interrupted her work in the National Union of Women's Suffrage Societies and the Women International League to take responsibility for the day-to-day operation of the NCF; Bertrand Russell, who spoke, wrote, and acted as Chairman of the fellowship until he was imprisoned in early 1918, and Edward Grubb, an elderly Quaker who, as NCF Treasurer, raised the money the fellowship needed to carry on its activities on behalf of imprisoned COs and against continuation of the war.

Throughout the last two years of the war the NCF remained a minor but troublesome irritant to the authorities, using its surprisingly resilient propaganda machinery to expose brutal or illegal treatment of conscientious objectors as well as to agitate, especially among the industrial working classes, for an end to the conflict. The government struck back, raiding NCF headquarters, prosecuting its leaders, and attempting, unsuccessfully, to halt the publication of its weekly paper, *The Tribunal*. But if the NCF managed to survive official persecution, it could claim no great victories, either in helping to shorten the war or even in securing the release of its imprisoned members.

For the individual war resister, its justification was perhaps that the fellowship made it easier for a small minority to follow the dictates of their consciences; for posterity, there was the fact that the injustices and abuses exposed by the NCF in its relentless pursuit of liberty of conscience had a significant impact upon the more humane and rational treatment of COs during the Second World War. Thus, the great achievement of the No-Conscription Fellowship was that in seeking to ensure freedom of conscience for one tiny and despised minority, it helped to establish an important precedent for protecting the civil liberties of all individuals in British society.

Thomas C. Kennedy

Bibliography

Kennedy, Thomas C. "Fighting about Peace: The No-Conscription Fellowship and the British Friends' Service Committee, 1915–1919," *Quaker History*, vol. 69 (1980), pp. 3–22.

———. *The Hound of Conscience: A History of the No-Conscription Fellowship, 1914–1919.* 1981.

Vellacott, Jo. *Bertrand Russell and the Pacifists in the First World War.* 1980.

Norman, Montagu Collet (1871–1950)

Montagu Norman, Governor of the Bank of England during the years 1920–44, was the most influential financial figure of the inter-war period. His reign at the Bank of England proved controversial, contentious, and critical to the events of the 1920s and 1930s.

Norman inherited a strong connection with the Bank of England as his maternal grandfather had been a Governor. After a stint at his grandfather's firm of investment bankers, Brown, Shipley, and Company, Norman joined the bank in a full-time capacity in 1915. The **First World War** was as much a turning point for the "Old Lady of Threadneedle Street," as the bank was called, as it was for Britain as a whole. The unprecedented financial demands of the conflict placed new demands on the bank and on Norman, who became Deputy Governor in 1918 and Governor in 1920. While the bank remained a private institution answerable to its shareholders, its efforts on behalf of the government intensified as Britain became increasingly reliant on American financing, both public and private, to meet the rising costs of the war.

The armistice left Norman in charge of an institution uneasily facing a brave new world. Virtually every European economy was in shambles while the destruction of the Austro-Hungarian and Turkish Empires together with the German and Russian Revolutions devastated the manufacturing and trading links upon which European prosperity depended. Most currencies had radically lost value during the war; all had been removed from the **gold standard**, which in the pre-war world had reigned supreme.

Against this backdrop Norman developed his principles of central banking. Central banks, he believed, should be independent entities entrusted with financial and fiscal questions, while governments could take care of budgetary and political issues. Central to Norman's position was the notion that all currencies must first be stabilized and then returned to the gold standard. Together with his counterparts, Benjamin Strong and George Harrison, the first two Governors of the Federal Reserve Bank of New York, and Hjalmer Schacht, Governor of the Reichsbank, Norman set out to make his goals into reality. British governments appreciated Norman's efforts while resenting his highhandedness and lack of accountability.

During the late 1920s it seemed that Norman's program would be a success. Together with his counterparts he presided over currency stabilizations in France, Belgium, and Germany after first restoring the British gold standard at the pre-war level of £1=$4.86. However, the American stock market boom and crash, followed by the Great Depression, ended the chimerical recovery. By the summer of 1931 Norman knew he faced the prospect of world financial chaos. The failure of the Austrian Credit Anstalt triggered banking catastrophes across Central Europe. With the collapse on 14 July of the Darmstadter und Nationalbank, one of Germany's largest banks, and the subsequent freezing of German banking assets, came a massive British credit exposure and a run on the pound. Suddenly at the beginning of August the survival of British financial stability seemed in question.

Norman, who had long suffered from intermittent nervous exhaustion, found himself unable to cope with the stress of this crisis. However, instead of retreating to South Africa, a frequent choice in such cases, Norman journeyed to Canada. While there, he remained in steady contact with Harrison, advising the American central banker as to the efficacy of the newly formed National government's attempt to rescue the gold standard.

When this effort failed, on 20 September, Norman was en route to Britain. On his arrival he found a changed economic world. He no longer sought to tie British finance to the gold standard; the establishment and nurturing of the Sterling Area became an acceptable substitute. As the 1931 financial crisis had exposed the defects in Norman's control over major financial decisions, he lost autonomy, the Treasury increasing its control over international financial transactions.

At the beginning of the Second World War Norman, who had already served longer in his position than any other Governor, postponed his retirement. An illness in 1944 forced his departure, with a peerage as a reward; thereafter, until his death in 1950, he remained completely isolated from public affairs.

Diane B. Kunz

Bibliography

Boyle, Andrew. *Montagu Norman: A Biography.* 1967.
Clay, Sir Henry. *Lord Norman.* 1957.
Kunz, Diane B. *The Battle for Britain's Gold Standard in 1931.* 1987.
Sayers, R.S. *The Bank of England, 1891–1944.* 1976.

Northcliffe, Lord (Alfred Charles William Harmsworth) (1865–1922)

Lord Northcliffe, the great newspaper proprietor, born Alfred Harmsworth, was the son of an unsuccessful barrister who soon moved the family from his birthplace near Dublin to England. Northcliffe's younger siblings included Harold, who became Northcliffe's business partner and the future Lord Rothermere. The premature death of their father forced Northcliffe to leave school and seek work in 1880. Over the next four decades he created a press empire and became one of the most powerful figures in the overlapping worlds of British journalism and politics. In due course he received a baronetcy (1903), a barony (1905), and a viscountcy (1917).

After free-lancing as a boy journalist and working for a Coventry publisher, Northcliffe launched a weekly, *Answers to Correspondents* (1888). This successful venture was followed by other weeklies, including *Comic Cuts*, which were both entertaining and informative. They addressed a popular rather than a gentlemanly readership, composed of schoolboys and girls, housewives, and men and women employed in lower-middle-class and even working-class occupations. The expanding circulation of these publications enabled the Harmsworth brothers to amass the necessary financial resources to enter the competitive field of daily evening and morning newspapers. They first purchased the *Evening News* (1894) and then founded the *Daily Mail* (1896). The *Daily Mail* broke the mold of mass journalism by offering readers a very inexpensive and attractive morning newspaper. Its circulation soared during the **Boer War**. The steady success of Northcliffe's weekly and daily publications created and sustained the impression that he understood the mind and mood of the masses, primarily the lower middle classes.

Historians have cut Northcliffe's larger than life figure down to size, but his commercial and political achievement remains extraordinary. Although not the only innovator on Fleet Street, he was able to divine which stories, advertisements, contests, and other features would hold the attention of his readers. Sometimes, however, he came close to overreaching himself. The *Daily Mirror* (1903), launched as a woman's newspaper, had to be salvaged by the introduction of photographic illustrations. Less than a decade later, however, it had reached a circulation of 1 million. Northcliffe was not satisfied with his commanding lead over his competitors in the realm of "cheap," or popular, mass journalism. With the acquisition of the Sunday *Observer* (1905), he entered the realm of "quality," or elite, journalism. Many in the **press** and political worlds shuddered when he became the proprietor of *The Times* (1908), but he maintained its special position as a fairly moderate voice of the national and imperial interest. Both the journalistic and financial sides of *The Times* improved under Northcliffe, even if the price for these changes was increased management from the top, directly from the proprietor or indirectly through his new editor, **Geoffrey Dawson** (1912).

In politics Northcliffe was a relatively straightforward imperialist and patriot. After standing unsuccessfully as a Conservative candidate for Portsmouth (1895), he never entered the fray again. Although sometimes seen as the epitome of a press baron whose newspapers forwarded his own party-political views, Northcliffe served the **Conservative Party** without becoming bound to it. Indeed, for a time around the turn of the century he inclined toward the Liberal Imperialist Lord Rosebery. Northcliffe was prepared to abandon unpopular Conservative causes like **tariff reform** and to cultivate some Liberal politicians. His newspapers, for example, gave the benefit of the doubt to the accused Liberal ministers during the pre-war **Marconi scandal** (1912–13). In any case, his business interests took precedence over his party loyalties. His unabashed **imperialism** probably flowed from the fact that the newsworthiness of the Empire benefited his newspapers.

If Northcliffe deserved his reputation for partisanship, it was due to the pressure he applied to governments during the **First World**

War. His newspapers campaigned against the alleged pro-Germanism of **Lord Haldane** and the alleged incompetence of **Lord Kitchener,** and for the creation of an all-party government of national defense. That government emerged in stages, beginning with **H.H.** Asquith's first coalition government (1915), and then, upon the resignations of Asquith and his friends from the **Cabinet,** with **David Lloyd George's** second coalition government (1916). Although he never forfeited the right of his newspapers to criticize the government, Northcliffe cooperated with Lloyd George during the remainder of the war. He served as Minister Plenipotentiary in charge of the British war mission to the United States (1917) and then as Director of Propaganda in Enemy Countries (1918). Northcliffe's fall from political grace was as rapid as his rise. Resigning his directorship when the armistice was agreed, Northcliffe argued with Lloyd George about the composition of the post-war government. Consequently, Lloyd George refused to include him in the British delegation to the Paris Peace Conference and publicly denounced him (1919). Northcliffe expended what little political capital he retained on promoting an Irish settlement (1921). Increasingly mentally unstable, he died soon after completing a world tour.

Northcliffe's drive for success and respectability found its main outlet in the commercial world of journalism, not the political world of parties and parliaments. Perhaps his greatest accomplishment, underlying the relentless acquisition of newspapers and perfection of their "copy," was the simple incorporation of millions of readers into his press empire.

Ian Christopher Fletcher

Bibliography

Koss, Stephen E. *The Rise and Fall of the Political Press in Britain.* 2 vols. 1981–4.

Pound, Reginald, and Geoffrey Harmsworth. *Northcliffe.* 1959.

Taylor, A.J.P. "The Chief" in *Essays in English History.* 1976. pp. 190–5.

Northern Ireland

See ULSTER

Novel, English, 1900–1945

The prestige of British fiction from the early part of the century is associated with innovative artistic aims, which are commonly referred to under the term "modernism." The meaning of the term is vexed by enduring controversy. Usually modernism in literary criticism designates the antagonism of artists flourishing between 1900 and 1930 to most or to all conventions—not just aesthetic, but social, religious, political, and ethical as well—which they identify with a superseded past. In literary production, modernism thus means a break with formerly customary form and content in art—for example, a break with linear, continuous, and unified storytelling, with consistent "life-like" characters, with art's intention to mime or represent history or reality, and with meaning itself. Abstraction of artistic form and of life from ordinary appearances and significances, and a heightening of artistic form for its own sake, are modernist hallmarks.

Simultaneously, in a way that makes palpable the controversial complexity and indeed the self-contradiction of the term and of its reference points, modernism may also stand not for the rejection of the past but for a radical transformative use of past traditions: a way, sometimes, of invoking the importance of history, even if only to announce history's end; a way, at other times, of claiming for modern art a hitherto unprecedented fidelity to history and to history's problematic nature. Modernism may also claim an unprecedented fidelity to reality or to the phenomenology of experience or to being itself. Perhaps the one unifying thread amid such manifold characteristics is the constant intention to produce what is unprecedented. The literary art resulting from modernism's complex of aims is, not surprisingly, highly various. The experimental techniques that compose the celebrated novels *Ulysses* (1922) by **James Joyce** or *The Waves* (1931) by **Virginia Woolf** can be read as the product of the modernist emphasis on form for the sake of form. The momentariness and immediacy of authentic experience that are evoked in *Nostromo* (1904) or *Chance* (1913) by **Joseph Conrad** or in *Pilgrimage* (1913–67) by **Dorothy Richardson** can be read as the product of the modernist emphasis on unexampled fidelity to history and being. But such ways of reading would be more limited in nature than the works themselves. The various characteristics of modernism typically are in play, no matter how self-contradictorily, in any one modernist text. In works by Joyce, Woolf, Conrad, and Richardson one finds equal traces of the intentions to heighten the artifice of art, to heighten the fidelity of art to historical life, and to doubt (no less than to celebrate) the reality or the intelligibility of art, history, and life together.

For a typical example of modernist impulses in fiction one might refer to *Howards End* (1910) by **E.M. Forster**, although this work lacks the glamor and obvious experimentation of Joyce and Woolf. Forster's two heroines, upper-middle-class orphans, inherit the house called Howards End in a way that represents the victorious undermining by feminist impulses of male patriarchy and of British **imperialism**. In the fact that one sister becomes an unashamedly unwed mother, whose child's father has working-class origins and has lost his life to class conflict, Forster suggests the interconnected political ascendancy of women and workers. The forging of hitherto repressed political and social alliances and connections becomes the novel's motto: "Only connect . . ." Nevertheless, *Howards End*, in spite of its motto, exhibits ironic self-consciousness about the real possibilities of novel connections. The story about creating newly liberating collective interests is pervaded by abrupt discontinuities. Indeed, without the latter, no new connections or collectives can come into being. The lifeline of the narrative itself is gaps in sequence, a constant pressure exerted upon unity and coherence. In the more celebrated modernist classics, *Ulysses*, Forster's own later *A Passage to India* (1924), and Woolf's *To the Lighthouse* (1927), a similar pressure is writ large.

A baffled political search for new forms of collective life might account for the constant perplexing of formal unity and continuity in modernist works. One basis for the bafflement is a persistent (if unfulfilled) attempt to theorize a place in nineteenth-century political theories and practices for new twentieth-century responses to gender and sexuality. *The New Machiavelli* (1910) by **H.G. Wells** illustrates the problem. The novel's protagonist searches for a theory of politics that intends to surmount the factitiousness of current ideological distinctions. As he cobbles together features of conservative, anarchist, and socialist thought, the protagonist also turns against the nation-state, in favor of accepting the global interdependencies that are an irreversible inheritance of global imperialism. Yet the obstacle to the political search is the current insufficiently thought-out place of eros in the world order. Traditional

heterosexual norms, including monogamous **marriage**, are identified by Wells with a destructive order of jealousy, a stumbling block in all modern political ideologies. But in *The New Machiavelli* the attempt to theorize sex and gender anew, in a way that will politicize them without at the same time victimizing either conventional or unconventional erotic desires, fails. To come to terms with the failure, or to reverse it, becomes the thematic as well as the formal basis of some of the era's most distinguished novelistic careers.

In Richardson and Woolf **feminism** mediates the opposing claims of eros and politics. Richardson suggests that both political theory and sexual psychology need to revise themselves, by taking as a starting point for change the experience of a unique, transcendental female selfhood. Woolf's polemic *Three Guineas* (1938) solicits feminism's critique of compulsory gender division to urge her readers to opt out of gender and political business-as-usual, and to insist on international **pacifism** as the key to a new collectivity. In Woolf's *Orlando* (1928), and in novels by **Ronald Firbank** and **Sylvia Townsend Warner**, as well as in suppressed work by Forster, transexualism, transvestism, and **homosexuality** are enlisted as forms of liberation from political and imperialist oppressions. Meanwhile, Wells' criticism of the jealous god that is heterosexuality is shared by Joyce and, more complexly, by **D.H. Lawrence**. Lawrence's novels and stories, highly sensitive to the role played by class and race differences and conflicts in the construction of **sexuality**, try to formulate a radically original ethos for heterosexual conduct. But although Lawrence newly locates in bodily eros the sources of tenderness, of personal autonomy, and of a passion for justice, he laments his inability to attach his sexual ethos to a satisfyingly collective political purpose. Similarly, **Ford Madox Ford**, surveying in *Parade's End* (1924–8) the murder of modern democracy by callous national and international interests, represents the ironic history of a pair of lovers whose public-minded virtues have no public political sphere on which to operate and are driven in upon a purely private domain. In all of these novelists, the engagement with the politics and antipolitics of eros (arising, not surprisingly, alongside the ascent of Freud's thought) remains an open tradition of puzzled inquiry, handed on to the century's latter half.

The novels of **Ivy Compton-Burnett, Elizabeth Bowen,** and **Henry Green** typify most powerfully the second generation of modernism and modernism's extension into mid-century. Compton-Burnett's dramas erode the boundary between realism and antirealism, even as her novels play up their high, pure artifice. Their artificiality inheres in their unspecified historical time and in their exactingly subtle dialogue (spoken with equal facility by bourgeois families and their servants). Yet the emotional medium of the novels is real enough: the familiar atmosphere of "family values." *Parents and Children* (1941) typically exhibits Compton-Burnett's picture of these values, which amount to a horrible self-perpetuating selfishness, promulgated in the father's name, constraining even when the patriarch is withdrawn by absence or death. The horror is registered coldly, however, as if the writer wants partly to concede that an artistic representation is not to be strictly identified with any social or historical reality.

Similar contradictory oscillations of attitude toward art's relation to reality inform Bowen and Green. On the one hand, Bowen's work is minutely realistic, both in its concentration on the daily domestic life of **women** and children and in its attention to world history. In *The Heat of the Day* (1949) the personal lives of two women of different classes are inescapably caught up in the conflict with **Fascism.** The story of one of them, who finds out that her English lover is a Nazi spy, symbolically discovers a disturbing political possibility: that Fascism is the inveterate double, and not the opposite, of modern democracy. But the novelist's aim to make fiction serve the investigation of real history goes hand in hand with her production of tales in which she portrays history itself as merely a ghost story. Spectral, both real and unreal, the ghostly nature of history in Bowen results partly from the Second World War's uncanny revival of the experiences of the First. In Henry Green's work the multiple characteristics of modernism (of what might be more accurately called various modernisms) are even more strikingly on show than in the other "second-generation" modernists. Green's *Living* (1929), one of the best modern fictions about urban industrial employers and workers, protests economic inequity, in terms of searching sociological realism. However, Green's career also encompasses, in marked contrast to realism, the fantastic narrative *Concluding* (1948),

set in a girls' school in a welfare-state future. *Concluding* plays an elaborate puzzle-like game with the reader (some of the game's pieces are deliberately left out), in a manner predicting the experimental novels, beginning with **Samuel Beckett's** *Molloy.* But written in a style midway between the aesthetic polarities of *Living* and *Concluding* is Green's *Party-Going* (1939), in which fog-bound passengers in a major London railway station figure the communal and erotic liberation that comes from the ruin of everyday routines. Not incidentally, "party-going" in Green repeats a narrative event and a motif that turns up repeatedly in modernist fiction, most prominently in Woolf and in **Wyndham Lewis,** because of its apparent convenience for dramatizing collective partisan movements, no less than social partying.

Clearly, English experiments with the forms of fiction remain the order of the day in the century's first half. At times the experiments change the genre beyond recognition. The narrative form of novels and histories dissolves into an illogic of fantasies and puns in Joyce's *Finnegans Wake* (1922–39), which represents novel writing and history writing alike as opaque lyric dream-work. Wells' novels about sex and politics eschew the novel's traditional ambition to show life rather than tell it: Wells insists that novels become *essays* about the need for social change. The work of **Aldous Huxley** is similarly antinovelistic. It derides the novel form for stimulating the reader's sense of subjectivity, at the expense of personal and social change, and complains of "the wearisomeness . . . of all those merely descriptive plays and novels, which critics expected one to admire" (*After Many a Summer Dies the Swan,* 1939).

Antinovel novels in the period are complemented by an equally antinovelistic resurgence of romance and fantasy writing, which burgeons alongside the growth of science fiction. Principal among the romance writers is **John Cowper Powys.** *Weymouth Sands* (1934), a typical Powys work, shows how the previous century's realism and naturalism can shade into romance. *Weymouth Sands'* cultural landscape is rooted in the elemental seaside meeting of earth and water, but its story is also about persons who oppose nature by means of intellectual and artistic aims, utopian political aspirations, struggles against the Oedipal structure that has become our second nature, and mysticism. In Powys both nature and culture are the grotesque masks of underlying mysterious cosmic forces, which Powys labors to house in narratives that strain the limits of literary form.

Nowadays it is a critical commonplace that modernism and what follows it—postmodernism—are radically different in character. Yet postmodernism is associated with precisely the mixing of realist and historical aims alongside antirealist and antihistorical ones (and in the same self-conscious, questioning way) exhibited by both generations of modernist novelists. Nowadays it is also claimed that postmodernist writing is acutely conscious, in a way modernism is not, of the political bearings of art. If the latter claim is true, present-day critics may yet have something to learn from the way modernist practices demonstrate that no aesthetic form carries the guarantee of one sort of politics rather than another, and vice versa.

The political antitype of most of the modernist figures mentioned here is **Rudyard Kipling**, whose name remains a byword for the British Empire at its most bloated. Yet Kipling's political conservatism is not matched by aesthetic conservatism, and Kipling's innovative storytelling form issues sometimes in conservative political morals—and sometimes not. Kipling's art exploits foreshortened and elliptical means of narration in order to produce the startling ambiguities that are characteristic of modernism. In "Little Foxes" (1909) these techniques flatter imperialism; in "The Church That Was at Antioch" (1929) these techniques condemn all imperialism (Christianity's especially) for not respecting the multiplicity of human cultures. Frequently Kipling's aesthetic is the ally of promiscuous or illicit sexual passion: "The Wish House" (1924) turns away as much as do the anti-imperialists Joyce and Wells from what Joyce's heroine Molly Bloom calls "stupid husbands jealousy." Of course, the restless play of myriad forms of art that structures Joyce's work makes us expect an alliance of such play with liberal or radical politics, if only because they appear in the work of an Irish rebel against religious and political tyrannies. Yet one finds similarly restless formal novelties structuring Wyndham Lewis' *The Apes of God* (1930) and *The Revenge of Love* (1937), where aesthetic innovation provides—in contrast to Joyce—a conservative rather than liberal perspective on the allegedly bottomless political factitiousness of the **General Strike** of 1926 and the **Spanish Civil War**.

Thus, given the way modernist aesthetic innovation guarantees no fixed accompanying (or even fully legible) political position, it is not surprising that traditional modes of fiction in the early twentieth century also resist easy translation into political terms. The art and politics of writers who were contemporaries of modernism but were not touched by its prestige have been unfairly obscured in literary history. Woolf attacked her senior contemporaries, the popular novelists **Arnold Bennett** and **John Galsworthy**, for their old-fashioned realism and their putative conservatism. But Bennett's *Clayhanger* series (1910–18) uses a conservative aesthetic means to portray the abrupt discontinuities that constitute history, no less than Woolf uses a radical means to portray the same in *The Years* (1937). And Galsworthy's study of a domestic rapist, the "hero" of *A Man of Property* (1906), uses a narrative form reminiscent of Thackeray's to express a feminism that is in line with *Three Guineas*.

Robert L. Caserio

Bibliography

Caserio, Robert L. *The English Novel, 1900–1950: Theory and History* (forthcoming).

Eysteinsson, Astradur. *The Concept of Modernism*. 1990.

Gilbert, Sandra, and Susan Gubar. *No Man's Land: The Place of the Woman Writer in the Twentieth Century*. 1988.

Green, Martin. *The English Novel in the Twentieth Century*. 1984.

Levenson, Michael. *A Genealogy of Modernism*. 1984.

Nash, Christopher. *World Postmodern Fiction*. 1991.

Novel, English, since 1945

During the strife-torn 1940s British publishers averaged 1,419 new novels a year; during the 1980s, this figure had risen to 3,183, approximately one work for each of the estimated 3,400 active novelists in Great Britain. These figures, however, disguise the fact that post-war British fiction has had to struggle as never before to find and to maintain its audience and its dominance in the publishing world. In 1939, 12.5 percent of all books published were fiction; by 1989, this number had declined to 6 percent. Other forms—film, **television**, music video, compact discs, "audiotape books"—have appropriated large portions of the audience. Moreover, the very notion of a literate culture has often been aggressively devalued since the 1960s. As a result, a number of schemes have been evolved to publicize and to support fiction, among them the 1979 Public Lending Right Act, which distributed more than £3 million to 14,149 authors in 1990, and literary prizes, with the prestigious Booker McConnell Award becoming a media event almost eclipsing the Whitbread, W.H. Smith, Somerset Maugham, and other awards.

Throughout the upheavals in the market, novelists have struggled to reinvent their genre, to adopt traditional forms to contemporary culture, and to give a uniquely British shape to the forces of postmodernism. Each decade has given the world an indisputably major work of fiction: L.P. Hartley's *The Go-Between* (1953), John Fowles' *The French Lieutenant's Woman* (1969), **Margaret Drabble**'s *The Realms of Gold* (1975), D.M. Thomas' *The White Hotel* (1981), and Graham Swift's *Waterland* (1983). While it is perhaps too early to discern the cultural dominant of the post-war years, one can see a new and intriguing interaction among high, mass, and emerging cultures.

The moralists and social activists who came to prominence in the 1930s at first dominated the serious fiction market in the decade following Allied victory. **Evelyn Waugh** and **Graham Greene** explored religious dimensions they thought had been missing from British fiction: Waugh's *Brideshead Revisited* (1945) and Greene's *The Heart of the Matter* (1948) and *The End of the Affair* (1951) depicted numinous worlds transformed by miracles and characterized by the paradoxes of love. Greene's pursuits put him on the cover of *Time* magazine and brought censure from the Vatican. The representation of political nightmares, from which the reader was to infer the necessity of maintaining the best in British humanist thought and action, was epitomized in **George Orwell's** *Nineteen Eighty-Four* (1949), whose title immediately became synonymous with the essence of the totalitarian state. It remains the most frequently read and taught novel from this period. Similar political inferences can be drawn from **Aldous Huxley's** *Ape and Essence* (1948), a protest against the arrival of the Atomic Age. Meanwhile, Hartley completed his *Eustace and Hilda* trilogy (1947) and *The Go-Between* (1953), both of which rigorously argued that Freudian and Marxist explanations of guilt and evil should be displaced by a renewal of concepts of individual responsibility. In offering

their religious, political, and humanistic perspectives, this generation of novelists continued and reaffirmed the directions they had taken in the 1930s. Greene remained an active voice in British fiction until his death in 1991.

The mid-1950s and early 1960s brought new sociological voices in those novelists often labeled the "angry young men." The novels of William Cooper, John Wain, Kingsley Amis, John Braine, and Alan Sillitoe addressed the **Labour** government's failures to reshape British society to benefit all of its citizens, the persistence of class struggles, the alienation of the worker in the work place, and the psychological helplessness felt by individuals during the Cold War. The novelists' charges constituted a global anger directed, often misdirected, toward the Establishment. In Cooper's *Scenes from Provincial Life* (1950), Wain's *Hurry on Down* (1953), Amis' *Lucky Jim* (1954), Braine's *Room at the Top* (1957), and Sillitoe's *Saturday Night and Sunday Morning* (1958), virile, aggressive, often amoral protagonists use cunning and **sexuality** as survival skills necessary to wage their picaresque adventures against the post-war world. The characters show a comic sensibility often overlooked by readers more intent on the sociological and political implications of their authors' works. That these novels were often brilliantly adapted by the revitalized British **film industry** helped earn them wide recognition. By the early 1960s, however, new winds were sweeping fiction in other directions. The "angries" continued to publish into the 1980s, but they never achieved the dominance they enjoyed for a few years in the 1950s and 1960s. Such later writers as Barry Hines and David Storey, who emphasized the dignity of craftsmanship and talent on the playing field and in the workshop, tempered the earlier anger, even as they maintained the class focus of fiction.

Sociological and historical ambitions for fiction are represented also in popular *roman fleuves* such as **Anthony Powell's** *A Dance to the Music of Time* (1951–75) and Lawrence Durrell's *The Alexandria Quartet* (1957–60). But telling blows against the sociological focus came from **Anthony Burgess'** *A Clockwork Orange* (1962), Fowles' *The Collector* (1963) and *The Magus* (1965), and B.S. Johnson's *Albert Angelo* (1964). These works savaged especially the moralist's and the activist's fiction and spoke urgently of reinstating the modernist projects of **James Joyce, Virginia Woolf**, and others. Burgess' fifteen-year-old Alex, Fowles' almost neurasthenic Ferdinand Clegg, and Johnson's Mr. Albert quickly unmasked the anger of the earlier novels by exhibiting the antisocial thug, the anarchistic kidnapper incapable of intellectual growth, and the reforming teacher overwhelmed by the social forces unleashed by the late 1950s in ways that neither the fashions of Carnaby Street, the music of The Beatles, nor a plethora of consumer goods could contain. By foregrounding language directly descended from Joyce's *Finnegans Wake* (1939), existential thought directly imported from Jean-Paul Sartre, and rebellion against the traditional look of the written page, Burgess, Fowles, and Johnson announced that postmodernism had arrived in British fiction. The announcement would be completed by Michael Moorcock's *Breakfast in the Ruins* (1971), which deconstructed the very form of the novel by unraveling its historical, subjective, mythic, and thematic tendencies, and Johnson's *Christie Malry's Own Double Entry* (1973, but planned in 1964), a hilarious send-up of the angry young hero.

Postmodernism has taken many forms in British fiction since the 1960s, some of them topical, some formal, some thematic. Experimental, iconoclastic engagement with the past and with ideas of history, or with fantasies of the future, has shaped the works of such novelists as Drabble, Swift, Fowles, Peter Ackroyd, Alasdair Gray, Brigid Brophy, Muriel Spark, J.G. Ballard, and even William Golding. Between the publication of *Lord of the Flies* (1954) and the awarding of the Nobel Prize in 1983, which was Great Britain's first such award since 1953, Golding seemed ambiguously independent of literary fashions, yet his "counterbooks"—Jorge Luis Borges' term for a book that invades, escapes from, or replies to an earlier book—mark one of the major tendencies in postmodern British fiction, seen in such works as David Lodge's *The British Museum Is Falling Down* (1965), Jean Rhys' *Wide Sargasso Sea* (1966), Angus Wilson's *No Laughing Matter* (1967), Brian Aldiss' *Frankenstein Unbound* (1973), George MacDonald Fraser's *Flashman Papers* (1969–90), and Drabble's *The Gates of Ivory* (1992). The best-known representative work, though, remains Fowles' *The French Lieutenant's Woman* (1969), which folds an existential parable and concerns with the "death of the author" and the "death of the subject" around a loving simultaneous re-creation and interroga-

tion of every aspect of the Victorian realistic novel. Fascination with works, figures, and fashions of earlier centuries, without turning to historical fiction, remains strong in Ackroyd's *Hawksmoor* (1985) and Antonia S. Byatt's extremely popular *Possession* (1990). The pasts of individuals have been brilliantly explored by **Doris Lessing**'s *The Golden Notebook* (1962), Drabble's *The Realms of Gold* (1975), and Swift's *Waterland* (1983), whose narrators' quest for meaning, purpose, and shape in their lives (within the issues raised by **feminism** in the cases of Lessing and Drabble). The experimentalism of Johnson, Rayner Heppenstall, Fowles, Brophy, and Spark has been fruitfully extended by Thomas' *The White Hotel* (1981), an extraordinarily powerful novel that both uses and abuses Freud, and by Julian Barnes' *Flaubert's Parrot* (1984) and *A History of the World in 10½ Chapters* (1989), both of which test the very boundaries of narrative, moving, as they do, toward the spatial rather than the more usual temporal and historical features of narrative. A "French connection" has been nurtured by Christine Brooke-Rose, who lives and teaches in France and who has written some of the most challenging postmodernist works, from *Such* (1966) to *Textermination* (1991).

One need only look at the names of a number of recently published authors to realize the importance of postcolonialist **Commonwealth literature** in contemporary British fiction: J.M. Coetzee, Kazuo Ishiguro, Hanif Kureishi, Timothy Mo, V.S. Naipaul, and Salman Rushdie. While these authors bring issues of pluralism in race, religion, family, and even diet to British fiction, lesbian and gay authors such as Neil Bartlett, Patrick Gale, Alan Hollingshurst, and Jeanette Winterson have placed the sexually marginalized worlds before the readers in *Ready to Catch Him Should He Fall* (1990), *The Aerodynamics of Pork* (1986), *The Swimming Pool Library* (1988), and *Oranges Are Not the Only Fruit* (1985).

Of course, the postmoderns also keep company with a number of authors more traditional in matters of forms and topics: **Iris Murdoch**, Anita Brookner, Penelope Lively, and Ian McEwan. Also, contemporary British fiction continues the earlier traditions of fantasy, **detective fiction**, and science fiction in authors such as Richard Adams, P.D. James, and Ballard.

David Leon Higdon

Bibliography

Higdon, David Leon. *Shadows of the Past in Contemporary British Fiction.* 1985.

Massie, Allan. *The Novel Today: A Critical Guide to the British Novel, 1970–1989.* 1990.

McEwan, Neil. *The Survival of the Novel: British Fiction in the Later Twentieth Century.* 1981.

Scanlan, Margaret. *Traces of Another Time: History and Politics in Postwar British Fiction.* 1990.

Stevenson, Randall. *The British Novel since the Thirties.* 1986.

Nuclear Power

Judged against the hopes with which civil nuclear development began in the 1950s, the outcome has been disappointing. A fuel-cycle business has been built up and the overall safety record has been good, but efforts to establish indigenous reactor types and to achieve exports with them have failed. If nuclear power has any immediate future in the United Kingdom, it must now be based on the American Pressurized Water Reactor (PWR). In the mid-1990s, however, nuclear power is still not really popular with either the public or the political parties, and with a major government review having begun in 1994, a question mark continues to hang over the industry.

Nuclear power in Britain effectively began with Calder Hall. Designed as a power station, it was re-optimized as a plutonium producer to meet an increased military demand for this fissile material. Even so, when Calder began to operate in 1956, it was hailed as a power station and a world first. The U.K. Atomic Energy Authority (UKAEA), half public corporation, half government department, had meanwhile been created in 1954. In 1955 a government White Paper announced a first nuclear power program of 1,500–2,000 megawatts, and, as a third major initiative, private industry was encouraged to organize itself into all-purpose consortia to construct nuclear stations on a turn-key basis—and five such consortia came into being. The commitment to a first nuclear program was made amid optimism about nuclear economics and against the background of a **coal industry** barely able to meet demand.

If the government's 1955 decision was bold, that of 1957 to expand to 5,000–6,000 megawatts was rash. The 1957 decision was taken following the successful opening of Calder Hall, and also the 1956 **Suez crisis**, which briefly interrupted oil supplies. However, the coal situation was already easing, oil became abundant, and the size of conventional power stations rapidly increased and their economics correspondingly improved, forcing nuclear to address a moving cost target. The 1957 program was almost immediately cut, and a more severe reduction followed in 1960.

Although several reactor types were planned for the first nuclear program, its nine stations all eventually used the same Magnox reactor, though the designs differed in detail so that there were no advantages from replication. Magnox reactors had a graphite moderator to slow the neutrons produced by fission of the fuel (which was contained in Magnox alloy cans); they were cooled by carbon dioxide under pressure; and, since the United Kingdom had at first no source of enriched uranium, they were fueled with natural uranium. In the late 1950s the UKAEA decided on a "mark II" of Magnox. This was the Advanced Gas Cooled Reactor (AGR), which uses slightly enriched uranium fuel. The UKAEA also decided to develop the Steam Generating Heavy Water Reactor (SGHWR) and joined with European partners to develop the High Temperature Reactor (HTR), a "mark III" of the basic line. Because all of these reactors could utilize only a small percentage of the energy potentially available in natural uranium, the UKAEA also developed the Fast Breeder Reactor (FBR), fueled with a mixture of the uranium-238 that was useless in other types of reactor and the plutonium produced by those other reactors. Experimental SGHWR and HTR reactors were built, as were a prototype and a demonstration FBR.

In the early 1960s the government was asked to approve a second nuclear program. The UKAEA wanted this based on its AGR, but the Central Electricity Generating Board (CEGB), the public utility for electricity supply in England and Wales, indicated it wished to consider all reactor types. After the American breakthrough to economic nuclear power at Oyster Creek in 1963, the CEGB insisted on considering American reactors. The result was a major argument between the UKAEA and the CEGB.

To resolve this the government announced a formal appraisal of competing tenders for a second (B) power station at Dungeness. Few outside Britain thought the 1965 appraisal—of the AGR's claims versus those of the American Light Water Reactors (LWRs)—was objective. The winner was held to be one particular AGR design, with the runner-up an American Boiling Water Reactor (BWR). Unfortunately, serious shortcomings emerged in the winning AGR design, and Dungeness B took almost twenty years to complete. Constructing it forced the winning consortium out of business; and even afterward the station proved unreliable.

The 1965 appraisal was represented as constituting Britain's own breakthrough to economic power, but whereas Oyster Creek led to a boom in nuclear ordering both in the United States and internationally, no AGRs were exported—even the Magnox design had managed two such sales.

After the 1965 appraisal, economic nuclear power seemed to threaten coal. This precipitated arguments with the National Coal Board, but these eased when AGR performance fell short of expectation. Reorganization of the construction industry, begun with a reduction from five to three consortia in the early 1960s, was a more protracted problem that eventually left just one construction organization.

Another issue precipitated by the switch to enriched-uranium reactors concerned the source of this enrichment. In 1969 the United Kingdom, West Germany, and the Netherlands agreed to develop the centrifuge as an alternative to diffusion, the enrichment method used earlier for nuclear weapons. This tripartite agreement was much criticized as possibly facilitating the proliferation of nuclear weapons. In a related move, the UKAEA's fuel business was transferred to a separate public company, British Nuclear Fuels Limited, in 1971.

In the early 1970s, with the CEGB briefly seeking a large tranche of nuclear power, the only British candidate was the SGHWR, and in 1974 the government decided in favor of this and against the PWR, which the CEGB then wanted. However, by 1976 it was clear the SGHWR was unsuitable and must be canceled, and in 1978 the government decided to build two further AGRs. This made seven AGRs in all, but again there were no advantages from design replication. This (Labour) government also ordered further studies of the PWR, and in 1979 a new (Conservative) government confirmed that it wished Britain to switch to PWRs. This required a public inquiry. One major nuclear inquiry had already been held in 1977 to approve construction of a spent-fuel reprocessing plant at Windscale (Sellafield). The PWR inquiry for the Sizewell B station proved exceptionally protracted. It ran from 1983 to 1985, with the Secretary of State's final approval coming only in 1987. The £2 billion plant is now expected to commission in February 1995.

Despite a serious accident with a military reactor at Windscale in 1957, nuclear power remained popular until the late 1960s, but opposition gradually grew, centering on issues of need, safety, decommissioning, and nuclear weapon proliferation raised in the Windscale and Sizewell inquiries. There was also much concern about, and study of, possible links between radiation releases at Sellafield and Dounreay and increased cancer incidence at these sites. Public opposition also manifested itself during efforts to establish disposal facilities for both high- and intermediate-level radioactive waste, responsibility for this area having been placed in 1982 with a new organization, the Nuclear Industry Radioactive Waste Executive (NIREX).

The Conservative governments of the 1980s initially supported nuclear power strongly—a White Paper provided for at least one nuclear station a year in the decade from 1982—but when in 1989 it proved impossible to include the nuclear stations in the privatization of the electricity industry, this support turned to skepticism, and the government decided to place a moratorium on the construction of three further nuclear stations provisionally planned to follow Sizewell B until after the 1994 review. In 1992 the government also decided to abandon further research on the FBR, the receding prospects of FBR commercialization having led in the 1980s to the United Kingdom joining a collaborative European FBR program. There was even a suggestion at the end of 1992 that the reprocessing plant being built at Windscale following the 1977 inquiry might not be allowed to operate, because the plutonium it would produce would no longer be wanted for FBRs, and permanent storage of spent fuel was by 1992 at least as attractive an option, but commissioning began in 1994.

In 1992, despite an enormous investment, whether measured financially or in scientific and engineering talent, the United Kingdom generated only about 20–25 percent of its electricity from nuclear power, a figure that will drop significantly over the next decade as more

Magnox reactors reach the end of their operational lives.

Roger Williams

Bibliography

Chesshire, John. "Why Nuclear Power Failed the Market Test in the UK," *Energy Policy*, vol. 20 (1992), pp. 744–54.

Gowing, Margaret. *Independence and Deterrence: Britain and Atomic Energy, 1945–1952*. 2 vols. 1974.

Hall, Tony. *Nuclear Politics: The History of Nuclear Power in Britain*. 1986.

Williams, Roger. *The Nuclear Power Decisions: British Policies, 1953–1978*. 1980.

Nuclear Weapons

After the United States and the Soviet Union, Britain became the world's third nuclear weapon state. Britain's weapon program draws attention to the specific problems confronted by a medium power in trying to sustain a military capability at the leading edge of technology: While policy has been driven by both political and military needs for independence, practically Britain's program has been characterized by high levels of reliance on American weapon systems.

British interest in the military potential of the atom was sparked during the **Second World War** by the fear that Germany might be working on such a project. A study by two scientists working in Britain (Frisch-Peierls memorandum) led to the establishment in 1940 of the official Maud Committee, which recommended in July 1941 the development of an atomic bomb. By secret wartime agreements between Prime Minister **Winston Churchill** and President Franklin D. Roosevelt, signed at Quebec in August 1943 and at Hyde Park in September 1944, Britain joined in a collaborative program of research with the United States.

British expectations that a joint British-American atomic venture would be continued in the post-war period were dashed by the McMahon Act of 1946, which prohibited sharing of sensitive nuclear information with foreign countries. In any case, there was a widespread assumption at the highest levels of British government that a British atomic bomb should be manufactured, and, after decisions in 1945 and 1946 to establish a research establishment and a nuclear reactor, a **Cabinet** subcommittee formally decided on 8 January 1947 to proceed to develop a British weapon. Simultaneously, work was commenced on design of a new generation of strategic bombers (V-bombers—Valiant, Victor, and Vulcan).

The first British device was tested on the Monte Bello Islands off Northwest Australia in October 1952. This success was marred by the fact that the United States and the Soviet Union were already embarking on tests of the much more powerful hydrogen bomb, and in mid-1954 the Cabinet decided that Britain, too, must have the most-up-to-date weapons possible. A British thermonuclear device was tested at Christmas Island in 1957.

Britain began to acquire an operational atomic capability from 1956 but discovered that the technological competition of the two superpowers was already pressing into the missile age. The fear was that Britain's V-bombers would become progressively vulnerable either to attack by Soviet missiles before they could leave the ground or to new surface-to-air missiles that would defend Soviet territory. Accordingly, Britain had also begun to develop its own medium-range ballistic missile, known as Blue Streak, and, as an interim measure, had also decided in March 1957 to deploy American Thor missiles at bases in Britain. Both of these missiles were liquid-fueled, which would mean a fueling delay before they could be launched, and fears grew that this would render them vulnerable to attack on the ground.

Increasingly, the British government sought assistance from the United States. Despite an official statement on defense in 1957 that emphasized Britain's need for an independent deterrent, efforts were redoubled to secure information from the United States about warhead design that would permit Britain to produce a lighter weapon that made more efficient use of scarce fissile material. This objective was achieved in July 1958 with the signing of a bilateral agreement on atomic energy that made Britain a privileged partner of the United States as far as nuclear information was concerned. In 1960 the Cabinet decided to cancel the Blue Streak program, but, before doing so, Prime Minister **Harold Macmillan** secured initial American agreement to sell to Britain the Skybolt missile that was then under development for the U.S. Air Force. This missile could be launched from the V-bombers and, having a range of 1,000 miles, would avoid the need for the bombers to enter into heavily defended air space.

A crisis was created for the British nuclear deterrent when, in December 1962, the Kennedy administration announced cancellation of the Skybolt program. At an emotional and difficult meeting between Macmillan and President John F. Kennedy at Nassau in the Bahamas in December 1962, the President agreed, against the wishes of many senior State Department advisers, to sell to Britain the Polaris missile, which would be launched from a submarine. Under the terms of the agreement, Britain would build its own **submarines** and design its own warheads, but much of the technical information for this effort was supplied by the Americans.

The fleet of four submarines carrying Polaris submarine-launched ballistic missiles has been the mainstay of the British strategic deterrent since 1969. In the 1970s the government undertook a secret program, known as Chevaline, to enhance the ability of Polaris to evade the anti-ballistic missile system the Soviet Union was deploying around Moscow. It was believed that a combination of three warheads, and various decoys, would penetrate Soviet defenses, but the cost of Chevaline, estimated at £1 billion, was very high. Accordingly, when planning commenced for the eventual replacement of the Polaris fleet, there was financial pressure to buy from the United States rather than develop a purely British weapon. In 1980 the United States agreed to sell to Britain the C4 Trident 1 missile, and in 1982 this was changed to allow Britain to acquire the more advanced D5 Trident 11 version.

British determination to acquire nuclear weapons was driven by a combination of military and political considerations, each of which changed over time. During the Second World War the fear of facing an atomic-armed Germany was the determining factor, but even then it was recognized that an atomic weapon would be vital in the post-war period. Early British strategic thinking was obsessed with the potential vulnerability to Soviet atomic attack of the small British Isles, with dense population, and hence with the need to have a deterrent against such attack. By the first half of the 1950s the military case for an independent British deterrent was being expressed primarily in terms of having the capacity to destroy targets in the Soviet Union that directly, and much more immediately, threatened Britain and that might not be given such high priority in American war plans. However, the endeavor to target Soviet

air bases and atomic installations became increasingly unrealistic by the late 1950s with the growth of Soviet nuclear power, and henceforth British doctrine rested largely on being able to mount an effective threat against Soviet population and industrial centers.

Underlying British policy statements has undoubtedly been the concern not to be wholly dependent upon the nuclear guarantee offered by the United States through the North Atlantic Treaty Organization (NATO). Absolute confidence in the willingness of the United States to put itself at nuclear risk for the sake of its European allies was questioned once the Soviets developed intercontinental missiles capable of reaching the continental United States and the two superpowers attained broad strategic parity. Independent deterrents have, therefore, been argued to contribute to British security; in recent years, the official doctrine justifying maintenance of a British nuclear force has been that of the "second center of decision."

Politically, the British program has reflected both specific and general motivations. Much of this has been associated with the special relationship with the United States. Early post-war British concerns were a somewhat contradictory determination to avoid undue dependence upon the United States and at the same time to prove to the United States that Britain was a worthwhile nuclear partner and thereby hasten the reestablishment of wartime collaboration. Additionally, in the first half of the 1950s British leaders thought that a deterrent would give Britain influence over American policy at a time when there was much anxiety over American policy in Korea and Indochina. In the late 1950s there was also some political incentive to emphasize the nuclear aspects of Britain's defense policy as a less costly alternative to conventional defenses, thus permitting some reduction in the overall costs of British defense, which had touched 10 percent of the gross national product during the Korean War. Finally, at a time when Britain was in relative political and economic decline, some saw political value in a British deterrent as a symbol of international status.

British nuclear policy became controversial in the late 1950s as people became concerned about the effects of atmospheric testing, and during this period the **Campaign for Nuclear Disarmament** became a vocal champion of opposition to the country's policy. Renewed disquiet about the British deterrent emerged in the early 1980s with large-scale demonstrations. Despite this, and despite the **Labour Party** having periodically favored unilateral nuclear disarmament, the British deterrent has been maintained by both Labour and **Conservative** governments when in power.

Ian Clark

Bibliography

Clark, Ian, and Nicholas J. Wheeler. *The British Origins of Nuclear Strategy, 1945–1955.* 1989.

Freedman, Lawrence. *Britain and Nuclear Weapons.* 1980.

Gowing, Margaret. *Britain and Atomic Energy, 1939–1945.* 1964.

———. *Independence and Deterrence: Britain and Atomic Energy, 1945–1952.* 2 vols. 1974.

Pierre, Andrew J. *Nuclear Politics: The British Experience with an Independent Strategic Force, 1939–1970.* 1972.

Nursing

If viewed from the vantage point of the history of professions, the history of the nursing profession in twentieth-century Britain can be considered as the history of failure. Nurses have never achieved the degree of self-regulation or autonomy traditionally associated with the **medical profession.** Nor are they likely to do so, so long as the dominance of medicine depends upon the subordination of nurses. Although they may at times have been among the fiercest critics of doctors and lawyers, sociologists have also paradoxically legitimized the privileged position of doctors and lawyers by setting them up as the standard by which all other professions are judged.

Sociologically informed analyses of nursing have dominated the historiography of the profession. Abel-Smith was the first to break the influence of internalist accounts of nursing history in the 1960s. His was very much an account of nursing as case study in the politics of professional closure between 1800 and 1948. He argues that attempts to set and maintain the purity of professionally set standards for entry into the profession were overridden by the pragmatic demands of politics and economics. Davies, in a more thorough-going sociological study of the professions, tested the validity of critiques of the professions that emerged in the 1970s against the historical

record of nursing and concluded that nurses' quest for autonomy was a "constant casualty" of government policy and wider social and political pressures.

Both Abel-Smith and Davies assume the antagonism and opposition between the interests of the state and those of professions. Nursing historians now argue that not only should nursing as a profession be considered as a contested sociological category, but that reform in nursing can best be understood in the context of convergence between nursing and the state.

This can be illustrated by the struggle for occupational licensing by nurses through the Nurses' Registration Act of 1919. The achievement of state registration has been explained as the product of sophisticated lobbying tactics by nurses, growing consensus in favor of registration within pressure groups, and the connections with **women's suffrage.** But the role of the government, and particularly the establishment of a Ministry of Health in 1919 and its plans for reconstructing health services, have been relatively neglected. These were crucial contributory factors to nurses securing the regulatory changes in the governance of their affairs and practice that registration might deliver. Standardizing the qualifications of nurses was likely to play an important part in creating a mobile nursing work force for use in the coordinated health service that was envisaged by the architects of **David Lloyd George's** coalition government's social reconstruction package. However, attempts to reconstruct the health services and unify the various branches of nursing fell prey to economic retrenchment. Nursing services throughout the inter-war period remained divided according to gender, class, specialty, and national and political identity.

The introduction of a **National Health Service** (NHS) in 1946 promised to break down the professional and organizational barriers to co-operation between nurses working in different branches of the health services. But political horse-trading and vested interests ensured that the organization of the NHS retained certain traditional features that militated against the radical reconstruction of service organization; the tripartite structure of local authority, hospital, and general practitioner services was left intact.

Anticipated changes in the structure and delivery of health services stimulated attempts to harmonize nursing with such changes and in particular to rethink the place that nursing education might have within an integrated system of health care in 1948 and 1974. The most recent expression of this trend can be found in what have come to be known as the Project 2000 proposals. These aim to de-institutionalize nurse training and create a flexible and mobile work force through a common foundation program and specialist branches of nursing. Such proposals can be seen as a strategy designed to prepare nursing for an increasingly competitive and differentiated health care market and to move nursing education into a closer relationship with institutions of higher education.

It is ironic that the radicalism of Project 2000 recapitulates some of the central features of an earlier model of nursing reform in terms of its entry criteria, curricular organization, and educational objectives. This strategy has its roots in the registrationist program of nursing reform canvassed by Mrs. Bedford Fenwick and her allies at the turn of the century. Thus it would appear the legacy of the past is very much in evidence in the present.

Anne Marie Rafferty

Bibliography

Abel-Smith, Brian. *A History of the Nursing Profession.* 1960.

Davies, Celia, ed. *Rewriting Nursing History.* 1980.

Dingwell, Robert, Anne Marie Rafferty, and Charles Webster. *An Introduction to the Social History of Nursing.* 1988.

Webster, Charles. *The Health Services since the War: Problems of Health Care: The National Health Service before 1957.* 1988.

White, Rosemary. *Social Change and the Development of the Nursing Profession.* 1978.

Nutrition

See DIET AND NUTRITION

Observer, The

The *Observer*, launched in 1791, is Britain's oldest Sunday newspaper. Under a succession of editors and proprietors it has enjoyed periods of considerable influence during the twentieth century, particularly under its two most celebrated editors, **J.L. Garvin** and David Astor.

Founded by W.S. Bourne, the *Observer* had an undistinguished Victorian history, and by the end of the nineteenth century the paper was under the uninspired direction of the Beer family, with a net sale of between only 2,000 and 4,000 copies a week. By the early 1900s the Beers were looking for a buyer to relieve them of a property that was losing £15,000 a year. In 1905 they sold the paper for £4,000 to **Lord Northcliffe**, a journalist of genius, if at times an overpowering and interfering proprietor, who was determined to, as he put it, rescue the *Observer* from the "Fleet (Street) ditch." To this end, he appointed J.L. Garvin as editor in 1908. Garvin, probably the most gifted journalist of his generation, was born in 1868 in humble circumstances in Birkenhead and largely self-educated. In politics, Garvin's early political hero was the Irish nationalist Charles Stewart Parnell, but he transferred his allegiance to Joseph Chamberlain in 1903 when he helped campaign for Chamberlain's program of **tariff reform** and imperial unity. He remained attached to Chamberlain's brand of Liberal Imperialism, within the Unionist Party, for the rest of his life.

Under Garvin the fortunes of the *Observer* improved rapidly, both in journalistic and financial terms. Garvin can be credited with the invention of modern Sunday journalism on the *Observer*, and as the Victorian sabbath was giving way to the Edwardian weekend, so the middle classes responded to a paper that sought,

in Garvin's own words, to be "half a newspaper; half a magazine or serial." His trenchant weekly signed column on the editorial pages soon became required reading for the political classes and became the most famous feature of the paper until he left the *Observer* in 1942. Garvin established the *Observer*'s reputation for informed and independent political comment with a series of campaigns such as his warnings of the German danger and the need for naval rearmament in 1908–11 and his principled defense of the **House of Lords** during the 1911 **constitutional crisis**.

So independent a writer as Garvin, however, could not have been expected to survive too long in harmony with a proprietor such as Northcliffe, a man of equally strong view, and the inevitable irreconcilable disagreement came in 1911. Northcliffe generously allowed Garvin three weeks to find an alternative buyer for the paper before he would buy Garvin's share in the paper and own it outright. Garvin, however, found William Waldorf Astor, who bought the *Observer* for £45,000 in 1911, beginning the paper's connection with the Astor family that would last until 1976. The moving spirit behind William Waldorf Astor's purchase of the paper was, in fact, his son Waldorf Astor, who, from the start, was the *de jure* proprietor, becoming the *de facto* proprietor on his father's death in 1919. It was during the early years of the Astor proprietorship that Garvin's *Observer* reached the peak of its influence and commercial success—the paper was selling 200,000 copies a week by the early 1920s.

During the 1930s, however, Garvin's powers began to wane, and the reputation of the *Observer* began to suffer. The paper also attracted criticism for its support of the **Neville**

Chamberlain government's appeasement of Nazi Germany during the late 1930s. Garvin and Astor began to disagree seriously on this issue after the Munich conference and on the support that the paper gave to Chamberlain from 1939 to 1940 and to Winston Churchill from 1940 to 1942. Garvin's enthusiasm for, and Astor's reservations about, Churchill's competence as a war leader led to Garvin's enforced resignation amidst considerable bitterness in February 1942.

Garvin's peremptory departure plunged the paper into crisis, and a series of temporary editors brought the paper out for the rest of the war, most notably the paper's drama critic, Ivor Brown, from 1942 to 1948. However, the most important figure in the history of the post-Garvin era was David Astor, Waldorf's second son. Astor was, politically, a Liberal strongly interested in foreign affairs, and through his recruitment of a number of new, often émigre, writers, he had transformed the *Observer* from the largely Conservative paper that it had become under Garvin to the leader of liberal opinion in Britain from the late 1940s through to the 1960s. Astor attracted a high caliber of writer, like George Orwell, Sebastian Haffner, Isaac Deutscher, and Anthony Sampson, who gave the paper an intellectual distinction greater than any of its rivals. In 1945 a trust was created to run the paper, and in 1948 David Astor was appointed editor, although he had been effectively determining policy since 1942.

Under Astor the *Observer* enjoyed a period of influence that surpassed Garvin's "golden age" during the First World War. The paper became widely known for its principled progressive campaigns, most notably against the continuation of white minority rule in Africa (and particularly in South Africa) and against capital punishment in Britain. The paper was involved in the founding of such organizations as Amnesty International. Its most important political intervention under Astor was its attack on Anthony Eden's government during the Suez crisis in 1956; the *Observer*'s editorial of November 4 did much to undermine confidence in Eden's handling of the crisis.

However, from the early 1960s onward, with increasing competition from the *Sunday Telegraph* and a revitalized *Sunday Times*, the *Observer* experienced increasing financial difficulties, which, in 1976, led to its sale to the American oil company, Atlantic Richfield, controlled by Robert Anderson. Astor retired as

editor in 1975 and was replaced by his deputy, Donald Trelford, who was still editor in the 1990s. After investing a lot of money in the paper for little return, Anderson, a patron of Liberal causes throughout the world, sold the paper to "Tiny" Rowland's Lonrho corporation in 1981. The sale to Lonrho aroused considerable controversy, as it was feared that Lonrho's extensive commercial interests in Africa would compromise the *Observer*'s capacity to speak out independently on African affairs. In 1993 the *Observer* was taken over by the *Guardian*, the one quality daily lacking a Sunday publication, and seemed likely to revive its flagging liberal reputation.

Richard Cockett

Bibliography

Ayerst, David. *Garvin and the* Observer. 1985.
Cockett, Richard. *David Astor and the Ob-server*. 1991.
Gollin, Alfred M. *J.L. Garvin and the Ob-server, 1908 to 1914: A Study in a Great Editorship*. 1960.

Official Secrets Act

Dating from 1889, the Official Secrets Act, amended several times, has been the government's legal weapon against espionage throughout the twentieth century. Portions of the act dealing with the disclosure of official information, however, have given rise to considerable controversy. Freedom of the press, government accountability, and the rights of the citizen have been used by critics in arguing that the act is anachronistic and open to abuse by the state.

The Official Secrets Act of 1889 was drawn up after it became clear that existing laws were inadequate to deal with suspected spies and the problem of civil servants leaking confidential information to the press. Section one of the act dealt with espionage, while section two made it an offense for any Crown servant or contractor "corruptly or contrary to his official duty" to reveal anything learned at work to someone to whom "it ought not, in the interests of State or otherwise in the public interest, to be communicated at that time."

In 1911, amidst growing fears of German spies, the government amended the act to increase its scope and make it more effective. The 1911 Official Secrets Act made it an offense not only to communicate official information, but also to receive it knowingly. In 1920 further amendments were introduced, chief among them a shifting of the burden of proof from the prosecution to the accused: The defendant, rather than the Crown, now had to demonstrate that no "guilty intent" was involved. A new section six, furthermore, made it a crime to withhold information concerning any offense under the act.

Public controversy has continually dogged section two of the act, especially when particular cases are at issue. Most notable for the criticism they generated have been the case of Duncan Sandys in 1938 (centering on public disclosure of sensitive information on the state of anti-aircraft defenses), the 1971 *Sunday Telegraph* affair (over Nigerian arms sale leaks), the 1978 "ABC" trial (in the wake of investigation by journalists into the actions of army intelligence), and three major cases in the mid-1980s involving unauthorized disclosures by various civil servants: Sarah Tisdall on the introduction of cruise missiles to Greenham Common, Clive Ponting on the sinking of the *Belgrano*, and Peter Wright on MI5 in *Spycatcher* (1986).

Such high-profile cases—many of them unsuccessfully prosecuted—have highlighted either the iniquities or the inadequacies of the act, depending on opinions as to the degree to which the state ought to restrict public access to information. Various attempts were made to overhaul the act after a government-appointed departmental committee under Lord Franks confirmed in 1972 that serious problems existed. It was only at the end of the 1980s, however, that the law was further amended under the **Conservative** government of **Margaret Thatcher**. The strengthening of section two in the 1989 Official Secrets Act has generated its own share of controversy, being regarded by its critics as a measure designed to muzzle civil servants once and for all, irrespective of the nature of the material they might leak and regardless of whether or not the disclosure is in the public interest.

S.P. Mackenzie

Bibliography

Griffith, John. "The Official Secrets Act, 1989," *Journal of Law and Society*, vol. 16 (1989), pp. 273–90.

Hooper, David. *Official Secrets: The Use and Abuse of the Act.* 1987.

Michael, James. *The Politics of Secrecy.* 1982.

Old-Age Pensions

A system of state old-age pensions was first introduced in Britain by the 1908 Old-Age Pensions Act. Prior to this, most old people had supported themselves by working—in the early 1900s two-thirds of males over age sixty-five were gainfully occupied—or by reliance on the Poor Law; a small and fortunate minority lived off savings or the few company pension schemes that had developed in the nineteenth century.

The campaign for old-age pensions between 1878 and 1908 aroused the interest of both Conservatives and socialists, but for different reasons. For the former, pensions (if funded from contributions) would remove old people from the Poor Law. For the latter, a tax-funded, noncontributory pension scheme would fund an honorable retirement for working people, redistributing wealth to the elderly poor. Thus by the early 1900s the labor movement was spearheading the campaign through organizations such as the National Committee of Organised Labour for the Promotion of Old-Age Pensions.

In eventual response to these pressures the 1908 act, sponsored by **David Lloyd George** as Chancellor of the Exchequer, was passed by the **Liberal** government. The scheme set up was very limited in both generosity and coverage. The pension was only five shillings per week (about one-quarter of the average unskilled urban wage), paid at the age of seventy, and subject to strict eligibility criteria relating to means, character, and nationality. However, in some ways the scheme was quite radical: It primarily benefited **women** (who comprised 63 percent of pensioners); it targeted the poor; it carried no retirement condition (thus acting as a wage subsidy); and, being tax-funded, it was highly redistributive. When old-age pensions were first paid in 1909, they covered 490,000 pensioners. By 1912 this number had risen to 642,500, largely because of increased number of applicants and a relaxation of some of the eligibility criteria.

For the next fifteen years old-age pensions were a source of political controversy. Sections of the labor movement envisaged a universal, tax-funded state pension of £1 per week, paid to all from the age of sixty, unfettered by any means tests. Pensioners were beginning to add their voice to these demands, and in 1916 an important pressure group, the National Conference on Old-Age Pensions, was formed.

O

Conservative opinion—especially within the Treasury—viewed such a prospect with alarm, since it would have cost (in 1919) an estimated £214 million in contrast to the existing scheme's £17.7 million. Discussion of this and other policy disagreements dominated the deliberations of the 1919 Ryland Adkins Committee. The immediate outcome was a doubling of the pension level to ten shillings per week.

The issue of pension funding was resolved by the Conservative government in its 1925 Widows', Orphans', and Old-Age Contributory Pensions Act. This introduced a new contributory scheme for those aged 65–70; it was a supplement to the 1908 plan, designed eventually to replace it. By this act (for which Neville Chamberlain as Minister of Health must be given credit) the labor movement's challenge was deflected and pension funding made less directly redistributive.

Demographic pressures inexorably increased the proportion of old people: Those age sixty-five or over rose from 5.3 percent of the population in 1911 to 10.9 percent in 1951. By the mid-1930s there was much discussion of the fiscal burden of future pension costs, and even a belief in certain quarters that the presence of older workers in the heavy industries was a factor hindering economic recovery. To this pessimistic view was added the support of trade union leaders (such as Ernest Bevin) for the introduction of a new, improved pension, which, by carrying a retirement condition, would encourage older workers to leave the labor market and hence reduce unemployment.

By the late 1930s pressure for pension reform was mounting again—for example, a campaign by the National Spinsters' Pensions Association succeeded in lowering women's pension age to sixty in 1940, and the newly formed National Federation of Old-Age Pensions Associations demanded that the basic pension be doubled (to £1 per week) and made universal without a means test. Essentially, the 1942 Beveridge Report recommended the amalgamation of the 1908 and 1925 schemes into a new universal, contributory scheme, with pensions conditional upon retirement from work. The levels proposed by Beveridge were relatively ungenerous: Full "subsistence" pensions were attainable only after twenty years of gradual increments. However, these low rates were unacceptable to both the wartime coalition and the post-war Labour government, and the new scheme, introduced in 1946, paid pensions of twenty-six shillings (single pensioner) and forty-two shillings (pensioner couple). The attachment of a retirement condition, though having little measurable effect on the steady, labor market-driven spread of retirement, marked the end of pensions paid solely by virtue of old age and financial need. From 1946, therefore, there began a new system of state retirement pensions.

John Macnicol

Bibliography

Blaikie, Andrew. "The Emerging Political Power of the Elderly in Britain, 1908–1948," *Ageing and Society*, vol. 10 (1990), pp. 17–39.

Macnicol, John, and Andrew Blaikie. "The Politics of Retirement, 1908–48" in Margot Jefferys, ed. *Growing Old in the Twentieth Century*. 1989. pp. 21–42.

Thane, Pat. "Non-Contributory versus Insurance Pensions, 1878–1908" in Pat Thane, ed. *The Origins of British Social Policy*. 1978. pp. 84–106.

Wilson, Sir Arnold, and G.S. Mackay. *Old Age Pensions: An Historical and Critical Study*. (1941).

Old Vic

The Old Vic, on the corner of the New Cut and Waterloo Road in London, has, since its opening in 1818, been linked with many important developments in British theater. It was built, on a site south of the Thames within reach of the recently constructed Waterloo Bridge crossing, to serve the rough but appreciative audiences for "transpontine" melodrama. At first named the Coburg, its affectionate cognomen "Old Vic" originated as an abbreviation of the change of name to the Royal Victoria following extensive renovations in 1833.

An unsavory reputation among respectable critics was redeemed by its reopening in 1880 as a concert hall *cum* coffee tavern by a stalwart of the mid-Victorian temperance movement, Emma Cons, whose niece Lilian Baylis assumed control of the theater in 1912. Thereafter, for half a century the Old Vic became the main London venue for the production of Shakespeare's plays, Baylis managing the theater after 1931 in tandem with Sadler's Wells, which she made the home for opera in English. A project for the presentation of all thirty-seven plays in the Shakespearean First Folio was initiated in 1915 under the direction of Ben Greet and completed in 1923 by Robert Atkins. While Sybil Thorndike was the first to achieve stardom with the Old Vic company, from the 1930s it included most of the great names in English acting, among them John Gielgud, **Laurence Olivier**, Ralph Richardson, Edith Evans, Michael Redgrave, and Peggy Ashcroft.

The Old Vic suffered extensive damage from wartime bombing. However, a company playing from 1941 at the New Theatre kept the name alive, from 1944 to 1949 under the leadership of Olivier, at first in a collaboration with Richardson. When the rebuilding of the Old Vic was completed in 1950, a new director, Michael Benthall, initiated a five-year plan for a second presentation of all of the First Folio plays, and this was duly completed in 1958.

By 1963 the quality of the productions had become unreliable, and the Old Vic company was disbanded to facilitate the temporary tenure of the **National Theatre**, during its fruitful fledgling period under Olivier before the opening of its purpose-built structure nearby in 1976. The trustees then offered the theater as a permanent London venue for the widely respected touring company Prospect Productions, which formed itself into a regenerated Old Vic company in 1979, only to be forced into liquidation in 1981 following the loss of its **Arts Council** subsidy. The theater then passed into the hands of a Canadian entrepreneur, Ed Mirvish, who undertook a lavish, two-year restoration of its interior, which, however, rather outshone many of the ensuing productions.

Although a "British institution," in its various passages from commercial to nonprofit management and back, the Old Vic has never become safely institutionalized. But, while it retains a strong place in the affections and memories of older theatergoers, various factors—including its inconvenient location relative to the West End and the emergence of smaller, "fringe" theaters as alternative centers of neighborhood work—have left it without a clear purpose, overshadowed as it is to the west by a grimy railway terminus, to the east and south by the impoverished back streets that once provided its audiences, and to the north by the subsidized South Bank arts complex.

Simon Trussler

Bibliography

Dent, Edward J. *A Theatre for Everybody.* 1945.

Findlater, Richard. *Lilian Baylis: The Lady of the Old Vic.* 1975.

Roberts, Peter. *The Old Vic Story: A Nation's Theatre, 1818–1976.* 1976.

Rowell, George. *The Old Vic Theatre: A History.* 1993.

O

Olivier, Laurence Kerr (1907–1989)

The most celebrated English actor of the century, Laurence Olivier performed on the stage and in films during the course of a career that lasted nearly sixty years and served as the first Artistic Director of the **National Theatre** from 1963 to 1973. Knighted in 1947 for his achievements as an actor, he was created a life peer (the first actor ever so honored) in 1970 and received the Order of Merit in 1981.

The son of a clergyman, Olivier was born on 22 May 1907 in Dorking, Surrey, and enrolled in the Central School of Speech and Drama in London at the age of seventeen. His earliest professional roles were with the Birmingham Repertory Company and at the Royal Court Theatre. In the late 1920s he made frequent appearances in commercial West End theaters, where he hoped to achieve popularity as a matinee idol. Olivier married the actress Jill Esmond in 1930, the same year that he appeared with **Noel Coward** and Gertrude Lawrence in Coward's *Private Lives* and made his film debut in *Too Many Crooks*. His first successful film was Samuel Goldwyn's production of *Wuthering Heights* in 1939 in which he portrayed Heathcliff. Olivier next worked with **Alfred Hitchcock**, playing Maxim de Winter in the adaptation of Daphne du Maurier's *Rebecca* (1940), and with Michael Powell in *The 49th Parallel* (1941).

These film triumphs paralleled forays into more serious stage drama. His first major Shakespearean roles were Mercutio and Romeo (alternating the parts with John Gielgud) in 1935, and, after joining the **Old Vic** in 1937–8, he undertook a range of parts that established his pre-war reputation as a Shakespearean actor: Sir Toby Belch in *Twelfth Night*, Henry V, Macbeth, Hamlet, and Iago (to Ralph Richardson's Othello).

During the **Second World War** Olivier served in the naval air force but was released in 1943 to direct a film production of *Henry V*, in which he reprised his title role performance, deliberately evoking strong patriotic sentiments in wartime. From 1944 to 1949 Olivier codirected the Old Vic company, initially at the New Theatre, essaying such varied parts as Richard III, Lear, Astrov in *Uncle Vanya*, Hotspur in *Henry IV, Part I*, and Oedipus. Films of *Hamlet* (1947) and *Richard III* (1954) brought him further international acclaim.

During the 1940s and 1950s Olivier frequently acted with his second wife, Vivien Leigh, including alternating productions of *Antony and Cleopatra* and **George Bernard Shaw**'s *Caesar and Cleopatra* in London during the **Festival of Britain** in 1951 and *Macbeth*, *Twelfth Night*, and *Titus Andronicus* at Stratford in 1954–5. Earlier, in 1941, they had also made a film adaptation of the life of Lord Nelson entitled *That Hamilton Woman*, which like his *Henry V*, was designed to boost national morale during the war years.

Olivier's distinctive acting style, which relied heavily on physical mannerisms, worked effectively in the modern idiom, and he achieved notable success as the down-and-out music hall performer Archie Rice in **John Osborne**'s *The Entertainer* (1957), playing opposite Joan Plowright, who became his third wife in 1961. Other modern plays in which he starred were Ionesco's *Rhinoceros* (1960) and Anouilh's *Becket* (1960–1). In 1961 he became the first Director of the Chichester Festival Theatre, and in 1963 he was appointed the Artistic Director of the newly formed National Theatre at the Old Vic. As an actor and director at the Old Vic, Olivier gave landmark and sometimes controversial performances as Astrov in *Uncle Vanya* (1963), Brazen in *The Recruiting Officer* (1963), Othello (1964), Edgar in Strindberg's *Dance of Death* (1967), Shylock (1970), James Tyrone in *Long Day's Journey into Night* (1971), and John Tagg in Trevor Griffiths' *The Party* (1973).

After worsening health compelled him to relinquish the artistic directorship of the National Theatre in 1973, he ceased to perform on the stage but continued to act in films and on television. Among his last films were *Sleuth* (1972), *Marathon Man* (1976), and *The Boys from Brazil* (1978), but he also made memorable appearances in *Brideshead Revisited* (1981) and in John Mortimer's *A Voyage Round My Father* (1982). He died in 1989, hailed as the preeminent actor of his generation and one of the last great actor-managers in the British theater.

Martha A. Schütz

Bibliography
Cottrell, John. *Laurence Olivier*. 1975.
Gourlay, Logan, ed. *Olivier*. 1973.
Holder, Anthony. *Olivier*. 1988.
Olivier, Laurence. *Confessions of an Actor*. 1982.

Open University

The Open University was founded in 1969 to serve the needs of British men and women who had missed the chance of a university education. It offers professional, academic, and self-enrichment courses to students in their homes via a combination of correspondence, group tutorial meetings at local study centers, residential summer schools, radio, and televised lectures broadcast by the **British Broadcasting Corporation** (BBC). By the early 1990s the Open University had 9 percent of all British students enrolled in higher education. It has justly attained public recognition for the high quality of its multimedia courses, but its real historical significance may prove to be its ability to provide mass access to **university education** at a modest cost to state and students alike.

Between 1964 and 1970 **Harold Wilson**'s **Labour** government increased access to higher education, creating the **polytechnics** and expanding the university system according to the recommendations of the **Robbins Report**. It was Wilson's idea to use **television** to create a truly democratic university serving older men and women without formal educational qualifications, whose work and family obligations forced them to study intermittently at home. Academics were originally critical of an idea that violated cherished assumptions about the nature of higher education: Universities were expected to be small-scale, academically selective, personalized, residential, and socially elite institutions, such as **Oxford** and **Cambridge**. Under the leadership of its first Vice Chancellor, Sir Walter Perry, the Open University attempted to ensure its acceptance as a university by recruiting an outstanding academic staff and by an extensive publicity campaign. It allowed for variations in students' preparation and ability by designing its curriculum to progress from the basic elementary "foundation courses" to more-specialized and demanding advanced courses, the successful completion of which indicated a high level of achievement. Unlike the other British universities, it employed a system of credits that enabled students to take time out from the course and to combine courses in ways designed to reflect their individual needs and interests.

By the early 1990s the Open University had become a respected institution and a model for the provision of adult university education. It has not, however, proved to be an avenue to higher education for the most poorly trained student. Instead, it has been an avenue for professional retraining, in particular for teachers to improve their qualifications and women to study while raising families. Although it has retained its policy of access without admissions requirements, it has established a selective graduate program. In the climate of economic privation of the 1980s, the Open University reluctantly made some places available to eighteen-year-olds, and will almost certainly continue to do so, functioning increasingly as a conventional university but retaining its character as the first British university fully to utilize the media to promote study for older men and women working at home.

Elizabeth Morse

Bibliography

Ferguson, John. *The Open University from Within.* 1975.

McIntosh, Naomi E. *A Degree of Difference: The Open University of the United Kingdom.* 1977.

Perry, Walter. *The Open University.* 1977.

Tunstall, Jeremy, ed. *The Open University Opens.* 1974.

Opera and Opera Companies

Before 1914 efforts to promote opera in English at the Royal Opera House, Covent Garden, ended in failure. Even such a successful plan as that launched by the conductors Hans Richter and Percy Pitt, and that culminated in the first performance of Wagner's *Ring* in English (1908), did not lead to the establishment of a national opera. Nonetheless, this period was noteworthy for the London debuts of Enrico Caruso and Luisa Tetrazzini, as well as the first performances in England of Puccini's *Tosca* (1900) and *Madama Butterfly* (1905), Debussy's *Pélleas et Mélisande* (1909), and Wagner's *Parsifal* (1914). **Thomas Beecham** introduced Strauss' *Salome* and *Elektra* in 1910, succeeded by Diaghilev's Ballets Russes the following year, but his 1920 season of international opera ended in liquidation, although

he was tempted to return to Covent Garden from 1932 to 1939, conducting Concita Supervia in Rossini, Richard Tauber in Mozart, and Kirsten Flagstad and Lauritz Melchior in Wagner. Meanwhile, German opera had been flourishing under Bruno Walter (1924–31) with such singers as Lotte Lehmann, Elisabeth Schumann, and Friedrich Schorr.

After the Second World War plans were adopted to establish Covent Garden as a permanent national home for opera and **ballet** and to place its running on a firm financial footing. Sir David Webster became General Administrator (1945–70) with Karl Rankl, Musical Director (1945–51), and an annual grant from the newly formed **Arts Council of Great Britain** was forthcoming. At first, opera in English was preferred, although by the mid-1950s the original language was often used. During the 1960s Sir Georg Solti confirmed its international status; among the highlights of his period as Music Director was the British premiere of Schoenberg's *Moses und Aron* (1965). Before succeeding Solti in 1971, Sir Colin Davis directed new productions of Berlioz's *Les Troyens* (1969) and of **Michael Tippett's** *The Midsummer Marriage* (1970), together with the premiere of Tippett's *The Knot Garden* (1970), one of the ten British operas that had their first performances at Covent Garden between 1945 and 1977. Others included **Ralph Vaughan Williams'** *Pilgrim's Progress* (1951), **Benjamin Britten's** *Billy Budd* (1951), Peter Maxwell Davies' *Taverner* (1972), and Tippett's *The Ice Break* (1977).

In contrast to the sporadic attempts to stage opera in English at Covent Garden, other companies such as the Carl Rosa Opera Company (1875–1960) and the Moody-Manners Company (1897–1916) specialized in its promotion, providing London seasons as well as provincial tours. Both also acted as a training ground for British artists. The Carl Rosa Company gave the first performances in English of Wagner's *Siegfried* (1901) and Verdi's *La forza del destino* (1909), and by the 1930s it was providing most of the opera heard outside London. Opera in English was also staged for two nights a week at the **Old Vic** by **Lilian Baylis**, who, in 1931, moved her company to the Sadler's Wells Theatre, subsequently renaming it Sadler's Wells Opera. Her repertory of almost thirty operas was gradually expanded and the company enlarged, so that by 1939 its reputation as the leading provider of opera in English in London was assured. Deprived of a permanent home during the Second World War, the company, under the direction of Joan Cross (1900–93), was forced to spend most of its time on tour, but it continued to extend its repertoire. Its reputation was further enhanced when Sadler's Wells was reopened after the war with the first performance of Britten's *Peter Grimes* (1945), with Peter Pears and Cross in the leading roles. A particularly adventurous period followed as several operas of Janácek were introduced—Davis, Musical Director in the years 1961–4, conducted the first British performance of *The Cunning Little Vixen* (1961). In 1968 the problems associated with the move to the Coliseum, which possesses the largest stage in London, were surmounted, and major triumphs followed with the production of Wagner's *Ring* conducted by Reginald Goodall (completed in 1973) and the first British stage production of Prokofiev's *War and Peace* (1972). Mark Elder, during his first ten years as Musical Director (1979–89), conducted many new productions, including Tchaikovsky's *Mazepa* (British premiere, 1984) and Busoni's *Doktor Faust* (British stage premiere, 1986); first British performances also included Philip Glass' *Akhnaten* (1985) and Harrison Birtwistle's *The Mask of Orpheus* (1986). In 1974 the company was renamed the English National Opera.

Outside London, John Christie (1882–1962) established an opera house at Glyndebourne, near Lewes, Sussex, in 1934, with the intention of mounting operas by both Mozart and Wagner, although under the guidance of his wife, he adopted the sensible plan of concentrating on the former. With Fritz Busch as Musical Director and Carl Ebert as Producer, new standards of performance and production of Mozart's operas were established and have been pursued ever since. To mark the reopening of Glyndebourne following the Second World War, the English Opera Group gave the first performances of Britten's *The Rape of Lucretia* (1946) and *Albert Herring* (1947); the repertoire was further expanded to include Rossini under the musical directorship of Vittorio Gui (1951–64). By the mid-1950s a policy of including a new work each year was implemented—the first French opera to be performed was Debussy's *Pélleas et Mélisande* in 1962—and subsequently Strauss' operas became a specialty, particularly those on a smaller scale. Among first performances of British operas, Glyndebourne has staged Nicholas Maw's *The Rising of the Moon*

(1970), Nigel Osborne's *The Electrification of the Soviet Union* (1988), and Tippett's *New Year* (1990).

The demand for opera in the regions led to the formation of two national companies, Welsh National Opera (WNO) at Cardiff in 1946 and Scottish National Opera (SNO) at Glasgow, formed by Sir Alexander Gibson in 1962. The reputation of the former was originally built on its fine chorus and Verdi productions, although more recently such successes as the first British performance of Berg's *Lulu* (1971) and a new production of Tippett's *The Midsummer Marriage* have broadened its repertoire considerably. Both companies have been keen to commission operas by native composers—the WNO, Alun Hoddinott's *The Beach of Falesá* (1974); and the SNO, Thea Musgrave's *Mary, Queen of Scots* (1977), for instance.

Other regions have also benefited from having their own company. The Kent Opera, formed in 1969 by Norman Platt (Artistic Director) and Roger Norrington (Musical Director until 1984), is an example of a regionally based English opera company funded by the Arts Council. Playing principally in theaters at Canterbury and Tunbridge Wells, but also touring throughout the southern counties, Kent Opera built up a repertoire with a broad appeal but enlivened with less well-known works and some commissions. Unfortunately, the withdrawal of its grant in 1989 led to its demise. Opera North, formed in 1977 and centered on Leeds, provides a similar service for the north of England, as does Opera East for East Anglia. The regions have also benefited from the touring companies of the major opera houses, together with Phoenix Opera (1965–80); Birmingham Touring Opera, which uses reduced forces and community venues; and Travelling Opera, founded in 1986 by Peter Knapp, possibly the most active of the smaller groups. Opera for All, formed by the Arts Council in 1949, was the first of these small companies created specifically to take opera in English to towns and villages unlikely to experience the art form live. Although it originally consisted of a group of four singers, a pianist, and a stage manager *cum* compère, it had expanded to three groups of twelve members by 1966. Its role was subsequently taken over by similar groups run by the main houses and by Opera 80, founded by the Arts Council in 1980 with similar aims but with its own orchestra.

Increasingly historical awareness produced a whole series of revivals of previously unknown pre-nineteenth-century operas—the Intimate Opera Company, formed in 1930 by Frederick Woodhouse, specializing in this field and being launched with Thomas Arne's 1760 opera *Thomas and Sally*. Subsequently, early English opera has been the specialty of the touring company Opera Restor'd, founded in 1985. The Handel Opera Society (1955; since 1977, Handel Opera), inspired by E.J. Dent, began its productions with *Deidamia* (in Dent's translation) and during its first twenty years of existence staged revivals of nearly the same number of Handel's operas, including *Ariodante*, *Orlando*, and *Theodora*. Some university opera societies, too, have been enthusiastic to explore not only the byways of earlier opera but also of the nineteenth- and twentieth-century repertoire. Cambridge University Opera Society, for instance, staged within a few years such different operas as Smetana's *The Kiss* (1969, a revival), Dessau's *The Trial of Lukullus* (1970), and Philidor's *Tom Jones* (1971), both British premieres.

Finally, dissatisfaction with the lack of enthusiasm shown by the main houses for promoting new British operas led to the formation of both the English Opera Group (1947) and the New Opera Company (1957). The former commissioned five operas from Britten, Lennox Berkeley's *Ruth* (1956), **William Walton's** *The Bear* (1967), and Birtwistle's *Punch and Judy* (1968), among others; the latter, Arthur Benjamin's *Tartuffe* (1964), Gordon Crosse's *Purgatory* (1966), Musgrave's *The Decision* (1967), and Elisabeth Lutyens' *Time Off? Not a Ghost of a Chance!* (1972). By 1975, the New Opera Company had also staged fifteen British premieres of operas from abroad, including Schoenberg's *Erwartung*, Henze's *Boulevard Solitude*, Shostakovich's *The Nose*, and Szymanowski's *King Roger*. In both companies, leading British singers took most of the roles—Janet Baker, Heather Harper, Owen Brannigan, Peter Pears, John Shirley-Quirk, and Robert Tear regularly appearing with the English Opera Group. Indeed, since the Second World War a considerable number of British singers have pursued distinguished careers in opera, some, like Geraint Evans and Gwyneth Jones, elevated to international stardom.

Trevor Bray

Bibliography
Donaldson, Frances. *The Royal Opera House in the Twentieth Century.* 1982.
Higgins, John, ed. *Glyndebourne: A Celebration.* 1984.
Northouse, Cameron. *Twentieth Century Opera in England and the United States.* 1976.
White, Eric Walter. *A History of English Opera.* 1983.

Orchestras

The founding of the Queen's Hall Orchestra (QHO) in 1895 marked a new departure in London's musical life. Hitherto, orchestras, including those for the many theaters, had been drawn on an *ad hoc* basis from a pool of professional musicians who lived and taught in the capital. However, although the QHO was not originally constituted on a permanent basis, it became so, benefiting from a corporate identity and a stable management (initially Robert Newman). In 1904 a dispute with Henry Wood, its conductor, over a long-standing right to send a deputy if a player had a prior engagement, led around fifty players to break away and form the London Symphony Orchestra, which from the outset was self-governing. Hans Richter became the orchestra's first principal conductor, succeeded more recently by Pierre Monteux (1961), André Previn (1969), and Claudio Abbado (1979). A tour of the United States and Canada in 1912 was the first by a British orchestra, as was the world tour of 1964.

In 1927 the **British Broadcasting Corporation** (BBC) took over the QHO (since 1915, New QHO), and its players became the nucleus of the BBC Symphony Orchestra (BBCSO), formed in 1930 and conducted by Adrian Boult, who rapidly brought it to the front rank. Players were salaried on a year-round contract, thereby gaining greater security, although this new arrangement was never adopted on a permanent basis by other orchestras (except those at the Royal Opera House, Covent Garden, and the English National Opera), players usually being paid a fee for each engagement. Soon after the BBCSO's inception, guest conductors included Richard Strauss, Felix Weingartner, and Bruno Walter, and it was the first British orchestra to be conducted by Arturo Toscanini (in 1935). Other BBC orchestras were formed in the regions, the three most important being the BBC Northern Orchestra at Manchester in 1934 (renamed the BBCN Symphony Orchestra in 1967), and, in the following year, the BBC Scottish Orchestra at Glasgow (the BBCS Symphony Orchestra, 1967) and the BBC Welsh Orchestra at Cardiff (the BBCW Symphony Orchestra, 1974).

Both the London Philharmonic Orchestra (1932) and Royal Philharmonic Orchestra (1946) were founded by Sir **Thomas Beecham**, testifying to his great entrepreneurial flair. The LPO soon rose to preeminence among London orchestras and, despite financial troubles in the 1950s, regained its corporate identity during the 1960s and 1970s under such principal conductors as John Pritchard (from 1962), Bernard Haitinck (1967) and Sir Georg Solti (1979). Finance for the RPO's launching was generated from substantial recording contracts, a similar arrangement funding the formation of the Philharmonia Orchestra (New PO, 1964–77) in 1945 by Walter Legge. Its considerable reputation, created through recordings, was consolidated in the 1960s when Otto Klemperer became its principal conductor.

Two orchestras had already been formed in the provinces before 1900—the Hallé at Manchester (1857) and the Bournemouth Municipal Orchestra (1897, renamed Bournemouth Symphony Orchestra, 1954)—and these were joined by the City of Birmingham Orchestra (1920, City of Birmingham Symphony Orchestra, 1948), the Royal Liverpool Philharmonic Orchestra (which became a full-time body in 1943), and orchestras for Scotland, the Scottish National Orchestra (1951) at Glasgow, and for Northern Ireland, the Ulster Orchestra (1966) at Belfast. All of these orchestras have gained considerable reputations, particularly when directed by such visionary **conductors** as Sir John Barbirolli (Hallé, from 1943), Sir Simon Rattle (CBSO, 1979), Sir Charles Groves (Liverpool PO, 1963), and Sir Alexander Gibson, the first Scotsman to conduct the SNO (1959).

In response to the growing awareness of how music written before 1800 was performed, a significant number of chamber orchestras were established, an early example being the London Chamber Orchestra (1921), founded by Anthony Bernard to specialize in seventeenth- and eighteenth-century repertoires. Both the Boyd Neel Orchestra (1932) and the Jacques Orchestra (1936) concentrated on baroque and twentieth-century works; the Goldsborough Orchestra (1948), originally fo-

cusing on the eighteenth century, broadened its scope in 1960 when it was renamed the English Chamber Orchestra, becoming associated in particular with the English Opera Group, the Aldeburgh Festival, and **Benjamin Britten's** music. The discipline and musicianship evident in the performances and recordings of the Academy of St. Martin-in-the-Fields (1959), formed and directed by the violinist Neville Marriner, set new standards, as did those of the London Sinfonietta (1968), conducted by David Atherton, an ensemble specializing in contemporary music and capable, because of the flexibility of its constitution, of coping with almost any instrumental combination. The regions could also support new chamber ensembles, most notably the Northern Sinfonia (1961) at Newcastle-upon-Tyne and the Scottish Chamber Orchestra (1974) at Edinburgh. During the 1970s and 1980s, the quest for authenticity led to the formation of yet further specialist ensembles, but using period instruments (and some of the same players)—most significantly, the Academy of Ancient Music (conducted by Christopher Hogwood), the English Baroque Soloists (John Eliot Gardiner), the English Players (Trevor Pinnock), the Hanover Band (Roy Goodman), the London Classical Players (Roger Norrington), and the Taverner Players (Andrew Parrott). These groups testified to the continued richness and diversity of British musical life and confirmed London's position as one of the most important musical capitals of the world.

Trevor Bray

Bibliography

Kennedy, Michael. *The Hallé, 1858–1983: A History of the Orchestra.* 1983.

Kenyon, Nicholas. *The BBC Symphony Orchestra: The First Fifty Years, 1930–1980.* 1980.

Pearton, Maurice. *The LSO at Seventy: A History of the Orchestra.* 1974.

Pettitt, Stephen J. *Philharmonia Orchestra: A Record of Achievement, 1945–1985.* 1985.

Orwell, George (1903–1950)

George Orwell was the wintry conscience not only for England, but for much of the world through his two most influential books, *Animal Farm* (1945) and *Nineteen Eighty-Four* (1949). He was born Eric Arthur Blair in India, where his father was a civil servant engaged in supervising the opium trade. In 1907 Eric, his older sister, Marjorie, and his mother returned to Henley in England, where his younger sister, Avril, was born. Orwell characterized himself, with that exactness of observation that would become his hallmark, as a member of the lower-upper-middle class. By that he meant that his father was a member by descent of the "established" classes, justifying the "upper" in his class designation, but that the family was not well off, justifying the term "lower." The family was determined that their son would have as many advantages as possible, and at the age of eight he was sent away to St. Cyprian's, a "prep" school in Eastbourne. This was a traumatic experience as he believed, whether rightly or wrongly, that he was scorned by the formidable headmistress and his fellow students because of his comparative poverty. The years at St. Cyprian's were also important in shaping his attitude toward his country, as he was swept up in the intense **patriotism** of the **First World War**. The value of his education was that in his writings at the time of the Second World War he was able both to be a patriot and to call for a radical transformation of British society.

St. Cyprian's served its purpose and gave him the sort of education that won for him a position as a King's Scholar at Eton. There he would mix with the rich and the grand, as well as the extremely intelligent who were his fellow members of College, the home of the Scholars. He was at Eton from 1917 to 1921, but, rather unusually for a member of College, he did not go to university or into a prominent profession. Rather he became a police officer in Burma—in a sense going into his father's business. The beginning of his career was rather conventional, although less distinguished than one might have expected considering his education. What was unusual was that when he returned to England on leave in 1927, he decided to abandon his secure position in order to be a writer.

The first five years of this attempt were extremely difficult, but he used his partially self-inflicted experience of poverty to provide the material for his first book, *Down and Out in Paris and London*, published in 1933. Partially not to embarrass his family, and partially because he felt a need to distance himself from his past, he chose to write under a pseudonym, choosing that most English of first names,

George, and as a last name, the name of the river Orwell in Suffolk, near where his parents were now living in Southwold. Orwell was developing an extremely effective plain style that convinced the reader of the truthfulness of his account. During the 1930s he became a fairly well-known minor novelist. His first novel, *Burmese Days* (1934), drew upon his police experience. What was unusual in the book, as well as one of the most famous essays in the language, "Shooting an Elephant" (1936), was that he pointed out the illegitimacy of **imperialism** without feeling sentimental about those who were "oppressed." In 1935 he published *A Clergyman's Daughter*; in 1936, *Keep the Aspidistra Flying*. Both of these novels, of which later he was not particularly proud, dealt with the effects of poverty on members of the middle class. He himself was barely surviving financially, although he was doing an increasing amount of journalism. He came to the attention of **Victor Gollancz**, the publisher and proprietor of the **Left Book Club**, and was commissioned to write an account of poverty in England. The result, *The Road to Wigan Pier* (1937), was a powerful account of the ravages of the Depression. Contrary to the wishes of the club, it was also an idiosyncratic autobiographical essay combining a critique of the pretensions of middle-class socialists, whose crankiness would keep them at a distance from the working class, with an attractive, but also a romantic, vision of the warmth and positive values of working-class life.

As a reporter, he went to Spain shortly after the outbreak of the **Spanish Civil War**. The new socialist world that he found in Barcelona was one that he believed he must fight for, and he joined the militia of the POUM, a dissident semi-Trotskyite group. He was almost killed at the front by a bullet through his throat, and on his return to Barcelona he was caught up in the betrayal of the revolution by the Communists. Through his experience in Spain he became a committed socialist, but he also discovered that the socialist dream was as likely to be betrayed by those who claimed to be on the Left as by those who were on the Right of the political spectrum. He wrote a magnificent account of his Spanish experience, *Homage to Catalonia* (1938), which received scant attention when it was originally published and did not become well known until it was reissued in 1952. Upon his return to England he published one further traditional novel, *Coming Up for Air* (1939),

O

which contrasted the false values of contemporary English society with what Orwell considered the greater genuineness of life before the First World War.

The Spanish experience, and his marriage to Eileen O'Shaughnessy in 1936, made him better able to come to terms with himself and his ideas. He now had become George Orwell, and thus he was known to those whom he met for the rest of his short life. He became much more prolific as a writer, with innumerable essays and reviews. He was a founder of a new sort of approach to society, a combination of literary and sociological values that provided new insights, such as his famous essay on Charles Dickens (1940), and his non-patronizing and insightful approach to popular culture in his essays on Boy's Weeklies (1940) and on the significance of the slightly smutty postcards that were sold at seaside resorts, "The Art of Donald McGill" (1941). With great effectiveness, he drew attention in his essay "Politics and the English Language" (1946) to the ways in which language can be used to manipulate thought and hide truths. With the outbreak of the **Second World War,** he wanted to help the war effort, but his age and health meant that he could only be active in the **Home Guard.** He worked at the **British Broadcasting Corporation** (BBC), organizing broadcasts to India, and he wrote regular columns for the socialist weekly, *Tribune.* In *The Lion and the Unicorn* (1941) he put forward his analysis of England as a family but "with the wrong members in control." It was a family that needed to be both preserved in its respect for individualism and liberty and transformed into a more egalitarian society.

In Spain he had observed the Communists' betrayal of the socialist dream. The idea of the betrayal of the revolution crystalized in his brilliant fable, *Animal Farm* (1945), which he had difficulty getting published while the Soviet Union was still an ally. The book was a powerful indictment in its accuracy of what had happened in Russia but also fitted into the development of the Cold War in the aftermath of the Second World War. It made Orwell an internationally famous author. That was even more true four years later when he published *Nineteen Eighty-Four* (1949), his account of what has happened to England, now called Airstrip One, an outpost of the West, now known as Oceania, which is in constant battle with the East, although sides change easily, and the past is constantly rewritten to conform with the party line, the job of the very minor official, Winston Smith, who is the central figure in the novel. Orwell made permanent contributions in his conceptions of Big Brother, the Thought Police, Newspeak, "two plus two equals five." He remained his own special sort of socialist and saw the book as a warning of what might happen. Those on the Right chose to see it as a prophecy of what was the inevitable result of socialism. The book has had a continual influence and was much remarked upon around the world when the actual year 1984 came and went.

Orwell died of **tuberculosis** in 1950, at the very beginning of his greatest fame. It was not until the years after his death that many of his essays were generally made available. He and his wife had adopted a son, but shortly thereafter she died unexpectedly in 1945 after a minor operation. Orwell married Sonia Brownell in 1949.

For such a short life, particularly considering that he did not start writing until 1927 and did not publish his first book until 1933, he was amazingly prolific. Of his traditional novels, *Burmese Days*, which had the longest period of gestation, was his best. All of his books of reportage are excellent, with *The Road to Wigan Pier* being written with the most sense of personality and *Homage to Catalonia* with the greatest moral authority. *Animal Farm* is a gem, and *Nineteen Eighty-Four*, although crude at times (having been written by a dying man), has tremendous and memorable power. He was a great artist who created what at the same time was a plain prose in the great English tradition but also reflected the personality he wished to project: a teller of truth.

Peter Stansky

Bibliography

Crick, Bernard. *George Orwell.* 1980.

Meyers, Jeffrey, and Valerie Meyers. *Orwell: An Annotated Bibliography of Criticism.* 1977.

Shelden, Michael. *Orwell: The Authorized Biography.* 1991.

Slater, Ian. *Orwell: The Road to Airstrip One.* 1985.

Stansky, Peter, and William Abrahams. *The Unknown Orwell.* 1972.

———. *Orwell: The Transformation.* 1979.

Woodcock, George. *The Crystal Spirit.* 1967.

Osborne, John James (1929–1994)

Born in Fulham, the son of a barmaid and a commercial artist, John Osborne came from the impoverished lower-middle-class background he depicted in his plays. He worked as a journalist, stage manager, and actor before achieving fame with the production of his play *Look Back in Anger* by the English Stage Company at the Royal Court Theatre in 1956, which ushered in a new wave of playwrights and theater practitioners. They sought to create a theatrical vocabulary to replace the conventions that had prevented mainstream theater from reflecting the current social and political realities of twentieth-century history. Jimmy Porter, the play's famous protagonist, gave voice to the discontent of Osborne's generation: the play's title was used to label a group of young writers, including Osborne himself, as "angry young men."

Set in a shabby Midlands bedsitting room, the play exposes Jimmy's merciless attempts to undermine his wife Alison's upper-middle-class complacency, a Strindbergian battle witnessed by Jimmy's peace-loving university chum, Cliff. The power of *Look Back in Anger* resides in its rhetoric, which integrates Osborne's naturalistic portrait of marital discord with an expressionistic attack on inertia and moral bankruptcy in the post-war British Establishment.

This stylistic tension became a fundamental principle of structure in Osborne's next successful stage play, *The Entertainer* (1957), in which the death of the British music hall symbolizes the decline of post-war Britain. The pathetic philanderings of the failed comedian Archie Rice are revealed in a series of short naturalistic scenes, while the the the music hall routines express the "state of Britain" theme, performers and audience alike revealed as "dead behind the eyes." The play provided a vehicle for **Laurence Olivier**, whose seedy and tragic portrayal of Archie Rice was one of the highlights of the London theater in the 1950s and a successful film as well.

Osborne's next successful ventures turned away from the contemporary world. *Luther* (1961) emphasizes Osborne's identification with heroes who are temperamentally unable to compromise their faith. In 1963 he wrote the screenplay for the highly successful film *Tom Jones*.

In 1964 the Royal Court staged *Inadmissible Evidence* with Nicol Williamson in the role of Maitland, a divorce lawyer who might be Jimmy Porter at forty. Many critics regard this as Osborne's finest play, pointing out that he has here provided a more balanced perspective on the protagonist's rage against the world. By presenting the action of the play as a series of cinematic flashbacks framed by Maitland's tirade against a world of compromise and double standards, Osborne allows his audience to question the validity of Maitland's views without sacrificing its sympathy for his situation. The strategy reveals the play's overt theme to be the tragic failure of individuals to connect with the passion and suffering of others. The play was revived by the **National Theatre** to mixed reviews in 1993.

A Patriot for Me (1965), *Time Present* and *The Hotel in Amsterdam* (1968), and *West of Suez* (1971) all enjoyed successful runs and a measure of critical acclaim, but Osborne lost touch with the left-wing audiences who had thrilled to the rhetoric of Jimmy Porter. By the early 1970s his plays had begun to seem both dated and reactionary. But his two volumes of autobiography, *A Better Class of Person* (1981) and *Almost a Gentleman* (1991), achieved critical and popular success.

Robert Gordon

Bibliography

Carter, Alan. *John Osborne*. 2nd ed. 1973.
Goldstone, Herbert. *Coping with Vulnerability: The Achievement of John Osborne*. 1982.
Hayman, Ronald. *John Osborne*. 2nd ed. 1970.
Hinchliffe, Arnold P. *John Osborne*. 1984.
Northouse, Cameron, and Thomas P. Walsh. *John Osborne: A Reference Guide*. 1974.
Trussler, Simon. *The Plays of John Osborne*. 1969.

Owen, Wilfred Edward Salter (1893–1918)

Wilfred Owen is the youngest of the war poets whose writing inspired the protest of trench conditions and slaughter on the Western Front of the **First World War**, and whose death in the final week of the war became (like **Rupert Brooke**'s) a symbol of the fate of a generation of "doomed youth."

Born in Oswestry, Shropshire, of Welsh descent, Owen failed to win a university scholarship and, after some months as an unpaid church worker in Berkshire, went to Bordeaux as a language tutor, remaining in France until autumn 1915 when he enlisted. He arrived on the Somme as a platoon commander in January 1917. After three months in the front line he was sent home due to hysterical "neurasthenia," or shell shock. He said that it was not the fighting that caused his collapse but having to hold a position for several days alongside a dead fellow officer whose body "lay in various places around and about." He was treated at Craiglockhart War Hospital, Edinburgh, under the holistic regime of Dr. A.J. Brock. Owen returned to the Western Front in September 1918 and was awarded a Military Cross in October. He was killed in action 4 November, and the news of his death reached the family as church bells announced the armistice.

Owen's early verse was influenced by Keats, Swinburne, Decadence, and French symbolism, and it is strongly flavored by narcissistic homoeroticism, encouraged in Owen by Laurent Tailhade (1854–1919), the Decadent poet and anarchist poseur. When Owen met **Siegfried Sassoon** at Craiglockhart, where Owen edited the hospital magazine, Sassoon inspired him to merge his poetic sensibilities with response to the horrors of trench warfare and with angry protest (shared by **Robert Graves** as well as Sassoon) at civilian failure to understand what frontline soldiers were enduring. This gave purpose and sinew to Owen's poetry. His return to the front was for the sake of both leadership and witness. Blending the purple diction of Decadence with the realism and homely language adopted by the pre-war Georgian poets, he produced some of the most striking literature of the First World War, in tragic satires like "Strange Meeting, "Spring Offensive," "Mental Cases," "Futility," "Disabled," "Smile, Smile, Smile," and "Dulce et Decorum Est."

Owen's reputation began posthumously with the publication in 1920 of *Poems*, edited by Sassoon. Unlike Sassoon and Graves, who survived, Owen came to represent the young men sacrificed in the cause of absolute but futile "victory" and the gulf between old and young.

The blend of disgusting detail and tender feeling in Owen's verse resonated with the mood of **T.S. Eliot**'s *The Waste Land* (1922) and influenced inter-war writers like **W.H. Auden, Louis MacNiece,** and **Stephen Spender.** Technically, Owen's experimental use of heavily stressed lines and pararhyme (such as

silent/salient) remains accessible to the general reader whom modernism's more rigorous experiments deter.

Increasingly, the younger generation saw the First World War through the eyes of Owen. His life and work had renewed impact in the 1960s, with the publication of *Collected Poems*, edited by **Cecil Day Lewis** (1963), and of his complete family letters and his brother Harold Owen's memoir, *Journey from Obscurity* (1963–5). Through inclusion in war poetry anthologies studied in schools and colleges Owen's writing contributed to the widespread "antiwar" culture in Britain at the time of the Vietnam conflict.

Most recently, his idealizing response to the male body (previously unmentioned at the family's behest) has been recovered and integrated into the long British tradition of homoerotic literature. Owen remains the most powerful and best-known war poet of the century, still able to rouse horror and pity in new readers.

Jan Marsh

Bibliography

Bergonzi, Bernard. *Heroes' Twilight.* 1965
Fussell, Paul. *The Great War and Modern Memory.* 1975.
Hibberd, Dominic. *Owen the Poet.* 1986.
Owen, Harold. *Journey from Obscurity.* 3 vols. 1963–5.
Owen, Harold, and John Bell, eds. *Wilfred Owen: Collected Letters.* 1967.
Stallworthy, Jon. *Wilfred Owen.* 1974.

Oxford, University of

In 1900 Oxford was one of the two principal seats of learning in England. This dominant position was maintained in the late twentieth century despite changes in the structure of English education following the creation of **new universities** and a considerable expansion of student numbers. State intervention in the Victorian period had created in Oxford an essentially self-governing university. The age of state funding, which began in 1919 and which by 1950 accounted for more than half of the university's income, barely altered this picture. A Royal Commission appointed in 1919 under the chairmanship of **H.H. Asquith** took an evolutionary approach to university reform. A later internal commission of inquiry chaired by Lord Franks, set up in response to a growing body of criticism leveled at Oxford's traditional structures, represented one of the most extensive exercises in self-scrutiny undertaken by a university in modern times. But its report, published in 1966, and its aftermath, while leading to significant modernization of the university's administrative machinery, left Oxford essentially a collegiate university.

In 1900 there were twenty fully fledged colleges; new colleges, notably St. Catherine's (1960), the foundation of graduate colleges, and the full recognition of the existing women's halls had raised the total to thirty-five by 1990. The majority were primarily concerned with undergraduate education. The colleges' strongly pedagogic emphasis was associated with the tutorial system, a method of individual tuition developed at Oxford and **Cambridge** in the previous century.

Undergraduate studies continued to be dominated by the demands of the honor schools (as the various courses of studies leading to the examinations for the B.A. degree were called). In 1900 the range comprised *Literae Humaniores* ("Greats") comprising Greek and Latin literature, philosophy, and ancient history (established in 1800); Mathematics (1807); Natural Sciences (1850); Jurisprudence (1850); Modern History (1850); Theology (1869); Oriental Studies (1886); and English (1894). To these were added Modern Languages (1903); Philosophy, Politics, and Economics (1920); Geography (1932); Psychology, Philosophy, and Physiology (1947); and Music (1950). The Natural Sciences, envisaged by the Victorians as a totality, divided into the various disciplines comprising the physical and biological sciences. Combinations of honor schools were introduced in the 1960s and following decades.

The Oxford curriculum had some markedly conservative tendencies. A knowledge of Greek remained compulsory until 1920, and Latin until 1960, while an examination in Divinity, a vestige of Oxford's earlier character as an exclusively **Church of England** institution, remained obligatory for Anglicans until 1932. *Literae Humaniores* remained the most prestigious of the arts diciplines until the second half of the century, despite the numerical predominance of Modern History. But the modern course of Philosophy, Politics, and Economics (PPE) rapidly established itself both in standing and numbers. In their formative years both English and Modern Languages were hindered by tensions between the competing claims of philology and literature.

The growth of science, while perhaps the most significant change in curricular patterns in twentieth-century Oxford, was slow to take effect, and well into the second half of the century sixth-formers considering university entrance were advised, "Oxford for Arts, Cambridge for Science." In 1923 80 percent of students were reading arts and social sciences, and only 20 percent science and medicine; in 1958 scientists remained heavily in a minority (27 percent). The most rapid growth in science came in the following thirty years (42 percent of Oxford students were studying science disciplines in 1990).

The weakness of Oxford science in the early part of the century, though often exaggerated, was undeniable. The revival of the Clarendon laboratory through research in the field of low-temperature **physics** took place between the wars and was strengthened by the arrival of academic **refugees** from Nazism. **Chemistry** had traditionally been the strongest area of Oxford science; for most of the period it had the largest number of students among the science disciplines, and its reputation was confirmed by Nobel Prize-winning research. But the most celebrated achievement of Oxford science was the development of penicillin in the Pathology laboratory, for which a Nobel Prize was awarded in 1945.

Oxford scholarship in the arts was sustained by the Bodleian Library, which by 1987 had 5 million books, and disseminated by the Oxford University Press, which became a model for other university presses. A New York branch opened in 1896. Its publications—notably the *Oxford English Dictionary* (1933)—became standard throughout the English-speaking world. Dictionaries came to replace bibles as the flagship publications of the press.

Although the scholarly output of Oxford's dons was often considerable, the local academic style in the first half of the century, particularly in the arts disciplines, was resistant to what was regarded as the teutonic pedantry of organized research. Research degrees (the B.Sc. and B.Litt.) were first introduced in 1895, but a doctoral-level credential (the D.Phil.) was not created until 1917. This was done mainly to attract overseas students, especially Americans, who had traditionally sought research training in Germany. Numbers of research students rose slowly; there were only 200 in 1939. By 1970 this figure reached 3,000; and in 1990, 3,700 (27 percent of the student population). Six new colleges were established to cater for graduate students: Green (1979), Linacre (1962), Nuffield (1937), St. Antony's (1948), St. Cross (1965), and Wolfson (1964).

Women's education at Oxford dated from the creation in the late nineteenth century of residential single-sex colleges, of which the earliest were Lady Margaret Hall and Somerville (both founded in 1879). Although permitted to enter university examinations, women were not admitted as full members of the university until 1920. Thereafter assimilation seemed to be the dominant theme, culminating in the constitutional changes that brought the five women's colleges into line with the men's colleges in 1959. Numerically, however, Oxford was still predominantly a male university; women represented 16 percent of students in 1965. Five of the men's colleges began to admit women in 1974; the remainder soon followed, while three of the women's colleges started to admit men. By 1986 only St. Hilda's and Somerville survived as single-sex colleges. The results of this sudden transformation to coeducation were much debated. Meanwhile, the proportion of women students at Oxford doubled from 19 percent in 1968 to 38 percent in 1988.

Oxford continued to be a nursery for future politicians; it educated nearly half of the Prime Ministers who held office between 1900 and 1987, a third of **Cabinet** ministers, and a fifth of MPs. Institutions such as the Oxford Union Society (a student debating society) had traditionally acted as a preparation for political life. New developments, such as the university's extramural work, and the establishment in 1899 of Ruskin College for working-class students, provided the basis for links with the **Labour Party**.

For much of the century the university was best known to the British public for its sporting activities: Annual fixtures with Cambridge, especially the boat race and rugby match, and individual feats, such as the breaking of the four-minute mile record by Roger Bannister in 1954, commanded national attention. The essence of Oxford sport, however, was participation; university clubs were self-financing and run by the students themselves, while professionalism had been eschewed at an early date.

Oxford's position as an international university of the Anglophone world was reinforced by the scholarships founded by Cecil Rhodes to bring students from the Empire and the United States. These came into effect in 1903. By 1964 overseas students at Oxford were still predominantly drawn from the Commonwealth and the United States. **Decolonization** and Britain's entry into the **European Community** (EC) suggested a change in the pattern, though in 1990 students from other EC countries still represented only 3 percent of the 13,948 students at Oxford (the total from overseas being over 18 percent). The creation, in 1992, of European Rhodes scholarships raised the possibility that in the next century Oxford might more fully reclaim its medieval inheritance as one of the original network of European universities.

M.C. *Curthoys*

Bibliography

Halsey, A.H. *Decline of Donnish Dominion: The British Academic Professions in the Twentieth Century.* 1992.

Harrison, Brian H., ed. *History of the University of Oxford: The Twentieth Century.* vol 8. 1994.

———. "Oxford and the Labour Movement," *Twentieth Century British History,* vol. 2 (1991), pp. 226–71.

Hibbert, Christopher, ed. *The Encyclopaedia of Oxford.* 1988.

University of Oxford: Report of Commission of Inquiry. 2 vols. 1966.

P

Pacifism

While pacifism was certainly extant as a distinctive ideology in British society prior to the twentieth century, the **Society of Friends** being a prime example, scholars tend to see its modern manifestation beginning with the **First World War**. It was the issue of **conscription** that galvanized pacifists into action, leading to the formation of the **No-Conscription Fellowship** in late 1914 under the leadership of **Fenner Brockway** and **Clifford Allen**. The Fellowship of Reconciliation (FOR) was also founded that same year by an energetic group of Christian pacifists, including Henry T. Hodgkin, the Rev. Richard Roberts, and Lucy Gardner, most of whom emerged out of a Free Church or Quaker tradition. While the number of young men who defied the state and went to prison rather than fight was relatively small, their courage, suffering, and dignified witness became important in the developing mythology of the peace movement.

After the war the No-Conscription Fellowship was abolished and the FOR experienced a decline in membership. The latter's problems were no doubt due in part to the founding of two new organizations, the War Resisters' International and the No More War Movement, both of which tended to attract pacifists who believed that socialism was a necessary prerequisite to achieving peace. By far the most successful peace organization during the 1920s was the **League of Nations Union**, which was not strictly pacifist. Headed by **Lord Robert Cecil** and **Gilbert Murray**, it eventually claimed over 400,000 members devoted to the concept of international order and collective security. Its popularity was probably due to the fact that the favorable state of international relations during the 1920s led people to believe that the **League of Nations** was the organization best positioned to secure disarmament and international security, and that its authority to impose economic, financial, and even military sanctions would deter potential aggressors.

Ironically, as the international scene deteriorated in the early 1930s, interest in peace quickened. Pacifist books and plays enjoyed immense popularity; peace rallies could attract large crowds; famous personalities announced their conversion to pacifism; and antiwar resolutions were adopted by universities, trade unions, women's groups, and even major political parties. Not surprisingly the 1930s has sometimes been referred to as the heyday of British pacifism. However, this peace sentiment was the product of an uneasy coalition of several disparate groups, and its unity was put to the test by the rise of the Fascist dictators. An important turning point occurred in 1935 when Fascist Italy invaded Abyssinia. A number of peace advocates rallied to the League of Nations, calling for economic sanctions to be imposed upon Italy, even at the risk of war. Then in the following year, the **Spanish Civil War** broke out, and many British socialists, previously committed to peace, rallied to the cause of Spanish republicanism, calling for arms and volunteers in the struggle against **Fascism**. The fragility of the peace coalition stood starkly exposed.

But those peace societies that resisted the call for economic sanctions or military assistance experienced much growth. For them pacifism had always implied unconditional opposition to all wars and taking of human life, regardless of the issues involved. The Fellowship of Reconciliation saw membership almost triple to 9,800 between 1934 and 1939, and the Council of Christian Pacifist Groups was founded to coordinate the ever-increasing activity of pacifists within the various Christian denominations. But the real success story of the 1930s was the phenomenal growth of the **Peace Pledge Union** (PPU), founded by the Rev. Dick Sheppard in 1936. Its members signed a pledge to renounce war and never support another one, and within a short time the PPU claimed over 100,000 members, a figure that would eventually rise to 136,000. Another important development was the creation of the Embassies of Reconciliation in 1936, which pioneered in the field of personal diplomacy by sending noted pacifists abroad to meet with heads of state and present to them the Christian call for peace and a Christian program of peacemaking. **George Lansbury**, a former leader of the **Labour Party**, visited a number of European leaders, including Adolf Hitler and Benito Mussolini, and secured publicity for the pacifist cause in the process.

When war broke out in 1939, many pacifists defected and supported the war effort, among them such names as Maude Royden, **Bertrand Russell**, Storm Jameson, Cyril Joad, Rose Macaulay, and A.A. Milne. Significantly, many of these ex-pacifists belonged to the Peace Pledge Union, while the Fellowship of Reconciliation, on the other hand, experienced few defections. None of the existing peace societies attempted seriously to obstruct the war effort; instead, these societies offered dignified witness to their belief and engaged in a variety of religious, humanitarian, and service projects, and some individuals even participated in civil defense schemes. It should also be emphasized that Christian pacifists from many denominations established close ties with one another during the war, and this cooperation and goodwill contributed substantially to the success of the world ecumenical movement in the post-war period.

After the war some societies ceased to exist while others went into a period of swift and noticeable decline. Occasionally, certain issues could galvanize large segments of the British public into action, notably the **Campaign for Nuclear Disarmament**, opposition to America's involvement in Vietnam, and the attempt during the 1980s to install and maintain American Cruise missiles on British soil. Admittedly, these issues were not always strictly pacifist in nature, but the younger generation found it difficult to separate pacifism from other causes, such as **imperialism**, sexism, racism, social injustice, gay liberation, and ecological concerns.

David C. Lukowitz

Bibliography
Ceadel, Martin. *Pacifism in Britain, 1914–1945: The Defining of a Faith.* 1980.
———. *Thinking about Peace and War.* 1987.
Moorehead, Caroline. *Troublesome People: The Warriors of Pacifism.* 1986.
Robbins, Keith. *The Abolition of War: The Peace Movement in Britain, 1914–1919.* 1976.
Wallis, Jill. *Valiant for Peace: A History of the Fellowship of Reconciliation, 1914 to 1989.* 1991.

Palestine

The three decades of British rule in Palestine after 1917 crucially changed the demographic and political shape of the country, paving the way for the establishment of the state of Israel upon the British departure in 1948.

The British administration in Palestine was inaugurated in December 1917 when General Sir Edmund Allenby entered Jerusalem after ousting the Ottoman Turks from southern Palestine. The remainder of the country was occupied by the British in the autumn of 1918. Until 30 June 1920 a British military administration ruled Palestine under the military law of occupation, which called for the maintenance, so far as practicable, of the status quo *ante bellum.*

Even before the British occupation the question of the post-war disposition of Palestine had been the subject of dispute among the Allied governments as well as the Zionists and the Sherifian Arab regime in the Hejaz. In 1915 the British-Arab exchange of letters known as the McMahon-Hussein correspondence provided an ambiguous basis for later Arab claims that Palestine was within the area promised by the British for a future pan-Arab state. In 1916 secret Anglo-French discussions resulted in the Sykes-Picot agreement, which provided for the partition of the central Middle East into zones of British and French dominance; central Palestine, under this scheme, was assigned to a vaguely defined international regime. In November 1917 the British government, after lengthy discussions with the Zionists, issued the

Balfour Declaration, which promised to facilitate the establishment of a Jewish national home in Palestine. Later statements by the Allied governments promised that the liberated peoples of the Ottoman Empire would be granted the right to self-determination.

At the Paris Peace Conference in 1919 both Zionist and Arab delegations appeared. On 3 January 1919 a tentative agreement was signed by the Zionist leader, Dr. Chaim Weizmann, and the Emir Faisal, leader of the Hejazi delegation, which seemed to indicate Hejazi acquiescence in the establishment of a Jewish national home in Palestine. But it was later repudiated by Faisal and rejected by Arab nationalists in Palestine itself.

The British, convinced that they were the only suitable rulers for Palestine, persuaded the French and other powers to grant Britain a "mandate" under the authority of the **League of Nations** to rule Palestine until it was fit for independence. Sophisticated lobbying by the Zionists secured the insertion into the mandate of several clauses that furnished guarantees in international law for the establishment and development of the Jewish national home.

Meanwhile, anti-Jewish riots in Jerusalem in April 1920 led the British government to replace the military by a civil administration prior to finalizing the mandate. On 30 June 1920 **Sir Herbert Samuel**, a former **Liberal** minister, took office as first High Commissioner. The first of seven holders of the post and the only one who was a Jew, Samuel embarked on efforts to persuade the Arab nationalist leadership, drawn mainly from the notable class, to acquiesce in the establishment of the Jewish national home. Further anti-Jewish riots in Jaffa and elsewhere in May 1921 led him to issue a reformulation of British policy in 1922 in a White Paper. This sought to balance support for the Jewish national home with assurances of safeguards for the Arab majority. Samuel also tried to establish an elected legislative council, but the elections were boycotted by the Arabs. Subsequent attempts to set up an unelected Advisory Council and an Arab Agency on a par with the recognized Jewish Agency (at that time identical with the Zionist Organization) also failed. As a result, from 1917 to 1948 Palestine was, in effect, an unfettered British colonial autocracy.

Under Samuel's rule, which continued until 1925, immigration, mainly from Eastern Europe, gradually increased the Jewish proportion of the population. Large tracts of cultivable land, particularly in the Valley of Jezreel, were purchased for Jewish settlement, mainly from absentee Arab landlords. Jewish institutions, such as the *Vaad Leumi* (National Council), the *Histadrut*, the Zionist labor union, and the underground *Haganah* (Zionist defense force) created the embryo of the national institutions of the Jewish state.

In an effort to provide some institutional counterweight for the Arab majority, Samuel established the Supreme Muslim Council, which was given charge of all Muslim *awkaf* (religious trusts), mosques, and other Muslim bodies in Palestine. He selected Haj Amin al-Husseini to serve as President of the council and in early 1921 engineered his appointment as Mufti of Jerusalem. Husseini's additional office as head of the Supreme Muslim Council endowed him with unparalleled authority, and by the end of the 1920s he had emerged as the leading figure of Arab Palestine. His prestige was enhanced by a controversy between Arabs and Jews in 1928–9 over religious rights on the Temple Mount (*Haram al-Sharif*) and the Western ("Wailing") Wall in Jerusalem, culminating in severe riots in Jerusalem in August 1929.

In the early 1930s Jewish immigration, mainly from Poland and Nazi Germany, reached unprecedented levels. By 1935 the 355,000 Jews in Palestine constituted 27 percent of the total population. The Arabs now feared that, if the influx continued unchecked, they might soon become a minority in their own country. In 1936 an Arab general strike in protest against Jewish immigration developed into a nationwide revolt against British rule and against the Jewish national home. When efforts of the High Commissioner, Sir Arthur Wauchope, to conciliate the Arabs failed, the British turned instead to repression. Military forces, eventually amounting to 40 percent of the entire field strength of the British **army**, were deployed to put down the rebels. Over 100 captured Arab rebels were hanged before the revolt collapsed in early 1939.

Meanwhile the Mufti, whose Arab Higher Committee was regarded as the chief inspiration of the revolt, had evaded arrest and fled the country. In 1937 a Royal Commission, headed by Earl Peel, reported in favor of partition of Palestine into separate Jewish and Arab states, with a residual British mandatory area. The government at first accepted the report but, in the face of Arab opposition to partition, eventually backed away from the idea. In February-

P

March 1939 a conference in London failed to produce agreement. The government felt an overriding need, given the dangerous international situation, to reduce its military commitment in Palestine. The policy announced in May 1939 limited Jewish immigration to no more than 75,000 over the next five years and sought to restrict land transfers from Arab to Jews.

This policy was maintained throughout the war, the British authorities resorting to extreme measures, including force, to prevent boatloads of Jewish refugees from Nazi Europe from landing in Palestine. Jewish resentment led to the rise of terrorist organizations such as the *Irgun Zvai Leumi*, headed by Menahem Begin, and the Stern Gang. In 1944 members of the Stern Gang assassinated the British Minister in the Middle East, Lord Moyne, in Cairo. Thereafter an escalating conflict between the Jewish terrorist organizations and the British army inflamed the politics of Palestine.

When the **Labour** government assumed office in Britain in 1945, British policy did not change. In spite of earlier pro-Zionist party policy statements, Labour in power, and particularly the Foreign Secretary, **Ernest Bevin**, resisted pressure to admit large numbers of Jewish immigrants to Palestine or to permit the establishment of a Jewish state. The government found itself caught between conflicting pressures: In Palestine the mainstream Zionist underground, the *Haganah*, joined forces with the terrorist groups to try to compel the British to admit Jewish immigrants; in the United States, on which Britain was now heavily dependent for economic aid, the Zionists mobilized effectively as a political lobby; but the newly formed League of Arab States demanded that Britain concede the Palestinian Arab demand for an independent Arab state in Palestine; the government feared that the entire British position in the **Middle East**, including vital assets such as the Suez Canal and the oil fields of Iraq, might be endangered if it acceded to Zionist demands; and it feared the consequences for **Anglo-American relations** if it yielded to the Arabs.

The result was a long period of irresolution and drift. In the autumn of 1945 the British and American governments agreed on the appointment of a joint Anglo-American Committee of Inquiry to look into the problems of Palestine and of the Jewish "displaced persons," as the survivors of Adolf Hitler's death camps in Europe were called. The committee reported in April 1946, but its major immediate recommendation, to admit 100,000 Jewish refugees to Palestine, was rejected by the British government. Prime Minister **Clement Attlee** announced that an essential precondition would be the disarming of all illegal forces in Palestine, a proposal the Zionists rejected.

Meanwhile, the military situation on the ground deteriorated in spite of the deployment of huge British forces. Terrorist incidents such as the massive bomb explosion in 1946 at the King David Hotel, the British military headquarters in Jerusalem, which killed ninety British, Jewish, and Arab victims, led to a partial breakdown of morale in the British army in Palestine and counterterrorism against Jewish targets. At the same time Arab-Jewish violence also increased.

After further efforts to obtain a settlement by agreement failed, the government announced in 1947 that it would return the mandate to the **United Nations** and withdraw from Palestine. The United Nations sent a committee to Palestine to investigate the position, and on the basis of its proposals the UN General Assembly, on 29 November 1947, voted by the necessary two-thirds majority in favor of the partition of Palestine into separate Jewish and Arab states.

The remaining five-and-a-half months of British rule were a descent into chaos. British authority collapsed as the rivals for the succession attempted to take over power on a local level in advance of the British withdrawal. By early 1948 the British army made no pretense of doing more than protecting British installations and personnel. By April full-scale civil war was in progress between Jewish armed forces and Arab irregulars supported by the armies of surrounding Arab states. A massive flight began of the Palestinian Arab population, in some areas forced to leave by the Zionists.

On 14 May the Zionist leader, David Ben Gurion, declared the establishment of the state of Israel. At midnight on the same day British rule ended when the last High Commissioner, Sir Alan Cunningham, embarked on a British warship at Haifa. Thirty years of British rule collapsed in ignominy and historic recriminations of which echoes resound to the present day.

Bernard Wasserstein

Bibliography
Hurewitz, J.C. *The Struggle for Palestine.* 1950.
Morris, Benny. *The Birth of the Palestinian*

Refugee Problem, 1947–1949. 1987.

Stein, Leonard. *The Balfour Declaration.* 1961.

Sykes, Christopher. *Crossroads to Israel: Palestine from Balfour to Bevin.* 1965.

Wasserstein, Bernard. *The British in Palestine: The Mandatory Government and the Arab-Jewish Conflict, 1917–1929.* 1978.

Pankhurst, Emmeline (1858–1928), Christabel (Harriette) (1880–1958), (Estelle) Sylvia (1882–1960)

Known primarily for their instigation of militancy on behalf of **women's suffrage**, the Pankhursts injected vitality and imagination into the politics of the early twentieth century. Emmeline (née Goulden) and her daughters Christabel and Sylvia contributed their considerable energies to progressive causes, though only Sylvia would remain constant to the beliefs instilled in her from childhood by her parents.

Emmeline Pankhurst, hailing from a Radical family in Manchester and marrying at the age of twenty a prominent Radical lawyer, Richard Marsden Pankhurst (1835–98), became involved in suffrage and feminist politics at an early age. The birth of her children, Christabel, Sylvia, Frank, Adela, and Harry, did not deter her from an active political life, which included organizing for suffrage and for married women's property rights, membership in the socialist **Independent Labour Party** (ILP), and a stint as a Poor Law Guardian in the 1890s. When the ILP refused to espouse votes for women, Emmeline formed the **Women's Social and Political Union** (WSPU) in 1903 to mobilize working-class women on behalf of suffrage.

Christabel Pankhurst, while still a law student at Owens College, first initiated WSPU acts of militancy in 1905, when she and Annie Kenney (1879–1953) were ejected from Free Trade Hall in Manchester for heckling Sir **Edward Grey**. Christabel spat at a policeman in an effort to force her arrest; she was fined and, upon refusing to pay, put in prison. The ensuing publicity brought the cause of women's suffrage into the public eye as never before. The WSPU moved to London where it pursued a policy of spectacular public protest. In 1907 the WSPU organized a "Mud March," in which 3,000 women carrying banners and stepping to the beat of **brass bands**, proceeded from Hyde Park to Exeter Hall demanding votes for women. Such activities succeeded beyond all expectations in focusing the public spotlight upon the women's cause and in increasing the ranks of suffragists, but much of that success depended upon the willingness of suffragettes, as WSPU members were called, to follow the Pankhursts without question. Many were unable to do so. In 1907 Teresa Billington-Greig (1877–1964), Charlotte Despard (1844–1939), and others, disillusioned by Christabel and Emmeline Pankhurst's antidemocratic ways and their abandonment of the ILP and of socialism, broke away and formed the **Women's Freedom League**. Sylvia Pankhurst, who had interrupted her art studies to work for the WSPU, shared their disillusionment but remained loyal to her mother and sister until 1912.

Until the summer of 1909 the Pankhursts eschewed violence. Suffragettes heckled **Cabinet** ministers and obstructed political meetings; they marched on Parliament to demand meetings with MPs. Often they were met with violence at the hands of the **police** and civilian bystanders before being arrested. In the summer of 1909 the militants turned to stone throwing to protest against politicians who refused their demands. Their symbolic protests also served to cut short the sometimes brutal struggles with police before they were arrested. Also during the summer of 1909 militant suffragists began hunger strikes in prison, demanding that their sentences be reduced to reflect more accurately the nature of their crimes and that they be treated as political prisoners rather than as criminals. The authorities responded with forced feedings, whose violence led both sympathizers and opponents of women's suffrage to decry the government's actions.

By 1910, with a large measure of support for women's suffrage within Parliament, it appeared that a bill enfranchising women had a good chance of passing, and the WSPU ceased its militancy. When, however, Prime Minister **H.H. Asquith** torpedoed a Conciliation bill designed to appeal to all parties, the WSPU abandoned its truce. On November 18, a day that became known as "Black Friday" in the annals of suffrage history, Emmeline Pankhurst led suffragettes on a march from Caxton Hall to Parliament Square, where they were attacked and sexually molested by police and civilian bystanders in a confrontation that lasted six hours. The vivid demonstrations of sexual violence against women acted as powerful recruiting agents.

P

In 1911 the Conciliation bill was revived, and again the Pankhursts halted their militant activities. But when the government appeared to sink the bill for a second time, the WSPU erupted in acts of intentional lawbreaking. In March 1912 Emmeline Pankhurst joined in smashing windows at 10 Downing Street, while coordinated attacks left countless windows shattered elsewhere in London. In the aftermath, 217 suffragettes were arrested, including Emmeline Pankhurst and Emmeline (1867–1954) and Frederick (1871–1961) Pethick Lawrence, who were charged with inciting to riot and sentenced to nine months in prison. Embarking upon a hunger strike, they became so ill that officials were forced to release them. Emmeline Pankhurst announced her intention of continuing violent acts and of expanding them to include arson. The Pethick Lawrences, who had financed the activities of the WSPU since its earliest days, resigned in protest, taking their newspaper, *Votes for Women*, with them. Christabel, meanwhile, had fled to Paris and began to edit the *Suffragette* in its stead. In it she published a series of articles on **venereal disease**, later compiled in a volume entitled *The Great Scourge and How To End It* (1913), that reflected on the direct connections between women's political powerlessness and their vulnerability to the sexual depredations of men. Sylvia, who could no longer countenance the behavior of her mother and sister, broke with them and devoted all of her energies to the East London Federation of Suffragettes, a working-class women's organization that retained its affiliation with the ILP. She also began a newspaper called *The Woman's Dreadnought*, which featured the concerns of working-class women.

In 1913 the WSPU embarked upon another round of lawbreaking, again in response to the government's betrayal of a promise to bring in a women's suffrage provision. **David Lloyd George**'s country house was set afire, prompting authorities to arrest Emmeline Pankhurst for inciting to commit a felony. She received three years' imprisonment. In anticipation of her cutting short her prison term by embarking on a hunger strike, the government passed the Cat and Mouse Act (1913), which enabled it to release a hunger-striking prisoner and reincarcerate her after she had recovered from her ordeal. Under the Cat and Mouse Act, Emmeline Pankhurst was released and reimprisoned numerous times, so that she had

served only thirty days of her sentence between April 1913 and April 1914.

The split between Sylvia and her mother and sister worsened during the **First World War**. While Emmeline and Christabel devoted their energies to the war effort, Sylvia, denouncing the war, concentrated on socialist rather than on feminist issues, changing the name of her newspaper to *The Worker's Dreadnought* and welcoming wholeheartedly the Russian Revolution. In 1920 she helped form the **Communist Party of Great Britain** and was tried and sentenced to a five-month term for sedition for an article she published in the *Dreadnought*. Her refusal to marry Sylvio Corio, an Italian exile who was the father of her son, Richard Pankhurst (1927–), completed the estrangement of her mother. With Corio, Sylvia Pankhurst continued to pursue radical causes, engaging in anti-Fascist activity in the 1920s and 1930s and devoting her life after 1936 to the cause of Ethiopia.

Emmeline and Christabel Pankhurst, by contrast, abandoned their **feminist** activity, although they did help organize a demonstration demanding "women's right to serve" in munitions factories and other jobs that would support the war effort in 1915. In 1917 they transformed the WSPU into the Women's Party but did not involve themselves in the negotiations that resulted in a measure of women's suffrage in 1918. Christabel's failure to win election to Parliament in 1918 and 1919 resulted in the demise of the Women's Party. She joined the Second Adventist movement, seeing in the second coming of Christ the solution to the ills she had hoped suffrage would alleviate. Withdrawing from politics, she spent most of her later years in the United States, where she died in 1958.

Emmeline, in 1918, embarked for **Canada**, where she lectured on behalf of the National Council for Combating Venereal Disease for seven years. In 1925 she returned to England, joined the **Conservative Party**, and was adopted as a parliamentary candidate for Whitechapel, much to the distress of Sylvia, but did not live long enough to contest the seat.

Although the women's suffrage campaign had existed for almost forty years before the WSPU burst upon the scene, and the victory won in 1918 owed at least as much to the efforts of the constitutional suffragists within the National Union of Women's Suffrage Societies, there can be no doubt that the provocative tactics of the Pankhursts brought to the cause of votes for women an energy and visibility that transformed the movement and helped to challenge the whole gender system of the early twentieth century.

Susan Kingsley Kent

Bibliography

Mitchell, David. *Queen Christabel.* 1977.

Pankhurst, Emmeline. *My Own Story.* 1914.

Pankhurst, E. Sylvia. *The Suffragette Movement.* new ed. 1977.

Raeburn, Antonia. *The Militant Suffragettes.* 1973.

Romero, Patricia W. *E. Sylvia Pankhurst: Portrait of a Radical.* 1987.

Sarah, Elizabeth. "Christabel Pankhurst: Reclaiming Her Power, 1880–1958," in Dale Spender, ed., *Feminist Theorists.* 1983. pp. 256–84.

Pasmore, Victor (1908–)

When, in 1948, Victor Pasmore exhibited his first abstract paintings (apart from four dating from 1934 that he had destroyed), he turned his back on the material and critical success he had achieved over a period of ten years for the uncertainties of abstract experimentation as a Constructivist who believed that art should have a role to play in the formation of everyday life. Pasmore's example in renouncing figurative painting encouraged a small group of artists in the early 1950s who included Terry Frost, Adrian Heath, Robert Adams, Anthony Hill, and Kenneth and Mary Martin.

By 1948 Pasmore was enjoying the patronage and influential support of Sir **Kenneth Clark** among others (support that was to fall away in the coming years) and had established himself as a leading figure of that approach to figurative painting in Britain founded on the analysis and lyrical representation of objective visual reality. In 1937 he had helped found (with William Coldstream, Claude Rogers, and Graham Bell) the **Euston Road School**, which adhered to these aims. Although short-lived—it closed with the outbreak of war in 1939—its influence is still felt in some quarters of art education in Britain.

Following an exhibition of Picasso and Matisse at the Victoria and Albert Museum in 1945 that underlined what Pasmore saw as a crisis in modern art, he started to shift his allegiances from **W.R. Sickert**, Degas, and Manet (whose work had underpinned the Euston Road

Group) toward the work of Klee, Kandinsky, and the Bauhaus for inspiration. His last figurative paintings of 1945–8, such as the series of paintings of Hammersmith Gardens, exhibit this mood of uncertainty. His shift toward abstraction was reflected in his changing attitude to teaching, which crystalized at the Central School of Arts and Crafts from 1949 and, from 1954, in Newcastle with **Richard Hamilton**. These foundation "Basic Form" courses, inspired by the Bauhaus model, used a set of formal problems, rather than objective transcription from nature, as a means of instruction.

Pasmore located his own development within the field of experimentation, and his evolution through collage and painting toward the relief format and use of industrial materials was swift. Although allied to the impersonal materials of science and industry, Pasmore's reliefs, all constructed on an empirical and intuitive basis, reveal a lyrical choice of color and surface that was at variance with the mathematically inspired work of Hill. By the end of the 1960s the distinction between relief and painting had broken down, and he moved toward a largely two-dimensional and more free-flowing expression that often seems to be searching for the tranquil humor of Klee. By this time he had represented Britain at the XXX Venice Biennale and had been able to give up teaching to concentrate on his work full-time. The increasing freedom of his approach can also be explained by his move to Malta in 1966.

Andrew Wilson

Bibliography

Alley, Ronald. *Victor Pasmore: Retrospective Exhibition, 1925–1965.* 1965.

Bell, Clive. *Victor Pasmore.* 1945.

Bowness, Alan, and Luigi Lambertini. *Victor Pasmore: With a Catalogue Raisonné of the Paintings, Constructions, and Graphics, 1926–1979.* 1980.

Grieve, Alastair. *Victor Pasmore.* 1980.

Lynton, Norbert. *Victor Pasmore, Nature into Art.* 1990.

Passchendaele (Third Battle of Ypres)

During the First World War the British Commander-in-Chief, Sir **Douglas Haig**, had planned an attack against German forces from the Ypres salient in Belgium as early as 1916. However, the **Somme** operation in that year and the British role in the Nivelle offensive the following spring delayed the plan until the summer of 1917. The operation called for an attack by fifteen British divisions from the salient. They would first capture the Passchendaele Ridge and then advance on Roulers and Thourout. Finally, in conjunction with a force attacking from Nieuport, the Belgian coast would be cleared, the German U-boat bases there captured, and German lateral communications to the south cut, ensuring a general German withdrawal from the entire northern section of the Western Front.

The operation was misconceived from the outset. Haig had to capture the Messines Ridge to deny the Germans observation over the section of the salient from which his main operation was to be launched. In an action brilliantly planned by General Sir Herbert Plumer, this was achieved on 7 June. But Haig had never intended launching his main strike until the end of July. Thus the Germans were given seven weeks to prepare their defenses for the coming battle. By the time the main attack began on 31 July 1917, they had created a checkerboard defense to a depth of 10,000 yards.

Nevertheless, after a sixteen-day artillery bombardment of unprecedented ferocity, the first day of battle was a partial success for the British. General Sir Hubert Gough's Fifth Army, aided by a French Corps, gained good ground in the northern section of the salient, penetrating almost halfway to the Passchendaele Ridge. Little ground was gained, however, on the Gheluvelt Plateau from which the Germans overlooked the remainder of the British Front. During August hardly any progress was made by the British. Operations were hampered by the rain but were in any case ill-thought-out, hastily conceived affairs that would have stood little chance whatever the weather.

In September Haig turned the battle over to Plumer, who determined that no further progress was possible until the Gheluvelt Plateau was captured. In three successful battles conducted in fine conditions on 20, 26 September and 4 October, he managed to capture most of the Gheluvelt Plateau and advance within striking distance of the Passchendaele Ridge. Poor weather then set in again, and the time for further operations seemed over. Haig was undeterred. During the next six weeks British troops were driven by the Commander-in-Chief, with Plumer's approval, through some of the worst conditions ever experienced by the British army on the Western Front. This period

(the Battles of Passchendaele), with the armies struggling through the bog, came in the popular mind to characterize the whole battle. With the capture of the ruins of Passchendaele village and part of the ridge on 12 November the operation was finally called off. For a cost of more than 200,000 casualties the British had not even taken their first objective. Given the strength of the German defense, a grand advance on the Belgian coast was always chimerical, and in any case the small coastal **submarines** operating from its ports were of little consequence. All that was possible at this stage were more cautious step-by-step advances such as those achieved by Plumer in September. Haig never accepted these tactics, and the Third Battle of Ypres was just one of a series of costly campaigns in which, while striving for grandiose objectives, he achieved little but the attrition of his own army.

Robin Prior
Trevor Wilson

Bibliography

Terraine, John. *The Road to Passchendaele.* 1977.
Wilson, Trevor. *The Myriad Faces of War: Britain and the Great War, 1914–1918.* 1986.

Patriotism

Far from being an eternal, unchanging, universal sentiment, patriotism has assumed different forms and meanings over the past two centuries. In the eighteenth century patriotism was associated with a radical critique of the corruption and ostentation of Court life and politics, and it implied, therefore, independence and opposition. It was not until the late nineteenth century, perhaps during the Eastern Crisis involving Turkey and the Balkans in the late 1870s, that patriotism acquired more Conservative connotations, such as the elevation of the idea of national solidarity at the expense of dissent or the chauvinistic emphasis upon national superiority as an absolute priority. At the turn of the century, in the midst of the **Boer War**, the British Left regarded patriotism with distaste, and its articulate spokesmen, such as **J.A. Hobson,** interpreted patriotic celebrations as manifestations of irrational mass behavior, fuelled by an irresponsible cheap press and the degenerate tendencies of urban squalor. Hobson and others deplored the jingoism and xenophobia that figured prominently in the Conservatives' avowedly patriotic electioneering strategies and in that party's legislation, such as the 1905 act to restrict alien **immigration**. In English regions with significant **Irish** communities, such as Lancashire, the Conservatives exploited ethnic politics and successfully appealed to native religious and cultural prejudices.

Indeed, the very notion of some broader, all-embracing British patriotism was problematic. Although nationalist or separatist movements ultimately proved weaker in Wales and Scotland than in Ireland, they all reflected the fact that the patriotism of the **Conservative Party** was a largely English affair. The acknowledged master in this regard was **Stanley Baldwin**, who evoked a rustic, organic England in which the simple decency and stable hierarchy of the rural life of southern England underwrote a Conservative appeal that appeared conciliatory and not bounded by class. Of course, Baldwin was no country bumpkin, but a calculating politician who shrewdly recognized the impact of radio and prudently prepared the ground for more-strident class appeals in the face of a **General Strike** in 1926. All the same, the linkage of celebratory patriotism to a very partial vision of the English past struck a responsive chord, for there was strong tradition within the British Left of distaste for the ugliness of industrialism and the harshness of unfettered market capitalism.

That broader resonance was one indication that patriotism amounted to more than an artificial notion induced by manipulative parties; another was the increasing range of institutions or agencies seeking to promote a common culture, and thereby, even if indirectly or implicitly, a wider basis for patriotic consensus. The advent of compulsory **primary education**, the growing penetration by the state of civil society (not least through the provision of **old-age pensions** and insurance), and (somewhat later) the emergence of the **British Broadcasting Corporation** (BBC), with its attendant conceptions of taste and standard usage, all operated as centralizing influences. So, too, did the monarchy, which reached new heights of popularity after it had withdrawn from active political involvement and simultaneously renovated and extended its ceremonial role. Patriotism's attraction as an idiom of cohesion may also have been enhanced by the steadily declining influence, as an established church, of **Anglicanism**; its privileged position had

occasioned much bitterness with various Nonconformist denominations as well as the **Roman Catholic** and **Jewish** communities. By the inter-war period the idea of Britain as a Christian nation commanded general assent without generating the acrimony characteristic of the previous century over forms of worship, frequency of attendance, or the relationship between church and state.

In short, by the 1930s there were grounds for presuming that patriotism as an overtly public form of loyalty was taking precedence over a variety of competing, often more private, forms of identification, whether confessional, regional, or economic in character. For the Left, whose conception of the nation was rooted less in unity and order through universal authority than in liberty and progress through the articulation of minority rights, in the assertion of the periphery rather than of the center, the challenge was to articulate an alternate view of patriotism. One response was the **Mass-Observation** movement, one of whose objectives was to document the wide variation in popular attitudes ignored by less-subtle observers who extolled the unanimity of public opinion (a prime example being the claims of the undiminished veneration of the monarchy in the midst of the abdication crisis of 1936).

Another response was **George Orwell's** *The Lion and the Unicorn*, published in 1941. Far from dismissing patriotism as irrational or merely manipulative, Orwell conceded that "as a positive force there is nothing to set beside it." He detected the patriotism of ordinary people, however, not in royal ritual, or even in the familiar symbols of Britannia or John Bull, but in the humbler, often private, fundamentally decent events of ordinary life, whether in the garden, the pub, or by the fireside. The wartime sense of popular unity in the face of Adolf Hitler's onslaught, therefore, was built upon more permanent foundations than temporary danger or **Winston Churchill's** stirring oratory. The great Conservative statesman's failure to recognize the peacetime political implications of this unofficial patriotism meant that the election loss to **Labour** in 1945 that he characterized as an unparalleled act of ingratitude in fact signaled a different popular conception of the state's obligations to its patriotic citizens.

In the post-war era the context for appeals to patriotism has shifted again. While English patriotism may have been largely insular, it had been sustained by the widespread sentiment that even if one did not know much about the Empire, one at least took pride in its possession. But after 1945 Britain as a whole had to adjust both to the rapid contraction of that Empire (and to a consequent diminution of its status as a great power) and to the equally rapid expansion of nonwhite immigration. Few politicians have made such allegedly grave changes in the nation's social fabric an explicit issue, and those who have, such as Enoch Powell, have eventually been relegated to the margins of public life. A deeper, if more diffuse, current of unease about national decline, though, was tapped by **Margaret Thatcher**, who consciously strove to restore the adjective "great" to Britain, and for whom the "**Falklands** factor" (the appeal to patriotic unities in the face of military conflict with Argentina over the Falklands Islands) was instrumental in resuscitating her flagging administration in 1982–3. Whether the Conservatives can continue to benefit from that approach remains to be seen; certainly the historical record suggests that patriotism is too protean a sentiment to fulfill that role for long.

Frans Coetzee

Bibliography

Colls, Robert, and Phillip Dodd, eds. *Englishness: Politics and Culture, 1880–1920.* 1986.

Grainger, J.H. *Patriotisms: Britain, 1900–1939.* 1986.

Samuel, Raphael, ed. *Patriotism: The Making and Unmaking of British National Identity.* 3 vols. 1989.

Peace Ballot

The Peace Ballot of 1934–5 marked a high point of British popular support for the **League of Nations** and played a key role in the response to the challenge to the League and world order posed by Fascist Italy in **Abyssinia**.

In April 1934 the **League of Nations Union** under the leadership of **Lord Robert Cecil** and **Gilbert Murray** had organized a National Declaration Committee to muster support for the League cause. It proposed to poll the public on whether it supported British membership in the League, the reduction of armaments, the abolition of military aircraft by international agreement, and the end to the private manufacture of arms. The critical fifth question it posed was: "Do you consider that, if a nation insists on attacking another, the other nations should combine to compel it to stop by (a) Economic and nonmilitary measures? (b) If necessary, military measures?"

These questions were framed to elicit positive answers, and as the 11.5 million answers came in, it was clear that they did. More than 90 percent of the answers were in the affirmative, except for 5(b), and even this got a majority of positive replies, with only 20 percent voting against military measures. When the final results were announced on 27 June 1935, it provided an impressive display of public opinion to Prime Minister **Stanley Baldwin**. From denouncing a collective peace system as "perfectly impracticable," he reversed himself and now proclaimed the League of Nations "the sheet anchor of British policy."

There was still opposition to a policy of sanctions imposed through the League from **Conservatives** as well as from **pacifists** and the extreme Left, and other polls were soon conducted to counter the Peace Ballot. They attracted little attention, however, and the British government took the lead in mustering League support for imposing sanctions against Italy in October 1935 when its forces invaded Abyssinia. Economic sanctions were incompletely applied and failed to stop the Italian conquest. The episode confirmed Peace Ballot supporters in their view that a historic opportunity to make collective security work had been wasted. The National government, meanwhile, concluded that a sanctions policy was risky and ineffective.

Donald S. Birn

Bibliography

Birn, Donald S. *The League of Nations Union.* 1981.

Livingstone, Adelaide, and Marjorie Scott Johnston. *The Peace Ballot: The Official History.* 1935.

Waley, Daniel. *British Public Opinion and the Abyssinian War.* 1975.

Peace Pledge Union

The Peace Pledge Union was the largest **pacifist** society in modern British history. It was formed under dramatic circumstances by the Rev. Dick Sheppard, a popular and well-known **Anglican** priest who was one of the few truly charismatic personalities produced by the pacifist movement. Alarmed by the deteriorating international situation, Sheppard sent a letter to several newspapers in October 1934, requesting those who agreed with his pacifist position to send him a postcard stating their willingness to support the following resolution: "We renounce war and never again, directly or indirectly, will we support or sanction another." The response was overwhelming. Within weeks thousands of postcards poured in, and by December 1935 he had received 100,000. In May 1936 he proceeded to organize this powerful expression of peace sentiment into a new body, the Peace Pledge Union (PPU).

During its early years a number of famous novelists, scientists, poets, philosophers, clergy, and politicians joined its ranks, including **Aldous Huxley, Bertrand Russell, Vera Brittain,** Rose Macaulay, **Siegfried Sassoon,** Storm Jameson, **George Lansbury,** and Lord Ponsonby. The PPU acquired its own weekly paper, *Peace News*, formed over 1,100 local and regional groups, held mass rallies, distributed pamphlets, and organized demonstrations and street corner speeches. The society suffered a grievous setback when Sheppard died suddenly on 31 October 1937, but membership, which was subsequently opened to women, continued to climb and peaked at 136,000 in early 1940.

When hostilities broke out in 1939, the PPU decided not to oppose war efforts, but rather to offer dignified witness to its pacifist beliefs. Still, the society did provide assistance to **conscientious objectors**, engage in relief work to alleviate suffering, explore new forms of communal living, encourage any initiatives to secure an armistice or negotiated peace, and offer fellowship and solace to pacifists who felt isolated and demoralized.

After the war the PPU entered a period of swift and noticeable decline. By 1947 the society claimed only 16,000 members; the connection with *Peace News* was severed; and the organization no longer commanded the public attention and respect it once did. The society was debilitated by internal wrangling, disagreement over both tactics and policy, and the tendency of the younger generation to broaden their interests from simply war resistance to more fashionable causes, such as racial justice, anticolonialism, ecological concerns, and unilateral nuclear disarmament. Lacking funds, members, and a distinctive ideology, the PPU, while still in existence in the early 1990s, had become weak and ineffective.

David C. Lukowitz

Bibliography

Ceadel, Martin. *Pacifism in Britain, 1914–1945: The Defining of a Faith.* 1980.

Lukowitz, David C. "British Pacifists and Appeasement: The Peace Pledge Union," *Journal of Contemporary History*, vol. 9 (1974), pp. 115–27.

Morrison, Sybil. *I Renounce War: The Story of the Peace Pledge Union.* 1962.

Roberts, R. Ellis. *H.R.L. Sheppard: Life and Letters.* 1942.

Scott, Carolyn. *Dick Sheppard: A Biography.* 1977.

Penal Reform

In 1900 penal reform had little effect upon a philosophy of imprisonment that called for hard time, hard labor, and hard beds. Prisoners lived under a regime that stressed discipline, silence, and isolation on the theory that prison life must act as both deterrent and punishment. In the course of the twentieth century the assumptions behind imprisonment have changed dramatically, although public debate about the purposes of incarceration continues.

Among the issues that have dominated discussion of penal reform is whether prison should serve primarily for punishment or as an instrument of behavioral reformation. Further inquiry focused on the actual physical conditions under which prisoners lived and their effects. Finally, questions have been raised as to whether prisons lead to greater recidivism and, if so, whether the entire system was a failure if it generated increased criminal activity.

In the Probation of Offenders Act (1907) prison became the last alternative as punishment, not a first resort. The Prevention of Crime Act (1908) addressed juvenile crime by initiating what became the Borstal system, training for those between sixteen and twenty-one years old who would be guided away from the criminal life. The rationale behind these changes was that deprivation of individual liberty constituted the greatest punishment. Sir Alexander Paterson (1884–1947), a prominent member of the Prison Commission (1922–45), expressed this assumption best when he wrote that individuals came to prison as punishment, not for punishment.

The lot of the individual prisoner has also altered remarkably. The Criminal Justice Act (1948) abolished corporal punishment once and for all. Many petty regulations that imposed needless humiliations upon prisoners have vanished. Supervision that undermined the dignity of the prisoner has in many, but not all, cases disappeared. The attempt to provide a more humane prison environment has faltered because of the overcrowding that afflicts the system in the 1990s. The noble idea of prison as a place for rehabilitation of the offender has not prevailed. Rates of recidivism have not changed noticeably throughout the century.

Two notable lobbying organizations for penal reform have been instrumental in the gradual adoption of more humane treatment of prisoners: the Penal Reform League (founded in 1908) and the Howard League for Penal Reform (founded in 1921). Among the achievements eventually obtained in part through their efforts were the introduction of shorter sentences, diagnosis and treatment of mental illness, and the abolition of **capital punishment**. While prisons have not become institutions that a person would willingly inhabit, they are far less degrading to the prisoner than in 1900.

Failure to carry penal reform further may be attributed to several intractable problems. The hope that a person's behavior will improve while in prison has remained a utopian goal, for most empirical evidence suggests that prison life enhances the chances of repeat offenses. Overcrowding, as proven by numerous prison riots in the 1980s, still represents a major problem. The British public wants more prisoners in jail but is reluctant to provide the tax revenue necessary for additional facilities. By any standard Britain has made significant progress toward a more humane penal system but has yet to realize its ambition to make the system a symbol of its own civilized standards.

Richard A. Cosgrove

Bibliography
Blom-Cooper, Louis, ed. *Progress in Penal Reform.* 1974.
Cross, Rupert. *Punishment, Prison, and the Public.* 1971.
Rose, Gordon. *The Struggle for Penal Reform: The Howard League and Its Predecessors.* 1961.
Ryan, Mick. *The Politics of Penal Reform.* 1983.

Periodicals

British periodicals in the twentieth century have gradually shifted from expressing the ideas of a relatively unified elite culture to addressing the interests of a much wider, but more fragmented, popular culture. As a result, they have lost something of the prestige they inherited from the Victorian period, while gaining in circulation and profitability. Moreover, the story of periodicals in the twentieth century is intertwined with the story of **advertising**, and the success of a British magazine came to depend on its value as a marketing tool.

A number of nineteenth-century magazines and reviews survived well into the twentieth. The *Cornhill Magazine* (1860–1975), for example, whose distinguished early editors included Anthony Trollope, William Makepeace Thackeray, and Leslie Stephen, continued to attract prominent writers through the 1940s. But in the 1950s its circulation was cut in half, a victim of the rise of **television** and cheap mass-market competitors, and the magazine's prestige waned along with its circulation. Similar fates awaited other great Victorian periodicals like *Quarterly Review* (1809–1967) and *Blackwood's Edinburgh Magazine* (1817–1980), which slowly lost their vitality and traditional audience.

Though many older magazines stagnated, the periodical as such became increasingly important with the rise of modernism after the **First World War**. A new generation of writers and intellectuals first exploded upon the scene in the pages of **Wyndham Lewis'** ground-breaking but short-lived *Blast* (1914–15). **T.S. Eliot**, Ezra Pound, and **James Joyce** were among those who found a home in Richard Aldington's *Egoist* (1914–19). Perhaps the most influential of modernist periodicals was the *Criterion* (1922–39), edited by Eliot himself, which attracted not only major British and American writers, but also European contributors, such as Hermann Hesse, Marcel Proust, Benedetto Croce, and André Malraux. Next to the *Criterion* in importance as a showcase for modernist writing was the *Calendar of Modern Letters* (1925–7). The **Bloomsbury** sensibility found its expression in *Life and Letters* (1928–50), which featured the work of **Virginia Woolf, E.M. Forster,** and **Bertrand Russell.**

There were also important periodicals that expressed the views of the antimodernist opposition. J.C. Squire's *London Mercury* (1919–39) saw its duty as combatting the pernicious influence of literary "abnormalities"—that is, writers like Eliot and Pound. Squire attracted the work of many of the Georgian, traditionalist writers, including Thomas Hardy and Hilaire Belloc. Other magazines proliferated to defend tradition, one of the most notable being the regionalist *Decachord* (1924–46). But Squire's *London Mercury* remained the periodical the new generation loved to hate; several new magazines were founded solely in order to satirize or attack it, notably Jack Lindsay's *London Aphrodite* (1928–9).

The 1930s saw periodicals founded or adapted to articulate the opinions of the new Left. John Middleton Murry's *Adelphi* (1923–55) reveals the temper of the changing times, as it adapted itself from a purely literary publication (with an emphasis on Murry's version of the ideas of **D.H. Lawrence**) to a primarily political one of Marxist orientation. The *Left Review* (1934–8) devoted itself to the proposition that all good art must serve the purposes of revolution; it also argued vigorously against war with Germany and for supporting the Soviet Union. And the once-conservative *London Mercury* shifted gears in 1934 with a new editor who emphasized politics, publishing left-wing writers like **Stephen Spender** and **W.H. Auden**. One of the more unusual of the many leftist periodicals was the *Bermondsey Book* (1923–30), whose pages mingled work by both middle-class intellectuals and ordinary workers. John Lehmann's important *New Writing* (1936–46) likewise opened its doors to proletarian writers but avoided dogmatism in its political orientation, publishing not only Spender and Auden, but Woolf and Forster.

With the coming of the war in 1939, a new era also began in periodicals. As if to signal this, the two antagonists, the *Criterion* and the *London Mercury*, both ceased publication in that year. In 1940 the government instituted a ban on new publications due to the paper shortages; the shortages and wartime crisis in the economy forced the closing of dozens of other magazines in the early 1940s. In spite of these obstacles, some important new publications were founded, notably Cyril Connolly's *Horizon* (1939–50). At the beginning of the war the indefatigable editor and publisher John Lehmann approached **Allen Lane**, founder of Penguin Books, and their collaborative effort resulted in *Penguin New Writing* (1940–50), a literary anthology with phenomenal sales, the circulation of nearly every issue hovering between 75,000 and 100,000.

The post-war period in Britain saw dramatic changes in the content and orientation of periodicals. Alongside well-established weeklies like the *Economist*, the *Spectator*, and the *New Statesman*, new magazines tried to reach an audience of intellectuals and common people with a mixture of literary and political opinion, but such periodicals became fewer and less vital in the second half of the century. One important example is *Encounter*, founded in 1953 by Spender and Irving Kristol as a voice of anti-Communist and pro-American thought. It achieved initial success and influence, with contributions from celebrated writers on literature, politics, and economics. But when in 1967 it was revealed to have been secretly funded by the CIA from its inception, Spender resigned, most of *Encounter's* array of contributors abandoned it, and the magazine lost its standing as an influential forum.

A more specialized, but equally significant periodical, *Scrutiny*, was published at **Cambridge** by **F.R. Leavis** from 1932 to 1953. Leavis argued for the centrality of literature and **literary criticism** in modern culture, but *Scrutiny* appealed mainly to the academic community in Britain and the United States. An exception to the trend toward greater specialization in intellectually oriented periodicals is the *Times Literary Supplement*, published on its own since 1914 and still providing a forum for intellectual debate across the various academic disciplines.

The periodicals that try to reach a wide audience are the slick magazines featuring a great deal of color and less-challenging content. Because serious discussions of issues are largely confined to academic journals of limited readership, the field has been left to magazines emphasizing primarily entertainment, and these have been shaped by market forces. Advertising revenue supports most such magazines, so that success is defined in terms of sales figures. One of the more profitable magazines of recent years has been the glossy *Harpers and Queen*, formed in 1970 by the merger of *Harper's Bazaar* and *Queen*. Each copy is said to cost £1.80 to print; it sells for £1 and brings in £2.50 in advertising revenue.

Magazine consumption per capita has generally risen in recent decades, but more and more titles compete for the buying public. One large category that has blossomed in recent years is the woman's magazine (although magazines aimed specifically at women have enjoyed popularity in Britain since the early nineteenth century). In 1981 nine of the top ten magazines in Britain were women's magazines; *Woman's*

Weekly alone reported a circulation of nearly 1.5 million. In 1986 there were over 120 different women's magazines being published, and new titles continue to be launched.

The recessions of the early 1980s and early 1990s claimed many casualties among magazines. In 1991 over 130 titles ceased publication, with 1,000 writers and editors losing their jobs, a clear indication that the economics of the marketplace dominate British periodical publishing. For the immediate future, there seems little reason to foresee a revival of periodicals that either reflect or help create a coherent and homogeneous culture.

Raymond N. MacKenzie

Bibliography

Hewison, Robert. *Under Siege: Literary Life in London, 1939–1945.* 1977.

Mulhearn, Francis. *The Moment of "Scrutiny."* 1979.

Sullivan, Alvin, ed. *British Literary Magazines.* Vol. 4: *The Modern Age, 1914–1984.* 1986.

White, Cynthia L. *The Women's Periodical Press in Britain, 1946–76.* 1977.

Pevsner, Nikolaus (1902–1983)

Nikolaus Pevsner was a historian, educator, architectural critic, and England's preeminent author of architectural guidebooks. A model of the Central European tradition of rigorous and perceptive scholarship, Pevsner was an indomitable researcher whose ultimate intention was to exhaust an inquiry to its definitive source, convey the facts, and document accurately the history of architecture, albeit interpreted in terms of the spirit of the times. His most significant contributions as a writer include extensive studies of industrial arts, modern architecture and design, Victorian architecture, and the history of building types.

Born in Leipzig and educated at the universities of Leipzig, Munich, Berlin, and Frankfort, Pevsner wrote his doctoral dissertation on German baroque architecture. But his love was almost from the start England, and his reputation would be made there. Pevsner left Germany in 1935 to take a position at the University of Birmingham researching contemporary design standards in British industries. He had already written, prior to leaving Germany, his first English book, *Pioneers of the Modern Movement* (1936), which traces the functionalist tradition

and machine aesthetic from the nineteenth century to the modern movement. Through this work, he became a spokesman for modernism. His *An Enquiry into Industrial Art in England* (1937) called for English designers to adopt Bauhaus forms. He would expand upon *Pioneers* through the pages of *Architectural Review* during the following years with a series of essays on contemporary industrial design. *Studies in Art, Architecture, and Design: Victorian and After* (1968) is a collection of essays republished from various architectural journals on designers, architects, and themes: Matthew Digby Wyatt, William Morris, C.F.A. Voysey, Charles Rennie Mackintosh, George Walton, **Frank Pick**, Gordon Russell, and the DIA (Design and Industries Association), often the earliest serious scholarship on these individuals and subjects.

Additional contributions to Victorian-era scholarship by Pevsner include his extensive reappraisal of Richard Norman Shaw in *Architectural Review* (1941), his lectures at Birkbeck College, and his preservationist activities as Director for thirteen years of the Victorian Society. The changed attitude toward Victorian architecture is evidenced by Pevsner's own admission that in his inaugural lecture as Slade Professor at **Cambridge** (1949), in which he analyzed the buildings of Matthew Digby Wyatt, the students thought his lecture "a huge joke." Twenty years later, in his 1968–9 Slade Lectures at **Oxford**, Pevsner would provide a significant critical discussion of the architectural writing of the last century. A later essay on Ruskin and Viollet-le-Duc, subtitled "Englishness and Frenchness in the Appreciation of Gothic Architecture," discloses an interest in identifying national characteristics in art and architecture, brought to fruition in his book *The Englishness of English Art* (1956), published from the 1955 Reith Lectures for the **British Broadcasting Corporation** (BBC).

Three further works that have become standard texts deserve mention. Pevsner's *An Outline of European Architecture* (1942) surveyed architecture viewed as space, not as building form and style, a perspective new to England at the time. Pevsner's *Dictionary of Architecture* (1966), written with John Fleming and Hugh Honour, is a standard reference. His Mellon Lectures in the Fine Arts (1970), published as *A History of Building Types*, with its reorganization of architectural history by typology rather than country or historic style, was another seminal work.

In his critical appraisals of architecture Pevsner returned again and again to basic principles of good design and his sense of quality. As a writer in an adopted language, Pevsner consistently demonstrated an extraordinary facility, joining skill and clarity of English expression with perceptive understanding of the innuendos and connotations of word meaning; in his own way he mastered the artistic form and function of written communication.

In his editorship of the *Pelican History of Art* series Pevsner required work that conformed to the exacting example set by his own scholarship, and he attracted scholars of art and architecture of international reputation: Heinrich Wofflin, Richard Krautheimer, Kenneth John Connant, John Summerson, Henry Russell Hitchcock, Anthony Blunt, Paul Frankl, and George Kubler. Through the prodigious output of his twenty-five-year *Buildings of England* series Pevsner lent his name inextricably to the English language, for the phrase, "look it up in Pevsner" has become a standard for countless building watchers and architecture lovers touring significant buildings of note in every town, city, or countryside landscape of every county in England.

Robert M. Craig

Bibliography

Watkin, David. *Morality and Architecture: The Development of a Theme in Architectural History and Theory from the Gothic Revival to the Modern Movement.* 1977.

Philanthropy

No nation can lay claim to a richer charitable past than Great Britain. And philanthropy in twentieth-century Britain has shown itself to be remarkably resilient in the face of the vast expansion in state health and welfare provision. Although the **welfare state** has overshadowed the voluntary sector since the Second World War, it has not altered many of its traditions or undermined its flow of funds. Indeed, in recent years British charities have shown a steady increase of financial support, which in 1991 reached an estimated £17 billion. Innovation and cost effectiveness are thought to be among the principal virtues of contemporary charity, and these have become increasingly apparent

against the background of government economies and the spiraling costs and bureaucratic inefficiencies of the state welfare services. The virtues of democratic action inherent in voluntarism have also become increasingly apparent. In the first half of the century philanthropists did their best to limit the expansion of state power; in the second half of the century, many campaigning charities, from Friends of the Earth to Save the Children, have turned their attention to government deceits and limitations.

The Victorian years were the heyday of British philanthropy, but by the end of the nineteenth century the consensus in favor of voluntary social action came under increasing attack. Given the philanthropic world's love of local autonomy and *ad hoc* remedies, and its tendency to sectarian rivalry, muddle and confusion proliferated. Across the spectrum of charitable activity, competition and imbalances in provision were rife. In the Edwardian years the criticism of charity mounted, fueled by the social investigations of Charles Booth and Seebohm Rowntree and the evidence of the Royal Commission on the Poor Laws (1905–9). To many social reformers, such as **Beatrice and Sidney Webb**, those age-old charitable remedies of self-help and personal service looked rather threadbare. What was needed, they argued, was a radical overhaul of the social services and greater state intervention.

From the late nineteenth century onward philanthropists responded to the criticism by a variety of means, including the introduction of social casework and better charitable coordination. Among the leaders in the field were the Charity Organisation Society (1869), which prided itself on its "scientific" outlook, and the King Edward's Hospital Fund for London (1897), a pioneering foundation in hospital provision. Such institutions sought to put charity's house in order before further government action sapped erstwhile philanthropic campaigns. But the social reforms of the **Liberal** administration in the years 1905–11, albeit piecemeal, further challenged charitable predominance and altered the relationship between voluntary and state welfare provision. Perhaps greater government involvement was inevitable as the focus of social policy shifted from what could be done to help "the poor" to what could be done to abolish "poverty."

The **First World War** further unsettled the philanthropic movement, for it undermined religious faith and fractured those pillars of charitable activity, family and parish life. Nor were the charities assisted by the record tax levels at the end of the war, which reduced the amount of disposable wealth available for philanthropic purposes. But while the First World War exposed the shortcomings of voluntarism and pointed to the need for greater state involvement, it also offered the voluntary movement fresh opportunities. Over 10,000 new societies were set up before its close, including the National Federation of Women's Institutes (1915) and King George's Fund for Sailors (1917). The government, reluctant to expand state welfare projects at the end of the war, welcomed their activities. In the inter-war years some in the welfare field looked to a "new philanthropy," in which charities would work in closer partnership with government departments. In practice, partnership worked most effectively in causes such as family planning and infant welfare. In the hospital world, with its long-standing rivalries between voluntary and state-aided institutions, it failed to live up to expectations.

While small, parish societies continued to typify the charitable world, they were joined in the early decades of the century by a host of large trusts and foundations, whose commissions allowed them to deal with a wide range of issues. The model for them came from America, as did much of the money. Among the premier British foundations were the Carnegie United Kingdom Trust (1913), the Wellcome Foundation (1924), the Pilgrim Trust (1930), the King George's Jubilee Trust (1935), and the Nuffield Foundation (1943). Most of them saw themselves as pioneering experimental projects. They would provide the "venture capital," but once a scheme had passed through its pilot stage, the expectation was that other voluntary bodies or government agencies would take it over. The Carnegie United Kingdom Trust, for example, established libraries throughout the country, but in 1935 it concluded that public bodies were sufficiently committed to library provision and moved into other fields. Foundations were unique institutions in having sizable capital reserves and freedom of operation. Without being accountable to the electorate or to annual subscribers, they were able to take risks in a way that was impossible for public agencies of unendowed charities.

The trend to bigger institutions in the twentieth century was shaped in part by the criticism that charities in the past were too small in scale to be effective and too unstable and understaffed to provide adequate care. But the larger the institution the more likely it was to distance individual philanthropists from beneficiaries. This posed a threat to charity's much-heralded quality of personal service, which was all the more evident in those organizations that worked with government agencies where utility and cost efficiency were at a premium. Still, in a relatively informal and secular society, charities continued to play a crucial role as repositories of moral and ethical values.

The impact of the **Second World War** on philanthropy has been obscured by the attention given to state social policy. As in 1914, the crisis both threatened and challenged voluntarists, and it accelerated the process of cooperation with state officials. While the number of civil servants rose dramatically, a problem for charities was how to cope with the continual calling-up of their personnel for the forces. The answer was for **women** to fill many of the places formerly held by men, which further strengthened their already powerful position within the voluntary world. Some of the charities came and went with the war. The "Bundles for Britain" campaign, for example, provided American money and supplies for voluntary **hospitals** during the **Blitz**. Other projects had more-enduring responsibilites, such as the Women's Voluntary Service and the Association of Jewish Refugees in Great Britain. The emergency also gave important work to established charities: The British Red Cross and the Order of St. John of Jerusalem ran the auxiliary hospitals on behalf of the Ministry of Health. In short, the war disrupted the work of most charities, killed off some, and promoted a host of others.

In the atmosphere of "total war," with the government making inroads on every front, the philanthropic world was bound to look diminished even where it thrived. In creating and exposing scarcity and deprivation, the war made traditional charitable remedies look inadequate. Compared to the prospect of universal state provision offered by the **Beveridge** Report, published in 1942, the charitable emphasis on local initiative did not appear very compelling, nor did appeals to self-help after all of the sacrifice the war itself demanded. With the vast expansion of the post-war social services, voluntarists had to take stock. Government absorbed many of philanthropy's health and welfare functions and nationalized many charities, most notably the voluntary hospitals. But other societies soldiered on. Many had a welfare role peripheral to government concerns. Others transformed into new institutions with a stronger social element in their makeup. Some shifted their priorities and changed their names. The Charity Organisation Society became the Family Welfare Association in 1946 and concentrated on social casework. Others still started up to fill the gaps in state social provision. MIND (1946), War on Want (1951), the Samaritans (1953), and Help the Aged (1963) are just a few prominent examples.

Despite signs that the philanthropic establishment could respond successfully to the new social environment, it was unsettled by the creation of the welfare state and uncertain about its future in a semi-collectivist society. To some extent it was the victim of changed public expectations. It was not obvious at the time that government could never fully satisfy them. The years from 1960 to the mid-1970s were the heyday of state-directed health and social services in Britain. Few people doubted that the central government had a primary responsibility for welfare provision, and most commentators assumed that it was well-equipped to administer the system devised by Parliament. The consensus did little to enhance the status of philanthropists, whose impulses were to decentralize, to break a problem down into pieces. As they settled into a decent anonymity, they had the consolation that charity was its own reward.

The strategic planning in state welfare provision that characterized the 1960s and 1970s ended in doubts and recrimination. The drift of opinion away from statutory provision in the 1980s widened the public's awareness of philanthropic influences and stimulated voluntary campaigns. With collectivism in retreat, voluntarism began to be taken much more seriously by politicians. But while charities welcomed the publicity, they had to cope with greater pressure on their services. In the hospital sector, for example, they had long provided amenities and thousands of volunteer workers; now they were being asked to fund capital projects, including the building of new **National Health Service** hospitals. Just what privatization meant for welfare provision was unclear, but it suggested a primary role for philanthropy that it had largely abdicated. After decades of state supremacy in welfare it was doubtful whether there was a cultural basis for a dramatic expansion of charity, or that charity was a suitable way of providing basic services according to need.

There has been a transformation in philanthropic attitudes since the nineteenth century. The change is perhaps most remarkable in regard to perceptions of the role of the state. Though they remain chary of state power, most philanthropists now look to government for greater expenditure on health and welfare and for leadership in tackling the causes of social deprivation. For its part, the government, aware that voluntary bodies are an effective way of delivering a range of health and social services, increasingly contributes to charitable campaigns. In its various guises, government increased its payments in the 1980s to such an extent that it is now the single largest contributor to charitable causes. Britain has reached a stage in the evolution of social policy in which the philanthropic sector wants the state to do more and the state wants the philanthropic sector to do more. There are signs that the long-standing battle between philanthropists and collectivists, which many assumed to have been won by the latter, now appears to be heading for the ropes, with the combatants holding each other up.

Frank Prochaska

Bibliography
Owen, David. *English Philanthropy, 1660–1960*. 1964.

Prochaska, Frank. "Philanthropy" in F.M.L. Thompson, ed. *The Cambridge Social History of Britain, 1750–1950*. vol. 3. 1990. pp. 357–93.

———. *The Voluntary Impulse: Philanthropy in Modern Britain*. 1988.

Philosophy and Philosophers
All of the traditional branches of philosophy are well represented in twentieth-century British philosophy. In retrospect there appear to be five phases of British philosophy that seem most salient. One is a neo-Hegelian idealist and metaphysical phase, exemplified by T.H. Green (1836–82), F.H. Bradley (1846–1924), Bernard Bosanquet (1848–1923), and John Ellis McTaggart (1866–1925), lasting into the 1920s. The second, a phase in which a nonidealist metaphysics is reconciled with science, is exemplified by the work of **Alfred North Whitehead** and **Bertrand Russell**. This phase is predated by the landmark work of Russell and

Whitehead, which culminated in the publication of their *Principia Mathematica* (1910–13). The third period, lasting from the early 1930s until the early 1960s, is dominated by the linguistic philosophy of Ludwig Wittgenstein (1889–1951). Wittgenstein's techniques of linguistic analysis were applied in several branches of philosophy by Gilbert Ryle (1900–76) (philosophy of mind), J.L. Austin (1911–1960) (philosophy of language), R.M. Hare (1919–) (moral philosophy), and Peter Winch (1926–) (philosophy of social science). The work of this phase finds important precursors in the German mathematician and logician Gottlob Frege (1848–1925) and the English philosopher **G.E. Moore**. The **logical positivism** of **A.J. Ayer**, approximately contemporary with British linguistic philosophy in its influence, is sometimes mistakenly assimilated to it. In fact, Ayer and his followers took as their paradigms of knowledge formal logic and the exact sciences, while ordinary language philosophers such as Wittgenstein, Austin, and Ryle took as theirs the uses of ordinary language. Ayer's most influential work, the manifesto of logical positivism, was *Language, Truth, and Logic* (1936). The latest phase, which began in the early 1970s, has seen a growth in interest in cognitive science, artificial intelligence, applied ethics, and modern Continental philosophy. During this period, too, British philosophy has increasingly been influenced by North American philosophers, especially John Rawls and Robert Nozick (political philosophy), Saul Kripke (philosophical logic), Donald Davidson (metaphysics and philosophy of language), and Thomas Nagel (metaphysics and moral philosophy).

Between the early phase of metaphysical idealism and the later phase of American influence, British philosophy in the twentieth century has been essentially German and Austrian in derivation. Frege, the father of linguistic philosophy, was a German. Logical positivism was the philosophy of the Austrian movement in the 1920s and 1930s, known as the Vienna Circle. Wittgenstein, the influential exponent of linguistic philosophy, was an Austrian who moved to **Cambridge**. J.L. Austin, professor at **Oxford** in the 1950s, was a translator of Frege. Michael Dummett (1925–), currently professor at Oxford, is the author of a number of massive studies of Frege's philosophy. The official and sophisticated opposition to both logical positivism and linguistic philosophy comes from the Austrian emigré Karl Popper (1902–1994), for many years professor at the **London School of Economics**.

From a wider historical perspective it is clear that the seemingly competing movements in twentieth-century philosophy are all species of neo-Kantianism. In sharing in this common neo-Kantianism, twentieth-century British philosophy has been antimetaphysical, has tended to identify what is with what may be known (especially observed) to be, has engaged deeply in conceptual and linguistic analysis, and has retained a deep, even when not overtly positivistic, respect for science. When the neo-Kantian nature of Western philosophy is more fully recognized, there will appear fewer differences between British and Continental philosophy than are presently believed to exist. Progress in philosophical problem solving in British philosophy, as in Western philosophy generally, will require shedding the neo-Kantian framework.

Stephen Priest

Bibliography

Ayer, A.J. *The Central Questions of Philosophy.* 1973.
Magee, Bryan. *Modern British Philosophy.* 1986.
Priest, Stephen. *The British Empiricists.* 1990.
Warnock, Geoffrey J. *English Philosophy since 1900.* 2nd ed. 1969.

Physics

Physics could be used as an indicator of Britain's international standing generally throughout the twentieth century. In 1900 Germany and France rivaled Britain in numbers of physicists and support for physics research. By the 1930s the United States overtook European nations, a lead dramatically emphasized by the events of the Second World War and the development of **radar** and atomic weapons, which owed much to the work of American physicists. While physicists from Britain still contribute to such fields as high-energy physics, they now participate internationally through CERN (the European Organization for Nuclear Research), near Geneva, one of the many such collaborations that have developed since 1945.

At the beginning of the twentieth century only a few hundred of those trained in physics were involved in some aspect of the field, the main center being the **Cavendish Laboratory** in

Cambridge, where fifty physicists worked under J.J. Thomson (1856–1940). Cambridge connections dominated British physics until the Second World War. Growing numbers and professional sensitivities, particularly in relation to chemists, led to the founding of the Institute of Physics in 1919. By the end of the century its membership approached 20,000, the majority working in industrial or government-funded laboratories. The National Physical Laboratory, established in 1900 outside of London with R.T. Glazebrook (1854–1935) as its first Director, undertook work on standards, which was particularly important for industry.

Early in the century the most significant work was on the structure of matter. In 1911 **Ernest Rutherford,** then in Manchester, proposed that the atom had a nucleus, or core. His collaborator, H.G.J. Moseley (1887–1915), helped determine the electrical charge on the nucleus. In 1912, during a stay in Britain working in Rutherford's laboratory, Niels Bohr (1885–1962) developed these ideas into a model of atoms in which he assumed that the electrons moved round the nucleus in orbits with fixed energies. This model became one of the foundations of quantum mechanics. While the main development of quantum mechanics took place on the Continent, P.A.M. Dirac (1902–84), made fundamental contributions to the field at Cambridge in the late 1920s, providing a theory of emission and absorption of radiation and a prediction of the positron and antimatter, and developing the relativistic wave equation for the electron.

During the **First World War** Rutherford and others, on behalf of the Admiralty Board of Invention and Research, used sonar to detect submarines. The wartime experience, which demonstrated the technical inferiority of British industry, led to the setting up of the Department of Scientific and Industrial Research (DSIR) in 1917, the forerunner of the present-day Science and Engineering Research Council (SERC), to support research.

During the 1920s and 1930s physicists at the Cavendish Laboratory played a remarkable role in the development of nuclear physics. Shortly before he moved to the Cavendish in 1920, Rutherford had observed disintegrations of nuclei. At the same time, F.W. Aston (1877–1945), also at Cambridge, showed that chemical elements had isotopes; while all atoms of an element had the same chemical properties they did not all have the same masses. Such evidence suggested that the nuclei of atoms were made from a small number of components. Aston won the Nobel Prize in 1922. Further clues came from the work of C.T.R. Wilson (1869–1959), another Cambridge physicist, who developed the cloud chamber, which allowed fragments nuclear reactions to be observed. Wilson shared a Nobel Prize in 1927.

In 1932, the pinnacle of Cavendish achievement in nuclear physics, James Chadwick (1891–1974) discovered the neutron, a component of the nucleus long predicted by Rutherford. J.D. Cockcroft (1897–1967) and E.T.S. Walton (1903–) carried out the first successful experiments using a particle accelerator, and **P.M.S. Blackett** and G.P. Occialini extended work on the positron, a positive counterpart to the electron. New electrical methods of counting particles were also developed. In the case of the new accelerators, the Cavendish physicists had relied on the assistance of the Metropolitan-Vickers industrial laboratory in Manchester, where the problems of high voltages had been investigated as part of the research encouraged by the development of the national grid for distributing electricity.

In the early 1930s N.F. Mott, another Cambridge product, moved to Bristol, where one of the first groups to study the problems of solid-state physics came into being. W.H. Bragg (1862–1942) and W.L. Bragg (1890–1971), the only father-and-son pair to share a Nobel Prize (1915), variously working in Leeds, London, and Cambridge, developed x-ray diffraction, which could be used for investigating the structure of crystals and later organic molecules. In 1927 G.P. Thomson, Professor of natural philosophy at Aberdeen (1892–1975), demonstrated the wave-nature of the electron, which could be used to probe even finer details of atomic structures. Thomson shared a Nobel Prize in 1937.

During the Second World War two important areas of research were radar and atomic weapons. The development in 1940 of the cavity magnetron by J.T. Randall (1905–84) and H.A.H. Randall at Birmingham was important for radar. After the discovery of nuclear fission in the winter of 1938–9, the early experiments had suggested that it was not practicable to build a weapon using the energy released in this process. However, early in 1940 O. Frisch (1904–79) and R. Peierls (1907–), **refugee** physicists in Britain, recognized that by using one rare isotope of uranium, a weapon might be practicable. On this basis the Tube Alloys project was set up to investigate the matter further. Though they made progress, it became clear the only option in wartime conditions was to join in with the Manhattan Project in the United States.

After the war there was more generous funding for physics. The decision to build **nuclear weapons** in Britain led to new government laboratories at Harwell and Aldermaston, where nuclear reactors were designed, initially for the production of weapons plutonium, later for the production of electricity.

Research on nuclear fusion was undertaken, although since the late 1980s this has been carried out at Culham as part of a European project, JET, the Joint European Torus.

During the post-war years many university physicists returned to the problems of the structure of matter. The techniques developed for radar during the war could be adapted to make more-powerful accelerators. In the few years this took to happen, studies of cosmic rays came to the fore. Government funding allowed the development of new photographic emulsions for detecting cosmic rays. In 1947 C.F. Powell (1903–69) and his group in Bristol discovered the pion in this way. Later that year G.D. Rochester (1908–) and C.C. Butler (1922–) discovered the K meson.

However, physicists working new larger accelerators soon displaced cosmic ray research. The largest accelerator in Britain, Nimrod, a proton synchrotron, operated from 1964 to 1978, when it was closed to allow support for CERN.

Alan Q. Morton

Bibliography
Crowther, James G. *The Cavendish Laboratory, 1874–1974*. 1974.
Forman, P., J.L. Heilbron, and S. Weart. *Physics c. 1900: Historical Studies in the Physical Sciences*. vol. 5. 1975.
Gowing, Margaret. *Britain and Atomic Energy, 1939–1945*. 1964.
Hendry, John, ed. *Cambridge Physics in the Thirties*. 1984.

Pick, Frank (1878–1941)

Frank Pick brought the worlds of business and art together through his roles as a ranking official of the London Underground (1906–33), vice chairman and chief executive officer of the London Passenger Transport Board (1933–40), Chairman of the government's Council for Art and Industry (1934–9), and longtime member and President (1932–4) of the Design and Industries Association (DIA). Pick admired the aesthetic and social goals of William Morris and believed that the transport system could shape London into an artistic and integrated civic community uniting art and industry, creativity and commerce. To further this goal Pick hired modern artists and architects to fashion a unified corporate design for the Underground, encompassing everything from trash bins to tube stations; he also commissioned **advertising** posters designed in post-impressionist styles, in order to increase revenues and to introduce the public to visual modernism. Under Pick's supervision the Underground became known as "the people's picture galleries," and Pick himself was hailed widely as one of the greatest art patrons of the age.

Pick was born on 23 November 1878 at Spalding, Lincolnshire, to a lower-middle-class family; his father was a draper who moved the family to York in 1883. Pick was raised as a Nonconformist, and although he abandoned any formal adherence to religion later in life he continued to be devout, calling himself a "Christian agnostic" and associating art with spirituality. He received a scholarship to St. Peter's School in York and upon graduation worked for a solicitor. In 1902 he went to work for the North Eastern Railway Company, and in 1906 he moved to London to work for the London Underground, rising to the position of Managing Director by 1928.

Pick was such an effective administrator that the General Manager of the Underground, Albert Stanley (Lord Ashfield, 1920), gave him wide latitude to pursue his aesthetic projects, especially since Pick argued persuasively that a beautiful transport system would be a lucrative transport system. He also believed that if the public were exposed to modern art they would become more aesthetically discerning and demand better-designed consumer goods; industries and the government would have to respond to the public's demand, thereby leading to the gradual transformation of England into an Earthly Paradise.

Pick shared this philosophy with fellow members of the Design and Industries Association, which had been formed in 1915. He hired an architect from the DIA, Charles Holden, to design many of the new stations in the International Style, and he commissioned Edward Johnston to design a special typeface to be used throughout the transport system in 1913. Pick also commissioned modern artists, such as E. McKnight Kauffer, to design **posters** and fixtures for the system. Controversial modern sculptors like **Jacob Epstein** and **Henry Moore** were given prominent exposure when Pick commissioned them to carve figures directly onto the new Underground headquarters designed by Holden, which opened in 1929 to a heated debate in the **press** over the merits of modernism.

Pick continued to play a commanding role within the transport system when the Underground became part of the London Passenger Transport Board (LPTB) in 1933. He resigned from the LPTB in 1940, briefly became Director of the Ministry of Information, and later worked for the Ministry of Transport before his death of a cerebral hemorrhage on 7 November 1941. Through his patronage, Pick introduced a generation to modern art and **architecture** and turned the London Underground into the culminating project of the arts and crafts movement: a union of the arts created for the service and pleasure of the common person.

Michael Saler

Bibliography

Barman, Christian. *The Man Who Built London Transport*. 1979.

Pevsner, Nikolaus. "Frank Pick" in *Studies in Art, Architecture, and Design*. vol. 2. 1968. pp. 190–209.

Saler, Michael. *Medieval Modernism: The Legitimation and Social Function of Modern Art in England, 1910–1945*. Ph.D. dissertation, Stanford University, 1992.

Pinter, Harold (1930–)

Since the mid-1960s Harold Pinter has been regarded as a preeminent British playwright. Although employing a typically British form of theatrical naturalism, his art derives equally from the traditions of Continental modernism as exemplified in Kafka and **Samuel Beckett.**

Pinter grew up as a **Jew** in London's East End, and his experience of **anti-semitism** during the **Second World War** may lie behind the powerful images of intimidation and violence in early plays like *The Room* (1957), *The Dumb Waiter* (1957), and his first full-length play, *The Birthday Party* (1957). Although *The Birthday Party* failed in its first London production, it was favorably reviewed by Harold Hobson in the *Sunday Times*, and Pinter was accordingly commissioned by **BBC** radio to write *A Slight Ache*, broadcast in 1959.

The television production of *A Night Out* (1960) and the success of the West End production of *The Caretaker* (1960) brought him recognition as a major new dramatist. *The Caretaker* received numerous productions around the world over the next few years, acquiring the status of a modern classic.

The influence of Beckett may be discerned in Pinter's redefinition of plot. Instead of employing conventional exposition to give the audience a privileged perspective on the action, Pinter presents the dramatic situation as a series of unresolved—and possibly unresolvable—mysteries. Denied a straightforward explanation of the contradictions and indeterminacies of character, an audience comes to realize that objective truth in human relationships collapses into a drama of conflicting subjectivities, a power struggle that is the basis of all human behavior.

His savage anatomy of the terms of English social behavior satirizes the tradition of comedy of manners inherited from **Noel Coward**. The adjective "Pinteresque" was coined in recognition of his theatrical style, which relies on pregnant pauses and silences.

Although more naturalistic than the preceding plays, *The Caretaker* is typical of Pinter's "comedies of menace." Its presentation of the struggle of a tramp (Davies) to secure possession of a squalid room in a house that is owned by Mick and looked after by Mick's brother Aston becomes a darkly comic emblem of the problem of authenticating one's identity.

The battle for living space gives way to an exploration of the dynamics of sex as power in *The Collection* (1962), *The Lover* (1963), and *The Homecoming* (1964). The deconstructed naturalism of these plays is replaced in *Landscape* (1968), *Silence* (1969), *Night* (1969), and *Old Times* (1971) by a looser, more expressionistic structure in which the static image of a group of characters motivates interwoven interior monologues through which men and women battle to establish the truth of their memories as a way of validating their identities. In these plays Pinter for the first time makes women the subject of the drama.

A new phase of his work began with the production of *One for the Road* in 1984. From

P

this point his drama has begun to reflect his liberal left-wing engagement with world politics. It employs the Pinteresque language of menace and ambiguity to explore the banal terrors created by the abusers of political power.

Pinter's many screenplays have received acclaim, as has his handling of scripts for radio and television. He has also pursued a successful career as a director and occasional actor.

Robert Gordon

Bibliography

Dukore, Bernard Frank. *Harold Pinter.* 1982.
Esslin, Martin. *Pinter: The Playwright.* 4th ed. 1982.
Gale, Steven H. *Harold Pinter: An Annotated Bibliography.* 1987.
Hayman, Ronald. *Harold Pinter.* 4th ed. 1980.
Thompson, David T. *Pinter: The Player's Playwright.* 1985.

Piper, John Egerton Christmas (1903–1992)

John Piper exerted considerable influence on the taste of his times at least as much through his writing, stage design, and craftwork as through his genuinely popular paintings and graphic works. His career also dramatizes more sharply than that of any of his contemporaries the conflicting artistic influences of European modernism and the insular romantic English tradition.

Piper was born in Epsom, Surrey, in 1903, the son of a solicitor. After being articled as a solicitor himself, he studied at the Richmond School of Art and the Royal College of Art before launching his career in 1929. His work as a reviewer for the *New Statesman* brought him into contact with Ivon Hitchens and Ben Nicholson, who invited him to join their 7 and 5 Society, a group sympathetic to modern French art. In the mid-1930s he produced fully abstract compositions, experimenting with collage, and these works, contemporary with Nicholson's White Reliefs and the carving of Barbara Hepworth, are considered important landmarks in the development of abstract art in Britain. Equally influential was *Axis*, a quarterly review of abstract art edited by his second wife, Myfanwy Evans, with Piper's help, which appeared in the years 1935–7. By the end it was less belligerently loyal to abstraction, seeking instead to encompass the modern movement in its complexity. Piper, meanwhile, extended his journalistic activities, contributing articles to the *Architectural Review* and later helping to produce the first television arts documentary films for the British Broadcasting Corporation (BBC).

In 1935 the Pipers moved to Henley-on-Thames, where he began to paint the surrounding countryside. By 1938 he had abandoned his abstract style, and in 1942 he published *Romantic British Artists* in the *Britain in Pictures* series. Looking back to William Blake, Samuel Palmer, and the British preoccupation with landscape, this text was a decisive factor in the resurgence of landscape painting and imaginative, picturesque composition painting with a literary, mystical bent, the movement known as neo-romanticism. Paul Nash was regarded as a mentor of this tendency, along with Graham Sutherland, while a younger generation attracted to it included John Minton, Michael Ayrton, John Craxton, Keith Vaughan, Leslie Hurry, and Lucian Freud. Poets associated with the movement included Geoffrey Grigson and John Betjeman, both of whom were closely identified with Piper. But while the insularity and nostalgia of the movement related to the apocalyptic mood engendered by the Second World War and Britain's initial isolation, landscape and English heritage were much earlier preoccupations of Piper's. As a child he had visited every church in Surrey, which served him well in his association with Betjeman, the chronicler of English rural churches. The two of them produced the *Shell Guide* for Shropshire together, and later Piper took over the editorship of this popular tourist series from Betjeman.

A celebration of England's architectural heritage, suffused with a wistful, elegiac romanticism, became the hallmark of Piper's imagery, whether in painting, stage design, or printmaking. He sought to capture what he once termed "pleasing decay," the sense of ancient stones taken over by, and settling into, the land, a symbiosis of nature and nationhood. In series after series of prints, he set out to document country churches, chapels, follies, and country houses. One of the first country houses he drew was Renishaw Hall, the ancestral home of the Sitwells, to illustrate the autobiography of the English author Osbert Sitwell. Piper's style entailed a combination of brooding, dark treatment shot through with unexpected bursts of strong color. He also developed a particular way of highlighting architectural details that risked making all his images look like preparations for stage scenery.

Piper's preoccupation with theater began in 1937 with his design for the Group Theatre production of **Stephen Spender**'s *Trial of a Judge*. It continued in 1942 with his contribution to *Façade*, the Edith Sitwell/**William Walton** collaboration, and after the war with his sets for **Frederick Ashton**. Piper's involvement reached its apogee in his collaboration with **Benjamin Britten**, for whose operas between 1946 and 1973 he designed all of the sets. This association with Britten was reinforced by Piper's wife Myfanwy's role as librettist for *The Turn of the Screw* and *Death in Venice*. Another aspect of applied art in which Piper excelled was stained-glass making, which was appropriate in view of the influence of medieval windows on his own work. His work with stained glass artist Patrick Reyntiens reached its climax with the glass designed for the rebuilt Coventry Cathedral in the early 1960s. This was particularly poignant because, as an official **war artist**, Piper had sketched the still smoldering ruins of this church after its destruction by bombing in November 1940.

David Cohen

Bibliography

Ingrams, Richard, and John Piper. *Piper's Places*. 1983.
Levinson, Orde. *John Piper: The Complete Graphic Works*. 1987.
Museum of Modern Art. *John Piper: Fifty Years of Work*. 1979.
Tate Gallery. *John Piper*. 1984.
West, Anthony. *John Piper*. 1979.

Poetry, English

The moribundity of English poetry at the turn of the century might be inferred from the number of groups committed to its reform—the Georgians and the Imagists being the most prominent. Despite strong individual efforts, like **Rudyard Kipling**'s *Barrack Room Ballads* (1892), Thomas Hardy's (1840–1928) *Wessex Poems* (1898), A.E. Housman's (1859–1936) *A Shropshire Lad* (1896), and **William Butler Yeats**' *The Wind among the Reeds* (1899), English poetry in the 1890s seemed to have lost historical relevance, craftsmanly rigor, and intellectual purpose. Aestheticism had given rise to a highbrow poetics of impressionistic sensualism and decadence, as in poetry by Arthur Symons (1865–1945) and Ernest Dowson (1867–1900). On the other hand, the poetry familiar to most readers reasserted Victorian moral certainties. Stephen Phillips (1865–1915), Alfred Austin (1835–1913), Henry Newbolt (1862–1938), and Alfred Noyes (1880–1958) delivered in didactic fashion generalizations about a moral universe that Darwinism and agnosticism had already thrown into doubt.

The term "Georgian poetry" refers to the anthologies edited by Edward Marsh (1872–1953) and published by Harold Monro (1879–1932) between 1912 and 1922, which represented a prevailing dissatisfaction with both moralism and precious artificiality. Contributors included **Rupert Brooke**, Lascelles Abercrombie (1881–1938), Walter de la Mare (1873–1956), Edmund Blunden (1896–1974), Gordon Bottomley (1874–1948), William H. Davies (1871–1940), **Robert Graves, D.H. Lawrence**, Edward Thomas (1878–1917), and **Wilfred Owen**.

Though the anthologies included poets representing different techniques and sensibilities, Georgian poetry has recognizable characteristics: a return to the sounds of English song and speech and to love of the English countryside. The principal boast of its supporters was the realism of Georgian poetry, its insistence upon narrating experience without referring to abstract categories (like the beautiful and the lofty) and without overt intellectual biases (like supernaturalism or socialism). Georgians wrote in traditional poetic forms and created an air of dreamlike unreality, a good example of which is "Adlestrop" by Edward Thomas. Based on such a general definition, Hardy, Housman, and the American Robert Frost—who lived in England in the years 1912–15 and published his first two volumes there—might be thought the best of the Georgian poets. Hardy's poetry, with its rugged metrical irregularities and gutteral phonetic conglomerations, its blend of deeply felt emotion and philosophically principled irony, has had a continuing influence on British poetry greater than that of any other poet of the period except Yeats, whose influence stems mostly from the poetry he wrote after 1914.

After the success of the Georgian experiment, publishing poetry in London became, to a significant extent, a group activity. This marketing device has hardened into an academic habit of lumping poets into schools that obscure their crucial individualities. No one took better advantage of this new way of presenting poetry than the Imagists, who used small, exclusively avant-garde publications to promote their movement.

Georgians and Imagists alike insisted that the poet should keep his eye upon the object itself and maintain direct contact with experience. The differences between the two movements concerned subject matter, attitude toward the world, and verse form. The Imagists described the concrete details of circumscribed objects (natural and rural, or urban and technological). They wrote in free verse (like some French symbolists) and imported other foreign verse forms such as Japanese *tanka* and *haiku*.

Imagism was begun in 1909 by T.E. Hulme (1883–1917) and F.S. Flint (1885–1960), along with the American Ezra Pound, who arrived in London that year. The group published yearly anthologies between 1914 and 1917. More stridently experimental, revolutionary, modern, and intellectual than the Georgians, the Imagists published essays and manifestos explaining the substance and importance of their work. Flint wrote the most definitive statement of Imagist principles for *Poetry* (March 1913): "1. Direct treatment of the 'thing' whether subjective or objective. 2. To use absolutely no word that did not contribute to presentation. 3. As regarding rhythm: to compose in sequence of the musical phrase not in sequence of a metronome." Pound, Flint, and Hulme published their own poems alongside contributions from **James Joyce, Ford Madox Ford,** and D.H. Lawrence, as well as American poets William Carlos Williams and H.D. (Hilda Doolittle).

The principal claim of Hulme and of Imagism under his influence was that the late-romantic poets had overrefined the expression of emotion and lost touch with living speech. Imagism attempted to restore immediacy to poetry by turning from the clichés of sentimental late romanticism to sharper perceptions of reality.

Imagism was a contained movement, of interest mainly to people professionally writing, reviewing, and publishing poetry. Not so the poetry of the First World War that described events affecting the nation as a whole. The war's history is reflected in the shifting moods of English poetry about the conflict. In 1914 and 1915 the most popular poetry was still nationalistic and militaristic. Housman's *A Shropshire Lad* became more popular at this time, along with more shoddy nationalistic stuff, such as the anthology called *For England's Sake* (1900), from which Henley's lines are typical: "What if the best of our wages be/ An empty sleeve, a stiff-set knee, / A crutch for the rest of life—who cares, / So long as the One Flag floats and dares?" Henley's poem exemplifies what First World War poets reacted against.

The first stage of war poetry written by participants was marked by Brooke's hugely popular five war sonnets (published posthumously in *1914 and other Poems* [1915]), which stress the pathos of homesickness, fear of death, and hope of personal redemption. The second phase of war poetry was written by the men who endured the prolonged horrors of trench war in Belgium and France. The antiwar poetry of Owen, **Siegfried Sassoon,** and Isaac Rosenberg (1890–1918) tells how far the actualities of gas attacks and filthy trenches were from heroic notions of soldiering. The poems of Owen and Sassoon are sometimes elegiac, sometimes satiric, and sometimes polemical demystifications of war. Their poems are deliberately choked with pathetically realistic descriptions of the battlefield, intended to educate civilians about the ugliness and moral stupidity of the war. Rosenberg's poems, written from the point of view of the common soldier, express the gallows humor of the trenches. His address to a rat in "Break of Day in the Trenches" anticipates the renewed taste for the grotesque tropings of Donne and Marvell that **T.S. Eliot** would valorize after the war. Rosenberg's use of rapidly juxtaposed images and staccato syntax to depict the mechanization of bodies in "Marching" also anticipates high-modernist descriptions of mechanized bodies and depersonalized human beings in urban life, such as in Eliot's "Preludes" (1917).

Interest has been greatest in the war poetry by men who witnessed the events first-hand. Catherine Reilly's anthology, *Scars upon My Heart* (1981), has brought to light war poems by **women** that have unfortunately been neglected. Nosheen Khan's *Women's Poetry of the First World War* (1988) is dedicated to examining the politics and emotions of women poets who experienced the war from the homefront. Such studies have created new interest in the work of Charlotte Mew (1869–1928), Alice Meynell (1846–1922), Frances Cornford (1886–1960), **Sylvia Townsend Warner,** and Valentine Ackland (1906–69).

The main drama in English poetry after the war was the conflict between modernist and traditional modes, a conflict incipient in the differences between Imagist and Georgian approaches to realism. At the end of the war Yeats, Hardy, de la Mare, and Robert Bridges (1844–1930), all writing in traditional forms, were the central British poets for most critics and readers. But the post-war era, which seemed to usher in a new age of international, mechanized, and dehumanized urban life, brought with it the perception that a new kind of poetry was needed to address the modern age relevantly. Eliot argued in "Tradition and the Individual Talent" (1917) that the unparalleled complexity of the age required unparalleled complexity of poetic form. Whether or not one believes in such historical necessity, the high-modernist mode produced brilliant and innovative books in the 1920s and 1930s such as Pound's *Hugh Selwyn Mauberly* (1920), Lawrence's *Birds, Beasts, and Flowers* (1921), Eliot's *The Waste Land* (1922), and Edith Sitwell's (1887–1964) *Façade* (1922).

The high-modernist mode, which dominated English and American poetry from the early 1920s to the early 1950s, incorporated *vers libre*, French symbolism, imagistic detail, realistic dramatic speech, jazz syncopations, and Freudian free association of words and images. Eliot's *Prufrock and Other Observations* (1917) created a sensation with its witty clichés. Sitwell's *Façade* uses many of these techniques to experiment with synesthesia and cadence, and Pound, Eliot, and Yeats emerged as the central figures of high modernism when they used these techniques to develop a prophetic overview of their culture.

The expatriate Americans in particular, Eliot and Pound, wrote fragmented, montage-like poems that attempt to embody the confusion into which these poets felt European culture had fallen. Pound in *Hugh Selwyn Mauberly* and Eliot in *The Waste Land* give the impression that the poem is not a description of the world from a personal perspective, but a collection of shards dug up by the objective poet-archeologist who, on the strength of his erudition and understanding, can begin the process of reforming cultural coherence. Like all avant-garde movements, modernism was largely an attack on "bourgeois complacency" and upon its own bourgeois roots.

Yeats' relationship to modernism was more complicated. His poetry of the 1890s, combining the delicate effects of late-Victorian verse and French symbolism with Irish folklore, creates a dreamy alternative to worldly interests. But with *Responsibilities* (1914) and *The Wild Swans at Coole* (1919) Yeats showed an ability to engage the world of contemporary reality, especially Irish politics, using sharper idiom and imagery. Yet Yeats was, from beginning to end, a mystical rather than a modernist poet. He wrote always in traditional forms and eschewed the metrical experimentations of other modernists. His greatest gift was that he could be at once a shrewdly modern, politically engaged poet, yet write of life as a drama of supernatural, mythical, and spiritual forces.

Lawrence's departure from his own Georgian beginnings was as radical and revolutionary as Eliot's or Pound's departure from late romanticism. But where Pound and Eliot advocated a "modern" poetry of craftsmanship, tradition, and "impersonality," Lawrence strove for an intensely personal union of poetic form and feeling. If Lawrence felt as much as Eliot or Pound that modern culture was painfully fragmented, he saw the relief from fragmentation not in artistic or intellectual control, nor in political discipline, but in recovery of a primally libidinal self.

The most important development of English poetry between the wars was the emergence of the Auden group at Oxford: **W.H. Auden, Stephen Spender, Louis MacNeice,** and **Cecil Day Lewis.** Their poetry is as conventional in verse forms as the Georgians had been, but as unconventional in its ideas as the most innovative modernists. Politically, the group was openly leftist whereas Yeats, Pound, and Eliot had been conservative. They combined a Georgian love of England with a modernist awareness of the international scene. From the modernists they learned to describe urban and technological subjects; from the Georgians, how to place those subjects in and against the English landscape. In contrast to the prophetic and high-pitched literary voices of modernism, Auden develops the tone of a sophisticated conversationalist and invents a poetry in which he can discuss Marx, Freud, and Kierkegaard equally with labor strikes, **cricket,** lunch counters, and traffic jams. He is a brilliant parodist of sermons, ballads, public announcements, and popular songs, and he uses these forms to expose the alienation of the proletariat. He is unsurpassed in English as a poet of public address; his "Letter to Lord Byron" (1937), which uses the device of a letter to the dead poet as an excuse for a survey of modern

P

culture, is an amalgam of serious poetry and light verse. Auden's match of radical inspirations with traditional form and with the decorum of Hardy and the Georgians has become central to English verse in the latter half of the century.

While the Auden group was emerging, modernism in Britain changed from being the practice of foreigners—Pound, Eliot, and Yeats—to the practice of natives. In the 1930s David Jones, Hugh MacDiarmid, Basil Bunting (1900–85), and William Empson (1906–84) emerged as native practitioners. To Bunting's modernist eye for images and ear for language both colloquial and literary, is added a Wordsworthian feeling for the Northumbrian countryside. Empson's greatest contributions may have been his literary criticism, especially *Seven Types of Ambiguity* (1930), which shows how the investigatory eye of science can be brought to bear upon the complex structures of poetic language. Empson's poetry itself uses image, syntax, and sound effects to produce arguments rather than impressions. Like early Donne, whom Empson imitates, his meanings are convoluted, his subject matter psychological, his rhythms bumpy.

During the 1940s Pound, Eliot, and Auden shared the limelight. In *Four Quartets* (1943) Eliot developed from his satiric, theatrical, modernist style an incantatorily liturgical and philosophical one. Although Pound discredited himself by broadcasting Fascist propaganda during the Second World War, his *Pisan Cantos* (1948) is a distinguished heir to *The Waste Land*. Auden, having abandoned his Marxist stance of the 1930s, reinterpreted *The Tempest* in a lyric *ars poetica, The Mirror and the Sea* (1945).

Many of the new poets of the 1940s belonged to a "neo-romantic" reaction against modernism in a way that included even Auden among its modernist targets. The reluctant guru behind this movement was the Welshman Dylan Thomas, who, during his short career, evinced a knack for profuse imagery and for hurling words together in a weirdly suggestive eldritch keen of sexual symbols and earthly magic.

The poets of the 1940s who followed Thomas' lead included a group that called itself "The New Apocalypse": J.F. Hendry (1912–86), Norman MacCaig (1910–), Henry Treece (1912–66), and G.S. Fraser (1915–80). Their use of myth as a means of personal reintegration characterizes what some have called the introspective turn of neo-romanticism away from the more public poetries of modernism and the Auden group. Hendry and Treece later explained their movement as a reconciliation between the tyrannies of modernist subjection of the personality to objects and surrealist subjection of personality to dream images. They proposed rather that poetry should allow conscious intelligence to shape the spontaneous images of dream into narrative and organic unity.

Somewhat more enduring poets of mystical or introspective turn during the 1930s and 1940s are David Gascoyne (1916–) and Kathleen Raine (1908–). Surrealist Gascoyne attempted to follow André Breton's method of allowing images from the unconscious to cluster about a subject by free association. In the introduction to her collected poems, Raine, much influenced by Yeats and Neoplatonism, explains why poetry must turn away from social history: "The ever-recurring forms of nature mirror eternal reality; the never-recurring productions of history reflect only fallen men, and are therefore not suitable to become a symbolic vocabulary for the kind of poetry I have attempted to write." Other neo-romantics were Thomas' friend Vernon Watkins (1906–67), George Barker (1913–91), and Lawrence Durrell (1912–90).

Some poets whose work was largely unaffected by modernism, Audenism, or neo-romanticism succeeded in writing in traditional modes between 1930 and 1950, among them Graves and Edwin Muir (1887–1959). Graves' mature style tends toward the Augustan: neat and carefully witty, lucid despite syntax that withholds a noun or verb through several subordinate clauses. The drama of many of his other poems is of critical intelligence examining the passions of emotional man. Muir's early poems express nostalgia for the Orkney farm life his parents were forced to abandon in 1900. His verse, syntactically straightforward but allegorically complex, fuses his lost childhood home and the decline of agrarian life in Britain with biblical myths of Eden and the great flood. He wrote his two most famous poems after the Second World War, "One Foot in Eden," about divine redress of evil by a great, post-historical harvest; and "Horses," a narrative of nuclear holocaust fitted to the pattern of the seven-day biblical creation.

Spender began by imitating Auden's confidently ironic, intellectual style, but in the 1940s he discovered his own dreamier, emotionally liquid persona. Where Auden ridiculed the absurdities of his culture, Spender seemed to suffer its wounds. John Betjeman (1906–84) was also of Auden's generation, but his popular, unintellectual social satire, seen from the point of view of the amiable, hypochondriacal everyman, was quite unlike Auden's Marxist-Freudian outlook. He became very popular in the 1950s alongside poets of "the Movement," who also cultivated self-mocking, anxiety-ridden, man-in-the-street personae. Stevie Smith (Florence Margaret Smith) (1902–71) was also of Auden's generation but belonged to no school or movement. Like Betjeman, she gained a large readership, especially in the 1950s, among people unaccustomed to reading poetry. Idiosyncratic and bitterly sardonic, Smith used the voice and viewpoint of a child to sharpen the satirical edge of her poems.

The experience of the Second World War, so different from the Great War, was reflected in the character of the poetry. This time Britons were disillusioned with war before it broke out, and there was no pompous nationalistic rhetoric to be answered. Some thought that mechanized weaponry made fighting more impersonal, a matter of technological competence or sheer victimization. Moreover, much of the war, endured on British soil, affected the civilian population directly. There was no longer a naive populace needing to be made aware, by some new Wilfred Owen, of the actualities of war. Eliot portrayed bombing raids in *Four Quartets*, Day Lewis responded to the war with Virgilian contemplations of England, and Sitwell used Christian symbolism to write about Hiroshima. Several single poems about the war have become celebrated anthology pieces, such as F.T. Prince's (1912–) "Soldiers Bathing," Gavin Ewart's (1916–) "Officer's Mess," and Henry Reed's (1914–86) "Lessons of War."

Keith Douglas (1920–44) and Alun Lewis (1915–44) are recognized as the most important of the poets who described the war and died during it. They do not remark the shocking, cataclysmic tragedy of the conflict, but its depressing dullness, its idiotic repetition of horror. Both poets, but particularly Douglas, feel the futility of writing war poetry in the shadow of Owen and Rosenberg. In Lewis' poetry, written from the Indian subcontinent—he died in Burma—the destructiveness of the war serves as background for lamentation over the diminished role of the soldier-hero and moral-objec-

tor, and over the fate of moral choice in a world where choices have become ineffectual. The neo-romantic poet Sidney Keyes (1922–43) deserves mention as another war poet complaining of the boredom of war. In contrast, poems by Roy Fuller (1912–91) are bitter in tone but light in form; they express the assumption that "verse in our time must try to comprise the experience of the majority, despite working in minority terms."

In the post-war period skeptical, humorous, deflatingly anti-romantic poets were gathered together in what came to be called "the Movement," celebrated in Robert Conquest's 1956 anthology, *New Lines*. Its character was not based on any distinct program of technical innovation or ideological statement, reflecting instead a pervasive dispiritedness and self-ironizing post-war humor. The nine poets chiefly identified with the Movement are **Philip Larkin**, Kingsley Amis (1922–), Donald Davie (1922–), Elizabeth Jennings (1926–), D.J. Enright (1920–), John Holloway (1920–), Robert Conquest (1917–), Thom Gunn (1929–), and John Wain (1925–94). Beyond a shared disdain for the romantic afflatus of the 1940s and its rhetorical excesses, these are poets of strongly different characters.

Larkin, who never claimed membership in "the Movement," is nevertheless its poetic exemplar. The persona of his most popular poems is an affably self-critical defeatist, not entirely unlike Larkin himself, whose awkwardness, ineffectualness, and anxiety are consonant with a national mood of postimperial letdown. Yet because the poems are deft, sure-footed performances, a complex tension between poet and persona emerges. "Church Going" (1954) is a fine example of Larkin's ambivalence toward English customs and institutions, which he both yearns for and rejects. His range of tones is wide and dynamic. Larkin can begin a poem with "he's fucking her and she's on the pill," yet rise to the guarded apotheosis of "High Windows" (1967).

Davie has been the most willing of the Movement poets to acknowledge its existence and to claim membership. For him the Movement is a return from neo-romanticism to controlled craftsmanship, moral responsibility, and civilized intelligence. Like Graves, his style can be Augustan, and his subject matter intense self-scrutiny. Davie's poetry is assertive yet also alertly self-conscious and self-questioning.

P

Gunn, the youngest poet included in the *New Lines* anthology, is rarely associated with that group now. His career since the 1950s has been a process of artistic growth that has followed the course of pop culture from writing about leather-jacketed "Rockers," motorcycle toughs, and Elvis Presley in the 1950s to tripping on LSD in the 1960s, to watching friends in San Francisco die of AIDS in his latest book, *The Man with Night Sweats* (1992).

Since the 1960s Gunn's name is more often linked with that of the controversial Ted Hughes (1930–), a tough-minded realist with romantic inclinations. In poems about animals Hughes confronts the brutality of life and seems to admire animal vitality for its unalterable violence. His blunt syntax and diction are well suited to his subject. His imagery is concrete, but the poems are philosophical considerations of general categories of the primal and the natural.

Charles Tomlinson (1929–), like Gunn and Davie, is one of the English poets who has praised the Americans William Carlos Williams, Edward Dorn, and Charles Olson, recommending them as models for British poets. (All three British poets have taught in America, although only Gunn has made it his permanent residence.) Tomlinson's poems are descriptions of landscapes viewed with an analytic, compositional eye. Unlike the emotional, "free-spirited" poets he praises, Tomlinson's persona is coldly aesthetic, like that of another American poet, Wallace Stevens. Like Stevens, he has a gift for making small matters of description into deep questions of human perception. Since the popular thrust of the Movement, no poet has been as antithetically unconcerned about public taste, or as impenetrably difficult, as Geoffrey Hill (1932–). His fierce contemplations of spiritual and political power are placed in remote and obscure historical frameworks such as King Offa's Mercia, or in invented historical ones like that of the poet "Sebastian Arrurruz." Even when Hill writes of actual historical figures such as Adolf Hitler, Joseph Stalin, or Idi Amin, his dense punning and allegorical conflations are uncompromisingly opaque. Nevertheless, his authoritative voice is in the line of Yeats, and his weaving together of historical moments with mythological symbols recalls Eliot and David Jones.

Seamus Heaney (1939–) is the most recent of Irish poets to play a central role in English poetry, and his impact has been greater than that of Austin Clarke (1896–1974) or Patrick Kavanagh (1904–67). A Catholic from Northern Ireland, Heaney has had to reconcile his gift for writing a universal poetry with his feelings of political allegiance to his countrymen. In *Death of a Naturalist* (1965) and *Door into the Dark* (1969) Heaney writes the best narratives of physical, country work since Frost. His descriptions of physical labor are parables of sexual and moral initiations. Since the 1970s Heaney's poetry has become more political, but not shallowly or propagandistically so.

Lewis Klausner

Bibliography

Corcoran, Neil. *English Poetry since 1940.* 1993.

Davie, Donald. *Under Briggflatts: A History of Poetry in Great Britain, 1960–1988.* 1989.

Morrison, Blake. *The Movement: English Poetry of the 1950s.* 1980.

O'Neill, Michael. *Auden, MacNeice, Spender: The Thirties Poetry.* 1992.

Parfitt, George A.E. *English Poetry of the First World War.* 1990.

Press, John. *A Map of Modern English Verse.* 1969.

Ross, Robert H. *The Georgian Revolt, 1910–1922: Rise and Fall of a Poetic Ideal.* 1965.

Shires, Linda. *British Poetry of the Second World War.* 1985.

Police

The civil police were created between 1829 and 1839 to enforce the law, prevent and detect **crime**, and maintain public order. By the mid-1990s, there were fifty-one separate police forces (forty-three in England and Wales, eight in Scotland), employing 135,000 police officers, 10 percent of whom were **women**. For the first two-thirds of the twentieth century the British police were regarded as a model of successful policing. Official histories celebrated the tradition of "policing by consent," the main constituent of which was unarmed policemen benignly enforcing the law, restrained in their response to **strikes** and political demonstrations, and accepted, not to say lionized, by all social classes. Recent decades, however, have witnessed a major crisis in the history of relations between police and policed. Despite the greater number of better-paid police officers than at any time in British history, the proportion of crimes solved has declined each year. The clear-up rate for burglary, for example, fell from 40 percent in 1951 to 28 percent in 1984. To inefficiency must be added both corruption, notably in the detective branch of the London Metropolitan Police, and criminal behavior, on the part of some West Midlands and Surrey policemen in fabricating evidence against innocent people accused of Irish Republican Army (IRA) terrorism. Furthermore, in the control of urban riots (1981 and 1985) and the miners' strike (1984–5), the police seem to have abandoned "policing by consent" in favor of policing by coercion. This drift toward adversarial policing has contributed to the decline in the level of public confidence in the police, particularly among inner-city ethnic minorities, who are more frequently stopped and searched, arrested and charged, and to a vigorous public debate concerning the principles and practices of policing.

In 1900 policing was an essentially local function with minimal central direction. There was little or no cooperation among the 200 police forces, no common standards of pay or pension, no special police department within the Home Office. The First World War and extensive industrial unrest transformed this want of system in policing. The increased duties imposed on the police during the war led to closer links between senior police officers and the Home Office, notably through the Central Conference of Chief Constables. The war also worsened working conditions, provoking the formation of the National Union of Police and Prison Officers and the outbreak of two police strikes. This militancy led, in turn, to the Desborough Committee and the 1919 Police Act, which introduced improved and uniform pay scales, a tame representative body (the Police Federation), and a centrally guided, federal structure of local police forces. The rise of a police force national in spirit if not in form was promoted, secondly, by the wave of strikes between the labor unrest of 1910–14 and the General Strike of 1926. The national scale of these industrial disputes prompted increasing government direction of policing. The outcome was increasing central-government influence over the organization and strategies of local police forces, an erosion of local responsibility for law enforcement, and (owing to continued government disinclination to take formal charge of a national police service) a greater degree of operational independence on the part of chief constables.

Already in the inter-war years, then, British pride in maintaining a decentralized police system and in rejecting the idea of a national force—an idea associated with government tyranny—was on its way to becoming a national myth. The trend since 1945 has been in the same direction. The 1964 Police Act, which defined the respective functions of Home Secretary, local police authorities (a mix of councilors and magistrates) and chief constables, did nothing to slow the *de facto* nationalization of the police, the marginalization of the police authorities, or the operational independence of chief officers. This was graphically confirmed by the events of the 1980s.

In 1981, an intensive "stop and search" operation in Brixton, London, spearheaded by the Special Patrol Group, aroused the most extensive national breakdown of civil order since the General Strike. The riots in London, Liverpool, and Manchester, characterized by bitter hostility toward the police, posed a direct challenge to the notion of "policing by consent" and lay bare the fact that police chiefs were acting without regard to the views of the elected representatives of local communities. Moreover, in response to the report of the public inquiry on the riots under Lord Scarman (1981), which criticized "hard" policing and advocated more police accountability, chief constables intervened publicly in the ensuing debate to push Scarman's blueprint for future policing off the political agenda. Paramilitary tactics were in evidence again in 1984–5, when antiriot squads from a number of forces were mobilized by the National Reporting Centre (set up to coordinate police movements and intelligence) to defeat the miners' strike. The medieval-style battle between police and pickets at the Orgreave coking plan, near Sheffield, was but one of many indications that Britain has a *de facto* national police force, that the police are vulnerable to being used for partisan political objectives, and that they are beyond the control of democratic government. Yet without an effective element of democratic control, the public support essential to "policing by consent" will be denied.

Victor Bailey

Bibliography

Critchley, T.A. *A History of Police in England and Wales.* 2nd ed. 1978.
Emsley, Clive. *The English Police: A Political*

and Social History. 1991.

Martin, J.P., and Gail Wilson. *The Police: A Study in Manpower.* 1969.

Morgan, Jane. *Conflict and Order: The Police and Labour Disputes in England and Wales, 1900–1939.* 1987.

Reiner, Robert. *The Politics of the Police.* 1985.

Political Thought

Political thought addresses the immediate and the longer-term problems and possibilities facing a society. In twentieth-century Britain the setting of those problems has been transformed. Government massively extended its responsibilities, its powers, and the number of its personnel, and in two World Wars mobilized larger and larger sections of society until the whole population and economy were drawn in. At the beginning of the century less than half of the adult population had the parliamentary vote; by its mid-point each adult had one vote, and none more than one. A country that began the century as an imperial power ended it as an auxiliary to the dominant United States and a troublesome and sometimes peripheral partner in the **European Union.** The decline in Britain's international importance was paralleled by an increase in the importance of international events and foreign intellectual influences: the years after 1917 saw as many transmutations in the influence of Karl Marx as had occurred in the Christian Church after the conversion of the Emperor Constantine. Political thought had been carried on in 1900 by a diverse collection of dons, dilettantes, politicians, and men of letters. By the end of the First World War it had become largely the preserve of academics.

At the beginning of the century, while conservatism may have been the most pervasive political doctrine, liberalism was the most sophisticated. The history of political thought in Britain in the twentieth century is the history of the transformations of liberalism. The commitment to individual liberty had been faced with the evident restrictions on the lives of even those adult males who had been given new political powers by the franchise reforms of the nineteenth century. Poverty among the mass of the people seemed to deny what political rights promised, while educational deprivation was a danger to democratic politics. The response of the **New Liberals** such as L.T. Hobhouse was to

argue that the state, no longer in privileged or aristocratic hands, could at last be trusted and could be used to equalize the material opportunities of ordinary citizens. The foundations were thus laid for a split between a liberalism that saw the state as regulating and redistributing in order to promote the spread of liberty, and a liberalism that, in classical economic mode, saw liberty as a matter of minimizing what government did. One branch of liberalism thus began to move toward an alliance, political rather than intellectual, with conservatism; the other, toward an association with socialism.

Socialism at the start of the century had two principal forms: one, **Fabian** socialism, rationalist and technical, the other visionary and moralistic. The Fabians, of whom the most prominent were **Beatrice and Sidney Webb** and **George Bernard Shaw,** anticipated the slow but inevitable extension of state responsibility for the management, by trained experts, of what capitalism could do only in a random and inefficient manner. Visionary socialism, on the other hand, appealed to a sense of justice or fairness, advocating the enjoyment by all of the opportunities—economic, educational, and cultural— that were at the time limited to a privileged minority. Visionary socialism shared with much Edwardian political thought a religious or semi-religious frame of reference, Christianity exercising an influence sufficient to make an appeal to its values a frequent support of political argument.

The most dramatic challenge to pre-1914 British politics was that of the suffrage campaigners. **Feminism** posed a challenge equally radical within political thought. The public face of feminism was a demand for votes for women, but the arguments of women like feminist writer Cicely Hamilton struck at the root of male economic power within both the public sphere of employment and the private one of the family. The threat to a liberalism that saw the household as the secure realm of individual freedom was especially great.

The First World War jolted religious belief, illustrated the possibilities of an economically active state, and, in making possible the Bolshevik Revolution of 1917, established a new hagiography and a new demonology. But while the opponents of socialism now saw it as the thin end of a Leninist wedge, socialists themselves became more firmly committed to democratic politics than ever, and the only lesson they took from the Soviet Union was that the central economic planning seemed preferable to **unemployment** and depression.

Between the wars, while the principal domestic issues were economic, the grand issues were increasingly dramatized abroad in Russia, Germany, Italy, and Spain. Political thought reflected this either in being resolutely domestic, as in the work of **George Orwell**, who based his socialism on the existing decencies of the working class, or in invoking the transcendental values of Christianity, as in the socialist egalitarianism of **R.H. Tawney** or the assertive conservative elitism of **T.S. Eliot**.

The Second World War, even more than the First, required a mobilization of human capital. Both the physical well-being and the active support of the population were necessary, and government became committed both in **propaganda** and in policy to a wider responsibility, with the achievement of peace, for the well-being of the population. When this was combined with a sweeping electoral victory for Labour in the 1945 general election, social democracy seemed firmly established. The "revisionist" socialism of **Anthony Crosland** widened the conception of equality and replaced public ownership with more indirect Keynesian economic management. The principles on which a social democratic society might be based were elaborated in the work of the social administrator **Richard Titmuss**, who saw the state as the agent of a publicly responsible use of resources and as the agency for economic equality. The advances of social democracy provoked a reformulation of conservatism. The political theorist Michael Oakeshott argued against "rationalism" and recommended a politics based on the pursuit of the "intimations" of tradition. A more vigorous reaction to social democracy came from F.A. von Hayek, who presented the alternatives of either a free market (or "catalaxy") or economic planning and totalitarianism. The experience of Nazism and Stalinism was being increasingly invoked to discredit social reform. By the 1950s the Cold War had provided for the critics of socialism and reform a ready polemical association of egalitarianism with East European despotism, and an "end of ideology" was being either described or advocated, expressing in more propagandist terms Karl Popper's preference for "piecemeal social engineering."

It was in response to this new orthodoxy that the "New Left" of the 1960s and 1970s argued for decentralization, pluralism, and the radical questioning of all forms of authority. E.P. Thompson attempted to construct a case for socialist humanism, which drew on indigenous traditions as much as on abstract principle, while feminists from the 1960s onward developed an analysis that, in its dissection of economic and sexual exploitation within the family, was as disconcerting for the traditional Left as for the traditional Right. The work of Juliet Mitchell, Sheila Rowbotham, and Carole Pateman presented the oppression of women as a fundamental social division that socialism did not adequately address and that liberalism and conservatism sustained.

The "New Right" of the 1980s and 1990s, while drawing on both Hayek and Oakeshott, and through him Burke, allied economic liberalism and political and social conservatism in a way that had more tactical than intellectual coherence. So while Samuel Brittan argued the case for the state to interfere as little as possible across the whole range of social and economic life, the tory Roger Scruton submerged the individual in the cultural, sexual, and moral traditions of society.

The end of the Cold War and the abdication of Communist autocracies after 1989 changed the demonology of British politics. As Britain approached the close of the twentieth century, the landmarks that had served to position political thought for the last three-quarters of a century had vanished. In Europe conservatism could now mean anything from old-style bureaucratic Marxism to vicious nationalism, while socialism had lost the association, whether justified or not, with the ponderous despotisms of Eastern Europe. The advocacy of both market socialism and citizenship drew on liberal ideals of individual autonomy, but also represented an openness to the various claims of ethnicity and gender, as well as the more traditional ones of class, and a mix of values that was more adaptable to the environmental, or **Green, movement** than either of its originating constituent parts. Liberalism as a coherent and comprehensive theory had begun to fragment before the First World War. But by the century's close it was informing a wide range of arguments. Feminists had taken its claims for individual rights at face value and used them to anatomize the family; liberal economic theories were taken up by the New Right; market socialism depended on the pursuit of maximum individual choice; the campaign for citizenship was steeped in a belief in

P

political rights and the value of active political participation. The life cycle of liberalism was complete.

Rodney Barker

Bibliography
Barker, Rodney. *Political Ideas in Modern Britain.* 1978.
———. *Politics, Peoples, and Government.* 1994.
Greenleaf, W.H. *The British Political Tradition.* vol. 2: *The Ideological Heritage.* 1986.

Polytechnics

In 1966 **Anthony Crosland**, the **Labour** government's Secretary of State for Education and Science, announced a plan to create a network of thirty colleges of technical education, to be known as polytechnics. The polytechnics were designed to be responsive to local needs, vocational rather than academic, and inexpensive to run. The establishment of a second educational tier resulted in a "binary system": universities, which enjoyed high status, had large budgets, and taught liberal arts and pure sciences; and polytechnics, which were under the control of local government, sparsely funded, and taught vocational and professional courses. This segregation of elite liberal education from the lower-status technical and vocational studies reflected cultural attitudes toward the disciplines that date from the nineteenth century and have persisted to the present day. Historically, institutions providing **technical education** added liberal arts to the curriculum in an effort to raise their status, while those that retained their vocational orientation were condemned to low prestige and lack of resources. Like their predecessors, the urban university colleges in the nineteenth century and the Colleges of Advanced Technology in the twentieth, the polytechnics immediately began a process of upward mobility, discontinuing their precollege courses, until by the end of the twentieth century they attained university status.

The polytechnics were eventually to number thirty-five, including seven in London. The technical colleges from which they grew had been founded by local initiative in the nineteenth century to promote working people's education, and they included the London institutions already called polytechnics. Their major periods of growth reflected the nation's anxiety about the state of its technical expertise and its ability to compete in trade, commerce, and war with its major industrial rivals. After 1945 there was a vast increase in demand for all forms of higher education. Although the universities expanded to meet this demand, the government decided to create a second sector offering business training and applied science, while the universities retained their traditional specialties in the liberal arts and pure sciences. The new polytechnics were less costly to run than the universities since they had neither elegant buildings nor expensive research programs, and the government hoped that their vocational curriculum and less socially elite atmosphere would make them attractive to the working-class student. In the late 1960s the polytechnic sector of the binary system seemed to be an exciting experiment in democratic access to higher education, and observers noted similarities with the comprehensive schools, an innovation in **secondary education**.

By the early 1970s it was obvious that the institutions themselves had outgrown the constraints of the binary system. The polytechnics were offering more of the traditional university subjects and creating the ambience of residential colleges by building halls of residence and student unions. Despite these advantages, the polytechnics were unable to alter their depressing image, and potential students continued to prefer the universities. Their inability to compete for the best undergraduates, together with chronic lack of funds, hampered the polytechnics' ability to reach the high status that they believed the quality of their staff and programs deserved. The polytechnics had almost six times as many part-time students as the universities, reflecting their original commitments to their local regions and to the working man and woman, but they lacked the amenities for student life that raise the experience of higher education above the functional level. It had become clear that the only way for the polytechnics to enjoy the status they desired and to obtain a greater share of available resources was to follow the example of earlier technical training institutions and take the name of universities.

Under the provisions of the 1992 Further and Higher Education Act, the polytechnics were permitted to assume the title of university, and all thirty-five of them chose to do so. The expanded university system was placed under a single funding body, and the polytechnics were allowed to award their own degrees. Although the government intended this act to expand the number of university places and raise the status of technical education, it was also a way to limit total investment in higher education. In the future, the old and new universities will compete among themselves for scarce research funding, as well as for students. Meanwhile, the polytechnics' nondegree courses have increasingly fallen to the Colleges of Further Education, which, in turn, aspire to the title of polytechnic. Despite the inherent justice of the 1992 act to the polytechnics, it has not solved the fundamental contradiction between technical and university-level education.

Elizabeth Morse

Bibliography

Halsey, A.H. *Decline of Donnish Dominion: The British Academic Professions in the Twentieth Century.* 1992.

Henry, Elaine. *Oxford Polytechnic: Genesis to Maturity, 1865–1980.* 1981.

Pratt, John, and Tyrrell Burgess. *Polytechnics: A Report.* 1974.

Robinson, Eric. *The New Polytechnics.* 1968.

Popular Culture

If, as many historians argue, the first decades of the nineteenth century in Britain witnessed the development of a radical popular culture by self-taught artisans, the twentieth century has seen the demise of that culture and the triumph of a commercial culture that has as much to do with business as with pleasure or politics. The commercialization of popular culture has led to many laments for a declining, yet more "authentic," culture of "the people." Nevertheless, although the leisure industries have transformed popular culture in the twentieth century, their products have often been creatively appropriated by individuals eager to maintain those very forms of popular creativity that critics argue have been lost.

In urban communities in Victorian Britain workers developed a rich associational life that flourished well into the twentieth century. Centered around communal activities like choral singing, club membership, betting, **brass band** competitions, **drink**, **football** games, pigeon racing, and going to fairs, the culture of the home, the street, and the neighborhood offered a crucial sense of belonging to many workers. Although activities were often segregated along gender lines, they served to bind members of the working class together in a cohesive community. Captured in Kathleen Woodward's *Jipping Street* (1928) and Robert Roberts' *The Classic Slum* (1971), this culture has more recently become central to televised representations of traditional working-class life in programs like *Coronation Street.*

In the late nineteenth and early twentieth centuries this culture was penetrated by newer forms of commercial entertainment. A significant rise in real wages, coupled with a gradual decline in working hours, solidified the division between work and **leisure** and afforded many workers the opportunity to purchase hitherto unavailable pleasures. The advent of the cheap excursion train led to the rapid growth of working-class resorts like Blackpool, which attracted 1 million visitors in 1883, 4 million in 1914, and 7 million in 1939. Major investment in football teams, music halls, and the popular **press** also transformed popular culture. While music halls emerged in the 1850s, it was only after the 1880s that they became highly capitalized ventures, attracting a mass audience. Likewise, readership of the popular press expanded rapidly, particularly with the advent of new papers like the *Daily Express* and the *Daily Mail* around the turn of the new century. While one adult in five or six read a daily newspaper in 1900, that number had climbed to one in two by 1920.

While working-class culture was largely an urban phenomenon, rural communities were also subject to commercial penetration. The increasing erosion of traditional rural culture led turn-of-the-century **folk song** collectors like Cecil Sharp to preserve the musical artifacts of a decaying way of life. This fueled the idealization of the popular culture of a once "Merrie England," which intensified as the last vestiges of traditional rural life were marginalized by newer forms of mass entertainment. By the 1940s the decline of traditional rural popular culture was almost complete, occasioning many elegiac laments for a lost way of life, of which Flora Thompson's trilogy, *Lark Rise to Candleford* (1945), is perhaps the best.

The inter-war years were marked by the development of new forms of popular culture. Although the cinema expanded rapidly after 1906—there were 400 million tickets sold in 1914—it only came to dominate popular culture after the First World War. In 1936 there were 903 million cinema admissions, a number that climbed to a peak of 1.6 million in 1946.

Most popular films were made in the United States, leading the government to establish a quota system in 1927 that called for 20 percent of all films exhibited in British cinemas to be made in Britain by 1936. Although this led to the production of inexpensive "quota quickies," it also aided the development of a highly successful British **film industry** in the 1930s and 1940s.

During the 1920s and 1930s the influence of the United States on popular culture in Britain was enormous. Not only were American films ubiquitous, but dance halls were dominated by American jazz, and American consumer goods were in great demand. These trends alarmed many intellectuals, who bemoaned the loss of national identity brought about by Americanization. They argued that popular culture should be more British, that it should be grounded in the concerns and traditions of local communities. Although this was often at odds with the cosmopolitan modernism of contemporary popular tastes, it led to the encouragement of indigenous forms of popular culture. Music hall entertainment, which had been attacked in the late nineteenth century, was now championed as an "authentic" voice of the British people, while in the 1930s a **documentary film** movement emerged that attempted to capture the uniqueness of those voices. **Mass-Observation** also began to study the popular culture of local communities, culminating in such publications as *The Pub and the People* (1943) and *The Press and Its Readers* (1949).

Between the wars popular culture was increasingly organized around the home and family, a tendency that was intensified by the growth of radio listening. By 1928 radios existed in a quarter of all British homes, and by the 1940s few homes were without one. Established early in the 1920s, the **British Broadcasting Corporation** (BBC) enjoyed a monopoly over the airwaves until commercial television was licensed in 1956. Under the direction of **John Reith**, who viewed radio as a source of cultural enlightenment in the battle against the dark forces of mass culture, the BBC was devoted to moral and cultural improvement. Classical music dominated the BBC's offerings in the 1930s, although the corporation began to capitulate to its listeners' preferences, particularly during the **Second World War** with the advent of the Forces Programme, which entertained British troops. After the war, the BBC played a greater role in reflecting the nation's popular taste, especially through its new Light Programme.

Although working-class culture was traditionally male-centered, many activities like radio listening were shared by men and women alike. A separate female world of popular culture also developed between the wars, in part due to the influence of Women's Institutes (established in 1915) and the continuing strength of the Women's Co-operative Guild. In addition—and despite the increasingly commercial nature of popular culture—a number of new voluntary organizations attracted both men and women in their pursuit of recreation, including the Holiday Fellowship (established in 1913), the Workers' Travel Association (1921), and the Youth Hostels Association (1930). Following the passage of the Holidays with Pay Act in 1938, more workers began to enjoy annual holidays. While this encouraged the growth of traditional resorts, it also led to the advent of the new holiday camp, which, under the entrepreneurial initiatives of Billy Butlin, flourished, especially in the later 1940s and 1950s.

During the twentieth century the state has come to play a major role in the regulation and provision of popular culture. Local authorities had always been responsible for licensing places of entertainment and providing amenities like parks and swimming pools; before the First World War the London County Council was particularly well known for its active, municipal culture. By the 1940s, however, the national government had also become a major purveyor of popular culture, especially through the **Entertainments National Service Association** (ENSA), which provided entertainment for the armed forces and in war-production factories, and the **Council for the Encouragement of Music and the Arts** (CEMA), which promoted amateur music, drama, and painting in Britain. Although the latter organization inspired the establishment of the **Arts Council of Great Britain** in 1946, which turned increasingly to the funding of artistic excellence, the state has continued to promote popular culture, largely through the National Film Finance Corporation (created in 1949), and the Sports Council (1964).

The late 1940s witnessed a surge in the number of people who enjoyed the cinema and football matches, although traditional working-class culture declined rapidly in the 1950s. By the end of the decade a number of writers lamented that decline, most notably Richard

Hoggart, whose *The Uses of Literacy* (1957) evoked a whole way of life that was in the process of disintegrating. The rapid advance in ownership of cars and television sets hastened the decline of the cinema and drove much popular culture into the home. In addition, traditional working-class neighborhoods, with their rich associational life that revolved around the street, the corner shop, the pub, and the club, were the target of urban redevelopment schemes in the 1950s and 1960s, leading to the destruction of the built environment in which much popular culture had once flourished.

Real disposable income in Britain doubled between 1951 and 1972, unleashing an unprecedented consumer boom that transformed popular culture, especially for the young. By the end of the 1950s, critics were noting the existence of the new "teenage consumer" who rebelled against traditional forms of working-class culture and engaged in the consumption of fashionable clothes, records, and entertainment in night clubs. With the advent of the teenager came the development of new **youth cultures**—the Teddy Boys in the 1950s, the Mods and the Rockers in the 1960s, and the more ominous Skinheads in the 1970s. They rejected traditional forms of popular culture, along with the homogeneity increasingly associated with highly commercialized forms of mass culture. In the "swinging London" of the 1960s, the style of the new youth culture pervaded society, especially after the **Beatles** were catapulted to fame and Britain began to make a major contribution to an increasingly global popular culture.

The post-war emphasis on personal choice in the uses of leisure undermined communal forms of popular culture, as did the emergence of ethnic cultures. **Immigration** to Britain from nations of the Commonwealth grew rapidly from the 1950s, each group bringing its own cultural baggage with it. On the one hand, this enriched dominant forms of popular culture: Jamaican reggae soon entered the British musical mainstream, while eating out, an increasingly popular pastime, often included the patronage of ethnic establishments. On the other hand, cultural diversity has been viewed by many as a threat to native forms of popular culture and to established idioms of national identity. Although Skinhead violence against immigrants peaked in the late 1970s and early 1980s, many white Britons have become increasingly nostalgic for traditional forms of

British popular culture, fueling the growth of the heritage industry in the 1980s.

Present-day popular culture in Britain cannot be understood without taking note of the importance of shopping and video arcades, of **television** and **travel**, and of the rapid emergence of a global entertainment market. By the 1980s leisure consumed more than 25 percent of consumer spending in Britain, much of it devoted to personal consumption and home-centered leisure activities. But other activities have also become popular, including overseas package holidays to places like the Spanish Costa Brava, which has led to the demise of Blackpool and other traditional British resorts. Although Blackpool has often tried to regain its reputation, largely through skillful advertising ("Costa Notta Lotta" was the mid-1980s rallying cry), traditional forms of popular culture in Britain have been transformed beyond recognition since the 1950s. Once defined by the communities that often made—and always enjoyed—it, popular culture has become a more complex and more fragmented phenomenon, increasing the opportunities for individual expression while undermining the social cohesiveness with which earlier forms of popular culture were often associated.

Chris Waters

Bibliography
Chambers, Iain. *Popular Culture: The Metropolitan Experience.* 1986.
Clarke, John, and Charles Critcher. *The Devil Makes Work: Leisure in Capitalist Britain.* 1985.
Davies, Andrew. *Leisure, Gender, and Poverty: Working-Class Culture in Salford and Manchester, 1900–1939.* 1992.
Jones, Stephen G. *Workers at Play: A Social and Economic History of Leisure, 1918–1939.* 1986.
Walvin, James. *Leisure and Society, 1830–1950.* 1978.

Popular Fiction

Throughout the century reading has been one of the most popular and accessible **leisure** activities among all ages and classes. The preferred choice has been popular or "light" fiction—romances, thrillers, Westerns—in book and magazine form. The desire to "escape" with a good story has rarely waned and during wartime has intensified. Because popular fiction is a commercial venture, it is susceptible to changing tastes and to external influences, particularly from the cinema.

At the turn of the century **publishing** was expanding along with the reading public, one result of the spread of education and the rise in literacy. By 1900 publishers responded to increasing demand by giving readers what they apparently wanted—weekly magazines filled with tales of romance and adventure, and inexpensive editions of best-selling novels. In 1900 there were two acknowledged best-selling authors of popular fiction: Marie Corelli and Hall Caine. Corelli wrote lush romances laden with religion and morality; Caine, romantic adventures set in exotic locales. Each author had average annual sales of 100,000 copies at a time when 5,000 qualified as a runaway best-seller. They inspired many, including Florence J. Barclay, whose purpose in writing was "the joy of helping people along the road to heaven." An estimated 20 million people read Barclay's *The Rosary* (1909), her biggest success. Charles Garvice and Nat Gould were also popular, as were more secular, romantic novelists, like the Baroness Orczy (1865–1947), author of the swashbuckler *The Scarlet Pimpernel* (1905). The more daring Ethel M. Dell's erotic, violent love stories were in the tradition of the Gothic novel, while E.M. Hull's *The Sheik* (1919) inspired legions of harem romances. Elinor Glyn's 1907 novel, *Three Weeks*, the story of an affair between a Balkan princess and her younger English lover, sold over 2 million copies.

The magazine leader was the Amalgamated Press, founded by Alfred Harmsworth, **Lord Northcliffe**, who built an empire of ninety titles targeted at working women, housewives, and children. *Woman's Weekly* (1911) is still one of Britain's best-selling magazines. Two titles for boys, the *Gem* (1907) and the *Magnet* (1908), set the standard for school stories, featuring the adventures of Tom Merry and Billy Bunter. Several prolific children's authors got their start in the serial world, including the adventure writer Percy Westerman and Angela Brazil, the mistress of the girls' school story.

Surveys showed the broad popularity of murder mysteries as well. The leader by far was Edgar Wallace, nicknamed "The Fiction Factory," who wrote 170 books, including *The Four Just Men* (1905). By 1939 one in four books bought in Britain were written by him. During the **First World War** soldiers and housewives alike read E. Phillips Oppenheim's detective novels, escapist fantasies often set in the French Riviera.

In the 1920s and 1930s publishing expanded and was commercialized, with advertising used as never before to promote new books. Radio and the cinema did not detract from reading; adaptations were common, and Hollywood glamor, "cops and robbers," and the Wild West inspired new writers. The new leader in popular weekly magazines was the Scottish firm D.C. Thomson. Its "Big Five" boys' papers (*Adventure, Wizard, Rover, Skipper, Hotspur*) took boys out of the classroom for thrilling international adventures. The firm also cornered the expanding comics market (*The Beano* and *The Dandy*) and dominated magazines for middle- and working-class women, with romance papers (including current best-sellers *The People's Friend* and *My Weekly*), and the so-called "erotic bloods" (*Red Letter, Red Star,* and *Secrets*), which contained graphic morality tales with good, clean violence.

The three most popular children's authors of the 1920s and 1930s are still read: Enid Blyton, Richmal Crompton, and Captain W.E. Johns. Blyton's success with the "Famous Five" and "Secret Seven" adventure series preceded her hit "Toyland" books, featuring Little Noddy and Big Ears, in the 1950s. Crompton's "William Brown" series was launched in 1922 with *Just William*. Johns' "Biggles" and "Worrals of the WAAF" series taught boys and girls lessons in sportsmanship and loyalty to both monarchy and parents.

Given the Depression, and the frequency of novel reading, borrowing books was preferred over buying. The commercial, or "tuppenny," libraries were the popular alternative to the public libraries, which tended not to stock lighter fare. Several firms, including the romantic fiction publishers Mills and Boon, became library houses, targeting novels to specific readers. Collins' enormously successful "Crime Club" detective series, featuring **Agatha Christie**, and Hodder and Stoughton's "Yellow Jackets" popular novels are other examples of commercial publishing ventures.

Popular inter-war detective writers included **Dorothy L. Sayers**, Peter Cheyney, John Creasey, Dornford Yates, and Nicholas Blake (**Cecil Day Lewis**). "Sapper" (Herman Cyril McNeile) launched his "Bulldog Drummond" series in 1920, and Leslie Charteris' "Saint" made his first appearance in 1928. Ruby M.

Ayres and Denise Robins penned romances; P.G. Wodehouse dominated comedy with 120 novels; and the American author Zane Grey's Westerns were sell-outs. Daphne du Maurier's novels, including *Jamaica Inn* (1936) and *Rebecca* (1938), have never been out of print.

During the **Second World War** reading choice was restricted by paper rationing, but blackout hours increased the demand. The best-sellers of the war years were both thrillers: James Hadley Chase's *No Orchids for Miss Blandish* (1939), and *Who Killed Oliver Cromwell?* (1937) by Leonard Gribble. Since 1945 the influence of cinema and **television** has been profound. Magazines, for example, became more visual and less text-intensive. Color and photography were used extensively. Fiction also broadened; romances reflected the improved status of **women** with more independent heroines and familiar situations. Mass-market weeklies, launched before the war, were redesigned in the 1950s and still dominate the market, with circulations near the million mark: *Woman* (1937), *Woman's Own* (1938), *Woman's Weekly*, and *My Weekly*. Children's magazines also evolved into "picture-story papers." One of the first, the *Eagle* (1950), was an instant success, selling over a million copies per week. Its companion paper, *Girl*, started in 1951, followed by D.C. Thomson's girls' publications *Bunty* (1958) and *Judy* (1960). D.C. Thomson also launched a Second World War nostalgia craze with its popular *Commando* and *Warlord* library novelettes (1974).

The decline of the commercial libraries inspired innovative schemes, including book clubs, to get people to buy books. Mills and Boon, for example, launched a successful direct-market subscription service in the 1960s. But it was the introduction of the mass-market paperback that would have the greatest impact. Penguin Books (1935), the first paperback venture, was joined after the war by the Pan, Corgi, Panther, Sphere, and Fontana paperback imprints, publishers of romance, crime, and war stories. At sixpence or less, books were now accessible, inexpensive, and as disposable as a weekly magazine.

Overall, it is striking to note how little reading tastes have changed since the Second World War, with the exception of Westerns, which declined in popularity both in print and on the screen. School stories, for example, continue to be popular among girls. Old favorites like Dorita Fairlie Bruce's "Dimsie" books and Elinor Brent-Dyer's "Chalet School" series endured, alongside novels spun off from the popular television series *Grange Hill* in the 1970s. Romantic fiction is still dominated by Mills and Boon. Behind the firm's longevity lies aggressive market research and a willingness to change with the times. The once-chaste Mills and Boon romance, for example, now includes premarital sex scenes. Barbara Cartland, the most visible British symbol of romance, may hold the world's record for the most novels written (over 600), but her dated tales of virginal heroines are no longer popular. More respectable—and marketable—romantic fiction is written by Catherine Cookson and Barbara Taylor Bradford.

The reading public still enjoys crime fiction and adventure thrillers. Novelists like Ian Fleming (*Casino Royale*), Frederick Forsyth (*The Day of the Jackal*), and Jeffrey Archer (*Kane and Abel*) have achieved celebrity status at home and abroad and sell in the millions. Ruth Rendell, P.D. James, and Elizabeth Ferrars are among those who have followed in Agatha Christie's footsteps.

Joseph McAleer

Bibliography

Cadogan, Mary, and Patricia Craig. *You're a Brick, Angela! The Girls' Story, 1839–1985*. 1976.

Hoggart, Richard. *The Uses of Literacy*. 1958.

McAleer, Joseph. *Popular Reading and Publishing in Britain, 1914–1950*. 1992.

Symons, Julian. *Bloody Murder: From the Detective Story to the Crime Novel*. 1985.

Turner, E.S. *Boys Will Be Boys*. 1975.

Popular Front

The Popular Front campaign aimed to unite all political forces opposed to the government's policy of appeasing the Fascist dictatorships. It was first advocated by the **Communist Party of Great Britain** (CPGB) in 1935 and was endorsed by many leading Liberals. Despite official opposition from the **Labour Party**, which nursed a profound distrust of the Liberals and the Communists and discounted the claim that a united effort would help defeat the government, the Popular Front slowly gathered support among Labour leftists. In April 1938 Sir **Stafford Cripps, Aneurin Bevan**, and other left-wing leaders launched a campaign to change Labour's position. They failed but continued the campaign publicly. Cripps was consequently expelled from the Labour Party in January 1939; Bevan and four others followed in March. Thus denied the essential objective of Labour Party participation, the campaign rapidly fizzled out.

The immediate inspiration for the Popular Front campaign in Britain was the election of Popular Front governments in France and Spain in 1936. In line with Soviet foreign policy, which aimed to form alliances with the democracies in order to contain Germany, the Communist International endorsed the strategy in 1935 following the formation of the French Popular Front in the previous year. This led the CPGB to broaden its earlier aim of forming a United Front consisting only of socialist organizations. As a first step the CPGB applied for affiliation to the Labour Party in 1936. The application was resoundingly defeated at the Labour Party conference in October despite the support of the **Socialist League** (the official organization of the Labour Left), which at that stage supported socialist unity but opposed the Popular Front on the grounds that nonsocialists could not be reliable allies.

In June the Socialist League's Secretary, J.T. Murphy, left the league to form the People's Front Propaganda Committee, which gained support from individuals of all parties and sponsored some well-attended public meetings, but made little real political headway. The outbreak of the **Spanish Civil War** in July 1936 lent the Popular Front further support, but it took Germany's annexation of Austria in March 1938 to bring wholehearted endorsement from the Labour Left.

In October and November 1938 the Labour Party refrained from nominating candidates against "Independent Progressive" candidates in two by-elections. In the first, A.D. Lindsay—a member of the Labour Party—considerably reduced the Conservative majority in Oxford; in the second, Vernon Bartlett, a Liberal, won at Bridgwater. Such passivity was as near as the Labour leadership ever came to accepting Popular Front forms of action.

Although the Popular Front is often seen simply as a Communist ruse, it struck deep chords among some Liberals and socialists, many of whom had advocated and practiced cross-party collaboration intermittently for de-cades, particularly in times of international political crisis.

D.P. Blaazer

Bibliography

Blaazer, David. *The Popular Front and the Progressive Tradition: Socialists, Liberals, and the Quest for Unity, 1884–1939.* 1992.

Cole, G.D.H. *The People's Front.* 1937.

Jupp, James. *The Radical Left in Britain, 1931–1941.* 1982.

Pimlott, Ben. *Labour and the Left in the 1930s.* 1977.

Popular Music

Britain's most lasting exports in its long years of decline as a manufacturing power since the Second World War have been the commodities associated with the popular music industry. Various "British waves" have hit the shores of other countries since Beatlemania led the first pop invasion of the United States in the early to mid-1960s, which included Herman's Hermits, the Rolling Stones, the Kinks, and many more. New pop (in the form of Boy George and the Culture Club, Spandau Ballet, and Duran Duran) repeated the exercise in the early 1980s, while the madcap imagery of "Madchester," the global media name for music supposedly associated with the region around Manchester in the late 1980s, made the cover of *Newsweek* without guaranteeing automatic stateside success for bands like Happy Mondays, Stone Roses, and 808 State. However, it is arguable that the British recording industry has never really regained its position after the economic crisis in the industry immediately after punk in the late 1970s.

In 1976–7 punk ideology managed, fleetingly, to discredit the rock myths that were manifestly decaying in Britain by the mid-1970s. It did so by laying bare the business techniques and tactics involved in its own production. One of the many contradictory effects of punk on the pop music industry was that it better prepared subsequent pop stars for the task of attempting to control their own destinies to a greater degree than before.

Alongside the musical form of punk itself came a resuscitation of rock meanings: what the music stood for, what, and whom, it represented. Politicization of pop in Britain in the period from the mid-1970s to the mid-1980s depended, mainly, on the notion of pop as an art form, rather than, as in pre-punk days, rock as a folk form. Whether, as consumers of the music press mythologies have claimed, it was indeed U2, or Simple Minds, or The Smiths, or Stone Roses that constituted the last great rock monument in pop culture remained, largely, beside the point. The influence of rock culture lies beyond any simple analysis of its political economy—in other words, it involves analysis of more than just its market potential, its part in patterns of profitability. Music industry corporate strategies have shifted significantly since the late 1970s, necessitating the creation and targeting of multiple new consumer categories, as well as the exploitation of rights in intellectual property (copyright in songs, for instance) rather than merely the orthodox reliance on selling as many units as possible.

Rock's late-1960s myths, amalgamating counterculture with a certain melange of musical styles, have provided the raw material for a host of young bands and performers to reference pop (and youth culture) pasts even though they were not personally present in the making of such popular memory. They also sustain older musicians and singers who first built their styles and reputations in those years and could not realistically have expected a prosperous, lifelong career in an industry that had institutionalized the notion of "permanent teenage." Recycling the 1970s for the compact disc 1980s frequently demanded a rather partisan reconstruction of the pop signs of that decade: This view tends to play down glam-rock's androgyny and punk's garage and pub rock roots. There is, though, always ample scope for rewriting the narrative for different audiences at different times to meet various consumer markets. The sight of a cluster of aging rock stars rattling their jewelry for royalty on Prince's Trust concert stages and records not only recalls the Beatles' moral dilemmas of the 1960s, but also emphasizes the historical development of the formularization of rock as "rebellion" and underscores the respectable face of rock and pop that has constantly been present. The sheer healthiness of the popular music industry was what stood out for the casual pop consumer in the mid- to late 1980s, just as it did in the mid-1970s prior to punk's emergence in 1976–7. In the shop window were the familiar selling points: the quality of digital production, the vitality of the speed and energetic movement on stage or video, and the super-efficiency of much of the playing, however simulated. It was this context that prompted a younger generation to develop what has become labeled as rave culture in the 1990s, promoting the role of the DJ, mixer and engineer, and dance culture as more radical than mere pop or rock.

Steve Redhead

Bibliography

Chambers, Iain. *Urban Rhythms: Pop Music and Popular Culture.* 1985.

Lee, Edward. *Music of the People: A Study of Popular Music in Great Britain.* 1970.

Taylor, Paul. *Popular Music since 1955: A Critical Guide to the Literature.* 1985.

Population

In contrast to the nineteenth century, when the population of Great Britain increased by more than 350 percent, the twentieth century has been characterized by diminishing fertility and a much slower rate of population growth. The 1901 census counted 38 million people in the country compared to 10.5 million a hundred years earlier. These figures reflected an increase of nearly 14 percent every ten years. They were closely associated with a higher incidence of **marriage** than in most other Western countries and an unprecedentedly high crude birthrate of nearly 35 births per 1,000 of the population.

Although the closing years of the century were marked by the beginning of a protracted decline in the birthrate and steady diminution in the number of children born per marriage, the increase in population remained high (10.9 percent) in the pre-First World War decade before it began to fall precipitously after 1911. Indeed, the population grew by less than 5 percent in the next ten years, a diminished rate of increase compounded to some extent by the disruptions and losses of the **First World War**, but which, despite minor fluctuations, continued in subsequent decades. An influx of **immigrants** from the Commonwealth in the 1950s and 1960s resulted in a modest surge in the decennial rate of growth to about 5.5 percent before plummeting at times to a nearly static 0.83 percent in the 1970s and 1980s. Instead of rising to the 76 million that planners predicted in the comparatively fertile post-Second World War decade when the population stood at approximately 50 million, the figure as Great Britain entered the last decade of the century was closer to 57 million. If current trends continue,

P

it is not likely to reach even 60 million until the year 2025.

The much slower rate of population growth in the twentieth century as compared to the nineteenth was closely correlated with the at first gradual and then precipitous decline in fertility that began in the 1880s. It has, despite temporary surges after the First and Second World Wars, more or less continued to the present day. At its peak in the 1870s the crude birthrate of 35 per 1,000, when corrected, translated into nearly 290 offspring per 1,000 women between the childbearing ages of fifteen and forty-four. By the First World War the birthrate had fallen 33 percent, to 24 per 1,000, and the corrected rate stood at 191 per 1,000. The large Victorian family of five or six children per marriage was fast being replaced by its more modern counterpart of three or four.

Contemporaries were often puzzled and distressed by this rapid reversal of demographic patterns that had persisted for more than a century, and they began a process of prognostication and inquiry that continued off and on throughout the remainder of the century. Their anxieties focused upon the inverse correlation between family size and social status as middle- and upper-class birthrates fell much more rapidly than those of the unskilled laboring poor— a phenomenon that allegedly threatened the "quality of the race." Others fearful of "race suicide" warned of the possibility of an absolute decline in population that would imperil Great Britain's economic and imperial position in the world.

The First World War only compounded these worries as casualties soared while fertility fell another 30 percent. Despite a brief recovery after the war stimulated by a temporary surge in marriages, the birthrate started down again in 1922, reaching a low of around 15 per 1,000 in the 1930s. Women who married in the post-war decade gave birth to an average of 2.2 children, well below the 3.5 produced by their parents in the first decade of the century.

Although the mean age at which women married has increased steadily throughout the century from around twenty-five years to nearly twenty-eight today, the overall rate of marriage in Great Britain, despite numerous fluctuations, remains, as it has been since the nineteenth century, the highest in Europe. If since the 1980s the number of marriages per 1,000 people fell from around 15 to 14, the figures are not re-markably different from those that prevailed at various times in the preceding decades. What has changed dramatically is the number of these marriages that end in **divorce**, up from only 7,000 before the Second World War to nearly 150,000 a year since the 1980s, the second-highest rate in Europe. Whatever the marital problems of the twentieth century, it is clear that couples, however long they were together, increasingly determined for a variety of economic, social, and cultural reasons to limit the number of children they were willing to have and families grew smaller with each succeeding generation.

Initially there were heated disputes about the causes of the falling birthrate; to resolve them the government authorized the taking of a unique Fertility of Marriage Census in 1911 that was not made public until after the war. It confirmed what by then was obvious—whatever their reasons, British couples were rapidly adopting **birth control** as an important facet of domestic culture. The first voluntary birth control facility, **Marie Stopes'** Mother's Clinic, was opened in 1921; by 1939 there were seventy such facilities, most of them allied with the newly established Family Planning Association. In addition, with the grudging acquiescence of the Ministry of Health, contraceptive advice was being provided in more than 280 local welfare centers. Most of the clinics were established to assist the working classes, whose greater fertility was a source of numerous concerns and complaints as well as an explanation for the persistence of poverty. In reality, the clinics and welfare centers were visited by a very small proportion of the population between the wars while birth control practices were increasingly adopted by people at every level of society, a pattern that has continued to the present day.

By the mid-1930s the birthrate had fallen so far that there were serious fears that the current generation was no longer even replacing itself and that at some point in the not-to-distant future the population of Great Britain would begin to decline precipitously. This "depopulation panic" preoccupied social reformers and demographic planners throughout the remainder of the decade and on into the Second World War. It stimulated numerous pronatalist schemes to encourage larger families and led to the appointment in 1943 of a Royal Commission on Population, which, when it finally reported in 1949, provided the most comprehensive survey of demographic patterns since the Fertility of Marriage Census of 1911.

As if to demonstrate the unpredictability of determining the domestic strategies of married couples, by the time the commission's findings began to appear the birthrate was already on the rise again from a record low of around 14 per 1,000 in 1941. During the post-war "baby boom" fertility hovered around 20 per 1,000 into the mid-1960s before it began a steady decline toward what some described as a "birth dearth." By the mid-1970s birthrates approached 12.5 per 1,000 before gradually creeping back up to around 13.5 per 1,000, a rate that has persisted more or less to the present day. As a result, the general fertility of women age fifteen to forty-four remains at near 62 per 1,000, while the average number of children born has fallen from 2.4 to 1.8 since the boom ended in 1971, a figure that remains below the replacement level of 2.1 estimated as necessary to sustain the population at its current level.

The effects of diminishing fertility on population size have been moderated by parallel century-long declines in mortality and improvements in longevity. Fueled by striking advances in the reduction of **infant** and childhood **mortality,** overall deathrates fell from 17 to 18 deaths per 1,000 of the population at the end of the Victorian era to approximately 11.5 in recent years. The result has been an increase in life expectancy from fifty-five years to seventy-eight years for women and from fifty-one years to seventy-two years for men. When coupled to the low fertility of modern marriages, these trends have resulted in an aging population in which the percentage of people under fifteen years of age has declined by 3 percent since before the Second World War while the percentage of those over sixty-five years of age has nearly doubled.

The integration of birth control instruction into the family welfare system and the **National Health Service** since the Second World War, coupled to the remarkable technological and biological developments in contraception such as the ubiquitous "pill," have greatly facilitated recent trends in reproduction. But in the broader context of twentieth-century developments the evidence seems to confirm that the post-war baby boom was but a temporary reversal in the decline of family size that began a hundred years ago as part of a social-demographic revolution characteristic today of all Western industrialized countries.

Richard A. Soloway

Bibliography

Coleman, David, and John Salt. *The British Population.* 1992.

Mitchison, Rosalind. *British Population Change since 1860.* 1977.

Soloway, Richard Allen. *Birth Control and the Population Question in England, 1877–1930.* 1982.

———. *Demography and Degeneration: Eugenics and the Declining Birthrate in Twentieth-Century Britain.* 1990.

Teitelbaum, Michael S. *The British Fertility Decline: Demographic Transition in the Crucible of the Industrial Revolution.* 1984.

Tranter, Neil. *Population since the Industrial Revolution: The Case of England and Wales.* 1973.

P

Poster Art

The design and display of posters improved considerably in the late nineteenth and early twentieth centuries, and the advertising posters of the inter-war period deserve special notice as an important channel for the introduction of visual modernism to the public. Beginning with the London Underground, several corporations and government agencies commissioned artists to design posters in "modern" as well as more traditional styles, thereby exposing the public to abstract designs at a time when few museums or galleries would display the new art. Many of these businesses and agencies scaled down their poster production following the Second World War, relying more heavily on **television** and radio as **advertising** media. But by introducing modernist styles of art to a wide public, the seemingly ephemeral advertising poster is assured of a lasting place in histories of British art as well as commerce.

Until the 1880s and 1890s advertising posters tended to be more verbal than pictoral. The development of colored lithography in the 1870s expanded the visual possibilities of the poster; in the 1890s these possibilities, in turn, were influenced by the contemporary vogue for Japanese art, particularly the simple, two-dimensional shapes and pure colors of the Japanese woodblock prints. The new technology and foreign styles were exploited by French poster artists like Toulouse-Lautrec, as well as by several British poster artists at the turn of the century. Among the most famous were the "Beggarstaff Brothers," William Nicholson (1872–1949) and James Pryde (1869–1941), whose collaborative designs of 1893–9 emphasized simple silhouettes and large, flat masses of color. Their efforts to aestheticize advertising posters were supported by members of the arts and crafts movement, such as Walter Crane and W.R. Lethaby, as well as art periodicals such as the *Studio*. Nevertheless, these "artistic" posters remained in the minority, and most advertising posters continued to be displayed in a chaotic fashion across any available free space, leading some artists and critics to form the Society for Checking the Abuses of Public Advertising (SCAPA) in 1893.

The golden age of British poster art really commenced when **Frank Pick** was put in charge of publicity for the London Underground in 1908. Pick, an adherent of the arts and crafts movement, balanced his concern for revenues with his commitment to creating a more aesthetic environment. He hired modern artists to design posters that would convey information about transport services, as well as to educate the public to appreciate the new styles of post-impressionist art. While not all of the posters Pick commissioned were modernist, a substantial number were designed in fauvist, cubist, and surrealist styles, particularly those by artists like E. McKnight Kauffer (1891–1954), **Paul Nash**, and **Graham Sutherland**. Pick supervised the posters' display as well as their design, and the Underground became widely known as "the people's picture gallery."

Pick continued to promote poster art when he directed the poster campaign of the Empire Marketing Board in the years 1926–31. The popularity of the Underground's posters also spurred other corporations and agencies to hire artists like **Ben Nicholson**, Frank Newbold (1887–1951), Austin Cooper (1890–1964), and Tom Purvis (1888–1959) to design posters: Shell-Mex, the Cunard Liners, and the General Post Office were among those organizations that promoted artistic posters during the inter-war period. Although the London Underground's poster production dwindled substantially in the post-war years, the idea that posters could be works of art, and that new styles of art could be conveyed beyond the walls of museums through posters, had become well established.

Michael Saler

Bibliography
Ades, Dawn. *Posters*. 2nd ed. 1990.
Green, Oliver. *Underground Art*. 1990.

Postmodernism in Architecture

Architecture in the last quarter of the twentieth century has manifested two trends, both of which emerged in the 1960s: a modern technological and structural expression, principally in steel and glass, embodied in high-tech design; and a return to premodern historicism, especially evidenced in a postmodern classicism and the neo-vernacular.

Work in the 1960s by James Stirling demonstrated the transition to an industrial aesthetic that consciously expressed the structural and techtonic elements of a building. Stirling and (James) Gowan's Leicester Engineering Laboratories (1959–63) borrowed forms from a factory vernacular, including traditional brick construction and industrial windows. The closed forms of the brick lecture theaters jutted dramatically from either side of the entrance and contrasted with the glass-enriched towers in a composition reminiscent of Constructivist projects. Stirling's History Faculty Library, **Cambridge** (with Michael Wilford, 1964–9), and his Foley Building, Queen's College, **Oxford** (1968), presented greenhouse walls of steel and glass as expressive declarations of the aesthetic potential of the materials of modernism.

Such displays of steel and glass would characterize two phases of late-modern design: a high-modern Miesian aesthetic, as evidenced by American architects' 1960s work in England and by the early work of Norman Foster, and a high-tech structural expressionism promoted initially by popular images of the Archigram Group and evidenced in executed work in Britain from the 1970s on. Eero Saarinen's 1964 Chrysler-Cummins Factory at Darlington continued the late high modernism of Mies Van der Rohe. Kevin Roche and John Dinkaloo's 1965 companion Cummins Factory was a classical steel-and-glass temple with columns and full entablature in cor-ten steel (its first use in Britain) on a steel sylobate. Norman and Wendy Foster (with Richard Rogers) directly expressed the frame and cross-shaped wind bracing at the Reliance Controls Factory, Swindon (1967), a work with corrugated steel cladding in a building that was fast and cheap to erect and American in appearance. In 1974, however, Foster built a highly expressive late-modern steel-and-glass curtain wall that he wrapped around the curved face of the Willis Faber and Dumas Insurance Building in Ipswich.

While the structural histrionics of the Archigram Group envisioned such fanciful mechanistic images as Peter Cook's Plug-In City (1964) or Ron Herron's Walking City (1964), few built works immediately brought to fruition such cartoon-inspired futuristic images of high technology. At the London Zoo, Cedric Price and Lord Snowdon had built an aviary (1962) constructed of steel tubes and glass, with pedestrian paths penetrating the volumes; the resulting experiences in the birds' environment recalled Price's Fun Palace project (1961) with its changeable stage sets for high-technology "happenings." The closest approximation to Archigram's high-tech imagery in a constructed work in London during the 1960s was the Ministry of Public Buildings and Works' Post Office Radio Tower of 1965. However, a dozen years later, a postmodern high-tech presence on the British urban landscape, comparable to Rogers and Renzo Piano's Pompidou Center in Paris (1974–6), was evidenced in London at Rogers' Lloyds' Bank Building (1978–86).

In Britain, the shift from the late-modern Miesian aesthetic to a high-tech display of a building's constructional and service elements was especially evidenced in the work of Norman Foster and is prefigured in his IBM Head Office, Hampshire (1971). Foster's Warehouse and Showroom for Modern Glass Ltd., Thamesmead (1973), more expressively displayed blue stove-enameled corrugated-steel skin enclosing steel portal frames and served as a prototype for the architect's more famous 1978 addition of the Sainsbury Center at the University of East Anglia. Subsequent high-tech works of note include Rogers' Inmos Microprocessor Factory in Gwent, Wales (1982), Foster's Renault Building, Swindon (1982), and Rogers and Michael Hopkins' Schlumberger Research Institute, Cambridge (1984).

The postmodern era also ushered in a return to a history-based aesthetic, finding inspiration in vernacular forms, classical traditions, and premodern British freestyle design. The pastiche dimensions of postmodern historicism are evidenced by the dream-world traditionalism of Clough Williams-Ellis, who at Portmeirion built a Mediterranean resort town in North Wales, and by the "dress up" history (cladding modern office buildings with classical

garb) of the Richmond Development, London (1989), by Quinlin Terry.

An accomplished exercise in postmodern classicism is Robert Venturi's Sainsbury Wing of the National Gallery of Art (1990), whose colossal pilastered facade and staircase succeed as more monumental gestures than William Wilkins' weak dome, the classical focus of the original National Gallery Building of 1832–8. A second postmodern classical work of note is Stirling and Wilford's One Poultry (1989), which employs the same V-windows that Stirling introduced at his Clore Gallery (1987). Both works are remarkable in scale, relating a large but well-proportioned building mass to neighboring classical structures.

On the enlarged urban scale, the pluralism of postmodernism is seen at Broadgate (1986–92), a redevelopment project larger than anything seen in London since the days of Christopher Wren's rebuilding after the Great Fire. At Broadgate (Phases 1–4 by Arup Associates, remaining phases by Skidmore, Owings, and Merrill), various architectural styles cluster around pedestrian squares and maintain a more human scale through what has been called "groundscrapers," skyscrapers turned horizontally. Canary Wharf (Phase 1, 1992), with master planning also by SOM and designs by I.M. Pei, Cesar Pelli, and Kohn Pederson Fox, brings to London an American urbanism of unprecedented scale.

When the more traditional and freestyle languages of recent British architectural history are revived—the Queen Anne, arts and crafts, and Edwardian forms—then the high tech/late modern finds a more humanistic and urbane aesthetic. Contemporary postmodern work by John Melvin broadens the historicist references beyond neo-classicism and Palladianism to artisan mannerism and the English baroque, and British architecture in the 1990s looks once again to Richard Norman Shaw, or even earlier to Wren and John Vanbrugh, for inspiration.

Robert M. Craig

Bibliography
Jencks, Charles. *AD Profile 91: Postmodern Triumphs in London.* 1991.
———. *The Language of Postmodern Architecture.* 1977.
Sudjic, Deyan. *Norman Foster, Richard Rogers, James Stirling: New Directions in British Architecture.* 1986.

Post-War Reconstruction (1916–1922)

Formal planning for post-war Britain began in March 1916 when Prime Minister **H.H. Asquith** appointed several **Cabinet** ministers to a newly created Reconstruction Committee. Its mandate was to coordinate investigations of how the end of the war would affect British society. Senior civil servants on the committee, particularly Vaughan Nash (1861–1932), its Secretary, extended its focus to social reform, especially health care, **housing** needs, and labor-management relations.

After **David Lloyd George** became Prime Minister, he restructured the committee to include such nongovernmental figures as **Beatrice Webb** and Seebohm Rowntree. **Edwin Montagu** proved ineffective as its new Secretary, inhibiting the formulation of reconstruction plans. In July 1917 a new Ministry of Reconstruction under the leadership of one of Lloyd George's political advisers, Christopher Addison (1869–1951), supplanted the committee. Addison recognized that reconstruction issues were crucial to Lloyd George's political future, but his organizational skills were deficient. The Ministry, barely surviving the end of the war, saw its projects reallocated to other departments in January 1919.

After government controls were dismantled in the course of 1919, few social reform schemes remained of the grandiose reconstruction plans. The Housing Act of 1919 funded 60 percent of all new houses built between January 1919 and March 1923. The new Ministry of Health, stemming from Addison's concern with **health** questions, was created, in part, to centralize control of the government's financial commitment to health care and the Poor Law. The **Whitley Council** scheme, designed to improve industrial relations by creating labor-management panels, gained public attention in 1917 and 1918, but neither owners nor labor leaders were enthusiastic about it, and the government appeared to withdraw support during meetings of the National Industrial Conference in the spring of 1919.

Ultimately, reconstruction proposals ran afoul of budgetary constraints, and after the budget crisis of 1922 only the Ministry of Health attempted fitfully to foster social reforms. In contrast to the determination of the Labour government after 1945 to maintain controls and implement post-war planning, Lloyd George yielded to popular and political pressures to scrap regulations and curtail government intervention in the private sector.

James W. Stitt

Bibliography

Johnson, Paul. *Land Fit for Heroes.* 1968.

Lowe, Rodney. *Adjusting to Democracy: The Role of the Ministry of Labour in British Politics, 1916–1939.* 1986.

Morgan, Kenneth O. *Consensus and Disunity: The Lloyd George Coalition Government, 1918–1922.* 1979.

———. *Portrait of a Progressive: The Political Career of Christopher, Viscount Addison.* 1980.

Wrigley, Chris. *Lloyd George and the Challenge of Labour: The Post-War Coalition, 1918–1922.* 1990.

Powell, Anthony Dymoke (1905–)

Anthony Powell is most noted for his vast and intricate sequence novel, *A Dance to the Music of Time* (1951–75). Both comic and melancholy, the work's twelve volumes follow the intersecting lives of colorful British acquaintances from 1914 to 1971 as they drift apart and come together again, most often unexpectedly, until death thins their ranks. Some of *A Dance*'s complex temporal patterns resemble those of Marcel Proust's *A la recherche du temps perdu*, but Powell's sense of humor more closely resembles that of major British comic writers such as Jane Austen and **Evelyn Waugh**.

Powell was descended on his father's side from Welsh princes of the twelfth and thirteenth century and on his mother's from English squires and parsons. Because of his father's military career—a disappointing one that left him at the rank of lieutenant colonel—Anthony Powell and his mother lived through many nomadic moves. Young Powell received his first schooling at Bordon Camp near Aldershot from a female tutor who arrived on a bicycle. He went next to a London day school, to a preparatory boarding school in Kent, to Eton, and finally to Balliol College, **Oxford**.

In 1926 Powell began a three-year editorial apprenticeship at the publisher Duckworth. He sold Duckworth his own first novel, *Afternoon Men* (1931), as well as *Venusberg* (1932), *From a View to a Death* (1933), and *Agents and Patients* (1936). He left publishing to write film scripts for "quota quickies," movies churned out in England by Hollywood studios to meet the protectionist requirement of a certain percentage of British-made films. Next he supported himself by reviews in the *Daily Telegraph* and occasionally the *Spectator*. He also published a fifth pre-war novel, *What's Become of Waring?* (1939).

Powell's 1930s novels have merit. In *Afternoon Men*, a Hemingway-like brevity merges with a nonchalant mockery reminiscent of **Ronald Firbank** to produce subacid comedy about mindless pleasure seekers. The ironic *Venusberg* deals with a seemingly casual love affair that deepens unexpectedly just before the heroine's sudden death. *From a View to a Death* resembles a sexier and grubbier Meredith's *The Egoist*: Powell's ultimately thwarted fortune hunter, Zouch, seduces one woman and proposes to another in the course of twenty-four hours. *Agents and Patients* creates humor out of accidental meetings and aimless moving to and fro, rather like the movements of a silent film comedy. From this pre-war period, only *What's Become of Waring?* disappoints the reader, because of its excessively elaborate farcical plot.

The **Second World War** halted Powell's fiction for six years. He requested and got assignment to a Welsh battalion. But in spite of his effort to plunge into combat, this middle-aged officer participated only in military paper shuffling. Shifted away from his battalion before it saw action, he served as liaison for Allied attachés at the War Office in London. Yet war itself enriched Powell's later fiction by showing him the transitory nature of all that he had known.

After writing the antiquarian *John Aubrey and His Friends* (1948) and supporting himself in subsequent years by book review editorships with the *Times Literary Supplement* and *Punch* and also by his own reviewing, Powell at age forty-five began his largest undertaking—*A Dance to the Music of Time*. In addition, he published two minor comic plays: *The Garden God* (1971) and *The Rest I'll Whistle* (1971). Having completed *A Dance* at age sixty-nine, in his seventies and eighties Powell continued writing: an amusing four-volume memoir, *To Keep the Ball Rolling* (1976–82); a comic novella, *O, How the Wheel Becomes It!* (1983); and an impressively ironic one-volume novel, *The Fisher King* (1986).

Robert L. Selig

Bibliography

Powell, Anthony. *To Keep the Ball Rolling: The Memoirs of Anthony Powell.* 4 vols. 1976–82.

Selig, Robert L. *Time and Anthony Powell: A Critical Study.* 1991.

Spurling, Hilary. *Invitation to the Dance: A Guide to Anthony Powell's Dance to the Music of Time.* 1978.

Powell, Michael (1905–1990)

As a filmmaker, Michael Powell rose to fame during the Second World War after making a series of "quota quickies" during the 1930s. Rejecting the dominant realist mode of British cinema, he maintained that film is a medium more suited to fantasy, and he distrusted the claims of contemporary **documentary film** makers that film could mirror life. As such, his films explore surreality, super-reality, and the practice of filmmaking itself.

His career started in Rex Ingram's (1893–1950) film unit near Nice. Moving to Britain, he worked as a stills photographer on **Alfred Hitchcock's** *Champagne* (1928) and as screenwriter on Hitchcock's first talkie, *Blackmail* (1929). Powell's first major film was *On the Edge of the World* (1937). Set on a Scottish island, it already contained elements of the mystic relationship of people and nature that emerged in his later films. During 1939 he was introduced to Emeric Pressburger (1902–88) by Alexander Korda (1893–1956), for whom he was then working, in order that Pressburger could tighten the script of *The Spy in Black* (1939). The partnership with Pressburger, lasting until 1956, produced a series of films that achieved prominence during the war, including *49th Parallel* (1941) and *One of Our Aircraft Is Missing* (1942).

Their most significant achievements were *A Matter of Life and Death* (1946), chosen as the first Royal Command film; *The Red Shoes* (1948); and the wartime epic *The Life and Death of Colonel Blimp* (1943), their most controversial film, which **Winston Churchill** tried to have banned.

Films like *A Canterbury Tale* (1944) and *I Know Where I'm Going* (1945) explored the interconnectedness of history, tradition, nature, and human nature, which also helped keep *Gone to Earth* (1950) from being a conventional melodrama. Powell's films seemed to cross traditional genre boundaries, none of them fitting comfortably within precise categories. The sublimation of the erotic into the *mise-en-scène* of *Black Narcissus* (1947) created an intensely powerful film, equally notable for its re-creation of the Himalayas in a studio by photographing landscapes painted onto grass.

Powell and Pressburger, releasing their movies under the Archers' signature, made one film each year during the war but seemed to lose touch with popular taste in the post-war years. *The Red Shoes*, their last success, earned an Oscar for Art Director Hein Heckroth, who deserves credit for the visually stunning effects of several Archers' films. It followed the fortunes of a ballerina torn between a career and marriage, symbolically playing out the dilemma of many other women during that period; the ballet dancer also reflected the prominence that British **ballet** had achieved during the war. The morbidity of the fairy tale story was reassessed and reviled in 1960 when Powell released his first major film without Pressburger for twenty years. *Peeping Tom* is self-consciously about filmmaking and film viewing. A powerful study of voyeurism in its plot of a young photographer/filmmaker who uses a camera with a spike to stab young women so that he may film them as they die, it has been taken up as the subject of **feminist** debate about the gendered psychological processes of cinema viewing.

After the shocked reception of *Peeping Tom* (made at the same time as Hitchcock's *Psycho*), Powell found it increasingly difficult to secure financial backing, although he did make two films in Australia, one of which was written by Pressburger under the pseudonym Richard Imrie. However, during the 1970s a number of British critics and film theorists helped revive Powell's reputation, which eventually led to the reprinting of some films for the National Film Archive, a season at the National Film Theater, and a series on **British Broadcasting Corporation** (BBC) television.

Initially Powell was rediscovered within auteur theories of the cinema, but later the uniquely shared roles were acknowledged. In their films between 1943 and 1956, the credits read: written, directed, and produced by Michael Powell and Emeric Pressburger. A number of American filmmakers of the 1980s acknowledged the significant impact of the Archers' films on their own craft. Francis Ford Coppola made *One from the Heart* (1982) as a homage to Powell, who was then working in his Hollywood studio, and Martin Scorcese has consistently cited Powell's influence on his work. Powell died in February 1990 while completing the second volume of his autobiography, *A Life in Movies.*

Nannette Aldred

Bibliography
Aldred, Nannette. "A Canterbury Tale: Powell and Pressburger's Film Fantasies of Britain" in David Mellor, ed. *A Paradise Lost*. 1987. pp. 117–25.
Christie, Ian. *Arrows of Desire: The Films of Michael Powell and Emeric Pressburger*. 1985.
Durgnat, Raymond. *A Mirror for England*. 1970.
Powell, Michael. *A Life in Movies*. 1986.
———. *Million Dollar Movie*. 1990.

Powys, John Cowper (1872–1963)

John Cowper Powys, English novelist, essayist, and poet, is most celebrated for the massive novel *A Glastonbury Romance* (1932), which portrays the contemporary political, erotic, and visionary conflicts that environ the staging of a pageant about Christ's passion and the Holy Grail on the island-city of Glastonbury. Typical of all of Powys' voluminous work, *A Glastonbury Romance* blurs distinctions between history and myth, reality and magic, in a way that has attracted readers and writers but has baffled **literary criticism**. However, the distinguished critic G. Wilson Knight persuasively argues a minority opinion steadily gaining ground: that Powys' work belongs in the company of modernist classics such as **D.H. Lawrence**'s *Women in Love*, **James Joyce**'s *Finnegans Wake*, and **Virginia Woolf**'s *Between the Acts*.

Powys' father, a puritanical **Anglican** priest, settled his family in Weymouth, whose associations with the life and work of Thomas Hardy early influenced John Cowper Powys. The eldest of seven children, he studied **history** at **Cambridge** and aspired to be a poet. After Cambridge he became an itinerant tutor and, more formatively, an employee of a lecture bureau, which sent him in 1905 to address American audiences on literary and cultural topics.

Success on the American lecture circuit kept Powys traveling and delivering inspiration talks for the better part of thirty years, during which time the work of American writers Edgar Arlington Robinson and Theodore Dreiser might have especially influenced him. Although he married in 1896 and fathered a son, his long absences from England helped dissolve the marriage. Powys did not return to live in England until 1934, when he settled in Dorset with Phyllis Plater, his companion until his death.

Powys' second novel, *Rodmoor* (1916), published in America, is his first distinguished work. Suggesting that destruction is "the ultimate essence of life," *Rodmoor* launches Powys' lifelong meditation (both Freudian and anti-Freudian) on the role of sadism and masochism in cultural life and visionary experience. Other works written in America include *Wolf Solent* (1929), a rewriting of Hardy's *Jude the Obscure*; a critical study, *Dorothy M. Richardson*, which celebrates **Richardson's feminism** and her assertion of "the desirability of bisexual awareness"; *A Glastonbury Romance*; Powys' *Autobiography* (1934); and *Weymouth Sands* (1934), a sociological and erotic panorama that includes portraits of the novelist-artist as a vaudeville clown, a puppet-master, and a fetishist.

With *Maiden Castle* (1936) Powys took up an interest in Welsh culture, history, and mythology that shaped the remainder of his career. "No-man," an unworldly historical novelist and researcher of Welsh legends in *Maiden Castle*, stands for Powys, whose *Owen Glendower* (1942) might well have been the fruit of No-man's research. *Porius* (1951) and *The Brazen Head* (1956) extend the series of historical novels about Wales, even as they experiment with the form of historical fiction and stretch the boundaries of the genre. In 1955 Powys moved to Blaenau Festiniog in Wales, where in 1962 he was awarded an honorary doctorate by the University of Wales. But in spite of his focus on Welsh materials, throughout the same period Powys was prolific in other directions. His critical studies, *Dostoievsky* (1947) and *Rabelais* (1948), are important statements of his own poetics of the novel and further develop ideas about fiction found in *Morwyn* (1937), a fantasia about vivisection and the afterlife, dominated by the Marquis de Sade and Rabelais. Pure fantasia rules Powys' last works, *Up and Out* (1957) and *All or Nothing* (1960).

In 1947, in a collection of critical essays, *Obstinate Cymric*, Powys writes enthusiastically about *Finnegans Wake*, a work whose obvious modernist experimentation seems antithetical to his romances, which are in a tradi-

tion as old as Spenser's *The Faerie Queene*. Not just Powys' form, but his very language looks premodernist next to Joyce's, but these are deceiving appearances. Under the guise of traditional patterns, Powys' language and structures innovate no less than *Ulysses*. His works pursue an internal disjunctiveness and resistance to coherence that is both modernist and postmodernist, and their excess of narrative complication becomes a parody of narrative tradition.

The importance Powys explicitly assigns to infantile sexuality, to allegedly non-normative sexual desires and fixations, and to scatology mark him as a modernist explorer of eros. Mistakenly evaluated as to his place in literary history, Powys has also been wrongly assessed as a writer whose mystical and fantastic components cannot come to terms with sociological and political realities. Yet the power of his work lies in its suggestion that political society cannot be created in purely political and social terms, but needs a supplementary constitution by means of erotic and mystical elements, no matter how perverse the latter elements might appear to be.

Robert L. Caserio

Bibliography
Collins, H.P. *John Cowper Powys.* 1966.
Graves, R.P. *The Brothers Powys.* 1983.
Knight, G. Wilson. *Neglected Powers.* 1971.
———. *The Saturnian Quest.* 1964.
Lane, Dennis, ed. *In the Spirit of Powys.* 1990.

Prayer Book Revision

The Book of Common Prayer contains the liturgical rites of the **Church of England** and is of literary, historical, and theological importance within English culture. Its revisions in the twentieth century have been controversial, revealing much about the character of the Church and its relationship with state and society.

For 250 years the authorized prayer book was *The Book of Common Prayer*, adopted by Parliament in 1662. Liturgical controversy led in 1904 to the creation of a Royal Commission that called for prayer book reform. Work officially began in 1906, and discussion focused on questions about ritual and liturgy left vague after the Reformation, but little consensus was achieved. Then, in 1925, amid conflicting comments from the several theological "parties," Anglo-Catholic, liberal, and evangelical, concrete proposals for reform emerged, which were finally adopted by the Church Assembly in 1927. However, opposition remained, surfacing in Parliament, where the proposed prayer book was sent for approval, only to be narrowly defeated in the House of Commons.

Further revisions, adopted by the Church Assembly in 1928, were again defeated in the Commons. This provoked a minor crisis in Church-state relations, the bishops claiming that the Church alone had the right to determine its forms of worship. Accordingly, they authorized the new prayer book. However, lacking official parliamentary sanction, and rejected by major theological wings of the Church, the 1928 version did not greatly prosper, leaving 1662 as the official prayer book.

The second major phase of reform began in earnest following the 1958 Lambeth Conference, not least because the 1662 book was by now 300 years old. In 1965 approval was finally given, both by the Church Assembly and the Parliament, to authorize the 1928 book as an official alternative to the 1662 book for seven years beginning in 1966. Thus was created the *Alternative Services: First Series* prayer book, or Series One. This opened floodgates of liturgical renewal, spurred by Parliament finally granting the Church a degree of autonomy in regulating liturgy in 1974.

Series One was followed immediately by a further set of alternative liturgies between 1966 and 1971 collectively known as Series Two. Then a third set, Series Three, began to appear in 1973, in which modern English was first used on a substantial scale, ending with a new Communion service in 1979. All three sets were then gathered into an *Alternative Service Book* (1980), authorized by the General Synod for use, alongside the 1662 book, initially for ten years, but then until 2000. Although controversy was stirred again, the provision of alternative liturgies eased the situation. Since 1980 the Church has operated with the two prayers books of 1980 and 1662.

George Moyser

Bibliography

The Alternative Service Book, 1980. 1980.
Cuming, G.J. *A History of Anglican Liturgy.* 2nd ed. 1982.

Pregnancy and Childbirth

Women's experience of pregnancy and childbirth at the end of the twentieth century in Britain, as in other Western countries, is associated with a high degree of medical and **hospital** involvement. In 1985 99 percent of all women in England and Wales gave birth in hospitals. This contrasts with the pattern at the beginning of the century. In 1900 the majority of women gave birth at home. By 1927, however, 15 percent of all births took place in an institution; by 1946, 53.7 percent. While the number of hospital births remained constant at approximately 65 percent during the 1950s, the figure increased substantially in the 1960s and 1970s. The shifts that have taken place in the location of births also reflect the wider changes that have occurred in women's experience of pregnancy and childbirth in the twentieth century.

At the beginning of the century childbirth was primarily a private domestic affair between mothers and those they chose to attend them. During succeeding decades, however, childbirth has increasingly become a public event, which no longer relies solely on the decisions of a mother and her birth attendant but involves a range of medical and lay experts, municipal and hospital bodies, as well as charitable and government authorities. This has had far-reaching implications for the social and cultural perceptions surrounding pregnancy and childbirth. Indeed, pregnancy and childbirth, formerly viewed as a natural physiological phenomenon, has increasingly become regarded as a hazardous and dangerous event, necessitating expert medical attention and intervention.

Much of this change was linked to anxiety over the persistently high rates of maternal mortality. Unlike other forms of mortality, which began to diminish from the 1870s, and **infant mortality**, which had begun to fall after 1906, maternal mortality remained high, and even rose in the 1920s and 1930s. Before the late 1930s, after **tuberculosis**, deaths in childbed were the most common cause of death among women of childbearing age. Between 1855 and 1934 the maternal death rate in England and Wales averaged 4.6 per 1,000 live births, amounting to 3,000 to 4,000 deaths a year. The major cause of these deaths was puerperal sepsis, followed by hemorrhages and toxemia. There has been extensive debate by historians about the determinants of high maternal mortality in these years, but most agree that before the late 1930s the quality of obstetric care was probably more important than social and economic factors.

While maternal mortality was the subject of a number of medical reports in the 1870s, it became a national concern for many statesmen and medical experts in the years following the First World War. What was particularly worrying was that, unlike infant mortality, maternal mortality had not declined, despite measures taken to train and regulate midwives (through the Midwives' Act of 1902), the provision of a range of maternal and infant welfare services, and the introduction of maternity benefit in 1913. Their concern was reinforced by a massive public outcry over the sharp rise in maternal mortality in the 1920s and 1930s.

The debate during these years centered on the influence on maternal mortality of social and economic factors, such as poor **nutrition** and bad **housing**, or clinical practice. The need for more preventive action, including better prenatal care, hospital provision, more clinics, and improved training of midwives and doctors, was stressed. This policy change was not only promoted by many medical professionals, but also requested by women campaigners, who called for improved social and economic conditions alongside greater hospital provision and pain relief.

The 1936 Midwives Act answered some of these demands, making it obligatory for every local authority to provide an adequate salaried domiciliary service. Together with the introduction of sulfonamides, this played a vital part in reducing maternal mortality. Maternity services were extended during the Second World War, when consultant services were made more widely available, and blood transfusion and penicillin were introduced. After 1948 the **National Health Service** also provided a well-coordinated and high standard of obstetric care free to all mothers.

Yet despite these advances and the fall in maternal mortality, disputes have continued over jurisdiction in the management of childbirth. While much of the earlier tension was between the midwife and the obstetrician, recently many women, particularly those involved in the National Childbirth Trust, have also begun to argue for greater control over their own bodies, control that they see as having been diminished by increased medical intervention and hospital care since the 1960s.

Lara Marks

Bibliography

Campbell, R., and A. Macfarlane. *Where to be Born? The Debate and the Evidence.* 1987.

Garcia, Jo, Robert Kilpatrick, and Martin Richards, eds. *The Politics of Maternity Care: Services for Childbearing Women in Twentieth Century Britain.* 1990.

Loudon, Irvine. *Death in Childbirth: An International Study of Maternal Care and Maternal Mortality, 1800–1950.* 1992.

Oakley, Ann. *The Captured Womb: A History of the Medical Care of Pregnant Women.* 1984.

Tew, M. *Safer Childbirth? A Critical History of Maternity Care.* 1990.

Press, British

The United Kingdom in the 1990s can still boast twelve daily and nine Sunday newspapers available nationwide. In addition, Scotland, Northern Ireland, and, to a lesser degree, Wales retain their own titles and traditions. Regular and substantial advertising revenue supports an extensive regional press; local evening newspapers are complemented by a few surviving morning editions in the Midlands, the north, and the west of England. A century earlier, local daily and weekly newspapers were a common phenomenon, but improved distribution methods during and after the **First World War** facilitated easier access to the metropolitan press. The same period witnessed the demise of the "newspapers of opinion": London-based daily and evening forums of Liberal debate, their readers scarcely evident beyond the clubland of St. James. The disappearance of titles such as the *Westminster Gazette* reflected not only the rise of **Labour** at the expense of the **Liberal Party**, but also the emergence of heavily subscribed, genuinely national newspapers, each tailored to a mass audience happy to accept less copy, larger headlines, more photographs, and maximum **advertising**.

Throughout the twentieth century the British press has played a uniquely central role in the political process. Prominent and powerful proprietors have not been averse to assuming office, particularly during the two World Wars, while in peacetime Conservative **Cabinets** have invariably included ministers whose wealth is based upon extensive media interests. No less than three Labour leaders— **Ramsay MacDonald, George Lansbury,** and

Michael Foot—have edited newspapers, their Parliamentary Party since the 1920s boasting a disproportionate number of journalists. Governments, particularly if **Conservative**, liaise regularly with the owners and editors of sympathetic newspapers, relying on the honors system to reward loyalty and obeisance. During and after the First World War, **David Lloyd George** proved that neither was the Liberal Party averse to cultivating Fleet Street, even to the extent of his purchasing the *Daily News*.

In no other liberal democracy does the impact of editorial bias upon public opinion, and in particular voting behavior, generate such intensity of debate, most recently in the aftermath of the 1992 general election. Similarly, the tension between what government judges the public "needs to know," and what the media assumes people are "entitled to know," highlights an historic concern over the control and management of information. Uniquely British institutions survive, battered but intact, most notably the Lobby: Westminster and Whitehall's elite of authorized correspondents, heavily dependent upon unattributable leaks and briefings delivered "off the record" by ministers, opposition leaders, or their spokespersons.

Three facets of the modern British press are evident: the unusual degree of partisanship, the consolidation of newspaper ownership, and the continuing importance of personality. Countless correspondents, columnists, and cartoonists have become celebrities in their own right, respective examples being the *News Chronicle*'s James Cameron, the *Daily Mirror*'s "Cassandra" and the *Evening Standard*'s **David Low**. Yet, the dominant personalities since 1900 have been proprietors, and, to a much lesser degree, their editors. The golden age for editors was between the wars: the *The Times*' Geoffrey Dawson and the *Observer*'s J.L. Garvin were nearly as famous as their newspapers. Yet interwar contemporaries such as Express Newspaper's **Lord Beaverbrook** or Associated Newspapers' Lord Rothermere were, rightly or wrongly, seen as the power brokers of high politics. Newspaper groups were under the *de facto* control of individuals or families that held majority shareholdings. These companies in a few cases became trusts, of which the *Manchester Guardian* was the best-known example (transfer to London in 1959 saw "Manchester" dropped from the masthead). More often they became absorbed into large holding companies

with diverse interests, witness the *Observer*'s sale to Atlantic Richfield, and then to Lonrho, but then to the *Guardian*.

Nevertheless, the chief executive or chairman still wielded extensive management and editorial powers, enjoying the high profile secured by running a famous title. Thus, the original "press barons" made way for "multimedia" tycoons, some of whom were themselves ennobled. Those who were not, notably Rupert Murdoch and Robert Maxwell, reveled in their influence and notoriety across at least three continents. Just as the Harmsworth brothers—the future **Lords Northcliffe** and Rothermere—had exploited late-Victorian technology to pioneer a mass-circulation popular press via the *Daily Mail*, so a century later Murdoch harnessed a favorable political climate, and a revolution in telecommunications and printing/publishing, to pursue equally aggressive marketing methods.

The **Boer War** and then the **First World War** had fueled the British public's hunger for news, albeit massaged by a largely voluntary system of **censorship**, and Fleet Street's enthusiasm for xenophobic **propaganda**. The popular press consolidated the advances made during the "Northcliffe Revolution" of the 1890s, and in the inter-war years the *Daily Express*, *Daily Mail*, and initially Labour-controlled *Daily Herald* relied on ever-more outrageous promotions to maintain individual circulations in the millions. The **Second World War** and after saw the tabloid *Daily Mirror* secure its position as the principal working-class newspaper for the next twenty-five years. Merger and closure resulted in the *Daily Mirror* after 1970 being Labour's only guaranteed supporter in Fleet Street, the *Daily Herald* ultimately metamorphosizing into Murdoch's stridently pro-Tory *Sun*. With the *Daily Express* and *Daily Mail* striving to widen their primarily lower-middle-class readership with only modest success, efforts to secure and retain average sales of 4 million focused upon the two major tabloids (and Express Newspapers' 1980s attempt to go down-market, the *Daily Star*).

The *Daily Mirror* boasted a laudable record of campaigning and hard news reporting, but the challenge of the *Sun* forced it to move away from reportage to personality features and show business gossip. News International's repackaging of the *News of the World* as a *de facto* sister tabloid to the *Sun* had a similar impact upon the *Sunday Mirror*. By the

1990s the priority given to soap opera stars or royalty, and the total lack of balance in reporting in domestic politics, led to hefty libel awards against allegedly intrusive tabloids, and the establishment of the popularly perceived "independent" **British Broadcasting Corporation** (BBC) and ITN as the principal sources of hard news. The general public's continuing respect for the integrity of terrestrial public-service broadcasting antagonized Murdoch and the present Lord Rothermere, major shareholders in the BSkyB satellite television service. Relentless promotion of News International's nonprint interests is most evident in its tabloids, the aforementioned *Sun* and *News of the World*, and *Today* (bought from the original pioneer of information technology [IT]-based national newspaper production in the United Kingdom, Eddie Shah); but mass advertising and "loaded" copy extends to its upmarket "quality" newspapers, *The Times* and the *Sunday Times*.

Internationally if perhaps no longer at home, *The Times* retains its "Establishment" image, while the *Sunday Times* remains the market leader, despite having moved sharply to the Right since Murdoch's purchase in 1981. Previously, under the editorship of Harold Evans, the *Sunday Times* was the first weekend broadsheet to promote in-depth investigative journalism, multisections, and color supplements. Ironically, Evans' equally professional and innovative successor, Andrew Neill, is now more widely known as a maverick figure of the Right unconcerned by accusations of having sullied his newspaper's reputation in its unashamed promotion of Sky and then BSkyB TV. The *Sunday Times*' traditional rival is the *Observer*, but further competition comes from the all-week *Independent* and the *Daily/Sunday Telegraph*. The recent emergence of cost-conscious seven-days publishing parallels a move to Saturday as the main focus of multisectioned reading, witness the *Guardian*'s larger weekend format and continued absence on Sundays. As in the 1960s the volume of review and opinion available on Sundays heralded a dramatic decline in sales of major weeklies such as the *Spectator* and **New Statesman**, so thirty years later the *Observer* and others struggle to retain sales and advertising at a time when even Saturday's *Financial Times* boasts saturation sports and arts coverage. Bucking the trend is the tabloid *Mail on Sunday*, which in the early 1990s initiated a modest move upmarket and in so doing nearly doubled its circulation. Skillful editing ensured the retention of older lower-middle-class readers and the recruitment of a younger, well-educated audience with a level of disposable income such as to generate substantial advertising revenue.

The *Mail on Sunday*'s success in not alienating readers shared with its sister paper, the *Daily Mail*, demonstrates that title loyalty (if not necessarily identification with the opinions and values espoused by the particular title) remains a distinct feature of the British newspaper industry. It also highlights the potential for recruiting fresh readers, and not simply at the expense of rival's circulations. The unique variety of newspapers in the United Kingdom notwithstanding, there still exists a large pool of potential new readers. Despite exaggerated fears of a future semiliterate society, courtesy of multiple television channels, video films, and computer games, the future for the British press looks by no means bleak. A decade of industrial upheaval in the 1980s ended with a reasonably efficient and cost-effective industry ready to embrace the next generation of media-related information technology. The price of such stability had been hundreds of print workers' jobs, journalists who placed a high premium on integrity, independence, and individuality, and, above all, Fleet Street itself. Within high-tech plants scattered around or even beyond central London are cost-conscious managers and editors, their computer monitors revealing up-to-the-minute stories and up-to-the-minute spreadsheets. For most enterprises new technology and new methods brought the Holy Grail of sustained profitability. The price was—if it ever existed in the first place—romance.

Adrian Smith

Bibliography
Boyce, George, James Curran, and Pauline Wingate, eds. *Newspaper History from the Seventeenth Century to the Present Day*. 1978.
Curran, James, and Jean Seaton. *Power without Responsibility: The Press and Broadcasting in Britain*. 4th ed. 1991.
Koss, Stephen. *The Rise and Fall of the Political Press in Britain*. 2 vols. 1981–4.
Seaton, Jean, and Ben Pimlott, eds. *The Media in British Politics*. 1987.
Seymour-Ure, Colin. *The British Press and Broadcasting since 1945*. 1991.

Priestley, J(ohn) B(oynton) (1894–1984)

In the 1930s and 1940s few writers were as widely read and well loved in Britain as J.B. Priestley. The publication of *The Good Companions* (1929) catapulted him to fame, the book selling over 1 million copies. In the following decades he became a prolific broadcaster, essayist, novelist, playwright, screenwriter, and social critic, his voluminous output totaling more than 100 books. In the early 1940s he was second only to **Winston Churchill** as the public voice of the nation at war. A populist, a self-proclaimed socialist, and a fierce critic of mass culture and state regimentation, Priestley was a keen observer of social change and an avid storyteller of the lives of ordinary people who attempted heroically to keep their heads above water in an increasingly complex world.

Born in Bradford ("Bruddersfield" in his novels), Priestley grew up in a Nonconformist lower-middle-class household and immersed himself in the world of Edwardian, provincial **popular culture.** He wrote frequently for the socialist *Bradford Pioneer*, championing a whole way of life that he later claimed ended abruptly in the trenches of the First World War. After a brief career in the **army,** Priestley studied English literature at **Cambridge** and moved to London, where he became a free-lance writer. While he was praised for his topical essays, and while his first novel, *Adam in Moonshine* (1927), was a modest success, it was *The Good Companions* (1929), a novel about the fortunes of a third-rate traveling concert troupe, that placed his name on the literary map. Equally successful was his next major novel, *Angel Pavement* (1930), a brilliant fictional portrait of lower-middle-class life in London.

In the 1930s success followed success for Priestley. He spent much time in the United States, where he wrote screenplays for Hollywood while developing an intense dislike of American mass culture. His criticism of mass culture surfaced in many of his works, particularly *Journey down a Rainbow* (1955), written with his third wife, Jacquetta Hawkes. In Britain his reputation as a dramatist in the 1930s was established through a number of plays, ranging from conventional comedies to experimental plays that dealt with the philosophy of time. His most notable plays in this decade were *Dangerous Corner* (1932), *Laburnum Grove* (1934), *Eden End* (1934), *Time and the Conways* (1937), *I Have Been Here Before* (1937), *When We Are Married* (1938), and

Johnson over Jordan (1939). In addition to writing two screenplays for the popular working-class comedienne Gracie Fields and a comic novel dealing with similar themes, *Let the People Sing* (1939), Priestley wrote two serious, documentary novels in the 1930s, *Wonder Hero* (1933) and *They Walk in the City* (1936). He also became an outspoken social critic during the Depression, vividly describing the state of the nation in *English Journey* (1934). His attack on the class system, plutocrats, media moguls, and the policies of **Neville Chamberlain** won him a sympathetic following, although he remained suspicious of the **Labour Party** and championed a sentimental and populist brand of socialism that harked back to the patriotic radicalism of William Cobbett and **Robert Blatchford.**

During the **Second World War** Priestley became famous for his "Postscripts," broadcast on the radio on Sunday evenings following the nine o'clock news. In attempting to define the enduring qualities of Englishness for his many listeners, Priestley looked both back to the golden age of his remembered Edwardian childhood and forward to a more egalitarian future. Both themes later resurfaced in one of his most successful novels, *Bright Day* (1946). After a brief period of infatuation with Richard Acland's independent Forward March political movement and the independent Common Wealth Party, Priestley campaigned tirelessly for the cultural, political, and spiritual renewal of British society. In the polemical tracts he wrote, in plays like *They Came to a City* (1944), and in his demobilization novel, *Three Men in New Suits* (1945), Priestley imagined a bold new order in which all of the virtues he identified with the English people at their best would flourish.

After the war Priestley became a disillusioned critic of the post-war settlement, attacking the materialism, mass culture, and conformity of the age. Although he was one of the most enthusiastic supporters of the **Festival of Britain** and wrote *Festival at Farbridge* (1951), a comic novel about a town in the Midlands attempting to stage its own festival, Priestley's reputation began to fade. Following his brief involvement in the early days of the **Campaign for Nuclear Disarmament,** Priestley turned once again to fiction to dramatize his discontent with the post-war world, culminating in perhaps his best novel, *The Image Men* (1968), a satirical romp through the world of public relations, advertising, the press, and government. More and more, however, he retreated into a world of nostalgia for the past, captured poignantly in his novel of Edwardian music-hall life, *Lost Empires* (1965), in his illustrated social history, *The Edwardians* (1970), and in various essays, published in *The English* (1973) and *Lost and Found: The English Way of Life* (1976).

Despite his widespread appeal in the 1930s and 1940s, Priestley's literary reputation has declined significantly. Although some of his plays are still performed, virtually all of his novels are out of print. An immensely popular novelist with the middlebrow reading public, Priestley fared less well with the critics. F.R. Leavis, for example, championed modernist writers and often belittled Priestley's work; likewise, George Orwell viewed him as a blatantly second-rate novelist. And yet for many decades Priestley both entertained the nation and became one of its foremost social critics. *English Journey* still offers an evocative portrait of England during the Depression, while his better novels vividly capture the trials and tribulations of ordinary people in their attempts to make sense of the world around them and their roles in it.

Chris Waters

Bibliography

Brome, Vincent. *J.B. Priestley*. 1988.
Day, Alan Edwin. *J.B. Priestley: An Annotated Bibliography*. 1980.
Priestley, J.B. *Instead of Trees: A Final Chapter of Autobiography*. 1977.
———. *Margin Released: A Writer's Reminiscences and Reflections*. 1962.
Waters, Chris. "J.B. Priestley, 1894–1984: Englishness and the Politics of Nostalgia" in Susan Pedersen and Peter Mandler, eds. *After the Victorians: Private Conscience and Public Duty in Modern Britain*. 1994. pp. 209–26.

Primary Education

Before the First World War education for children between ages three and ten was provided free in elementary schools, which were run by a mixture of church and local authority bodies after the 1902 Education Act. In these schools children were taught in large groups by teachers who had begun to be qualified, under a formal regimented system. They sat on long benches, facing the teacher, and learned to read and write on slates by a process of verbal repetition. All days began with some formal religious assembly. Terms ran from September to July with breaks at Easter and Christmas. Teachers could and did use physical punishment to discipline their charges. All schools kept a record of the day's proceedings in logbooks, which have provided a valuable source for historical work on child life before 1918. Schools were mostly local, with one provided in almost every village.

Most reforms in schooling stemming from the 1918 Fisher Education Act were in secondary education. Primary schooling was changed by the eradication of child labor, which had been allowed before 1918 by license in individual cases provided children were attending some schooling, or collectively through half-time attendance for those over age ten. Reform without legislation was achieved by improving the training of teachers and relaxing some of the more formal aspects of instruction that were ineffective in eliminating illiteracy and in educating for work and adult life. Nature study and history became subjects in which children were encouraged to use imaginative skills. The Inspectorate of Schools, an independent body responsible to the Crown, helped spread good practice by encouraging it in their reports. However, the interests of higher goals also imposed some contraints upon teachers in the elementary system: The increasing significance of eleven-plus examinations meant that resources were often concentrated on children who might get scholarships and go on to special free places in secondary school. This exam concentrated on English, arithmetic, and verbal reasoning/intelligence tests, so schools were dominated by testing for ten-year-olds and nearly all schools were tracked by ability.

The biggest inequality between children of this age was the rural-urban divide. In cities elementary schools were improving educational quality by separating children into age specific junior and senior sections and providing a differentiated, progressive curriculum. Rural schools tended to place children of all ages together with one teacher and a common program of teaching across the ages, sometimes with low expectations on the part of teachers.

The Consultative Committee on Education, chaired by Sir Henry Hadow, published *The Primary School* in 1931, which suggested differentiation of children beyond that warranted by secondary-education selection through tracking within the primary school. It recommended that large schools follow a "triple-track system" of organization on the basis of ability. City children were then described according to their level of intelligence, usually as measured by tests. On the other hand, the same report argued for "activity and experience" rather than "facts" and "knowledge." Inspectors and teachers could interpret this statement either as a call for more attention to the highest achievers among children in primary education or a demand for a liberalized curriculum. Wartime arrangements were equally ambiguous in leaving teachers to get on with their task with limited central scrutiny or support.

In the post-war reorganization of education, primary schooling was ended at age eleven, although some authorities developed middle schools, which took nine- to thirteen-year-olds. Much of the new school building was in the primary sector since the rising birthrate fed an expanded population into the infant and junior schools from 1951 on. Architects developed open-plan classrooms where work was undertaken on tables rather than desks, and homework was reduced except for "scholarship" pupils. Art and craft teaching reflected increased concern for visual edcuation, with Marion Richardson-style writing becoming the norm.

Sociologists have contributed much on the procedures and effects of primary schooling. In J.W.B. Douglas' *The Home and the School* (1964), based on a longitudinal study of a large group of children, educational success or failure was attributed largely to the influence of the home. The Plowden Committee of 1967 investigated reading and encouraged mixed-ability teaching and learning as a means of encouraging higher levels of achievement for students at the lower end of the ability range. Disadvantage was attacked by introducing "educational priority areas," which were given extra staff and resources to iron out inequalities. Migration from the new Commonwealth nations was thus dealt with successfully, although rich migrant cultures tended to be treated as problems by educational administrators. Class rather than race remained the main theoretical concept explaining inequalities in outcome.

Educational standards became a political issue again after 1979 when the Conservative administration of Margaret Thatcher sought change in education, the largest component of local government expenditure. The government also moved against increasingly militant teaching unions, which were strongest in the primary schools and had been organizing strikes to reduce pay differentials. Governors were given increased power over their schools, and local financial management, introduced in the 1990s, detached the schools further from local government. The national curriculum introduced at the same time tried to standardize practice, while nationally administered tests for all seven- and eleven-year-olds ensured that educational performance was publicly accountable. However all of the careful understanding of educational experts was undermined by the government's disdain for expertise; scores were to be used without any contextual material that explained whether high performance was in fact attributable to well-prepared and resourced students. Concern for the underachievement of some groups in society was not reflected in any action. Schools continued to be held largely responsible for the educational success or failure of their charges. Classroom experience predominated in the training of teachers, just as it had in 1900.

Deborah Thom

Bibliography

Dent, Harold Collett. *Education in England and Wales*. 1982.
Gordon, Peter. *Education since the Second World War*. 1983.
Lowe, Roy, ed. *The Changing Primary School*. 1987.
Lowndes, G.A.N. *The Silent Social Revolution: An Account of the Expansion of Public Education in England and Wales, 1895–1965*. 2nd ed. 1969.

Propaganda

Propaganda played a major role in Britain's effort at sustaining morale at home, encouraging defeatism among its enemies, and appealing to neutral sympathies during both World Wars of the twentieth century. Britain entered the First World War with no propaganda department at all, but by war's end it had the most sophisticated such organization among the belligerents. Between 1914–18 the need to mobilize mass opinion in wartime became apparent, not just in Britain, but also in enemy countries, where propaganda could be deployed undermine morale, and among Britain's allies, who needed to be assured of

Britain's resolve. Neutrals were included as well, for their benevolence was needed in order to maintain supply lines.

Organization of British propaganda was haphazard, with agencies operating for several years without central coordination. A number of agencies were set up to deal with **censorship**, news management, military recruitment, appeals to allies, neutrals, and Dominions, and subversion of enemy morale, including the Parliamentary Recruiting Committee (PRC), formed to coordinate War Secretary **Lord Kitchener**'s appeal for volunteers; the Censorship and Press Bureau; the Neutral Press Committee; the Foreign Office News Department; and, from the War Office, MI7—all agencies responsible for managing the news as the government wanted. Reorganization in 1916 resulted in the Department of Information; the National War Aims Committee, whose duty it was to keep the public committed to the British cause; Crewe House, devoted to propaganda in enemy countries; and an overall coordinating body, the Ministry of Information.

These organizations employed a multitude of channels for dissemination. The PRC liked mass rallies and posters to get its message across, and others agencies deployed postcards, stamps, pamphlets, news items strategically placed in both domestic and foreign newspapers (Reuters News Agency was the primary overseas channel in this regard), and film. Newsreels and war-film grew in importance as the war progressed. In 1915 the War Office released *Britain Prepared*, which was shown as far away as Imperial Russia. For the enemy, Crewe House deployed clandestine tactics, including smuggled newspapers, pamphlets, and leaflets. The content varied, but the themes were generally the same: heroic British soldiers contrasted with cowardly **conscientious objectors**, supportive British wives and mothers, resolute leaders, and a display of German atrocities.

When the war ended, the antiwar reaction fostered repudiation of propaganda. It was only in the 1930s that the **Committee of Imperial Defence** (CID), albeit reluctantly, undertook to make provision for the dissemination of propaganda in the event of an emergency. A propaganda planning committee for wartime was established in 1936 to prepare for a Ministry of Information (MOI), which would spring into action should war come. In the meantime, it was to remain secret and avoid upsetting either Benito Mussolini or Adolf Hitler.

"You Never Know Who's Listening" (Fougasse). Kenneth Bird's posters were the most popular in the "Careless Talk Costs Lives" series.

In 1937 Parliament demanded a response to Italian anti-British broadcasts aimed at the Middle East, and the **Foreign Office** began to organize broadcasts in retaliation. A year later German success in Austria and Czechoslovakia convinced some officials that war was no longer avoidable, but the status of propaganda planning scarcely changed, a fact that became painfully clear the following September when war began.

In September 1939 the MOI was put into operation, but for the next year it achieved little if anything—the propagandists because they were trying to figure out how the machinery of the new organization was supposed to work, the military because, short of the **Royal Air Force** dropping propaganda leaflets, they had no real way to engage the enemy, save at sea. The MOI was reorganized in October 1939, again in 1940, and then again in 1943, after which it remained more or less intact, though never efficienct. After 1943 the MOI consisted principally of offices for censorship, relations with the **press**, supervising propaganda at home, in the Empire, and among neutrals and allies, and planning and executing this propaganda through broadcasting, film, and print media. Propaganda to enemy countries was under the Political Warfare Executive, administered jointly by the MOI, the Foreign Office, and the Ministry of Economic Warfare.

Compared to 1914, the objectives were clear: victory in a just cause over an evil adversary. With the advent of the bombing war of English cities, the home audience was assured that they could take it, a perception the government also imparted to the Empire and to neutral and friendly countries. After the Soviet Union, Japan, and the United States entered the war, and Britain won its first major victories, the new message was that Britain would win the war and become again a European, if not a world, leader.

Propaganda channels were similar, but more extensive, than those of the First World War. They included the press, broadcasting, posters, postcards, pamphlets, newsreels, film, talks by prominent figures, "whispering" campaigns, and leaflets dropped over enemy lines. "Black propaganda" was reserved for enemy and enemy-occupied countries. This was propaganda of dis- and mis-information, designed to disrupt military operations and undercut civilian and troop morale.

The content of propaganda was as varied as in the First World War. Posters warned soldiers and sailors against **venereal disease** and advised civilians to mind the blackout and to avoid spreading rumors or disclosing information. "Careless talk costs lives" was the theme of dozens of posters. Pamphlets described the importance of **rationing** and gave directions for air raid protection. Newsreels displayed and newspapers reported whatever good news about the war was available and, in order to avoid D (Defense) Notices from censors, kept quiet about the rest, especially about the extent of bomb damage, casualties, and tons of shipping lost to **submarines** in the Atlantic. Newsreels also provided reassurance about the courage and resourcefulness of the people at home. Much of this kind of propaganda was aimed at the United States or transmitted to neutral countries, who were encouraged either to join in the struggle against **Fascism** or at least to remain benevolently neutral toward Britain.

Robert Cole

Bibliography
Cole, Robert. *Britain and the War of Words in Neutral Europe, 1939–1945.* 1990.
Crofts, William. *Coercion or Persuasion? Propaganda in Britain after 1945.* 1989.
Cruickshank, Charles. *The Fourth Arm: Psychological Warfare, 1938–1945.* 1977.
McLaine, Ian. *Ministry of Morale: Home Front Morale and the Ministry of Information in World War II.* 1979.
Messinger, Gary S. *British Propaganda and the State in the First World War.* 1992.
Sanders, Michael, and Philip M. Taylor. *British Propaganda during the First World War.* 1982.
Taylor, Philip M. *The Projection of Britain.* 1981.

Prostitution

The general attitude in twentieth-century Britain toward prostitution has been marked by a trend toward toleration. By the beginning of the century reformer Josephine Butler's campaign against legal regulation had led to a worldwide movement for abolition of traffic in women and girls. The British Vigilance Society under the direction of W.A. Coote had organized the International Congress on White Slave Traffic in London in 1899, resulting in an international treaty ratified in May 1904. With the formation of the **League of Nations**, enforcement of this prohibition became part of its job, and it continued to be a function of the **United Nations** following the Second World War.

In Britain itself brothels had been officially illegal since the sixteenth century, although the prohibition was never strictly enforced. Providing such establishments were discreet, they were tolerated, but so was street prostitution. While this meant that prostitutes could earn much more than women employed in the more respectable jobs in Britain, it also gave **police** extraordinary discretion since any kind of disorderly, riotous, or indecent behavior was punishable. It became customary for British police periodically to arrest prostitutes, whereupon they paid their fine and returned to the street until the next time.

To deal more effectively with this, Parliament in 1954 appointed the Wolfenden Committee to study prostitution, which led to the Street Offenses Act of 1959. Under its provisions soliciting and loitering for the purpose of prostitution were made punishable, and penalties were increased for those aspects of prostitution that had always been punishable, such as procuring, managing a brothel, or living off the immoral earnings of a woman. While the modifications of the law compelled prostitutes to behave more discreetly, continuing prohibitions also meant that they were still vulnerable to gangsters, blackmailers, and extortionate landlords.

There has, however, been a growing reassessment of the role of the prostitute, motivated in part by a new generation of feminist scholars who view prostitutes as working women who are discriminated against, more victims than victimizers. Greater sympathy has not thus far translated into liberalization of the law, but neither have legal penalties done much to eliminate prostitution.

Vern L. Bullough

Bibliography

Bullough, Vern L., and Bonnie Bullough. *Women and Prostitution.* 1987.

Report of the Committee on Homosexual Offences and Prostitution (Wolfenden Report). Cmd. 247. *Parliamentary Papers,* vol. 14 (1956–7).

Scarlet, Iain. *The Professionals: Prostitutes and their Clients.* 1972.

Wilkinson, Rosalind. *Women of the Streets.* 1955.

Psychoanalysis

The British psychoanalytic movement began with the founding of the London Psycho-Analytic Society by Ernest Jones (1879–1958) in 1913, the year after he published *Papers on Psychoanalysis* (1912), the first book in English on the subject. The first work by Sigmund Freud to appear in Britain in an English translation was *Interpretation of Dreams* in 1913. The popularization of psychoanalysis also began at this time, primarily in the periodical press aimed at the intellectual and cultural Establishment. Before and during the First World War the elite publicizers of Freud were more receptive to his ideas than the mostly hostile majority of the medical and psychological communities. This cultural elite was sympathetic to Freud's theory of the unconscious, which many were convinced could be usefully employed to acquire greater self-knowledge. Some believed that the curative power of psychoanalytic therapy was demonstrated during the war by its use in the successful treatment of some soldiers who suffered from shell shock. But many who were receptive to Freudianism doubted that it was supported by empirical evidence. Even more believed that Freud had exaggerated the role of **sexuality** in the human mind and behavior. Despite such misgivings, the tolerance of Freudianism by the cultural elite facilitated the successful development of the psychoanalytic movement in England during its formative years.

In 1919 the London Psycho-Analytic Society was reconstituted by Jones as the British Psychoanalytic Society, and by 1925 it had over fifty members and associates, a number of whom lacked medical training. This high proportion of lay analysts remained a distinctive feature of the society. Led by Jones, it founded the *International Journal of Psychoanalysis* (1920), the International Psychoanalytical Library (1921), the Institute of Psychoanalysis (1924), and the London Clinic of Psychoanalysis (1926).

While the society flourished, a psychoanalytic craze emerged in the early 1920s among the general public. Extensive press reportage about psychoanalysis and the publication of scholarly and popular psychoanalytic books greatly increased the public's awareness of Freudianism and facilitated the process whereby psychoanalytic terms ultimately became commonplaces of British everyday speech. Some publicists championed Freud's therapy as a successful cure for nervous disorders. But critics charged more sharply than ever that Freud was unscientific and too reductionist in his emphasis on sex. The alternative theories of Carl Gustave Jung and Alfred Adler were often more sympathetically received by the educated public, who perceived them as less preoccupied than Freud with sexuality. Even more popular were the theories of the English eclectic psychologists and psychotherapists who de-emphasized the role of sexuality, borrowed freely from various psychological schools, and remained more respectful than the Freudians of traditional moral and religious beliefs. It was often such eclecticism rather than strict Freudianism that dominated the various attempts by those outside the Freudian community itself to apply psychoanalysis to literature, art criticism, **philosophy**, progressive education, and pastoral psychology. The British Psychoanalytic Society disapproved of the distortions of orthodox Freudianism during the psychoanalytic craze and felt threatened by the increased public hostility toward the movement itself. But in 1929 the society gained in public respectability when a report of the British Medical Association officially recognized psychoanalytic therapy without, however, endorsing its efficacy.

During the 1930s the British Psychoanalytic Society was torn by dissension between those who supported the theoretical innovations of Melanie Klein (1882–1960) and those who championed the views of Anna Freud (1895–1982), who in June 1938 settled in London, where Freud and his family took refuge from the Nazi persecution in Austria. Freud's exile in England prompted an outpouring of personal sympathy and honors for him from the British public, although, when he died in September 1939, there was still much criticism in the retrospective reviews of his work. Psychoanalysis never did become as popular in Britain as in some other European countries and the United States.

After the Second World War a compromise was reached in the British Psychoanalytic Society among the Kleinians, the Anna Freudians, and the majority in the middle known as the Independent Group. Much of the controversy among the factions had originated during the inter-war years over differing views of child analysis, one of the pioneering contributions of the society to the psychoanalytic movement. Among its other notable post-war achievements were the biography of Freud by Jones (1953–7), the twenty-four volume *Standard Edition* of Freud's works in English (1953–74), and the establishment of the Freud Museum (1986) in London.

Dean Rapp

Bibliography

Clark, Ronald W. *Freud: The Man and the Cause*. 1980.

Kohon, Gregorio, ed. *The British School of Psychoanalysis: The Independent Tradition*. 1985.

Ramon, Shulamit. *Psychiatry in Britain: Meaning and Policy*. 1985.

Rapp, Dean. "The Early Discovery of Freud by the British General Educated Public, 1912–1919," *Social History of Medicine*, vol. 3 (1990), pp. 217–43.

Timms, Edward, and Naomi Segal, eds. *Freud in Exile: Psychoanalysis and its Vicissitudes*. 1988.

Psychology

Psychology in its modern sense, the study of the nature, functions, and phenomena of the human mind, is almost entirely a twentieth-century growth in Britain. The basis of an institutional framework was laid in the Edwardian period: By 1914 there were eleven posts in psychology at Scottish and English universities. The *British Journal of Psychology* was founded in 1904 and the British Psychological Society in 1907; in 1914 the *Journal* became the official organ of the society. By 1920 psychology had its own section at British Association for the Advancement of Science meetings.

The applications of psychology have proved as important a source of employment as its academic study, particularly after the Second World War, and the authority conceded to the British Psychological Society to recognize—or withhold recognition from—training courses for clinical psychologists has made it effectively the governing body of the profession.

The development of psychology, like that of all of the human sciences in the English-speaking world, has been profoundly marked by evolutionary ideas—the post-Darwinian process that has been called "the biologizing of social thought." Within this general intellectual shift it grew from a multiplicity of roots: from the philosophy of mind, from the development of neurophysiology, and from the growth of mental measurement. These influences have made it an area of study particularly prone to fragmentation. One of the standard texts of the 1980s lists no less than seven subspecialties: cognitive, physiological, social, developmental, and comparative psychology, along with psychometrics and psychopathology.

In common with other British social scientists, psychologists have tended to pride themselves on their empiricist and positivist approach. They have perhaps been less swept by wholesale enthusiasms than their European or North American counterparts, although both Gestalt theory and, more important, behaviorism, have had their ardent supporters. Conversely, the applications of psychology in industrial and educational fields have proved major growth points. The National Institute of Industrial Psychology was founded in 1922 and by 1930 was attracting £30,000 per annum in funding from companies. The mass **conscription** of the Second World War greatly expanded demand for aptitude testing, profiling, and vocational guidance, and for improved efficiency in working practices at all levels. The mass upheavals brought by the Second World War, **evacuation** and the repeated bombing of civilian populations, focused attention on the disturbances of childhood and the child victims of the destruction of families as never before.

In addition, the inter-war period saw the employment of psychologists to advise on the identification and treatment of children with mental handicaps and on the treatment of children and adolescents with behavioral problems or otherwise deviant. To the category "delinquent" was added that of "maladjusted," although the former tended to be used of working-class children and the latter of middle-class children.

Educational psychologists were also engaged to test and profile "normal" schoolchildren and thus drawn into the competitive selection of children for **secondary education.** The income generated by providing this service for local education authorities enabled Godfrey Thomson, Professor of education at the University of Edinburgh, to create a testing service and research trust, known initially as Moray House and subsequently as the Godfrey Thomson Unit for Educational Research. Testing and test production also proved a major source of income for the National Foundation for Educational Research, established in 1945. The Educational Reform Act of 1988 linked a national program of assessment to the introduction of a national curriculum for children aged seven to sixteen; and the efforts of government to put a complex and elaborate structure in place fast have provoked a considerable backlash among teachers and parents, from which psychologists as well as politicians and administrators have suffered.

Gillian Sutherland

Bibliography

Flugel, John Carl, and Donald J. West. *A Hundred Years of Psychology, 1833–1933.* 1964.

Hearnshaw, Leslie Spenser. *Cyril Burt, Psychologist.* 1979.

Lloyd, Peter, Andrew Mayes, et al. *Introduction to Psychology: An Integrated Approach.* 1984.

Sampson, Olive. *Child Guidance: Its History, Provenance, and Future.* 1980.

Sutherland, Gillian. *Ability, Merit, and Measurement: Mental Testing and English Education, 1880–1940.* 1984.

Public Health

Public health as a form of state regulation has a long history. In Britain in the nineteenth century state intervention was more extensive in the area of health than in any other, largely because of the threat of disease to the whole population. Environment and health were seen as interconnected; questions of **housing** and of sanitation were normally included within the public health remit.

C.E.A Winslow, the early-twentieth-century American authority on public health, identified three phases in its development. The first, from 1840, was characterized by environmental sanitation; the second, from 1890 to 1910, by developments in bacteriology and germ theory, resulting in an emphasis on isolation and disinfection; and the third, beginning around 1910, by an emphasis on education and personal hygiene, referred to as personal prevention. This chronology is broadly applicable to developments in Britain. Germ theory brought a realization that it was not dirt as such that caused infectious disease; the broad mandate of public health to deal with housing and sanitation disappeared. During the years of **Liberal** welfare reforms before the First World War the health and welfare aspects of policy were more firmly separated than previously. The focus of public health work shifted to personal hygiene and health education. There was increasing concern about the apparent deterioration of the race and the high **infant mortality** rate. The revelations of the Select Committee on Physical Deterioration (1904) about the poor physical condition of Britain's recruits in the **Boer War** resulted in the establishment of a school medical service. A variety of infant welfare clinics were established, and local authorities were given statutory authority for services for mothers and infants by the Maternity and Child Welfare Act of 1918. Medical Officers of Health focused on improving the quality of maternal care to the virtual exclusion of factors such as low incomes, poor housing and sanitation, and contaminated milk.

In the years from 1929 to 1948 public health departments in local authorities delivered a wide range of health services. Chief among these was responsibility for municipal hospitals, transferred to public health departments by the Local Government Act of 1929. Medical Officers of Health in local authorities could also provide maternity and child welfare services, the school medical service, dentistry, school meals and milk, **tuberculosis** schemes, infectious disease, ear, nose and throat, and **venereal disease** services; and health centers. Some commentators have seen these years as the "golden age" of public health. But an opposing point of view has criticized this expansion of functions for its lack of a clear vision of what was distinctive about public health. There has been further criticism of inter-war Medical Officers of Health for failing (with some exceptions) to address the relationship between **unemployment**, poverty, and ill health.

The coming of the **National Health Service** in 1948 represented a considerable setback for public health. **Aneurin Bevan**, as Minister of Health, achieved consultant support for the new service through the nationalization of the **hospitals**, a victory for the voluntary hospitals and a clear defeat for the idea of a state medical service based on local authorities and public health. Public health doctors in local authorities lost their hospital empires and were left with a substantially reduced range of responsibilities. Attempts were made in the 1940s to reorient public health practice round a new academic discipline of "social medicine," an attempt to link the planning of health and social services to the needs of the population. It was remote from the practice of public health and failed to have much impact on **medical education**.

From the 1950s to the 1970s public health was increasingly fragmented, at both organizational and conceptual levels. Parts of the public health sphere in the local authorities began to break away—first sanitary inspectors in the 1950s, then social workers, transferred to separate social work departments following the Seebohm Committee report of 1968. "Community medicine" replaced what was seen as the outdated concept of public health. The 1974 reorganization of the National Health Service transferred public health (as community medicine) into the Health Service with a twin function of epidemiology and medical administration. The community physician became preoccupied more with administration than with the health of the population and its determinants.

A new focus on the prevention of ill health became government policy in Britain in the 1970s and 1980s. But the emphasis was again on individual responsibility for health, and the focus was on single-issue campaigns (smoking, alcohol, heart disease) rather than an analysis of structural determinants of public health. The Black Report on Inequalities in Health (1979) and the subsequent Whitehead Report (1987), which drew attention to questions of class and poverty in relation to health, were not popular with the **Conservative** government.

The 1980s saw a revival of public health concerns. The desire to integrate personal prevention and environmental perspectives became associated with the World Health Organization's *Health for All by the Year 2000* strategy (1981) and the "new public health." In Britain the revival of infectious disease (legionella, salmonella, AIDS) led to a determined effort in the 1988 Acheson Report to upgrade the status of public health medicine. The future of public health in Britain remained uncertain even after this report, not least because of its primary focus on public health as a *medical* specialty. This has been a distinctive feature of British public health, in contrast to the multidisciplinary American approach; but by the 1990s a broader range of disciplines were also laying claim to expertise in public health.

Virginia Berridge

Bibliography

Draper, Peter, ed. *Health through Public Policy: The Greening of Public Health.* 1991.

Fee, Elizabeth, and Roy Acheson, eds. *A History of Education in Public Health.* 1991.

Lewis, Jane. *What Price Community Medicine? The Philosophy, Practice, and Politics of Public Health since 1919.* 1986.

Publishing and Publishers

Publishing has been subject to both commercial and cultural change in twentieth-century Britain. At the beginning of the century it was still largely based on small, family-owned businesses, but by the 1990s it had become dominated by multinational corporations. Even so, the greatest influence was exerted by individuals, whose importance should never be underestimated in a business that, because of the unique cultural and educational significance of its product, can never be a neutral commercial enterprise. Indeed, there is a recurrent pattern of firms founded by individual publishers that, if successful, needed to look for the large capital base provided by a corporate owner.

In 1900 the industry embarked upon a new phase of its history when the Net Book Agreement came into operation. This agreement, which determines the conditions of sale under which publishers sell books to retail booksellers, allowed publishers to fix the minimum retail price of British books sold in the United Kingdom. In effect, it has prescribed the basic economic structure of the trade for much of the century. It gave the publishers a predominant position in the book trade, and it survived largely intact until the late 1980s. It gave the industry an apparent stability and a sense of security, for one of its effects was to guarantee profit margins. It also helped ensure that comparatively low-profit books could be published, since a reasonable, if modest, profit could be expected provided that about three-quarters of even a very short print run were sold. This helped preserve the reputation of British publishers for issuing scholarly and literary works that might not have found a commercial outlet in other countries. It was also a factor in the most obvious statistical phenomenon of British publishing in the twentieth century: the great and steady increase in the number of titles published. From about 6,000 new titles a year at the beginning of the century, annual output rose to about 70,000 by the late 1980s. Although this was partly a reflection of social and educational change—more readers, more leisure time, and greater disposable incomes—it was also a consequence of the comparatively well-protected commercial environment in which the publishers operated. The greatest challenge to the Net Book Agreement came in the late 1980s, when entrepreneurial booksellers insisted on their right both to fix any price they thought the market could bear and to reduce prices in order to sell more books. The issue seems likely to be resolved when the agreement is overriden by the provisions of **European Union** law on competition.

The Net Book Agreement emerged from the self-contained and self-confident world of late-Victorian publishing. The great nineteenth-century publishing houses, such as Macmillan, John Murray, and Longmans, with their accumulated prestige (and copyrights) dominated the industry, although a few were already beginning to feel the need for change. As early as 1895 Chapman and Hall, who had once been Dickens' publishers, were forced to look for British agencies for American publishers to help to revive their declining business. This pattern was to be repeated many times after the First World War and again from the 1970s onward. The industry was, however, continuously renewed by the entry of new blood and new ideas. Despite the general economic problems of the 1920s and 1930s, many important new publishing houses were established, some to become a permanent feature of the scene. Of these, the best-known, and the most influential, were perhaps **Victor Gollancz** (founded 1928), Jonathan Cape (founded 1920); Faber and Faber (founded 1929 by Geoffrey Faber); Michael Joseph (founded 1935); and Stanley Unwin (George Allen and Unwin Ltd., bought, reformed, and renamed 1914). All of their founders were individualists who brought to publishing their own tastes and interests. Perhaps the most important cultural achievement was that of **Allen Lane**, whose Penguin Books (founded 1935), the first true paperback house, was one of the great influences on **popular culture** and education before, during, and long after the Second World War.

Small businesses, in which the owner-founder played an important day-to-day part, characterized British publishing until the 1960s. Perhaps as a consequence, the quality of the management was not always equal to the quality of the product. There was great reluctance to change, and the death of the founder often heralded the demise of the company in its original form. As publishing houses became larger, the need for management skills became more obvious and usually had to be found outside the industry. This led to tensions between the commercial and cultural aspects of the business and often to strained relations with authors and their agents. Although some firms, such as Faber and Faber, remained independent and ploughed a lonely furrow of cultural excellence, more were subsumed in the bland generality of commercial publishing.

The crisis of the 1960s and 1970s was further exacerbated by the loss of part of the industry's traditional overseas' markets. Since the beginning of the century, about 30–40 percent of all British books had been sold as exports, principally in Britain's colonies and Dominions. The Australian and New Zealand markets were opened to American publishers after 1976, when the informal arrangement to restrict their operation in the British Commonwealth was successfully challenged by the American government. The development of domestic publishing industries in those countries also had a serious effect on British exports and coincided with the growth of indigenous publishing industries in newly independent countries in Asia and Africa, beginning with India in 1947. Exports declined dramatically, and although there was a recovery in the 1980s, it was achieved only by far more aggressive marketing techniques than had traditionally been employed by the agents of British publishers, and by switching to a heavy dependence on texts for English language teaching and teaching English as a second language.

The same period, however, saw other great changes from which the publishing industry was able to benefit. The expansion of higher education following the publication of the **Robbins Report** in 1963 led to the growth of existing institutions and the creation of new ones. Both their libraries and their students, in those comparatively affluent times, provided a vast new market that was met by the proliferation both of the reprint industry (to supply new libraries with out-of-print books and journals) and of small academic publishing houses. Many of these firms (like the expansive phase of the education system that spawned them) were a short-lived phenomenon, but a number of important ideas and people came into the industry in this way. The new publishers of the 1960s pioneered the use of new technologies of book production. Offset-lithography, a cheaper, cleaner, and more efficient printing system than traditional letterpress, was ideally suited to their short print runs of specialized texts. Combined first with the products of the electric typewriter, and then with computer output, it enabled small quantities of a great number of specialized titles to be produced at affordable prices.

A second change in the same period arose from the growing influence of **television**, which, like cinema and radio before it, had a generally beneficial effect on the book industry, stimulating rather than inhibiting the sales of certain kinds of books. In the late 1960s, however, the concept of the "TV tie-in" was developed. Expensively produced documentary series and historical costume dramas were linked to the publication of books consisting either of the text of the work dramatized or of production stills from the documentaries combined with a text based on the script. Some of these books were phenomenally successful, not least in the United States where the television programs on which they were based attracted large audiences. While this development emphasized the primacy of television as a mass medium, it also stimulated welcome new sales and probably broadened the historically narrow socioeconomic base of the domestic book market in Britain.

The TV tie-ins heralded a new style in British publishing, which was to be market-oriented and unashamedly popular. Lacking the massive domestic base that supported the American publishing industry (especially for "blockbuster" **popular fiction** in paperback), British publishers sought to combine popularity with quality. To some extent this ploy was a success, but by the end of the 1980s, the best-seller lists reflected current social trends as much as literary taste, with a proliferation of books on cookery, gardening, travel, and other fashionable pastimes. Even this was achieved only with great infusions of capital from outside the publishing industry, some from the United States, some from **Australia**, and only a comparatively small part from Britain. Literary quality and academic merit were never entirely abandoned as the criteria for publication, but they were increasingly subordinated to commercial pressures.

At the beginning of the 1990s British publishing consisted of a few very large companies, with many different imprints that were formerly independent publishers, who dominated the industry; about ten companies accounted for perhaps 80 percent of the total output of new titles, and almost all of the popular best-sellers in both hardback and paperback. Yet there are about 5,000 publishing organizations in the United Kingdom, many of them operating on a commercial basis, however limited. Diversity survives, and with it the spirit of both entrepreneurial and literary independence, which characterizes a healthy publishing industry.

John Feather

Bibliography

Curwen, Peter J. *The U.K. Publishing Industry.* 1981.

Feather, John. *A History of British Publishing.* 1988.

Lane, Michael, and Jeremy Booth. *Books and Publishers.* 1980.

Norrie, Ian. *Mumby's Publishing and Bookselling in the Twentieth Century.* 6th ed. 1982.

Punch

Punch, an illustrated humorous weekly, appeared in 1841 and ceased publication in April 1992. By the 1890s it had shed its original radicalism and become a national institution—a complacent repository in prose, verse, and cartoons of late-Victorian middle- and upper-class values and views. It blended wry and whimsical commentary with illustrated reviews of the media. Many of the finest comic artists, caricaturists, and illustrators of the twentieth century enlivened its pages. Circulation was 105,000 in 1905, topping out at 175,000 in 1948. Advertisers used *Punch* from 1908 on to reach its affluent readers. Once the austere 1940s were over, color-filled advertisements flanked genteel, eccentric humor and satire in prose and cartoons. *Punch* is a primary source of the vagaries of fashion, mores, and moods of the Home Counties upper and middle classes in the twentieth century.

Punch's Edwardian tone was slight and safe; it rarely, if ever, gave offense. What Owen Seaman (editor, 1906–32) wanted was lucidity, intelligibility, and "soundness"—that is, conservative political reliability. What he got was a self-satisfied, stodgy, increasingly right-wing, often unfunny weekly. Light stories, even lighter verse and social cartoons, mostly of middle- and upper-class activities, interspersed with *Charivari*—a page of "humorous" clippings—two full-page political cartoons, usually by Bernard Partridge from 1910 to 1945, reviews of stage plays, some concerts, and "the Essence of Parliament" kept an aging readership reassured. Aside from the contributions of **P.G. Wodehouse** and A.A. Milne, most *Punch* prose and verse before and during the First World War is unmemorable. During the war *Punch* sought to sustain morale, while it trivialized the trenches and demonized the enemy.

In the 1920s *Punch* contributors groused about flappers, jazz, cocktails, the Charleston, upstart Americans, and the servant problem, hoping somehow that the pre-war certainties would return. The exception to the prevailing mediocrity were such gems as A.P. Herbert's witty *Misleading Causes* and singable verses, Milne's whimsical rhymes, *When We Were Very Young*, and Seller and Yeatman's burlesque history text, *1066 and All That*. Seaman's last years were redeemed by H.M. Bateman's irate colonels, Fougasse's comic abstractions, Lewis Baumer's lissome flappers, George Belcher's cockneys, Bert Thomas' **caricatures**, and Arthur Watts' slightly crazed panoramas. Under the formidable Marion Jean Lyon, *Punch* became a "shop window" for the **advertising** industry and increased in size, with some color, especially in the annual almanac.

EVOE (E.V. Knox) (editor, 1932–49) and Fougasse (Kenneth Bird) (art editor, 1937–49, editor, 1949–52) gradually modernized the magazine. New contributors such as Richard Mallett, Eric Keown, Basil Boothroyd, and R.G.G. Price brought it topicality and wit. Verbal and visual humor about tennis, ski holidays, broken plumbing, bridge playing, the **British Broadcasting Corporation** (BBC), domestic and foreign **Fascists** remain informative and amusing. In the late 1930s *Punch* became a showcase for sophisticated comic art and illustration. Thomas Derrick's modernistic energy, E.H. Shepard's decorative illustrations, Rowland Emmet's eccentric trains, Paul Crum's (Roger Pettiward) pensive hippos, David Langdon's lively, linear gags, and Anton's (Antonia Yeoman) elegant spivs can still be appreciated. Pont's (Graham Laidler, 1908–40) series "The British Character" and "Popular Misconceptions" aptly captured the bemused English in decline, muddling through the Depression, the looming war, and the **Blitz**. Leslie Illingworth's post-war political cartoons were moderately Tory, gently critical of **Labour** and the **welfare state**. In the late 1940s *Punch* reached its highest circulation.

In 1953 Bradbury Agnew brought in the iconoclastic outsider Malcolm Muggeridge. To give *Punch* topicality and style Muggeridge enlisted, among others, Claude Cockburn, John Betjeman, and **Anthony Powell** and coaxed P.G. Wodehouse to contribute again. Russell Brockbank, art editor in the 1950s, enhanced what was already a showcase for cartooning. Ronald Searle's zany line, exclusively in *Punch* for several years, influenced a generation of artist-caricaturists, especially Ralph Steadman and Gerald Scarfe. Robert Sheriffs' caricatures, Osbert Lancaster, and Mark Boxer's pocket cartoons, the exuberant Giovanetti, Andre François, and Gerard Hoffnung's zaniness added to the comic spirit of the *Punch* regulars.

Between 1957 and 1988 the editors, Bernard Hollowood, William Davis, Alan Coren, and David Taylor, struggled with mixed results to find a role for *Punch*. Aimed at an educated, middle-class, mature audience, *Punch* sought to be literate and witty. Cartoonists such as Trog (Wally Fawkes), Bill Hewison, Quentin Blake,

(Michael) ffoukes, Larry (Terry Parkes), Bill Tidy, John Jensen, Steadman and Scarfe, Norman Thelwell, Ken Mahood, Michael Heath, Ed Mclachlan, and Mike Williams, among others, sustained it as an arena for satirical commentary and eccentric comic art.

Despite its considerable efforts, *Punch* never redefined itself effectively in the increasingly competitive media environment. When readership and revenues fell in the late 1980s, United Newspapers ordered the youthful David Thomas to "reposition" *Punch* down-market. This change and an infusion of money to celebrate its 150th year, however, could not staunch *Punch*'s losses, as advertising revenues and circulation dropped dramatically. United Newspapers closed *Punch* on 8 April 1992 and put it up for sale. Mr. Punch died of circulation failure, it was said, brought on by trying to be youthful and vulgar, something it never was.

Peter Mellini

Bibliography

Prager, Arthur. *The Mahogany Tree: An Informal History of* Punch. 1979.
Price, R.G.G. *A History of* Punch. 1957.

Quakers

See FRIENDS, SOCIETY OF (QUAKERS)

Quiller-Couch, Arthur Thomas (1863–1944)

A popular novelist, poet, and anthologist from the 1890s, Arthur Thomas Quiller-Couch (Q, as he signed most of his writings) set the standard of mainstream poetical taste in the first half of the twentieth century with *The Oxford Book of English Verse* (1900, new ed. 1939). Knighted in 1910, Quiller-Couch was appointed two years later the second King Edward VII Professor of English Literature at **Cambridge**, where he was instrumental in establishing English studies. Two collections of his lectures, *On the Art of Writing* (1916) and *On the Art of Reading* (1920), widely influenced students and the reading public.

Quiller-Couch, son of a Cornish doctor, was born on 21 November 1863 and educated at Clifton and Trinity College, **Oxford**. After the publication of his first novel, *Dead Man's Rock* (1887), he became a prominent man of letters through an impressive outpouring of novels, criticism, anthologies, and verse. Even though he retired to Cornwall for his health in 1892, Quiller-Couch was an assistant editor of the *Speaker*, providing each week short stories, causeries, or book reviews and working with other contributors such as **William Butler Yeats**, J.M. Barrie, George Moore, and Henry James.

After Robert Louis Stevenson died in 1894, Quiller-Couch finished the adventure story "St. Ives" (1898) at the estate's behest. About the same time he finished one of his finest novels, *The Ship of Stars* (1899), and compiled *The Oxford Book of English Verse*, which was reprinted twenty times and sold nearly half a million copies during his lifetime. Between *English Verse* and his professorship in 1912, Quiller-Couch continued to publish prolifically: a volume of poetry, three anthologies, a collection of essays, several children's books, and twenty volumes of fiction, including thirteen novels.

After his move to Cambridge in 1912, Quiller-Couch quickly overcame critics of his appointment with a series of wildly popular lectures characterized by deep learning, wide reading, and the sensitivities of an accomplished craftsman. In 1917 his standing with the public and members of academia enabled him and like-minded colleagues to argue successfully for the creation of an English School and examination (tripos) at Cambridge. In addition to his academic duties, he was active during the **First World War** in raising troops in Cornwall.

The sheer volume of his work remained prodigious: coeditor of the *New Cambridge Shakespeare* until 1931; editor of scores of *The King's Treasury of Literature*; three biblical anthologies and coeditor of *The Cambridge Shorter Bible* (1928); lecturer and essayist in *Studies in Literature, Charles Dickens and Other Victorians* (1925), *The Poet as Citizen and Other Papers* (1934); and dozens of introductions to works by others. During the Second World War he spent part of his time on an autobiography, but he had only carried the narrative through his Oxford years when he died after an accident on 12 May 1944.

Quiller-Couch belonged to the era of the British "man of letters" that included Stevenson, Barrie, Andrew Lang, Austin Dobson, G.A. Henty, and Oscar Wilde. His was an athletic, Christian-humanist view of the world, and he had little sympathy for the aesthete or the jaundiced, alienated artist.

Michael Douglas Smith

Bibliography

Brittain, Frederick. *Arthur Quiller-Couch: A Biographical Study of Q.* 1947.

Roberts, Sydney C., ed. *Memories and Opinions: An Unfinished Autobiography by Q.* 1944.

Rowse, A.L. *Quiller-Couch: A Portrait of Q.* 1988.

R

Race Relations

Although it is impossible to comprehend the contemporary shape of race relations in Britain without reference to the legacy of the slave trade and the experience of British **imperialism**, it is nevertheless clear that the era of a racial "question" in British society and politics commenced no earlier than the late 1940s. With the arrival of 800 Jamaican immigrant workers between December 1947 and October 1948 and the eventual settlement of tens of thousands of others from the West Indies and the Indian subcontinent over the next decade and a half, a race relations "problem" and, hence, the foundations for a "politics of race" in Britain became firmly established.

Since the late 1950s race-related conflict and state policies that regulate the **immigration** of nonwhites into Britain have persisted as socially divisive and politically charged issues that have challenged the capacity of Britain's political system to respond. Since the arrival of the initial wave of new Commonwealth immigrants, racial disturbances have flared periodically; a racist, neo-Fascist political movement, the **National Front**, has surged and declined; and successive British governments, in responding to illiberal public attitudes, have radically altered the country's immigration and nationality statutes. An unseen mover of votes, race is believed to have influenced the outcome of at least two general elections during the 1970s and contributed to eroding the long-held attachments of many voters to the **Conservative** and **Labour** parties. Moreover, pervasive conditions of racism and economic disadvantage among nonwhites are almost universally recognized as partial causes of a series of **urban riots** that rocked several English cities during the 1980s.

The main response of Britain's political elites to the evolution of a multiracial society has been to extricate race-related subjects from the political arena. Particularly between 1964 and 1975 the principal parties forged an implicit consensus to depoliticize race. The simplest and least effective strategy the parties pursued to depoliticize race-related issues was to deny their political relevance. During the 1964 general election campaign, for example, only eight Conservative, fourteen Labour, and three **Liberal** candidates for Parliament cited the subjects of immigration or race relations in their campaign addresses despite the acute concern of the British public about the overall number of immigrants entering Britain and the difficulties that even long-settled immigrants were experiencing in assimilating into British society. This trend continued; immigration was cited in the election addresses of only 6 percent of all parliamentary candidates in 1966 and 14 percent in 1970. Although the national manifestos of the parties cited this area of public policy more frequently, such discussions were often purposely vague.

The second strategy pursued to depoliticize race was to enact cosmetic antidiscrimination legislation in conjunction with the implementation of even tighter immigration controls. For every piece of restrictive immigration legislation adopted between 1965 and 1976, an accompanying Race Relations Act either preceded or shortly followed its passage. Labour was especially adept at this game of political football; in 1965 and again in 1968 a Labour government successfully introduced both restrictive legislation and an antidiscrimination statute. The genesis of the 1965 Race Relations Act can be traced to the fear that racial issues were then beginning to influence the outcome of parliamentary contests in a number of local constituencies.

The third strategy adopted by the parties to depoliticize race-related issues was to create "racial buffers," quasi-governmental, bureaucratic bodies designed to assume the primary responsibility of addressing race-related problems. By establishing the National Committee for Commonwealth Immigrants (1965–8), the Race Relations Board (1965–76), the Community Relations Commission (1968–76), and the Commission for Racial Equality (1977–), the parties shielded politicians from the political hazards of addressing race-related issues squarely and also inhibited nonwhites from participating in conventional interest group and party politics. By bureaucratizing race-related issues, buffer institutions, at least until the late 1970s, acted as political roadblocks for **Black people** rather than as bridges between the nonwhite community and the government.

Buffeted over time by the pressures of public opinion dissatisfied with the approach of the parties to race-related issues and of party-affiliated pressure groups clamoring for change, the Conservative Party, and then Labour, eventually disengaged from the racial consensus. Since the mid-1970s race-related subjects have become more frequent topics of intra-party discussion, inter-party differences on race have visibly widened, and the race relations and immigration policies of the post-1979 Conservative governments have been challenged by the opposition.

Throughout the 1960s and 1970s public opinion polls revealed that a substantial percentage of citizens thought that too many immigrants had been admitted into Britain and that immigration constituted one of the most urgent problems confronting the country; even into the early 1980s, more than 80 percent of the electorate expressed the view that controlling immigration was very important, and, despite a series of immigration measures passed by successive governments, almost half of all voters believed that the political parties were not addressing the immigration issue adequately. Although issues of race relations appeared less salient at the beginning of the 1990s than a decade before, such issues have far from disappeared from the consciousness of the British public. Heated debates in British society and politics persist over the political representation of Black people—there were only four nonwhites among the 650 members of the House of Commons in 1991, despite the fact that nonwhites account for more than 4 percent of the total population—as well as over the necessity for affirmative action laws, the alleged decline of law and order in inner-city areas where there are large concentrations of immigrants, and other issues.

In the 1990s, forty-five years after the initial wave of new Commonwealth immigration, Britain's new ethnic and racial minorities, most of whom are full citizens, are still not fully integrated into the mainstream of British politics, racial discrimination persists at all levels of society, and racial violence perpetrated against nonwhites is a recurrent feature of the British urban experience.

Anthony M. Messina

Bibliography

Foot, Paul. *Immigration and Race in British Politics.* 1965.

Katznelson, Ira. *Black Men, White Cities: Race, Politics, and Migration in the United States, 1900–30, and Britain, 1948–68.* 1973.

Messina, Anthony M. *Race and Party Competition in Britain.* 1989.

Panay, Panikos. *Racial Violence in Britain, 1882–1958.* 1993.

Rich, Paul B. *Race and Empire in British Politics.* 1986.

Radar

The term radar—an acronym for *radio detection and ranging*—refers to the means of locating distant objects by radio. Although several countries were investigating the use of radio waves to locate obstacles at sea, it was Britain that decided to develop radar for defense purposes in 1935. One of its strongest advocates, Robert Watson-Watt (1892–1973), staged a trial in February 1935 in which the progress of a bomber, flying through the beam of a short-wave radio transmitter, was successfully plotted by detecting the small amounts of energy reflected from it. This, and the government's concern over the worsening situation in Europe, prompted the decision to equip Britain with an early warning system against aerial attack.

A development program of unprecedented urgency and secrecy was initiated. By 1939 many "Chain Home" radar stations were in service on the eastern fringes of Britain, and by 1941 most of the coastline had radar coverage.

With their large antennas supported by 300-foot-high towers, the radar stations were conspicuous, illuminating the sky with high-power pulses of radio energy. Radar operators observed echoes on the screens of cathode-ray tubes and determined the position and height of intruding aircraft by adjusting the line of sight of the directional receiving aerials. Since their screens did not provide any sort of map, operators could only guess the numbers of the attackers from the nature of the echoes.

This system played a crucial role in the **Battle of Britain** in September 1940, when outnumbered defenders took to the skies and repulsed waves of German attackers. Despite the excellence of the British aircraft and the skill of the **Royal Air Force**, the battle would have been lost without the warnings provided by radar, fed in to the fighter squadrons by a highly developed communication and control network. Daytime raids diminished in frequency and intensity, and the threatened invasion of Britain was halted. The emphasis turned to night raids and the war in the Atlantic, calling for smaller, more mobile radar systems that could be fitted to aircraft and ships.

By this time the Chain Home system was already out of date. All radar engineers knew that more accurate, sensitive, and, above all, transportable radar sets would have to operate at centimetric, rather than metric, wavelengths. Crude mobile radars for gunnery and for airborne interception had already been constructed, operating at wavelengths of around a meter. A University of Birmingham group commissioned by the Admiralty undertook a program to develop components for centimetric radar. The result was a thermionic tube called the cavity magnetron, which could give pulses of tens of kilowatts at wavelengths of a few centimeters. Manufacturing this device in quantity proved problematical until a British mission under **Sir Henry Tizard** secured an agreement for the American Bell Telecommunication Laboratories to produce improved copies of the magnetron.

By early 1942 warships defending North Atlantic convoys were beginning to moderate the losses suffered by merchant ships carrying war material to Europe, thanks to the improved performance of radar using the magnetron. At the same time, centimetric radars for aircraft were being designed with two main functions in mind. Forward-looking radars for airborne interception were urgently needed to replace the earlier metric sets. This would improve the interception of attacking aircraft in cloud and at night, following their earlier detection by ground radar. Their other function was to look downward from the aircraft. For maritime reconnaissance aircraft, the ASV (air-to-surface vessel) radars were so successful that they finally rendered the North Atlantic uninhabitable for the German **submarines**. Over land a radar using similar technology gave bomber crews a picture of the ground at night and through cloud, allowing them to bomb specific targets accurately, assisted by navigation systems based hundreds of miles behind them in the United Kingdom.

A less glamorous role for radar was in directing antiaircraft guns. In this field, the United States had an enviable lead, and supplies of the now-celebrated SCR-584 radar, which could track fast-flying targets and aim guns at them automatically, were supplied to Britain and proved themselves in the fight against the V1 flying bombs.

Fighter control in the form of Ground Controlled Interception (GCI) followed from the 1940 success of the Chain Home system. One of the weaknesses of that system had been its inability to plot individual aircraft in detail, especially if they were flying at low altitudes. Smaller rotating-antenna radars, known as Chain Home Low (CHL), were installed at many sites to overcome the deficiency. More-compact radars, eventually adopting centimetric techniques, evolved from these and were installed separately from the main Chain Home stations for fighter direction. GCI radars, compact enough to be transportable, proved invaluable in the theaters of war beyond the British coastlines.

The techniques developed, both electronic and operational, presaged the peacetime role of radar and air navigation. Modern air traffic control now relies upon the methods that were effective in combat during the Second World War. Ground-based radars, airborne "weather" radar, short- and long-range radio navigation systems, and ways of identifying individual aircraft all had their origins in the frantic battle for electronic superiority in 1939–45.

Eryl Davies

Bibliography
Bowen, E.G. *Radar Days.* 1987.
Brown, R. Hanbury. *Boffin: A Personal Story of the Early Days of Radar and Radio*

R

Astronomy. 1991.

Lovell, Bernard. *Echoes of War: The Story of H2S Radar.* 1991.

Pritchard, David. *The Radar War: Germany's Pioneering Achievement, 1904–45.* 1989.

Railways

Britain inherited from the nineteenth century a densely built, efficiently operated, and privately owned railway network, which, in the days before substantial development of the automobile and modern highways, provided through 9,000 stations the country's primary transport system for both passengers and freight. In mid-century every spot in England was still within eighteen miles of railway line. By the closing decade of the twentieth century the system, nationalized and drastically pruned, offered on its remaining routes a modernized service arguably no longer an economic necessity because of the dominance of road transport.

In 1910 about 150 railway companies operated within Britain; the most important included the Great Western, running westward from Paddington Station, London, to destinations arching from Cornwall to Chester; the London and North Western, from London's Euston Station through Lancashire, connecting with the Caledonian into Scotland; and the Great Northern, from London's King Cross to Yorkshire, connecting with Scotland via the North Eastern and the North British. Passenger service was frequent and often competitive. Between London and Manchester there were sixteen trains daily on the London and North Western, twelve on the Midland, and six on the Great Central. During the **First World War** the government assumed temporary ownership of the railways. The Railways Act of 1921 forced a major consolidation. Most of the railways south of London were grouped into the new Southern. The London, Midland and Scottish was created from the former London and North Western, Midland, Lancashire and Yorkshire, Caledonian, and other smaller lines. The London and North Eastern included the former Great Northern, Great Central, Great Eastern, North Eastern, and North British. The fourth of the post-grouping lines was the original Great Western, augmented by acquisition of previously independent lines in South Wales. Grouping was intended to help the railways cope with increasing highway competition, which between the wars began to erode receipts and forced closure of some rural lines. Of the new companies only the Southern, which undertook extensive electrification in its commuter territory south of London, made major changes in its physical plant, while the London and North Eastern attracted public attention by developing, under the direction of Sir Nigel Gresley (1876–1941), a series of handsome express locomotives for nonstop London-Edinburgh service. One achieved a speed of 126 miles per hour in 1938.

Railways were again temporarily nationalized during the **Second World War**, when freight traffic rose 50 percent and passenger traffic 68 percent over pre-war levels. Definitive and permanent governmental purchase came from the Transport Act of 1947, which created in theory a unified national transportation system, including not only railways, but also air, canal, and highway freight and passenger services. In 1962, when the attempt to coordinate all transport under single management was abandoned, British Rail began to function as a distinct entity. For operational purposes it was divided into six semiautonomous regions: Southern, Western, Eastern, London Midland, North Eastern, and Scottish. True integration of the railway network was achieved hesitantly; ten years after **nationalization** there continued to be London-to-Manchester service on three separate routes. Modernization came only slowly. In the late 1950s the majority of freight cars were still not equipped with air brakes, and horse-drawn British Rail vans still plodded the streets of London bearing the slogan "British Rail—Safe, Fast, Efficient." It was hoped that eventually the railway might operate profitably, but soon governmental subsidies, to supplement inadequate revenues, became a continuing reality, justified as the cost of maintaining socially necessary but inherently unremunerative lines.

The Beeching Report (1963), by British Railways Chairman Richard Beeching (1913–85), resulted in a major cutback of lines and service, as the Victorian ideal, with a nearby station for almost everyone, was abandoned, to be replaced by a relatively sparse network offering frequent service between major points but conceding rural services to local bus lines. The report called for the elimination of 5,000 miles of route along with about one-third of all stations. The Beeching cuts allowed abandonment of steam, only five years after construction of British Rail's last steam engine in 1960. In the

1960s the west-coast line from London through Lancashire toward Scotland was rebuilt and electrified, with a consequent speed-up of service, and in the 1980s new equipment brought similarly fast service to the old Great Western and the east-coast line from London to Scotland, electrified in 1991.

At the beginning of the 1990s the railway network constituted 10,307 route miles, of which 2,825 were electrified, with 2,483 passenger stations and a staff of approximately 130,000. Passenger service dominated, freight traffic accounting for less than 13 percent of total train miles. But less than 7 percent of British passenger miles were rail-generated, the same percentage as that produced by long-distance buses, whereas 84 percent of passenger miles came from private automobiles. Statistics such as these fueled the tendency of **Margaret Thatcher's** administration to regard the railway as an expensive and unnecessary luxury and accounted for the government's reluctance to finance construction of a projected high-speed line from London to connect with the new Channel tunnel. **Labour** politicians continued to be more sympathetic to the railways than the **Conservatives,** in part a reflection of an ideological bias toward the collectivity of mass transport rather than the individuality of the private automobile, and in part to assure the maintenance of jobs for the dwindling number of railway workers. Supporters of railways resented public concentration on rail deficits, unbalanced by similar attention to far greater highway costs. In 1971, for example, while British Rail was spending only £26 million on maintenance or construction of roadbed, £687 million was spent on maintaining or building highways. As the 1990s began, public debate continued on the future role, if any, of railways in Britain, with the Conservatives pledged to the goal of privatization.

John Ranlett

Bibliography

Aldcroft, Derek H. *British Railways in Transition.* 1968.

Bagwell, Philip S. *The Transport Revolution, 1770–1985.* 1988.

Ellis, C.H. *British Railway History.* vol. 2. 1959.

Freeman, Michael, and Derek H. Aldcroft. *The Atlas of British Railway History.* 1985.

Gourvish, T.R. *British Railways, 1948–73: A Business History.* 1986.

Ottley, George. *A Bibliography of British Railway History.* 2nd ed. 1983.

Ramsey, (Arthur) Michael (1904–1988)

Michael Ramsey was a major leader of the **Church of England.** He initially rose to prominence as a theologian, being appointed Professor of divinity at the University of Durham in 1940 and then to a similar post at **Cambridge** in 1950. Less than two years later Ramsey was consecrated Bishop of Durham, a post traditionally held by a scholar. In 1956 he became Archbishop of York, and in 1961 Archbishop of Canterbury, where he served for thirteen years until his retirement in 1974. He was given a life peerage as Lord Ramsey of Canterbury and died in 1988.

Ramsey gained influence through his powerful mind and his warm, pastoral personality rather than his administrative skills. While still at school, and then as a Cambridge student, he came under the influence of Liberal Anglo-Catholicism, ultimately emerging as one of its most renowned modern exponents. From that theological position, he reached out to Protestant, Orthodox, and **Roman Catholic** leaders alike, making personal ecumenical dialogue one his archepiscopal priorities. He thus became an international and much-traveled public figure, meeting, for example, the Ecumenical Patriarch of Constantinople, whom he visited in Istanbul in 1962, and Patriarch Alexei of Moscow. In 1966 Pope Paul VI accorded Ramsey the first official reception (though not the first meeting) of an Archbishop of Canterbury. With Protestants he had many dealings, notably the Lutherans in Sweden and East Germany and, at home, the **Methodists.** The latter were partners during Ramsey's primacy in a reunion scheme that ultimately fell through in 1972.

Domestically, Ramsey emphasized lessened state control. This bore fruit in the establishment of a more powerful General Synod to replace the old Church Assembly (1970) and in the Worship and Doctrine Measure (1974) granting autonomy in liturgy. Politically, Ramsey identified with liberal causes and played a considerable role in the spate of legislation on moral issues that went through Parliament during the 1960s. Thus, he supported the abolition of **capital punishment** (1965) and decriminalization of **homosexuality** (1967). He also favored widening the grounds for **divorce** and **abortion**. He was a leader in addressing racism in English society, serving as Chairman of a National Committee for Commonwealth Immigrants and opposing the **immigration** acts of 1962 and 1968.

Despite time pressures Ramsey wrote numerous works, including *The Gospel and the Catholic Church* (1936), *From Gore to Temple* (1960), *The Christian Priest Today* (1972), and *Be Still and Know* (1982), in which he revealed himself as a master of Christian spirituality.

George Moyser

Bibliography
Chadwick, Owen. *Michael Ramsey: A Life.* 1990.

Rathbone, Eleanor Florence (1872–1946)

Eleanor Rathbone is remembered today as the leader of the thirty-year campaign for **family allowances** and as the most important feminist politician of her generation. In her own day, however, she also had a formidable reputation as a social thinker. Her classic work, *The Disinherited Family* (1924), remains the most lucid critique of a distributive system organized around a male family wage, and an eloquent plea for a comprehensive family policy.

Rathbone was born into a Liverpool shipbuilding family with a distinguished record of public service. Her father, William Rathbone IV (1829–1902), was an MP, prominent in philanthropic and reforming circles; his daughter would write his biography and succeed to his positions. In 1893 Rathbone entered Somerville College, **Oxford**, where she was remembered as serious and as a "fierce feminist." She returned to Liverpool after taking a second-class degree in 1896, and over the next twenty-five years she built a career in local politics and social work. Her work as a charitable visitor, **settlement** worker, and social investigator gave her an intimate knowledge of the social problems of the city, and she published studies of dock workers (1909), women's wages (1912), and the condition of widows under the Poor Law (1913). She was elected the first woman member of the City Council in 1909, a position she held until 1935.

Through her pioneering social investigations Rathbone became aware of the devastation wrought in working-class families by the cyclical nature and occasional failure of wages; even before 1914 she was developing a critique of a distributive system, which left the support of women and children to the vagaries of the male wage. After helping organize a comprehensive system of state aid to soldiers' wives and children during the **First World War**, she became convinced that only similar peacetime policies could improve the status of mothers and children. By destroying men's claim to a "family wage," she argued, direct state support for dependents could also make the **equal pay** of men and women possible. In 1917 she formed a Family Endowment Committee, and over the next thirty years she devoted much of her time, energy, and private resources to the campaign for family allowances.

Rathbone also came to hold an important place within feminist politics in the inter-war years. Initially involved in the **women's suffrage** movement in Liverpool, she supported the "pro-war" wing of the National Union of Women's Suffrage Societies and in 1919 succeeded **Millicent Garrett Fawcett** as President of the renamed National Union of Societies for Equal Citizenship. NUSEC suffered a sharp decline in its membership and fortunes after 1919, largely because of the war and the partial achievement of the vote, but some adherents also disagreed with Rathbone's leadership, especially with her espousal of a "new **feminism**" aimed less at the achievement of strict equality than at the improvement of conditions for wives and mothers. In 1929 Rathbone was elected to the House of Commons as an Independent for the Combined English Universities, a seat she held until her death. Although she continued to argue for social supports for mothers and children, she devoted much of the 1930s to a series of campaigns aimed at raising the status of **women** in the British colonies. Her interventions were sometimes tactless and not always welcomed by their purported beneficiaries, but in some cases she was able to force the Colonial Office to consider women's issues and to establish contacts between women across national lines.

If a single thread united Rathbone's many writings and interests, it was her concern to mitigate women's subordination to men—whether legal, customary, or economic—within the family. Convinced of the dignity and worth of "women's work" of childbearing and **childrearing**, she tended to attribute all opposition to her campaigns simply to the desire of men of all classes and races to preserve their domestic and sexual privileges—a predilection she notoriously labeled the "Turk Complex" in *The Dis-*

inherited Family. This belief in men's universal disposition toward familial tyranny is intriguing, particularly in light of her close relations with her own father and her strong identification with the Rathbone heritage. Perhaps the key to this puzzle, and the source of her ability to imagine that marriage need not entail economic dependence, is to be sought in her lifelong relationship with Elizabeth Macadam, a feminist and social worker with whom she lived until her death. Eleanor Rathbone died on 1 January 1946, barely six months after the passage of the Family Allowances Act.

Susan Pedersen

Bibliography

Land, Hilary. "Eleanor Rathbone and the Economy of the Family" in Harold L. Smith, ed. *British Feminism in the Twentieth Century.* 1990. pp. 104–23.

Pedersen, Susan. "Eleanor Rathbone, 1872–1946: The Victorian Family under the Daughter's Eye" in Susan Pedersen, and Peter Mandler, eds. *After the Victorians: Private Conscience and Public Duty in Modern Britain.* 1994. pp. 105–25.

Stocks, Mary D. *Eleanor Rathbone: A Biography.* 1949.

Rationing

Rationing, the sharing of food and other necessities among the population through controls imposed by the government during the **First World War** and the **Second World War**, was an essential element in homefront war policy.

At the onset of both wars the country produced only about one-third of its food, measured in calories. The rest was imported by ship. This put the nation at risk of starvation in wartime, when merchant vessels came under attack by the enemy and when more cargo space was needed for munitions and other war materiel. Rationing reduced pressure on shipping by compulsorily lowering demand for imported foodstuffs and by limiting imports to the most economical in terms of nutrition and shipping space. It also prevented one region or social group going short while others had plenty by distributing available supplies fairly.

At the start of the First World War there were no plans to ration civilians. Despite German **submarine warfare**, shipments of most foods remained adequate for the first two years of the war. By mid-1916, however, dwindling imports necessitated control of distribution. The British public got its first taste of rationing in July 1916 when "datum period rationing" went into effect for sugar. Shopkeepers were allotted amounts equal to 65 percent of their 1915 sales. It was their responsibility to share supplies among customers. In February 1917 other shortages forced the government to announce "voluntary rationing." The public was asked to eat no more than four pounds of breadstuffs, two-and-one-half pounds of meat, and three-quarters of a pound of sugar each week. Since most working people ate much more bread and less meat than this and could not afford to substitute other foods for bread, the cheapest staple of the day, there was much resistance to voluntary rationing as unfair pressure on those least able to economize. In June the government acknowledged the importance of safeguarding the diet of industrial workers by promising that, whatever other foods might have to be rationed, bread would not. Moreover, the price of bread would be subsidized.

The public reacted positively when compulsory rationing began in January 1918. It was first intended to use a complex five-tier scheme based on calorie needs according to sex, age, and occupation. Instead, because of the need to move quickly, coupons were issued that provided equal rations to all adults, with extra supplies for men on heavy industrial work. To start with, weekly rations were one-half pound of sugar; four ounces of butter or margarine; two ounces of lard; and varying amounts of tea, cheese, jam, and other items, depending on supplies. In a popular move, meat was rationed by price, not weight, which left working-class consumption virtually unchanged. Milk was not rationed, but expectant and nursing mothers and children under age five received priority tickets that gave them first call on supplies. Vegetables, like bread, remained unrationed. Those who could afford it were free to buy whatever unrationed items remained in the stores and **restaurants**.

Rationing satisfied public demands for equality of treatment and maintained the **diet** of most people at a caloric level similar to pre-war while reducing consumption practices of wealthier people to a level closer to the norm.

With the lessons of the past and inter-war nutritional research to draw on, rationing in the Second World War was more efficient and scientifically designed. Plans formulated before the war went into effect in January 1940. The key policy that distinguished British rationing from that of other countries was, again, that of leaving cereals and vegetables unrationed and subsidizing the price of bread. Individuals thus determined their own calorie intake by eating more or less of these items in addition to their rations. This made possible the division of the population into just three groups for ration books: "normal consumers" age eighteen and over, children age six to seventeen, and children under age six. Only about 50 percent of the average person's calories were controlled by coupons. These allowed each person fixed quantities of protective foods needed in similar amounts by all adults, such as meat, cheese, milk, fats, and eggs, with extra milk for children. Sugar, jam, tea, and coffee were also shared equally. In 1943 weekly basic rations provided eight ounces of sugar, four ounces of fats, three ounces of cheese, two ounces of tea, and one and a half dried eggs. Meat was again rationed by price. In 1943 the coupon bought about eight ounces of bacon and a pound of other meat. In addition, each person was allotted a monthly number of "points" that could be "spent" on such foods as canned fish or biscuits, as the consumer wished. Extra food for people engaged in heavy labor was provided through communal feeding. About 12 million people a day ate a coupon-free meal in canteens at large industrial plants or in "British restaurants" (public, government-run cafés) near smaller factories. Children were served additional food and milk at school, free if the family could not afford to pay. Preschool children and expectant and nursing mothers benefited from priority tickets for highly nutritious foods in short supply, such as milk, fresh eggs, fruit, and juice. The milk was free, if necessary. Rationing continued after the war, with bread added to the coupon book from mid-1946 to mid-1948. Starting with milk in 1950, controls were gradually dismantled and ended in 1954.

Britain's wartime experience with rationing was probably the most successful in Europe. Average calorie intake remained close to prewar levels and for the lowest-income groups rose. Health improved due to the increased consumption of milk and vegetables and the special care paid to the diet of children and pregnant women. Rationing thus contributed not only to national survival in wartime but to narrowing the socioeconomic gap between classes.

L. Margaret Barnett

Bibliography

Barnett, L. Margaret. *British Food Policy during the First World War.* 1985.

Beveridge, William H. *British Food Control.* 1928.

Hammond, R.J. *Food.* 3 vols. 1951–62.

Reddaway, W.B. "Rationing" in D.N. Chester, ed. *Lessons of the British War Economy.* 1951. pp. 182–99.

Rattigan, Terence Mervyn (1911–1977)

Between 1936 and 1956 Terence Rattigan was the one West End playwright who achieved both critical acclaim as a serious writer and huge commercial success. The son of a diplomat, educated at Harrow and Trinity College, **Oxford**, he became a celebrated playwright at the age of twenty-five. The light comedy *French without Tears* (1936) was his first hit, running for 1,030 performances. *Flare Path* (1942), his drama about a **Royal Air Force** bomber squadron during the **Second World War**, ran for 679 performances, and *While the Sun Shines* (1943), a comedy, ran for 1,154 performances.

Beneath the lighthearted surface of *French without Tears*, an awareness of the pain and humiliation of unrequited love is interwoven with well-observed if exaggerated social comedy. Throughout his career, Rattigan's output alternated between light comedies and dramas of pathos. His critical reputation rests on the darker side of his output: the studies of individuals or groups of characters whose heroism consists in courageously facing a world in which injustice, intolerance, and unreciprocated sexual infatuations are the norm, moral integrity and fullfilment of romantic passion mere ideals. Rattigan's identification as a writer with the outsider or the underdog may have been a consequence of the tension he experienced as a pillar of the upper-middle-class theatrical Establishment forced to keep his own **homosexuality** a secret until the partial decriminalization in 1967 of homosexual relations among men.

All of his critical successes from *The Winslow Boy* (1946) to *Cause Célèbre* (1977) were written as variations on the formulaic well-made play, which constituted the dominant tradition of British drama from 1890 to 1956 (the year of *Look Back in Anger* by **John Osborne**). His persistent themes are the suffering endured by principled but reticent individuals in conflict with a dishonest and repressive society and the inequalities that characterize sexual relationships as a consequence of class or gender differences. However limited in their treatment of social and intellectual issues, plays such as *The Browning Version* (1948) and *The Deep Blue Sea* (1952) are characterized by a Strindbergian relentlessness in plumbing the depths of human misery.

The Deep Blue Sea is a harshly realistic study of a middle-class woman's struggle to come to terms with living alone after realizing that circumstances condemn her to a comfortable but passionless marriage or a relationship with a lover who is incapable of reciprocating her intensity. At the beginning of the play she has attempted suicide; the end of the play makes it clear that she is facing up to life with no illusions.

Although Rattigan was criticized in the 1950s and 1960s for the middlebrow quality of his plays, *The Winslow Boy*, *The Browning Version*, *The Deep Blue Sea*, and *Separate Tables* (1954) have become classics of the British theater, and his reputation, having waned, now seems to be undergoing a revival. Most of Rattigan's popular plays were made into films, and he also wrote a number of successful screenplays. He was knighted in 1971 for his contribution to the theater.

Robert Gordon

Bibliography

Darlow, Michael, and Gillian Hodson. *Terence Rattigan: The Man and His Work*. 1979.

Taylor, John Russell. *The Rise and Fall of the Well-Made Play*. 1967.

Young, B.A. *The Rattigan Version: Sir Terence Rattigan and the Theatre of Character*. 1986.

Read, Herbert Edward (1893–1968)

Herbert Read was a prominent critic, poet, editor, and anarchist whose activities helped introduce the public to the bewildering varieties of visual and literary modernism, and whose support of many British modern artists helped them weather the initial incomprehension that often greeted their work. Read thought of himself as an heir to the social aesthetic of John Ruskin and William Morris. Like them, he sought to break down the distinction between art and life and to heighten the public's aesthetic sensibility at a time when art and art education were undervalued by many. Read devoted his popular art criticism and lectures to this end and also became extensively involved in the fields of art education, industrial **design**, and museum display. In addition to his attempts to unify art and life, Read tried to merge classicism and romanticism in his poetry and to unite an anarchist's commitment to individual freedom with a romantic (and at times Tory) idealization of "organic" communities that he thought had existed in England prior to the Industrial Revolution.

Read was born on 4 December 1893 in North Yorkshire. He attended the University of Leeds and was a captain in the **army** during the **First World War**. He wrote poetry (collected in *Songs of Chaos*, 1915; *Naked Warriors*, 1919) and edited the avant-garde journal *Art and Letters* with Frank Rutter. When he returned to London after the war Read became associated with many modernists, including **T.S. Eliot** and T.E. Hulme. He married Evelyn Roff in 1919. Read worked for the Treasury (1919–22) and then became an Assistant Keeper in the Ceramics Department of the Victoria and Albert Museum (1922–31). During these years he wrote for many publications on literary modernism as well as romanticism (*Reason and Romanticism*, 1926; *The Sense of Glory*, 1929). He also began to write more frequently about the visual arts, based on his experience with ceramics. He was appointed Professor of fine art at the University of Edinburgh (1931–3), but for professional and personal reasons (including an affair with Margaret Ludwif, whom he married in 1936), he returned to London and assumed the editorship of the *Burlington Magazine* (1933–9). Among his significant publications on art during this decade were *Art Now* (1933); *Art and Industry* (1934); and *Art and Society* (1937). He was one of the organizers of the 1936 surrealist exhibition in London and became a Director of Routledge and Sons in 1939, a position he held for the next twenty-five years.

Read was pragmatic as well as romantic and attempted to turn his aesthetic ideals into practical projects. His interest in industrial art led him to become a founder and President of the Design Research Unit in 1943, and he was also an active member of the Design and Industries Association. During the Second World War he organized exhibitions of children's art and presented his own plan for an aesthetic education in the influential *Education through Art* (1943). In terms of promoting avant-garde art, he was one of the founders of the collective of modernist painters, designers, and architects known as Unit One in 1934 and a cofounder of the **Institute of Contemporary Arts** in 1948.

Read's own strenuous advocacy of modern artists prevented him from writing as much of his own poetry as he wished, but he nevertheless continued to publish a number of well-received poems (assembled in *Collected Poems*, 1966), a series of autobiographical works (notably *The Contrary Experience*, 1963), and one novel, *The Green Child* (1935). Many of his essays and talks were collected in numerous volumes; among these were *Icon and Idea* (1955), based on his Charles Eliot Norton Lectures at Harvard University, and *The Art of Sculpture* (1956), based on his Andrew Mellon Lectures at the National Gallery of Art in Washington, D.C. Read's writings were often tinged with his anarchist sentiments, although these did not prevent him from accepting a knighthood in 1953. His later writings, particularly those of the 1960s, expressed less hope for the aesthetic salvation of mankind: Read had become disillusioned with several of the new schools of art, such as pop art, and expressed his fear of the gradual dehumanization of the individual through the spread of technology and the threat of nuclear destruction. He became ill with cancer in the early 1960s and died on 12 June 1968. Like Ruskin, Read not only introduced new art to the public, but connected it to a romantic, "English" ideal of life that made the new more palatable; his humane vision and pellucid prose proved attractive to readers all over the world.

Michael Saler

Bibliography

King, James. *The Last Modern: A Life of Herbert Read.* 1990.

Read, Herbert. *The Contrary Experience.* 1963.

Woodcock, George. *Herbert Read: The Stream and the Source.* 1972.

Refugees

There is a tradition of **immigration** into Britain, despite the fact that in the recent past the country has been a net exporter of population. Within this wider process of immigration can be found a constant flow of refugees. In the nineteenth century Britain became a haven for many fleeing from persecution, although eventual reluctance to admit more refugees manifested itself in restrictive legislation. The 1905 Aliens Act, together with the acts of 1914 and 1919, allowed the government to exercise tight control over the entry, movement, and deportation of all aliens. In spite of such controls, imposed by whichever party was in power and reinforced by subsequent restrictions, refugees continued to come to Britain throughout the century. A small number of émigrés arrived from Russia after 1917, while the advent of Benito Mussolini's Fascist regime brought Italian exiles to Britain from the 1920s onward.

The decisive period for the arrival of refugees, however, was the 1930s when a significant number came from Germany and, following the *Anschluss* in 1938, from Austria. After the **Munich** agreement and the continued penetration of Czechoslovakia, refugees also arrived from that part of Central Europe. The advent of Adolf Hitler in 1933 did not initially result in a large-scale exodus from Germany, but emigration grew as the nature of Nazism became clearer. A significant increase in Jewish emigration followed *Kristallnacht* in November 1938. With restrictive immigration controls already in place, refugees encountered little official encouragement and widespread public opposition to their entry. Between 1933 and 1939 an estimated 56,000 refugees from the German Reich, 95 percent of them Jewish, entered Britain. Such figures suggest that Britain was generous in its welcome, but official policy remained cautious.

Many refugees from Germany found it difficult to make a new beginning. The British government required that Jewish refugees would not become a public charge, and the **Jewish** community had to provide guarantees on this score. Moreover, refugees in general encountered opposition to their employment: Architects, doctors, and university teachers were among those occupational groups who reacted with antipathy. As a result, some refugees departed to the United States, which they perceived as a more open, less selective society. Some refugees who remained in Britain gradually made a significant impact, notably in business and the academic world. But other refugees, often invisible to historians, never fully adjusted to life in exile.

Apart from German refugees, the 1930s witnessed the arrival of groups fleeing from the impact of the **Spanish Civil War**, including a number of Basque children whose entry was assisted by the National Joint Committee for Spanish Relief.

Since the 1930s other refugees have come to Britain, such as Poles and Hungarians fleeing from repressive Communist regimes. Increasingly, however, refugee problems have become worldwide; the arrival in Britain of groups from Chile in the 1970s and from Vietnam in the 1980s revealed merely the tip of an international problem. The issue of asylum for refugees and government proposals to tighten entry laws continue to be the subjects of impassioned debate.

Colin Holmes

Bibliography

Holmes, Colin. *John Bull's Island: Immigration and British Society, 1871–1971.* 1988.

Kushner, Tony. *The Persistence of Prejudice: Anti-Semitism in British Society during the Second World War.* 1989.

Sword, K., with Norman Davies, and Jan Ciechanowski. *The Formation of the Polish Community in Great Britain, 1939–1950.* 1989.

Tannahill, John Allan. *European Volunteer Workers in Britain.* 1958.

Reith, John Charles Walsham (1889–1971)
The first Director-General of the British Broadcasting Corporation (BBC), John Reith was a seminal figure in the development of twentieth-century mass communication. A figure of enormous energy and ambition, Reith helped shape the structure of broadcasting in Great Britain. His notion of public service, most forcefully enunciated in the 1920s, provided the BBC with an institutional identity and national purpose it never wholly abandoned.

Reith was born in Scotland in July 1889, the seventh and youngest child of George and Adah Reith. A minister in the Free Church of Scotland, George Reith had served the College Church in Glasgow since 1866. Educated at Glasgow Academy and Gresham's School in Norfolk, John Reith was withdrawn from school under mysterious circumstances at age seventeen and apprenticed as an engineer to the North British Locomotive Company. From 1906 to 1914 he studied and worked as an engineer, first in Glasgow and then for a brief period in London. Long interested in the military, Reith served with valor in the **First World War**, where in 1915 a sniper's wound left his

face scarred. Prohibited from returning to the front, Reith was sent to the United States in 1916 to help organize the manufacture and supply of rifles for the British **army**. His managerial skills and deep moral seriousness greatly impressed American and British authorities. Three years after the war ended, while manager of a factory, Reith married Muriel Odhams, the daughter of a wealthy publisher.

In 1922 Reith was offered the leadership of the newly formed BBC, a tiny company of limited resources and no fixed identity. Distressed by the commercialism of American broadcasting and mass communication generally, Reith struggled hard for the ideals of public service broadcasting. Demanding and receiving monopoly powers for the BBC in 1923 and then again in two subsequent renewals of the charter (1926, 1936), Reith argued that high culture need only be made available for most people to embrace it. With its emphasis on classical music, instructional talks, and Sunday religious programs, the BBC became the embodiment of cultural respectability during the inter-war period and gained wide support across the political spectrum as a successful experiment in public ownership and control.

A prominent national figure in the 1930s, Reith longed for greater authority and responsibility in national affairs. In 1938 he resigned from the BBC to become head of Imperial Airways, an audacious gesture that proved a mistake for his career and a disaster for him personally. Never again would he occupy an office of such power, prestige, and access. During the Second World War he served in a variety of posts, including Minister of Information, but his authoritarian manner, self-absorption, and personal bitterness, especially toward **Winston Churchill**, soured the considerable achievements of this period. From 1950 to 1959 Reith led the Colonial Development Corporation, retiring at age seventy with many honors, not least the peerage granted in 1942, but also with an abiding sense of personal failure that haunted his later career and bewildered his admirers. His monument remained the BBC, which despite enormous changes after his departure retained the sense of mission bequeathed by its first Director-General.

D.L. LeMahieu

Bibliography

LeMahieu, D.L. "John Reith, 1889–1971: Entrepreneur of Collectivism" in Susan

Pedersen, and Peter Mandler, eds. *After the Victorians: Private Conscience and Public Duty in Modern Britain.* 1994. pp. 189–206.

Reith, John (Lord). *Into the Wind.* 1949.

Stuart, Charles, ed. *The Reith Diaries.* 1975.

Reparations (1919–1930)

The reparations question—how much Germany should pay as compensation for damage done during the First World War—was a central and divisive issue in European international relations in the 1920s. As such, it was one of the focal points of British diplomacy in the postwar years, as successive governments sought to achieve a final settlement acceptable to all parties concerned.

The reparations dispute began at the 1919 Paris Peace Conference. To the German delegation and public the vast sums being discussed by Allied statesmen, and still more the wording of Article 231 of the Treaty of Versailles, which gave the impression that Germany was being burdened with the entire moral responsibility for the war, came as a profound shock. Under the threat of renewed hostilities the treaty was signed, but German politicians considered the reparations clauses—and indeed the treaty as a whole—a *diktat* that ought to be circumvented as soon as possible. Even before a final reparations bill of 132 billion gold marks was announced by the Allied Reparations Commission in May 1921, Germany was falling behind on the interim payments set at Versailles and claiming an inability to pay.

The French were outraged: Reconstruction and war debts had to be financed, and Germany should be kept weak so as to prevent a future war, all of which necessitated the rigid enforcement of the reparations schedule. The British position, however, was more ambivalent. Despite the Germanophobia of the 1918 election campaign, various civil servants and ministers—Prime Minister David Lloyd George among them—were increasingly concerned about the potential effect of reparations on the British economy. If reparations were too high, there would be no German market for British goods. Influenced by John Maynard Keynes' *The Economic Consequences of the Peace* (1919), which argued that reparations beyond Germany's capacity were being demanded and that unless they were reduced a worldwide depression would result, British statesmen and diplomats soon began to argue strongly in favor of scaling down reparations.

No compromise proved acceptable to all sides, however, and in January 1923 French troops marched into the Ruhr in retaliation for Germany defaulting on reparations payments. The German government responded with a campaign of passive resistance. The British government of Andrew Bonar Law deplored the Ruhr occupation but made no effort to block French access via the British occupation zone in the Rhineland. With hyperinflation rampant and the German economy in ruins as a result of the Ruhr crisis, passive resistance was finally called off in August 1923.

British coal exports had soared during the Ruhr occupation, but the British government, in conjunction with the United States, seized the opportunity provided by the ending of passive resistance to force the French to accept a new deal and pull out of the Ruhr. The German economy had to be allowed to prosper in order to facilitate the recovery of Anglo-German trade, and also to enable Germany to pay reparations sufficient to allow Britain to pay off its war debts to the United States. The result was the 1924 Dawes Plan, in which the size of reparations payments was recognized as being tied to the health of the German economy. Payments would be low to begin with and then gradually increase, so that by 1928—when full yearly payments of over 2.5 billion gold marks would come into effect—Germany would possess a healthy economy and be able to pay.

As a result of large-scale private loans from the United States, the Dawes Plan appeared to be working: U.S. funds poured into Germany, the scaled-down reparations payment schedule was met, and the Allies in turn paid their war debts to America. With the full payment schedule coming back into force in the latter 1920s, however, the German government once more began to protest that it was unable to pay. The British government of Ramsay MacDonald would have preferred at this point a general reduction of war debts and reparations, but to this the United States and France would not agree, and a new reduced payment schedule— the Young Plan—was negotiated in 1929. This compromise was less than satisfactory to most of the participants, but the effects of the Great Depression soon submerged the reparations issue permanently. With the German economy once more at a virtual standstill, it was agreed at the Lausanne Conference of April 1932 that in order to revive European trade, reparations would have to be canceled entirely.

S.P. MacKenzie

Bibliography

Bunselmeyer, Robert E. *The Cost of the War, 1914–1919: British Economic War Aims and the Origin of Reparation*. 1975.

Kent, Bruce. *The Spoils of War: The Politics, Economics, and Diplomacy of Reparations, 1918–1932*. 1989.

Trachtenberg, Marc. *Reparation in World Politics: France and European Economic Diplomacy, 1916–1923*. 1980.

Restaurants

In 1900 London had about a dozen grand West End restaurants, such as Verrey's or the Trocadero, all French style, serving elaborate multicourse dinners for which patrons were required to wear full evening dress and pay upwards of £2 with wine. One could dine for less at the old English chop houses like Rule's or the Cheshire Cheese, and the growing hordes of clerks and shoppers made the fortunes of the Lyons' Corner House and ABC chains. The continuing influx of Italian **immigrants** increased the number of more modest cafés and restaurants that they tended to open, particularly in Soho. Some of the very best restaurants were in **hotels** such as the Cavendish, the Savoy, and the Carlton, where Auguste Escoffier was chef. They also offered grill rooms for quicker, less formal dining favored particularly by American tourists. Outside London virtually the only first-class restaurants were in the major **railway** hotels.

First World War **rationing** encouraged a vogue for lighter meals than the twelve-course standard set by **Edward VII**. The post-war period saw the opening of a new generation of restaurants such as the Berkeley, beloved of **P.G. Wodehouse**'s Bertie Wooster, and Quaglino's, offering cocktails, cabarets, and dancing for the smart young crowd led by the dashingly informal Prince of Wales. Boulestin's offered serious French cooking in an unintimidating setting. Its owner-chef, Marcel Boulestin, did much to demystify and popularize French cooking as an author and as the **British Broadcasting Corporation**'s (BBC) first TV chef in 1937–9. But the 1940s were grim years for gastronomy. The **Second World War** brought food rationing that lasted until 1950, and even the best restaurants were forbidden to charge over 25p for a meal. At the government-run British restaurants scientifically nourishing meals of snoek (whale meat) potato pie and turnips could be had very cheaply.

The 1950s and 1960s witnessed a surge of pent-up interest in good food. Raymond Postgate's *Good Food Guide*, which first appeared in 1951, used the criticism of independent diners in its judgment of restaurants and, with the work of other critics like Egon Ronay, did much to raise the expectations of diners and the standards of restaurants. In the twilight of Empire, Cypriots, Indians, and Chinese immigrants and **refugees** contributed to the restaurant scene. Belated imperialists could prove their mettle on hot curries, while Cantonese, joined later by Pekinese, Szechuan, and Dim Sum, cuisine proved popular with middle- and even working-class diners out, for whom it offered an exotic alternative to fish and chips.

A particularly notable feature of the post-1950 restaurant boom was the emergence of a novel force: The British amateur spirit took the form of gastronomic entrepreneurship. Army officers, academics, and physicians found an outlet for their creative urges by becoming owner-chefs. Frequently they were inspired by the Penguin cookbooks of Elizabeth Davis, as was Dr. Hilary James, a psychotherapist who opened Le Matelot in 1952, followed by La Bicyclette in 1954. Bill Staughton's Hungry Horse and Nick Clarke's Nick's Diner are two other early examples. The point of these restaurants, as their names suggest, was not just good food but good fun in a relatively informal setting. Provincial and Mediterranean food, particularly scampi, were made popular by these sorts of place, to the point that journalists took to calling the newly gentrified inner-ring suburbs where such restaurants tended to proliferate the "scampi belt." Newspaper journalism played an important role in the good-food boom, especially the quality Sunday papers: The American-born Robert Carrier, another important chef-journalist-*restaurateur* was the first food editor of the *Sunday Times Magazine*. The cheapening of the Continental holiday, general upward mobility, and the vague but powerful dictates of trendiness were also important factors. So, too, was the great extension of car ownership, since a lot of the smart amateur restaurants were located in the country, where real estate was cheap and kitchen gardens possible. The darker side of the post-war picture, particularly from the 1970s onward, was the relentless spread of American fast-food chains.

Christopher A. Kent

Bibliography
Baedeker, Karl. *London and Its Environs: Handbook for Travellers.* 1900.
Boniface, Priscilla. *Hotels and Restaurants, 1830 to the Present Day.* 1981.
Bowden, Gregory H. *British Gastronomy: The Rise of Great Restaurants.* 1975.

Richards, I(vor) A(rmstrong) (1893–1979)
In a career spanning sixty years I.A. Richards made major contributions to semantics, literary theory and practice, linguistics, and education. *Practical Criticism* (1929) revolutionized the academic study of literature and dominated classrooms in the English-speaking world from the 1940s to the 1960s. Its method of "close reading" remains a continuing influence. His programs in beginning reading and second-language training embraced the use of modern media, from slide, recording, and filmstrip to television, video, and cassette.

Richards was born in Sandbach, Cheshire, and was educated at Clifton and Magdalene College, **Cambridge,** where he read moral sciences under **G.E. Moore** and received first-class honors in 1915. Shortly thereafter he suffered a serious attack of **tuberculosis** and recuperated by climbing mountains in North Wales. There he met his future wife, Dorothea Elinor Pilley, a journalist and mountaineer. In 1919 the new English School at Cambridge invited him to teach courses on contemporary literature and the theory of criticism. His first book was *The Foundations of Aesthetics* (1922, coauthored by C.K. Odgen and James Wood), in which he outlines sixteen aesthetic theories, with a preference for psychological "synaesthesis," a harmonious state of thought and feeling together with an equilibrium that prevents any immediate tendency to action. In *The Meaning of Meaning* (1923, with C.K. Ogden) he presents a contextual theory of meaning in which context is given a psychological and physical definition; though the authors are rooted in British philosophical psychology, they borrow elements of behaviorism in constructing a model of interpretation. They postulate two broad uses of language, the emotive and the referential (or symbolic), as well as five separate functions, each more or less present in a given speech-act.

In later books Richards raises the number to seven: indicating, charactering, realizing, valuing, influencing, controlling, and purposing.

The nature of the literary text and the reader's response are the subjects of his next books. *Principles of Literary Criticism* (1924) elaborates theories of communication and value, defined in terms of the enrichment of the mental personality. The treatment of poetic texts places a strong emphasis on balance and attitudinal equilibrium in which irony is seen as a literary device for bringing in opposed or complementary attitudes to ensure complexity and wholeness. In *Practical Criticism* (1929), his masterpiece and one of the most famous experiments in the history of criticism, he examines hundreds of undergraduate reports on poems of varying quality, categorizes the types of misreading, and proposes a corrective method of textual "close reading" (sense, irony, ambiguity, metaphor, feeling, tone, intention, and the like). *The Philosophy of Rhetoric* (1936) advances a revolutionary theory of metaphor, defined as a "transaction between contexts." *Interpretation in Teaching* (1938) rounds out his theory of criticism, applying his method to the study of critical or expository prose.

The influence of these books has been deep and lasting. One of his pupils was William Empson, whose *Seven Types of Ambiguity* (1930) had its origins in tutorial. Richards is often acknowledged as the "father" of American New Criticism, an academic movement stressing the objectivity of the work of art, contextualism, and "close reading."

During the 1930s Richards turned his attention from higher education to problems in beginning reading and language training. He spent several years in China promoting Ogden's "Basic English," a normal version of English based on an initial knowledge of 850 key words and grammatical patterns. Of the books that emerged from his experience in China *Mencius on the Mind* (1931) and *A First Book of English for Chinese Learners* (1938) are particularly noteworthy. In 1939, after twenty years at Cambridge, he accepted a post at Harvard where he became University Professor (1944–63). He pioneered the use of audiovisual media in the teaching of reading and second-language learning. *English through Pictures* (1945, with Christine M. Gibson) was the first of a series of *Language through Pictures* in seven languages. He also translated Homer, Plato, and the Book of Job into simplified English so that students could have major works among their first literary experiences in the language.

In 1974 Richards published *Beyond*, which examines the dialogues with deities in Homer, Plato, Job, Dante, and Shelley. In the same year he returned to Cambridge, England. At the age of sixty he had begun writing poetry, eventually bringing out four collections and three verse-plays. In his eighty-seventh year he undertook a tour of China, lecturing on the teaching of English. He fell seriously ill and was brought back to England, where he died on 7 September 1979.

John Paul Russo

Bibliography

Hotopf, W.H.N. *Language, Thought, and Comprehension: A Case Study of the Writings of I.A. Richards.* 1965.

Needham, John. *The Completest Mode: I.A. Richards and the Continuity of English Literary Criticism.* 1982.

Russo, John Paul. "A Bibliography" in Reuben Brower, Helen Vendler, and John Hollander. *I.A. Richards: Essays in His Honor.* 1973. pp. 319–65.

———. *I.A. Richards: His Life and Work.* 1989.

Schiller, Jerome P. *I.A. Richards' Theory of Literature.* 1969.

Richardson, Dorothy Miller (1873–1957)

Dorothy Richardson is best known for her sequence-novel, *Pilgrimage*, published in twelve parts between 1915 and 1938, with a thirteenth part found among her papers when she died and added to the sequence in 1967 when the entire novel was reprinted. The early "chapter-volumes" of *Pilgrimage* were recognized at once as a radical departure from tradition in both form and content. Not only did the narrative proceed from the limited consciousness of one central character as though there were no author behind the text, but in addition the single protagonist—Miriam Henderson—was a young, naive, inexperienced yet opinionated British girl, whose developing thoughts and feelings constituted the "story" of *Pilgrimage*. In other words, Richardson was defying the expectations of early twentieth-century novel readers in two revolutionary ways: by eliminating a standard plot and by insisting on the cultural value and significance of a female consciousness.

Miriam's fictional time was Richardson's historical reality. At least in outline and often in detail, *Pilgrimage* took up the life of its author from the age of seventeen, when she was forced by her father's financial reverses to seek employment, first as a pupil-teacher in a school for girls in Germany, then as a teacher in a north London private school and a governess in a wealthy suburban family—all of which provided the material for *Pointed Roofs* (1915), *Backwater* (1916), and *Honeycomb* (1917). These three "chapter-volumes"—a thematic unit—trace Miriam's gradual separation from the confines as well as the security of her family. *Honeycomb* ends with the bankruptcy of Mr. Henderson and the suicide of Mrs. Henderson, events whose repercussions are felt throughout the rest of *Pilgrimage*, as Miriam (like Richardson herself) moves into the London—and centrally formative—phase of her life.

Alone in the city, employed as a receptionist-secretary by several dental surgeons in the West End and living in an attic room on the outskirts of Bloomsbury, Miriam absorbs all that an expanding and heterogeneous **London** had to offer. London becomes her university, as it had been for Richardson, and each succeeding "chapter-volume" of *Pilgrimage* explores yet another stage in the education of its heroine and the re-creation of its author's past: *The Tunnel* and *Interim* (1919); *Deadlock* (1921); *Revolving Lights* (1923); *The Trap* (1925); *Oberland* (1928); *Dawn's Left Hand* (1931); *Clear Horizon* (1935). With *Dimple Hill* (1938), Miriam's London life comes to an end, along with the multiple—and tangled—relationships she has formed with various men, women, and ideologies. London is replaced by Sussex, where Miriam experiments with living among **Quakers**, learning from them some valuable lessons about her own self and its expressive needs. Again like Richardson, Miriam has already begun to write reviews and essays for little magazines, but by the time she leaves the Quaker household at the close of *Dimple Hill*, she is contemplating the much larger work that would turn into *Pilgrimage*. And in the posthumously published *March Moonlight* (1967), Miriam considers the benefits and the liabilities of the demanding project she is about to undertake—a novel about herself as a representative woman of her time.

Although *Pilgrimage* would play its part in changing the contours of modern fiction and win for Richardson a place among the great experimentalists of the twentieth century, the critical estimates—with a few exceptions—have been grudging, if not downright hostile. Yet there is no doubt that the work poses formidable difficulties by virtue of its size as well as its problematic content. In addition, Richardson's letters indicate that she may not have initially conceived of *March Moonlight* as the final "chapter-volume" that many critics take it to be. A further sequel would have been influenced in part by Miriam's meeting with the artist clearly modeled on Alan Odle (1888–1948), whom Richardson met soon after *Pilgrimage* began to appear and whom she married in 1917. But enough evidence certainly exists to warrant reaching no conclusion about the state of *Pilgrimage* as a finished or unfinished work. Recently, however, under the influence of French **feminist** theory, especially that of Hélène Cixous, critics have begun to portray *Pilgrimage* as an open-ended plotless precursor of *écriture féminine*. Other critics are engaged in "naturalizing" *Pilgrimage* as a *roman fleuve* rather than autobiography or stream-of-consciousness narrative. Still others, expanding the range of the critical treatment of Richardson even further, are looking at the entire body of her work—sketches, reviews, essays (including her film criticism), short stories, poems—in an effort to show the unity and consistency of her aesthetic and the evolution of her social and political thought. Contemporary critics, then, are coming to terms with Richardson by discarding old restrictive clichés and bringing into focus the genuinely original nature of her work.

Gloria G. Fromm

Bibliography
Fromm, Gloria G. *Dorothy Richardson: A Biography.* 1977.
———. *Windows on Modernism: Selected Letters of Dorothy Richardson.* 1994.

Robbins Report (1963)

In the first half of the twentieth century higher education in Britain consisted of three distinct segments: universities, teacher training colleges, and institutions of further education, which included technical, commercial, and art colleges. After 1945 the priority of economic recovery and an unprecedented number of university-qualified secondary-school graduates signaled the need for a coordinated system of higher education in Britain. In 1961 a subcom-

mittee of the University Grants Committee was established to analyze the current state of higher education and provide recommendations for its future. Lionel Robbins, a leading academic economist known for his interest in liberal education, was invited to be Chairman.

As no comprehensive picture of the status of higher education yet existed, the committee undertook a thorough stocktaking of the nation's educational system. Four hundred written submissions of evidence were solicited from individuals and organizations, and a series of statistical surveys was commissioned. Surveys of full-time undergraduates, postgraduates, students in teacher training programs, members of academic staff, and twenty-one-year-olds formed the bulk of the research. The surveys revealed a sizable scholastic potential and untapped ability in students aged above sixteen, particularly among girls. It was apparent that Britain, like the Continent in general, lagged behind the United States in student enrollment and would benefit by providing more opportunities for higher education.

The Committee on Higher Education published its findings in 1963. The Robbins Report focused criticism on the uncoordinated state of British higher education, concluding that without systematic reform there was little chance of "maintaining an adequate position in the fiercely competitive world of the future." With reform, the committee predicted an increase in the number of postgraduates from 9,500 in 1961 to 32,000 by 1980–1.

The seven-volume report offered both general strategies and specific proposals for educational reform. In all, it set forth 178 recommendations touching on every aspect of university organization: staffing, student life, research, teaching, finance, academic coverage, and governance. Four principal objectives for higher education were cited. First, educational institutions should help prepare students for the marketplace by providing the means to specialization. Second, there should be no sacrifice of liberal learning and cultivation of the mind. Third, a new emphasis should be placed on teaching and research. Fourth, common citizenship values should be inculcated in higher education.

The Robbins Report provided guidelines for the fledgling **new universities** of the 1960s and came to be associated with the method for selecting university students. The concept that all young Britons qualified by ability and achievement (based on sixth-form Advanced-level exams) were entitled to a full-time course of higher education if they chose became known as the Robbins principle.

Martha A. Schütz

Bibliography

Anderson, Sir David. *Robbins Report on Higher Education.* 1964.

Carswell, John. *Government and the Universities in Britain: Programme and Performance, 1960–1980.* 1985.

Report of the Committee on Higher Education, 1961–3 (Robbins Report). Cmnd. 2154. 1963.

Stewart, W.A.C. *Higher Education in Postwar Britain.* 1989.

Roman Catholicism

Numerical growth, institutional development, social and intellectual advance, and national acceptance have been the principal characteristics of Roman Catholicism in Britain throughout much of the twentieth century. It was only in 1850 that a Catholic hierarchy was restored in England and Wales, with Cardinal Nicholas Patrick Wiseman (1802–65) appointed to head the Archdiocese of Westminster and its twelve suffragan sees. The restoration resulted in an outburst of anti-Catholic criticism and even rioting. Wiseman and his immediate successors, Henry Edward Manning (1808–92) and Herbert Vaughan (1832–1903), were successful, however, in winning increased acceptance of the growing Catholic community. The twentieth century has been a period of further development, growth, and consolidation to the point where Roman Catholics are found in virtually every walk of life.

Within two decades after the turn of the century, there were over 2 million Catholics in England and Wales, almost three times the number assessed at the time of the hierarchy's restoration. They were served by 4,000 priests, double the number recorded just thirty years earlier. Catholic schools educated 400,000 students, significant in accounting for the cohesion of the Catholic body. By 1951 there were 2.8 million Catholics, served by nearly 7,000 priests. At the turn of the century Catholic landed families still played a dominant role in Church life as they had in the nineteenth century. They were overwhelmingly outnumbered, however, by Irish **immigrants** and their descendants, most of whom belonged to the working class in cities such as Liverpool and, to a lesser extent, Birmingham, and **London**. This explains the fact that in 1911 the Holy See divided the Archdiocese into three ecclesiastical provinces—Birmingham, Liverpool, and Westminster. In 1916 the Diocese of Newport was raised to archepiscopal rank as well, under the title of Cardiff. Scotland's hierarchy was restored in 1878 and today consists of two provinces, St. Andrews-Edinburgh and that of Glasgow.

As their educational opportunities increased at every level, Catholics became increasingly affluent, with a large proportion soon numbered among the middle class. The growing diversity within the Catholic population meant that increasing numbers were no longer confined to the large industrial cities. In 1915, for example, 58.4 percent of the Catholic population lived in the Archdiocese of Liverpool, while 26.2 percent lived in the Archdiocese of Westminster and the Diocese of Southwark, the two sees that divided London. By 1951 Liverpool's share of the Catholic population was down to 37.8 percent, while Westminster and Southwark claimed 51 percent. In recognition of the population shift, the Holy See, in 1965, raised Southwark to the status of an archdiocese.

In spite of the creation of new provinces, the archbishops of Westminster have retained a unique status, especially in dealing with the Holy See. For the most part they have been recognized primarily for their pastoral and administrative skills rather than their erudition or social presence. Francis Bourne (1861–1935), who succeeded Cardinal Vaughan in 1903, quietly presided over the Westminster Archdiocese until his death. These were years of steady progress for Catholics, with landmarks such as an International Eucharistic Congress (1908); the opening of Oxford theological degrees to non-Anglicans (1920); the beatification of the English martyrs (1929); and the restoration of the shrine of Our Lady of Walsingham (1935). Bourne was succeeded by Arthur Hinsley (1865–1945), who thoroughly endeared himself not only to the Catholic community, but also to the British public at large, for his promotion of social reform and his leadership in support of the war effort. He also had the honor of welcoming the first apostolic delegate for Britain since the Reformation, William Godfrey (1888–1963), who later succeeded William Griffin (1899–1956) as Archbishop of Westminster. Godfrey's successor was John Carmel Heenan (1905–75), an able communicator and a man already recognized for his commitment to Catholic social teaching. It was his responsibility to implement the liturgical reforms after the Second Vatican Council. Heenan's popular successor, George Basil Hume (1923–), an Oxford graduate and Ampleforth Benedictine, has, in many respects, followed the policies of his predecessor, especially in matters of social justice and a commitment to ecumenism.

While the English and Welsh bishops have not encouraged specific political positions in Britain, they have struggled consistently to obtain and retain government funding for the support of Catholic schools. There has not been a Catholic political constituency, as such, so that in the last Parliament prior to the independence of southern Ireland in 1918, there were ten Catholic MPs from England and seventy-eight from Ireland. The *Catholic Directory* for 1990 listed forty-three Catholic MPs and seventy-eight peers.

Catholics have been allowed by their hierarchy to attend **Oxford** and **Cambridge** since 1895. This has certainly been a factor in their intellectual as well as their social advance. No discussion of Catholicism in twentieth-century Britain would be complete without reference to some of the more famous authors and scholars who have either converted to, or been born into, the Church. Among them have been **G.K. Chesterton**, Hilaire Belloc (1870–1953), Ronald Knox (1888–1957), **Evelyn Waugh**, Martin D'Arcy (1888–1976), J.R.R. Tolkien (1892–1973), and **Graham Greene**. A similar listing could be made of Catholics identified with other professions.

Following the Second Vatican Council there has been some controversy and unrest among Catholics, particularly with regard to liturgical reform and the introduction of the vernacular. Certainly Britain has shared the religious problems that have been commonplace in the West. Yet a National Pastoral Congress in Liverpool (1980) urged even further liturgical reform. A decline in the number of vocations to the priesthood and religious congregations of both men and women is a serious setback, especially for Catholic education. Yet Catholics can no longer be accused of nursing a "fortress mentality," as is commonly alleged to have been the case in the past. Cooperation with and acceptance by other churches has been one of the more noteworthy characteristics of Roman Catholicism in recent years.

R.J. Schiefen, CSB

Bibliography

Beck, George Andrew, ed. *The English Catholics, 1850–1950*. 1950.
Hastings, Adrian. *A History of English Christianity, 1920–1990*. 3rd ed. 1991.
Hornsby-Smith, Michael P. *Roman Catholics in England: Studies in Social Structure since the Second World War*. 1987.

Round Table Conference (1930–1932)

The Round Table Conference was an attempt to engage Indian nationalists and British politicians in a cooperative effort to fashion responsible government in India. It failed largely because of deep divisions among Indian participants and because of a resurgence of hardline views among British Conservatives.

The idea for the conference came from the Viceroy, Lord Irwin (subsequently **Lord Halifax**), who wished to break a recently unified Indian nationalist movement by offering moderates the opportunity to cooperate with the British. Backed by the new **Labour** government, Irwin announced in 1929 that the British goal was Dominion status for India, and that a conference would be held in London, where Indian and British delegates would work together to make this possible.

The first session of the conference was held in the waning months of 1930. The Indian National Congress refused to attend and instead conducted a campaign of civil disobedience under Mohandas Gandhi's leadership. Representatives of most other important Indian political organizations did attend, as did representatives of the princely states. All three major parties were represented in the British delegation. The one major advance made at this session was the consensus reached on the idea of a federal structure. Communal differences, especially between Muslim and Hindu interests, proved to be an insurmountable obstacle to any lasting agreement.

In early 1931 Irwin agreed to meet with Gandhi, and the two signed a pact ending civil disobedience. Gandhi agreed to attend the next session of the Round Table Conference, as the sole representative of the Congress. This session, which began in September 1931, ended in the same deadlock as the previous one, because of deep divisions among Indian delegates over both the communal problem and the details of a federal structure. Within a week of his return to India, Gandhi was again in jail, as the recently elected National government embarked on a new policy of suppression of militant nationalism.

A final session of the conference was held at the end of 1932. Representatives of the Congress, again, did not attend, and neither did many of the Indian princes. Little progress was made in solving the old problems associated with communal representation and federalism. Interest in future sessions of the conference dissipated quickly. The next constitutional step was a unilateral one by the British government, which drafted a White Paper in 1933 outlining a new constitution for India. Conservative dissenters, especially **Winston Churchill**, beat the drum of **imperialism** loudly enough to delay its implementation for nearly two years.

The conference was clearly a failure, since Irwin's hopes for a cooperative venture to shape a new constitution for India were dashed. **Indian nationalism**, while less unified than in the late 1920s, was yet a troubling force in Indian politics. The forces of repression had the upper hand in British administrative circles. Still there were some fruits from the conference: The federal idea remained a lasting contribution to India's constitutional development, and Dominion status was put on the political agenda for good.

Lynn Zastoupil

Bibliography
Moore, R.J. *The Crisis of Indian Unity, 1917–1940.* 1974.
Peele, Gillian. "Revolt over India" in Gillian Peele, and Chris Cook, eds. *The Politics of Reappraisal, 1918–1939.* 1975. pp. 114–45.

Royal Air Force
The Royal Air Force (RAF) was the world's first independent air force, not merely separate from the **army** and the **Royal Navy**, but on an equal footing with them in the councils of government and represented by its own Secretary of State and the Air Ministry. Established in April 1918, the RAF was preceded as a fighting service in Britain by the Royal Flying Corps (RFC), which was formed in May 1912 and included both Military and Naval Wings. In 1914, when Brit-

ain entered the **First World War,** the Naval Wing became separate as the Royal Naval Air Service (RNAS).

In those early days the airplane's role in warfare was undeveloped, and it was regarded merely as an adjunct to military and naval operations, a machine to be used in support of an army in the field or a fleet at sea. Air power, in any strategic aspect, did not play a decisive role in the conflict of 1914–18. Nevertheless there were already those who realized that the aircraft had the potential to wage an entirely new, "independent" warfare in its own element. But the views of the existing services dominated military and strategic thinking, and the ideas of the visionaries were not welcome.

This situation changed profoundly in 1917, when German Gotha four-engined aircraft bombed London. Up to that time there had been only a few scattered raids by Zeppelin airships, causing negligible damage. In the Gotha raids nearly 500 people were killed. This was the advent of war in a new dimension, both spatially and conceptually. It ignored frontiers and battle lines, the division between land and sea, and the distinction betweeen the fighting servicemen and the noncombatant civilian. In response to public outcry a **Cabinet** committee was formed under General Jan Christian Smuts (1870–1950) to examine defense arrangements and the organization of the air services. The committee quickly saw that the existing organization had two serious limitations. First, if air power was tied to the needs of armies and navies, its potential to operate independently, whether in offense or defense, was unlikely to receive the attention it demanded. Second, the air itself was a single entity covering both land and sea; the separation of the air services was an anomaly. The committee recommended the formation of a third service, to be responsible for all the military applications of air power. And so the Royal Air Force was created, on 1 April 1918, absorbing both the RFC and the RNAS.

The early years of the RAF were precarious. At the end of the war there was strong sentiment, backed by the Royal Navy and the army, in favor of disbanding the third service. It was suggested that the Air Ministry be disestablished and the component parts of the RAF returned to the Admiralty and the War Office. The lobby reckoned without the enigmatic Sir Hugh Trenchard (1873–1956), the Chief of the Air Staff. His early military career was undistinguished, but he had a vision of a new service and managed to carry it to reality.

There was nothing Trenchard could do to increase the size of the RAF, but he saw to the establishment of Boy Entrants and Apprentice schemes, the Royal Air Force College at Cranwell for Officer Entrants, and the Royal Air Force Staff College. If the numbers at his disposal were few, he wished to ensure that they were highly trained and imbued with distinctive *esprit de corps*. He also created University Air Squadrons, Reserves, Auxiliary Squadrons, and Short Service Commissions—all schemes that would foster air-mindedness in the population at large and provide a cadre of skilled people on whom any sudden expansion of the RAF could be based, should that ever become necessary.

But without a role for it, the case for the continued existence of an independent air force would have been hard to sustain. Opportunely, such a role emerged very quickly, one quite unlike anything that had been envisaged. It came to be called "Air Control" and entailed the policing of immense areas of Britain's colonial and mandated territories in Africa, the Near and Middle East, and India. It was **Winston Churchill**, Air Minister in 1919, who decided that it would be the first duty of the RAF to garrison the British Empire.

This would previously have been a role for the army, but the cost of covering this vast commitment by stationing troops on the ground would have been crippling and unsustainable. In 1921 Churchill, by then Colonial Secretary, convened a conference in Cairo to settle the regional affairs and insisted that Trenchard be there, confirming Air Control as a major role for the RAF. In parts of the world where hostilities had been endemic, Air Control fostered greater peace and stability. This was done with a considerable saving in lives and money, and in a way that tended to win respect from the local populations. It may also have been instrumental in ensuring the survival of the RAF as an independent service.

It was not until the latter half of the decade of the 1930s that the threat from Germany came to be recognized. It was at this time that the RAF placed orders for the Hurricane, the Spitfire, and the Lancaster bomber. Various schemes to enlarge the service were initiated but foundered or were delayed through lack of money. The buildup did not gain real momentum until almost the last moment. During the years from 1920 to 1935 the RAF rarely numbered above 30,000. By 1939 it was over 100,000, and by 1943 over 1 million.

The RAF's first real test came early in the **Second World War**, with the **Battle of Britain** in the summer of 1940. Since Adolf Hitler could not launch his invasion fleet while it was vulnerable to air attack during the channel crossing, the first stage of his plan was the neutralization of the RAF. But RAF Fighter Command, under Sir Hugh Dowding (1882–1970), fought back doggedly, while aircraft of Bomber Command and Coastal Command attacked the German invasion fleets gathering in the French ports. Hitler had to delay his decision to launch the invasion, and on 17 September 1940 he was forced to postpone it indefinitely.

The Battle of Britain has historical significance not only as one of the turning points of the Second World War, but because it was the first—and probably the last—major battle to be fought exclusively in the air.

As the war progressed, the RAF played a key part in all of the major campaigns: the Battle of the Atlantic, which was the long campaign against German **submarine warfare** to keep open the vital sea lines of supply with the North American continent; North Africa, where the principles of land-air warfare were thoroughly consolidated; the Strategic Bombing Offensive against Germany, which claimed more RAF lives than all other campaigns put together; the Far East, where air transport was essential to supply the forces fighting in the jungles; and the final campaign in Northern Europe, which led to the defeat of Germany.

For about twenty-five years after the end of the Second World War the RAF maintained a major presence in the Far East, the Middle East, and in Germany. It participated in the long Malayan Campaign (1948–60) leading to the defeat of the Communist insurgency, in "confrontation" with Indonesia (1962–6), in most of the recurring crises in the Middle East, in the **Falklands War** in 1982, and in the Gulf War of 1991. For a large part of the period of the Cold War it also covered Britain's contribution to the strategic nuclear deterrent until this role was assumed by the Royal Navy with Polaris submarines.

The RAF numbers about 75,000 men and women. It is based mainly in Britain, with a few squadrons in Germany. With the exception of long-range bombers, it covers all of the roles of air power—offensive, defensive, maritime, transport, and reconnaissance—and operates worldwide. The three services in Britain no longer have their separate Departments of State; since 1964 all are under a single Ministry of Defence.

Ian Madelin

Bibliography
Armitage, Michael. *The Royal Air Force: An Illustrated History.* 1993.
Boyle, Andrew. *Trenchard.* 1962.
Dean, Maurice. *The Royal Air Force and Two World Wars.* 1979.
Richards, Denis, and Hilary St.G. Saunders. *The Royal Air Force, 1939–1945.* 3 vols. new ed. 1993.
Terraine, John. *A Time for Courage: The RAF in the European War, 1939–1945.* 1985.
Trevenen, James. *The Royal Air Force: The Past Thirty Years.* 1976.

Royal Institution of Great Britain

During the nineteenth century the Royal Institution (founded 1799) achieved immense fame through the scientific research work of its professors and as a center for the diffusion of scientific knowledge to the public. It entered the twentieth century during James Dewar's (1842–1923) tenure as Fullerian Professor of **Chemistry**, fully committed to both of these aspects of scientific work.

Twentieth-century Britain witnessed a great expansion of scientific laboratories, yet the quality of research at the Royal Institution under successive Professors and Directors remained high and worthy of its nineteenth-century antecedents. This standard was facilitated by Ludwig Mond's (1839–1909) endowment of the Davy-Faraday Laboratory, which opened in 1896.

The comparatively small size of the Royal Institution has meant that the direction of research in the Davy-Faraday Laboratory has been that of the interests of the Director. Thus when William Henry Bragg (1862–1942) became Director in 1923, x-ray crystallography became the chief subject of research. He built up a formidable team of researchers, including his son William Lawrence Bragg (1890–1971), as well as Kathleen Lonsdale (1903–71) and **J.D. Bernal**. All of these scientists were to have considerable influence on the development of science in Britain during the middle years of the century. Following the elder Bragg's death

Henry Dale (1875–1968) acted as caretaker Director for the remainder of the Second World War. After his retirement Eric Rideal (1890–1974), Director between 1946 and 1949, built up a team of colloid chemists. Following Edward Neville da Costa Andrade's (1887–1971) controversial directorship, Lawrence Bragg took over in 1953. During his period, research reverted to x-ray crystallography. He retired in 1966, and his place was taken by George Porter (1920–), whose research concentrated on investigating high-speed chemical reactions using photochemical methods. After he was elected President of the **Royal Society** in 1985, the dominant topics of research became solid-state chemistry under the direction of John Meurig Thomas (1932–) and, since 1991, materials science under Peter Day (1938–).

Parallel with the research activity, the Royal Institution has continued and expanded its activities in the popularization and public understanding of science to as many audiences as possible. Throughout the century this outreach has occurred through the two series of lectures initiated by Michael Faraday during the 1820s and continued to this day—the Friday Evening Discourses and the Christmas Lectures. At the instigation of George Porter, the lectures have been televised since 1966 and so reach an audience of millions in Britain and elsewhere.

In addition, during the directorship of Lawrence Bragg the lecture program was increased by the establishment of the Schools Lectures whereby schoolchildren come to hear about science and see experimental demonstrations from distinguished scientists. This program has been greatly expanded in recent years, as have other educational activities, and many lectures are now taken overseas.

Part club, part research institute, part educational establishment, the Royal Institution, as it approaches its bicentenary, retains its unique position in British life.

Frank A.J.L. James

Bibliography
Caroe, Gwendy. *The Royal Institution: An Informal History.* 1985.

Royal Shakespeare Company

Along with the **National Theatre**, the Royal Shakespeare Company (RSC) is one of the two major state-subsidized institutional theater companies to have emerged in post-war Britain.

But the Royal Shakespeare Theatre in Stratford-upon-Avon, the company's original home and a continuing artistic and administrative base, is of earlier origins; dating from 1932, it was, as the Shakespeare Memorial Theatre, successor to the first permanent playhouse in Shakespeare's birthplace, built in 1879 and burned down in 1926.

Seating around 1,500 spectators, the present Stratford theater has a proscenium-arched stage that, despite recurrent modifications, remains stubbornly closer in spirit to the traditions of nineteenth-century pictorialism than to the conventions of the Elizabethan period. Here, from the 1930s through the 1950s, five or six of Shakespeare's plays were presented during short summer seasons by an acting company freshly assembled each year. Then, in 1961, Peter Hall, newly appointed as Artistic Director, reformed the company under its present name, also acquiring for it a London home—first at the Aldwych Theatre, off the Strand, while plans for a purpose-built base within the new Barbican Centre began their long gestation.

With a policy of cross-fertilizing Shakespeare's plays with other classics as well as with plays from the modern British and European repertoires, Hall recruited a semipermanent ensemble, placing actors on extended contracts, to work under a team of regular directors that at first included Peter Brook and Michel St-Denis. In 1968 Hall was succeeded as Artistic Director by his protégé, Trevor Nunn, who after 1978 worked in harness with his close associate Terry Hands. When Hands, by then sole Director, retired in 1990, he was succeeded by yet another Director whose reputation had been made within the company, Adrian Noble.

This continuity of leadership has been reinforced artistically by the continuing association with the company of directors such as John Barton and Clifford Williams, from the earlier generation, with Howard Davies, Ron Daniels, Bill Alexander, and John Caird among more recent recruits—a male dominance only briefly challenged by the tragically brief tenure of Buzz Goodbody as inaugural Director of The Other Place. This prefabricated former rehearsal room in Stratford was converted for smaller-scale work in 1974, and three years later the company opened The Warehouse in Covent Garden as a metropolitan counterpart.

In 1982 the London operation was at last transferred to the new Barbican Centre, where it employs both a flexible main stage and a studio space, The Pit. With the opening in 1986 of the Swan Theatre in Stratford, constructed within the shell of the original burned-out theater, the company in 1986 gained a fifth, medium-size space, designed in a fluent mix of Elizabethan and contemporary idioms especially for the staging of the work of Shakespeare's more neglected contemporaries and immediate successors.

In addition to sustaining for these venues a complex repertoire system, with seasonal interchanging between Stratford and London, the company also makes regular small-scale tours to places normally denied access to theater, and it plays an annual northern season in Newcastle-upon-Tyne. Even by comparison with the National Theatre, which only irregularly ventures beyond the confines of its three London stages, the RSC has thus within thirty years of its formation established a formidable presence within the British theatrical scene, and this requires a constant juggling of artistic, economic, and logistic considerations.

To an extent, the artistic work of the company has reflected the changing sensibilities of the times. Hall's pacifistic version of *Troilus and Cressida* in 1963 was thus as true to the year of the Cuban missile crisis as was Hands' version, strongly emphasizing the sexuality of the play, for the later "permissive" years of that decade. Similarly, the early, strongly politicized approach to *The Wars of the Roses* sequence of Shakespeare's histories reflected the company's original impulses as surely as the vivid narrative drive behind such happy collaborative blockbusters as the day-long adaptation of Dickens' *Nicholas Nickleby* served, in 1981, as an impressive summation of the Nunn directorship.

Arguably the blander theatricalist ingenuities of the musical *Les Miserables* were no less redolent of the escapist aesthetics and technocratic trappings of the Thatcherite decade. Certainly, the continued shortage of subsidy during this period required resolutely "safe" Shakespearean programming, geared to tourist audiences. Varyingly advantageous deals have also had to be struck with commercial managements.

The RSC represents to its enemies the dangers of allowing a company of initially modest function to build an empire that deprives funding to humbler supplicants. Its friends would respond that its growth has been logical and inspired by identified needs, that its use of funding is modest relative to its output. While it has kept faith with new writing, especially in the studio spaces, its cross-fertilization of the Shakespearean and the contemporary repertoire has, for all of the flexibility and occasional retrenchment involved, been nonetheless in keeping with the company's original spirit.

Simon Trussler

Bibliography
Beauman, Sally. *The Royal Shakespeare Company: A History of Ten Decades.* 1982.
Chambers, Colin. *Other Spaces: New Theatre and the RSC.* 1980.

Royal Society of London

The Royal Society (founded 1660) is the oldest continuously existing learned and scientific society in the world. Although originally it drew its Fellowship from all of those interested in scientific knowledge, by the beginning of the twentieth century its Fellows were overwhelmingly distinguished men of science (women were not admitted until the election of Kathleen Lonsdale [1903–71] and Marjory Stephenson [1885–1948] in 1945). From its foundation the society had close links with government, while maintaining its independent status as a learned society. During the twentieth century, however, the Royal Society's role in the formation of national policy on scientific and technical matters has, without compromising its status, increased greatly.

The number of Fellows has increased considerably during the century, from 456 at the beginning to just over 1,100 in 1992. During the century the number of new Fellows elected annually has grown from fifteen in 1900 to forty in 1992. The larger Fellowship since 1945 reflects the expansion of scientific activity during the past fifty years. Election signifies the highest honor that can be bestowed on a British or Commonwealth scientist by his or her peers. The society also elects approximately six foreign members each year from among those who have made outstanding contributions to the advancement of scientific thought.

To be elected President (a post normally held for a term of five years) is to occupy the highest position that a scientist can achieve in Britain. The Presidents of the Royal Society in the twentieth century have been among Britain's most distinguished scientists and have included:

Lord Rayleigh (1842–1919; President 1905–8), Joseph John Thomson (1856–1940; 1915–20), **Ernest Rutherford** (1925–30), Frederick Gowland Hopkins (1861–1947; 1930–5), William Henry Bragg (1862–1942; 1935–40), Howard Walter Florey (1896–1968; 1960–5), **P.M.S. Blackett** (1965–70), Andrew Huxley (1917– ; 1980–5), George Porter (1920– ; 1985–90), and from 1990 Michael Atiyah (1929–).

Throughout the century the Royal Society has directly supported scientific research. At the beginning of the century most of this research was financed from the society's own funds, in addition to £5,000 from a grant awarded annually by Parliament. Indeed, the society supported scientific research before the formation of any of the research councils. The parliamentary grant has risen to more than £17 million and now forms the society's largest source of income that is devoted to research. Most of this increase has happened since 1945 and reflects not only the expansion of the scientific community, but also the important function that science occupies in everyday life.

The society publishes several journals, including *Philosophical Transactions*, which is the oldest surviving continuously published scientific journal. The society awards medals such as the Copley and Royal to individuals who have obtained the highest merit in their scientific work.

During the century the Royal Society has been active in promoting international scientific relations. It took a leading role in forming, following the First World War, the International Research Council, later the International Council of Scientific Unions.

Frank A.J.L. James

Bibliography
The Record of the Royal Society of London for the Promotion of Natural Knowledge. 4th ed. 1940.
The Yearbook of the Royal Society.

Russell, Bertrand (1872–1970)

No British intellectual in the twentieth century spanned as many decades, filled as many pages, provoked as many arguments, enraged as many worthies, launched as many crusades, inspired as many disciples, or served as much jail time as did Bertrand Russell. Born into one of the proudest families of the Whig aristocracy, Russell died a social renegade; accepted into the highest reaches of the British intellectual elite by virtue of his astonishing philosophical creativity, he ended his days outside the academy and at war with dominant philosophical fashions; championed by conventional **pacifists** and unorthodox dissenters, he died at the head of a bitterly divided and divisive protest movement. From the **Boer War** to Vietnam, from neo-Hegelianism to linguistic philosophy, from nuclear disarmament to **birth control**, there was no public issue, scholarly fashion, intellectual preoccupation, or political question on which he flinched from offering a heretical opinion.

Russell was born on 18 May 1872 to John and Kate Stanley Russell, Lord and Lady Amberley. Members of the radical wing of the late-Victorian Whig aristocracy, the Amberleys both died tragically young—she in 1874, he in 1876—and the young Russell was left in the care of his paternal grandparents, the Earl and Countess Russell. The only child in a world of adults, Russell was carefully inculcated with the hereditary aristocratic Whiggism embodied by his grandfather and prepared for an inevitable political career devoted to continuing those principles into the twentieth century. Educated by private tutors, Russell gave early evidence of both a formidable intelligence and a consuming passion for mathematics, and in October 1890 he went to Trinity College, **Cambridge**, intending to study mathematics. Almost immediately Russell blossomed both intellectually and socially. Not merely did he place in the first class in Part 1 of the mathematical tripos in 1893 and in Part 2 of the moral science tripos in 1894, but he was elected to the celebrated undergraduate discussion society the **Apostles**, where he made intimate friends among the brethren, such as J.M.E. McTaggart, **G.E. Moore**, Robert Trevelyan, and **Alfred North Whitehead**. In their company Russell—lonely and friendless upon his arrival—flourished, and under their encouragement and guidance he turned his interests to questions of the logical foundations of mathematics, to the study of which he was elected to a prestigious Trinity College Prize Fellowship in 1895.

In even his earliest writings Russell demonstrated those traits that would come to characterize his entire intellectual life: an enviable lucidity, an astonishing fertility, a brave iconoclasm, an irrepressible wit, and limitless energy. His initial work, such as *An Essay on the Foundations of Geometry* (1897), was well within the confines of the dominant neo-Hegelian orthodoxy in which he had been schooled. By the turn of the century, however, Russell had joined Moore in launching an ultimately fatal challenge to that orthodoxy. In a mood of exhilaration and liberation Russell entered the most creative period of his career, writing a dazzling series of papers and books—such as "On Denoting" (1904) and *The Principles of Mathematics* (1903)—culminating in the three collaborative volumes of *Principia Mathematica* (1910–13). His technical mastery of logic, unparalleled command of mathematics, sparkling virtuosity of style, and incomparably wide reading in contemporary Continental thought all combined to enable him to achieve a commanding intellectual ascendancy. Elected to the **Royal Society** in 1907 and to a Trinity College lectureship in logic and the philosophy of mathematics created especially for him in 1910, Russell was by the summer of 1914 at the peak of his scholarly reputation and intellectual prestige.

The outbreak of the **First World War** transformed Russell's life. Although never an archetypically cloistered Cambridge don—he had been active in the **tariff reform** campaign of 1903 and the **women's suffrage** movement from 1907—Russell had nonetheless not been a public man in the sense his grandfather would have approved. But as Britain lurched toward war in the summer of 1914, Russell threw himself first into the pro-neutrality and then into the antiwar movement—speaking, writing, organizing, and counseling. No pacifist, Russell passionately believed that this particular war—not all war—was a mistake; indeed, it offended his every political instinct and principle. And as the war lengthened and Britain's commitment extended, Russell's opposition sharpened—to mistreatment of **conscientious objectors**, to the suppression of civil liberties, and to the arrogant wastefulness of British commanders. This opposition—strident, unrelenting, and deeply unpopular—was the defining experience of Russell's life; not merely did emotions run so high on all sides that he alienated friends, exasperated allies, and nettled enemies, but his opposition cost him his Trinity College lectureship and a six-month spell in prison.

In the years after 1918 Russell was at once intellectually unwilling and emotionally unable to return to his former life. Satisfied with his work in **philosophy**, prepared to allow his former pupils (especially Ludwig Wittgenstein) to make the running for the next philosophical generation, and determined to do all he could to reconstruct society and to regenerate individuals so as to eliminate war, Russell turned his attention in the 1920s and 1930s to lecturing, writing, teaching, and traveling (to Russia in 1920 and China in 1920–1). Although much of his writing proved evanescent, it nonetheless reached a wide audience and served to heighten his notoriety; indeed, for all that his liberal views on religion, science, and **sexuality** attracted the young, independent, and free-thinking, they also offended the comfortable, conforming, and established.

The outbreak of the Second World War found Russell teaching in America. Eager to return to Britain, he was prohibited from doing so by a British government willing to remember his earlier antiwar activities but not to believe his current—and genuine—support for this conflict. He therefore remained in America until 1944—writing, lecturing, teaching, and preparing the manuscript for what would become his most widely known book, *A History of Western Philosophy* (1945). Russell returned to considerable acclaim and, in the 1940s and 1950s, unaccustomed respectability. Reconciled to Trinity College, he was a popular teacher and lecturer at Cambridge and, indeed, to all of Britain as a **British Broadcasting Corporation** (BBC) broadcaster and pundit. The award of the Order of Merit in 1949 and the Nobel Prize for Literature in 1950 was further evidence of the healing of old wounds.

In the end, this quiet proved only temporary, for by the late 1950s Russell had entered a new period of even greater controversy that would continue until the end of his life. Convinced of the irresistible threat of nuclear annihilation and of the absolute necessity of Britain's unilateral renunciation of its nuclear deterrent, Russell was one of the founders of the **Campaign for Nuclear Disarmament** in 1958 and, beginning in 1960, of the more radical Committee of 100. With an astounding robustness for a man now in his mid-eighties, Russell once again threw himself headlong into a contentious and divisive public campaign—writing, marching, lecturing, and getting arrested. It was a course of action he repeated, in his nineties, in the late 1960s in opposition to American and British involvement in the war in Vietnam.

Russell died, on 2 February 1970, in the midst of bitter recrimination. Convinced of the criminality of the war in Vietnam, of the irresistible slide toward nuclear holocaust, of the wrong-headedness of contemporary philosophy, and of the incapacity of any of Britain's political leaders to arrest his beloved nation's apparently inexorable decline, Russell died railing like Lear against the storms about him. To many contemporaries, he appeared to have been a man who squandered his gifts and betrayed his position in a series of unnecessarily offensive and wholly quixotic ventures. But to Russell himself, his life had been, if not a success, at least a worthy effort—to help mankind save itself from its own extinction, to speak directly to the deepest sources of human spirituality, to search for the truth of philosophy and mathematics, and to appeal to wellsprings of humanity and generosity.

Kirk Willis

Bibliography

Clark, Ronald W. *The Life of Bertrand Russell*. 1975.
Moorehead, Caroline. *Bertrand Russell*. 1992.
Russell, Bertrand. *The Autobiography of Bertrand Russell*. 3 vols. 1967–9.
———. *My Philosophical Development*. 1959.
Ryan, Alan. *Bertrand Russell: A Political Life*. 1988.

Rutherford, Ernest (1871–1937)

Ernest Rutherford became the most prominent physicist in Britain, known for his work on radioactivity and the structure of the atomic nucleus. He received the Nobel Prize for **Chemistry** in 1908 for showing that radioactivity involved the change of an atom of one chemical element into an atom of another. In 1911 he proposed that atoms had a central core, or nucleus, and in 1919 he reported he had disintegrated the nucleus. He built successful schools of research in both Manchester and later **Cambridge**. He was President of the **Royal Society**, 1925–30. In 1931 he became Lord Rutherford of Nelson.

Rutherford was born in **New Zealand** to a family of Scottish extraction. After graduating from Canterbury College, Christchurch, he became a research student at the **Cavendish Laboratory**, Cambridge, under J.J. Thomson in 1895. There Rutherford worked on the electrical conductivity of gases and radioactivity. He identified and named two types of radioactive decay, alpha and beta. It was an exciting time, for x-rays and the electron were also discovered in the last few years of the nineteenth century.

Leaving Cambridge, in 1898 Rutherford became Professor of **physics** at McGill University, Montreal, where he continued to work on radioactivity. There Rutherford, in collaboration with Frederick Soddy, showed that radioactive change involved the transmuting of an atom of one chemical element into an atom of another, quite unlike the more familiar chemical changes.

In 1907 he moved to Manchester, entering a fruitful period of collaboration with James Chadwick, Hans Geiger, Niels Bohr, and Henry Moseley. Rutherford, investigating the internal structure of the atom, argued in 1911 that an atom had a central nucleus, containing most of its mass and with a positive electrical charge. These ideas were extended by Bohr to account for the properties of simple atoms, such as hydrogen. The Rutherford-Bohr model of the atom became one of the foundations of quantum mechanics, the modern theory of atomic behavior.

In 1919 he published the results of the first experiments on nuclear disintegration. He had caused nitrogen nuclei to emit particles with a single positive electrical charge, which he took to be a constituent of all nuclei and to which he later gave the name proton. That year he succeeded J.J. Thomson as Cavendish Professor of Physics at Cambridge. There he assembled a group of researchers, including Chadwick, **P.M.S. Blackett**, and John Cockcroft, who profoundly influenced the course of nuclear research, and Peter Kapitsa, who worked on magnetic research until he returned to Russia. Chadwick discovered the neutron, Cockcroft and Walton built the first particle accelerator, and electronic methods of counting particles were built, advances that owed much to the vision of Rutherford.

From 1930 until his death Rutherford was Chairman of the Advisory Council of the Department of Scientific and Industrial Research (DSIR). He also was head of the Academic Assistance Council, which provided assistance to **refugee** scholars from Germany between 1933 and 1936.

Alan Q. Morton

Bibliography
Chadwick, James. *The Collected Papers of Lord Rutherford of Nelson.* 3 vols. 1962–5.
Eve, A.S. *Rutherford.* 1939.
Wilson, David. *Rutherford, Simple Genius.* 1983.

S

Samuel, Herbert (1870–1963)

Herbert Samuel, created first Viscount Samuel in 1937, statesman, philosopher, and leading figure in the Jewish community, served as a government minister (1905–16), as High Commissioner in Palestine (1920–5), and as leader of the Liberal Party (1931–5).

Samuel was born in Liverpool, the son of a wealthy Jewish banker, but lived most of his life in London. He was educated at University College School, London, and Balliol College, Oxford, where he gained a first-class degree in modern history. Even as a student he was active on the radical wing of the Liberal Party. His book, *Liberalism* (1902), foreshadowed many of the social reforms enacted by Liberal governments after 1905.

Samuel entered Parliament in 1902 as Liberal MP for Cleveland, retaining the seat until 1918. He made his name as a debater in 1903 by denouncing the "barbarism" of the autocracy of King Leopold of the Belgians in the Congo. In 1904–5 Samuel was among those who attacked the Conservative government's scheme for the importation of Chinese labor to work in gold mines in South Africa. The controversy helped bring down the Conservative government of Arthur Balfour in December 1905.

As Undersecretary at the Home Office in the Campbell-Bannerman and Asquith governments between 1905 and 1909, Samuel helped devise, draft, and defend social reform legislation. He was particularly identified with the Probation Act (1907), which established a national system of probation officers, and the Children Act (1909), which extended state responsibility for the welfare of children. With his appointment in 1909 as Chancellor of the Duchy of Lancaster, Samuel became the first unconverted Jew to hold Cabinet office. As Postmaster-General (1910–14 and May 1915 to January 1916) he presided over the nationalization of the telephone service. But his plans for social reform as President of the Local Government Board (February 1914 to May 1915) were cut short by the outbreak of the First World War. His brief tenure as Home Secretary (January to December 1916) brought him into conflict with former radical allies over such civil liberties issues as conscientious objection.

When David Lloyd George formed his coalition government in December 1916, Samuel refused a post, remaining with Asquith on the opposition front bench. His main preoccupation now was Zionism. In early 1915 he had been the first to propose to the Cabinet the creation of a British-sponsored Jewish home in Palestine and played an essential behind-the-scenes role in the discussions that led to the pro-Zionist Balfour Declaration in 1917. He was, therefore, a natural choice in 1920 to serve as first High Commissioner in Palestine under the League of Nations mandate. His five years there laid the groundwork for the Jewish national home, although Arab anti-Zionist riots in 1921 led him to restrict Jewish immigration according to the principle of "economic absorptive capacity."

Samuel had hoped to spend the rest of his life writing philosophy, but he was called back to public life to head a Royal Commission on Coal, which reported in March 1926. The report failed to end strife in the coal industry that led to the General Strike of May 1926. Samuel, acting as an unofficial mediator, helped persuade the Trades Union Congress to call off the strike on 12 May.

As Liberal organization chief before the 1929 election, Samuel reinvigorated the party in its last serious bid for power. He himself triumphed at Darwen, but the party's 5.3 million votes earned it only fifty-nine seats. In 1931, deputizing for an ailing Lloyd George, Samuel led the Liberals into the National government in which he became Home Secretary. But in the October 1931 election the Liberals suffered further setbacks. Cabinet disagreements over the return to protection were papered over in January 1932 by the "agreement to differ." In September, however, Samuel and his supporters (but not those Liberals who followed Sir **John Simon**) withdrew from the government. In 1933 he carried thirty Liberals with him to the opposition benches. But in the 1935 election the Liberal Party was reduced to only nineteen seats, and Samuel himself was defeated.

Samuel never held office again. In retirement he wrote extensively on philosophy, broadcast on the **British Broadcasting Corporation** (BBC), and after 1937 spoke frequently in the **House of Lords**.

The Liberal Party probably owed to Samuel, more than to any other person, its survival as a distinctive, albeit attenuated, element in British politics. He lived just long enough to witness the revival of party fortunes in the early 1960s. His most lasting historic achievement must be reckoned his contribution to the advancement of Zionism and to the laying of the foundations for the state of Israel.

Bernard Wasserstein

Bibliography
Samuel, Viscount. *Memoirs*. 1945.
Wasserstein, Bernard. *Herbert Samuel: A Political Life*. 1992.

Sankey Commission (1919)

The Sankey Commission was constituted in February 1919 to deal with a crisis in the **coal** industry. Its origins lay in the wartime experiences and consequent expectations of miners. Their industry had been taken under state control with generally positive results for them. The **Miners Federation of Great Britain**'s post-war program demanded a 30 percent wage increase, the reduction of the underground working day from eight hours to six, and public ownership.

Although the **Lloyd George** coalition had won an overwhelming election victory in December 1918, ministers felt nervous about the destabilizing consequences of any large-scale industrial conflict. On 10 February 1919 a government offer of one shilling a day increase and a committee of inquiry was rejected by the miners; a subsequent strike ballot favored a stoppage by a margin of almost six to one. Lloyd George anticipated this result by offering a Royal Commission with miners' participation. Initially a Miners' Conference seemed hostile to the proposition, but pressure from their President, Robert Smillie, and other advocates of involvement eventually won the day.

The composition of the commission was three miners' officials, three intellectuals sympathetic to the union (including **R.H. Tawney** and **Sidney Webb**), three coal owners and three other industrialists. The Chairman was Sir John Sankey, a cautious, formerly Conservative, lawyer. The appointment of the commission was a device to lessen the risk of industrial confrontation at what was for the government a worrying time. Proceedings began on 3 March 1919, with a commitment that the questions of wages and hours should be the subject of an interim report by 20 March. The hearings, held in the Robing Room of the House of Lords, soon acquired the trappings of political theater as the pro-miner members of the commission, seizing the initiative, subjected their adversaries to vigorous cross-examination.

The commission's membership guaranteed conflicting conclusions. In the middle, Sankey and the industrialists argued for a two-shilling-a-shift increase, the reduction of the working day to seven hours with a further cut to six hours in July 1921 if warranted by the industry's situation. These proposals became the effective offer and were strongly endorsed in a miners' ballot on 5 April.

The public ownership question remained. Further hearings of the commission were held for almost two months beginning 23 April. Once again conflicting reports emerged. The pro-miners section backed public ownership; the coal owners and two industrialists were adamantly against. The other industrialist, Sir Arthur Duckham, backed a scheme for unification under private ownership. Sankey's decision to support public ownership, albeit with minor differences from his pro-**nationalization** colleagues, gave a majority of seven to six.

For two months the government made no public pronouncement. Then, on 19 August, Lloyd George rejected any possibility of public ownership. There had never been any prospect of a unanimous report, and there were few within the **Cabinet** who would accept public ownership. There was certainly no Commons majority for the appropriate legislation. The Miners Federation, already with a wages and hours settlement, found it impossible to mobilize sufficient support for any industrial action on public ownership. If the miners had a moment of opportunity, it had been in the spring when they chose an inquiry rather than a strike. Yet the Sankey Commission left one major legacy: The organization of the industry became a political question that required responses by successive governments.

David Howell

Bibliography

Arnot, R. Page. *The Miners: Years of Struggle.* 1953.

Cole, G.D.H. *Labour in the Coal-Mining Industry, 1914–1921.* 1923.

Heuston, R.F.V. *Lives of the Lord Chancellors, 1885–1940.* 1964.

Supple, Barry. *The History of the British Coal Industry, 1913–1946: The Political Economy of Decline.* 1987.

Wrigley, Chris. *Lloyd George and the Challenge of Labour: The Post-War Coalition, 1918–1922.* 1990.

Sassoon, Siegfried (1886–1967)

Siegfried Sassoon's career as a poet spanned almost six decades (1903–60), but he is best known for his bitter antiwar poetry, which first appeared in the pacifist *Cambridge Magazine* and later in two collected editions, *The Old Huntsman* (1917) and *Counter-Attack* (1918). In the early stages of the **First World War** Sassoon, serving with distinction as an officer in the Royal Welsh Fusiliers, was awarded the Military Cross for valor. But in July 1917 he openly allied himself with **pacifists** and **conscientious objectors** in a reckless statement of "willful defiance of military authority," which invited a court martial and imprisonment. The War Office wisely decided not to press the issue as a disciplinary case. Sassoon was examined by a medical board, declared unfit for active duty, and transferred to the convalescent home for neurasthenics at Craiglockhart in Scotland, where he was a patient of the psychologist W.H.R. Rivers. Sassoon's poetry and defiant, if futile, gesture against the war made him a national symbol of disillusionment. His name was

soon linked with two other war poets, **Robert Graves** and **Wilfred Owen**.

In spite of his instant fame Sassoon was temperamentally ill-suited for the brave new post-war world. He initially took up the cause of socialism and launched a poetic assault on capitalist exploitation, the **press** lords, mob **patriotism**, and the injustice of privilege in general, but his attack was vague and fragmented. He hated violence, distrusted revolutionary change, and was more than half in love with the world that the socialists sought to reform or destroy. Despite his pacifism, in 1940 he published a poem, entitled "The English Spirit," that might have come from the pen of **Rudyard Kipling**, whom he had satirized as late as 1935. The post-war "political" Sassoon is usually confused, illogical, and inconsistent. After his brief period of notoriety, he wisely withdrew from public debate. The major theme of the poetry of Sassoon's mature years is a tortuous search for religious belief, which culminated in his formal conversion to **Roman Catholicism** in 1957. Beyond his opposition to the First World War, Sassoon was never a rebel. He was in many ways a tragic figure, a living survivor of a lost generation and a lost way of life.

Sassoon's poetry, like his temperament, seems old-fashioned and out of step with the major events and intellectual currents of the turbulent times in which he lived. He was oblivious to Freud and, in spite of his initial rebelliousness, ignored Marx, the Russian Revolution, and the **Spanish Civil War**. Sassoon was one of the last of the Georgian poets, a Wordsworthian nature poet in the era of **T.S. Eliot** and **W.H. Auden**. In an age of analysis, social criticism, and political commitment, he chose to celebrate the beauty of nature and the tragic mysteries of life.

Ironically, a deepening sense of alienation from the present and ever-growing nostalgia for the past led logically to Sassoon's major literary achievement, his memoirs: *The Sherston Trilogy* (*Memoirs of a Fox-Hunting Man,* 1928; *Memoirs of an Infantry Officer,* 1930; and *Sherston's Progress,* 1936), which was followed by *The Old Century* (1938), *The Weald of Youth* (1942), and *Siegfried's Journey* (1945). Sassoon's fictionalized memoirs are likely to be read long after his poetry is forgotten. His war volumes, *Memoirs of an Infantry Officer* and *Sherston's Progress,* compare favorably with the accounts of Robert Graves and C.E. Montague. But Sassoon is at his best when he takes us back

S

to the innocent, rustic, lost world of his youth, although his sentimental account of the years "before the war" cannot be read as history. Foreign affairs, Ireland, industrial strife, and the angry suffragettes do not intrude upon the seasonal rituals of these contented fox-hunting provincials. Sassoon himself recognized that they were blissfully unaware the "the next twenty-five years would be a cemetery for the civilized delusions of the nineteenth century." Perhaps because his autobiography is so long and intimate, there is as yet no full-length biography of Siegfried Sassoon.

Gordon B. Beadle

Bibliography

Fussell, Paul. *The Great War and Modern Memory*. 1975.
Keynes, Geoffrey. *A Bibliography of Siegfried Sassoon*. 1962.
Thorpe, Michael. *Siegfried Sassoon: A Critical Study*. 1967.

Sayers, Dorothy L(eigh) (1893–1957)

Dorothy L. Sayers, the creator of the fictional detective characters Lord Peter Wimsey and Harriet Vane, is regarded as one of the most important writers of modern British **detective fiction**. Although Sayers was not as prolific as **Agatha Christie**, the twelve detective novels she published between 1923 and 1937, extremely successful at the time, remain popular in the late twentieth century. Recent televised serializations of her books have brought Sayers a new audience.

Sayers was born in Oxford, to upper-middle-class parents—her father was a **Church of England** clergyman—and she was educated at the Godolphin School and Somerville College, **Oxford**, where she completed her studies in medieval French literature in 1915 with first-class honors. When Oxford finally admitted women to degrees in 1920, Sayers took part in the first degree-granting ceremony in which women participated.

After leaving Oxford, she taught school but soon abandoned an occupation unsuited to her temperament. By 1917 she was employed as an editor for the young Oxford publishing firm Basil Blackwell's, and by 1922 she was working in London for Benson's, one of the country's largest advertising agencies, a connection that lasted until 1931. A talented copywriter, she was responsible for several celebrated advertising campaigns.

Meanwhile, as early as 1920 she was attempting to write detective fiction. Her first Lord Peter Wimsey novel, *Whose Body?*, completed in 1921, did not find a publisher at first, but once it was published in Britain and the United States in 1923, it was immediately successful, and from then until the publication of the final Wimsey-Vane novel, *Busman's Holiday*, in 1937, Sayers' detective fiction brought its author popular fame and financial success.

About her difficult personal life, she was intensely private. In 1923 Sayers and a man whose identity is not generally known—the authorized biography refers to him only as "Bill"—became lovers. Sayers never publicly acknowledged John Anthony, born in 1924, as her natural son, and while she supported him financially, he was reared by her cousin Ivy Shrimpton. In 1934 she did, however, informally "adopt" Anthony, who took the surname of Oswald Atherton "Mac" Fleming, the ex-army Captain she had married in 1926.

Sayers always regarded her detective fiction as entertainment, and from the late 1930s until her death she concentrated on what she believed to be literary work of a more serious nature. She wrote plays and essays reflecting her deep religious faith—for example, *The Man Born to be King* (1941)—and published works of **literary criticism** and translation, the most important being her work on Dante. (Her translation of the *Inferno* was published in 1949.) But her lasting literary reputation rests on the charm and wit of the Wimsey novels, with their debonair, insouciant hero, Lord Peter, and their independent, "strong-minded" heroine, detective-novelist Harriet Vane. In the late twentieth century the best of them—for example, *Gaudy Night* (1937)—survive not only as first-rate detective fiction, but as evocative expressions of the mores of the inter-war period.

Deborah Gorham

Bibliography

Brabazon, James. *Dorothy L. Sayers: A Biography*. 1981.
Brunsdale, Mitzi. *Dorothy L. Sayers: Solving the Mystery of Wickedness*. 1990.
Reynolds, Barbara. *Dorothy L. Sayers: Her Life and Soul*. 1993.
Tuschler, Nancy M. *Dorothy L. Sayers: A Pilgrim Soul*. 1980.

Science and Government

During the course of the twentieth century the government has funded between one-half and one-third of total expenditures on scientific research and development (R&D) in Britain. Indeed, its only rivals in the proportion of state-funded research have been Germany, France, Japan, the United States, and the former Soviet Union. The first government estimates for national expenditure date from the 1950s, when it was found that 1.5 percent of the gross domestic product (GDP) was devoted to research and development. That figure rose to 2.32 percent in 1964 but fell to 2.09 percent in 1975. However, with the exception of wartime and the 1940s and 1950s, government has spent less on R&D than private industry, even though it has indirectly borne much of the cost of training R&D personnel, especially after 1945. Most government-funded R&D has been performed by external contractors, above all, private firms.

In the United Kingdom research and development has been the responsibility almost exclusively of the central government, although the principal funding departments have gone through many changes of name and function. With the exception of the Ministry of Technology (1964–70)—but only in its last years when, under Tony Benn, it was really a Ministry of Industry and Defence Procurement—no single government department has been dominant in this area.

Until the 1960s most government funding of R&D went to develop of weapons of war. Before the First World War the Admiralty and the War Office each maintained R&D establishments. During the war the **Ministry of Munitions** temporarily became the major factor, and subsequently the two service ministries were joined by the Air Ministry, the heaviest spender in the inter-war period. The R&D and production responsibilities of the War Office and the Air Ministry were tranferred to the new Ministries of Supply and of Aircraft Production in 1939–40, but the Admiralty remained autonomous. After the war a single Ministry of Supply was responsible for most defense-oriented R&D, replaced by the Ministry of Aviation in 1959 and merged into the Ministry of Technology in 1967. In 1970 a Ministry of Aviation Supply was formed, which in 1973 became the major part of the Ministry of Defence's Procurement Executive. In real terms defense R&D was probably higher in the inter-war years than before 1914; it increased rapidly in the **Second** World War and fell slightly thereafter, only to increase sharply in the 1950s and remain at high levels since then. Although most government-funded work has been performed in the laboratories and workshops of private arms manufacturers, the state also maintained its own research establishments, the most famous of which are located at Farnborough, Porton Down, Aldermaston, Harwell, and Malvern.

Official support for R&D for industrial purposes and to improve energy supply, transportation, **health**, and agriculture has been carried out mainly through government departments, despite funding before 1964 of nondepartmental organizations devoted exclusively to R&D. These reported to the Lord President of the Council, effectively Minister for Science in the years 1959 and 1964. The two most significant such bodies were the Department of Scientific and Industrial Research and the **Medical Research Council**, although in the years 1954–7 and 1959–64 the United Kingdom Atomic Energy Authority was also responsible to the Lord President. Each research council maintained its own laboratories and funded its own university research. Since 1964 they have reported to the Department of Education and Science.

The scientific community, especially in the years 1900–18 and 1957–64, has been critical of an alleged lack of government interest in science and technology; the 1930s saw an important socialist-inspired critique of capitalist and military control of science. Unfavorable comparisons were made with different countries in each period: Germany in the Edwardian years; the Soviet Union in the 1930s; and the United States and the Soviet Union in the 1950s and 1960s. Only more recently have favorable comparisons been made with Germany once again, and with France and Japan. British scientists and engineers may not have run the country, but senior scientific advisers like Sir **Henry Tizard**, Lord Cherwell, and Sir Solly Zuckerman have been influential at the highest levels of the civil and military apparatus.

David E.H. Edgerton

Bibliography

Alter, Peter. *The Reluctant Patron: Science and the State in Britain, 1850–1920.* 1987.

Gummett, Philip J. *Scientists in Whitehall.* 1980.

Ince, Martin. *The Politics of British Science.* 1986.

Vig, Norman J. *Science and Technology in British Politics.* 1968.

Science Education and Training

In England and Wales the regulations issued under the 1902 Education Act confined elementary-school science to nature study, a limitation that was to survive the reorganization of the educational system in 1944 and remain unchallenged until the accommodation of programs of primary science in the 1960s. Within the highly selective secondary schools, laboratory-based science teaching became a condition of support from public funds, but, influenced by examinations controlled by the universities, the science curriculum was highly academic and preprofessional in character. The First World War encouraged a rejection of an earlier overemphasis on the teaching of scientific method and led to the development of broad courses of general science. The inter-war years also saw some expansion of biology teaching, although the medical influence remained strong, and, as with general science, the curriculum status of the subject was relatively low.

The secondary curriculum established in the early twentieth century excluded and, thereby, devalued technical and vocational education. Responsibility for this work lay with a bewildering variety of under-resourced and usually badly housed junior and senior technical schools, continuation schools, and technical centers. In general, the attitudes of employers to technical and vocational education was apathetic, although there were important exceptions. The need to rationalize courses and qualifications led to local, then regional, and, finally, to national arrangements, of which the scheme of National Certificates and Diplomas was particularly important. By 1918 the future pattern of **technical education**—part-time evening instruction combined with practical experience—was set. Until 1944, however, the dominant features of technical education and training were its voluntaryism and the enduring lack of commitment of most of British industry to investment in human capital.

The early years of the century also brought full university status to newer "civic" universities, located in the large manufacturing and commercial centers such as Birmingham and Manchester, which provided advanced training and research in applied disciplines such as metallurgy, brewing, textile chemistry, naval archi-

tecture, and food science. Between 1918 and 1939 science-based research in the universities benefited significantly from funds disbursed by the Department of Scientific and Industrial Research (DSIR), set up in 1915 as the first venture of the central government into the funding of large-scale research. By 1939 scientific and technological studies were well established within British higher education, although disputes about the nature and purpose of university education persisted.

The **Education Act of 1944** established a strongly class-based, tripartite system of secondary grammar, modern, and technical schools. Grammar-school science remained academic and preprofessional in form and function and attracted most of the scarce resources and the best of the teachers. In the modern schools science was often topic based and quasi-vocational, but the science education of most students was severely handicapped by a chronic shortage of teachers. The technical schools, few in number, struggled to find a distinctive identity and curriculum.

During the 1960s secondary- and primary-school science curricula underwent major reform and incorporated new techniques of assessment. Biology gained an established place in the secondary curriculum, but attempts to accommodate technology met initially with little success. Legislation establishing nonselective **secondary education** from 1965 onward led to attempts to derive a "science for all" from the different curriculum traditions of the tripartite system, and to rationalize the associated systems of public examinations [Certificate of Secondary Education (CSE) and General Certificate of Education (GCE)]. The introduction in 1988 of the General Certificate of Secondary Education (GCSE) examination for students at sixteen-plus confirmed a significant role for science teachers in the school-based assessment of their students' competence at practical science. The Education Reform Act of 1988 compelled schools to offer a broad and balanced science course as a core element of a national curriculum in England and Wales and introduced standardized forms of assessment at four "key stages" between the ages of five and sixteen. (There were parallel but significantly different developments in Scotland and Northern Ireland.) The relationship of the science and technology components of this subject-based national curriculum remains problematic. The 1980s also witnessed a variety of attempts to foster links between education, industry, and the world of work, notably the Technical and Vocational Education Initiative (1982). More recent developments have been concerned with articulating academic (GCSE, GCE) and technical/vocational [for example, Business and Technology Education Council (BTEC)] courses and qualifications and with reducing specialization for students at eighteen-plus.

Post-war scientific and technical education and training were strongly influenced by the Percy (1945) and Barlow (1946) Reports. The former led, although only gradually, to the development of a national system of technical colleges, some of which became Colleges of Advanced Technology and, subsequently, independent universities.

The **Robbins Report** (1963) led to the creation of **new universities** and laid the foundation for a large increase in undergraduate numbers, although the relative unpopularity of courses in physical and engineering sciences remained a cause for concern. The early 1990s were marked by a further, rapid expansion in student numbers and the granting of independence and university status to the **polytechnics** established during the 1960s. However, these developments, coupled with a commitment by the central government to accountability and selectivity, call into question the sustainability of research in the science-based disciplines within a number of institutions of higher education and raise important questions about the appropriateness of the science education traditionally provided.

Edgar W. Jenkins

Bibliography

Argles, Michael. *South Kensington to Robbins: An Account of English Technical and Scientific Education since 1851.* 1964.

Jenkins, E.W. *From Armstrong to Nuffield: Studies in Twentieth-Century Science Education in England and Wales.* 1979.

McCulloch, Gary, Edgar Jenkins, and David Layton. *Technological Revolution? The Politics of School Science and Technology in England and Wales since 1945.* 1985.

Scott, C(harles) P(restwich) (1846–1932)

C.P. Scott acquired an unusual eminence in the opening decades of the twentieth century. He was not a politician (apart from an undistinguished spell as a back-bench MP), and the newspaper he edited and subsequently owned was not a London-based or mass-circulation journal. Yet he enjoyed ready access to leading political figures (and kept an illuminating account of some of his interviews with them). And the journal over which he presided evolved into a newspaper of international reputation.

Scott came from a commercial, dissenting background. Graduating from **Oxford**, he was appointed in 1872—when he was only twenty-five years old—editor of the *Manchester Guardian*, then owned by his cousin. Scott ran the paper with a firm hand, skimped on salaries to himself and others, and brought in a succession of literate, perceptive writers.

Under his direction the *Manchester Guardian* soon became distinguished for its cogent and principled views on political and international affairs, often maintained in defiance of prevailing tastes and at cost to circulation and revenue. In the 1880s, coincident with Gladstone's conversion to Irish home rule, Scott's formerly Whiggish views moved decisively to the Liberal Left. Thereafter the paper espoused a succession of radical causes, at least some of which reached fulfillment: **women's suffrage, Irish nationalism,** protection of trade unions, free trade, amelioration of the lot of the needy, hostility to aggressive **imperialism,** and retrenchment on naval expenditure.

In Parliament from 1895 to 1905 Scott had formed associations with up and coming Liberals that persisted thereafter. They sought his endorsement and respected his opinions—even when failing to act on them. Longest-lasting, if often brought near a breaking point, was his relationship with **David Lloyd George,** which went back to mutual opposition to the **Boer War.**

Until the last moment, Scott seemed prepared to oppose another war, that of 1914–18. Under the myopic guidance of Lord Loreburn (another one-time associate in Parliament), he attributed the deteriorating international relations to "imperialist" elements in the Liberal government rather than to external challenge. But with the outbreak of war he espoused its vigorous and devoted prosecution—if not such draconian measures as military **conscription.** On grounds of energy as against lethargy, he campaigned for the ousting of **H.H. Asquith** by Lloyd George in 1916—but in 1918 he utterly condemned Lloyd George's jingoist campaign and disruption of the **Liberal Party** in the notorious "coupon" election.

In the 1920s the disintegration of the Liberals, **Labour's** rejection of the pre-war radical alliance, and the bleak **Conservative** dominance diminished Scott's influence. His stature as a great moral force, identified with social reform and international reconciliation, received wide recognition.

Robin Prior
Trevor Wilson

Bibliography

Ayerst, David. Guardian: *Biography of a Newspaper.* 1971.
Hammond, J.L. *C.P. Scott of the Manchester Guardian.* 1934.
Wilson, Trevor ed. *The Political Diaries of C.P. Scott, 1911–1928.* 1970.

Scottish Literature

In 1919 T.S. Eliot asked: "Is there a Scottish Literature?" The implication, that there was no identifiable or readable literature from Scotland, points to the necessity of marking Scotland's vexed national history in any consideration of its literary traditions.

One might begin dating the modern period in Scottish literature in the 1920s with what is now referred to as the Scottish Literary Renaissance. The movement, dubbed, it is said, in 1924 by Denis Saurat, Professor of English at the University of Bordeaux, is most closely associated with **Hugh MacDiarmid** (Christopher Murray Grieve). He is counted along with Ezra Pound, **T.S. Eliot**, and **James Joyce** as one of the premiere English modernists. It is, of course, revealing of the problematics of the category of modernism and of the differences among the writers that, of these so-called English literary innovators, two were American, one Irish, and the other Scottish—all former or approximate British colonials.

The thing that perhaps most distinguishes and at the same time obscures MacDiarmid is his self-conscious revival of Scots in his work. Though Gaelic is identified as Scotland's native language, akin to Irish Gaelic, Scots, often referred to as a dialect of English, was dominant in the fourteenth century in almost all areas east and south of the Highlands and has prevailed as the local vernacular since the seventh century. MacDiarmid did not see his revival of Scots as a nostalgic act, in line with **William Butler** Yeats' reconstruction of Irish mythology for the "Celtic Twilight"; he saw the revival, rather, as an effort to bring modern Scottish literature into the realm of linguistic experimentation associated with modernist writers in Europe and the United States. MacDiarmid's work is also associated with the resurgence of **Scottish nationalism** and with the rise of the National Party of Scotland (1928), later to become the SNP (Scottish National Party). These two readings would suggest a link between modernism and a nationalist impulse, in the sense that cultural and linguistic dispossession underwrites linguistic innovation. MacDiarmid believed that the Scottish spirit was repressed through English cultural and political domination and that the way to restore the Scottish psyche was through the use of the vernacular. His most famous expression of this is "The Drunk Man Looks at the Thistle" (1926), identified as a nationalist poem and written very much in the modern epic form of Joyce's *Ulysses*. In "In Memoriam James Joyce" (1955) MacDiarmid makes this tribute clear. And like Joyce's work, MacDiarmid's problematizes rather than romanticizes national identity.

The immediate contemporaries of MacDiarmid are Violet Jacob, Marion Angus, Helen Burness Cruikshank, William Soutar, and Lewis Spence. Successive decades claim poets such as Robert Garioch Sutherland and Maurice Lindsay and eventually novelists Neil M. Gunn and Eric Linklater, Naomi Mitchison (also a poet), and James Leslie Mitchell (1901–35), author under the pen name Lewis Grassic Gibbon of the trilogy *A Scots Quair* (*Sunset Song,* 1923; *Cloud Howe,* 1933; *Grey Granite,* 1934). The trilogy, like some of MacDiarmid's work, proffers socialism as a remedy for the oppressive system identified with the British state.

The Scottish Renaissance writers—in particular, Gibbon—are also credited with the reaction against the *kailyard* school of Scottish literature (*kailyard* means cabbage patch), representative of rural sentimentality and of conformity to the romantic stereotypes of Scotland (the gentle Highlander, with kilt and spade, lumbering in the croft). The *kailyard* period precedes the Renaissance, beginning in the late nineteenth century and including, however arguably, writers like J.M. Barrie. Some prefer to link Barrie with Robert Louis Stevenson, the nineteenth-century writer who is certainly better known for his horror story *Dr. Jekyll and Mr. Hyde* (1886) than for his Scottishness, and whose adventure novels (such as *Treasure Island*, 1883) line up with Barrie's fantasy works for and/or about children. Like Gibbon, George Douglas Brown has written a classic anti-kailyard novel, *The House With Green Shutters* (1901).

A Scottish writer with one of the more international reputations who does not fall neatly into any category is Edwin Muir. His best-known works, *We Moderns* (1918), a collection of aphorisms, *The Labyrinth* (1949), a collection of poetry, and with his novelist wife, Willa Muir, his many translations of Kafka and other writing in German, have given him modernist standing in European letters; at the same time, his conclusion that "Scotland can only create a national literature by writing in English" alienated him from fellow Scottish writers like MacDiarmid. Another maverick figure, considered within Scottish letters to be one of its greatest living poets, is Norman MacCaig (*Collected Poems* 1985, 1990). MacCaig takes up where both MacDiarmid and Muir leave off by using English in a way that, however formal the semantic and structural elements, however pastoral the setting, represents the inflections of a Scots cultural vernacular.

Since the time of Muir's death (1959) there has been an explosion of writing in Scotland in English, Scots, and Gaelic. Poets like Tom Leonard and Edwin Morgan, in keeping with immediate literary ancestors, have made language the metaphorical subjects of their investigations into national (literary) identity. Morgan, recently one of Scotland's few self-acknowledged gay writers, writes a poem like "The First Men on Mercury" (*From Glasgow to Saturn*, 1973) to underscore the linguistics of imperialism. In Leonard's "Jist Ti Let Yi No," from his collection *Bunnit Husslin* (1975), he pays linguistic tribute to the American modernist William Carlos Williams by rewriting an imagist poem, "This is Just to Say" (1934), from a Glaswegian cultural and phonetic point of view.

Leonard has been identified as part of the movement dubbed the Glasgow school of artists, although this label was conceived to designate the fine art emerging from Glasgow alongside the recent revivification of the city. The Renaissance of painting has spread to the other arts, especially to poetry and theater. The writer Liz Lochhead bridges the genres, though since the 1980s she has become identified almost exclusively with drama. Lochhead has vocalized what has been true of Scottish writing, that the literary Establishment has excluded **women**. Having begun as a painter, Lochhead moved on to producing poetry whose cadences and themes redress and retell the gendering of fairy tales and myth (*Dreaming Frankenstein and Collected Poems*, 1984). She has produced performance poetry in which she provides what she calls "new clichés" (*True Confessions and New Clichés*, 1985), and she has written and performed in more than ten plays and several revues since 1985. Her play *Mary Queen of Scots Got Her Head Chopped Off* (first performed in 1987 in Edinburgh) creates a dialogue between country and gender, and between past and present, in a Scottish historical and literary context. The play also takes up the clash of religions, whose political import is not confined to the Irish conflict. Lochhead has remarked on her work's journey from "my country of gender" to a recognition of the necessity for dialogue between nationality and **sexuality**, such as the one between Mary and Elizabeth in her play, and the one implicitly between herself and a male writer like MacDiarmid. In fact, several women writers—Jessie Kesson (*The White Bird Passes*, 1987) and Agnes Owens (*Gentlemen of the West*, 1984), as did their female Renaissance predecessors—have, like Lochhead, turned to Scots, perhaps in an effort to reverse the belief that country and language are "male-centered" domains. Lochhead has also been engaged in translating "classic" texts of other languages into Scots, such as Moliere's *Tartuffe* (1985). Other women writers who contribute to the dialogue are poets Carol Ann Duffy, Kathleen Raine, Kathleen Jamie, and Jackie Kay, and fiction writers Dylis Rose (who also writes poetry), Janice Galloway (author of *The Trick Is to Keep Breathing*, 1990; and *Blood*, 1991). Even the more established writer **Muriel Spark** is lately being considered within a Scottish and **feminist** literary context. If the women writers are not in every case confronting the issues of gender and nationality as directly as Lochhead, they are fortifying the dialogue by being visible and readable.

Two fiction writers and sometime poets identified with the Glasgow school whose work has traveled to the United States are James Kelman and Alasdair Gray. Such travel is not only difficult, but uncharacteristic of Scottish writing not undertaken under the auspices of the British/English **publishing** industry. The use of the Scots vernacular that is associated with the Glasgow school cannot be separated out for the most part from attention to class and urban life in most of this work, attention for which both of these writers are particularly noted. Gray is perhaps the first writer since MacDiarmid to be compared specifically with Joyce. In his case the comparison is most justified by virtue of the narrative innovations of Gray's texts, which are a cross between Joyce, Laurence Sterne, and Thomas Pynchon—the characters are (Leopold) Bloomian, the tone and graphics are (Tristram) Shandyish, and the atmosphere is surreal. Kelman's work, on the other hand, is relentlessly "real" in subject and style (*Greyhound for Breakfast,* 1987; *A Dissaffection,* 1989).

It has been as true of Scotland as of Ireland that the nation harbors a small but enduring Gaelic speaking and writing population. And it is true of both places that the literature has experienced a kind of revival since about 1980 among the younger generation. In Scotland this is more remarkable since there is no national policy, as in Ireland, requiring students to learn Gaelic in school. In the 1990s approximately 80,000 of the 5 million inhabitants of Scotland are Gaelic speaking. The name most often associated with Gaelic writing in a bardic tradition is Somhairle MacGilleain/Sorley Maclean; he is grouped with MacDiarmid in terms of the magnitude of contribution to Scottish letters in the twentieth century. As is true of many of the island populations of Scotland, MacLean's community of Osgaig on the Isle of Raasay is Gaelic speaking. His poems are like lyrical histories. They recall in Scotland's first language its cultural monuments. A poem like "Hallaig" (*Selected Poems, 1945–1972)* commemorates and laments the Highland clearances of the eighteenth century. This event, in which thousands of inhabitants were displaced to make way for grazing sheep, has become a tragic marker of English domination. But Maclean is also affected by the socialist vision of MacDiarmid and the circumstances of national communities in the world around Scotland. In his poem "The Cry of Europe" he places himself as artist in a national tradition in relation to writers who died in the **Spanish Civil War.** Maclean studied English literature at the University of Edinburgh, which until recently included almost no writing by Scots in its curriculum (this was reserved for the School of Scottish Studies); he does his own translations. Iain Crichton Smith, another writer of Gaelic poetry, is one of the most versatile of Scottish writers, in all genres, in each of three British languages; he is praised for his deftness in all. He also has contributed to the critical literature and has helped bring Gaelic writing to international attention. Among the younger writers in Gaelic are Roderick Watson, Christopher Whyte, and Meg Bateman.

Marilyn Reizbaum

Bibliography
Cairns, Craig, ed. *The History of Scottish Literature.* vol. 4: *Twentieth Century.* 1987.
Dunn, Douglas, ed. *The Faber Book of Twentieth Century Scottish Poetry.* 1992.
Kerrigan, Catherine. "The Ugsome Thistle: Hugh MacDiarmid and the Nationalism of the Modern Literary Revival" in Horst W. Drescher, and Hermann Volkel, eds. *Nationalism in Literature-Literarischer Nationalismus: Literature, Language, and National Identity.* 1989. pp. 181–9.
Royle, Trevor. *The Macmillan Companion to Scottish Literature.* 1983.
Smith, Iain Crichton. "The Internationalism of Twentieth Century Gaelic Poetry," *Scottish Literary Journal,* vol. 18 (1991), pp. 82–6.

Scottish Nationalism

Broadly defined, Scottish nationalism has been a movement geared to the political and cultural expression of Scotland's national identity. It has made a significant, if episodic, impact on twentieth-century British politics, and can be given credit for the re-emergence of devolution and constitutional change as an important issue of political debate since the late 1960s.

The demand for self-government for Scotland within the United Kingdom was a central feature of the wider constitutional debate in British politics before 1914. Then, ideas of "Home Rule All Round"—separate parliaments for Scotland, England, Ireland, and Wales along with an Imperial Assembly—were current. However, Irish problems took precedence, and a combination after the First World War of their resolution and changed political circumstances, notably the decline of the **Liberal Party,** thwarted the federalist-style devolution schemes. Between 1919 and 1928 successive bills allowing for varying measures of self-government for Scotland failed to make headway in Parliament.

In the belief that a separate party was required to fight for self-government, the National Party of Scotland (NPS) was formed in 1928. The NPS absorbed, among other groups, the Scottish National League (SNL), which had been in existence since 1920. The SNL promoted Gaelic cultural concerns and was the first organization to advocate complete independence and separation from England. The 1920s, moreover, saw the flowering of a literary "renaissance" in Scotland in which leading figures such as the poet **Hugh MacDiarmid** (Christopher Murray Grieve) came to prominence and robustly enforced the SNL line. However, the NPS included people of differing views on the national question: from those in favor of a mild degree of devolution to outright separatists, with federalists and supporters of Dominion status in between. In 1934 it merged with the moderate Scottish Party (a Conservative breakaway group set up in 1933) to form the Scottish National Party (SNP), and the balance of the new organization shifted decidedly away from the extremists. The SNP pursued a policy of self-government within the Empire, and cultural nationalists like MacDiarmid were ousted.

The apparent popularity among Scots of at least some measure of administrative devolution saw the transfer of the Scottish departments of state from London to Edinburgh in 1939; the office of Secretary of State for Scotland had been established in 1885. These governmental arrangements buttressed the enduring sense of distinctive national identity enshrined in the separate Scottish educational, legal, and church establishments.

The SNP split during the Second World War and a secessionist movement made the political running into the 1950s with a national covenant campaign for Home Rule. When this ran out of steam, the SNP gradually reasserted its claim to represent the only realistic way forward: through the ballot box. In 1967 this strategy finally paid off when the SNP won a by-election in the Labour seat of Hamilton. In the views of most commentators this was a protest vote against Labour's failure to rebuild the Scottish economy. In the 1970s the SNP held out the hope of a prosperous future if, through independence, Scotland took advantage of the recently discovered North Sea oil. Unprecedented success followed in the general elections of 1974,

the latter of which saw the SNP win eleven seats.

The revived constitutional debate eventually produced a commitment by the Labour government to devolution, conditional on the endorsement of at least 40 percent of the Scottish electorate in a referendum to be held in March 1979. The required threshold was not reached, although a majority did vote in favor. Amid anticlimax and disillusionment the SNP, which viewed devolution as a first step to ultimate independence, suffered electoral decline. The 1980s were a period of infighting and rebuilding.

The **Thatcher** era saw increasing political divergence between Scotland and England. The arousal of social resentments in Scotland benefited the **Labour Party**; class loyalties remained stubborn. But the antigovernment mood was also increasingly nationalistic; cultural nationalism revived in a fusion of literary, artistic, and popular music developments. By the 1990s the Scottish question was pivotal to a new decentralist movement for constitutional modernization, and the SNP's policy of "Independence in Europe" signaled the salience to this debate of the **European Union**.

Scottish nationalism in the twentieth century has encompassed a variety of positions on the constitutional issue, a range of ideological tendencies, and a broad, if insufficiently concentrated, social base of support. It has largely been free of any association with physical force to achieve its aims.

Graham Walker

Bibliography

Brand, Jack. *The National Movement in Scotland*. 1978.
Gallagher, Tom, ed. *Nationalism in the Nineties*. 1991.
Hanham, H.J. *Scottish Nationalism*. 1969.
Harvie, Christopher. *Scotland and Nationalism*. 1977.

Scouting Movement

Robert Baden-Powell capitalized on his reknown as the **Boer War** hero of Mafeking first to establish, and then to promote, scouting as a scheme for character building among the boys of Britain, beginning with an experimental camp on Brownsea Island, off the coast of Dorset, in 1907. A year later he published his hugely popular *Scouting for Boys* (1908), which in its many editions ranks third among best-sellers in English during the twentieth century, behind only the Bible and Shakespeare. Above all, he wanted to promote **patriotism** and manliness through scouting, so that the British Empire would not go the way of the Roman Empire. A movement that initially received its stimulus from Edwardian anxieties about degeneration and decline spread not only in Britain, but around the globe as a vehicle for the socialization of adolescents.

Youth groups had existed before the scouting movement. Some of these included the Boys' and Girls' Life Brigade, the **Catholic** Lads' Brigade, and the **Anglican** Church Lads' Brigade, all of them more concerned with the religious deterioration of youth than with physical exercise and rejuvenation, so vital to scouting. The Jewish Lads' Brigade attempted to "Anglicize" and assimilate into British society immigrant boys from Eastern Europe living in the ghettos of the East End of London, making them good **Jews** and good British subjects. To reach this goal, British public-school ethics and military drill and discipline were to be imposed on the boys. But none of these groups had the success of the Boy Scouts. By 1910 the scouting movement claimed 100,000, more than the other youth groups in Britain combined. By 1913 there were 140,000 scouts, in addition to 14,500 scout masters and assistants.

During the early years of scouting Baden-Powell received generous financial assistance from newspaper publisher Sir Arthur Pearson, who funded a publicity campaign on behalf of scouting, including a national lecture tour by Baden-Powell himself. Through a combination of patriotism, good citizenship, the worship of nature, and the healing qualities of the outdoors based largely on the woodcraft scheme of training established by the American Ernest Thompson Seton, scouting was to stop the decadence of urban life, while generating class unity and bolstering imperial defense. Scouting as conceived by Baden-Powell might have had as its goal the creation of a good citizen, not necessarily a good soldier. Baden-Powell hated what he termed mindless military drill, but there seems little doubt that the War Office, the National Service League, and Empire enthusiasts tried to militarize the scouts since Britain lacked any scheme of universal training or military service.

When Baden-Powell first established scouting, he had only boys in mind, but thousands of girls joined the scouting movement, probably as many as 6,000 by 1909. Baden-Powell and his sister Agnes organized the British Girl Guides in 1910, a movement that had as its primary goal the creation of good wives and mothers for the British Empire, halting the deterioration of the so-called "imperial race." The Girl Guides grew rapidly, with both the scouting and the guide movements becoming permanent social institutions in twentieth-century Britain.

Richard A. Voeltz

Bibliography

Dedman, Martin. "Baden-Powell, Militarism, and the 'Invisible Contributors' to the Boy Scout Scheme, 1904–1920, *Twentieth Century British History*, vol. 4 (1993), pp. 201–23.

Reynolds, Ernest E. *The Scout Movement.* 1950.

Rosenthal, Michael. *The Character Factory: Baden-Powell and the Origins of the Boy Scout Movement.* 1986.

Springhall, John. *Youth, Empire, and Society: British Youth Movements, 1883–1940.* 1977.

Warren, Allan. "Mothers for the Empire? The Girl Guides Association in Britain, 1909–1939" in J.A. Mangan, ed. *Making Imperial Mentalities.* 1990. pp. 96–109.

Second World War: Homefront

Historians formerly viewed the Second World War's effect on Britain as an example of how "total war" permanently altered a society. But recent studies have undermined this "war and social change" model by drawing attention to the pre-war origins of reforms attributed to the war, by challenging the belief that the post-war **welfare state** was the result of a wartime consensus on social policy innovations, and by demonstrating that few of the wartime changes in class, gender, and demographic structures continued beyond the end of the war.

Public support for greater state intervention to promote social welfare increased during the war. The evacuation of British troops from **Dunkirk** and the subsequent **Battle of Britain** contributed to a heightened sense of social solidarity that strengthened public pressure for social reform, although the degree and duration of this sentiment should not be exaggerated.

This benefited the **Labour Party**, perceived as more committed to reform than the Conservatives, and contributed to the Labour victory in the 1945 general election.

Although the December 1942 Beveridge Report became a watershed in the history of social policy, this was not the government's intent in appointing **William Beveridge** to chair what was considered a minor committee reviewing the social insurance system. Beveridge seized the opportunity to produce proposals that went far beyond what the government desired. He recommended a comprehensive social insurance scheme providing a subsistence-level income to protect members of all classes from poverty, and insisted that the scheme would be effective only if accompanied by **family allowances**, full employment, and a free **National Health Service**. The social insurance proposal was an extension of the pre-war system rather than a radical departure; it also continued the insurance principle, financing the scheme by regressive flat-rate contributions from employers and employees rather than from general taxation as socialists preferred. It was novel in being comprehensive, universal, and, as there was no **means test**, in providing benefits as a right of citizenship.

Beveridge's report embarrassed the government because it drew attention to the disagreement between the major parties on social reform. Conservative backbenchers privately informed **Winston Churchill** of their opposition to the proposals, reinforcing the Prime Minister's preference for avoiding a commitment to reform. But confronted with strong public support for Beveridge's report and a Labour backbench revolt, the government reluctantly issued a White Paper on social insurance in September 1944 that accepted the main features of Beveridge's scheme.

The 1944 White Paper, *Employment Policy*, has been viewed as implying government responsibility for maintaining full employment and for using Keynesian economic policies to achieve it. In fact, the government issued the White Paper because it knew Beveridge was planning to publish employment proposals more radical than it could endorse and hoped that by publishing first it could deflect the public support for his recommendations that followed his report on social insurance. Whereas Beveridge sought a government commitment to maintain full employment—that is, that unemployment would not be allowed to rise above 3

percent—the White Paper only proposed maintaining a high level of employment, defined as limiting unemployment to no more than 8 percent. While the White Paper did imply a greater degree of government responsibility for sustaining high employment than pre-war governments had accepted, it did so in order to avoid endorsing full employment and Keynesian economic policies.

There was wide agreement before 1939 on the need to reform the health services. The Labour Party had been committed since 1934 to establishing a National Health Service financed by the central government; even the British Medical Association (BMA) was urging during the 1930s that the health insurance system be expanded to include nearly all adults and their dependents. At the onset of war the government set up the Emergency Medical Service to care for civilians injured by enemy action. But it was not until Beveridge included a National Health Service as part of his report that the government addressed the issue. In February 1944 it issued a White Paper outlining its proposals for a reformed health service. While there was agreement on the need for change, the two major parties differed as to its form. Under pressure from the BMA the Tory Minister of Health, Henry Willink, abandoned several key features in the White Paper scheme, including the proposal for a salaried service. At the time the coalition government ended in 1945, he was preparing a new White Paper with proposals significantly different from the system Labour instituted after the war.

Eleanor Rathbone had been campaigning for family allowances for nearly two decades prior to the Second World War, but it was not until Beveridge included this reform in his report that implementation seemed likely. Athough the government preferred to postpone the matter until after the war, it reluctantly agreed to proceed with reform because of strong public support. It delayed two years before introducing a bill strikingly different from what Rathbone and Beveridge desired. Whereas Beveridge intended the allowance to provide subsistence-level maintenance for a child, and calculated it must be no less than eight shillings weekly to achieve this end, the government viewed the allowances as a means of avoiding demands for higher wages. Since the government considered the benefit to be a general subvention toward family needs rather than subsistence for a child, the 1945 Family Allow-

Building an Anderson shelter in the back garden. Notoriously damp, these shelters were effective in protecting families from anything except a direct bomb attack.

London schoolchildren with gas masks, 1941.

ances Act provided only five shillings weekly for each child beginning with the second one.

The 1938 Spens Report recommended free secondary education be provided up to age fifteen through three different types of schools: secondary modern, technical, and grammar. This was incorporated into the **Education Act of 1944** after **R.A. Butler**, President of the Board of Education, overcame Churchill's initial resistance to introducing an education bill. Treasury officials viewed the legislation as a less expensive alternative to Beveridge's proposals and hoped it would satisfy the public pressure for reform. It was the most important social legislation enacted during the war; the percentage of fourteen-year-olds in school rose from 38 in 1938 to nearly 100 after 1947 when the school leaving age was raised to fifteen.

Due primarily to a steady decline in the birthrate, population growth during the interwar period slowed to less than one-half the pre-First World War rate. The war strengthened concern over this trend and encouraged a revival of pro-natalism. Beveridge's report included proposals intended to encourage a higher birthrate by making the roles of housewife and mother more attractive to **women**. Parliamentary concern led to the appointment of a Royal Commission on Population in 1944. Although policymakers feared the high level of wartime **women's employment** would further reduce the birthrate, the war had the opposite effect. In 1941 the birthrate fell to the lowest level since official records had been kept (13.9 per 1,000 population), but it then rose steadily until it peaked in 1947 (at 20.6 per 1,000). This wartime change proved temporary, however; in the 1950s the birthrate resumed its pre-war decline.

The wartime rise in the **marriage** rate was partially responsible for the increase in the birthrate. This trend was well established by 1939 rather than being initiated by the war. The change in the marital status of young women was especially striking: 42 percent of all women age twenty-five to twenty-nine were single in 1931, but by 1951 only 22 percent of this age cohort were unmarried. Although some historians have suggested the war emancipated women, the changes in birth and marriage rates suggest that it reinforced traditional roles.

The wartime labor shortage became an important pressure for change by forcing Britain to make greater use of female workers. The December 1941 National Service (No. 2) Act granted the government the power to conscript women into industry or military service. Britain's use of womanpower far exceeded that of other belligerent nations; by September 1943, 46 percent of all women between the ages of fourteen and fifty-nine were engaged in some form of national service. But this trend did not undermine the sex segregation of jobs; women who undertook wartime jobs were considered temporary workers and at the end of the war were usually either dismissed or transferred to traditional women's work.

During the war's first year back-bench women MPs from all parties joined with the leaders of influential women's organizations to form the Woman Power Committee. The committee pressed the government to establish equal employment opportunities and to eliminate sex-differentiated policies. Although they succeeded in forcing the government to grant sex equality in the rates of compensation paid civilians injured by enemy action (women originally received two-thirds of the rate paid men), in other areas women's reform efforts were usually unsuccessful. An attempt to secure **equal pay** for women teachers was defeated when the government threatened to resign rather than accept reform; it then prevented further action on the matter by appointing a Royal Commission to study the issue.

The belief that the post-war welfare state should be attributed to a wartime consensus on reform pays insufficient attention to Conservative concern with the nation's financial position. During the war Churchill had privately expressed doubts that Britain would emerge from the war in a position to finance costly social reforms. Since Britain was virtually bankrupt by 1945, the election of a Conservative government in that year would likely have meant the subordination of social legislation to the improvement of the nation's financial position. The 1945 general election thus seems more directly responsible for the post-war welfare state than wartime developments; the shock of overwhelming defeat in that election should not be underestimated in explaining the **Conservative Party**'s subsequent acceptance of the main features of the welfare state.

Harold L. Smith

Bibliography
Addison, Paul. *The Road to 1945: British Politics and the Second World War.* 1975.

Calder, Angus. *The People's War: Britain, 1939–45.* 1969.

Harris, Jose. "War and Social History: Britain and the Home Front during the Second World War," *Contemporary European History,* vol. 1 (1992), pp. 17–35.

Jefferys, Kevin. *The Churchill Coalition and Wartime Politics, 1940–1945.* 1991.

Smith, Harold L., ed. *War and Social Change: British Society in the Second World War.* 1986.

Titmuss, Richard M. *Problems of Social Policy.* 1950.

Second World War: Military

Britain was a belligerent throughout the Second World War as it struggled to prevent Germany, Italy, and Japan from dominating Europe, Africa, and Asia. The principal theaters of war were the Atlantic, the English Channel, the skies over Europe, North Africa, northwest Europe, and Burma. Although suffering initial defeat on the Continent, submarine blockade, bombing, and economic strain, Britain ended the war victorious through a combination of its own exertions, Russian efforts and sacrifices, and military and economic aid from the Commonwealth and the United States.

Britain went to war on 3 September 1939 in order to prevent German domination of Eastern Europe and the consequent threat to Anglo-French security. The specific cause of war was Germany's invasion of Poland on 1 September. The Allies could not save Poland from quick defeat and, in fact, made little effort to do so. They did impose a blockade on Germany, but the latter could still obtain supplies from neutral Sweden, Russia, and other Continental areas. Meanwhile, the First Lord of the Admiralty, **Winston Churchill,** proposed to interrupt Germany's iron ore imports from Sweden by mining Norwegian waters, a violation of Norway's neutrality—which, to be sure, had been violated by both sides before. Adolf Hitler, however, beat Churchill to the punch by an audacious invasion of Denmark and Norway in April 1940; a subsequent Anglo-French expedition to Norway had to be withdrawn some weeks later.

The Germans' next move was a *blitzkrieg* attack on the Lowlands and France beginning on 10 May 1940. Allied forces, unaccustomed to modern tank warfare, were quickly outmaneuvered. As France fell, the British Expedition-ary Force had to be evacuated from **Dunkirk** and elsewhere in May and June. This left Britain alone, its **army** shattered. Fortunately, an immediate German invasion was impracticable since the enemy had first to secure control of the channel skies in order to have any hope of neutralizing the **Royal Navy.** Churchill, as Prime Minister, refused Hitler's offer to negotiate; therefore, the Germans began an aerial bombing campaign, soon to be called the **Battle of Britain** (July-October 1940). **Royal Air Force** fighter planes, assisted by a well-developed **radar** system, blunted the German air attack, thereby frustrating Germany's plans for a landing on England's southern coast in September. Subsequent German night bombing of Britain from that month until May 1941—the **Blitz**—did not cause the British to yield.

Yet Britain was still in grave danger. German **submarine warfare,** and to a lesser extent attacks by surface raiders, seriously threatened the economy from 1940 until mid-1943. In this phase of the war the British employed a code- and cipher-breaking system nicknamed ULTRA for the reading of German radio messages. The British, Canadian, and—after 1941—the U.S. navies eventually defeated the German submarines with the help of ULTRA, increased long-range aerial patrols, aircraft-carrier protection of convoys, advanced antisubmarine radar, American mass production of cargo ships, and an increased supply of escort vessels.

At the same time Britain had to deal with Italy, which had entered the war just before the fall of France. During 1940–1 British forces trounced the Italians in Ethiopia, Libya, and the Mediterranean only to face German air attacks against the British base on Malta and an expeditionary force in North Africa under General Erwin Rommel. Although Africa was always of secondary interest to Hitler—gearing up for his campaign against the Soviet Union—to the British it was a vital area of the world where important bases in Gibraltar, **Malta, Cyprus, Palestine,** Alexandria, and Suez were endangered. In June 1941 Hitler invaded Russia, thereby draining German resources away from both Africa and the Atlantic.

Meanwhile, President Franklin D. Roosevelt was leading the United States in a policy of helping Britain with measures just short of co-belligerency. In 1940 the Americans sold guns and ammunition to Britain and traded fifty old U.S. destroyers for the right to build bases on British islands in the western Atlantic. In 1941

Lend-Lease began, and the American navy waged a quiet, undeclared, quasi-war against German submarines in support of Lend-Lease convoys. When the Japanese attacked Pearl Harbor on 7 December 1941, Hitler declared war on the United States; American factories henceforth poured even more of their output into the hands of the British, the Russians, and the other Allied powers.

The Japanese, questing for riches in Southeast Asia, attacked the British Empire and Commonwealth immediately after going to war with the United States. Britain now had to pay for its previous support of American opposition to Japanese imperialism. Hong Kong, Malaya, most of Burma, and other British holdings were soon lost. Worst of all in terms of strategy and prestige was the ignominious fall of the great naval base at **Singapore** in February 1942. Preoccupied with Europe and North Africa, the British thereafter could do little more than guard India from a possible Japanese invasion, or an Indian uprising, or both, leaving the United States to carry on most of the war against Japan.

Yet by late 1942 and early 1943, the tide of war was turning all over the world. In addition to the great Russian victory at Stalingrad and American victories in the Pacific, there were accomplishments more closely related to Britain's war effort. Although Rommel had driven the British back into Egypt in the summer of 1942, that proved to be the worst he could do at the end of his overstretched supply line. British naval and air forces now gained the upper hand, mangling Italian convoys carrying such supplies to Rommel as Hitler could spare. The British Eighth Army in Egypt grew stronger, and by September 1942, a new commander, General Sir **Bernard L. Montgomery**, had checked a fresh German offensive at **El Alamein**; on 23 October he attacked in the same area, grinding down the Axis by weight of men and materiel until Rommel had to retreat. In November Anglo-American forces landed in western North Africa, violating the neutrality of French Morocco and Algeria; these landings threatened the Axis forces from the west while the Eighth Army threatened them from the east. By May 1943 all of North Africa was free of the enemy.

The Americans had at first resisted an African campaign, believing that sideshows in the Mediterranean area would only prolong the war. They had wanted a cross-channel invasion of France as soon as possible. The British, on the other hand, argued that the Allies should postpone the risky and difficult task of invading France until better prepared. Thus the British urged Africa upon the Americans, and with reason: the French and Italians could easily be defeated, thus knocking the props out from under Rommel's forces; inversely, for the Allies to do nothing against Hitler except stockpiling for an eventual invasion of France would damage public morale as well as anger the hard-pressed Russians.

Roosevelt had been convinced by such arguments, but when he and Churchill met in Casablanca in January 1943, the President's staff renewed its demand for an early invasion of France. They were disappointed to find the British staff again recommending a possible postponement of the harder task, using many of the same kinds of arguments as before. Now the British wanted to attack Italy, another relatively easy target, thereby gaining control of both the Italian peninsula and the central Mediterranean. Among other reasons for such a strategy, it was crucial to open the route from Gibraltar to Suez so that Allied shipping, always scarce, would not have to go all the way around southern Africa. Since the British were still carrying most of the burden of the war against Hitler, they got their way yet again—and many historians believe rightly so. The result was an Anglo-American invasion of Sicily in July 1943 and of the Italian mainland in September, leading to Italy's surrender; German troops, however, prevented an Allied conquest of the entire peninsula until the end of the war.

Another decision made at Casablanca involved British acceptance of Roosevelt's unconditional surrender policy, placing the war more than ever on the level of a crusade against **Fascism**. This suited the psychological needs of the Allied peoples and made it possible for the American, British, and Russian governments to postpone serious arguments among themselves as to the ultimate fate of Europe.

The conferees also agreed to continue the strategic bombing of Europe—America by day, the British by night. The Royal Air Force had turned to night bombing early in the war as a way of reducing bomber losses, but with an inevitable cost in accuracy. By 1943-4, Britain had inflicted serious damage on German cities, as witness, for example, the destruction of Hamburg (July-August 1943). Although the Allied bombing program did not fulfill the ex-

S

pectations of bomber enthusiasts, it did force the Germans to expend resources on counter-measures such as night fighters—the latter costing Britain's bomber fleet tremendous losses despite the cover of darkness.

Churchill had wanted to reinforce the bogged-down Italian campaign and even open up new theaters in the eastern Mediterranean; he was willing to postpone the landing in France until Mediterranean operations, the Russians, and the strategic bombers could do so much damage to Germany as to guarantee an easy conquest of northwest Europe. The United States and Russia, however, insisted on a cross-channel attack in 1944, and Churchill acquiesced at the Tehran Conference in Iran in November and December of 1943. By that time Britain's role was diminishing, its resources becoming overstrained, while the United States and Russia were just then achieving full mobilization. General Dwight D. Eisenhower was chosen as Supreme Commander for Operation Overlord, the Anglo-American landing at Normandy in northern France, which began on 6 June 1944. Even so, British and Canadian troops were responsible for three out of five of the beaches, and British officers commanded all of Eisenhower's air, sea, and land invasion forces. After the breakout from the beachheads in August 1944, however, Eisenhower assumed direct management of the land war in France.

The British and Canadian armies, led by Montgomery, held the north end of the line facing Germany, while the Americans, with the help of pro-Allies French forces, held the rest. Montgomery's idea was to annex most of the supplies and ground forces—even the Americans among them—to his command for a concentrated thrust into northern Germany. The Americans, however, regarded Montgomery as arrogant, quarrelsome, and too slow-moving for such a daring, "narrow" thrust; moreover, he seemed to Eisenhower to be oblivious to logistical imperatives. Eisenhower maintained a more or less "broad front," while giving Montgomery only some of what he wanted. The American view of Montgomery seemed to be vindicated when he failed to secure a bridge-head over the Rhine in September 1944, while Montgomery's frustrated claims to overall direction of the land war seemed to be justified when American troops got into serious trouble during the Battle of the Bulge (December 1944). At that point Eisenhower gave Montgomery temporary command over yet more American troops; but the Supreme Commander secured from Montgomery what amounted to an apology for the latter's arrogance.

The war in Europe ended on 8 May 1945 with British forces in control of northwestern Germany. Britain's contribution to the Asian war had increased somewhat by then: In 1944 General William J. Slim had led Empire and Commonwealth forces in the successful defense of India; in spring 1945 he carried out a brilliant reconquest of southern Burma. On 2 September Japan surrendered to the United States and the other Allied powers, Britain among them.

Karl G. Larew

Bibliography

Barnett, Correlli. *Engage the Enemy More Closely.* 1990.
Calvocoressi, Peter, and Guy Wint. *Total War.* 1972.
Churchill, Winston S. *The Second World War.* 6 vols. 1948–53.
Lewin, Ronald. *Ultra Goes to War.* 1978.
Liddell Hart, Basil H. *History of the Second World War.* 1970.
Parker, R.A.C. *Struggle for Survival: The History of the Second World War.* 1989.

Secondary Education

Secondary schooling debates have been the mainstay of the perennial English enthusiasm for discussions of class and social change, and their history has followed the same pattern, concentrating on organization rather than curriculum, legislation rather than practice. In 1900 grammar-school pupils received a secondary education, and those in elementary schools received what later became primary schooling. Thus the pattern of secondary education was organized in the interests of the few for an academic education for professional middle-class or white-collar employment. About 10 percent of children received such schooling. Its curriculum, reflecting the practice of the great public schools, emphasized classical languages and arts, which ensured that the educated product of such schooling was eloquent in speech and on paper but not well versed in science or technology. Girls were included in secondary education but in smaller numbers. The universities had established their dominance over the content and structure of secondary education, and the higher education offered to girls precluded much emphasis on their academic development.

Secondary education was constructed in the interests of academic excellence of young men. Secondary schools were administered locally through the structure of government set up by the 1902 Education Act and the interpretative regulations of 1904.

The central government regulated, inspected, and funded secondary education through the Education Committee of the local council, which constituted the local education authority. Children of respectable artisans were encouraged to enter secondary schools with government help under the special-places regulations of 1907, providing those children who could demonstrate ability the education for which the rest of the secondary-school population paid fees. Social mobility was to be promoted by this "ladder of opportunity," through a mixture of national regulation and local initiative, with secondary schools partly funded through the rates (local property tax) as well as from the central government. They had some autonomy over their curriculum despite regulations that insisted on three hours of English, another language (usually Latin), some mathematics and science, and housewifery for girls. Teaching had to reflect the demands of a standardized assessment of school leavers through the system of matriculation by examination—the schools certificate.

The post-war (Fisher) Education Act of 1918 compelled local authorities to develop a national system of secondary as well as elementary education. Fisher attacked the idea of the "half-timer" who attended school while working and advocated compulsory part-time education for children age fourteen to eighteen. The proportion of twelve- to fourteen-year-olds in secondary schools was roughly 10 percent rising to 20 percent by 1938. The content of secondary education changed little until the late 1930s, although its organization and funding were subject to frequent change. The "Geddes axe" (1922) on expenditure cut salaries and meant few new buildings for secondary schools. Yet education was a subject of intense, vigorous debate in the inter-war years. The association of curricular change with social reform took a back seat, except over questions of gender, and the dominant argument became one about access to, rather than content of, education. Yet commercial or **technical education** expanded slightly in day continuation schools for apprentices in which engineering, printing, or building trades were taught in classes rather than on the job, as well as in a few central or technical high schools for clerical or artisan trades.

Public debate on education in the 1930s concentrated on the physical state of schools. The Board of Education listed inadequate schools in a "black book," including even some of the elite secondary schools. The building stock was decayed, investment was insufficient, and there was little interest in renovation. Selection for secondary schools was increasingly based on standardized examinations taken at age eleven by all potential secondary students, or sometimes, by all eleven-year-olds. Some local authorities were making all of their secondary-school entrants behave as if they were applying for a "scholarship"—that is, a free place, which became "special" (means-tested) places in 1932, subject to entry by examination. In other words, although pupils still paid for their secondary education, they were also all academically selected and assessed. Assessment increasingly followed a standardized pattern of English, arithmetic, and verbal reasoning or "intelligence" test, the so-called eleven-plus examination.

In 1936 the school leaving age was ostensibly raised to fifteen, but implementation of this provision was deferred, initially to 1939. Once again an educational principle was accepted but not enacted because of financial constraints. The outbreak of war in 1939 both encouraged and inhibited further change. The development of a free secondary-education system for all did not include the expansion of building programs, and most of the additional school population was housed in huts known by their acronym of HORSA. In 1947 the leaving age was finally raised to fifteen.

Historical debate has focused on the question of parity of esteem between schools, enjoined by the **Education Act of 1944**, in relation to their tripartite structure. The Norwood Committee Report in 1943 described three types of child—the academic, the technically minded, and the rest, for whom there should be three types of education, which Ministry of Education officials interpreted as three types of school. Of the senior children of the elementary school, about 70 percent of eleven-year-olds were to go to secondary modern schools, 25 percent to grammar schools, and 5 percent to technical schools. It was not until the late 1950s that London was able to build new comprehensive schools and educate all under the same roof. Education in schools after the 1944 act

S

was highly stratified, particularly for the most academic children in the grammar schools, where they were "streamed" by ability.

The other historical debate has been about equality of opportunity and Britain's industrial decline. Education absorbed a large part of governmental welfare expenditure and pursued egalitarian aims, it was argued, at the expense of efficiency, accelerating the relative failure of the technical schools to compete with the grammar and secondary modern schools. The technology of selection that used standardized test batteries to place children in rank order allowed for a single scale of merit, seeing technical ability as inseparable from the general. Technical schools took second place to the education offered by the grammar schools. They did not, then, generate a large group of technically accomplished engineers or craftsmen with high public esteem.

In the 1950s the selective system was challenged, and local authorities began to move toward comprehensive systems of secondary education. In 1965 the **Labour** government insisted that local authorities reorganize along comprehensive lines. The number of students sitting the General Certificate of Education (GCE) Ordinary (O) and Advanced (A) levels rose slowly from 1965 onward, so comprehensive education appears to have widened access to secondary qualifications. Many grant-maintained schools went independent at this period rather than lose the power of selection.

After 1987 the **Conservative** government made it possible for schools to be centrally funded, thereby diminishing the local-authority contribution to governing schools. Tests were to be used to establish schools' success or failure, administered to cover the topics of the new national curriculum. Centralization thus replaced local autonomy, and the content of secondary education reentered the debate.

Deborah Thom

Bibliography

Fenwick, I.G. Keith. *The Comprehensive School, 1944–1970.* 1976.
Halsey, A.H., A.F. Heath, and J.M. Ridge. *Origins and Destinations: Family, Class, and Education in Modern Britain.* 1980.
Judge, Harry. *A Generation of Schooling: English Secondary Schools since 1944.* 1984.
Simon, Brian. *Education and the Social Order, 1940–1990.* 1991.
———. *The Politics of Educational Reform, 1920–1940.* 1974.
Sutherland, Gillian. *Ability, Merit and Measurement.* 1984.

Settlement Movement

The settlement movement began in **London** in the 1880s as an attempt to build bridges of personal sympathy and mutual knowledge between rich and poor. Throughout its first decades the movement was closely associated with Samuel Barnett, Rector of St. Jude's, Whitechapel, and his wife, Henrietta Barnett, whose followers at **Oxford** and **Cambridge** joined them in establishing Toynbee Hall in December 1884. Settlements were communities of educated men and, after 1887, women who temporarily "settled" in poor urban neighborhoods to provide social, educational, charitable, and recreational services. Most settlement houses consisted of a residence hall for the exclusive use of settlers (as the residents were called) and nearby buildings that served as headquarters for clubs, societies, lectures, classes, and concerts catering to local working-class men, women, and children. Initially, the leaders of the movement were animated by a belief that by sharing their culture with their poor neighbors they could promote social and political solidarity and orderly class relations. The movement also originally focused on the salutary effects of cross-class relationships—"friendships"—between individuals as the basis for broader changes in social relations. However, by the early twentieth century, social policy formulation, social scientific investigation, and training in social work joined personal service as expressed goals of settlers. Many distinguished leaders of the twentieth-century church, state, and social reform worlds began their careers in settlements, including **Clement Attlee, William Beveridge,** William Mackenzie King, **Eleanor Rathbone,** and **R.H. Tawney.**

Historians have so closely identified the settlement movement with Toynbee Hall and the "new **philanthropy**" of the 1880s that they have overlooked its variety and legacy to twentieth-century Britain. The movement expanded geographically and redefined its goals, ideology, and practices during the first decades of the twentieth century. By the eve of the First World War settlements were located in nearly every major city in Britain, including Birmingham, Bristol, Edinburgh, Glasgow, Liverpool, and

Manchester, where they adapted to suit the needs and political cultures of their local communities. While Toynbee Hall was officially nondenominational and nonpartisan, most settlements followed the example of Oxford House settlement (also founded in 1884) and had an explicitly religious basis. The High Church Oxford House trained more than a dozen bishops of the **Church of England** in the first half of the century. Mansfield House in West Ham, supported by **Methodists**, allied itself to municipal socialism and labor politics. After the establishment of the Women's University Settlement in 1887, women enthusiastically joined the movement and probably outnumbered men by 1900. While most settlements remained single-sex institutions, a few, including Browning House in Camberwell, were mixed-sex and encouraged marriages between committed workers.

The Poplar Labour leader **George Lansbury** disparagingly asserted that the movement's only real accomplishment was not to enrich the lives of the poor but to launch many settlers on successful careers in public service. He was correct only insofar as experiences in settlements did shape the agendas of many influential civil servants, reformers, and politicians who worked together to produce landmark state welfare measures such as national insurance (1911). The eccentric Warden of Browning House Settlement, Herbert Stead, spearheaded the early stages of the national campaign for **old-age pensions**. Contrary to Lansbury's assertions, working-class autobiographers and activists, including Albert Mansbridge (founder of the Workers' Educational Association) and Frederick Rogers (Chairman of the **Labour Representation Committee**), overwhelmingly praised settlements for providing them with scarce intellectual and cultural resources.

Women made several distinctive contributions to the movement. Working in concert with the Charity Organisation Society, the Women's University Settlement in Southwark and, somewhat later, the Victoria Women's Settlement in Liverpool helped establish the first two schools of **sociology** in Great Britain. Many of the leaders of social work education in the first half of the century, including Hilda Cashmore and Elizabeth Macadam, spent their formative years after college living in women's settlements. Others such as Grace Kimmins, Eleanor Rathbone, Mary Danvers Stocks, and Mary Ward called attention to the health and educational needs of women and children.

Settlements played important roles in their adopted neighborhoods as places of refuge and community life during the two World Wars. However, in the decades following the Second World War the residential component of many settlements contracted. The impact of most settlements is now largely confined to specific localities where they encourage grass-roots citizens organizations as well as continue their traditional work running clubs and programs for children, adolescents, and pensioners. Some settlements have been absorbed into local Citizens Action Bureaus. Others have retained their separate identities as voluntary organizations and work closely with local government and education authorities in developing community-based programs such as literacy training for new **immigrants**. Many settlements provide free legal advice, continuing the work of the Poor Man's Lawyer, which was created by Frank Tillyard during his residence at Mansfield House in the early 1890s. If the origins of the settlement movement lie embedded in the social and cultural preoccupations of the late-Victorians, many of its most illustrious members and innovative accomplishments date from the first decades of the twentieth century.

Seth Koven

Bibliography

Ashworth, Mandy. *The Oxford House in Bethnal Green: One-Hundred Years of Work in the Community.* 1984.
Briggs, Asa, and Anne Macartney. *Toynbee Hall: The First Hundred Years.* 1984.
Meacham, Standish. *Toynbee Hall and Social Reform, 1880–1914: The Search for Community.* 1987.
Picht, Werner. *Toynbee Hall and the English Settlement Movement.* 1914.
Vicinus, Martha. *Independent Women: Work and Community for Single Women, 1850–1920.* 1985.

Sexuality

Over the course of the twentieth century public attitudes toward sex have undergone major changes. As the century began, Victorian attempts to deny and control sexuality were still prevalent. Popular medical literature subscribed to the idea of masturbatory insanity and held that uncontrolled sex and nonprocreative sex was dangerous. Learned sexologists such as Richard von Kraft-Ebbing emphasized the dangers of unbridled sexuality. Inevitably there was an effort to desensualize sex, limit eroticism, and insist that marital sex be for purposes of procreation. **Marriage** itself was regarded as a means of controlling sex by emphasizing the importance of spiritual love between individuals. Such a view appealed strongly to the middle class, partly because self-control and restraint were seen as virtues that rendered them superior to the lower classes, who were more likely to be motivated by impulse and desire. It also served to empower **women**, whose supposedly more spiritual natures found justification in elevating men morally by helping them to control their sexuality.

A series of challenges to this view was launched at the start of the twentieth century by reformers and researchers such as **Havelock Ellis**, who regarded sex as indispensable to the fullest human development and who appealed for passion rather than restraint. Ellis saw sex as central to marriage and sexual love as enabling two individuals to share a united life. He became an apostle of the new woman who accepted her own sexuality and sought to control her own destiny through more effective contraception, greater economic opportunity, and higher levels of education.

Ellis expressed the reaction against the failed efforts to spiritualize sex and restrict eroticism. Evidence of this failure could be found in the growth of the sexual underground and the efforts of the purity crusades to abolish **prostitution**, curb obscene literature, outlaw **abortion**, and eliminate the double standard that justified such a sexual underground. Advice literature, much of it written by women, helped redirect the battleground from a negative crusade against the dangers of sex to an attempt to re-eroticize marriage. One of its leaders was **Marie Stopes,** whose marriage manual had sold over 900,000 copies by 1940. Stopes, concerned with the number of failing marriages and unhappy wives, blamed the perceived marital crisis on sexual dissatisfaction, which she believed could be remedied. The new basis of marriage, according to Stopes and others, had to be sexual compatibility. Once woman's sexual needs were accorded an equal status with those of men, the norms of companionship and mutuality in marriage would extend into domain of sex.

Gradually, the ubiquity of contraception, the Kinsey studies on human sexuality, and such

documents as the 1957 **Wolfenden Report** fostered shifts in attitudes about premarital sex and led to greater public discussion about sexuality. **Advertising**, which always exploited sexual themes, became more overt in doing so. The growth of **leisure** time, the campaign to legalize abortion, and the increasing emancipation of women undermined the sexual double standard. While traditional marriage manuals had emphasized the pleasurable, communicative, and expressive qualities of sex within marriage, there was a growing realization that the enjoyment of sex did not necessarily presuppose the rites of marriage. The prominence of sex in **popular culture** was illustrated by the British-American writer Alex Comfort whose book *The Joy of Sex* (1972) sold millions of copies on both sides of the Atlantic.

Once sex for pleasure became acceptable, there was no compelling need to limit it to monogamous heterosexual sex. **Homosexuality**, too, came to be recognized as a legitimate form of expression both popularly and legally, and a variety of unconventional sexual activities and groups began to proliferate on the social fringes. These ranged from group sex to special clubs for sadomasochists, transvestites, and others. In the process, what constituted pornography was redefined, and erotic publications gained wider circulation. Perhaps, the most radical challenge to the past has been the growth of transsexualism, signaled in England by the case of Roberta Cowell in the late 1940s.

Obviously, many of these changes were class based, with the higher social classes defining the norms. The working class proved slower to change, although it had always been less subject to the inhibitions of Victorian morality. Moreover, none of these changes took place uncontested, the opposition intensifying with the appearance in the 1980s of AIDS and the widespread dissemination of other sexually transmitted diseases. The result in the 1990s was a renewed emphasis on "safe sex," which to many implied a return to abstinence and sex only within marriage. This was coupled with an attack on female sexuality as evidenced in some areas by the reaction to abortion and the fear of female sexuality. Still, the existence of politically potent groups of gays and lesbians, as well as the growing empowerment of women in general, coupled with the development of new forms of contraception and abortifacients, would indicate that the changes wrought during the century in attitudes toward sexuality and in sexual practices will not be easily abandoned.

Vern L. Bullough

Bibliography

Bullough, Vern L. *Sexual Variance in Society and History.* 1977.

Ellis, Havelock. *Studies in the Psychology of Sex.* 2 vols. 1936.

Robinson, Paul. *The Modernization of Sex.* 1976.

Seidman, Steven. *Romantic Longings.* 1991.

Stopes, Marie Carmichael. *Married Love.* 1918.

Weeks, Jeffrey. *Sex, Politics, and Society: The Regulation of Sexuality since 1800.* 2nd ed. 1989.

Shaw, George Bernard (1856–1950)

The playwright Bernard Shaw (the name by which he preferred to be known) was born into a lower-middle-class Protestant family in Dublin in 1856. When his parents separated in 1876, the young Shaw came with his mother to London where, as he put it, he did not throw himself into the battle of life but threw his mother in instead. He was determined to write and made his way into journalism. He wrote five novels that remained unpublished for many years, but, by the end of the century, he had established a reputation as a critic of music, painting, drama, and all forms of literature and had become known as a formidable political publicist, debater, and controversialist. An energetic campaigner for socialism, he was active in politics, becoming an elected member of the St. Pancras Vestry in London.

The twentieth century brought two great changes in Shaw's life. In 1898 he had married Charlotte Payne-Townshend, whom he called "a green-eyed Irish millionairess." This union, although childless, was one of lasting affection, which gave stability to a personal life that was previously unsettled. The other great change was the beginning of his career as a dramatist. Shaw had started to write plays in the early 1890s and had written ten by the end of the century, but none of them had met with success. Shaw then met a young dramatist and producer, Harley Granville Barker, who cooperated with J.E. Vedrenne, the manager of the Court Theatre in the west of London, to present seasons of new plays. The new and exciting repertory attracted large audiences; of the 988 separate performances presented by Barker and Vedrenne between October 1904 and June 1907, 701 were of plays by Shaw. Several of the earlier plays were produced but, in addition, in a most fertile period Shaw wrote new plays for the new enterprise. *Man and Superman* (1903), the first play that Shaw wrote in the twentieth century, was given the description, "A Comedy and a Philosophy." The comedy consisted in Shaw's taking the theme of Don Juan, the great seducer, and turning it upside down. In the play it is woman, the embodiment of the "life force," who pursues, and man who is "the marked-down victim, the destined prey." Underlying the comedy is Shaw's enunciation of his own theory of "creative evolution," in which he attempted to improve on Charles Darwin. The Don Juan theme is linked with Mozart's *Don Giovanni*, and, in an act that the author did not originally intend for stage performance, characters in the comedy are translated in a dream into the figures of Mozart's opera.

Other plays had more contemporary political subjects. The problems of Shaw's native country were the theme of *John Bull's Other Island* (1907). *Major Barbara* (1907) showed the conflict in society between religious vision and the hard facts of material power in terms of the personal relations between the Salvationist Barbara and her father, the munitions manufacturer Undershaft. In *The Doctor's Dilemma* (1911), the "tragedy" of the death of a gifted but unprincipled artist, Shaw made a persuasive plea for the establishment of a National Health Service. The plays, while undoubtedly polemic, were never crudely propagandist. Shaw, indeed, often showed a readiness to present a stronger case for those characters with whom he himself was less in sympathy. Some audiences found the plays excessively wordy, but this potential fault was offset by Shaw's humor. On the eve of the war in 1914 he had one of his greatest successes in *Pygmalion* (published 1916), which combined an original treatment of the Galatea story with commentary on the effect of English speech on the class system.

Shaw's political activities had been subordinated to his work in the theater, but he had continued to be active in the **Fabian Society**, in close collaboration with **Sidney and Beatrice Webb** and others. With them he had cooperated in founding the weekly journal the *New Statesman*, which first appeared in April 1913. The outbreak of war in 1914 provoked him into powerful attacks on the mentality and policies that had made the conflict inevitable, and, while convinced that once the war had come it had to be fought, he had contempt for those who had blundered into the war and were now blundering through it. This attitude, expressed in precisely marshaled arguments and with an attitude of lofty superiority to his opponents, lost him friends.

After the war he returned to the stage with three important plays, all of which were presented first in New York. *Heartbreak House* (1919) was an attempt to combine his own style with that of Chekhov, of whom he had become a great admirer. In this "fantasia in the Russian manner on English themes," Shaw purported to show the ineffectiveness of the upper classes in England when confronted with the problems of a declining civilization. The play combines farce and apocalyptic vision with, at the center, a strange enigmatic figure, Captain Shotover, described by the critic James Agate as "Ibsen and Shaw, Whitman and General Booth rolled into one." This was followed by an even stranger and more controversial creation, *Back to Methuselah* (1921). With the descriptive subtitle, "A Metabiological Pentateuch," this was five plays in one and traced the course of human history from the Garden of Eden to "As Far as Thought Can Reach," in the year A.D. 31920. In this work Shaw returned to his doctrine of creative evolution, but here he was concerned to warn that, if human beings did not learn to live longer and more wisely, life itself would tire of them and look elsewhere for a new experiment. The next play brought unanimously favorable responses from critics and playgoers. This was *Saint Joan* (1924), a chronicle of the life, death, and canonization of Joan of Arc, called by Shaw "the most notable warrior saint in the Christian calendar and the queerest fish among the eccentric worthies of the Middle Ages." Shaw was awarded the Nobel Prize for Literature for 1925, which he accepted despite previous refusals to receive any kind of award or title.

Shaw continued to write plays up to the time of his death at the age of ninety-four, but few of his later works have been considered among his best. Nevertheless, *The Apple Cart* (1930) contains sharp observations on the political scene in the United Kingdom, and *In Good King Charles' Golden Days* (1939) is an elegant presentation of King Charles II and his entourage, in which the "merry monarch" is shown as a kind of Shavian version of a Platonic

philosopher-king. Some of the plays of the 1930s, such as *Too True to Be Good* (1934), which Shaw described as "a political extravaganza," have been seen as forerunners of the "theater of the absurd" of such writers as **Samuel Beckett** and Eugene Ionesco.

Although Shaw wrote over fifty plays, he was prolific in other fields. He was a voluminous correspondent. He threw himself into every public campaign: the opposition to the censorship of plays (several of his own works had suffered); the campaign for a **National Theatre**; all of the problems of Ireland; international politics and the issues of peace and war (his writings during the First World War were collected in a volume called *What I Really Wrote about the War*, 1930); **feminist** causes; electoral reform; and his lifelong championing of socialism, explaining his own idiosyncratic interpretation of that creed in a long treatise, *The Intelligent Woman's Guide to Socialism and Capitalism* (1928). Shaw insisted on the improvement of society as a whole rather than on individual satisfaction. *Everybody's Political What's What?* (1944), written as he approached the age of ninety, remains remarkably stimulating. In addition to these more public causes, Shaw was always calling for reform in a multitude of directions: religion, the marriage laws, the education of children, standards of dress, food and drink, the language and the alphabet itself. Between the wars Shaw's continuing admiration for Joseph Stalin caused many of his admirers to question the soundness of his political judgment.

Shaw had no time for "fine writing" and declared that "effectiveness of assertion" was the basis of style. Even such an unsympathetic critic as **T.S. Eliot** considered Shaw one of the greatest of English prose stylists. Humor was an essential part of his method of writing. Shaw maintained that humor strengthened his arguments and called laughter "my sword, my shield, and spear."

T.F. Evans

Bibliography
Holroyd, Michael. *Bernard Shaw*. 3 vols. 1988–91.

Sickert, W(alter) R(ichard) (1860–1942)

W.R. Sickert, born in Munich of a Danish father and an Anglo-Irish mother, is admired both as a British successor to Degas and as a precursor of Andy Warhol. During the 1930s he painted from photographs and on a large scale. This practice had begun in 1906 with the portrait *Lady in Red: Mrs. Swinton*, now in the Fitzwilliam Museum, Cambridge.

He was for a time the most modern of British artists, in that his work was consistently topical, determined by artistic developments in France and by British life and times. Although his father was a painter and illustrator, the young W.R. Sickert began in 1879 as an actor and maintained an interest in theatrical subjects throughout his career. He was introduced to painting by Whistler in 1879, entered the **Slade School of Art** in 1881, and became Whistler's assistant in 1882. The next year Whistler introduced him to Degas, a decisive turn in his career. He remained a follower of Degas all of his life, using the same beige palette and reporting on similar subjects: theaters, entertainments, sequestered models. Summers were mainly spent in Dieppe, and between 1898 and early 1905 he settled in Dieppe, with visits to Paris and Venice.

A Degasian modernist, he enjoyed a heyday in the first decade of the century, before being sidelined by the great Post-Impressionist exhibitions of 1910 and 1912. Having learned in one school, he was unable to adapt and entered on a course of eccentricity, which resulted in the photographically based work of his later years. However, on his return to London from Dieppe in 1905 he confidently pursued a role as innovator both as a painter and as a reviewer. His subjects were the music hall and intimate domestic scenes, sometimes with a topical slant, as in the *Camden Town Murder* pictures of 1908 and 1909. These pictures, of reclining female nudes and seated clothed men, were studies of the quotidian, of boredom and of postcoital *tristesse*, culminating in his celebrated renderings of *Ennui* in 1914. Always a publicist and teacher, he gathered young artists around him, including Spencer Gore (1878–1914) and Harold Gilman (1876–1919). In 1907 these artists formed the Fitzroy Street Group, which in 1911 became the **Camden Town Group**. By 1914 that group had expanded to become the London Group and to include **Jacob Epstein**, **Wyndham Lewis**, and Frederick Etchells (1886–1973). Sickert resigned on the grounds of Epstein's pornography.

In 1914 he parted company with convention in a way that anticipated his "topical" work of the 1930s. He painted two patriotic Belgian subjects, *The Soldiers of King Albert the Ready* and *The Integrity of Belgium*. After the vanguard, *intimiste* years they represent an abrupt accommodation with the status quo.

Immediately after the First World War he moved back to Dieppe where he remained until 1922. He was, through the 1920s, a prolific etcher, and in 1925 he was elected an Associate of the Royal Society of Painters, Etchers, and Engravers. His painting practice as outlined in letters to **Winston Churchill**, to whom he gave lessons in 1927, and to other students involved transfers from photographs and the use of very deliberated, even automated, painting practices. In 1927 he began a series of self-portraits in which he appeared variously as Lazarus and as *The Servant of Abraham* (1929). In the same year he also appeared on a large scale as Christ in *The Raising of Lazarus*.

By 1929 Sickert was entering the most inexplicable, postmodern phase of his career, characterized by his "English Echoes" series, based on Victorian illustrations and designs. These later pictures, including several theater and news images, represent Sickert overcollaborating with the status quo, putting himself almost entirely in the hands of the media and of popular taste. Having pledged himself to the accurate rendering of real life in his Camden Town years, he now committed himself wholeheartedly to mediated topicality. In 1932, for example, he celebrated the arrival of the American aviatrix Amelia Earhart in London after a transatlantic flight. An equally celebrated picture of *King George V and His Racing Manager: A Conversation Piece at Aintree* (1929–30) also derived from the newspaper. Another picture, of a miner being embraced by his wife, owed a lot to the attention in the mid-1930s to the plight of miners in Wales and in the North. In fact, Sickert appeared to nominate himself as a kind of national laureate, responsible for rendering such major subjects as *Sir Thomas Beecham Conducting* (1938). In this respect he was merely putting into effect another implication of the automated procedures he had consistently applied to the act of painting, almost from the beginning, or from the moment when he exchanged Whistler's *alla prima* manner for the planning of Degas (1885). The final results, in his old age, are paintings that stand as uncanny prefigurations of the *pittura buffa* of the international art scene in the 1980s and 1990s.

Ian Jeffrey

Baron, Wendy. *Sickert*. (1973).
Baron, Wendy, and Richard Shone. *Sickert: Paintings*. 1992.
Emmons, Robert. *The Life and Opinions of Walter Richard Sickert*. 1941.
Sitwell, Osbert. *A Free House; or, the Artist as Craftsman: The Writings of Walter Richard Sickert*. 1947.

Simon, John Allesbrook (1873–1954)

John Simon was born of Welsh parents in Manchester on 28 February 1873. Leaving Fettes College in 1892, he went to Wadham College, Oxford, as a classics scholar. After being elected President of the Oxford Union, he took a first-class degree in 1896 and was elected a Fellow of All Souls. Called to the Bar two years later, he advanced rapidly, becoming a King's Counsel after only nine years. Enormously successful in his practice, he was soon one of the most sought-after barristers in London and, in 1909, standing counsel to the **University of Oxford**.

Simon's true ambition was for a political career. He won a seat in the landslide election of 1906 as Liberal MP for the Walthamstow Division of Essex. In 1910 he first held office when Prime Minister **H.H. Asquith** appointed him Solicitor-General, accompanied by a knighthood. In 1912 he became a Privy Councillor and the following year joined the **Cabinet** as Attorney General.

Simon, uneasy about British participation in the **First World War,** considered resignation but was convinced to remain in office. After the formation of Asquith's multiparty government in May 1915, he refused the offer of the post of Lord Chancellor and became Home Secretary instead. The decision to introduce a **conscription** bill in January 1916 offended Simon's classical Liberal values, and he resigned office, serving for the remainder of the war with the Royal Flying Corps in France.

Simon opposed the **Lloyd George** coalition and lost his seat in the "coupon" election of 1918. He returned to Parliament four years later representing the Spen Valley. The failure of the second Labour ministry of **Ramsay MacDonald** and the creation of the National government in 1931 provided Simon the opportunity for a second term in office. By this time he led a faction of the splintered **Liberal Party** and accepted the post of Foreign Secretary in this **Conservative**-dominated coalition.

Simon's foreign policy, oriented toward disarmament and noninterventionism, entirely suited MacDonald. He took no steps to impede the aggressiveness of the Fascist dictators and can be considered one of the architects of the policy of **appeasement**. In 1935, when the Conservative **Stanley Baldwin** replaced MacDonald, Simon returned to the Home Office. When **Neville Chamberlain** replaced Baldwin in 1937, he recognized a kindred spirit and appointed Simon Chancellor of the Exchequer. For the remaining years of peace, Simon enjoyed Chamberlain's full confidence and was one of the small number of ministers who made up the inner Cabinet. Only after Adolf Hitler struck the first blow against Poland did Simon accept the need to resist the Nazis and lead a delegation of ministers to Chamberlain demanding a war declaration.

Simon took little part in the direction of the war. With the advent of **Winston Churchill's** coalition in May 1940, he was appointed Lord Chancellor, with the title Viscount Simon of Stackpole Elidor. He retired from office in 1945 and died in 1954.

R.J.Q. Adams

Bibliography

Adams, R.J.Q. *British Politics and Foreign Policy in the Age of Appeasement, 1935–39*. 1992.
Dutton, David. *Simon: A Political Biography of Sir John Simon*. 1992.
Heuston, R.F.V. *Lives of the Lord Chancellors, 1940–1970*. 1987.
Simon, Viscount. *Retrospect: The Memoirs of the Rt. Hon. Viscount Simon*. 1952.

Singapore

The British colony of Singapore, an island of about 200 square miles, was founded by Sir Stamford Raffles about 1820. Its strategic geographic location at the southern tip of the Malay Peninsula and across trade routes ensured its development into a major commercial and naval center in the Far East. A naval coaling station was established in the 1880s. "Main Fleet to Singapore" described the strategic plan formulated for the Commonwealth immediately after the First World War. The objective envisioned was a base in the Far East that could accommodate a major contingent of the battle fleet, up to twenty battleships, for the purpose of protecting the British Empire and its extensive interests east of the Suez Canal. A dockyard that could service the largest units of the fleet was an essential component. An impregnable base, secure from naval attack, would safeguard imperial outposts in Asia.

After several years of discussion the British **Cabinet** approved construction of the base, but progress was impeded by financial constraints and unforeseen delays, so that it was not until 1938 that the dockyard was finally completed and opened. Debate began about sending the "Eastern Fleet" out to its base, but crises in the Mediterranean precipitated by Italy and in the North Sea by Germany prevented deployment. Ultimately, an advance contingent, Force Z, comprising the battleships *Prince of Wales* and *Repulse*, was sent out to appease the Commonwealth, arriving on 2 December 1941. These ships were soon sunk by Japanese planes from bases in French Indochina, the first confrontation in which air power overwhelmed unprotected naval power. The Japanese, who landed in northern Malaya, initiated a seventy-day campaign that led to the capture of the island by landing in northern Malaya. Singapore fell on 15 February 1942 as 85,000 British imperial troops surrendered and were incarcerated for the duration. The loss of Singapore to the Japanese was widely regarded as a military disaster and a national humiliation, the greatest blow to British self-esteem since **Dunkirk**. Clearly, British racial arrogance and underestimation of the potential of Japanese forces had been factors in the defeat, as had the lack of preparation for a nonnaval attack on the base.

Subsequently Singapore evolved from colony into self-governing state. It has become a thriving international commercial hub for trade, banking, and industry.

Eugene L. Rasor

Bibliography

Callahan, Raymond. *The Worst Disaster: The Fall of Singapore.* 1977.
Kirby, S. Woodburn. *Singapore: The Chain of Disaster.* 1971.
McIntyre, W. David. *The Rise and Fall of the Singapore Naval Base, 1919–1942.* 1979.

Slade School of Art

The Slade School of Art, founded in 1871, introduced French art education practices into Britain. At the Royal Academy Schools, which monopolized art education in the 1850s, students made elaborate copies from ornamental designs and drawings after casts. At the Slade, by contrast, life models were employed, and artists were encouraged to copy the old masters. Remarkably, this emphasis on drawing survived for well over a century and came to characterize the Slade style. The school's exhibiting wing was the New English Art Club, founded in 1886.

Although the Slade came to be regarded as a conservative influence on British art, its firmly held views on the priority of drawing and on the centrality of the old masters stood as a reliable ground against which newer radicalisms might be judged. Draughtsmen and colorists, ancient and modern, its students dominated British painting in the years 1900–50. In the 1880s these students included **W.R. Sickert**, and in the school's heyday in the 1890s it was attended by **Augustus John**, by his sister Gwen John (1876–1927), by Ambrose McEvoy (1878–1927), and by William Orpen (1878–1931). Thereafter it educated many of Britain's major modernists, including **Wyndham Lewis**, Harold Gilman (1876–1919), Dickson Innes (1887–1914), Matthew Smith (1879–1959), **Duncan Grant**, Edward Wadsworth (1889–1949), **C.R.W. Nevinson, David Bomberg, Stanley Spencer,** Mark Gertler (1891–1939), and **Paul Nash**.

Later pupils included William Coldstream (1908–87) and Claude Rogers (1907–79), both of whom were instrumental in the 1937 founding of the **Euston Road School**, remarkable for its earnest teachers of drawing very much along Slade lines. The Slade's other great influence was through David Bomberg, who taught in London at the Borough Polytechnic and whose vitalist drawing style influenced both Leon Kossoff (1926–) and Frank Auerbach (1931–). The illustrator-painter Rex Whistler (1905–44) was a prize winner at the Slade in 1925, and the major late modernists **Richard Hamilton** and Eduardo Paolozzi (1928–) were both graduates. More recently its Department of Theater Design was attended by the filmmaker Derek Jarman (1942–94).

The Slade itself was endowed by the wealthy lawyer Felix Slade, who also endowed professorships in **Oxford, Cambridge,** and London. The school was attached to University College, London, and its first Slade Professor was Sir Edward Poynter (1836–1919), a devotée of Ingres and of drawing. He was succeeded in 1876 by the Frenchman Alphonse Legros (1837–1911), who turned the school toward French naturalism. He was followed by Fred Brown in 1892, and then between 1919 and 1930 Henry Tonks was in charge. In 1930 an ex-student, Randolph Schwabe (1885–1948), was appointed; he was succeeded by another ex-student, William Coldstream, in 1949 and then by Lawrence Gowing in 1975. It is a school that somehow succeeded in remaining true to its origins through a period of convulsive vanguardism, much of which was promoted by restive ex-students.

Ian Jeffrey

Bibliography
Hone, Joseph. *The Life of Henry Tonks.* 1939.
The Slade Tradition (catalog). 1971.
The Slade, 1871–1971 (catalog). 1971.

Slums

Slums are poor urban districts characterized by extreme overcrowding, badly maintained residential properties, and unsanitary living conditions that have been represented by nonresidents as socially dangerous and unacceptable. "Slum" signified not only a physical space, but also a set of attitudes defining that space and its inhabitants as problems demanding intervention. Once reformers and politicians labeled an area a "slum," they were able to justify a range of often coercive interventions into heretofore private landlord-tenant relations. The history of "slums" and "slumming"—casual, often voyeuristic visits to slum districts by the well-to-do—is closely intertwined with elite ideas and policies toward the poor, criminality, **public health, housing** and property ownership, **race relations**, and sexual morality. Debates about the nature and meaning of slums and attempts to respond to their problems lie at the heart of modern British social policy and help to demarcate the economic, social, and ideological contours of party politics in the twentieth century.

The word "slum" acquired its modern usage by the mid-nineteenth century; however, it was popularized in the 1880s by sensational journalistic exposés depicting the slums of East and South London as haunts of criminality, deviant or immoral **sexuality**, and extreme poverty. While earlier social investigators like Thomas Chalmers and J.P. Kay publicized the squalor of Glasgow and Manchester, from the 1880s onward the slums of **London** dispropor-

tionately dominated national discussions about how the poor lived. The London slums were the destination for large numbers of Irish and Jewish **immigrants** in the nineteenth century followed by immigrants from Britain's former colonies in the Caribbean, Africa, and the Indian subcontinent. Throughout the twentieth century slums have been touchstones for anxieties about Britain's declining imperial fortunes (Mafeking riots, May 1900) as well as scenes of racist conflict (**Oswald Mosley's** British Union of Fascists demonstrations in Bethnal Green in 1936; Brixton and Toxteth race riots, 1981).

Twentieth-century reformers, bureaucrats, and politicians inherited a rich legacy of Victorian philanthropic and legislative approaches to slums, which influenced their own policy choices. Victorian philanthropic ventures such as the **settlement movement**, the Salvation Army, and slum missions, for example, survived and sometimes even flourished well into the new century; however, their initial aspirations to transform society were often tempered by their limited achievements.

Whereas nineteenth-century discussion of slums was usually couched in terms of disease and sanitary reform, on the one hand, and cultural and moral elevation, on the other, in the late nineteenth and in the twentieth centuries, public and private remedies favored transforming the physical environment of slums. Twentieth-century slum policy emphasized population densities and the character of housing for the poor. Clearance, renovation, and redevelopment debates revolved around several concrete issues reflecting the interests of landlords and tenants and the pressures of municipal and national politics: financing (level of compensation for landlords, public and private funding); location (central urban, suburban, **garden city**, or **new town**); physical layout (vertical multistory flats, cottages); and qualitative amenities (elevators, toilets, balconies, sculleries). These housing concerns became increasingly important electoral issues in inter-war politics after the enfranchisement of women, usually to the benefit of the **Labour Party**.

Slum clearance and redevelopment schemes in the twentieth century drew on a variety of models, each deriving in part from earlier initiatives. Following the lead of the Victorian housing reformer and charity organizer Octavia Hill, **Neville Chamberlain** in the 1920s advocated reconditioning existing dwellings along with

Ainstey Street, Rotherhithe, 1903: A typical pre-war slum.

personal supervision of tenants by lady property managers. Such programs combined attention to the physical condition of buildings with concern for the behavior and use of them by occupants. Others, drawing on Ebenezer Howard's late-Victorian vision of **garden cities**, called for dispersing slum populations and integrating them into cross-class garden suburbs and cities (Bournville, Hampstead Garden Suburb). Still others called for municipal purchase and demolition of large blocks of derelict properties. Most proponents of slum clearance in the twentieth century, unlike their nineteenth-century predecessors, insisted that new housing specifically be set aside for displaced tenants.

While "slums" continue to carry many negative late-Victorian connotations, an alternative tradition of social commentary emerged after the First World War celebrating slums as sites of tightly knit, indigenous working-class communities threatened by rationalizing urban planners. This "countertradition" was fueled in part by commentaries written by "slum dwellers" themselves as well as by critics of large-scale **council housing** for the poor. In the early twentieth century, reformers condemned as soulless and degrading model housing

erected by **philanthropies** such as the Peabody Trust. Similarly, the sprawling, multi-story council estates erected before and after the Second World War are today often blamed for reproducing a demoralized, permanent underclass. Ironically, solutions to the problems of slum life implemented by one generation have often been identified as problems by the next.

Seth Koven

Bibliography

Chapman, Stanley D., ed. *The History of Working-Class Housing*. 1971.

Gaskell, S. Martin, ed. *Slums*. 1990.

Roberts, Robert. *The Classic Slum: Salford Life in the First Quarter of the Century*. 1971.

White, Jerry. *Rothschild Buildings: Life in an East End Tenement Block, 1887–1920*. 1980.

———.*The Worst Street in North London: Campbell Bunk, Islington, between the Wars*. 1986.

Yelling, J.A. *Slums and Redevelopment: Policy and Practice in England, 1918–1945*. 1993.

Young, Michael, and Peter Willmott. *Family and Kinship in East London*. 1957.

Snowden, Philip (1864–1937)

Philip Snowden was a profoundly controversial figure in the early years of the British labor movement. His name is closely associated with that of **Ramsay MacDonald** in the "betrayal" of 1931, which saw the collapse of the second Labour government, an event that many contemporaries saw as having arisen from his policies as Labour's first Chancellor of the Exchequer. Between 1906 and 1931 Snowden was certainly a prominent Labour leader, comparable to MacDonald and **Keir Hardie** in political importance.

Snowden was born on 18 July 1864 in the remote Pennine moorland parish of Cowling, near Keighley, in the West Riding of Yorkshire. He was raised in a small textile community where Nonconformity, particularly Wesleyan **Methodism**, shaped the life of the community. He received a basic elementary education but, as a bright boy, was destined to become a schoolmaster. Changed family circumstances led him to become a clerk and, eventually, to join the **civil service**. An accident and illness in the early 1890s forced him out of employment, and while he was recuperating he became involved in **Liberal** and then socialist politics, joining the **Independent Labour Party** (ILP), which was active in the West Riding, in January 1895.

At the local level, Snowden became prominent in Keighley politics, being elected to the Cowling School Board in 1895, acting as editor of the *Keighley Labour Journal* between 1898 and 1902, and winning seats on both the Keighley School Board and the Keighley Town Council in 1899. He was also involved in the Labour Church movement, soon becoming recognized as a fine orator on ethical socialism. It was evident that Snowden was a rising man in the independent Labour movement, and it surprised few when he became a member of the National Administrative Council of the ILP in 1898.

Parliamentary politics was to be Snowden's real forte. He stood, unsuccessfully, for Blackburn in 1900 and Wakefield in 1902 before being elected as MP for Blackburn in 1906 and twice in 1910. Snowden represented Blackburn from 1906 to 1918 when, due to his opposition to the First World War, he lost his seat. Subse-quently, he was MP for Colne Valley from 1922 until 1931, being returned at four general elections, before being raised to the **House of Lords** as Viscount Snowden of Ickornshaw in November 1931. During his time in the Commons, he was Chancellor of the Exchequer of the first and second Labour governments in 1924 and between 1929 and 1931. As Viscount Snowden he was briefly a member of MacDonald's National government, acting as Lord Privy Seal until his resignation on 28 September 1932.

Throughout his life Snowden adhered to radical Liberal sentiments and was particularly concerned to oppose war, to support free trade, and to discourage borrowing. Indeed, he was a good old-fashioned Gladstonian Liberal in his economic policies. His wife, Ethel Annakin, whom he married in 1905, also directed him toward the need to press for **women's suffrage**. It was these policies and forces that shaped his political career. They helped him rise within the ILP, of which he was Chairman (1903–6 and 1917–20) and Treasurer (1920–1). His staunch radical Liberal ideas also led him to attack Britain's involvement in the First World War and to mount the ILP's Peace Campaign in 1917. From 1916 onward he attacked the use and abuse of military tribunals against **conscientious objectors**, and by the end of the war he was demanding that the **Lloyd George** government declare its war aims in order to secure the peace more speedily. He also attended the Workmen's and Soldier's Council Convention held at Leeds in June 1917, where a mixture of Marxists and socialists sought to force international peace in the wake of the first Russian Revolution of 1917. Not surprisingly, he was vilified for his actions and opposition to the war.

Snowden's commitment to Liberal radicalism helped to move him out of the ILP in the early 1920s, when it became committed to left-wing socialism. From 1922 onward, having been returned as MP for Colne Valley, he made the **Labour Party** his political home. He was frustrated by the return of MacDonald as Labour's parliamentary leader but served under him as Chancellor of the Exchequer and Shadow Chancellor. In the former role he gave full vent to his notions of balancing the budget, reducing the national debt, and, if necessary, deflating the economy. Although his tenacity brought him some personal success, and Britain some economic saving at The Hague conference on **reparations** in 1929, it is clear that his policies were inappropriate in the economic climate of 1929–31, which saw **unemployment** and government expenditure rise, the pound sink under pressure from the money markets, and the Labour government split on the issue of cutting unemployment benefits by 10 percent. The Labour split was a result of MacDonald's support for Snowden's economic policies and the reluctance of a substantial minority of the **Cabinet** to accept such views. Thus it was not surprising that Snowden was obliged to support MacDonald's National government and to ditch Labour, claiming two months later in the October 1931 general election that Labour's economic policies, which he himself had forged, were "Bolshevism run mad."

After less than a year in the National government Snowden resigned because he could not accept its abandonment of free trade. Subsequently, although a spent force in British politics, he engaged in making personal attacks on MacDonald. He died of a heart attack, following a long illness, on 15 May 1937.

Keith Laybourn

Bibliography

Cross, Colin. *Philip Snowden.* 1966.
Laybourn, Keith. *Philip Snowden: A Biography, 1864–1937.* 1988.
Laybourn, Keith, and David James, eds. *Philip Snowden.* 1987.
Snowden, Philip. *An Autobiography.* 1934.

Social Democratic Party

The Social Democratic Party (SDP) was founded in 1981, largely as a breakaway from the **Labour Party** at a time when it had fallen under the influence of a left-wing and trade union compact. The SDP, as it was generally known, enjoyed a remarkable surge of initial popularity, reaching a peak in the winter of 1981–2. Its first leader, Roy Jenkins, was instrumental in forming the Alliance with the **Liberal Party**, and together the Alliance parties polled over 25 percent of the vote in the 1983 general election. Thereafter its fortunes fluctuated under the leadership of Dr. David Owen, and tensions with the Liberals became more apparent in the run-up to the 1987 general election. After it, the party voted for a merger with the Liberals and became a constituent part of the new Social and Liberal Democrats (though Owen for a time led his own faction, which continued to use the name SDP).

For most of the twentieth century the term social democrat had Continental European rather than British connotations. Only in the 1970s did the revisionist right wing of the Labour Party become generally known as social democrats. One reason was their own strong European credentials. As deputy leader, Jenkins had led sixty-nine Labour MPs into the lobby to vote for British accession to the **European Community** in 1971, in defiance of the party line. A further reason for the adoption of the social democratic terminology was to draw a distinction between the essentially Liberal, parliamentary, and moderate outlook of this section of the Labour Party and the strident, purist, militant socialism proclaimed by an increasing number on the Left.

It was not so much the rise of the Left that produced the friction, however, as its new-found support from the trade unions, on whom the right wing had been able to rely in the days of former leaders like **Clement Attlee** and **Hugh Gaitskell**. This highlighted trade union control of the Labour Party through the "block vote" system (whereby trade unions had historically affiliated their millions of members to the party and cast their blocks of proxy votes at the party conference accordingly). It was on the issue of "one member, one vote" that the SDP finally split from the Labour Party at the beginning of 1981, after its special conference at Wembley (January 1981) had granted the trade unions the major say in electing the parliamentary leadership.

In another sense, however, the SDP could trace its origin to the Dimbleby Lecture Jenkins gave on television in 1979. Jenkins spoke now as an exile from British politics, having served since 1976 as President of the European Commission. His message was that the Labour Party no longer offered a relevant vehicle for reformist politcs in Britain. This was an unashamed plea for the strengthening of the political center. As such it cut no ice with the leaders of the social democratic faction within the Labour Party. Here the key figures were Jenkins's old lieutenant, William Rodgers, and two former **Cabinet** ministers, Shirley Williams and David Owen.

Williams had become one of the representatives of the women's section on Labour's National Executive Committee from 1970; Owen had had a brilliant career as a Labour MP, rising to become Foreign Secretary in 1977 at the age of thirty-eight. Following Labour's swing to the left after losing the 1979 general election, Williams' decision to work in concert with Owen and Rodgers—the "Gang of Three"—was indispensable in rallying solid support from within Labour ranks for what became the SDP, but their initial rebuff to Jenkins' initiative showed the strategic gap between them. It was only the inexorable slide of the Labour Party under trade union control during the course of 1980 that brought all of these forces together. In a move Owen subsequently regretted, the Limehouse Declaration (January 1981) signaled full cooperation with Jenkins. Initially pledged only to a campaign for social democracy, the "Gang of Four" quickly moved during the next few weeks to set up a new party.

Many saw Williams as its natural leader, but she could not or would not press this claim. It was Jenkins who, meanwhile, consolidated his position by taking on the first by-election challenge in the northern industrial borough of Warrington, which he almost won from Labour in July 1981. No longer could the SDP be dismissed as a maneuver by the parliamentary elite; its burgeoning popular support now made the running and the headlines. The Alliance with the Liberals was forged at this stage, and opinion polls showed it having more support than either the Labour Party or the **Conservative Party**. The zenith came in the sensational by-election victory Williams achieved over the Conservatives at Crosby in November 1981. In the House of Commons she joined twenty-six MPs who had now defected from Labour, plus one former Conservative MP.

Jenkins, too, resumed his parliamentary career when, in March 1982, he won the Glasgow constituency of Hillhead for the SDP. But the tide was on the turn, and the invasion of the Falkland Islands (April 1982) created a new situation. What made—and left—an impression was Owen's firm support for the government in mounting a military expedition. When he stood for the leadership of the SDP shortly afterward, he ran Jenkins a fairly close second. Indeed, the new leader not only failed to command the House of Commons from his back-bench seat, but also lagged behind Owen's popular ratings.

Parliamentary constituencies were to be divided between the Liberals and the SDP as part of the Alliance strategy. Naturally the Liberals took the most immediately promising prospects, as a result of their previous strength on the ground; what the SDP needed was a broad-based breakthrough to surmount the crucial threshold imposed by the electoral system. But no longer was the Alliance ahead in the opinion polls, now that **Margaret Thatcher** had established her post-**Falklands War** ascendancy and could point, moreover, to increasing signs of economic recovery. The 1983 general election saw an impressive vote for the Alliance, which polled 25.4 percent of the national vote as compared with Labour's 27.6 percent. But this gave the Alliance only twenty-three MPs to Labour's 209. It was worst of all for the SDP, which won only six seats.

On Jenkins' resignation at this point, Owen was unanimously elected to the leadership. He succeeded in making the SDP presence felt at Westminster; if it was, as critics alleged, a one-man band, it was still a virtuoso performance, against all numerical odds. But the Alliance with the Liberals in the country entered a more traumatic phase. Owen resisted moves toward closer affiliation. He wanted the SDP to maintain a distinctive image, notably upon issues like defense, on which he took a hard line in favor of Britain's independent nuclear deterrent. Owen's talk of a "social market" also suggested to some that his economic views were disconcertingly close to **Thatcherism**.

Owen's relations with David Steel as Liberal leader were civil but not as close as they had been in Jenkins' day. In the 1987 general election the double leadership of the Alliance was widely seen as a disadvantage, especially when Steel seemed to incline toward the Left, Owen toward the Right. The Alliance poll slipped (though not as badly as it had feared) to 22.6 percent, electing twenty-two MPs. In the aftermath, Steel's prompt initiative for merger was met by Owen's dismissive rejection. Williams worked effectively for closer cooperation with the Liberals and voiced the wish of most SDP members for a full merger. Repudiated by the bulk of SDP members voting in a national ballot, Owen resigned the leadership in August 1987. There was no reconciliation, and in 1988 Owen rallied his own followers in a tightly organized movement of uncertain size, which perpetuated the old SDP name for a couple of years.

Constitutionally the SDP had become merged into a new party, the Social and Liberal Democrats, which a majority of its old members joined. Their efforts to break the mold had come up against the bias in the electoral system, the stubborn resilience of traditional Labour support (especially in Scotland), and the impact of events (notably the Falklands factor). Electorally the SDP missed the boat, but ideologically it caught the tide. Its stance in favor of the European Community and electoral reform, and against unilateral disarmament and large-scale **nationalization**, posed fundamental differences with Labour during the early 1980s.

Peter Clarke

Bibliography
Bradley, Ian. *Breaking the Mould? The Birth and Prospects of the SDP.* 1981.
Harris, Kenneth. *David Owen.* 1987.
Jenkins, Roy. *A Life at the Center.* 1991.
Stephenson, Hugh. *Claret and Chips: The Rise of the SDP.* 1982.

Socialist League (1932–1937)

The Socialist League was founded in 1932 as an affiliate organization of the **Labour Party** and dissolved itself in 1937 under pressure from the Labour leadership. The League was the chief organization of Labour's intellectual Left, a role that brought it into frequent conflict with the party's moderate mainstream. The League was closely identified with the views and policies of Sir **Stafford Cripps**, who led it from the death of its founding Chairman, E.F. Wise, in November 1933. Its membership included virtually every prominent intellectual in the Labour Left.

The immediate trigger for the foundation of the Socialist League was the decision of the **Independent Labour Party** (ILP) to disaffiliate itself from the Labour Party in 1932. A substantial minority of ILP members believed that the ILP would lose all influence as a result and accordingly formed a "National ILP Affiliation Committee" led by Wise and **H.N. Brailsford**. This group soon entered into negotiations with **G.D.H. Cole** to amalgamate with the **Society for Socialist Inquiry and Propaganda** (SSIP), a recently formed Labour discussion circle. Despite the disquiet of some members of the SSIP, who feared that any new body would repeat the ILP's history of perpetual conflict with the Labour Party leadership, the amalgamation was concluded and the League launched in October 1932. Some members of the SSIP, notably **Ernest Bevin**, never joined the Socialist League. Others, such as **Clement Attlee**, J.A. Hobson, and Cole, left it within twelve months.

The Socialist League enjoyed its greatest success in its early days, while the Labour Party, still recovering from the shock of **Ramsay** MacDonald's "betrayal" of 1931, sought to repudiate the gradualist tradition that MacDonald represented. League speakers were well received at Labour's 1932 conference, which passed a number of the Socialist League's radical motions, including one for the **nationalization** of banking. It was somewhat less successful at the 1933 conference, and not a single League-sponsored motion was accepted by the Labour Party thereafter.

The pattern of estrangement between the League and the Labour Party became obvious during 1933, when Cripps and other prominent League spokesmen advocated the use by the next Labour government of an Emergency Powers Act to counter capitalist resistance to socialist measures. The proposals caused outrage in the **press**, and an embarrassed Labour leadership publicly condemned the League.

The final crisis in the Socialist League's life was precipitated by its involvement in the **Unity Campaign** of 1937. In January the League published a "Unity Manifesto" jointly with the **Communist Party of Great Britain** and the ILP. The Labour Party, which at its 1936 conference had banned collaboration with Communists, disaffiliated the League within the month and shortly after declared that the League would be proscribed after 1 June. In May, in order to avoid its members' expulsion from the Labour Party, the Socialist League dissolved itself at a poorly organized and sparsely attended meeting. A few dissenters immediately attempted to resurrect the League as the Socialist Left Foundation, but with no success.

D.P. Blaazer

Bibliography
Jupp, James. *The Radical Left in Britain, 1931–1941.* 1982.
Pimlott, Ben. *Labour and the Left in the 1930s.* 1977.
Seyd, Patrick. "Factionalism within the Labour Party: The Socialist League, 1932–1937" in Asa Briggs, and John Saville, eds. *Essays in Labour History, 1918–1939.* 1977. pp. 204–31.

Society for Socialist Inquiry and Propaganda (1931–1932)

The Society for Socialist Inquiry and Propaganda (SSIP) was a left-wing pressure group within the **Labour Party** in the 1930s. It was founded in June 1931 by a variety of Labour

Party supporters concerned about the lack of socialist initiative demonstrated by the second MacDonald government of 1929–31. With the Fabian Society in a moribund state and the Independent Labour Party (ILP) threatening secession, the need was felt for a new organization to provide Labour with a group of "loyal grousers." The prime movers in this enterprise were G.D.H. Cole and his wife, Margaret. From a series of weekend conferences at Easton Lodge, Essex, the country home of Lady Warwick, they gathered together a circle of like-minded socialists, including G.R. Mitchison, George Lansbury, Raymond Postgate, Ellen Wilkinson, Clement Attlee, Stafford Cripps, R.H. Tawney, D.N. Pritt, the economist Colin Clark, and, notably, two trade unionists, Ernest Bevin of the Transport and General Workers' Union (TGWU) and Arthur Pugh of the Iron and Steel Confederation. With the ideal of establishing an organization loyal but stimulating to Labour, providing "inquiry and propaganda," rather than posing as a rival faction, fourteen branches of the SSIP, or "Zip," were established. Its most important members were Cole himself and its Chairman, Bevin. Lectures and conferences were held and a dozen pamphlets published, including a collaboration between Cole and Bevin entitled *The Crisis*.

In 1931 the Independent Labour Party disaffiliated from the Labour Party. ILP affiliationists such as E.F. Wise and H.N. Brailsford sought the creation of a new organization loyal to the Labour Party, to be achieved in part, they hoped, by amalgamation with the SSIP. Cole opposed the move, but the SSIP executive agreed to proceed with talks. The new body, the Socialist League, was established in September 1932. The former ILP contingent insisted upon Wise being made Chairman, which infuriated Bevin and led to his resignation from the League and a strong reluctance to have any further dealings with intellectuals. The birth of the new organization also alienated a substantial number of former SSIP members. Led by Evan Durbin, they decided not to join the new Socialist League and to stay instead with the New Fabian Research Bureau.

The potential of the SSIP was largely unrealized. It had filled a vacuum in 1931–2, when there was no active socialist organization within the Labour Party. It also promised to bring two often conflicting sides of the Labour movement, intellectuals and unionists, together.

Stephen Brooke

Bibliography
Cole, Margaret. *The Story of Fabian Socialism*. 1961.
Pimlott, Ben. *Labour and the Left in the 1930s*. 1977.

Society of Friends
See FRIENDS, SOCIETY OF (QUAKERS)

Sociology
Sociology in twentieth-century Britain has largely followed the guidelines laid down in the nineteenth century. That has meant two things: one, that sociology has been closely allied to social and public policy; and two, that it has remained peripheral to the national culture.

That sociology has been so much concerned with the making of policy is at first sight surprising. The most famous British sociologist of the nineteenth century was Herbert Spencer, who was most distinctly a theorist. His *Principles of Sociology* (1874–96) dealt in the most general terms with the evolution of human society. Spencer's lead was followed not simply by early British social anthropologists, such as E.B. Tyler and J.F. McLennan, but by some major British sociologists at the end of the nineteenth century, L.T. Hobhouse and Edvard Westermarck being the most prominent. In this century Spencer has continued to have disciples. Morris Ginsberg, Professor of sociology at the London School of Economics from 1929 to 1954, wrote extensively on ideas of progress and evolution, typically Spencerian themes.

But it was another strand of nineteenth-century British social thought that proved the dominant influence on twentieth-century sociology. This was the strand that began with the Report of the Poor Law Commission (1834), continued with various reports on the work, health, housing, and education of the working classes, and culminated at the end of the century in the social surveys of Charles Booth and Seebohm Rowntree on the life and labor of the poor. Paralleling this very public activity were the more scholarly initiatives: the founding of the Statistical Society of London (1834), the National Association for the Promotion of Social Science (1857), and the Sociological Society (1903).

The other main fact about British sociology, its marginality to British culture, is plain from its painfully slow progress in the academy.

While other new subjects—history, English, even economics—were finding a secure place in the universities, sociology had to wait until the late 1950s before it was generally available as an undergraduate degree. The University of London had a professor of sociology—L.T. Hobhouse—since 1907, and Ginsberg taught later at the London School of Economics. But they were lone pioneers whose brand of evolutionary sociology found few followers and left little legacy in the culture as a whole. More important was the studied refusal of Oxford and Cambridge to entertain sociology as a degree subject. It was left largely to the new universities and the polytechnics in the 1960s to promote the discipline—a task they pursued with vigor. But this served only to associate sociology with fashionable novelties and left-wing lecturers, thereby making its status even more problematic. Finally, first Cambridge and then Oxford established chairs of sociology—in the latter's case, in close association with social statistics and social policy. By that time—the 1980s—sociology was reasonably secure as a university subject, but it remained on the margins of the general culture, a favorite target of ridicule by the mass media and abuse by politicians.

Why has sociology found it so difficult to find a place in the national culture? Probably because it has come to be identified with particular policies and programs of reform. More damaging, it has appeared very often simply as the intellectual arm of the Labour Party. Some of the major works of British sociology—Brian Jackson and Dennis Marsden's *Education and the Working Class* (1962), Michael Young and Peter Willmott's *Family and Kinship in East London* (1957)—were closely related to Labour policies of educational reform and urban renewal. British sociology's claim to fame may indeed rest on its contribution to the introduction of "comprehensive" schooling under the Labour government of 1964–70. Even more striking, the most important work of empirical sociology to date—John Goldthorpe and David Lockwood's *The Affluent Worker* (1968–9)—was directly inspired by Labour's repeated failure to win office in the 1950s. The unspoken premise of the study was to determine whether changes in the nature and composition of the British working class had undermined the traditional social basis of the Labour Party. A similar question, though differently phrased, underlay the highly sophisticated study by W.G.

Runciman, *Relative Deprivation and Social Justice* (1966).

In this way sociology continued in the nineteenth-century tradition that stressed its role as the handmaid of reform. From Poor Law reform to the origins and development of the welfare state, sociology has put its techniques of social investigation at the service of reformist parties and movements. Usually the impulse has been compassionate: the desire to ameliorate the condition of the poor and the powerless. This has been true even at those times, as in its flirtation with eugenics and Social Darwinism at the end of the nineteenth century, when its thinking has appeared harsh and unfeeling. Here, as in its advice on Poor Law reform, it has tried to preserve the dignity and independence of the "deserving" poor by separating them from the "residuum" of the profligate and idle "undeserving" poor.

Where social theory was concerned, British sociology for long lived in the shadow of its powerful American counterpart. Talcott Parsons and Erving Goffman were especially influential. But since the 1970s British sociology has at last come to engage with some of the central questions of social theory in its own way. Much of this change has been due to the prolific output of Anthony Giddens, Professor of sociology at Cambridge (*The New Rules of Sociological Method,* 1974; *The Constitution of Society,* 1984). There has also been a revival of historical sociology, in such works as Michael Mann's *The Sources of Social Power* (1986). Reflections on the long-term future of industrial societies, in the spirit of the original founders of European sociology, have also appeared, such as Krishan Kumar's *Prophecy and Progress* (1978) and John Urry and Scott Lash's *The End of Organised Capitalism* (1987). The work of Michel Foucault and Jacques Derrida has inspired an outpouring of books on modernity and "postmodernity" (for example, Zygmunt Bauman's *Intimations of Postmodernity,* 1991). Feminism, too, has notably contributed to a rethinking of the family and gender relationships, in such works as Michelle Barrett's *The Anti-Social Family* (1983) and Mary Evans' *The Woman Question* (1987).

Nevertheless, there are no signs yet of a distinctive "British school" of sociology. One could say that British sociology missed its moment. In its formative years it was dominated by the preoccupations of social policy and social reform. By the time it achieved due recognition in the universities, and had established itself professionally, the discipline was fragmenting worldwide. Sociology was becoming an amalgam of history, political theory, economics, even **psychoanalysis**; its practitioners were finding more in common with colleagues in other disciplines than with their fellow sociologists.

Krishan Kumar

Bibliography

Abrams, Philip. *The Origins of British Sociology, 1834–1914*. 1968.

Bulmer, Martin, ed. *Essays on the History of British Sociological Research*. 1985.

Giddens, Anthony. *Sociology*. 1989.

Kent, Raymond A. *A History of British Empirical Sociology*. 1981.

Marshall, T.H. *Sociology at the Crossroads*. 1963.

Somme, Battle of the

The Battle of the Somme in France was devised late in 1915 as part of an Allied offensive on all fronts intended for mid-1916. The French were seen as the senior partners in this Anglo-French battle, contributing forty-one divisions to the British twenty-five. Nevertheless, this would be Britain's largest military undertaking so far, employing the men who had volunteered in the opening phase of the war.

There were good reasons for attacking in the Somme region. The Anglo-French armies met there. They would not be confronting imposing high ground. And, as long as the weather held, the clay soil would constitute good campaigning territory. Certainly the district had disadvantages. As was true all along the Western Front, the Germans occupied what raised ground was available. They had enjoyed ample time to prepare their defenses. And the firm soil had enabled them to construct a complex system well below the surface. Nevertheless, the notion that the Somme was manifestly a silly region at which to attack is unfounded. It ignores the advantages of the district and the painful lack of a better alternative.

The Somme campaign was not launched as planned. It did coincide, roughly, with a Russian offensive on the Eastern Front. But from February 1916 the French had been subjected to a murderous blood-letting at Verdun (which also took heavy toll of the Germans). Hence the twenty-five British divisions became the major contributor to an attack whose first purpose had become relief of the pressure on Verdun.

Yet the wider purpose remained, despite the reduced Allied force. Sir **Douglas Haig**, the British Commander-in-Chief, hoped to rupture the enemy line with guns and infantry and pour his cavalry into open country. Whether he possessed sufficient ammunition to crush the German defenses nobody seemed to be calculating.

The ensuing campaign, of 141 days, falls into six pieces. The attack of 1 July 1916 was a bloody failure. The preliminary bombardment had been too meager and was spread too wide to achieve its purpose. Of the 120,000 Britons who went forward, 57,000 became casualties, including 19,000 killed. No ground was gained except on the right, which was not the main objective.

Phase two occupied 2–13 July. It consisted of sporadic attacks by small units. Then on 14 July (phase three) a considerable attack was launched at night, after an appropriately heavy bombardment. It enjoyed initial success, until the cavalry—called in for exploitation—outran their artillery and were cut down.

Phase four was the longest and most confused episode of the campaign. From 15 July to 14 September small sections of Haig's army were thrown into uncoordinated attacks for limited objectives. They attracted disproportionately heavy artillery resistance. The casualties suffered and the negligible ground gained were equivalent to the disastrous opening day.

More dramatic, and even somewhat rewarding, were the operations of phase five (15–25 September). On 15 September the British employed tanks for the first time. Regrettably, to facilitate the new weapon they restricted the role assigned to artillery. Hence not very much was gained. More profitable was an operation ten days later, making highly effective use of artillery—not least in the form of a creeping barrage moving just ahead of the attacking infantry.

After this, meaningful campaigning became impossible, as bucketing rain turned the clay soil into a quagmire. Haig, nonetheless, persisted in attacking. Apart from a minor closing success at Beaumont Hamel, this sixth phase (October-November) is the sorriest episode of all.

For the British, the Somme campaign was not entirely barren. It ended the pressure on Verdun, killed many Germans, saw the birth of a new weapon, and witnessed noteworthy developments in artillery techniques. But overall it was a failure. It did not break the German line, or capture strategically important territory, or destroy the German will to persevere. Most of all, it did not inflict on the enemy casualties as great as those sustained by the Allies. (British casualties numbered 420,000 and French 200,000; those of Germany, 500,000.)

The Somme casualties reduced whole towns in Britain to mourning, ended the political authority of the **Asquith** coalition, and raised doubts about the wisdom of Britain's military command.

Robin Prior
Trevor Wilson

Bibliography
Farrar-Hockley, A.H. *The Somme.* 1964.
Keegan, John. *The Face of Battle.* 1976.
Prior, Robin, and Trevor Wilson. *Command on the Western Front: The Military Career of Sir Henry Rawlinson, 1914– 1918.* 1992.

South Africa
The twentieth century began with the British colonies in South Africa and the Boer republics located to the north embroiled in the last of the Victorian colonial wars. The Anglo-**Boer War** tarnished the concluding years of Queen Victoria's reign and shattered the image of British imperial supremacy. The terms of the subsequent Treaty of Vereeniging (1902) established a pattern of race relations that continued to plague South Africa throughout the century.

The treaty provided that Boers who took a loyalty oath were to be released, their language was to be safeguarded, and self-government was to be restored. Voting rights for Blacks in South Africa were not to be considered until the stated terms had been implemented, and even then votes for the Black inhabitants were not to be raised until the two Boer territories had become again self-governing. A large degree of local autonomy was granted to the former Afrikaner republics after the British **Liberal** government took office in 1905. When British South Africa and Boer South Africa were united in 1910 into the Union of South Africa, Black voting rights were excluded.

Once self-government was restored in the former Boer republics, elections were held within constituency boundaries drawn to the advantage of the Afrikaner farmers. The result was that former Boer leaders Louis Botha and Jan Christian Smuts were voted into power and quickly attempted to ally themselves with the Johannesburg mining interests as the basis of a political partnership. By skillful negotiation, the Transvaal leadership was able to gain practically all it desired during the discussions that led to the creation of the Union of South Africa. When political leaders combined to form that union, all delegates except those from British Cape Colony represented all-white constituencies. A "South African Native National Congress," created in 1912, could do little but express dismay about government policy.

The subsequent political history of South Africa revolved around the concerted effort of Afrikaner nationalism to recover from military defeat and to protect the principle of white supremacy. Gradually the franchise for nonwhites was whittled away and finally abolished, paving the way for apartheid, the system that from 1948 until recently promulgated the view that white and colored should be completely separated. When South Africa became a republic in May 1961, it was committed to the exclusion of all nonwhites from its political process and the relegation of Blacks to separate areas that were styled "Black homelands."

In South Africa a definite shift to the Right occurred in 1948 with the defeat of Smuts' moderate government by a determined Afrikaner-dominated National Party. During the Second World War a number of Blacks had moved into the urban areas, becoming fully a part of the white economy. As white concern increased, the Nationalists exploited the fear to underpin their apartheid strategy. By introducing a system of internal passports, for example, Black mobility and Black economic strength could be limited. By the 1950s, therefore, the National Party had established apartheid and had excluded Blacks from a proportionate share of economic prosperity. Black enmity was evidenced by episodes such as the one at Sharpeville in 1960, in which police fired into a crowd, killing sixty or seventy persons, and revolt seemed imminent until forestalled by increased police efficiency and severity.

In May 1961 South Africa proclaimed itself a republic, but it was told it could not remain in the British Commonwealth unless it condemned apartheid. Offended by the requirement, South Africa withdrew its application for Commonwealth membership. Its pariah status within the world community caused Afrikaner Nationalists such as the *Broederbond* (brotherhood) membership to "laager the wagons" (circle the wagons) and ignore the almost universal international contempt.

By the early 1960s African National Congress leader Nelson Mandela had become a hero of mythic proportion within the Black community. After the Sharpeville massacre he was hunted by the police, as he and other revolutionary leaders planned disruption and sabotage of the South African government. By the use of torture and infiltration, the police were able to capture Mandela in August 1962 and sentence him along with several others to life imprisonment. The treatment of Mandela and other Black leaders such as Steve Biko, who died in prison, solidified world condemnation of the South African government, and a political, social, and economic boycott was undertaken by most of the nations of the world. White South African "laager" mentality continued even beyond the release of Mandela in 1990 and the dismantling of apartheid.

By the end of 1991 international pressure and the impact of economic boycott combined to prod the government toward full-scale negotiations with the goal of ending white-minority rule. African National Congress leaders campaigned with President F.W. de Klerk and nationalist politicians to win support for a provisional constitution based on a democratic electorate and majority rule. Unanimity is still a distant goal, however. Both rightist white conservatives from the *Broederbond* and Black nationalists from the Pan African Congress boycotted preliminary discussions. Likewise, Black support remains fragmented between the African National Congress and the Inkatha Party, which seeks to maintain the integrity of Zulu homelands. After the African National Congress victory in the April 1994 elections, progress toward a multiracial republic appears irreversible despite opposition from separatist elements. The approval of world opinion was reflected in the award of the Nobel Peace Prize in 1993 to Nelson Mandela and F.W. de Klerk for their contribution to ending the most intractable racial conflict of the twentieth century. In April 1994 Mandela became President, and in May South Africa rejoined the Commonwealth.

Newell D. Boyd

Bibliography
Austin, Dennis. *Britain and South Africa.* 1966.
Barber, James. *The Uneasy Relationship: Brit-ain and South Africa.* 1983.
Davenport, T.R.H. *South Africa: A Modern History.* 1981.
Pyrah, Geoffrey B. *Imperial Policy and South Africa, 1902–1910.* 1955.
Wilson, Monica H., and Leonard M. Thompson, eds. *The Oxford History of South Africa.* 2 vols. 1969–71.

Spanish Civil War (1936–1939)

The outbreak of civil war and revolution in Spain in the summer of 1936 coincided with the sharpening of tensions in the international arena. In March German troops brazenly violated the Treaty of Versailles and the **Locarno Pact** of 1925 by reoccupying the Rhineland, and, in May, the Italians marched into Addis Ababa, thereby demonstrating the impotence of the **League of Nations** as an instrument of diplomacy. Notwithstanding these developments, the prevailing view at the time was that another European war could be averted. So potent was this belief that from 1936 until the war ended in April 1939 it conditioned British reaction to events in Spain.

British public opinion was deeply divided. Many saw Spain as the stage on which the major political and ideological struggles of the period were being played out. Those who sided with the Republican cause—a group that embraced middle-class professionals, intellectuals, and rank-and-file trade unionists—tended to be sympathetic to the left-wing coalition of Popular Front parties resisting the rebels. On the other hand, the predominantly middle- and upper-class supporters of Francisco Franco and his Nationalist forces regarded the rebellion as a struggle against Bolshevism and were inclined to see **Fascism** in a positive light. Among those who favored Franco were some of Britain's most prominent businessmen, diplomats, army and naval officers, and Conservative politicians, as well as the relatively small community of British **Roman Catholics.**

To members of the British government the idea of a "Red" Spain was anathema, but all were highly alarmed at the possibility that the Spanish conflict might ignite another European conflagration. Immediately following the outbreak of the Spanish Civil War the **Baldwin** government adopted a "wait and see" policy. If at all possible, Britain wanted to maintain Spain's territorial integrity and secure the benevolent neutrality of whichever side emerged victorious. How the government was to pursue these goals remained unclear until the end of July, when it became clear that both Germany and Italy were openly assisting the insurgent cause. Britain then joined the French in promoting the idea of a multilateral nonintervention agreement.

In August 1936 a Nonintervention Agreement (NIA) was signed by twenty-seven countries, and, one month later, a nonintervention committee, the NIC—officially known as the International Committee for the Application of Nonintervention in Spain—was set up to monitor outside interference in Spanish internal affairs. Based in London, the NIC was convened under the auspices of the British **Foreign Office** and chaired by Lord Plymouth, the Parliamentary Undersecretary. From its inception until its formal disbandment in April 1939, the committee's effectiveness was diminished by its lack of powers to stop or control even the most obvious forms of intervention. Flagrant violations of the NIA, especially by Germany, Italy, and the Soviet Union, further undermined the credibility of the committee. Ironically, what the NIC did succeed in doing was to obstruct the legitimate Republican government from securing desperately needed materiel from countries that might otherwise have come to its aid.

One particularly pressing problem facing the British was how to respond to the naval blockades imposed by the Nationalists. Unwilling to compromise its neutrality and fearing an overwhelmingly negative public reaction to the use of force, the government initially opted for a policy of restraint. Then, following a series of submarine attacks on neutral commercial shipping vessels in the summer of 1937, some high-ranking officials, including Foreign Secretary **Anthony Eden**, felt compelled to take a firmer stand. To stop the unidentified **submarines**, generally known to be Italian, France and Great Britain recommended the use of multinational naval patrols. At the Nyon Conference convened in September 1937, their plan was formally adopted and, for a brief while, the sinkings stopped.

Meanwhile, on the domestic front in Britain, the Spanish Civil War deepened existing political and class divisions. Like no other event of the period, the war mobilized the forces of the Left and, to a lesser extent, of the Right. Spain's troubles inspired countless public rallies and street demonstrations, and debates over the nature and significance of the war filled news-

paper columns, books, and pamphlets. An informal survey taken by *Left Review* during 1937 revealed that nearly every major British artist, writer, and intellectual held strong convictions about the war. The vast majority, like **W.H. Auden, Stephen Spender**, and **George Orwell**, favored the Republicans, whereas **Evelyn Waugh** and a handful of lesser-known authors sided with the Nationalists.

The Spanish Civil War not only served to polarize national politics, it also divided parties among themselves. Most **Conservatives** instinctively supported the Nationalists, but a few, like **Winston Churchill** and other "antiappeasers," came to believe that a pro-Axis Spain would threaten British interests in the Mediterranean. For different reasons the leadership of the labor movement was divided over the question of intervention. In the early stages of the war, union leaders like **Walter Citrine** and **Ernest Bevin** advocated a cautious approach toward Spain, a position at first overwhelmingly endorsed by the rank and file of the **Trade Union Congress** (TUC). What guided their thinking was the belief that direct British involvement would most likely split the labor movement and thereby destabilize trade unionism. One of their greatest fears was that the Communists, spearheading a United Front campaign to provide active aid to Spain, might gain control of organized labor. But clearly the main preoccupation of the leadership was the threat of another war: Both Citrine and Bevin rightly sensed that few workers were prepared to sacrifice the fragile European peace for the sake of the Spanish Republic.

As it became increasingly apparent that non-intervention was working in the interests of the Nationalists, the pro-Republican passions of the labor movement became more difficult to restrain. In the autumn of 1937 both the TUC and the **Labour Party**, though still opposed to directly intervening in Spain, began pressuring the British government to lift its embargo on arms to the Republican forces. For its part, the National Council of Labour expressed its disapproval of nonintervention by providing humanitarian aid. Food, clothing, medical supplies, and other forms of assistance were generously provided by such groups as the Socialist Medical Association as well as many other organizations affiliated with the labor movement. Perhaps the most successful relief programs were those aimed at helping children displaced by the war: mineworkers contributed over £55,000 to orphaned children of Asturian miners, and a publicly supported adoption scheme brought 4,000 Basque orphans to England by the time the war had ended.

The **Communist Party of Great Britain** launched an even stronger initiative aimed at supporting Republican Spain. Obeying the Communist International's (Comintern) call for the formation of an international contingent to be sent to Spain, British Communists actively recruited volunteers. Thanks to their efforts, between 1936 and 1939 over 2,000 men and women served in the **International Brigades** of the Republican army. Though they came from different social backgrounds and represented a variety of left-wing opinions, these mostly young and idealistic volunteers went primarily because they were convinced that if Adolf Hitler and Benito Mussolini could be stopped in Spain another general war could be averted.

On arriving in Spain, the volunteers underwent an intensive, if extremely brief, military training program. Most were then assigned to combat units, although some served in noncombatant roles as ambulance and truck drivers and as medical assistants. Despite their lack of military training and limited wartime experience, the British volunteers displayed considerable valor and courage. The 600 members of the British Battalion attached to the XV International Brigade were used as shock troops in some of the bloodiest engagements of the war, such as the Battles of Jarama and Brunete. By the time the International Brigades were obliged to withdraw from Spain late in 1938, the casualty figures for the British contingent was staggeringly high: Of the approximately 2,000 combatants who served, over 500 had been killed and 1,200 had been wounded.

Public interest in the fate of Spain remained high throughout 1937 and 1938, not least because the tragedy of the Spanish war was kept alive in the printed media. The vicious destruction of the small Basque town of Guernica in 1937, for example, commanded the headlines of the British press for several weeks. No less disturbing—at least for those on the Left—were the eyewitness reports from George Orwell, **Fenner Brockway**, and other representatives of the **Independent Labor Party** (ILP), which disclosed that deep-seated animosities between the left-wing parties were seriously undermining Republican unity.

In any case, by the autumn of 1938 Spain's problems were almost completely overshad-

owed by events taking place elsewhere in Europe. As far as Spain was concerned, it was now clear that the European powers were not prepared to go to war over its domestic crisis. By the winter of 1938 the Republicans were all but defeated, although, for the next few months, the Negrín government clung to the slender hope that the war would be absorbed into a general one. On 27 February 1939 the British and French governments recognized Franco, thus hastening the conclusion of the war, which came on 1 April 1939.

George Esenwein

Bibliography

Buchanan, Tom. "'A Far Away Country of Which We Know Nothing'? Perceptions of Spain and Its Civil War in Britain, 1931–1939," *Twentieth Century British History*, vol. 4 (1993), pp. 1–24.

———. *The Spanish Civil War and the British Labor Movement*. 1991.

Cunningham, Valentine, ed. *Spanish Front: Writers on the Civil War*. 1986.

Edwards, Jill. *The British Government and the Spanish Civil War, 1936–1939*. 1979.

Fyrth, Jim. *The Signal Was Spain: The Spanish Aid Movement in Britain, 1936–1939*. 1986.

Watkins, K.W. *Britain Divided: The Effect of the Spanish Civil War on British Public Opinion*. 1963.

Spark, Muriel Camberg (1918–)

Ever since the publication of *The Comforters* in 1957, Muriel Spark has been one of the most highly regarded novelists writing in English. Although she has published critical and biographical works on the Brontës, **John Masefield**, and Mary Shelley in addition to two collections of poetry, numerous short stories, a play, and a children's book, Spark is primarily recognized for the nearly twenty novels she has written over the past four decades. Scottish by birth, Spark achieved her greatest recognition with the film, stage, and television adaptations of the novel based upon her years at James Gillespie's High School for Girls in Edinburgh, *The Prime of Miss Jean Brodie* (1961). She was awarded the James Tait Black Memorial Prize for her novel *The Mandelbaum Gate* (1965). *Curriculum Vitae* (1993) traces her life to the moment of her conversion to **Roman Catholicism** in 1954.

Born Muriel Camberg in 1918, Spark is the daughter of Jewish-Scottish parents. She was married briefly to Sydney Oswald Spark, with whom she traveled to Southern Rhodesia, the setting of many of her short stories. During the **Second World War** Spark worked with the secret intelligence service. She has spent most of her life as an expatriate and currently lives in Tuscany.

According to Spark, the world of fiction is a lie, but it is also a reference, however parodic, to the world outside the fiction. Both the real world and fiction are alike for Spark, because they are equally mysterious realms of fabrication and manipulation. In Spark's novels, as in the world outside them, what happens is often more apparent than why.

Such elusiveness has led critics to interpret Spark's work in a variety of ways. Her fiction has been labeled postmodern, metafictional, satiric, metaphysical, and, at the very least, paradoxical. Her deadpan tone and use of present tense are unsettling, leaving it up to readers to discriminate between the trivial and the essential in her narratives, between the artistic lie and the anagogical truth in them, and to determine for themselves Spark's intention and stance.

Jennifer L. Randisi

Bibliography

Bold, Alan. *Muriel Spark*. 1986.
Massie, Allan. *Muriel Spark*. 1979.
Randisi, Jennifer Lynn. *On Her Way Rejoicing: The Fiction of Muriel Spark*. 1991.
Spark, Muriel. *Curriculum Vitae: Autobiography*. 1993.
Whittaker, Ruth. *The Faith and Fiction of Muriel Spark*. 1982.

Spence, Basil Urwin (1907–1976)

Basil Spence was born in Bombay, India, to British parents, raised in Edinburgh, and trained in **architecture** both there and in London. Most significant was his association with **Edwin Lutyens** in 1929–30 while Lutyens was engaged in designing the government buildings for New Delhi, India. From Lutyens, Spence learned both an appreciation for traditional materials and for monumental form and composition, carrying that sensitivity into his own work of the third quarter of the twentieth century.

Noted as both architect and designer of exhibitions, furniture, and decorative arts and interiors, Spence executed a few houses in the late 1930s but turned chiefly to exhibition design during the 1940s. Best known is his *Britain Can Make It* exhibition, London (1946) and his work for the *Scottish Industries* (Glasgow, 1949) and *Heavy Industries* (1951), the latter for the **Festival of Britain** in London.

Spence came into international prominence in 1951 when he won the competition for the rebuilding of Coventry Cathedral. The great church of St. Michael was destroyed by fire bombs on 14 November 1940, when Coventry sustained the longest air raid on any one night on any British city during the **Second World War**. At Coventry Spence was to redefine the character of British cathedral architecture in the twentieth century; it became his most personal work as architect and craftsman and the project by which his name is still best remembered. Spence preserved the ruins of the noble perpendicular parish church but declared the new Coventry a distinctly modern phoenix rising from the ashes of the past.

In the spirit of medieval cathedral builders Spence gathered together a team of artists and craftsmen to decorate the work in stained glass, sculpture, tapestry, metalwork, woodwork, and pottery. Sir **Jacob Epstein**'s bronze sculpture of *St. Michael Fighting Lucifer* references not only the patron saint of the historic church but also the symbolic victory of good over evil, both eternal salvation and the Allied forces' defeat of the Nazis. Stained glass by various artists is most breathtaking in the *Holy Spirit Window of the Baptistry* by **John Piper**. Finally, behind the main altar and Lady Chapel is the great tapestry, the largest in the world and here replacing the traditional great east window. It was designed by **Graham Sutherland** and depicts the traditional Christ in Majesty, enthroned in the mandorla and surrounded by the tetramorph.

Spence is also noted for his university designs, most especially his monumental Falmer House, University of Sussex (1962), which translates the cloistered medieval traditions of university designs to a celebration in modern materials of sweeping arches, strong forms, and noble proportions. During the same years Spence designed buildings for the University of Southampton (1960–73), for the University of Liverpool (1959–60), and for the University of Sussex (1964–75).

Spence planned housing for Basildon New Town in 1958 and 1962, and in 1959 he built his first major office building in London, Thorn House (with Andrew Renton), a slab-on-po-

Coventry Cathedral (Basil Spence, completed 1962). Spence's fusion of the medieval ruin with a modern church attracted wide attention.

dium design inspired by Gordon Bunshaft's Lever House (1951) in New York. A public library and a swimming pool were all that was built of a larger scheme designed for the Civic Center, Hampstead, London (1964). Other libraries (University of Edinburgh, 1967; University of Sussex, 1964, 1971; Newcastle-upon-Tyne (1969) and Civic Centers (Sunderland, County Durham, 1970; and Kensington and Chelsea, London, 1977) were to follow.

Although his Household Cavalry Barracks in London (1970) intrude on Hyde Park and add little to the Knightsbridge streetscape, his Chancery, British Embassy, Rome (1971), is a highly successful building and a model of contextualism and scale.

Creating designs of individual character in an age of anonymity, works executed in the spirit of an artisan craftsman in an era of increased technology and mass production, Spence found at Coventry his greatest celebration of architecture; the cathedral is one of the best-known British works of the century and Spence's most significant accomplishment as an architect.

Robert M. Craig

Bibliography

Spence, Sir Basil. *Phoenix at Coventry: The Building of a Cathedral.* 1962.

Spencer, Stanley (1891–1959)

Stanley Spencer belonged to the last generation in Britain that believed in the possibility of a great art continuous with tradition. His own style harks back to that of Giotto, whom he admired during his time at the **Slade School of Art** (1909–12). His other major debt was to Post-Impressionism, which he saw at the first exhibition organized in 1910 by **Roger Fry** for the Grafton Gallery. In 1912, at the second of these exhibitions, Spencer himself was included with a picture of *John Donne Arriving in Heaven.*

Like William Blake—another influence—Spencer was a visionary capable of redeeming local life, of which he was also a scrupulous observer. Commonplace sites, especially the village of Cookham in Berkshire where he was brought up, became settings for miracles and for religious events. In 1937, for example, he represented Cookham Moor with its war memorial as a stage for *A Celebration of Love in*

Heaven. The war memorial is as priapic as it is commemorative and points to a pantheistic and unorthodox element in Spencer's quasi-religious art.

The **First World War** was formative. After service in the Royal Army Medical Corps he went to Macedonia as an orderly, before joining a frontline unit in 1917. Although briefly appointed an official **war artist** in 1918, his true war work came later. Engrossed by memories of the front, he sought patrons and a space, and in 1923 he entered into negotiations to decorate the Sandham Memorial Chapel at Burghclere in Hampshire, a work finally completed in 1932. Painted on canvas, it is a comprehensive record of the practicalities of soldiering life, and it established Spencer as the artist of British laboring vernacular. On its east wall is a scene of *The Resurrection of the Soldiers*, characteristic of an artist who visualized the present in biblical terms.

Spencer's other great project, *Shipbuilding on the Clyde*, was the result of an official commission awarded in January 1940 that took him to the shipyards of Port Glasgow in May of that year. The first image, *Burners*, was completed in 1940 and was successful when shown at the National Gallery. He continued to work on such other scenes as *Plumbers, Riveters*, and *Bending the Keel Plate* until 1943. The pictures, now in the Imperial War Museum, London, recall the murals of Diego Rivera painted in the United States in the early 1930s.

Spencer's tendency was to think, in the medieval manner, in terms of cycles and series, and at Burghclere and in the Lithgow shipyard, commission and inclination coincided. Otherwise he was obliged to imagine an overall scheme that might give sense to his production. After Burghclere he envisaged a notional chapel: "The Village Street of Cookham was to be the nave and the river which runs behind the street was a side aisle." The idea of the chapel was more suggestive than programmatic; it helped him envisage Cookham as a sacred site. Spencer's thinking at this time anticipates *arte povera* aesthetics of the 1960s to a quite surprising degree. After the Port Glasgow commission he imagined another project based on the Resurrection. Between 1945 and 1950 he painted four triptychs and the vast *Resurrection: Port Glasgow*, now in the Tate Gallery, London.

Although known as an appreciative documentarist of British folk life, Spencer is famous for his unsparing portraits of 1936 and 1937 of himself and his second wife, Patricia Preece. He was, for a while, a practitioner of a kind of pitiless New Objectivity. He either acceded to or denied time. The self-portraits dwell on human ageing. The many Resurrection scenes reiterate moments of joyful return. Intent on confronting and on denying time he, for instance, maintained a correspondence with his first wife, Hilda Carline, long after her death in 1950. His visualizations of Cookham as a paradise on earth, and of suburban cemeteries as sites of the Resurrection also helped dissolve strictly quotidian concepts of time, involving the present in a mythic past.

He earned his living mainly as a landscape painter, where his manner was strict and objective. His preference was for quite unspectacular park landscapes and suburban scenes, notable for an orderliness that was at odds with his often turbulent married lives. Despite controversy, however, he was established in the 1950s as Britain's senior painter, marked by the award of a knighthood in 1958.

He can be compared to the sculptor **Eric Gill**, with whom he shared a pantheistic and carnal view of religion and an affinity for Indian art. On the other hand, he can also be compared to his contemporary, the photographer **Bill Brandt**, who also envisaged Britain in near-mythic terms, as an apocalyptic space newly cleared for the business of the Last Judgment.

Ian Jeffrey

Bibliography

Bell, Keith. *Stanley Spencer: A Complete Catalogue of the Paintings.* 1992.
Carline, Richard. *Stanley Spencer at War.* 1978.
Robinson, Duncan. *Stanley Spencer.* 1990.
Rothenstein, John. *Stanley Spencer the Man: Correspondence and Reminiscences.* 1979.

Spender, Stephen (1909–)

Stephen Spender, poet, critic, and essayist, was born into a Liberal family of comfortable means. His father was a journalist and an unsuccessful candidate for Parliament; his uncle was the legendary J.A. Spender, editor of the *Westminster Gazette.* Both of Spender's parents died while he was a troubled and sickly adolescent. The most important figure in his early intellectual development was his maternal grandmother, an affluent second-generation

German Jewish immigrant of advanced opinions and artistic tastes.

The shy Spender was an indifferent student at University College School, a London day school, Gresham's School, the Lycée Clemenceau in Nantes, and finally Oxford. Withdrawn and initially unpopular, Spender declared himself to be unpatriotic, "a pacifist and a socialist, a genius." He later believed that his Oxford years were a waste of time because he simply wanted to write. But at Oxford Spender first met W.H. Auden, a major force behind his subsequent literary and political views. At the age of twenty, Auden was already the center of an emerging literary movement, which included Christopher Isherwood, Cecil Day Lewis, and Louis MacNeice. Auden introduced Spender to Isherwood, who convinced him to go to Germany.

Spender arrived in Hamburg in July 1929, determined to leave Oxford and fulfill his literary aspirations. He was initially enchanted by the freedom and hedonism of the young Germans, but the misery of Weimar Germany in its last years aroused profound feelings of guilt. Spender saw himself as a member of the exploiting class that had brought on the economic disaster that it was unable or unwilling to alleviate. Democracy had failed, Fascism was on the rise, and the only hope seemed to lie in the east, where a new egalitarian society was emerging. Spender was by nature an outsider, a contemplative observer of life, a poet. But Adolf Hitler and the nature of the times drove him inexorably in the direction of Communism as the only answer to "The Waste Land." The turning point for Spender and many others was the Spanish Civil War.

By 1936 Spender had become a man dedicated to the cause. In Forward from Liberalism (1937), a Left Book Club selection, he argued that "Liberals must reconcile Communist social justice with their liberal regard for social freedom, and that they must accept the methods which it might be necessary to use in order to defeat Fascism." Spender toured the Spanish Front, wrote for the Daily Worker, and attended the Writers' Congress in Madrid in the summer of 1937. But Spender was always more of a liberal than a dogmatic Marxist; his Communism was "a matter of conscience, not of belief." The comrades bitterly criticized his work, even when he attempted to write Communist propaganda, as in the case of Trial of a Judge (1938). He soon drifted away from the Communist Party of Great Britain (CPGB).

Spender's political soul-searching did not inhibit the rise of his literary reputation. By the end of the 1930s he was part of New Writing and a recognized member of the "Auden Generation." When the Second World War began, he joined Cyril Connolly to edit Horizon, the most influential English periodical of the war years. After the war, Spender continued to write poetry and criticism and was knighted in 1982 for his contribution to literature, but his literary reputation went into a long decline. He is still most often thought of as a young writer of the 1930s. Spender's memoirs—World within World (1951), The Thirties and After (1978), and Journals, 1939–1983 (1985)—are likely to be read by critics and historians after his poetry is out of print. Nevertheless, Spender's poems—like Auden's—movingly commit themselves to the "invention of the human city" ("Explorations"); in other words, to civic poetry and to the renewal of public life. One aspect of the project is an attempt to redefine personal subjectivity (as in "Subject: Object: Sentence"); another is to wed private erotic experiences to public order.

Gordon B. Beadle

Bibliography

Hynes, Samuel. The Auden Generation. 1976.

Kulkarni, H.B. Stephen Spender: Poet in Crisis. 1970.

———. Stephen Spender, Works and Criticism: An Annotated Bibliography. 1976.

Pandey, Surya Nath. Stephen Spender: A Study of Poetic Growth. 1982.

Sport

Sport is a singular noun in Britain, but under its large umbrella it shelters many different activities. At the turn of the century, sport, like the British climate, had its seasons. The year began with winter and football (soccer), two versions of rugby, union and league, cross-country running, boxing, and horse racing over the jumps. Spring signaled the start of the flat-racing season; summer, sports of track and field athletics, bowls, cricket, golf, tennis, and rowing. Angling had its own particular seasons. These were the sports that most players played, that most spectators watched, and that took up most of the space in the newspapers and later on the air time of radio and television. There may have been some slight shifts in popularity and support between the major sports, and badminton, squash, snooker, and swimming have all enjoyed popularity since the 1970s. The transport and communications revolution may have distorted the idea of the sporting season, but what sports are played and watched in Britain in the 1990s showed a stubborn similarity to the 1890s.

If sport is not a single thing, Britain is not a single place. England, Northern Ireland, Scotland, and Wales all have particular sporting preferences. Curling remains a largely Scottish game. Golf remains strongly associated with Scotland, some districts having four or five times the British average per capita number of golf clubs. Professional rugby league called itself the Northern Union until 1922, and its strength remains in the northern counties of Lancashire and Yorkshire, though it has been played for fun more widely in the last twenty years. Cricket is most popular in the southeastern counties of Kent, Surrey, Oxfordshire, Cambridgeshire, Sussex, and Essex and in the north, in Yorkshire. Sport in twentieth-century Britain has contributed to and reflected local, regional, and national identities. Many sports had separate national organizations, English, Irish, Scottish, and Welsh. The England-Scotland football match, one of the first international sporting events, was played almost every year from 1872 until 1989. It increasingly became an opportunity to celebrate Scottishness and to express dislike of the economically, numerically, politically, and socially dominant English. The same opportunity was provided by Rugby Union in Wales.

Sport also played an important role in the British Empire, both cementing ties with the Mother Country and fuelling local national feeling. Cricket Test Matches began with **Australia** in 1876–7, **South Africa** 1888–9, the West Indies 1928, **New Zealand** 1929–30, India 1932, and Pakistan in 1954. In track and field the British Empire Games was founded in 1930. As the British Empire and Commonwealth Games, from 1952 and, since 1970, the Commonwealth Games, it takes place every four years in a different Commonwealth country. Sport became an important British export and an ideological package. Fair play and sportsmanship were regarded as making sports worthwhile. These ideas were accompanied by an amateur tradition that is in decline but still capable of occasional vigor.

At the beginning of the twentieth century it was only a slight exaggeration to say that sport was played, run, and written about by gentlemen. It had long been important in public schools, where sport was thought to shape character by stressing the sacrifice of self-interest for the good of the team in a context of competition. Fair play meant sticking not only to the letter of the rules but to their spirit as well. It involved self-control and accepting winning or losing with equal modesty. Sporting clubs could exclude all those who had not been to the right schools and did not know how to play the game.

There were many working-class amateurs, but they rarely mixed with their better-off colleagues off the field or the track. And gentlemen did not need to play for money. The man who did found himself either totally excluded or rigorously controlled. Before the 1960s hired hands were never allowed anywhere near the Jockey Club, the MCC (Marylebone Cricket Club), the National Sporting Club, and rarely the Football Association (FA). English rowing was split into two organizations largely because the Amateur Rowing Association adhered to a draconian definition of amateurism that excluded working men. The two bodies did not merge until 1956. In track and field athletics the professional was outlawed and marginalized. In English football he was confined by a maximum wage, and his freedom to change employers was severely restricted. In county cricket most of the hard work—the bowling—was done by professionals. Many batsmen and all captains before 1945 were amateurs. The amateur gentlemen were called Mr. and often had a separate dressing room. The professionals had inferior accommodation and were known by their family names. A professional did not captain the English cricket team until 1952. The categories of amateur and professional, or Gentlemen and Players, were not abolished until 1962.

Such class distinctions seemed somewhat anachronistic after the Second World War and the ideas of a fairer society that had generated the **welfare state**. Fewer gentlemen could afford the time to practice and train in order to play at the highest level. Some took generous expense allowances, yet still maintained their amateur status. "Shamateurism" provoked much criticism, which gradually had its effect. The year 1968 saw the first open Wimbledon. The FA amateur cup, which started in 1894, was competed for in 1974 for the last time. In 1982 track and field athletes were allowed trust funds to store appearance money, sponsorship, and advertising fees. By 1992 even the elite of the aggressively amateur Rugby Union were being allowed to exploit their fame and prowess for money. The amateur tradition at its best stood for a more balanced approach to sport and a better way of playing it. But at its worst it promoted snobbery and hypocrisy. In Britain it also held back the tide of commercialization of sport until the 1970s.

Sport was and has remained a voluntary activity. But several factors combined to attract the attention of the state. Local governments were able to spend taxpayers' money on public parks, but playing sport in them was not usually allowed. It was not until the Public Health Act of 1907 that facilities for cricket and football specifically and "any other games or recreation" were mentioned as worthy items on which local authorities might spend their money. In the next half-century or so many did so. But there was never enough supply of playing fields to meet the demand.

By the 1930s sport was becoming more international. The Fascist governments in Germany and Italy made it clear that sport was the business of the state and deliberately sought the prestige that success in international sport could bring. Anxieties about the condition of the nation during the Great Depression also contributed to the first tentative action by the British Parliament, the Physical Training Act of 1937. Money released under this act paid for some of the first generation of post-war athletic coaches. Perhaps more significant was that the Education Act of 1944 made it compulsory for state schools to include sport in the curriculum.

Sport itself also began to clamor for a greater share of state resources. For much of the twentieth century there was no organization that represented British sport as a whole. The British Olympic Association was founded in 1905, but its sole concern was to liaise with the bodies that ran individual sports in order to select Olympic teams. In 1935 a number of these organizations joined together in the Central Council of Recreative Physical Training—later renamed the Central Council of Physical Recreation (CCPR). It was the CCPR that set up its own inquiry into the state and future of British sport in 1957. It followed twelve post-war years of underachievement on the field and erosion of facilities off it. The 1957 Wolfenden Report suggested a Sports Development Council, and the reforming Labour government set up the Sports Council in 1965. By 1971 it had received a Royal Charter and was trying both to encourage participation in sport and to improve the standards of British elite performers. It dispensed taxpayers' money to individual sports and presided over a considerable increase in facilities with, for example, the twenty-seven Sports Centers of 1972 becoming 770 in 1981. Margaret Thatcher's governments showed that there was a price to be paid for state aid when she asked the leaders of the various sports to support her government's protest of the Soviet invasion of Afghanistan by boycotting the Moscow Olympics in 1980. Most competitors defied her, as did some Sports Council officials, who later lost their jobs.

At the end of the twentieth century more men, and especially women, were enjoying sport than ever before. Although it is unlikely that crowds at sporting events will return to the heights of 1945–9, only outdoor pop concerts attract more people—and on many fewer occasions. Color television has altered the relationship between sport and the public, especially by its encouragement of commercial sponsorship, only £2.5 million in 1971 but more than £200 million in 1992. Gambling also makes a large financial contribution, notably to horse racing and football. Sport is an industry; the making of sporting goods, big business. But sport is also a passion among a significant minority of the British population and remains an important part of the British way of life.

Tony Mason

Bibliography

Holt, Richard. *Sport and the British*. 1989.
Mason, Tony, ed. *Sport in Britain: A Social History*. 1989.

Spy Novel, British

The origins of the modern British spy novel, which has enjoyed best-seller status since 1900, can be traced to a confluence of developments: the rise of mass literacy in nineteenth-century Britain; the emergence of new forms of popular literature, especially serialized stories in mass-circulation newspapers and journals; and a climate of fear surrounding Britain's global security and future as a great power. The subject matter of the spy novel was uniquely a product of the political climate in Britain at the turn of the century. That climate was a compound of anxieties about the societal implications of fast-paced economic and political change at home and the destabilizing effects of the rise of foreign powers such as Germany. The spy hero emerged as a fictional device that built on the existing genres of adventure and **detective fiction** but operated as a new kind of hero with a political mission: nothing less than the rescue of British civilization from the destruction of war and from foreign barbarisms. Obviously functioning as a form of political escapism as well as a form of political anxiety, the spy genre has been the product of British writers primarily.

The first generation of spy-fiction writers, most notably Erskine Childers (1870–1922), William le Queux (1864–1927), E. Phillips Oppenheim (1866–1946), and John Buchan (1875–1940), established some of the genre's trademark features in the decade before the outbreak of the First World War. They wrote male adventure stories with a strongly patriotic and moralizing bent. Their heroes belonged to imagined intelligence communities whose scope and power far surpassed the historical reality. The fiction preceded the reality and began that process that saw the intertwining of **popular culture** images of **espionage** with revolutionary changes in the nature of intelligence services themselves. The bridge between the fiction and the reality has subsequently been sustained by the intermingling of careers in writing and espionage, first seen in the case of John Buchan.

But even before writers like Buchan could bring a degree of earned verisimilitude to their fiction, pioneers like William le Queux, with his prodigious output, had established one of the enduring features of British spy fiction—namely, the deliberate blurring of fiction and fact, using some of the standard devices of the historical novel, but more blatantly foregrounding the hero, and often the author, as narrator of a thinly disguised reality. Le Queux loudly proclaimed himself a master spy and had his characters, in novels such as the dramatic *Spies of the Kaiser* (1909), narrate tales supposedly freshly gathered from the secret chancelleries of Europe.

Fantasies of espionage as a symbol of darker fears of societal survival were displaced in the years after the First World War by a literature that fed on both sensationalized memoir accounts of spy missions during the conflict and on more personally grounded experience. John Buchan contributed the Hannay series of four novels (The *Thirty-Nine Steps*, *Green-mantle*, *Mr. Standfast*, and *The Three Hos-*

tages), the writing of which spanned the years 1915 to 1924, and which allowed him to build on his experience of imperial politics, on personalities such as Aubrey Herbert and General Ironside (models for Hannay), and on Buchan's wartime involvement with British intelligence. Writers such as **Compton Mackenzie** and **Somerset Maugham** drew even more directly than Buchan on an insider's knowledge of British espionage—Mackenzie served with the wartime British secret service in Greece, while Maugham was engaged on an improbable mission to spy out the nature of the new Bolshevik leadership in Russia in 1918.

It was Maugham who first established higher literary credentials for the spy novel, in his set of linked stories, *Ashenden* (1927). Arguably, Maugham's effort to undermine the device of "faction" (the overlaying of fact and fiction) had little impact on the development of the genre as a whole; the double act of the espionage agent and the spy writer remained potent. Of more significance was the way in which Maugham introduced a new element to the spy narrative—namely, a concern with the ethics of spying. His depiction of a world of spy master Machiavellis, and their oppressed and sometimes innocent victims, established a troubling discourse with which spy writers since Maugham's day have struggled, often unsuccessfully. Indirectly, *Ashenden* also helped lay the foundation for the most significant development in inter-war spy fiction.

The 1930s novels of Eric Ambler (1909–) and **Graham Greene** transformed the political landscape against which previous British spy fiction had been written. Moving beyond Maugham's Machiavellian world, Ambler and Greene fashioned a new kind of spy novel out of political struggle between the forces of Left and extreme Right, often fought out on the homefront, as in Greene's *The Confidential Agent* (1939). The heroes in Ambler and Greene were figures on the political Left, acting out the drama of the **Popular Front** strategy of the 1930s. Political oppression at home, creeping totalitarianism, and fear of war gave the new spy novel of the 1930s a darker tone, with radically altered definitions of what constituted global threats and political decency, as compared with the spy novel of pre-1914 days.

A post-war reaction to Ambler and Greene was heralded by the popular success of the Ian Fleming (1908–64) series of James Bond novels. Fleming's writing was untroubled by moral

S

concerns; his political backdrop, a hearty and patriotic caricature of the Cold War. The Bond novels attempted, very successfully, to return the genre to its roots in simple political adventure and civilization-saving. The Bond novels also featured large dollops of exotic travel, sex, and brand-name consumerism.

Fleming's monopoly on the spy-fiction market was destined to be brief, not least because the genre already contained a historical reminder of alternative narratives. The 1960s saw the takeover bids of Len Deighton (1929–), starting with *The Ipcress File* (1962), and John le Carré (1931–), with *The Spy Who Came in from the Cold* (1963), both rooted in echoes of Ambler and Greene of the 1930s. Deighton and Le Carré reintroduced morality, left-wing politics, and angst into the spy novel, while retaining the sure foundations of adventure, cautionary tale, and heroic endeavor by individuals who prove to be historic forces in their own right. Le Carré's most enduring fictional hero, George Smiley, battles on the literal front lines of the Cold War while growing ever more reflective about the role of human agency, morality, and political purpose, a trend that culminates in *The Secret Pilgrim* (1991). Le Carré remains the standard by which contemporary spy-fiction writing is judged; he has also proclaimed fiercely that spy fiction has a future in the post-Cold War world. The proof he offers is *The Night Manager* (1993), which targets the arms traders and the Thatcherite *nouveau riche* as the new villains and the new conspirators against order and good.

Wesley K. Wark

Bibliography

Bennett, Tony, and Janet Woollacott. *Bond and Beyond: The Political Career of a Popular Hero.* 1987.

Cawelti, John G., and Bruce A. Rosenberg. *The Spy Story.* 1987.

Denning, Michael. *Cover Stories: Narrative and Ideology in the British Spy Thriller.* 1987.

Stafford, David. *The Silent Game: The Real World of Imaginary Spies.* 1988.

Wark, Wesley K., ed. *Spy Fiction, Spy Films, and Real Intelligence.* 1991.

Standard of Living

Sustained and almost continuous economic growth in Britain since 1900 has led to a great increase in average real incomes. These higher incomes have allowed people to buy more and better food, **housing, leisure,** and good **health,** all of which have contributed to an overall rise in living standards. This improvement in living standards has led to the virtual disappearance from Britain of diseases associated with malnutrition, such as rickets, but there remain great differences between the living standards of the richest and poorest groups in society.

Direct measures of changes in living standards over time are problematic because many goods and services that contribute to today's overall standard of living, such as television or air travel, have no direct equivalents in the early years of the century. One common way to circumvent this problem is to compare the monetary value of national income per capita, adjusted for changes in the price level over time. Using constant 1990 prices, national income per capita has risen from around £2,000 in 1900 to £2,500 in 1930, £4,000 in 1960 and £9,000 in 1990. By this measure, the average Briton was over four times better off in 1990 than in 1900.

This improvement has not meant that spending power has increased at the same rate. The average weekly earnings of an adult male manual worker in 1900 were £1 8s. (£1.40), which equals £63 in 1990 prices, whereas the average male manual worker in 1990 actually earned £214 per week. Until 1940, however, manual workers paid no direct (income) tax, but since then virtually all earners have had to pay tax on their income, which has reduced their spending power. The post-tax income of the representative manual worker in 1990 was about £160, or two-and-a-half times greater than in 1900. Some economic growth appears to have been "lost" from the worker's earnings, but this has mainly been paid in taxes and used by governments to extend the range of services provided by the state, services that have played a major role in increasing living standards. Better and more extensive education and health care, together with comprehensive income support for the sick, the old, and the unemployed, are the most obvious manifestations of this public provision, but tax revenue has also been used to extend the road network, construct the electricity supply system, and so on.

Higher incomes have allowed people much more choice over spending, and so have provided the necessary economic foundation for a modern consumer society. Yet this consumer society is not simply a consequence of economic growth; it has also been encouraged by a profound demographic change, which has seen average family size (fertility) fall from 3.4 children per woman in 1900 to 2.0 children in 1940 and 1.8 in 1990. In 1900 over a quarter of married women under age forty-five had five or more children, but by 1940 fewer than one in ten had very large families. Since largeness of family was found by Seebohm Rowntree in his social study of York in 1900 to be the second-most-important cause of poverty (after low wages), it is clear that the decline in fertility has contributed to the overall improvement of family living standards. Smaller families have also allowed more married women to engage in paid employment and so contribute to family income. Up to 1940 about 10 percent of married women worked outside the home, but this figure increased sharply during the war and stood at 26 percent in 1951, rising to 62 percent by 1981. Higher family incomes have resulted, but this may have been at the cost of other, less easily measurable, welfare criteria; by the mid-1970s most mothers with dependent children were in paid (usually part-time) employment, and an increasing amount of child care was being carried out by paid helpers.

Smaller families and higher incomes together have led to a substantial improvement in housing conditions. Overcrowding—defined as more than 1.5 persons per room—affected one in six households in England and Wales in 1911, but by 1966 it was a problem for only one in eighty. The quantitative increase in living space has been matched by a qualitative improvement in housing amenities, which itself reflects both higher incomes and technical change. In 1951 over one-third of households possessed neither a bath nor a shower, but thirty-five years later these fittings were practically universal. Such changes have had a significant impact on the way people live their lives; homes are now more comfortable, and allow more privacy for all family members, than ever before. Homes are also more likely to be owned by their occupiers. Before the First World War the great majority of people, whatever their income level and social class, rented their homes, and even in 1961 it was still more normal to rent than to own. By 1990, however, two-thirds of houses were owner-occupied, and real estate had become the most valuable of all personal assets.

The improvement in housing conditions has been permitted in part by a reduction in the proportion of income that has had to be spent on food. In the late nineteenth century it seems that working-class households spent over half of their weekly income on food, compared with 30 percent in 1957 and less than 20 percent by 1990. At the same time **diet** has become more varied, not only because of higher income but also because of new food technology, new sources of overseas supply, and new tastes. More extensive **foreign travel** since the 1960s, particularly for Mediterranean holidays, has introduced many people to a less-bland cuisine than was the norm in post-war Britain, and the simultaneous development of local Indian, Chinese, and Italian restaurants has made exotic flavors available on almost every high street. High streets themselves have changed as rising incomes have transformed shopping from a necessary subsistence chore into a major leisure activity focused on the purchase of **fashion** clothes, consumer durables, cars, and holidays.

Not everyone has shared to the same degree in this overall improvement in living standards. There are still large differences in the economic resources and living standards of different groups in Britain, and although welfare provision has prevented the old, the sick, and the unemployed from becoming even poorer, it has certainly not made them rich. The poorer half of the population in 1949 received about one-quarter of total after-tax income, and after forty years of comprehensive welfare provision and redistributive taxation they still receive almost exactly the same proportion. There have, however, been some changes within this poorer group. Until the early 1970s, to be old in Britain meant to be poor, with the elderly dominating poverty statistics; in 1990 it was young families headed by unemployed males or by single parents who were the worst off. Although these groups have living standards much higher than the poorest people in 1900, nevertheless their income is not sufficient to allow them to engage in the modern consumerist activities of dining out, traveling abroad, buying a home, or accumulating durable goods.

The substantial increase in real incomes in twentieth-century Britain has not necessarily made people more satisfied with life. At an individual level the rising ownership rates of consumer durables such as video recorders or washing machines may have reduced the relative contentment of that diminishing proportion of the population whose poverty precludes purchase. At the national level the relatively poor performance of the British economy since the Second World War compared with that of France and Germany may have created a more general dissatisfaction with living standards. Since there is no necessary or direct relationship between affluence and happiness, it is not appropriate to draw conclusions about living standards simply from quantitative evaluations of income or spending patterns. There is, however, one indicator that is unambiguous—life expectancy. In 1900 154 of every 1,000 infants died within a year of their birth. By 1939 better nutrition, housing conditions, and medical care had reduced this number to 51, and by the mid-1980s it had fallen to only 10. Over this same period life expectancy at birth has risen from an average of forty-eight to seventy-five years. Whether people in 1990 were happier than people in 1900 we cannot say, but they were certainly better clothed, better housed, better fed, and longer lived.

Paul Johnson

Bibliography
Burnett, John. *Plenty and Want.* 3rd ed. 1989.
———. *A Social History of Housing, 1815–1985.* 2nd ed. 1986.

Statute of Westminster (1931)

The Statute of Westminster codified concretely the transformation of the self-governing parts of the British Empire into the Commonwealth of Nations. It embodied the decisions that had been arrived at during the Imperial Conferences of 1926 and 1930 involving Britain and those colonies formally designated as Dominions after 1907. By the legislation the predominantly Caucasian settler colonies Canada, Australia, and New Zealand, or in South Africa's case, a Caucasian-dominated colony, and the new Irish Free State were freed from most aspects of surviving imperial subordination. The statute illustrated graphically that although Dominion patriotism had led to major colonial participation in the First World War, such collaboration had accelerated the centrifugal forces that had been present before 1914.

The many crises of the First World War and the 1920s had threatened to destroy what was constructive in the imperial connection. After 1918 Dominion premiers who had participated in Prime Minister David Lloyd George's Imperial War Cabinet, and whose countries suffered extraordinarily high casualties, resented being overruled by British ministers. In the immediate post-war period, Canada and most other Dominions were determined not to be pulled into a conflict initiated by Britain, as Lloyd George found out to his cost over the Chanak crisis of 1922 with the new Turkish state. By 1923 Canada had begun to sign agreements independently of Britain, notably the Halibut treaty with the United States. More dramatically, by 1921 Britain had been forced to recognize the Irish Free State, made up of all of Ireland except for Ulster and run by politicians determined systematically to eliminate remaining British power by creating a republic. In addition, South Africa was ruled by Boer leaders not especially favorable to Britain.

It was in this tense atmosphere that in 1926 the Colonial Secretary, L.S. Amery, asked the elder statesman Arthur Balfour to devise a formula that might maintain certain imperial links and preserve some form of working international body that would coexist with the increasingly ineffective League of Nations. The result was the famous formulation by Balfour that was accepted by the Imperial Conference of that year and from which the central ideas contained in the Statute of Westminster were derived. His words were:

> The Commonwealth is made up of autonomous communities within the British Empire, equal in status, in no way subordinate one to another in respect of their domestic or external affairs, though united by a common allegiance to the Crown, and freely associated as members of the British Commonwealth of Nations.

This conception was accepted by the Dominions—reluctantly by some such as New Zealand, which thought that the formula attenuated the kinship values associated with the imperial relationship, and enthusiastically by others such as South Africa, where most Boers detested the idea of any continued imperial domination.

Since 1931 many aspects of the statute have been modified to adapt to the constitutional evolution of various countries in the Commonwealth. For example, by dropping the adjective "British" after 1945, the concept of "equality of status," embodied in the statute for the Dominions, has been extended to mean that all former Dominions and colonies that have since become independent states have "equality of function." Thus, the statute arrested the collapse of the Commonwealth, which, while now much diminished in sentiment and effectiveness, still exists, although Britain's entrance into the **European Community** as of January 1973 symbolized the end of the United Kingdom's imperial epoch. Nevertheless, the post-Statute of Westminster imperial evolution has allowed most of the developed states of the former Empire and many of the former colonies to continue to participate in Commonwealth gatherings for common political, economic, and, especially, athletic activities.

Richard A. Rempel

Bibliography

Hancock, W.K. *Survey of Commonwealth Affairs*. 2 vols. 1937–42.
Mansergh, Nicholas. *Survey of British Commonwealth Affairs*. 2 vols. 1952–8.
Wheare, K.C. *The Constitutional Structure of the Commonwealth*. 1960.

Steamship Travel

The advent of the steamship in the nineteenth century facilitated the phenomenon of the passenger liner. Between 1838 and the 1990s over 1,300 relatively large liners were built for such companies as Peninsular and Oriental Steam Navigation (P&O), White Star, Cunard, and Royal Mail. Between the 1880s and 1940s Great Britain was the principal maritime power of the world, carrier of goods and people. In 1914 the British merchant fleet consisted of 12 million tons. After the turn of the century Cunard and White Star engaged in competition for the biggest, best, and most luxurious passenger liners. One of the best-known Cunard ships was the *Aquitania*, in service thirty-six years and traveling over 3 million miles. Others were the *Mauretania* and the *Lusitania*, the latter sunk by a German U-boat off Ireland in May 1915, a catastrophe that affected developments in the war. The White Star response in the competition involved three superliners: the 45,000-ton *Olympia* in 1910; followed by the *Titanic*, completed and sunk in 1912; and a third, first to be called the *Gigantic*, but changed to the *Britannic* after the *Titanic* was lost.

A long slump prevailed during the 1920s and 1930s. Cunard-White Star superliners *Queen Mary* and *Queen Elizabeth*, built in the late 1930s, each weighing over 80,000 tons and capable of speeds of over thirty knots, had a peacetime capacity of about 2,000 passengers and 1,200 crew. During the **Second World War** they were converted to troop carriers. By resorting to extraordinary arrangements—bunks, called "hot sacks," stacked five high and used continuously over eight-hour shifts, they could accommodate 16,000 troops, the size of a division. They crossed the Atlantic alone at high speed carrying a total of 2 million persons during the war. Notable post-war liners included the *Canberra* and the new *Queen Elizabeth II* (*QE2*). Both were temporarily requisitioned by the government in April 1982 and converted for use as troop ships during the **Falklands War.** In recent years, with rising costs and diminishing demand in the transatlantic route, the passenger liner has been used increasingly as a cruise ship. The latest type of modern steamship has been a new generation of super ferry, operating mostly in the English Channel and in the Baltic, North, and Mediterranean seas.

Eugene L. Rasor

Bibliography

Braynard, F.O., and William H. Miller. *Fifty Famous Liners*. 3 vols. 1982–7.
Brinnin, John Malcolm. *The Sway of the Grand Saloon: A Social History of the North Atlantic*. 1971.
Gibbs, C.R.V. *British Passenger Liners of the Five Oceans*. 1963.

Steel Industry

In 1900 Britain ranked third among the world's steel producers, having been surpassed in turn during the previous decade by the United States and Germany; Britain's and their respective shares of world tonnage were 36 percent, 23 percent, and 18 percent. By 1990 Britain ranked tenth in the world, with 2.3 percent of the output; the United States produced 11.6 percent; Germany, 5.4 percent. Throughout the century the British industry has struggled to reshape its inheritance of too many, too small, and sometimes inadequately equipped works operating in locations better suited to nineteenth-century conditions. Although steel continued to be regarded as one of the "commanding heights" of the national economy, its leaders lacked opportunity, capital, or sometimes resolution to change all of these adverse conditions at the same time or sufficiently. Even so, by the end of the 1980s, the British steel industry was again one of the most technically efficient in the world.

Since the Industrial Revolution the steel industry had benefited from abundant, easily accessible mineral resources. Home ore and fuel supported iron production in distinct districts from central Scotland to South Wales. In wrought iron and later in steel there was strong regional product specialization. Northeast England, Scotland, and Lincolnshire concentrated on heavy products, notably plate, angles, and structurals. South Wales made rails for world markets throughout the Victorian age, but then gradually concentrated on its old specialty of tinplate, to which were added sheet and strip. The northwest coast district of Cumbria, always prominent in steel rails, now contains the only rail mill in Britain. South Lancashire and West Yorkshire had major portions of the wire trade. Tubular products came mainly from the Black Country of the West Midlands and from central Scotland. Sheffield has always been exceptional, not so much for the forms of its finished products as for their quality. It has had a quite disproportionate share of special and alloy steel production. Since 1900 it has normally turned out only 11 to 14 percent of national output by tonnage, but about half by value. During the twentieth century some of these regional specializations have been modified. In the 1930s, for instance, the search for lower-cost material brought much of the bulk tube trade to the ore fields of Northamptonshire where the Basic Bessemer process was reintroduced; thirty years later the development focus for tubes shifted to Teesside in Northeast England. In the late 1950s, as shipbuilding declined, and in the hope of encouraging new, consumer durable industries, the traditionally heavy emphasis of Scottish steel was lightened by the construction of a hot-strip mill.

Throughout the first third of the century, with the exception of the First World War, a persistent problem was foreign competition. This was not confined to traditional outlets overseas, but involved large imports to home markets. In 1932 the free-trade principles under which the industry had always operated were abandoned, and an *ad valorem* import duty of 33.33 percent was imposed. In return for protection, the industry committed itself to create a new, stronger, central organization, the British Iron and Steel Federation (BISF), and to a rationalization program. The goal was to maximize efficiency through coordinated reconstruction, financed by private companies. Mergers, concentration of production, plant closures, and a good deal of new construction were carried through before the outbreak of the Second World War. However, most old companies survived, and the limited nature of their cooperation as well as the large number of plants suboptimal in location, size, and equipment limited the achievement. The plans of those who, usually from the outside, had advocated massive demolition and a new start proved to have been far too simplistic. By 1939 twenty-two integrated steelworks, and many more not linked with iron making, were involved in that year's record production of 13.4 million tons.

Well before the war ended, active planning for more far-reaching and fully coordinated reconstruction was underway. A series of development plans was carried through between 1945 and the mid-1960s. The first fifteen years of this period were in some ways uniquely favorable: Demand was rising, indeed apparently insatiable, and for a time the industry was operating in world markets from which some leading competitors had been removed by war and its aftermath. Production rose rapidly, though still largely within the old constraints of companies and locations. In 1955 20.1 million tons of steel were produced. The industry still had twenty-two integrated works as well as at least twenty-seven other plants, each making more than 100,000 tons of steel. In these post-war programs there were a number of major "brownfield" developments, essentially new works grafted onto existing complexes of plants, though sometimes far exceeding in size what was there before—Port Talbot, Ravenscraig, Lackenby, and redevelopment at Scunthorpe. There was only one wholly new, "greenfield" development, the works at Newport, South Wales, built between 1959 and 1962.

At the end of the 1950s trade recession and revived competition from old rivals brought the first serious check to increasing output. Matters then improved, so that by 1964, at 26.6 million metric tons, Britain was producing twice as much steel as in any pre-war year and over five times the output of 1900. Shortly after, the industry's organization was dramatically changed. Long a subject of keen political dispute, it was first nationalized in 1951; there was a speedy return to private ownership under the incoming **Conservative** administration. In the summer of 1967 the fourteen major companies—defined as those producing over 500,000 tons of steel annually—were again nationalized under the title of the British Steel Corporation (BSC). The remaining firms, producing over 2 million tons of steel but in a multitude of generally small works, remained privately owned. This sector contained much of the Sheffield special steel industry. Over the next few years, the independent industry grew more rapidly than British Steel, with which it collaborated in a few joint ventures.

BSC began operations with thirty-nine works making steel, of which twenty-two were integrated with blast furnaces. In a world that already contained works of 12 million tons' annual capacity or more, British Steel was recognized as needing still more concentration. For its first seven or eight years it was believed that progress toward a planned system of fewer, bigger, better-located works would be eased by an overall large-scale expansion of capacity. Instead, deep recession led to abandonment of these plans, to reductions of national capacity, and to plant and other closure programs more radical than any that had gone before. The twenty-two integrated works with which BSC had begun work were reduced to five by the mid-1980s. By the end of 1992 there were only four. Home production of iron ore, which reached a twentieth-century peacetime peak of 17.4 million metric tons in 1960, shrank rapidly after the mid-1960s and has practically ceased. Coking coal came wholly from British mines until 1970; now it is procured mainly from overseas. The British Steel work force fell from 257,000 at the time of **nationalization** to 47,000 by the first half of 1991. Production has fallen much less, from 23.3 million metric tons in 1967 to 17 million in 1990.

Despite its traumatic twentieth-century career, the industry's heritage is still important. Only one of the five sites for integrated works with which it entered the 1990s had been developed from a greenfield since 1900. Steel making began around Ravenscraig in the 1870s; Scunthorpe derives from an iron-making site of the mid-1860s; Teesside, from 1851; and there has been iron making and later a steel industry in the neighborhood of Port Talbot since the mid-nineteenth century. The ideal location for today's bulk steel plants is at a deepwater ore dock, but of the present plants only Port Talbot and Redcar have ore docks next to their furnace stockyards. Scunthorpe and Ravenscraig must haul their ore from ore terminals twenty-two and forty-seven miles, respectively, from the ironworks. Newport is at tidewater but has no terminal of its own, instead drawing its ore through the Port Talbot docks forty-five miles away.

As a result of the draconian changes of the last fifteen years, Britain's steel industry has become one of the most efficient in the Western world. BSC was returned to private ownership in 1988. Having suffered heavy losses in the late 1970s and early 1980s, for a time in the late 1980s it made large profits, but then, in the sharp recession of the early 1990s, it again fell into the red. Study of its longer-term development shows that it is difficult but not impossible to modernize an old industrial structure. When the task is carried through, the result may be a revitalized, even a world-competitive, industry. However, its economic history and past geography cannot be wholly erased.

Kenneth Warren

Bibliography

Burn, Duncan L. *The Economic History of Steel Making, 1867–1939.* 1961.

Carr, James C., and Walter Taplin. *History of the British Steel Industry.* 1962.

McCloskey, Donald N. *Economic Maturity and Entrepreneurial Decline: British Iron and Steel, 1870–1913.* 1973.

Tolliday, Steven. *Business, Banking, and Politics: The Case of British Steel, 1918–1939.* 1987.

Vaizey, John. *The History of British Steel.* 1974.

Stopes, Marie Charlotte Carmichael (1880–1958)

The preeminence of Marie Stopes in shaping a new cultural consensus about sex and reproduction in the 1920s can hardly be overestimated, as she herself would have been quick to agree. Her flair for public controversy and her numerous books on **birth control, sexuality,** and motherhood made her the best-known British champion of women's right to birth control and marital satisfaction. Her works include *Married Love* (1918), *Wise Parenthood* (1918), *A Letter to Working Mothers* (1919), and *Radiant Motherhood* (1920).

Stopes was born in Edinburgh into a middle-class family dedicated to learning. Her father, Henry Stopes (1851–1902), was an enthusiastic amateur archaeologist whose work failed to find approval in the academy. Her mother, Charlotte Carmichael Stopes (1840–1929), a passionate suffragist, attained considerable distinction as a Shakespeare scholar, writer, and literary lecturer. Stopes' own career as a paleobotanist and her doctoral degrees from both London and Munich were perhaps undertaken to win the academic laurels denied her parents. She quickly gained a reputation as an able scientist, in 1904 becoming the first woman appointed Lecturer in botany at the University of Manchester.

Convinced by her unconsummated first marriage that the majority of men and women were ignorant of the endless possibilities for conjugal bliss—as she had been before reading up on the subject in the **British Museum**—Stopes published *Married Love* in 1918. This paean to marital sexuality included little information on contraception, but it evoked so many inquiries that she wrote and published *Wise Parenthood* later the same year. The latter, besides supplying practical birth control information, argued that contraception was an essential component of Christian marriage, social harmony, and progress for the British "race."

Both books were sensationally successful. Almost overnight Stopes became Britain's foremost arbiter of sexual knowledge. During the next four decades she received, and answered, thousands of letters asking for advice on sexual matters, published the *Birth Control News*, and wrote about a dozen books on related subjects. In 1921, with her prosperous second husband, aviation pioneer H.V. Roe (1879–1949), she opened the Mother's Clinic in North London to provide birth control to poor women. She also launched the Society for Constructive Birth Control and Racial Progress to pressure the Ministry of Health to give contraceptive services at maternal and infant welfare centers.

Stopes and her organization ceased to be a political force by the 1930s, but her cultural influence persisted through book sales and her knack for self-publicity. Although most of her ideas were not new, she combined disparate elements in original ways. Erotic rapture was expressed in religious images of spiritual bonding, while advice on sex technique was proffered in the frank (and, at the time, shocking) vocabulary of scientific discourse. Moreover,

Stopes' message of the "radiant motherhood" that would result from women's freedom to determine when to bear children was conventional enough to fit within the inter-war renewal of a domestic ideology; it also included a strong element of pro-natalism to assuage fears of population decline.

Stopes' idiosyncratic and sometimes confused social philosophy enabled her to represent a number of contradictory strands. Her vision appealed not only to women seeking reproductive freedom and enhanced health but to physicians, eugenists, clergymen, population scientists, and "respectable" people on all sides of the political spectrum. She saw no reason to doubt that all of these constituencies would follow her once they understood the scientific, social, and religious bases of her "new gospel." Yet, in the end, Stopes was more successful at changing private attitudes toward women's sexuality than she was at influencing public policy.

Roberta A. Clark

Bibliography

Hall, Ruth. *Marie Stopes: A Biography*. 1977.
Leathard, Audrey. *The Fight for Family Planning: The Development of Family Planning Services in Britain, 1921–74*. 1980.
Rose, June. *Marie Stopes and the Sexual Revolution*. 1992.
Soloway, Richard Allen. *Birth Control and the Population Question in England, 1877–1930*. 1982.
Weeks, Jeffrey. *Sex, Politics, and Society: The Regulation of Sexuality since 1800*. 2nd ed. 1989.

Stoppard, Tom (1937–)

The playwright Tom Stoppard, born Tomas Straussler in Zlin, Czechoslovakia, is the author of *Rosencrantz and Guildenstern Are Dead* (1967), *Jumpers* (1972), *Travesties* (1974), *Night and Day* (1978), *The Real Thing* (1982), and *Arcadia* (1993). His plays have earned commercial and critical success and have won Tony and New York Drama Critics Circle awards in the United States; the Shakespeare Award, and the Laurence Olivier and *Plays and Players* awards in Britain; and the Prix Italia. Stoppard has also won an Oscar nomination as coauthor of the original screenplay of *Brazil* (1990). He has written numerous radio and **television** plays and several other screenplays, including the adaptations of Vladimir Nabokov's *Despair* (1978), **J.G.** Ballard's *Empire of the Sun* (1987), John le Carré's *The Russia House* (1989), and E.L. Doctorow's *Billy Bathgate* (1991); he has also freely adapted several stage plays: Ferenc Molnár's *Rough Crossing* (1984) and Arthur Schnitzler's *Undiscovered Country* (1984) and *Dalliance* (1986). Stoppard's attempt at film direction, his adaptation of *Rosencrantz and Guildenstern* (1991), won the Grand Prize at the Venice Film Festival. Since 1989 he has served on the Royal **National Theatre** Board.

In 1939 Eugene Straussler, Stoppard's father, moved the family from his native Czechoslovakia to **Singapore** where, in 1942, he was killed. His wife and sons were evacuated to India. In India, Stoppard's English mother, Martha, met and married a Major with the British **army**, Kenneth Stoppard. The family moved to Nottinghamshire after the war and later to Bristol. After leaving school, Stoppard worked as a newspaper reporter and reviewer, experience that likely figured in his writing of *Night and Day* (1978), which deals with journalistic responsibility. He did not attend university.

Stoppard's youthful career as a theater reviewer left him with an encyclopedic knowledge of theater and stagecraft. Influenced equally by Oscar Wilde and **Samuel Beckett**, he offers the unlikely combination of entertainment and intellectuality in his works, which are characterized by pyrotechnic wordplay and a highly allusive, self-referential exploitation of dramatic traditions. His early plays interpolate dialogue and characters from the canon of great drama: *Rosencrantz and Guildenstern* draws directly upon *Hamlet*; *Travesties*, upon Wilde's *The Importance of Being Earnest*. His later plays are comedies of ideas: Philosophy is the subject of *Jumpers*; aesthetics, of *Travesties*; and physics, of *Hapgood* (1988).

Unlike mainstream post-war British writers and dramatists, Stoppard does not chronicle the decline and despair of Britain but affirms what he identifies as the traditions of "Western liberal democracy, favouring an intellectual elite and a progressive middle class and based on a moral order derived from Christian absolutes." Stoppard has actively campaigned for human rights in Eastern Europe, a commitment that appears in *Cahoot's Macbeth* (1979), the television play *Professional Foul* (1977), and *Every Good Boy Deserves Favour* (1977).

Joan FitzPatrick Dean

Bibliography

Corballis, Richard. *Stoppard: The Mystery and the Clockwork.* 1984.

Dean, Joan FitzPatrick. *Tom Stoppard: Comedy as a Moral Matrix.* 1981.

Tynan, Kenneth. *Show People.* 1979.

Whitaker, Thomas R. *Tom Stoppard.* 1983.

Strachey, John (1901–1963)

In the 1930s John Strachey was preeminent as a pro-Communist propagandist and theorist. He was the most widely read Marxist writing in English, almost as well known in the United States as in Britain. However, he had already changed his political affiliations several times, and subsequently shifted again. He rejoined the **Labour Party** in 1942 and became Undersecretary of State for Air, then Minister for Food, and finally Secretary of State for War, in the **Attlee** governments of 1945–51. During the 1950s he gradually moved toward the "revisionist" right-wing of the party, and, had he not died prematurely, he would certainly have achieved high office in the **Wilson** government in 1964.

Educated at Eton and **Oxford**, and the son of the editor and owner of the *Spectator*, Strachey was brought up in a conventional "Establishment" environment. However, he joined the Labour Party in 1923 and was adopted as a candidate for a Birmingham constituency the next year. He was unsuccessful in the election, and observed, with dismay, the failure of the short-lived Labour government to make any real impact on the stagnating economy. He collaborated closely with **Oswald Mosley** in campaigning for a more radical, expansionist approach, and his first book, *Revolution by Reason* (1925), provided a theoretical rationale for such ideas. In this book he argued that, by combining increases in the money supply with economic redistribution and the establishment of a state planning body, it was possible both to provide an incentive to manufacturers and to help the working classes. The book revealed Strachey's unusual qualities as a popularizer of complex theories and established him as a thinker who was attempting to find a new strategy for democratic socialism.

The 1926 **General Strike** affected him deeply, and he immersed himself in the workers' cause, becoming the editor of both the **Independent Labour Party**'s *Socialist Review* and the *Miner*. He was elected to Parliament when the second Labour government assumed office in 1929, and served as Parliamentary Private Secretary for Mosley, who now had special responsibility for **unemployment** policy. Both of them resigned in May 1930, when the **Cabinet** rejected Mosley's expansionist program in favor of economic orthodoxy, and early the next year they left the Labour Party to form the New Party. However, Strachey wanted to establish a left-wing movement, and he abandoned the New Party in July 1931 when he discerned Mosley's growing sympathy for **Fascism**. This episode, and the subsequent collapse of the Labour government, led him to reject reformist ideas. He had been attracted to Marxism since the latter half of the 1920s and now embraced it as the solution to the problems of the era. His application to join the **Communist Party of Great Britain** (CPGB) in the summer of 1932 was rejected—because he was regarded as an unreliable intellectual—but for the rest of the decade he effectively wrote and worked as a Communist.

The essential factor in Strachey's outstanding success as a propagandist in these years was his extraordinary ability as a writer. He was able to mount a compelling argument on a theme that addressed the most fundamental problems of the times. For example, in *The Coming Struggle for Power* (1932) he conveyed one urgent message across a vast range of subject matter: that capitalism would lead to barbarism, while Communism was the hope for the world. In 1936 he secured a still wider audience when he joined **Victor Gollancz** and **Harold Laski** in forming the **Left Book Club** and became its most popular author. *The Theory and Practice of Socialism* (1936) was the most influential book ever produced by the Club, and *Why You Should Be a Socialist* (1938) sold more than 250,000 copies within two months of its publication.

Yet by 1938 Strachey was beginning to change course again, for Keynesian economic theory and the experience of the New Deal led him to believe that capitalism might be reformed. He expressed this view in *A Programme for Progress* (1940)—a book that was criticized by the CPGB hierarchy. When he thought that the Communists were prepared to see Britain defeated by Nazism, he could stand it no longer, and in April 1940 he broke with the party. Shortly afterward, he joined the **Royal Air Force** and spent the latter part of the war as a propagandist for the Air Ministry.

As Minister of Food from 1946 Strachey was unlucky to bear the brunt of the criticism for the abortive attempt to grow groundnuts in East Africa. He returned to writing after the **Conservatives** were returned to power in 1951, and his *Contemporary Capitalism* (1956) was a major work of democratic socialist theory that combined **John Maynard Keynes** and Karl Marx to explore the current situation. He concluded that the inherent conflict between capitalism and democracy could be contained and controlled by a purposeful government that understood the dynamics of the economic system. This text was complemented by *The End of Empire* (1959), a timely book that sought to demonstrate that **imperialism** was unjust to its victims and unnecessary for the economies of its beneficiaries. However, in his final years Strachey became more conventional in his political outlook. A supporter of Anglo-American **nuclear weapons** policy, he was a bitter opponent of the **Campaign for Nuclear Disarmament**, and his last book, *On the Prevention of War* (1962), was influenced by current deterrence theories.

Strachey's reputation has suffered because of his volatility and because his work did not fit neatly into the reformist or Marxist traditions. However, he was consistently preoccupied with the problem of **unemployment**, and in each of his phases he explained his current thinking to his contemporaries with brilliant clarity. His writing was at its most powerful during his Communist years, but the works in which he tried to find a synthesis between differing theories were more original. In particular, *Contemporary Capitalism* remains an important text of "revisionist" socialism that still deserves to be read alongside **Anthony Crosland**'s *The Future of Socialism* (1956).

Michael Newman

Bibliography

Newman, Michael. *John Strachey.* 1989.
Thomas, Hugh. *John Strachey.* 1973.
Thompson, Noel. *John Strachey: An Intellectual Biography.* 1993.

Strachey, (Giles) Lytton (1880–1932)

Lytton Strachey, biographer, critic, and member of the **Bloomsbury Group**, is best known for his iconoclastic *Eminent Victorians* (1918), in which he questioned the reputations of the Victorian worthies Cardinal Manning, Florence

Nightingale, Dr. Thomas Arnold, and General Gordon. In writing these lives he pioneered a form of "new biography," challenging the standard Victorian two-volume life and letters with a more psychologically penetrating approach. His *Queen Victoria*, more fully researched and more sympathetic, followed in 1921. The notably psychologically-oriented *Elizabeth and Essex* (1928) was influenced by his brother James' interest in Freud, whom Strachey heard speak in Berlin in 1922 and who praised the book for being "steeped in the spirit of psychoanalysis."

Strachey was born in Clapham, London, on 1 March 1880. In 1884 he moved with his parents (retired colonial administrators) to Lancaster Gate, London, the family home until 1907. After attending schools at Poole, Abbotsholme, and Leamington, Strachey entered Liverpool University College in 1897, and then transferred to Trinity College, **Cambridge,** in 1899. In 1902 he was elected the 239th **Apostle** of the elite Cambridge Conversazione Society. The same year he received the Chancellor's Medal for his "Ely: An Ode." Strachey's Cambridge friends included **John Maynard Keynes, G.E. Moore,** and **Leonard Woolf.** Failing twice to be elected a Fellow of Trinity, Strachey joined the staff of his cousin St. Loe Strachey's *Spectator* as drama critic in 1907.

On 17 February 1909 Strachey proposed marriage to **Virginia** Stephen (later **Woolf**) and on the same day withdrew his proposal. Ensuing relationships with painters **Duncan Grant** and Henry Lamb both ended unhappily. *Landmarks in French Literature* (1912) was Strachey's first book. The same year he conceived the idea of *Victorian Silhouettes* (later *Eminent Victorians*). He worked on the four historical portraits during the **First World War,** and they can be read as an expression of Strachey's antipathy for the war and the shrill **patriotism** associated with it. In 1916 he requested exemption from military service on grounds of **conscientious objection.** Though his request was rejected, he was exempted following a medical examination. In 1915 Strachey began a friendship with the painter (Dora) Carrington. They lived together at the Mill House, Tidmarsh, where they were joined by Ralph Partridge in a *ménage à trois*. It was at the Mill House until 1924 that Strachey enjoyed the happiest years of his life and achieved his greatest success. In 1923 Carrington and Par-tridge, who had married two years earlier, separated, and Strachey and Carrington moved to Ham Spray House, Hungerford, in 1924.

A prominent man of letters, Strachey received numerous honors. He delivered the Leslie Stephen Lecture on Pope at Cambridge in 1925 and the next year received an honorary doctorate from the University of Edinburgh. Strachey began *Elizabeth and Essex* in 1925 and a final, and ultimately unhappy, relationship with Roger Senhouse in 1926. Strachey became ill in January 1930. Though specialists diagnosed typhoid, colitis, and an ulcer, he died of stomach cancer on 21 January 1932. His friend Carrington committed suicide within two months of Strachey's death.

Strachey's historical essays show the irony of personal and social impulses that have created "modern" life. In *Eminent Victorians*, for example, Thomas Arnold's and Florence Nightingale's passions aimed at modernization are shown to be rooted in their willful and unavowed intellectual and spiritual muddles; the realizing of their passions creates a modern order at once improved and worsened, free and yet more oppressively disciplined than what precedes it. Moreover, in a way characteristic of the paradoxes of literary modernism, Strachey's histories pair his distrust of the eminent authors of modernity with his self-reflexive doubts about the possibility of writing reliable stories and interpretations about history.

John Ferns

Bibliography

Edmonds, Michael. *Lytton Strachey: A Bibliography.* 1981.
Ferns, John. *Lytton Strachey.* 1988.
Holroyd, Michael. *Lytton Strachey: A Biography.* 1971.

Strikes

Elections, petitions, and mass mobilizations give Western publics numerous means of voicing their objections and demands, and they provide at least the hope of change and redress. Many ordinary people, particularly manual workers, add another method to this repertoire—the strike—and have seen fit to make repeated use of it. In no country has this been more true than in Britain, where workers seem to have been proficient at putting together effective unions, normally the prerequisite for sustained strike activity. Just as unions have been key to strikes, however, so the history of strikes has provided many of the turning points in the history of trade unionism.

Sporadic use of the strike can be found back in the eighteenth century, and the infamous Combination Act of 1799 banning combinations of workers was testimony to its increased frequency in the era of the Napoleonic Wars. From the 1850s, however, workers could make use of the financial and organization backing of the so-called "new model" unions that were established by skilled workers, especially in large cities. Gradually, unions became adept at choosing when and against whom to strike, and when their efforts were underpinned by a buoyant labor market they could be extremely effective. During the prosperous years 1871–3, for example, there was a large explosion of highly successful strikes that had the effect of enrolling large numbers of previously unorganized workers into unions. The Depression of 1873–96 quickly tipped the balance of power back toward the employers, and workers suffered bitter defeats, particularly in **coal mining** and in textiles.

The late 1880s witnessed yet another outburst of strikes and union organization. This "new unionism" emerged in 1889, with major strikes in London on the part of matchgirls, dockers, and gas workers. Advocates of the "new unionism" were particularly concerned to bring the unskilled within the orbit of trade unionism. To do that required the creation of more-inclusive unions with lower qualifications and appropriately lower dues, inevitably providing fewer benefits as well. It was further held that to be effective these broader unions would have to adopt a more aggressive approach toward employers and also make demands upon the state.

The period of the **First World War** was the most strike-prone in British history. A number of very large strikes broke out before the war, as the effort to bring unionization to the less skilled revived with great intensity. The miners engaged in bitter strikes aimed at securing a national minimum wage, railwaymen and port workers sought recognition from employers, and many other groups sought redress for declining real wages. The pre-war battles witnessed increasing involvement by the state, either as conciliator or—more controversially—as policeman, and also more-effective organization on the part of workers. Particularly impressive, at least on paper, was the Triple Alliance of miners, dockers, and railwaymen that threatened to strike in concert over issues of mutual interest.

The war postponed confrontation but served also to change the terms on which employers and workers contended. Union membership jumped massively from just over 4 million in 1914 to 8.3 million by 1920, and government became even more implicated in setting wages, controlling prices, and fixing working conditions, and hence more easily drawn into conflict. Employers also became more organized during the war, and by its end they were firmly resolved to resist the encroachments of unions and of the state. After the war, therefore, there was a series of bitter strikes that swept up workers in one industry after another. For about two years workers succeeded in winning recognition, higher wages, and shorter hours in a number of industries. By mid-1920 the post-war boom had ended, and **unemployment** had begun to spread into the staple industries, such as coal, shipbuilding, and textiles. From 1921, therefore, employers began to take back many of the concessions granted during and just after the war. The Triple Alliance was revealed as a "paper tiger" on Black Friday (23 April 1921) when the **transport workers** and the railwaymen refused to back up the miners. The worst defeat came in 1926, when the **General Strike** was called off after nine days and the miners were left to carry on their ultimately unsuccessful strike alone.

The losses of the 1920s had a sobering effect on the unions and the workers they represented. To begin, the Trade Disputes Act of 1927 narrowed the political rights that the unions thought they had secured in 1906. While the framework of laws governing industrial conflict remained much the same after 1926, so, too, did the depressed state of the labor market, which discouraged strikes throughout the interwar years. The **Second World War** shifted the balance of advantage in the labor market back to the workers, but the war also brought political changes whose effect was to convince many workers to refrain from striking. Unions used their leverage within the state to press for economic policies more favorable to working-class interests, and the unions themselves grew rapidly. By the end of the war the membership losses incurred during the inter-war decades had been made up, and a **Labour** government, pledged to a major program of reform, was in power. Thus strikes remained infrequent throughout the 1940s, as workers gained through politics much of what they had previously sought through industrial action.

What the organizational gains of the 1940s did, however, was to give workers the shop-floor strength with which to wage a different sort of strike later on. This new pattern did not emerge immediately, but as prices began to climb and growth to falter in the late 1950s, workers began to employ small, "unofficial" strikes aimed at local management. The coming of mass production in the **automobile industry** gave greater clout to small groups of workers and to shop stewards, who used this leverage to press for improvements in wages and conditions. Prolonged full employment increased the bargaining power of other workers as well, and from the late 1950s strikes began to spread across a wide range of industries. Miners, dockers, and car workers invoked the strike most often and effectively, but by the mid-1960s the habit had caught on much more broadly. Successive governments during the 1960s became fixated on strikes, seeing them as responsible for inflation and lagging productivity, and the Labour government moved to impose statutory control over "unofficial action" with the publication of *In Place of Strife* in 1969.

The effort to reshape the legal framework for strikes was a sign that the question of industrial conflict and trade union rights had taken center stage in British political debate. The issues would be kept there throughout the 1970s and into the 1980s by continued high levels of strike activity, worsening inflation, and the nation's deepening economic malaise. Despite government efforts to discourage disputes, workers found them to be the most effective means of improving their **standard of living**. The Labour government backed off from its plan to legislate a new order in industrial relations, but the **Conservatives** under **Edward Heath** were less cautious. The Industrial Relations Act of 1971, however, met with sustained resistance from the unions and was made inoperative before being repealed by the **Wilson** government in 1974. In the meantime, strikes became more frequent and massive: Between 1970 and 1975 there were on average more than 3,000 strikes per year, involving approximately 1.3 million workers and costing over 12.5 million working days annually. These disputes also were waged with novel tactics that met with considerable success: sympathy strikes and boycotts, flying pickets—pioneered by the miners in 1972—and factory occupations, as at

Upper Clyde Shipbuilders. The climax came with the miners' strike of 1973–4, which led the government to impose a three-day week on the industry and to call an election that, they hoped, would provide popular backing for their stance against the unions. The Tories lost, however, and Labour was returned to office with a narrow majority, pledged to restore, and even increase, the legal rights of workers and of unions.

Labour was unable, however, to cope with the enormous economic problems of the 1970s. The oil price increases of 1973–4 and 1979 fueled inflation while slowing growth, and workers were almost forced to demand compensating wage increases. Labour was able to use its influence with union leaders to moderate wage claims and to avert a major wave of strikes until the fall of 1978, when a dispute broke out at Ford. That proved the signal for what came to be known as the "winter of discontent," when truck drivers and a number of public-sector workers went out on strike. Labour paid dearly for its failure in the election of May 1979, when **Margaret Thatcher** led the Conservatives to a major victory. Thatcher came into office resolved to avoid the industrial-relations failures of previous governments, to tame the unions, and to restrict strikes. Overall, the Conservatives were remarkably successful, though the price was very high. Aided no doubt by the sharp recession of 1981–2, from which the older industries in the north never truly recovered, the Tories inflicted a series of defeats upon the unions. The national steel strike of 1980 was a bitter loss for the unions and confirmed the long-term decline of the **steel industry** and its work force; civil servants lost a long-running dispute in 1981, **National Health Service** staff and railway workers in 1982; workers in the public utilities were beaten in 1983; and the miners were brutally crushed in a dispute over pit closures that began in March 1984 and dragged on for more than a year.

The Conservatives also transformed the legal framework of trade unionism through a series of Employment Acts that restricted secondary picketing, made unions liable to civil actions by employers over strikes, mandated secret ballots prior to official strike action and for union elections, and weakened the closed shop. In this increasingly inhospitable environment, union membership declined from nearly 13.3 million in 1979 to less than 10.5 million in 1985, or from 54.4 percent to 43.3 percent of the work force. Inevitably, strike activity lan-

S

guished as well. Between 1979–80 and 1989–90 strike activity declined by more than half, and neither the legal framework, nor the economic climate, nor the recent evolution of union-management relations suggests that an early revival is imminent.

Strikes thus remain an important means by which workers can make their grievances and demands heard, but they are unlikely in the near future to play so prominent a role in the nation's social and economic life as they did earlier in this century.

James E. Cronin

Bibliography

Cronin, James E. *Industrial Conflict in Modern Britain*. 1979.
———. "Strikes and Power in Britain, 1870–1920" in L. Haimson, and C. Tilly, eds. *Strikes, Wars, and Revolutions in an International Perspective: Waves in the Late Nineteenth and Early Twentieth Centuries*. 1989. pp. 79–100.
Durcan, J.W., W.E.J. McCarthy, and G.P. Redman. *Strikes in Post-War Britain*. 1983.
Phelps Brown, E.H. *The Origins of Trade Union Power*.
Price, Richard. *Labour in British Society*. 1986.

Also see GENERAL STRIKE (4–12 MAY 1926); MINERS' STRIKE (1984–1985)

Submarine Warfare

Submarine warfare, a revolutionary form of naval warfare in the twentieth century, provided the only real danger of naval defeat for Britain in both World Wars.

The invention of the first practical submarine by the Irish-American John Holland in 1898 initially left admirals unsure what, if any, use the new warship might have. In the first decade of the twentieth century the world's navies experimented with submarines as coastal patrol units and fleet auxiliaries without great enthusiasm. When the **First World War** broke out in 1914, Britain and Germany each possessed a few dozen submarines. The German navy, as the weaker naval power, was more aggressive in its employment of the new giant-killer. In the first months of the war German submarines, known as U-boats, sank several major warships of the **Royal Navy**. The British Grand Fleet was temporarily forced out of its main base by the submarine threat, and its operations were severely constricted.

It was against British trade, however, that German submarines were nearly decisive. At first the Germans divided their submarine resources between fleet operations and attacks on trade, hesitating to abandon international law entirely. Sinkings of civilian vessels such as the *Lusitania* (1915) outraged British and neutral (particularly American) opinion, and each time the Germans retreated. But early in 1917, convinced by the Battle of Jutland (1916) that they could not defeat the Royal Navy in conventional combat, the Germans declared unrestricted submarine warfare, threatening to sink without warning any ship approaching European waters. For a time in 1917 it appeared that an unbreakable submarine blockade might force Britain to make peace. But unrestricted submarine warfare brought American naval resources into the war, and the adoption of a convoy strategy allowed escorts and land-based patrol aircraft to protect merchant shipping against submarine attack. By 1918 the submarine menace had been defeated.

Between the wars the Royal Navy viewed the submarine threat with misplaced confidence due to the 1918 invention of sound-detection equipment (known as asdic or sonar), efforts to tighten international law regarding submarine warfare, and the ultimate failure of submarines in the First World War. The Germans had learned better lessons, however. U-boat Captain Karl Doenitz had experimented in 1918 with night surface attacks (making detection by patrol aircraft or asdic impossible) and "wolfpacks" of several submarines working together (enabling them to overwhelm a lightly escorted convoy). In 1939, as commander of the German submarine service, he quickly put his new techniques to effective use in the **Second World War**. After 1940 bases on the French coast allowed German submarines to patrol farther out into the Atlantic for longer periods than ever before, and by 1942 Britain once again faced defeat by blockade. Fortunately, increased escort resources provided by American intervention, **radar**-equipped patrol aircraft able to find and attack submarines at night, escort carriers giving convoys their own integral airpower, and successful decoding of German naval communications allowed the Allies to defeat the U-boats by 1943.

In both World Wars British submarines successfully attacked enemy warships and sea lines of communication, but against Continental powers whose fleets rarely left port and whose lines of communication were mostly on land, submarines could not hope to be decisive. In the First World War Royal Navy submarines attacked the German ore trade in the Baltic until the defeat of Russia eliminated their bases, and they made several daring forays into Turkish coastal waterways and the Sea of Marmara. In the Second World War they played an important role in cutting supply lines to the *Afrika Korps* and contributed to the American submarine blockade of Japan.

In the post-war era, however, new opportunities for submarines appeared. With the invention of nuclear propulsion in the 1950s, the submarine became capable of remaining submerged for weeks or months at a time. Fittingly, the first British nuclear submarine (1963) was named HMS *Dreadnought*, in honor of another warship that had revolutionized naval warfare a half-century earlier. These nuclear attack submarines were not only extremely effective hunters of surface ships, as HMS *Conqueror* proved by sinking the Argentine cruiser *Belgrano* in the **Falklands War**, but also became the preferred escorts against enemy submarines. The most significant submarine mission of all, however, arrived in the 1960s with the development of nuclear ballistic missile submarines. British submarines, such as HMS *Resolution* (1967), and their American, Soviet, French, and Chinese counterparts, cruised the ocean depths with a deadly cargo of nuclear missiles, providing an undetectable and thus invulnerable deterrent to nuclear attack.

David MacGregor

Bibliography

Grove, Eric J. *Vanguard to Trident: British Naval Policy since World War II.* 1987.

Lipscomb, Frank W. *The British Submarine.* 1954.

Marder, Arthur J. *From the Dreadnought to Scapa Flow: The Royal Navy in the Fisher Era, 1904–19.* 5 vols. 1961–70.

Roskill, Stephen W. *The War at Sea.* 3 vols. 1954–61.

Tarrant, V.E. *The U-Boat Offensive, 1914–1945.* 1989.

Suez Crisis (1956)

From the British perspective the Suez crisis began in July 1956 when the Egyptian government nationalized the Paris-based Suez Canal Company. The British government, led by Sir **Anthony Eden**, feared that this move would sooner or later be followed by an Egyptian refusal to allow passage to vessels headed for Great Britain, with catastrophic implications for British industry in an era when most of the country's oil was imported from the Middle East via the Suez Canal. But members of the **Cabinet** did not feel able to respond with any immediate military action and hence, against their better judgment, found themselves drawn into international negotiations aiming at a compromise diplomatic solution. By mid-October this began to look as if it would be the ultimate outcome, but in a surprising development Eden and a few senior colleagues decided to join with France in "arranging" for a second crisis to occur. This took the form of an Israeli attack on Egypt, thereby giving the British and the French the pretext to send forces to occupy the canal, not ostensibly to reverse the nationalization decree but simply to separate the combatants. But the operation had to be aborted in the face of overwhelming pressure from many quarters. The upshot was that the Suez canal remained nationalized, and the British government was widely perceived to have been humiliated.

When Egypt, led by Gamal Abdel Nasser, announced that the Canal Company would be nationalized the British Cabinet's initial reaction was to resolve that "while our ultimate purpose was to place the canal under international control, our immediate objective was to bring about the downfall of the present Egyptian Government." But the view of the Chiefs of Staff was that the immediate objective could not be achieved rapidly, since many weeks would be needed to assemble an expeditionary force in **Malta** capable of landing in strength at Alexandria. Orders were accordingly given to make the necessary preparations for what was code named "Operation Musketeer." And agreements were made to enable France to take part in an essentially subordinate role.

Meanwhile, however, the Americans had concluded that Egypt's action, however unfriendly, did not constitute a sufficient provocation to justify the use of armed force. They accordingly sought to draw the British and the French into diplomatic negotiations aimed at securing a compromise solution. Eden and his colleagues reluctantly recognized that they had no practical alternative to going through the motions of seeking a peaceful outcome while preparations proceeded for use of force as "a last resort." The upshot was many weeks of essentially unwelcome discussion at two successive international conferences held in London and then under the auspices of the **United Nations** in New York. Gradually it became clear to most members of the Cabinet, including Eden himself, that the planned assault on Alexandria ("Musketeer") or even just the Suez Canal itself ("Musketeer Revise," as it had become known) had ceased to be practical politics unless and until Egypt actually proved itself unwilling or unable to permit British shipping to use the canal. For diplomacy had revealed that too many countries (including both superpowers and several members of the Commonwealth) were in favor of a solution involving vague international "guarantees" of the canal's future status. Moreover, the opposition **Labour Party**, after an initial outburst of hostility toward Egypt, had now moved decisively into a position where it would oppose the use of force in the absence of the approval of the United Nations.

By mid-October, therefore, Eden appeared to be reconciled to accepting a compromise formula (known as the "Six Points") in the process of being made final in discussion between British Foreign Secretary Selwyn Lloyd and his Egyptian counterpart, Mohammed Fawzi. But the Prime Minister had been left in no doubt by the **Conservative Party** conference, held in Llandudno in early October, that he would be widely condemned by party activists as an "appeaser" if he consented to any compromise deal. And his Chancellor of the Exchequer, **Harold Macmillan**, indicated that he might resign and attempt to play **Winston Churchill** to Eden's **Neville Chamberlain**. In these circumstances Eden proved unwisely receptive to a plan presented to him by French representatives on 14 October at Chequers.

The French proposed that the Israelis should be secretly induced to attack Egypt, thereby enabling the British and the French, pretending lack of foreknowledge, to send forces to occupy the canal in order to protect it by separating the combatants. Once Eden had expressed an interest in this approach the French invited the Israeli leaders to Sèvres on the outskirts of Paris. The upshot was that Lloyd met David Ben-Gurion, the Israeli Prime Minister, on 22 October, and in the ensuing days the three countries negotiated what amounted to a collusive bargain as to how each

would play its hand after Israel had invaded Egypt on 29 October.

Several leading Cabinet ministers were informed about every aspect of the plan, and even the entire Cabinet was given a broad hint of what was afoot. Some of Eden's colleagues were undoubtedly uneasy either on practical or moral grounds, but none resigned. It does not seem, therefore, that the Prime Minister can be accused of acting alone or even "unconstitutionally"; on the other hand, few civil servants or diplomats were in the picture, and ministers undoubtedly deceived the House of Commons and the country when the scenario unfolded.

Perhaps more important was that the Americans were not consulted about the devious plan. For in the event President Dwight D. Eisenhower simply did not believe the rather threadbare public justification offered by London and Paris. With great alacrity, therefore, he set out to wreck the operation. American delegates at the United Nations helped mobilize an overwhelming vote of condemnation—forcing the use of British and French vetoes on the Security Council. U.S. diplomats ruthlessly exploited the British need for oil supplies that became acute when the Egyptians blocked the canal with sunken vessels, and refused to allow the British to draw on the resources of the International Monetary Fund when sterling came under acute selling pressure.

The decisive day was 6 November when the Cabinet met to review the position. The military aspect was satisfactory: Anglo-French forces were ashore in Egypt and were in control of about one-third of the canal, and bombing of airfields on the edge of Cairo was proceeding—necessitated by the vulnerability of Israeli cities to possible Egyptian bombing. The political-diplomatic outlook, however, was grim. Macmillan reported on the vulnerability of sterling; concern was expressed lest conventional Soviet forces intervene in the Middle East—something apparently taken more seriously than Soviet threats to use nuclear weapons on London; the position at the United Nations was deeply disturbing; several members of the Commonwealth were expressing opposition—with threats of resignation being mooted; the Labour Party had reflected passionate divisions in the country—even leading to a Commons sitting having to be suspended owing to disorder; and, above all, Eisenhower had spoken on the telephone to Eden in unmistakably vigorous terms: The operation must be halted. Facing a Cabinet that had earlier revealed potential splits, Eden took the initiative in proposing a ceasefire. By midnight, Anglo-French forces were accordingly halted in their progress down the canal.

In the ensuing weeks the British government strove desperately to persuade the United Nations (and the United States in particular) that the Anglo-French force should be allowed to form the nucleus of a U.N. peacekeeping operation. But the Americans remorselessly used economic pressure (and secret dealings with several treacherous British Cabinet ministers willing to go behind Eden's back) to enforce an unconditional and humiliating withdrawal, which was duly announced on 30 November.

From that day onward London tacitly accepted that the Egyptian nationalization of the Suez Canal Company could not be reversed. And Eden, after brazenly lying to the House of Commons on 20 December ("There was not foreknowledge that Israel would attack Egypt"), resigned on 9 January 1957, citing ill health. The whole affair had been "no end of a lesson" not only for him but for the entire British nation.

David Carlton

Bibliography

Carlton, David. *Britain and the Suez Crisis.* 1988.

Epstein, Leon D. *British Politics in the Suez Crisis.* 1964.

Kunz, Diane B. *The Economic Diplomacy of the Suez Crisis.* 1991.

Kyle, Keith. *Suez.* 1991.

Lucas, W. Scott. *Divided We Stand: Britain, the U.S., and the Suez Crisis.* 1991.

Thomas, Hugh. *The Suez Affair.* 3rd ed. 1986.

Sutherland, Graham Vivian (1903–1980)

Although at the height of his career Graham Sutherland was feted as one of Britain's great modern artists, his reputation began to dwindle before the end of his life, and it no longer seems as credible as it once was to speak of him in the same breath as **Henry Moore** and **Francis Bacon**. In the last decades critical attention was stronger on the Continent than in Britain, although interest in the artist has revived more recently along with the neo-romantic movement with which his name is now closely associated. It is a fascination with transformations in nature and a tendency toward spiritual subjects that made him an exemplary member of this school, drawing as it does on insular British concerns. Peers included **Paul Nash** and **John Piper**, as well as younger artists such as Michael Ayrton and Keith Vaughan.

Sutherland staked his affiliation with the British romantic tradition at the very outset of his career, which began as an engraver heavily indebted to Blake's follower, Samuel Palmer. A student at Goldsmiths' School of Art (1921–6), he adopted a pastoral image in his intaglio prints of the 1920s, with an abundance of churchyards and thatched cottages, although technically they were innovative with their deep creative use of overbiting. The 1929 Wall Street crash brought the post-war print boom to an abrupt halt, forcing a change of direction upon Sutherland.

He turned to oils and watercolors, but it needed the shock of nature to launch his painting career in earnest. In 1934 he visited Pembrokeshire; his experience of the landscape there was, according to his own testimony, an epiphany of Wordsworthian proportions. Significantly, however, he chose to live in Kent, where the landscape of the surrounding North Downs was not allowed to influence his painting in the same way. He needed his inspiration to be in some remote place, or to be discovered in chance encounters. A painter of nature, rather than landscape, he was disposed to incorporate geographically disparate elements in single pictures.

Eager to bridge the gap between romanticism and avant-garde art, Sutherland briefly associated with the English surrealists, taking part in their 1936 exhibition at the Burlington Galleries. The boldly imaginative commercial posters he was designing at the time were surreal fantasies, but what attracted him to surrealism was the idea of the "*objet trouvé*" a commonplace object rendered exotic and marvelous by its chance discovery. Like Nash and Moore, but unlike Continental surrealists, his inspiration lay in nature, not man-made objects. His vision of nature was neither benign nor lyrical, and he always sought exotic and disturbing phenomena. What excited him were hybrids, anthropomorphic characteristics in stones and plants, threatening conglomerations of tree roots, upturned trunks, and unruly vegetal growths.

In common with other artists of the 1930s Sutherland's brooding, apocalyptic canvases reflected the mood of impending conflict. He was among the first to be enlisted by **Kenneth**

Clark as an official **war artist** with the outbreak of hostilities. Sutherland's experiences as a war artist were almost as significant as his epiphany in the Welsh landscape. Recording bomb damage in Wales and sketching among the ruins of the London **Blitz** stimulated his fascination with the violence of growth and change, as twisted girders and shattered walls began to assume the mysterious life hitherto detected in plants and rocks.

Toward the end of the war Sutherland undertook his first religious commission, a *Crucifixion* for St. Matthew's Parish Church, Northampton, whose vicar, Walter Hussey, had already commissioned Moore's *Madonna and Child* and a cantata by **Benjamin Britten**. Sutherland had never attempted such a large work before, but his poignant interpretation of the theme, which combines the influence of Grunwald and the recently published photographs of concentration camp victims, marked a major departure in his career. For most of the 1950s he was engaged in designing the tapestry *Christ in Glory in the Tetramorph*, which was unveiled in 1962 in the rebuilt Coventry Cathedral. A convert to **Roman Catholicism**, Sutherland used his religious paintings to express his personal artistic preoccupations. Arising from the Northampton commission was a series exploring thorns both as a Christian symbol of the passion of Christ and as a metaphor of threatening nature.

A visit to the Picasso Museum in Antibes in 1947 encouraged the introduction of totemic figures, a development also indebted to Moore and Bacon although rooted in his own practice. It was as though the upturned trees and bombed houses, imbued with a life of their own, had given birth to ambiguous amalgams of animal, human, and vegetal elements. His mural for the **Festival of Britain**, *The Origins of the Land* (1951), populated by such threatening beings, and his series of standing forms in garden settings can be related to contemporary expressions of neo-romantic angst like John Wynd-

ham's novel *The Day of the Triffids*. The climax of Sutherland's international career was marked with a retrospective exhibition at the Venice Biennale (1952), which then transferred to the Musée National d'Art Moderne in Paris.

After **Somerset Maugham** invited him to paint his portrait in 1949, commissions came from many celebrated personalities of the day, including Kenneth Clark, Konard Adenauer, Helena Rubinstein, and **Winston Churchill**, whose portrait was a gift from Parliament. Churchill never hid his dislike of the painting, which like all of Sutherland's best portraits focuses on psychological strain in the face of the sitter. Some critics argue that the conventional, naturalistic portraits detract from Sutherland's reputation as an original artist. Others attribute a decline in the quality of his work to his move to the south of France, where he was cut off from the English landscape. In 1967 he renewed contact with Pembrokeshire when he returned to make a **documentary film**. He later bequeathed much of his work to the gallery that bears his name at Picton Castle in Pembrokeshire. Sutherland was admitted to the Order of Merit in 1960, was awarded a D.Litt. by **Oxford**, and was the first artist to receive the Shakespeare Prize in Hamburg in 1974.

David Cohen

Bibliography
Berthoud, Roger. *Sutherland: A Biography.* 1982.
Cooper, Douglas. *The Work of Sutherland.* 1961.
Sackville-West, Edward. *Sutherland.* 1943.
Stansky, Peter, and William Abrahams. *London's Burning: Life, Death, and Art in the Second World War.* 1994.
Sutherland in Wales: A Catalogue of the Collection at the Graham Sutherland Gallery, Picton Castle, Haverfordwest, Dyfed. 1976.
Tassi, Roberto. *Sutherland: Complete Graphic Work.* 1978.

T

Taff Vale Judgment (July 1901)

The Taff Vale judgment undercut trade unions' immunity from legal action to secure financial compensation for losses arising from **strikes**, an immunity that had hitherto been presumed to have been conferred by trade union legislation in 1871. This had major political effects, for many more trade unions turned to the newly formed **Labour Representation Committee** (LRC) to secure through Parliament legal changes to reverse this judgment by the Law Lords.

The legal case arose from a railway strike in South Wales in August 1900. It began as an unofficial action by workers on the Taff Vale Railway to gain union recognition at a propitious time, there being high demand for the local coal and less labor in the area because of the **Boer War**. The executive of the Amalgamated Society of Railway Servants (ASRS) made it an official dispute. Throughout the dispute the general manager of the railway company repeatedly used the law against the strikers, and after its settlement he moved against the ASRS. Legal opinion was surprised when the **House of Lords** overturned a Court of Appeal verdict that would have prevented the Taff Vale Company from taking action for damages against the union. By December 1902 the ASRS had incurred a total of £42,000 in settlement with the company and in legal costs.

In the year following the Taff Vale judgment the numbers of trade unionists affiliating with the LRC roughly doubled. This proved to be an important point in the move of British trade unionism away from Liberal politics. The case was also one of several factors that contributed to relative industrial peace between 1899 and 1907.

C.J. Wrigley

Bibliography

Bagwell, Philip S. *The Railwaymen: The History of the National Union of Railwaymen.* 1963.

Brown, Kenneth D. "Trade Unions and the Law" in C.J. Wrigley, ed. *A History of British Industrial Relations, 1875–1914.* 1982. pp. 116–34.

Clegg, H.A., Alan Fox, and A.F. Thompson. *A History of British Trade Unions since 1889.* vol. 1: *1889–1910.* 1964.

McCord, Norman. "Taff Vale Revisited," *History,* vol. 78 (1993), pp. 243–60.

Tariff Reform

Often dismissed as a mere euphemism for protection, tariff reform amounted to much more than a revival of the agitation for fair trade that had characterized the 1880s. Its emergence is conventionally dated to May 1903 when Joseph Chamberlain (1836–1914), the Unionist Colonial Secretary, called for the reevaluation of Britain's existing tariff policy, even if this meant challenging the prevailing dogma of free trade to which, it was widely believed, national prosperity was due. For the next decade, and again in the early 1920s, no issue in domestic politics would prove more controversial.

Manufacturers, especially in the iron and **steel industry,** had longed for protective tariffs against foreign competition, and to their voices were added many from the agricultural interest, which had suffered from the depressed prices and cheap imports of the preceding three decades. Ranged against them in defense of free trade were those sectors that relied on the freest exchange of raw materials or services (such as banking or the textile trades) and those individuals who feared either an unprecedented tariff war with heightened international tensions, an unwarranted extension of state interference, or an unpopular rise in the cost of living.

Yet tariff reform's controversial nature lay not just in the conflicting economic interests it galvanized, but also in its centrality as the touchstone of **Conservative Party** commitment. Chamberlain himself regarded tariff reform not as a protectionist end in itself, but as a means to reinvigorate the British polity. Accordingly, he stressed the fundamental importance of binding the Empire together through a preferential remission of duties for the colonies, conceding that to do so would elevate the price of agricultural imports (thus leading his critics to label tariffs as "food taxes"), but insisting that such transient sacrifices were essential to a constructive policy that would secure fuller employment, raise additional revenue to fund social reforms, and prompt greater Anglo-Saxon imperial solidarity in commercial and military matters. But the Prime Minister, **Arthur Balfour**, resisted Chamberlain's policies, because he feared that food duties would be electorally disastrous and that Chamberlain's avowed intention to convert the party to tariffs would shatter it, much as Sir Robert Peel's repeal of agricultural protection in 1846 had done during the 1840s. Initially, Balfour's fears were justified. A number of prominent Unionist free traders defected to the **Liberals** (including **Winston Churchill**), while even more chose to retire from politics. The party entered the 1906 election divided, with Balfour attempting to steer a middle course, endorsing only the idea of enacting tariffs as a means of retaliation designed to elicit more equitable treatment from Britain's protectionist trading partners. Not surprisingly, this compromise satisfied nobody and undoubtedly magnified the party's crushing defeat in the 1906 election.

Over the next four years, however, tariff reform grew more attractive to the Conservatives as a form of indirect taxation they could propose as an alternative to the Liberal government's measures of direct, redistributive taxation aimed directly at affluent, propertied Tory supporters. Defensive and domestic-centered, tariff reform was now shorn of the more radical, constructive, and imperial agenda that Chamberlain had originally envisioned. By 1913 Balfour's successor, **Andrew Bonar Law**, judged that other issues, such as strident opposition to Irish Home Rule, would better serve his party's defensive posture, and tariff reform was shifted to the back burner.

Back-bench sentiment in favor of tariffs persisted, however, and the issue resurfaced in the Conservative Party's program for the election of 1923. It would not be until 1932, though, in the very different climate of economic depression, that the British government finally committed itself to a full policy of tariffs.

Frans Coetzee

Bibliography
Coetzee, Frans. *For Party or Country: Nationalism and the Dilemmas of Popular Conservatism in Edwardian England.* 1990.
Semmel, Bernard. *Imperialism and Social Reform: English Social-Imperial Thought, 1895–1914.* 1960.
Sykes, Alan. *Tariff Reform in British Politics, 1903–1913.* 1979.

Tawney, R(ichard) H(enry) (1880–1962)
He may have been christened Richard Henry Tawney, but to the world he became simply "Tawney" (sometimes also "Harry" to a few intimates). He was a major social philosopher of the British Left, perhaps *the* major social philosopher, for much of the first half of the twentieth century. His writings, especially *The Acquisitive Society* (1921) and *Equality* (1931), came to exercise a profound and enduring influence, continuing long after his death.

He was born, as many others of his class and generation were, in India, but was soon returned to England for a conventionally classical education (at Rugby and Balliol). At Oxford, his own deep religious faith—he was to become a leading apostle of a social **Anglicanism**—combined with a prevailing ethic of social service to point him in the direction of both social action and social reflection. There followed a period at Toynbee Hall, the Oxford **settlement** in London's East End; a spell running a charity to provide country holidays for poor city children; a short bout of **economics** lecturing at the University of Glasgow; and (in 1908) an adult education tutorship under the joint scheme between the University of **Oxford** and the Workers' Educational Association (WEA) that was the origin of university extramural education.

This last experience was an important moment both for Tawney and for the working-class **adult education** movement. His classes (in the Staffordshire Potteries and the North) were landmarks in the history of this movement. They also turned Tawney into an economic historian, his professional discipline thereafter (his first book, *The Agrarian Problem in the Sixteenth Century* (1912), was a product of this period), but an economic historian with a clear and contemporary social purpose. It only needed a final experience, of the **First World War** trenches (he was badly, nearly fatally, wounded on the **Somme**), to give the rest of his life and work a clear pattern and direction.

There were three books, all essentially the products of the first post-First World War decade, that expressed his social philosophy and established his reputation. *The Acquisitive Society* (1921) excoriated the growth of an atomic, possessive individualism and embraced a new communalism of social purpose and responsibility. In *Religion and the Rise of Capitalism* (1926) the economic historian and Christian moralist sought to demonstrate how the loss of a moral reference for social and economic affairs had come about, combined with a passionate argument on the need for the retrieval of such a reference. Most influential of all, his *Equality* (1931) marshaled an elegantly ruthless assault on the English "religion of inequality" and its baneful consequences for social life. In its place, Tawney advanced a social philosophy of equal worth (in which equality of treatment was not to be confused with identity of treatment), which he presented as the precondition of a "common culture" of social unity and shared participation.

These books had a vast influence, not just on British socialists but on the wider currents of thought and opinion. For a generation of British socialists, those who grew up in the inter-war period and inhabited the post-1945 world, Tawney's work was the predominant philosophical influence. It represented the authentic and distinctive voice of English ethical socialism.

His influence and activity were evident in more specific and practical directions, too. Within Anglicanism it was his voice (along with that of his friend **William Temple**) that constantly sought to confront the Church with its social mission. He remained a leading spokesman for the adult education movement in general and for the Workers' Educational Association in particular. He was a prolific writer on educational issues, especially for the **Manches-**ter *Guardian*, and his prospectus for the **Labour Party** on *Secondary Education for All* (1922) decisively shaped the party's education policy. In 1919 he had represented the trade union side on the **Sankey Commission** on the **coal mining** industry, to wide acclaim, and he had a hand in many of Labour's policy statements, including a decisive hand in *Labour and the Nation* (1928).

This document is a reminder that Tawney was a resolutely party man, sometimes critical but always a loyalist as far as Labour was concerned. His political loyalties, and activities on their behalf, coexisted with his professional work as an economic historian who did pioneering studies of the sixteenth and seventeenth centuries. A chair at the **London School of Economics** in 1931 might have come sooner but for his other engagements. There was a remarkable unity to all his work, whether as economic historian, adult educator, churchman, social theorist, or party intellectual, and he remains a central reference point for the British socialist tradition.

Anthony Wright, MP

Bibliography

Terrill, Ross. *R.H. Tawney and His Times.* 1973.
Wright, Anthony. *R.H. Tawney.* 1987.

Taylor, A(lan) J(ohn) P(ercivale) (1906–1990)

A.J.P. Taylor was a historian, political commentator, and radical dissenter over five decades. A gifted journalist, he wrote for the "popular" and the "quality" **press**, appeared regularly on **television**, challenged orthodoxy, and became the "traitor within the gates." Taylor was the most controversial and widely-read English historian of his time, perhaps the only one, with the possible exception of **G.M. Trevelyan**, whose name was universally recognized.

Born in Lancashire into a family of well-to-do cotton manufacturers, Taylor was educated at **Quaker** schools and at Oriel College, **Oxford**, where he took a first-class degree and joined the **Communist Party of Great Britain**. After Oxford he learned research in diplomatic history from A.F. Pribram in Vienna, and in 1930 he was appointed as a Lecturer at the University of Manchester, where he was strongly influenced by **Lewis Namier**. He published his first studies in European diplomatic history, *The Italian Problem in European Diplomacy, 1847–1849* (1934) and *Germany's First Bid for Colonies* (1938), and began to work as a reviewer and editorial writer on the *Manchester Guardian*. Meanwhile, he left the Communist Party and became an "out-of-hand radical."

In 1938 Taylor was appointed a Fellow of Magdalen College, Oxford. It was the year of the **Munich** agreement, and he was soon speaking out against **appeasement**. Although he remained at Oxford throughout the Second World War, Taylor broadcast frequently and was employed to lecture for the Ministry of Information (MOI). However, his talks challenged government policy in the Mediterranean, for which he was criticized in the House of Commons, and MOI soon found it could do without him.

In that period, Taylor addressed himself to issues involving the war, in part as a result of his association with Slav refugees in Oxford. These included ethnic issues in Central Europe, the subject of various articles and of *The Habsburg Monarchy, 1815–1918*, published in 1941, and German aggression, treated in *The Course of German History* in 1946, the latter earning him a reputation as an anti-German. After the war Taylor expanded his research in diplomatic history and in 1954 published *The Struggle for Mastery in Europe, 1848–1918*, a masterpiece of synthetic scholarship that enhanced his reputation as a serious historian. He followed this *magnum opus* with an impressively succinct study of *Bismarck* (1955).

Never satisfied with being respectable, Taylor turned from European to English diplomacy with an eye toward exploring its relationship to populist dissent. This began with his 1956 Ford Lectures at Oxford, published as *The Troublemakers: Dissent over Foreign Policy, 1792–1939* (1958), always his "favorite brainchild." In the same year, when England became embroiled in the **Suez crisis**, Taylor took to the stump in protest, remaining there after Suez to agitate for the **Campaign for Nuclear Disarmament**. In 1956 the politically heterodox Taylor was passed over for appointment as Regius Professor of Modern History, a slight by his own university that continued to rankle, although Oxford remained his academic base until 1976, when he retired as an honorary Fellow of Magdalen.

The year 1956 began Taylor's "English Period." He started writing for the populist *Daily Express* and *Sunday Express* radical pieces usually on British political or social subjects, and in the process he formed a close friendship with the proprietor, **Lord Beaverbrook**, who became Taylor's mentor and patron.

In 1961 Taylor published *The Origins of the Second World War*, his most controversial work. In it he argued that no one and everyone was responsible for the outbreak of war in 1939, and that Adolf Hitler was "no more wicked than any other statesman." For questioning the most sacred of modern historiographical sacred cows, Taylor was soon accused of everything from mere perversity to neo-**Fascism**. Though it threatened his reputation, the book did not destroy it, and he was asked to write the twentieth-century volume in the Oxford History of England. *English History, 1914–1945* was published in 1965; an idiosyncratic account of his own time, its theme was the "rise of the people." It was his last major work of serious scholarship, enthralling but hardly judicious, his passionate involvement with his own history coupled with skepticism about the motives of politicians.

In 1967 Taylor was named Director of the Beaverbrook Library and began his biography of Beaverbrook, which appeared in 1972 to a cool critical reception. *Beaverbrook* was overly long, and its blatant hero-worship did little to enhance Taylor's scholarly reputation. Thereafter, until the debilitating illness began that presaged his death, he wrote, lectured, and published collections of his essays, remaining actively engaged with both **history** and political commentary. In addition he became something of a television celebrity, dazzling audiences with his lucid exposition of the international history of the twentieth century.

Robert Cole

Bibliography

Cole, Robert. *A.J.P. Taylor: The Traitor within the Gates*. 1993.

Sisman, Adam. *A.J.P. Taylor: A Biography*. 1994.

Taylor, A.J.P. *A Personal History*. 1983.

Wrigley, Chris. *A.J.P. Taylor: A Complete Annotated Bibliography*. 1980.

Technical Education

Controversy has surrounded technical education in Britain since the mid-nineteenth century, when its importance for economic success was first urged. At the Paris Exhibition in 1867 Britain won prizes in only ten categories of goods displayed in contrast to 100 at the Great Exhibition held in London in 1851. The first government grants for technical education in 1852 were supposed to aid local initiative rather than provide central direction, so no guidance was given about the balance between theory and practice. The institutions that made use of these Science and Art Department grants ranged from mechanics institutes, elementary and grammar schools, and teacher training colleges, to lyceums and atheneums. The variety became even wider after the passing of the Technical Instruction Act of 1889 to enable local authorities to supply or aid technical instruction from the local property taxes. They included the City and Guilds of London Institute established in 1881, **polytechnics** set up in London from 1891, and technical classes and colleges established by local authorities. Technical instruction under the 1889 act ruled out the teaching of a trade as such, though it was to involve some manual instruction as well as general principles. But in practice the emphasis was on a general and relatively abstract approach, seen as supplementing rather than mirroring practical experience in employment.

Any association of higher education, in secondary schools as well as universities, with technical education was contested. The most prestigious occupational destinations of their products were in politics, home and colonial administration, and the liberal professions. Such ends would be achieved by devotion to liberal education dominated by the classics, other literary subjects, and nonapplied sciences. The achievement of this ideal through the secondary system required a more interventionist role than the state had formerly taken. In particular local initiatives to develop a technical and vocational curriculum in the higher-grade (elementary) schools were stifled, even though they were popular locally. They were accused both of threatening "genuine" secondary education based on the liberal curriculum by deflecting middle-class children from it, and of offering working-class children an education above their station. In 1900 Sir Robert Morant, shortly to become Permanent Secretary at the Board of Education, issued guidelines constraining the development of these schools, and in 1904 he produced Regulations for Secondary Schools, which explicitly ruled out technical and vocational subjects from their curricula, though science was given a prominent place.

Nevertheless, a combination of local demand and perceived need in government for the continuing provision of technical and vocational education produced a number of developments, many of which challenged the liberal hegemony. These included central schools from 1904 and junior technical schools from 1907, and secondary modern and secondary technical schools after 1944. Central schools aimed to prepare their pupils for employment by offering them a curriculum with either an industrial or a commercial bias. Although they had the kudos of selecting their pupils, they were funded as advanced elementary schools, with inevitable consequences in terms of the quality of facilities and teaching. Junior technical schools were also of two types. They either taught specific trades such as cabinetmaking and the needle trades, or they prepared pupils to take up apprenticeships in particular industries (mainly engineering and building). Industrial training for girls in central schools was defined as domestic economy and needlework; in junior technical schools the preapprenticeship courses were entirely confined to boys. Commercial training in bookkeeping, shorthand, typing, and office work was offered to both sexes, but with subtle differences of emphasis. Commercially trained boys were expected to become salesmen and managers, whereas girls were earmarked as future shorthand-typists. After the **Education Act of 1944** the central-school tradition was absorbed into the secondary modern school with even lower status, in that these schools were no longer selective but were required to take the 70–80 percent of eleven-year-olds who had "failed" to get grammar-school places. The junior technical school was absorbed into the secondary technical school in an attempt to upgrade the trade schools. They provided general secondary education with a vocational bias, toward housecraft and commercial subjects for girls and building and engineering for boys. But the secondary technical schools lacked supporters. In 1958 only 3.7 percent of the secondary-school population attended them. From the mid-1960s they were absorbed, like the secondary modern schools, into comprehensive secondary schools, where the liberal/academic curriculum tended to prevail.

Some of the opponents of secondary technical schools believed that the education they offered was better provided after school-leaving age. From the 1920s technical colleges for adults offered nationally recognized certification, but there was deliberate avoidance of a national policy where technical colleges were concerned. There was a strong tendency for these institutions to seek higher status by departing from the practical and the applied and moving toward the abstract and the advanced. Technical colleges in the 1950s offered a wide range of courses from the most elementary to the most advanced, to both full- and part-time students. Some became Colleges of Advanced Technology, leaving local-authority control in 1962 and attaining university status in 1966; others became locally managed polytechnics in 1966 but followed the same path over the next twenty years, most becoming universities in 1992, oriented increasingly to degree-level and postgraduate work and research.

In the 1980s, in the context of a perceived skills shortage, fierce economic competition from abroad, recession, and high levels of **unemployment,** the government for the first time started to make efforts to achieve a closer rapprochement between education and employers, particularly at the secondary-school level. The Technical and Vocational Education Initiative (TVEI) and the City Technology Colleges (CTC) were attempts to address the needs of industry and to draw employers into education and education into the workplace. The TVEI, introduced in 1982, was meant to strengthen the technical and vocational content of secondary education by inviting schools to bid for resources for curriculum development. The CTCs, launched in 1986, were intended as a new sort of selective secondary school, funded by both government and private-sector sponsors, offering a broadly based secondary education with a technological element (as the secondary technical school had tried to do). But the problem of how to define and promote technical education remained. By the end of the decade official understanding of TVEI had moved away from the delineation of a specific curriculum to a more general commitment to learning experiences beyond the classroom—that is, in the world of paid work.

Thus, while there have been changes in attitudes to, as well as provision of, technical education in the twentieth century, many of the nineteenth-century problems of definition and status remain unresolved.

Penny Summerfield

Bibliography
Argyles, Michael. *South Kensington to Robbins: An Account of English Technical and Scientific Education since 1851.* 1964.
Cotgrove, Stephen F. *Technical Education and Social Change.* 1958.
McCulloch, Gary. *The Secondary Technical School: A Usable Past?* 1989.
Summerfield, Penny, and Eric J. Evans. *Technical Education and the State since 1850: Historical and Contemporary Perspectives.* 1990.

Television

British broadcasters pioneered television technology as well as the public service broadcasting model. British television, like that of other European countries, began with a public service philosophy, which later grew to encompass commercial broadcasting.

The British model, in which a public corporation is franchised by the government and funded out of users' license fees, has been widely copied. This arrangement, which initially provided the **British Broadcasting Corporation** (BBC) with autonomy over programming, developed from an earlier tradition in radio broadcasting begun by the BBC's first Director-General, **John Reith.**

The BBC began broadcasting television signals in 1936 and televised King **George VI**'s coronation the next year. Although suspended during the Second World War, television broadcasts were resumed in 1946. The BBC lost its monopoly with the creation of the Independent Television Authority in 1954 and the introduction of commercial television the following year. The legislation divided Britain into regions, with regional companies licensed to broadcast commercially supported programming within a single region. Commercial broadcasters did not compete directly with each other, as they did in the United States, but they did challenge the BBC, which quickly lost a large share of its audience to commercial television. In general, BBC programming was more conservative, often failing to attract younger viewers as readily as commercial television's faster-paced shows. In the 1960s the BBC made a concerted effort to regain some of its lost audience by producing popularly oriented series such as *Z-Cars,* which succeeded in wooing back disaffected viewers. The advent of BBC 2, the second public channel, also permitted the corporation to separate "highbrow" and arts-oriented programming from mainstream popular programming and helped noncommercial television maintain a larger share of the audience.

Beginning in the 1960s, with the dramatization of **John Galsworthy**'s *The Forsyte Saga*, the BBC acquired an international reputation for high-quality dramatic series. Many of these were produced with an eye to the international, and especially American, market. Today, many British drama series are made in conjunction either with other European broadcasters or American public television affiliates. Under **Margaret Thatcher**, the BBC was mandated to shed much of its production capacity, so that today a large proportion of BBC programming is produced by independent companies.

Commercial television has flourished, extending the number of hours broadcast daily. In 1982 a second commercial network, Channel Four, began broadcasting, its brief being to produce arts and cultural programming. Channel Four has become Britain's largest independent film producer. In 1983 American-style morning television was introduced into Britain. In recent years the number of options offered to viewers has increased with the emergence of satellite-based channels, including Sky Television and British Satellite Broadcasting. This technology, potentially providing access to signals from other European broadcasters as well as the United States, promises to alter dramatically the face of British television.

Paul Swann

Bibliography

Briggs, Asa. *History of Broadcasting in the United Kingdom.* vol. 4: *Sound and Vision.* 1979.

Burns, R.W. *British Television: The Formative Years.* 1986.

Corner, John, ed. *Popular Television in Britain.* 1991.

Davis, Anthony. *Television: The First Forty Years.* 1976.

Sendall, Bernard. *The History of Independent Television in Britain.* 4 vols. 1982–9.

Temple, William (1881–1944)

William Temple is widely regarded as Britain's greatest religious leader of the twentieth century. Rising rapidly in the **Church of England**, he was appointed a Canon of Westminster Abbey in 1919 and Bishop of Manchester in 1921. He became Archbishop of York in 1928 and of Canterbury in 1942. In these two decades he established an international reputation as a philosopher-theologian, reformer, churchman, and ecumenical leader. He was widely mourned when he died in office in 1944.

Temple was born the second son of Frederick Temple, at the time Bishop of Exeter and later also Archbishop of Canterbury (1897–1902). The paternal influence was a strong one, Temple attending Rugby School where Frederick had been headmaster (1857–69). William then attended **Oxford** where he received a first-class degree and was elected President of the Oxford Union. While at Oxford, he became an avowed socialist, which, with his Anglican commitments, established the intellectual basis for his future contribution. This was first expressed through his membership (1904) and then presidency (1908–24) of the Workers' Educational Association (WEA). To Temple, education was the means of individual cultural and spiritual emancipation. Initially, he followed an academic career, first at Queen's College, Oxford (1904–10), and then, after ordination, as headmaster of Repton School (1910–14).

His growing ecclesiastical stature was signaled by his appointment in 1914 as Rector of St. James's Piccadilly, London, and also, in 1915, as Honorary Chaplain to King **George V**. He established lasting fame when he became full-time Chairman in 1917 of the newly formed Life and Liberty Movement. Dedicated to internal church reform, it was one of the pressures that led to the creation of the Church Assembly in 1919.

After Temple served briefly as a Canon of Westminster Abbey, his growing reputation was confirmed by appointment to the Bishopric of Manchester in 1921. Here he emerged as a church leader of the first rank. Notable among his many activities was his chairmanship of the Conference on Christian Politics, Economics, and Citizenship (COPEC) in 1924, which established influential principles for the Church's social and ecumenical engagement. In the latter area he became a major figure, acting as a leader for the 1927 Lausanne World Conference on Faith and Order. He also led the Committee on Unity of the 1930 Lambeth Conference and in 1938 chaired a committee that laid the basis for the World Council of Churches. In 1942 Temple helped form the British Council of Churches and supported the unity scheme for the Church of South India finally approved just after his death.

He continued to emphasize the social relevance of Christianity. Following his work for the WEA and COPEC, he chaired the influential Pilgrim Trust inquiry on **unemployment** (*Men without Work*, 1938). His legacy for the post-war period was assured through his chairmanship of the 1940 Malvern Conference on Reconstruction and his help in passing the **Education Act of 1944** to reform secondary education.

Among his many publications are *Mens Creatrix* (1917), *Christus Veritas* (1924), and *Christianity and Social Order* (1942). It is difficult to underestimate his contribution as teacher, prophet, thinker, church leader, and man of God.

George Moyser

Bibliography

Iremonger, F.A. *William Temple, Archbishop of Canterbury*. 1948.

Kent, John. *William Temple*. 1992.

Tennis, Lawn

The exploits of Fred Perry apart, British tennis has little international success of which to boast. As in the case of soccer, Britain invented and developed a sport only to find it taken over and perfected by more skillful opponents in other countries. Though tennis has a long history, stretching back to the late Middle Ages, the version played today originated in England in the 1870s. A retired army officer, Major Wingfield, patented a game called "Sphairistike" in 1874, and from this tennis quickly emerged. In 1875 the Marylebone Cricket Club drafted rules, while in the same year tennis was included in the program of the All England Croquet Club at Wimbledon. Two years later the first Wimbledon championships were held, using the rectangular court and scoring system known today. In 1888 the Lawn Tennis Association was formed to oversee the activities of tennis clubs, which at this time were to be found almost entirely in an upper-class milieu.

Of the major British sports, tennis is the one that has remained the most socially restricted. By the early twentieth century it had become vitually synonymous with middle-class status—the popular saying "Anyone for tennis?" instantly denoting social privilege and a leisured lifestyle. This image, together with a series of financial constraints—the cost of equipment, the high ratio of land to participant, the preference for expensive grass courts— which also account for the absence of tennis in the educational curriculum outside a small group of private schools, ensured the sport's continuing exclusivity. Municipal authorities did begin making tennis courts available to the general public in the inter-war years, and since the Second World War there have been several attempts to promote it more widely, especially among the young. In spite of this, tennis is still far short of being a "national game."

Nevertheless, Britain has made one outstanding contribution to world tennis—Wimbledon. As the senior event of the international tennis calendar, Wimbledon is familiar, through **press** and **television,** to millions of people who otherwise know little of the sport. Following the first competition of 1877 (and the introduction in 1884 of one for women) Wimbledon gradually established its eminence, still under the control of the All England Club. It was not until the 1920s that the dominance of overseas players became apparent, the French star Suzanne Lenglen being the first of many. But the marginalization of British players (Perry's triumphs of 1934–6 being the outstanding exception) did nothing to affect Wimbledon's popularity. To accommodate a massive increase in interest immediately following the First World War the present stadium was opened in 1922, incorporating the famous Center Court (15,000 spectators) and the No. 1 court (5,000). Other innovations have been relatively few. Seeding (to prevent the meeting of star players in early stages of the tournament) was introduced in 1924. The "tie break" to curtail excessively long matches, arrived in the 1970s. The principal change, however, has been the recognition of professionals, a move in which the Wimbledon authorities took the lead. The first "open" Wimbledon came in 1968. By thus attracting the world's leading players the event's future as an international sporting occasion was secured, and continuing fees for television coverage have helped ensure appropriate prize money. Maria Bueno received £20 for winning the ladies' title in 1960; almost a quarter of a century later Martina Navratilova earned £90,000 for the same achievement. Wimbledon's awareness of the need to move with the times is as keen as ever.

Jeffrey Hill

Bibliography
Barrett, John. *One Hundred Wimbledon Championships: A Celebration.* 1986.
Robertson, Max. *The Encyclopedia of Tennis.* 1974.
Walker, Helen. "Lawn Tennis" in Tony Mason, ed., *Sport in Britain: A Social History.* 1989. pp. 245–75.

Territorial Army

The embarrassments of the **Boer War** at the turn of the century made military reorganization a priority for the British government. The **Liberal** Secretary for War, **R.B. Haldane**, proposed achieving greater military efficiency at reduced cost by reorganizing the **army** into a bipartite structure: Regular Army and Territorial Army. The role of the territorials would be home defense, and at the mobilization of the regulars they would also be mobilized to undergo systematic training for war. Since this reorganization would mean the abolition of the militia and volunteers, Haldane provided that the volunteers could be absorbed into the territorials, while militiamen would be urged to join a new special reserve of the regulars. Though his plan met determined and emotional opposition, Haldane was able to push through Parliament a Territorial Reserve Forces bill providing for a territorial force to serve anywhere in Britain but not abroad, under the administration, but not the command, of a country association headed by the Lords-Lieutenant. The first of April 1908 marked the official establishment of the Territorial Army. Though Haldane had wanted twenty-eight divisions, the government reduced the force to fourteen divisions with fourteen cavalry brigades and corps staff. Some volunteer units joined immediately, while seventy militia battalions went into the special reserve.

On the eve of the First World War the Territorial Army numbered 268,777 men, 85 percent of its established strength of 316,094. Provision having been made that territorials might volunteer for overseas service, by December 1914 nearly 70,000 of them were serving on the Continent. By mid-1917 more than 500,000 territorials were serving abroad, and by war's end the territorials had provided a total of twenty-four divisions for overseas service. At the beginning of 1939, with another World War threatening, the Territorial Army was at a peacetime strength of twelve infantry divisions, five antiaircraft divisions, one tank brigade and three cavalry brigades. In March Prime Minister **Neville Chamberlain**, without consulting the Chiefs of Staff, announced an immediate increase to twenty-six divisions. Called up for training in May, the territorials were merged with the Regular Army at the onset of hostilities in September. At war's end, the Territorial Army was given responsibility for the antiaircraft defense of Britain, though it embraced an airborne division as well as armor and infantry. Most of its officers and men were drawn from persons who had completed the active portion of their National Service and were now doing their reserve stint. It was not up to full strength until 1952.

With changing military technology and needs came alterations in the Territorial Army's shape and mission. Its antiaircraft role was abolished in 1955, its airborne unit disbanded but for a single brigade, its armor downgraded. Two divisions were charged with reinforcing North Atlantic Treaty Organization (NATO) troops in any European conflict. By 1960 it had been cut to 123,000 persons with a reserve to add 70,000 on mobilization. In the 1960s the Territorial Army suffered from recruiting difficulties stemming from the perceived lack of mission and training, and the Reserve Forces Act of 1966 merged it with the Army Emergency Reserve in a Territorial Auxiliary and Volunteer Reserve of 50,000 to flesh out the army for small conflicts. In 1985 a Home Service Force of 5,000 was linked to the territorials to guard important civilian and military sites.

Joseph M. McCarthy

Bibliography
Blaxland, Gregory. *The Regiments Depart: A History of the British Army, 1945–1970.* 1971.
Dennis, Peter. *The Territorial Army, 1907–1940.* 1987.
Dunlop, John K. *The Development of the British Army, 1899–1914.* 1938.
Strawson, John. *Gentlemen in Khaki: The British Army, 1890–1990.* 1989.

Terrorism

Terrorism has been primarily an Irish phenomenon in twentieth-century Britain. There was a short, ineffective campaign of indiscriminate bombing in England shortly before the Second World War; this was linked with a campaign in Northern Ireland aimed at achieving unity.

Much more serious, and much more prolonged, was the campaign that emerged from the civil rights troubles beginning in Northern Ireland in 1969.

In January 1970 the Irish Republican Army (IRA) split between the "Officials" and the "Provisionals"; the latter, cast in the mold of traditional nationalists, were determined on a military campaign to end what they saw as the British occupation of Northern Ireland and to unite the province with Eire. The military campaign began in Northern Ireland, but by 1972 it had spread to the mainland with terror bombings of military targets—notably, in that year, a bomb at the Parachute Regiment headquarters in Aldershot that killed seven and injured nineteen. In 1974 civilian targets were also attacked: Bombs in two Guildford pubs killed five and injured sixty-two, while bombs in two pubs in the city center of Birmingham killed seventeen and injured 120. Four men were convicted for the former offense and six for the latter; all were sentenced to life imprisonment, but, on appeal, the "Guildford Four" were released after fifteen years and "the Birmingham Six" after sixteen.

The terror campaign continued with some spectacular successes in the terrorists' terms, in particular the murders of **Earl Mountbatten** (1979) and of the MPs Airey Neave (1979) and Ian Gow (1990), and the bombing of the Grand Hotel in Brighton during the **Conservative Party** conference in 1984. But some of the tactics have been counterproductive, such as the attack on the Remembrance Day service at Enniskillen (1987) and the attempts in 1990 to use human bombs, compelling private individuals to drive vehicles loaded with primed explosives. In addition the terrorists themselves split; the Irish National Liberation Army broke with the Provisionals and a bloody feud followed. Nationalist terror also fostered loyalist terror: Paramilitary murder gangs of the Ulster Freedom Fighters targeted IRA sympathizers, Sinn Fein councillors, and sometimes simply **Catholics**; Catholic murder gangs responded with retaliatory killings.

While the terrorist campaign failed to force successive British governments to withdraw from Ireland it has, arguably, eroded some democratic freedoms. On the recommendation of the English judge, Lord Diplock, the "Diplock Courts" were established in 1973 enabling suspected terrorists in Northern Ireland to be tried before senior judges acting without a jury. The Prevention of Terrorism Acts (1976 and 1984) enable the **police** in Britain to detain a suspect for seven days before being charged or released.

In addition to Irish terrorism, during the 1970s and 1980s there were minor bombings and arson attacks by **Scots** and **Welsh nationalists**, and, once or twice, **Middle East** conflicts have brought another brand of terrorism to British shores, most tragically in the destruction of an American airliner over the small Scottish town of Lockerbie (December 1988). The proclamation of an IRA ceasefire in September 1994 brought to an end the worst phase of terrorism in Britain.

Clive Emsley

Bibliography

Bell, J. Bowyer. *The Secret Army: The IRA, 1916–1979*. rev. ed. 1979.
Crozier, Brian. "Ulster: Politics and Terrorism," *Conflict Studies*, vol. 36 (1978), pp. 1–20.
Lee, A. McLung. *Terrorism in Northern Ireland*. 1983.
Wilkinson, Paul, ed. *British Perspectives on Terrorism*. 1981.

Thatcher, Margaret Hilda Roberts (1925–)

During her eleven-year tenure as Prime Minister, from May 1979 to November 1990, Margaret Thatcher was the most controversial, most discussed, and perhaps most effective of Britain's post-war leaders. She was the first woman in European history to be Prime Minister, the longest continuously serving Prime Minister since 1827, and the first since then to win three successive elections without intervening loss of office.

She rejected the post-war consensus, sold most **nationalized industries** to the public, showed that direct taxation could be sharply reduced, abolished incomes policy, encouraged economic liberalism, and reduced the power of the unions. Yet in defense, social security, **health**, and education, she left matters largely as she found them, and public attitudes to social questions changed little during her premiership.

In foreign policy she maintained close relations with the United States, and especially with President Ronald Reagan. As the Cold War ended, she developed good relations with the Soviet Union. In the **Falklands War** (1982), caused by Argentine invasion, she exhibited resolve not only over a local issue, but in the wider context of the final phase of the Cold War. She presided over perhaps the last war to be fought by the United Kingdom on its own, the last to evoke intense **patriotism**, and the first **television** war. Her greatest failure lay in her relations with the **European Community**, where gradual erosion of national sovereignty occurred against her will.

Thatcher was the daughter of an ex-Liberal **Methodist** lay preacher, a grocer who was Mayor of the small Midlands town of Grantham. Ambitious as a schoolgirl, she went from local day school to **Oxford**, where she studied **chemistry**. Excluded from speaking in the all-male Oxford Union debates, she went unnoticed at university, becoming a research chemist (1947–51) until she married fellow-Methodist Denis Thatcher, by whom she had twins (1954).

After qualifying as a lawyer, she was elected in 1959 as **Conservative** MP for the North London constituency of Finchley, which she never lost. Soon promoted to a minor post (October 1961), she was, successively, a party spokesman on pensions, housing, energy, transport, education, and environment (1961–70), entering the Shadow Cabinet in 1967. However, when appointed Education Minister (1970–4) in **Edward Heath**'s Cabinet, she was almost unknown to the public. On resigning in 1990, she had had twenty-nine years of continuous official responsibility, twenty-three of them at the **Cabinet** level.

As Education Minister, she espoused policies on higher public spending and the creation of comprehensive schools that reflected the progressive orthodoxy of the day. A minor transfer of funds from school milk to science created a furor about "Thatcher the milk-snatcher," so that when Heath's government fell, Thatcher appeared unpopular as well as unimportant. A second Conservative election defeat in 1974 caused a leadership election in which she stood, for want of anyone else, as the nominee of a backbenchers' revolt. Her victory (1975), by 130 votes to 119, was less a vote for her than a vote for removing Heath. Of the Shadow Cabinet, all but one opposed her.

Thus, as opposition leader (1975–9) Thatcher saw herself as leader on sufferance. At first, she had no definite following or policies. She did not reconstruct the front bench with her own supporters. Nevertheless, by 1979 she had marginalized Heath, prevented Scottish devolu-

tion, imbued an intellectual "New Right," whose role is highly controversial, with a sense of her leadership as a mission, and defeated the Labour government of **James Callaghan** first in Parliament, then at the polls.

The 1979 election saw the largest swing between one major party and another since the Second World War, and the highest Conservative lead in votes cast since 1935. Yet the Conservative share of the vote was the lowest of any winner since 1922, and Thatcher was personally less popular than Callaghan. This showed how much **Thatcherism** depended on a divided opposition.

Thatcher's first year lacked sureness of touch, with the economy not under control, until monetarism, involving hitherto unthinkable levels of **unemployment**, became a central issue in 1980. Politically, this was the first episode to publicize Thatcher's will to succeed at all costs. The most conspicuous single episode was the 1981 budget, which, contrary to Keynesian orthodoxy, raised taxes during a recession and was denounced by 364 economists in a letter to *The Times*. In fact a tighter tax policy was accompanied by an easier monetary policy, the two together producing a sharp fall in inflation (from 21.8 percent in April 1980 to 3.7 percent in June 1983, the lowest for fifteen years) and a mild economic recovery prior to the 1983 election.

In 1980–1 the picture was grim, with antipolice **urban riots**, hunger strikes by Irish Republican Army (IRA) prisoners (March-August 1981), and unemployment reaching 3 million. Yet Thatcher gained some ground politically, winning control of the Cabinet by dropping five dissenting colleagues.

In the Falklands War, Thatcher gained greatly in stature, her popularity briefly rising to 80 percent. She succeeded in ensuring a national consensus, unlike over Suez in 1956. Within the small War Cabinet, she is thought to have provided the necessary political backing for the aims of the armed forces and to have recognized that a compromise with Argentina was unattainable. The extent to which the "Falklands factor" affected the 1983 election is highly disputed, the poor state of Labour, the improving economy, and the division between the opposition parties being also important.

Thatcher's second Parliament (1983–7) lacked a legislative program. Instead, privatization became an unexpected success, decisively changing the balance between the public and private sectors. Dominating all else, however, were two political dramas: the **miners' strike** (10 March 1984–5 March 1985) and the unrelated Westland affair.

The coal strike changed the structure of British politics. Faced with a militant leader, Arthur Scargill, who had already done much to destroy one Conservative government, Thatcher had little choice but to resist. Preparations were good; there were no power cuts. Neither the long struggle nor the final victory brought electoral advantage, for the middle class did not rally in defense of stability. As with the Falklands, Thatcher was extremely lucky to win, and win unconditionally; only Scargill's intransigence saved her from a disconcerting compromise.

In the midst of this episode, an IRA bomb exploded (12 October 1984) at the Grand Hotel, Brighton, during the Conservative conference, killing five people and injuring thirty-two. Thatcher escaped narrowly and by chance, but carried on undeterred the next day at the conference.

The other critical event of Thatcher's second Parliament was the resignation (9 January 1986) of Defense Secretary Michael Heseltine, following a prolonged dispute over the future of the Westland helicopter firm. The resignation itself was not damaging; it was the subsequent escalation over secondary points that made the question of Thatcher's allegedly presidential style of government a central issue.

Not until late summer 1986 did it become clear that the Westland affair had changed nothing. Thereafter, with good economic news, falling unemployment, and a cut in the income tax, Thatcher was unassailable, as the June 1987 general election indicated. The Conservative share of the vote, 42.3 percent, was almost exactly the same as in 1983. In other ways, the election was traumatic, as that of 1983 had not been. It showed the Conservatives virtually eliminated in the major cities, and Labour virtually eliminated in the South.

The "British economic miracle" of 1987–8 appeared at the time to be Thatcher's crowning glory and a matter for national pride. The budget of spring 1988 reflected this, with higher-rate income taxes cut dramatically to 40 percent, the lowest top rate in Europe, combined with increased public spending and a public-sector surplus. Yet within two years this winner of three elections had gone, for four reasons: the unpopularity of the poll tax, the inevitable

downturn in the economic cycle, her resistance to closer links with the European Community (EC), and less support from senior colleagues.

Nothing has aroused more bitter opposition in post-war Britain than the poll tax, a direct result of Thatcher's personal commitment to abolishing property-based rates. The principle of the poll tax, that each adult should pay the same for the same local services, was widely seen as unjust. In addition, local authorities used the change as a smokescreen for an exceptional spurt in spending, and the Conservative Party conference insisted on the poll tax being implemented in one year instead of being phased in gradually over four years as planned.

The European issue concerned fewer people but in higher places. Since 1985 the EC had regained momentum. In a famous speech at Bruges (20 September 1988) Thatcher declared her wholehearted opposition to any diminution of U.K. sovereignty, thus placing herself in conflict with a tacit coalition of business, Labour, the media, much of her party and Cabinet, and the general trend of articulate public opinion. After Bruges, Europeanism was a particularly effective form of anti-Thatcherism.

Despite all of this, Thatcher's policies showed continuing confidence; indeed, it was perhaps only in her third Parliament that one could truly speak of a coherent **Thatcherism** not confined to narrowly economic issues. Thus the 1988 Education Reform Act, introducing a national curriculum, and changes in the **National Health Service** in 1989 led to difficulties with the teachers and the doctors.

In 1989, and still more in 1990, inflation reappeared, and with it high interest rates. The year 1990 saw Thatcher an isolated figure, facing a newly credible **Labour Party**, at issue with a pro-European consensus, associated with high mortgages, and without a natural constituency, even her claim to be the leader who kept inflation down no longer holding good. In London, the riots (31 March 1990) against the poll tax were the worst since 1886, with 339 arrests.

Thatcher's downfall was dramatic. Under party rules, the leadership may be contested annually. Thatcher was unchallenged until 1989, when a back-bench candidate lost by a vote of 314 to 33. In November 1990, after a sensational attack on Thatcher by her closest former colleague, Geoffrey Howe, Michael Heseltine stood, and although he lost in the first ballot by a vote of 204 to 152, under party rules, Thatcher was four votes short of the majority required for outright victory in the first round.

Thatcher, then in Paris, announced her intention to fight on, but on returning to London and meeting Cabinet ministers individually, she decided under some pressure to resign once a new leader was elected. John Major, the candidate hailed by Thatcher as her natural heir, won the second round (with 185 votes, against Thatcher's 204 in the first round). Her departure was followed by a temporary sharp rise in Conservative support, thus seeming to justify her opponents. In 1992 Margaret Thatcher accepted a life peerage and took her seat in the House of Lords as Baroness Thatcher of Kesteven.

Her impact on British life remains a matter of controversy. Some would argue that she changed the way the country was run; others, that she changed the way people thought. Both views stress her achievement. Another, more skeptical school asserts that the United Kingdom remained a typical West European state in its pattern of social security, health, education, and taxation. Skeptics would also cite poll evidence showing that Thatcher had not changed social attitudes, as proof of the persistence of the post-war consensus.

In some areas, she redrew the map. The removal of trade unionism from its place at the heart of government was not only her greatest feat, but the greatest change in the structure of politics since 1940. It cannot be said that it would have occurred anyway. Privatization folded back the frontiers of the state to a quite unexpected extent, while introducing, again unexpectedly, a much higher degree of regulation in the public interest. Her liberalization of the economy and rejection of incomes policy decisively rejected the policy consensus of the 1970s and 1980s. Thatcher demonstrated that mass unemployment did not spell political disaster. She also showed, perhaps for the first time since Gladstone, that highly visible cuts in direct taxation were possible. In both cases, she overthrew central assumptions of post-war politics.

Thatcher rose to the top despite being a woman, being of modest social origin, being a scientist, and not being good with words. In power, she was rarely popular with the public or much of her party. She owed her two greatest successes, the Falklands War and the coal strike, to the folly of her opponents. Her most serious opponents were extra-parliamentary:

the trade unions, the media, the churches, the arts world, the intelligentsia and the educational establishment, the public-sector payroll vote, parts of the **civil service** (after 1983), the doctors and lawyers (intermittently), the pro-European consensus of the later 1980s, a pervasive sense of social guilt among the gently bred, and simple inertia. No previous Conservative leader had encountered such strong middle-class opposition.

John Vincent

Bibliography

Jenkins, Peter. *Mrs. Thatcher's Revolution.* 1987.

Young, Hugo. *The Iron Lady: A Biography of Margaret Thatcher.* 1989.

Young, Hugo, and Anne Sloman. *The Thatcher Phenomenon.* 1986.

Thatcherism

British politics in the 1980s were dominated by the **Conservative Party** and by its leader, **Margaret Thatcher**, Prime Minister from 1979 to 1990. She established a rare personal ascendancy over her party and in some ways over the nation—although it should be remembered that in an era in which Britain's two-party system fragmented, her governments never rested on as much as 50 percent of the votes cast. Thatcher combined a forceful style of leadership with an eclectic set of values hard to locate within any one of Britain's main political traditions; hence the use of "Thatcherism" to denote the ideas and approach to government that she represented.

It is true that in the 1980s many other liberal democracies shifted rightward as governments tried to defeat inflation, control public spending, and promote economic growth, and as disillusionment with state power was matched by a resurgent faith in markets. Within that context, however, Thatcherism was a distinctive blend of ideas and policies. It is variously seen as a break with the pragmatism of modern British Conservatism, as a radical rejection of the bipartisan foundations of post-1945 politics, and as an approach to politics founded on Thatcher's confrontational, assertive temperament.

By the usually undoctrinaire standards of British Conservatism, Thatcherism was an intensely ideological movement. It was founded upon a belief in the virtues of economic markets and a distrust of managed economies, public ownership, and the **welfare state**. Few British institutions were to escape its reformist ambitions, while Thatcher and her supporters envisaged a change in cultural values, hoping to create a more self-reliant, entrepreneurial spirit. Thatcherism rejected basic elements of the bipartisan and elite consensus that had, since 1945, sustained a commitment to a mixed economy of private and public ownership, the maintenance of full employment, and the comprehensive provision of welfare services as a matter of right. Government was regarded as a positive force, able effectively to intervene in the economy and to reconcile competing social interests without compromising its own authority.

By the late 1970s this consensus was in tatters. A mediocre long-term economic performance had further degenerated. Industry seemed sluggish and uncompetitive, labor relations disastrous, demands on government greater than could be met. Thatcherism claimed to offer an alternative. Thatcher's rise to power was not initially seen as an ideological crusade; her election as party leader in 1975 was more a rejection of her predecessor, **Edward Heath**, than an endorsement of radical change. She had, however, given some signs of her distinctive outlook, and by 1979 the main outlines were in place. Although described by many commentators as "instinctive," her beliefs, which sometimes seemed at odds with one another, and sometimes gave way in the face of party or popular resistance, were nonetheless an animating force. Some were bolstered by the arguments of neo-classical economists such as F.A. von Hayek or of monetarists such as Milton Friedman. These and other intellectual strands were woven together in the institutions of a British "New Right"—a network of policy institutes in which long-term dissenters from the old consensus were joined by zealous converts.

Thatcher had little sympathy with traditional conservative views of society as an organic, interdependent (if also hierarchical) entity. Her individualist stress on personal freedom and choice sustained her faith in markets, hostility to labor unions, and distrust of government as an instrument of economic planning or social engineering. Her belief in the "Victorian values" of self-help, thrift, and hard work underpinned her critique of the welfare state, which she saw as not only impossibly costly and inefficient but as encouraging dependence and passivity. She was, perhaps, an economic liberal and social conservative, whose individualism coexisted with a conventional Tory stress on law and order and traditional moral values, and certainly did not extend to tolerance for such causes as **feminism** or **homosexual** rights.

Thatcherism's economic strategy began with a strong commitment to monetarist policy, enthusiastically inherited from the preceding Labour government, as the main weapon against inflation—at a price of **unemployment** levels not seen since the 1930s. The monetarist experiment fell by the wayside in the early 1980s, although the tolerance for high unemployment did not. Much of inherited economic policy was swept aside. The Thatcher governments abandoned exchange controls, prices and incomes policies, subsidies for weak companies, large state investment programs, and regional development projects. A tough stance on public-sector strikes (notably the **miners' strike** of 1984–5) was combined with a careful, incremental legislative approach to shifting the balance of power between unions and management, and with a dismantling of machinery that had previously given union leaders a voice in many policy areas. The return of **nationalized industries** to the private sector redrew the boundaries of the economy and was increasingly seen to have an electoral by-product. The sale of shares linked with the sale of **council housing** to occupiers enlarged the social groups that, Thatcherites assumed, would adopt a more thoroughly middle-class aversion to socialism.

In social policy areas Thatcherism did not achieve the aims of its most devoted advocates, yet attracted great hostility from the other political parties. The welfare state was not subject to wholesale demolition but underwent numerous changes that were widely—but not universally—seen as diminishing its scope, reducing its standards of provision, and in such areas as health care and education as widening the gap between public and private services.

Thatcherism arguably included a distinctive approach to foreign affairs, although given Thatcher's strength of will and her supporters' primarily domestic concerns, this aspect is perhaps best seen in personal terms. It is questionable whether another Prime Minister would have undertaken the **Falklands War** or displayed the same mixture of aggression and skepticism toward the **European Community** (EC). Thatcher was deeply attached to British sovereignty, although this did not prevent her from signing the Single European Act in 1987, which propelled Britain further along the path to a more integrated Europe. She was more at home sustaining Britain's relationship with the United States, not least because she was more ideologically in step with President Ronald Reagan than with the social democrats whom she saw as dominating the EC.

The effects of Thatcherism are hotly disputed. In at least two main areas it cannot be judged a success on its own terms. Government expenditure as a proportion of the national product was not significantly reduced, although the burden of taxation was redistributed by a greater reliance on indirect taxation and less-progressive direct taxes. The state of the British economy in the early 1990s does not suggest an economic miracle: Many commentators believe that the Thatcher governments allowed the nation's manufacturing base to decline, showing an excessive faith in "postindustrial" sources of wealth while underinvesting in education and training. The suggestion that society became more materialist and selfish during the 1980s must be balanced against the failure of Thatcherism to attract a majority of votes, in an electoral system producing exaggerated Parliament majorities, and against a striking consistency of opinion poll evidence on such issues as public health care.

Although her own party turned against her increasingly idiosyncratic leadership in 1990, and the government led by John Major often provoked her private anger and public criticism, it continued to operate largely within the parameters of Thatcherism. Whatever its particular successes and failures, Thatcherism profoundly altered the direction of contemporary British politics.

Steven Reilly

Bibliography

Jenkins, Peter. *Mrs. Thatcher's Revolution.* 1987.

Kavanagh, Dennis. *Thatcherism and British Politics: The Age of Consensus?* 1987.

Riddell, Peter. *The Thatcher Decade: How Britain Has Changed during the 1980s.* 1989.

Skidelsky, Robert, ed. *Thatcherism.* 1988.

Theater Management and Ownership

Most British theaters were in individual or family ownership until, during the 1870s, specula-tive companies began to emerge to run single theaters or circuits. Investors with capital in hand met the need to spread the risks involved in the building of large new playhouses and to comply with more stringent safety requirements in the old.

By the end of the nineteenth century managers of the prestigious theaters of London's West End were catering largely to the respectable, wealthier sections of society, eliminating the cheap pit section of the house in favor of more-expensive stalls seats, discouraging other than formal attire, limiting **advertising** to the "quality" **press**, and opening booking offices only during the daytime, when ordinary people were at work. The plays presented tended to have high initial production costs for scenery and costume, but, with a small operating cost, a long run could produce considerable profits.

By contrast, London suburban and provincial managers, though often presenting the same plays as in the West End, needed to fill theaters that often seated over 2,000, and so retained lower admission prices and a more populist policy. Increasingly, such theaters became grouped into regional or national circuits, often touring the same play in many venues, in some cases for years after its initial London run; and any independent productions were largely imitative of the West End style. Such theaters were most successful in expanding industrial cities such as Liverpool, Manchester, and Leeds—audiences from the surrounding countryside being encouraged to make use of the new public transport to visit these cities, as tours to smaller towns had become uneconomic.

In 1908 was formed the Society of West End Theatre Managers (SWET), whose members, including the Moss, Stoll, and Tennant managements still active today, owned or leased not only most West End theaters but also many of the venues on the regional touring circuits. By keeping rental costs at artificially high levels, and so discouraging nonmember managements from developing their own productions, they succeeded in controlling and standardizing the quality and format of plays in most British theaters.

Also in 1908 Annie Horniman opened the first theater, the Gaiety in Manchester, to develop a modern repertory theater system, whereby a permanent company of actors performed a diverse range of plays for one or two weeks only, primarily for local audiences. Such "reps" opened in most major towns until, by the beginning of the Second World War, there were approximately fifty such theaters, and by 1950 over 400.

An entertainment tax on theater tickets was introduced in 1916, initially to support the war effort but retained until the late 1950s, making cheap theater tickets artificially higher in price than in the highly competitive cinema. Additionally, the ever more elaborate sets required for London productions and their subsequent tours led West End managers to seek investment from independent backers, or "angels," leading to a policy of "safe" productions calculated to provide an early return on capital invested. Costs were also increased by the success of Equity, the actors' union, in securing a minimum wage for its members.

By 1940 approximately 200 theaters were owned and run by local authorities, a movement given impetus by the authorization after the Second World War of a sixpenny tax rate for arts purposes and also by the emergence of the **Arts Council of Great Britain** as the body responsible for allocating state subsidy.

A period of economic growth in the 1950s and 1960s saw the planning and opening of many new civic venues, better equipped though smaller in size than the old circuit theaters, which, if not already converted into cinemas, were increasingly falling victim to office or supermarket development. By 1992 fourteen large regional theaters remained as "receiving houses" for touring productions, against thirty-three regional theaters sustaining part of their program with a repertory company. In addition to these there were at least 700 small-scale municipal theaters and halls used to receive tours and also as the main venues for fringe and amateur productions.

Of the thirty active West End theaters remaining in London by the mid-1990s, the majority were owned by large entertainment companies such as Maybox and the Stoll-Moss combination, with a few in the hands of private individuals. A recent phenomenon in commercial management and ownership, made possible by the huge profits derived from large-scale musicals such as *Cats* and *Les Miserables*, has seen their producers, Cameron Mackintosh and **Andrew Lloyd Webber**, purchase the theaters that house their shows.

The Arts Council takes responsibility for funding Britain's two institutional companies, the Royal **National Theatre** and the **Royal Shakespeare Company**. A further significant development since the 1960s—although anticipated by the "little theater" movement that flourished in the inter-war years—has been the growth in the number of smaller, fringe venues, 250 of which, in London, are owned by breweries, clubs, local councils, and small charitable bodies.

Gerald Lidstone

Bibliography
Lewis, Justin. *Art, Culture, and Enterprise: The Politics of Art and the Cultural Industries.* 1990.
Myerscough, John. *The Economic Importance of the Arts in Britain.* 1988.
Pick, John. *Managing the Arts? The British Experience.* 1986.
———. *The Theatre Industry.* 1985.

Thomas, Dylan Marlais (1914–1953)
A writer whose work ranged from obscure quasi-religious poetry to comic essays, plays, and short stories, Dylan Thomas was born and brought up in Swansea, in Wales, and was educated at the Swansea Grammar School. He was an inattentive student, but his literary talent appeared early as he took part in school publications and dramatic performances. After leaving school in 1931, Thomas worked as a reporter on a local newspaper for about a year and a half and moved to London toward the end of 1934.

He had begun writing poetry when he was fifteen, preserving his poems in a series of notebooks. His first publications were a version of "And death shall have no dominion," which appeared in the London magazine, *New English Weekly,* in May 1933 and some poems in the Poet's Corner column of the *Sunday Referee.* But his poetic career had its real start in 1934 when the *Sunday Referee* awarded Thomas its semiannual book prize, which meant the publication of a book of verse. Despite the obscurity of this first volume, *Eighteen Poems,* it was favorably received. Apparently, the reviewers could not miss the poetic authority the poems projected, even if their meanings were not clear. Many of the poems came from Thomas' notebooks, and for some years afterward Thomas would continue to draw material for his books from poems he had written between the ages of fifteen and nineteen.

In 1933 he began to exchange letters with Pamela Hansford Johnson, herself a young poet, who had written to him after reading one of his poems. The two met, became lovers, and spoke of marriage, but Thomas' drunkenness, poverty, and bohemian life made it impossible. He moved to London toward the end of 1934 and survived there on very little money, bedding down with any friend who would take him in, spending much time in bars, and incidentally meeting London literary figures.

Thomas continued to publish poems and book reviews in periodicals, and in September 1936 a second collection, *Twenty-Five Poems*, appeared. He had gained the influential poet Edith Sitwell as an advocate, and her enthusiastic review of this volume made it a great success. By this time, Thomas' poetry had made a strong impression on the literary community, in spite of its obscurity and unfashionable romanticism.

In July 1937 Thomas married Caitlin Macnamara, and the couple, after living with others for time, took a cottage in Laugharne, the Welsh village that was eventually to be their permanent home. In the first years of his marriage Thomas had no regular source of income and no settled home, and he struggled to live on the poems, short stories, and book reviews he published and on what he could borrow from friends and relatives.

The two books Thomas produced during this period earned little because the outbreak of the Second World War interfered with their sales. *The Map of Love* (1939), a collection of material that had been appearing in **periodicals**, contained some of his best-known poems, including "After the Funeral," and seven fantastic short stories with surrealistic overtones. The stories of *Portrait of the Artist as a Young Dog* (1940), on the other hand, are well controlled, realistic narratives set in Swansea and the nearby countryside. Thomas next attempted, but never finished, a full-length comic novel, *Adventures in the Skin Trade*, published posthumously in 1955.

He was rejected for military service on medical grounds, and he and Caitlin continued to move about in the turmoil of wartime England and Wales, partly in order to avoid creditors. In 1941, however, he obtained employment as a scriptwriter for a cinema company, and in the following years he wrote a number of dramatic and **documentary films**. The best of the dramatic films, *The Doctor and the Devils*, was the only one actually produced, but not until 1985, long after Thomas' death. Thomas had occasionally spoken on the Third Programme of the **British Broadcasting Corporation** (BBC) since 1937, and during the war he began to work regularly as a broadcaster and to write his own scripts. Sketches and essays on poetry from these broadcasts were published posthumously in 1954 under the title *Quite Early One Morning*. The radio and cinema work produced a comfortable income, but Thomas, unable to keep up with his expenses, was invariably in debt.

The war years were a productive time for Thomas. In spite of the hack work he had to do and the confusion of the times, he published two books that contain the bulk of his mature poetry, *New Verse* (1943) and *Deaths and Entrances* (1946). In 1949, after a friend bought him the Boat House on the bank of the river Towy that has since become a Thomas memorial, he moved back to Laugharne with his family, which now included two children, with a third soon expected. By this time Thomas had become well known in America as well as in Britain, and in 1950 he was invited to go to the United States to do a well-paid reading tour. In the following years, he undertook four of these American tours, giving dozens of performances, usually at colleges, and impressing his audiences with his sonorous reading style. But he also became drunk, misbehaved on social occasions, had affairs with several women, and gained a reputation as an amusingly disreputable figure.

These tours were intended to earn money, but Thomas, as usual, spent what he earned and was still in debt, and his relations with Caitlin, always difficult, deteriorated. He was still writing, but America tempted him as an escape from both work and home life in Wales as well as a way of earning money.

During these last years Thomas was in poor health and his drinking increased. But in spite of these handicaps and his strenuous tours, his radio play, *Under Milk Wood*, gradually came into shape and had a first reading with a full cast, with Thomas as one of its voices, in New York in the spring of 1953. When he came back to New York later in the year, he began to drink and to exhibit signs of mental disturbance. He fulfilled a few engagements and saw friends, but then, after drinking heavily, he collapsed, fell into a coma, and died on 9 November 1953.

Thomas' most popular and accessible work is *Under Milk Wood*. However, he is best represented by the body of verse in his *Collected*

Poems, 1934–1952 (1952). These poems, densely packed with verbal ingenuities and personal mysticism, anticipated a brief mid-century neo-romantic revival in English poetry and are among the most important lyric poems of the century.

Jacob Korg

Bibliography

Ferris, Paul. *Dylan Thomas: A Biography*. 1977.

Fitzgibbon, Constantine. *The Life of Dylan Thomas*. 1965.

Maud, Ralph N. *Entrances to Dylan Thomas' Poetry*. 1963

Moynihan, William T. *The Craft and Art of Dylan Thomas*. 1966.

Rolph, J. Alexander. *Dylan Thomas: A Bibliography*. 1956.

Thomas, James Henry ("Jimmy") (1874–1949)

Jimmy Thomas was for long a very bright star in Labour's firmament. He was the dominant figure in the National Union of Railwaymen (NUR) as its General Secretary (1916–31), a major moderate member of the General Council of the **Trades Union Congress** (TUC) in the 1920s, and at the forefront of the Parliamentary **Labour Party** from 1914 until 1930, holding major office in the 1924 and 1929–31 Labour governments and subsequently in the 1931–6 National governments.

Thomas had a hard upbringing in Newport. The illegitimate son of a domestic servant, he was raised by his widowed grandmother, a washerwoman. Leaving school at age twelve, he was employed in a series of unskilled jobs, culminating, at fifteen, in being an engine cleaner for the Great Western Railway. From this he graduated to engine driver, only leaving shunting in the freight yards in early 1906 when he became a full-time trade union official.

Thomas' political impact stemmed from his leadership of a major trade union. He had risen fast: From being elected a delegate to its 1898 Congress, he was President in 1904–6, Organizing Secretary in 1906–10, and Assistant General Secretary in 1910–16 before winning the post of General Secretary by a three-to-one majority. The NUR grew rapidly during the **First World War**, its membership rising by 80 percent and its funds by 150 percent between 1913 and 1919. From 1914 the NUR's potential industrial strength had been enhanced by an alliance with the **miners** and transport workers. In the turbulent post-war years this Triple Industrial Alliance posed a challenge to the government, with clashes threatened or occurring over these unions' various demands, which ranged from wage increases to **nationalization**. Though Thomas and the NUR took on the government in the national rail strike in the fall of 1919, he was generally seen as a figure urging compromise and moderation. He was vilified by the Left when the NUR and the transport workers declined to provide sympathy strikes for locked-out miners in 1921 and when the TUC leadership called off the 1926 **General Strike**.

Thomas was a Labour councillor in Swindon (1901–6) and MP for Derby (1910–36), both railway towns. In 1916 he declined office under **David Lloyd George**. In **Ramsay MacDonald's** Labour governments he was Colonial Secretary (1924), Lord Privy Seal (1929–30) and Dominions Secretary (1930–1). His unsuccessful attempts to grapple with mass **unemployment** in 1929–30 undermined his reputation and ended talk of him as a likely successor to MacDonald. His links with the labor movement ended when he joined MacDonald in the National governments, serving again in the Colonial and Dominion Offices. His career ended ignominiously after an inquiry into a budget leak in 1936.

Thomas was a colorful personality who often outraged the Left by his willingness to make secret deals and to fraternize with opponents. Yet as a union leader he took great pains to represent individual union members at tribunals, and he frequently emerged from collective bargaining with substantial gains. Politically, he was often astute and as a speaker frequently won over hostile audiences by his personality, rhetoric, and considerable wit.

C.J. Wrigley

Bibliography

Bagwell, Philip S. *The Railwaymen: The History of the National Union of Railwaymen*. 1963.

Blaxland, Gregory. *J.H. Thomas: A Life for Unity*. 1964.

Thomas, James H. *My Story*. 1937.

Thompson, E(dward) P(almer) (1924–1993)

E.P. Thompson, English historian and radical, ranks as one of the great historians of the twentieth century, and his book *The Making of the English Working Class* (1963) is arguably the most influential work of social history ever written. It has informed and inspired the labors of a generation and more of social historians not only in Britain, but around the world, perhaps most especially in the United States. Thompson provided a poetic manifesto for radical historians to pursue the recovery of the lives and agencies of the laboring classes and the oppressed.

Thompson was born 3 February 1924, the second son of Edward John and Theodosia Jessup Thompson, who had been **Methodist** educational missionaries in India. Raised near Oxford, the younger Edward went to **Cambridge** to study literature but eventually switched to **history**. At this time he also joined the **Communist Party of Great Britain**. Like most of his generation, Thompson saw his studies interrupted by the **Second World War**. Commissioned an officer, he was given command of a tank unit and served in Italy.

Following the war, Thompson returned to Cambridge where he met his wife and fellow historian-to-be, Dorothy Sale. Completing their undergraduate degrees in 1946, they went with other young volunteers to Yugoslavia to work on the building of a railway. Returning to England, Thompson was appointed an **adult education** lecturer in the Leeds University Extramural Department. He and Dorothy remained active in both the Communist Party and the Communist Party Historians' Group, which included Christopher Hill, Eric Hobsbawm, John Saville, Victor Kiernan, and George Rudé, who, with Thompson, were the founding figures of the British Marxist historical tradition and the approach to the past known as "history from the bottom up." An important project of the group was the creation of the journal *Past and Present*, on whose editorial board Thompson later served for many years. His own writings of the time include his first book, *William Morris: Romantic to Revolutionary* (1955).

In 1956 Thompson left the party—as did many of his historian comrades—in protest against the Soviet invasion of Hungary. Still, he remained a committed and engaged democratic socialist and a founding figure of the early British New Left and the journals *New Reasoner* and *New Left Review*. Also, he became energetically involved with the **Campaign for Nuclear Disarmament** (CND).

The publication of *The Making of the English Working Class* led to Thompson joining the faculty of the newly established University of Warwick as Reader in the Center for Social History in 1968. His scholarly investigations turned to eighteenth-century English class relations and struggles, especially aspects of **popular culture, crime**, and the law. These studies significantly revised historical understanding of modes of power and authority and rebellion and resistance and resulted in the publication in 1975 of *Whigs and Hunters* and, with his students (British and North American), *Albion's Fatal Tree*—plus a remarkable set of articles only recently published as *Customs in Common* (1992). Also, Thompson continued to be engaged as a public intellectual, as evidenced in such works as *May Day Manifesto 1968* (1968) and *Warwick University Ltd.* (1970).

Thompson left Warwick in the mid-1970s to write full-time; however, during the next fifteen years he took up visiting professorships at Brown University and Rutgers University in the United States, and at Queen's University in Canada. Among his writings of the late 1970s was *The Poverty of Theory* (1978), a powerful defense of the historical discipline and of human agency in the making of history against the claims of French structuralist philosophers.

Increasingly, Thompson's historical imagination and commitments propelled him into full-time political labors. Concerned about what he recognized to be threats to the rights and liberties of "free-born Britons," he directed his broadsides and public speeches at the power and abuses of the British state and Establishment in *Writing by Candlelight* (1980) and *Beyond the Cold War* (1982). And, in the face of the "Second Cold War" of the 1980s, Thompson penned the pamphlet *Protest and Survive*, which mobilized hundreds of thousands to the cause of nuclear disarmament, and joined with other peace activists to establish END (European Nuclear Disarmament). To the lament of many academics, he put aside his historical scholarship for almost a decade, though he did find time to write a satirical work of science fiction, *The Sykaos Papers* (1988).

With the end of the Cold War, Thompson was able to return to historical study. Although he suffered a series of debilitating illnesses he continued his scholarly output. In addition to putting in order the eighteenth-century collection, *Customs in Common*, and writing *Alien Homage: Edward Thompson and*

Rabindranath Tagore (1993) about his father, Thompson completed his long-promised book on the romantic poets, *Witness against the Beast: William Blake and the Moral Law* (1993), and prepared another collection of historical essays, which he delivered to the publishers just weeks before his death. He died on 28 August 1993 at his home Wick Episcopi, for many years a gathering place for historians and writers from around the globe.

Harvey J. Kaye

Bibliography
Bess, Michael D. *Realism, Utopia, and the Mushroom Cloud: Four Activist Intellectuals and Their Strategies for Peace, 1945–1989.* 1993.
Kaye, Harvey J. *The British Marxist Historians.* 1984.
Kaye, Harvey J., and Keith McClelland. *E.P Thompson: Critical Perspectives.* 1989.
Palmer, Bryan D. *The Making of E.P. Thompson: Marxism, Humanism, and History.* 1981.

Also see Marxist Historians

Times, The

The Times is Britain's oldest surviving daily newspaper and, certainly from the Victorian period to the 1970s, remained the country's primary journal of record. It also attained a reputation for independent, intelligent, and informed opinion, expressed through its famous editorials, or "leaders," that has probably never been rivaled.

John Walter founded the *Daily Universal Register* in 1785, changing the name of the paper to *The Times* three years later. However, the prosperity and reputation of the paper were only secured by his son, John Walter II. It was he who appointed Thomas Barnes as editor in 1817, and Barnes and Walter succeeded in establishing *The Times* as a paper of "independent" conviction, not beholden to any party or government. Barnes was succeeded by the other great Victorian editor of *The Times*, John Delane, in 1841. Under Delane, who served as editor until 1877, the influence and prestige of the paper reached its zenith.

After the death of Delane in 1877, a series of editors maintained the paper's reputation, although increasing competition from a new generation of alternative newspapers meant that *The Times* lost its unchallenged position in the marketplace. Increasing financial losses forced the Walter family to sell the paper to **Lord Northcliffe** in 1908 (although the Walter family retained a minority shareholding in the paper until the 1960s). Northcliffe, founder of the *Daily Mail* in 1896, brought a somewhat unsavory reputation as the creator of the "yellow press" to *The Times*, which provoked a certain amount of anxiety among some of the staff. However, the character of the paper survived Northcliffe and contributed significantly to the course of British politics during the **First World War**, playing an important role in the political process the led to **H.H. Asquith** being replaced by **David Lloyd George** as Prime Minister in 1916. On Northcliffe's death in 1922, *The Times* was bought by J.J. Astor, and it remained in the Astor family until 1966.

The most important editor of *The Times* during the first half of the twentieth century was **Geoffrey Dawson** (1912–19 and 1922–41). He dominated the paper in the tradition of Barnes and Delane, but, unlike his Victorian predecessors, he failed to keep *The Times* independent of government. Through his frequent and close contacts with members of successive British governments during the inter-war years, he may have enhanced the level of intelligence that *The Times* was able to call on when its writers sat down to pen their editorials, but by the same token he was at least in part responsible for making *The Times* too dependent on the government for its views and, indeed, often its news as well. The process reached its peak with the close collusion between Dawson and **Neville Chamberlain**'s government over the policy of **appeasement** toward Germany in the late 1930s, an episode that damaged the reputation of *The Times* for honest and informed independence. Indeed, the close links that *The Times* had sought to cultivate with the government, just as all governments had sought to gain the support and cooperation of *The Times*, led to the charge that *The Times* was the official mouthpiece of the British government; under Dawson there was some truth in this allegation. *The Times'* close relationship to the government was only really broken with the **Suez crisis** in 1956, when the editor, Sir William Haley, refused to support Prime Minister **Anthony Eden**'s military action against Egypt despite being one of the very few people privy to Eden's secret plan of military collusion between Britain, France, and Israel for the attack on Egypt.

The most important editors of the postwar era were Haley (1952–66) and Sir William Rees-Mogg (1967–81). Rees-Mogg, in particular, did much to maintain the intellectual distinction of *The Times*: The paper was, for instance, important in introducing the economic doctrine of monetarism to a wider audience during the early 1970s. However, the cost of producing *The Times*, which always had a relatively small, if affluent, readership, grew dramatically in the 1960s and 1970s. These rising costs led in 1966 to the sale of the paper by the Astor family to Lord Thomson, who combined the paper with the *Sunday Times* (previously a separate title) in one newspaper group. However, after a series of protracted union disputes in the late 1970s, the Thomson group was obliged to sell both papers to Rupert Murdoch's News International company in 1981.

The position of *The Times* as Britain's preeminent newspaper was threatened by several factors during the 1980s. Under Murdoch's management, *The Times* sought to appeal to a wider readership in order to make the paper financially viable, which inevitably led to a deterioration of its standards, both as a journal of record and as a leader of intellectual opinion. Furthermore, in 1986 *The Independent* was launched to try to capitalize on this by utilizing the old journalistic strengths of *The Times* to replace the latter as Britain's most important daily newspaper. In 1985–6 *The Times* was also at the center of a bitter industrial dispute arising from the move of all of Murdoch's papers to a new, central location in Wapping, East London. The close identification of *The Times* with the rest of Murdoch's newspaper empire meant that the paper lost, in some people's eyes, its reputation for intellectual and political independence that other proprietors, such as the Astors, had struggled to maintain.

In the mid-1990s, no paper in Britain played the role that *The Times* once played in public life during its heyday, and the place of *The Times* as Britain's primary journal of record and opinion was in doubt. However, given the paper's checkered financial history during the twentieth century it may also be considered a small miracle that the paper still exists at all, let alone that it has continued to play an important, if diminished, role in the public life of contemporary Britain.

Richard Cockett

Bibliography

Evans, Harold. *Good Times, Bad Times.* 1984.

McLachlan, Donald. *In the Chair: Barrington-Ward of* The Times, *1927–1948.* 1971.

The Official History of The Times. 6 vols. 1935–93.

Woods, Oliver, and James Bishop. *The Story of* The Times. 1983.

Wrench, John Evelyn. *Geoffrey Dawson and Our Times.* 1955.

Tippett, Michael Kemp (1905–)

The output of English composer and conductor Michael Tippett reveals in retrospect a majestic progression of five **operas** interspersed with five string quartets, and four each of piano sonatas, concertos, and symphonies. Although a late developer musically, he has created a highly individual neo-classical style, drawing on rhythmic techniques found in English Renaissance music and Stravinsky, and strongly influenced by his admiration for Beethoven's music and for jazz, particularly the blues. His initial visit to the United States in 1965, a liberating experience, led to his first American commission, the Fourth Symphony, which was given its world premiere in Chicago in 1977. Subsequent American world premieres have included the first performances of *The Mask of Time* (Boston), the Fourth Piano Sonata (Los Angeles), and the opera, *New Year* (Houston). Among official honors Tippett has received several doctorates as well as a knighthood (1966) and the Order of Merit (1983).

Born in London, the son of an entrepreneur of Cornish stock, Tippett had little formal musical instruction while at school except piano lessons, but by the time he left, he had made up his mind to become a composer. Following a period of study at the Royal College of Music, London (1923–8), with Charles Wood and then Charles Kitson as composition teachers (the latter uncongenial), as well as help with conducting from Adrian Boult and Malcolm Sargent, Tippett settled in Oxted, Surrey, teaching French part-time. There he gained much useful practical experience from local music making, conducting a choir and staging operas, but a concert of his own music in 1930 demonstrated the need for further instruction, which he received from R.O. Morris (1930–2). In 1933 he was invited to conduct the South London (Morley College)

Orchestra for professional unemployed musicians, and he subsequently became the Director of Music at Morley College, serving from 1940 to 1951. His **pacifist** convictions were put to the test during the Second World War when, as a registered **conscientious objector**, he was sentenced to three months' imprisonment. Following the war he could devote himself more fully to composition, although he acted as the Musical Director of the Bath Festival for a five-year period (1969–74). In 1951 he left Oxted, subsequently settling in the West Country, where he now lives.

With the completion of the First String Quartet (1935) and First Piano Sonata (1938), Tippett withdrew or destroyed all of his earlier compositions, thereby marking the emergence of his mature style. Indeed, the finale of the quartet contains the first example of his highly individual use of asymmetrical rhythms, more fully explored in the virile counterpoint of the exultant Concerto for Double String Orchestra (1939) and the presto scherzo of the Second String Quartet (1942). In contrast to Tippett's self-confessed preoccupation with form in these works, the oratorio *A Child of Our Time* (Tippett, 1941) reveals his commitment to expressing fundamental truths about the contemporary human condition, in this case, man's inhumanity to man, inviting our understanding and compassion. Although the subject matter of the opera *The Midsummer Marriage* (Tippett, 1952) is different—two lovers can be united only after having attained self-knowledge—the *raison d'etre* is the same. The opera's "images of abounding, generous, exuberant beauty" are conveyed in a luminous opulence that also pervades the subsequent *Fantasia Concertante on a Theme of Corelli* for strings (1953) with its rich profusion of arabesques, and the glittering textures of the Piano Concerto (1955).

A move, already evident in the Second Symphony (1957), toward greater concentration, with the music evolving as the statement of many contrasting ideas in different juxtapositions rather than the lengthy development of a few, gains fuller expression in the mosaic-like structures of the Second Piano Sonata (1962) and the more sophisticated "collage" treatment in the Concerto for Orchestra (1963). The complex, multilayered textures of *The Vision of St. Augustine* (1965) for baritone, chorus, and orchestra, Tippett's most radical work, form the climax of this development.

The opera *King Priam* (Tippett, 1961) gains its starkness from the accumulation of often brutally juxtaposed gestures, but in his next opera, *The Knot Garden* (Tippett, 1969), a contemporary comedy of forgiveness influenced by Shakespeare's *The Tempest*, Tippett draws on a synthesis of his earlier styles to portray the characters' separations and reconciliations. Tippett's inclusion of blues at the end of Act I, together with the blues sequence in the second part of the Third Symphony (1972), point to his renewed enthusiasm for the United States, which forms the implied setting for his fourth opera, *The Ice Break* (Tippett, 1976), although the plot's themes of racial conflict (including mob violence), the generation gap, and the polarity of Communist and capitalist political systems have resonances worldwide. Tippett's preoccupation with the New World led him to reassess his attitude to the Old World, symbolized by the music of Beethoven, quoting the "Ode to Joy" in the Third Symphony, both to assert values and to criticize them. A similar process can be heard in the Fourth String Quartet (1978), with the rhythmic allusions to Beethoven's *Grosse Fuge*.

Tippett's most recent works, while continuing to explore new sound worlds, also relate back to earlier developments. The warm lyricism of the radiant Triple Concerto (1979) echoes to a certain extent that of the *Fantasia Concertante on a Theme of Corelli*; in the opera *New Year* (Tippett, 1988), the portrayal of the tension that exists between our dream worlds and their inevitable conflict with reality reminds us of the personal problems confronting Jenifer and Mark in *The Midsummer Marriage*. *The Mask of Time* (1982) for four soloists, chorus and orchestra, "fragments or scenes from a possible epiphany for today," is a rich musical metaphor of the multifaceted nature of contemporary humanity that celebrates reconciliation.

Trevor Bray

Bibliography

Kemp, Ian. *Tippett: The Composer and His Music.* 1984.

Tippett, Michael. *Moving into Aquarius.* 1974.

———. *Those Twentieth Century Blues: An Autobiography.* 1991.

Whittall, Arnold. *The Music of Britten and Tippett.* 1982.

Titanic, Sinking of the (1912)

RMS *Titanic* was a superliner built for the White Star Line by Harland and Wolff of Belfast to participate in the keen competition for luxury and steerage passengers crossing the Atlantic Ocean during the early twentieth century. It was over 850 feet long and displaced 52,300 tons, making it one of the largest liners. "Unsinkable" was a descriptive term touted by some. There were over 2,200 passengers and crew aboard on its maiden voyage in April 1912. Four days out of Southampton, about 390 miles east of Newfoundland, on 14 April 1912, at a speed of twenty-one knots, *Titanic* struck an iceberg and sank in two-and-a-half hours with the loss of more than 1,500 lives; over 700 were saved: 63 percent of first-class passengers, 41 percent of those in second class, 38 percent of third class, and 24 percent of the crew; 20 percent of male passengers, 74 percent of female passengers, and 52 percent of the children aboard.

Investigations abounded. There had been specific warnings about dangerous ice fields in the area. The ship's speed under such conditions was seemingly reckless. Clearly the number of lifeboats was insufficient by as much as two-thirds. The acclaimed engineering design of the watertight bulkheads was suspect. Fictional, dramatic, literary, film, and documentary accounts of events surrounding the disaster have been numerous. During the 1970s and 1980s an intensive search proved successful—the wreck was found two-and-a-half miles below the surface—reviving interest in the ill-fated liner.

Eugene L. Rasor

Bibliography

Ballard, Robert D. *The Discovery of the Titanic.* 1987.

Lord, Walter. *A Night to Remember.* 1955.

———. *The Night Lives On.* 1986.

Wade, Wyn Craig. *The Titanic: End of a Dream.* 1992.

Titmuss, Richard Morris (1907–1973)

Richard Titmuss occupies a deservedly important place in the study of social policy in Britain. Many of his contemporaries would share Margaret Gowing's verdict that, by the time he died, Titmuss had "created a new discipline and was one of the few truly original social scientists of his generation." Given all of the obstacles he had to overcome, his rise to academic eminence was remarkable. Born in 1907, he was forced by the pressure of family finances to leave school at age fourteen and take an office job, eventually becoming a clerk in an insurance firm. The work was unremittingly dull, but it taught Titmuss actuarial skills and developed in him a fascination for the vital statistics of demography. Possessed of a lively and inquiring mind, Titmuss became interested in politics and gradually in the 1930s began to cultivate an ever-widening circle of important friends who later were to act as useful patrons.

It was these autodidact leanings that impelled him to write his first important book, *Poverty and Population* (1938). It made skillful use of mortality statistics to argue trenchantly against the government's apparent lack of concern over differential mortality rates by social class and region. Two more part-academic, part-polemical works followed in quick succession: *Birth, Poverty, and Wealth* (1943) and (with his wife, Kay) *Parents Revolt* (1943). He also joined the **Eugenics** Society, editing the *Eugenics Review* for a time, and advised the government on a variety of **health** and demographic matters during the Second World War.

Such activities attracted public attention and led to Titmuss' appointment as one of the official historians of the **Second World War.** The resultant volume, *Problems of Social Policy* (1950), was an exploration of how the social services coped with the human consequences of bombing, **evacuation**, homelessness, and other social disruptions of wartime. A central tenet of the book was the belief that universal, state-provided welfare was not only efficient but socially integrative. The plaudits earned led to Titmuss' appointment as Professor of social administration at the **London School of Economics** in 1950—a remarkable achievement for one who had left school with no formal academic qualifications.

For the next two decades Titmuss established himself as the personification of social policy studies in Britain. In an number of important publications, such as *Essays on "The Welfare State"* (1958) and *Commitment to Welfare* (1968), he argued the case for a social democratic, universal **welfare state** that would protect its weakest citizens and bestow equality of rights. One of his most imaginative books, *The Gift Relationship* (1970), was a study, using criteria taken from both **economics** and moral **philosophy**, of the superiority of an unpaid, state-run system of blood donating over one organized on free-market principles. Indeed, one of his strengths was the combination of a strong moral commitment to greater equality with a mastery of statistical detail—as in his study of inequality, *Income Distribution and Social Change* (1962).

Since his death in 1973 Titmuss' work has been subject to the criticism that it was often dilettantish or that it failed to explore the realities of political power. Nevertheless, his status as a modern "founding father" of social policy remains unchallenged.

John Macnicol

Bibliography

Gowing, Margaret. "Richard Morris Titmuss," *Proceedings of the British Academy*, vol. 61 (1975), pp. 401–28.

Reisman, David A. *Richard Titmuss: Welfare and Society*. 1977.

Wilding, Paul. "Richard Titmuss and Social Welfare," *Social and Economic Administration*, vol. 10 (1976), pp. 147–66.

Tizard, Henry Thomas (1885–1959)

Henry Tizard was a senior civil servant, scientific adviser, and academic administrator, concerned above all with the application of science to war, especially in aviation. He was the son of a naval officer and Fellow of the Royal Society, and was educated at public school and Magdalen College, Oxford. In 1911 he was elected a Fellow of Oriel College, where he taught chemistry. He volunteered for the army in 1914 and the following year transferred to the Royal Flying Corps, where he developed testing procedures for a new aircraft. He ended the war as a Lieutenant-Colonel and second in command of the new Air Ministry's scientific and technical branch. After a brief interlude at Oxford he returned to government as a senior civil servant in the new Department of Scientific and Industrial Research in 1920, at first with responsibility for coordinating research for the services. In 1927 he became the Permanant Secretary of the department. He left the civil service in 1929 to become Rector of Imperial College, London; in 1942 he became President of Magdalen College, Oxford. He returned full time to the civil service in 1946 as Chairman of the Defence Research Policy Committee and the Advisory Council on Scientific Policy and retired in 1952.

While outside the civil service he undertook many important advisory roles in military aviation, operating at the highest official and political levels. He was from the early 1930s to the middle of the Second World War the most senior scientific adviser to the Royal Air Force (RAF) and to the Ministry of Aircraft Production. As such he was closely involved with advising on the development of radar, jet engines, atomic weapons, and much else. Tizard's associations were primarily with the air war, not with the naval or land wars. He did not have the ear of Prime Minister Winston Churchill, who relied on Lord Cherwell as his scientific adviser. However, Tizard did chair an inter-service committee of scientific advisers on weapons of the future in 1944–5, which was in effect a prelude to becoming scientific adviser to the Ministry of Defence after the war. For all of his wide-ranging responsibilities Tizard did not have responsibility for nuclear weapons.

Tizard became known to a wider public soon after his death, largely through C.P. Snow's misleading picture of him as an opponent of strategic bombing. That analysis has been thoroughly rebutted by evidence that Tizard did not object in principle to strategic bombing, but only to what he saw as a diversion of bombers away from where they were most needed in 1942. It would indeed have been extraordinary if the RAF had had as its adviser an opponent of its primary strategy since 1918. Tizard was at the center of Britain's military-scientific complex for decades, in peace and in war. But unlike other scientist-civil servants and advisers like Lord Cherwell, Lord Hankey, Sir John Anderson, or Sir John Grigg, he achieved neither ministerial office nor a peerage, although he received a knighthood in 1937.

David E.H. Edgerton

Bibliography

Clark, Ronald W. *Tizard*. 1965.

Town and Country Planning

The most urbanized country in the world in 1900, Britain was also a world leader in thinking about the rational planning of cities, but its strong political traditions respecting the sanctity of private property meant that theory remained well ahead of practice until mid-century. A comprehensive planning system embracing both town and country was erected in the late 1940s and was widely envied and imitated abroad. The system was most successful in protecting the countryside from creeping suburbanization, but it was only halfheartedly implemented in the towns. Planners were blamed for the soulless building boom of the 1950s and 1960s, and toward the end of the century physical planning was just as politically unpopular as it had been at the beginning.

Limited elements of town planning, such as regulation of the layout and density of private housing, had in the nineteenth century been justified on public health grounds. The first modern town planning acts derived from this tradition but also pointed the way toward a more deliberate and comprehensive system. An act of 1909 encouraged local authorities to link their disparate powers to regulate land use, density, roadbuilding, and sanitary and amenity provision in the drawing up of local plans. A few did, and town planning departments emerged in some cities, notably Birmingham. A professional association, the Town Planning Institute, was in place by 1914. But at this stage the practice of statutory planning was rudimentary by the standards being set by theorists like Ebenezer Howard or Patrick Geddes and by philanthropic efforts such as the Cadbury family's Bournville or William Lever's Port Sunlight. Even the First World War, a catalyst for government growth in so many other areas, had relatively little impact. The post-war Housing and Town Planning Act of 1919 contributed more to housing than to town planning. It did, however, make compulsory the development plans for towns permitted by the 1909 act. The 1932 Town and Country Planning Act extended these plans to all local authorities, rural as well as urban, and to all kinds of land (whether or not ripe for development), but in other respects was looser and more permissive.

Planning between the wars therefore proceeded on a piecemeal and local basis. A few central-government officers—Raymond Unwin, a veteran of Howard's **Garden Cities** movement who became chief planner at the Local Government Board, and George Pepler at the Ministry of Health—provided encouragement and pooled expertise, but they had little funding to provide and no powers of compulsion. Ambitious local authorities such as the London County Council achieved much under this regime, such as regional coordination, open-space reservation, and transport schemes, but little pressure was applied to laggards. In consequence, the face of Britain changed dramatically

in this period without much conscious direction: Countryside was eaten up by suburban extension and disfigured by ribbon development and the mushrooming road and electricity supply networks, cities sprawled yet remained congested, and industry and employment became increasingly maldistributed.

Probably this chaos would have triggered an environmental planning revolution even if the **Second World War** had not popularized planning in all spheres. During the war environmental planning came to be seen as a national task, linked to other forms of planning, taking into account social, economic, and cultural needs as well as **public health** and **housing**. The Barlow, Scott, and Uthwatt Reports on planning matters had an effect on public opinion parallel to that of the **Beveridge** Report on social security. Their principal fruit was the 1947 Town and Country Planning Act, supplemented by legislation facilitating the creation of **new towns** and national parks. Planning powers were concentrated in the larger local authorities (counties and county boroughs) and coordinated by a central Ministry of Town and Country Planning (Housing and Local Government from 1951; Department of the Environment from 1970). A complicated "compensation and betterment" mechanism was established that enabled local authorities to direct land use without having to pay ruinous compensation to private owners: Development rights had essentially been nationalized. A land-use map for the whole nation could gradually be compiled and lightly guided from the center. Historic buildings were protected, cities were ringed by "greenbelts" of undeveloped land to prevent sprawl, and the road network and the distribution of industry and population were now matters of national policy.

Under this regime, physical planning improved on the national and regional level but probably deteriorated locally, especially in cities. City planning departments were overwhelmed both by their new powers and by pressure from developers and politicians not to use them lest they dampen housing and commercial growth, booming in the 1950s and 1960s. **Conservative** governments responded to these pressures by de-nationalizing development rights, which put a question mark over local authorities' ability to plan land use compulsorily. "Planning blight"—nondevelopment for fear that planning powers *might* be applied in future—resulted regardless. Thus, planners tended to be blamed for developments they had not controlled and for nondevelopment they had not planned, against which credit for their positive achievements paled.

In the 1970s the momentum given by the 1947 act ran out. By this time the building boom had ended anyway. Local planning ground to a halt, and central planning had largely attained its stated goals. The election of an anti-planning Conservative government in 1979 only capped this process. The 1947 machinery largely remained in place, but its public profile and popularity had melted away: No change was preferred to planned change. Just as before the First World War, urban renewal was largely the work of the private sector; London's Docklands and other riparian schemes were deliberately exempted from normal planning controls.

Peter Mandler

Bibliography

Cherry, Gordon E. *Cities and Plans: The Shaping of Urban Britain in the Nineteenth and Twentieth Centuries*. 1988.

Cullingworth, J.B. *Town and Country Planning in Britain*. 10th ed. 1988.

Hall, Peter et al. *The Containment of Urban England*. 2 vols. 1973.

Sheail, John. *Rural Conservation in Inter-War Britain*. 1981.

Trade Union Legislation

For more than two centuries the exercise of trade union power has been a matter of political controversy in Britain. During the nineteenth century many of the legal restrictions that had been placed on the trade unions by the Combination Acts of 1799 and 1800 and by earlier legislation were removed. However, from the 1890s there was a series of legal decisions hostile to the unions, most famously the **Taff Vale judgment** (1901), which fueled trade unionists' demands for legislative action to restore what they saw as their rights under 1871 and 1875 legislation.

Such legislation came soon after the **Liberal Party**'s landslide victory in the 1906 general election. Prime Minister Sir **Henry Campbell-Bannerman** went further than many of his ministerial colleagues wished when he supported giving unlimited legal immunity to trade unions for damages incurred during the course of trade disputes rather than simply providing limited protection for union funds, as his **Cabinet** initially had agreed. The Trade Disputes Act (1906) enabled unions to organize **strikes** without fear of backruptcy and thereby restored to them their most important card in collective bargaining.

The Liberals redressed another trade union grievance in 1913. The Osborne judgment (1910) had banned trade unions from funding political activity, a decision that was very damaging to the young **Labour Party**. The Trade Union Act (1913) permitted trade unions to use their funds for political purposes providing that a majority of members agreed and that those who did not wish to support such expenditure were entitled to contract out.

During both World Wars trade union action, along with most economic activity, was restricted. In the **First World War** the most important measure was the Munitions of War Act (1915). This substituted arbitration for strikes and lockouts, controlled war industries and set up special courts (munitions tribunals) to enforce good working practices within them, suspended trade union restrictive practices, and indirectly controlled labor mobility. The definition of "munitions" was wide—and was later extended by the Munitions of War (Amendment) Act (1916) and by the courts so that compulsory arbitration was also applied to groups such as textile workers and dockers. During the **Second World War** the government again took a range of exceptional powers. The most important in regard to labor were Defence Regulation 58A, which gave the Minister of Labour full control over civilian manpower, and Order 1305, which banned strikes and lockouts and established a National Arbitration Tribunal.

After the First World War the number and nature of strikes led many in governing circles to believe that the extraordinary wartime powers under the **Defence of the Realm Act** should be continued to enable governments to deal with any future labor unrest that threatened to undermine the political system. Hence **David Lloyd George**'s government put on the statute book the Emergency Powers Act (1920), which gave governments virtually unlimited powers should they declare a national emergency. This act has been used by several governments, most notably **Edward Heath**'s (1970–4).

The labor unrest of 1910–20 brought the issue of trade union power to the forefront of British politics. During the years 1910–14 the Conservative leadership considered proposing legislative curbs. After the First World War the party's right wing became increasingly restless. In early 1925 **Stanley Baldwin** persuaded Tory backbenchers to withdraw a bill to reinstate the Osborne judgment. In the aftermath of the 1926 **General Strike** he found that Conservative pressure for trade union legislation was irresistible. The Trade Disputes and Trade Unions Act (1927) banned general strikes and strikes by local government workers, made picketing more difficult, forbade central and local government employees from joining unions that could affiliate to the **Trades Union Congress** (TUC), and shifted the onus of effort in the trade union political levy on members to the Labour Party from contracting out to contracting in (which immediately cut the Labour Party's funds from this source by a third). The **Attlee** government repealed this legislation with the Trade Disputes and Trade Unions Act (1946).

In the 1960s higher levels of inflation, declining competitiveness of much of British industry, and growing concern about strikes in export industries brought trade union legislation back as a major issue in British politics. With the *Rookes v. Barnard* case (1964) the courts threw doubt on the legal immunity of trade union officials, which had hitherto been believed to have been given by the Trade Disputes Act (1906). Following the election in 1964 of **Harold Wilson**'s Labour government, the Royal Commission on Trade Unions and Employers' Associations (1965–8) under Lord Donovan was set up to investigate British industrial relations. The resulting report argued against major legislation. However, with the **Conservative Party** demanding legislation and public opinion being critical of many strikes, Wilson and Barbara Castle, the Employment Secretary, produced the White Paper *In Place of Strife*, which proposed legislation that exceeded the Royal Commission's suggestions. The trade union movement reacted strongly against the proposals that the employment secretary should have the power to impose a twenty-eight-day cooling-off period before a strike occurred, to settle inter-union disputes, and to order strike ballots. The Wilson government was humiliated when its industrial relations bill, which included the first two of these proposals, had to be withdrawn because of a revolt by Labour backbench MPs.

In the 1970 general election the Conservatives were returned to power with a commitment to trade union legislation. Heath's Industrial Relations Act (1971) went further than *In Place of Strife*. While it gave a special court, the National Industrial Relations Court, the power to order cooling-off periods and to require a strike ballot, it also gave this court the power to fine unions for "unfair industrial practices," to award compensation to workers unfairly sacked, and to require union recognition. The act also dealt with the closed shop, gave workers the right to belong or not to belong to a union, and made collective agreements legally binding (unless specified in the agreements that they were not). Under the act a new Registrar of Trade Unions and Employee Associations was appointed, who had some powers of regulation over such unions as registered with him. The passage of this legislation was marked by large hostile demonstrations, organized by the TUC and the Labour Party. Well before the miners' strike that led to the early general election of February 1974 that the Conservatives lost, much of the act's provisions were becoming ineffective. Organized labor was hostile, the imprisonment of five dockers under the act gave its opponents martyrs, employers often were unwilling to risk worsening industrial relations by taking their workers to court, and Heath's own government came to see trade union legislation as secondary to securing union cooperation for its prices and incomes policy.

With the return of Labour under Wilson (1974–6) and **James Callaghan** (1976–9), Heath's trade union legislation was repealed by the Trade Union and Labor Relations Acts (1974, 1976). These acts took up what the unions regarded as the more positive aspects of the 1971 legislation, notably on unfair dismissals. Working people were given further safeguards in the Health and Safety at Work Act (1974) and the Employment Protection Acts (1975, 1978).

Margaret Thatcher's victory in the 1979 general election began an era of trade union legislation that aimed to weaken the unions. Unlike in 1971, this was carried out in a step-by-step manner that did not arouse the united opposition that Heath's legislation had done. Moreover, in the 1979, 1983, and 1987 general elections many trade unionists voted Conservative, probably more than voted Labour. The Conservative attack on the trade unions was also buttressed by monetarist economic thinking, which views unions as a restriction on an ideal free market where wages go down as unemployed people compete to do, for lower wages, the work currently being done by those who are employed. Between 1980 and 1992 the Conservatives enacted a considerable amount of trade union legislation: the Employment Acts (1980, 1982, 1988, 1989, 1990), the Trade Union Act (1984), and the Trade Union and Labor Relations (Consolidation) Act (1992).

The main feature of the 1980–92 legislation was to take trade union law back to before 1906. Trade unions, not just individual trade unionists, were again liable for damages arising from collective action. Unions lost their immunity from legal action if they called strikes without first holding a secret ballot or if a dispute involved secondary action. Picketing was limited to those directly involved and to their workplace. The closed shop was banned except where a ballot showed 85 percent of those voting supported it. The legislation helped union members who disregarded majority verdicts in their union: Unions could not discipline members who crossed picket lines or refused to strike. It also provided advice and funds to members who took legal action against their own union. There were also public funds for union secret ballots. There had to be ballots for union officers and executive committee members and, every ten years, for unions to maintain political funds. All in all the 1980–92 legislation shifted the legal balance in industrial relations to the benefit of employers and to the detriment of the unions.

C.J. Wrigley

Bibliography

Brown, Kenneth D. "Trade Unions and the Law" in C.J. Wrigley, ed. *A History of British Industrial Relations, 1875–1914.* 1982. pp. 116–34.

Ewing, K.D. *Trade Unions, the Labour Party, and the Law.* 1982.

Kessler, Sidney, and Fred Bayliss. *Contemporary British Industrial Relations.* 1992.

McCarthy, W., ed. *Legal Intervention in Industrial Relations.* 1992.

McIlroy, J. *The Permanent Revolution? Conservative Law and the Trade Unions.* 1991.

Wedderburn, K.W. *The Worker and the Law.* 3rd ed. 1986.

Trades Union Congress (TUC)

By 1900 the TUC was well established as the collective voice of much of the British trade union movement. Some 70 percent of trade unionists were members of unions that were affiliated to the TUC. Set up in 1868, the TUC provided a national forum for the unions and acted as a pressure group on the central government. Through its Parliamentary Committee, which was made up of the main trade union leaders of the day, the TUC lobbied ministers and MPs. Until the 1890s the TUC leadership, like most trade unionists, had been predominantly **Liberal** or Lib-Lab in politics. This changed in the twentieth century.

Indeed the 1899 Congress passed a resolution calling on the Parliamentary Committee to arrange a conference that would ensure more Labour members of Parliament. The resulting conference of February 1900 marked the establishment of a separate **Labour Party**, initially the **Labour Representation Committee** (LRC). A major reason for this action by the TUC was dismay at the adverse decisions on trade union law that were being made in the law courts. The **Taff Vale judgment** (1901) turned a slow flow of unions affiliating with the LRC to a flood. Between 1901 and 1906 the proportion of the TUC membership affiliated with the LRC doubled from 29 to 58 percent. In the 1906 general election nine members of the thirteen-strong Parliamentary Committee of the TUC were elected to Parliament, three still as Lib-Labs but six through the LRC. By the early stages of the First World War the TUC and the Labour Party were very close, a situation helped by the latter being led by such prominent trade unionists as **Arthur Henderson**, J.R. Clynes, and William Adamson.

The **First World War** greatly strengthened British trade unionism and thereby the TUC. During the course of the war, nearly 5.7 million men joined the armed forces from a male labor force at the war's outbreak of 15 million. Thus labor generally, and skilled labor in particular, was in a potentially very powerful position in "a war of production." The TUC and the leaderships of most unions backed the war and did not try to exploit fully their much-enhanced position in the labor market. Indeed, the TUC was a major party to the declaration on 28 August 1914 of an industrial truce for the duration of the war and to the Treasury Agreement of March 1915, a voluntary agreement that included the suspension of trade union restrictive practices as well as various schemes to move labor to war priority work and to curtail labor benefiting from free-market forces.

However, while the TUC did not take advantage of the wartime labor market, it nevertheless emerged stronger from the war and the post-war economic boom. For one thing it benefited from the doubling of trade union membership from 4.1 million in 1914 to 8.3 million in 1920 (with the proportion affiliated with the TUC rising from 65 to 77 percent). For another, it gained in prestige as the wartime governments needed to pay attention to its views on a wide range of industrial and social matters.

The TUC became a more efficient pressure organization after the First World War. It moved into a bigger building, began appointing full-time officials, and began providing its affiliates with information on industrial relations. Most

PUNCH, OR THE LONDON CHARIVARI.—MAY 12, 1926.

UNDER WHICH FLAG?

JOHN BULL. "ONE OF THESE TWO FLAGS HAS GOT TO COME DOWN—AND IT WON'T BE MINE."

"Under Which Flag?" (Bernard Partridge, Punch, 12 May 1926). Published as the General Strike ended.

important, in 1921 it replaced its Parliamentary Committee with the General Council, which was elected on a more representative basis than its predecessor, taking into account industrial groupings and union size. Within the limits that individual trade union autonomy would permit, the General Council had much potential for giving direction to the whole trade union movement.

The TUC also took on an international role from the later stages of the First World War when it felt the need to be involved in discussing the post-war world. In 1920 the TUC elbowed aside the General Federation of Trade Unions (GFTU), which until the middle of the war had been allowed to be the sole collective voice overseas of British trade unionism.

In 1924 the General Council was given powers to intervene to try to achieve settlements in industrial disputes and, where such mediation failed, to organize the whole resources of the movement to support the trade union involved. In 1925 the TUC became embroiled in the affairs of a large, militant union when the **miners** were faced with wage cuts, longer working hours, and an end to national collective agreements. This led in May 1926 to the General Council calling a **General Strike** in support of the miners, intended to affect government policy, not to overthrow constitutional government. After nine days the General Council called off its action, leaving the miners to their fate. The bitter experience of the 1926 General Strike reinforced most trade union leaders in their hostility to "direct action." Thereafter, until the Second World War, the TUC was willing to work with moderate employers (as shown in the **Mond**-Turner Talks of 1928–9) and with governments, regardless of their political complexion. In this **Walter Citrine**, its General Secretary (1926–45), and the General Council were following a strong tendency that had always been present in the TUC, even during the tumultuous years of 1917–26.

The TUC was fully behind Britain's effort during the **Second World War**. When **Winston Churchill** formed a coalition government in May 1940 he appointed **Ernest Bevin**, a major figure in the TUC for nearly the whole inter-war period, as Minister of Labour. Bevin saw that the TUC and the unions were actively involved in the organization of the war. Nevertheless, controls in the labor market and in industrial relations were as rigorous as during the First

World War. As in the earlier conflict the TUC benefited not only from its enhanced status but also from increased trade union membership, which rose from 6.3 million in 1939 to nearly 8.9 million in 1946 (with the proportion affiliated with the TUC rising from 77 to 86 percent).

After 1945 the TUC continued to be much consulted by government officials when their management of the economy involved incomes policies. The relative success of **Clement Attlee's** government in holding wage levels down in 1948–50 owed a great deal to the support of the General Council. Economists have suggested that as a result weekly wage rates were 2 percent lower than they would have been. When **Harold Macmillan's** government brought in a pay freeze in 1961 followed by a pay norm in 1962, the TUC refused to cooperate with these policies, complaining in particular of the lack of prior consultation, the policies' effect on collective bargaining, and the failure to deal similarly with prices and profits. With the return to office of Labour in 1964 under **Harold Wilson**, the General Council reluctantly agreed to support a national economic plan and to cooperate in a voluntary prices and incomes policy. At the annual Congresses, however, the trade union representatives made clear their opposition to both voluntary and statutory policies, and the General Council subsequently refused to support either a voluntary or a statutory policy on wages, prices, and incomes when **Edward Heath's** government (1970–4) pursued them. It did, however, support Labour's wider mix of measures (covering not only wages, prices, and profits but also rent freezes, increased pensions, and tax benefits) in the "Social Contract" of 1975–7, brought in to deal with soaring inflation. Again the General Council found, as in the late 1940s and mid-1960s, that it could only deliver support for a limited period. Trade union unrest over **James Callaghan's** government's (1976–9) policy to allow 5 percent pay raises was an important element in Labour's 1979 electoral defeat.

The TUC continued to play a major public role on other trade union matters. It campaigned vigorously against proposals for trade union legislation under Wilson in 1969, Heath in 1971–2, and **Margaret Thatcher** and John Major in 1979–92. It also took a lead in many major industrial disputes, including over cuts in **National Health Service** expenditure in 1983 and closing coal mines in 1992.

During the post-1945 period until 1979 the TUC was frequently consulted by governments and sent representatives to government-appointed committees. Even during the premiership of Margaret Thatcher (1979–90) Chancellors of the Exchequer discussed economic policy with both sides of industry on the National Economic Development Council (set up in 1962, abolished in 1991). However, outside the World Wars few historians have found that the TUC had a major and sustained influence over central-government policy. Nevertheless, on occasions the TUC, as the voice of the British trade union movement, has had a marked impact on British politics since 1914.

C.J. Wrigley

Bibliography

Lovell, John, and B.C. Roberts. *A Short History of the TUC*. 1968.

Martin, Ross M. *TUC: The Growth of a Pressure Group, 1868–1976*. 1980.

Middlemas, Keith. *Politics in Industrial Society*. 1979.

Nicholson, Marjorie. *The TUC Overseas: The Roots of Policy*. 1986.

Pelling, Henry. *A History of British Trade Unionism*. 4th ed. 1987.

Roberts, B.C. *The Trades Union Congress, 1868–1921*. 1958.

Transport and General Workers' Union (TGWU)

Britain's largest trade union represents inland transport workers, other than railways, and has manual-worker membership in engineering, motors, aircraft, oil refining, chemicals, wool textile, food processing, drink and tobacco, national and local government, and milling industries. It has a semiautonomous section for nonmanual workers.

The TGWU was founded in 1922 by an amalgamation of eighteen sectional unions of dockers, carters, tram and busmen, and general laborers. Their origins lay in the "new unionism" of the 1880s, which created permanent organization in the poorest layers of society neglected by the craft-dominated Victorian unions. The TGWU's forerunners also turned the trade union movement away from its adherence to the **Liberal Party** and played a role in the creation of the **Labour Party** and its adoption of socialist objectives.

Between 1911 and 1921 these unions won recognition from the employers, leading to national bargaining over wages and conditions, and from the state, for conciliation and arbitration services. In this process, they used both the mass **strike**, associated with syndicalist advocacy, and political pressure for legislative reforms deriving from **Guild Socialist** doctrine.

In the inter-war years the TGWU was led by its first General Secretary, **Ernest Bevin**. The formative influence on its founding structure, he was driven by a large vision of the role of trade unions in a democratic socialist society. He created a strong executive authority but also a system of internal Trade Group Committees to manage the union's diverse industrial interests. Yet there were sectional revolts against central authority in the Docks' Group and among London busmen, which were often supported by the **Communist Party of Great Britain**.

After the defeat of the 1926 **General Strike** Bevin took the leading role in discussions between the **Trades Union Congress** (TUC) and prominent industrialists on trade union functions and industrial rationalization (the **Mond-Turner Talks**). After the fall of the Labour government of 1929–31 he worked to strengthen trade union influence in the Labour Party from his powerful position in the TUC. He advocated Keynesian economics and greater authority for the International Labour Office.

Following its merger with the Workers' Union in 1929, the TGWU recruited widely, both men and women, in assembly-line factories. Its numbers grew from 300,000 in 1922 to 750,000 in 1940, and to 1.5 million in 1966. Bevin used his powers, conferred when **Winston Churchill** appointed him Minister of Labour in the wartime coalition government, to achieve a greater degree of mobilization of the civilian workforce than in either the United States or Nazi Germany, by combining state manpower planning with the promotion of trade union influence in industry.

On Bevin's departure to the **Foreign Office** in 1945, the union confirmed the acting General Secretary, Arthur Deakin, in office. He used his authority to provide loyal support for the Labour government of 1945–51. Its wage-restraint policies, intended to fight inflation and the balance-of-payments crisis (the dollar shortage), collided with workers whose bargaining power was enhanced by full employment. As the Cold War intensified, Deakin came to interpret industrial militancy as Communist-inspired. In 1949, he persuaded the union's Delegate Conference to ban members of the Communist Party from holding union office.

These tensions continued until the election of Frank Cousins to the general secretaryship (1956–69). Cousins provided a more militant, left-wing leadership and placed the TGWU in the vanguard of the **Campaign for Nuclear Disarmament**. He joined the Labour **Cabinet** of 1964 as Minister for Technology but resigned in 1965 in opposition to its policies of wage restraint.

His successor as General Secretary, Jack Jones (1969–78), restructured the union and extended the role of the shop steward, whom he saw as "the instrument of industrial democracy." He lifted the ban on Communists. Bargaining was decentralized to plant level, and the union became the principal opponent of state regulation of wages and legal constraints on strike action. Yet Jones, in the tradition of TGWU leadership, was the architect of the voluntary "Social Contract," designed to harmonize relations between the unions and the Labour government of 1974–9. He negotiated many mergers with other unions, and in 1977 membership reached 2 million, one in six of all trade unions, as overall trade union density surpassed 50 percent of the working population.

During the 1980s Moss Evans (1978–85) and Ron Todd (1985–92) led the TGWU in more conflicts with the **Thatcher** government's trade union laws than any union other than the miners and the printworkers. High **unemployment** and the collapse of manufacturing industries combined with the hostile political and social climate to drive membership down to 1.2 million by 1991. In 1992 Bill Morris was elected, the first black General Secretary of any British union.

Tony Topham

Bibliography

Allen, V.L. *Trade Union Leadership: Based on a Study of Arthur Deakin*. 1957.
Bullock. Alan. *The Life and Times of Ernest Bevin*. vol. 1–2. 1960–67.
Coates, Ken, and Tony Topham. *The Making of the Transport and General Workers' Union: The Emergence of the Labour Movement*. 1991.
Goodman, Geoffrey. *The Awkward Warrior: Frank Cousins: His Life and Times*. 1979.
Minkin, Lewis. *The Contentious Alliance: Trade Unions and the Labour Party*. 1991.

Trevelyan, C(harles) P(hilips) (1870–1958)

C.P. Trevelyan was a politician associated first with the radical wing of the **Liberal Party** and later with the Left of the **Labour Party**. He became a junior minister in 1908 but resigned in protest at Britain's entry into the First World War. He was a cofounder of the **Union of Democratic Control** (UDC), joined the **Independent Labour Party** (ILP) in 1920, and was a member of both of **Ramsay MacDonald's** governments. He resigned office in February 1931 and retired after losing his seat in the House of Commons in the general election in October the same year. He became Sir Charles on inheriting his father's baronetcy in 1928.

Trevelyan was born into a famous family of Liberal politicians and intellectuals. His father, George Otto Trevelyan, had served in Gladstone's and Rosebery's ministries, and his younger brother was the noted historian **G.M. Trevelyan**. By 1894 he was moving in progressive intellectual circles that included the leaders of the **Fabian Society** and the ILP, and by 1899 he had won election to Parliament on his second attempt. He supported the **Boer War**, and when his fellow Liberal Imperialist **H.H. Asquith** became Prime Minister in 1908, Trevelyan became Parliamentary Secretary to the President of the Board of Education.

Trevelyan believed that the **First World War** was largely due to Russian ambition, and that Britain's participation stemmed from an irrational dislike of Germany. When his efforts to keep Britain neutral failed, he became one of a small group of Liberals and socialists who formed the UDC in order to promote a negotiated peace. The UDC's position incurred widespread hostility, and in the "coupon" election of 1918 Trevelyan was overwhelmingly defeated in his Elland constituency, where he stood as an independent.

Trevelyan joined the ILP mainly because of its foreign policy but made it clear that he strongly supported Labour's social program. He won Newcastle Central for Labour in 1922 and in 1924 became President of the Board of Education in the first Labour government. He implemented some minor reforms but was severely constrained by the government's financial caution and its dependence on Liberal parliamentary support. In 1929 he was given the same post in the second Labour government. Acutely dissatisfied with the government's timidity, he resigned after a series of defeats in the Cabinet and Parliament on educational measures.

Trevelyan remained on the National Executive Committee of the Labour Party until 1934 and campaigned for left-wing causes throughout the 1930s. After visiting the Soviet Union he wrote *Soviet Russia: A Description for British Workers* (1935), an enthusiastic account of the Stalin regime, whose foreign and domestic policies he supported until its rapprochement with Germany in 1939. Despite repeated urgings from friends who believed that he could lead Labour to success, Trevelyan remained content to devote most of his energies to improvement and reform on his family estate and to his duties as Lord-Lieutenant of Northumberland.

Circumstances dictated that Trevelyan's concrete achievements in government would be modest, but his political conviction and courage in support of unpopular causes provided inspiration for two generations of socialists and progressives.

D.P. Blaazer

Bibliography

Morris, A.J.A. *C.P. Trevelyan, 1870–1958: Portrait of a Radical*. 1977.

Trevelyan, C.P. *From Liberalism to Labour*. 1921.

Trevelyan, G(eorge) M(acaulay) (1876–1962)

A historian of immense fame during his lifetime, G.M. Trevelyan wrote some of the most popular works of the twentieth century; many titles are still in print and have sold hundreds of thousands of copies. Many professional historians, however, questioned his approach to evidence and decided that he was not asking the right questions, while a devoted minority followed his example. Although Trevelyan acknowledged scientific elements in research, he devoutly believed in the artistic nature of historical writing and argued that style is as integral as substance in accomplishing the historian's primary task, the presentation of the past to the public.

Born the third son of the historian and Liberal politician Sir George Otto Trevelyan and his wife, Caroline, a grandniece of the British historian and statesman Thomas Babington Macaulay, Trevelyan was educated at Harrow and Trinity College, Cambridge. After achieving first-class honors in history (1896), he wrote a dissertation on late medieval English Lollardy and was awarded Trinity's first history fellowship in 1898. The dissertation was published the next year as *England in the Age of Wycliffe* (1899).

Trevelyan left Cambridge in 1903, having decided that London was a more congenial place to write "literary" history and to continue his interest in social reform and the Working Men's College. The next year he married Janet Penrose, younger daughter of Humphry and Mary Ward (the novelist), and published *England under the Stuarts* (1904), a textbook that has had twenty-one editions and was still in print in the 1990s.

A wedding present inspired Trevelyan to write a trilogy on the Italian patriot Giuseppe Garibaldi (1907, 1909, 1911) that made him famous. As preparation Trevelyan retraced the steps of his hero and talked with survivors of Garibaldi's campaigns. The result was a romantic narrative full of excitement and beautifully written. A biography of Victorian Radical statesman John Bright followed in 1913; that same year *Clio: A Muse*, a defense of literary history, established Trevelyan as a principal opponent of the dominant "scientific" approach to writing history.

Declared unfit for combat at the outset of the First World War, Trevelyan accepted the command of a British ambulance unit in Italy and served with distinction. In 1920 he was awarded a CBE and published *Lord Grey of the Reform Bill*. Ten years later he received the Order of Merit.

During the 1920s Trevelyan increased his popularity with the public with *British History in the Nineteenth Century* (1922) and the *History of England* (1926), though his return to Italian history, *Manin and the Venetian Revolution of 1848* (1923) was not a success. The Lowell Lectures at Harvard University (1924) were followed by the Romanes Lectures at Oxford (1926) and a happy return to Cambridge as Regius Professor of Modern History (1927). The final years of the decade were occupied with another trilogy, entitled *England under Queen Anne* (1930, 1932, 1934), which he considered his best work along with the Garibaldi trilogy. A laudatory biography of his friend and former Foreign Secretary Sir Edward Grey was published in 1937.

Even as the Queen Anne trilogy was coming out, many professional historians saw Trevelyan's approach as irrelevant. The principal attack came from **Lewis Namier**, who denied Trevelyan's belief in the continuity of party history, and from Herbert Butterfield, who chastised historians who take sides in history.

In 1940 Trevelyan was named Master of Trinity College, Cambridge, where he remained until 1951. During the Second World War he published *English Social History* (1944)—a continuation of Macaulay's famous third chapter on the State of England in 1685 in his *History*—which became his most popular work, though it was denigrated by many professional historians. At the end of the decade he offered a short autobiography in *An Autobiography and Other Essays* (1949), in which he proclaimed himself to be "not an original but a traditional kind of historian" with a passion for poetry in history. He died in Cambridge on 21 July 1962.

There are still historians who denounce Trevelyan's "simplistic" optimism, views on morality, and Liberal humanist outlook, but most professionals at least acknowledge the need to write well, even if they disagree on "why" they should care about writing at all. Trevelyan ardently believed that these attributes were not shortcomings but virtues and were the basis for his popularity with the public.

Michael Douglas Smith

Bibliography

Cannadine, David. *G.M. Trevelyan: A Life in History.* 1992.

Moorman, Mary. *George Macaulay Trevelyan: A Memoir.* 1980.

Plumb, J.H. *Trevelyan.* 1951.

Tuberculosis

Tuberculosis was acknowledged as a major health problem in Britain in the early twentieth century. Although it was already on the decline, a national antituberculosis campaign was launched that gained momentum in the following decades. A dramatic decline in tuberculosis occurred, although the role played by the campaign itself is questionable.

It was estimated in the early twentieth century that up to 90 percent of the urban population of Britain had been infected with the tubercle bacillus, but that only 1 percent developed the disease. It has never been determined precisely who was most likely to contract tuberculosis. The question of the influence of heredity remains unresolved; environment appears to have been a far more important factor. Studies indicate that the geographical distribution of the disease coincided with less-prosperous areas, with generally higher rates in Scotland and Wales than in England. Death rates are shown to have been inversely related to socioeconomic status.

In 1900 the death rate was about 2 per 1,000 population, but it was much higher among young adults. It caused one in every three deaths among men age fifteen to forty-four and one-half of the deaths of women age fifteen to twenty-four. Attacking people in their prime of life, tuberculosis attracted attention in the cause of "national efficiency." The fitness of the nation as it affected Britain's military and economic strength was at the forefront of political consciousness early in the century, particularly in view of the decline of Britain as a world power compared with Germany, America, and Japan.

The death rate from tuberculosis was believed to be declining faster in Germany than in Britain, and the reason was thought to be that since the 1880s Germany had established a network of institutions for the treatment of tuberculosis.

In Britain, under the 1911 National Insurance Act (which introduced health and **unemployment** benefits) tuberculosis was the only disease for which all insured workers and their dependents were entitled to free institutional treatment. From 1921 such treatment was available for everyone and was the responsibility of local authorities.

Treatment in sanatoria consisted of good plain food, rest, and exercise. Patients were to be educated in leading a healthy life-style. The sanatoria were not seen primarily as places of isolation of the source of infection. With a total of 27,000 beds provided for tuberculosis treatment in England and Wales in 1929 and about 300,000 cases (estimated at ten times the mortality figure), it was not possible to isolate all sources of infection.

By the 1920s the results of sanatorium treatment were seen to be disappointing. Increasingly, surgical intervention was introduced into tuberculosis treatment—in the form of operations on the chest or lungs—although there was no evidence of the superiority of surgical intervention over more traditional methods.

BCG (Bacillus Calmette-Guerin) vaccination against tuberculosis, described in France in 1921, was widely adopted as a preventive measure in the Scandinavian countries in the following two decades with apparent success. The use of BCG vaccination was rejected in Britain, where authorities preferred to focus on treatment and education until after the Second World War, when BCG vaccination of schoolchildren was introduced following a controlled trial by the Medical Research Council.

After the war mass radiographical surveys were also launched to discover early cases. These, combined with effective drugs (chemotherapy) discovered in the 1940s and 1950s, reduced the disease substantially, so that by the 1960s institutions for the treatment of the disease were no longer needed. By 1974 the death rate from tuberculosis was 14 per 1 million population (0.7 percent of the 1900 death rate). Yet, chemotherapy accounted for only the final dropping off in the mortality rates from tuberculosis. Most of the decline had occurred before the 1940s and was probably related not to active medical intervention but to improvements in housing and diet.

Linda Bryder

Bibliography
Bryder, Linda. *Below the Magic Mountain: A Social History of Tuberculosis in Twentieth-Century Britain.* 1988.
Dubos, René, and Jean Dubos. *Tuberculosis, Man, and Society.* new ed. 1987.
McKeown, Thomas. *The Modern Rise of Population.* 1976.
Smith, F.B. *The Retreat of Tuberculosis.* 1988.

U

Ulster

Britain's solutions to its "Irish question" have never fared well, partly because of naivete regarding the divergent political, religious, and cultural elements ingrained through Irish and especially Ulster history. The anomaly of Northern Ireland—six counties incorporating most of ancient Ulster—created in 1920 was an expedient rather than a viable settlement. Thus, Ulster's history predicted its reappearance on the British political scene in the 1960s.

Ulster Unionism, born with the 1886 Home Rule effort, was formalized by the creation of the Ulster Unionist Council in 1904, led by **Sir Edward Carson**. Militant Protestants opposed to Home Rule launched the Ulster Volunteer Force in 1912, the first of many Ulster paramilitary organizations that relied upon the threat of force to obtain political objectives. Protestant fears of becoming a persecuted minority in a **Roman Catholic** Irish state have shaped Protestant politics in Northern Ireland throughout the twentieth century.

The threat of an Irish civil war during the 1912–14 Home Rule debates caused the **Liberal** government to consider dividing the predominantly Protestant north from the Catholic south. Partition satisfied Ulster Unionists and was popular with British public opinion. **H.H. Asquith** in 1914 and **David Lloyd George** in 1916 pledged to Unionist leaders that the government would not coerce Ulster into a unified Ireland. As a result, Carson, anxious for Protestant majority rule in a northern state, agreed to renounce three Catholic-majority counties in Ulster.

Since the Irish conflict was the dominant political issue in Britain after the First World War, the Lloyd George government sought to end the crisis in December 1920 through passage of the Government of Ireland Act. The measure implemented the principles of partition and devolution with separate Parliaments in the north and south, while both divisions retained a limited number of MPs at Westminster. Ulster Protestants opposed the inclusion of a Council of Ireland representing both Irish governments, intended by the British to facilitate Irish unity. Although the republican south rejected the proposal and signed a 1921 treaty that created the Irish Free State as a Dominion, Ulster Unionists accepted the 1920 act as the basis of their new state.

Sir James Craig (1871–1940) succeeded Carson in 1921 as leader of the Ulster Unionist Council. Unionists won forty seats in the first Commons, while nationalists and the separatist group Sinn Fein each elected six members. All twenty-four Senate seats were filled by Unionists. Craig (later Lord Craigavon) became the first Prime Minister of Northern Ireland. The 1920 act, however, retained important links with Westminster, including a Lord-Lieutenant with veto power over the Northern Ireland Parliament, headquartered at Stormont outside Belfast. Britain anticipated that its "excepted," or reserved, powers—foreign policy, the military, foreign trade, currency, postal service, and certain taxes—would later be transferred to a unified Irish government. Also, the Stormont Parliament shared governance with local councils. Hence, it was caught in a vise between British and local authorities, with no constitutional autonomy.

The egregious structural problems of Northern Ireland's government compounded rule by a Protestant majority, representing about 60 percent of the population, over a Catholic minority. Convinced of Catholic disloyalty to the United Kingdom and support for Sinn Fein, Unionists rationalized the suspension of proportional representation in local government (1922) and Parliament (1929), which contravened the 1920 legislation. The British Home Secretary, overseer of civil and religious protections, ignored discrimination against Catholics in political representation, employment, and housing. Unionists used the Irish Republican Army (IRA) violence in 1922 as an excuse to employ *carte blanche* police authority permitted by the Special Powers Act (1922). Repression of Catholics resulted from instruments such as the "B" Specials auxiliary police, an exclusively Protestant body used to assist the integrated Royal Ulster Constabulary (RUC).

Ulster Unionists were also backed by Britain during the Boundary Commission's 1925 deliberations. The commission, created by the 1921 Anglo-**Irish Treaty** to redraw the Northern Ireland border, encouraged nationalist hopes for unification. Yet, when the commission's proposals proved anathema to the Free State, **Stanley Baldwin's Conservative** government pressured the Free State leader, William T. Cosgrave, to accept the 1920 boundary. In return, Britain agreed to rescind certain Irish financial obligations, and Craig promised to release political prisoners and relax the repression against Ulster Catholics. Also, the Council of Ireland was terminated, which pleased Protestants but disappointed Britain.

In addition to Britain's reluctance to moderate Unionist policies, the British taxpayer heavily subsidized Northern Ireland's economy and unemployed. Economic depression in farming and in the linen and shipbuilding industries between the wars was offset only partially by a spurt of economic activity during the Second World War. Catholic and Protestant workers alike suffered as residents of the United Kingdom's poorest region. British subsidies not only made Northern Ireland dependent upon the imperial government, but also frustrated economic and hence political unity with the Irish Free State.

When Eamon de Valera (1882–1975) succeeded Cosgrave in 1932 as head of the Free State, he quickly pressed for changes in the imperial connection, including an end to partition. During British negotiations with de Valera in 1937–8, Lord Craigavon refused to allow Northern Ireland's status to enter the discussion. Notwithstanding British **press** criticism

and a fainthearted investigation by the Home Office into anti-Catholic discrimination charges, the Ulster Unionist government again emerged from the episode with virtually no British interference.

The stagnant economy, religious divisions, and political inequities ultimately forced the British as well as Stormont governments to face the consequences of unattended issues. In the mid-1950s, the long-quiescent Irish Republican Army launched a new campaign of violence along the divided Irish border. When IRA appeals to Catholic nationalists failed to energize support, the strategy ended in 1962. Yet, the door for possible reform was opened with the accession in 1963 of the moderately liberal Unionist Prime Minister Terence O'Neill (1914–90).

O'Neill's government drafted a new economic policy, a six-year plan to stimulate new industry and modernize economic infrastructure. O'Neill also opened a dialogue with Catholic communities regarding education and **civil service** reform as well as jobs. Full of symbolism but lacking substance, O'Neill's policy at least modified the historic mold. The economic plan generated only 5,000 of the 65,000 jobs O'Neill predicted, and Northern Ireland continued to have the highest **unemployment** rate in the United Kingdom. Virtually no progress was made in dismantling the religiously segregated schools. In fact, the Education Act of 1968 actually increased funding for private schools. Public **housing** remained under the control of gerrymandered local councils. Thus, O'Neill's program failed to satisfy Catholics. Instead, it encouraged them to launch a new campaign patterned after the civil rights movement in the United States.

A unique organization, the Northern Ireland Civil Rights Association, founded in February 1967, de-emphasized Catholic nationalist goals and disavowed violence. The Association sought equal opportunity for Catholics under the existing Northern Ireland government in education, housing, jobs, and voting rights as well as the end of the Special Powers Act and the "B" Specials. When the Association resorted to public marches in Ulster communities in the summer of 1968, demonstrators clashed with Protestant mobs and the RUC. **Harold Wilson's** Labour government, less sympathetic toward Unionism, favored a reconciliation between Northern and southern Ireland and urged Stormont to institute reforms. O'Neill responded to the pressure with a five-point reform program that undercut the authority of local councils.

Extremists on both sides sabotaged potential negotiations. Catholic civil rights advocates split, some wanting further pressure upon the government. Stirred by the Presbyterian Reverend Ian Paisley (1926–), radical Unionists portrayed reform as a prelude to the Irish Republic's annexation of Ulster. Such fears were rampant especially in Protestant working-class neighborhoods. The 1969 elections to the Northern Ireland Parliament revealed an electorate more polarized than ever.

Circumstances overwhelmed O'Neill's government, and he resigned in April 1969. The new Prime Minister, ex-army officer James Chichester-Clark (1923–), pursued the single-minded objective of law and order. Yet, Britain was compelled increasingly to direct Northern Ireland's affairs. In August Wilson proposed various reforms but assuaged Protestant fears by insisting that any changes must receive majority support.

Hard-core violence exploded during 1970, beginning with the creation of the "Provisional" Irish Republican Army committed to the use of force and largely funded by American sympathizers. Although British troops separated Catholic and Protestant mobs, put the RUC under British authority, and disbanded the infamous "B" Specials, chaos continued. The new policy produced little success in the early 1970s under Conservative Prime Minister Edward Heath and Northern Ireland Prime Minister Brian Faulkner (1921–77), an experienced civil servant. Britain instituted its controversial "internment" policy in August 1971, which allowed the military to arrest and detain suspects without bringing them to trial.

Two new parliamentary parties made their appearance in 1970: The Catholic Social Democratic and Labour Party (SDLP) favored a socialist economic program and a peaceful union with the Republic, while the Alliance Party appealed to liberals among Catholics and Protestants, a scarce commodity in Northern Ireland. Protesting the lack of progress, the SDLP members withdrew from Parliament in July 1971. When violence peaked in 1972 with 467 deaths, Heath suspended the Northern Ireland Parliament, and Britain began "direct rule," with William Whitelaw as Secretary of State for Northern Ireland. Britain intended direct rule to be temporary, with restoration of a devolved, proportionally represented government to follow in due course.

A March 1973 White Paper proposed a "power-sharing" assembly and executive based upon proportional representation. Although extremists on both sides condemned the idea, Parliament created a seventy-eight-seat assembly and a plural executive. At the 1973 Sunningdale Conference in England, Heath obtained the Republic's concurrence in majority determination of Northern Ireland's future and established another Council of Ireland to foster an Anglo-Irish exchange.

In May 1974 the Protestant Ulster Workers' Council's successful strike combined with Paisley's anti-power-sharing Democratic Unionist Party to undermine Faulkner's power-sharing government. The assembly was suspended, and direct British rule reasserted. Parliament's Northern Ireland Act in July sanctioned a constitutional convention based on proportional representation, which met from May 1975 to March 1976, but it could not agree upon the type of government. Yet another power-sharing attempt in 1982 by Margaret Thatcher's Conservative government launched a proportional assembly. The SDLP members refused to take their seats, leaving only Unionists participating. To break the impasse, Thatcher held face-to-face meetings in 1986 with Unionist leaders James Molyneaux (1920–) and Paisley as well as with SDLP leader John Hume (1937–). When Hume appeared flexible, clashes with police followed another Unionist strike and led to the dissolution of the assembly in June 1986.

The Thatcher government resumed attempts at cooperation with the Republic of Ireland, both to quell violence and to initiate a dialogue between north and south. The Anglo-Irish Agreement of 1985, signed at Hillsborough Castle by Thatcher and Republic Taoiseach (Prime Minister) Dr. Garret Fitzgerald reiterated that the majority must approve changes in Northern Ireland's status. An Anglo-Irish Intergovernmental Conference cochaired by the British Secretary of State for Northern Ireland and the Irish Foreign Secretary regularly discussed matters such as border security, protecting Catholic rights, and stimulating the Irish economy. Formal discussions between Britain and the Republic concerning Ulster caused Protestants considerable uneasiness. Unionist MPs at Westminster resigned en

U

masse to protest the Anglo-Irish Agreement, but the SDLP supported the pact and undercut Sinn Fein's Catholic support.

British nonpolitical measures have been instituted with modest success in Ulster. Labour's Fair Employment Act (1976) aimed at elimination of job discrimination, but loopholes prevented adequate enforcement. Thatcher's government enacted a new fair-employment law in 1989 to eliminate "indirect or unintentional discrimination" against Catholics through a Fair Employment Commission that monitored hiring practices. The Thatcher government also concentrated upon job creation. The 1986 joint Anglo-Irish International Fund solicited investment funds for an all-Ireland economic development. Still, Northern Ireland's unemployment rate, at more than 17 percent in 1987, was much higher than Britain's.

Since the 1970s, Britain has learned difficult lessons about law enforcement in Northern Ireland, such as that simple repression could not end either violence or hatred. Even though the infamous Special Powers Act was repealed in 1973, the Emergency Provisions Act replaced it with controversial "Diplock Courts," which tried terrorists without a jury. Catholics criticized the denial of constitutional protections and the treatment of republican prisoners. Several deaths resulting from a 1981 hunger strike at the infamous Maze Prison in Belfast refocused world opinion on Northern Ireland and sensitized Britons to human rights issues in their police and prison policies.

By the 1990s Britain's commitments seemed certain: a devolved government with proportional representation and majority bipartisan support, no changes in Northern Ireland's status without a clear majority, and a formal dialogue between the governments of the Republic and Britain for an acceptable solution to Northern Ireland's future. Among trends in Northern Ireland, the growing strength of the SDLP in elections reflected greater disenchantment among Catholics with IRA terrorist acts. Unionists were not sanguine about cooperation with the Republic, but internal divisions skewed an accurate reading of Protestant opinion. Finally, the changing tone of nationalist rhetoric in the Republic favored a peaceful, broadly-backed settlement in Northern Ireland. A September 1994 IRA cease fire finally signaled a willingness to abandon violence for a negotiated settlement. The beginning of talks between Britain and the IRA offered the hope that peace could ultimately be achieved.

Daniel W. Hollis III

Bibliography

Buckland, Patrick. *A History of Northern Ireland.* 1981.

Darby, John, ed. *Northern Ireland: The Background to the Conflict.* 1983.

Miller, David W. *The Queen's Rebels: Ulster Loyalism in Historical Perspective.* 1979.

Moody, T.W. *The Ulster Question, 1603–1973.* 1974.

Wilson, Tom. *Ulster: Conflict and Consent.* 1989.

Unemployment

Unemployment, in the general sense of being without work, has been around for much of human history, but it was not until the turn of the twentieth century that the term was widely used. It was only in the 1920s in Britain and in the 1940s in the United States that governments began to collect statistics of unemployment on any regular basis. It had been clearly recognized throughout the nineteenth century that fluctuations in the business cycle threw people out of work, but one reason for the lack of recognition of unemployment as a major problem was that its existence was ascribed to a defect in character. Industrialization, it was believed, had generated work for all of those who needed it. Idleness or want of employment, therefore, had to be the result of the moral failure of the individual.

This view of unemployment was challenged by Karl Marx, who regarded unemployment as the result of the capitalist need for a reserve army of labor to keep wages low relative to profits. Other investigators produced evidence of large-scale involuntary unemployment, the result of fluctuations in the business cycle over which individuals had little control whatever their moral qualities. The title of one of the most influential investigations, **William Beveridge**'s *Unemployment: A Problem of Industry*, published in 1909, recognized that imperfections in the demand for, and supply of, labor were the result of market forces and the business cycle. By the end of the first decade of the century unemployment was seen as both an industrial and a social problem.

The word unemployment was not introduced into the language of political economists until 1888, and its first formal definition, in terms of involuntary idleness of the able bodied, was advanced by **J.A. Hobson** in 1895. The term unemployment is generally subdivided into frictional unemployment (temporary unemployment inevitably suffered by those moving from one job to another); cyclical unemployment (the loss of jobs caused by the downswing of the trade cycle); seasonal unemployment (displaying regular and fairly predictable fluctuations); and structural unemployment (the result of longer-term changes in demand or technology and frequently affecting particular groups of workers or industrial regions). In the period 1910–40 neo-classical theory produced a view of unemployment as an inevitable product of the business cycle. The overriding perception, therefore, was that there was little that governments could or should do about it. It was recognized that some unemployment was necessary for economic growth; the necessary unemployment rate was normally presumed to be about 2 percent in the skilled trades, but if it persisted at higher levels, as it did in Britain in the 1930s in particular, it was believed to be the result of interferences with the free working of the market, either from monopolistic employers, trade unions, or government legislation. There was a profound conviction that if the free market were left to its own devices, it would push the economy toward equilibrium at the level of full employment. All that social policy could do was reduce the pain that the business cycle caused to the unemployed. Employers and workers, meanwhile, would strive to contact each other through the operation of labor exchanges, while government would ease the financial hardships of short-term unemployment through the implementation of insurance schemes.

From 1940 to the late 1970s this neo-classical view was replaced by the Keynesian message that unemployment was caused by deficiencies of aggregate demand and, therefore, subject to manipulation and control by the activities of the state. While consumption might be fairly stable in the short run, investment was liable to erratic fluctuations. In a cyclical downturn, business confidence recedes and less investment takes place as businessmen's expectations of future profits become depressed. **John Maynard Keynes** saw no reason why, when employment failed in a recession, it should be followed by a fall in wages to create a demand for more labor. At a time of rising unemployment Keynes deemed it essential to maintain or increase the level of investment in order to increase the demand for labor. With careful management by the state, high levels of unemployment could be eliminated.

The concept of Keynesian full employment was able to gain hold on both sides of the Atlantic for a number of reasons. The **Second World War** demonstrated the possibility of running the economy effectively with virtually no unemployment and pushing political leaders toward an acceptance of full employment as a policy goal. The 1945 election, giving power to the **Labour Party**, helped strengthen the commitment to full employment. Governments were able to sustain this commitment through most of the 1950s and 1960s because of the growth of international trade and the rising levels of investment.

Circumstances changed dramatically in the late 1970s when the Keynesian view was replaced by the concept of monetarism, which again saw unemployment as a product of market forces over which the state had little direct control. Against a background of continued relative economic decline, financial instability, and a dramatic increase in inflation that started in the early 1970s following a substantial rise in commodity, particularly oil, prices, Britain embarked on a policy of deflation. Unemployment started to rise substantially above the levels to which the country had become accustomed in the post-war period. The rate of unemployment, which had generally stayed below 2 percent between 1948 and 1966, rose from 5.6 percent (1.3 million) in the United Kingdom in 1979 to 13.2 percent (over 3.1 million) at its peak in the third quarter of 1983. The combination of rising inflation and rising unemployment led to a questioning of Keynesian employment policies. For decades past, the prevailing view had been that higher unemployment meant lower inflation, and lower unemployment meant higher inflation. As unemployment decreased, the argument ran, the bargaining power of trade unions increased, enabling them to obtain higher wages. In a buoyant market employers could easily pass on these increased costs as higher prices. However, in the 1970s inflation accelerated independently of the level of unemployment. As a consequence the control of the accelerating rate of inflation became a policy priority. Under the **Thatcher** administration particular emphasis was placed upon controlling the money supply. If there was no control over the money supply, then inflation would follow as more money expenditure would be chasing a given amount of goods and services. Such expenditure could be contained by keeping a tight rein over the medium term on the growth of the money supply. Although it was recognized that this might cause unemployment in the short run, monetarists believed that employment would gravitate to its natural level if the market was left to operate with minimum interference by the state.

With unemployment in the 1980s reaching levels reminiscent of the 1930s (even though its occupational, industrial, and spatial characteristics were often quite different from the interwar years), the problem became a major political issue. Debate raged over whether high unemployment-benefit rates and the actions of the trade unions were more responsible for the prevailing state of affairs than the monetarist doctrine allowed for, with its emphasis on the power of government to influence only the inflation rather than the unemployment rate. There were those who argued that a determined attack on the power and legal status of trade unions and on particular features of the social security system would be an effective response to the persistent unemployment that had come to characterize the mid- to late 1980s.

The unemployment rate in 1990 was only half that of 1982, but there were serious doubts as to the comparability of official statistics over time. The basis of the figures were subjected to numerous changes over the decade after 1979, and most of the changes were judged to have understated the real rate of unemployment. For example, the restriction of the category of the unemployed to those receiving relief, at a time when the regulations for receipt of such relief were tightened, is said to have reduced the official count substantially.

W.R. Garside

Bibliography

Constantine, Stephen. *Unemployment in Britain between the Wars.* 1980.

Garside, W.R. *British Unemployment, 1919–1939.* 1990.

Gordon, Alan. *The Crisis of Unemployment.* 1988.

Harris, Jose. *Unemployment and Politics: A Study in English Social Policy, 1886–1914.* 1972.

Layard, Richard, R. Jackman, and Stephen Nickell. *Unemployment, Macroeconomic Performance, and the Labour Market.* 1991.

Showler, Brian, and Adrian Sinfield, eds. *The Workless State.* 1981.

Union of Democratic Control

The Union of Democratic Control (UDC) was a peace organization whose principal aim was to replace "secret diplomacy" with a foreign policy controlled by Parliament. It was formed in 1914, at the beginning of the First World War, by **C.P. Trevelyan, E.D. Morel** (its secretary and driving force), **Ramsay MacDonald,** Arthur Ponsonby, and **Norman Angell.** Although some of its members were absolute pacifists, the UDC's mainstream advocated a negotiated peace without annexations or indemnities. As the most important single vehicle of criticism of the government's war policy, the UDC was extremely unpopular, but its ideas came to exert considerable influence on interwar thinking, particularly within the **Labour Party.** It is also significant because it acted as a conduit for disaffected **Liberals** who joined the **Independent Labour Party** (ILP) during or shortly after the war. Although the UDC survived until the 1960s as a discussion group and occasional publisher, it lost its momentum and importance after 1924.

The UDC in its early years was frequently condemned as "antiwar" or even "pro-German." It was neither. Its members differed over who was to blame for the war and whether an Allied victory was desirable. It published a wide range of opinions on these questions in its signed pamphlets and its monthly journal, *UDC* (1915–19; continued until 1924 as *Foreign Affairs*). The UDC propounded four cardinal points: (1) there should be no annexations of territory without indigenous popular consent; (2) the British government should make no agreements with foreign powers without parliamentary approval; (3) the balance of power should be abandoned in favor of a council to resolve international disputes; and (4) armaments production should be both nationalized and severely curtailed.

All the leaders of the UDC, except Angell, had criticized the conduct of British foreign policy along these lines in their pre-war writings. Angell, who did not regard armaments manufacturers as blameworthy and was skeptical about the benefits of open diplomacy, argued that wars were caused by irrational beliefs that were at least as widespread among the population at large as among the ruling classes. He therefore took little active part in the UDC's affairs, since its propaganda placed heaviest emphasis upon the evils of secret diplomacy—Morel's consuming passion.

Although some of the UDC's members had previously collaborated in political campaigns, they began the First World War with diverse opinions and political affiliations. Ponsonby and Trevelyan were Liberals, the latter a junior minister until he resigned upon Britain's entry into the war. Morel and Angell were nonparty liberals; the former had made his name campaigning against Belgian atrocities in the Congo before turning his attention to secret diplomacy. MacDonald was Secretary of the ILP and Chairman of the Parliamentary Labour Party. Among other leaders, **H.N. Brailsford** and **J.A. Hobson** had developed the influential thesis that imperialism and international rivalry were the results of capitalism's search for outlets for surplus capital; Helena Swanwick was a moderate leader of the **women's suffrage** movement; and **Leonard Woolf** was a prominent member of the **Fabian Society**. By 1924, however, all of the leaders of the UDC had joined the ILP, the only party officially to oppose not only the war, but also the punitive peace terms.

The UDC's fortunes began to improve in 1917 when the United States entered the war. President Woodrow Wilson's peace proposals resembled those of the UDC, thus making the latter respectable. In the same year, the revolutionary Soviet government published the "secret treaties," a series of pre-war agreements between the Allied powers, which appeared to validate UDC allegations that the war was an imperialist venture. Finally, the post-war economic slump lent credence to UDC arguments against war reparations.

Between the wars, the UDC dominated the Labour Party's Advisory Committee on International Questions. While this increased its influence, it greatly reduced the necessity for separate activity, which virtually ended with the advent of MacDonald's first Labour government in 1924. Although Morel criticized its foreign policy, most other UDC members were reluctant to campaign against a government whose Cabinet included nine of their own members. Morel's death in 1924 effectively finished the UDC as a significant, independent pressure group.

D.P. Blaazer

Bibliography
Cline, Catherine Ann. *E.D. Morel, 1873-1924: The Strategies of Protest.* 1980.
Swanwick, H.M. *Builders of Peace.* 1924.
Swartz, Marvin. *The Union of Democratic Control in British Politics during the First World War.* 1971.

United Nations

Britain was one of the founder members of the United Nations and was made one of the five permanent members of the Security Council at San Francisco in 1945. Accordingly, Britain has a veto over the decisions of the Security Council, the most important aspect of which is action under Chapter VII of the Charter concerning the enforcement of international peace and security. Britain is one of the two members of the **European Union** that is in this position, the other being France.

It has been argued that the changes in the relative power of Britain since 1945 justify some modification of the permanent membership of the Security Council. Since 1945 a number of other states, such as Germany and Japan, could claim greater power and, therefore, a right to permanent membership and the veto. Britain and France have come under pressure to yield their seats to the European Union, and the closer the Union gets to a common defense and foreign policy the stronger that becomes. But there is little indication that the British are prepared to accept this. In the Maastricht treaty (1991), however, there was a sign of movement in that they accepted an obligation to discuss with the other members of the European Union in the United Nations relevant issues that came before the Security Council.

There is, however, a strong case for the view that Britain should retain the seat because of the special contribution it can make to U.N. business. The United Nations is a forum the British take very seriously in their diplomacy, and British diplomats, unlike many Americans, regard promotion to a U.N. post as career enhancement. One of the United Nation's advantages for Britain is that it has become a way of enhancing a declining power, rather than reflecting, as was the case in 1945, an actual power. Since it is treated seriously, Britain's ambassadors to the United Nations have often been distinguished and able; Sir John Thomson was followed by Sir Crispin Tickell, and most

U

recently David Hannay, who came to New York from Brussels.

It was evident in the early 1990s that the British were unique in the United Nations in combining quality in their personnel, with experience and skill in the arts of multilateral diplomacy, and a global vision. The Americans were seen as not to take the United Nations very seriously, and American diplomats, with some exceptions, do not like a U.N. posting. One reason is that the State Department insists upon too detailed and close a control over its people in New York. British diplomats, on the other hand, are allowed a greater freedom for maneuver by the **Foreign Office**. The British also possess a strong global interest and experience, which gives them a unique perspective on, and knowledge about, all of the continents and the wide range of U.N. business. For all of these reasons, therefore, the British have something positive to contribute to the United Nations that no other state can offer—strong justification for retaining their permanent membership of the Security Council.

In recent years they have initiated a number of new developments in the United Nations and played a leading part in its work. An important procedural change was the introduction, by Sir John Thomson in 1986, of a resolution creating a special coordinating committee of the Permanent Five. The group was to meet prior to the full Security Council and attempt to reach a consensus among the Five on issues that were to be discussed. The British also pushed hard for international cooperation on environmental policy through the United Nations. The lead was taken in this by Sir Crispin Tickell, who had **Margaret Thatcher**'s strong support. He proposed that the Security Council should have responsibility in this area, but this suggestion was rejected.

Of particular importance was the leading role of the British, with the Americans, in responding through the United Nations to the invasion and annexation of Kuwait by the forces of Iraqi leader Saddam Hussein in August 1990. The United States and Britain were the two activist states and between them managed the diplomacy around the Security Council, which produced a high degree of agreement in a succession of resolutions against Iraq. The British played a leading role in the drawing up and approval of Resolution 678, which was the legal basis of the opening of the military campaign against Hussein in January 1991, and of

Resolution 687, which established the conditions of peace in February-April 1991.

The British government has dealt with the United Nations positively in recent years. Though it supported a policy of zero growth in the budget of the organization, it has worked to persuade the United States to pay the sums that it owed. Though there was a case for making the British more sensitive to the views of the other members of the European Union in the U.N. context, the value of their contribution could be lost to the world organization if Britain were to lose its position as a permanent member.

Paul Taylor

Bibliography

Hughes, E.J. "Winston Churchill and the Formation of the United Nations Organization," *Journal of Contemporary History*, vol. 9 (1974), pp. 177–94.

Goodwin, Geoffrey Lawrence. *Britain and the United Nations*. 1957.

Jensen, Erik, and Thomas Fisher, eds. *Britain and the United Nations*. 1991.

Taylor, Paul, and A.J.R. Groom. *The United Nations and the Gulf War*. Discussion paper no. 38, Royal Institute of International Affairs, 1992.

Unity Campaign

The Unity Campaign of early 1937 aimed to create a "United Front" of the **Labour Party**, the **Communist Party of Great Britain** (CPGB), and the **Independent Labour Party** (ILP) in order to oppose **Fascism** in Britain and abroad. The campaign was conducted by the ILP, the CPGB, and the **Socialist League**—the official organization of the Left within the Labour Party. It was launched on 17 January 1937 with the publication of a brief Unity Manifesto. The leadership of the Labour Party vehemently opposed the campaign, and, armed with a resolution of the 1936 party conference banning collaboration with Communists, disaffiliated the Socialist League in January. A few weeks later they declared that membership of the League and the Labour Party would become incompatible on 1 June. The League dissolved itself in May. This effectively doomed the campaign, although it continued until after the United Front was decisively rejected by the Labour Party conference in October.

The basis of the Unity Campaign was a set of shared theoretical beliefs about the nature of

Fascism and the dynamics of international politics. The participants held that Fascism was merely capitalism's political response to a profound international economic crisis. They concluded that the British government—with its overwhelming parliamentary majority, its apparent hostility to the working class, its acquiescence in Italian and German intervention in the Spanish Civil War, and its attempts to suppress revolutionary socialist propaganda while tolerating the British Union of Fascists—was evolving toward Fascism.

Despite their common ground the participants had divergent aims. The Communist Party sought socialist unity as a preliminary to the formation of a Popular Front of all opponents of Fascism. The Socialist League and the ILP, by contrast, wanted a United Front in order to prevent a Popular Front. The Socialist League, in particular, was worried that right-wingers in the Parliamentary Labour Party were secretly lobbying for united action with Liberals and Conservatives opposed to the government's foreign policy. Consistent with their theoretical analysis, the Socialist League and the ILP feared any such development, arguing—as the CPGB had also argued before 1935—that only socialists could lead an effective and committed anti-Fascist movement.

Despite an intensive propaganda effort, some of it conducted through the popular Left Book Club, the campaign failed to attract mass support and was clearly doomed from the start. Not only was Labour officially opposed, but there was also considerable mutual antagonism among its supporters. The CPGB had long engaged in vitriolic abuse of the Labour Party, and especially of the Labour Left. The ILP and CPGB's previous attempts at collaboration had ended bitterly, with the CPGB poaching some of the ILP's rapidly dwindling membership. The ruthless suppression of the POUM (the ILP's sister party in Spain) at the behest of the Spanish Communists in May 1937, as well as the 1936-7 Moscow show trials of alleged Trotskyists, further poisoned relations among the British parties.

D.P. Blaazer

Bibliography

Jupp, James. *The Radical Left in Britain, 1931–1941.* 1982.
Pimlott, Ben. *Labour and the Left in the 1930s.* 1977.

Universities, New

Charters were granted in the first half of the twentieth century to thirteen new British universities. Nine more sprang up in the 1960s in the wake of concerns about higher education in the post-war era. Following in the tradition of the dissenting academies of the eighteenth century and the university colleges of the nineteenth, the new universities of the twentieth century were established to fulfill civic needs that the great humanist centers of learning, Oxford and Cambridge, did not satisfy. They were also intended to accommodate an anticipated increase in demand for higher education that the older universities could not meet.

In the first half of the century many existing regional colleges achieved university status under charters granted by the Chancellor of the Exchequer through an Advisory Committee on Grants. In 1919 the University Grants Committee was established jointly by the Treasury and the Board of Education to administer these funds. The early recipients of these funds were civic universities that were largely associated with the industries of their area—Birmingham with engineering and mining; Liverpool with architecture and commerce; Manchester with machining and cotton; Reading with agriculture.

The establishment in North Staffordshire of Keele in 1949–50 set a new course for the twentieth-century British university. Unlike the "red brick" universities, which were haphazard outgrowths of earlier institutions only latterly given state sponsorship, the new universities were public enterprises: pre-approved and carefully sited by the government. As the first of the "white brick" universities, Keele was intended to be both fully residential and coeducational. In contrast to its precursors, it would not simply supplement the Oxford and Cambridge curricula, but actually endeavor to reformulate the shape and content of higher education.

At Keele the primary focus was providing for careers in the post-war world by producing well-rounded students, schooled in both the sciences and the humanities. A compulsory foundation course ensured that students were exposed to both subject areas from the outset of their university careers. Influenced by contemporary German university theorists, Keele's founders underlined the importance of research but at the same time emphasized good teaching. Future universities would make use of the Keele model, refashioning it to their own requirements.

University of East Anglia (Denys Lasdun, 1970).

In 1959 the University Grants Committee (UGC) appointed a subcommittee to examine twenty-eight applications, from which six were chosen to open as new universities. Sussex, already approved in 1958, opened in 1961; York and East Anglia (approved 1960), in 1963; Essex and Lancaster (approved 1961), in 1964; and Kent and Warwick (approved 1961), in 1965.

The choice of these six sites was partly determined by geographical factors. The eastern and mid-eastern areas were served by Kent at Canterbury, Essex at Colchester, and East Anglia at Norwich, while the West Midlands and northwest were covered by Warwick and Lancaster, respectively. With the founding of Stirling and Ulster in 1967, new universities expanded to Scotland and Northern Ireland.

Space was another factor in the site selection. A priority of the new universities was the provision of campus residence for as many students as possible. As such, the UGC chose locations with potential expansion in mind; most of the universities were situated in the outskirts of towns, where land was not at so great a premium. It was left to the individual institutions to devise their residential systems. Kent, Lancaster, and York each based their social and academic plans on a college structure, and the remaining universities established residential hall schemes.

Each of the new universities was dedicated to some combination of general and specialized education. In keeping with the recommendations of the **Robbins Report** of 1963, all of them hoped to avoid confining a student too early in a prescribed course of study. At Sussex—the most experimental of the new university programs—a team of experts devised a "multisubject" system of learning that exchanged individual departments for "Schools" of inter-disciplinary studies in which related subjects overlapped. "Schools" of European Studies, English and American Studies, and Social Studies were soon followed by Physical, Biological, and Applied Sciences. Essex and East Anglia were similarly based on fields of study, with varying subject disciplines included under the broader category of "Schools."

From their founding, the new universities set out to establish themselves as centers of research as well as teaching. By its third year, 20 percent of Warwick's student population of 1,384 were graduate students and nearly a quarter of the faculty were research staff. Within their first few years Essex and East Anglia had employed in a range of departments senior professors whose reputations for research were already well established.

To keep pace with the Robbins Report estimates of demand for higher education in the decades ahead, the new universities prepared themselves for rapid growth. Though existing civic universities and Oxbridge bore much of the brunt of the 1960s student explosion, the newly founded universities underwent unprojected expansion. Between 1964 and 1967, Sussex grew from 1,500 to 3,000 students; Essex and Kent, too, were to reach a 3,000 student target over the course of the decade. Robbins had anticipated a need to accommodate 197,000 students by the year 1968; all combined, nearly 220,000 places were available in institutions of higher education by that year.

Expansion continued at a steady rate over the course of the next decade. The total number of full-time students in higher education rose to 307,000 by 1980. In the 1980s, however, the new universities experienced their first significant drop in enrollment as the over-all average student growth rate fell from 5.1 percent annually to 1.1 percent. At the same time student-staff ratios improved, and an ever-increasing percentage of graduates were immediately joining the workforce upon graduation. The pace of student enrollment and degree completion in the new universities appears to have recovered in the early 1990s.

Martha A. Schütz

Bibliography

Beloff, Michael. *The Plateglass Universities.* 1968.

Birks, Tony. *Building the New Universities.* 1972.

Blin-Stoyle, Roger, and Geoff Ivey, eds. *The Sussex Opportunity: A New University and the Future.* 1986.

Stewart, W.A.C. *Higher Education in Post-War Britain.* 1988.

Truscot, Bruce. *Red Brick University.* 1943.

University Education

University education in Britain at the beginning of the twentieth century was an elite affair and has remained so for much of the century, although provision began to expand and to change significantly from the end of the 1950s.

There were eighteen institutions and clusters of institutions using the name "university" in 1900. The four Scottish universities, Edinburgh, Glasgow, St. Andrews and Aberdeen, cherished lineages nearly as long as those of **Oxford** and **Cambridge**. But all of the remainder, the constituent colleges of the University of London, and of the University of Wales, the universities of Durham, Manchester, Leeds, Newcastle, Birmingham, Bristol, Sheffield, and Reading, and the university colleges of Nottingham and Southampton, were nineteenth-century creations.

Their funds came from three sources: student fees, endowments, and the state. The Scottish universities had received some government funding throughout the nineteenth century; and in 1889 the Treasury finally conceded the principle of grant aid to English and Welsh institutions outside Oxford and Cambridge, few of whom had anything substantial in the way of endowments. By 1906 this had been pushed up to £100,000 per annum.

In 1900–1 full-time students at all British universities, including the medical schools, totaled 20,249, just under 1 percent of the appropriate age group. Although London had pioneered the external, part-time degree and nineteenth-century Scottish universities had contained students of widely varying ages, the dominant model for the composition of the student body was one derived from Oxford and Cambridge, or "Oxbridge" as the composite was known: resident, full-time, and largely between the ages of eighteen and twenty-two.

There were some scholarships, but fees and full-time residence meant that this elite was as much a social as an intellectual one. No child born to an unskilled or semiskilled father before 1910 could expect to get to university. The children of the professional middle classes were the dominant group. However, the children of the lower-middle classes and of skilled workers were beginning to appear in student bodies outside Oxford and Cambridge, in particular those in Scotland. The elite was also largely male; only 3,284 of those students of 1900 were women.

Despite grand statements by politicians about the importance of investment in education during the last years of the First World War, the university sector grew only slowly in the inter-war period. The loss of fee income during the war hit all universities badly. In 1919 Oxford and Cambridge joined those seeking government funding, followed in the 1920s by four more new university colleges, Exeter, Swansea, Hull, and Leicester. From 1919 the Treasury was advised by the University Grants Committee (UGC), which endeavored to make its allocations on a quinquennial cycle. Yet even by the mid-1930s, government grants to the universities were running at only £2 million per annum, representing about one-third of their income.

Their student populations remained small and exclusive. In 1938–9 there were just under 50,000 full-time students, one-quarter of whom were women. Almost all came from upper-middle- and middle-class backgrounds. Of children born to an unskilled or semiskilled father between 1920 and 1929, 0.5 percent could expect to find their way to university. With social exclusiveness went intellectual traditionalism. At Oxford and Cambridge the vast majority of students—80 percent and 70 percent, respectively—were in the arts faculties. Science dominated only in London, Manchester, Leeds, and Edinburgh. The first research degrees had been developed in the 1890s, in an effort to challenge the German universities. But the numbers of research students grew only very slowly.

The **Second World War** finally pushed universities into financial dependence upon the state. It also brought manpower planning on an unprecedented scale, preparing the ground for a radical review of the nature and extent of higher education as a whole. However, the pressures of this, coupled with the demand represented by the post-war "baby boom," were slow to make themselves felt. Although in the four years after the end of the war numbers were swelled by returning servicemen, they fell back again. In 1954 only 3.2 percent of the relevant age group were going to university, 3.8 percent of boys and 1.5 percent of girls.

The first clear sign of growth came at the end of the 1950s, with the foundation of the first of the **new universities**, Sussex, in 1958. In 1960, the recommendation of the Anderson Committee, that everyone who could secure a place at a university should, subject to a parental **means test**, get a grant to attend, was accepted. Expansion and wider access were then both signaled and legitimated by the **Robbins Report** on Higher Education in 1963. It recommended that all students who wished to attend university and could achieve the requisite standard should be found a place, envisaging a student population in 1980 two-and-a-half times the size of that in 1962. The lion's share of the extra places were to be provided in science and technology. By 1967 already 6.3 percent of the age group were entering university. Simultaneously, the development of the "binary system" with the expansion and upgrading of **polytechnics**, offering degree-earning courses of far greater variety, including the vocational, to a far more varied student population, including mature part-time adults, sometimes with very few formal qualifications, began the redefinition of notions and expectations of higher education as a whole.

The pace of expansion was checked, however, in the 1970s. In part this was a consequence of the deteriorating national and international economic situation; in part it was a function of the spiraling cost element to which the Robbins Committee had paid little attention, that of the system of mandatory student support recommended by the Anderson Committee. By the end of the decade quinquennial planning had collapsed. The full-time university student population in 1980 was 45,000 short of that envisaged by Robbins.

The end of the 1980s saw a reconstruction of university funding and government more concentrated and thoroughgoing than any that had preceded it. Student grants were phased out and replaced by loans. The Education Reform Act of 1988 replaced the UGC by the Universities Funding Council (UFC) and created a parallel Polytechnics and Colleges Funding Council (PCFC). The Education Act of 1992 then replaced both with a single Higher Education Funding Council (HEFC), and 44 polytechnics were designated universities.

The increase of demand for places generated by the post-war demographic surge and the rapidity of the financial seesaw meant that the Robbins-led expansion altered the composition and activities of the student population less than might have been expected. The expansion of numbers in science and technology was far less than the Robbins Committee had hoped. Between 1962 and 1980 it envisaged the numbers of students working in these fields in universities and other institutions of higher education increasing over threefold. In the event they barely doubled.

By 1990 women students made up more than 40 percent of the full-time student population of universities, but very few of these were working-class girls. The chances of access to university education for all social classes improved, but the middle and upper classes preserved, indeed even enhanced, their position of advantage. In 1962 4 percent of the sons of skilled manual workers could expect to get to university; the sons of unskilled manual workers statistically did not figure at all. By 1992 4 percent of them could expect to do so, while the daughters of unskilled manual workers still did not feature in the statistics. By contrast, while in 1962 15 percent of the daughters and 29 percent of the sons of professional fathers could expect to go to university, in 1992 the respective percentages were 22 and 33 percent.

By 1991 just over 20 percent of eighteen-year-olds were entering some form of higher education, roughly half of them going to universities. The elite was larger than that of 1900, but still recognizably its descendant.

Gillian Sutherland

Bibliography

Berdahl, Robert O. *British Universities and the State.* 1959.

Carswell, John. *Government and the Universities in Britain: Programme and Performance, 1960–1980.* 1985.

Halsey, A.H., A.F Heath, and J.M. Ridge. *Origins and Destinations: Family, Class, and Education in Modern Britain.* 1980.

Layard, Richard, John King, and Claus Moser. *The Impact of Robbins.* 1969.

Report of the Committee on Higher Education, 1961–3 (Robbins Report). Cmnd. 2154. 1963.

Urban Riots

Urban rioting has been spasmodic throughout the twentieth century in Britain, but only in the last quarter has it appeared to acquire new dimensions, with violent disorders in inner-city areas met by **police** outfitted with new riot control equipment and informed by a tactical manual originating in the colonial experience.

In keeping with the research into crowds during earlier periods and in other countries, it is probably true to say that urban riots in twentieth-century Britain have often had some kind of legitimizing notion behind them, though these are not always such that subsequent generations can sympathize; for example, those critical of the conduct of the **Boer War** at the turn of the century were the objects of ferocious Crown hostility, and the early stages of the **First World War** were marked by anti-German riots in several cities. While the **General Strike** of 1926 was relatively free of serious unrest, during the inter-war years urban disorder was often linked with economic problems and/or politics. In one or two instances the police appear to have overreacted to demonstrations by the **unemployed** before any manifest disorder, and in Birkenhead in September 1932 there was what can only be described as a riot by police in the poorer districts of the town following a protest against the **means test**. The British Union of **Fascists**' decision to conduct politics on the streets also led to violence, most notably the Battle of Cable Street (4 October 1936), which provided the climax to **Oswald Mosley's** attempt to lead a Black Shirt parade through London's East End. This confrontation provided the occasion for the introduction of the Public Order Act (1936), which prohibited the wearing of uniforms for political purposes in public places or meetings and also gave chief constables powers to regulate marches and processions and, with the Home Secretary's approval, to ban any such if it was considered that it would lead to disorder.

Two decades following the Second World War witnessed little serious urban disorder, though with hindsight it could be argued there were ominous pointers to the future with the race riot in London's Notting Hill (1958), the battles between youth gangs of Mods and Rockers on bank holidays generally at seaside resorts in the mid-1960s, and the clashes between police and anti-Vietnam War demonstrations. During the 1970s demonstrations by the neo-Fascist **National Front** brought counterdemonstrations by antiracist groups; they also fostered the development of paramilitary policing in the form of Special Patrol Groups (SPGs) organized to clamp down on **crime** and to provide units trained for riot control. Clamping down on crime invariably meant that an area was flooded with SPG units for several weeks stopping and searching suspects. A massive police presence along these lines during the Notting Hill Carnival in 1976 resulted in a confrontation with predominantly Black youths who forced the police to retreat under a hail of stones and bricks. More serious rioting in the St. Paul's district of Bristol in April 1980 was the result of an inept, strong-arm anticrime swoop on a café patronized largely by young **Blacks**. In the spring and summer of 1981 a series of similar riots swept through inner-city areas, notably Brixton in South London,

Toxteth (Liverpool), and Moss Side (Manchester). Four years later there was a similar wave of rioting again in Brixton, but also in Handsworth (Birmingham) and on the Broadwater Farm Estate, Tottenham, North London. The latter incident was sparked by a police raid during which an innocent woman had a heart attack and died; the riot became particularly notorious for the savage killing of P.C. Keith Blakelock, who became separated from his police squad during the disturbance.

As ever with popular disturbance, it was a commonplace for some senior police officers, politicians, and sections of the media to speak of agitators behind the trouble, but no such agitators were ever arrested or prosecuted. More probably, as the Scarman official enquiry into the 1981 Brixton riots concluded, the trouble is best understood as the boiling over of the frustration and anger of the underprivileged youth who believed themselves to be victimized by authority, and, most obviously, authority personified by the police. The training of the police in paramilitary tactics, together with a decline in their public accountability, arguably exacerbated the potential for violence, though in the rioting in Cardiff, Oxford, and Newcastle during the late summer of 1991 the police preferred to contain the conflict in a small area rather than seek to suppress it with force.

Frustration and anger on the part of a wider cross section of the population than just inner-city youth, and possibly, too, the handling of paramilitary police, contributed to the last major urban riot in London in the period of **Margaret Thatcher**'s government. On 31 March 1990 a massive demonstration against the new poll tax degenerated into a riot centering on Trafalgar Square; cars and shops were burned, shops were looted, police vans drove at crowds, mounted police charged them, and the crowds responded by throwing bricks, stones, and pieces of scaffolding. Again there were accusations of agitators and hooligans, yet none were prosecuted and charges were dropped against several of those charged with rioting because of the unreliability of police evidence.
Clive Emsley

Bibliography

Benyon, John, ed. *Scarman and After: Reflecting on Lord Scarman's Report, the Riots, and Their Aftermath.* 1984.

Benyon, John, and John Solomos. "The Simmering Cities: Urban Unrest during the Thatcher Years," *Parliamentary Affairs.* vol. 41 (1988), pp. 402–22.

Edwards, E., R. Golland, and S. Leach. *Urban Riots and Public Order: A Select Bibliography, 1975–1985.* 1986.

Gaskell, George, and Robert Benewick, eds. *The Crowd in Contemporary Britain.* 1987.

Kettle, Martin, and Lucy Hodges. *Uprising: The Police, the People, and the Riots in Britain's Cities.* 1982.

Pilkington, Edward. *Beyond the Mother Country: West Indians and the Notting Hill Riots, 1958.* 1988.

Urban Transport

In 1900 an unusually high proportion (80 percent) of Britain's population already lived in towns; but only in **London**, by far the largest of them all, where the world's first steam Underground had been started in 1863 and the world's first deep electric tube added in 1890, did **railways** play a significant part in passenger movements. And even in London the 400 million passengers carried per year in the Underground or by suburban surface railway were considerably fewer than the total who traveled by road: 300 million by bus and 280 million by tramcar. Of Britain's four other main cities, only Glasgow had opened a small, cable-hauled Underground (1896), and, as these cities covered a much more limited surface area, they relied much less than London on suburban trains. Most journeys were made either on foot—some remarkably long walks to work were recorded—or in horse-drawn vehicles, usually double deckers because of a mid-nineteenth-century change in the method of vehicle taxation. The growing number of slow-moving passenger (and even slower freight) vehicles struggling to get along the often narrow streets created more congestion, street filth, and atmospheric pollution.

Relief was at hand in the form of the electric motor and the internal combustion engine. The first commercially viable electric tramway system, benefiting from earlier U.S. experience and with American equipment, was introduced in Bristol in 1895. By 1902 782 route miles of electrified track had been laid in a total route mileage of 1,321, most of it within or, to encourage building, just outside towns. A peak of 2,599 route miles was reached in 1923, most of it municipally owned and operated, the London

County Council (LCC) being the main operator in the capital. There, but not elsewhere, electric trams were kept out of the central streets but offered faster services from the suburbs. They were cheaper, too, for horses were costly to feed and maintain, and eleven or twelve were needed to keep each vehicle on the road throughout the day. The number of passengers carried by tram throughout the country grew from just under 1 billion per year in 1899–1900 when electric systems were augmenting the horse-hauled, to a peak of just over 4.7 billion in 1927–8. Motor buses also started to appear early in the century, but it was not until the advent of the London General Omnibus Company's (LGOC's) X-type in 1908, and more particularly its B-type in 1910, that these vehicles were capable of constantly starting and stopping in traffic without shaking themselves to pieces. Hackney carriages and cabs were motorized at about the same time. By 1913 few horse-drawn passenger vehicles were to be seen in Britain's towns, though many carts, each pulled throughout the day by the same horse and often with much standing and waiting while freight was loaded and unloaded, were in evidence in the 1920s and some even survived the 1930s. Private companies played a more notable part than municipalities in the spread of motor buses: They required less fixed capital than the tramways, were more flexible in operation, could make money on more lightly trafficked routes, and were generally more profitable.

In London, unlike most other towns, private capital played a larger role, despite the tramway activities of the LCC, mainly because of the more heavily capitalized tube railways that came into use in, and soon after, 1900. The Central London Railway (now known as the Central Line), running under the main east-west thoroughfare between Shepherd's Bush and the City and originally charging a flat fare of 2d, was an immediate financial success (unlike its predecessor, the City and South London, in 1890) and encouraged the well-known American urban transport speculator Charles Tyson Yerkes to raise the funds (mainly from American sources) to electrify part of the existing steam Underground and to build three more electric tubes: from Baker Street to Waterloo and the Elephant and Castle; from Charing Cross to Hampstead with a branch to the foot of Highgate Hill (Archway); and from South Kensington via Piccadilly Circus to Finsbury Park. These lines, together with the other part of the steam Underground, electrified by its owner, the Metropolitan Railway, opened for traffic between 1905 and 1907, adding greatly to London's passenger-carrying capacity just as an effective motor bus was also to become available. They added too greatly, in fact, for the new Underground Electric Railways of London (UERL) had to struggle hard to win enough passengers to avoid liquidation. Albert Henry Stanley (1874–1948), then Superintendent of the Public Service Corporation of New Jersey, was sent over by the American shareholders in 1907 to save their investment. This he gradually did, and then, at the beginning of 1912, he made to the LGOC, with large profits from its new motor bus, an offer it could not refuse. The combine so created became profitable overall, the motor buses supporting the less profitable—but for London and Londoners enormously important—Underground system. The new electric railways and the faster motor buses and trams eased the urban road congestion despite the survival of the slower-moving freight vehicles, still horse drawn. The combine remained in private shareholders' hands, with Stanley (created Lord Ashfield in 1920) in charge. In the early 1930s he turned to advantage political experiences gained during the war as President of the Board of Trade by coming to terms with the London County Council, other local tramway authorities outside central London, and the Metropolitan Railway to form the London Passenger Transport Board (LPTB), a public corporation that, from 1 July 1933, ran all of the capital's Underground and tramways and almost all of its buses. Only the taxicabs, many still privately owned by their drivers, and the suburban services of the main-line railways remained independent, the latter pooling their receipts with the LPTB.

As the profitable petrol bus, and its oil engine successor, was allowed by the authorities to run on pneumatic, instead of solid, tires, received a covered top deck, and became altogether larger, more comfortable and efficient, it began to win more traffic from the electric tramways, which reached peak carryings in 1927–8. By 1937 London's road services were responsible for 2 billion journeys by bus and a further 203 million journeys by trolley bus, the capital having taken to these hybrids in a big way after 1930. LPTB railways were responsible for 480 million journeys. Between the wars much more spacious subsurface central stations had been opened on the Underground, and more lines had been extended to the suburbs and beyond, **Frank Pick**, the Managing Director, earning a well-deserved reputation for his encouragement of modern, functional design in these new stations.

The spread of private cars, from 2 million licensed in 1950 (roughly the same number as in 1938) to 19.75 million in 1990, has caused a great decline in the excellent urban public transport system, which has been used by people in all walks of life. In the 1930s even the middle-class minority who could afford cars used them mainly for "pleasure motoring" and not for traveling by day to and from work. It was then more of the wage earners, not the salaried, who went to work by private vehicle: The pedal cycle, still a popular mode of travel until the early 1950s, has since then been used less and less, especially in congested, fume-laden city centers. Motor bicycles, too, often with sidecars attached, were popular among some better-off wage earners in the 1930s; 462,000 motor bicycles were registered in Britain in 1938. With the advent of mopeds after the war, this form of transport was even more widely supported by younger people, peaking at 1.7 million in 1962. By 1990, however, only half this total was registered.

When electric tramways were finally phased out—the last of them ran in Manchester in 1949, London in 1952, and everywhere else apart from the seaside promenade in Blackpool, Lancashire, by 1960—soon to be followed by trolley buses, urban passenger transport by road came to depend wholly upon the motor bus. But bus traffic fell as more people stayed at home in the evening to watch **television**, went to work five, instead of six, days a week, and increasingly used their own cars. Bus operators cut services, which encouraged more use of private transport and increased congestion. Urban bus services became unreliable for users and unprofitable for operators, who became increasingly reliant upon tax concessions and public subsidies. In London, two new tube railways (the Victoria and Jubilee lines) were opened (1968–72 and 1979), and refugees from the unreliable buses took to the Underground even for shorter journeys. Its traffic grew remarkably, from 498 million to 815 million journeys a year between 1982 and 1989, encouraged by the introduction of daily and weekly contract tickets. The elderly Underground became seriously overloaded, and a disastrous escalator fire at King's Cross tube station in 1987 drew national attention to the urgent need for renovation. Tyneside linked its suburban railways by a new Underground line, Glasgow modernized its old subway, and Manchester brought back a street tramway along which small suburban trains passed through the city center. Elsewhere, however, all cities relied entirely for their public transport upon the bus, once again struggling hard to make its way along roads becoming increasingly congested. Many towns had been diverting through traffic with bypass roads since the inter-war years and more recently with ring roads. Other attempts to encourage the bus by discouraging the car were parking meters, first introduced into British towns in 1958; bus lanes; the setting up of passenger transport authorities in the main conurbations outside London (1969); and, in 1986, the freeing of buses outside London of certain aspects of public regulation to which they had been subjected since 1930. But, as in 1900, the true solution is likely to be found in new technology: sophisticated forms of road pricing whereby private cars and commercial traffic can be charged for using urban roads at busy times, the sums involved being directly related to the extent of congestion. With urban roads once again sufficiently clear for them to operate a fast service, buses of various sizes, from small runabouts to large double deckers capable of carrying up to seventy passengers at a time, would dispel public transport's tarnished image and allow people to move about in urban centers more freely once again—and at fares subsidized by the income from the road pricing of cars and commercial vehicles.

T.C. Barker

Bibliography

Barker, T.C. *Moving Millions: A Pictoral History of London Transport.* 1990.

Barker, T.C., and C.I. Savage. *An Economic History of Transport in Britain.* 1974.

Collins, Michael F., and Timothy M. Pharoah. *Transport Organisation in a Great City: The Case of London.* 1974.

Munby, Denys Lawrence. *Inland Transport Statistics: Great Britain, 1900–1970.* 1978.

Utopian Thought

Ever since Thomas More's communistic *Utopia* (1516), utopian thought has flourished in Britain. Francis Bacon's *New Atlantis* (1627) added a fresh strand to the British contribution, with its depiction of a utopian society ruled by scientists. In the eighteenth century Jonathan Swift's *Gulliver's Travels* (1726) mocked this vision, and so enriched the utopian tradition with a new ingredient: the satirical dystopia or anti-utopia. Samuel Butler used this form to telling effect in his anti-utopian satire on Victorian society, *Erewhon* (1872).

The Morean tradition was also revitalized in the nineteenth century by the rise of a powerful British school of utopian socialism. Robert Owen's *A New View of Society* (1816) laid the foundation stone; numerous contributions followed, such as John Bray's *Labour's Wrongs and Labour's Remedy* (1839). At the end of the century William Morris produced the most vivid and effective utopia of socialism to date in his *News from Nowhere* (1891).

There have been significant developments of this tradition of utopian socialism in the twentieth century. **H.G. Wells'** many scientific utopias—for example, *A Modern Utopia* (1905), *The World Set Free* (1914), *The Shape of Things to Come*, (1933)—married the socialism of More to the science of Bacon. But Wells also creatively worked in the vein of anti-utopia, in his compelling science fantasies *The Time Machine* (1895) and *The War of the Worlds* (1898). Ironically it was this anti-utopian aspect of Wells' writing that was drawn upon to attack the scientific, "Wellsian" utopia in the two most famous anti-utopias of the twentieth century: **Aldous Huxley's** *Brave New World* (1932) and **George Orwell's** *Nineteen Eighty-Four* (1949). Huxley's book satirized the hedonism and soullessness of modern scientific civilization; his sojourn in California in the 1920s had given him a vision of a frivolous materialist society that he saw as increasingly the future of the world. Orwell's inspiration was nearer home, in the totalitarian societies of Nazi Germany and Stalinist Russia. But he, too, saw these as merely the portents of a world that seemed to be moving inexorably in a totalitarian direction.

Anti-utopias—"utopias in the negative"—continued to figure strongly in the post-1945 period of the Cold War and the threat of nuclear annihilation. **William Golding's** *Lord of the Flies* (1954), ostensibly a fable about the inherent evil in human nature, as illustrated by the reversion to barbarism of a group of English schoolboys shipwrecked on an island, actually was a comment on the aggressive and warlike propensities of the society of their parents.

Anthony Burgess' science-fiction novel, *A Clockwork Orange* (1962), also used the example of a group of young people—in this case violent delinquents—to draw attention to the violence of the state and the danger of the new methods of "behavioral conditioning" that it increasingly employed. Part of the effectiveness of the novel came from Burgess' invention of a future form of street language, meant to illustrate the degeneracy of contemporary culture.

But the climate of the 1960s also encouraged optimism and hope. Fittingly it was Aldous Huxley—then a resident of southern California, the original *Brave New World*—who marked the turn of the tide with his utopia *Island* (1961). In this work Huxley blended Eastern religion with Western science—including some of the scientific techniques of *Brave New World*—to portray a gentle anarchistic, ecological utopia. There were strong echoes of William Morris in this vision, a feature also of Robert Van de Weyer's *Wickwyn* (1986). The ecological perspective was also a leading characteristic of the **feminist** utopia that, launched in the United States, found a ready response in Britain. Increasingly many of the women's presses, such as Virago, established special series to promote this new, or newly revived, genre. British women writers did not produce such compelling examples as Marge Piercy's *Woman on the Edge of Time* (1975), but works such as Miranda Miller's *Smiles and the Millennium* (1989) and Fay Weldon's *Darcy's Utopia* (1990) were engaging and effective uses of the genre.

At the end of the twentieth century the future of utopia, in Britain as elsewhere, is uncertain. The breakup of the Communist world has weakened, perhaps destroyed, one of the most important bases of modern utopia, the vision of a socialist society. At the same time the threat of ecological disaster hangs over the planet, and utopia has frequently been a response to crises—in the fifth century B.C., in the sixteenth century, and at other times. It would be surprising if this were not also to be the case in our time.

Krishan Kumar

Bibliography

Armytage, W.H.G. *Heavens Below: Utopian Experiments in England, 1560–1960.* 1961.

Davis, J.C. *Utopia and the Ideal Society.* 1981.

Kumar, Krishan. *Utopia and Anti-Utopia in Modern Times.* 1987.

Morton, A.L. *The English Utopia.* 1952.

V

Vaughan Williams, Ralph (1872–1958)
An English composer, conductor, writer and folk-song collector, Ralph Vaughan Williams succeeded **Edward Elgar** as the leading British composer of his generation. Of central importance to his output is a series of nine highly individual symphonies, interspersed with large-scale choral and orchestral works, **operas**, concertos, and some chamber music. His melodic writing, when influenced by his enthusiasm for **folk song**, imparts a nationalist flavor to several of his works, although others are more cosmopolitan in nature, sharing to a certain extent in the development of modernism. No type of music making, however humble, was shunned by Vaughan Williams; he was equally at home composing for local musicians as for the *cognoscenti*. His involvement with the community found expression in his conductorship of the Leith Hall Festival (Dorking) during the period 1905–53. Following the award of an honorary doctorate from the **University of Oxford** (1919), he received many other official honors, including the Order of Merit (1935), although he declined a knighthood.

Born in Down Ampney, Gloucestershire, Vaughan Williams, a vicar's son with distinguished forebears on both sides of his family, lived for most of his life in or near Dorking, Surrey, and in London. He was slow to develop musically, and two years at the Royal College of Music, London (1890–2), led to three at Trinity College, **Cambridge** (1892–5), before he returned to the Royal College—his composition teachers were Hubert Parry, Charles Wood and Charles Villiers Stanford. At the Royal College in 1895 he met and befriended **Gustav Holst**, and on "field days," which were held regularly until Holst's death, they would discuss the progress of each other's compositions. Further encouragement was provided by lessons with Max Bruch in Berlin (during 1897 on his honeymoon with his first wife, Adeline Fisher), but more significant for the development of his style was a deepening interest in folk song, culminating in the collection of more than 800 examples beginning with "Bushes and Briars" in 1903. The adaptation of folk songs as hymns was an important part of his task as music editor of the *English Hymnal* (1904–6), as well as writing new tunes himself—for instance, *Sine nomine* ("For all the saints") and *Down Ampney* ("Come down, O Love Divine")—and subsequently he made many folk-song arrangements. The first works to include folk songs were the three *Norfolk Rhapsodies* (1905–6), but a more integrated use comes in three pieces dating from 1908–9, the String Quartet in G minor; the song cycle *On Wenlock Edge* for tenor and piano quintet; and the incidental music to *The Wasps* (Aristophanes). All three also exhibit evidence of Vaughan Williams' lessons in instrumentation with Ravel (1908). Bestriding this early period and crowning it is Vaughan Williams' first symphony, *A Sea Symphony* (Whitman, 1903–9) for soloists, chorus, and orchestra, a visionary exploration of humanity's place in the universe.

Vaughan Williams' interest in the contemporary revival of Elizabethan and Jacobean music can be heard in his first masterpiece, the *Fantasia on a Theme by Thomas Tallis* (1910) for double string orchestra, where passages of mystical tenderness contrast with others of spiritual ardor and exaltation. Similar feelings pervade the *Five Mystical Songs* (Herbert, 1911) for baritone, chorus, and orchestra, but in *A London Symphony* (1913), the more down-to-earth existence of city life is portrayed in some of the most colorful orchestration Vaughan Williams ever wrote. An attempt in *Hugh the Drover* (H. Child, 1914) to compose an opera, "written to *real* English words, with a certain amount of *real* English music and also a *real* English subject," was equally colorful if not as successful because of its inadequate libretto, whereas the romance for violin and orchestra, *The Lark Ascending* (1914), a meditative, unclouded idyll, is a gem.

Because Vaughan Williams felt duty-bound to enroll for military service during the First World War, seven years separate *The Lark Ascending* from his next important work, the *Pastoral Symphony* (1921). This is a bleaker portrait of nature, at time forbidding and austere, characteristics further explored in the oratorio *Sancta Civitas* (Revelation, 1925) and the suite *Flos Campi* (1925) for viola, small (wordless) chorus and small orchestra, which opens bitonally. Turning to the stage, Vaughan Williams drew on the expanded harmonic and melodic resources contained in these works to produce spiritually numbing portrayals of a woman almost defeated by nature in the opera *Riders to the Sea* (Vaughan Williams, after Synge, 1932), and of Job almost defeated by Satan in the "Masque for Dancing," *Job* (1930). Despite the noble strains of the triumphant Galliard of the Sons of the Morning in the latter, it is Satan's music, brutal and angular, that is most memorable, a type fully developed in the harshly discordant and violent Fourth Symphony (1934).

With the death of Holst in 1934, the warmth of Vaughan Williams' earlier style returned. The opera *Sir John in Love* (Vaughan Williams, after Shakespeare, 1928), from which Ralph Greaves arranged the *Fantasia on Greensleeves*, had kept this quality alive during the 1920s, and in the next decade it was amply demonstrated in the sensuously ravishing *Serenade to Music* (Shakespeare, 1938) for sixteen soloists, chorus, and orchestra and the rich, glowing textures of the *Five Variants of "Dives and Lazarus"* (1939) for string orchestra and harp(s). This development culminated in the splendor and spiritual security of the Fifth Symphony (1943). That Vaughan Williams, now in his seventies, could follow this symphony with another, the Sixth (1947), which from its opening minor-major clash to its desolate, antihuman epilogue negates the message of the Fifth, is evidence of a remarkable range of expression.

Although bitterly disappointed by the failure of the morality opera *The Pilgrim's Progress* (Vaughan Williams, after Bunyan, 1949) at its premiere at Covent Garden in 1951, Vaughan Williams found new reserves of energy to marry a second time (Ursula Wood in 1953), to undertake a lecture tour in the United States in 1954, and to continue composing. His involvement with film music, which had begun in 1940 with *49th Parallel* (1941) and *Coastal Command* (1942), now impinged on his symphonic writing when he transformed his score for *Scott of the Antarctic* (1948) into his seventh symphony, *Sinfonia Antartica* (1952), characterized by a renewed interest in unusual sounds, particularly those of the tuned percussion. This feature he explored further in the lighthearted and exuberant Eighth Symphony (1955). Finally, conflicts similar to those in the Sixth Symphony can be heard in the sombre, tough Ninth Symphony (1957), but here they find a hard-won resolution of qualified hope.

Trevor Bray

Bibliography

Kennedy, Michael. *The Works of Ralph Vaughan Williams.* 1964.

Mellors, Wilfrid. *Vaughan Williams and the Vision of Albion.* 1989.

Vaughan Williams, Ralph. *National Music and Other Essays.* 1963.

Vaughan Williams, Ursula. *R.V.W.: A Biography of Ralph Vaughan Williams.* 1964.

Venereal Disease

Responses to venereal disease have been defined by the inter-relationship of three issues—sex, disease, and medicine—and have been dependent on social fears about class, **sexuality**, and the family. These complex tensions were apparent in nineteenth-century attempts to control the spread of venereal disease (primarily syphilis and gonorrhea) and continued to underpin the interventions of the twentieth century.

The reservoir of venereal disease in the nineteenth-century British population was large. The connection with **prostitution** meant that the diseases were seen particularly as threats to the armed services, which led to the passage of the Contagious Diseases Acts (1864–9). The example of the failure of state regulation of vice powerfully shaped the twentieth-century response to venereal disease: the establishment of a tradition of voluntarism.

Early in the century significant discoveries in German laboratories revolutionized the medical ability to deal with syphilis. Both prevention and cure became possible, the former by means of the Wassermann test (1906), a diagnostic test for syphilis, the latter through Paul Ehrlich's discovery in 1909 of salvarsan, the first effective treatment. These issues were complicated in Britain, as elsewhere, by the medico-moral politics of venereal disease. Discussion of VD formed part of the debates over "national deterioration" associated with the aftermath of the **Boer War**. It was, however, the **First World War** and the association between VD and military efficiency that brought matters to a head.

The Royal Commission on Venereal Disease, set up in 1913, quickly became a focus for social-purity activity. By the time it reported in 1916, the issue had become urgent because of the rapid spread of venereal disease among the troops. In 1917 nearly 55,000 British soldiers were hospitalized with VD. A primary concern of government policy was to avoid appearing to condone immorality through the measures it adopted. The resistance to the state regulation of vice also remained strong. The main recommendations of the Royal Commission were accepted: State-funded pathology laboratories were established; free supplies of salvarsan were given to doctors; and local authorities were encouraged to set up free special clinics in general hospitals with substantial government funding.

The issue that had affected the Royal Commission debates, and that persisted in the inter-war years, was whether to provide proper prophylaxis and risk encouraging immorality, or to urge moral restraint and risk disease. These debates affected sex education, which the government was content to relegate to a voluntary body, the National Council for the Control of Venereal Disease (NCCVD), founded in 1914. This organization, subsequently the British Social Hygiene Council (BSHC), favored early treatment of infected persons but opposed the provision of prophylaxis. The Society for the Prevention of Venereal Disease (SPVD), established in 1919, took an opposite stance for eugenic reasons, advocating the use of prophylactic disinfectants.

The outbreak of the **Second World War** again brought the issue to the fore, especially after the arrival of American troops in 1942 prompted a steep rise in venereal infection. Warnings about VD appeared in the **press** (although modified to suit the moral concerns of newspaper proprietors) and on radio, and compulsory medical examination and treatment were introduced for those who had infected others.

The post-war availability of penicillin led to a period of optimism about the eventual disappearance of venereal diseases. A decline in infection after the war was followed by a substantial increase from the mid-1950s. This increase mainly involved gonorrhea, since the incidence of syphilis continued to fall, and came to be associated in the 1960s with **youth culture** and the "permissive society." A major area of increase was among male **homosexuals**. Despite the series of reforms in the late 1960s of laws relating to sexual behavior, discussions of venereal diseases targeted gay men, **Black immigrants**, and young single women as "risk groups" for disease. This was the context in which the AIDS epidemic burst on the scene in the early 1980s. Historians drew parallels between AIDS in the 1980s and syphilis in the early twentieth century, although the response to AIDS was informed by its own particular social and historical context.

Virginia Berridge

Bibliography

Austoker, Joan. "AIDS and Homosexuality in Britain: A Historical Perspective" in M. Adler, ed. *Diseases of the Homosexual Male*. 1988. pp. 185–97.

Berridge, Virginia, and Philip Strong, eds. *AIDS and Contemporary History*. 1993.

Davenport-Hines, Richard. *Sex, Death, and Punishment: Attitudes to Sex and Sexuality in Britain since the Renaissance*. 1990.

Mort, Frank. *Dangerous Sexualities: Medico-Moral Politics in England since 1830*. 1987.

Weeks, Jeffrey. *Sex, Politics, and Society: The Regulation of Sexuality since 1800*. 2nd ed. 1989.

Veterans' Organizations (1916–1945)

The inter-war history of the British veterans' movement calls into question several commonplaces about the politics and social behavior of veterans' groups. Far from embodying the emotional alienation of **First World War** veterans from post-war society, organizations like the British Legion evolved into institutions that were closely integrated into patterns of local community and national political life. And despite its social and political Conservatism, the Legion eschewed the paramilitary rituals and overt antileftist posture of its more notorious Continental counterparts.

Britain's first veterans' associations—chief among them the National Federation of Discharged and Demobilised Sailors and Soldiers—were formed in 1916 and 1917 by soldiers discharged from the armed forces because of war-related disabilities. Closely allied to the labor movement, these groups came into being to articulate the men's dissatisfaction with existing government policies on **housing**, war pensions, and job training for the disabled. Their strident rhetoric and labor movement connections convinced many in political circles that they constituted a grave danger to public order. Events soon blunted their radicalism, however. In November 1917 a group of prominent senior military officers founded a rival veterans' body, the Comrades of the Great War, which attracted discharged men disenchanted with the National Federation's implicit challenges to state authority. The relationship between organized veterans and the labor movement gradually soured over conflicts in their respective interests; in turn, the veterans movement's geographic base shifted to rural areas. Once the war was over, the government instituted major reforms of war pensions and unemployment insurance policies, while giving veterans' groups the responsibility for aiding those veterans who fell through gaps in the system. Branches of the rival groups turned their energies to running mutual aid societies and social clubs and sponsoring commemorative ceremonies; as they did so, their political and ideological differences began to dissolve. The culmination of this process of institutional and doctrinal convergence occurred in July 1921, when the National Federation, the Comrades, and two smaller groups merged to form the British Legion.

The course charted by the Legion after its foundation reinforced the shift in the veterans' movement's social and political orientation. Based primarily in rural villages and country towns, and led by middle- and upper-class former officers, the Legion devoted itself to charitable work and social activities rather than political activism. Alone among veterans' groups in Europe and the United States, it supplemented state assistance for veterans with its own sizable relief programs, funded primarily through its annual Armistice Day sale of red paper poppies. It thus became part of an existing private charitable network dedicated to the care of needy veterans. Members of the Legion's affiliated Women's Section played an especially vital role in Legion affairs as fund-raisers, propagandists, and volunteer workers.

Politically, the Legion claimed to be a nonpartisan organization. In practice it tended to embrace the politics of the Right but fully accepted parliamentary democracy and the rule of law. Prohibited by its constitution from engaging in partisan activity, the Legion by and large adhered to this stricture and disavowed both extra-parliamentary and antileftist violence. As the threat of another European war arose in the 1930s, however, the group plunged into foreign affairs, driven by its members' revulsion at the thought of any repetition of their war experiences. Branches forged contacts with German veterans, and Legion spokesmen propagandized tirelessly on the duty of Britain's First World War veterans to prevent the outbreak of another war. During the **Munich** crisis of September 1938 the Legion even sent a volunteer force of 10,000 members to Czechoslovakia to police the transfer of the Sudetenland into German hands, although it was recalled while crossing the English Channel. Only with Adolf Hitler's seizure of the rest of Czechoslovakia in March 1939 did the Legion abandon its peacemaking efforts.

Since the Second World War the state has appropriated many of the welfare responsibilities that the Legion once undertook. Nonetheless, the group continues to assist needy veterans out of its funds, act as an advocate for veterans claiming war pensions from the state, operate business enterprises that employ disabled veterans, and run Legion clubs. "Poppy Day" is still held every Remembrance Sunday throughout Britain.

Charles Kimball

Bibliography
Ward, Stephen R. "Great Britain: Land Fit for Heroes Lost" in Stephen R. Ward, ed. *The War Generation: Veterans of the First World War*. 1975.
Wootton, Graham. *The Official History of the British Legion*. 1956.
———. *The Politics of Influence: British Ex-Servicemen, Cabinet Decisions, and Cultural Change, 1917–57*. 1963.

Vorticism

Despite **Wyndham Lewis'** retrospective assertion that "Vorticism, in fact, was what I personally, did, and said, at a certain period," and given that Lewis was the animating force behind Vorticism, there is no doubt that it constituted a recognizable movement that, however short-lived, can probably claim to have been the first coherently modernist group of artists in Britain.

Initially impressed by the work of the Italian Futurists, who had first exhibited in London in 1912, and their celebration of the machine in the flowering of the industrial age, by 1914 these artists were unhappy about becoming co-opted into the Italian movement. Ultimately, Vorticism and their publication, *Blast* (which ran to two issues published in 1914 and 1915), was formed as a statement of independence from the Italians and what was perceived as their misguided, romanticized view of the machine. Although differences between Lewis and the Italian Futurists had been visible for some time, the catalyst had been the publication of **C.R.W. Nevinson's** *Vital English Art: Futurist Manifesto* in June 1914, to which he penned the signatures of Lawrence Atkinson, **David Bomberg, Jacob Epstein,** Frederick Etchells, Cuthbert Hamilton, William Roberts, Edward Wadsworth, and Wyndham Lewis, not only without their permission, but also as if they were under the direction of Nevinson and the Italian Futurist, Filippo Marinetti.

The address used without authorization by Nevinson for his manifesto had been the Rebel Art Center, founded in March 1914 as a rival to the Omega Workshops for which Lewis had worked. Four months earlier that group (Lewis, Nevinson, Wadsworth, Epstein, Etchells, Hamilton, and Bomberg) had declared its independence from the impressionism of **W.R. Sickert's Camden Town Group,** the **Bloomsbury Group,** as well as the Futurists by exhibiting in a separate "Cubist" room at *The Camden Town and Others* exhibition.

Although Nevinson claims to have invented the title of their magazine, *Blast*, before joining the Futurist camp, the theorist of Vorticism was initially the poet Ezra Pound. He built on the philosophy of T.E. Hulme, whose belief in the rebirth of a geometric art was a formative influence on the nascent Vorticists, and especially on Epstein and Bomberg, whom he particularly championed. For Pound, Vorticism's birth was to be found in Imagism—a literary movement that might be akin to nonrepresentational painting. In the first issue of *Blast* Pound held that "the vortex is the point of maximum energy. It represents in mechanics the greatest efficiency." Lewis explained this "point of maximum energy" by recourse to the metaphor of the whirlpool: "At the heart of the whirlpool is a great silent place where all the energy is concentrated. And there, at the point of concentration, is the Vorticist."

This belief sought an art that could be identified with the new machine age in which technology and rationality ruled, an art that echoed the characteristics of the machine through its formal simplification and coherence of vision. The paintings produced by the Vorticists, although often severely abstract, operate on a number of levels: as reflection, vision, and criticism of a predominantly urban life of present and future. This vision was unable to survive the First World War, in whose mechanized slaughter Vorticism was seen to be implicated. The two Vorticist exhibitions, in 1915 at London's Doré Galleries and in 1917 at New York's Penguin Club (organized by Pound and the American collector John Quinn), were both unsuccessful. The sculptor Henri Gaudier-Brzeska had been killed at the front, and many of the others were psychologically affected by military service or by the demands placed on them through the commissions they received as **war artists,** and so welcomed the post-war aesthetic "Call to Order." Lewis' ultimately unfruitful attempts with McKnight Kauffer to regroup some of the artists under the banner of Group X were symptomatic of this changed situation. Nevertheless, the roll call of those who signed the Vorticist manifesto—Richard Aldington, Malcolm Arbuthnot, Lawrence Atkinson, Jessica Dismorr, Henri Gaudier-Brzeska, Cuthbert Hamilton, Wyndham Lewis, Ezra Pound, William Roberts, Helen Saunders, and Edward Wadsworth—testifies to a moment that set the modernist agenda and, through its ambitious energy and dynamic experimentation, changed the history of British art.

Andrew Wilson

Bibliography

Cork, Richard. *Vorticism and Abstract Art in the First Machine Age.* 2 vols. 1976.

Wees, William. *Vorticism and the English Avant-Garde.* 1974.

Wilson, Andrew, ed. *Vorticism.* 1988.

Wallas, Graham (1858-1932)

Overshadowed by the reputation of Shaw and the Webbs, Graham Wallas remains the forgotten man of the early **Fabian Society**. Not only did he play a leading part in forming it, he retained a lifelong connection with its offshoot, the **London School of Economics**, where he served as Professor of political science (1914–23). His academic interests produced a seminal book, *Human Nature in Politics* (1908), which was widely influential in bringing the insights of social psychology to bear upon the study of politics.

Wallas was the son of an Evangelical clergyman of the **Church of England** and, after a conventional education at public school (Shrewsbury) and **Oxford**, took a post as a classics teacher at a London public school. In 1885 the break came: He rejected Christianity on rationalist grounds, resigned accordingly from his teaching post, and threw himself into the study of socialism. Like his friends Sydney Olivier, **George Bernard Shaw**, and **Sidney Webb**, Wallas found in the Fabian Society the sort of intellectual milieu in which he felt at home. With them he elaborated the theory of evolutionary collectivism, which *Essays in Fabian Socialism* (1889), edited by Shaw, proclaimed to a wider public. Critical of Marxism, Wallas remained a **Liberal** in party politics, committed to a strategy of permeation rather than to an independent socialist or workers' party.

Wallas worked for years on *The Life of Francis Place* (1898), analyzing the activities of an early-nineteenth-century radical who played a notable part in changing the labor legislation of his day. This readiness to take "a great deal of trouble to find out how things were really done before we began trying to do them" won high praise from Shaw. It was this practical, dispassionate, empirical aspect of Fabianism that really appealed to Wallas. In 1895 he was strongly in favor of the scheme for using a bequest to the Fabian Society, not for political propaganda, but for academic research and teaching—the origin of the London School of Economics, of which he was appointed the first Director. He declined to serve in this post but remained associated with the LSE for the rest of his life.

In the process, his Fabian commitment waned. One influence upon him came through his years of service in local government, first on the London School Board and subsequently on the Education Committee of the London County Council. He thus knew local politics from the inside and was thrown, moreover, into opposition to the **Conservatives'** Education Act of 1902, which Webb supported on administrative grounds. Wallas finally resigned from the Fabian Society in 1904 because of Shaw's attempt to associate it with protectionism, another Conservative policy. The root cause was a divergence between the manipulative and authoritarian temper that Shaw and the Webbs increasingly displayed and Wallas' Liberal outlook. **Beatrice Webb** adjudged Wallas less "democratic" than themselves; Wallas had another concept of democracy altogether.

The political thinking of Wallas' mature years was associated with **New Liberalism**, as propagated by his friends and colleagues L.T. Hobhouse and **J.A. Hobson**. Like them he argued for a democratic collectivism in social policy to be implemented through a progressive alliance between the Liberal and **Labour** parties. Yet in *Human Nature in Politics* (1908), he sought to inject some worldly skepticism into idealistic notions of how a democratic political system actually worked. The critical impact of the book is admittedly more powerful than its constructive suggestions. Wallas sought to remedy this deficiency in later works like *The Great Society* (1914) and *Our Social Heritage* (1921), but they lack the cutting edge of his masterpiece. For all that his insights into irrationalist trends had made him fearful of war, the events of August 1914 came as a shock to Wallas. He worked with Hobson in organizing a British Neutrality Committee, but the German invasion of Belgium doomed their efforts. By 1915 he was telling American readers that "I intensely desire victory for the Allies," and, like many other Liberals, his hopes were now pinned upon the prospects of post-war international cooperation.

It was the attempt to rethink democratic theory in the light of modern findings in social **psychology** that became Wallas' lifework. He pointed to the strong irrational—or, at any rate, nonrational—forces that influenced political attitudes and to the role of party in mediating electoral opinion. Yet he manifested a strong faith in democracy. Wallas' point was that progressives needed a clear-eyed understanding of the frailties of the democratic process. The influence of his ideas was felt particularly in the United States, which he frequently visited.

Peter Clarke

Bibliography

Clarke, Peter. *Liberals and Social Democrats.* 1978.

Qualter, Terence H. *Graham Wallas and the Great Society.* 1980.

Wiener, Martin J. *Between Two Worlds: The Political Thought of Graham Wallas.* 1971.

Walton, William Turner (1902–1983)

Largely self-taught, William Walton was an English composer who, despite a relatively small output, produced at least one major work in almost every genre. Although he was at first considered something of an *enfant terrible*, Walton's fundamental traditionalism soon became apparent, his style, characterized by its unique lyricism and the use of traditional structures invigorated by modernistic harmonies, forming a parallel with Prokofiev's later idiom. Among official honors he received were seven doctorates, a knighthood (1951) and the Order of Merit (1967).

Born in Oldham, Lancashire, the son of a local choirmaster and singing teacher, Walton won a place as a chorister at Christ Church Cathedral, Oxford, in 1912. He began to compose two years later, and such was his promise that he was accepted as an undergraduate at Christ Church at the early age of sixteen, although he left **Oxford** in 1920 without completing his degree. At Oxford he met Osbert and Sacheverell Sitwell and for many years lived under their protection. By the age of twenty Walton had already completed a Piano Quartet (1919), which received a Carnegie Award, a String Quartet (1922), according to the composer "full of undigested Bartok and Schoenberg," and *Façade* (Edith Sitwell, 1922), for reciter and chamber ensemble. The langorous Southern melancholy and witty use of parody [including the (mis-) quotation of popular song] provide *Façade* with a Gallic sensibility, at once knowing and fresh, that was virtually unique in English music of the time. Having drawn on and developed characteristics of *Façade* in the robust, jazz-inspired rhythms of the overture *Portsmouth Point* (1925) and in the lassitude of *Siesta* for small orchestra (1926), Walton finally felt prepared to tackle a full-scale instrumental work in the *Sinfonia Concertante* for orchestra with obbligato piano (1927), themes from its three movements, which are portraits of the Sitwells, exhibiting a suitable family likeness. Stylistic maturity came with the richly poetic Viola Concerto (1929) and the ultravirtuosic Violin Concerto (1939), between which Walton wrote two other masterpieces, the oratorio *Belshazzar's Feast* (Osbert Sitwell, after Bible, 1931), pagan in tone, violent and savage, and the First Symphony (1935). In both works Walton revitalized traditional genres, and in the latter he provided a twentieth-century counterpart to the Beethovenian symphonic model of initial conflict finally resolved in triumph.

The Second World War marks a watershed in Walton's output, because, although he gained in fluency through being involved in film music—he completed six film scores between *Major Barbara* (1941) and *Henry V* (1944)—there is a loss of conviction, and the quality of the masterpieces of the 1930s is attained only in such works as the String Quartet in A Minor (1947), the Cello Concerto (1956), and the *Variations on a Theme of Hindemith* (1963). Other works, like the *Improvisations on an Impromptu of **Benjamin Britten***, for orchestra (1969), where manner takes precedence over matter, are less inspired. Even the opera *Troilus and Cressida* (C. Hassell, 1954), grand and sumptuous, betrays a lack of depth.

Trevor Bray

Bibliography
Howes, Frank. *The Music of William Walton.* 2nd ed. 1974.
Kennedy, Michael. *Portrait of Walton.* 1989.
Tierney, Neil. *William Walton: His Life and Music.* 1984.
Walton, Susana. *William Walton: Behind the Façade.* 1988.

War Artists
The **First World War** provided the first instance of state sponsorship of art in Britain. Under the Ministry of Information (from 1917) various schemes were implemented to provide pictorial **propaganda** and a historic record of the experience of war, and later, under the Canadian War Memorials Scheme (CWMS), to commemorate the war on a large scale. At the beginning of the **Second World War**, the Ministry of Information was reinstated to counter the German propaganda machine, to record the war, and to provide employment opportunities for artists. The establishment of the Imperial War Museum in 1917 has provided a permanent archive of the sketches, prints, paintings, photographs, films, and written documentation of Britain's involvement in war during the twentieth century.

When war broke out in August 1914, a number of artists of different generations formed an artists' regiment that drilled in front of the Royal Academy. Two years later the government formed the Official War Artists' Schemes (OWAS), which undertook commissions for painters and printmakers and purchases of appropriate works. Those commissioned ranged from artists like Richard Caton-Woodville (1856–1927), who had been one of Queen Victoria's favorite painters, to the Vorticist **C.R.W. Nevinson**, an indication of the wide diversity of style.

The OWAS was an indirect result of the 1914 **Defence of the Realm Act**, which provided for a Press Bureau to disseminate official war correspondence. In 1916, when **conscription** was introduced, employment of professional artists within the services was suggested by the etcher Muirhead Bone (1876–1953), who argued that he could be more profitably employed in propaganda than in combat. Official recognition resulted in an increasing number of artists employed in all theaters of war and all aspects of the war effort. After the Ministry of Information was disbanded in 1918, the War Memorials Commission granted a number of commissions for paintings to be exhibited in a planned Hall of Remembrance. Artists from the older generation included George Clausen (1852–1944), Wilson Steer (1860–1942), Henry Tonks (1862–1937), and John Singer Sargent (1856–1925); among the younger artists were **Stanley Spencer**, Laura Knight (1877–1970), and Bernard Meninsky (1891–1950). In addition to the British government scheme, a number of artists worked for the Canadian War Memorials Commission (CWMC), sponsored by **Lord Beaverbrook**. They included **Augustus John**, Harold Gilman (1876–1919), Charles Ginner (1878–1952), **Wyndham Lewis**, William Roberts (1895–1980), William Nicholson (1872–1949), **David Bomberg**, Edward Wadsworth (1882–1949), **Paul Nash**, and Nevinson.

An exhibition of their works, held in the Royal Academy in 1919, brought together for the first time a full spectrum of contemporary painting styles. The public response suggests disappointment at the results and disapproval over the spending of public money. Between 1920 and 1923 the War Museum collection was seen at Crystal Palace by 5–6 million visitors. A high proportion of the modernist paintings have entered our consciousness as representations of the First World War, works like Lewis' *A Battery Shelled* (1918), Nevinson's *Returning to the Trenches* (1914–15), Sargent's *Gassed* (1918), and Bomberg's *Sappers at Work: A Canadian Tunnelling Company* (1918–19).

The Ministry of Information was reinstated at the outbreak of the Second World War, with **Kenneth Clark**, the Director of the National Gallery, in charge of pictures. Clark's initiative led to the establishment of the War Artists' Advisory Committee (WAAC), with representatives from each of the services and from the Royal College of Art and the **Slade School of Art**, as well as Bone representing artists and serving as a link with the earlier scheme. During the war years it commissioned and bought 5,500 paintings. In contrast to the modernist language employed to describe the experiences of trench warfare, the Second World War provided a larger number of figurative and romantic works. This change was probably fueled by two considerations. In the

First World War most of the artists were involved militarily before being commissioned; in the Second World War artists were were employed without prior combat experience and remained as artists not soldier-artists. In the second place the homefront played a more significant role, and Britain itself was under greater threat. A number of artists, like Paul and John Nash, Nevinson, Spencer, Knight, and Roberts, were war artists in both wars.

The WAAC met for the first time on 23 November 1939 and then weekly at the National Gallery until 28 December 1945. Its first task was to draw up lists of suitable subjects, artists, and working agreements. A later decision increased the range of subject matter from the war to cover the impact of the war. Artists like **John Piper** recorded the devastation of English cities like London and Coventry, **Henry Moore** produced drawings of the inhabitants of the underground shelters, and Laura Knight painted a series of women working for the war effort before she was commissioned to record the war trials.

By 1941 there was a sufficient number of works to mount an exhibition at the Museum of Modern Art in New York to encourage support for the British war effort. The exhibition included work by Edward Ardizzone (1900–79), Eric Ravilious (1903–42), Edward Bawden (1903–89), and **Graham Sutherland**. Other commissions provided a steady stream of exhibitions at the National Gallery in London, whose permanent collection had been removed for storage at the start of the war.

Nannette Aldred

Bibliography

Fuglie, Gordon L., and Lucinda H. Gedeon eds. *Images of the Great War, 1914–1918.* 1983.

Harries, Meirion and Susie. *The War Artists: British Official War Art of the Twentieth Century.* 1983.

Ross, Alan. *The Colours of War: War Art 1939–1945.* 1983.

Sillars, Stuart. *British Romantic Art and the Second World War.* 1991.

Warner, Sylvia Townsend (1893–1978)

Sylvia Townsend Warner, novelist, short-story writer, poet, musicologist, and biographer, is best known for three of her novels, each of which is markedly **feminist**: *Lolly Willowes* (1926), a fantasia about a spinster whose quest for emancipation leads her to become a witch and to consort with Satan; *Summer Will Show* (1936), a historical novel in which an English gentlewoman and a Lithuanian Jewish actress meet in Paris, come to love each other passionately, and participate together in the Revolution of 1848; and *The Corner That Held Them* (1948), another historical novel, in which a community of English nuns attempts to survive the Black Death of the fourteenth century.

Warner, an only child whose mother wished she had been a boy, grew up among the boys at Harrow School, where her father, George, was a master from 1903 until his death in 1915. Warner was educated privately by her father, and her first love (after her father) was music. She intended to study composition on the Continent, but her plans were diverted by the First World War. She began work in 1917 as an editor of a multivolume edition of Tudor church music, a twelve-year project. She started to write poems in 1921 and published her first volume of them in 1925. *Lolly Willowes*, her first novel, was the original selection offered to subscribers of the new Book-of-the-Month Club in America.

In 1913 Warner had become the mistress of her music teacher (and her father's best friend), Percy Buck, a married man and father. The relation, which Warner came to call her "pretext of troth," was ended in 1930 by Warner. She then fell in love with a young poetess, Valentine Ackland. From 1931 on, Warner considered herself and Ackland married. A trip to Paris with Ackland in 1932 crystalized plans for *Summer Will Show*. The two poets published a joint collection of poems in 1933, *Whether a Dove or Seagull*, dedicated to Robert Frost, whose privately expressed homophobic distaste for the authorial couple perhaps hurt the book's reception.

In 1935 Warner and Ackland joined the **Communist Party of Great Britain**; committed to the Spanish Republican cause, they visited Spain twice in 1936-7, first on behalf of the Red Cross, then as delegates to the Second International Congress of Writers in Defense of Culture. Warner's staunch Communism (in Spain she found **Stephen Spender** too soft politically) endured into the mid-1950s; she seems never to have lost sympathy with Joseph Stalin. Ackland's leftist loyalty eroded much earlier; by the end of the Second World War, to Warner's disappointment, she had become preoccupied with religion. This abetted earlier deep strains on the women's marriage, between 1938 and 1950, resulting from Ackland's liaison with an American woman. But the marriage survived, in spite of constant tensions over politics and religion, until Ackland's death in 1969.

Warner's work remarkably conjoins artistic and political modes that critics (and even artists) have often considered incompatible. On the one hand, *Summer Will Show*, *The Corner That Held Them*, and *The Flint Anchor* (1954) are minutely historical and realistic. The realism of the latter two novels especially eschews conventional novelistic focus on one or two characters, and instead presents as primary the economic, patriarchal, and circumstantial relations that constitute entire historical communities. Yet although Warner's ideological inspiration is historical realist fiction and Marxism, her aesthetic inspiration comes from romance fantasy, surrealism, and fairy tale, no less than from history and Marx. Among the formative influences on her style were the English fantasists and romance writers Arthur Machen (1863–1947), T.F. Powys (1875–1953, brother of **John Cowper Powys**, another fantasist novelist), and T.H. White (1906–64), famous for his Arthurian romances; and works like *Lady into Fox* (1924) by David Garnett (1892–1981).

Her mixture of analytic socioeconomic scrutiny and fable produced, in addition to *Lolly Willowes*, *The Cat's Cradle-Book* (1940) and *Kingdoms of Elfin* (1977), both about amoral, anarchic, "inhumanized" creatures. The 1977 book was inspired by White, whose biography Warner wrote in 1967. Outside of *Lolly Willowes*, Warner's fullest blending of realism and fantasy occurs in *The True Heart* (1929), a retelling of the Cupid and Psyche story in a late Victorian milieu, and in *After the Death of Don Juan* (1938), a Marxist allegory of the **Spanish Civil War**, in which Don Juan stands for fascist capitalism.

The combination of traditionally antithetical aesthetic modes in Warner's work perhaps accounts for a lag in posthumous critical attention to her. Although her work regularly appeared in the *New Yorker* for more than thirty years, it is largely out of print in the United States. And the large body of poems she wrote throughout her life—unfashionably antimodernist, but major—still await full critical response.

Robert L. Caserio

Bibliography
Davie, Donald. *Under Briggflatts: A History of Poetry in Great Britain, 1960–1985.* 1989.
Harman, Claire. *Sylvia Townsend Warner: A Biography.* 1989.
———, ed. *The Diaries of Sylvia Townsend Warner.* 1994.

Washington Naval Conference (1921–1922)

The Washington Conference represented a watershed in British naval and strategic history. At the end of the First World War the **Royal Navy** was probably as strong as, if not stronger than, the rest of the world's navies combined. With forty-two **Dreadnought**-class capital ships, the British outnumbered the next-largest naval power, the United States, by twenty-eight such vessels and was allied with the third-ranking naval power, Japan, under the terms of the Anglo-Japanese alliance. At the Washington Conference, however, the British formally accepted naval parity with the United States and agreed, for all intents and purposes, to emasculate the alliance with Japan.

While on the surface this might seem like a foolhardy move on the part of the **Lloyd George** government, it was motivated by realistic concerns. In the first place, the United States was threatening to complete construction of sixteen capital ships of post-Jutland design, which would have left the Americans in 1925 with twenty-five capital ships less than ten years old. The Royal Navy, given the relative age of its ships, would have only eighteen such vessels at that time, and the cost of building eight more capital ships to match the United States' total was estimated to be £75 million, a figure only slightly less than the entire Admiralty budget for 1920–1, which contained provision for no capital ship construction. As the cost of attaining parity was so high, few British officials realistically contemplated maintaining naval superiority over the Americans. Only **Winston Churchill** continued to strongly press for naval superiority, but even he was more than willing to accept capital ship parity at Washington.

While the British had tried to assure the Americans that the Anglo-Japanese alliance would never be invoked against them, the United States made it very clear that it wished the agreement terminated. The Admiralty urged the government to work more closely with the

United States at the expense of the Japanese. The **Foreign Office**, on the other hand, was slightly more committed to the agreement, but its own special committee favored replacing the pact with a tripartite treaty involving the United States. Certain Dominions, most notably **Australia** and **New Zealand**, endorsed the extension of the alliance during the 1921 Imperial Conference, but they, too, were unwilling to continue an agreement that antagonized the United States.

The British went into the Washington Conference meetings hoping to achieve the following goals: the cessation of all American capital ship building after the completion of the 1916 program, an agreement establishing parity between the two powers, the abolition of the **submarine**, a 50 percent superiority for the Royal Navy over the Japanese Imperial Fleet, freedom of action in developing a naval base in **Singapore** and, lastly, restraint on the Japanese building new naval bases south of Formosa (Taiwan).

When the conference opened in November 1921, the American Secretary of State, Charles Evans Hughes, promised to terminate the 1916 program in exchange for large-scale reductions in the size of the three main naval powers' forces. He proposed that Britain, the United States, and Japan should regulate the size of their fleets on the basis of the 5–5–3 ratio, and that all further building of capital ships should be suspended for ten years to free the respective countries from the burden of excessive armaments spending. Despite Admiralty misgivings about the ten-year rule, the British delegation in Washington, led by **Arthur (Earl) Balfour**, and the **Cabinet** realized that they were in sight of their most important objectives. As such, they worked hard to calm American anxieties over the Anglo-Japanese alliance by their efforts to obtain a Three-Power Pact, later extended to a Four-Power Pact with the inclusion of the French, in the Pacific. The eventual treaty signing took place on 6 February 1922, and for the most part the pact satisfied British hopes. The 5–5–3 ratio of naval power, which gave the Royal Navy a 60 percent superiority over the Japanese, was accepted, and the French and Italians were included at a ratio of 1.75 each. The ten-year rule was confirmed, with the proviso that the British alone would be allowed to construct two more capital ships in the upcoming years to match slightly more modern American and Japanese fleets. A Four-Power Treaty

was signed in place of the Anglo-Japanese alliance, and powers were forbidden from constructing new naval facilities outside of their immediate home territories, with the singular exception of Australia, New Zealand, and Singapore. The only area in which the British were unsuccessful was in banning submarines, since the French refused to accept such limitations after agreeing to a relatively small ratio for capital ships.

The treaty itself was greeted enthusiastically at the time but has since been subjected to criticism. If anything, the conference served to illustrate the primacy of **Anglo-American relations** in the naval sphere and allowed for a more comprehensible world naval situation than would have been the case had there not been any restrictions on the construction of naval craft.

Phillips Payson O'Brien

Bibliography

Hall, Christopher. *Britain, America, and Arms Control, 1921–37.* 1986.
Richardson, Dick. *The Evolution of British Disarmament Policy in the 1920s.* 1989.
Roskill, Stephen W. *Naval Policy between the Wars.* vol. 1. 1968.

Waugh, Evelyn Arthur St. John (1903–1966)

Evelyn Waugh, satiric novelist, was the son of Arthur Waugh, Managing Director of the publishing firm Chapman and Hall, and Catherine Raban Waugh. After attending Lancing, he went to **Oxford**, where he led a life he described as "idle, dissolute, and extravagant," and he left in 1924 without taking a degree. Within a few years, however, he began to establish a literary reputation. In 1928 he published two books: a critical and biographical study of Rossetti and his first novel, *Decline and Fall*. In the same year, he married Evelyn Gardner. The marriage lasted barely a year; his wife left him, in August 1929, to live with a mutual friend.

After the shock of this marital breakup, Waugh embarked on a series of travels, all of which provided material for his books. In 1930 he went as a *Times* correspondent to Emperor Haile Selassie's coronation in Abyssinia; out of this came a travel book, *Remote People* (1931), and a novel about the clash of cultures, *Black Mischief* (1932). An assignment to cover the Italo-Abyssinian War in 1935 for the *Daily Mail* yielded another travel book, *Waugh in Abyssinia*, and a satire of the newspaper world, *Scoop* (1938).

Following a period of instruction by Jesuit priest and author Martin D'Arcy, Waugh was received into the **Roman Catholic** Church in 1930. One effect of his conversion was his biography of an Elizabethan Jesuit martyr, Edmund Campion, in 1935. In 1936 the Church annulled his first marriage, enabling him to marry a Catholic, Laura Herbert, the following year. In time they had five children, one of whom, Auberon, became a journalist—as acerbic a commentator on the contemporary scene as his father before him.

When the war began, Waugh received a commission in the Royal Marines. He joined the Commandos and underwent parachute training even though he was approaching forty, but his military career was anything but distinguished. He was assigned to the British military mission for Marshal Tito's partisans in Yugoslavia, where he attempted unsuccessfully to save a large number of Jewish refugees from deportation and certain death.

One further journey took him to Hollywood to prepare a film script for his novel *Brideshead Revisited* (1945); the film was never made, but the experience led to a satire on California burial customs, *The Loved One* (1948). As he grew older, he assumed the guise of a crotchety country gentleman who had abandoned the modern world. But the *Sword of Honour* trilogy (1952–61) mingles comic inventiveness with its theme of moral decency adrift in the Second World War.

In his early novels Waugh creates an Alice-in-Wonderland type of world, in which outrageous actions are performed by characters with names like Tantamount and Pastmaster. Yet the title *Decline and Fall* creates the suspicion that the fantasy is anchored in reality, that he is writing of a civilization in decline. His second novel, *Vile Bodies* (1930), describes the amusing social whirl of the Bright Young People in London, of which Waugh was very much a part; yet, by ending on the biggest battlefield so far in world history, the story stresses the price of the fun.

His best novel of the 1930s, *A Handful of Dust* (1934), contains a farcical account of divorce proceedings such as he himself had gone through but reflected his conversion only indirectly: Religion in the novel is emphasized through its absence. The book borrows from

T.S. Eliot's *The Waste Land*; there are many correspondences between book and poem, and they are handled with great subtlety.

In a *New Yorker* assessment in 1944 Edmund Wilson stated that Waugh was the only first-rate comic and satiric genius to emerge in English literature since **George Bernard Shaw**, and praised him for his detachment: Waugh was known to have Conservative political, religious, and moral opinions, but these, Wilson said, did not mar his comedy. However, when Waugh published *Brideshead Revisited* the following year, he made his Conservatism so decidedly clear and serious a motive for the new novel's historical realism that Wilson was bitterly disappointed—as were many other critics. *Brideshead* marked a watershed in Waugh's career; as a Book-of-the-Month Club selection, it gained him a much larger following in the United States than he had had, but many of his admirers wished that his novel writing had remained in the realm of comic or satiric fantasy. Some reviewers claimed that snobbery rather than religion was at the heart of the work; Kingsley Amis ridiculed the deathbed conversion of the novel's Lord Marchmain in an article entitled "How I Lived in a Very Big House and Found God." Like other critics of the book, he overlooked the importance in the story of a representative of simple and ordinary religious faith, Nanny Hawkins.

Religion and satire mingle in a macabre way in *The Loved One*, based on the premise that the decline of Western civilization is first made obvious in the graveyard. A similar mixture of religious feeling, decline, and disillusionment is at the heart of *Sword of Honour*, published as a trilogy in 1965 after appearing in separate volumes. When the war begins, the novel's hero, Guy Crouchback, views it as a noble crusade through which he can vindicate himself after a life of failure. By the end of the story the crusade, too, has failed; the sword of Stalingrad, presented to Soviet Russia by Great Britain, has become a symbol of Soviet oppression. In the last volume of the trilogy, *Unconditional Surrender* (*The End of the Battle* in the American edition), the surrender is not just Germany's surrender but Guy's—his surrender to the will of God. He finds vindication, not as he expected, but through his penitent admission that he has been part of "a will to war, a death wish, everywhere."

The novel is especially convincing in conveying the political and moral fog of war, particularly in the narrative of the defeat of the British on Crete. The unifying vision behind *Sword of Honour* is an ironic one, especially in regard to justice in the modern world. Yet the novel concludes that it may still be possible for a Christian to keep his own house in order and to find meaning in life.

Waugh's published letters and diaries—some of which are more fabulous than his novels—provide a picture of the circle in which he moved. On his death his friend **Graham Greene** wrote that "a writer of Evelyn's quality leaves us an estate to walk through: We discover unappreciated vistas, paths are left for our discovery at the right moment."

D.J. Dooley

Bibliography

Carens, James F. *The Satiric Act of Evelyn Waugh.* 1966.

Carpenter, Humphrey. *The Brideshead Generation: Evelyn Waugh and His Friends.* 1989.

Hastings, Selina. *Evelyn Waugh: A Biography.* 1994.

Heath, Jeffrey. *The Picturesque Prison: Evelyn Waugh and His Writing.* 1982.

Stannard, Martin. *Evelyn Waugh: The Early Years, 1903–1939.* 1986.

———. *Evelyn Waugh: The Later Years, 1939–1966.* 1992.

Wavell, Archibald Percival (1883–1950)

Wavell was a **Second World War** theater-level commander in the Middle East, Southeast Asia, and India. He also served as Viceroy of India. Noted for his victories over the Italians, he suffered defeats at the hands of the Germans and Japanese. He became a Field Marshal and a Viscount in 1943 and was named Earl Wavell in 1947.

Wavell was born into a military family and entered the Black Watch Regiment in 1901 after graduating from Sandhurst. He served in the **Boer War** and in the **First World War**, losing an eye in 1915; by 1918 he was a brigadier in Palestine. During the 1920s and 1930s he made his reputation as a student of military thought, but he was also a literary scholar, publishing a collection of poetry in 1944 entitled *Other Men's Flowers*.

He began the Second World War as Commander-in-Chief, Middle East, where his responsibilities included everything from Kenya

to the northern shores of the Mediterranean and Iraq as well. In 1940–1 his forces, although outnumbered, defeated the Italians in Somaliland, Ethiopia, and Libya. He also secured French Syria for the Allies and put down an anti-British movement in Iraq. But his resources were spread too thin to prevent German victories in Greece (including Crete) and Libya in 1941. In the case of the Axis attack on Greece, he had recommended British intervention—it was not forced upon him by Prime Minister **Winston Churchill**, as legend would have it. In the case of Libya, General Erwin Rommel took advantage of the scarcity of British troops first to defeat and then block a counterattack by Wavell's men in June 1941. Churchill had unwisely urged this counterattack upon Wavell before the British were ready; yet the Prime Minister subsequently blamed his theater commander for the failure. Wavell was then sent to India where he became Commander-in-Chief.

In early 1942 he commanded Allied forces in Southeast Asia in a hopeless attempt to stem the tide of Japanese advance; troops under his distant supervision surrendered **Singapore** in February 1942, one of the greatest disasters in British military history. Wavell soon returned to India, becoming Viceroy in 1943; as such, he helped pave the way for Indian independence. He retired in 1947, yielding his post to **Lord Louis Mountbatten**, the last Viceroy.

It was Wavell's misfortune to face the Germans and Japanese at a time early in the war when they held most of the advantages. He was also unfortunate in lacking the full confidence of his Prime Minister.

Karl G. Larew

Bibliography

Barnett, Correlli. *The Desert Generals.* 1960.

Connell, John. *Wavell: Scholar and Soldier to June 1941.* 1964.

Lewin, Ronald. *The Chief: Field Marshal Lord Wavell, Commander-in-Chief and Viceroy, 1939–1947.* 1980.

Webb, Beatrice Potter (1858–1943) and Sidney (1859–1947)

The partnership of Sidney and Beatrice Webb, which formally dates back to their marriage on 23 June 1892, was to develop into an extraordinarily fruitful professional and intellectual relationship. The couple became eminent collaborators in a number of fields: in historical research into various social and political institutions (culminating in the publication of such monumental works as *The History of Trade Unionism* (1894), the two-volume *Industrial Democracy* (1897), and the multivolume history of *English Local Government* (1906–29); in social investigation (especially of the problems of poverty and methods of relieving it); in the reform of education at various levels; in local and national politics (mainly, though not exclusively, from behind the scenes); and in the sponsorship of independent journalism (the most notable example of which was their creation of the weekly periodical the *New Statesman* in 1913).

Some of their joint efforts had come to fruition before the end of the nineteenth century. They had already made an enduring contribution to tertiary education with their founding of the **London School of Economics and Political Science** in 1895. By the turn of the century they were busy hobnobbing in top parliamentary circles in order to secure legislative support for the expansion and reorganization of **technical** and **secondary education**. The government in power at this time was a **Conservative** one, while their own politics were steadfastly socialist, albeit of the nonrevolutionary middle-class variety associated with the **Fabian Society**, of which they had become the recognized leaders.

According to their long-serving secretary, F.W. Galton, the Webbs' minds worked "so closely and harmoniously that it is hard to disentangle the parts played by each of them" in their joint writings or other ventures. Their social backgrounds and their personalities were very different, however, and the roles they played, though usually complementary, were never identical.

Beatrice's father, Richard Potter, was a railway magnate, her mother, Laurencina Heyworth, the daughter of a wealthy mill owner. Beatrice herself was educated at her family home in rural Gloucestershire, in the manner of most Victorian upper-middle-class girls. Though widely accomplished, articulate, and beautiful, she was never to push herself forward in the political arena, except during her appointment as a member of the Royal Commission on the Poor Laws (1905–9) and in the subsequent campaign—abortive in the short run—to overturn the old legislation and replace it with a cohesive system of state-run welfare services.

Sidney had not been a member of this commission, though he vigorously assisted Beatrice in the campaign. Up to 1910 the focus of his own political activity, apart from the Fabian Society, was the London County Council, of which he had been an active member since 1892, representing the Progressive Party, a Liberal-Labour alliance. In a sense he was the archetype of the self-made professional who figured so prominently in the Fabian ranks. He had been born into a lower-middle-class family in London, though he had enjoyed some unusual advantages: a spell of schooling in Switzerland and Germany; and early exposure to the world of radical politics through some contacts that his father (a hairdresser-turned-accountant) had made when serving on committees supporting the liberal theorist and MP John Stuart Mill. Sidney went into the **civil service** soon after leaving school, and it was as a committee man that he was to shine, whether in the Fabian Society, on the London County Council, or during his later years with the **Labour Party**. He was chiefly responsible for drafting the "socialist" **Clause Four** in the party's constitution of 1918, and he served as an effective advocate of the miners' cause when appointed a year later to the **Sankey Commission** investigating the condition of the **coal mining** industry. Self-effacing in temperament, and physically undistinguished, he lacked the requisite charisma for more-public political roles; yet he allowed himself to be thrust into these roles when Labour first came to power in Britain in the 1920s. In the first Labour government of 1924 he served as President of the Board of Trade, and in the second of 1929–31 (having been elevated to the peerage as Lord Passfield) he became Secretary of State for Dominion Affairs and Colonial Secretary.

Following the disappointments of her anti-Poor Law campaign and the calamities of the First World War, Beatrice's usual introspection was to take a more depressive turn for a while. As always, however, she continued to find a creative outlet for such moods in her now-famous diaries (extracts of which were first published in 1926, as *My Apprenticeship*, and in 1948 as *Our Partnership*). By the 1920s she had recovered her spirits sufficiently to play an active, if rather condescending, role as political hostess in Sidney's mining constituency of Seaham Harbour in Durham.

With the collapse of **Ramsay MacDonald's** administration of 1929–31, both partners suffered disillusionment with the Labour Party over its inability to respond in a creative socialist way to the economic crisis of the time. They placed their hopes in the example of the Soviet Union. A visit there in 1932 helped convert them from the deep skepticism they had been expressing about the Communist experiment throughout the 1920s to near-adulation. They published their observations in another joint work, *Soviet Communism: A New Civilisation?* (2 vols., 1935).

This last major work may not have shown them at their sober, steady-sighted best. But for all of its more blinkered enthusiasms about Stalinist Russia, it was not entirely oblivious or uncritical of the authoritarian excesses now commonly identified with the regime. And the most impressive qualities of the Webbs' earlier historical and social investigations—intensive research and encyclopedic range—were still clearly in evidence. Whatever their own political achievements, the record of the Webbs as scholarly writers on all manner of issues connected with the labor or socialist movements is far too solid ever to be ignored, even by the most vehement of their detractors.

Ian Britain

Bibliography

Cole, Margaret, ed. *The Webbs and Their Work.* 1949.

MacKenzie, Norman, ed. *The Letters of Sidney and Beatrice Webb.* 3 vols. 1978.

MacKenzie, Norman, and Jeanne MacKenzie, eds. *The Diary of Beatrice Webb.* 4 vols. 1982–5.

McBriar, A.M. *An Edwardian Mixed Doubles: The Bosanquets versus the Webbs: A Study in British Social Policy, 1890–1929.* 1987.

Radice, Lisanne. *Beatrice and Sidney Webb.* 1984.

Seymour-Jones, Carole. *Beatrice Webb: Woman of Conflict.* 1992.

Welfare State

The term "welfare state," which became part of the everyday British vocabulary after 1945, means a state that defines as an essential part of its role the prevention of absolute poverty and, somewhat more contentiously, the maintenance of an adequate standard of life for all of its citizens. It may seek to achieve this goal by a variety of means, including the provision of cash benefits and/or services and the regulation of the fiscal system or the labor market in order to maximize incomes.

During the twentieth century such activities have certainly grown in size, range, cost, and complexity. Central and local government expenditure on social welfare services in the United Kingdom was 4.1 percent of the gross national product (GNP) in 1913, 10.15 percent in 1921, 9.5 percent in 1929, 11.3 percent in 1938, 17.5 percent in 1951, 23 percent in 1967, and 22.5 percent in 1987. This growth has not simply been the result of a benevolent state choosing to levy taxes in order to promote social equality. The objectives of state welfare must be considered in relation to other agencies (the family, voluntary and private institutions, the labor market) that provide support. The state has not necessarily displaced other agencies as providers of welfare; rather their roles have developed complementarily.

At the end of the nineteenth century central and local governments were already responsible for a significant range of welfare functions. Apart from a growing state responsibility for education, the Poor Law provided a framework of benefits and services for those in acute need: institutionalized care of increasingly specialized and less punitive character for an expanding range of categories of need—the sick, the elderly, orphaned and abandoned children—and minimal cash benefits for the "deserving poor," most frequently the elderly and widowed mothers and their children.

The central government came under increasing pressure to extend welfare activities. As institutional provision for such deserving groups as the sick improved, it became less obvious why they should remain within the unpopular framework of the Poor Law. **Unemployment** was acknowledged to be not always the fault of the unemployed, yet the jobless had no right to assistance other than in the punitive workhouse. The family and voluntary agencies could not meet all needs. Many of the elderly poor in particular had no relatives willing to support them because they had never married, were childless, or because their families had emigrated, died, or were simply too poor to help. Throughout the century there is strong evidence that kin have given what they could to those in need. Another striking feature of the early years of the century is the large sums that were redistributed annually through charitable donations, but the demands on charitable funds exceeded the available supply.

Hence the state came under pressure to provide **old-age pensions**, assist the unemployed, and to support mothers and children by less punitive means. In addition, fears were expressed that appalling urban conditions were leading to degeneration of the national physique. At the same time levels of **infant mortality** remained high and the birthrate was falling—fastest among the better off and, it was assumed, most physically fit specimens. Concern about what were seen as indicators of national decline was the more acute at a time when Britain faced overseas competition economically and militarily from such rivals as Germany. Welfare was seen as desirable not purely for humanitarian reasons but to achieve "national efficiency." The market and private mechanisms could not maintain that efficiency unaided; only the state had the necessary resources and access to information. However, the resulting pressure to improve the **health** and welfare, especially of infants and children, also faced opposition from those who still believed in minimal state intervention in family life. Poor families themselves often resented official interference in their lives.

Few people at this time, even in the emerging labor movement, favored the state taking complete responsibility for welfare. They believed that voluntary action should be encouraged but supplemented by the vastly greater resources of the state, which would regulate the labor market to ensure full employment and adequate wages. This would enable more people to help themselves and to escape from the low pay and underemployment that the poverty surveys of the period showed to be the main cause of deprivation. Governments were slow to respond to interventionist pressures largely because both major political parties were committed to low levels of taxation. The **Liberals** had a progressive wing and, as the chief beneficiaries of the working-class vote, were induced to enact reform measures that established some of the principles on which the welfare state later developed. These measures, neither costly nor notably redistributive, included free school meals for needy children (1906), medical inspection in schools (1907), and a comprehensive Children Act (1908), all stemming from concern about the physical condition of the nation. Old-age pensions were introduced in 1908. The first cash benefit to be paid by the state outside the Poor Law, it nonetheless imposed on claimants **means** and character **tests** similar in spirit from the Poor Law. The Trade Boards Act (1909) introduced a minimum wage and improved conditions into some of the lowest paid, mainly female, occupations. The Housing and Town Planning Act (1909) sought to limit existing and future urban overcrowding and pollution. Successive budgets rendered the system of direct taxation somewhat more progressive. National insurance, introduced in 1911, provided health and unemployment benefits outside the Poor Law, but mainly for the regularly employed and in return for compulsory weekly contributions. Collectively this was a significant leap in the state's responsibility for welfare. However, there was no underlying intention to establish the state as the permanent primary provider of welfare. It was intended to support self-help and voluntary effort.

These measures were limited and tentative, and their effects are hard to assess due to the onset of the **First World War**, which greatly extended the range of responsibilities of the state and popular expectations. In general, living standards improved because of full employment, and expectations about living standards in the future rose. Fear of political disorder lest these expectations be dashed led the government from 1916 to plan for **post-war reconstruction**.

Recession and continuous heavy unemployment followed, and the government responded by cutting public expenditure. However the long-term picture of the inter-war years is one of expanded welfare services and mounting expenditure. The government, fearing political unrest, maintained subsistence-level payments to the unemployed throughout. Although often subject to humiliating tests of need, for the first time most of the unemployed could be sure of a regular payment, which for some meant a steadier income than they had earned before the war. Large amounts of subsidized **council housing** were built and bad housing pulled down. Local-authority health care improved, especially for mothers and children. The main beneficiaries of these improvements were members of the manual working class. An important force behind the changes was the growing power of the **Labour Party**. The inter-war years also saw employers providing on a larger scale such benefits as pensions, especially for their white-collar employees, who were largely excluded from state welfare.

Demands for an increased role for the state, already strong in the 1930s, were realized during the **Second World War**, when many argued in favor of rewarding the people for their sacrifices in wartime. Despite the sacrifices and loss of life, living standards improved for those who survived, due partly to full employment, partly to effective government planning to ensure adequate supplies of necessities.

The post-war Labour government was committed to full employment and to extending the welfare state. Using modified Keynesian techniques, assisted by high levels of world demand, it achieved full employment that lasted (with occasional mild recessions) until the oil crisis of 1973. This brought significant improvements in the **standard of living** for most of the population, but, as social surveys continually revealed, not the abolition of severe deprivation among those excluded from, or on the margins of, the labor market, such as old people or single mothers.

Economic policy and the operation of the market did more to improve overall living standards than did the development of welfare policies. These made a major contribution to improving conditions even for those on the margins and the quality of life more generally. The Labour government significantly extended welfare provision, introducing the principle that the major benefits and services were available to all social classes. Old-age pensions, as well as health and unemployment insurance benefits were much improved, though less generously than was proposed in 1942 by **William Beveridge**. The **National Health Service**, which provided free medical (including hospital) care for all was established in 1948, and **family allowances** were introduced in 1945 for all children other than first children. There were also major improvements in **housing**, education, and community social services.

An effect of this universalization of services has been that the better off have benefited disproportionately. This was the price that was paid to encourage taxpayers to fund the new services. It has been argued that this welfare expenditure diverted resources from industrial investment and constrained economic growth. However, it must be noted that higher levels of social expenditure had no such effects on the German economy in this period.

Labour's **Conservative** successors continued the expansion of welfare services, while encouraging the growth of private and business-based forms of welfare—occupational pensions and health care schemes, for example. In the 1950s and 1960s many even in the middle classes felt unable to provide for themselves at the standard provided by the state. The most rapid period of expansion of public expenditure on welfare, in Britain as in most developed countries, came in the 1960s, with large programs of **hospital** and house building begun under Conservative governments and continued by Labour.

Conservatives in the 1980s sought to cut state services, to transfer them to the private sector, and to encourage all forms of private insurance and private care (for example, for the elderly). Legislative protection of lower-paid (often female) workers was eroded. In a period of high unemployment, unemployment benefits were less severely cut, except for the very young, because governments still feared the political consequences of unemployment. Also, further cuts were restrained by the **European Union** (EU), which sought to set standards of welfare provision throughout the Community higher than those prevailing in Britain in the early 1990s. Pressure from the EC is one reason why public expenditure on welfare did not fall as a percentage of GNP through the 1980s, despite the attempts to reduce it. Difficult as it is to measure precisely, public welfare expenditure absorbed about 22.2 percent of GNP (compared, for example, with 19.4 percent in the United States) at the end of the 1980s. This was also partly due to the costs of supporting the large numbers of the unemployed, elderly people, and single parents. The major client groups of the welfare state changed somewhat, or reverted to older patterns, while the better off remained heavy consumers of publicly financed education and health care, though larger numbers of them by this time felt able to provide for themselves independent of the state. The state remained the most efficient available mechanism for remedying the failings of the market and for providing basic minimum standards for all, although not social equality. Statistically it was clear by the early 1990s that one effect of changes in social and economic policies was marked social polarization: The rich grew richer and the poor poorer.

Pat Thane

Bibliography
Crowther, M.A. *British Social Policy, 1914–1939.* 1988.

Deakin, Nicholas. *The Politics of Welfare.* 1987.

Lowe, Rodney. *The Welfare State in Britain since 1945.* 1993.

Mommsen, W.J., ed. *The Emergence of the Welfare State in Britain and Germany, 1850–1950.* 1981.

Thane, Pat. *The Foundations of the Welfare State.* 1982.

Wells, H(erbert) G(eorge) (1866–1946)

H.G. Wells originated most of the themes that have dominated science fiction in the twentieth century, including interplanetary warfare, time travel, and genetic engineering. He was also one of the most celebrated novelists and social critics of his day.

Born into the lowest stratum of the middle class, Wells escaped from poverty via a scholarship to the Normal School of Science. There he studied under T.H. Huxley, from whom he absorbed Darwinian theory and some deep forebodings about the evolutionary process. Wells came to fear that humans might regress to their animal ancestors and become the ape-like Morlocks of *The Time Machine* (1895) or the beast-men of *The Island of Dr. Moreau* (1896). But young Wells had also read Plato, and he attended socialist gatherings at William Morris' Kelmscott House; from these influences he developed a passionate faith in a scientifically planned society. Apocalypse or utopia: Wells spent the rest of his life warning humanity that it had to choose one or the other.

His early novels were pessimistic. *The Time Machine*, which made his reputation, predicted that the upper and working classes would evolve into two distinct species, one preying on the other, while the whole universe descended into entropic decay. Wells admitted that *The War of the Worlds* (1898) was an exercise in wish fulfillment—he wanted to blast Victorian civilization with Martian heat rays. *The First Men in the Moon* (1901) conjured up a lunar race of highly evolved social insects as a Swiftean satire on British society.

Wells' mood changed with *Anticipations* (1901), which offered his forecasts for the new century. He now placed his hopes in a dictatorship of technocrats who would establish universal peace and plenty through central planning and **eugenics. George Bernard Shaw** and **Sidney and Beatrice Webb** were very taken with Wells'

elitist socialism, and in 1903 they brought him into the **Fabian Society.**

Wells would attempt to commandeer the Fabians and transform them into a well-funded mass political organization. He might have succeeded, but he sabotaged himself through his childish personal attacks on Shaw and the Webbs, whom he later ridiculed in his novel *The New Machiavelli* (1911). That episode set a pattern for Wells: He was always talking up schemes for saving the world, but he habitually provoked quarrels with his friends and lacked the patience for sustained political work.

Nor could Wells commit himself to one woman. He married his cousin Isabel Mary Wells (1866–1931) in 1891, and early in 1894 he took up with Amy Catherine Robbins (1872–1927). His advocacy of sexual liberation in *In the Days of the Comet* (1906) and *Ann Veronica* (1909), as well as his affairs with Amber Reeves and Rebecca West, made him the center of a series of public scandals.

Wells foresaw armored warfare in the story "The Land Ironclads" (1903), strategic bombing in *The War in the Air* (1908), and nuclear weaponry in *The World Set Free* (1914). Leo Szilard, who worked on the Manhattan Project, claimed that *The World Set Free* led him to the idea of an atomic chain reaction in 1934. Wells' genius lay not so much in predicting gadgetry as in projecting the impact of future technology: He knew in advance how tanks, bombers, and nuclear science would transform warfare.

He was less farsighted about the **First World War,** which he proclaimed "The War That Will End War." Convinced that the conflict would bring about a technocratic revolution, he fell headlong into war hysteria. In *The Research Magnificent* (1915), *Mr. Britling Sees It Through* (1916), and *God the Invisible King* (1917) he proclaimed his faith in a Wellsian deity who was somehow leading mankind toward the World State. Wells was an early advocate of the **League of Nations** but was equally quick to become disillusioned with it.

After the war Wells synthesized his whole worldview in a grand universal chronicle: *The Outline of History* (1920) sold in the millions and made him wealthy. In collaboration with his son George ("Gip") and **Julian Huxley** he produced a similarly popular survey of biology, *The Science of Life* (1930).

Meanwhile, Wells continued to search for a visionary elite that would give his visions reality. In *The World of William Clissold* (1926) he looked to an "Open Conspiracy" of enlightened capitalists, and later he turned hopefully to Franklin D. Roosevelt's New Dealers. In 1934 he went to Russia and tried to convert Joseph Stalin; he left disgusted with the Soviet regime and its Marxist dogmatism. In the late 1930s he badgered scientists to assemble a world encyclopedia, but by then Wells was too old and impatient to carry out such a grandiose project. He grew increasingly cranky and scolding, rehashing old ideas, lashing out at politicians and other writers. In disgust with the entire human race, he composed his epitaph: "God damn you all, I told you so."

The younger generation was no longer listening. **Virginia Woolf** dismissed him for not being a modernist, Christopher Caudwell denounced him for not being a Marxist. The Art Deco futurama of Wells' film *Things to Come* (1936) looked sterile and chilling in the age of Henry Ford and the Five-Year Plans. **E.M. Forster's** story "The Machine Stops" (1908), Evgeny Zamyatin's *We* (1920), **Aldous Huxley's** *Brave New World* (1932), and **George Orwell's** *Nineteen Eighty-Four* (1949) all rewrote Wells' dreams as nightmares.

Although Wells was an international cultural celebrity, he has never been admitted to the first rank of novelists. In his 1914 essay "The Younger Generation," Henry James bemoaned Wells' slapdash methods of writing, which only worsened in later years. There is, however, honest workmanship in his novels of lower-middle-class life: *Love and Mr. Lewisham* (1900), *Kipps* (1905), and *The History of Mr. Polly* (1910) have a humorous realism that has been called Dickensian, though they rely less on broad caricature. *Tono-Bungay* (1909) was one of the first novels to confront those twin horrors of the twentieth century, radioactive pollution and mass media **advertising**. Counterpointing nuclear disintegration with the imminent crack-up of Victorian society, Wells might have had good artistic reasons to ignore Jamesean unities. His rationale—"The splintering frame began to get into the picture"—sounds almost postmodern, coming from a writer who was always straining to leap ahead of modernity.

Jonathan Rose

Bibliography

Hammond, John R. *Herbert George Wells: An Annotated Bibliography of His Works.* 1977.

MacKenzie, Norman, and Jeanne MacKenzie. *H.G. Wells.* 1973.

Ray, Gordon N. *H.G. Wells and Rebecca West.* 1974.

Scheick, William J., and J. Randolph Cox. *H.G. Wells: A Reference Guide.* 1988.

Smith, David C. *H.G. Wells, Desperately Mortal.* 1986.

Welsh Music

Three broad categories of Welsh music have coexisted in the twentieth century: music drawn from the folk traditions of Wales; the amateur music of the industrial areas, which favored large-scale communal music making; and art music, which has developed in a separate institutional infrastructure from the rest of British music.

Traditional music is most popular in the Welsh-speaking heartland. The most enduring genre in this category is penillion, an improvisatory form for harp and voices. Interest in penillion and other traditional music has grown through systematic study by organizations such as the Welsh Folk Museum and the Welsh Folk Music Society and through its promotion at the National *Eisteddfodau* and smaller *eisteddfodau*. *Eisteddfodau* are festivals of the arts, usually based entirely on the Welsh language and usually competitive. Schools and youth movements, particularly *Urdd Gobaith Cymru* (the Welsh League of Youth), hold *eisteddfodau* annually, and they have served to foster Welsh music as well as other arts.

Eisteddfodau also act as focal points for choral singing, which is particularly popular in Wales. Choral singing was fostered in the first half of the century by the Nonconformist chapels, which emphasized hymn singing. Many chapels held *cymanfa canu* (festivals of singing), usually at Eastertime, which drew communities together for music making. The most distinctive large-scale choral singing has probably been that of male voice choirs. The Rhondda choirs at Treorchy and Ferndale (Pendyrus) have been particularly successful, as well as those at Morriston, Rhosllanerchrugog, and Llanelli.

The principal developments in Welsh art music, to the extent that it differs from mainstream British music, have been in its institutional infrastructure. In the 1920s Sir Walford Davies' Council of Music for Wales was prominent in promoting art music. In 1936 the **British Broadcasting Corporation** (BBC) established its own **orchestra** in Wales with twenty-nine players; expanded to forty-five in 1945, it became a full symphony orchestra in the 1970s. The Welsh National Opera was founded in 1946 and became a permanent, full-time company in 1972–3. Both organizations were encouraged by the Welsh Arts Council, the main source for public funding of the arts in Wales in the second half of the century.

Wales has never produced a composer to equal **Edward Elgar, Benjamin Britten,** or **Michael Tippett,** but a number of notable figures have emerged, such as Grace Williams, Daniel Jones, William Mathias, and Alun Hoddinot. Among Welsh singers who have forged international reputations and been exemplars for succeeding generations are Geraint Evans, Stuart Burrows, Gwyneth Jones, and Margaret Price.

Trevor Herbert

Bibliography

Allsobrook, David Ian. *Music for Wales.* 1992.
Stephens, Meic. *The Arts in Wales, 1950–75.* 1979.

Welsh Nationalism

National feeling in Wales has found expression historically in a variety of ways, including cultural, religious, and political movements; these have rarely been exclusively or explicitly nationalist associations, but they have to varying degrees possessed a Welsh national dimension since the early nineteenth century. A more explicit nationalism has made a distinctive impact on Welsh and British politics since the election of the first *Plaid Cymru* (the Welsh nationalist party) member of Parliament in 1966.

It is particularly difficult in the case of Wales to disentangle nationalism from those religious and cultural, especially linguistic, factors that have fed into it. The survival of the Welsh language, still spoken by 44 percent of the Welsh population in 1911, and its distinctive literature combined with a predominant Nonconformity to create a widespread consciousness of a Welsh *gwerin*: a people with a common culture opposed at every point to what was conceived of as an English church and an anglicized, Tory squirearchy. This consciousness found political articulation in an increasingly radical Welsh Liberalism, especially after the election of 1868, for which the disestablishment of the "alien" **Church of England** in Wales was a keynote demand with obvious nationalistic connotations. By the 1890s Welsh politicians such as **David Lloyd George** were advocating Home Rule for Wales and proselytizing in the *Cymru Fydd* movement, a nationalist Young Wales movement founded in 1886 within the **Liberal Party** but with ambitions to create a Welsh party in Parliament on the Irish model.

This political ferment came to an end effectively in 1896, but it did achieve the establishment of an impressive number of Welsh institutions, including the federal University of Wales. Following the First World War nationalistic Liberalism was eclipsed by socialism. There were voices within the **Labour Party,** which became, after 1922, the dominant political force in Wales, who argued for devolved Welsh structures, but these were largely overwhelmed by the social struggle of the inter-war years. In the post-Second World War period, however, the Labour Party did accept demands for some degree of devolved government in Wales, which resulted, in 1964, in the establishment of the Welsh Office with a Secretary of State for Wales with a seat in the U.K. **Cabinet,** a development that was greatly to increase the political visibility of Wales. A Welsh Language Act, granting equal validity to the Welsh language in certain circumstances, was passed in 1967. (In 1981 Welsh was spoken by 19 percent of the Welsh population, over half a million persons.)

However, this Welsh national strategy, which found expression first in Home Rule Liberalism and then in some Labour policies, was never nationalist in any explicit sense. That specific political project was to become (following some early ambivalence) associated with the Welsh National Party, which later adopted the name *Plaid Cymru* (Party of Wales). The party was launched in 1925, and the key figure in its development until the war was the English-born Welshman Saunders Lewis. In an impressive creative effort, he devised an intellectual justification for a self-governing and Welsh-speaking Wales, which, surprisingly in such a Protestant country, relied in large measure on a return to a medieval European **Roman Catholicism** as an escape from the English nationalism of the Reformation and the consequent industrialization of Wales. His appeal to Welsh-speaking intellectuals was profound, but the party made virtually no progress outside such confined circles despite the development of a more socialistic economic policy by D.J. Davies and a celebrated direct-action protest and court case in 1936.

During the Second World War the party argued for Welsh neutrality in a conflict that they claimed was of England's making. The party did succeed in broadening its base marginally and in changing to a more pragmatic leadership under Dr. Gwynfor Evans, who became President in 1945. The party retained a modest presence in Welsh politics, but its fortunes were transformed by the victory of Evans at the Carmarthen by-election of 1966. This success followed the establishment in 1963 of the Welsh Language Society (*Cymdeithas yr Iaith Gymraeg*), which initiated a direct-action campaign for equal status for the Welsh language. Despite the unwelcome publicity attracted by some violent protests and a bombing campaign, Welsh nationalism succeeded in the late 1960s in establishing broad support in some parts of Wales and among certain social groups; the party performed well in a number of further by-elections and, in 1974, succeeded in electing three members of Parliament. This was in part responsible for the devolution legislation and the subsequent referendum of 1979. The referendum result in Wales, however, witnessed a substantial anti-devolution majority.

This was a setback for nationalism, but, under the then-socialist leadership of Dr. Dafydd Elis Thomas, MP, the party succeeded in regaining some of the ground during the 1980s. In the April 1992 election it gained only 8.8 percent of Welsh votes but did, nevertheless, succeed in electing four members of Parliament. This phenomenon explains the strength and the weakness of Welsh nationalism—its electoral strongholds have been provided by the still strongly Welsh-speaking west of the country, and the party has found it extremely difficult to break out of the confines of its language base and create a wider nationalist politics in industrialized and urban Wales. In the elections for the European Parliament in 1989 the party adopted a new strongly pro-Europe stance and argued for the creation of democratic institutions to achieve a Europe of the regions.

R. Merfyn Jones

Bibliography

Davies, Charlotte Aull. *Welsh Nationalism in the Twentieth Century: The Ethnic Option and the Modern State.* 1989.
Davies, D. Hywel. *The Welsh Nationalist Party, 1925–45: A Call to Nationhood.* 1983.
Morgan, Kenneth O. *Rebirth of a Nation: Wales, 1880–1980.* 1981.

Wheatley, John (1869–1930)

John Wheatley was Minister of Health (with responsibility also for housing) in the 1924 **Labour** government and is often regarded as that administration's most effective member. More broadly, he was a man of the Labour Left and became a principal critic of **Ramsay MacDonald's** leadership.

He was born in County Waterford in 1869. His family migrated to the west of Scotland, and, probably in 1881, he became a miner. He left the industry in the early 1890s and after a series of business ventures established himself in 1908 as a partner in a printing business that prospered. This social mobility was combined with increasingly radical politics. Early involvement with the United Irish League was followed, probably in 1906, by a move to the **Independent Labor Party** (ILP). Wheatley was a devout Catholic whose attempts to demonstrate that **Roman Catholicism** and socialism could be reconciled led to the founding of the Catholic Socialist Society and to a series of controversies with clerics. Within the labor movement he wrote pamphlets in which he used his mining experiences to indict capitalism, and he became a municipal politician. He joined the Glasgow City Council in 1912 and established a reputation as an expert on housing.

Wheatley responded cautiously to the outbreak of war in 1914. He adopted a critical position but concentrated on issues of immediate relevance to the Glaswegian working class. The city's prominence in the munitions industry intensified the demand for housing, and the labor movement became involved in a campaign of rent strikes and attempts to prevent evictions. This paralleled and sometimes interacted with the emergence of a strong shop stewards movement concerned to block dilution of skilled workers by women and unskilled workers. The combination produced the image—some would say misleading—of the Red Clyde. Wheatley played a prominent role in the rent agitations and gave advice and support to the shop stewards. He was concerned to offer a campaigning alternative to the revolutionary section in the workshops.

The Glasgow ILP emerged from the war with an enhanced reputation, and Wheatley only narrowly missed election to the House of

Commons in 1918. Industrial defeats, the start of the inter-war depression, and the continuing salience of the housing issue all helped to send Wheatley to Westminster in November 1922. At that election Glasgow returned ten Labour MPs. Most were orthodox backbenchers, but a few—most notably Wheatley and **James Maxton**—established themselves as left-wing critics and earned the sobriquet the "Clydesiders." In June 1923 Wheatley, Maxton, and two colleagues were suspended from the Commons for unparliamentary behavior. It was a protest, partly instinctive, partly deliberate, against staid parliamentary mores.

Nevertheless, Wheatley was appointed to the first Labour **Cabinet** in January 1924. He achieved prominence because he produced a significant piece of legislation despite the government's minority status. His Housing Act extended the provision of subsidies for public-sector **housing** projects. This was not innovative; it built upon the earlier legislation by post-war coalition and **Conservative** ministries. Yet for a government concerned to establish Labour's credibility, it demonstrated a reassuring competence. In other spheres Wheatley's record was more ambiguous. He encountered difficulties in reconciling labor movement demands with legal and administrative proprieties. He met vehement opposition from **birth control** campaigners over his refusal to allow publicly funded organizations to give contraceptive advice. It was the one issue on which Wheatley's Catholicism seemingly affected his political judgment.

Following Labour's loss of office in October 1924 Wheatley became increasingly hostile to Labour's leadership. He passionately supported the miners in their 1926 dispute and attacked their "betrayal" by both party and trade union leaders. His criticism of party policy deepened: He became a somewhat distinctive advocate of the ILP's "Living Wage" policy, and he advocated a planned economy and protectionism. When the second Labour government was formed in 1929, he was not considered for office. Instead he and Maxton led a small group of left-wing critics. He died in May 1930, a respected but isolated figure.

Wheatley evades easy categorization—the radical businessman and devout Catholic who was also a Glasgow machine politician, a widely admired minister, and eventually a socialist rebel. His contemporaries generally found him an intellectually impressive figure; they also found him elusive. Perhaps this reflected a failure to appreciate the significance of his Glasgow Catholic base, which remained fundamental to his political identity.

David Howell

Bibliography

Howell, David. *A Lost Left: Three Studies in Socialism and Nationalism.* 1986.

McLean, Ian. *The Legend of Red Clydeside.* 1983.

Middlemas, Robert Keith. *The Clydesiders: A Left-Wing Struggle for Parliamentary Power.* 1965.

Wood, Ian. *John Wheatley.* 1989.

Whitehead, Alfred North (1861–1947)

Brilliant mathematician, inspirational teacher, gifted philosopher, and unwearying administrator, Alfred North Whitehead was one of Britain's most versatile and admired intellectuals. As close to a Victorian polymath as it was possible to be in the twentieth century, he wrote two dozen books, ranging from the orthodox *A Treatise on Universal Algebra* (1898) to the revolutionary *Principia Mathematica* (3 vols., 1910–13), from the critical *An Enquiry Concerning the Principles of Natural Knowledge* (1919) to the inspirational *Process and Reality* (1929). Revered by his students, esteemed by his colleagues, and worshiped by his disciples, Whitehead became one of Britain's best-known and most respected thinkers.

Born into a family that had produced a succession of **Church of England** clergymen and schoolmasters on the Isle of Thanet, Whitehead was educated at Sherborne School and Trinity College, **Cambridge**. An accomplished mathematician—albeit with wide-ranging intellectual interests—Whitehead was elected a Fellow of Trinity in 1884 and quickly established himself as a teacher of uncommon dedication and an academic administrator of rare humility. It was at Trinity that he encountered his most famous pupil, **Bertrand Russell**, and proved instrumental in turning Russell's interests to problems of the philosophy of mathematics. Their friendship quickly ripened into a collaboration, culminating in the *Principia Mathematica*, a heroic effort of scholarship aimed at establishing the logical foundations of mathematics.

In 1910 Whitehead stunned his colleagues by resigning his Trinity College fellowship and moving to London. The next year he took up a position at University College, and from 1914 to 1924 he held a chair of applied mathematics at Imperial College. At Cambridge Whitehead had been almost exclusively a pure mathematician, writing a series of remarkable papers—such as "On Mathematical Concepts of the Material World" (1906). In London, by contrast, he turned his scholarly energies away from mathematics and toward **philosophy** and the philosophy of science, publishing many papers and books, most prominently *The Concept of Nature* (1920) and *The Principle of Relativity* (1922).

In 1924 Whitehead again mystified his friends by resigning his London appointment and—at age sixty-three—accepting a position as Professor of philosophy at Harvard University, a post he held until his retirement in 1937. At Harvard Whitehead once again proved an inspiring teacher and once again shifted his interests, this time toward cosmology and what he termed the "philosophy of organism." Such writings as *Process and Reality: An Essay in Cosmology* (1929) and *Nature and Life* (1934) presented the mature expression of his thought.

Whitehead died—on 30 December 1947—rich with honors: a Fellow of both the **Royal Society** and the British Academy, a member of the Order of Merit, and the recipient of the Sylvester Medal of the Royal Society and the Butler Medal of Columbia University. His enduring intellectual reputation rests with his earliest and latest work—with his contributions to the *Principia* and his meditations on the nature of God and the universe. Judged by admirers, skeptics, and critics alike as an estimable man of intelligence, humanity, and wisdom, Whitehead set a standard of personal conduct and intellectual distinction rarely matched in this century.

Kirk Willis

Bibliography

Kuntz, Paul Grimley. *Alfred North Whitehead*. 1986.

Lowe, Victor. *Alfred North Whitehead: The Man and His Work*. 2 vols. 1985–90.

Schilpp, Paul Arthur. *The Philosophy of Alfred North Whitehead*. 1941.

Whitley Councils

The **Lloyd George** coalition government proposed the creation of joint industrial councils, commonly known as Whitley Councils, in 1917 as a central component of post-war planning. Although originally intended for private industry, the scheme was extended to the **civil service** in the 1920s, and today the councils exist only in the civil service. Whitley Councils were composed of representatives of unions and industry in equal numbers who would meet regularly to discuss trade-related issues in the hope to reducing the number of strikes and improving conditions for growth.

The name Whitley Council came from John H. Whitley (1866–1935), who chaired the Subcommittee on Relations between Employers and Employed that drafted the plan. The plan borrowed ideas from many industrial reform schemes proposed before and during the war. Arthur Greenwood (1880–1954), one of the two Secretaries of Whitley's committee, probably drafted the Whitley Council plan. The Minister of Reconstruction, Dr. Christopher Addison (1869–1951), supported Whitley Councils but relied on Ernest Benn (1875–1954), a temporary civil servant, to encourage industry to adopt Whitley Councils. The Ministry of Labour provided significant personnel support until budget retrenchment in 1922 cut available funds, and by the 1930s it had distanced itself entirely from Whitley Council activity.

Despite official efforts, few highly organized industries were persuaded to undertake what was perceived as a risky experiment in industrial relations. Nor were influential labor leaders much less suspicious of Whitley Councils, preferring instead to restore traditional pre-war mechanisms for the settlement of disputes. More-radical labor leaders believed that Whitley Councils were an insufficient step toward their goal of industrial democracy. The most successful Whitley Councils were in industries in which unionization was weak. Established in early 1918, the National Council of the Pottery Industry was the first and the most famous of the more than thirty industrial Whitley Councils, which were still functioning in 1939. All of them were absorbed into other government schemes for industrial relations during the Second World War.

James W. Stitt

Bibliography

Charles, Roger. *The Development of Industrial Relations in Britain, 1911–1939*. 1973.

Johnson, Paul. *Land Fit for Heroes*. 1968.

Lowe, Rodney. *Adjusting to Democracy: The Role of the Ministry of Labour in British Politics, 1916–1939.* 1986.

Morgan, Kenneth. *Portrait of a Progressive: The Political Career of Christopher, Viscount Addison.* 1980.

Wilkinson, Ellen (1891–1947)

Ellen Wilkinson was one of Britain's most important female politicians, becoming Minister of Education in **Clement Attlee's** post-war **Labour** government. She was also a trade union organizer, partly responsible for the **Jarrow** March, a journalist, a brilliant orator, and a prominent member of the Labour national executive.

Wilkinson was born in Manchester on 8 October 1891 into a respectable upper-working-class family. She was raised a **Methodist**, valued education, and worked her way through school until, winning a scholarship, she entered the University of Manchester in 1910, where she obtained an upper-second-class degree in **history** and an M.A. At university she joined the **Fabian Society** and was active in the University Socialist Federation, which brought her into contact with leading socialists of the day, including J.T. Walton Newbold, the first Communist MP, to whom she was briefly engaged, and **Herbert Morrison.**

During these years, and subsequently, she gained a reputation for being a fiery personality. The fact that she was red-haired and small led to the epithets "elfin fury," the "Fiery Atom," and later, "Red Ellen." For a time she worked for the National Union of Women's Suffrage Societies; she was active in the Women's International League and, in 1915, became the national women's organizer of the Amalgamated Union of Cooperative Employees. She was a powerful and tireless speaker and ubiquitous crusader. Although initially active in the **Communist Party of Great Britain**, she won her political spurs for Labour when she was returned as a City Councilor for Manchester in November 1923. She lost her first parliamentary contest at Ashton-under-Lyne in 1923 but was eventually returned for Middlesborough East in 1924 and became one of only four women in the House of Commons. She held that seat until the crushing Labour defeat in the 1931 general election but was returned for Jarrow in 1935, holding the seat until her death.

From 1924 until 1939 Wilkinson was closely associated with the British Left, active in the ill-fated **Socialist League,** involved in **pacifist** and anti-Fascist movements, and contributing to the socialist weekly *Tribune.* She also aspired to be a journalist and a novelist. But her claim to fame was the fact that she helped to organize the Jarrow March to pressure the National government to provide jobs for Jarrow, a town suffering mass **unemployment.** She later wrote of her experiences and the unemployment and poverty problems of Jarrow in *The Town That Was Murdered* (1939). From 1939 onward, however, she moved more into the center of Labour politics. In **Winston Churchill's** wartime coalition government she was appointed Parliamentary Secretary to the Ministry of Pensions in May 1940, Parliamentary Secretary at the Home Office in October 1940, and was made a Privy Councilor at the beginning of 1945. In August 1945 she became Minister of Education in Attlee's post-war Labour government. It was in this capacity that she pressed ahead with campaigns for free school milk and **secondary education** for all. Unfortunately, her educational work was cut short by her untimely death, of heart failure following bronchitis, on 6 February 1947.

Keith Laybourn

Bibliography

Morgan, Kenneth O. *Labour People.* 1987.

Rubinstein, David. "Ellen Wilkinson Reconsidered," *History Workshop Journal,* vol. 7 (1979), pp. 161–9.

Vernon, Betty D. *Ellen Wilkinson.* 1982.

Wilkinson, Ellen. *The Town That Was Murdered.* 1939.

Williams, Raymond Henry (1921–1988)

Raymond Williams was one of the most important literary and cultural critics of his generation. Born into a Welsh working-class family, he was educated at Abergavenny grammar school and Trinity College, **Cambridge** (B.A., 1946). During the Second World War he served in the Guards Armoured Division (1944–5). He worked as an **adult education** tutor for fifteen years before joining the Cambridge English faculty in 1961. A Fellow of Jesus College, he became a Professor in 1974 and taught at Cambridge until his retirement.

In a series of highly influential books, including *Culture and Society, 1780–1950*

(1958), *The Long Revolution* (1961), *Modern Tragedy* (1966), *The English Novel from Dickens to Lawrence* (1971), and *The Country and the City* (1973), Williams set forth a new definition of the study of literature for the British tradition by his demonstration of the power of a social-historical analysis at the service of a socialist consciousness. He shared with **F.R. Leavis** an interest in "culture" as a key component of human interaction, and a belief in the power of literature both to embody and to disseminate (as well as to critique) the national imagination. But he broke down Leavis' carefully maintained barrier between high culture and mass culture in a radically democratic extension of the franchise; after Williams, every expressive medium, from comics to classics, could be seen to involve a serious imagination and to deserve a careful critical analysis. His pioneering work on **popular culture**, film, and **television**, in countless articles and in such books as *Communications* (1962, revised 1968 and 1976) and *Television* (1974) was a major factor in the acceptance of communications research by humanists and historians. Reciprocally, it informed social scientists of the importance of nonquantitative analyses of culture and literature to their own developing disciplines.

In *Keywords* (1976) Williams set out to examine, in dictionary style, the important terms in the vocabulary of modern British culture and society and thereby stimulated an increased awareness, within and well beyond the universities, of the power of words and of their historical and political associations. And in *Marxism and Literature* (1977) he answered those who had accused him of ignoring the European theoretical tradition by producing a masterpiece of literary theory, a field in which he had become more seriously interested after meeting French Marxist philosopher Lucien Goldmann in 1970. Williams kept an untypically clear head throughout the debates for and against Louis Althusser and his brand of theoretical Marxism that dominated the humanities and social sciences in Britain during the 1970s. He never embraced the excesses of what was then called "theory," nor did he endorse the often anti-intellectual extremes of British common sense that were invoked to fend off its challenges. In similar spirit, his interpretations of mass culture avoided both populist celebration, which assumed that whatever was popular was also good, and the equally inflexible

critiques mounted by the theorists of the Frankfurt School, who saw in mass culture only the deformed ideological workings of a repressive capitalism.

Williams' life was never that of a mere scholar and university teacher. He wrote several plays and five novels, among them *Border Country* (1960), *Second Generation* (1964), and *The Fight for Manod* (1979), in which he attempted a fictional representation of the social and psychological stresses he saw attending the processes of modernization and class struggle in his native Wales. From his earliest years his life was that of a public intellectual. Whether inside or outside the **Labour Party**, he was constantly pressuring it toward a socialist agenda. He worked for his local Labour candidate at age fourteen and at seventeen spoke out against the **Munich** agreement. In his years as an adult tutor he worked for and edited various magazines and journals and was an important figure in the foundation and evolution of *New Left Review*. He was only briefly a member of the **Communist Party of Great Britain** (in 1939–41), and in 1966 he resigned from five years of official membership of the Labour Party, after which he maintained the role of an oppositional socialist intellectual working within the broad Left but with a consistently independent and original perspective. In 1967 he coedited, with Stuart Hall and **E.P. Thompson**, *May Day Manifesto* (revised and expanded, 1968), in which he and his contributors, many of them at the center of the "New Left," denounced the Labour government as the agent rather than the critic of late capitalism and called for an end to the "deadening language of a false political system."

In his last years Williams remained as energetic as ever in his challenges to the parochialisms and cruelties of the British (and, above all, the English) Establishment, even as he remained immensely loyal to what he saw as the best of the national tradition embodied in a working-class, nonmetropolitan culture. In *Towards 2000* (1983) he made a major effort to extend and update the analysis begun in *Culture and Society*. His own thoughts and opinions about his long career in criticism and politics can be found in *Politics and Letters* (1979). Since his death, various collections of his essays and reviews have been published, among them *Resources of Hope* (1988) and *What I Came To Say* (1989). In person as in print, he was and continues to be an inspiration for the new generations of oppositional intellectuals in the English-speaking world.

David Simpson

Bibliography
Eagleton, Terry. *Criticism and Ideology: A Study in Marxist Literary Theory.* 1976.
———, ed. *Raymond Williams: Critical Perspectives.* 1989.
Gorak, Jan. *The Alien Mind of Raymond Williams.* 1988.
O'Connor, Alan. *Raymond Williams: Writing, Culture, Politics.* 1989.
Prendergast, Christopher, ed. *Cultural Materialism: On the Work of Raymond Williams.* 1994.

Wilson, Angus Frank Johnstone (1913–1991)

Angus Wilson is among the important British novelists to have emerged in the latter half of the twentieth century, not only because of the artistic quality of his fiction but because much of it provides a detailed, shrewd reflection of British society before and after the Second World War in gradual and sometimes painful transition toward a more egalitarian order.

Wilson was born in August 1913 in Bexhill, Sussex, the sixth and last child of a Scottish father and a South African mother, both well into their forties. He spent his earliest childhood in England and 1920–4 with his mother's relatives in Durban, South Africa. After three years at a preparatory school run by one of his brothers, Wilson entered Westminster School as a day pupil in 1927, moving from there to Merton College, Oxford, in 1932. He graduated from Oxford in 1935 with a degree in history and from 1936 to 1955 was employed at the British Museum, first as a cataloger of books and in 1949 as Deputy Superintendent of the Reading Room. For almost four years of the Second World War he worked for the Foreign Office at Bletchley Park, in the operations that successfully decoded material transmitted by the German "Enigma Machine." It was the isolation and uncongeniality of his wartime work that led Wilson to his career as a writer. In 1944 he suffered a nervous breakdown, for which writing was suggested as therapy. He did not immediately take up the suggestion, but when in 1946 he started to write, producing his first short story, "Raspberry Jam," in a single weekend, he found he had liberated a fully formed talent. It was quickly recognized in two prestigious magazines, *Horizon* and the *Listener*.

His first two books were collections of short stories: *The Wrong Set* (1949) and *Such Darling Dodos* (1950). Their mixture of satirical observation and human sympathy established Wilson's reputation, though a third collection, *A Bit Off the Map* (1957), was less successful, and Wilson's only stage play, *The Mulberry Bush*, performed at the Royal Court Theatre in London in 1956, proved to be no match for the new wave of drama inaugurated in the same theater a few weeks later by **John Osborne**'s *Look Back in Anger*. Wilson's position as a writer of fiction, however, was by this time incontestable, having been made so by the first two of his eight novels, *Hemlock and After* (1952) and the much longer and Dickensianly rich *Anglo-Saxon Attitudes* (1956). Each book centers on the self-discovery of an aging male protagonist, the first a "Grand Old Man" of English letters, the second a distinguished historian. Both novels display acute awareness of the mixed motives of heart and mind in a wide range of characters from recent and contemporary society, and both novels courageously depict **homosexuality**. Wilson's third novel, *The Middle Age of Mrs. Eliot* (1958), presents the slow adjustment to widowhood and reduced circumstances of its middle-class protagonist and shows Wilson to be a writer as sensitive to the lives of women as to those of men. This empathy is also evident in *Late Call* (1964), set in a post-war British **new town**, which Wilson presents with his characteristic care for social detail. His two other novels of the 1960s are more technically experimental: *The Old Men at the Zoo* (1961) takes place in a future in which civilized order and liberal values are in the process of breaking down; *No Laughing Matter* (1967) is a panoramic novel covering the lives of six siblings from 1912 to the present, in which the conventions of "realistic" narrative are diversified by interior monologue, dramatic interludes, and functional stylistic parody. Wilson's last two novels, *As If by Magic* (1973) and *Setting the World on Fire* (1980), though generally felt to lack the cogency of their predecessors, nevertheless display considerable vitality in their depiction, respectively, of Third World conditions and of noble risk-taking in artistic enterprise.

In addition to writing his own fiction, Wilson commented on the fiction and the lives of other writers, most notably in *Emile Zola*

(1952), *The World of Charles Dickens* (1970), and *The Strange Ride of Rudyard Kipling* (1977). From 1966 to 1973 he was a part-time Professor of English literature at the University of East Anglia (where he was also Public Orator), and he lectured at many universities in the United States. He chaired the Literature Panel of the **Arts Council of Great Britain** (1966) and the National Book League (1971–4), and was President of the Royal Society of Literature of Great Britain (1983–6). These posts recognized his personal distinction as a writer and his commitment to the cause of literature, as did the many honors awarded him in Britain and abroad, including CBE (1968), Chevalier de l'Ordre des Arts et des Lettres (1972), and Honorary Member of the American Institute and Academy of Arts and Letters (1980). He was awarded a knighthood in 1980. After having spent three decades, from 1955 onward, living in a cottage in Suffolk, Wilson spent the later 1980s in St. Remy de Provence. He died, after a long illness, in a nursing home in Suffolk on 31 May 1991.

An inheritor of the realist and liberal-humanist traditions of the English novel—in which capacity he has influenced such younger writers as **Margaret Drabble** and Malcolm Bradbury—Wilson was at the same time always aware of "the dangerous edge of things" and of the need for literature to keep pace with the modernist and postmodernist experiment and to encompass fresh and challenging modes of communication.

Averil Gardner

Bibliography

Drabble, Margaret. *Angus Wilson.* 1995.
Faulkner, Peter. *Angus Wilson: Mimic and Moralist.* 1980.
Gardner, Averil. *Angus Wilson.* 1985.
Stape, John Henry. *Angus Wilson: A Bibliography, 1947–1987.* 1988.

Wilson, (James) Harold (1916–1995)

A dominant figure in British politics for over a decade, Harold Wilson is the first **Labour Party** leader to win three general elections and was Prime Minister from 1964 to 1970 and from 1974 to 1976. He became Baron Wilson of Rievaulx in 1983. His career attracts mixed assessments: although a partial rehabilitation has begun, the balance is unfavorable. While recognized as shrewd and tactically adroit,

Wilson is also condemned as a mere survivor and political "fixer"; a faint aura of seediness and duplicity surrounds his career. He combined a fierce urge for achievement and status with an insecurity that made him constantly suspicious of colleagues and vulnerable to press criticism. Wilson had an agile intelligence but seemed more at home with processes than outcomes, happier finding short-term solutions than pursuing a political vision.

These characteristics, and his poorly articulated belief in a roughly defined set of social democratic values, can be discerned in his upbringing, education, and early career. Wilson grew up in a lower-middle-class family in Yorkshire. Its strong work ethic and Nonconformist religious faith left an imprint, although critics see more evidence of the former than the latter. At **Oxford** he studied hard and competitively; he dabbled in Liberal politics but had no contact with the heady social and intellectual atmosphere of the Labour Club and the Oxford Union, frequented by many future colleagues, rivals, and opponents whose loftier social background and assured manner unnerved Wilson throughout his career. As a junior academic he worked with **William Beveridge**, whose ideas influenced the development of the post-1945 **welfare state**. Wilson was attracted to the Labour Party by **G.D.H. Cole**, one of its foremost intellectuals, perhaps partly because it offered a more plausible route than did the **Liberals** to the political career he already coveted.

The Second World War drew Wilson from academic life into several **civil service** posts in London; the experience increased his faith in government planning. Elected MP for Ormskirk in 1945 (he moved to the Huyton seat in 1950 and retained it throughout his career in the House of Commons), Wilson was quickly promoted to a series of government positions. His resignation from office in 1951 over budgetary priorities coincided with that of **Aneurin Bevan**, a hero of the Left; Wilson exploited or underplayed the association as circumstances required. His ability to maneuver among the Labour Party's factions sustained his rise through its ranks in the 1950s and secured his election as its leader in 1963. He was seen essentially as a pragmatist, a moderate who did not alienate the party's left wing and who had little time for abstract or electorally damaging ideological debates. He led the party to a very narrow election victory in 1964 (consolidated by another victory in 1966), sidestepping bitter arguments by redefining socialism as the planned management of technological progress and economic efficiency. Although the Wilson government inherited serious economic problems, it began with a self-conscious burst of energy. He appeared committed to modernization, technocracy, and growth, and sought to establish Labour as the more forward-looking, less class-based party. To economic promises were added hopes for an expanded welfare state and rejection of Establishment values in favor of a more open, dynamic society. However, the government and its 1966 successor offered more than they could deliver. For three years the defense of sterling limited their freedom of action, but this and the restoration of a healthy trade balance were articles of faith to Wilson. The belated decision to devalue the pound in November 1967 constrained growth-oriented policies, while the commitment to planned expansion was also undermined by tensions between the Treasury and the newly created Department of Economic Affairs. Although Wilson was able to bequeath to his **Conservative** successor a revived trade balance and stable currency, underlying economic problems and patterns of rising public expenditure remained. So did Britain's archaic system of industrial relations; in 1969 an attempt to modernize it was beaten back by the trade unions and much of the rest of the labor movement, despite Wilson's commitment to reform.

It was Wilson's fate to hold office during a difficult period in foreign affairs. Britain was adjusting slowly to its diminishing role in world affairs. The burgeoning **European Community** had previously denied British entry, and did so again in 1967. The "special relationship" with the United States increasingly seemed less special to Washington than to London. Wilson's efforts to act as a mediator in the Vietnam War showed him to be naively optimistic about his personal influence and underlined the decline of British power. The same may be said of the Rhodesian crisis: The white government unilaterally declared independence from the Commonwealth and the Crown. Wilson genuinely disliked racism and had a deep regard for a renewed, postcolonial Commonwealth. He identified himself closely with the issue but could neither prevent independence nor effectively impose punitive measures.

Wilson's overall record as Prime Minister in the 1960s was mixed. For a while the nation

seemed reinvigorated and optimistic, although this may have had more to do with changes in **popular culture** than with politics. The government did, however, introduce or facilitate a series of reforms, in such areas as **capital punishment, abortion, homosexuality,** and **divorce,** which made for a somewhat more humane and liberal society. It also entered the fields of **race relations** and **equal pay.** Wilson's personal style seemed suited to the times; he was witty, informal, and at home on **television,** in contrast to his recent Conservative predecessors. His manner emphasized rather than disguised his background; it reflected and perhaps helped quicken something of a thaw of a permafrost of the class structure. Other aspects of Wilson's style drew criticism. He was constantly aware of the need to balance factions in the Labour Party, yet he often treated them with disdain. He seemed increasingly to see government in terms of external crises and internal threats. Suspicious of senior colleagues (sometimes with good reason), he kept his cards close to his chest while nervously watching his ministers. His use of small committees to circumvent the full **Cabinet,** his manipulation of the **press,** and his reliance on a small circle of personal aides and advisers prompted exaggerated talk of a semipresidential system of "Prime Ministerial government."

Wilson seemed traumatized by Labour's defeat in 1970. He survived as leader of a party that he found increasingly hard to control as its balance tilted leftward. Particular skill was needed to deal with divisions over European Community membership, which was generally opposed by the Left and favored by the Right, and which acted as an ideological litmus test to both. Wilson's mixture of evasion and compromise was to some observers a necessary display of great dexterity; to others, a cynical defense of his own position. It did, at least, take a remarkable politician to paper over the deepening cracks while being attacked from both sides for doing so.

In 1974 Wilson became Prime Minister again at a time of intense industrial unrest and mounting economic problems. The February election produced a Labour government lacking a parliamentary majority; it barely acquired one in October. Wilson's approach differed from that of a decade earlier. He treated the Cabinet as a more collegial body and lacked the restless energy of his earlier years. He described himself disingenuously as the "custodian of the Manifesto," having helped reduce it to a brief agenda shorn of left-wing items. He strove to sustain the "Social Contract," a grandiose term for the horse trading between government and unions over wage claims and social policy. He provided one vintage performance, using the unprecedented device of a national referendum to secure continued British membership in the European Community (achieved during the 1970–4 Conservative administration) while preventing an irreconcilable split in the Labour Party, in which a majority favored withdrawal.

In 1976 Wilson unexpectedly resigned as Prime Minister. Rumors then and since link his departure to an alleged long-term campaign by members of the security services, said to believe him to be a Soviet stooge. There had indeed been something of a vendetta, but with no proven justification, and neither this nor a worsening economic situation explains Wilson's departure. He was deeply fatigued and had planned his departure for some time. His final Honors List did not help his reputation; some of its beneficiaries' contribution to national life was hard to identify. Wilson retired to the back benches until 1983; he was then elevated to the **House of Lords** and largely withdrew from politics. His health failing, he became a somewhat isolated figure, pilloried by the Labour Left for abandoning the party's socialist principles and by Labour moderates for sticking to them.

Wilson was a superb political tactician whose limited strategic sense was further diminished by the pressure of events. His achievements may come to look less meager as the record of the **Thatcher** years becomes clearer. It may also be that the rickety state of Britain's economy, the archaic nature of its institutions, and the divisiveness of the labor movement required a leader best suited to crisis management, the blurring of issues, and postponement of hard decisions.

Steven Reilly

Bibliography
Morgan, Austen. *Harold Wilson*. 1992.
Pimlott, Ben. *Harold Wilson*. 1992.
Tiratsoo, Nick. *The Wilson Governments, 1964–1970*. 1993.
Wilson, Harold. *Memoirs: The Making of the Prime Minister, 1916–1964*. 1986.
———. *The Labour Government, 1964–70*. 1971.
———. *Final Term: The Labour Government, 1974–76*. 1979.
Ziegler, Philip. *Harold Wilson: The Authorised Life*. 1993.

Wodehouse, P(elham) G(renville) (1881–1975)

P.G. Wodehouse was one of the masters of the English language, beguiling it into doing improbable things with grace and charm. He enjoyed an equally rare comic genius and commendable industry. These gifts combined to produce ninety-eight books (mostly novels, but including sixteen volumes of short stories, two of collected articles, three of "autobiography," and one posthumous collection of letters); all or part of the book and lyrics for thirty-one produced musicals, mostly smash hits; seventeen staged plays that he wrote or co-wrote; and a vast amount of journalism. He is best known for creating Bertie Wooster, his valet Jeeves, and the Wodehousian Elysium where it is always glorious summer. But Wodehouse also created a host of other stars in the galaxy of English literature such as Bertie's Aunt Agatha who—her nephew suspects—wears barbed-wire next to the skin, kills rats with her teeth, and sacrifices her young by the light of the full moon. Other notables include Clarence, Earl of Emsworth and his prize pig, The Empress of Blandings; Uncle Fred, fifth Earl of good old Ickenham; Stanley Featherstonehaugh Ukridge; Honoria Glossop, whose laugh is like cavalry charging over a tin bridge; Psmith, "The 'p' is silent as in psittacosis;" and that wondrous raconteur of golf stories, The Oldest Member.

Wodehouse (pronounced Woodhouse) was born into a cadet branch of one of England's great landed families, which gave him his knowledge of the aristocracy. He was educated at Dulwich College, which gave him a thorough grounding in Latin and Greek and a deep understanding of the English language.

After Wodehouse left Dulwich there was no money to send him to university, and his father placed him with the Hong Kong and Shanghai Bank in London as a trainee manager. After two years trainees were sent out East, a fate Wodehouse dreaded as all he wanted to do was write. So on evenings and weekends he wrote every sort of journalism for every sort of periodical in a frantic effort to earn enough money from his pen to save him from the luxurious life of a Hong Kong bank manager in Asia. He succeeded.

Wodehouse first came to popular notice as a writer of "school stories" such as *Tales of St. Austin's* (1903) and *Mike* (1909), accepted as among the finest of the genre. In 1904 he first visited America, which he instantly loved, and became an Anglo-American author living in, writing for, and selling all of his work to, both countries.

If Wodehouse had never written a word of prose he would be remembered, in America at least, as one of the greatest lyric writers for Broadway musicals. His successes, often with Jerome Kern writing the score, included *Oh Boy!* and *Leave It to Jane* (both 1917), although his best-known song is "Bill," interpolated into Kern and Oscar Hammerstein's *Show Boat* (1927).

In the late 1920s Wodehouse concentrated on his novels and short stories, which became better and better appreciated around the globe and which assure his fame throughout the English-reading world. From 1929 with *Summer Lightning* to 1963 with *Stiff Upper Lip, Jeeves* he produced book after book that had reviewers desperate for new superlatives. Sir **Compton Mackenzie** gave up and wrote: "To criticise him is like taking a spade to a souffle." Only in Wodehouse's last years did his work become slightly self-derivative and fall below his best.

In 1940 the advancing German armies captured Wodehouse and his wife, Ethel, at Le Touquet on the north French coast. Later that year, as a civilian internee, Wodehouse made some innocent broadcasts to neutral America. The Nazis rebroadcast these to England, and Wodehouse was subjected to intense obloquy. His knighthood, just before his death in 1975, officially confirmed what had long been recognized: Those broadcasts were no more than an unworldly error of judgment.

Wodehouse influenced every subsequent novelist writing in English—whether they realize it or not—and is cited 1,255 times in *The Oxford English Dictionary*. Laymen were amazed when, in a pre-war broadcast in America, Hilaire Belloc described Wodehouse as "the best writer of English now alive, the head of my profession." Fellow writers treated this as no more than a statement of fact. They, at least, knew how difficult it was to create such sublime prose.

Barry Phelps

Bibliography
Donaldson, Frances. *P.G. Wodehouse: The Authorized Biography.* 1982.
McIlvaine, Eileen, et al. *P.G. Wodehouse: A Comprehensive Bibliography.* 1990.
Phelps, Barry. *P.G. Wodehouse: Man and Myth.* 1992.
Wodehouse on Wodehouse. 1980.

Wolfenden Report

In 1954, in the wake of several trials of public figures charged with various homosexual offenses, the government appointed a committee, chaired by John Wolfenden (1906–85), Vice Chancellor of the University of Reading, to examine the existing laws pertaining to **homosexuality** and **prostitution**. The committee's report, published in 1957, urged stricter control over public solicitation by prostitutes and recommended that homosexual acts between two consenting adults (over the age of twenty-one) in private should cease to be a criminal offense. The appearance of the report initiated a major public discussion of homosexuality and led to the creation of the Homosexual Law Reform Society, which worked to garner support for legal change. The report's recommendations regarding prostitution were implemented in the Street Offences Act of 1959. However, because opposition to the committee's position on homosexuality was widespread, the government was reluctant to change the laws concerning homosexuality. Only in 1967, with the passage of the Sexual Offences Act, was homosexuality in England and Wales finally decriminalized.

The Wolfenden Report was a landmark in the struggle for gay rights. By suggesting that it was not the business of the state to act as the guardian of private morality, it prepared the ground for the "permissive legislation" of the 1960s. Nevertheless, although the report called for the decriminalization of homosexual acts, it did not condone homosexuality, and it suggested the need for stricter controls over the public manifestation of what it considered irregular sexual conduct.

Chris Waters

Bibliography
National Deviancy Conference, ed. *Permissiveness and Control: The Fate of Sixties Legislation.* 1980.
Report of the Committee on Homosexual Offences and Prostitution (Wolfenden

Report). Cmnd. 247, Parliamentary Papers, vol. 14 (1956–7).

Wolfenden, Sir John. *Turning Points: The Memoirs of Lord Wolfenden.* 1976.

Women

In the first years of the twentieth century there were an unprecedented number of campaigns to achieve for women respect, influence, and independence comparable to that normally accorded to men, and there were changes of fundamental importance for women's lives that occurred independently of any conscious campaigning.

Most significant for most women in the long run was the falling birthrate. Beginning in the later nineteenth century, it eventually affected all social groups, though on a significant class gradient: The fall was greatest among the higher social classes; least, though still observable, among miners. Around 1900 women gave birth to an average of three children in the highest social class, seven in the lowest. Thereafter family size gradually declined and became increasingly socially homogeneous. Women born in the 1880s and having their children in the early twentieth century had only half as many children as their mothers; their own children in the inter-war years averaged two-thirds as many as themselves (around two). The birthrate reached its lowest point in the early 1930s (15.8 per 1,000 women of reproductive age, compared with 28.7 in 1901), and the trend moved rapidly toward the two-child family norm throughout society. After an upturn during and after the Second World War (to 20.7 in 1947), the birthrate stabilized and then fell again from the mid 1960s.

This change meant liberation from repeated **pregnancy**, miscarriage, **childbirth**, and associated ailments that had been the common lot of women. Throughout the first half of the century working-class women's organizations, such as the Women's Co-operative Guild, and middle-class philanthropic bodies campaigned for better conditions in pregnancy, childbirth, and **child-rearing**, especially for poor women. Death in childbirth was the one form of mortality that did not decline from the later nineteenth century; indeed it increased sharply during the First World War, then, after falling back to pre-war levels, rose again during the inter-war Depression. The figures did not fall until the introduction of penicillin and the sulfonamide drugs in the later 1930s facilitated the cure of previously fatal puerperal infection. From a little under 5 maternal deaths per 1,000 live births in 1911, and a peak of about 7.6 in 1918–9, the rate fell to less than 4 in 1939 and thereafter dwindled to tiny numbers. **Tuberculosis** was a much more significant cause of female deaths, accounting for 25 percent of deaths of women age fifteen to forty-four between 1911 and 1930.

Accompanying these changes was a trend to concentrate childbirth into relatively few years of **marriage**. By the 1950s most women had completed childbearing by their mid-thirties while still young enough for active involvement in life outside the family, again changing the age-old pattern of most women's lives. At the same time, a higher proportion of women married, at least once. At the beginning of the century about 15 in 100 women did not marry; of women born around 1940 only 5 in 100 have not married at least once. Women have come to have fewer children, but more of them do so.

The reduction in family size appears to have been a result of conscious limitation, although contraceptive devices were hard for any but the prosperous and well-informed to obtain before the 1960s, despite campaigns by women's groups in the inter-war years to make them more readily available. From the 1960s the birth control pill, free **birth control** clinics established by the **Labour** government, and access to **abortion** further increased women's control over reproduction.

The partnerships within which children are born have changed. Marriage was a matter of intense debate among women in all classes at the beginning of the century as an institution unduly restrictive of women. **Divorce** was difficult to obtain. The annual average number of divorces was 582 around 1900, about half of them among working-class people. There were active campaigns by women to give women equal rights with men to end unhappy marriages, resulting in legislation in 1918, 1923, and 1937. Divorce became significantly easier to obtain for both sexes after a further change in the law in 1984.

At the beginning of the century there was still the likelihood that marriage would terminate in middle age due to the death of one of the partners. By the 1930s longevity had changed this pattern, and, for a while, the long-surviving marriage became the norm. From the 1950s divorce replaced death as the cause of broken marriages. However, in the 1980s a significant trend toward cohabitation, often stable, to replace marriage began. In 1991 almost one-third of babies in Britain were born to unmarried parents. Many were in stable cohabiting relationships, but large numbers of women were bringing up children alone, and such women were disproportionately poor.

Power to change the law to improve women's position within marriage was one of many reasons why women campaigned for the vote and other political rights. One million women already possessed the vote in local elections in 1900 as legal householders and rate (local tax) payers, and several thousand were elected to local authorities. Their effective use of political rights at the local level and their active involvement in all political parties made their lack of voting rights at the national level the more absurd.

A peaceable but determined campaign for the vote, which became more active in the 1900s, largely grew out of such political activism. The militant and constitutionalist strands complemented each other more than either realized, putting both public and private pressure upon the government. The concession of the vote in 1918 was much influenced by the fact that the franchise was at the same time extended to all men at age twenty-one. Women, however, were initially granted the vote only at age thirty. In 1928 the danger of a majority female electorate was judged to have receded, and women were granted the vote on the same terms as men. The women's movement became more active especially in the 1920s in encouraging women to use their new citizenship rights and in campaigning for **equal pay** and improved welfare facilities.

The delayed progress of women in elective politics was just one aspect of their slowness to reach the top in any sphere of influence or paid employment. In 1900 women were beginning to be admitted to the professions, but their numbers were small (212 doctors for example). The **First World War** opened the way for middle-class women to undertake paid employment at least until marriage. After the war such women, no longer chaperoned, could lead much freer lives. The **Second World War**, which took female labor to the point of limited conscription, extended this process. But in 1946 only 7,198 medical practitioners out of 44,341 were female, as were 325 of 9,375 architects and 164 of 17,102 solicitors. By 1961 women repre-

sented 15.9 percent of the **medical profession** (concentrated in its less prestigious specialties), 3.5 percent of the **legal profession**, and 2.3 percent of architects. By 1988 21 percent of lawyers and 22 percent of general practitioners in medicine were female, but only 3.2 percent of surgeons and 0.5 percent of engineers. These changes indicate a new expectation among middle-class families that their daughters might enter professional careers. Accompanying this is a pattern of delayed childbirth and employment of full-time child care for professional women.

If there is some progress in paid employment of middle-class women, there is much less for lower-middle- and working-class women. The range of manual and (especially) lower-level white-collar occupations open to women has increased, though the prospects of career opportunities, pay, and promotion for women comparable with men have scarcely begun to be realized. At the beginning of the century the largest female occupation was **domestic service**, but a high proportion of working-class women have continued to be concentrated in low-paid, routinized employment. The First World War created demand for women in paid work, though often in hazardous occupations like making ammunition. After the war working-class women were expected to revert to pre-war occupations, including domestic service, which had sharply diminished during the war and continued to decline into the 1930s. Although many women suffered in the Depression, some found opportunities in the new light industrial occupations that developed in the inter-war years.

Before 1939 middle-class women would rarely take paid employment after marriage; poorer women were obliged to augment household resources throughout their life cycle. At the end of the Second World War the government, anticipating a manpower shortage, campaigned to keep women in the labor force. Many left to have or to care for young children, but the total numbers of women in paid employment rose from the later 1940s. Since then a pattern has been established in all social classes for women to cease work for a few years when children are young and then return to paid work, often part-time. Part-time work is a notable feature of the modern female labor market in Britain, accounting for about one-third of all paid **women's employment**.

Sexual inequality in paid employment survived a campaign on the part of the trade unions and white-collar occupations, from the 1930s, for comparable pay for women; a Royal Commission in 1946 that confirmed the facts of inequality; a revived women's movement, again with complementary moderate and radical wings; the Equal Pay Act (1970); and the establishment of the Equal Opportunities Commission under the Sex Discrimination Act (1975). In the 1980s and 1990s the European Commission and the European Court of Justice have supported some British women's appeals against discriminatory practices. The process, slow and costly, has established valuable precedents.

Unpaid work in the home has been improved by the demographic changes outlined above, by improved housing for working-class people since the 1920s, and generally smaller, servantless housing for the better-off. Domestic technology has replaced servants and has filtered down the social scale at increasing speed since the 1950s. The effect has not been to reduce average hours spent on housework, but to eliminate the heavy, debilitating physical labor that housework previously implied.

The experiences of women have differed by class, by age group, and, importantly from the 1950s, by ethnic background. Just as the lives of Orthodox Jewish women among immigrants early in the century differed from those of the non-Orthodox and non-Jewish women, so some Muslim and Hindu women live within the customs of their own cultures, though their experience also varies with age, class, and region of origin, as does that of the large numbers of women of Caribbean origin and the somewhat smaller numbers from Africa.

Pat Thane

Bibliography

Anderson, Michael. "The Social Implications of Demographic Change" in F.M.L. Thompson, ed. *The Cambridge Social History of Britain, 1750–1950*. vol. 2. 1991. pp. 1–70.

Lewis, Jane. *Women in England, 1870–1950: Sexual Divisions and Social Change.* 1984.

Meehan, Elizabeth. *Women's Rights at Work: Campaigns and Policy in the United States and Britain.* 1984.

Pugh, Martin. *Women and the Women's Movement in Britain, 1914–1959.* 1992.

Reid, Ivan, and Erica Stratta, eds. *Sex Differences in Britain.* 2nd ed. 1989.

Thane, Pat. "Towards Equal Opportunities? Women in Britain since 1945" in Terry Gourvish, and Alan O'Day, eds. *Britain since 1945.* 1991. pp. 183–208.

Women in Wartime (1914–1918 and 1939–1945)

Both World Wars have been seen by historians as emancipating for British women. Greater freedom was ostensibly expressed through consumption and personal style: Women in war work had their own incomes to spend, wore shorter skirts or even trousers, and smoked cigarettes in public. Enfranchisement in 1918 and the establishment of a Royal Commission on Equal Pay in 1944 appeared to give official encouragement to political and economic equality. But feminist historians have questioned whether women's labor-market gains were permanent and whether changes of style indicated a readjustment of the relationship between the sexes. In addition they have argued that the vote was granted to women over age thirty in 1918 mainly because of suffragist activity and pressure to revise the male franchise, rather than as a reward for war service. They also note that the only outcome of the equal-pay debate of 1944–6 was a recommendation that equal pay might be introduced for a small group of workers in the public services, and this was not acted upon until 1955.

In both wars there were large rises in the numbers of women employed. These were temporary, though they took place in the context of an overall upward trend between 1911 and 1951 in the number and proportion of British women in paid work. Between 1914 and 1918 there was an increase of about 1.5 million women in the industrial labor force, from 5.3 million in 1911 to nearly 7 million in 1918. But numbers then fell to 5.7 million in 1921. Unemployment was rising and there was political pressure to give job preference to ex-servicemen. Women were expected to return to traditional jobs in domestic service and the textiles and clothing industries or to stay at home. Between the wars, however, the women-employing sectors of some industries, such as electrical assembly, expanded. So did clerical work for women. In 1931 6.2 million women were in paid employment. The Second World War saw another increase of about 1.5 million women, but once again there was a decrease at the end of the war, from about 7.7 million to 6 million between 1943 and 1947. In part this was a temporary post-war readjustment and in part the result of demographic factors. By 1951 the census recorded 6.9 million women in paid work, and the proportion in industries like engineering and transport and in government service was higher than it had been pre-war. As in the case of the inter-war trend, this was not because women took men's jobs, but because women-employing sectors expanded more than those that employed men.

So the wars themselves contributed to a long-term process of enlarging **women's employment** within gender-stereotyped sectors of the economy. But wartime expansion also appeared to threaten gender boundaries at work and at home. There were four aspects to this problem.

First, in both wars women used the wartime opportunities to obtain relatively well-paid work in industries and occupations that were previously male-dominated, like munitions, engineering, transport, and office work. Most women had done paid work at some point in their lives before, usually in industries like textiles and clothing or in services like laundry work, waitressing, shopwork, and personal domestic service. They included married women, who were customarily expected to be supported by a male breadwinner and not to seek paid work. In 1918 40 percent, and in 1943 43 percent, of women workers were married, compared with only 15 percent in 1911 and 16 percent in 1931. The fact that women rarely did exactly the same jobs as men, and were in the main employed on work that had been simplified, was not as publicly visible as their entry in large numbers into unfamiliar territory. Male workers responded to the influx with varying degrees of hostility. In both wars there were incidents of workplace sabotage by men who opposed women's presence because it meant in the short term that the men were likely to be called up into military service, and in the long term that they might lose their jobs to this cheaper work force. Trade unions endeavored to protect their male members. A Munitions Act, passed in 1915, stipulated that women should be allowed into work from which trade union agreements had excluded them before the war, on the condition that their wages did not undercut those of men and that they would be removed at the end of the war. In 1940 individual union-employer agreements were signed on the same lines: Women should be allowed

into men's work for the duration of the war provided they received equal pay after a specified period. In both wars the implementation of these rules was problematic. Women struck for an equal war bonus on the London trams and buses in 1918 and for equal pay in a Scottish engineering factory in 1943. Men were prepared to help if they thought it would protect their jobs and pay rates, but they did not support women's long-term claims to jobs and fair pay. The unions actively promoted women's redundancies at the end of both wars.

"Women of Britain, Come into the Factories" (Zec): One of the best-known examples of propaganda targeted at women during the Second World War.

Second, in both wars women were recruited into various uniformed services, an apparent challenge to gender norms that caused considerable public alarm. In 1917 the women's auxiliary services to the armed forces (the Women's Army Auxiliary Corps, the Women's Royal Naval Service, and the Women's Royal Air Force) were formed on a cautious, experimental basis, recruiting around 40,000 women. A Women's Land Service Corps, later renamed the Women's Land Army, was founded in 1916 and recruited 23,000. In addition a few thousand women joined the Voluntary Aid Detachments as nurses. In the Second World War all of these organizations were enlarged and sometimes renamed. The three military services for women were the Auxiliary Territorial Service, the Women's Royal Naval Service, and the Women's Auxiliary Air Force. They recruited 450,000 women, while 80,000 women joined the Women's Land Army. In addition 500,000 women were employed in civil defense, and a million worked in the Women's Voluntary Services for Air Raid Precautions, established in 1938. Single women age nineteen to thirty were conscripted into the armed forces, industry, or civil defense following the National Service (No. 2) Act of December 1941. All the same, panic was expressed in the **press** and in Parliament about the effects a uniform might have on a woman's morals.

Third, steps were taken in both wars to alter the organization of domestic work in order to make women available for war work. In the First World War 108 day nurseries attached to large government-run factories, and a small number of municipal and private creches, were established for about 4,000 children of women war workers. Child care was greatly extended in the Second World War when 1,500 nurseries taking nearly 72,000 children were set up by local authorities with subsidies (and regulation) from the central government. Fears that nurseries would tempt women to desert their proper role of motherhood in favor of paid work were rife in the First World War. In the Second the Ministry responsible for nurseries (Health) saw them as a temporary necessity when alternative home-based arrangements (such as minding) could not be made, but a mother's place was still perceived to be in the home with her own children. In both wars the government responded to food shortages by introducing **rationing** (though not until 1918 in the First World War). But the woman worker faced the problem of missing a meal or absenting herself from work in order to queue for food in short supply. In the Second World War government ministries discussed the shopping problem, but the favored solution was to give women unpaid time off to shop, or to introduce schemes of part-time work, rather than to relieve the women of the work of shopping itself.

Fourth, in both wars there were anxieties that the family was under threat because of the large numbers of women in paid work and of men away from home in the armed forces. The illegitimacy rate rose by 30 percent in the First World War and more than doubled in the Second. In 1914 surveillance of servicemen's wives was introduced. If they were drunk or engaging in "irregular conduct," their army separation allowances were stopped. The **divorce** rate rose between 1918 and 1920 from 0.2 to 0.8 per 10,000 of the population, and between 1938 and 1947 from 1.5 to 13.6 per 10,000. The disruption of the Second World War undoubtedly contributed to this huge increase, but so, too, did legislation between the wars that made divorce cheaper and easier to obtain. After a rash of "khaki" weddings, there was a slump in the **marriage** rate in the middle of both wars, followed by a recovery at the end.

Investigation of these aspects of women's experiences in wartime indicates that the appearance of gender boundaries being under threat may have been much greater than the reality.

Penny Summerfield

Bibliography

Braybon, Gail. *Women Workers in the First World War: The British Experience.* 1981.

Braybon, Gail, and Penny Summerfield. *Out of the Cage: Women's Experiences in Two World Wars.* 1987.

Smith, Harold L. "The Effect of the War on the Status of Women" in Harold L. Smith, ed. *War and Social Change: British Society in the Second World War.* 1986. pp. 208–29.

Summerfield, Penny. "Women, War, and Social Change: Women in Britain in World War II" in Arthur Marwick, ed. *Total War and Social Change.* 1988. pp. 95–118.

———. *Women Workers in the Second World War: Production and Patriarchy in Conflict.* 1984.

Thom, Deborah. "Women and Work in Wartime Britain" in Richard Wall, and Jay Winter, eds. *The Upheaval of War: Family, Work, and Welfare in Europe, 1914–1918.* 1988. pp. 297–326.

Woollacott, Angela. *On Her Their Lives Depend: Munitions Workers in the Great War.* 1994.

Women's Education

The history of women's education in twentieth-century Britain has been a story of progress.

Women, as well as men, have benefited from the expansion and democratization of the educational system. On the other hand, gender bias—like class bias and racism—has affected access to equality in education. While there have been some changes since the 1970s, women have experienced the same disadvantages in education that they have had to confront more generally in British society throughout the century.

How did conceptions of gender difference influence the development of **primary** and **secondary education** in the period up to 1944? The fact that those with money and power almost invariably selected single-sex schools for their own children reflected the dominant belief that different educational needs of boys and girls should be reinforced through schooling. An ideological commitment to a conception of femininity that encouraged in girls and women not only dependence, but an acceptance of male dominance and masculine privilege, affected the curriculum and the mores of elementary education.

The central Board of Education (created in 1899) developed policies and programs designed to ensure that girls would receive training in domesticity through sewing, cookery, and laundry classes. Moreover, as resources expanded, sex segregation within schools increased. Where possible, schools provided separate entrances for girls and boys and separate play areas. The idea that the state school system should be used to train girls to be good wives and mothers, while their brothers were to be trained to be responsible wage earners, was accepted by the great majority of educational policymakers, men and women alike. Thus, elementary education in the first half of the century was extended relatively equally to girls and boys. However, schooling reflected and reinforced dominant beliefs about the differing roles of women and men explicitly through the formal curriculum (girls and not boys were trained for domesticity) and through less obvious informal mechanisms.

Until the **Education Act of 1944**, while the numbers of free places in secondary schools were increasing, secondary education was only available to a small minority of working-class children. By 1939 80 percent of the children educated in the state system left school at age fourteen. More boys than girls went on to secondary school: 14.5 percent of boys as against 13 percent of girls. Whether secondary-school pupils from the state system occupied free places in established schools, or whether they attended secondary schools created by local education authorities, they entered a middle-class milieu. One feature of this milieu was that, in contrast to primary education, secondary education almost invariably meant single-sex education. Thus, girls entering secondary schools from the state system were indeed being offered a chance to expand their horizons but not the same opportunities as their brothers. When they entered secondary school, they became part of a *female* middle-class milieu.

The foundations for girls' secondary education were laid by those pioneers of women's education who had established schools for the daughters of the middle classes designed to expand opportunities and prepare women for activities beyond the scope of domesticity. These pioneers, for the most part identified with the conservative wing of the women's movement, had struggled with conflicting objectives. On the one hand, they wished to provide their pupils with sound training, a liberal education, and skills that would allow them to earn their livings in a dignified manner, should that be necessary. On the other hand, as a group they also wished to develop and reinforce in their pupils the values of Victorian and Edwardian femininity.

Such middle-class girls' schools, whether private proprietary bodies or "public" schools, had developed as independent institutions. After the 1902 Education Act, there was some blurring of boundaries between the state system and the independent schools, as secondary schools serving children from the state system came under the aegis of the Board of Education's Secondary Branch. Its policymakers took the position that while girls, like boys, should be provided with a liberal education, schooling at the secondary level should also reinforce perceived inherent differences between the sexes. A tangible result of this policy was that from 1905, "housewifery" was made compulsory in those girls' secondary schools over which the board exercised authority.

Thus, the state-supported secondary system created during the first half of the century did incorporate into its structure some significant gender differences. While girls did share in the standard curriculum and were prepared for the School Certificate Examinations introduced in 1917, in crucial ways girls were also taught that their primary purpose was to fulfill their womanly role.

How did girls fare after the passage of the Education Act of 1944? Until the 1960s, when "secondary education for all" meant in practice a two-tier system in which only the 20 percent of children passing the eleven-plus examination were given access to a secondary education that would prepare them for skilled nonmanual work or university entrance, clear sex differences in educational opportunity emerged. Although as a group girls did at least as well as boys at eleven-plus, girls' grammar schools were not as successful as those for boys in retaining their pupils. Significantly fewer girls than boys stayed on in school past the age of sixteen: 66 percent of the eighteen-year-old school population was male in 1965.

Since the 1970s there has been a marked improvement in the retention rate for girls at the secondary level. By the 1980s girls had overtaken boys in General Certificate of Education "ordinary"-level passes achieved, in Certificate of Secondary Education passes, and in the unified General Certificate of Education examination introduced in 1986. Girls are also more likely than boys to attain at least one Advanced (A)-level pass. However, in the late 1980s boys still exceeded girls by a small margin in achieving the minimum two "A" levels needed for university entrance.

It is not clear that these improved opportunities for girls at the secondary level can be attributed to the restructuring of the secondary system. More likely they reflect the influence of the partial success of feminism. It is certainly the case that only since the 1970s have sociologists of education, educational psychologists, and historians of education begun to recognize the extent to which the educational system has served to perpetuate inequalities of gender, and only more recently have serious attempts been made to counteract such inequities.

Although the state system educates the great majority of Britain's children, 6.7 percent continue to be educated in independent schools and continue to attain a disproportionate number of university places. Some believe that such schools, while offering girls as well as boys undoubted advantages, reinforce outmoded notions of correct feminine behavior. In contrast, others argue that the academic successes of girls attending independent schools can be attributed to the fact that most of them remain single-sex institutions. Such observers believe that state-mandated coeducation, a feature of the state secondary-school system since the in-troduction of comprehensive schools—nearly all of which are coeducational—is in fact damaging to girls, given that the wider culture remains male-dominated. The debate about the relative merits of coeducation and single-sex education for girls at the secondary level remains unresolved. In the early years of the century postsecondary education was virtually restricted to those educated in the elite, independent stream. Women could attend and receive degrees from most British universities, but a majority of university students were male, and for both sexes **university education** remained the preserve of an elite minority. With the end of the Second World War a commitment to expand access to higher education became part of social policy. Changes were implemented through an expansion of university and college places and through a program of financial aid to postsecondary students. In the course of this expansion women have made striking advances. Whereas in the 1940s only 20 percent of the postsecondary population was female, by the 1980s this figure had risen to 40 percent. The number of women receiving degrees has increased eightfold since the 1940s, whereas the number for men has increased fourfold. However, women still receive slightly fewer degrees than men and hold only a small minority (10 percent) of teaching posts at British universities.

Deborah Gorham

Bibliography

Blair, Gage. "Great Britain" in Gail P. Kelly, ed. *International Handbook of Women's Education*. 1989. pp. 285–322.

Hunt, Felicity, ed. *Lessons for Life: The Schooling of Girls and Women, 1850–1950*. 1987.

Jones, Carol, and Pat Mahony. *Learning Our Lines: Sexuality and Social Control in Education*. 1989.

Purvis, June, and Margaret Hale, eds. *Achievement and Inequality in Education*. 1983.

Wilson, Maggie. "England and Wales" in Maggie Wilson, ed. *Girls and Young Women in Education: A European Perspective*. 1989. pp. 41–66.

Women's Employment

Women's economic activity attained a statistical high-water mark in the mid-Victorian years, with women working outside the home principally in the textile and clothing industries, domestic service, and laundressing. Yet women fully engaged at home with domestic chores were also considered to be productively employed and were so tabulated. In the census of 1881 housewives were still counted, but only as "unoccupied." By the census of 1911 they were no longer counted at all. Census figures indeed reveal an overall decline in female employment from 1871 to 1911. An increase in real wages in the closing decades of the nineteenth century fueled this trend by allowing more married women to remain at home full-time.

Prior to the First World War, a good deal of married women's economic activity escaped the official reports. For many working-class women with dependent children, home work done at piece rates away from the workshop provided a means of adding to meager family incomes. Home work constituted sweated labor performed under unregulated and often unsanitary conditions; it involved long hours, the frequent use of child labor, and was done for very little pay. Nevertheless, home work could be done sporadically, in the event of a financial crisis, by women who could not work outside the home. Sweated occupations included cardboard box making, sewing, chain making, carding hooks and eyes, brush making, and fur pulling. Production forces coupled with a vigorous public outcry effectively ended most sweated labor by the second decade of the twentieth century.

With the decline of home work, the cleft between the home and workplace was complete. A direct result of this separation was that young single women overwhelmingly comprised the female work force. By the 1920s married women without children increasingly continued their employment until the birth of their first child. But in virtually all events, women considered their jobs to be of short duration. They intended to resign at the first opportunity, usually upon **marriage**. Indeed, some occupations such as teaching and **nursing** enforced a marriage bar compelling a married woman to relinquish her job. This restriction remained in force in a number of fields until the Second World War. Not until 1946 was the marriage bar removed for female **civil servants**.

Given the perception of women's employment as transitory by both women and employers, the jobs offered were low-status, low-paying, tedious, and often unskilled or semiskilled. Job training was minimal. Further, women's participation in trade unions was but a fraction of men's involvement, further reinforcing their low status and pay. Over the decades, the proportion of women to men among trade unionists had remained smaller, despite a solid increase in the absolute numbers of women joining unions.

As the traditional female occupations declined in the twentieth century, other industries sprang up to absorb women workers. Technological advances in many industries made for lighter tasks requiring less skill. As a result, women entered such areas as mining and metallurgy, printing, papermaking, bookbinding, the chemical industry, and food processing. While **domestic service** continued to employ almost a quarter of the female labor force as late as the 1930s, a significant number of women left service for factory jobs that offered greater freedom, privacy, and higher wages.

Despite women's role in manufacturing, female employment in the twentieth century has been characterized by a shift toward white-collar work with the development of the distributive and service sectors. Large shops and department stores were established in response to the needs engendered by growing urban populations and the problems of distribution that resulted from new methods of mass production. These large stores replaced smaller family-run businesses and created a sharp demand for shop assistants. The growth of telephone and telegraph services required a large number of semiskilled and unskilled workers, as did the post office. A series of Education Acts, coupled by the raising of the school-leaving age, increased the demand for teachers and also provided a higher degree of literacy within the female work force. Clerical work for women received a stimulus with the growth of large offices and the expansion of the insurance and banking industries. Office work evolved into a series of discrete jobs such as typewriting, stenography, filing, and reception, many of which required little or no training. Women entered these occupations on the lower echelons in such numbers that whole segments of these industries became feminized, with the attendant depreciation in status and pay.

With the rise of the **welfare state**, government bureaucracy increased dramatically, further fueling the demand for female office personnel. The welfare state is also responsible for the provision of more social services to the public. More vigorous health care demanded more nurses and other **hospital** personnel. Protective legislation created the need for an army of inspectors. Various public programs required social workers and administrators. Along with elementary-school teachers, these occupations were characterized as the low professions (as distinct from the "high professions" of medical doctor, lawyer, and other careers requiring advanced degrees) and were, therefore, considered fit work for women.

The character and composition of the female work force was dramatically influenced by war. Many women were temporarily displaced from their jobs at the start of the **First World War** when a number of industries contracted in the face of economic restrictions. However, they were soon recruited as a reserve army of labor to supply desperately needed workers in munitions and essential industries. The lines between women's and men's work blurred during the war effort as women proved themselves capable of performing more skilled and heavier tasks than they had hitherto been hired to undertake.

The occupational advances made by women during the First World War were short-lived. Trade union agreements to protect men's jobs at the beginning of the war, along with the pressure of public opinion, led to mass resignations of women from the industrial ranks at the war's conclusion. Economic adversity in the inter-war years prevented the reabsorption of many women, particularly married women with children, back into the work force. There continued to be cherished a strong conviction, which most women shared, that mothers should remain at home with dependent children. Married women without young children, however, worked in increasing numbers from the 1920s on, signaling an important shift in the composition of the female labor force.

The **Second World War** provided a massive stimulus to women's employment, with 80 percent of married women working. Women with children were also employed on a part-time basis. In contrast to the experience following the First World War, women at the end of the Second World War did not abandon their jobs to the extent that an earlier generation of women workers had done. This was due to a variety of factors operating in the post-war economy. The need to reconstruct the economy, followed shortly by the mobilization for the Korean War, required a constant supply of labor. Attitudes toward women in the workplace were finally revised, with employers and gov-

ernment planners actively encouraging women to remain in industry. The bar to married women in many fields was abolished, and employers, prompted by the government, made some efforts to provide work convenient to the needs of married women. Part-time positions and shift work flourished.

Social changes also contributed to married women taking jobs. By the 1950s over 50 percent of married women were employed. Family planning, labor-saving devices in the home, greater literacy levels, and higher economic expectations made work more desirable and respectable. Gradually, more women with children returned to the workplace once their youngest child reached school age.

Despite the transitions that women's employment has undergone in the course of the century, certain elements have been slow to change. Women stay clustered in the lower levels of occupations, and, for most of the century, they have remained concentrated in separate occupations. For much of the period under study, women have received at best 50 to 60 percent of men's pay for equal work. Though much improvement has been wrought by the **Equal Pay** Act of 1970, the goal of equality in the workplace has yet to be fully realized.

Donna Price Paul

Bibliography
Braybon, Gail. *Women Workers in the First World War: The British Experience.* 1981.
Joseph, George. *Women at Work: The British Experience.* 1983.
Lewis, Jane. *Women in England, 1870–1950: Sexual Divisions and Social Change.* 1984.
Soldon, Norbert C. *Women in British Trade Unions, 1874–1976.* 1978.
Tilly, Louise A., and Joan W. Scott. *Women, Work, and Family.* 2nd ed. 1987.

Women's Freedom League (1907–1961)

In October 1907 a significant portion of the membership of the **Women's Social and Political Union** broke away from the leadership of **Christabel and Emmeline Pankhurst** to form a more broadly based, democratically governed militant suffrage organization, the Women's Freedom League (WFL). Key figures in the split were Charlotte Despard (1844–1939), Teresa Billington-Grieg (1877–1964), and Edith How

Martyn (1875–1954). Under the direction of Billington-Grieg, the WFL undertook protests illustrating women's lack of political representation in Britain. These included resistance to man-made laws (1907–9), to taxation (1907–18), and to registration by the census (1911). The WFL pursued a limited parliamentary measure for **women's suffrage**, although it disagreed with the age restriction—limiting voting to women over age thirty—established by the Representation of the People Act (1918). In the 1920s the WFL agitated for the extension of fuller voting rights to women. Upon passage of the Representation of the People (Equal Franchise) Act (1928), the WFL worked for the full equality of women with men, emphasizing the need for equal access to the professions and **equal pay** for equal work. The WFL was the only militant suffrage organization to transform its pre-war agenda into one that appealed to **feminists** in the 1920s and beyond.

Two WFL protests had far-reaching implications for the Edwardian suffrage movement. The Grille Protest on 28 October 1908 resulted in the partial dismantling of the metal screen rendering the Ladies' Gallery invisible to the House of Commons. The Siege of Westminster, a fifteen-week vigil outside Parliament, culminated in the Bermondsey Protest on 28 October 1909, an attempt to invalidate a by-election by destroying ballots. In 1909 a number of members formed the Women's Tax Resistance League. The WFL undertook no active militancy after 1909, continuing tax and other forms of passive resistance until 1918. It remained officially nonparty, although particular branches maintained ties to the **Labour Party**.

During the **First World War** the WFL agitated for women's suffrage, resisted government restrictions of women's civil liberties—such as the attempted reinstatement of the Contagious Diseases Act to regulate **prostitution**—and provided aid to women and children via the Women's Suffrage National Aid Corps, the Nine Elms **Settlement** House, and Brackenhill Hospital. In 1914 the WFL formed the Women Police Volunteers under the direction of C. Nina Boyle. In 1915 the WFL National Service Organization operated a labor exchange for middle-class women, and the North London branches opened a pub in Hampstead, the Despard Arms, serving nonalcoholic beverages and providing affordable housing for single working women.

Membership consisted primarily of lower-middle-class women, many of whom were employed as teachers, clerks, and nurses, and was split evenly between single and married women. The WFL maintained ties to women's professional organizations, notably the National Federation of Women Teachers and its successor, the National Union of Women Teachers. Between 1909 and 1920 membership remained at approximately 5,000. In 1909 the WFL had sixty-six branches in England, Scotland, and Wales; in 1929, twenty-four; and in 1943, thirteen. The WFL newspaper, *The Vote* (1909–33), was replaced by the *Women's Freedom League Bulletin* (1934–61).

From 1918 to 1961 the WFL lobbied for the equal access of women to the professions, equal pay for equal work, an equal moral standard for women and men, and an increase in the numbers of women magistrates and members of Parliament. With financial assistance from Dr. Elizabeth Knight (1870–1933), the WFL opened the Minerva Club, a meeting place for feminists in London for many years. WFL Presidents included Charlotte Despard, Alice Schofield Coates, Anna Munro, Emmeline Pethick-Lawrence, Lady Pares, Margery Corbett Ashby, Mavis Tate MP, and Marian Reeves. The WFL voted to disband in 1961.

Laura E. Nym Mayhall

Bibliography

Garner, Les. *Stepping Stones to Liberty: Feminist Ideas in the Women's Suffrage Movement, 1900–1918*. 1984.

Leneman, Leah. *A Guid Cause: The Women's Suffrage Movement in Scotland*. 1991.

Linklater, Andro. *An Unhusbanded Life: Charlotte Despard, Suffragist, Socialist, and Sinn Feiner*. 1980.

Mayhall, Laura E. Nym. "'Dare to Be Free': The Women's Freedom League, 1907–1928," Ph.D. dissertation, Stanford University, 1993.

McPhee, Carol, and Ann FitzGerald, eds. *The Non-violent Militant: Selected Writings of Teresa Billington-Grieg*. 1987.

Nevinson, Margaret Wynne. *Life's Fitful Fever: A Volume of Memories*. 1926.

Women's Labour League (1906–1918)

The Women's Labour League (WLL) was founded in 1906 at a time of great social and political unrest in Britain. It was established with the support of the **Labour Party** leadership, which had received a number of requests from wives and daughters of Labour men to create an organization that would help the women understand the politics of independent Labour representation.

The League counted among its founding members activist women who were successful trade union organizers, ardent suffragists, and socialist propagandists. They quickly expanded the League's scope to include all working-class women, not simply the relatives of party men, and pressed for a comprehensive representation of their social and political interests. More important, they taught working-class women to play an active role in political events.

Many women responded to the challenge, gathering practical political experience, first by running their local WLL branches and then by serving their communities in a variety of appointed and elected capacities. The group energetically participated in the battle for the vote. Members spearheaded many social reforms that affected the working-class family, such as the provision of free school meals, free medical inspection and treatment of schoolchildren, and the establishment of state insurance for widows. They also helped organize working women and agitated for industrial reforms on their behalf.

The WLL differed from other contemporary organizations by focusing completely on the objectives of serving and empowering the women of the working class. The WLL functioned as a constituent member of the Labour Party until 1918, when it relinquished its separate identity by merging with the party. It continues to exist in this capacity as the Women's Section of the Labour Party.

Donna Price Paul

Bibliography

Collette, Christine. *For Labour and for Women: The Women's Labour League, 1906–1918.* 1989.

Middleton, Lucy, ed. *Women in the Labour Movement: The British Experience.* 1977.

Paul, Donna Price. "The Women's Labour League of Great Britain, 1906–1918," Ph.D. dissertation, University of North Carolina, Chapel Hill, 1988.

Women's Social and Political Union (1903–1917)

The Women's Social and Political Union (WSPU) galvanized the women's suffrage movement. Its policy of militant action—"Deeds Not Words"—riveted the attention of the British public, giving the suffrage campaign a visibility and mass base that it had hitherto lacked.

Organized by **Emmeline Pankhurst** in 1903, the WSPU burst into prominence in 1905, when **Christabel Pankhurst** and Annie Kenney (1879–1953) were bodily thrown out of the Free Trade Hall in Manchester for heckling Sir **Edward Grey**. Seeking imprisonment, Christabel Pankhurst spat on a policeman, was arrested and tried, refused to pay her fine, and went to jail. The publicity aroused the country, and the women's suffrage ranks began to swell.

In contrast to the constitutional tactics pursued by the National Union of Women's Suffrage Societies (NUWSS), the WSPU adopted a policy of spectacular public protest. Until the summer of 1909 militancy remained nonviolent. Suffragettes, as WSPU followers were called, heckled **Cabinet** ministers and obstructed political meetings; they converged on Parliament to meet with MPs who refused to see them. Often, they were met with violence at the hands of the **police** and civilian bystanders before being arrested. In the summer of 1909 the militants began to throw stones, protesting against politicians who refused their demands by breaking government windows and—not incidentally—thereby cutting short the sometimes brutal struggles with police before they were arrested.

Upon imprisonment, militant suffragists embarked on hunger strikes, insisting that they be treated as political prisoners and their sentences be reduced to reflect more accurately the nature of their crimes. The authorities responded with forced feedings, a painful and intrusive procedure involving the insertion of a tube through the nasal passage into the stomach.

In 1912 and 1913, in response to the government's repeated refusals to honor its promises of a women's suffrage provision, militancy intensified. Coordinated attacks shattered windows all over **London**. Christabel Pankhurst, in hiding from British authorities, directed the campaign from Paris, ordering her followers to step up their attacks on windows throughout London, to cut telegraph wires, to pour acid into letter boxes, to slash paintings in public galleries, and to commit arson. **David Lloyd George**'s country house was set afire, prompting authorities to arrest Emmeline Pankhurst for inciting to commit a felony. She received three years' imprisonment. In anticipation of her hunger striking and thereby cutting short her prison term, the government passed the "Cat and Mouse Act" (1913), which enabled it to release a hunger-striking prisoner and reincarcerate her after she had recovered from her ordeal. On 31 May 1913 Emily Wilding Davison (1872–1913) threw herself in front of the King's horse at the Derby and was trampled to death, providing the militant suffragists with their first true martyr to the cause.

This kind of behavior could have mixed results. On the one hand, it may have turned many people away from the cause of women's suffrage, perhaps delaying the enfranchisement of women. On the other hand, militancy served to challenge and contest dominant cultural norms of femininity that were mobilized to deny women equality with men and to exclude them from public life. In conjunction with the writings of Christabel Pankhurst in the WSPU's *Suffragette*, the visible and provocative behavior of militant suffragists helped focus the public spotlight on the grievances of women.

With the outbreak of war in 1914, the WSPU devoted its energies and talents to recruitment for the armed forces. Paradoxically, it did not participate in the negotiations that led to the partial enfranchisement of women in 1918. In 1917 the WSPU renamed itself the Women's Party, but little remained of the feminist agenda that had characterized its pre-war existence. When in 1918 Christabel Pankhurst's

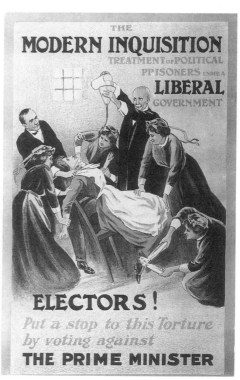

"The Modern Inquisition" protests the forcible feeding of imprisoned suffragettes.

The Funeral of Emily Wilding Davison, June 1913: The martyrdom of a WSPU militant.

bid for a parliamentary seat failed, the Women's Party, too, faded away.

Susan Kingsley Kent

Bibliography

MacKenzie, Midge. *Shoulder to Shoulder.* 1975.

Pankhurst, E. Sylvia. *The Suffragette Movement.* new ed. 1977.

Rosen, Andrew. *Rise Up, Women! The Militant Campaign of the Women's Social and Political Union, 1903–1914.* 1974.

Tickner, Lisa. *The Spectacle of Women: Imagery of the Suffrage Campaign, 1907–1914.* 1988.

Women's Suffrage

The campaign for women's suffrage has generally been considered a purely political and often conservative movement. But women's demands for enfranchisement were understood by contemporaries to constitute a radical challenge to the patriarchal order. Suffragists intended to transform the lives of women and men, to redefine and re-create by political means the sexual culture of Britain.

An important key to understanding the persistence of the demand for suffrage lies in comprehending not only the political, social, and economic developments of the nineteenth and early twentieth centuries, but ideological developments as well. The ideology of separate spheres promulgated during this period assigned women to the household and endowed them with biological characteristics that objectified them as "the Sex." By raising women to the level of angels, Victorian ideology conferred upon them superhuman status; by reducing them to sexual, animal characteristics, it presented them as subhuman. Dehumanization justified women's exclusion from positions of power and legitimated their continued subjugation to men in all aspects of life. The suffrage campaign aimed to change that perception so that women could no longer be objectified or defined essentially in terms of their biology and would no longer be victims of what they identified as male sexual tyranny. Suffragists struggled for over fifty years to obtain votes for women. Their campaign, while continuous, was divided into three phases. During the first phase, from 1866 to 1870, suffrage activity revolved around the Reform Act of 1867, which enfranchised large numbers of working-class men. The women's suffrage campaign emerged in 1866, when Barbara Bodichon (1827–91), Emily Davies (1830–1921), and Elizabeth Garrett (1836–1917) began a petition drive to demand votes for women. That same year, in Manchester, Lydia Becker (1827–90) formed the Manchester Women's Suffrage Committee; soon after suffrage societies in London, Edinburgh, and Bristol were organized. Aware that activities and policy needed to be coordinated, the four independent societies formed the London National Society for Women's Suffrage.

When the effort to enfranchise women failed, however, suffragists tended to direct their attention to other feminist reforms; from 1870 to 1905, the suffrage movement *per se* became somewhat quiescent, though suffragists worked actively to expand educational and employment opportunities to women, to obtain women's property and custody rights, and to end government regulation of prostitution. In 1897, sixteen suffrage societies federated themselves in the National Union of Women's Suffrage Societies (NUWSS), headed by **Millicent Garrett Fawcett.**

With the appearance of militancy in 1905, the campaign for women's enfranchisement erupted into public view; the Cause, as it was called by its proponents, took on an intensity and fervor unmatched in earlier years. Adopted by the **Women's Social and Political Union** (WSPU) under the direction of **Emmeline and Christabel Pankhurst,** militancy had the effect of energizing the entire women's suffrage movement. Between 1897 and 1903, when the WSPU was formed, the NUWSS comprised only sixteen women's suffrage societies. By 1909 fifty-four more societies had emerged and joined the constitutional group, as the NUWSS was called to distinguish it from the militants. In 1911, 305 societies belonged to the NUWSS; that number grew to 400 by 1913. The **Women's Freedom League** (WFL), headed by Charlotte Despard (1844–1939), broke off from the WSPU when it became clear that Emmeline and Christabel Pankhurst would not permit challenges to their decisions or to their increasingly dictatorial rule, but it continued to follow a militant course. Partially as a consequence of militant tactics, the campaign for votes for women became a mass movement, commanding the attention of the British public and the energies of thousands of men and women.

The creation of a mass movement depended on other factors, however, most importantly the ability of the suffrage campaign to attract large numbers of working-class adherents. While upstaged by the militant organizations, working-class suffrage organizations such as the North of England Society for Women's Suffrage, led by Esther Roper (1868–1938), and the East London Federation of Suffragettes, led by Sylvia Pankhurst (1882–1960), contributed mightily to the growth and vitality of the suffrage campaign. In 1912, responding to the pressures of working-class women for the right to vote and to Prime Minister **H.H.** Asquith's betrayal of the women's cause, the **Labour Party** overcame its reservations about women's suffrage and joined forces with the NUWSS to establish the Election Fighting Fund; this alliance between labor and suffrage marked the creation of a truly democratic, egalitarian organization. Because women of all classes faced the potential of sexual and economic exploitation within the institutions of **marriage and prostitution,** a shared consciousness of women's wrongs enabled suffragists to create an ethos of sexual solidarity among women from diverse backgrounds and to establish a mass movement.

Christabel Pankhurst's "Great Scourge" articles, published in the WSPU's *Suffragette* in 1913, provide a vivid example of the kind of grievances women's suffrage was intended to end. Pankhurst argued that from 75 to 80 percent of all men in England suffered from **venereal disease,** and she pointed out the consequent dangers of marriage for women. The solution, she asserted, was "Votes for Women, Chastity for Men." Historians have generally dismissed her views with scorn, but her concerns pervaded and informed the entire suffrage movement.

Suffragists maintained that men's monopoly on power extended beyond the economic and political realms into that of the personal, which helps explain why they focused so much of their attention on sexual issues and self-consciously associated them with their demand for the vote: They were convinced of the intimate connection between their exclusion from political power and their sexual powerlessness and vulnerability. Sexual equality as symbolized by the vote constituted one of the means by which feminists hoped to undermine the power of men in both the public and the private spheres, and to challenge the cultural constructions of masculinity and femininity and male and female **sexuality** that served to justify separate spheres for men and women.

As a badge of civic equality, a symbol of women's humanity and equality with men, the vote had a great deal of appeal. But feminists also intended to use it as a tool to raise the status of women, to increase their welfare, and to protect them from the depradations of men. Their ultimate goal was to effect a profound transformation in the sexual culture and gender hierarchy of Britain, to bring about a society characterized by equality between and respect for men and women.

The outbreak of war in August 1914 brought suffrage activity to a halt. In 1916, when the government became concerned about the need to call a new election, franchise reform once again became an issue. At this point, the NUWSS stepped in, demanding that women be included in any reform that enfranchised new male voters on the basis of service to the country, claiming that women's contributions to and sacrifices for the war effort entitled them, no less than men, to full citizenship. A Speaker's Conference was convened to deal with these thorny issues; its recommendations, issued in 1917, included a measure of women's suffrage.

In 1918 Parliament granted the vote to women over the age of thirty. Contemporary observers attributed the government's willingness to enfranchise women to its appreciation of the work women performed during the war. But other factors influenced the outcome as well. Several MPs hinted that the militancy of the pre-war years might very well resurface after the war if women were not enfranchised; this contingency persuaded many former anti-suffragists in Parliament to reverse their position. But it was not so much the actual reality of militancy that had so significant and visceral an impact on politicians as what it represented.

A not so subtle undercurrent informed the debates over women's suffrage: that a sex war had, prior to August of 1914, been raging throughout the land, that it had been subsumed in the larger international conflagration, and that failure to resolve the suffrage issue would result in its flaring up again. The conflation of **feminism** with sex war was not new, but the context in which the equation was made was entirely different now. Feminism soon became linked in the public mind not merely with sex war, but with armed conflict, death, and destruction, and it was given greater force by the existence of large numbers of women in uniform. It raised the specter of combat in the streets of England—combat between men and women.

Fear of renewal of the sex war so characteristic of the pre-war period, but raised now to intolerable levels, determined the terms under which women would be admitted to the franchise. The age requirement ensured that women would not enjoy a majority over men, whose numbers had been greatly reduced in the slaughter of war. Fawcett and other NUWSS leaders explained to their unhappy Labour followers, most of whom would not be eligible to vote because they were under age, that they did not want to jeopardize their chances for partial success by insisting upon full equality with men.

The capitulation of suffragists on so vital an issue as the age restriction resulted from the terms in which the debates over suffrage were framed and conducted between 1914 and 1918: At one level, MPs and suffragists asserted women's right to vote as a function of wartime service, defining them, at least in part, as warriors; on another, feminists' recruitment and relief efforts and debates over peace utilized rhetoric that ultimately served to conflate the suffrage cause with the cause of the war. The NUWSS' complicity in the war had a distinct bearing on its cautious stance in the debates over suffrage in 1916 and 1917. Fawcett and the other members of the Executive Committee of the NUWSS could be held responsible, in holding out for greater representation for women, for perpetuating the war between the sexes. Compromise on the issue of age limitations, by contrast, would reduce the tensions between men and women and help bring the sex war to a halt for good.

In 1928, when women's participation in the political arena no longer seemed to pose a threat to men's power, Parliament eliminated the over-thirty age restriction and gave the vote to women on the same lines as for men.

Susan Kingsley Kent

Bibliography

Holton, Sandra Stanley. *Feminism and Democracy: Women's Suffrage and Reform Politics in Britain, 1900–1918.* 1986.
Hume, Leslie Parker. *The National Union of Women's Suffrage Societies, 1897–1914.* 1982.
Kent, Susan Kingsley. *Sex and Suffrage in Britain, 1860–1914.* 1987.
Liddington, Jill, and Jill Norris. *One Hand Tied Behind Us: The Rise of the Women's Suffrage Movement.* 1978.
Morgan, David. *Suffragists and Liberals: The Politics of Women's Suffrage in Britain.* 1975.
Tickner, Lisa. *The Spectacle of Women: Imagery of the Suffrage Campaign, 1907–1914.* 1988.

Woolf, Leonard Sidney (1880–1969)

Although overshadowed by his wife, Virginia, Leonard Woolf was an important writer and political activist in his own right as well as a prominent original member of the **Bloomsbury Group**. The author of more than twenty books, including a five-volume autobiography published in his eighties, and hundreds of articles, Woolf was also a celebrated publisher, as cofounder with **Virginia Woolf** of the Hogarth Press, one of the most innovative small presses in England.

The son of a **Jewish** barrister who died when Leonard was twelve years old, leaving the family in reduced circumstances, Woolf attended St. Paul's School and Trinity College, **Cambridge** (1899–1904), where he developed a lifelong fascination with classical Greek civilization and came under the influence of the philosopher **G.E. Moore**. Elected to the select secret society known as the **Apostles**, he formed intimate friendships among his university contemporaries, notably with **Lytton Strachey**, Thoby Stephen (1880–1906), and Saxon Sydney-Turner (1880–1962). These formative years at Cambridge were perhaps the happiest of his life. From Moore, whose *Principia Ethica* (1903) was published during his student years, Woolf acquired a commitment to duty and moral rectitude that, reinforcing the Jewish ethical values of his childhood, dominated his life; Cambridge gave him not only a classical education, but a belief in rationalism; from his Apostle friends he derived a skepticism toward dogma and a disdain for status that became ingrained in his character.

After receiving only second-class honors and doing poorly in the **civil service** examinations, Woolf decided to accept a cadetship in the Ceylon colonial service, where he was to spend seven rewarding, if rather lonely, years, promoted rapidly from Cadet, to Superintendant, to Assistant Government Agent before returning to London in 1911. An efficient, conscientious, if somewhat rigid, administrator, he developed an affection for those under his authority but a strong distaste for **imperialism.**

In 1912 he resigned from the colonial service, married Virginia Stephen, and launched his career as a writer. His first publications, the novels *The Village in the Jungle* (1913) and *The Wise Virgins* (1914), while interesting autobiographically, proved to be an abortive start and failed to win an audience. Woolf shifted increasingly to political writing, becoming active in the Women's Co-operative Guild and the **Fabian Society,** which commissioned him to write a report on international machinery for the peaceful settlement of disputes. Appearing first as a *New Statesman* supplement, it was subsequently published as *International Government* in 1916 and had considerable influence on the British proposals for a **League of Nations.**

In 1917 the Woolfs established the Hogarth Press, publishing not only many of their own works, but also such significant writers as Sigmund Freud, **T.S. Eliot,** and Vita Sackville-West. While Leonard was preoccupied with selecting manuscripts, managing the finances of the small company, and, at first, with the actual printing, he was also fully engaged politically by the end of the First World War. A member of the **Independent Labour Party,** he was appointed Secretary to the **Labour Party's** Advisory Committee on International Questions and helped coordinate the reports that were to shape Labour's policy on foreign affairs during the inter-war decades. In addition Woolf wrote extensively on co-operation and on imperialism, producing in rapid succession a series of seminal studies: *Co-operation and the Future of Industry* (1918); *Empire and Commerce in Africa* (1919); *Economic Imperialism* (1920); and *Socialism and Co-operation* (1921). He served as editor of the *International Review* (1918–19), as literary editor of the *Nation* (1923–30), and as coeditor of *Political Quarterly* (1931–59). During the 1930s and 1940s he was also a frequent contributor, occasional substitute editor, and longtime member of the board of the *New Statesman.*

In his political writings Woolf sought to promote a socialism based on the noncompetitive objectives of the **co-operative movement,** which would enable the community, constituted as consumers, to control production. But if he was concerned to eliminate capitalist exploitation, he was equally concerned to preserve the individuality and tolerance that he cherished in English society as well as in ancient Greek culture. An outspoken opponent of imperialism, striving to accelerate self-government in British dependencies, Woolf broke with many of those on the Left who clung to **pacifism** during the 1930s, like his friend **Kingsley Martin.** He became a strong advocate of collective security and of mandatory sanctions and warned Labour against sterile opposition to rearmament in the face of a mounting **Fascist** threat. By the late 1930s, in books like *Quack, Quack!* (1935) and his **Left Book Club** selection *Barbarians at the Gate* (1939), Woolf began to criticize the Soviet Union almost as vociferously as he condemned Nazism for creating an irrational tyranny and betraying the civilized ideals implicit in socialism.

After the Second World War Woolf increasingly withdrew from political involvement, devoting himself to the literary estate and reputation of Virginia Woolf and, in his last years, to writing memoirs. After the critical failure of his political *magnum opus,* published in three volumes over twenty-two years—*After the Deluge* (1931, 1939) and *Principia Politica* (1953)—he was both surprised and gratified at the enormous success of his autobiography, written amid the rising tide of popular and scholarly interest in Virginia Woolf and the Bloomsbury Group. Composed in the comparative serenity of his last decade, the five volumes—*Sowing* (1960), *Growing* (1961), *Beginning Again* (1964), *Downhill All the Way* (1967), and *The Journey Not the Arrival Matters* (1969)—represent a return to the personal dimension of his earliest works, revealing its author as austere, stoical, and rigorous in his moral and political standards but engagingly human to the end.

F.M. Leventhal

Bibliography

Leventhal, F.M. "Leonard Woolf, 1880–1969: The Conscience of a Bloomsbury Socialist" in Susan Pedersen, and Peter Mandler, eds. *After the Victorians: Private Conscience and Public Duty in Modern Britain.* 1994. pp. 149–68.

Meyerowitz, Selma S. *Leonard Woolf.* 1982.

Spater, George, and Ian Parsons. *A Marriage of True Minds: An Intimate Portrait of Leonard and Virginia Woolf.* 1977.

Spotts, Frederic, ed. *Letters of Leonard Woolf.* 1989.

Wilson, Duncan. *Leonard Woolf: A Political Biography*. 1978.

Woolf, (Adeline) Virginia Stephen (1882–1941)

Born Adeline Virginia Stephen on 25 January 1882 at 22 Hyde Park Gate, Kensington, London, the daughter of Sir Leslie Stephen (1832–1904) and Julia Jackson Duckworth (1846–95), Virginia Woolf has no letters standing for honored titles after her name. She refused all official honors on political principle, including the coveted Companion of Honour, accepting only the *Femina Vie Heureuse* prize. Though her family was strongly connected to **Cambridge**, she was not allowed to attend classes and saw herself as deprived of a university education, a fact that contributed to the development of her concept of the "outsider," most notably in the pacifist, socialist, and feminist polemic *Three Guineas* (1939). Some biographers and critics, however, believe that the private education she received in her father's library was superior to any formal education available to women at the time. Leslie Stephen, Victorian man of letters, founding editor of the *Dictionary of National Biography*, and a leading member of the so-called "intellectual aristocracy," came from a family of public servants remarkable for their reforming zeal and instrumental in shaping British government, education, and the law. Many of the Prinseps and Pattles on her mother's side also served in colonial India, a fact that doubtless served to inspire the writer's insistent critique of **imperialism**. Her cousin Katherine Stephen (1856–1924) became Principal of Newnham College, Cambridge. Virginia was tutored in languages and continued to read Greek with her tutor, Janet Case, until late in life, believing that knowledge of the classics was necessary for the educated person. She had many close women friends, including Violet Dickinson, Margaret Llewelyn Davies, and the composer Dame Ethel Smyth. Her powerful originality as a writer is often attributed to the fact that she was self-educated and had a chip on her shoulder about her lack of formal education. As a young woman she taught working-class men and women at Morley College in London for three years and also worked in the **women's suffrage** movement.

Always close to her sister **Vanessa (Bell)**, the painter who was married to art critic Clive Bell but lived with painter **Duncan Grant**, Virginia Stephen married a Cambridge **Apostle** friend of her brother and a fellow **Bloomsbury Group** intellectual, **Leonard Woolf**, in 1912. He is credited both with his wife's successes and with her failures in their companionate marriage, caring for her fragile mental health by taking the advice of doctors who urged them not to have children. Her breakdowns and suicide have been attributed alternately to child abuse, neurasthenia, anorexia, genetic madness, and, most recently, to "bipolar affective disorder."

In addition to her status as a major twentieth-century English novelist, Virginia Woolf is considered to be one of the most important feminist theorists of what is called the "Second Wave" of the modern movement for women's rights. *A Room of One's Own* (1929), a set of anti-lectures given at Newnham and Girton and written in the style of suffrage pamphlets, is often called the Bible of the women's movement. When university literary canons began to include women writers in the 1970s, *A Room of One's Own*, with its tragic martyr, an imaginary figure of Shakespeare's sister, was the text most often read. Feminist literary criticism began in a struggle over whether Woolf was an exemplary foremother as a feminist critic. The author of several volumes of critical essays on literary and cultural matters, including *The Common Reader* (1925) and *The Common Reader*, Second Series (1932) and the posthumously published *The Death of the Moth and Other Essays* (1942), *The Moment and Other Essays* (1947), *The Captain's Deathbed and Other Essays* (1950), *Granite and Rainbow* (1958), *Contemporary Writers* (1965), and four volumes of *Collected Essays* (1966–7), Virginia Woolf earned a reputation as a formidable modern literary critic. Before her death in 1941 she had also produced many serious reviews for journals like the *Times Literary Supplement*. A new edition of the *Essays*, complete in six volumes in chronological order, collects many of these reviews and corrects errors in the earlier editions. Leonard Woolf also published her short fiction as *A Haunted House and Other Short Stories* (1943), now superseded by *Collected Short Stories*, edited by Susan Dick. Leonard Woolf's edition of excerpts from her diaries, *A Writer's Diary* (1953), has been replaced by the five-volume *Diary of Virginia Woolf*, edited by Anne Olivier Bell with the assistance of Andrew McNeillie (1977) and regarded as one of the major personal and autobiographical documents in English literature.

The *Early Diaries* and journals were subsequently published in one volume, edited by M. Leaska and including the "1897 Diary," in which the fifteen-year-old Virginia Stephen, upset by the early and tragic death of her mother and her just-married stepsister Stella Duckworth soon afterward, invented an alterego called "Miss Jan." The diary is notable for its expression of the wish to mourn her mother in some kind of religious ceremony, a gesture forbidden by Leslie Stephen's aggressive agnosticism and the memory of Julia Stephen's similar views on the subject of religion. Later she showed great interest in the mysticism of her Quaker aunt, Caroline Emelia Stephen, called "Nun." It was this aunt who nursed her after her breakdown after nursing Leslie Stephen on his deathbed (1904), who encouraged her to write, and who got her her first professional paid writing assignments for *The Guardian-Church Weekly*, thereby inaugurating Virginia Stephen's career. Caroline Emelia also left her niece the legacy that allowed her to become independent, famously recalled in *A Room of One's Own* as the "£500 a year" needed for the emancipation of the woman intellectual. Leonard Woolf also published some of the correspondence between Virginia Woolf and Lytton Strachey in 1956. Six volumes of *The Letters of Virginia Woolf* have also appeared, edited by Nigel Nicolson and Joanne Trautmann (Banks) (1975–80) as well as a one-volume edition, *Congenial Spirits: Selected Letters* (1990), establishing Woolf's reputation as one of the finest letter writers of the twentieth century in her concern to please her correspondents rather than give vent to petty egotistical concerns. The official biography by her nephew Quentin Bell, *Virginia Woolf* (1972), is the standard work.

In addition to the nine novels, five volumes of the *Diary*, six volumes of *Letters*, six volumes of *Essays*, the political pamphlets, *A Room of One's Own*, and *Three Guineas*, Woolf also published *Flush: A Biography* (1933), a comic spoof about Elizabeth Barrett Browning's dog, and *Roger Fry: A Biography* (1940).

A brilliant experimental novelist, Virginia Woolf is ranked internationally with James Joyce, Gertrude Stein, and Marcel Proust as a genius of literary modernism, although the English critic F.R. Leavis and his wife, Queenie, denigrated her writing and her feminism, comparing her unfavorably with D.H. Lawrence and undermining her reputation for at least a generation on the false grounds of her alleged "Bloomsbury elitism" and class distance. The style and structure of each of her nine novels is entirely different from the others. *To the Lighthouse* (1927), her much beloved elegy to the Victorian patriarchal family, is regarded as a modern classic. *Mrs. Dalloway* (1925), an evocation of one day in the life of a London society hostess, Clarissa Dalloway, and her spiritual counterpart, Septimus Smith, a lower-middle-class shell-shocked soldier returned from the battlefields of the First World War, is often read in relation to her friend T.S. Eliot's modern classic poem, *The Waste Land* (1922), a work for which Virginia Woolf herself hand-set the type and published at the Hogarth Press (founded in 1917 with her husband, Leonard Woolf). *The Voyage Out* (1915), her first novel, a female *Bildungsroman* ending with the death of the heroine, and *Night and Day* (1918), the fairly traditional social comedy experimenting with plot structure and reversals as in Shakespeare's plays and Mozart's opera *The Magic Flute*, were published by Duckworth, her half-brother's press. But her future independence and creativity were assured and protected by the decision to publish the rest of her work, novels, several volumes of **literary criticism**, and biographies, at the Hogarth Press. *Jacob's Room* (1922), considered a modernist masterpiece and Woolf's first attempt at long fiction in nontraditional, often called "stream-of-consciousness," style, is an elegy for the lost promise of the youthful generation of elite English boys dead in the war. The novel was inspired, it is said, by the loss of her own brother Thoby.

Orlando (1928), an illustrated fictional "fantastic biography" of her friend and sometime lover, the writer and gardener Vita Sackville-West, and of the historic Sackville estate Knole, which Vita's gender prevented her from inheriting, is a spectacular literary *tour de force*, a triumph over the conventions of realism and the limits of historical time in lifewriting. The novel extends the actions of its sex-changing man-woman hero-heroine over 360 years of English history and mocks by imitation and spoof the literary and social conventions of each period traversed by the narrative. Some passages—the description of the skating parties on the Thames during "The Great Frost," for example—are often cited as examples of Woolf's immense powers of "scene making"; not surprisingly, *Orlando* has been made into a film (Sally Potter, 1993) and dramatized often for the stage. By contrast *The Waves* (1931) is a deeply serious philosophical and historical "play-poem" for six characters conceived of as one. It questions, as Woolf had in *To the Lighthouse*, "the meaning of life," exploring the social meaning of Einstein's theory of relativity and the absence of God in modern life through repeated figures of waves of light and sound. The interior monologues of the characters Ginny, Susan, Neville, Bernard, Rhoda, and Louis take the six friends from childhood through the ignominious death of their common friend, Percival, who fatally falls from a donkey in India to Bernard's chivalric protest against death. *The Waves* quotes extensively from the romantic poets and is read both as a celebration of English culture and an example of the "postcolonial carnivalesque." While critics have traditionally ranked the novel as Woolf's masterpiece and have seen in her Bernard the modern poet as hero, postmodern readings now point to the novel's mockery of the Parsifal myth of the quest for the Holy Grail and to its critique of imperialism and of the role of the English in colonizing India. *The Waves'* chapters of alternating interior monologues during a generation's lifetime, ending in 1930, are surrounded by brief italicized sections describing the movements of the sun from dawn to dusk in the manner of Hindu prayers to the sun. This device suggests the limitations of Western ideologies and English life and culture, at the same time as it celebrates them.

The Years (1937), a great popular success on both sides of the Atlantic, is a family saga that follows an upper-class family and their servants in the social upheavals from the 1880s through the 1930s. It caused Woolf a great deal of trouble, and much of the historical material of the original sections was used in *Three Guineas*. An edition published by the New York Public Library and the Hogarth Press in 1978 contains the original version of Woolf's famous 1931 speech to the National Society for Women's Service, often cited for its invention of that inhibitor of women's creativity "the angel in the house," a figure taken from Coventry Patmore's Victorian poem about ideal womanhood and used by Woolf to embody the concept of the social pressure on women to sacrifice their artistic creativity and desire to outmoded and destructive notions of propriety, virtue, and chastity, often imposed by mothers on their daughters' lives. The speech urges women to kill the "angel in the house" by throwing their inkpots at her and emancipating their imaginations.

Between the Acts (posthumous, 1941), Woolf's last novel, depicts a village historical pageant during the buildup to the Second World War. The pageant's dramatic form emphasizes the destruction of culture and values in war; its speakers' unfinished sentences and broken bits of dialogue show persons failing to communicate across gender, class, age, and religious gaps, which the text calls "scraps, orts, and fragments." Charged with sexual violence, the novel connects rape with war and uses the ancient theme of the myth of Procne and Philomel, the swallow and the nightingale, to suggest that sexual violence is the root of war and that the history of imperialism is implicated in twentieth-century European wars.

Who could measure the genius of the artist "when caught and tangled in a woman's heart?" Woolf asks in her classic *A Room of One's Own*, anticipating the day when working-class writers would produce Shakespeares from their own ranks. "For masterpieces are not single and solitary births," but "the product of thinking by the people," Woolf claims, radically attacking English pride in individualism. Even more radically her pacifist masterpiece, *Three Guineas*, argues that **Fascism** did not originate in nationalism or in Italian or German class ideology, but in the patriarchal family. Increasingly recognized as an important twentieth-century intellectual figure and as a theorist of **feminism** and **pacifism**, Virginia Woolf, always valued by writers for her "difficult" technical innovations in narrative, has gained new readers and new popularity as her fiction has begun to be read from a postmodern perspective.

Jane Marcus

Bibliography

Bell, Quentin. *Virginia Woolf.* 2 vols. 1972.
Briggs, Julia, ed. *Virginia Woolf: Introductions to the Major Works.* 1994.
Homans, Margaret, ed. *Virginia Woolf: Twentieth Century Views: A Collection of Critical Essays.* 1992.
Marcus, Jane. *Virginia Woolf and the Languages of Patriarchy.* 1987.
Minow-Pinkney, Makiko. *Virginia Woolf and the Problem of the Subject.* 1987.
Zwerdling, Alex. *Virginia Woolf and the Real World.* 1986.

Y

Yeats, William Butler (1865–1939)

William Butler Yeats, one of the finest poets in English during the twentieth century, won the Nobel Prize for Literature in 1923. He was born in Dublin in 1865. His father, John Butler Yeats (1839–1922), a brilliant conversationalist and a portrait artist, soon moved the family to London, but in 1881 the family returned to Dublin, where Yeats finished high school and spent two years studying drawing. His first poems were published in 1885. The next year, when his dramatic poem *Mosada* was published as a pamphlet, he began full-time writing; he returned with his family to London in 1885. London would remain his principal residence until he settled in Dublin in 1919. But he wrote very much as an Irishman, as is apparent from the titles of his first two full volumes of poetry, *The Wanderings of Oisin and Other Poems* (1889) and *The Countess Kathleen and Various Legends and Lyrics* (1892). During the early 1890s Yeats edited collections of Irish folklore and literature and wrote reviews, and he had some success as a fiction writer, with a novella, *John Sherman and Dhoya* (1891), and with three short-story collections published in 1897: *The Secret Rose*, *The Tables of the Law*, and *The Adoration of the Magi*. The title of his folklore collection, *The Celtic Twilight* (1893, expanded 1902), has been used to caricature the shadowy remoteness of the Irish folk materials that predominate in Yeats' verse of those years and in his earliest dramas, *The Countess Cathleen* (1892, performed 1899) and *The Land of Heart's Desire* (1894).

Yeats was from his early years active in the study of spiritualism and occultism, as a member first of Madame Blavatsky's Theosophical Society (1887–90) and then of the Hermetic Order of the Golden Dawn (1890–1922). The monument of his occultism is *A Vision* (1925, revised 1937), which describes a spirit system that determines cosmic history and individual personality.

In London in 1889 he met and fell in love with Maud Gonne (1866–1953), an ardent Irish nationalist of independent means who lived in Paris and who, unknown to Yeats, maintained until 1898 a secret liaison with a French journalist. Yeats' frustrated courtship of her, which inspired a number of his poems, lasted until 1903 when she married an exiled Irish patriot, Major John MacBride; the courtship revived briefly in 1916 when MacBride was executed for his role in the Easter Rising.

Yeats' support of Irish cultural nationalism intensified when he first visited Lady Augusta Gregory's country home, Coole Park, in County Galway in 1897. He and Lady Gregory collected folklore and provided leadership and plays for the Irish National Theatre Society, which, with generous patronage from Annie E.F. Horniman, an Englishwoman, gained a permanent home at the Abbey Theatre, Dublin, from 1904. The opening production at the Abbey Theatre included plays by Yeats, Lady Gregory, and John Millington Synge, the three directors of the company. Yeats' play was *On Baile's Strand*, one of his finest. It was the first of his several plays about the ancient Irish heroic warrior Cuchulain. During the first decade of the century Yeats was extremely active in the management of the Abbey Theatre, choosing plays, hiring and firing actors and managers, and arranging tours.

Partially as a result of his interest in drama, which requires direct, comprehensible language, and partially perhaps because of the inspiration of the new century, Yeats began a radical simplification of his poetic diction and adopted the rhythms of ordinary speech for his verse. His changes in literary style were cheered on by Ezra Pound, who became a close friend in 1909. When Yeats looked back on those years in which he contributed to the beginning of the modernist reform of poetry, he said, "In 1900 everybody got down off his stilts." His transformation of poetic style developed in *In the Seven Woods* (1903), *The Green Helmet and Other Poems* (1910, 1912), and *Responsibilities* (1914).

Throughout these years Yeats maintained his permanent residence in London, although he traveled frequently to Ireland. The 1916 Easter Rising, an unsuccessful, six-day armed rebellion in Dublin by Irish republicans against the British, dramatically reasserted **Irish nationalism** in public history and in Yeats' life. His poem "Easter, 1916" eloquently expresses Yeats' complicated reaction, a mixture of surprise, admiration for Irish romanticism, and clear-eyed realism.

In October 1917, at age fifty-two, Yeats married Georgie Hyde-Lees (1892–1968), an occultist twenty-seven years younger than he. Yeats traveled with his bride to Coole Park, where he proudly showed her a nearby medieval stone tower, Thoor Ballylee, that he had purchased along with two cottages in 1916 for £35. The tower became a summer residence for Yeats, his wife, and their two children, Anne (1919–) and Michael (1921–). His next two volumes of poetry, *The Wild Swans at Coole* (1917, 1919) and *Michael Robartes and the Dancer* (1921, title page 1920), show a consolidation of his style into poised, mature works that characterize his "middle" period in the 1920s and the early 1930s.

Although England and Ireland signed a treaty at the end of 1921, bitter controversies erupted within the new Irish Free State over the partition of Northern Ireland and over the wording of a formal oath of allegiance to the British Crown; those issues led to a civil war, which ended in 1923 with the Irish Free State's victory over the anti-treaty rebel forces. Yeats emphatically cast his lot with the Irish Free State. In 1922 he bought a house in Dublin, where he took up permanent residence, and accepted a six-year appointment to the Senate of the Irish Free State. He relished the aristocratic overtones of his public role as senator. The Nobel Prize in December 1923 further

heightened Yeats' public stature. The energy of the poems written in response to the disturbing times in Ireland and to the ageing poet's awareness of his own decrepitude gave astonishing power to his collection *The Tower* (1928), which can justly be considered the best single book of poems in the twentieth century. The high level of accomplishment continued in *The Winding Stair* (1929, 1933) and *Words for Music Perhaps and Other Poems* (1932).

In 1924 Yeats was cautioned about his high blood pressure and told to reduce his public speaking and to avoid Irish winters, so he spent eight of his remaining fifteen winters in the Mediterranean. In spite of continuing bouts of serious illness, Yeats' life and writings in his last decade were marked by activity and enjoyment of life. He presided over a circle of young artists, poets, and playwrights in Dublin. He continued to write plays, including two translations of Greek tragedies, *Sophocles' King Oedipus* (performed 1926; 1928) and *Sophocles' Oedipus at Colonus* (performed 1927; 1934), and a full-length play about spiritualism and the eighteenth-century Irish writer Jonathan Swift, *The Words upon the Window Pane* (performed 1930; 1934).

In 1929, after recovering from illness, he wrote a series of brash poems narrated by "Crazy Jane," a fictitious old Irish peasant woman. His pose as "The Wild Old Wicked Man"—the title of one of his poems from 1938—has at least some basis in the rejuvenation that he felt after a vasectomy in 1934 at age sixty-eight. His poetical vitality was reflected in the title of his 1938 volume, *New Poems*.

In the 1930s Ireland changed in ways that displeased Yeats. His Anglo-Irish Protestant minority no longer controlled Irish society and culture. He turned for inspiration to his eighteenth-century Anglo-Irish predecessors, particularly to Swift, to the philosopher Bishop George Berkeley, and to the statesman Edmund Burke. Their intellectual talent, independence of spirit, and respect for traditional social forms were admired by Yeats. According to his unblushingly antidemocratic views, their greatness contrasted sharply with the undistinguished commonness of contemporary Irish merchants and workmen. He stated his unpopular opinions in the essays of *On the Boiler* (1939) and in his later plays, such as *Purgatory* (performed 1938; 1939).

Yeats' last poems are enriched by conflicting responses to the approach of death. He had courage that was founded partly on a vague hope for reincarnation and partly on the bold heroism that he admired in Ireland in earlier times. In that courageous mood he could speak in the stern voice of his famous epitaph "Under Ben Bulben": "Cast a cold eye / On life, on death. / Horseman, pass by!" But the stoic coldness is complicated by the terror that distracts the poet's thoughts at the end of another late poem, "The Man and the Echo," and also by the poignantly frivolous desire for life in the closing lines of the poem "Politics," which Yeats placed as the last in his final collection: "But O that I were young again / And held her in my arms."

Yeats' imagination remained very much his own, isolated to a remarkable degree from the successive fashions of modern poetry, despite his extensive contacts with other poets. Literary modernism held no inherent attraction for him except in its general association with vigorous expression. He admired a wide range of traditional English poetry and drama, and he plainly was unconcerned that, during the last two decades of his life, his preference for using rhyme and strict stanza forms would set him apart from the vogue of modernism.

William H. O'Donnell

Bibliography

Adams, Hazard. *The Book of Yeats' Poems.* 1990.
Ellmann, Richard. *The Identity of Yeats.* 1964.
———. *Yeats: The Man and the Masks.* 1979.
Jeffares, A. Norman. *A New Commentary on the Poems of W.B. Yeats.* 1984.
Jeffares, A. Norman, and A.S. Knowland. *A Commentary on the Collected Plays of W.B. Yeats.* 1975.
Jochum, K.P.S. *W.B. Yeats: A Classified Bibliography of Criticism.* 1990.
Rosenthal, M.L. *Running to Paradise: Yeats' Poetic Art.* 1994.

Youth Culture

Youth cultures appear to have succeeded each other in Britain since the mid-1940s. There are histories of previous youth subcultures before this era, but something marks out the distinctive post-war British youth styles. In this period a specifically youth "style" became commodified as consumer culture progressively swamped the advanced economies of the West. By the 1980s youth culture had become an industry in itself, and it was even argued by some that youth was no longer about rebellion or revolt but constituted merely a marketing device and advertisers' fiction. For others this had always been the case. Whether or not this is true, youth cultural tourism in Britain is rife; it is seen as part of Britain's heritage, and cities vie for tourists on the basis of their respective **popular music** and youth culture past—for instance, Merseyside and the **Beatles**.

Beginning, initially, with the Teddy Boy style (culled largely from the late 1940s Edwardian look) in the early to mid-1950s, working-class subcultures have been retrospectively mapped back onto British cultural history every few years by fashion and music journalists and entrepreneurs eager to perpetuate some enduring myths about spectacular subcultures. The Mods, seen to spring from a more semiskilled and white-collar social base than the Teds, came on to the youth cultural landscape to clash, metaphorically and literally, with unskilled Rockers especially at holiday beaches (Clacton, Brighton, Hastings) in the mid-1960s. Greasers, bikers and other variants of bike boys in leather jackets (epitomized first by Marlon Brando in the 1950s film *The Wild One*) emerged eventually, though without the legendary menace of the American Hell's Angels. Mod, itself, on the other hand, prefigured many varieties of British youth culture for the foreseeable future. Skinheads, metamorphosed "hard" Mods, were spotted fighting other teams' "Crews" at **football** matches in the season after England's World Cup soccer victory in 1966, before they, too, splintered—eventually, in the early 1970s—into crombies, suedeheads, and other groupings, but not before the Skinheads had become infamous for their attacks on gays and **Blacks** as well as a penchant for ska music, the precursor of reggae. Glamrock united these remnants with a hippie style that itself had been created from "soft" Mod styles in 1967. Perhaps most controversially of all, punks in 1976–7 were held to be the natural inheritors of a dole-queue ethos. Punk style was much more likely to have originated in the art schools rather than the "street," however. Around the time punk was promoting "ripped and torn," Nazi insignia, and bondage gear, the casuals, emphasizing "smart," expensive clothes from sports or menswear, took their place in this youth culture museum from a complex of Mod, "soulboy," and a look modeled on the influential singer David Bowie. Casual style was mainstream and ubiquitous in Britain by the late 1980s, but such one-dimensional freeze-framing hid a complex and ever-changing street style that has rarely been documented outside fanzines (fan magazines produced independently) or, much later, by style magazines like *Blitz*, *The Face*, or *i-D*.

More middle-class styles such as the beats in the 1950s as well as the hippies in the late 1960s were on the same historical plane. These youth subcultural fashions were usually read as white styles; some urban Black styles—rudies, rastas, B-Boys and ragga(muffin)s—did receive a similar kind of treatment in pop histories on a parallel timescale. In truth, British youth styles always owed as much a debt to developments in Black styles or Black music as they did to changes in gay culture. The absence of **women** in these youth culture narratives began to be remedied from the mid-1970s both in terms of previous subcultural histories that could be revised to include their previously hidden presence and a more observant notation of their role in post-punk subcultures. Subsequent revivals of these "original" youth styles failed to disturb the orthodoxy that this was an unfolding progression of youth style upon youth style. Only in the 1980s did this linear process receive a critical look. Music-led styles such as heavy metal boys (and girls), goths, new romantics, and Acid House or "Ravers" dominated the 1980s as Britain constantly sought the "new punk." Acid House or Rave culture was misread in this fashion, when in reality it looked to roots in the club-based northern soul of the 1970s and was in fact notorious for mixing all kinds of youth styles on the same dance floor and attracting a range of previously opposed subcultures, from football hooligans to New Age hippies.

As the end of the century approached, a "hedonism in hard times" was perhaps the best way to describe a sea of youth styles circulating and recirculating in a harsh economic and political climate where youth were increasingly seen as a source of fear for "respectable" society and a "law and order" problem for the **police**.

Steve Redhead

Bibliography

Brake, Mike. *The Sociology of Youth Culture and Youth Subcultures*. 1980.

Cohen, Stanley. *Folk Devils and Moral Panics: The Creation of Mods and Rockers*. 1972.

Hall, Stuart, and Tony Jefferson, eds. *Resistance through Rituals: Youth Cultures in Postwar Britain*. 1976.

Hebdige, Dick. *Subculture: The Meaning of Style*. 1979.

Willis, Paul E. *Profane Culture*. 1978.

Z

Zinoviev Letter (1924)

The **Labour** government of **Ramsay Mac-Donald** had opened diplomatic relations with Soviet Russia in early 1924 and signed several treaties with Moscow in August of the same year designed to improve trade and reduce Comintern (Communist International) sedition in Britain and the Empire. Labour's **Liberal** allies refused to accept the treaties, and a general election was called for in late October. During the campaign the **Foreign Office** intercepted a letter purporting to be from Grigori Zinoviev, President of the Comintern, to the Central Committee of the **Communist Party of Great Britain**, instructing members to stir up revolt in the British armed forces and in factories. The Foreign Office published a copy of the letter on 25 October in *The Times*, along with a note of protest to the Soviet Ambassador in London. The *Daily Mail* and other newspapers also printed a copy. There have been extensive debates ever since as to the letter's authenticity and the role of the Foreign Office and *Daily Mail* in its publication. Most writers now accept that Labour's defeat was due more to the decline of the Liberal vote than to the letter. There have been many theories about authorship, although the Foreign Office believed that it was authentic at the time. The incident made the Labour Party suspicious of Foreign Office officials' motives for publication and soured **Anglo-Soviet relations** at a delicate moment.

Andrew J. Williams

Bibliography

Crowe, Sybil. "The Zinoviev Letter: A Reappraisal," *Journal of Contemporary History*, vol. 10 (1975), pp. 407–32.

Gorodetsky, Gabriel. *The Precarious Truce: Anglo-Soviet Relations, 1924–27.* 1977.

Lyman, Richard W. *The First Labour Government, 1924.* 1957.

Guide to Further Research

Bibliographies

Catterall, Peter, ed. *British History,
1945–1987.* 1990.

Chaloner, W.H., and R.C. Richardson, eds.
*Bibliography of British Economic
and Social History.* 2nd ed. 1984.

Fraser, A.G.S. *A Subject Bibliography
of the First World War: Books
in English, 1914–1978.* 1979.

Furber, Elizabeth Chapin, ed. *Changing
Views on British History.* 1966.

Hanham, H.J., ed. *Bibliography of British
History, 1851–1914.* 1976.

Havighurst, Alfred, ed. *Modern England,
1901–1984.* 2nd ed. 1987.

Howard-Hill, T.H., ed. *Bibliography
of British Literary Bibliographies.*
2nd ed. 1987.

Schlatter, Richard, ed. *Recent Views
on British History.* 1984.

Smith, Harold, ed. *The British Labour
Movement to 1970: A Bibliography.*
1981.

Westergaard, John, Anne Weyman, and Paul
Wiles, eds. *Modern British Society:
A Bibliography.* 2nd ed. 1977.

Labour History Review publishes an annual
bibliography of books and articles
published in British labor history.

Guides to Sources

Aster, Sidney, ed. *British Foreign Policy:
A Guide to Research and Research
Materials.* 1984.

Barrow, Margaret. *Women, 1870–1928:
A Select Guide to Printed and Archival
Sources in the United Kingdom.* 1981.

Cook, Chris, ed. *Sources in British Political
History, 1900–1951.* 6 vols. 1975–85.
Vol. 1: *A Guide to the Archives
of Selected Organisations and Societies.*
Vol. 2: *A Guide to the Private Papers of
Selected Public Servants.* Vol. 3: *A Guide
to the Private Papers of Members of
Parliament, A-K.* Vol. 4: *A Guide to the
Private Papers of Members of
Parliament, L-Z.* Vol. 5: *A Guide to the
Private Papers of Selected Writers,
Intellectuals, and Publicists.* Vol. 6: *First
Consolidated Supplement.*

Cook, Chris, and David Waller, eds.
*St. Martin's Guide to Sources
in Contemporary British History.* vol. 1:
Organisations and Societies. 1993.

Cook, Chris, Jane Leonard, and Peter Leese,
eds. *St Martin's Guide to Sources in
Contemporary British History.* vol. 2:
Individuals. 1994.

Foster, Janet, and Julia Sheppard. *British
Archives: A Guide to Archive Resources
in the United Kingdom.* 1982.

Hazlehurst, Cameron, and Christine Wood-
land. *A Guide to the Papers of British
Cabinet Ministers, 1900–1951.* 1974.

Kanner, Barbara, ed. *Women in English
Social History, 1800–1914.* 3 vols.
1987–90.

*Record Repositories in Great Britain:
A Geographical Directory.* 9th ed. 1991.

Walford, A.J. *Guide to Reference Material.*
3 vols. 4th ed. 1980–7.

Reference Works

Barnes, Philip. *A Companion to Post-War
British Theatre.* 1986.

Bergonzi, Bernard, ed. *History of Literature in the English Language.* vol. 7: *The Twentieth Century.* 1970.

Butler, David E., and Gareth Butler. *British Political Facts, 1900–1985.* 1986.

Craig, F.W.S., ed., *British Electoral Facts, 1832–1987.* 5th ed. 1989.

——. *British Parliamentary Election Results, 1885–1918.* 2nd ed. 1989.

——. *British Parliamentary Election Results, 1918–1949.* 3rd ed. 1983.

——. *British Parliamentary Election Results, 1950–1973.* 1983.

——. *British Parliamentary Election Results, 1974–1983.* 1984.

——. *Chronology of British Parliamentary By-elections, 1833–1987.* 1987.

——. *Conservative and Labour Party Conference Decisions, 1945–1981.* 1982.

——. *Minor Parties at British Parliamentary Elections, 1885–1974.* 1974.

Doughan, David, and Denise Sanchez. *Feminist Periodicals, 1855–1984.* 1987.

Drabble, Margaret, ed. *The Oxford Companion to English Literature.* 5th ed. 1985.

Farr, Dennis. *English Art, 1870–1940.* 1978.

Ford, Boris, ed. *The Cambridge Guide to the Arts in Britain: The Edwardian Age and the Inter-War Years.* 1989.

——. *The Cambridge Guide to the Arts in Britain: Since the Second World War.* 1988.

——. *The New Pelican Guide to English Literature.* vols. 7–8. 1983.

Gifford, Denis. *The British Film Catalogue, 1895–1985: A Reference Guide.* 2nd ed. 1986.

Hamilton, Ian, ed. *The Oxford Companion to Twentieth-Century Poetry in English.* 1994.

Hartnoll, Phyllis, ed. *The Oxford Companion to the Theatre.* 4th ed. 1983.

Mitchell, B.R. *British Historical Statistics.* 1988.

Noyce, John, ed. *The Directory of British Alternative Periodicals, 1965–1974.* 1979.

Ousby, Ian, ed. *The Cambridge Guide to Literature in English.* 2nd ed. 1994.

Sadie, Stanley, ed. *The New Grove Dictionary of Music and Musicians.* 20 vols. 1981.

Thompson, F.M.L. *The Cambridge Social History of Britain, 1750–1950.* 3 vols. 1990.

Trussler, Simon. *The Cambridge Illustrated History of British Theatre.* 1994.

Biography

Banks, Olive, ed. *The Biographical Dictionary of British Feminists.* 2 vols. (1800–1945). 1985–90.

Baylen, Joseph O., and Norbert J. Gossman, eds. *Biographical Dictionary of Modern British Radicals.* vol. 3 in 2 vols. (1870–1914). 1988.

Bellamy, Joyce M., and John Saville, eds. *Dictionary of Labour Biography.* vols. 1–9. 1972–93.

Biographical Memoirs of Fellows of the Royal Society. 1955– .

Briggs, Asa, ed. *Dictionary of Twentieth Century World Biography.* 1992.

Dictionary of National Biography. 1908– (with supplements to 1980). This will eventually be superseded by the projected *New Dictionary of National Biography*, edited by H.C.G. Matthew.

Jeremy, David J., ed. *Dictionary of Business Biography.* 5 vols. 1984–6.

Robbins, Keith, ed. *The Blackwell Biographical Dictionary of British Political Life in the Twentieth Century.* 1990.

Dissertations

Comprehensive Dissertation Index. 1973– .

Gilbert, Victor F., ed. *Labour and Social History Theses: American, British, and Irish University Theses and Dissertations in the Field of British and Irish Labour History Presented between 1900 and 1978.* 1982.

Index to Theses Accepted for Higher Degrees in the Universities of Great Britain and Ireland. 1953– .

Periodicals

Contemporary Record: The Journal of the Institute of Contemporary History. 1987– .

Labour History Review (formerly *Bulletin of the Society for the Study of Labour History*). 1960–.

Twentieth Century British History. 1990–.

Contributors

Hazard Adams
University of Washington
Cary, (Arthur) Joyce Lunel
    (1888–1957)

R.J.Q. Adams
Texas A&M University
Cliveden Set
Conscription
Ministry of Munitions
Munich Conference
Simon, John Allesbrook
    (1873–1954)

Roger Adelson
Arizona State University
Balfour, Arthur James (1848–1934)
Balfour Declaration
Lawrence, T(homas) E(dward)
    (1888–1935)
Middle East Policy

Geoffrey Aggeler
University of Utah
Burgess (Wilson), (John) Anthony
    (1917–1993)

Nannette Aldred
University of Sussex
Bomberg, David (1890–1957)
Camden Town Group (1911–1913)
Institute of Contemporary Arts (ICA)
    and Independent Group (IG)
Powell, Michael (1905–1990)
War Artists

Victor Bailey
University of Kansas
Juvenile Delinquency
Police

Norman Baker
State University of New York, Buffalo
History

Stuart Ball
University of Leicester
Baldwin, Stanley (1867–1947)
Beaverbrook, Lord (William Maxwell
    Aitken) (1879–1964)
Butler, R(ichard) A(usten)
    (1902–1982)
Churchill, Winston Spencer
    (1874–1965)
Conservative Party
1922 Committee, The

Rodney Barker
London School of Economics
Political Thought

T.C. Barker
London School of Economics
Urban Transport

L. Margaret Barnett
University of Southern Mississippi
Defence of the Realm Act (DORA)
Diet and Nutrition
Rationing

G.C. Baugh
Victoria History of Shropshire
Garden Cities
Milton Keynes
New Towns

J.O. Baylen
Georgia State University
Gardiner, A(lfred) G(eorge) (1865–1946)
Massingham, H(enry) W(illiam) (1860–1924)
Nation (1907–1931)

Gordon B. Beadle
State University College of New York,
*   Cortland*
Brooke, Rupert Chawner (1887–1915)
Sassoon, Siegfried (1886–1967)
Spender, Stephen (1909–)

Madeleine Beard
Cambridge, England
Landownership

Alan Beattie
London School of Economics
London School of Economics and Political
    Science

G.H. Bennett
University of Plymouth
Curzon, George Nathaniel (1859–1925)
Locarno Pact (1925)

Virginia Berridge
London School of Hygiene
*   and Tropical Medicine*
Drug Addiction
Public Health
Venereal Disease

Donald S. Birn
State University of New York, Albany
British Council
League of Nations
League of Nations Union
Murray, (George) Gilbert (Aimé)
    (1866–1957)
Peace Ballot

D.P. Blaazer
Australian National University
Angell (Lane), (Ralph) Norman
    (1872–1967)
Cripps, (Richard) Stafford (1889–1952)
Ethical Societies
Guild Socialism
Popular Front
Socialist League (1932–1937)
Trevelyan, C(harles) P(hilips)
    (1870–1958)
Union of Democratic Control
Unity Campaign

T.M. Boon
Science Museum, London
Bernal, J(ohn) D(esmond) (1901–1971)
Haldane, J(ohn) B(urdon) S(anderson)
    (1892–1964)
Huxley, Julian Sorell (1887–1975)

Newell D. Boyd
Houston Baptist University
Boer War (1899–1902)
Milner, Alfred (1854–1925)
South Africa

Trevor Bray
Cardigan, Dyfed, Wales
Britten, (Edward) Benjamin
    (1913–1976)
Composers and Music
Conductors
Delius, Frederick Theodore Albert
    (1862–1934)
Elgar, Edward William (1857–1934)
Folk Song and Dance
Holst, Gustavus Theodore von
    (1874–1934)
Lloyd Webber, Andrew (1948–)
Opera and Opera Companies
Orchestras
Tippett, Michael Kemp (1905–)
Vaughan Williams, Ralph
    (1872–1958)
Walton, William Turner
    (1902–1983)

Laurence A. Breiner
Boston University
Commonwealth Literature

Ian Britain
University of Melbourne
Webb, Beatrice Potter (1858–1943)
    and Sidney (1859–1947)

Stephen Brooke
Dalhousie University
Attlee, Clement Richard
    (1883–1967)
Dalton, (Edward) Hugh John Neale
    (1887–1962)
Durbin, Evan Frank Mottram
    (1906–1948)
Labour Party
New Fabian Research Bureau
Society for Socialist Inquiry
    and Propaganda (1931–1932)

Olga R.R. Broomfield
Mount Saint Vincent University
Bennett, (Enoch) Arnold
    (1867–1931)

Linda Bryder
University of Auckland
Medical Research Council
New Zealand
Tuberculosis

Vern L. Bullough
*State University College
    of New York, Buffalo*
Prostitution
Sexuality

James M. Cahalan
Indiana University of Pennsylvania
Irish Literature

David Cantor
Johns Hopkins University
Fleming, Alexander
    (1881–1955)
Medawar, Peter (1915–1987)

Roger Cardinal
University of Kent at Canterbury
Nash, Paul (1889–1946)

David Carlton
University of Warwick
Eden, (Robert) Anthony (1897–1977)
Suez Crisis (1956)

Robert L. Caserio
Temple University
Firbank, (Arthur Annesley) Ronald
    (1886–1926)
Green, Henry (1905–1973)
Huxley, Aldous Leonard (1894–1963)
Novel, English, 1900–1945
Powys, John Cowper (1872–1963)
Warner, Sylvia Townsend (1893–1978)

Youssef Cassis
University of Geneva
Big Bang
City of London
Clearing Banks
Merchant Banks

David Childs
University of Nottingham
Communist Party of Great Britain

Ian Clark
Selwyn College, Cambridge
Nuclear Weapons

Roberta A. Clark
Chapel Hill, North Carolina
Birth Control
Stopes, Marie Charlotte Carmichael
    (1880–1958)

Peter Clarke
St. John's College, Cambridge
Hammond, John Lawrence Le Breton
    (1872–1949) and Barbara (1873–1961)
Keynes, John Maynard (1883–1946)
Social Democratic Party
Wallas, Graham (1858–1932)

Catherine Ann Cline
Catholic University of America
Morel, E(dmund) D(ene)
    (1873–1924)

Richard Cockett
Royal Holloway and Bedford
  New College, London
Dawson, Geoffrey (1874–1944)
Garvin, J(ames) L(ouis) (1868–1947)
Observer
Times, The

Frans Coetzee
George Washington University
Bonar Law, Andrew (1858–1923)
Constitutional Crisis (1909–1911)
Patriotism
Tariff Reform

David Cohen
London, England
Freud, Lucian (1922–)
Hepworth, Barbara (1903–1975)
Kitaj, R(onald) B(rooks) (1932–)
Moore, Henry Spencer (1898–1986)
Piper, John Egerton Christmas
  (1903–1992)
Sutherland, Graham Vivian (1903–1980)

Robert Cole
Utah State University
Censorship
Propaganda
Taylor, A(lan) J(ohn) P(ercivale)
  (1906–1990)

Stephen Constantine
University of Lancaster
Emigration

Richard A. Cosgrove
University of Arizona
Capital Punishment
Judicial System
Legal Profession
Penal Reform

Robert M. Craig
Georgia Institute of Technology
Architecture
Gardens and Landscape Architecture
Lutyens, Edwin Landseer (1869–1944)
Pevsner, Nikolaus (1902–1983)

Postmodernism in Architecture
Spence, Basil Urwin (1907–1976)

Don M. Cregier
University of Prince Edward Island
Black and Tans
Carson, Edward Henry (1854–1935)
Irish Land Purchase Act (1903)
Irish Nationalism
Irish Treaty (1921)
Liberal Party
Lloyd George, David (1863–1945)

James E. Cronin
Boston College
Strikes

Hugh Cunningham
University of Kent at Canterbury
Leisure

M.C. Curthoys
Christ Church, Oxford
Oxford, University of

Eryl Davies
London, England
Radar

John H. Davis
The Queen's College, Oxford
London
London Government since 1900

Joan Fitzpatrick Dean
University of Missouri, Kansas City
Stoppard, Tom (1937–)

Charles Dellheim
Arizona State University
Marks and Spencer

David R. Devereux
St. John Fisher College
Aviation
Canada

Fram Dinshaw
St. Catherine's College, Oxford
Clark, Kenneth Mackenzie (1903–1983)

Michael Dintenfass
University of Wisconsin, Milwaukee
Entrepreneurship
Gold Standard
Mond, Alfred Moritz (1868–1930)

D.J. Dooley
University of Toronto
Mackenzie, (Edward Morgan) Compton
    (1883–1972)
Waugh, Evelyn Arthur St. John
    (1903–1966)

Ruth Dudley Edwards
London, England
Gollancz, Victor (1893–1967)

Bryan Dyson
University of Hull
Cooperative Movement

David E.H. Edgerton
Imperial College, London
Blackett, P(atrick) M(aynard) S(tuart)
    (1897–1974)
Science and Government
Tizard, Henry Thomas (1885–1959)

Duane Edwards
Fairleigh Dickinson University
Lawrence, D(avid) H(erbert)
    (1885–1930)

Clive Emsley
The Open University
Crime
Terrorism
Urban Riots

George Esenwein
University of Florida
International Brigade
Spanish Civil War (1936–1939)

T.F. Evans
Stone, Staffordshire
Shaw, George Bernard (1856–1950)

John Feather
University of Loughborough
Publishing and Publishers

John Ferns
McMaster University
Strachey, (Giles) Lytton (1880–1932)

Anthony Field
London, England
Arts Council of Great Britain

Ian Christopher Fletcher
Georgia State University
Grey, Edward (1862–1933)
Haldane, R(ichard) B(urdon)
    (1856–1928)
Montagu, Edwin Samuel (1879–1924)
Marconi Scandal (1912–1913)
Northcliffe, Lord (Alfred Charles
    William Harmsworth) (1865–1922)

Richard Flynn
Georgia Southern University
Children's Literature

Aaron Fogel
Boston University
Conrad, Joseph (1857–1924)

Dennis A. Foster
Southern Methodist University
Ballard, J(ames) G(raham) (1930–)

Michael Freeden
Mansfield College, Oxford
Hobson, J(ohn) A(tkinson)
    (1858–1940)

Gloria G. Fromm
University of Illinois, Chicago Circle
Richardson, Dorothy Miller (1873–1957)

Averil Gardner
Memorial University of Newfoundland
Wilson, Angus Frank Johnstone
  (1913–1991)

W.R. Garside
University of Birmingham
Dole, The
Means Test
Unemployment

Kathy Justice Gentile
University of Missouri, St. Louis
Compton-Burnett, Ivy (1884–1969)

Julie S. Gibert
Canisius College
Domestic Servants

Nancy K. Gish
University of Southern Maine
MacDiarmid, Hugh (Christopher Murray
  Grieve) (1892–1978)

Robert Gordon
Goldsmiths' College, London
Actors and Acting
Fringe and Noncommercial Theater
Osborne, John James (1929–1994)
Pinter, Harold (1930)
Rattigan, Terence Mervyn (1911–1977)

Deborah Gorham
Carleton University
Brittain, Vera Mary (1893–1970)
Sayers, Dorothy L(eigh) (1893–1957)
Women's Education

Ira Grushow
Franklin and Marshall College
Beerbohm, Henry Maximilian "Max"
  (1872–1956)

David Gullette
Simmons College
Joyce, James Augustine Aloysius
  (1882–1941)

Peter L. Hahn
Ohio State University
Anglo-American Relations
Cyprus
Lend-Lease
Malta

Peter H. Hansen
Worcester Polytechnic Institute
Mountaineering

Anne Hardy
*Wellcome Institute for the History
  of Medicine*
Hospitals

Cameron Hazlehurst
Queensland University of Technology
Asquith, H(erbert) H(enry) (1852–1928)
Campbell-Bannerman, Henry (1836–1908)

Trevor Herbert
The Open University
Beecham, Thomas (1879–1961)
Brass Bands
Early Music Revival, The
Welsh Music

Andrew Hewitt
State University of New York, Buffalo
Lewis, (Percy) Wyndham (1882–1957)

David Leon Higdon
Texas Tech University
Greene, (Henry) Graham (1904–1991)
Novel, English, since 1945

Jeffrey Hill
Nottingham Trent University
Boxing
Cricket
Horse Racing
Tennis, Lawn

Daniel W. Hollis III
Jacksonville State University
Ulster

Colin Holmes
University of Sheffield
Anti-Semitism
Fascism
Immigration
Mosley, Oswald Ernald
(1896–1980)
Refugees

Frank Honigsbaum
London, England
Medical Profession

David Howell
University of York
Hardie, (James) Keir (1856–1915)
Independent Labour Party
Miners Federation of Great Britain
National Union of Mineworkers (NUM)
Sankey Commission (1919)
Wheatley, John (1869–1930)

Joan B. Huffman
Macon College
Hyndman, Henry Mayers
(1842–1921)
Marshall Plan (1948–1951)

Jeffrey A. Hughes
University of Manchester
Cavendish Laboratory

Christopher T. Husbands
London School of Economics
National Front

Frank A.J.L. James
Royal Institution of Great Britain
Royal Institution of Great Britain
Royal Society of London

Ian Jeffrey
Rodmell, East Sussex
Beaton, Cecil Walter Hardy
(1904–1980)
Brandt, Hermann Wilhelm "Bill"
(1904–1983)
Euston Road School

Gill, (Arthur) Eric Rowton
(1882–1940)
John, Augustus Edwin (1878–1961)
Sickert, W(alter) R(ichard) (1860–1942)
Slade School of Art
Spencer, Stanley (1891–1959)

Edgar W. Jenkins
University of Leeds
Science Education and Training

Nicholas Jenkins
Brooklyn, New York
Auden, W(ystan) H(ugh) (1907–1973)

Paul Johnson
London School of Economics
Hours of Work
Standard of Living

Geoffrey Jones
University of Reading
Multinational Corporations
Nationalization and Nationalized Industries

R. Merfyn Jones
University College of North Wales, Bangor
Welsh Nationalism

Tudor Jones
University of Coventry
Clause Four
Crosland, (Charles) Anthony "Tony" Raven
(1918–1977)
Gaitskell, Hugh Todd Naylor
(1906–1963)
Labour Revisionism

Heather Bryant Jordan
Harvard University
Bowen, Elizabeth Dorothea Cole
(1899–1973)

Sydney Janet Kaplan
University of Washington
Mansfield (Beauchamp), Katherine
(1888–1923)

Harvey J. Kaye
University of Wisconsin, Green Bay
Marxist Historians
Thompson, E(dward) P(almer) (1924–1993)

Brenda Keegan
Newton North High School, Newton, Massachusetts
Drabble, Margaret (1939–)

Thomas C. Kennedy
University of Arkansas
Allen, (Reginald) Clifford (1889–1939)
Conscientious Objection
No-Conscription Fellowship (1914–1919)

Christopher A. Kent
University of Saskatchewan
Clubs
Drink
Hotels
Restaurants

Susan Kingsley Kent
University of Colorado
Pankhurst, Emmeline (1858–1928),
    Christabel (Harriette) (1880–1958),
    (Estelle) Sylvia (1882–1960)
Women's Social and Political Union
Women's Suffrage

Frank Kersnowski
Trinity University
Graves, Robert von Ranke (1895–1985)

Charles Kimball
Lyon College
Veterans' Organizations (1916–1945)

Lewis Klausner
University of Utah
Poetry, English

Jacob Korg
University of Washington
Jones, David (1895–1974)
Thomas, Dylan Marlais (1914–1953)

Seth Koven
Villanova University
Masterman, C(harles) F(rederick) G(urney)
    (1874–1927)
Settlement Movement
Slums

Charles Krantz
New Jersey Institute of Technology
Namier, Lewis Bernstein (1888–1960)

Krishan Kumar
University of Kent at Canterbury
Sociology
Utopian Thought

Diane B. Kunz
Yale University
Norman, Montagu Collet (1871–1950)

Karl G. Larew
Towson State University
Blitz and Battle of Britain
Dunkirk (26 May–4 June 1940)
El Alamein, Battle of
Montgomery, Bernard Law (1887–1976)
Second World War: Military (1939–1945)
Wavell, Archibald Percival (1883–1950)

Christopher Lawrence
Wellcome Institute for the History of Medicine
Chemistry
Health of the Population

Keith Laybourn
University of Huddersfield
Bevan, Aneurin "Nye" (1897–1960)
Jarrow
Labour Research Department
MacDonald, (James) Ramsay (1866–1937)
Morrison, Herbert Stanley (1888–1965)
Snowden, Philip (1864–1937)
Wilkinson, Ellen (1891–1947)

D.L. LeMahieu
Lake Forest College
British Broadcasting Corporation (BBC)

British Broadcasting Corporation (BBC)
  Overseas Service
Leavis, F(rank) R(aymond) (1895–1978)
Reith, John Charles Walsham (1889–1971)

Van Michael Leslie
Union College, Barbourville, Kentucky
Abyssinian Crisis (1935–1936)
Chamberlain, (Joseph) Austen
  (1863–1937)
Chamberlain, (Arthur) Neville
  (1868–1940)
Hoare, Samuel John Gurney
  (1880–1959)
Hoare-Laval Pact (1935)

F.M. Leventhal
Boston University
Baylis, Lilian Mary (1874–1937)
Brailsford, H(enry) N(oel) (1873–1958)
Council for the Encouragement
  of Music and the Arts (CEMA)
Festival of Britain (1951)
Henderson, Arthur (1863–1935)
Woolf, Leonard Sidney (1880–1969)

Wayne Lewchuk
McMaster University
Automobile Industry
Morris, William (1877–1963)

Jane Lewis
London School of Economics
Marriage

Gerald Lidstone
Goldsmiths' College, London
Theater Management and Ownership

Trevor Lloyd
University of Toronto
Electoral System
House of Lords

Roger D. Long
Eastern Michigan University
Decolonization
India, Partition of

W.C. Lubenow
Richard Stockton College of New Jersey
Apostles, The
Espionage

David C. Lukowitz
Hamline University
Appeasement
Halifax, Earl of (Edward Frederick
  Lindley Wood) (1881–1959)
Pacifism
Peace Pledge Union

Mary Lydon
University of Wisconsin, Madison
Beckett, Samuel (1906–1989)

Michael H. Macdonald
Seattle Pacific University
Lewis, C(live) S(taples) (1898–1963)

David MacGregor
Webster, New York
Dreadnought
Fisher, John Arbuthnot (1841–1920)
Jellicoe, John Rushworth (1859–1935)
Submarine Warfare

Raymond N. MacKenzie
University of St. Thomas, Minneapolis
Advertising
Lane, Allen (Williams) (1902–1970)
Manchester Guardian
Periodicals

S.P. MacKenzie
University of South Carolina
Army Education
Chatham House
Internment of Enemy Aliens
Lytton Commission (1931–1932)
Official Secrets Act
Reparations (1919–1930)

John Macnicol
*Royal Holloway and Bedford New College,
  London*
Beveridge, William Henry (1879–1963)

Eugenics
Evacuation of Children in the Second
    World War
National Health Service
Old-Age Pensions
Titmuss, Richard Morris (1907–1973)

Ian Madelin
Bracknell, Berkshire
Royal Air Force

John Maloney
University of Exeter
Economics and Economists

Peter Mandler
London Guildhall University
Country Houses
Historic Preservation
National Trust
Nicolson, Harold George (1886–1968)
Town and Country Planning

Jane Marcus
*Graduate Center, City University
    of New York*
Woolf, (Adeline) Virginia Stephen
    (1882–1941)

Lara Marks
Imperial College, London
Infant Mortality
Pregnancy and Childbirth

Jan Marsh
London, England
Owen, Wilfred Edward Salter
    (1893–1918)

Tony Mason
University of Warwick
Football
Sport

Laura E. Nym Mayhall
Millsaps College
Women's Freedom League (1907–1961)

Joseph McAleer
Stamford, Connecticut
Popular Fiction

Joseph M. McCarthy
Suffolk University
Army
Falklands War
Home Guard
Territorial Army

John McDermott
University of Winnipeg
Foreign Office
    and Foreign Service

Dorren McMahon
University College, Dublin
Irish in Britain

Arthur Mejia
San Francisco State University
Edward VII (1841–1910)
Edward VIII (1894–1972)
George V (1865–1936)
George VI (1895–1952)

Peter Mellini
Sonoma State University
Caricature and
    Political Cartooning
Low, David (1891–1963)
Punch

Anthony M. Messina
Tufts University
Race Relations

T.B. Millar
London School of Economics
Australia

Elizabeth Morse
Oxford, England
Cambridge, University of
Open University
Polytechnics

Alan Q. Morton
Science Museum, London
Physics
Rutherford, Ernest (1871–1937)

George Moyser
University of Vermont
Church of England
Lang, Cosmo Gordon (1864–1945)
Prayer Book Revision
Ramsey, (Arthur) Michael (1904–1988)
Temple, William (1881–1944)

Elizabeth Muther
Bowdoin College
Eliot, T(homas) S(tearns) (1888–1965)

John F. Naylor
State University of New York, Buffalo
Cabinet, The

Barbara Newman
London, England
Ballet
de Valois, Ninette (1898–)
Fonteyn, Margot (1919–1991)
Macmillan, Kenneth (1929–1992)

Michael Newman
University of North London
Laski, Harold Joseph (1893–1950)
Left Book Club
Strachey, John (1901–1963)

Phillips Payson O'Brien
Pembroke College, Cambridge
Washington Naval Conference
  (1921–1922)

William H. O'Donnell
Memphis State University
Yeats, William Butler (1865–1939)

Warren Olin-Ammentorp
Cazenovia College
Golding, William (1911–1993)
Lehmann, Rosamond Nina (1901–1990)

Donna Price Paul
Springfield, Virginia
Bondfield, Margaret (1873–1953)
Women's Employment
Women's Labour League (1906–1918)

Brian Pearce
Pinetown, Natal, South Africa
Ayckbourn, Alan (1939)
Civic and Repertory Theater
Drama

Susan Pedersen
Harvard University
Family Allowances
Feminism
Rathbone, Eleanor Florence
  (1872–1946)

Barbara Bennett Peterson
University of Hawaii
Foreign Travel
Holiday Travel

Barry Phelps
London, England
Wodehouse, P(elham) G(renville)
  (1881–1975)

Brian Phillips
Amnesty International, London
Brockway, (Archibald) Fenner (1888–1988)
Friends, Society of (Quakers)
Movement for Colonial Freedom

Stephen Priest
University of Edinburgh
Ayer, A(lfred) J(ules) (1910–1989)
Logical Positivism
Philosophy and Philosophers

Robin Prior
Australian Defence Force Academy, Canberra
First World War: Military (1914–1918)
Gallipoli
Passchendaele (Third Battle of Ypres)
Scott, C(harles) P(restwich) (1846–1932)
Somme, Battle of the

Frank Prochaska
London, England
Philanthropy

Anne Mary Rafferty
University of Nottingham
Nursing

Jennifer L. Randisi
California State University,
 San Bernardino
Spark, Muriel Camberg (1918–)

John Ranlett
State University College of New York,
 Potsdam
Railways

Dean Rapp
Wheaton College, Wheaton, Illinois
Psychoanalysis

Eugene L. Rasor
Emory and Henry College
Navy, Royal
Singapore
Steamship Travel
Titanic, Sinking of the (1912)

Steve Redhead
Manchester Metropolitan University
The Beatles
Popular Music
Youth Culture

Steven Reilly
University of Kent at Canterbury
Callaghan, (Leonard) James (1912–)
Campaign for Nuclear Disarmament
Foot, Michael (1913–)
Green Movement/Party
Heath, Edward Richard George
 (1916–)
Kinnock, Neil Gordon (1942–)
Militant
Miners' Strike (1984–1985)
Thatcherism
Wilson, (James) Harold (1916–)

Marilyn Reizbaum
Bowdoin College
Scottish Literature

Richard A. Rempel
McMaster University
Imperial Preference
Statute of Westminster (1931)

Richard Rodger
University of Leicester
Council Housing
Housing

Jonathan Rose
Drew University
Adult Education
Ellis, (Henry) Havelock (1859–1939)
Fabian Society
Wells, H(erbert) G(eorge)
 (1866–1946)

Janice Rossen
Austin, Texas
Larkin, Philip Arthur (1922–1985)

David Rubinstein
University of Hull
Fawcett, Millicent Garrett
 (1847–1929)

John Paul Russo
University of Miami
Literary Criticism
Richards, I(vor) A(rmstrong)
 (1893–1979)

Charles J. Rzepka
Boston University
Detective Fiction

Michael Saler
University of California, Davis
Design
Pick, Frank (1878–1941)
Poster Art
Read, Herbert Edward (1893–1968)

Gail Savage
George Washington University
Astor, Nancy Witcher Langhorne
    (1879–1964)
Civil Service
Divorce and Divorce Law Reform

Margaret Scanlan
Indiana University, South Bend
Murdoch, Iris (1919–)

R.J. Schiefen, CSB
University of St. Thomas, Houston
Roman Catholicism

Jonathan Schneer
Georgia Institute of Technology
Lansbury, George (1859–1940)

Martha A. Schütz
Chapel Hill, North Carolina
Coward, Noel Pierce (1899–1973)
Entertainments National Service Association
    (ENSA)
Musical Revues
Olivier, Laurence Kerr (1907–1989)
Robbins Report (1963)
Universities, New

Karl W. Schweizer
New Jersey Institute of Technology
Namier, Lewis Bernstein (1888–1960)

Robert L. Selig
Purdue University
Powell, Anthony Dymoke (1905–)

Peter Simkins
Imperial War Museum
Committee of Imperial Defence (1902–1939)
Haig, Douglas (1861–1928)
Kitchener, Horatio Herbert (1850–1916)

Madeleine Simms
Institute for Social Studies in Medical Care,
    London
Abortion

David Simpson
University of Colorado
Williams, Raymond Henry (1921–1988)

Adrian Smith
La Sainte Union College
    of Higher Education
Martin, (Basil) Kingsley (1897–1969)
New Statesman (1913–)
Press, British

Clyde Curry Smith
University of Wisconsin, River Falls
Archaeology
British Museum

Elton Edward Smith
University of South Florida
Day Lewis, Cecil (1904–1972)
MacNeice, Louis (1907–1963)

Harold L. Smith
University of Houston, Victoria
Equal-Pay Movement
Second World War: Homefront (1939–1945)

Michael Douglas Smith
Germantown, Maryland
Quiller-Couch, Arthur Thomas
    (1863–1944)
Trevelyan, G(eorge) M(acaulay)
    (1876–1962)

Richard A. Soloway
University of North Carolina
Population

Peter Stansky
Stanford University
Bloomsbury Group
Forster, E(dward) M(organ) (1879–1970)
Jennings, Humphrey (1907–1950)
Orwell, George (1903–1950)

Gary M. Stearns
Elizabethtown Community College
Cecil, Robert Gascoyne (1864–1958)

Sanford Sternlicht
Syracuse University
Galsworthy, John (1867–1933)
Masefield, John Edward (1878–1967)
Maugham, (William) Somerset (1874–1965)

James W. Stitt
High Point College
Post-War Reconstruction (1916–1922)
Whitley Councils

Steven W. Sturdy
University of Edinburgh
Medical Education
Medical Research

Penny Summerfield
University of Lancaster
Mass-Observation (1937–1949)
Technical Education
Women in Wartime (1914–1918
    and 1939–1945)

Barry Supple
The Leverhulme Trust
Coal Mining
Economic Performance

Gillian Sutherland
Newnham College, Cambridge
Psychology
University Education

Paul Swann
Temple University
Documentary Film
Film Industry
Hitchcock, Alfred (1899–1980)
Television

Laura Tabili
University of Arizona
Black People in Britain

Andrew Tadie
Seattle University
Chesterton, G(ilbert) K(eith) (1874–1936)

Lou Taylor
University of Brighton
Clothing and Fashion

Paul Taylor
London School of Economics
European Union
    (*formerly* European Community)
United Nations

Pat Thane
University of Sussex
Ageing
Welfare State
Women

Deborah Thom
Robinson College, Cambridge
Child-Rearing
Education Act of 1944
Primary Education
Secondary Education

Virginia Tiger
Rutgers University, Newark
Lessing, Doris May Tayler
    (1919–)

Tony Topham
Leven, North Humberside
Transport and General Workers' Union
    (TGWU)

Simon Trussler
Goldsmiths' College, London
National Theatre
Old Vic
Royal Shakespeare Company

James Urry
Victoria University at Wellington
Anthropology

Marina Vaizey
London, England
Epstein, Jacob (1880–1959)
Fry, Roger Eliot (1866–1934)

David Vaughan
Cunningham Dance Foundation, New York
Ashton, Frederick (1904–1988)

John Vincent
University of Bristol
Home, Alec Douglas- (1903–)
Macleod, Iain Norman (1913–1970)
Macmillan, (Maurice) Harold (1894–1986)
Thatcher, Margaret Hilda Roberts (1925–)

Richard A. Voeltz
Cameron University
Baden-Powell, Robert (1857–1941)
Imperialism
Kipling, (Joseph) Rudyard (1865–1936)
Lugard, Frederick John Dealtry
    (1858–1945)
Scouting Movement

Mary Wagoner
University of New Orleans
Christie, Agatha Miller (1890–1976)

A. Martin Wainwright
University of Akron
Mountbatten, Louis Francis Albert Victor
    Nicholas (1900–1979)

Graham Walker
Queen's University, Belfast
Labour Representation Committee
    (1900–1906)
Maxton, James (1885–1946)
Scottish Nationalism

Wesley K. Wark
University of Toronto
Spy Novel, British

Kenneth Warren
Jesus College, Oxford
Steel Industry

Bernard Wasserstein
Brandeis University
Jews

Palestine
Samuel, Herbert (1870–1963)

Chris Waters
Williams College
Blatchford, Robert Peel Glanville
    (1851–1943)
Homosexuality
Popular Culture
Priestley, J(ohn) B(oynton)
    (1894–1984)
Wolfenden Report (1957)

Peter Weiler
Boston College
Bevin, Ernest (1881–1951)
New Liberalism

James White
University of Southern Alabama
Isherwood, Christopher William Bradshaw
    (1904–1986)

Joseph Wiesenfarth
University of Wisconsin, Madison
Ford, Ford Madox (1873–1939)

Andrew J. Williams
University of Kent at Canterbury
Anglo-Soviet Relations (1917–1956)
Zinoviev Letter (1924)

Roger Williams
University of Reading
Nuclear Power

Kirk Willis
University of Georgia
Moore, G(eorge) E(dward)
    (1873–1958)
Russell, Bertrand (1872–1970)
Whitehead, Alfred North
    (1861–1947)

T. Mervyn Willshaw
Bromley, Kent
Methodism

Andrew Wilson
London, England
Bacon, Francis (1909–1992)
Bell, Vanessa Stephen (1879–1961)
Caro, Anthony (1924–)
Grant, Duncan James Corrowr
  (1885–1978)
Hamilton, Richard (1922–)
Heron, Patrick (1920–)
Hockney, David (1937–)
Nevinson, C(hristopher) R(ichard) W(ynne)
  (1889–1946)
Nicholson, Ben (1894–1982)
Pasmore, Victor (1908–)
Vorticism

Trevor Wilson
University of Adelaide
First World War: Military (1914–1918)
Gallipoli
Passchendaele (Third Battle of Ypres)
Scott, C(harles) P(restwich) (1846–1932)
Somme, Battle of the

Guil Winchester
*Wellcome Institute for the History
  of Medicine*
Crick, Francis (1916–)
Genetics
Molecular Biology

Angela Woolacott
Case Western University
First World War: Homefront
  (1914–1918)

Anthony Wright, MP
House of Commons
Cole, G(eorge) D(ouglas) H(oward)
  (1889–1959)
Tawney, R(ichard) H(enry) (1880–1962)

C.J. Wrigley
University of Nottingham
Citrine, Walter McLennan (1887–1983)
Clydesiders
General Strike (4–12 May 1926)
Taff Vale Judgment (July 1901)
Thomas, James Henry "Jimmy"
  (1874–1949)
Trade Union Legislation
Trades Union Congress (TUC)

Lynn Zastoupil
Rhodes College
Amritsar Massacre (1919)
Government of India Act (1935)
Indian Nationalism
Morley-Minto Reforms (1909)
Round Table Conference (1930–1932)

Index

Boldface indicates encyclopedia entry.

Abdication crisis, 57, 150, 254–5, 327, 438
Abercrombie, Patrick, 317–18, 470, 566
Abortion, **3–4**, 134, 285, 450, 674, 716, 841, 844;
    Abortion Law Reform Association, 3;
    Abortion Reform Act (1967), 3–4, 80,
    285
Abyssinian crisis, **4–5**, 23, 364–5, 445, 603, 612;
    Hoare-Laval Pact (1935), 5, 23, 56, 136,
    364–5
Actors, **5–7**
Addison, Christopher, 646, 836
Adult Education, **7–8,** see also Education
Advertising, **8–10**, 101, 257, 266, 274, 331, 447,
    502, 614, 622, 643, 655, 716, 773, 832
Ageing, **10–11**, 264, 351, 450
Aldermaston, 122, 622, 699
Allen, Clifford, **11–12**, 186, 392, 571, 603
Allingham, Margery, 224
Amery, L.S., 264, 519, 744
Amis, Kingsley, 216, 578, 629, 825
Amritsar massacre, **13**
Angell, Norman, **13–14**, 800
Anglican, see Church of England
Anglo-American Committee of Inquiry, 606
Anglo-American relations, **14–16**, 58, 151, 313,
    357, 517, 582–3, 604, 606, 750, 768;
    American loan (1945), 15, 214, 390,
    424, 431, 453; Atlantic Charter, 15;
    Lend-Lease, 15, 256, 390, 424, **452–3,**
    711; Marshall Plan, 15, 78, **496–7**; and
    war in Viet Nam, 432, 604, 841 Wash-
    ington Naval Conference (1921–2), 14,
    58, **823–4**
Anglo-Iranian Oil Company, 516–17, 558; British
    Petroleum, 517, 539, 559
Anglo-Soviet relations, 15, **17–18**, 150–2, 207, 250,
    465; Zinoviev letter (1924), 17, **867**
Anthropology, **18–20**
Anti-Semitism, **20–21**, 58, 110, 281–2, 366, 411–
    13, 456, 491, 493, 526, 536, 551, 623

Apostles, **21–2,** see also Cambridge, University of
Appeasement, 4, 11–12, **23–5**, 40, 55, 136, 138,
    163, 215, 346–7, 364, 541, 568, 720
Archaeology, 19, **26**
Architecture, **27–31**, 287, 360–1, 476–8, 567,
    616–17, 735–6; New Brutalism, 27, 30,
    399; postmodernism, 27, **644–5**
Army, **31–3**, 125, 293–7, 390, 397, 427, 486, 526–
    7, 561, 605, 687; British Expeditionary
    Force, 32, 241, 294, 297, 302, 343–4,
    710; Bureau of Current Affairs (ABCA),
    8, 34; Haldane reforms of, 31, 343, 345,
    767; Territorial, 31–3, 346, **767**
Army education, **33–4,** see also Education, army
Arts Council, **34–6**, 129–30, 159, 267, 311, 368,
    422, 426, 452, 591, 636, 840; and bal-
    let, 61–2; and CEMA, 196–7; and Festi-
    val of Britain, 287; and opera, 593–4;
    and theater, 155–6, 311, 774
Ashton, Frederick, **36–7**, 60–1, 225, 300, 398,
    488, 625
Asquith, H.H., **37–9**, 339, 345, 600; and coali-
    tion, 95, 523, 731; and conscription,
    185, 188; and Liberal leadership, 39,
    124, 457, 465; as Prime Minister, 58,
    172, 401, 427, 464, 607, 646, 720, 795;
    and women's suffrage, 607, 857
Astor, David, 587–8
Astor, Nancy, **39–40**, 79, 163
Astor, Waldorf, 39, 163, 321, 587
Atomic weapons, see nuclear weapons
Attlee, Clement, **40–2**, 171, 242, 442, 472, 533,
    563, 714, 727–8; as Prime Minister,
    115–18, 207, 214, 430–1, 605
Auchinleck, Claude, 255
Auden, W.H., **43–4**, 107, 215, 224, 230, 236, 407–
    8, 600, 615, 733, 738; and Auden
    group, 489, 627–9
Auerbach, Frank, 53, 94, 308, 426, 721
Australia, **44–7,** 49, 173, 204, 262–4, 351, 391,

401, 427, 525, 540, 544, 568, 664, 739, 744, 824

Automobile industry, **47–9**, 246, 468, 532, 753; British Leyland, 48, 532, 559–60

Aviation, **49–50**, 430, 558, 782; British Airways, 50, 560

Ayckbourn, Alan, **50–1**, 238

Ayer, A.J., **51–2**, 166, 467, 620

Bacon, Francis, **53–4**, 59, 129, 308, 367, 426, 757

Baden-Powell, Robert, **54–5**, 705–6

Baldwin, Stanley, **55–7**, 66, 128; advocates protection, 458, 525; and appeasement, 23; and General Strike, 322–3, 611; and patriotism, 611; as Prime Minister, 95, 133, 150, 172, 189, 192, 210, 254, 612, 785

Balfour, Arthur, **57–8**, 94, 126, 130, 191, 304, 370, 744, 824; as Prime Minister, 57, 171, 760

Balfour Declaration, **58–9**, 219, 491, 526, 605, 695

Ballard, J.G., **59–60**, 579, 749

Ballet, 36–7, **60–2**, 69, 108, 197, 225–6, 299–300, 488–9, 593, 648; *Ballets Russes*, 36, 60, 68, 225, 593; Royal Ballet, 36–7, 62–3, 225–6, 299–300, 488; Sadler's Wells, 36, 62, 225–6, 300, 488

Bank of England, 154, 214, 329, 430, 514, 558, 572

Banks, 540–1; clearing, 78, 154, **161–3**, 513; merchant, 78, 154, 161, **513–14**

Barbirolli, John, 182, 596

Barrie, J.M., 144, 236, 316, 667, 702

Barry, Gerald, 286–7

Battle of Britain, *see* Blitz and Battle of Britain

Bax, Arnold, 177, 265

Baylis, Lilian, 5, 61, **63–4**, 225, 311, 590, 593

Beatles, The, **64–5**, 289, 579, 637, 640–1, 865

Beaton, Cecil, 36, **65**

Beaverbrook, Lord, **65–6**, 126, 254, 762, 821; and Empire Free Trade, 66, 525; as government minister, 71; as press lord, 56, 475, 570, 652; and relations with politicians, 66, 152

Beckett, Samuel, **67**, 237, 406, 576, 623, 718, 749

Beecham, Thomas, **67–8**, 182, 225, 593, 596, 719

Beerbohm, Max, **68–9**, 71, 127–8

Bell, Clive, 90–1, 121, 222, 312

Bell, Vanessa, **69–70**, 90–1, 222, 273, 312, 334, 860

Belloc, Hilaire, 98, 110, 141, 615, 686, 843

Benn, Tony, 109, 539

Bennett, Arnold, **70–1**, 90, 236, 306, 474, 497, 550, 577

Bennett, Richard Rodney, 180

Berkeley, Lennox, 179

Bernal, J.D., 22, **71–2**, 175, 358, 524, 689

Betjeman, John, 360, 624, 629, 665

Bevan, Aneurin, 41–2, **72–3**, 278, 313, 430–1, 535, 639–40, 840; and Bevanites, 42,

72–3, 214, 301, 431; and National Health Service, 73, 484, 553, 662

Beveridge, William, **73–5**, 102, 278, 473, 494, 497, 707, 714, 798, 830, 840; Report, 74–5, 280, 430, 502, 590, 618, 707, 783

Bevin, Ernest, 41, **75–8**, 153, 430–1, 533, 727–8; as Foreign Secretary, 15, 18, 42, 207, 304, 327, 431, 496, 605; as Minister of Labour, 74, 187, 189, 788; as trade union leader, 73, 213, 434, 439, 497, 590, 733, 789

Big Bang, **78**

Birth control, **79–81**, 143, 285, 642, 692, 716, 747–8, 835, 844

Birtwistle, Harrison, 101, 180, 594–5

Black and Tans, **81**

Black people, 11, **81–4**, 97, 174, 282, 387, 470, 552, 670, 807, 865

Blackett, P.M.S., **85**, 132, 621, 691, 694

Blatchford, Robert, **85–6**, 654

Blitz and Battle of Britain, **86–9**; *see also* Second World War

Bloomsbury Group, 69, **89–91**, 307, 312, 333–4, 455, 527, 569, 817, 858–60

Blunden, Edmund, 110, 550, 625

Blunt, Anthony, 22, 269, 617

Boer War, 31, 45, 86, **91–3**, 125, 149, 171, 187, 343, 389–90, 457, 518–19, 567, 731; Mafeking, relief of (1900), 54, 92, 722; opposition to, 320, 350, 367, 386, 462, 491, 500, 692, 701, 807; physical condition of recruits, 226, 397, 661; Vereeniging, Treaty of (1902), 93, 518, 731

Bomberg, David, **93–4**, 721, 817, 821

Bonar Law, Andrew, 39, 55, 65–6, **94–5**, 130, 136; as Conservative leader, 135, 191–2, 390, 523, 760; as Prime Minister, 210

Bondfield, Margaret, **95–6**

Bone, Muirhead, 94, 821

Boult, Adrian, 182, 265, 595, 779

Bowen, Elizabeth, **96–7**, 449, 576

Boxing, **97**, 738

Boy Scouts, 54, 452, 705–6

Bracken, Brendan, 135, 152

Bragg, W.H., 140, 523, 621, 689, 691

Bragg, W.L., 132, 523, 621, 689

Brailsford, H.N., **98–9**, 109, 320, 392, 491, 550, 727–8, 801

Brandt, Bill, **99–100**, 737

Brass bands, **100–1**, 635

Bridge, Frank, 107, 177, 183

British Broadcasting Corporation (BBC), 8, **101–4**, 216, 451, 489, 545, 558, 570, 611, 623, 636, 679, 681; and censorship, 134; Colonial Service, 173, 598; and music, 68, 108, 182, 595, 832; and Open University, 8, 592; Overseas Service, 99, **104**; and Proms, 182; as source of news, 653; talks on, 159, 360, 454, 570, 616, 693, 696; television, 231, 360, 624, 648,

Economic planning, 242–3
Economics, 22, 119, 171, 213, **248–9**, 313, 366, 371, 421–4, 461, 601, 729–30, 760
Eden, Anthony, 113, 152, 163, 211, **249–51**, 490; as critic of appeasement, 138, 150, 192, 250; as Foreign Secretary, 18, 250, 304, 733; and Suez, 25, 250–1, 517, 588, 755–7, 778
Education, Act (1902), 457, 462, 655, 700, 713, 819, 849; Act (1918), 655, 713; Act (1944), 75, 112, **251–2**, 700, 709, 713, 740, 763, 766, 849; adult, **7–8**, 63, 313, 777, 837; army, 7–8, **33–4**, 172; comprehensive schools, 714; Education Reform Act (1988), 700, 770; Hadow Committee (1931), 655; Higher Education Funding Council (HEFC), 806; medical, **506–7**, 662; national curriculum, 656, 700, 714; new universities, 30, 256, 432, 600, 684, 701, 729, **803–5**, 806; polytechnics, **634–5**, 701, 729, 763–4; primary, 120, 611, **655–6**, 849; science, **700–1**; secondary, 120, 251–2, 634, 655, 661, **712–14**, 827, 837, 849; Spens Report (1938), 251, 709; technical, 634, 700, 713, **762–4**, 827; university, 22, 592, **805–7**, 850; University Grants Committee (UGC), 684, 803–4; women's, 119, 284, 593, 602, **848–50**; workers', 171
Edward VII, 13, 194, **252–4**, 377, 681
Edward VIII, 150, **254–5**, 325, 438
El Alamein, Battle of, **255–6**
Electoral system, **256–8**; Plural voting, 256; Representation of the People Act (1918), 256, 283–4, 293, 853; Representation of the People Act (1928), 853
Elgar, Edward, 100, 177, 182–3, **258–9**, 813
Eliot, T.S., 90–1, 224, **259–61**, 426, 455, 629–30, 633, 718, 859; as critic, 459–60, 626–7; edits *Criterion*, 460, 614; modernism of, 415, 447, 456, 627–8, 677, 702; as playwright, 236–7; as publisher, 335; and *The Waste Land*, 600, 627, 825, 861
Ellis, Havelock, **261–2**, 373, 716
Emergency Powers Act (1920), 784
Emigration, 46, **262–4**, 412
Empire Marketing Board, 230, 644
Empson, William, 460, 628, 682
Enemy aliens, internment of, **400–1**
Entertainments National Service Association (ENSA), 197, 201, **264–5**, 545, 636
Entrepreneurship, **265–6**
Epstein, Jacob, **266–8**, 358, 528, 623, 719, 735, 817
Equal pay, 39, **268–9**, 285, 674, 841, 845–6, 853; Equal Pay Act (1970), 266, 285, 846, 852
Esher, Lord, 172
Espionage, **269–70**, 338, 588, 741
Ethical societies, **270**, 365

Eugenics, 22, 262, **270–1**, 280, 366, 729, 831; Eugenics Society, 385, 781
European Community, *see* European Union
European Free Trade Area (EFTA), 265
European Union, 46, 49, 229, 265, **272–3**, 280, 380, 727; British attempts to join, 16, 355, 370, 437, 486–7, 602, 841; Common Agricultural Policy, 272, 437; elections to European Parliament, 257, 272, 834; Maastricht Treaty (1991), 273, 801; membership in, 123, 190, 227, 425, 725, 745, 769–70, 772–3; provisions of, 240, 268, 663, 830; referendum on (1975), 119, 272, 842; Single European Act (1987), 773
Euston Road School, **273–4**, 609, 721
Evacuation of children in the Second World War, **274–5**; *see also* Second World War
Evans, Edith, 5–6, 63, 591
Exhibitions: Britain Can Make It (1946), 735; Post-Impressionist, 69, 90, 121, 311, 333, 414, 736

Fabian Society, 171, **277–8**, 328, 341, 441, 472, 480, 497, 500, 563–4, 717, 728, 801, 819, 827, 831, 837, 859; Fabian Colonial Bureau, 278, 539; New Fabian Research Bureau, 171, 242, 278, **563–4**, 728; university Fabian societies, 11, 213
Falklands War, 16, 33, 103, 116, 148, 190, **278–9**, 491, 561–2, 688, 726, 745, 755, 768–9, 771–2
Family allowances, 74–5, 142–3, 227, **279–81**, 285, 674–5, 707, 830
Family Endowment Committee, 280, 674
Farjeon, Herbert, 545
Fascism, 20–1, 72, 171, **281–2**, 331, 455, 497–8, 570, 603, 750, 802–3
Fascists, British Union of, 20–1, 189, 281–2, 413, 534–6, 551, 722, 807
Fashion, *see* Clothing
Fawcett, Millicent Garrett, **282–3**, 284, 674, 856, 858
Federation of British Industries, 222, 525
Fellowship of Reconciliation, 603–4
Feminism, 39, 106, 235, 270, 280–1, **283–5**, 386, 453, 494, 575, 579, 608, 632–3, 649, 674, 772, 822, 850, 853, 857, 862; Open Door Council, 106, 284; Six Point Group, 106, 284–5
Festival of Britain (1951), 62, 216, **286–7**, 530, 533, 554, 592, 654, 735, 758
Festivals: Aldeburgh, 108, 287, 596; Edinburgh, 287
Fiction, detective, *see* Literature
Film, 61, 100, 184, 202, 224, 363–4, 647–8, 838; documentary, 107, **229–31**, 274, 288, 410–11, 501, 624, 636, 647, 758, 775; industry, 103, 134, 175, 231, **287–90**, 578, 636; quota quickies, 288

393–4; Cripps mission (1942), 208, 397;
Government of India Act (1919), 526;
Government of India Act (1935), 56,
332–3, 365, 391, 396; independence of,
42, 431, 538; Indian National Congress,
13, 217, 333, 391, 393–7, 538; Montagu-
Chelmsford Report (1918), 526; Morley-
Minto reforms (1909), 395, **531–2**; na-
tionalism, 13, 99, 217, **395–7**, 441, 531,
687; partition of, 217, 333, **393–5**, 538;
Quit India campaign, 397; Round Table
Conference (1930–2), 332, 396, **686–7**;
Rowlatt Acts (1919), 13, 396
Infant Mortality, **397–8**; *see also* Health
Institute of Contemporary Arts, 347, **398–9**, 678
International Brigade, **399–400**
International, Second, 351, 356, 386
Ireland, John, 177
Irish, **401–2;** Easter Rising (1916), 131, 404–5;
Land Purchase Act (1903), **403**; nation-
alism, 130, 194, 404, **405–6**, 701, 863;
Republican Army, 81, 405–6, 538, 631,
768–70, 796; Treaty (1921), 81, 257,
406–7, 574, 795–6; *see also* Literature,
Irish
Isherwood, Christopher, 43, 182, 236, 306, 335,
384, **407–8**, 489, 738
Ishiguro, Kazuo, 174, 234, 579
Ismay, Lord, 172

James, Henry, 71, 97, 182–3, 302–3, 306, 336,
447, 483, 667
James, P.D., 224, 579, 639
Jarrow, **409–10**, 837
Jay, Douglas, 214, 242, 435
Jekyll, Gertrude, 318, 476
Jellicoe, John, **410**, 561
Jenkins, Roy, 243, 432, 435, 725–6
Jennings, Humphrey, 230–1, 398, **410–11**, 501
Jews, 20–1, 58–9, 97, 331–2, 388, 401, **411–13**,
493, 516, 526, 547, 605, 611, 623, 678,
695, 858
Jinnah, Muhammad Ali, 217, 393–5
John, Augustus, 121, 273, **413–14**, 721, 821
Jones, David, 328, **414–15**, 628, 630
Jones, Thomas, 163, 196
Joseph, Keith, 193
Joyce, James, 174, 178, 236, 290, 303, 404–5,
414, **415–16**, 442, 456, 575–7, 614,
626, 648, 702, 861; and modernism, 90,
306, 384, 574, 578; and *Ulysses*, 437,
570, 574
Joyce, William, 281
Judicial system, **417–18**
Juvenile delinquency, **418–19**

Kauffer, E. McKnight, 623, 644, 817
Kenya, 84, 218
Keynes, John Maynard, 21, 61, 110, 197, 213,
248–9, 366, **421–4**, 473, 497, 751, 799;

and Bloomsbury, 89–91, 333, 421; criti-
cizes Versailles treaty, 422, 531; and
German reparations, 680; and Keynesian
economics, 112, 192, 242, 249, 278,
313, 422–3, 486, 535–6, 633, 707, 750,
769, 789; opposes return to gold stan-
dard, 168, 329, 422; supports public
works, 120, 422–3
Kinnock, Neil, 278, 301, **424–5**, 433, 518, 522
Kipling, Rudyard, 144, 183, **425–6**, 577, 625
Kitaj, R.B., 308, 367, **426–7**
Kitchener, Lord, 57, 209, **427–8**; and Boer War, 92,
427; as Secretary for War, 31–2, 39, 315,
427, 522, 574, 657
Knight, Laura, 821–2
Knox, Ronald, 686
Korda, Alexander, 288, 647
Kossoff, Leon, 53, 94, 308, 426, 721

Labour Party, 24, 41, 56, 76, 122, 127, 206–8,
213–14, 242, 254, 280, 300–1, 313–14,
355–7, 424–5, **429–33**, 439–42, 481–3,
498, 520, 530, 533, 539, 563, 840–2;
Advisory Committee on International
Questions, 98, 801; and Campaign for
Labour Party Democracy, 432; Clause
Four, **160–1**, 209, 314, 429, 435, 827;
and commitment to welfare state, 430,
707; constitution of, 277, 356; educational policy of, 761; enthusiasm for
February revolution, 17; and European
Union, 272, 314, 432; and House of
Lords, 380; Left, 72–3, 109, 207, 300,
304, 313, 424, 431–3, 517–18, 640,
727, 803, 837, 841–2; National Executive Committee of, 213–14, 301, 424,
429, 431–3, 441–2, 518, 533, 791;
opposes Popular Front, 639; opposes
rearmament, 25, 77; Party Conference,
73, 313–14, 431, 433; and public ownership, 161, 435, 558; refuses to allow
Communists to affiliate, 175; refuses to
serve under Chamberlain, 138, 430; Revisionism, 118, 208–9, 314, **435–6**; Social Democrats split from, 725–7; and
Spanish Civil War, 733; and Suez crisis,
756; and working class voters, 190
Labour Representation Committee, 277, 350, 355,
391, 429, **433–4**, 481, 759, 786
Labour Research Department, 171, 341–2, **434**
Labor Revisionism, **435–6**
Lambert, Constant, 36, 179
Landownership, 200–1, 379, **436–7**, 555
Lane, Allen, **437–8**, 615, 663
Lang, Cosmo Gordon, **438**
Lansbury, George, 41, 355, **438–40**, 651, 715, 728;
pacifism of, 439–40, 604, 613; Poplar
campaign, 40, 439
Larkin, Philip, **440–1**
Lasdun, Denys, 29–30, 555

Laski, Harold, 41, 170, **441–2**, 448, 472–3, 497, 550, 750
Lawrence, D.H., 71, 110, 236, 302, 306, 336, 384, **442–3**, 447, 484, 492, 575, 615, 625–7, 861; *Lady Chatterley's Lover* obscenity trial, 438; and modernism, 90, 648
Lawrence, T.E., 414, **444**
League of Nations, 45, 133, **445–6**, 544, 568, 658, 744, 831; and Abyssinia, 5, 250, 364, 732; and collective security, 12, 466; and Manchurian crisis, 478; mandates, 58, 218–19, 516, 605, 695; popular support for, 603, 612; proposals for, 277, 464, 859
League of Nations Union, 106, 133, 340, 356–7, 445, **446–7**, 544, 603, 612
Leavis, F.R., 22, 120, **447**, 460, 615, 655, 838, 861
LeCarré, John, 269, 742
Lee, Jennie, 35, 73
Leese, Arnold, 281–2, 551
Left Book Club, 331, 442, **448**, 597, 738, 750, 803, 859
Legal profession, 38, 207, 229, 417, **448–9**, 771, 845
Lehmann, John, 91, 96, 336, 407, 450, 615
Lehmann, Rosamond, 96, 216, **449–50**
Leisure, **450–2**, 635, 742
Lend-Lease, **452–3**
Lessing, Doris, 173, **453–4**
Lethaby, William, 27, 221, 644
Lewis, C.S., 144, 335, **454–5**
Lewis, Wyndham, 121, 291, 302, 312, 384, 414, 447, **455–6**, 576–7, 719, 721, 821; and *Blast*, 455, 614, 817; and Vorticism, 455, 460, 563, 817
Liberal Democrats, 459
Liberal Party, 24, 39, 124, 149–50, 190, 194–5, 340, 413, 422, **456–9**, 461–5, 493, 526, 564, 695–6; attacks landowners, 381; New Liberalism, 349, 367, 457, 502, **564–5**, 632, 819; opposes tariffs, 390; refuses to serve under Chamberlain, 138
Literary criticism, 119, 260, 308, 335, 447, 454, **459–61**, 628, 648, 682, 861
Literature: children's, **143–5**, 437, 454, 638; Commonwealth, **173–4**, 579; detective fiction, 141–2, 145–6, 216, **223–5**, 338, 503, 579, 698, 741; drama, 51, 66–7, 201–2, **235–8**, 261, 599, 717–18, 748–9; gay, 290, 307, 408, 579; Georgian poetry, 110, 178, 334, 625; Imagists, 626; Irish, **403–5**, 415–16, 863–5; poetry, 43–4, 110, 215–17, 259–60, 334–5, 440–1, 479–80, 489–90, 499–500, 599–600, **625–30**, 863–5; popular fiction, **637–9**, 664; science fiction, 59–60, 579; Scottish, 479–80, **702–4**; spy novel, **740–2**
Littlewood, Joan, 237, 311
Lloyd George, David, 73, 278, 340, 379, 422–3, **461–5**, 493, 501, 652, 854; advocates Welsh Home Rule, 833; budget of 1909, 38, 58, 194, 436, 462, 519; and German reparations, 680; and Irish settlement, 407; and land reform, 436, 464; and Liberal Party leadership, 458, 461, 465; as Liberal reformer, 149, 320, 457, 462, 502, 565, 589; as Minister of Munitions, 464, 522; and National Health Insurance, 552–3; and post-war coalition, 17, 55–7, 150, 209–10, 439, 503, 696; as pro-Boer, 92, 462, 701; replaces Asquith, 39, 66, 150, 172, 187, 192, 209, 215, 464, 525–6, 701, 778; as wartime Prime Minister, 58, 81, 94–5, 116, 131, 294–6, 304, 325, 344, 429, 646, 795
Lloyd Webber, Andrew, **465–6**, 774
Locarno Pact (1925), 135, **466–7**, 732
Logical Positivism, **467**; *see also* Philosophy
London, 9, 21, 28–31, 87, 89, 206, 265, 286–7, 382, 411–12, **467–71**, 722; City of, 78, **153–5**, 206, 245, 329, 437, 467, 513–14; Passenger Transport Board, 472, 558, 622–3, 809; Underground, 29, 222, 329, 387, 468, 529, 622–3, 643–4, 808–10; University of, 28, 51, 140, 507, 805
London Economic Conference, 14
London government, **471–2**; Greater London Council, 470, 472; Inner London Education Authority (ILEA), 470, 472; London County Council, 21, 207, 274, 439, 471–2, 533, 636, 783, 809, 819, 827
London School of Economics, 74, 277, 346, **472–4**, 728, 819, 827; faculty appointments at, 19, 213, 242, 441, 497, 761, 781
Long, Walter, 94, 130
Lonsdale, Kathleen, 689, 691
Lords, House of, 3, 37–8, 56, 57, 147, 194–5, 209, 253, 345–6, 370–1, **379–80**, 424, 438, 476, 493, 534, 587, 696, 724, 771, 842; as appeals court, 417, 759; life peers, 109, 380; Parliament Act (1911), 130, 191, 195, 209, 405, 457, 462, 519; Peerage Act (1963), 371, 380; reform of, 124, 133
Lothian, Lord, 163, 519
Low, David, 127–8, **474–5**, 652
Lubetkin, Berthold, 28–9
Lugard, Frederick, **475–6**
Lutyens, Edwin, 27, 318, **476–8**, 735
Lutyens, Elizabeth, 179, 595
Lytton Commission, 445, **478**

MacDiarmid, Hugh, **479–80**, 628, 702–5
MacDonald, Ramsay, 99, 365, 391, **480–3**, 651, 724, 834; and First World War, 392, 800; and Labour Party, 12, 355–6, 429, 434, 505, 727; as Prime Minister, 12, 13, 17, 40–41, 56, 96, 207, 326, 357, 430
MacGregor, Ian, 522, 557
Mackenzie, Compton, **483–4**, 741, 843